July 16-19, 2018
New York, NY, USA

Association for
Computing Machinery

Advancing Computing as a Science & Profession

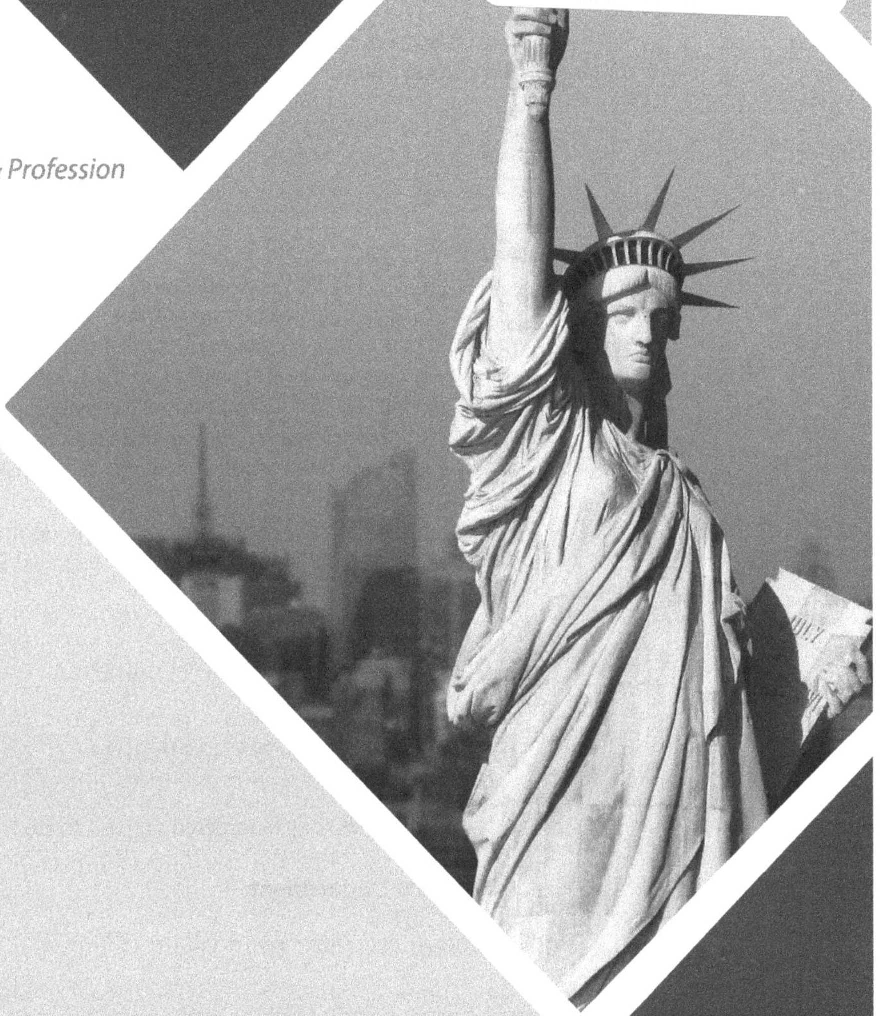

ISSAC '18

Proceedings of the 2018 ACM International Symposium on Symbolic and Algebraic Computation

Sponsored by:

ACM SIGSAM

In-cooperation with:

The Graduate Center of the City University of New York, National Security Agency, National Science Foundation, Maplesoft, and Fachgruppe Computeralgebra

Association for
Computing Machinery

Advancing Computing as a Science & Profession

The Association for Computing Machinery
2 Penn Plaza, Suite 701
New York, New York 10121-0701

ISBN: 978-1-4503-5550-6 (Digital)

ISBN: 978-1-4503-5957-3 (Print)

Additional copies may be ordered prepaid from:

ACM Order Department
PO Box 30777
New York, NY 10087-0777, USA

Phone: 1-800-342-6626 (USA and Canada)
+1-212-626-0500 (Global)
Fax: +1-212-944-1318
E-mail: acmhelp@acm.org
Hours of Operation: 8:30 am – 4:30 pm ET

Foreword

The International Symposium on Symbolic and Algebraic Computation (ISSAC) is the premier conference for research in symbolic computation and computer algebra. ISSAC 2018, to be held at the City University of New York, New York City, USA, is the 43rd meeting in this series. The series has been held annually since 1981. ISSAC is sponsored by the Association for Computing Machinery (ACM) and its Special Interest Group on Symbolic and Algebraic Manipulation (SIGSAM), and is generously supported by several other institutions and organizations, which are listed in the following pages.

This year's meeting takes place from the 16th to the 19th of July 2018. The ISSAC meeting is a showcase for original research contributions on all aspects of computer algebra and symbolic mathematical computation, including:

Algorithmic aspects:

- Exact and symbolic linear, polynomial, and differential algebra
- Symbolic-numeric, homotopy, perturbation, and series methods
- Computational algebraic geometry, group theory, number theory, quantifier elimination, and logic
- Computer arithmetic
- Summation, recurrence equations, integration, and solution of ODEs and PDEs
- Symbolic methods in other areas of pure and applied mathematics
- Complexity of algebraic algorithms and algebraic complexity

Software aspects:

- Design of symbolic computation packages and systems
- Language design and type systems for symbolic computation
- Data representation
- Considerations for modern hardware
- Algorithm implementation and performance tuning
- Mathematical user interfaces
- Use with systems for, e.g., digital libraries, courseware, simulation and optimization, automated theorem-proving, computer-aided design, and automatic differentiation

Application aspects:

- Applications that stretch the current limits of computer algebra algorithms or systems, use computer algebra in new areas or new ways, or apply it in situations with broad impact.

The conference presents a range of invited speakers, tutorials, poster sessions, software demonstrations, and vendor exhibits, with its centerpiece being peer-reviewed research papers.

The ISSAC program committee has adhered to the highest standards and practices in the evaluation of submitted papers, producing three or more referee reports per submission. All papers submitted to ISSAC were judged, and accepted or rejected, based solely on their scientific novelty, importance, non-triviality, and rigor. The program committee selected 47 papers for publication in these proceedings. We gratefully acknowledge the thorough and important work of the program committee members and external reviewers, whose names appear in the following pages, and thank all the authors of all the submitted papers, tutorials, and invited talks for their contributions.

Running a large conference such as ISSAC requires the work of many volunteers, and hopefully all of them are credited in the following pages. Without their contributions, the conference would not have been possible.

Finally, we want to take this opportunity to remember George E. Collins, one of the founders of our community, who passed away last November at the age of 90. Collins made seminal contributions to the field. Among his most influential works are his contributions to polynomial GCDs and (sub)resultant computation, and the cylindrical algebraic decomposition algorithm for quantifier elimination in the theory of real closed fields, to name just two. Collins advised more than 15 Ph.D. students, several of whom play prominent roles in the computer algebra community today. We will honor his memory.

Manuel Kauers and Alexey Ovchinnikov *(General Chairs)*

Éric Schost *(Program Committee Chair)*

Carlos Arreche *(Proceedings Editor)*

Table of Contents

ISSAC 2018 Organization

General Chairs: Manuel Kauers *(Johannes Kepler University, Austria)*
Alexey Ovchinnikov *(City University of New York, USA)*

Program Committee Chair: Éric Schost *(University of Waterloo, Canada)*

Local Arrangements Chair: Victor Pan *(City University of New York, USA)*

Treasurer: Alexander Hulpke *(Colorado State University, USA)*

Proceedings Editor: Carlos Arreche *(University of Texas at Dallas, USA)*

Tutorial Chair: Clément Pernet *(Université Grenoble Alpes, France)*

Poster Chair: François Lemaire *(Université de Lille, France)*

Software Presentations Chair: Adam Strzebonski *(Wolfram Research, USA)*

Publicity Chair: Gleb Pogudin *(New York University, USA)*

Program Committee: Fatima K. Abu Salem *(American University of Beirut, Lebanon)*
Anna Bigatti *(Università di Genova, Italy)*
Shaoshi Chen *(Chinese Academy of Sciences, China)*
Thomas Cluzeau *(Université de Limoges, France)*
Luca de Feo *(Université de Versailles, France)*
Matthew England *(Coventry University, UK)*
Gábor Ivanyos *(Hungarian Academy of Sciences, Hungary)*
Fredrik Johansson *(INRIA Bordeaux, France)*
Jeremy Johnson *(Drexel University, USA)*
Laura Kovacs *(Vienna University of Technology, Austria)*
Viktor Levandovskyy *(RWTH Aachen University, Germany)*
Hongbo Li *(Chinese Academy of Sciences, China)*
Susan Margulies *(United States Naval Academy, USA)*
Katsusuke Nabeshima *(Tokushima University, Japan)*
Daniel Perrucci *(Universidad de Buenos Aires, Argentina)*
Mohab Safey El Din *(Sorbonne Universités, France)*
Dave Saunders *(University of Delaware, USA)*
Éric Schost *(University of Waterloo, Canada)*
Arne Storjohann *(University of Waterloo, Canada)*
Jan Verschelde *(University of Illinois at Chicago, USA)*

Poster Presentations Committee: François Lemaire *(Université de Lille, France)*
Marc Moreno Maza *(University of Western Ontario, Canada)*
Gleb Pogudin *(New York University, USA)*
Clemens Raab *(Johannes Kepler University, Austria)*

Software Presentations Committee: Hidenao Iwane *(Fujitsu Laboratories Ltd and National Institute of Informatics, Japan)*
Daniel Roche *(United States Naval Academy, USA)*
Adam Strzebonski *(Wolfram Research, USA)*

Local Arrangements Committee: Richard Gustavson *(Manhattan College, USA)*
Delaram Kahrobaei *(City University of New York, USA)*
Victor Pan *(City University of New York, USA)*
Liang Zhao *(City University of New York, USA)*

Additional Reviewers:
Sergei Abramov
Martin Albrecht
Xavier Allamigeon
Carlos Arreche
Daniel Bates
Carlos Beltran
Kamal Bentahar
Jérémy Berthomieu
Markus Blaser
Mark Boady
Paola Boito
Yacine Bouzidi
Sándor Bozóki
Gabor Braun
Christopher Brown
Michael Burr
Francisco-Jesus Castro-Jimenez
Changbo Chen
Cyrille Chenavier
Jin-San Cheng
Frédéric Chyzak
Diego Cifuentes
Thomas Cluzeau
Robert Corless
Carlos D'Andrea
Xavier Dahan
Willem de Graaf
Christian Eder
Ruyong Feng
Claus Fieker
Xing Gao
Mark Giesbrecht
Gavin Harrison
David Harvey
Jonathan Hauenstein
Johannes Hoffman
Derek Holt
Hoon Hong
Nazeran Idrees
Maximilian Jaroschek
Gabriela Jeronimo
Xiaohong Jia
Erich Kaltofen
Deepak Kapur
Manuel Kauers
Franklin Kenter
Edward Kim
Christoph Koutschan
Daniel Krenn
Mario Kummer
Peter Kutas
George Labahn
Pierre Lairez
Guenter Landsmann
Markus Lange-Hegerman
Santiago Laplagne

Additional Reviewers (continued):

Robin Larrieu
Daniel Lazard
Viktor Levandovskyy
Anton Leykin
Ziming Li
Sergio R. Lopez-Permouth
David Lucas
Diane Maclagan
Victor Magron
Gregorio Malajovich
Scott McCallum
Gabor Megyesi
Johannes Middeke
Teo Mora
Guillaume Moroz
Bernard Mourrain
Kosaku Nagasaka
Simone Naldi
Vincent Neiger
Andrew Novocin
Yanbin Pan
Timothée Pecatte
Clément Pernet
John Perry
Marko Petkovsek
Gleb Pogudin
Sebastian Posur
Victoria Powers
Clemens G. Raab
Stanislaw Radziszowski
Georg Regensburger
Bruce Reznik
Lorenzo Robbiano
Daniel Robertz
Daniel Roche
Lajos Ronyai
Fabrice Rouillier
Timur Sadykov
Bruno Salvy
Josef Schicho
Carsten Schneider
Hiroshi Sekigawa
Changpeng Shao
Michael Singer
Pierre-Jean Spaenlehauer
Yann Strozecki
Agnes Szanto
Elias Tsigaridas
Tristan Vaccon
Marc Van Barel
Joris van der Hoeven
Leandro Vendramin
Joachim von zur Gathen
Paul Vrbik
Dingkang Wang
Mingsheng Wang
Jacques-Arthur Weil
Michael Wibmer
Bican Xia
Ichitaro Yamazaki
Zhengfeng Yang
Josephine Yu
Chunming Yuan
Zhonggang Zeng
Yi Zhang

ISSAC 2018 Sponsor and Supporters

Sponsor: ACM Special Interest Group on Symbolic and Algebraic Manipulation

Supporters: Ph.D. Program in Mathematics, and Initiative for the Theoretical Sciences

The Graduate Center of the City University of New York

National Security Agency

National Science Foundation

Maplesoft

Fachgruppe Computeralgebra

Algebraic Techniques in Geometry: The 10th Anniversary

Extended Abstract

Micha Sharir
Tel Aviv University
Tel Aviv, Israel
michas@tau.ac.il

ABSTRACT

This year we are celebrating the 10th anniversary of a dramatic revolution in combinatorial geometry, fueled by the infusion of techniques from algebraic geometry and algebra that have proven effective in solving a variety of hard problems that were thought to be unreachable with more traditional techniques. The new era has begun with two groundbreaking papers of Guth and Katz [14, 15], the second of which has (almost completely) solved the celebrated distinct distances problem of Paul Erdős [11], open since 1946.

In this talk I will survey, as time permits, some of the progress that has been made since then, including a variety of problems on distinct and repeated distances and other configurations, on incidences between points and lines, curves, and surfaces in two, three, and higher dimensions, on polynomials vanishing on Cartesian products with applications, and on cycle elimination for lines and triangles in three dimensions.

CCS CONCEPTS

• **Mathematics of computing → Combinatorics**; • **Theory of computation →** *Computational geometry*;

KEYWORDS

Combinatorial Geometry, Incidences, Polynomial method, Algebraic Geometry, Distances

ACM Reference Format:

Micha Sharir. 2018. Algebraic Techniques in Geometry: The 10th Anniversary: Extended Abstract. In *ISSAC '18: 2018 ACM International Symposium on Symbolic and Algebraic Computation, July 16–19, 2018, New York, NY, USA.* ACM, New York, NY, USA, 5 pages. https://doi.org/10.1145/3208976.3209028

Algebraic techniques in geometry: The revolution

One of the most ubiquitous hard problems in combinatorial geometry has been Erdős's distinct distances problem [11, 12]. Introduced in a paper in 1946, the problem asks for a lower bound on the number of distinct distances determined by any set of n points in the plane. The set of vertices of a $\sqrt{n} \times \sqrt{n}$ grid determines $\Theta(n/\sqrt{\log n})$ distinct distances, and Erdős conjectured that this is the correct lower bound. For nearly 65 years (and for that matter, somewhat also today) the problem has been open, and resisted many attempts by the brightest minds to solve it. The best lower bound that was obtained was $\Omega(n^{0.8641})$ by Katz and Tardos [24], using a fairly involved analysis.

This problem has been the crown jewel in the recent developments, in which sophisticated machinery from algebra and algebraic geometry has been introduced into combinatorial geometry, and has lead to dramatic progress, manifested in the solution of numerous hard problems, many of which seemed totally out of reach by standard combinatorial approaches. This technique was pioneered by Larry Guth and Nets Hawk Katz in two groundbreaking papers, in 2008 and 2010. In their second work [15], they have almost completely solved the distinct distances problem, establishing the nearly-tight lower bound $\Omega(n/\log n)$ on the number of distinct distances in any set of n points in the plane.

In this survey talk, I will attempt to review some of these developments. More comprehensive reviews, covering also related topics, can be found, e.g., in Guth's recent book [13], Tao's survey [46], and the author's recent survey [39].

The early stages. The revolution has started two years earlier, in 2008, in the first groundbreaking work of Guth and Katz [14]. Extending ideas that Dvir [7] has developed for finite fields, they have obtained a complete solution of the *joints problem*, posed in [4] in 1992, which seeks a sharp upper bound on the number of points that can be incident to at least three non-coplanar lines, in a set of n lines in three dimensions; these points are called *joints*. Simple constructions show that the number of joints can be $\Omega(n^{3/2})$, and the goal was to obtain a matching upper bound. After 15 years of frustrating research, the best upper bound that one could obtain, with the "traditional" machinery, was $O(n^{1.623})$.

Guth and Katz obtained the tight upper bound $O(n^{3/2})$, using several reasonably simple tools from algebra and algebraic geometry. Here is a brief, rough, and informal description of their analysis. Given a set L of n lines in $\mathbb{R}^3$, they "force", in a preliminary pruning and sampling step, most of the joints of L to lie on the zero set $Z(f)$ of a polynomial f of degree $D \le cn^{1/2}$, with a sufficiently small constant c, and then only consider lines of L that are also fully contained in $Z(f)$ (the other lines do not contain too many joints). Now a joint incident to three non-coplanar lines, all contained in $Z(f)$, must be a *singular* point of f, and lines that contain more than D such joints must consist exclusively of singular points (each of the three first-order derivatives of f must vanish identically on

ISSAC '18, July 16–19, 2018, New York, NY, USA

ACM ISBN 978-1-4503-5550-6/18/07...$15.00
https://doi.org/10.1145/3208976.3209028

such a line). Lines that contain fewer than D joints contribute a total of at most $nD = O(n^{3/2})$ joints, so they can be ignored. Now, assuming f to be irreducible, one can show, using an argument based on Bézout's theorem, that the number of singular lines contained in $Z(f)$ is $O(D^2)$, which we can make smaller than, say, $n/2$. An inductive argument on n then completes the proof.

The actual proof in [14] is more involved and technical. It has been greatly simplified in two subsequent papers by Kaplan, Sharir and Shustin [19] and by Quilodrán [36]; the bound has also been extended, in both papers, to any dimension $d \geq 3$; the worst-case bound is $\Theta(n^{d/(d-1)})$.

Incidences. Although the joints problem might appear, on the face of it, just a curiousity, it is actually a significant pillar in the study of *incidences* between points and lines, curves, (hyper)planes or surfaces, as well as of several other related fields, both combinatorial and algorithmic. We briefly mention the highlights of the topic of incidences, extensively studied during the past 35 years, and considered as one of the main active areas in combinatorial geometry; see Pach and Sharir [35] for a comprehensive (albeit somewhat outdated) survey.

In the simplest form of the problem, we are given a set P of m points and a set L of n lines in the plane, and we wish to obtain sharp upper and lower bounds for the maximum possible value of $I(P, L)$, the number of *incidences* between the points of P and the lines of L, where an incidence is a pair $(p, \ell) \in P \times L$ with $p \in \ell$.

The 1983 celebrated Szemerédi–Trotter theorem [45] asserts that $I(P, L) = O(m^{2/3}n^{2/3} + m + n)$, and that this bound is tight in the worst case. Many extensions of the problem have been studied, in which one considers, instead of lines, other curves in the plane (e.g., circles) or planes, hyperplanes, or surfaces in higher dimensions. In most of these extensions, though, tight bounds on the maximum number of incidences are not known. Incidence problems, besides being a fascinating topic of study in its own right, show up in many applications in combinatorial geometry, including Erdős's distinct distances, and the equally famous *repeated distances* problems (see below). They are strongly related to algorithmic problems such as range searching in computational geometry, arise in the study of additive combinatorics, and reach as far as the *Kakeya problem* in harmonic analysis; see the title "Algebraic methods in discrete analogs of the Kakeya problem" of Guth and Katz's first work [14].

If one considers incidences between m points and n lines in higher dimensions, say in $d = 3$ dimensions, the problem, on first sight, seems totally uninteresting. Indeed, one can project the points and lines onto some generic plane, observe that incidences are preserved in the projection, and apply the Szemerédi–Trotter bound. Since the bound is worst-case tight in the plane, it continues to be so in any higher dimension. The joints problem, in retrospect, was an attempt to remove the triviality from this extension, by forcing the input, in a sense, to be "truly three-dimensional". As follows from the results of Guth and Katz (and even from the weaker previous results), one does indeed get improved bounds in truly three-dimensional scenes, in which the amount of coplanarity of the input points and lines is kept under control.

As we will shortly discuss, truly three-dimensional point-line incidences are a key step in the solution of the planar distinct distances problem in [15].

Distinct distances. The next developments took place in an attempt to apply the new machinery to the planar distinct distances problem of Erdős [11]. As we recall, in this celebrated problem the goal is to establish a sharp lower bound on the minimum possible number of distinct distances between the elements of a set S of n points in the plane.

About 10 years earlier, György Elekes, perhaps the real hero behind all the new developments, had come up, in an unpublished note, with an ingenious program to reduce the planar distinct distances problem to an incidence problem between points and curves in three dimensions. (As it turned out in [15], Elekes's curves are actually lines, with a suitable parameterization.) To tackle the latter problem, though, Elekes needed a couple of fairly deep conjectures, which neither he nor anybody else knew how to solve at that time. If these conjectures could be established, they would have lead to the almost tight lower bound $\Omega(n/\log n)$ on the number of distinct distances.

In a joint paper with Elekes [9], written after his passing away in 2008, I have laid out and somewhat developed Elekes's program. Having thus become public, it was immediately seized by Guth and Katz, who, in their second (and major) breakthrough [15], in November 2010 (the paper was eventually formally published five years later), they introduced new algebraic machinery, based on the *polynomial ham sandwich theorem* of Stone and Tukey, which allowed them to establish Elekes's conjectures and thereby obtain the aforementioned lower bound $\Omega(n/\log n)$ for distinct distances. Specifically, their main result, an extension of the main conjecture of Elekes, is: Given N lines in three dimensions,[1] the number of points that are incident to at least $k \geq 3$ of these lines is $O(N^{3/2}/k^2)$, provided that no plane contains more than $N^{1/2}$ lines. (Compare this with the bound $O(N^{3/2})$ on the number of joints.) The case $k = 2$ is also treated in [15]. There one needs to assume that no plane or *regulus* (doubly ruled quadric) contains more than $N^{1/2}$ lines (which holds for the lines in Elekes's transformation), and the analysis is based on algebraic properties of *ruled surfaces*, established by Salmon and Cayley in the 19th century [38]; see also Monge [29].

Another, slightly more general formulation of the results in [15] is as follows. Let P be a set of m points and let L be a set of n lines in $\mathbb{R}^3$. Then the number of incidences between P and L satisfies:

$$I(P, L) = O\left(m^{1/2}n^{3/4} + m^{2/3}n^{1/3}q^{1/3} + m + n\right),$$

where q is the maximum number of lines of L in any common plane. The 'leading term' $m^{1/2}n^{3/4}$ is smaller than the leading term $m^{2/3}n^{2/3}$ in the Szemerédi-Trotter planar bound (for $m \geq n^{1/2}$; both terms are sublinear for smaller values of m). The second term $m^{2/3}n^{1/3}q^{1/3}$ arises from the Szemerédi-Trotter bound. For $q = n^{1/2}$ (the assumption made in [15]), it is subsumed by the other terms. Another point worth noting is that the two terms $m^{1/2}n^{3/4}$ and m 'compete' for dominance, where the first (resp., second) term dominates when $m \leq n^{3/2}$ (resp., $m \geq n^{3/2}$). This threshold is not accidental (recall the bound on the number of joints).

The application of the polynomial ham sandwich theorem in [15] results in a so-called *polynomial partitioning* scheme, a new and major tool then, that has become by now a standard staple. Its power has been demonstrated time and again, with some highlights

[1] The number of lines in Elekes's transformation is $N = \Theta(n^2)$.

mentioned below. It nicely complements and strengthens the nearly 30-years-old arsenal of "traditional" geometric partitions based on *cuttings* and on *simplicial partitions*. Roughly, it states that, given a set P of m points in $\mathbb{R}^d$, and a parameter $t < m$, one can find a d-variate polynomial f, of degree $D = O(t^{1/d})$, such that each connected component ("cell") of $\mathbb{R}^d \setminus Z(f)$ contains at most m/t points of P; the number of cells is $O(D^d) = O(t)$. This partitioning of P is not exhaustive, as some (perhaps many, or all) points of P may lie on the zero set $Z(f)$, and they require a special treatment, depending on the specific problem at hand. Handling these points in a systematic manner appears to be a missing fundamental ingredient of the infrastructure of the new paradigm, although certain general tools have since been developed—see, e.g., [6, 20, 28].

The power of the new polynomial partitioning technique has quickly been recognized by the community, and has lead to numerous new results, 'cracking' many hard-nut problems one after the other. Many of these problems were deemed hopeless to solve by 'standard' means, so it is doubly pleasing to see them succumb to the new machinery.

In the remaining part of this brief survey, we review some of the developments that took place after the initial surge reviewed above. This review is certainly incomplete, and somewhat biased, reflecting the author's own personal taste. Apologies are due to the many authors and their amazing results that are not mentioned below.

Algebraic techniques in geometry: Partial review of the progress

Applications of the polynomial partitioning technique. There have been many recent works that successfully applied the technique to a variety of problems in combinatorial geometry. Some of these results are listed below. One of the most basic areas in which the new machinery has been applied involves incidences between points and lines, curves, or surfaces, in three and higher dimensions. As already noted, incidences pop up in many other problems, including Erdős's classical problems of repeated and distinct distances. Incidences arise naturally in the repeated (or unit) distance problem, in which we seek an upper bound on the number of pairs in a set of n points in the plane (or in higher dimensions) at distance exactly 1 from each other. For example, given a set P of n points in $\mathbb{R}^3$, we draw a sphere of radius 1 around each $p \in P$. Now the number of pairs $(p, q) \in P \times P$ at distance 1 from each other is precisely half the number of incidences between the n points of P and the n unit spheres, so a bound on the number of these incidences is all we need.

It is less obvious how incidences enter the distinct distances problem. A major ingredient of Elekes's program, mentioned above, is a reduction that transforms the distinct distances problem in the plane to a question concerning incidences between points and lines in three dimensions. Concretely, we used three-dimensional space to represent rigid motions in the plane, which indeed have three degrees of freedom. Each of the lines is defined in terms of two original points p, q, and is the locus of all rigid motions that take p to q. A point τ incident to k lines representa a rigid motion that maps k input points to k other input points, and an upper bound on the number of such "k-rich" points (motions) leads, via a clever application of the Cauchy-Schwarz inequality, to a lower bound on the number of distinct distances. Similar transformations have been introduced and exploited for other problems.

Incidences, distances, and the like. Some of the progress on these problems include the following results. (i) New proofs (simpler, different) of old results (the Szemerédi-Trotter incidence bound in the plane, spanning trees with small crossing number); see Kaplan et al. [18]. (ii) Improved bounds for unit distances in three dimensions. The bound $O(n^{3/2})$ was obtained independently by Zahl [49] and by Kaplan, Matoušek, Safernová, Sharir [20]. A slightly improved bound was recently obtained by Zahl [48]. (iii) Improved bounds for point-circle incidences in three dimensions; see Sharir, Sheffer, Zahl [27], Sharir, Solomon [41]. (iv) The point-line Szemerédi-Trotter incidence bound in the complex plane and related bounds. It is in fact a special case of incidences between points and two-dimensional surfaces in $\mathbb{R}^4$; see Solymosi, Tao [44], Zahl [50], Sheffer, Szabó, Zahl [1]. (v) Incidences between points and lines in four dimensions, extending the Szemerédi-Trotter and the Guth-Katz bounds for point-line incidences one dimension higher; see Sharir, Solomon [40]. (vi) General bounds for incidences between points and algebraic curves in higher dimensions; see Sharir, Sheffer, Solomon [25], Sharir, Solomon [41]. (vii) Incidences in general and semi-algebraic extensions: bounds on the number of pairs $(p, q) \in P \times Q$, for two sets P, Q of objects, that satisfy some semi-algebraic predicate, under the assumption that the resulting graph of such pairs does not contain a large complete bipartite subgraph; see Fox, Pach, Sheffer, Suk, Zahl [22]. (viii) Bounds on the number of 2-rich points (points incident to at least two curves) in a set of n algebraic curves, with interesting connections to the theory of doubly-ruled surfaces; see Guth, Zahl [16, 17]. (ix) A lower bound of $\Omega(n^{4/3})$ on the number of distinct distances between two sets, each contained in a line, where the lines are non-parallel and non-orthogonal; see Sharir, Sheffer, Solymosi [26]. (x) Extensions of the previous result on distinct distances to other special configurations; see Sharir, Solymosi [42], Pach, de Zeeuw [34], Charalambides [5], Raz [37], Sharir, Solomon [41].

Polynomials vanishing on grids: The Elekes-Rónyai-Szabó theory. Let A, B, C be three sets, each of n real numbers, and consider their Cartesian product $A \times B \times C$. Let F be a trivariate polynomial of constant degree. How many zeros can F have on $A \times B \times C$? This problem has been studied by Elekes and Rónyai [8] for the special 'bivariate' case where F is of the form $F(x, y, z) = z - f(x, y)$, and by Elekes and Szabó [10] for the general case. The number of zeros is always $O(n^2)$, and they have shown that the number can be quadratic only when F has some special group-like structure: In the bivariate case the special form is

$$f(x, y) = \varphi(g(x) + h(y)) \quad \text{or} \quad f(x, y) = \varphi(g(x) \cdot h(y)),$$

for suitable *polynomials* g, h, and φ. A similar, more involved characterization holds for the general case. When F does not have the special form, the number of zeros is subquadratic. The same question can also be asked, and handled, over the complex field.

The Elekes–Rónyai–Szabó theory has recently been revisited: In several recent works (Raz, Sharir, Solymosi [31], Raz, Sharir, de Zeeuw [32, 33]), the proofs were simplified, and the subquadratic bounds were significantly improved to $O(n^{11/6})$; related bounds are also provided when the sizes of A, B, C are not equal, and over the complex field. The theory is strongly connected to several interesting problems in combinatorial geometry. Two such examples yield (a) a subquadratic bound on the number of triple intersections of three families of unit circles where all the circles in the same family pass through some fixed point; see Raz, Sharir, Solymosi [30], and (b) an improved lower bound on the number of distinct distances from three points [42]. We note though that direct application of the Elekes–Rónyai–Szabó theory is problematic mainly because it is not easy to verify that the relevant polynomial F does not have the special form, so often one has to use ad-hoc, problem-specific arguments instead.

Eliminating depth cycles and applications. A recent significant progress involves the fairly old problem of eliminating depth cycles in a set of n pairwise disjoint triangles in $\mathbb{R}^3$. The problem is motivated by the so-called Painter algorithm in computer graphics, but is fascinating in its own right. Even the simpler special case of eliminating depth cycles among n pairwise disjoint lines in $\mathbb{R}^3$ has been notoriously hard to approach without the algebraic machinery. The *depth relation* among n lines, say for simplicity in general position, is defined so that $\ell_1 \prec \ell_2$ if the unique vertical line that meets both ℓ_1 and ℓ_2 meets ℓ_1 below ℓ_2. In general, this relation can have cycles, and, in the case of lines, we want to cut them into a small number of pieces (segments, rays, lines) so that the resulting depth relation among the pieces be acyclic. With a bit of care, this problem can be extended to the case of pairwise disjoint triangles—see below.

One can show, using a variant of the lower bound construction for joints, that $\Omega(n^{3/2})$ cuts might be needed in the worst case, and the challenge is to eliminate all cycles with a number of cuts close to this lower bound. A quadratic number of cuts is easy to show, but, over more than 30 years of research, only very weak subquadratic bounds were obtained, and only for special cases. The case of triangles has been essentially untouched.

Using polynomial partitioning, in a rather "unconventional" manner, we have shown (Aronov, Sharir [2]) that one can eliminate all depth cycles for n lines in three dimensions with $O(n^{3/2}\text{polylog}(n))$ cuts, thus almost matching the lower bound. We have also extended the technique to show that, for n pairwise disjoint triangles in three dimensions, one can eliminate all the depth cycles among them by cutting them, along constant-degree algebraic arcs, into $O(n^{3/2+\varepsilon})$ simply-shaped pieces, for any $\varepsilon > 0$, where each piece is a semi-algebraic set of constant complexity; see Aronov, Miller, Sharir [3]. This solution for the case of triangles is less satisfactory, because one would actually like to cut them by straight cuts, into a collection of sub-triangles. To do this with close to $n^{3/2}$ cuts is still open, but a solution with roughly $n^{7/4}$ cuts has recently been obtained by de Berg [?].

The same technique also works (with some extra care) to eliminate depth cycles in a set of n algebraic curves or arcs of constant degree. This can be combined with a recent clever transformation offered by Ellenberg, Solymosi, Zahl [21] (which yields, again using the algebraic machinery, new bounds on curve tangencies and orthogonalities in the plane). This transformation lifts a set of curves in the plane to curves in 3-space, essentially making the slope of the tangent at a point its third coordinate. In this way, if a pair of original curves γ_1, γ_2 cross twice, then the lifted curves form a depth 2-cycle. Hence, by eliminating all these cycles, we cut the original curves into close to $n^{3/2}$ arcs that are *pseudo-segments*—each pair of them intersect at most once. This has been a major open problem for close to 20 years. Its solution, by Sharir, Zahl [43], has lead to improved bounds for incidences between points and constant-degree alebraic curves in the plane.

In closing, While significant progress has been made, there are many open problems that are still waiting to be solved. Perhaps the most significant of them is to obtain a tight lower bound for distinct distances in three dimensions. A grid-based construction gives an upper bound of $O(n^{2/3})$, and the goal is to show that this is the correct general lower bound. Here Elekes's transformation leads to more involved incidence problems of higher-dimensional surfaces in higher-dimensional spaces, which currently still seem to be out of reach.

In addition, the overwhelming majority of the various known upper bounds for incidences, even in the plane, are not known to be tight, and are strongly suspected to be improvable. We therefore obtain a long list of open problems, all appearing to be very difficult. Maybe the most challenging is to obtain an improved upper bound for the repeated distances problem in the plane, or, equivalently, for incidences between m points and n unit circles. This is an especially intriguing (and difficult) question, because, as is known, the bound, which is $O(m^{2/3}n^{2/3} + m + n)$ [23] is worst-case tight if we replace unit circles by translates of a parabola [47]. One would therefore hope that the algebraic machinery would be effective here, somehow distinguishing between circles and other curves.

REFERENCES

[1] E. Szabó A. Sheffer and J. Zahl. 2015. Point-curve incidences in the complex plane. (2015). in arXiv:1502:07003.

[2] B. Aronov and M. Sharir. 2018. Almost tight bounds for eliminating depth cycles in three dimensions. *Discrete Comput. Geom.* 59 (2018), 725–741.

[3] E. Miller B. Aronov and M. Sharir. 2017. Eliminating depth cycles among triangles in three dimensions. *Proc. 28th ACM-SIAM Sympos. on Discrete Algorithms* (2017), 2476–2494.

[4] L. Guibas R. Pollack R. Seidel M. Sharir B. Chazelle, H. Edelsbrunner and J. Snoeyink. 1992. Counting and cutting cycles of lines and rods in space. *Comput. Geom. Theory Appl.* 1 (1992), 305–323.

[5] M. Charalambides. 2014. Distinct distances on curves via rigidity. *Discrete Comput. Geom.* 51 (2014), 666–701.

[6] M. de Berg. 2017. Removing depth cycles among triangles: An efficient algorithm generating triangular fragments. *Proc. 58th IEEE Sympos. Foundations of Comput. Sci.* (2017), 272–282.

[7] Z. Dvir. 2009. On the size of Kakeya sets in finite fields. *J. Amer. Math. Soc.* 22 (2009), 1093–1097.

[8] G. Elekes and L. Rónyai. 2000. A combinatorial problem on polynomials and rational functions. *J. Combinat. Theory Ser. A* 89 (2000), 1–20.

[9] Gy. Elekes and M. Sharir. 2011. Incidences in three dimensions and distinct distances in the plane. *Combinat. Probab. Comput.* 20 (2011), 571–608.

[10] G. Elekes and E. Szabó. 2012. How to find groups? (and how to use them in Erdős geometry?). *Combinatorica* 32 (2012), 537–571.

[11] P. Erdős. 1946. On a set of distances of n points. *Amer. Math. Monthly* 53 (1946), 248–250.

[12] P. Erdős. 1960. On sets of distances on n points in Euclidean space. *Magyar Tud. Akad. Mat. Kutató Int. Kozl.* 5 (1960), 165–169.

[13] L. Guth. 2016. *Polynomial Methods in Combinatorics.* University Lecture Series, Vol. 64. Amer. Math. Soc. Press, Providence, RI.

[14] L. Guth and N. H. Katz. 2010. Algebraic methods in discrete analogs of the Kakeya problem. *Advances Math.* 225 (2010), 2828–2839.

[15] L. Guth and N.H. Katz. 2015. On the Erdős distinct distances problem in the plane. *Annals Math.* 181 (2015), 155–190.

[16] L. Guth and J. Zahl. 2015. Algebraic curves, rich points, and doubly-ruled surfaces. *Amer. J. Math. (to appear)* (2015).

[17] L. Guth and J. Zahl. 2017. Curves in $\mathbb{R}^4$ and two-rich points. *Discrete Comput. Geom.* 58 (2017), 232–253.

[18] J. Matoušek H. Kaplan and M. Sharir. 2012. Simple proofs of classical theorems in discrete geometry via the Guth-Katz polynomial partitioning technique. *Discrete Comput. Geom.* 48 (2012), 499–517.

[19] M. Sharir H. Kaplan and E. Shustin. 2010. On lines and joints. *Discrete Comput. Geom.* 44 (2010), 838–843.

[20] Z. Safernová H. Kaplan, J. Matoušek and M. Sharir. 2012. Unit distances in three dimensions. *Combinat. Probab. Comput.* 21 (2012), 597–610.

[21] J. Solymosi J. Ellenberg and J. Zahl. 2016. New bounds on curve tangencies and orthogonalities. *Discrete Analysis* 22 (2016), 1–22.

[22] A. Sheffer A. Suk J. Fox, J. Pach and J. Zahl. 2017. A semi-algebraic version of Zarankiewicz's problem. *J. European Math. Soc.* 19 (2017), 1785–1810.

[23] E. Szemerédi J. Spencer and W. T. Trotter. 1984. Unit distances in the Euclidean plane. In *Graph Theory and Combinatorics*, B. Bollobas (Ed.). Academic Press, 293–308.

[24] N. H. Katz and G. Tardos. 2004. *Towards a Theory of Geometric Graphs.* Contemporary Mathematics, Vol. 342. Amer. Math. Soc., Providence, RI, Chapter A new entropy inequality for the Erdős distance problem, 119–126.

[25] A. Sheffer M. Sharir and N. Solomon. 2016. Incidences with curves in $\mathbb{R}^d$. *Electronic J. Combinat.* 23, 4 (2016), P4, 16.

[26] A. Sheffer M. Sharir and J. Solymosi. 2013. Distinct distances on two lines. *J. Combinat. Theory, Ser. A* 120 (2013), 1732–1736.

[27] A. Sheffer M. Sharir and J. Zahl. 2015. Improved bounds for incidences between points and circles. *Combinat. Probab. Comput.* 24 (2015), 490–520.

[28] J. Matoušek and Z. Patáková. 2015. Multilevel polynomial partitioning and simplified range searching. *Discrete Comput. Geom.* 54 (2015), 22–41.

[29] G. Monge. 1809. *Application de l'Analyse á la Geometrie.* Bernard, Paris.

[30] M. Sharir O. E. Raz and J. Solymosi. 2015. On triple intersections of three families of unit circles. *Discrete Comput. Geom.* 54 (2015), 930–953.

[31] M. Sharir O. E. Raz and J. Solymosi. 2016. Polynomials vanishing on grids: The Elekes–Rónyai problem revisited. *Amer. J. Math.* 138 (2016), 1029–1065.

[32] M. Sharir O. Raz and F. de Zeeuw. 2016. Polynomials vanishing on Cartesian products: The Elekes–Szabó theorem revisited. *Duke Math. J.* 165, 18 (2016), 3517–3566.

[33] M. Sharir O. Raz and F. de Zeeuw. 2018. The Elekes–Szabó theorem in four dimensions. *Israel J. Math. (to appear)* (2018).

[34] J. Pach and F. de Zeeuw. 2017. Distinct distances on algebraic curves in the plane. *Combinat. Probab. Comput.* 26 (2017), 99–117.

[35] J. Pach and M. Sharir. 2004. *Towards a Theory of Geometric Graphs.* Contemporary Mathematics, Vol. 342. Amer. Math. Soc., Providence, RI, Chapter Geometric incidences, 185–223.

[36] R. Quilodrán. 2010. The joints problem in $\mathbb{R}^n$. *SIAM J. Discrete Math.* 23 (2010), 2211–2213.

[37] O. E. Raz. 2016. A note on distinct distances. (2016). in arXiv:1603.00740.

[38] G. Salmon. 1915. *A Treatise on the Analytic Geometry of Three Dimensions* (5th ed.). Vol. 2. Hodges, Figgis and co. Ltd., Dublin.

[39] M. Sharir. 2017. Computational Geometry Column 65. *SIGACT News* 48, 2 (2017), 68–85.

[40] M. Sharir and N. Solomon. 2017. Incidences between points and lines in $\mathbb{R}^4$. *Discrete Comput. Geom.* 57 (2017), 702–756.

[41] M. Sharir and N. Solomon. 2017. Incidences between points and surfaces and points and curves, and distinct and repeated distances in three dimensions. *Proc. 28th ACM-SIAM Sympos. on Discrete Algorithms* (2017), 2456–2475.

[42] M. Sharir and J. Solymosi. 2016. Distinct distances from three points. *Combinat. Probab. Comput.* 25 (2016), 623–632.

[43] M. Sharir and J. Zahl. 2017. Cutting algebraic curves into pseudo-segments and applications. *J. Combinat. Theory Ser. A* 150 (2017), 1–35.

[44] J. Solymosi and T. Tao. 2012. An incidence theorem in higher dimensions. *Discrete Comput. Geom.* 48, 2 (2012), 255–280.

[45] E. Szemerédi and W. T. Trotter. 1983. Extremal problems in discrete geometry. *Combinatorica* 3 (1983), 381–392.

[46] T. Tao. 2014. Algebraic combinatorial geometry: the polynomial method in arithmetic combinatorics, incidence combinatorics, and number theory. *EMS Surveys in Mathematical Sciences* 1, 1 (2014), 1–46.

[47] P. Valtr. 2006. Strictly convex norms allowing many unit distances and related touching questions. (2006). manuscript.

[48] J. Zahl. Breaking the 3/2 barrier for unit distances in three dimensions. (????). in arXiv:1706.05118.

[49] J. Zahl. 2013. An improved bound on the number of point-surface incidences in three dimensions. *Contrib. Discrete Math.* 8, 1 (2013), 100–121.

[50] J. Zahl. 2015. A Szemerédi-Trotter type theorem in $\mathbb{R}^4$. *Discrete Comput. Geom.* 54 (2015), 513–572.

Polynomial Systems Arising From Discretizing Systems of Nonlinear Differential Equations

Andrew J. Sommese
University of Notre Dame
Notre Dame, Indiana
sommese@nd.edu

ABSTRACT

This article is an extended abstract of the ISSAC 2018 talk "Polynomial systems arising from discretizing systems of nonlinear differential equations" by Andrew Sommese.

CCS CONCEPTS

• **Mathematics of computing → Discretization; Nonlinear equations;**

KEYWORDS

discretizations; nonlinear differential equations; numerical solutions; polynomial systems

ACM Reference Format:
Andrew J. Sommese. 2018. Polynomial Systems Arising From Discretizing Systems of Nonlinear Differential Equations. In *ISSAC '18: 2018 ACM International Symposium on Symbolic and Algebraic Computation, July 16–19, 2018, New York, NY, USA.* ACM, New York, NY, USA, 3 pages. https://doi.org/10.1145/3208976.3209029

1 INTRODUCTION

Systems of differential equations arise from applications throughout engineering and science. Discretizations of nonlinear differential equations often lead to systems of polynomials. These discretizations, which often have thousands of equations in thousands of variables, are sparse with a fair amount of structure. For example, finite difference discretizations with related grids resemble each other, and in particular many of the solutions of a given discretization may be associated with solutions of discretizations that are "finer." The polynomial systems arising through discretization are a rich source of significant problems. In this talk, I give an overview of what I have learned working on these problems.

In §2, which might also be called "Truth in Advertising," I discuss issues, which (though for the most part standard for applied mathematicians) might not be expected by those used to exact computation and the certainty afforded by proofs.

In §3, I discuss some of the approaches we have used to investigate the polynomial systems that arise in discretizing systems of differential equations.

ISSAC '18, July 16–19, 2018, New York, NY, USA

ACM ISBN 978-1-4503-5550-6/18/07...$15.00
https://doi.org/10.1145/3208976.3209029

It is worth noting (and satisfying to this algebraic geometer) that many systems that at first appear "nonalgebraic" can be converted to (and often first arose from) systems of differential equations with polynomial discretizations. For example if e^x occurs in an equation, we can replace e^x by a new quantity v and add an equation

$$\frac{dv}{dx} - v = 0.$$

This same adjustment applies to the occurrence of many classical functions (such as Bessel functions), which satisfy "algebraic differential equations." Of course, in practice this is not necessarily a good fix since it significantly increases the number of variables and equations in discretizations.

I would like to here thank my many collaborators on this work and in particular Bei Hu, Wenrui Hao, and Jonathan Hauenstein.

2 RULES OF THE GAME

Relatively few systems of nonlinear differential may be solved exactly, and must instead be solved numerically. As a simple example (see [17] for more realistic examples), consider computing a function $y(x)$ on $[0, 1]$ that satisfies

$$y'' + p(y) = 0 \text{ with } y(0) = a \text{ and } y(1) = b, \tag{1}$$

where $p(y)$ is a polynomial and a and b are real numbers. For each positive integer N, choose $N+2$ points $x_j = jh$ where $h = 1/(N+1)$ and $j = 0, \ldots, N+1$. We would like to find numbers $y_1, \ldots, y_N$ such that there is a solution $y(x)$ of Eq.1 with y_j appropriately close to $y(x_j)$. One way to approach this is to set $y_0 = a$ and $y_{N+1} = b$ and try to solve the polynomial system

$$\frac{y_{i-1} - 2y_i + y_{i+1}}{h^2} + p(y_i) = 0 \;\; j = 1, \ldots, N. \tag{2}$$

If $p(y) = y$, then Eq.2 is a system on linear equations with a unique solution $(y_1, \ldots, y_N)$ and for large enough N, there is a constant $B > 0$ such that $|y(x_j) - y_j| \leq Bh^2$. Going from a solution of Eq.1 in this case to the conclusion that the solution of Eq.2 satisfies $|y(x_j) - y_j| \leq Bh^2$ is straightforward. It follows from the fact that given a function $y(x)$ with enough differentiability on $[0, 1]$, there is a positive constant C such that for all sufficiently large N and any $x \in (0, 1)$

$$\left| y''(x) - \frac{y(x-h) - 2y(x) + y(x+h)}{h^2} \right| \leq Ch^2.$$

Going the other way takes work (not much in the case of Eq.1 with $p(y)$ linear). For a wide variety of linear ordinary and partial differential equations, i.e., differential equations with y and its derivatives entering linearly, this sort of procedure works very well. The elementary text [21] is a good place for general information.

Most systems of differential equations are not linear. Discretization still makes sense and solutions of the original differential equations are "close" to solutions of the discretized equations, but there are some serious issues with going from the solutions of the discretized equations to the approximate solutions of the original system of differential equations. Let's enumerate them.

(1) Even for ordinary differential equations, it is often unknown in the nonlinear case how many solutions exists or even whether any solution exists.
(2) The discretization for any reasonable number of gridpoints often has more solutions than estimates of the number of atoms in the universe. (In fact, more than the square of the estimates.)
(3) It is not clear which solutions of the discretization are approximate solutions of the original system of differential equations.
(4) the discretization is numerically very difficult to work with when using double precision.

The first point is an ever present issue. As noted in [17], the system of differential equations in a simple two-dimensional tumor growth model [11] is more complicated than the classical Hele-Shaw problem with surface tension (with many works devoted to it in the literature, i.e., searching Hele-Shaw on the title alone on MathSciNet returns 517 entries).

For traditional polynomial systems arising in applications areas such as Theoretical Kinematics, sorting through all solutions for those that are physically realistic is standard. For nonlinear differential equations, this is rarely possible. For example, a discretization of a simple two-dimensional Lotka-Volterra population model with diffusion, that consists of two partial differential equations ([17, §1.1] and [18, §9.4]), has is a polynomial system with $2g$ equations of total degree 2^{2g} with 2^g complex solutions. A relatively coarse 20×20 grid gives $g = 324$ for a system with $\approx 3.4 \cdot 10^{97}$ solutions. This rules out finding all solutions as a viable option.

I know no absolutely certain solution for the third point about whether a solution of the discretization corresponds to a solution of the system of differential equations. What can be done is to interpolate to extend the solution on one grid to a finer grid and then check if the extension is near a solution of the analogous discretized system for the finer grid.

The last point about needing double precision is key. At typical nonsingular solutions, condition numbers of Jacobian matrices of the polynomial system in the range of 10^9 and larger as the grid size grows are common, e.g., [12]. If we restrict ourselves to double precision, the linear algebra is not trustworthy and continuation sometimes fails. Moreover deciding whether a numerical scheme is converging (and what the order of convergence is) seems hopeless with just double precision, e.g., see [19, Table 1]. In our work we used Bertini [4, 5] which uses adaptive multiprecision algorithms based on [6? , 7].

3 COMPUTING SOLUTIONS

The goal is to find solutions of the systems of differential equations. In light of the points raised in the last section, what can be done?

There are several approaches we have followed.

The simplest, which might be labeled the *brute force method* is to compute all solutions for a coarse grid and sort through them for possible solutions to the system of differential equation. We tried with some success for a system of four ordinary differential equations arising in a pattern formation problem [9]. In 2011, a discretization of this system with ten gridpoints took about eleven hours on a 200 core cluster. Each additional gridpoint add four new equations and four new variables, with the count of paths which need to be followed increased by a multiple of five. Software and hardware have improved since then, but the exponential growth of the number of solutions as the number of gridpoints increase means that at most a few more nodes could be added.

In [1] a *filtering* approach was proposed (see also [2, 3]). To understand the basic idea in the case of a single ordinary differential that has a discretization into a system of polynomials $F_n(y) = 0$ for n gridpoints $(x_1, \ldots, x_n)$ at which we want to compute solutions $(y_1, \ldots, y_n)$ giving approximations of solutions of the differential equation at gridpoints:

(1) start with a set S_{n_0} of isolated solutions of $F_{n_0}(y_1, \ldots, y_{n_0}) = 0$ for some n_0;
(2) construct a homotopy $H_{n_0}(y_1, \ldots, y_{n_0+1}, t) = 0$ with $H_{n_0}(y, 0) = F_{n_0+1}(y)$ and
$$H_{n_0}(y, 1) = \begin{pmatrix} F_{n_0}(y_1, \ldots, y_{n_0}) \\ g_{n_0}(y_1, \ldots, y_{n_0+1}) \end{pmatrix}$$
for a polynomial $g_{n_0}(y_1, \ldots, y_{n_0+1})$;
(3) for each solution s of S_{n_0}, compute the solutions (s, y_{n_0+1}) of $g_{n_0}(s, y_{n_0+1}) = 0$ and denote the union of these solutions when running over all $s \in S_{n_0}$ by T_{n_0+1};
(4) use $H_{n_0}(y, t) = 0$ to compute the continuations to $t = 0$ of the solutions T_{n_0+1} of $H_{n_0}(y, 1) = 0$ and denote the set of these solutions of $H_{n_0}(y, t) = 0$ by $\widehat{S}_{n_0+1}$; and
(5) remove from $\widehat{S}_{n_0+1}$ those solutions which are "far" from being discretizations of solutions of the differential equation and call the remaining solutions S_{n_0+1}.

Repeating this procedure, we can hopefully compute for large n the solutions of $F_n(y) = 0$ corresponding the solutions of the differential equation.

There are two main problems with this procedure. First, it is not easy to apply it partial differential equations. Second, the filtering procedure going from $\widehat{S}_{n_0+1}$ to S_{n_0+1} is not obvious, e.g., complex solutions in S_{n_0} can turn into real solutions of S_{n_0+1}. This said, there is a lot of flexibility in this approach, and it can be quite effective when applied to ordinary differential equations.

A third (and very powerful) approach [14] called the *bootstrap method* (related in spirit to the filtering approach and to domain decomposition methods in numerical partial differential equations) is to use the geometry of the chosen grid to find a homotopy to the given discretization from a nearby easier-to-solve system. For example, consider Eq.2

$$\begin{aligned} a - 2y_1 + y_2 + h^2 p(y_1) &= 0 \\ y_1 - 2y_2 + y_3 + h^2 p(y_2) &= 0 \\ y_2 - 2y_3 + b + h^2 p(y_3) &= 0 \end{aligned} \qquad (3)$$

with $N = 3$, which consists of 3 polynomials in the variables y_1, y_2, y_3 with $y_0 = a$ and $y_4 = b$ for the constants a, b. A choice of a nearby easier-to-solve system could consist of

$$\begin{aligned} a - 2y_2 + b + (2h)^2 p(y_2) &= 0 \\ a - 2y_1 + y_2 + h^2 p(y_1) &= 0 \\ y_2 - 2y_3 + b + h^2 p(y_3) &= 0. \end{aligned} \tag{4}$$

Note the first equation of the simpler system is just Eq.2 with the nodes x_0, x_2, x_4. After solving this for y_2, the second equation of the simpler system is Eq.2 with the nodes x_0, x_1, x_2 on $[x_0, x_2]$ and the third equation is just Eq.2 with the nodes x_2, x_3, x_4 on $[x_2, x_4]$. This will work an the same way when $N + 1 = km$ is a product of two integers $k \geq 2$ and $m \geq 2$. The simpler system would consist of

(1) Eq.2 for the nodes $0 = x_0, x_m, x_{2m}, \ldots, x_{km} = b$;
(2) Eq.2 on $[x_k, x_{(k+1)j}]$ for the nodes $x_{kj}, x_{kj+1}, \ldots, x_{kj+k}$ for $j = 0, \ldots, m-1$.

A fourth approach is to take a solution we know, which depends on a parameter, and change the parameter until a bifurcation occurs, and then follow the solution along a different branch occurring at the given bifurcation. This has been a surprisingly successful approach applied to a sequence of successively more complicated systems of differential equations arising in tumor growth (see [10–13, 16]). All of these examples have very nice bifurcations, i.e., the tangent cones consist of two reduced lines. A numerical algorithm to compute the tangent cone in general would be useful. For more complicated bifurcations, something along the lines of a local irreducible decomposition computed off local information is needed: the result [8] depends on global information that is not available on the large polynomial systems arising from differential equations.

Finally, I would like to mention a surprising success [15] that came from applying algebraic geometric ideas to the numerical solution of polynomial systems. Hyperbolic conservations laws are a class of differential equations that arise in many places often with discontinuous solutions, e.g., shockwaves from explosions. For these problems, there are often positive dimensional sets of solutions with the physically realistic time-invariant solution picked out by minimizing auxiliary quantities. For many of these a theoretical way to pick out the realistic solution is to add a term ϵD, where D is something like a Laplacian to the system. This perturbed system has a unique solution, which "theoretically" goes to the true solution when ϵ goes to zero. I say theoretically, because the discretization is very singular when $\epsilon = 0$, and the standard numerical method to find the physically realistic solution is time-marching. Of course, for numerical algebraic geometers, seeing a parameter, i.e., ϵ in this case, going to zero, the first thought is *use an endgame.* So as a "proof of concept," we used the Cauchy Endgame [20] in Bertini [5] to compute the limit when $\epsilon \longrightarrow 0$. This led to [15]. The surprise is that the endgame applied to the theoretical approach (not thought of as practical numerically) is remarkably better than the standard numerical approach.

ACKNOWLEDGMENTS

The work is supported in part by the National Science Foundation under Grant No. NSF ACI-1440607.

REFERENCES

[1] E. L. Allgower, D. J. Bates, A. J. Sommese, and C. W. Wampler. 2010. Solution of polynomial systems derived from differential equations. *Computing* 76 (2010), 1–10.

[2] E. L. Allgower, S. G. Cruceanu, and S. Tavener. 2009. Application of numerical continuation to compute all solutions of semilinear elliptic equations. *Adv. Geom.* 9, 3 (2009), 371–400. https://doi.org/10.1515/ADVGEOM.2009.020

[3] E. L. Allgower, S. G. Cruceanu, and S. Tavener. 2009. Turning points and bifurcations for homotopies of analytic maps. In *Interactions of classical and numerical algebraic geometry.* Contemp. Math., Vol. 496. Amer. Math. Soc., Providence, RI, 1–10. https://doi.org/10.1090/conm/496/09715

[4] D. J. Bates, J. D. Hauenstein, A. J. Sommese, and Charles W. Wampler. [n. d.]. Bertini: Software for Numerical Algebraic Geometry. Available at bertini.nd.edu with permanent doi: dx.doi.org/10.7274/R0H41PB5.

[5] D. J. Bates, J. D. Hauenstein, A. J. Sommese, and C. W. Wampler. 2013. *Numerically solving polynomial systems with Bertini.* Software, Environments, and Tools, Vol. 25. Society for Industrial and Applied Mathematics (SIAM), Philadelphia, PA. xx+352 pages.

[6] D. J. Bates, J. D. Hauenstein, A. J. Sommese, and C. W. Wampler, II. 2008. Adaptive multiprecision path tracking. *SIAM J. Numer. Anal.* 46, 2 (2008), 722–746. https://doi.org/10.1137/060658862

[7] D. J. Bates, J. D. Hauenstein, A. J. Sommese, and C. W. Wampler, II. 2009. Stepsize control for path tracking. In *Interactions of classical and numerical algebraic geometry.* Contemp. Math., Vol. 496. Amer. Math. Soc., Providence, RI, 21–31. https://doi.org/10.1090/conm/496/09717

[8] D. A. Brake, J. D. Hauenstein, and A. J. Sommese. 2016. Numerical Local Irreducible Decomposition. In *Mathematical Aspects of Computer and Information Sciences,* I. S. Kotsireas, S. M. Rump, and C. K. Yap (Eds.). Springer International Publishing, Cham, 124–129.

[9] W. Hao, J. D. Hauenstein, B. Hu, Y. Liu, A. J. Sommese, and Y.-T. Zhang. 2011. Multiple stable steady states of a reaction-diffusion model on zebrafish dorsal-ventral patterning. *Discrete Contin. Dyn. Syst. Ser. S* 4, 6 (2011), 1413–1428. https://doi.org/10.3934/dcdss.2011.4.1413

[10] W. Hao, J. D. Hauenstein, B. Hu, Y. Liu, A. J. Sommese, and Y.-T. Zhang. 2012. Bifurcation for a free boundary problem modeling the growth of a tumor with a necrotic core. *Nonlinear Anal. Real World Appl.* 13, 2 (2012), 694–709. https://doi.org/10.1016/j.nonrwa.2011.08.010

[11] W. Hao, J. D. Hauenstein, B. Hu, Y. Liu, A. J. Sommese, and Y.-T. Zhang. 2012. Continuation along bifurcation branches for a tumor model with a necrotic core. *J. Sci. Comput.* 53, 2 (2012), 395–413. https://doi.org/10.1007/s10915-012-9575-x

[12] W. Hao, J. D. Hauenstein, B. Hu, T. McCoy, and A. J. Sommese. 2013. Computing steady-state solutions for a free boundary problem modeling tumor growth by Stokes equation. *J. Comput. Appl. Math.* 237, 1 (2013), 326–334. https://doi.org/10.1016/j.cam.2012.06.001

[13] W. Hao, J. D. Hauenstein, B. Hu, and A. J. Sommese. 2011. A three-dimensional steady-state tumor system. *Appl. Math. Comput.* 218, 6 (2011), 2661–2669. https://doi.org/10.1016/j.amc.2011.08.006

[14] W. Hao, J. D. Hauenstein, B. Hu, and A. J. Sommese. 2014. A bootstrapping approach for computing multiple solutions of differential equations. *J. Comput. Appl. Math.* 258 (2014), 181–190. https://doi.org/10.1016/j.cam.2013.09.007

[15] W. Hao, J. D. Hauenstein, C.-W. Shu, A. J. Sommese, Z. Xu, and Y.-T. Zhang. 2013. A homotopy method based on WENO schemes for solving steady state problems of hyperbolic conservation laws. *J. Comput. Phys.* 250 (2013), 332–346.

[16] W. Hao, B. Hu, and A. J. Sommese. 2013. Cell Cycle Control and Bifurcation for a Free Boundary Problem Modeling Tissue Growth. *Journal of Scientific Computing* 56, 2 (01 Aug 2013), 350–365. https://doi.org/10.1007/s10915-012-9678-4

[17] W. Hao, B. Hu, and A. J. Sommese. 2014. Numerical algebraic geometry and differential equations. In *Future vision and trends on shapes, geometry and algebra.* Springer Proc. Math. Stat., Vol. 84. Springer, London, 39–53. https://doi.org/10.1007/978-1-4471-6461-6_3

[18] J. D. Hauenstein, A. J. Sommese, and C. W. Wampler. 2011. Regeneration homotopies for solving systems of polynomials. *Math. Comp.* 80 (2011), 345–377.

[19] A. E. Lindsay, W. Hao, and A. J. Sommese. 2015. Vibrations of thin plates with small clamped patches. *Proc. A.* 471, 2184 (2015), 20150474, 19. https://doi.org/10.1098/rspa.2015.0474

[20] A. P. Morgan, A. J. Sommese, and C. W. Wampler. 1991. Computing singular solutions to nonlinear analytic systems. *Numer. Math.* 58, 7 (1991), 669–684.

[21] J. Stoer and R. Bulirsch. 2002. *Introduction to numerical analysis* (third ed.). Texts in Applied Mathematics, Vol. 12. Springer-Verlag, New York. xvi+744 pages. Translated from the German by R. Bartels, W. Gautschi and C. Witzgall.

Thirty Years of Virtual Substitution

Foundations, Techniques, Applications

Thomas Sturm
CNRS, Inria, and the University of Lorraine, France
Max Planck Institute for Informatics and Saarland University, Germany
thomas@thomas-sturm.de

ABSTRACT

In 1988, Weispfenning published a seminal paper introducing a substitution technique for quantifier elimination in the linear theories of ordered and valued fields. The original focus was on complexity bounds including the important result that the decision problem for Tarski Algebra is bounded from below by a double exponential function. Soon after, Weispfenning's group began to implement substitution techniques in software in order to study their potential applicability to real world problems. Today virtual substitution has become an established computational tool, which greatly complements cylindrical algebraic decomposition. There are powerful implementations and applications with a current focus on satisfiability modulo theory solving and qualitative analysis of biological networks.

CCS CONCEPTS

• **Computing methodologies → Equation and inequality solving algorithms**; *Algebraic algorithms*;

KEYWORDS

Real quantifier elimination, virtual substitution

ACM Reference Format:

Thomas Sturm. 2018. Thirty Years of Virtual Substitution: Foundations, Techniques, Applications. In *ISSAC '18: 2018 ACM International Symposium on Symbolic and Algebraic Computation, July 16–19, 2018, New York, NY, USA.* ACM, New York, NY, USA, 6 pages. https://doi.org/10.1145/3208976.3209030

1 REAL QUANTIFIER ELIMINATION

The following formal statement φ over the reals asks whether or not one can find for all $x \in \mathbb{R}$ some $y \in \mathbb{R}$ such that a certain polynomial $p \in \mathbb{Z}[a, b, x, y]$ is strictly positive while another such polynomial q is not positive:

$$\varphi \doteq \forall x \exists y (p > 0 \land q \leq 0), \tag{1}$$

where $p \doteq x^2 + xy + b$ and $q \doteq x + ay^2 + b$. We have to expect that the validity of φ depends on the choices of real values for the *parameters* a and b. A solution is probably not easy to see right away. It gets easier when considering $\neg\varphi$, which is equivalent to $\exists x \forall y (p \leq 0 \lor q > 0)$. When $a \geq 0$, we can choose $x = -b + 1$ to satisfy $q > 0$. When $b \leq 0$, we can choose $x = 0$ to satisfy $p \leq 0$. Thus $a \geq 0 \lor b \leq 0$ implies $\neg\varphi$. Equivalently, φ implies

$$\varphi' \doteq a < 0 \land b > 0.$$

Vice versa, it is not too hard to see that φ' also implies φ.

Formally, we are considering interpreted first-order logic with equality over a finite language $L = (0, 1, +, -, \cdot, =, \leq, <, \neq)$ where all symbols have their usual interpretations over the reals. We assume w.l.o.g. that L-formulas are in *prenex normal form*

$$\varphi \doteq Q_n x_n \dots Q_1 x_1 \psi, \quad Q_i \in \{\exists, \forall\}, \quad \psi \text{ quantifier-free.}$$

If all variables occurring in ψ are quantified, in other words, if there are no parameters, φ is called an *L-sentence.*

Given a first-order L-formula φ, real *quantifier elimination (QE)* computes a quantifier-free L-formula φ' such that

$$\mathbb{R} \models \varphi \longleftrightarrow \varphi'.$$

When applying quantifier elimination to a sentence φ, the obtained quantifier-free formula φ' will not contain any variables and can be straightforwardly evaluated to either "true" or "false." This way, real quantifier elimination establishes in particular a *decision procedure.*

2 HISTORY AND SCIENTIFIC CONTEXT

The first real quantifier elimination procedure was developed by Tarski around 1930 [65] but, due to the war, published only in 1948 [66]. Tarski's procedure is not elementary recursive. As early as 1954, concluding remarks in a technical report by Davis to the US Army on an implementation of a corresponding procedure for Presburger arithmetic point at a surprisingly early interest in software implementations also of real quantifier elimination [16].

During the 1970s, Collins developed the first elementary recursive real quantifier elimination procedure [10], which was based on *cylindrical algebraic decomposition* (CAD). An implementation by Arnon was available around 1980 [3]. CAD has undergone many improvements since and establishes an active research area until today [7, 11, 43, 44]. The method is double exponential, more precisely double exponential in the number of *all* occurring variables [6]. A robust implementation is available in the interactive system Qepcad B, originally by Hong and now developed by Brown [5].

From the mid 1980s to the early 1990s there was a strong interest in the asymptotic worst-case time complexity of the real decision problem. In 1988, Davenport–Heintz [15] and Weispfenning [69] independently showed that it is doubly exponential. Weispfenning's article actually brought even stronger results: First, it showed that the decision problem is doubly exponential already for linear formulas, where there are no products between variables. Next, considering finer complexity parameters than the input word length it

ISSAC '18, July 16–19, 2018, New York, NY, USA

ACM ISBN 978-1-4503-5550-6/18/07...$15.00
https://doi.org/10.1145/3208976.3209030

showed that the problem for linear formulas is doubly exponential only in the number of quantifier alternations. Finally, it came with a corresponding quantifier elimination procedure, where the idea is for the elimination of an existential quantifier to formally substitute sufficiently many test terms derived from parametric zeros of polynomials contained in the input formula.

Subsequent research on complexity by Grigoriev, Renegar, Basu–Pollack–Roy, and others developed entirely new real quantifier elimination procedures with strong theoretical results taking into consideration even finer complexity parameters like polynomial degrees or coefficient sizes [4, 30, 48].

Virtual substitution was implemented by Weispfenning's students in the computer logic system Redlog [20, 23, 55, 56], which developed into an established tool with about 400 citations in the scientific literature pointing at quite a number of successful applications, mostly in the sciences. Such implementations require powerful heuristics, which by themselves establish significant research in symbolic computation [17, 18, 21, 25, 33, 35, 51, 58–60]. As the above-mentioned complexity results suggest, the focus is on problems with few quantifier alternations and with parameters.

We are going to discuss the development of virtual substitution from a linear method to higher degrees, which went surprisingly slow. This was caused by several factors. First, motivated by the success with real quantifier elimination, there was a focus on research on virtual substitution for various other theories, which we will address in Section 8. Second, from a practical point of view, plenty of meaningful problems have been solved with a degree bound of only 2. Third, on the one hand, the question for higher degrees had been theoretically answered already in 1997 [71], and, on the other hand, there was a strong belief that with higher degrees practical implementations would be outperformed by CAD. Recent work by Košta and his accompanying implementation paint a more positive picture [34].

3 THE LINEAR CASE FOR THE REALS

We start with Weispfenning's original result from 1988 [69]. Elimination takes place in an extended language $L' = L \cup \{\mathrm{inv}\}$ with a unary function symbol inv for multiplicative inverses. In order to avoid partial functions, one defines in the L'-structure $\mathbb{R}$ that $\mathrm{inv}(0) = 0$. Notice that, e.g., $2a^2b\,\mathrm{inv}(2a^3) = ab\,\mathrm{inv}(a^2)$ but one cannot further reduce to lowest terms without a case distinction on the vanishing of a. An L'-formula φ is called a *linear* in $x_1, \dots, x_n$ if it contains no products or multiplicative inverses of the x_i. Coefficients of the x_i are arbitrary L'-terms in the parameters. We use $\pm$ as a shorthand for listing multiple terms.

Theorem 3.1 (Linear real QE; Weispfenning, 1988). *Let ψ be a quantifier-free L'-formula linear in variables $x_1, \dots, x_n$. Write the set of atomic formulas occurring in ψ as*

$$\Psi = \{\, a_j x_1 + b_j \ \varrho_j\ 0 \mid j \in J \,\},$$

where J is a finite index set, a_j, b_j are L'-terms not containing x_1, and ϱ_j are relations from L'.

$$\mathrm{Sk}(x_1, \Psi) = \{\, -b_j\,\mathrm{inv}(a_j) \pm 1, -b_j\,\mathrm{inv}(2a_j) - b_k\,\mathrm{inv}(2a_k) \mid j, k \in J \,\}.$$

Then the following holds:

(i) *Fix real interpretations for all variables except x_1. Then for each interpretation of x_1 in $\mathbb{R}$ there is at least one $t \in \mathrm{Sk}(x_1, \Psi)$ such that all atomic formulas in Ψ evaluate identically for the considered interpretation of x_1 and t:*

$$\mathbb{R} \models \forall x_1 \bigvee_{t \in \mathrm{Sk}(x_1, \Psi)} \bigwedge_{\psi \in \Psi} (\psi \longleftrightarrow \psi[x_1/t]).$$

(ii) *This allows quantifier elimination of the innermost quantifier $Q_1 x_1$ from $Q_n x_n \dots Q_1 x_1 \psi$:*

$$\mathbb{R} \models \exists x_1 \psi \longleftrightarrow \bigvee_{t \in \mathrm{Sk}(x_1, \Psi)} \psi[x_1/t]$$

$$\mathbb{R} \models \forall x_1 \psi \longleftrightarrow \bigwedge_{t \in \mathrm{Sk}(x_1, \Psi)} \psi[x_1/t].$$

(iii) *The elimination results on the right hand sides of the bi-implications in (ii) are linear in $x_2, \dots, x_n$. Hence the theorem can be iteratively applied to $Q_2 x_2, \dots, Q_n x_n$.* □

For $j = k$ we have in particular $-b_j\,\mathrm{inv}(a_j) \in \mathrm{Sk}(x_1, \Psi)$. The set $\mathrm{Sk}(x_1, \Psi)$ is called a *Skolem set*, where Theorem 3.1(i) is the defining property of Skolem sets.

Consider the application of Theorem 3.1 for the elimination of several subsequent existential quantifiers. We can exploit the compatibility of existential quantifiers with logical disjunction to move subsequent quantifiers inside the disjunctions after each elimination step:

$$\exists x_2 \exists x_1 \psi \longleftrightarrow \exists x_2 \bigvee_t \psi[x_1/t] \longleftrightarrow \bigvee_t \exists x_2 \psi[x_1/t].$$

The same works with universal quantifiers and conjunctions. This observation has been made for Presburger arithmetic already by Reddy–Loveland in 1978 [47]. In our situation we obtain $\#\,\mathrm{Sk}(x_1, \Psi)$ many independent elimination steps for $\exists x_2$, where Skolem sets will be smaller and, more important, the terms of each Skolem set must be substituted only into the corresponding member of the disjunction. Whenever there is a *quantifier alternation*, i.e., a change between $\exists$ and $\forall$ in the prenex block, we will encounter $\forall$ in front of a disjunction or $\exists$ in front of a conjunction, and our optimization is not applicable.

Theorem 3.2 (Complexity, Weispfenning 1988). *Consider a prenex linear formula $\varphi \doteq Q_n x_n \dots Q_1 x_1 \psi$. Let a be the number of quantifier alternations, and let b be the longest occurring sequence of quantifiers without alternation. Denote by $\mathcal{T}(\mathrm{length}(\varphi))$ the time asymptotically required for the elimination of all quantifiers from φ using Theorem 3.1 as described. Then the following holds:*

(i) *$\mathcal{T}(\mathrm{length}(\varphi)) = 2 \uparrow 2 \uparrow O(\mathrm{length}(\varphi))$. This bound is tight in the sense that the corresponding time complexity of the problem is bounded from below by a function in $2 \uparrow 2 \uparrow \Omega(\mathrm{length}(\varphi))$.*
(ii) *If a is bounded, then $\mathcal{T}(\mathrm{length}(\varphi)) = 2 \uparrow O(\mathrm{length}(\varphi))$.*
(iii) *Assume that both a and b are bounded, say $a \le \alpha$ and $b \le \beta$. Then $\mathcal{T}(\mathrm{length}(\varphi)) = \mathrm{length}(\varphi) \uparrow \big((\alpha + 1) O(\beta)^{\alpha+1}\big)$. This applies in particular if n is bounded.*

Proof. The proof of the upper bounds is based on the following observations. For a term $t = a_0 + \sum_{i=1}^{n} a_i x_i$ define $\mathrm{rank}(t) = \max_{i=0}^{n} \mathrm{length}(a_i)$, which naturally extends to sets of atomic formulas. Then $\mathrm{rank}(\mathrm{Sk}(x_1, \Psi)) = O(\mathrm{rank}(\Psi))$, $\#\,\mathrm{Sk}(x_1, \Psi) = O(\#\Psi^2)$, and

$\mathrm{Sk}(x_1, \Psi)$ can be constructed in polynomial time. The result on the lower bound requires more extensive means and is only mentioned here for its importance. □

The existential decision problem had been shown to be in NP by von zur Gathen–Sieveking already in 1976 [67]. Fourier–Motzkin elimination [29, 45] is double exponential even without quantifier alternation. However, the single exponential complexity comes at a price. On input of a conjunction of atomic formulas, Fourier–Motzkin elimination preserves that form, while Theorem 3.1 produces a disjunction of conjunctions of atomic formulas (DNF). With a more algebraic choice of words, on input of a system of constraints, the theorem introduces unnecessary case distinctions.

Notice that Theorem 3.1 uses regular term substitution. The theorem was soon implemented in order to study its practical performance [9]. Two problems became apparent. First, although hardly relevant from the point of view of theoretical complexity bounds, the quadratic growth of the Skolem sets with the arithmetic means, which have the purpose to cover open intervals, significantly slowed down computation times and increased result sizes. Second, results contained nested occurrences of inv, hiding case distinctions and making them hard to understand for human readers.

For the first problem one moved to another extension language $L'' = L' \cup \{\varepsilon\}$, where ε is a constant for a positive infinitesimal, and used $-b_j \operatorname{inv}(a_j) \pm \varepsilon$ instead of $-b_j \operatorname{inv}(2a_j) - b_k \operatorname{inv}(2a_k)$. The results then contained also ε, which made the second problem even worse. It turned out that both inv and ε can be equivalently removed introducing suitable quantifier-free case distinctions. The question was then whether to remove those symbols from the final result in a post-processing step, or as early as possible during elimination. The early elimination performed way better than post-processing, and lifting this observation from an implementation detail to the mathematical level was the birth of *virtual substitution.*

Virtual substitution does not map terms to terms but atomic formulas to quantifier-free formulas. This relaxation is surprisingly strong. It not only solves both above-mentioned problems but, as we shall see soon, allows to generalize the method from the linear case to arbitrary higher degree bounds. From now on, our language is the original language L without any extensions. As an example, we give the virtual substitution of a quotient, which is not an L-term, into a linear weak inequality. The quotient comes in a pair with a *guard* guaranteeing that it is defined in $\mathbb{R}$. This pair is called a *test point.* We substitute formally and then multiply by the positive square of the denominator:

$$(\alpha x_1 + \beta \leq 0)\big[x_1 /\!\!/ \big(a \neq 0, -\tfrac{b}{a}\big)\big] \doteq a \neq 0 \wedge -\alpha a b + \beta a^2 \leq 0.$$

Virtual substitution of $t - \varepsilon$ treats the virtual substitution of t as a black-box and takes into consideration the derivative of the targeted polynomial:

$$(a x_1 + b < 0)[x_1 /\!\!/ (\chi, t - \varepsilon)] \doteq$$
$$(a x_1 + b < 0)[x_1 /\!\!/ (\chi, t)] \vee \big((a x_1 + b = 0)[x_1 /\!\!/ (\chi, t)] \wedge a > 0\big).$$

A complete set of virtual substitutions for the linear case can be found in [41].

Since $\forall x_1 \psi$ is equivalent to $\neg\exists x_1 \neg\psi$, we assume w.l.o.g. that $Q_1 = \exists$ from now on. A *positive* quantifier-free L-formula is an $\wedge$-$\vee$-combination of atomic L-formulas. L-formulas can be efficiently made positive by moving logical negations $\neg$ inside via de Morgan's laws and then eliminating them in front of atomic formulas by adapting relations and signs of terms. Language allowing this, like our L, are called *closed under negation.*

Theorem 3.3 (Improved linear real QE; Loos–Weispfenning, 1993). *Let ψ be a positive quantifier-free L-formula linear in variables $x_1, \dots, x_n$. Write the set of atomic formulas occurring in ψ as*

$$\Psi = \bigcup_{k=1}^{4} \{\, a_j x_1 + b_j \varrho_k 0 \mid j \in J_k \,\},$$

where J_k are finite index sets, a_j, b_j are L-terms not containing x_1, and $(\varrho_1, \dots, \varrho_4) \doteq (=, \leq, <, \neq)$ are relations from L. Denote $S_j = -\frac{b_j}{a_j}$ and define

$$E(x_1, \Psi) = \big\{(\mathrm{true}, \infty)\big\} \cup$$
$$\big\{\, (a_j \neq 0, S_j) \;\big|\; j \in J_1 \cup J_2 \,\big\} \cup \big\{\, (a_j \neq 0, S_j - \varepsilon) \;\big|\; j \in J_3 \cup J_4 \,\big\}.$$

Then $E(x_1, \Psi)$ allows quantifier elimination of an innermost existential quantifier $\exists x_1$ from $Q_n x_n \dots Q_2 x_2 \exists x_1 \psi$ via virtual substitution:

$$\mathbb{R} \models \exists x_1 \psi \longleftrightarrow \bigvee_{t \in E(x_1, \Psi)} \psi[x_1 /\!\!/ t].$$

The elimination result on the right hand side of the bi-implication is linear in $x_2, \dots, x_n$ so that the theorem can be iteratively applied to $\exists x_2, \dots, \exists x_n$.

Proof. Fix a real interpretation ι for all variables except x_1, and consider the set $S = \{\, r \in \mathbb{R} \mid \mathbb{R}, \iota \cup \{x_1 = r\} \models \psi \,\}$ of satisfying values with respect to ι for x_1. If $S = \emptyset$, then there is nothing to prove. Otherwise $E(x_1, \Psi)$ must contain at least one test term t such that $\mathbb{R}, \iota \models \psi[x_1 /\!\!/ t]$. If S is unbounded from above, then we have $t = \infty$. Assume now that $\sup S = s \in \mathbb{R}$. If $s \in S$, then $s = S_j$ with $j \in J_1 \cup J_2$, and we have $(\mathrm{true}, s) \in E(x_1, \Psi)$. If $s \notin S$, then $s = S_j$ with $j \in J_3 \cup J_4$, and we have $(\mathrm{true}, s - \varepsilon) \in E(x_1, \Psi)$. □

To illustrate the limitation to positive formulas, consider the non-positive L-formula $\exists x \psi$ with $\psi \doteq \neg(x \neq 0)$. Elimination would fail with $E(x_1, \Psi) = \{(1 \neq 0, -\varepsilon), (\mathrm{true}, \infty)\}$ from the theorem, because ψ holds for $x = 0$, which is not simulated by either of the two elements of E. This also shows that $E(x_1, \Psi)$ is not a Skolem set.

4 THE QUADRATIC CASE FOR THE REALS

An L-formula φ is *quadratic* in x_1 if all occurring terms can be written as $t = a x_1^2 + b x_1 + c$, where the coefficients a, b, c are polynomials not containing x_1. We discuss the virtual substitution of one root of such a quadratic polynomial t into an equation $g = 0$. Univariate division with remainder yields

$$g = q t + \alpha x_1 + \beta, \tag{2}$$

where α and β do not contain x_1. Since we are considering a root of t, we can as well substitute into the linear remainder:

$$(\alpha x_1 + \beta = 0)\big[x /\!\!/ \big(a \neq 0 \wedge -\Delta < 0, \tfrac{-b+\sqrt{\Delta}}{2a}\big)\big] \doteq \tag{3}$$
$$a \neq 0 \wedge -\Delta < 0 \wedge (-\alpha b + 2\beta a)^2 = \alpha^2 \Delta \wedge (-\alpha b + 2\beta a)\alpha \leq 0.$$

To understand this substitution consider the formal substitution

$$\alpha \frac{-b + \sqrt{\Delta}}{2a} + \beta = \frac{(-\alpha b + 2\beta a) + \alpha\sqrt{\Delta}}{2a}.$$

The L-formula in (3) expresses that the two summands of the numerator have equal absolute values and that their signs are opposite or both zero. A complete set of virtual substitutions for the quadratic case can be found in [71].

THEOREM 4.1 (QUADRATIC REAL QE; WEISPFENNING, 1997). *Let ψ be a positive quantifier-free L-formula at most quadratic in x_1. Write the set of atomic formulas occurring in ψ as*

$$\Psi = \bigcup_{k=1}^{4} \{ a_j x_1^2 + b_j x_1 + c_j \ \varrho_k \ 0 \mid j \in J_k \},$$

where J_k are finite index sets, a_j, b_j, c_j are L-terms not containing x_1, and $(\varrho_1, \dots, \varrho_4) \doteq (=, \leq, <, \neq)$ are relations from L. Denote $S_j = -\frac{c_j}{b_j}$, $\Delta_j = b^2 - 4ac$, $R_j^{\pm} = \frac{-b_j \pm \sqrt{\Delta_j}}{2a_j}$, and define

$$E(x_1, \Psi) = \{(\text{true}, \infty)\} \cup$$
$$\{(a_j \neq 0 \land -\Delta_j \leq 0, R_j^{\pm}), (a_j = 0 \land b_j \neq 0, S_j) \mid j \in J_1 \cup J_2\} \cup$$
$$\{(a_j \neq 0 \land -\Delta_j \leq 0, R_j^{\pm} - \varepsilon),$$
$$(a_j = 0 \land b_j \neq 0, S_j - \varepsilon) \mid j \in J_3 \cup J_4\}.$$

Then $E(x_1, \Psi)$ allows quantifier elimination of an innermost existential quantifier $\exists x_1$ from $Q_n x_n \dots Q_2 x_2 \exists x_1 \psi$ via virtual substitution:

$$\mathbb{R} \models \exists x_1 \psi \longleftrightarrow \bigvee_{t \in E(x_1, \Psi)} \psi[x_1 /\!\!/ t]. \qquad \square$$

The proof is analogous to the proof of Theorem 3.3. However, there is no guarantee that Theorem 4.1 can be iterated. In Equation (3) above one can see that degrees are doubled within α, β, a, b, which can all contain $x_2, \dots, x_n$. Applying the theorem to the inner $\exists y$ of our introductory example (1) we obtain in the output, e.g., $ab^2 + 2abx^2 + ax^4 + bx^2 + x^3$, which is not quadratic in the universally quantified x anymore. When applying suitable simplification heuristics during elimination, input formulas modelling real world situations, in contrast to random input, are surprisingly well-behaved concerning the increase of degrees.

Against this background, theoretical complexity results would have to weigh efficiency against incompleteness. Practical computing times appear compatible with Theorem 3.2 also in the quadratic case.

5 HIGHER DEGREES FOR THE REALS

The *real type* of a polynomial is the finite sequence of the signs assumed from $-\infty$ to ∞. For instance, $x_1^2 - 2$ has real type $(1, 0, -1, 0, 1)$, because both its leading coefficient and its discriminant Δ are positive. For a generic quadratic polynomial $a_j x_1^2 + b_j x_1 + c_j$ there are 6 possible real types when a_j does not vanish plus 2 possible real types when a_j does vanish. The former are characterized by the signs of a_j and Δ_j, and the latter are characterized by the sign of b_j. With this intuition we replace $E(x_1, \Psi)$ from Theorem 4.1 with the following variant, which establishes a case distinction on real types omitting two of them with $\Delta_j < 0$, where there are no real roots:

$$E'(x_1, \Psi) = \{(\text{true}, \infty)\} \cup \tag{4}$$
$$\{(-a_j < 0 \land -\Delta_j < 0, R_j^{\pm}), (-a_j < 0 \land \Delta_j = 0, R_j^{+}),$$
$$(a_j < 0 \land -\Delta_j < 0, R_j^{\pm}), (a_j < 0 \land \Delta_j = 0, R_j^{+}),$$
$$(a_j = 0 \land -b_j < 0, S_j), (a_j = 0 \land b_j < 0, S_j) \mid j \in J_1 \cup J_2\} \cup$$
"the same with $R_j^{\pm} - \varepsilon$, $R_j^{+} - \varepsilon$, and $S_j - \varepsilon$ for $j \in J_3 \cup J_4$".

We will now discuss a degree bound of 3 in such generality that our constructions work for arbitrary degree bounds. The first ingredient is the real types. There are still only finitely many of them, for which we need quantifier-free descriptions. To understand that this is possible consider a generic polynomial $f = ax_1^3 + bx_1^2 + cx_1 + d$ and, e.g., the real type $(-1, 0, 1, 0, 1)$. One can easily construct a first-order formula with parameters $a, \dots, d$ stating that f has that real type, viz. $\tau \doteq \exists r_1 \exists r_2 \forall x_1 \xi$, where

$$\xi \doteq r_1 < r_2 \land (x_1 < r_1 \longrightarrow f < 0) \land (r_1 < x_1 < r_2 \longrightarrow 0 < f) \land$$
$$(x_1 = r_2 \longrightarrow f = 0) \land (r_2 < x_1 \longrightarrow 0 < f).$$

Since Tarski gave us real quantifier elimination in 1948, we know that there is an equivalent quantifier-free description τ'. The second ingredient is the representation of the roots. They are simply numbered from left to right, like $(\tau', 1)$ and $(\tau', 2)$ in our example.

The third ingredient are the virtual substitutions. Recall from our discussion of (2) in the previous section that using division with remainder we must explain virtual substitution only into atomic formulas $g \ \varrho \ 0$, where $g = \alpha x_1^2 + \beta x_1 + \gamma$ is of degree less than our bound 3. There are only finitely many such atomic formulas. Here is an example with our generic polynomials f and g:

$$(g < 0)[x_1 /\!\!/ (f, \tau', 1)] \doteq \tau' \land \sigma',$$

where σ' is a quantifier-free equivalent of the first-order description $\sigma \doteq \exists r_1 \exists r_2 \forall x_1 (\xi \land g[x_1/r_1] < 0)$.

Virtual substitutions for generic polynomials can be used for arbitrary polynomials as follows. Let f^*, g^* be polynomials of x_1-degree 3 and 2, respectively. The coefficients of $x_1^3, \dots, x_1^0$ in f^* and g^* are multivariate polynomials not containing x_1. Let $\tau'[f/f^*]$ and $\sigma'[f/f^*, g/g^*]$ denote the substitution of the coefficients of f^* for $a, \dots, d$ and the coefficients of g^* for $\alpha, \dots, \gamma$. Then

$$(g^* < 0)[x_1 /\!\!/ (f^*, \tau', 1)] \doteq \tau'[f/f^*] \land \sigma'[f/f^*, g/g^*].$$

THEOREM 5.1 (REAL QE FOR DEGREE BOUND B; KOŠTA 2016). *Let ψ be a positive quantifier-free L-formula of degree at most B in x_1. Write the set of atomic formulas occurring in ψ as*

$$\Psi = \bigcup_{k=1}^{4} \{ f_j(x_1, \dots x_n, y) \ \varrho_k \ 0 \mid j \in J_k \},$$

where J_k are finite index sets and $(\varrho_1, \dots, \varrho_4) \doteq (=, \leq, <, \neq)$ are relations from L. Let T be a finite table of quantifier-free descriptions of real types for generic polynomials up to degree B. For a type $\tau \in T$ let $\mu(\tau)$ be the number of distinct real roots. Let $\Sigma = \{\sigma_{\varrho, b, \tau, r}\}$ for

$$\varrho \in \{=, \leq, <, \neq\}, \quad 1 \leq b \leq B - 1, \quad \tau \in T, \quad 1 \leq r \leq \mu(\tau)$$

be another finite table. Each $\sigma_{\varrho, b, \tau, r}$ is a quantifier-free description of the virtual substitution of the r-th root of a generic polynomial f of type τ into $g \ \varrho \ 0$, where g is another generic polynomial of degree b. Define

$$E(x_1, \psi) = \{(\text{true}, \infty)\} \cup \bigcup_{j \in J_1 \cup J_2} \bigcup_{\tau \in T} \bigcup_{1 \leq r \leq \mu(\tau)} (f_j, \tau, r)$$
$$\cup \bigcup_{j \in J_3 \cup J_4} \bigcup_{\tau \in T} \bigcup_{1 \leq r \leq \mu(\tau)} (f_j, \tau, r) - \varepsilon.$$

Then $E(x_1, \Psi)$ allows quantifier elimination of an innermost existential quantifier $\exists x_1$ from $Q_n x_n \dots Q_2 x_2 \exists x_1 \psi$ via virtual substitution:

$$\mathbb{R} \models \exists x_1 \psi \longleftrightarrow \bigvee_{t \in E(x_1, \Psi)} \psi[x_1 /\!\!/ t]. \qquad \square$$

The problem is, of course, to find suitable quantifier-free tables T and Σ. Furthermore, recall that with Equation (4) we have introduced case distinctions that were not necessary in Theorem 4.1. Accordingly, we actually want to find substitution formulas in Σ that work for several combinations of real types τ and root indices r simultaneously. This is known as *clustering*.

Košta has given such tables for $B = 3$, including clustering, and provided a generic implementation of Theorem 5.1, where T and Σ exist as isolated tables in software so that the implementation can be instantiated for arbitrary degree bounds without any further programming [34]. Having effectively separated logic from real algebraic geometry, the development of useful tables for higher degrees is now a challenging task for the entire community in the spirit of [40], where every progress will have considerable impact for application scenarios of real quantifier elimination.

6 ALGORITHMS AND APPLICATIONS

There are comprehensive experiences with implementations and practical computations for various domains, where the reals clearly dominate. Such computations are feasible only in combination with fast and strong heuristics. In the first place there is simplification of quantifier-free formulas, where the central method in use is still the *deep simplification* from 1997, which is based on the combination of *additive smart simplification* with *implicit theory* construction during recursion [21]. Black-box/white-box simplification [8] appears very interesting. It would be important to study how to integrate this with the current simplification framework.

Another aspect are heuristics for *degree reductions*. Those are equivalence transformations heuristically working against the increase of degrees with non-linear real virtual substitution, specifically polynomial factorization and degree shifts [25, 34, 35].

Modern implementations of virtual substitution do not naively compute elimination sets from sets of atomic formulas. Instead *structural elimination sets* are based on *prime constituents* and *co-prime constituents*. Those are arbitrary subformulas with finitely or co-finitely many solutions, respectively. Virtual substitutions are not applied to the original quantifier free formula ψ but before *condensing* is used to prune ψ based on the origin within ψ of the test point to be substituted [34].

For an overview of applications see, e.g., [19, 25–28, 52, 53, 57–62, 68] and citations of the Redlog standard reference [20], e.g., on Google Scholar.

7 IMPACT BEYOND COMPUTER ALGEBRA

Virtual substitution for the reals is well known in the satisfiability modulo theories (SMT) community. There it is typically employed in combination with DPLL(T) [46] as a component of theory solvers for linear and non-linear real arithmetic [1, 2, 13, 14]. Independently, Redlog took part in the SMT-COMP 2017 competition and won the section for non-linear real arithmetic using plain virtual substitution with CAD as a fallback option when exceeding the degree bound.

8 OTHER DOMAINS

Already in 1988, Weispfenning discussed Skolem sets for the linear theory of discretely valued fields [69]. In 1995, an improved version using positive formulas and virtual substitution was implemented in Redlog [50]. In 1999, deep simplification for discretely valued fields was developed and implemented [22]. In 2000, discrete valuations were supplemented with divisibility predicates and virtual substitution was introduced also for the linear theory of non-discretely valued fields [54]. In 2001, the methods and implementations for discretely valued fields were used as a component within a solver for parametric systems of linear congruences [24].

In 2002, virtual substitution was applied to term algebras over suitably expanded finite functional first-order languages [63], equivalent to Malcev's relational expansions [42]. The complexity is in the 4th class of the Grzegorcyk hierarchy [31], which is in a sense optimal, since the problem is provably not elementary recursive. The method is implemented in Redlog [32].

In 2003, virtual substitution was applied to *parametric quantified Boolean formulas (parametric QBF)*, i.e., propositional logic with existential and universal quantifiers over propositional variables [49]. The elimination sets are simply $\{\text{true}, \text{false}\}$, representing the entire finite domain. With the size of the elimination sets in $O(1)$ the overall complexity is single exponential even with unbounded quantifier alternation. The approach and the complexity result work for all finite domains where all domain elements can be expressed as terms. This rather naive approach to propositional reasoning turns out surprisingly strong when combined with a propositional variant of the deep simplification. For certain QBF benchmarks this combination turned out even superior to adaptions of context-driven clause learning (CDCL) to QBF [64]. There is an implementation in Redlog [49].

During 2005–2009, there was considerable research on virtual substitution for Presburger Arithmetic with several extensions. Most of this work has been implemented in Redlog [36–39]. In retrospect, earlier work by Weispfenning [70] in this area and maybe even Cooper's work [12] already resembled virtual substitution to some extent.

ACKNOWLEDGMENTS

This work has been partly supported by the European Union's Horizon 2020 research and innovation programme under grant agreement No H2020-FETOPEN-2015-CSA 712689 SC-SQUARE.

REFERENCES

[1] Erika Ábrahám, John Abbott, Bernd Becker, Anna M. Bigatti, Martin Brain, Bruno Buchberger, Alessandro Cimatti, James H. Davenport, Matthew England, Pascal Fontaine, Stephen Forrest, Alberto Griggio, Daniel Kroening, Werner M. Seiler, and Thomas Sturm. 2016. SC^2: Satisfiability Checking Meets Symbolic Computation. In *Proc. CICM 2016*. LNCS, Vol. 9791. 28–43.

[2] Erika Abraham, Jasper Nalbach, and Gereon Kremer. 2017. Embedding the Virtual Substitution Method in the Model Constructing Satisfiability Calculus Framework. In *Proc. of the 2nd International Workshop on Satisfiability Checking and Symbolic Computation*. CEUR Workshop Proceedings, Vol. 1974.

[3] Dennis S. Arnon. 1981. *Algorithms for the Geometry of Semi-Algebraic Sets.* Technical Report 436. Comput. Sci. Dept., University of Wisconsin-Madison.

[4] Saugata Basu, Richard Pollack, and Marie-Françoise Roy. 1996. On the Combinatorial and Algebraic Complexity of Quantifier Elimination. *J. ACM* 43, 6 (1996), 1002–1045.

[5] Christopher W. Brown. 2003. QEPCAD B: A Program for Computing with Semi-algebraic Sets Using CADs. *ACM SIGSAM Bulletin* 37, 4 (2003), 97–108.

[6] Christopher W. Brown and James H. Davenport. 2007. The Complexity of Quantifier Elimination and Cylindrical Algebraic Decomposition. In *Proc. ISSAC 2007.* ACM, 54–60.
[7] Christopher W. Brown and Marek Košta. 2014. Constructing a Single Cell in Cylindrical Algebraic Decomposition. *J. Symb. Comput.* 70 (2014), 14–48.
[8] Christopher W. Brown and Adam Strzeboński. 2010. Black-Box/White-Box Simplification and Applications to Quantifier Elimination. In *Proc. ISSAC 2010.* ACM, 69–76.
[9] Klaus-Dieter Burhenne. 1990. *Implementierung eines Algorithmus zur Quantorenelimination für lineare reelle Probleme.* Diploma Thesis. University of Passau, Germany.
[10] George E. Collins. 1975. Quantifier Elimination for the Elementary Theory of Real Closed Fields by Cylindrical Algebraic Decomposition. In *Automata Theory and Formal Languages. 2nd GI Conference.* LNCS, Vol. 33. 134–183.
[11] George E. Collins and Hoon Hong. 1991. Partial Cylindrical Algebraic Decomposition for Quantifier Elimination. *J. Symb. Comput.* 12, 3 (1991), 299–328.
[12] David C. Cooper. 1972. Theorem Proving in Arithmetic without Multiplication. In *Proc. 7th Annual Machine Intelligence Workshop.* Machine Intelligence, Vol. 7. Chapter 5, 91–99.
[13] Florian Corzilius. 2016. *Integrating Virtual Substitution into Strategic SMT Solving.* Doctoral Dissertation. RWTH Aachen University, Germany.
[14] Florian Corzilius and Erika Abraham. 2011. Virtual Substitution for SMT Solving. In *Proc. FCT 2011.* LNCS, Vol. 6914. 360–371.
[15] James H. Davenport and Joos Heintz. 1988. Real Quantifier Elimination is Doubly Exponential. *J. Symb. Comput.* 5, 1–2 (1988), 29–35.
[16] Martin Davis. 1954. *Final Report on Mathematical Procedures for Decision Problems.* Technical Report. Institute for Advanced Study, Princeton, NJ.
[17] Andreas Dolzmann. 2000. *Algorithmic Strategies for Applicable Real Quantifier Elimination.* Doctoral Dissertation. University of Passau, Germany.
[18] Andreas Dolzmann, Oliver Gloor, and Thomas Sturm. 1998. Approaches to Parallel Quantifier Elimination. In *Proc. ISSAC 1998.* ACM, 88–95.
[19] Andreas Dolzmann and Thomas Sturm. 1997. Guarded Expressions in Practice. In *Proc. ISSAC 1997.* ACM, 376–383.
[20] Andreas Dolzmann and Thomas Sturm. 1997. Redlog: Computer Algebra Meets Computer Logic. *ACM SIGSAM Bulletin* 31, 2 (1997), 2–9.
[21] Andreas Dolzmann and Thomas Sturm. 1997. Simplification of Quantifier-free Formulae over Ordered Fields. *J. Symb. Comput.* 24, 2 (1997), 209–231.
[22] Andreas Dolzmann and Thomas Sturm. 1999. P-adic Constraint Solving. In *Proc. ISSAC 1999.* ACM, 151–158.
[23] Andreas Dolzmann and Thomas Sturm. 1999. *Redlog User Manual, 2nd Edition.* Technical Report MIP-9905. FMI, University of Passau, Germany.
[24] Andreas Dolzmann and Thomas Sturm. 2001. Parametric Systems of Linear Congruences. In *Proc. CASC 2001.* Springer, 149–166.
[25] Andreas Dolzmann, Thomas Sturm, and Volker Weispfenning. 1998. A New Approach for Automatic Theorem Proving in Real Geometry. *J. Autom. Reasoning* 21, 3 (1998), 357–380.
[26] Andreas Dolzmann, Thomas Sturm, and Volker Weispfenning. 1998. Real Quantifier Elimination in Practice. In *Algorithmic Algebra and Number Theory.* Springer, 221–247.
[27] Hassan Errami, Markus Eiswirth, Dima Grigoriev, Werner M. Seiler, Thomas Sturm, and Andreas Weber. 2013. Efficient Methods to Compute Hopf Bifurcations in Chemical Reaction Networks Using Reaction Coordinates. In *Proc. CASC 2013.* LNCS, Vol. 8136. 88–99.
[28] Hassan Errami, Markus Eiswirth, Dima Grigoriev, Werner M. Seiler, Thomas Sturm, and Andreas Weber. 2015. Detection of Hopf Bifurcations in Chemical Reaction Networks Using Convex Coordinates. *J. Comput. Phys.* 291 (2015), 279–302.
[29] Joseph Fourier. 1827. Analyse des travaux de l'Académie Royale des Sciences pendant l'année 1824, Partie mathématique. In *Mémoires de l'Académie des sciences de l'Institut de France.* Vol. 7. Gauthier-Villars, Paris, France, xlvij–lv.
[30] Dima Grigoriev. 1988. Complexity of Deciding Tarski Algebra. *J. Symb. Comput.* 5, 1-2 (1988), 65–108.
[31] Andrzej Grzegorczyk. 1953. Some Classes of Recursive Functions. *Rozprawy Matematyczne* 4 (1953), 1–45.
[32] Christian Hoffelner. 2005. *Quantifier Elimination-based Parametric Solving in Term Algebras.* Diploma Thesis. University of Passau, Germany.
[33] Konstantin Korovin, Marek Košta, and Thomas Sturm. 2014. Towards Conflict-Driven Learning for Virtual Substitution. In *Proc. CASC 2014.* LNCS, Vol. 8660. 256–270.
[34] Marek Košta. 2016. *New Concepts for Real Quantifier Elimination by Virtual Substitution.* Doctoral Dissertation. Saarland University, Germany.
[35] Marek Košta, Thomas Sturm, and Andreas Dolzmann. 2016. Better Answers to Real Questions. *J. Symb. Comput.* 74 (2016), 255–275.
[36] Aless Lasaruk. 2005. *Parametrisches Integer-Solving.* Diploma Thesis. University of Passau, Germany.
[37] Aless Lasaruk and Thomas Sturm. 2007. Weak Integer Quantifier Elimination Beyond the Linear Case. In *Proc. CASC 2007.* LNCS, Vol. 4770.
[38] Aless Lasaruk and Thomas Sturm. 2007. Weak Quantifier Elimination for the Full Linear Theory of the Integers. *Appl. Algebr. Eng. Comm.* 18, 6 (2007), 545–574.
[39] Aless Lasaruk and Thomas Sturm. 2009. Effective Quantifier Elimination for Presburger Arithmetic with Infinity. In *Proc. CASC 2009.* LNCS, Vol. 5743. 195–212.
[40] Daniel Lazard. 1988. Quantifier Elimination: Optimal Solution for Two Classical Examples. *J. Symb. Comput.* 5, 1 (1988), 261–266.
[41] Rüdiger Loos and Volker Weispfenning. 1993. Applying Linear Quantifier Elimination. *Comput. J.* 36, 5 (1993), 450–462.
[42] Anatoliĭ I. Malcev. 1971. Axiomatizable Classes of Locally Free Algebras of Various Types. In *The Metamathematics of Algebraic Systems.* Studies in Logic and the Foundations of Mathematics, Vol. 66. Chapter 23, 262–281.
[43] Scott McCallum. 1988. An Improved Projection Operation for Cylindrical Algebraic Decomposition of Three-Dimensional Space. *J. Symb. Comput.* 5, 1–2 (1988), 141–161.
[44] Scott McCallum and Hoon Hong. 2016. On Using Lazard's Projection in CAD Construction. *J. Symb. Comput.* 72 (2016), 65–81.
[45] Theodore S. Motzkin. 1936. *Beiträge zur Theorie der linearen Ungleichungen.* Inaugural Dissertation. University of Basel, Switzerland.
[46] Robert Nieuwenhuis, Albert Oliveras, and Cesare Tinelli. 2006. Solving SAT and SAT Modulo Theories: From an Abstract Davis–Putnam–Logemann–Loveland Procedure to DPLL(T). *J. ACM* 53, 6 (2006), 937–977.
[47] Cattamanchi R. Reddy and Donald W. Loveland. 1978. Presburger Arithmetic with Bounded Quantifier Alternation. In *Proc. STOC 1978.* ACM, 320–325.
[48] James Renegar. 1992. On the Computational Complexity and Geometry of the First-Order Theory of the Reals. Part II. *J. Symb. Comput.* 13, 3 (1992), 301–328.
[49] Andreas M. Seidl and Thomas Sturm. 2003. Boolean Quantification in a First-Order Context. In *Proc. CASC 2003.* Institut für Informatik, TU München, Germany, 329–345.
[50] Thomas Sturm. 1995. *Lineare Quantorenelimination in bewerteten Körpern.* Diploma Thesis. University of Passau, Germany.
[51] Thomas Sturm. 1999. *Real Quantifier Elimination in Geometry.* Doctoral Dissertation. University of Passau, Germany.
[52] Thomas Sturm. 1999. Reasoning over Networks by Symbolic Methods. *Appl. Algebr. Eng. Comm.* 10, 1 (1999), 79–96.
[53] Thomas Sturm. 2000. An Algebraic Approach to Offsetting and Blending of Solids. In *Proc. CASC 2000.* Springer, 367–382.
[54] Thomas Sturm. 2000. Linear Problems in Valued Fields. *J. Symb. Comput.* 30, 2 (2000), 207–219.
[55] Thomas Sturm. 2006. New Domains for Applied Quantifier Elimination. In *Proc. CASC 2006.* LNCS, Vol. 4194. 295–301.
[56] Thomas Sturm. 2007. REDLOG Online Resources for Applied Quantifier Elimination. *Acta Academiae Aboensis, Ser. B* 67, 2 (2007), 177–191.
[57] Thomas Sturm. 2017. A Survey of Some Methods for Real Quantifier Elimination, Decision, and Satisfiability and Their Applications. *Math. Comput. Sci.* 11, 3–4 (2017), 483–502.
[58] Thomas Sturm and Ashish Tiwari. 2011. Verification and Synthesis Using Real Quantifier Elimination. In *Proc. ISSAC 2011.* ACM, 329–336.
[59] Thomas Sturm and Andreas Weber. 2008. Investigating Generic Methods to Solve Hopf Bifurcation Problems in Algebraic Biology. In *Proc. AB 2008.* LNCS, Vol. 5147. 200–215.
[60] Thomas Sturm, Andreas Weber, Essam O. Abdel-Rahman, and M'hammed El Kahoui. 2009. Investigating Algebraic and Logical Algorithms to Solve Hopf Bifurcation Problems in Algebraic Biology. *Math. Comput. Sci.* 2 (2009), 493–515.
[61] Thomas Sturm and Volker Weispfenning. 1997. Rounding and Blending of Solids by a Real Elimination Method. In *Proc. IMACS World Congress 1997.* Vol. 2. Wissenschaft & Technik Verlag, Berlin, Germany, 727–732.
[62] Thomas Sturm and Volker Weispfenning. 1998. Computational Geometry Problems in Redlog. In *Automated Deduction in Geometry.* LNAI, Vol. 1360. 58–86.
[63] Thomas Sturm and Volker Weispfenning. 2002. Quantifier Elimination in Term Algebras. The Case of Finite Languages. In *Proc. CASC 2002.* Institut für Informatik, TU München, Germany, 285–300.
[64] Thomas Sturm and Christoph Zengler. 2010. Parametric Quantified SAT Solving. In *Proc. ISSAC 2010.* ACM, 77–84.
[65] Alfred Tarski. 1930. The Completeness of Elementary Algebra and Geometry. (1930). Reprinted by CNRS, Institute Blaise Pascal, Paris, 1967.
[66] Alfred Tarski. 1948. *A Decision Method for Elementary Algebra and Geometry. Prepared for publication by J. C. C. McKinsey.* RAND Report R109, Revised 1951.
[67] Joachim von zur Gathen and Malte Sieveking. 1976. Weitere zum Erfüllungsproblem polynomial äquivalente kombinatorische Aufgaben. In *Komplexität von Entscheidungsproblemen.* LNCS, Vol. 43. Chapter 4, 49–71.
[68] Andreas Weber, Thomas Sturm, and Essam O. Abdel-Rahman. 2011. Algorithmic Global Criteria for Excluding Oscillations. *Bull. Math. Biol.* 73, 4 (2011), 899–916.
[69] Volker Weispfenning. 1988. The Complexity of Linear Problems in Fields. *J. Symb. Comput.* 5, 1–2 (1988), 3–27.
[70] Volker Weispfenning. 1990. The Complexity of Almost Linear Diophantine Problems. *J. Symb. Comput.* 10, 5 (1990), 395–403.
[71] Volker Weispfenning. 1997. Quantifier Elimination for Real Algebra—the Quadratic Case and Beyond. *Appl. Algebr. Eng. Comm.* 8, 2 (1997), 85–101.

Fast Algorithms for Displacement and Low-Rank Structured Matrices

Shivkumar Chandrasekaran
University of California Santa Barbara
Santa Barbara, California
shiv@ucsb.edu

Nithin Govindarajan
University of California Santa Barbara
Santa Barbara, California
ngovindarajan@ucsb.edu

Abhejit Rajagopal
University of California Santa Barbara
Santa Barbara, California
abhejit@ucsb.edu

ABSTRACT

This tutorial provides an introduction to the development of fast matrix algorithms based on the notions of displacement and various low-rank structures.

KEYWORDS

Fast matrix algorithms, displacement structure, low-rank, sequentially semi-separable, hierarchically semi-separable, Toeplitz, Hankel, Vandermonde, Cauchy, Hilbert, Fast multipole method

ACM Reference Format:
Shivkumar Chandrasekaran, Nithin Govindarajan, and Abhejit Rajagopal. 2018. Fast Algorithms for Displacement and Low-Rank Structured Matrices. In *ISSAC '18: 2018 ACM International Symposium on Symbolic and Algebraic Computation, July 16–19, 2018, New York, NY, USA.* ACM, New York, NY, USA, 6 pages. https://doi.org/10.1145/3208976.3209025

1 INTRODUCTION

In this tutorial we give a broad introduction to the class of displacement structured and other low-rank structured matrices that have come to recent prominence. Due to page limitations this paper only provides a short summary of the actual topics that will be explained in the tutorial itself.

As is well-known, it costs roughly $O(n^3)$ arithmetic operations to multiply two $n \times n$ generic matrices (as long as no Strassen-style fast multiplication algorithm is used[1]). Similarly, the solution to a generic linear system of of n equations in n unknowns requires $O(n^3)$ operations (again assuming we do not use a fast matrix multiplication algorithm).

However, when we consider a *structured* family of matrices it might be possible to find practically fast algorithms. Famous examples include the FFT method [10] for multiplying the discrete Fourier series matrix rapidly. As a fallout of the FFT, we get a fast method for convolution and as a result a large number of fast algorithms for polynomials [14], which in turn yield fast algorithms for Toeplitz matrices. However, many of these fast algorithms did not prove so useful in practice [17]. Some of them, were too slow for reasonable values of n, whereas others required large number of bits to hold intermediate values.

Eventually some of these shortcomings were over come by exploiting low-rank structures that are lurking in these problems (e.g. [6, 8, 30]). In this tutorial we focus on two aspects of this. The first is the *displacement structure* approach pioneered by Kailath et. al. [21, 22]. The second is the *low-rank structured* approach pioneered by Rokhlin [18, 26, 27], Hackbusch [19], Eidelman and Gohberg [13], Dewilde and van der Veen [12], and others.

[1]We discard Strassen style algorithms as they are slower than the standard algorithm for reasonable values of n.

ISSAC '18, July 16–19, 2018, New York, NY, USA

ACM ISBN 978-1-4503-5550-6/18/07...$15.00
https://doi.org/10.1145/3208976.3209025

2 DISPLACEMENT STRUCTURE

We eschew generality in this presentation and also do not worry about *superfast* algorithms. For simplicity we restrict ourselves to the real field.

Let the linear operator $\mathcal{L}[A, B] : \mathcal{R}^{n\times n} \to \mathcal{R}^{n\times n}$ be defined as

$$\mathcal{L}[A, B](T) = T - ATB^T,$$

where $A, B \in \mathcal{R}^{n\times n}$. We will call such a linear operator as a displacement operator. We say that the matrix T has a displacement structure (wrt $\mathcal{L}[A, B]$) if the rank of $\mathcal{L}[A, B](T)$ is small compared to n. The standard examples are Toeplitz, Hankel, Vandermonde, Cauchy and Pick matrices.

- Let Z denote the down-shift matrix
$$Z_{i,j} = \begin{cases} 0, & i \neq j - 1 \\ 1, & i = j - 1. \end{cases}$$
Then it is easy to check that if T is a Toeplitz matrix rank of $\mathcal{L}[Z, Z](T)$ is at most 2. Conversely, any T for which rank of $\mathcal{L}[Z, Z]$ is small is called a Toeplitz-like matrix.
- Let $x_i \in \mathcal{R}$ and let $D(x) = \text{diag}\{x_i\}$. Let V be the Vandermonde matrix: $V_{i,j} = x_i^j$. Then rank of $\mathcal{L}[D(x), Z](V)$ is at most 1.
- Let $0 \neq y_j \in \mathcal{R}$. Let C be the Cauchy matrix: $C_{i,j} = 1/(y_i - x_j)$. Then rank of $\mathcal{L}[D^{-1}(y), D(x)](C)$ is at most 1. Conversely any matrix C for which rank of $\mathcal{L}[D(y), D(x)](C)$ is small is called a generalized Pick matrix.

What is surprising is that the inverse has the same structure too. In fact

$$\text{rank}\,(\mathcal{L}[A, B](T)) = \text{rank}\left(\mathcal{L}[B, A]\left(T^{-1}\right)\right).$$

More trivially

$$\text{rank}\,(\mathcal{L}[A, B](T_1 + T_2)) \leq \text{rank}\,(\mathcal{L}[A, B](T_1)) + \text{rank}\,(\mathcal{L}[A, B](T_2)).$$

Unfortunately the result for products is not as nice:

$$\operatorname{rank}(\mathcal{L}[A,B](T_1T_2)) \leq \operatorname{rank}(\mathcal{L}[A,B](T_1)) + \operatorname{rank}(\mathcal{L}[A,B](T_2)) + \operatorname{rank}\left(B^TA - I\right).$$

In particular this is rather disastrous for generalized Pick (Cauchy) matrices, which will be rectified later.

We next look for fast algorithms that can exploit the displacement structure. Suppose that

$$T - ATB^T = PQ^T,$$

where $P, Q \in \mathcal{R}^{n \times p}$. If $\mathcal{L}[A,B]$ is invertible then the pair (P,Q) can be used as a more efficient representation of the matrix T as we would require only $O(np)$ numbers versus the usual $O(n^2)$ numbers. In this case the pair (P,Q) will be called **generators** for T. The question is: can we carry out the usual matrix operations faster using the pair (P,Q)? Surprisingly, this question is easier to answer for $T^{-1}x$ rather than for Tx, for $x \in \mathcal{R}^n$. In particular we will show that the LU factorization (Gaussian elimination) of T can be computed quickly in $O(n^2)$ arithmetic operations rather than the standard $O(n^3)$ operations, provided inverting $\mathcal{L}[A,B]$ itself is cheap.

We note that the displacement rank is invariant under similarity transformations

$$\operatorname{rank}\left(\mathcal{L}[VAV^{-1}, WBW^{-1}](VTW^T)\right) = \operatorname{rank}(\mathcal{L}[A,B](T)).$$

Therefore it is convenient to assume that A and B are lower triangular matrices from now on (say using the Schur decomposition). Note that for this to be effective in fast algorithms, the computation and application of V, V^{-1} W and W^{-1}, must cost less than $O(n^3)$ operations. There are extensions of the method to the case when A or B is a lower Hessenberg matrix [20], but we do not cover it here.

Let $\mathcal{L}[A,B](T)$ have low-rank with A and B lower triangular and let

$$T = \begin{matrix} 1 \\ n-1 \end{matrix} \overset{\begin{matrix} 1 & n-1 \end{matrix}}{\begin{pmatrix} T_{11} & T_{12} \\ T_{21} & T_{22} \end{pmatrix}}, \qquad S = T_{22} - T_{21}T_{11}^{-1}T_{12},$$

where S is the Schur complement of T and we have have assumed that $T_{11} \neq 0$. The key idea of fast Gaussian elimination is that S has a low-rank displacement structure that can be quickly computed from that of T. To see this, let

$$A = \begin{matrix} 1 \\ n-1 \end{matrix} \overset{\begin{matrix} 1 & n-1 \end{matrix}}{\begin{pmatrix} A_{11} & 0 \\ A_{21} & A_{22} \end{pmatrix}}, \qquad B = \begin{matrix} 1 \\ n-1 \end{matrix} \overset{\begin{matrix} 1 & n-1 \end{matrix}}{\begin{pmatrix} B_{11} & 0 \\ B_{21} & B_{22} \end{pmatrix}}.$$

Then it can be readily shown that rank of $\mathcal{L}[A_{22}, B_{22}](S)$ is at most rank of $\mathcal{L}[A,B](T)$, and furthermore the generators for S can be computed in $O(np^2)$ operations provided that the first column and row of T can be generated in $O(n)$ operations[2] from its generators (P,Q). The recursive application of this idea leads to the fast generalized Schur algorithm for computing the LU factorization of T in $O(n^2)$ operations.

For many applications already this speed-up is sufficient. However there is sometimes a need for more. For example if T is a Toeplitz matrix we can compute Tx in $O(n \log_2 n)$ operations using the FFT. The Gohberg-Semencul formulas [9, 16] show that there is a representation for T^{-1} (which might require some time to compute) such that $T^{-1}x$ can also be computed in $O(n \log_2 n)$ operations via the FFT. The displacement structure approach can also shed light on this situation.

First note that T^{-1} is a Schur complement of

$$M = \begin{bmatrix} T & I \\ -I & 0 \end{bmatrix}.$$

So we could compute the generators of T^{-1} by running the generalized Schur algorithm on M half-way through. This would be fast if M had a short displacement rank for an appropriate $\mathcal{L}[A_M, B_M]$. One potential choice is

$$A_M = \begin{bmatrix} A & \\ & A \end{bmatrix}, \qquad B_M = \begin{bmatrix} B & \\ & B \end{bmatrix},$$

provided rank of $I - AB^T$ is small. Another possibility is

$$A_M = \begin{bmatrix} A & \\ & B^{T\dagger} \end{bmatrix}, \qquad B_M = \begin{bmatrix} B & \\ & A^{T\dagger} \end{bmatrix},$$

provided the orthogonal projectors $I - BB^\dagger$ and $I - AA^\dagger$ have small rank.

For generalized Pick matrices P where the rank of $\mathcal{L}[D_1, D_2](P)$ is small, with D_i a diagonal matrix, we have a problem if $\mathcal{L}[D_1, D_2]$ is not invertible. In this case we can still make progress via a rank-1 perturbation of the form $\mathcal{L}[D_1 + uu^T, D_2](P)$ for a well-chosen column u, and exploiting the fact the eigenvector matrix of $D_1 + uu^T$ is an orthogonal Cauchy matrix, which can be multiplied rapidly using one of several techniques. This rank 1 perturbation will increase the displacement rank of P by at most 1 so the fast generalized Schur algorithm can still be deployed.

Once the generators for T^{-1} have been computed, the question naturally arises as to how to multiply $T^{-1}x$ quickly. If $|\lambda(A)| < 1$ and $|\lambda(B)| < 1$, then we have the series solution for $\mathcal{L}[A,B](T) = PQ^T$ as:

$$T = \sum_{l=0}^{\infty} \left(A^l P\right)\left(B^l Q\right)^T. \tag{1}$$

If T is the inverse of a Toeplitz matrix and $A = B = Z$, then this gives the celebrated Gohberg–Semencul formula as A and B are nilpotent. When A and B are diagonal then T is a generalized Cauchy (Pick) matrix and there are fast algorithms for matrix–vector multiply [15]. Some generalizations are available in [1]. However there seems to be no general approach for multiplying an arbitrary low displacement-rank matrix with a vector for a general class of *nice* A and B.

We do make the general observation that if the sum (1) is converging rapidly then one can easily construct a fast *approximate* matrix–vector multiplication algorithm. But those matters are better dealt with later in this tutorial.

It is easy to see how to compute the generators for $T_1 + T_2$ quickly from those of T_i provided they have low displacement-rank for the same displacement operators $\mathcal{L}[A,B]$. Similarly it is not difficult to quickly compute the generators of T_1T_2 provided that we can rapidly multiply by both A and B, and that a low rank factorization of $I - B^TA$ is quickly available.

The big draw back of displacement structure approach is that there has been no progress on generalizing it to nested structures

[2]This requires that A and B be specially structured lower-triangular matrices. The shift-down and diagonal matrices are good examples.

like Toeplitz-block-Toeplitz matrices. This might in turn be related to the fact that the inverses of higher-order Sylvester–Stein operators are not well-understood.

3 SEQUENTIALLY SEMI-SEPARABLE (SSS) REPRESENTATIONS

Just like displacement structure theory was born from *systems* theory (study of linear time-invariant [LTI] systems), another study of low-rank structured matrices was born from trying to generalize systems theory to time-varying systems [12]. We do not attempt a generalized approach in this tutorial. (More information can be found in [3, 6, 7].)

For any square matrix A consider partitions of the form

$$A = \begin{matrix} & m & n-m \\ m & \multicolumn{2}{c}{\multirow{2}{*}{}} \\ \end{matrix} \quad A = \begin{array}{c} \\ m \\ n-m \end{array}\!\!\begin{array}{c} \begin{array}{cc} m & n-m \end{array} \\ \begin{pmatrix} A_{11} & A_{12} \\ A_{21} & A_{22} \end{pmatrix} \end{array}.$$

We will call such off-diagonal blocks as A_{12} and A_{21} as Hankel blocks. Note that these off-diagonal blocks never cross the principal diagonal and always extend as far to the corners as possible. In this section we study families of matrices for which the ranks of all Hankel blocks are small compared to the matrix size n. In particular it turns out that there is a non-linear representation of the matrix that captures this structure precisely and permits a full spectrum of fast linear (in matrix size n) algorithms.

The key question is what constraints are placed on the matrix entries by the requirement that two overlapping Hankel blocks must have low rank? Consider the following partition of A:

$$A = \begin{bmatrix} A_{11} & A_{12} & A_{13} \\ A_{21} & A_{22} & A_{23} \\ A_{31} & A_{32} & A_{33} \end{bmatrix}$$

where both $\mathcal{H}_1 = \begin{bmatrix} A_{12} & A_{13} \end{bmatrix}$ and $\mathcal{H}_2 = \begin{bmatrix} A_{13}^T & A_{23}^T \end{bmatrix}^T$ are Hankel blocks. From the presence of the shared common block A_{13} we see that the column space of $\mathcal{H}_1$ must be related to the column space of $\mathcal{H}_2$, and similarly the row-space of $\mathcal{H}_2$ must be related to the row-space of $\mathcal{H}_1$. To that end, let:

$$\mathcal{H}_1 = U_1 \begin{bmatrix} V_{11}^T & V_{12}^T \end{bmatrix}, \qquad \mathcal{H}_2 = \begin{bmatrix} U_{21} \\ U_{22} \end{bmatrix} V_2^T,$$

be full column-rank factorizations of $\mathcal{H}_i$ conformally partitioned with $A_{13} = U_1 V_{12}^T = U_{21} V_2^T$. For a fixed choice of the two factorizations there is a unique matrix W, which we call a transition operator, such that

$$U_{21} = U_1 W, \qquad V_{12}^T = W V_2^T.$$

If the rank of $\mathcal{H}_i$ is r_i then $W \in \mathcal{R}^{r_1 \times r_2}$.

If we now choose $\sum_{i=1}^{p} n_i = n$, and use it to partition A into a block $p \times p$ matrix, such that the sub-block $A_{ij} \in \mathcal{R}^{n_i \times n_j}$, then we can use the above idea repeatedly on adjacent Hankel blocks to construct a representation of the blocks of A of the following form:

$$A_{ij} = \begin{cases} D_i, & i = j, \\ U_i W_{i+1} W_{i+2} \cdots W_{j-1} V_j^T, & i < j, \\ P_i R_{i-1} R_{i-2} \cdots R_{j+1} Q_j^T, & i > j. \end{cases}$$

A simple example is a banded matrix which clearly has the desired low-rank property for the Hankel blocks. In this case if we choose n_i to be equal to the band-width we can write down the components directly.

$$\begin{aligned} D_i &= A_{i,i} \\ U_i &= A_{i,i+1} \\ V_i &= I \\ P_i &= A_{i,i-1} \\ Q_i &= I \\ R_i &= 0 \\ W_i &= 0. \end{aligned}$$

To understand this representation better we look at how you can compute $Ax = b$ fast. A little bit of algebra reveals that the following recursions will do the job:

$$\begin{aligned} g_i &= V_i^T x_i + W_i g_{i+1} \\ h_i &= Q_i^T x_i + R_i h_{i-1} \\ b_i &= D_i x_i + U_i g_{i+1} + P_i h_{i-1}, \end{aligned} \tag{2}$$

where all undefined variables are assumed to be empty matrices of suitable size, and x_i and b_i are conformal partitions of x and b respectively. It is clear that if all Hankel block ranks are small compared with the matrix size then this is a linear time algorithm for computing Ax.

However there are more to these recursions. We make the notation, for example, that

$$D = \begin{bmatrix} D_1 & & & \\ & D_2 & & \\ & & \ddots & \\ & & & D_p \end{bmatrix} \qquad g = \begin{bmatrix} g_1 \\ g_2 \\ \vdots \\ g_p \end{bmatrix}.$$

The recursions can then be written in matrix form as

$$\begin{bmatrix} I - WZ^T & 0 & -V^T \\ 0 & I - RZ & -Q^T \\ UZ^T & PZ & D \end{bmatrix} \begin{bmatrix} g \\ h \\ x \end{bmatrix} = \begin{bmatrix} 0 \\ 0 \\ b \end{bmatrix}. \tag{3}$$

From this we get the *diagonal* representation of A as

$$A = D + UZ^T(I - WZ^T)^{-1}V^T + PZ(I - RZ)^{-1}Q^T. \tag{4}$$

In other words A is just the Schur complement of a large sparse matrix. In particular we will call (D, U, W, V, P, R, Q) as the SSS representation of A.

Furthermore there is a re-ordering of the unknowns in equation (3) into the sequence (g_i, h_i, x_i), and if the rows of the sparse matrix in (3) are also re-ordered the same way we can then see that the the sparse matrix will be a linear graph by referring to the original recursions in (2). Therefore it follows that in this ordering the sparse matrix has a no fill-in elimination order and that therefore there is a fast algorithm (sparse Gaussian elimination) to quickly compute x (and incidentally also g and h) from b. Some elementary calculations then reveal that the resulting algorithm wll be linear in the matrix size n.

However more operations involving SSS representations can be done in linear time. The key to understanding this is the simple fact that low-rank Hankel blocks imply short SSS representations and vice versa.

For example, since

$$\begin{bmatrix} A_{11} & A_{12} \\ A_{21} & A_{22} \end{bmatrix} \begin{bmatrix} B_{11} & B_{12} \\ B_{21} & B_{22} \end{bmatrix} = \begin{bmatrix} * & A_{11}B_{12} + A_{12}B_{22} \\ * & * \end{bmatrix}$$

it follows that the product of two SSS matrices will be another SSS matrix whose Hankel block ranks are at most the sum of the corresponding Hankel blocks of the original SSS matrices. With some effort a linear time algorithm can be constructed for producing the SSS representation of AB given those of A and B.

Similarly from

$$\begin{bmatrix} A_{11} & A_{12} \\ A_{21} & A_{22} \end{bmatrix}^{-1} = \begin{bmatrix} * & *A_{12}* \\ *A_{21}* & * \end{bmatrix},$$

where the $*$'s denote matrices that we do not care about, it follows that the Hankel block ranks of the inverse are at most those of the original matrix. It therefore follows, for example, that both banded matrices and their inverse have short SSS representations. Though not all matrices with short SSS representations are the inverses of banded matrices, the diagonal representation (4) shows that every SSS representation *is* the Schur complement of a larger banded matrix in the right ordering.

One way to quickly compute the SSS representation of the inverse is as follows. First we observe that since

$$\begin{bmatrix} A_{11} & A_{12} \\ A_{21} & A_{22} \end{bmatrix} = \begin{bmatrix} I & 0 \\ A_{21}A_{11}^{-1} & I \end{bmatrix} \begin{bmatrix} A_{11} & A_{12} \\ 0 & A_{22} - A_{21}A_{11}^{-1}A_{12} \end{bmatrix},$$

both L and U in the LU factorization of A will have exactly the same Hankel block ranks as A. From this with some algebra one can construct a linear time algorithm to compute the SSS representations of L and U from that of A. Then, using the diagonal representation and the Woodbury formula, we can compute in linear time the SSS representation of L^{-1} and U^{-1}. We can then use the aforementioned linear time multiplication algorithm to find the SSS representation of $U^{-1}L^{-1} = A^{-1}$.

We also note that there are linear time algorithms for the ULV factorization of A in SSS form, if growth factor becomes an issue.

Clearly the sum of two SSS matrices is another SSS matrix. So effectively matrix algebra is fast in the SSS representation and this has proven to be tremendously useful in practice.

4 HIERARCHICALLY SEMI-SEPARABLE (HSS) REPRESENTATIONS

There is another non-linear matrix representation that is also capable of providing a linear time matrix algebra. This was born independently from efforts to speed up the application of integral operators that arise in potential theory in the fundamental work of Greengard and Rokhlin on the fast multi-pole method (FMM). The representation we present now (HSS) is a special case of this more general class of FMM representations. The more general class is not *closed* under inversion and multiplication, but the HSS representation is. More detailed information can be found in [2, 5, 11, 23–25, 28, 29].

The HSS representation uses a slightly different definition of Hankel blocks. Let

$$A = \begin{bmatrix} A_{11} & A_{12} & A_{13} \\ A_{21} & A_{22} & A_{23} \\ A_{31} & A_{32} & A_{33} \end{bmatrix}.$$

Then we call $\begin{bmatrix} A_{21} & A_{23} \end{bmatrix}$ a row Hankel block, and we call $\begin{bmatrix} A_{12}^T & A_{32}^T \end{bmatrix}^T$ a column Hankel block. The HSS representation exploits the low-rank structure of these types of blocks, but not *all* of them. It restricts itself to a fixed set hierarchical set of blocks instead. (This is to be contrasted with the SSS representation which does capture the low-rank structure of all the relevant Hankel blocks.)

To this end we need some notation. Let $A = A_{0;0,0} \in \mathcal{R}^{n \times n}$, and let $n = n_{0;0}$. We assume that there is a partition tree associated to A, which is defined as follows. We assume that for each $0 \leq k < K$ there are non-negative integers $n_{k;i}$, for $i = 0, \ldots, 2^k - 1$, such that $n_{k;i} = n_{k+1;2i} + n_{k+1;2i+1}$. Note that these numbers can be naturally associated with a binary tree which we call the partition tree. (In general we do not need to have a complete binary tree, but we ignore that generalization here.)

Based on this partition tree we recursively partition A as follows:

$$A_{k;i,j} = \begin{matrix} & n_{k+1;2j} & n_{k+1;2j+1} \\ n_{k+1;2i} & \left(A_{k+1;2i,2j} \right. & \left. A_{k+1;2i,2j+1} \right) \\ n_{k+1;2i+1} & \left(A_{k+1;2i+1,2j} \right. & \left. A_{k+1;2i+1,2j+1} \right) \end{matrix},$$

and these sub-blocks can be viewed as edges on the partition tree.

We define the row Hankel blocks at each level as:

$$\mathcal{H}_{k;i} = \begin{bmatrix} A_{k;i,0} & \cdots & A_{k;i,i-1} & A_{k,i,i+1} & \cdots & A_{k,i,2^k-1} \end{bmatrix}.$$

That is, $\mathcal{H}_{k;i}$ is the i'th row at the k'th level with the block $A_{k;i,i}$ deleted. In analogous manner, one can define column Hankel blocks $\mathcal{V}_{k;i}$, where the block columns of A at the k-th level are considered instead. Next let the matrix $V_{k;i}$ be such that its columns form a basis for the row space of $\mathcal{H}_{k;i}$. Similarly let the matrix $U_{k;i}$ be such that its columns form a basis for the column space of $\mathcal{H}_{k;i}$.

Since $\mathcal{H}_{k,i}$ shares sub-matrices with $\mathcal{H}_{k+1;2i}$ and $\mathcal{H}_{k+1;2i+1}$, it follows that there are *translation* matrices $R_{k;i}$ such that

$$U_{k;i} = \begin{bmatrix} U_{k+1;2i}R_{k+1;2i} \\ U_{k+1;2i+1}R_{k+1;2i+1} \end{bmatrix}.$$

Similarly there are translation matrices $W_{k;i}$ associated with $V_{k;i}$. We define the *expansion coefficients* $B_{k;i,j}$ as follows:

$$\begin{aligned} A_{k;2i,2i+1} &= U_{k;2i}B_{k;2i,2i+1}V_{k;2i+1}^T \\ A_{k;2i+1,2i} &= U_{k;2i+1}B_{k;2i+1,2i}V_{k;2i}^T, \end{aligned}$$

for $0 < k \leq K$. We also define

$$A_{K;i,i} = D_{K;i}.$$

We next observe that the translation matrices can be much smaller than the basis matrices. Therefore in the HSS representation we store only $U_{K;i}$ and $V_{K;i}$. To recover the other basis matrices we use $R_{k;i}$ and $W_{:k;i}$ instead. Therefore the complete HSS representation of A is the partition tree $n_{k;i}$ along with the leaf-level matrices $D_{K;i}$, $U_{K;i}$, $V_{K;i}$, the translation matrices $R_{k;i}$, $W_{k;i}$, and the expansion coefficients $B_{k;2i,2i+1}$, $B_{k;2i+1,2i}$. With this we can check that every entry of A can be uniquely recovered from the HSS representation.

If $p_{k;i}$ denotes the rank of $\mathcal{H}_{k;i}$ and $q_{k;i}$ the rank of $\mathcal{V}_{k;i}$, then it can be verified, for example, that $R_{k+1;2i} \in \mathcal{R}^{p_{k+1;2i} \times p_{k;i}}$ and $B_{k;2i,2i+1} \in \mathcal{R}^{p_{k;2i} \times q_{k;2i+1}}$. So the ranks of the row and column Hankel blocks determines how small the HSS representation is.

Just as in the SSS case, there exists an $O(n^2)$ algorithm to construct an optimal HSS representation directly from the entries of the matrix [5]. However, in special cases we can do much better. For sparse matrices the construction can be done in linear time [5]. For matrices of the form $A_{i,j} = f(x_i, y_j)$, where $f : \mathcal{R}^d \to \mathcal{R}$ the FMM techniques of Greengard and Rokhlin can be used to compute the HSS representation of A in linear time provided f satisfies some nice properties [18]. However, in practice the HSS representation is most often computed quickly from the fact that matrix algebra in HSS form can be done quickly.

Just as in the SSS case, the key observation is that there is a short HSS representation as long as the row and column Hankel blocks have small rank. Then one observes for example, that the sum of two HSS matrices will have column (row) Hankel block ranks that are the sum of the corresponding column (row) Hankel blocks of the summands. Therefore it is not surprising that there is a linear time algorithm to add two HSS matrices.

The superfast multiplication of two HSS matrices is based on the following observation:

$$\begin{bmatrix} A_{11} & A_{12} & A_{13} \\ A_{21} & A_{22} & A_{23} \\ A_{31} & A_{32} & A_{33} \end{bmatrix} \begin{bmatrix} B_{11} & B_{12} & B_{13} \\ B_{21} & B_{22} & B_{23} \\ B_{31} & B_{32} & B_{33} \end{bmatrix} =$$

$$\begin{bmatrix} * & *B_{12} + A_{12} * + * B_{32} & * \\ A_{21} * + * B_{21} + A_{23}* & * & A_{21} * + * B_{23} + A_{23}* \\ * & *B_{12} + A_{32} * + * B_{32} & * \end{bmatrix},$$

where $*$'s denote matrices whose ranks are irrelevant. From this we see that the ranks of the column (row) Hankel blocks of the product are the sums of the ranks of the corresponding colum (row) Hankel blocks of the multiplicands. Again there is a linear time algorithm to compute the HSS representation of the product from the HSS representation of the multiplicands.

To give a flavor of how HSS algorithms are constructed we go back to the problem of fast matrix-vector multiplications $Ax = b$, where A is in HSS form. We will use the notation $x_{K;i}$ to denote the i-block of x when it is partitioned according to the cuts at the leaf level of the partition tree. Then with a little bit of algebra one can show that the following recursions will do the job:

$$\begin{aligned} g_{K;i} &= V_{K;i}^T x_{K;i} \\ g_{k;i} &= W_{k+1;2i}^T g_{k+1:2i} + W_{k+1;2i+1}^T g_{k+1;2i+1}, \qquad k < K, \\ f_{0;0} &= [] \\ f_{k;2i} &= R_{k;2i} f_{k-1;i} + B_{k;2i,2i+1} g_{k;2i+1}, \qquad 0 < k \le K, \\ f_{k;2i+1} &= R_{k;2i+1} f_{k-1;i} + B_{k;2i+1,2i} g_{k;2i}, \qquad 0 < k \le K, \\ b_{K;i} &= D_{K;i} x_{K;i} + U_{K;i} f_{K;i}. \end{aligned}$$

It is a clear that this leads to a linear time algorithm. Just like in the SSS case these recursions can also be used to give a diagonal representation of A and to also give a linear time solver for computing x given b via sparse Gaussian elimination.

Towards this define the pair, $Z_\downarrow$ and $Z_\leftrightarrow$, of linear operators on the binary partition tree, via the equations:

$$\begin{aligned} \left(Z_\downarrow x\right)_{k;i} &= x_{k-1;\lfloor \frac{i}{2} \rfloor} \\ (Z_\leftrightarrow x)_{k;2i} &= x_{k;2i+1} \\ (Z_\leftrightarrow x)_{k;2i+1} &= x_{k;2i}. \end{aligned}$$

Also define the linear projection operator P on the binary partition tree such that $P^T g$ restricts g just to the leaves of the tree, $(P^T g)_i = g_{K;i}$.

As before also define the block diagonal matrices D, U and V, which only consist of the entries $D_{K;i}$, $U_{K;i}$ and $V_{K;i}$ that are on the leaves of the binary partition tree. Also define the block diagonal matrices R and W that consist of the entries $R_{k;i}$ and $W_{k;i}$ which are defined on all nodes of the binary partition tree. Finally define the block diagonal matrix B which consists of the entries $B_{k;2i,2i+1}$ and $B_{k;2i+1,2i}$ by making a natural association with the nodes of the binary tree. Similarly we will use g to denote a column vector containing all the $g_{k;i}$'s.

Then we can re-write the fast recursions for the multiplication Ax as

$$\begin{aligned} g &= Z_\downarrow^T W^T g + P V^T x \\ f &= R Z_\downarrow f + B Z_\leftrightarrow g \\ b &= Dx + U P^T f. \end{aligned}$$

In matrix form this appears as:

$$\begin{bmatrix} I - Z_\downarrow^T W^T & 0 & -PV^T \\ -BZ_\leftrightarrow & I - RZ_\downarrow & 0 \\ 0 & UP^T & D \end{bmatrix} \begin{bmatrix} g \\ f \\ x \end{bmatrix} = \begin{bmatrix} 0 \\ 0 \\ b \end{bmatrix}.$$

This implies that the HSS diagonal representation of a matrix A is given by

$$A = D + UP^T (I - RZ_\downarrow)^{-1} BZ_\leftrightarrow (I - Z_\downarrow^T W^T)^{-1} PV^T,$$

which also shows that A is just the Schur complement of a larger block sparse matrix with the binary partition tree with edges *only* between siblings, as the incidence graph.

Since such a binary partition tree has a fill-in free elimination order, this also shows that we can get a linear time solver for constructing x given b, by first re-ordering the unknowns (and the equations) in the order: $(g_{K;i}, f_{K;i}, x_{K;i})$, followed by $(g_{k;i}, f_{k;i})$.

If numerical stability is a concern, it is also clear that a linear time sparse QR factorization algorithm can also be constructed by similar considerations.

If A has a short HSS representation then so does A^{-1} and this can be computed in linear time from that of A. To see how and why this is possible, first observe that:

$$\begin{bmatrix} A_{11} & A_{12} & A_{13} \\ A_{21} & A_{22} & A_{23} \\ A_{31} & A_{32} & A_{33} \end{bmatrix} =$$

$$\begin{bmatrix} I & 0 & 0 \\ A_{21}* & I & 0 \\ * & (A_{32} + *A_{12})* & I \end{bmatrix} \begin{bmatrix} * & A_{12} & * \\ 0 & * & A_{23} + A_{21}* \\ 0 & 0 & * \end{bmatrix},$$

where again $*$'s denote matrices whose ranks are irrelevant. From this it follows that the LU factors of A will have the same column and row Hankel block ranks as that of A itself. Furthermore, with a little bit bit of algebra, a set of fast linear time recursions can be worked out for computing the HSS representations of the LU factors from that of A.

From:

$$\begin{bmatrix} U_{11} & U_{12} & U_{13} \\ 0 & U_{22} & U_{23} \\ 0 & 0 & U_{33} \end{bmatrix}^{-1} = \begin{bmatrix} * & *U_{12}* & * \\ 0 & * & *U_{23}* \\ 0 & 0 & * \end{bmatrix},$$

we observe that the columns and row Hankel blocks of the inverse of a triangular matrix have the same ranks as those of the original matrix. Furthermore a linear time algorithm can be devised for computing the HSS representation of the inverse of a triangular HSS matrix.

We already know that the product of two HSS matrices will have short HSS representations, but the Hankel block ranks will add up. So when we multiply $U^{-1}L^{-1} = A^{-1}$ there is the danger that we will end up with larger column and row Hankel block ranks. However, we note that:

$$\begin{bmatrix} A_{11} & A_{12} & A_{13} \\ A_{21} & A_{22} & A_{23} \\ A_{31} & A_{32} & A_{33} \end{bmatrix}^{-1} =$$

$$\begin{bmatrix} * & (*A_{12} + *A_{32})S_v & * \\ S_h(A_{21} * + A_{23}*) & * & S_h(A_{21} * + A_{23}*) \\ * & (*A_{12} + *A_{32})S_v & * \end{bmatrix},$$

which shows that the column and row Hankel block ranks of A^{-1} are at most that of A itself. Therefore with a little algebra we can devise linear time algorithms to compute the HSS representation of A^{-1} from those of the LU factors of A. The above formula is also the reason for the definition of row and column Hankel blocks.

5 CONCLUSION

We have presented a basic outline of the displacement structured matrices and the construction of fast solvers for them. However the biggest open question in this area is whether this approach generalizes to dealing with Toeplitz–block–Toeplitz (TBT) matrices?

Currently the most efficient solvers convert Toeplitz matrices to Cauchy-like matrices via the FFT and exploit their HSS structure instead. However, even this approach does not seem to extend to TBT matrices, though in general the HSS approach does not do too badly if there is an underlying 2D kernel function (via the FMM representation).

For SSS and HSS type representations the biggest open question is the exact rank structure of the inverse of discrete 2D Laplace like matrices. There are several papers on the approximate low-rank structure in special cases, but the general question remains quite open.

We have made some remarks recently on this problem [4]. Our key observation is to note that the complexity of SSS algorithms depends critically on the underlying linear graph, while that of HSS depends on the special binary partition tree. Conversely the lack of a fast direct solver for FMM representations can be traced to the difficulty of doing Gaussian elimination quickly on a the more complicated FMM tree. This immediately raises the issue of tying the graph structure more intimately to the matrix representation and the associated fast algorithms.

This problem is important as our understanding of the inverse of discrete 3D Laplace like matrices is not sharp enough to yield fast enough practical solvers and the underlying graph is the 3D mesh.

REFERENCES

[1] Alin Bostan, Claude-Pierre Jeannerod, Christophe Mouilleron, and Éric Schost. 2017. On matrices with displacement structure: generalized operators and faster algorithms. *CoRR* abs/1703.03734 (2017). arXiv:1703.03734 http://arxiv.org/abs/1703.03734

[2] Shivkumar Chandrasekaran, Patrick Dewilde, Ming Gu, William Lyons, and Timothy Pals. 2006. A fast solver for HSS representations via sparse matrices. *SIAM J. Matrix Anal. Appl.* 29, 1 (2006), 67–81.

[3] Shivkumar Chandrasekaran, Patrick Dewilde, Ming Gu, T Pals, Xiaorui Sun, Alle-Jan van der Veen, and Daniel White. 2005. Some fast algorithms for sequentially semiseparable representations. *SIAM J. Matrix Anal. Appl.* 27, 2 (2005), 341–364.

[4] Shivkumar Chandrasekaran and Nithin Govindarajan. 2018. The exact fine structure of the inverse of discrete elliptic operators. In *SIAM Conference on Applied Linear Algebra (SIAM-ALA18).*

[5] Shivkumar Chandrasekaran, Ming Gu, and Timothy Pals. 2006. A fast ULV decomposition solver for hierarchically semiseparable representations. *SIAM J. Matrix Anal. Appl.* 28, 3 (2006), 603–622.

[6] Shivkumar Chandrasekaran, Ming Gu, X Sun, J Xia, and J Zhu. 2007. A superfast algorithm for Toeplitz systems of linear equations. *SIAM J. Matrix Anal. Appl.* 29, 4 (2007), 1247–1266.

[7] Shivkumar Chandrasekaran, Ming Gu, Jianlin Xia, and Jiang Zhu. 2007. A fast QR algorithm for companion matrices. In *Recent advances in matrix and operator theory.* Springer, 111–143.

[8] Shivkumar Chandrasekaran and Ali H Sayed. 1996. Stabilizing the generalized Schur algorithm. *SIAM J. Matrix Anal. Appl.* 17, 4 (1996), 950–983.

[9] J Chun and T Kailath. 1989. A constructive proof of the Gohberg-Semencul formula. *Linear Algebra Appl.* 121 (1989), 475–489.

[10] James W Cooley and John W Tukey. 1965. An algorithm for the machine calculation of complex Fourier series. *Mathematics of computation* 19, 90 (1965), 297–301.

[11] Patrick Dewilde and Shivkumar Chandrasekaran. 2006. A hierarchical semi-separable Moore-Penrose equation solver. In *Wavelets, multiscale systems and hypercomplex analysis.* Springer, 69–85.

[12] Patric Dewilde and Alle-Jan van der Veen. 1998. *Time-Varying Systems and Computations.*

[13] Yuli Eidelman, Israel Gohberg, and Iulian Haimovici. 2014. *Separable type representations of matrices and fast algorithms.* Springer.

[14] Joachim von zur Gathen and Jurgen Gerhard. 1999. *Modern computer algebra.* Cambridge University Press, Cambridge.

[15] Israel Gohberg and Vadim Olshevsky. 1994. Fast algorithms with preprocessing for matrix–vector multiplication problems. *Journal of Complexity* (1994).

[16] Israel Gohberg and A. Semencul. 1972. On the inversion of finite Toeplitz matrices and their continuous analogs. *Mat. Issled* (1972).

[17] Gene H Golub and Charles F Van Loan. 2013. *Matrix computations* (4 ed.). JHU Press.

[18] Leslie Greengard and Vladimir Rokhlin. 1987. A fast algorithm for particle simulations. *Journal of computational physics* 73, 2 (1987), 325–348.

[19] Wolfgang Hackbusch. 2015. *Hierarchical matrices: algorithms and analysis.* Vol. 49. Springer.

[20] G Heinig and V Olshevsky. 2001. The Schur algorithm for matrices with Hessenberg displacement structure. *Contemp. Math.* 281 (2001), 3–16.

[21] Thomas Kailath, Sun-Yuan Kung, and Martin Morf. 1979. Displacement ranks of matrices and linear equations. *J. Math. Anal. Appl.* 68, 2 (1979), 395–407.

[22] Thomas Kailath and Ali H Sayed. 1995. Displacement structure: theory and applications. *SIAM review* 37, 3 (1995), 297–386.

[23] K Lessel, M Hartman, and Shivkumar Chandrasekaran. 2016. A fast memory efficient construction algorithm for hierarchically semi-separable representations. *SIAM J. Matrix Anal. Appl.* 37, 1 (2016), 338–353.

[24] William Lyons. 2005. *Fast algorithms with applications to PDEs.* Ph.D. Dissertation. University of California, Santa Barbara.

[25] Timothy Pals. 2004. *Multipole for Scattering Computations: Spectral Discretization,Stabilization, Fast Solvers.* Ph.D. Dissertation. University of California, Santa Barbara.

[26] Vladimir Rokhlin. 1985. Rapid solution of integral equations of classical potential theory. *Journal of computational physics* 60, 2 (1985), 187–207.

[27] Vladimir Rokhlin. 1990. Rapid solution of integral equations of scattering theory in two dimensions. *J. Comput. Phys.* 86, 2 (1990), 414–439.

[28] Zhifeng Sheng, Patrick Dewilde, and Shivkumar Chandrasekaran. 2007. Algorithms to solve hierarchically semi-separable systems. In *System theory, the Schur algorithm and multidimensional analysis.* Springer, 255–294.

[29] Paige Starr. 1992. *On the numerical solution of one-dimensional integral and differential equations.* Ph.D. Dissertation. Yale University.

[30] Jianlin Xia, Yuanzhe Xi, and Ming Gu. 2012. A superfast structured solver for Toeplitz linear systems via randomized sampling. *SIAM J. Matrix Anal. Appl.* 33, 3 (2012), 837–858.

GAP 4 at Twenty-one – Algorithms, System Design and Applications

Stephen A. Linton
University of St Andrews
steve.linton@st-andrews.ac.uk

ABSTRACT

The first public beta release of GAP 4[6] was made on July 18 1997. Since then the system has been cited in over 2400 publications, and its distribution now includes over 130 contributed extension packages. This tutorial will review the special features of computational abstract algebra and how they are reflected in the system design; some areas of current algorithmic development, and some recent achievements.

ACM Reference format:
Stephen A. Linton. 2018. GAP 4 at Twenty-one – Algorithms, System Design and Applications. In *Proceedings of 2018 ACM International Symposium on Symbolic and Algebraic Computation, New York, NY, USA, July 16–19, 2018 (ISSAC '18)*, 2 pages.
https://doi.org/10.1145/3208976.3209026

1 COMPUTING WITH ELEMENTS TO ANSWER QUESTIONS ABOUT STRUCTURE

In 1945, Alan Turing, in his proposal of build one of the first general purpose electronic computers wrote:

> There will positively be no internal alterations to be made even if we wish suddenly to switch from calculating the energy levels of the neon atom to the enumeration of groups of order 720[7, p. 293]

In this he was referencing a tradition of (hand) computational investigation of finite groups that dated back decades [8, Ch. 1], and presaging the development of digital methods that would have a huge impact in decades to come. Note that he proposes computing abstract properties of mathematical structures, not just computing with their elements. This will be a recurring theme. Incidentally, there are 840 isomorphism classes of groups of order 720, and recalculating this list with generic methods using the `grpconst` package[3] in GAP takes my laptop about 30 seconds.

In 1993, Martin Schönert, the original technical architect of GAP prepared an example session showing how the system could be used to analyse the Rubik's cube, to answer such questions as "can all configurations be reached?", "how many reachable configurations are there?" and given a configuration, to find a reasonable short way of achieving (or undoing it)[1].

Even then, this was not an especially challenging computation, but it exhibits again a key characteristic of Computational Group Theory (and more broadly Computational Abstract Algebra): *computing with elements to answer questions about structures.* The Rubik's cube computation starts with six permutations (one for each face of the cube) and all of the actual computation (in this case) is done with permutations and small integers, but the results are mathematical properties that describe the whole group of 43 252 003 274 489 856 000 permutations, most of which have clearly never actually been realised.

One consequence of this is that one can often answer a question by computing not in the concrete structure defined by the input but in an abstractly isomorphic, but completely different one. A question about the structure of a permutation group may be best addressed by instead studying the action on an elementary abelian normal subgroup, realised as an equivalent action of matrices on a vector space. Equally, a question about matrix groups is sometimes best addressed by considering their permutation action on an orbit of vectors or subspaces. This approach has, perhaps, reached its culmination in so-called "black-box" group methods (introduced in [1]) which are completely independent of the form of the group elemnents, and in the "Trivial Fitting" methods for addressing a variety of problems in general finite groups using a purely group-theoretic decomposition (e.g. [9]) which will form a part of the tutorial.

2 SYSTEM DESIGN – THE GAP LANGUAGE AND TYPE SYSTEM

The freedom to choose which concrete realisation of an abstract problem to solve, makes it very difficult to implement many group-theoretical algorithms as stand-alone software. The best known methods for computing the order of the group given by two permutations may potentially involve computing with matrix groups and finitely-presented groups; using databases arising from the classification of finite simple groups and many other techniques.

This connectness drove computational group theorists to move quickly to the development of integrated systems on top of which new algorithms could be tested without reimplementing the huge body of prior art. The design of such a system to be both natural for mathematicians to use and powerful and flexible enough for state of the art algorithmic research is challenging. The structure of the GAP 4 system and its programming language and type system [4] are an attempt to address this, and a second part of this tutorial will

ISSAC '18, July 16–19, 2018, New York, NY, USA

ACM ISBN 978-1-4503-5550-6/18/07...$15.00
https://doi.org/10.1145/3208976.3209026

[1]A version for current GAP is available at https://www.gap-system.org/Doc/Examples/rubik.html.

explore them, combining a tutorial in extending GAP with some reflections on 21 years of experience and on future directions.

3 FUTURE PROBLEMS AND FUTURE SOLUTIONS

The tutorial will conclude with a review of some recent work that suggests where upcoming and future challenges and opportunities for computational algebra may be found, including new methods that can address questions about structures such as matrix groups over infinite domains [5], and hyperbolic finitely-presented groups.

One thing these new problems all have in common is the large scale of the computations required. For the last nine years, we have been exploring ways to allow GAP users to take advantage of modern multi-core computers [2]. I suspect we are not alone in the symbolic computation community in saying that this has been much harder than we expected. Nevertheless, a number of solutions exist in various stages of development, and the third part of the tutorial will conclude by showcasing some of these together with some recent examples of their use.

REFERENCES

[1] L. Babai and E. Szemeredi. On the complexity of matrix group problems i. In *25th Annual Symposium onFoundations of Computer Science, 1984.*, pages 229–240, Oct 1984. doi: 10.1109/SFCS.1984.715919.

[2] Reimer Behrends, Kevin Hammond, Vladimir Janjic, Alexander Konovalov, Steve Linton, Hans-Wolfgang Loidl, Patrick Maier, and Phil Trinder. Hpc-gap: Engineering a 21st-century high-performance computer algebra system. *Concurr. Comput. : Pract. Exper.*, 28(13):3606–3636, September 2016. ISSN 1532-0626. doi: 10.1002/cpe.3746. URL https://doi.org/10.1002/cpe.3746.

[3] H. U. Besche and B. Eick. GrpConst, constructing the groups of a given order, Version 2.6. `http://www.icm.tu-bs.de/~beick/so.html`, Mar 2018. Refereed GAP package.

[4] T. Breuer and S. Linton. The GAP 4 type system. organizing algebraic algorithms. In *ISSAC '98: Proceedings of the 1998 international symposium on Symbolic and algebraic computation*, page 38–45, New York, NY, USA, 1998. ACM, ACM Press. ISBN 1-58113-002-3. Chairman: Volker Weispfenning and Barry Trager.

[5] A. Detinko, D. L. Flannery, and A. Hulpke. Zariski density and computing in arithmetic groups. *Mathematics of Computation*, 87(310):967–986, 3 2018. ISSN 0025-5718. doi: 10.1090/mcom/3236.

[6] GAP. *GAP – Groups, Algorithms, and Programming, Version 4.9.1.* The GAP Group, 2018. URL https://www.gap-system.org.

[7] A. Hodges. *Alan Turing: The Enigma.* Vintage, 1992. ISBN 9780099116417. URL https://books.google.co.uk/books?id=VWvPIWm75XIC.

[8] D.F. Holt, B. Eick, and E.A. O'Brien. *Handbook of Computational Group Theory.* Discrete Mathematics and Its Applications. CRC Press, 2005. ISBN 9781420035216. URL https://books.google.co.uk/books?id=i2UjAASZ33YC.

[9] Alexander J. Hulpke. Calculation of the subgroups of a trivial-fitting group. In *Proceedings of the 38th International Symposium on Symbolic and Algebraic Computation*, ISSAC '13, pages 205–210, New York, NY, USA, 2013. ACM. ISBN 978-1-4503-2059-7. doi: 10.1145/2465506.2465525. URL http://doi.acm.org/10.1145/2465506.2465525.

What Can (and Can't) we Do with Sparse Polynomials?

Daniel S. Roche
United States Naval Academy
Annapolis, Maryland, U.S.A.
roche@usna.edu

ABSTRACT

Simply put, a sparse polynomial is one whose zero coefficients are not explicitly stored. Such objects are ubiquitous in exact computing, and so naturally we would like to have efficient algorithms to handle them. However, with this compact storage comes new algorithmic challenges, as fast algorithms for dense polynomials may no longer be efficient. In this tutorial we examine the state of the art for sparse polynomial algorithms in three areas: arithmetic, interpolation, and factorization. The aim is to highlight recent progress both in theory and in practice, as well as opportunities for future work.

KEYWORDS

sparse polynomial, interpolation, arithmetic, factorization

ACM Reference Format:
Daniel S. Roche. 2018. What Can (and Can't) we Do with Sparse Polynomials?. In *ISSAC '18: 2018 ACM International Symposium on Symbolic and Algebraic Computation, July 16–19, 2018, New York, NY, USA.* ACM, New York, NY, USA, 6 pages. https://doi.org/10.1145/3208976.3209027

1 SPARSE POLYNOMIALS

Sparse polynomials are found in the core of nearly every computer algebra system or library, and polynomials with many zero coefficients frequently occur in practical settings.

Mathematically, the dividing line between a sparse and dense polynomial is not well-defined. From a computer science standpoint, there is a clear distinction, depending on the *representation* of that polynomial in memory: A *dense* representation stores zero coefficients explicitly and exponents implicitly, whereas a *sparse* representation does not store zero coefficients at all, but stores exponents explicitly.

There are many variants of sparse representations [25]. This tutorial considers algorithms for the most compact representation, the so-called *distributed sparse* storage [72]. Let $f \in \mathsf{R}[x_1, \ldots, x_n]$ be an n-variate polynomial with coefficients in a ring R. The representation of f is by a list of t nonzero terms

$$(c_1, e_{1,1}, \ldots, e_{1,n}), (c_2, e_{2,1}, \ldots, e_{2,n}), \ldots, (c_t, e_{t,1}, \ldots, e_{t,n})$$

such that

$$f = c_1 x_1^{e_{1,1}} \cdots x_n^{e_{1,n}} + c_2 x_1^{e_{2,1}} \cdots x_n^{e_{2,n}} + \cdots + c_t x_1^{e_{t,1}} \cdots x_n^{e_{t,n}}$$

with each coefficient $c_i \in \mathsf{R}$ nonzero and all exponent tuples $(e_{i,1}, \ldots, e_{i,n}) \in \mathbb{N}^n$ distinct. We also assume that the terms are sorted according to their exponents in some consistent way.

ISSAC '18, July 16–19, 2018, New York, NY, USA
2018. ACM ISBN 978-1-4503-5550-6/18/07.
https://doi.org/10.1145/3208976.3209027

This sparse representation matches the one used by default for multivariate polynomials in modern computer algebra systems and libraries such as Magma [83], Maple [73], Mathematica, Sage [84], and Singular [81].

1.1 Sparse polynomial algorithm complexity

Sparse polynomials in the distributed representation are also called *lacunary* or *supersparse* [55] in the literature to emphasize that, in this representation, the degree of a polynomial could be exponentially larger than its bit-length. This exposes the essential difficulty of computing with sparse polynomials, in that *efficient algorithms for dense polynomials may cost exponential-time in the sparse setting.*

Specifically, when analyzing algorithms for dense polynomials, the most important measure is the degree bound $D \in \mathbb{N}$ such that $\deg f < D$. The size of the dense representation of a univariate polynomial is D ring elements, and many operations can be performed in $D^{O(1)}$ ring operations, or even $D(\log D)^{O(1)}$.

In the sparse representation, we need to also consider the number of nonzero terms t, and the *bit-length* of the exponents. For a multivariate (sparse) polynomial, the representation size is $O(t)$ ring elements plus $O(nt \log D)$ bits, where n is the number of variables and D is now an upper bound on the maximum degree. The goal, then, is to develop new sparse polynomial algorithms which minimize the cost in terms of n, t, and $\log D$.

The coefficient ring R makes a difference for some algorithms. In the general setting we let R be an arbitrary integral domain, and count ring operations. Another important setting is when $\mathsf{R} = \mathbb{Z}$, the ring of integers, in which case we also account for the size of coefficients. Write $\mathsf{H}(f)$ for the *height* of a polynomial, which is the maximum magnitude $\max_i |c_i|$ of its coefficients; then a fast algorithm on f should have a small running time in terms of $\log \mathsf{H}(f)$.

For simplicity of presentation, and because the algorithmic work with sparse polynomials is still at a much more coarse level than, say, that of integers and dense polynomials, we frequently use the soft-oh notation $\widetilde{O}(\gamma) := O\Big(\gamma \cdot (\log \gamma)^{O(1)}\Big)$, where γ is some running-time function.

1.2 Overview

The basic challenge of sparse polynomial algorithms is to match the complexity of dense polynomial algorithms for the same task. In some cases, interestingly, this is (provably) not possible — for a few problems, even a polynomial-time algorithm in the sparse representation size would imply that P = NP.

Where algorithms are possible, one interesting feature is that they must usually take into account not only the coefficient arithmetic over R, but also the *exponent arithmetic* over $\mathbb{Z}$. In fact, the latter frequently poses the most difficulty in the design of efficient algorithms.

This tutorial aims to outline the state of sparse polynomial algorithms, dividing roughly into the three areas of arithmetic, interpolation, and factorization. We highlight where essentially-optimal algorithms are already known, where they are known *not* to exist, and the numerous cases of open problems in between.

2 ARITHMETIC

Polynomials stored in the dense representation can be added and subtracted in linear-time. Dense polynomial multiplication costs $O(D^2)$ ring operations using the classical algorithm, but considerable research effort has gone to reducing this complexity, which we now denote as simply $\mathsf{M}(D)$. The most general result of [16] gives $\mathsf{M}(D) \in O(D \log D \operatorname{loglog} n)$, and more recent work [27, 44] reduces this even further for most commonly-used rings.

Many other polynomial computations can be reduced to multiplication. In particular, Euclidean division with remainder costs $O(\mathsf{M}(D))$, and (extended) gcd, multi-point evaluation, interpolation, Chinese remaindering, and rational reconstruction all cost $O(M(D) \log D)$ ring operations [14, §2–6] [32, §8–11]. Note that all these operations take quasi-linear time in the input size $\widetilde{O}(D)$.

As discussed previously, these algorithms are *not* polynomial-time in the size of the sparse representation.

2.1 Addition and subtraction

Adding or subtracting sparse polynomials is a matter of combining like terms, which amounts to a *merge* operation on the two lists of nonzero terms. From our assumption that terms are stored in sorted order, this costs $O(t \log D)$ bit operations and $O(t)$ ring additions, where t is the number of terms in the two input polynomials. This matches the size of the input and is therefore optimal.

Notice, however, that the size of the *output* can grow much more quickly than with dense polynomials. When adding two dense polynomials with degrees less than D, the cost is $O(D)$ and the output size is also D; the size does not increase. But when adding two t-sparse polynomials, the number of nonzero terms in the output may double to $2t$. Hence repeated addition of sparse polynomials (of which multiplication is a special case) requires more care.

2.2 Multiplication

A significant difference from case of dense polynomial multiplication is that the *output size* grows quadratically: the product of multiplying two t-sparse polynomials may have as many as t^2 nonzero terms.

In terms of input size, therefore, the best that one can hope for is $O(t^2)$ ring operations and $O(t^2 \log D)$ bit complexity. This is nearly achieved by the classical algorithm of repeated monomial multiplications and additions, which has bit complexity $O(t^2 \log D \log t)$ if the additions (merges) are done in a balanced way [23, 24, 52].

In practice, the *size of intermediate results*, and in particular the time to handle memory allocation and de-allocation, can dominate the complexity of multiplication. At least one specialized data structure was designed for this purpose [85], and [52] suggested a very simple idea of using a *heap* to simultaneously store and sort un-merged terms in the product.

Decades later, Monagan and Pearce [69, 70, 73, 74] rediscovered the heaps idea and developed extremely efficient implementations and a careful analysis. They point out that, while the asymptotic runtime is the same, the space for intermediate results is only $O(t)$, no matter how many terms are in the output. This has tremendous practical performance benefits, and it seems that many computer algebra systems now use this approach in at least some cases. In fact, there seems to be considerable interest in the fastest practical speeds for sparse polynomial multiplication on a variety of hardware platforms including parallel computing [10, 29, 30, 70, 77].

Still, this is unsatisfying from an algorithmic perspective since the number of ring and bit-operations is still quadratic in *every* case, meaning that even the heap-based algorithms will have a hard cut-off with the speed of dense multiplication as polynomials start to fill-in with nonzero coefficients.

Another approach is to consider the *size of the output* as a parameter in the complexity. In the worst case, this can be quadratic in the input size, but in cases where the output is smaller, we can hope for faster computation. Furthermore, considering the output size allows for a smooth transition to dense algorithms, where the output is guaranteed to have at most $2D$ nonzero terms.

Open Problem 1. Develop an algorithm to multiply two sparse polynomials $f, g \in \mathsf{R}[x]$ using $\widetilde{O}(t \log D)$ ring and bit operations, where t is the number of terms in f, g, and fg, and D is an upper bound on their degrees.

Considerable progress has been made toward this open problem, and it seems now *nearly* within reach. Some authors have looked at special cases, when the *support* of nonzero coefficients has a certain structure, to reduce to dense multiplication and achieve the desired complexity in those cases [45, 79, 80].

A more general solution approach is to use *sparse interpolation* algorithms, which we examine in further detail in the next section. First, [46] showed that the open problem is essentially solved *when the support of the product is already known.* More recently, [2, 5] solved Open Problem 1 under two conditions:

- The ring R is either the integers $\mathbb{Z}$, or some other ring such as $\mathbb{F}_p$ that can be reduced to that case with no loss of efficiency.
- The so-called *structural support* matches the size of the *actual support.* Which is to say (roughly) that there are not too many cancellations of coefficients in the product.

Removing the second condition seems to be the main remaining hurdle in solving Open Problem 1.

2.3 Division

When dividing sparse polynomials, it is *imperative* to consider the output size: for example, the exact division of two 2-term polynomials $x^D - 1$ by $x - 1$ produces a quotient with D nonzero terms.

Fortunately, the heaps idea which works well in practice for sparse multiplication has also been adapted to sparse division, and this method easily yields the remainder as well as the quotient [31, 71]. As before, this approach uses $O(t^2)$ ring operations, leaving us with another challenge:

Open Problem 2. Given two sparse polynomials $f, g \in \mathsf{R}[x]$, develop an algorithm to compute the quotient and remainder $q, g \in \mathsf{R}[x]$ such that $f = qg + r$, using $\widetilde{O}(t \log D)$ ring and bit operations, where t is the number of terms of f, g, q, and g, and $\deg f < D$.

Note that an efficient solution to Open Problem 2 is already available when $\deg g$ is small, *i.e.*, when f is sparse but g is dense. The algorithm in that case amounts to computing $x^{e_i} \bmod g$ for all exponents e_i that appear in the support of f, via repeated squaring, then multiplying by the coefficients c_i and summing.

In the more difficult case that g is also sparse, [22, §III] has a nice discussion of the problem. In particular, they point out that a seemingly-easier *decision problem* is still open:

Open Problem 3. Given two sparse polynomials $f, g \in \mathsf{R}[x]$, develop an algorithm which determines whether g divides f exactly, using $\widetilde{O}(t \log D)$ ring and bit operations.

Again, a solution is known only when g is dense.

3 INTERPOLATION

Polynomial interpolation is a problem of *model fitting*: given some measurements, find a (sparse) polynomial which (best) fits the data.

In the case of dense polynomials, this is a classical problem. Exact interpolation from an arbitrary set of points can be accomplished in $\widetilde{O}(D)$ ring operations. Even if the data is noisy or has outliers, classical numerical methods can recover the best polynomial fit (see, *e.g.*, [82, §4,13]).

The challenge of *sparse* polynomial interpolation is to fit a t-sparse polynomial to some small number of evaluation points $m \ll D$. Even the *decidability* of this question is non-trivial and depends on the choice of ring and evaluation points [12]. In fact, all efficient solutions require a stronger model that allows the algorithm to sample the unknown function at arbitrary points.

Definition 4. A *black box* for an unknown n-variate polynomial $f \in \mathsf{R}[x_1, \ldots, x_n]$ is a function which accepts any n-tuple $(\theta_1, \ldots, \theta_n) \in \mathsf{R}^n$ and produces the value $f(\theta_1, \ldots, \theta_n) \in \mathsf{R}$.

In this context, a *sparse interpolation algorithm* takes a black box for an unknown f as well as upper bounds D, T on its degree and number of nonzero terms, respectively. An efficient algorithm should minimize the number of evaluations, plus required ring and bit-operations, in terms of T and $\log D$.

Open Problem 5. For any ring R, given a black box for $f \in \mathsf{R}[x_1, \ldots, x_n]$ and bounds T, D on the number of nonzero terms and maximum degree of f, determine the nonzero coefficients and corresponding exponents of f using $\widetilde{O}(T \log D)$ ring operations, bit operations, and black box evaluations.

The methods for sparse interpolation have very strong connections to other techniques in coding theory and signal processing. In the first case, the support of the unknown sparse polynomial f corresponds to the error locations in Reed-Solomon decoding; the decoding algorithm of Blahut [11] can be seen as a sparse interpolation algorithm similar to Prony's method below [18].

In another viewpoint, the evaluations of a sparse polynomial at integer powers of some complex root of unity have a 1-1 correspondence with evaluations of a sum of exponentials at integer points: signal frequencies correspond to polynomial exponents and amplitudes correspond to polynomial coefficients. The recovery techniques come from multi-exponential analysis, the theory of Padé approximants, and tensor decomposition; see [21, 75] and references therein.

In the context of computer algebra, algorithms for sparse polynomial interpolation go back to the work of Zippel [86, 87], who developed a randomized algorithm which recovers a sparse polynomial in recursively, variable-by variable. However, the reliance on dense *univariate* interpolation makes it unsuitable for the setting of this tutorial.

For exact (super)sparse polynomial interpolation, we first consider the easier case of univariate polynomials where $n = 1$. There are are essentially two classes of algorithms here, which we discuss separately. Then we see how to reduce the multivariate case to the univariate one without changing the sparsity.

3.1 Prony's method

The classic numerical technique of Prony [78] from the 18th century was rediscovered by Ben-Or and Tiwari and adapted to the context of computer algebra nearly 200 years later [9]. The key idea is that any sequence of evaluations at consecutive values in geometric progression $(f(\omega^i))_{i \geq 0}$ form a linearly-recurrent sequence with degree t, where t is the actual number of nonzero terms in f. Furthermore, the minimum polynomial of the linear recurrence is a product of linear factors, and its roots are exactly of the form ω^{e_i}, where e_i is the exponent of a nonzero term in f.

Given a black box for unknown univariate sparse polynomial $f \in \mathsf{R}[z]$, plus degree and sparsity bounds D and T, the algorithm takes the following steps:

(1) Find a suitable element $\omega \in \mathsf{R}$ with multiplicative order at least D.
(2) Evaluate $f(1), f(\omega), f(\omega^2), \ldots, f(\omega^{2T-1})$.
(3) Use the Berlekamp-Massey algorithm (or a Toeplitz solver) to compute the minimum polynomial of the linear recurrence $\Lambda(z) \in \mathsf{R}[z]$.
(4) Find the roots ω^{e_i} of Λ.
(5) Compute the discrete logarithms of the roots to base ω to discover the exponents $e_1, \ldots, e_t$.
(6) Solve a transposed Vandermonde system from the first t evaluations to recover the nonzero coefficients $c_1, \ldots, c_t$.

The main benefit of this procedure is that it computes the minimal number of evaluations $2T$ in Step 2. Steps 3 and 6 involve well-known techniques from structured linear algebra and can be solved efficiently using $\widetilde{O}(t)$ ring operations [13, 58].

However, the other steps depend heavily on the coefficient ring R. In particular, the algorithm must find a high-order element $\omega \in \mathsf{R}$, perform root-finding of a degree-t polynomial, and then perform t discrete logarithms to the base ω.

When $\mathsf{R} = \mathbb{Z}$, these steps can be performed reasonably efficiently by working modulo p for a very carefully-chosen prime p. The first modular version of this approach [60] was not polynomial-time in the discrete logarithm step, but an idea from [53, 61] proposes choosing a prime p with $p \in O(D)$ such that $(p-1)$ is divisible by a large power of 2. This divisor means that $\mathbb{F}_p^*$ has a large subgroup with smooth order, facilitating fast discrete logarithms in only $\widetilde{O}\left(\log^2 D\right)$ field operations each. Because of the size of the prime, the resulting algorithm has total cost of $\widetilde{O}\left(T \log^3 D + T \log \mathsf{H}(f)\right)$ bit operations. This almost solves Open Problem 5, except it is cubic in the size of the exponents $\log D$.

Many important improvements have been made to this algorithm since it was developed in the 1990s. Early-termination techniques allow for only $O(t)$ evaluations instead of $O(T)$, where $t \leq T$ is the true sparsity of f [57]. The root-finding step was found to be the bottleneck in a practical implementation by [47]; a better root-finding algorithm in this case was developed [40] to improve the situation.

[51] adapt the algorithm to the case of finite fields with a parallel algorithm that has better complexity in terms of $\log D$ but becomes quadratic in the sparsity t; they also implemented their algorithm and performed some experiments. Earlier modular, parallel algorithms were also developed by [42, 48]. A more straightforward parallel algorithm over $\mathbb{Z}$ was developed and experimentally evaluated by [65].

3.2 Homomorphic imaging

As we have seen, the Prony approach to sparse interpolation does not perform well over arbitrary finite fields due to the cost of discrete logarithm computations, which in general cannot be performed in polynomial-time.

A radically different method was first proposed by [28], based on some earlier ideas of [41]. This does not directly use the black box model defined earlier, but instead assumes a more generous model that can be stated as follows:

Definition 6. A *modular black box* for an unknown polynomial $f \in \mathsf{R}[x]$ is a function which accepts any pair of dense polynomials $g, h \in \mathsf{F}[x]$ with $\deg h < \deg g$ and produces the value $f(h) \bmod g$.

If $g = x$ and $h = \theta$, this corresponds to the normal black-box evaluation $f(\theta)$. But when $\deg g > 1$, the setting is more general. It makes sense when interpolating a straight-line program or algebraic circuit for f, where each step of the evaluation can be performed modulo g. We must be careful with the cost model also, because for example if $\deg g > \deg f$, the problem is trivially solved with a single evaluation. To accommodate this, we say that each such evaluation costs $\widetilde{O}(\deg g)$ ring operations.

The first algorithm in this model by [28] was deterministic and works over any ring R, but with a high complexity of $\widetilde{O}\left(T^4 \log^2 D\right)$. A series of later improvements [6–8, 37, 49] has improved this to $\widetilde{O}\left(T \log^3 D\right)$ ring operations, largely by introducing numerous randomizations. Note that this is a similar cost to the best-known variants of Prony's method over $\mathbb{Z}$, but it still has the comparative shortcoming of requiring more expensive evaluations.

3.3 Kronecker substitution

Any n-variate polynomial f with maximum degree less than D is in one-to-one correspondence with a univariate polynomial g with degree less than D^n, according to a map introduced by Kronecker [66]. The forward map can be written as an evaluation of f at powers of a single variable z:

$$g(z) := f(z, z^D, \ldots, z^{D^{n-1}}).$$

The reverse map simply involves converting each integer exponent of g into an n-tuple of exponents of f via a D-adic expansion of the univariate exponent.

Because the forward map is simply an evaluation, this means that a multivariate f can be found via univariate supersparse interpolation of a single polynomial with degree less than D^n and the same number of nonzero terms. Supersparse algorithms have complexity in terms of the bit-length of the exponents, so the resulting complexity should be polynomial in T and $n \log D$, as desired.

Even so, the exponential increase in degree is to be avoided, since the cost of both approaches above is at least quadratic in $\log D$. A compromise approach was presented by [4], who showed how to use a randomization to reduce the multivariate polynomial to a set of $O(n)$ univariate polynomials, each of degree only $O(DT)$. When combined with the univariate supersparse interpolation algorithms above, this results in a better complexity in terms of n.

3.4 Problem variations and extensions

Numerous authors have focused on solving different useful variants of the sparse interpolation problem rather than improving the asymptotic complexity. One important consideration is the *basis*. So far we have assumed a monomial basis $1, x, x^2, \ldots$, and the *arithmetic* algorithms of the previous section work more or less the same over any basis. But interpolating into a different basis is more subtle. Sparse interpolation in Pockhammer, Chebyshev, and shifted power bases has been considered by [3, 35, 38, 50, 67].

Another interesting direction has been the development of more robust sparse interpolation algorithms, which can tolerate numerical noise in the evaluations, or completely-erroneous outliers, at the cost of performing more evaluations than in the exact setting [3, 15, 18, 59].

An even more difficult problem is *sparse rational function interpolation*, which is the same as sparse polynomial interpolation except that the unknown f is a fraction of two sparse multivariate polynomials. Interestingly, [62] showed that the sparsest rational function is not always reduced; see also [20, 63, 64].

4 FACTORIZATION

The development of efficient algorithms to factor dense polynomials has been widely celebrated [33, 43, 54]. Most notably for our current purposes, since the 1980s it has been possible to factor polynomials over $\mathbb{Z}[x]$ in polynomial-time. Ignoring the thorny issues with multivariate polynomials and finite fields for now, we ask the same question for sparse polynomials over $\mathbb{Z}[x]$.

This question is already addressed in some other surveys such as [22, 26, 54]. Because of this, and since this is the area in which the speaker has the least expertise, we give only a very cursory overview of the accomplishments and challenges here.

4.1 Impossibility results

Plaisted [76] showed that the problem of determining whether two sparse polynomials are relatively prime is NP-complete, via a reduction from 3-SAT. This means that even computing the gcd of two supersparse polynomials is (seemingly) intractable. However, as highlighted by [22], it is important to emphasize that the reduction only uses cyclotomic polynomials; hence there is a possibility that by excluding such polynomials more progress is possible.

Another impossibility is complete factorization, as illustrated by the (cyclotomic) example $x^D - 1$, which has an exponentially-large dense factor.

The best we can hope for is perhaps the following:

Open Problem 7. Suppose $f \in \mathbb{Z}[x]$ is a t-sparse polynomial with at least one sparse factor $g \in \mathbb{Z}[x]$ such that g has at most s nonzero terms. In polynomial-time in t, s, $\log \mathrm{H}(f)$, and $\log \deg f$, find any s-sparse factor of f.

4.2 Low-degree factors

One case in which supersparse polynomial factorization is possible is when the factors are dense and have small degree. The results in this category generally depend on *gap lemmas*, whose statements are of the following form: If $f \in \mathsf{F}[x]$ can be written as $f = f_0 + f_1 \cdot x^k$, where the "gap" ($k - \deg f_0$) is large, then every non-cyclotomic factor of f is a factor of both f_0 and f_1.

The actual gap lemmas are a bit more technical in specifying the gap and some other conditions, but what they tell us is that finding low-degree factors of a high-degree, sparse polynomial, can be reduced to finding factors of some dense sub-polynomial(s) of f and then checking divisibility. (Recall from Section 2.3 that sparse divisibility testing is tractable when the divisor has low degree.)

This technique has been applied to degree-1 factors in $\mathbb{Z}[x]$ [19], then to small degree over $\mathbb{Q}[x]$ [68], degree-2 in $\mathbb{Q}[x, y]$ [55], and finally small degree over $\mathbb{Q}[x_1, \ldots, x_n]$ [17, 39, 56].

4.3 High-degree factors

Finding high-degree sparse factors remains a challenge in almost all cases. Very recent work by [1] proves that essentially all bivariate high-degree factors of a bivariate rational polynomial must be sparse, which provides some new hope that this problem is tractable.

Otherwise, the only high-degree sparse factorizations that can be computed efficiently are perfect roots of the form $f = g^k$ for some $k \in \mathbb{N}$. As shown by [34, 36], such factors g can be computed when they exist and are sparse, and the power k can be computed unconditionally, in polynomial-time in the sparse size of f. Interestingly, it can be proven that the power k must be relatively small whenever f is sparse; conversely, a high power of any polynomial is necessarily dense.

ACKNOWLEDGMENTS

This work was performed while the author was graciously hosted by the Laboratoire Jean Kuntzmann at the Université Grenoble Alpes.

This work was supported in part by the National Science Foundation under grants 1319994 (https://www.nsf.gov/awardsearch/showAward?AWD_ID=1319994) and 1618269 (https://www.nsf.gov/awardsearch/showAward?AWD_ID=1618269).

REFERENCES

[1] F. Amoroso and M. Sombra. Factorization of bivariate sparse polynomials. online, 2017. URL https://arxiv.org/abs/1710.11479.

[2] A. Arnold. *Sparse Polynomial Interpolation and Testing*. PhD thesis, University of Waterloo, 2016. URL http://hdl.handle.net/10012/10307.

[3] A. Arnold and E. L. Kaltofen. Error-correcting sparse interpolation in the chebyshev basis. ISSAC '15, pages 21–28. ACM, 2015. doi:10.1145/2755996.2756652.

[4] A. Arnold and D. S. Roche. Multivariate sparse interpolation using randomized Kronecker substitutions. ISSAC '14, pages 35–42. ACM, 2014. doi:10.1145/2608628.2608674.

[5] A. Arnold and D. S. Roche. Output-sensitive algorithms for sumset and sparse polynomial multiplication. ISSAC '15, pages 29–36. ACM, 2015. doi:10.1145/2755996.2756653.

[6] A. Arnold, M. Giesbrecht, and D. S. Roche. Faster sparse interpolation of straight-line programs. In V. P. Gerdt, W. Koepf, E. W. Mayr, and E. V. Vorozhtsov, editors, *Proc. Computer Algebra in Scientific Computing (CASC 2013)*, volume 8136 of *Lecture Notes in Computer Science*, pages 61–74. Springer, September 2013. doi:10.1007/978-3-319-02297-0_5.

[7] A. Arnold, M. Giesbrecht, and D. S. Roche. Sparse interpolation over finite fields via low-order roots of unity. ISSAC '14, pages 27–34. ACM, 2014. doi:10.1145/2608628.2608671.

[8] A. Arnold, M. Giesbrecht, and D. S. Roche. Faster sparse multivariate polynomial interpolation of straight-line programs. *Journal of Symbolic Computation*, 2015. doi:10.1016/j.jsc.2015.11.005.

[9] M. Ben-Or and P. Tiwari. A deterministic algorithm for sparse multivariate polynomial interpolation. STOC '88, pages 301–309. ACM, 1988. doi:10.1145/62212.62241.

[10] F. Biscani. Parallel sparse polynomial multiplication on modern hardware architectures. ISSAC '12, 2012.

[11] R. E. Blahut. A universal reed-solomon decoder. *IBM Journal of Research and Development*, 28(2):150–158, March 1984. doi:10.1147/rd.282.0150.

[12] A. Borodin and P. Tiwari. On the decidability of sparse univariate polynomial interpolation. *Computational Complexity*, 1:67–90, 1991. doi:10.1007/BF01200058.

[13] A. Bostan, G. Lecerf, and E. Schost. Tellegen's principle into practice. ISSAC '03, pages 37–44. ACM, 2003. doi:10.1145/860854.860870.

[14] A. Bostan, F. Chyzak, M. Giusti, R. Lebreton, G. Lecerf, B. Salvy, and E. Schost. *Algorithmes Efficaces en Calcul Formel*. 1.0 edition, Aug. 2017.

[15] B. Boyer, M. T. Comer, and E. L. Kaltofen. Sparse polynomial interpolation by variable shift in the presence of noise and outliers in the evaluations. In *Electr. Proc. Tenth Asian Symposium on Computer Mathematics (ASCM 2012)*, 2012.

[16] D. G. Cantor and E. Kaltofen. On fast multiplication of polynomials over arbitrary algebras. *Acta Informatica*, 28:693–701, 1991. doi:10.1007/BF01178683.

[17] A. Chattopadhyay, B. Grenet, P. Koiran, N. Portier, and Y. Strozecki. Computing the multilinear factors of lacunary polynomials without heights. Manuscript (submitted), 2013. URL https://arxiv.org/abs/1311.5694.

[18] M. T. Comer, E. L. Kaltofen, and C. Pernet. Sparse polynomial interpolation and Berlekamp/Massey algorithms that correct outlier errors in input values. ISSAC '12, pages 138–145. ACM, 2012. doi:10.1145/2442829.2442852.

[19] F. Cucker, P. Koiran, and S. Smale. A polynomial time algorithm for Diophantine equations in one variable. *J. Symbolic Comput.*, 27(1):21–29, 1999. doi:10.1006/jsco.1998.0242.

[20] A. Cuyt and W. Lee. Sparse interpolation of multivariate rational functions. *Theoretical Computer Science*, 412(16):1445 – 1456, 2011. doi:10.1016/j.tcs.2010.11.050.

[21] A. Cuyt, W. shin Lee, and X. Wang. On tensor decomposition, sparse interpolation and Padé approximation. *Jaen journal on approximation*, 8(1):33–58, 2016.

[22] J. H. Davenport and J. Carette. The sparsity challenges. In *Symbolic and Numeric Algorithms for Scientific Computing (SYNASC), 2009 11th International Symposium on*, pages 3 –7, Sept. 2009. doi:10.1109/SYNASC.2009.62.

[23] R. Fateman. Comparing the speed of programs for sparse polynomial multiplication. *SIGSAM Bull.*, 37(1):4–15, March 2003. doi:10.1145/844076.844080.

[24] R. Fateman. Draft: What's it worth to write a short program for polynomial multiplication? Online, Dec. 2008. URL http://www.cs.berkeley.edu/~fateman/papers/shortprog.pdf.

[25] R. J. Fateman. Endpaper: Frpoly: A benchmark revisited. *LISP and Symbolic Computation*, 4(2):155–164, Apr 1991. doi:10.1007/BF01813018.

[26] M. A. Forbes and A. Shpilka. Complexity theory column 88: Challenges in polynomial factorization. *SIGACT News*, 46(4):32–49, Dec. 2015. doi:10.1145/2852040.2852051.

[27] M. Fürer. Faster integer multiplication. STOC '07, pages 57–66. ACM, 2007. doi:10.1145/1250790.1250800.

[28] S. Garg and É. Schost. Interpolation of polynomials given by straight-line programs. *Theoretical Computer Science*, 410(27-29):2659–2662, 2009. doi:10.1016/j.tcs.2009.03.030.

[29] M. Gastineau and J. Laskar. Development of TRIP: Fast sparse multivariate polynomial multiplication using burst tries. In V. Alexandrov, G. van Albada, P. Sloot, and J. Dongarra, editors, *Computational Science - ICCS 2006*, volume 3992 of *Lecture Notes in Computer Science*, pages 446–453. Springer Berlin Heidelberg, 2006. doi:10.1007/11758525_60.

[30] M. Gastineau and J. Laskar. Highly scalable multiplication for distributed sparse multivariate polynomials on many-core systems. In V. P. Gerdt, W. Koepf, E. W. Mayr, and E. V. Vorozhtsov, editors, *Computer Algebra in Scientific Computing*, pages 100–115, Cham, 2013. Springer International Publishing. doi:10.1007/978-3-319-02297-0_8.

[31] M. Gastineau and J. Laskar. Parallel sparse multivariate polynomial division. PASCO '15, pages 25–33. ACM, 2015. doi:10.1145/2790282.2790285.

[32] J. von zur Gathen and J. Gerhard. *Modern Computer Algebra*. Cambridge University Press, Cambridge, second edition, 2003.

[33] J. von zur Gathen and D. Panario. Factoring polynomials over finite fields: A survey. *Journal of Symbolic Computation*, 31(1-2):3 – 17, 2001. doi:10.1006/jsco.1999.1002.
[34] M. Giesbrecht and D. S. Roche. On lacunary polynomial perfect powers. ISSAC '08, pages 103–110. ACM, 2008. doi:10.1145/1390768.1390785.
[35] M. Giesbrecht and D. S. Roche. Interpolation of shifted-lacunary polynomials. *Computational Complexity*, 19:333–354, 2010. doi:10.1007/s00037-010-0294-0.
[36] M. Giesbrecht and D. S. Roche. Detecting lacunary perfect powers and computing their roots. *Journal of Symbolic Computation*, 46(11):1242–1259, 2011. doi:10.1016/j.jsc.2011.08.006.
[37] M. Giesbrecht and D. S. Roche. Diversification improves interpolation. ISSAC '11, pages 123–130. ACM, 2011. doi:10.1145/1993886.1993909.
[38] M. Giesbrecht, E. Kaltofen, and W. Lee. Algorithms for computing sparsest shifts of polynomials in power, chebyshev, and pochhammer bases. *Journal of Symbolic Computation*, 36(3-4):401 – 424, 2003. doi:10.1016/S0747-7171(03)00087-7. ISSAC 2002.
[39] B. Grenet. Bounded-degree factors of lacunary multivariate polynomials. *Journal of Symbolic Computation*, 75:171–192, 2016. doi:10.1016/j.jsc.2015.11.013. Special issue on the conference ISSAC 2014: Symbolic computation and computer algebra.
[40] B. Grenet, J. van der Hoeven, and G. Lecerf. Randomized root finding over finite FFT-fields using tangent Graeffe transforms. In *Proc. 40th International Symposium on Symbolic and Algebraic Computation*, ISSAC '15, page to appear, 2015.
[41] D. Y. Grigoriev and M. Karpinski. The matching problem for bipartite graphs with polynomially bounded permanents is in NC. In *Foundations of Computer Science, 1987., 28th Annual Symposium on*, pages 166–172, Oct. 1987. doi:10.1109/SFCS.1987.56.
[42] D. Y. Grigoriev, M. Karpinski, and M. F. Singer. Fast parallel algorithms for sparse multivariate polynomial interpolation over finite fields. *SIAM Journal on Computing*, 19(6):1059–1063, 1990. doi:10.1137/0219073.
[43] W. Hart, M. van Hoeij, and A. Novocin. Practical polynomial factoring in polynomial time. ISSAC '11, pages 163–170. ACM, 2011. doi:10.1145/1993886.1993914.
[44] D. Harvey, J. van der Hoeven, and G. Lecerf. Faster polynomial multiplication over finite fields. *J. ACM*, 63(6):52:1–52:23, Jan. 2017. doi:10.1145/3005344.
[45] J. van der Hoeven and G. Lecerf. On the complexity of multivariate blockwise polynomial multiplication. In *Proc. ISSAC 2012*, pages 211–218, 2012. doi:10.1145/2442829.2442861.
[46] J. van der Hoeven and G. Lecerf. On the bit-complexity of sparse polynomial and series multiplication. *Journal of Symbolic Computation*, 50:227–0254, 2013. doi:10.1016/j.jsc.2012.06.004.
[47] J. van der Hoeven and G. Lecerf. Sparse polynomial interpolation in practice. *ACM Commun. Comput. Algebra*, 48(3/4):187–191, Feb. 2015. doi:10.1145/2733693.2733721.
[48] M.-D. A. Huang and A. J. Rao. Interpolation of sparse multivariate polynomials over large finite fields with applications. *Journal of Algorithms*, 33(2):204–228, 1999. doi:10.1006/jagm.1999.1045.
[49] Q. Huang and X. Gao. Faster deterministic sparse interpolation algorithms for straight-line program multivariate polynomials. *CoRR*, abs/1709.08979, 2017. URL http://arxiv.org/abs/1709.08979.
[50] E. Imamoglu, E. L. Kaltofen, and Z. Yang. Sparse polynomial interpolation with arbitrary orthogonal polynomial bases. In *Proc. ISSAC'18*, 2018.
[51] S. M. M. Javadi and M. Monagan. Parallel sparse polynomial interpolation over finite fields. PASCO '10, pages 160–168. ACM, 2010. doi:10.1145/1837210.1837233.
[52] S. C. Johnson. Sparse polynomial arithmetic. *SIGSAM Bull.*, 8:63–71, August 1974. doi:10.1145/1086837.1086847.
[53] E. Kaltofen. Notes on polynomial and rational function interpolation. Unpublished manuscript, 1988.
[54] E. Kaltofen. Polynomial factorization: A success story. ISSAC '03, pages 3–4. ACM, 2003. doi:10.1145/860854.860857.
[55] E. Kaltofen and P. Koiran. On the complexity of factoring bivariate supersparse (lacunary) polynomials. ISSAC '05, pages 208–215. ACM, 2005. doi:10.1145/1073884.1073914.
[56] E. Kaltofen and P. Koiran. Finding small degree factors of multivariate supersparse (lacunary) polynomials over algebraic number fields. ISSAC '06, pages 162–168. ACM, 2006. doi:10.1145/1145768.1145798.
[57] E. Kaltofen and W. Lee. Early termination in sparse interpolation algorithms. *Journal of Symbolic Computation*, 36(3-4):365–400, 2003. doi:10.1016/S0747-7171(03)00088-9. ISSAC 2002.
[58] E. Kaltofen and L. Yagati. Improved sparse multivariate polynomial interpolation algorithms. In P. Gianni, editor, *Symbolic and Algebraic Computation*, volume 358 of *Lecture Notes in Computer Science*, pages 467–474. Springer Berlin / Heidelberg, 1989. doi:10.1007/3-540-51084-2_44.
[59] E. Kaltofen and Z. Yang. On exact and approximate interpolation of sparse rational functions. ISSAC '07, pages 203–210. ACM, 2007. doi:10.1145/1277548.1277577.
[60] E. Kaltofen, Y. N. Lakshman, and J.-M. Wiley. Modular rational sparse multivariate polynomial interpolation. ISSAC '90, pages 135–139. ACM, 1990. doi:10.1145/96877.96912.
[61] E. L. Kaltofen. Fifteen years after DSC and WLSS2: What parallel computations I do today [invited lecture at PASCO 2010]. PASCO '10, pages 10–17. ACM, 2010. doi:10.1145/1837210.1837213.
[62] E. L. Kaltofen and M. Nehring. Supersparse black box rational function interpolation. ISSAC '11, pages 177–186. ACM, 2011. doi:10.1145/1993886.1993916.
[63] E. L. Kaltofen and Z. Yang. Sparse multivariate function recovery from values with noise and outlier errors. ISSAC '13, pages 219–226. ACM, 2013. doi:10.1145/2465506.2465524.
[64] E. L. Kaltofen, C. Pernet, A. Storjohann, and C. Waddell. Early termination in parametric linear system solving and rational function vector recovery with error correction. ISSAC '17, pages 237–244. ACM, 2017. doi:10.1145/3087604.3087645.
[65] M. Khochtali, D. S. Roche, and X. Tian. Parallel sparse interpolation using small primes. PASCO '15, pages 70–77. ACM, 2015. doi:10.1145/2790282.2790290.
[66] L. Kronecker. Grundzüge einer arithmetischen Theorie der algebraischen Grössen. *Journal für die reine und angewandte Mathematik*, 92:1–122, 1882.
[67] Y. N. Lakshman and B. D. Saunders. Sparse polynomial interpolation in nonstandard bases. *SIAM Journal on Computing*, 24(2):387–397, 1995. doi:10.1137/S0097539792237784.
[68] H. W. Lenstra, Jr. Finding small degree factors of lacunary polynomials. In *Number theory in progress, Vol. 1 (Zakopane-Kościelisko, 1997)*, pages 267–276. de Gruyter, Berlin, 1999.
[69] M. Monagan and R. Pearce. Polynomial division using dynamic arrays, heaps, and packed exponent vectors. In V. Ganzha, E. Mayr, and E. Vorozhtsov, editors, *Computer Algebra in Scientific Computing*, volume 4770 of *Lecture Notes in Computer Science*, pages 295–315. Springer Berlin / Heidelberg, 2007. doi:10.1007/978-3-540-75187-8_23.
[70] M. Monagan and R. Pearce. Parallel sparse polynomial multiplication using heaps. ISSAC '09, pages 263–270. ACM, 2009. doi:10.1145/1576702.1576739.
[71] M. Monagan and R. Pearce. Sparse polynomial division using a heap. *Journal of Symbolic Computation*, In Press, Corrected Proof, 2010. doi:10.1016/j.jsc.2010.08.014.
[72] M. Monagan and R. Pearce. Sparse polynomial multiplication and division in maple 14. *ACM Commun. Comput. Algebra*, 44(3/4):205–209, Jan. 2011. doi:10.1145/1940475.1940521.
[73] M. Monagan and R. Pearce. POLY: A new polynomial data structure for maple 17. *ACM Commun. Comput. Algebra*, 46(3/4):164–167, Jan. 2013. doi:10.1145/2429135.2429173.
[74] M. Monagan and R. Pearce. The design of Maple's sum-of-products and POLY data structures for representing mathematical objects. *ACM Commun. Comput. Algebra*, 48(3/4):166–186, Feb. 2015. doi:10.1145/2733693.2733720.
[75] B. Mourrain. Fast algorithm for border bases of artinian gorenstein algebras. ISSAC '17, pages 333–340. ACM, 2017. doi:10.1145/3087604.3087632.
[76] D. A. Plaisted. New NP-hard and NP-complete polynomial and integer divisibility problems. *Theoret. Comput. Sci.*, 31(1-2):125–138, 1984. doi:10.1016/0304-3975(84)90130-0.
[77] D. A. Popescu and R. T. Garcia. Multivariate polynomial multiplication on gpu. *Procedia Computer Science*, 80:154 – 165, 2016. doi:10.1016/j.procs.2016.05.306. International Conference on Computational Science 2016, ICCS 2016, 6-8 June 2016, San Diego, California, USA.
[78] B. d. Prony. Essai expérimental et analytique sur les lois de la Dilatabilité des fluides élastique et sur celles de la Force expansive de la vapeur de lâĂŽeau et de la vapeur de lâĂŽalkool, à différentes températures. *J. de lâĂŽÉcole Polytechnique*, 1:24–76, 1795.
[79] D. S. Roche. Adaptive polynomial multiplication. In *Proc. Milestones in Computer Algebra (MICA)*, pages 65–72, 2008.
[80] D. S. Roche. Chunky and equal-spaced polynomial multiplication. *Journal of Symbolic Computation*, 46(7):791–806, July 2011. doi:10.1016/j.jsc.2010.08.013.
[81] H. Schönemann. Singular in a framework for polynomial computations. In M. Joswig and N. Takayama, editors, *Algebra, Geometry and Software Systems*, pages 163–176, Berlin, Heidelberg, 2003. Springer Berlin Heidelberg. doi:10.1007/978-3-662-05148-1_9.
[82] J. Solomon. *Numerical Algorithms.* AK Peters/CRC Press, 2015.
[83] A. Steel. Multivariate polynomial rings. In *The Magma Handbook.* Computational Algebra Group, University of Sydney, 2018. URL http://magma.maths.usyd.edu.au/magma/handbook/text/223#1924.
[84] W. Stein and T. Sage Development Team. Polynomial rings. In *Sage Reference Manual.* URL https://doc.sagemath.org/html/en/reference/polynomial_rings. v8.2.
[85] T. Yan. The geobucket data structure for polynomials. *Journal of Symbolic Computation*, 25(3):285–293, 1998. doi:10.1006/jsco.1997.0176.
[86] R. Zippel. Probabilistic algorithms for sparse polynomials. In E. Ng, editor, *Symbolic and Algebraic Computation*, volume 72 of *Lecture Notes in Computer Science*, pages 216–226. Springer Berlin / Heidelberg, 1979. doi:10.1007/3-540-09519-5_73.
[87] R. Zippel. Interpolating polynomials from their values. *Journal of Symbolic Computation*, 9(3):375–403, 1990. doi:10.1016/S0747-7171(08)80018-1. Computational algebraic complexity editorial.

Modular Algorithms for Computing Minimal Associated Primes and Radicals of Polynomial Ideals

Toru Aoyama
Kobe University
Department of Mathematics Graduate school of Science
Kobe, Japan
Rikkyo University
Department of Mathematics
Tokyo, Japan
taoyama@math.kobe-u.ac.jp

Masayuki Noro
Rikkyo University
Department of Mathematics
Tokyo, Japan
noro@rikkyo.ac.jp

ABSTRACT

In this paper, we propose algorithms for computing minimal associated primes of ideals in polynomial rings over $\mathbb{Q}$ and computing radicals of ideals in polynomial rings over a field. They apply Chinese Remainder Theorem (CRT) to Laplagne's algorithm which computes minimal associated primes without producing redundant components and computes radicals. CRT reconstructs an object in a ring from its modular images in the quotient rings modulo some ideals. In Laplagne's algorithm, ideals are decomposed over rational function fields by regarding some variables as parameters. In our new algorithms, we compute the minimal associated primes and the radical of $\langle \phi(G) \rangle$ for a given ideal $I = \langle G \rangle$, where ϕ is a substitution map for a parameter. Then we construct candidates of the minimal associated primes and the radical of I by applying CRT for those of $\langle \phi(G) \rangle$'s. In order for this method to work correctly, the shape of each modular component must coincide with that of the corresponding component of the ideal for computations of minimal associated primes, and radicals of modular images of given ideals must coincide with modular images of radicals of given ideals for radical computations . The former is realized with a high probability because a multivariate irreducible polynomial over $\mathbb{Q}$ remains irreducible after a substitution of integers for variables with a high probability and the latter is realized except for a finite number of moduli.

CCS CONCEPTS

• **Computing methodologies** → **Algebraic algorithms**; • **Mathematics of computing** → *Mathematical software*;

KEYWORDS

minimal associated primes; radicals; modular algorithms; Gröbner basis; polynomial ring

ACM ISBN 978-1-4503-5550-6/18/07...$15.00
https://doi.org/10.1145/3208976.3209014

ACM Reference Format:
Toru Aoyama and Masayuki Noro. 2018. Modular Algorithms for Computing Minimal Associated Primes and Radicals of Polynomial Ideals. In *ISSAC'18: 2018 ACM International Symposium on Symbolic and Algebraic Computation, July 16–19, 2018, New York, NY, USA.* ACM, New York, NY, USA, 8 pages. https://doi.org/10.1145/3208976.3209014

1 INTRODUCTION

This paper proposes modular algorithms for computing minimal associated primes of ideals in $\mathbb{Q}[X]$ and computing radicals of ideals in polynomial rings over a field. Modular algorithms avoid the swell of coefficients which makes ideal computations slow-down. For computational targets in a ring R, modular algorithms choose projection maps R to R', take projected images of targets and compute in R' with the images to avoid the swell of coefficients. Then they reconstruct the real computed results in R from the computed results in R'. For reconstructions, the projection images need to maintain information of the original targets. We call a projection lucky if its images are 'useful' for reconstructions. Luckiness depends on what computations we perform and in general, we can not decide whether a projection is lucky or not before computations. It means that the computation is probabilistic and that in many cases the computed results of modular algorithms are only candidates of the expected results and we should verify the correctness in some way. Therefore, it is important for modular algorithms to detect unlucky projections quickly and to guarantee the correctness of the computed results by efficient methods.

There are several researches about modular algorithms for ideal computations. Arnold [3] and Pauer [14] propose modular algorithms for computing Gröbner basis. Idrees-Pfister-Steidel [9] apply a modular algorithm for radical computations and computing minimal associated primes of zero-dimensional ideals. Noro-Yokoyama [13] summarize them, describe the relation among several notions of luckiness and illustrate applications of modular algorithms for saturations, intersections, radical computations and primary decompositions.

In this paper, we apply modular algorithms for Laplagne's algorithm. It deals with a rational function field $\mathbb{K}(U)$ as a coefficient field, for the sake of reductions to zero-dimensional case. This tends to produce huge coefficients at intermediate computations. Therefore we apply modular algorithms which suppress the swell of coefficients. On the other hand, modular algorithms for computing minimal associated primes and radicals of polynomial ideals have been proposed in [9]. The most significant difference between our algorithms and the algorithms in [9] is the setting of projection maps. The algorithms in [9] utilize projections $\mathbb{Q}$ to $\mathbb{F}_p$ where p is a prime number, while our algorithms utilize projections $\mathbb{Q}(u)$ to $\mathbb{Q}$ (u is a parameter). Our projections reduce the number of parameters and keep the characteristic of coefficient fields 0.

In Section 3, we introduce some tools on which our algorithms are based. Laplagne's algorithm computes minimal associated primes and radicals of ideals over polynomial rings. Chinese Remainder Theorem guarantees the existence of an inverse image for given projected images and we compute it by interpolations and rational function reconstructions. Then we give definitions of luckiness for computing minimal associated primes and radicals. Our definitions are based on the luckiness for computing Gröbner basis defined in [13].

Our main results are in Section 4. We construct modular algorithms for computing a subset of minimal associated primes of zero-dimensional ideals in $\mathbb{Q}(U)[X]$ and computing radicals of zero-dimensional ideals in $\mathbb{K}(U)[X]$. Then we apply them for Laplagne's algorithm. We show the correctness of our algorithms. We also show that the number of lucky moduli is sufficiently large so that we can obtain the correct result with a high probability. Then we show the results of our implementation of the new algorithms. We measure the time for computing minimal associated primes and radicals of some ideals. We see that our algorithms are efficient for ideals which take long time to compute minimal associated primes and radicals by the Laplagne's original algorithm.

2 PRELIMINARIES

Let R be a ring, $\mathbb{K}$ a field, $X = \{x_1, \ldots, x_n\}$ variables, $U = \{u_1, \ldots, u_l\}$ parameters, $R[X]$ a polynomial ring over R, $R(U) = \left\{ \frac{f}{g} \,\middle|\, f, g \in R[U] \right\}$ and $\mathcal{M}$ the set of all power products in X. We define a monomial as a member of $\mathcal{M}$. For a polynomial f, we denote the square-free part of f by $\sqrt{f}$. For $F \subset R[X]$, we denote an ideal generated by F over R by $\langle F \rangle_R$. We also denote the ideal by $\langle F \rangle$ when the coefficient ring R is clear. Fix a monomial ordering $<$. For a polynomial $f \in R[X]$, we denote its leading term, leading monomial and leading coefficient with respect to $<$ by $LT(f)$, $LM(f)$ and $LC(f)$, respectively. Note that we define a term as a product of a monomial and a coefficient. For a set $F \subset R[X]$, we define the leading monomial set of F with respect to $< LM(F) = \{LM(f) | f \in F\}$. In the following of this paper, we omit to specify a monomial ordering unless it is necessary.

Definition 2.1. (*general position*)

1) A maximal ideal $M \subset \mathbb{K}[X]$ is called in general position with respect to $x_i \in X$, if there exist $g_1, \ldots, g_n \in \mathbb{K}[x_i]$ such that $\{x_1 + g_1(x_i), \ldots, x_{i-1}+g_{i-1}(x_i), x_{i+1}+g_{i+1}(x_i), \ldots, x_n+g_n(x_i), g_i(x_i)\}$ is the reduced Gröbner basis of M with respect to lexicographic ordering where x_i is smallest in X.
2) A zero-dimensional ideal $I \subset \mathbb{K}[X]$ is called in general position with respect to $x_i \in X$, if all associated primes $P_1, \ldots, P_m$ are in general position with respect to x_i and if $P_j \cap \mathbb{K}[x_i] \neq P_k \cap \mathbb{K}[x_i]$ for $j \neq k$.

Definition 2.2. Let I be an ideal in $\mathbb{K}[X]$. $U \subset X$ is called an *independent set* of I if $I \cap \mathbb{K}[U] = \{0\}$. We say that an independent set U is *maximal* when $\#U = \dim(I)$.

3 FUNDAMENTAL TOOLS AND DEFINITIONS

In this section, we review tools and define luckiness of ideals for constructing our new algorithms.

3.1 Laplagne's Algorithm

There are two well-known algorithms for computing radicals and minimal associated primes of zero-dimensional ideals. The former is designed for a zero-dimensional ideal I in $\mathbb{K}[X]$. It computes univariate square-free polynomials f_i such that $\langle f_i \rangle = I \cap \mathbb{K}[x_i]$ then $\sqrt{I} = \langle I, \sqrt{f_1}, \ldots, \sqrt{f_n} \rangle$. We name this algorithm zeroRadical. The latter is designed for ideals in $\mathbb{K}[X]$ where $char(\mathbb{K}) = 0$. It makes a given zero-dimensional ideal in general position by random coordinate changes then decomposes it by factorizations of polynomials. More details are in [7, Subsection 4.2]. We name the algorithm zeroMinAss. Laplagne's algorithm makes ideals zero-dimensional by regarding maximal independent sets of ideals as parameters and utilizes zeroRadical and zeroMinAss (Algorithm 1). In every loop of Algorithm 1, new components PJ and MA are disjoint therefore it works without producing redundant components. We list a lemma and a proposition which are related to the proof of Algorithm 1 for convenience of reference. More details and proofs are in [11] and [12].

Lemma 3.1. (See [4, Exercise 1.12 iv)].) Let I be an ideal in $\mathbb{K}[X]$ and $\sqrt{I} = \bigcap_{i=1}^{m} P_i$ the prime decomposition. Then a polynomial $g \in \mathbb{K}[X]$ gives the prime decomposition $\sqrt{I : g^\infty} = \bigcap_{g \notin P_i} P_i$.

Proposition 3.2. (See [7, Exercise 4.3.3 and Proposition 4.3.1 (2)].) Let I be an ideal in $\mathbb{K}[X]$, U a maximal independent set of $I : g^\infty$ and the prime decomposition $\sqrt{I} = \bigcap_{i=1}^{m} P_i$ in the condition $P_i \cap \mathbb{K}[U] = \{0\}(1 \leq i \leq l), P_i \cap \mathbb{K}[U] \neq \{0\}(l+1 \leq i \leq m)$. Then we have the prime decomposition $\sqrt{I\mathbb{K}(U)[X \setminus U]} \cap \mathbb{K}[X] = \bigcap_{i=1}^{l} P_i$.

Algorithm 1 Laplagne

Input: an ideal $I \subset \mathbb{K}[X]$ ($char(\mathbb{K}) = 0$)
Output: minAss(I) and $\sqrt{I}$

```
1:  Int ← ⟨1⟩, MA ← ∅
2:  Rad ← ⟨1⟩
3:  while Int \ √I ≠ ∅ do
4:      choose g ∈ Int \ √I
5:      J ← I : g^∞
6:      U ← a maximal independent set of J
7:      J ← JK(U)[X \ U]
8:      {P_1, ..., P_m} ← zeroMinAss(J)
9:      PJ ← {P_1 ∩ K[X], ..., P_m ∩ K[X]}
10:     MA ← MA ∪ PJ, Int ← Int ∩ ⋂_{P∈PJ} P
11:     Rad ← Rad ∩ (zeroRadical(J) ∩ K[X])
12: end while
13: return MA, Rad
```

Remark 3.3. By Algorithm 1, when we compute only minimal associated primes, we can omit line 11 and return MA. Note that Rad and Int coincides at line 3. Therefore when we compute only radicals, we can omit line 8, 9, and 10, utilize Rad instead of Int at line 3 and return Rad.

3.2 Chinese Remainder Theorem

When we perform a computation of an object from an input $F \subset R$ utilizing Chinese Remainder Theorem (CRT), we choose some ideals $I_i \subset R$ and compute a modular image of the object from F mod I_i on R/I_i. Interpolating these computed results we try to reconstruct the true object. There are two well-known interpolation, Lagrange's and Newton's. See [8, Subsection 5.2] for details.

Definition 3.4. Let $r_1, r_2 \in \mathbb{K}[u]$ and $I_1, I_2 \subset \mathbb{K}[u]$ comaximal ideals. We name the interpolation r_1 modulo I_1 and r_2 modulo I_2 $\mathrm{CRT}(r_1, r_2, I_1, I_2)$. For $f = \sum_{m \in \mathcal{M}} c_m m, g = \sum_{m \in \mathcal{M}} d_m m \in \mathbb{K}[u][X]$, we define $\mathrm{CRT}(f, g, I_1, I_2) = \sum_{m \in \mathcal{M}} \mathrm{CRT}(c_m, d_m, I_1, I_2)m$. For $F = \{ f_1, \dots, f_s \}, G = \{ g_1, \dots, g_s \} \subset \mathbb{K}[u][X]$ where $LM(f_i)$'s and $LM(g_i)$'s are distinct respectively and $LM(f_i) = LM(g_i)$, we define $\mathrm{CRT}(F, G, I_1, I_2) = \{ \mathrm{CRT}(f_i, g_i, I_1, I_2) \mid 1 \leq i \leq s \}$. Moreover, for $\mathcal{F} = \{ F_1, \dots, F_t \}$ and $\mathcal{G} = \{ G_1, \dots, G_t \}$ where $\mathrm{CRT}(F_i, G_i, I_1, I_2)$'s are defined, we define $\mathrm{CRT}(\mathcal{F}, \mathcal{G}, I_1, I_2) = \{ \mathrm{CRT}(F_i, G_i, I_1, I_2) \mid 1 \leq i \leq t \}$. When we compute CRT of indexed sets, we reset indices of members implicitly in order to complete the computation unless there are two or more candidates of indices which are suitable for the computation.

3.3 Rational function reconstruction

Our main target in this paper is the reduced Gröbner basis G of a minimal associated prime (or the radical) of an ideal I over a rational function field $\mathbb{K}(u)$. If we apply CRT for the modular images computed over $\mathbb{K}$, what we obtain is an object G' over $\mathbb{K}[u]$. If a coefficient $c(u)$ appearing in G is not a polynomial we have to recover $c(u)$ from the corresponding polynomial coefficient in G'. This procedure is as follows. Suppose that we try reconstructing a rational function $\frac{g(u)}{h(u)} \in \mathbb{K}(u)$. Let $k_i \in \mathbb{K}$ such that $h(u) \notin \langle u - k_i \rangle$ and $\langle M \rangle = \cap_i \langle u - k_i \rangle$. Utilizing CRT, we obtain a polynomial $f(u) \in \mathbb{K}[u]$ such that $f(u) \equiv \frac{g(u)}{h(u)} \pmod M$. Then g, h can be recovered by the following theorem and algorithm (Algorithm 2).

Theorem 3.5. ([8, Theorem 5.16]) Let $f, M \in \mathbb{K}[x]$, $\deg(f) < \deg(M) = n > 0$ and $r_i, s_i, t_i \in \mathbb{K}[x]$ be the j-th row in extended Euclidean Algorithm for M, f ,where j is minimal such that $\deg(r_j) < k$. There exist polynomials $r, t \in \mathbb{K}[x]$ satisfying

$$r \equiv tf \pmod M, \ \deg(r) < k, \ \deg(t) \leq n - k,$$

namely $r = r_j, t = t_j$. If in addition $\gcd(r_j, t_j) = 1$, then r, t also satisfy

$$\gcd(t, M) = 1, rt^{-1} \equiv f \pmod M, \ \deg(r) < k, \ \deg(t) \leq n - k.$$

We also utilize the algorithm RFR for reconstructing coefficients of polynomials, ideals and a set of ideals.

Definition 3.6. Let $\langle M \rangle = \cap_i \langle u - k_i \rangle (k_i \in \mathbb{K}) \subset \mathbb{K}[u]$. For a polynomial $f = \sum_{m \in \mathcal{M}} c_m m \in \mathbb{K}[u][X]$, we define $\mathrm{RFR}(f, M) = \sum_{m \in \mathcal{M}} \mathrm{RFR}(c_m, M)m$. For a subset $F \subset \mathbb{K}[u][X]$, we define $\mathrm{RFR}(F, M) = \{ \mathrm{RFR}(f, M) \mid f \in F \}$. Moreover, for $\mathcal{F} = \{ F_1, \dots, F_s \}$ where $\mathrm{RFR}(F_i, M)$'s are defined, we define $\mathrm{RFR}(\mathcal{F}, M) = \{ \mathrm{RFR}(F, M) \mid F \in \mathcal{F} \}$.

Remark 3.7. According to Theorem 3.5, when we reconstruct $\frac{g(u)}{h(u)} \in \mathbb{K}(u)$ ($\gcd(g, h) = 1$) from $f(u) \in \mathbb{K}[u]$ by RFR, we need more than $\deg(g) + \deg(h)$ ideals $\langle u - k_i \rangle$ ($k_i \in \mathbb{K}$ and $h(k_i) \neq 0$).

Algorithm 2 RFR

Input: polynomials $f, M \in \mathbb{K}[x]$
Output: $g, h \in \mathbb{K}[x]$ s.t. $f \equiv g/h \pmod M$, h is monic and $\gcd(g, h) = 1$

```
r_0 ← M, r_1 ← f, t_0 ← 0, t_1 ← 1
i ← 1
while 2 deg(r_i) > deg(M) do
    R_i ← NF(r_{i-1}, {r_i})
    Q ← (r_{i-1} - R_i)/r_i
    r_{i+1} ← R_i, t_{i+1} ← t_{i-1} - Q t_i
    i ← i + 1
end while
return (r_i, t_i)
```

With a shortage of ideals, RFR can return a rational function which is different from $\frac{g(u)}{h(u)}$. We say that the output of RFR is *stable* if we have more than $\deg(g) + \deg(h)$ ideals. However, we can not decide $\deg(g) + \deg(h)$ before computation in general. Therefore we say that the output is *pseudo stable* if $\mathrm{RFR}(f(u), M) = \mathrm{RFR}(f(u), M')$, where $\langle M \rangle = \cap_{i=1}^{r} \langle u - k_i \rangle$, $\langle M' \rangle = \cap_{i=1}^{s} \langle u - k_i \rangle$ $(r < s)$. When the output becomes pseudo stable, we regard the output as a candidate of the unique rational function.

3.4 Luckiness

For constructing modular algorithms, we have to define several notions of luckiness of moduli. The following definitions are extensions of [13, Definition 2.1].

Definition 3.8. Let $u \notin X$ be a variable, F a subset of $\mathbb{K}(u)[X]$, G the reduced Gröbner basis of $\langle F \rangle$ and $k \in \mathbb{K}$, then $\langle u - k \rangle$ is a prime ideal in $\mathbb{K}[u]$.

1) $\mathbb{K}[u]_{(u-k)} := \{ \frac{f}{g} | f, g \in \mathbb{K}[u], g(k) \neq 0 \}$.
2) $\phi_{(u-k)} : \mathbb{K}(u) \to \mathbb{K}; f \mapsto f(k)$. We denote projection maps $\mathbb{K}[u]_{(u-k)} \to \mathbb{K}$ and $\mathbb{K}[u]_{(u-k)}[X] \to \mathbb{K}[X]$ by the same symbol $\phi_{(u-k)}$ such that $\frac{f}{g} \mapsto \frac{f(k)}{g(k)}$ and $\sum_{m \in \mathcal{M}} c_m m \mapsto \sum_{m \in \mathcal{M}} \phi_{(u-k)}(c_m)m$.
3) $I_{(u-k)}(F) := \langle \phi_{(u-k)}(f) | f \in F \rangle$.
4) $\langle u - k \rangle$ is said to be *weak permissible* for F if $F \subset \mathbb{K}[u]_{(u-k)}$. $\langle u - k \rangle$ is said to be *permissible* for F if $\langle u - k \rangle$ is weak permissible for F and $\phi_{(u-k)}(LC(f)) \neq 0$ for all $f \in F$.
5) Let H be the reduced Gröbner basis of $\sqrt{\langle G \rangle}$. $\langle u - k \rangle$ is said to be *effectively radical lucky* for G if $\langle u - k \rangle$ is permissible for G, H and $\phi_{(u-k)}(H)$ is the reduced Gröbner basis of $\sqrt{I_{(u-k)}(G)}$.
6) Let $\sqrt{\langle G \rangle} = \cap_{i=1}^{m} P_i$ be the prime decomposition and G_i the reduced Gröbner basis of P_i. $\langle u - k \rangle$ is said to be *effectively minass lucky* for G if $\langle u - k \rangle$ is permissible for G and G_i $(i = 1, \dots, m)$, $\sqrt{I_{(u-k)}(G)} = \cap_{i=1}^{m} Q_i$ is the prime decomposition and $\phi_{(u-k)}(G_i)$ is the reduced Gröbner basis of Q_i.

Note that Definition 3.8 1) to 4) are defined for computing Gröbner basis by Noro-Yokoyama [13]. Now, our goal is computing radicals and minimal associated primes. Therefore we define Definition 3.8 6), 7) as luckiness. The following lemma is fundamental.

Lemma 3.9. Let G be a Gröbner basis (respectively the reduced Gröbner basis) of $I \subset \mathbb{K}(u)[X]$ ($u \notin X$). If an ideal $\langle u-k \rangle$ is permissible for G, then $\phi_{(u-k)}(G)$ is a Gröbner basis (respectively the reduced Gröbner basis) of $I_{(u-k)}(G)$.

Proof. For $\overline{h} \in I_{(u-k)}(G)$, $\overline{h}$ is written as $\overline{h} = \sum_{g \in G} c_g \phi_{(u-k)}(g)$ where $c_g \in \mathbb{K}[X]$. Then $h = \sum_{g \in G} c_g g \in I \cap \mathbb{K}[u]_{(u-k)}[X]$ and $\phi_{(u-k)}(h) = \overline{h}$. Let $h_0 \in I \cap \mathbb{K}[u]_{(u-k)}[X]$ such that $\phi_{(u-k)}(h_0) = \overline{h}$ and $LM(h_0)$ is minimal. Since $h_0 \in I$, there exists $g \in G$ such that $LM(g) \mid LM(h_0)$. Since $\langle u-k \rangle$ is permissible for G, $\phi_{(u-k)}(LC(g)) \neq 0$. Set $h' = h_0 - \frac{LT(h_0)}{LT(g)} g$. Then $LM(h') < LM(h_0)$. If $\phi_{(u-k)}(LC(h_0)) = 0$ then $\phi_{(u-k)}(h') = \phi_{(u-k)}(h_0)$ and it contradicts the construction of h_0. Thus $\phi_{(u-k)}(LC(h_0)) \neq 0$ and $LM(h_0) = LM(\overline{h})$. Therefore $LM(\phi_{(u-k)}(g)) \mid LM(\overline{h})$ and $\phi_{(u-k)}(G)$ is a Gröbner basis of $I_{(u-k)}(G)$. If G is the reduced Gröbner basis of I, then $\phi_{(u-k)}(G)$ is a Gröbner basis of $I_{(u-k)}(G)$ consisting of monic polynomials. The permissibility implies $LM(G) = LM(\phi_{(u-k)}(G))$ and it is clear that $\phi_{(u-k)}(G)$ is the reduced Gröbner basis. □

4 NEW ALGORITHM

zeroMinAss contains factorizations of polynomials and it may cause a problem which does not occur in the case of Gröbner basis computation: a problem caused by extraneous factors. For example, if we try to apply the modular algorithm over $\mathbb{Q}$, in many cases, a factorization over $\mathbb{F}_p$ produces more factors than over $\mathbb{Q}$ and it is hard to reconstruct the correct result from the results of modular computations. [9, Algorithm 3] is a modular algorithm for computing minimal associated primes which contains factorizations of polynomials however it performs reconstructions before factorizations and avoids factorizations over $\mathbb{F}_p$.

Now, Algorithm 1 regards some variables $U \subset X$ as parameters. Therefore we propose to apply Chinese Remainder Theorem over $\mathbb{Q}(U)$ for Algorithm 1. We fix some $u \in U$ and we reconstruct the result over $\mathbb{Q}(U)$ from the results of modular computation over $\mathbb{Q}(U \setminus \{u\})$ by using CRT and RFR. Namely, for an ideal $I = \langle G \rangle \subset \mathbb{Q}(U)[X \setminus U]$ where G is the reduced Gröbner basis of I, we find $\langle u-z \rangle$ which is permissible for G and compute the minimal associated primes (or the radical) of $\langle \phi_{(u-k)}(G) \rangle$. We gather these results for sufficiently many moduli for reconstructing the results over $\mathbb{Q}(U)$. Applying $\phi_{(u-k)}$ is equivalent to substituting k for u. Thus we can reduce one parameter. We repeat this procedure recursively and finally we compute minimal associated primes (or the radical) in $\mathbb{Q}[X \setminus U]$. Then we reconstruct parameters one by one recursively and obtain some members of the minimal associated primes (or the radical) (Algorithm 3, 4). We describe how to apply modular algorithms for zeroRadical and zeroMinAss concretely.

For showing the termination and correctness of Algorithm 3, 4 we give several propositions. In the following let $U = \{u_1, \ldots, u_l\}$ be a set of parameters and $\mathbb{K} = \mathbb{Q}(U)$ a rational function field over $\mathbb{Q}$.

Proposition 4.1. Let $u \notin X$ be a parameter, $I \subset \mathbb{K}(u)[X]$ an ideal and G the reduced Gröbner basis of I. If $k \in \mathbb{K}$, $\langle u-k \rangle$ is permissible for G and $\overline{I} = I_{(u-k)}(G)$ is a prime ideal in $\mathbb{K}[X]$, then I is a prime ideal in $\mathbb{K}(u)[X]$.

Algorithm 3 modZeroRadical

Input: G is a Gröbner basis of a zero-dimensional ideal in $\mathbb{K}(U)[X]$, U a set of parameters
Output: $\sqrt{\langle G \rangle}$

```
if U = ∅ then
    return zeroRadical(⟨G⟩)
end if
M ← 1, K ← ∅, F ← ∅, F_R ← ∅
u ← an element of U
loop
    choose k ∈ K \ K s.t. ⟨u − k⟩ is effectively radical lucky for G
    K ← K ∪ {k}, m ← u − k
    ZR ← modZeroRadical(φ_(u−k)(G), U \ {u})
    F' ← the reduced Gröbner basis of ZR
    if F ≠ ∅ then
        F' ← CRT(F, F', ⟨M⟩, ⟨m⟩)
    end if
    F'_R ← RFR(F', mM)
    if F_R = F'_R then
        if ⟨G⟩ ⊂ ⟨F_R⟩ ⊂ √⟨G⟩ then
            return ⟨F_R⟩
        end if
    end if
    M ← mM, F ← F', F_R ← F'_R
end loop
```

Proof. From Lemma 3.9, $\phi_{(u-k)}(G)$ is the reduced Gröbner basis of $\overline{I}$. For $f, g \in \mathbb{K}(u)[X] \setminus I$, assume that $fg \in I$ ($m \in \mathbb{Z}$). We can regard f, g as G-reduced and $(u-k) \nmid f, g$ without loss of generality. Then $\phi_{(u-k)}(f) \neq 0$ and $\phi_{(u-k)}(g) \neq 0$. On the other hand, $\phi_{(u-k)}(fg) = \phi_{(u-k)}(f)\phi_{(u-k)}(g) \in \overline{I}$. When $\overline{I}$ is a prime ideal, $\phi_{(u-k)}(f) \in \overline{I}$ or $\phi_{(u-k)}(g) \in \overline{I}$. Since $\phi_{(u-k)}(f), \phi_{(u-k)}(g)$ are $\phi_{(u-k)}(G)$-reduced, $\phi_{(u-k)}(f) = 0$ or $\phi_{(u-k)}(g) = 0$. It is a contradiction. □

Proposition 4.2. ([10, Theorem 5.6 (2)]) Let $u \notin X$ be a parameter, $I \subset \mathbb{K}(u)[X]$ an ideal and G the reduced Gröbner basis of I. If $k \in \mathbb{K}$, $\langle u-k \rangle$ is permissible for G and $\overline{I} = I_{(u-k)}(G)$ is a radical ideal in $\mathbb{K}[X]$, then I is a radical ideal in $\mathbb{K}(u)[X]$.

Proof. We can prove in a similar manner as the proof of Proposition 4.1. □

Proposition 4.3. Let P, Q be ideals in $\mathbb{K}(u)[X]$, $G = \{g_1, \ldots, g_s\}$ the reduced Gröbner basis of P, $H = \{h_1, \ldots, h_r\}$ the reduced Gröbner basis of Q. If $k \in \mathbb{K}$ and $\langle u-k \rangle$ is permissible for G, H and $\langle \phi_{(u-k)}(G) \rangle \not\subset \langle \phi_{(u-k)}(H) \rangle$, then $P \not\subset Q$.

Proof. Take a polynomial $\overline{f} \in \langle \phi_{(u-k)}(G) \rangle \setminus \langle \phi_{(u-k)}(H) \rangle$. $\overline{f}$ can be written as $\overline{f} = \sum_{i=1}^{s} c_i \phi_{(u-k)}(g_i)$ ($c_i \in \mathbb{K}$). Set $f = \sum_{i=1}^{s} c_i g_i \in P$. If $P \subset Q$, then f can be written as $f = \sum_{i=1}^{r} d_i h_i$ ($d_i \in \mathbb{K}[u]_{(u-k)}$) because H is the reduced Gröbner basis of Q and $\langle u-k \rangle$ is permissible for H. Then $\overline{f} = \phi_{(u-k)}(f) = \sum_{i=1}^{r} \phi_{(u-k)}(d_i)\phi_{(u-k)}(h_i) \in \langle \phi_{(u-k)}(H) \rangle$. It is a contradiction. □

Theorem 4.4. Algorithm 3 terminates and outputs $\sqrt{\langle G \rangle}$.

Algorithm 4 modZeroMinAss

Input: G is a Gröbner basis of a zero-dimensional ideal in $\mathbb{Q}(U)[X]$, U a set of parameters

Output: a subset P of $\text{minAss}(\langle G\rangle) = \{P_1, \dots, P_m\}$ such that

$$P = \left\{ P_i \;\middle|\; j \neq i \Rightarrow LM(P_j) \neq LM(P_i) \right\}$$

1: **if** $U = \emptyset$ **then**
2: $MA \leftarrow$ zeroMinAss$(\langle G\rangle)$
3: $GB' \leftarrow \{$ the reduced Gröbner basis of $I \mid I \in MA \}$
4: $GB \leftarrow GB' \backslash \left\{ G_i \in GB' \;\middle|\; j(\neq i) \text{ exists s.t. } LM(G_i) = LM(G_j) \right\}$
5: **return** $\{ \langle G_i \rangle \mid G_i \in GB \}$
6: **end if**
7: $M \leftarrow 1, Z \leftarrow \emptyset, GB \leftarrow \emptyset, GB_R \leftarrow \emptyset$
8: $u \leftarrow$ an element of U
9: **loop**
10: choose $z \in \mathbb{Z} \backslash Z$ s.t. $\langle u - z\rangle$ is effectively minass lucky for G
11: $Z \leftarrow Z \cup \{z\}, m \leftarrow u - z$
12: $MA \leftarrow$ modZeroMinAss$(\phi_{(u-z)}(G), U \setminus \{u\})$
13: **if** $MA = \emptyset$ **then**
14: **return** $\emptyset$
15: **end if**
16: $GB' \leftarrow \{$ the reduced Gröbner basis of $I \mid I \in MA \}$
17: **if** $GB \neq \emptyset$ **then**
18: $GB' \leftarrow \mathsf{CRT}(GB, GB', \langle M\rangle, \langle m\rangle)$
19: **end if**
20: $GB'_R \leftarrow \mathsf{RFR}(GB', mM)$
21: **if** $GB_R = GB'_R$ **then**
22: **if** for all $G_i \in GB_R$, $\langle G_i\rangle \supset \langle G\rangle$ **then**
23: **return** $P = \{ \langle G_i\rangle \mid G_i \in GB_R \}$
24: **end if**
25: **end if**
26: $M \leftarrow mM, GB \leftarrow GB', GB_R \leftarrow GB'_R$
27: **end loop**

Proof. If $U = \emptyset$ then the algorithm simply calls zeroRadical and the output is correct. We assume that the algorithm terminates and outputs a correct result in the case $\#U = s$. Suppose $\#U = s + 1$. Let H be the reduced Gröbner basis of $\sqrt{\langle G\rangle}$. Since $\langle u - k\rangle$ is effectively radical lucky, $I_{(u-k)}(H) = \sqrt{I_{(u-k)}(G)}$. From the assumption on $\#U = s$, $ZR = \sqrt{I_{(u-k)}(G)}$. Therefore F_R will be eventually H after sufficient interpolations. In this case F_R satisfies the termination condition and the termination of the algorithm is guaranteed.
When the algorithm terminates, from Proposition 4.1, $\langle F_R\rangle$ is a radical ideal in $\mathbb{K}(U)[X]$. Then $\langle G\rangle \subset \langle F_R\rangle \subset \sqrt{\langle G\rangle}$ implies $\sqrt{\langle G\rangle} = \sqrt{\langle F_R\rangle} = \langle F_R\rangle$. □

Theorem 4.5. Algorithm 4 terminates and outputs a subset of $\text{minAss}(\langle G\rangle)$.

Proof. If $U = \emptyset$ then the algorithm simply calls zeroMinAss and the output is correct. We assume that the algorithm terminates and outputs a correct result in the case $\#U = s$. Suppose $\#U = s + 1$. Let $G_1, \dots, G_m$ be the reduced Gröbner bases of the minimal associated primes of $\langle G\rangle$. Set

$$\left\{ G_{i_1}, \dots, G_{i_k} \right\} = \left\{ G_i \;\middle|\; j \neq i \Rightarrow LM(G_j) \neq LM(G_i) \right\}.$$

Since $\langle u - z\rangle$ is effectively minass lucky,

$$\text{minAss}(\langle \phi_{(u-z)}(G)\rangle) = \{\langle \phi_{(u-z)}(G_1)\rangle, \dots, \langle \phi_{(u-z)}(G_m)\rangle\}$$

and $LM(G_i) = LM(\phi_{(u-z)}(G_i))$ $(i = 1, \dots, m)$. From the assumption on $\#U = s$,

$$GB' = \{\phi_{(u-z)}(G_{i_1}), \dots, \phi_{(u-z)}(G_{i_k})\}$$

at line 16 and for each $H \in GB'$ there exists the unique element G_i such that $LM(H) = LM(G_i)$. Thus we can combine the correct modular images by CRT and GB_R will be eventually the set $\left\{ \langle G_{i_1}\rangle, \dots, \langle G_{i_k}\rangle \right\}$ after sufficient interpolations. In this case GB_R satisfies the termination condition and the termination of the algorithm is guaranteed.
When the algorithm terminates, from Proposition 4.1, every $P_i \in P$ is a prime ideal in $\mathbb{Q}(U)[X]$ and $P_i \supset \langle G\rangle$. Then we have $\sqrt{P_i} = P_i \supset \sqrt{\langle G\rangle} = \cap_{i=1}^m \langle G_i\rangle$, which implies that $P_i \supset \langle G_j\rangle$ for some j. Since $\langle G\rangle$ is zero-dimensional $\langle G_j\rangle$ is maximal and we have $P_i = \langle G_j\rangle$. Thus every $P_i \in P$ is a member of $\text{minAss}(\langle G\rangle)$ and the result is correct in the case $\#U = s + 1$.

□

Remark 4.6. In Algorithm 4, the recursive application of Proposition 4.3 implies that the output P has no redundant components.

Remark 4.7. In Algorithm 4, depending on the input, some components of GB' can have the same leading monomial set at line 3. In such a case, we can not determine which pair of ideals we should interpolate. Therefore we do not perform interpolations for such components. If all of the components do not have unique leading monomial set unfortunately, we utilize zeroMinAss for computing the minimal associated primes of the zero-dimensional ideal.

Remark 4.8. In Algorithm 4, we cannot decide whether a modulus $\langle u - z\rangle$ is effectively minass lucky during the computation. If we choose a modulus which is permissible for G, we can obtain a subset of $\text{minAss}(\langle \phi_{(u-z)}(G)\rangle)$ by calling Algorithm 4 but the result may not be $\{\phi_{(u-z)}(G_{i_1}), \dots, \phi_{(u-z)}(G_{i_k})\}$. In this case the result is a noise for our modular algorithm and we have to add some additional criteria or preprocessing to avoid bad moduli as much as possible. However, even if we do not assume the effective minass luckiness of moduli, if the algorithm terminates then the result is a subset of $\text{minAss}(\langle G\rangle)$. This is ensured by the last part of the proof of Theorem 4.5. By a similar argument, if Algorithm 3 terminates, then the result is $\sqrt{\langle G\rangle}$ even if we do not assume the effective radical luckiness of moduli.

Utilizing Algorithm 3, 4 instead of zeroRadical and zeroMinAss in Algorithm 1, we can compute $\sqrt{I}$ and $\text{minAss}(I)$ of an ideal $I \subset \mathbb{Q}[X]$ (Algorithm 5, 6).

Theorem 4.9. Algorithm 5 works correctly.

Proof. (correctness) Since Algorithm 3 outputs $\sqrt{I : g^\infty}$ in $\mathbb{K}(U)[X \setminus U]$, Int is an intersection of prime components of $\sqrt{I}$ in $\mathbb{K}[X]$ by Lemma 3.1 and Int $\supset \sqrt{I}$. When the termination condition is satisfied, Int $= \sqrt{I}$.
(termination) Suppose Int $\neq \sqrt{I}$, $g \in \text{Int} \setminus \sqrt{I}$ and $\sqrt{I : g^\infty} = \bigcap_{i=1}^m P_i$

Algorithm 5 MODLRADICAL

Input: an ideal $I \subset \mathbb{K}[X]$
Output: $\sqrt{I}$
  Int $\leftarrow \langle 1 \rangle$
  while Int $\setminus \sqrt{I} \neq \emptyset$ **do**
    choose $g \in$ Int $\setminus \sqrt{I}$
    $U \leftarrow$ a maximal independent set of $I : g^\infty$
    $G \leftarrow$ a Gröbner basis of $I : g^\infty$ in $\mathbb{Q}(U)[X \setminus U]$
    Int $\leftarrow$ Int $\cap$ (MODZERORADICAL(G, U) $\cap \mathbb{K}[X]$)
  end while
  return Int

is the prime decomposition. For all $P_i (1 \leq i \leq m)$, $g \notin P_i$ by Lemma 3.1. Therefore Int $\not\supset$ Int $\cap (\sqrt{I : g^\infty} \cap \mathbb{K}[X])$. Since $\mathbb{K}[X]$ is Noetherian, this ascending chain becomes stable in finite steps. □

Algorithm 6 MODLMINASS

Input: an ideal $I \subset \mathbb{Q}[X]$
Output: minAss(I)
  Int $\leftarrow \langle 1 \rangle$, MA $\leftarrow \emptyset$
  while Int $\setminus \sqrt{I} \neq \emptyset$ **do**
    choose $g \in$ Int $\setminus \sqrt{I}$
    $U \leftarrow$ a maximal independent set of $I : g^\infty$
    $G \leftarrow$ a Gröbner basis of $I : g^\infty$ in $\mathbb{Q}(U)[X \setminus U]$
    $P \leftarrow$ MODZEROMINASS(G, U)
    if $P = \emptyset$ **then**
      $P \leftarrow$ ZEROMINASS$(\langle G \rangle)$
    end if
    $PG \leftarrow \{P_i \cap \mathbb{Q}[X] \mid P_i \in P\}$
    MA $\leftarrow$ MA$\cup PG$, Int $\leftarrow$ Int $\cap \bigcap_{P \in PG} P$
  end while
  return MA

Theorem 4.10. Algorithm 6 works correctly.

Proof. (correctness) Since Algorithm 4 outputs a subset of minAss$(I : g^\infty)$ in $\mathbb{Q}(U)[X \setminus U]$, PG is a subset of minAss$(I : g^\infty)$ in $\mathbb{Q}[X]$ by Proposition 3.2. Therefore MA is always a subset of minAss(I) by Lemma 3.1 and Int $\supset \sqrt{I}$. When the termination condition is satisfied, Int $= \sqrt{I}$ and $MA =$ minAss(I).
(termination) Let MA $\subset$ minAss(I) and Int $= \bigcap_{P \in MA} P$ (if MA $= \emptyset$, we define Int $= \langle 1 \rangle$). Suppose Int $\neq \sqrt{I}$, $g \in$ Int $\setminus \sqrt{I}$, $\sqrt{I : g^\infty} = \bigcap_{i=1}^{m} P_i$ is the prime decomposition and PG is a subset of minAss$(I : g^\infty)$. For all $P_i \in PG$, $g \notin P_i$ and $P_i \in$ minAss(I) by Lemma 3.1. On the other hand, since $g \in$ Int, for all $Q_i \in$ MA, $g \in Q_i$. Therefore for all $P_i \in PG$, $P_i \notin$ MA. In other words, Algorithm 6 obtains at least one new components in every loop. Since the number of components of minAss(I) is finite, Algorithm 6 terminates in finite steps. □

4.1 Existence of lucky moduli

In Algorithm 3, 4, we suppose all $\langle u - z \rangle$ (or $\langle u - k \rangle$) are effectively minass (or radical) lucky. However, effective luckiness is defined depending on the minimal associated primes (or the radical) of the given ideal. In general, we can not decide effective luckiness during the computation. Therefore we show that there are sufficiently many effectively minass (or radical) lucky ideals and we can obtain them with a high probability by random choice. Let G be the reduced Gröbner basis of a zero-dimensional ideal $I \subset \mathbb{K}(u)[X]$. $\sqrt{\langle G \rangle} = \cap_{i=1}^{m} P_i$ the prime decomposition, G_i the reduced Gröbner basis of P_i. If $\langle u - k \rangle$ is permissible for G and G_i's then $\phi_{(u-k)}(G)$ and $\phi_{(u-k)}(G_i)$'s are Gröbner bases of $\langle \phi_{(u-k)}(G) \rangle$ and $\langle \phi_{(u-k)}(G_i) \rangle$'s respectively, and $LM(G) = LM(\phi_{(u-k)}(G))$ and $LM(G_i) = LM(\phi_{(u-k)}(G_i))$ imply $\langle \phi_{(u-k)}(G) \rangle$ and $\langle \phi_{(u-k)}(G_i) \rangle$'s are zero-dimensional. For simplicity, we assume that I is in general position with respect to x_n. This implies that each $\langle G_i \rangle$ is in general position with respect to x_n. If the monomial order is the lexicographic order, then G_i is a shape basis, i.e. $G_i = \langle x_1 - c_1(u), \ldots, x_{n-1} - c_{n-1}$ $c_1(u), \ldots, c_{n-1}(u), g_i(x_n) \in \mathbb{K}(u)[x_n]$ and $g_i(x_n)$ is irreducible over $\mathbb{K}(u)$ because $\langle G_i \rangle$ is zero-dimensional and prime. Set

$$NP = \{k \in \mathbb{K} \mid \langle u - k \rangle \text{ is not permissible for } G \text{ or some } G_i\}.$$

Then NP is a finite set. A modulus $\langle u - k \rangle$ is effectively minass lucky for G if the following four conditions hold.

1) $k \notin NP$.
2) $\sqrt{I_{(u-k)}(G)} = I_{(u-k)}(G_1) \cap \cdots \cap I_{(u-k)}(G_m)$.
3) If $i \neq j$, then $I_{(u-k)}(G_i) \neq I_{(u-k)}(G_j)$.
4) Each $I_{(u-k)}(G_i)$ is prime.

First of all, we consider the condition 2).

Lemma 4.11. Let $G \subset \mathbb{K}(u)[X]$ be the reduced Gröbner basis of a zero-dimensional ideal $\langle G \rangle$ and $H \subset \mathbb{K}(u)[X]$ the reduced Gröbner basis of $\sqrt{\langle G \rangle}$. Except for a finite number of $k \in \mathbb{K} \setminus NP$, $\sqrt{I_{(u-k)}(G)} = I_{(u-k)}(H)$.

Proof. If $\langle u - k \rangle$ is permissible for G, H, then $G \subset \langle H \rangle$ implies $\phi_{(u-k)}(G) \subset I_{(u-k)}(H)$ and $H \subset \sqrt{G}$ implies $\phi_{(u-k)}(H) \subset \sqrt{I_{(u-k)}(G)}$. Thus we have $\sqrt{I_{(u-k)}(H)} = \sqrt{I_{(u-k)}(G)}$. Since $\langle H \rangle$ is zero-dimensional and radical, for each $x_i \in X$ there exists a univariate square-free polynomial $f_i(x_i) \in \langle H \rangle$. Then $r_i(u) = \text{resultant}_{x_i}(f_i, f_i') \neq 0$. If $\langle u - k \rangle$ is permissible for $f_i(x_i)$ and $r_i(k) \neq 0$ for all i, then $\phi_{(u-k)}(f_i) \in I_{(u-k)}(H)$ is square-free. Then $I_{(u-k)}(H)$ is radical and in this case $\sqrt{I_{(u-k)}(H)} = I_{(u-k)}(H) = \sqrt{I_{(u-k)}(G)}$. Since the number of $k \notin NP$ such that k is not permissible for $f_i(x_i)$'s, or $r_i(k) = 0$ for some i is finite, the assertion is proved. □

Corollary 4.12. Except for a finite number of $k \in \mathbb{K}$, $\langle u - k \rangle$ is effectively radical lucky for G.

Proposition 4.13. Except for a finite number of $k \in \mathbb{K} \setminus NP$, $\sqrt{I_{(u-k)}(G)} = I_{(u-k)}(G_1) \cap \cdots \cap I_{(u-k)}(G_m)$.

Proof. Set

$$\tilde{I} = \langle 1 - (t_1 + \cdots + t_m), t_1 G_1, \ldots, t_m G_m \rangle \subset \mathbb{K}(u)[t_1, \ldots, t_m, X].$$

If $\tilde{H}$ is the reduced Gröbner basis of $\tilde{I}$ with respect to an elimination ordering such that $\{t_1, \ldots, t_m\} >> X$, then $H = \tilde{H} \cap \mathbb{K}(u)[X]$ is the reduced Gröbner basis of $\sqrt{\langle G \rangle} = \langle G_1 \rangle \cap \cdots \cap \langle G_m \rangle$. If $\langle u - k \rangle$

is permissible for all intermediate polynomials appearing during the execution of Buchberger's algorithm for computing $\tilde{H}$, then the remainder computations in the execution can be mapped by $\phi_{(u-k)}$. This implies that the reduced Gröbner basis of

$$\langle 1-(t_1+\cdots+t_m), t_1\phi_{(u-k)}(G_1), \ldots, t_m\phi_{(u-k)}(G_m)\rangle$$

with respect to the same elimination ordering is $\phi_{(u-k)}(\tilde{H})$. Since $\langle u-k\rangle$ is permissible for $\tilde{H}$, $\phi_{(u-k)}(\tilde{H}) \cap \mathbb{K}[X] = \phi_{(u-k)}(H)$ and $\phi_{(u-k)}(H)$ is the reduced Gröbner basis of $I_{(u-k)}(G_1)\cap\cdots\cap I_{(u-k)}(G_m)$. By Lemma 4.11 $\sqrt{I_{(u-k)}(G)} = I_{(u-k)}(H)$ except for a finite number of $k \in \mathbb{K}$. Therefore $\sqrt{I_{(u-k)}(G)} = I_{(u-k)}(H) = I_{(u-k)}(G_1) \cap \cdots \cap I_{(u-k)}(G_m)$ except for a finite number of $k \in \mathbb{K} \setminus NP$. □

Next we consider the condition 3).

Proposition 4.14. Except for a finite number of $k \in \mathbb{K} \setminus NP$, $I_{(u-k)}(G_i)$'s are distinct.

Proof. If $i \neq j$ then $\langle G_i\rangle$ and $\langle G_j\rangle$ are comaximal and $1 \in \langle G_i\rangle + \langle G_j\rangle$. Thus if $\langle u-k\rangle$ is permissible for G_i, G_j and all the coefficients in the generating relation of 1 by G_i and G_j, then $1 \in I_{(u-k)}(G_i)+I_{(u-k)}(G_j)$, which implies $I_{(u-k)}(G_i) \neq I_{(u-k)}(G_j)$. Thus $I_{(u-k)}(G_i)$'s are distinct except for a finite number of $k \in \mathbb{K} \setminus NP$. □

Finally we consider the condition 4).

Proposition 4.15. ([15, Proposition 132, Proposition 133]) Let $F(X_1, \ldots, X_n, Y_1, \ldots, Y_m)$ be an irreducible polynomial over $\mathbb{Q}$ and let $R(N)$ denote the number of integer x_i with $|x_i| < N$ such that $F(x_1, \ldots, x_n, Y_1, \ldots, Y_m)$ is reducible. Then

$$R(N) < cN^{n-1/2}\log N$$

where c depends only on the degree of F.

Proposition 4.16. Set

$$N_i = \{k \in \mathbb{Z} \mid |k| < N, k \notin NP, I_{(u-k)}(G_i) \text{ is not prime}\}.$$

Then $\#N_i \leq cN^{1/2}\log N$ for a constant c.

Proof. If $\langle u-k\rangle$ is permissible for G_i, then $\phi_{(u-k)}(G_i)$ is the reduced Gröbner basis of $I_{(u-k)}(G_i)$. $I_{(u-k)}(G_i)$ is prime if and only if $\phi_{(u-k)}(g_i(x_n))$ is irreducible. $g_i(x_n)$ can be written as $g_i(x_n) = \tilde{g}(u, u_1, \ldots, u_l, x_n)/d(u, u_1, \ldots, u_l)$ with $\tilde{g} \in \mathbb{Q}[u, u_1, \ldots, u_l, x_n]$, with $d \in \mathbb{Q}[u, u_1, \ldots, u_l]$ and $\tilde{g}$ is irreducible over $\mathbb{Q}$. Then the irreducibility of $\phi_{(u-k)}(g_i(x_n))$ is equivalent to that of $\tilde{g}(k, u_1, \ldots, u_l, x_n)$ and Proposition 4.15 with the case $n = 1$ implies $\#N_i \leq cN^{1/2}\log N$ for a constant c. □

Theorem 4.17. Set

$$NEML = \{k \in \mathbb{Z} \mid |k| < N, k \notin NP, \langle u-k\rangle \text{ is not effectively minass lucky for } G\}.$$

Then there exist constants c_1, c_2 such that $\#(NP \cup NEML) \leq c_1 + c_2N^{1/2}\log N$.

Proof. Set

$$BAD_2 = \{k \in \mathbb{K}\backslash NP \mid \sqrt{I_{(u-k)}(G)} \neq I_{(u-k)}(G_1)\cap\cdots\cap I_{(u-k)}(G_m)\},$$

$$BAD_3 = \{k \in \mathbb{K}\backslash NP \mid I_{(u-k)}(G_i) = I_{(u-k)}(G_j) \text{ for some } i, j (i \neq j)\}.$$

Then BAD_2 and BAD_3 are finite sets by Proposition 4.13 and Proposition 4.14 respectively. Then Proposition 4.16 implies $\#(NP \cup NEML) \leq (\#NP + \#BAD_2 + \#BAD_3) + (mc)N^{1/2}\log N$. □

Corollary 4.18. If k is randomly chosen from $\{k \in \mathbb{Z} \mid |k| < N\}$, then the probability that $\langle u-k\rangle$ is effectively minass lucky tends to 1 as $N \to \infty$.

5 EXPERIMENTS AND TIMING DATA

We measure the timings for computing minimal associated primes and radicals by our algorithms and Laplagne's algorithm. Laplagne's algorithm is implemented as a function `minAssGTZ` and `radical` in Singular [6]. In this paper, the unit of timing is a second and all results have been rounded to no more than three significant digits. All of our algorithms were implemented in Singular [6] and measured on a 64-bit Linux machine with Intel Xeon E5-2650 v2, 2.60GHz and 256GB memory. The library file of algorithms will be available from the URL [2].

In Subsection 4.1, we have shown that there are sufficiently many effectively minass (or radical) lucky moduli. However, when we choose an unlucky modulus there is a possibility that our algorithms do not terminate. Therefore we should discard unlucky modular images during computations. We adopt following strategies to terminate Algorithm 3, 4 with a high probability.

Strategy 5.1. Let G be the reduced Gröbner basis of the given ideal.

1) Chose $z \in \mathbb{Z} \setminus Z$ (or $k \in \mathbb{K} \setminus K$) such that $\langle u-z\rangle$ (or $\langle u-k\rangle$) is permissible for G.
2) For z_i's (or k_i's) satisfying 1), compute ModZeroMinAss($I_{(u-z_i)}(G)$) (or ModZeroRadical($I_{(u-k_i)}(G)$)), classify them by leading monomial sets of their components and perform CRT for the class of largest cardinality.
3) In Algorithm 4, if GB_R is pseudo stable and there are some $G_i \in GB_R$ such that $\langle G_i\rangle \not\supset \langle G\rangle$, then we discard G_i's and return $\left\{ \langle G_j\rangle \,\middle|\, G_j \in GB_R, \langle G_j\rangle \supset \langle G\rangle \right\}$.

As explained in Remark 4.8, when Algorithm 3, 4 with Strategy 5.1 terminate, the output is correct even if we choose some moduli which are not effectively minass (or radical) lucky for G in the computational process. If Algorithm 3, (respectively Algorithm 4) with Strategy 5.1 terminates, then Algorithm 5 (respectively Algorithm 6) terminates and outputs the radical (respectively the minimal associated primes) of the input ideal.

Furthermore, there are three improvements for Algorithm 5, 6 which are not written in the pseudo codes for the sake of simplicity. The first one is recording the number of moduli for the reconstruction. For a parameter u and $z_1 \in \mathbb{Z}$ (or $k_1 \in \mathbb{K}$), the number of moduli which makes ModZeroMinAss($\phi_{(u-z_1)}(G)$) (or ModZeroRadical($\phi_{(u-k_1)}(G)$)) pseudo stable becomes a hint to decide how many moduli we should gather for ModZeroMinAss($\phi_{(u-z_i)}(G)$)'s where z_i's are distinct from z_1 (or for ModZeroRadical($\phi_{(u-k_i)}(G)$)'s where k_i's are distinct from k_1). The second one is utilizing modular computations for RFR. We do not need the exact value of RFR before the output become pseudo stable. Therefore we perform RFR over $\mathbb{F}_p$ where p is a prime number. We perform RFR over the original coefficient field only when we confirm pseudo stability of RFR over $\mathbb{F}_p$. The last one is the preprocessing proposed in [1, Algorithm 5.2].

It utilizes the square-free parts of generators of the given ideal in order to enlarge the given ideal without changing its radical. We name Algorithm 5, 6 with these improvements and Strategy 5.1 Algorithm 5', 6'.

We construct examples of ideals from ideals given in [5, 3 Examples]. We classify ideals in [5, 3 Examples] by their number of variables. For $I_i \in \mathbb{Q}[v_1, \ldots, v_n]$ and $I_j \in \mathbb{Q}[u_1, \ldots u_n]$, we set a map

$$\varphi_{u,v} : \mathbb{Q}[u_1, \ldots u_n] \to \mathbb{Q}[v_1, \ldots, v_n]; u_m \mapsto v_m (1 \leq m \leq n)$$

and denote that

$$I_{i \cap j} = I_i \cap \varphi_{u,v}(I_j)$$

For these examples, we measure the timings for computing minimal associated primes (or radicals) by Algorithm 6' and Laplagne's algorithm (Table 1, 2). We omit examples which are decomposed in a few seconds by Laplagne's algorithm or do not terminate in four hours by both algorithms and zero-dimensional ideals. For zero-dimensional ideals, our algorithms and Laplagne's algorithm simply call zeroRadical and zeroMinAss.

Remark 5.2. As a characteristic of modular algorithms, if there are no swells of coefficients in the original computations, then computations of modular algorithms have little advantages over the original one. Moreover, modular algorithms iterate modular computations for some moduli and reconstruct their results. They become extra times of computations.

Table 1: Computing minimal associated primes of examples

	$I_{3\cap 8}$	$I_{18\cap 31}$	$I_{18\cap 33}$	$I_{31\cap 33}$	$I_{7\cap 9}$	$I_{7\cap 12}$	$I_{5\cap 23}$	$I_{1\cap 4}$
Variables	3	4			6		8	
Algorithm 6'	1.2	34.4	28.4	34.9	54.9	240	5880	812
Laplagne's	$> 4h$	$> 4h$	$> 4h$	$> 4h$	284	87.1	12100	$> 4h$

Table 2: Computing the radical of examples

	$I_{3\cap 8}$	$I_{18\cap 31}$	$I_{18\cap 33}$	$I_{31\cap 33}$	$I_{7\cap 9}$	$I_{7\cap 12}$	$I_{5\cap 23}$	$I_{1\cap 4}$
Variables	3	4			6		8	
Algorithm 5'	1.01	32.1	25.5	30.7	53.2	122	269	645
Laplagne's	0.95	608	2580	$> 4h$	398	$> 4h$	80.9	$> 4h$

6 CONCLUDING REMARKS

Our algorithms are fast for some class of ideals and will be a choice when general-purpose algorithms can not finish the computation in practical time. In addition, our algorithms are suitable for parallelizations. In this paper, we have not yet implemented the parallel version of our algorithms and we expect further speed-up with parallelizations. It is a future project.

In Subsection 4.1, we have shown that there are sufficiently many effectively minass lucky moduli. However there are infinite moduli which are not effectively minass lucky in general. On the other hand, in the case of computing Gröbner basis by modular algorithms over $\mathbb{F}_p$, it is shown that the number of unlucky primes is finite [13, Section 3] and we can construct algorithms which terminate in finite steps even if we choose some unlucky primes in the computational process [13, Section 5]. In order to improve our algorithms, we need more researches of luckiness and moduli whose modular images of irreducible polynomials keeps their irreducibility. It will be closely related with Hilbert's irreducibility theorem and its applications.

ACKNOWLEDGMENTS

This work was supported by JSPS KAKENHI Grant Number 15K05008.

REFERENCES

[1] T. Aoyama. 2017. An Algorithm for Computing Minimal Associated Primes of Binomial Ideals Without Producing Redundant Components. *Proceedings of the 2017 ACM on International Symposium on Symbolic and Algebraic Computation* (2017), 21–27. https://doi.org/10.1145/3087604.3087644

[2] T. Aoyama. 2017. A Singular package of modular algorithms for Laplagne's algorithm. http://www.math.kobe-u.ac.jp/HOME/taoyama/singular/modLap.lib.

[3] E. A. Arnold. 2000. Modular algorithms for computing Gröbner bases. *Journal of Symbolic Computation* 35 (2000), 403–419.

[4] M.F. Atiyah and I.G. MacDonald. 1969. *Introduction to commutative algebra.* Westview Press.

[5] W. Decker, G-M. Greuel, and G. Pfister. 1999. Primary decomposition: Algorithms and comparisons. *Algorithmic algebra and number theory* (1999), 187–220.

[6] W. Decker, G-M. Greuel, G. Pfister, and H. Schönemann. 2016. Singular 4-1-0 — A computer algebra system for polynomial computations. http://www.singular.uni-kl.de.

[7] J. V. Z. Gathen and J. Gerhard. 2003. *Modern Computer Algebra.* Cambridge University Press New York.

[8] G-M. Greuel and G. Pfister. 2008. *A Singular introduction to commutative algebra.* Springer-Verlag Berlin Heidelberg.

[9] N. Idrees, G. Pfister, and S. Steidel. 2011. Parallelization of modular algorithms. *Journal of Symbolic Computation* 46 (2011), 672–684.

[10] M. Kadota. 2009. Decomposition algorithms for polynomial ideals by modular computation (in Japanese). *Master's thesis, Kobe university* (2009).

[11] S. Laplagne. 2006. An algorithm for the computation of the radical of an ideal. *Proceedings of the 2006 international symposium on Symbolic and algebraic computation* (July 2006), 191–195. https://doi.org/10.1145/1145768.1145802

[12] S. Laplagne. 2006. Computation of the minimal associated primes. *Challenges in Symbolic Computation Software* 06271 (2006). https://doi.org/10.1145/1145768.1145802

[13] M. Noro and K. Yokoyama. 2017 online. Usage of Modular Techniques for Efficient Computation of Ideal Operations. *Mathematics in Computer Science* (2017 online). https://doi.org/10.1007/s11786-017-0325-1

[14] F. Pauer. 1992. On lucky ideals for Gröbner basis computations. *Journal of Symbolic Computation* (1992).

[15] R. Zippel. 1993. *Effective Polynomial Computation.* Springer US.

Desingularization of First Order Linear Difference Systems with Rational Function Coefficients

Moulay A. Barkatou
XLIM UMR 7252 , DMI, University of Limoges; CNRS
123, Avenue Albert Thomas, 87060 Limoges, France
moulay.barkatou@unilim.fr

Maximilian Jaroschek*
Technische Universität Wien,
Institute for Logic and Computation
Favoritenstraße 9-11, 1040 Vienna, Austria
Johannes Kepler Universität Linz, Institute for Algebra
Altenberger Straße 69, 4040 Linz, Austria
maximilian@mjaroschek.com

ABSTRACT

It is well known that for a first order system of linear difference equations with rational function coefficients, a solution that is holomorphic in some left half plane can be analytically continued to a meromorphic solution in the whole complex plane. The poles stem from the singularities of the rational function coefficients of the system. Just as for differential equations, not all of these singularities necessarily lead to poles in solutions, as they might be what is called removable. In our work, we show how to detect and remove these singularities and further study the connection between poles of solutions and removable singularities. We describe two algorithms to (partially) desingularize a given difference system and present a characterization of removable singularities in terms of shifts of the original system.

KEYWORDS

systems of linear difference equations, apparent singularities, desingularization, removable singularities.

ACM Reference Format:

Moulay A. Barkatou and Maximilian Jaroschek. 2018. Desingularization of First Order Linear Difference Systems with Rational Function Coefficients. In *ISSAC '18: 2018 ACM International Symposium on Symbolic and Algebraic Computation, July 16–19, 2018, New York, NY, USA.* ACM, New York, NY, USA, 8 pages. https://doi.org/10.1145/3208976.3208989

1 INTRODUCTION

First order linear difference systems are a class of pseudo-linear systems [4, 9, 15] of the form $\phi(Y) = AY$, where ϕ is the forward- or backward shift operator and A an invertible matrix with, in our case, rational function coefficients. To study properties of possible solutions Y, it is not always necessary to explicitly compute the solution space, but one can rather obtain the information from the system itself. Properties that can be derived in this fashion comprise, among others, the asymptotic behavior [5, 6, 13], positive/negative (semi-) definiteness [1, 22], holomorphicity, and closure properties of (a class of) solutions [18].

In the center of attention when analyzing difference and differential systems lie the poles of the rational function coefficients. It is well known that, like in the case of differential equations and systems, not all poles of the coefficients of a difference system lead to singularities for solutions. These apparent singularities can therefore distort the properties of solutions and should be circumvented in the analysis. One technique to do so is *desingularization*—transforming a given system (or operator) in a way that removes as many poles of the system as possible to discard apparent singularities. In this paper we describe the first algorithm to desingularize first order linear difference systems with rational function coefficients. Our main tool in the treatment of these systems are polynomial basis transformations. We show how to achieve desingularization by composing several basic and easy to compute transformations, and our procedure results in the provably "smallest possible" such desingularizing transformation in the sense that any other desingularizing transformation can be obtained as a right multiple.

The main contributions of this paper are:

(1) The first algorithm to desingularize—partially, or, if possible, completely—first order linear difference systems with rational function coefficients.
(2) A non-trivial necessary and sufficient condition for a given system to be desingularizable at a given singularity.
(3) With the help of (2), an analysis of the connection between removable and apparent singularities of difference systems and their meromorphic function solutions.
(4) An algorithm for reducing the rank of the leading matrix at a singularity of a linear difference system.

In the context of single linear difference equations [1, 2], linear differential equations [21] and, more general, Ore operators [10, 11, 17], desingularization and the effects of removable singularities have been extensively studied in recent years. In [22], the author presents an extension of the idea of desingularization that also takes into account the leading number coefficients of Ore operators. For first order differential equations, a first algorithm for desingularization was given in [7].

It is possible to convert any first order linear difference system to a difference operator of higher order and vice versa [3, 5, 6, 8]. Desingularization of systems could therefore be done by computing for a given system the corresponding operator, use existing

*The author is supported by the ERC Starting Grant 2014 SYMCAR 639270 and the Austrian research projects FWF Y464-N18 and FWF RiSE S11409-N23.

ISSAC '18, July 16–19, 2018, New York, NY, USA

ACM ISBN 978-1-4503-5550-6/18/07...$15.00
https://doi.org/10.1145/3208976.3208989

techniques to desingularize the operator and then constructing the desingularized system from the new operator. While this is possible, the procedure comes with at least two caveats:

(1) It can be observed that the coefficients grow very large in the conversion process which has severe negative impact on the computation time.
(2) Desingularization on operator level is done by finding a suitable left-multiple of the given operator. In general, this leads to an increase in order, and thus to an increase in the dimension of the solution space.

Both problems are avoided when dealing directly with systems instead of operators, making the results presented in this paper an essential tool for analyzing difference systems.

The paper is organized as follows. In Section 2 we remind the reader of the formal definition of linear difference systems with rational function coefficients, well known results about meromorphic function solutions and the notion of apparent singularities. In Section 3, we present an algorithm to remove poles of difference systems and give a necessary and sufficient condition for a singularity to be removable. Lastly, the connection between removable poles and apparent singularities is established in Section 4 before concluding the paper in Section 5.

2 DIFFERENCE SYSTEMS AND REMOVABLE SINGULARITIES

Let C be a subfield of the field $\mathbb{C}$ of complex numbers, $C(z)$ the field of rational functions over C and ϕ the C-automorphism of $C(z)$ defined by $\phi(z) = z+1$. A homogeneous system of first-order linear difference equations with rational function coefficients is a system of the form

$$\phi(Y) = AY, \tag{1}$$

where Y is an unknown d-dimensional column vector, $\phi(Y)$ is defined component-wise, and A is an element of $\mathrm{GL}_d(C(z))$, the group of invertible matrices of size $d \times d$ with entries in $C(z)$. Throughout the paper, we always suppose $A \in \mathrm{GL}_d((C(z))$. We denote the set of matrices of size $d \times d$ with entries in $C[z]$ as $\mathrm{Mat}_d(C[z])$. A (block) diagonal matrix with entries (respectively blocks) $a_1, \ldots, a_d$ is denoted by $\mathrm{diag}(a_1, \ldots, a_d)$. We will refer to system (1) as $[A]_\phi$.

Given a matrix $T \in \mathrm{GL}_d(C(z))$, we can apply a basis transformation

$$Y = TX,$$

and substitute TX into system (1) to arrive at an equivalent system

$$\phi(X) = T[A]_\phi X,$$

where $T[A]_\phi$ is defined as

$$T[A]_\phi := \phi(T^{-1})AT.$$

A difference system $[A]_\phi$ can be rewritten as

$$\phi^{-1}(Y) = A^* Y, \tag{2}$$

where $A^* := \phi^{-1}(A^{-1})$. We will refer to system (2) as $[A^*]_{\phi^{-1}}$. A transformation $Y = TX$ yields the equivalent system

$$\phi^{-1}(X) = T[A^*]_{\phi^{-1}} X,$$

with

$$T[A^*]_{\phi^{-1}} := \phi^{-1}(T^{-1})A^* T.$$

The set of meromorphic solutions of $[A]_\phi$ form a vector space of dimension d over the field of 1-periodic meromorphic functions. It is well known [19] that any difference system $[A]_\phi$ possesses a fundamental matrix of meromorphic solutions. If F is a holomorphic solution of (1) in some left half plane ($\mathrm{Re}\, z < \lambda$ for some $\lambda \in \mathbb{R}$), then it can be analytically continued to a meromorphic solution in the whole complex plane $\mathbb{C}$ using the relations:

$$\begin{aligned} F(z) &= \phi^{-1}(A)\phi^{-2}(A)\cdots\phi^{-n}(A)\phi^{-n}(F)(z) \\ &= A(z-1)A(z-2)\cdots A(z-n)F(z-n), \end{aligned}$$

which are valid everywhere except at the points of the form $\zeta + n$ where ζ is a pole of A and n is a positive integer ($n = 1, 2, \ldots$). If F is a holomorphic solution of (1) in some right half plane ($\mathrm{Re}\, z > \lambda$), then it can be analytically continued to a meromorphic solution in the whole complex plane $\mathbb{C}$ using the relations:

$$\begin{aligned} F(z) &= \phi(A^*)\phi^2(A^*)\cdots\phi^n(A^*)\phi^n F(z) \\ &= A^*(z+1)A^*(z+2)\cdots A^*(z+n)F(z+n), \end{aligned}$$

which are valid everywhere except at the points of the form $\zeta - n$ where ζ is a pole of A^* and n is a positive integer ($n = 1, 2, \ldots$).

We will denote by $\mathcal{P}_r(A)$ (respectively $\mathcal{P}_l(A)$) the set of poles of A (respectively A^*). The elements of $\mathcal{P}_r(A)$ (respectively $\mathcal{P}_l(A)$) will be called the r- (respectively l-) singularities of the system (1). A point $\zeta \in \mathbb{C}$ is said to be *congruent* to a given r- (respectively l-) singularity ζ_0 of $[A]_\phi$ if $\zeta = \zeta_0 + k$ (respectively $\zeta = \zeta_0 - k$) for some positive integer k.

The finite singularities of the solutions of $[A]_\phi$ are among the points that are congruent to the singularities of the system.

Definition 2.1. Let ζ be a pole of A (respectively pole of A^*). It is called

(1) a removable r- (respectively l-) singularity if any solution of $[A]_\phi$ which is holomorphic in some left (respectively right) half-plane can be analytically continued to a meromorphic solution which is holomorphic at $\zeta + 1$ (respectively $\zeta - 1$).
(2) an apparent r- (respectively l-) singularity if any solution of $[A]_\phi$ which is holomorphic in some left (respectively right) half-plane can be analytically continued to a meromorphic solution which is holomorphic at each point of $\zeta + \mathbb{N}^*$ (respectively $\zeta - \mathbb{N}^*$), with $\mathbb{N}^* = \mathbb{N} \setminus \{0\}$.

Example 2.2. A 2×2 system of linear difference equations is given by

$$Y(z+1) = AY = \begin{pmatrix} 0 & 1 \\ \frac{-2(z+1)}{z-2} & \frac{3(z-1)}{z-2} \end{pmatrix} Y(z), \quad A^* = \begin{pmatrix} \frac{3(z-2)}{2z} & \frac{3-z}{2z} \\ 1 & 0 \end{pmatrix}.$$

Here $\mathcal{P}_r(A) = \{2\}$ and the points that are congruent to $\zeta = 2$ are $3, 4, 5, \ldots$. We have $\mathcal{P}_l(A) = \{0\}$ and the corresponding congruent points are $-1, -2, -3, \ldots$. It can be easily verified that a fundamental matrix of solutions of this system is given by

$$F(z) = \begin{pmatrix} 2^z & z^3 + 5z + 6 \\ 2^{z+1} & z^3 + 3z^2 + 8z + 12 \end{pmatrix}.$$

We focus on studying r-singularities. L-singularities can be removed in the same way by considering A^* and ϕ^{-1} instead of A and ϕ.

We give an algebraic characterization of removable singularities. Let $q \in C[z]$ be an irreducible polynomial. For $f \in C(z) \setminus \{0\}$, we define $\mathrm{ord}_q(f)$ to be the integer n such that $f = q^n \frac{a}{b}$, with $a, b \in C[z] \setminus \{0\}$, $q \nmid a$ and $q \nmid b$. We put $\mathrm{ord}_q(0) = +\infty$. Let $O_q = \{f \in C(z) : \mathrm{ord}_q(f) \geq 0\}$ be the *local ring* at q and O_q/qO_q the residue field of $C(z)$ at q. Let π_q denote the canonical homomorphism from $C[z]$ onto $C[z]/\langle q\rangle$. It can be extended to a ring-homomorphism from O_q onto $C[z]/\langle q\rangle$ as follows: let $f \in O_q$; by definition of O_q, f can be written $f = a/b$ where $a, b \in C[z]$ and $q \nmid b$. We can find $u, v \in C[z]$ such that $ub + vq = 1$, *the value* of f at q, denoted by $\pi_q(f)$, is then defined as $\pi_q(ua)$. Sometimes we write $f \,\mathbf{mod}\, q$ for $\pi_q(f)$. It is clear that π_q is well-defined on O_q and is a surjective ring-homomorphism. The kernel of π_q is qO_q, so O_q/qO_q and $C[z]/\langle q\rangle$ are isomorphic.

If $A = (a_{i,j})$ is a finite-dimensional matrix with entries in $C(z)$, we define the *order* at q of A by $\mathrm{ord}_q(A) := \min_{i,j}(\mathrm{ord}_q(a_{i,j}))$. We say that A has a pole at q if $\mathrm{ord}_q(A) < 0$. We define the *leading matrix* of A at q (notation $\mathrm{lc}_q(A)$) as the leading coefficient $A_{0,q}$ in the q-adic expansion of A:

$$A = q^{\mathrm{ord}_q(A)}(A_{0,q} + qA_{1,q} + q^2 A_{2,q} + \dots).$$

Here the coefficients $A_{i,q}$ are matrices with entries in the field $C[z]/\langle q\rangle$. Note that the matrix $A_{0,q}$ is the value of the matrix $q^{-\mathrm{ord}_q(A)}A$ at q.

For a rational function $r = p/q$ with p monic and $\gcd(p, q) = 1$, we write $\mathrm{num}(r) := p$ and $\mathrm{den}(r) := q$. Similarly, for a matrix $M \in \mathrm{Mat}_d(C(z))$ we denote by $\mathrm{den}(M)$ the least common denominator of all the entries of M and denote by $\mathrm{num}(M)$ the polynomial matrix $\mathrm{num}(M) := \mathrm{den}(M)M$.

Definition 2.3. Let $q \in C[z]$ be an irreducible polynomial. We say that q is a ϕ-minimal pole of A if $q \mid \mathrm{den}(A)$ and for all $j \in \mathbb{N}^*$, $\phi^j(q) \nmid \mathrm{den}(A)$.

We can now give an algebraic definition of desingularizability of difference systems in an inductive fashion.

Definition 2.4. Let $q \in C[z]$ be an irreducible pole of A.

(1) If q is ϕ-minimal, we say that the system $[A]_\phi$ is partially desingularizable at q if there exists a polynomial transformation $T \in \mathrm{GL}_d(C(z)) \cap \mathrm{Mat}_d(C[z])$ such that $\mathrm{ord}_q(T[A]_\phi) > \mathrm{ord}_q(A)$ and $\mathrm{ord}_p(T[A]_\phi) \geq \mathrm{ord}_p(A)$ for any other irreducible polynomial $p \in C[z]$. If moreover, $\mathrm{ord}_q(T[A]_\phi) \geq 0$ then we say that $[A]_\phi$ is desingularizable at q and we call T a desingularizing transformation for $[A]_\phi$ at q.
(2) If q is not ϕ-minimal, then we call $[A]_\phi$ (partially) desingularizable at q if there exists a desingularizing transformation T for all poles of A of the form $\phi^k(q)$, $k \geq 1$, and $T[A]_\phi$ is either (partially) desingularized at q or (partially) desingularizable at q.

While it is immediate that, for a ϕ-minimal pole q, the algebraic notion of desingularization implies that the roots of q are removable in the sense of Definition 2.1, the converse is not obvious and is proven later in Section 4. Consequently, the roots of q are apparent singularities if (and only if) the system A is desingularizable at all poles of A of the form $\phi^{-k}(q)$, $k \geq 0$. In practice, in order to desingularize a system at a non-ϕ-minimal pole q, one first removes the ϕ-minimal pole congruent to q. The resulting system then has a new ϕ-minimal pole 'closer' to q. One can repeat this process until q itself is ϕ-minimal and eventually removed. A desingularizing transformation for q is then given by the product of all the transformations obtained during this process.

Let us illustrate in the next example why we require removing all singularities left of a given pole, thus making it ϕ-minimal, before considering it eligible for desingularization.

Example 2.5. The system $[A]_\phi$ given by

$$A = \mathrm{diag}\left(\frac{(z+1)^2}{z}, \frac{1}{z+1}\right),$$

can be transformed via $T = \mathrm{diag}(z, 1)$ to $T[A]_\phi = \mathrm{diag}(z+1, \frac{1}{z+1})$. The transformed system still does not enable analytic continuation at 0 of solutions that are holomorphic in the left half-plane with $\mathrm{Re}(z) < 0$.

3 REMOVING R-SINGULARITIES

3.1 ϕ-Minimal Desingularization

We begin our discussion of removing r-singularities by deriving a method for shifting a factor in the denominator of a given system in a way that allows, if possible, cancellation with zeroes of the system. For this we bring the leading matrix of A into a specific form.

Lemma 3.1. *Let $q \in C[z]$ be an irreducible pole of A. Set $n := -\mathrm{ord}_q(A)$ and $r := \mathrm{rank}(\mathrm{lc}_q(A))$, the rank of the leading matrix of A at q. There exists a unimodular polynomial transformation S such that $S[A]_\phi$ is of the form*

$$\begin{pmatrix} \frac{1}{q^n}A_1 & \frac{1}{q^{n-1}}A_2, \end{pmatrix}, \tag{3}$$

where A_1, A_2 are matrices with entries in O_q of size $d \times r$ and $d \times d - r$ respectively with $\mathrm{rank}(A_1) = r$.

Proof. The leading matrix $\mathrm{lc}_q(A)$ of A at q is a matrix with entries in the residue field $C[z]/\langle q\rangle$. There exists a non-singular matrix Q with entries in $C[z]/\langle q\rangle$ such that $\mathrm{lc}_q(A) \cdot Q$ is in a column-reduced form, i.e. the last $d - r$ columns of $\mathrm{lc}_q(A) \cdot Q$ are zero, and Q is of the form $Q = C \cdot (I_d + U)$, where C is a non-singular constant matrix, I_d the identity matrix of dimension $d \times d$, and U is a strictly upper triangular matrix. Taking $S = Q$ as a matrix in $\mathrm{Mat}_d(C[z])$ will result in $S[A]_\phi$ as desired. □

Example 3.2 (Example 2.2 continued). If we set $q = z - 2$, then the leading matrix of the system in Example 2.2 at q is

$$\mathrm{lc}_q(A) = (qA) \,\mathbf{mod}\, q = \begin{pmatrix} 0 & 0 \\ -6 & 3 \end{pmatrix}.$$

A suitable transformation to bring this matrix into a column-reduced form is

$$S = \begin{pmatrix} 1 & \frac{1}{2} \\ 0 & 1 \end{pmatrix}.$$

Applying S to A gives

$$S[A]_\phi = \begin{pmatrix} \frac{z+1}{z-2} & 0 \\ \frac{-2z-2}{z-2} & 2 \end{pmatrix}.$$

Lemma 3.3. *Let $q \in C[z]$ be a ϕ-minimal pole of A. Suppose that A is of the form (3) and let $r = \mathrm{rank}(\mathrm{lc}_q(A))$. If $[A]_\phi$ is partially* *desingularizable at q then any desingularizing transformation T for $[A]_\phi$ can be written as*

$$T = D \cdot \tilde{T}, \text{ where}$$

$$D = \operatorname{diag}(\underbrace{q, \dots, q}_{r \text{ times}}, \underbrace{1, \dots, 1}_{d-r \text{ times}}) \text{ and } \tilde{T} \in \mathrm{GL}_d(C(z)) \cap \mathrm{Mat}_d(C[z]).$$

Proof. Let $n = -\mathrm{ord}_q(A)$. Suppose we are given a desingularizing transformation $T \in \mathrm{GL}_d(C(z))$ and let $B = T[A]_\phi$. Then we have that $\phi(T)B = AT$ and hence

$$\phi(T)(q^n B) = (q^n A)T.$$

Since $\mathrm{ord}_q(q^n B) > 0$ and the orders at q of the other matrices involved in the equality are non-negative, we get

$$\pi_q(q^n A)\pi_q(T) = 0.$$

By assumption, the matrix $\pi_q(q^n A)$ is of the form

$$\pi_q(q^n A) = \begin{pmatrix} A_1 & 0 \end{pmatrix},$$

where A_1 is a $d \times r$ matrix with linearly independent columns. Thus, the first r rows of $\pi_q(T)$ must be zero, i.e. the first r rows of T have to be divisible by q. This yields the claim. □

Remark 3.4. *Note that the determinant of any desingularizing transformation T of A at q, not necessarily ϕ-minimal, is divisible by q; in fact $q^r \mid \det(T)$. It then follows that $\phi(q)$ divides $\det(\phi(T))$; in fact $\phi(q)^r \mid \det(\phi(T))$.*

Lemma 3.5. *Let $q \in C[z]$ with $q \mid \mathrm{den}(A)$ be an irreducible pole. If $[A]_\phi$ is (partially) desingularizable at q then there exists a maximal positive integer ℓ such that $\phi^\ell(q) \mid \mathrm{num}(\det(A))$.*

Proof. First, suppose q is ϕ-minimal. There are only finitely many factors of $\mathrm{num}(\det(A))$ of positive degree because $\det(A) \neq 0$. Thus it suffices to show that there exists a positive integer ℓ_0 such that $\phi^{\ell_0}(q) \mid \mathrm{num}(\det(A))$. Let T be a desingularizing transformation of A at q. Put $B := T[A]_\phi$ and denote $\det(T)$ by t. Then, due to the desingularization property, we have that

$$\phi(T)^{-1}\mathrm{num}(A)T = \frac{\mathrm{den}(A)}{\mathrm{den}(B)}\mathrm{num}(B) \in \mathrm{Mat}_d(C[z]).$$

Hence

$$\frac{\det(\mathrm{num}(A))t}{\phi(t)} \in C[z].$$

Let ℓ_0 be the largest integer such that $\phi^{\ell_0}(q) \mid \phi(t)$. By Remark 3.4, ℓ_0 is strictly positive. Since $\phi^{\ell_0}(q) \nmid t$, it follows that $\phi^{\ell_0}(q) \mid \det(\mathrm{num}(A))$. Now from the relation $\det(\mathrm{num}(A)) = \mathrm{den}(A)^d \det(A)$ and since we assumed that $\mathrm{den}(A)$ has no factor of the form $\phi^j(q)$ with $j \in \mathbb{N}^*$ we can conclude that $\phi^{\ell_0}(q) \mid \mathrm{num}(\det(A))$. To see that the theorem holds for non-ϕ-minimal poles, let $\tilde{q}$ be a non-ϕ-minimal pole congruent to q, i.e. there exists a positive integer k such that $\phi^k(\tilde{q}) = q$. Then $\phi^{k+\ell_0}(\tilde{q}) = \phi^{\ell_0}(q) \mid \mathrm{num}(\det(A))$. □

Definition 3.6. Let $q \in C[z]$ be an irreducible pole of A. We define the ϕ-dispersion of A at q as :

$$\phi\text{-}dispersion(A, q) = \max\{\ell \in \mathbb{N}^* \text{ s.t. } \phi^\ell(q) \mid \mathrm{num}(\det(A))\}.$$

When the latter set is empty we put ϕ-dispersion$(A, q) = 0$.

Note that by Lemma 3.5, a necessary condition that $[A]_\phi$ can be (partially) desingularized at q is that ϕ-dispersion$(A, q) > 0$.

Example 3.7 (Example 3.2 continued). The determinant of $S[A]_\phi$ in Example 3.2 is $\frac{2(z+1)}{z-2}$. Therefore the ϕ-dispersion of $S[A]_\phi$ at $q = z - 2$ is equal to 3.

We will now describe an algorithm for desingularizing a given system $[A]_\phi$ at a ϕ-minimal pole q. By repeatedly applying the algorithm to $[A]_\phi$, it is then possible to desingularize the system at all removable singularities. It is sufficient to treat the case where q is a single and simple pole of A (i.e. qA has polynomial entries). This is stated in the following lemma.

Lemma 3.8. *Let $q \in C[z]$ be a ϕ-minimal pole of A. Set $h = \frac{\mathrm{den}(A)}{q}$ so that the matrix $hA = q^{-1}\mathrm{num}(A)$ has a single and simple pole at q. Then the system $[A]_\phi$ is (partially) desingularizable at q if and only if the system $[hA]_\phi$ is desingularizable at q. More precisely, a polynomial matrix $T \in \mathrm{GL}_d(C(z))$ is a desingularizing transformation for $[hA]_\phi$ at q if and only if T (partially) desingularizes $[A]_\phi$ at q.*

Proof. It is a direct consequence of the following (trivial but interesting) property: for all $T \in \mathrm{GL}_d(C(z))$ and $h \in C[z] \setminus \{0\}$, one has $T[(hA)]_\phi = h \cdot (T[A]_\phi)$. □

Remark 3.9. *With the notation of the above lemma, the ϕ-dispersion of $[hA]_\phi$ at q is greater than or equal to the ϕ-dispersion of $[A]_\phi$ at q, and equality holds if q is ϕ-minimal. It follows from the fact that $\det(hA) = h^d \cdot \det(A)$.*

Lemma 3.10. *Suppose that A has a single, simple, irreducible pole at $q \in C[z]$. If $[A]_\phi$ is desingularizable at q with ϕ-dispersion ℓ, then there exist a unimodular polynomial matrix S and a diagonal polynomial matrix D such that $(S \cdot D)[A]_\phi$ is either desingularized (with respect to q) or desingularizable at $\phi(q)$ with ϕ-dispersion $\ell - 1$.*

Proof. We first take S as in Lemma 3.1 so that $S[A]_\phi$ has the form

$$S[A]_\phi = \begin{pmatrix} \frac{\tilde{A}_{1,1}}{q} & \tilde{A}_{1,2} \\ \frac{\tilde{A}_{2,1}}{q} & \tilde{A}_{2,2} \end{pmatrix},$$

where the $\tilde{A}_{i,j}$ are blocks with polynomial entries, the diagonal blocks are of size $r = \mathrm{rank}(\mathrm{lc}_q(A))$ and $d - r$ respectively. Take $D = \mathrm{diag}(qI_r, I_{d-r})$ as in Lemma 3.3. Then the matrix $B := (S \cdot D)[A]_\phi$ has the form

$$B = \begin{pmatrix} \frac{\tilde{A}_{1,1}}{\phi(q)} & \frac{\tilde{A}_{1,2}}{\phi(q)} \\ \tilde{A}_{2,1} & \tilde{A}_{2,2} \end{pmatrix}.$$

The resulting system $[B]_\phi$ has at worst a simple and single pole at $\phi(q)$ with ϕ-dispersion $\ell - 1$. □

Example 3.11 (Example 3.7 continued). The rank of the leading matrix in Example 3.2 is 1. We apply the transformation

$$D_1 = \begin{pmatrix} z-2 & 0 \\ 0 & 1 \end{pmatrix},$$

to $S[A]_\phi$ of Example 3.7 and arrive at the system

$$(S \cdot D_1)[A]_\phi = \begin{pmatrix} \frac{z+1}{z-1} & 0 \\ -2z-2 & 2 \end{pmatrix}.$$

The determinant of $(S \cdot D_1)[A]_\phi$ is $\frac{2(z+1)}{z-1}$. The new ϕ-dispersion is 2.

Theorem 3.12. *Let A be desingularizable at a single, simple, irreducible pole q. Then there exists an integer n, unimodular polynomial matrices $S_1, \ldots, S_n$ and diagonal polynomial matrices $D_1, \ldots, D_n$ such that*

$$T = S_1 \cdot D_1 \cdots S_n \cdot D_n,$$

is a desingularizing transformation for A at q. Furthermore, any other desingularizing transformation T' for A at q can be written as

$$T' = T \cdot \tilde{T} \text{ with } \tilde{T} \in \mathrm{GL}_d(C(z)) \cap \mathrm{Mat}_d(C[z]). \tag{4}$$

Proof. By Lemma 3.5, a desingularizable system $[A]_\phi$ has strictly positive ϕ-dispersion ℓ. Applying the transformation $S \cdot D$ as in Lemma 3.10 gives a system equivalent to $[A]_\phi$ having at worst a pole at $\phi(q)$ (instead of q) but with reduced ϕ-dispersion. After at most ℓ such transformations, the resulting matrix $T[A]_\phi$ has to be desingularized at q. This shows that T can be chosen as in the statement of the theorem. To see that any other desingularizing transformation T' of $[A]_\phi$ at q can be written as in (4), we first note that since S_1 is unimodular, for any such T' we have

$$T' = S_1 \cdot (S_1^{-1} \cdot T'),$$

with $=: T'' \in \mathrm{GL}_d(C(z)) \cap \mathrm{Mat}_d(C[z])$. Therefore we can assume that A is of the form (3). Then, as was shown in Lemma 3.3, we can write

$$T'' = D_1 \cdot \tilde{T},$$

with $\tilde{T} \in \mathrm{GL}_d(C(z)) \cap \mathrm{Mat}_d(C[z])$). Again, we can repeat this reasoning n times until we arrive at the desired form. □

Example 3.13 (Example 3.11 continued). The leading matrix of $(S \cdot D_1)[A]_\phi$ as in Example 3.11 at $\phi(q) = z - 1$ is already in column-reduced form and of rank 1. We apply the transformation $D_2 = \mathrm{diag}(z - 1, 1)$, and get

$$(S \cdot D_1 \cdot D_2)[A]_\phi = \begin{pmatrix} \frac{z+1}{z} & 0 \\ -2z^2 + 2 & 2 \end{pmatrix}.$$

Again, the leading matrix of this system at $\phi^2(q) = z$ is column-reduced and of rank 1. Finally, after applying the transformation $D_3 = \mathrm{diag}(z, 1)$, we get the desingularized system

$$(S \cdot D_1 \cdot D_2 \cdot D_3)[A]_\phi = \begin{pmatrix} 1 & 0 \\ -2z^3 + 2z & 2 \end{pmatrix}.$$

Collecting all the transformations, we see that a desingularizing transformation for A at $q = z - 2$ is given by

$$T = S \cdot D_1 \cdot D_2 \cdot D_3 = \begin{pmatrix} z^3 - 3z^2 + 2z & \frac{1}{2} \\ 0 & 1 \end{pmatrix}.$$

As was already shown in Lemma 3.5, a positive ϕ-dispersion is a necessary condition for a removable singularity. For a given system $[A]_\phi$ and an irreducible polynomial q, the ϕ-dispersion can be obtained by computing the largest integer root of the resultant $\mathrm{res}_z(q(z + y), \mathrm{num}(\det(A)))$ with a new indeterminate y. This, together with Theorem 3.12 and its proof gives rise to Algorithm 1.

Algorithm 1: desingularize_A(A, q)

Input: $A \in \mathrm{GL}_d(C(z))$ with a single, simple, irreducible pole $q \in C[z]$.

Output: $(T, T[A]_\phi)$ s.t. $T[A]_\phi$ is desingularized at q, or (I_d, A) if desingularization is not possible.

1 $T \leftarrow I_d$

2 **WHILE** (ϕ-dispersion(A, q) > 0 **AND** den(A) $=$ 0 **mod** q) **DO**

2.1 $A_0 \leftarrow \mathrm{lc}_q(A)$

2.2 $S \leftarrow$ as in the proof of Lemma 3.1.

2.3 $D \leftarrow \mathrm{diag}(q, \ldots, q, 1, \ldots, 1)$ with $\mathrm{rank}(A_0)$ many elements equal to q.

2.4 $A \leftarrow \phi(S \cdot D)^{-1} \cdot A \cdot (S \cdot D)$

2.5 $T \leftarrow T \cdot S \cdot D$

2.6 $q \leftarrow \phi(q)$

3 **IF** (den(A) $= 0$ **mod** q) **RETURN** (I_d, A)

4 **ELSE RETURN** (T, A)

3.2 Characterization of Desingularizable Poles

We can give a necessary and sufficient condition for a pole to be desingularizable. It can be seen as the shift analogue of the nilpotency of the leading matrix at the considered pole of the system, which is a necessary condition for an apparent singularity in the differential setting [7].

Proposition 3.14. *Let $q \in C[z]$ be a ϕ-minimal pole of the system $[A]_\phi$. Let $\tilde{A} = q^n A$, so that $\mathrm{ord}_q(\tilde{A}) = 0$ and $\pi_q(\tilde{A}) = \mathrm{lc}_q(A)$. If A is (partially) desingularizable at q then there exists a positive integer k such that*

$$\pi_q(\tilde{A}\phi^{-1}(\tilde{A}) \ldots \phi^{-k}(\tilde{A})) = 0. \tag{5}$$

Proof. Let T be a desingularizing transformation for $[A]_\phi$ at q and $B = T[A]_\phi$. Then for all non-negative integers k one has

$$\phi(T)B\phi^{-1}(B) \ldots \phi^{-k}(B) = A\phi^{-1}(A) \ldots \phi^{-k}(A)\phi^{-k}(T),$$

and hence

$$\phi(T)(q^n B)\phi^{-1}(q^n B) \ldots \phi^{-k}(q^n B) = \tilde{A}\phi^{-1}(\tilde{A}) \ldots \phi^{-k}(\tilde{A})\phi^{-k}(T).$$

As $\mathrm{ord}_q(q^n B) > 0$ and

$$\mathrm{ord}_q(\phi^{-j}(q^n B)) = \mathrm{ord}_{\phi^j(q)}(B) \geq \mathrm{ord}_{\phi^j(q)}(A) \geq 0, \text{ for all } j \in \mathbb{N}^*,$$

we get that

$$\pi_q(\tilde{A}\phi^{-1}(\tilde{A}) \ldots \phi^{-k}(\tilde{A})\phi^{-k}(T)) = 0.$$

Now we conclude by remarking that for k large enough $\pi_q(\phi^{-k}(T))$ is invertible. □

We will now show that the factorial relation (5) is a sufficient condition for a matrix A to be partially desingularizable at q.

Proposition 3.15. *Let $q \in C[z]$ be a ϕ-minimal pole of $[A]_\phi$. Let $\tilde{A} = q^n A$, so that $\mathrm{ord}_q(\tilde{A}) = 0$ and $\pi_q(\tilde{A}) = \mathrm{lc}_q(A)$. If $[A]_\phi$ is such that the factorial relation (5) holds for some integer $k \geq 1$ then $[A]_\phi$ is (partially) desingularizable at q.*

Proof. Let k be minimal so that (5) holds. Put

$$M := \pi_q(\tilde{A}\phi^{-1}(\tilde{A}) \cdots \phi^{-k+1}(\tilde{A})) \quad \text{and} \quad N := \pi_q(\phi^{-k}(\tilde{A})).$$

By definition of k, the matrix M is nonzero (but singular) and we have $M \cdot N = 0$. With $d := \dim(A)$ it follows that

$$0 < \operatorname{rank}(M) \leq s := d - \operatorname{rank}(N) < d.$$

Let $P \in \mathrm{GL}_d(C[z]/\langle q\rangle)$ such that $P \cdot N$ has its last $(d-s)$ rows linearly independent over $C[z]/\langle q\rangle$ while its s first rows are zero. Consider the matrix : $U = \phi^{k-1}(P^{-1})$ as an element of $\mathrm{Mat}_d(C[z])$ then by applying the unimodular transformation $Y = UX$, we can assume that the matrix N has the following form:

$$N = \begin{pmatrix} 0_s & 0_{s,d-s} \\ N_{2,1} & N_{2,2} \end{pmatrix},$$

where $N_{2,1}$ and $N_{2,2}$ are matrices with entries in $C[z]/\langle q\rangle$ of size $(d-s)\times s$ and $(d-s)\times(d-s)$ respectively, so that the last $d-s$ rows of N are linearly independent over $C[z]/\langle q\rangle$. As $M \cdot N = 0$ we have that the $d-s$ last columns of M are zero. Let $\tilde{A} = (\tilde{A}_{i,j})_{1\leq i,j\leq 2}$ be partitioned in four blocks as N. Then $\pi_q(\phi^{-k}(\tilde{A}_{1,j})) = 0$ for $j = 1, 2$. In other words, the s first rows of $\tilde{A}$ are divisible by $\phi^k(q)$. Using the substitution $Y = DX$ where $D = \operatorname{diag}(\phi^{k-1}(q)I_s, I_{d-s})$, we get a new system which still has a pole at q of multiplicity at most n. Indeed, we have

$$\begin{aligned} B := \phi(D)^{-1}AD &= q^{-n}\begin{pmatrix} \frac{\phi^{k-1}(q)\tilde{A}_{1,1}}{\phi^k(q)} & \frac{\tilde{A}_{1,2}}{\phi^k(q)} \\ \phi^{k-1}(q)\tilde{A}_{2,1} & \tilde{A}_{2,2} \end{pmatrix} = \\ & q^{-n}\begin{pmatrix} \phi^{k-1}(q)\tilde{A}'_{1,1} & \tilde{A}'_{1,2} \\ \phi^{k-1}(q)\tilde{A}_{2,1} & \tilde{A}_{2,2} \end{pmatrix}, \end{aligned} \tag{6}$$

for some matrices $\tilde{A}'_{1,1}, \tilde{A}'_{1,2}$ with entries in O_q. It is clear that $\operatorname{den}(B) \mid \operatorname{den}(A)$ and that $\operatorname{ord}_q(B) \geq \operatorname{ord}_q(A)$. Now we will prove that the factorial relation (5) holds for $\tilde{B} := q^n B$ with $k-1$ instead of k. For this we remark first that

$$\phi(D)\tilde{B}\phi^{-1}(\tilde{B})\cdots\phi^{-k+1}(\tilde{B}) = \tilde{A}\phi^{-1}(\tilde{A})\cdots\phi^{-k+1}(\tilde{A})\phi^{-k+1}(D).$$

It then follows that

$$\pi_q(\phi(D))\pi_q(\tilde{B}\phi^{-1}(\tilde{B})\cdots\phi^{-k+1}(\tilde{B})) = M \cdot \pi_q(\phi^{-k+1}(D)).$$

We have that

$$\pi_q(\phi^{-k+1}(D)) = \pi_q(\operatorname{diag}(qI_s, I_{d-s})) = \operatorname{diag}(0_s, I_{d-s}),$$

hence $M \cdot \pi_q(\phi^{-k+1}(D)) = 0$ (since the $d-s$ last columns of M are zero). Now $\pi_q(\phi(D)) = \pi_q(\operatorname{diag}(\phi^k(q)I_s, I_{d-s}))$ is invertible (since q and $\phi^k(q)$ are co-prime), it then follows that

$$\pi_q(\tilde{B}\phi^{-1}(\tilde{B})\cdots\phi^{-k+1}(\tilde{B})) = 0.$$

If $k-1$ is still positive then we can repeat this process for the matrix B and the polynomial q until we arrive at $k = 1$. When $k = 1$ the above factorial relation reduces to $\pi_q(\tilde{B}) = 0$ which means that $\operatorname{ord}_q(\tilde{B}) > 0$ and therefore $\operatorname{ord}_q(B) \geq -n + 1 > \operatorname{ord}_q(A)$. □

This proof motivates the following alternative desingularization algorithm. In contrast to Algorithm 1, instead of shifting a singularity towards a zero of the system, it performs the analogous task of moving a zero towards the singularity until they cancel each other

An implementation of Algorithm 1 and Algorithm 2 in the computer algebra system Sage [12] can be obtained from

http://www.mjaroschek.com/systemdesing/

Algorithm 2: desingularize_B(A, q)

Input: $A \in \mathrm{GL}_d(C(z))$ with a single, simple, irreducible pole $q \in C[z]$.

Output: $(T, T[A]_\phi)$ s.t. $T[A]_\phi$ is desingularized at q.

```
T ← I_d
WHILE (den(A) = 0 mod q) DO
    ℓ ← φ − dispersion(A, q)
    IF (ℓ ≤ 0) THEN RETURN (T, A)
    n ← ord_q(A) ; Ã ← q^n A
    k ← 0 ; M ← I_d ; N ← π_q(Ã)
    WHILE (M · N ≠ 0 AND k ≤ ℓ) DO
        M ← M · N; k ← k + 1 ; N ← π_q(φ^{-k}(Ã))
    U ← as in the proof of Proposition 3.15.
    D ← diag(φ^{k-1}(q)I_s, I_{d-s}) with s = d − rank(N).
    A ← φ(U · D)^{-1} · A · (U · D)
    T ← T · U · D
RETURN (T, A)
```

Remark 3.16. *All systems that are desingularizable via Algorithm 1 are also desingularizable via Algorithm 2 and vice versa.*

Example 3.17. For A as in Example 2.2 and $q = z - 2$ we have

$$\tilde{A} = (z-2)A = \begin{pmatrix} 0 & z-2 \\ -2(z+1) & 3(z-1) \end{pmatrix},$$

$$M = \pi_q(\tilde{A}(z)\tilde{A}(z-1)\tilde{A}(z-2)) = \tilde{A}(2)\tilde{A}(1)\tilde{A}(0) = \begin{pmatrix} 0 & 0, \\ -12 & 6 \end{pmatrix} \neq 0$$

$$N = \pi_q(\phi^{-3}(\tilde{A})) = \tilde{A}(-1) = \begin{pmatrix} 0 & -3 \\ 0 & -6 \end{pmatrix},$$

$$\pi_q(\tilde{A}(z)\tilde{A}(z-1)\tilde{A}(z-2)\tilde{A}(z-3)) = \tilde{A}(2)\tilde{A}(1)\tilde{A}(0)\tilde{A}(-1) = 0,$$

so $k = 3$. If we chose

$$U = \begin{pmatrix} \frac{1}{2} & \frac{1}{2} \\ 0 & 1 \end{pmatrix},$$

then

$$\phi(U)^{-1}AU = U^{-1}AU = \frac{1}{(z-2)}\begin{pmatrix} (z+1) & 0 \\ -(z+1) & 2(z-2) \end{pmatrix}.$$

We have $s = 1$, so with $D = \operatorname{diag}(\phi^2(q), 1) = \operatorname{diag}(z, 1)$ we get

$$B = \phi(D)^{-1}(\phi(U)^{-1}AU)D = \frac{1}{(z-2)}\begin{pmatrix} z & 0 \\ -z(z+1) & 2(z-2) \end{pmatrix}.$$

Note that, as expected, we have that

$$\tilde{B}(2)\tilde{B}(1)\tilde{B}(0) = 0.$$

Here we can repeat the above process on B to desingularize as much as possible the matrix A at $q = z - 2$. In this particular example q is removable by the transformation $T = U \cdot \operatorname{diag}(z(z-1)(z-2), 1)$. Indeed, one can see that

$$T[A]_\phi = \phi(T)^{-1}AT = \begin{pmatrix} 1 & 0 \\ -z(z^2-1) & 2 \end{pmatrix},$$

has polynomial entries. The transformation T is the same as in Example 3.13 up to a right factor $\operatorname{diag}(\frac{1}{2}, 1)$.

3.3 Rank Reduction

Consider a system $[A]_\phi$ and let q be a ϕ–minimal factor of $\operatorname{den}(A)$ with multiplicity $n \geq 1$, such that $[A]_\phi$ is not partially desingularizable at q. This implies that there is no positive integer k such that relation (5) holds. As the quantity n cannot be reduced, it is natural to ask if it is possible to reduce the rank of the leading matrix $\mathrm{lc}_q(A)$ by applying a polynomial transformation T to $[A]_\phi$. We shall give a criterion for the existence of a polynomial transformation T such that $\mathrm{ord}_q(T[A]_\phi) = \mathrm{ord}_q(A)$ and $\mathrm{rank}(\mathrm{lc}_q(T[A]_\phi)) < \mathrm{rank}(\mathrm{lc}_q(A))$.

PROPOSITION 3.18. *Let $q \in C[z]$ be a ϕ-minimal pole of $[A]_\phi$ such that $[A]_\phi$ is not partially desingularizable at q. Let $\tilde{A} = q^n A$, so that $\mathrm{ord}_q(\tilde{A}) = 0$ and $\pi_q(\tilde{A}) = \mathrm{lc}_q(A)$. Then a necessary and sufficient condition for the existence of a polynomial transformation T such that $\mathrm{ord}_p(T[A]_\phi) \geq \mathrm{ord}_p(A)$ for all $p \in C[z]$ and $\mathrm{rank}(\mathrm{lc}_q(T[A])) < \mathrm{rank}(\mathrm{lc}_q(A))$ is that there exists a positive integer k such that*

$$\mathrm{rank}(\pi_q(\tilde{A}\phi^{-1}(\tilde{A})\dots\phi^{-k}(\tilde{A}))) < \mathrm{rank}(\mathrm{lc}_q(A)). \tag{7}$$

PROOF. *Necessary condition*: Suppose first that there exists a polynomial matrix T with the desired properties and let $B = T[A]_\phi$. Similarly to the proof of Proposition 3.14, one gets for all non-negative integers k:

$$\phi(T)(q^nB)\phi^{-1}(q^nB)\dots\phi^{-k}(q^nB) = \tilde{A}\phi^{-1}(\tilde{A})\dots\phi^{-k}(\tilde{A})\phi^{-k}(T).$$

Since $\mathrm{ord}_q(q^nB) = 0 = \mathrm{ord}_q(\tilde{A})$ and all the other factors in both sides of this equality have non-negative orders at q we get that

$$\pi_q(\phi(T))\pi_q((q^nB))\pi_q(\phi^{-1}(q^nB)\dots\phi^{-k}(q^nB)) = \pi_q(\tilde{A}\phi^{-1}(\tilde{A})\dots\phi^{-k}(\tilde{A}))\pi_q(\phi^{-k}(T)).$$

By using the fact that the rank of a product of matrices is less or equal to the rank of each factor we get that the rank of the product in the right hand side of the previous equality is bounded by $\mathrm{rank}(\pi_q((q^nB))) = \mathrm{rank}(\mathrm{lc}_q(B))$ and hence

$$\mathrm{rank}(\pi_q(\tilde{A}\phi^{-1}(\tilde{A})\dots\phi^{-k}(\tilde{A}))\pi_q(\phi^{-k}(T))) \leq \mathrm{rank}(\mathrm{lc}_q(B)) < \mathrm{rank}(\mathrm{lc}_q(A)).$$

Now let k be the smallest positive integer such that the matrix $\pi_q(\phi^{-k}(T))$ is of full rank. Then

$$\mathrm{rank}(\pi_q(\tilde{A}\phi^{-1}(\tilde{A})\dots\phi^{-k}(\tilde{A}))) = \mathrm{rank}(\pi_q(\tilde{A}\phi^{-1}(\tilde{A})\dots\phi^{-k}(\tilde{A}))\pi_q(\phi^{-k}(T))) < \mathrm{rank}(\mathrm{lc}_q(A)).$$

Sufficient condition: Let $r = \mathrm{rank}(\mathrm{lc}_q(A))$ and let k be minimal so that (7) holds. Put

$$M := \pi_q(\tilde{A}\phi^{-1}(\tilde{A})\cdots\phi^{-k+1}(\tilde{A})) \quad \text{and} \quad N := \pi_q(\phi^{-k}(\tilde{A})).$$

By definition of k, the matrix M is nonzero, has the same rank r as $\mathrm{lc}_q(A)$ and we have the strict inequality

$$\mathrm{rank}(M \cdot N) < r = \mathrm{rank}(M).$$

This implies in particular that $\mathrm{rank}(N) < d = \dim(A)$. Let $s := d - \mathrm{rank}(N)$. As in the proof of Proposition 3.15, we can assume that N has the following form:

$$N = \begin{pmatrix} 0_s & 0_{s,d-s} \\ N_{2,1} & N_{2,2} \end{pmatrix},$$

where $N_{2,1}$ and $N_{2,2}$ are matrices with entries in $C[z]/\langle q\rangle$ of size $(d-s)\times s$ and $(d-s)\times(d-s)$ respectively, so that the last $d-s$ rows of N are linearly independent over $C[z]/\langle q\rangle$. Let $M = (M_{i,j})_{1\leq i,j\leq 2}$ be partitioned in four blocks as N. Then we have

$$M \cdot N = \begin{pmatrix} M_{1,2} \\ M_{2,2} \end{pmatrix} \cdot \begin{pmatrix} N_{2,1} & N_{2,2} \end{pmatrix}.$$

As the matrix $(N_{2,1} \ \ N_{2,2})$ is of full rank, we get that

$$\mathrm{rank}\begin{pmatrix} M_{1,2} \\ M_{2,2} \end{pmatrix} = \mathrm{rank}(M \cdot N) < r.$$

Let $\tilde{A} = (\tilde{A}_{i,j})_{1\leq i,j\leq 2}$ be partitioned in four blocks as N. Then $\pi_q(\phi^{-k}(\tilde{A}_{1,j})) = 0$ for $j = 1, 2$. Using the substitution $Y = DX$ where $D = \mathrm{diag}(\phi^{k-1}(q)I_s, I_{d-s})$, we get a system $[B]_\phi$ of the form (6) with $\mathrm{den}(B) \mid \mathrm{den}(A)$ and $\mathrm{ord}_q(B) \geq \mathrm{ord}_q(A)$. Note that

$$\pi_q(q^nB) = \begin{pmatrix} \pi_q(\frac{1}{\phi^k(q)})I_s & 0_{s,d-s} \\ 0_{d-s,s} & I_{d-s} \end{pmatrix} \cdot \begin{pmatrix} \pi_q(\tilde{A}_{1,1}) & \pi_q(\tilde{A}_{1,2}) \\ \pi_q(\tilde{A}_{2,1}) & \pi_q(\tilde{A}_{2,2}) \end{pmatrix} \cdot \begin{pmatrix} \pi_q(\phi^{k-1}(q))I_s & 0_{s,d-s} \\ 0_{d-s,s} & I_{d-s} \end{pmatrix}.$$

It follows that if $k \geq 2$, then $\mathrm{rank}(\pi_q(q^nB)) = \mathrm{rank}(\mathrm{lc}_q(A))$, but we will prove that the factorial relation (7) holds for $\tilde{B} := q^nB$ with $k-1$ instead of k. As in the proof of Proposition 3.15, we have that

$$\pi_q(\phi^{-k+1}(D)) = \pi_q(\mathrm{diag}(qI_s, I_{d-s})) = \mathrm{diag}(0_s, I_{d-s}),$$

hence

$$M \cdot \pi_q(\phi^{-k+1}(D)) = \begin{pmatrix} 0_s & M_{1,2} \\ 0_{d-s} & M_{2,2} \end{pmatrix},$$

whose rank is less than r. Now $\pi_q(\phi(D)) = \mathrm{diag}(\pi_q(\phi^k(q))I_s, I_{d-s})$ is invertible (since q and $\phi^k(q)$ are co-prime), it then follows that

$$\mathrm{rank}(\pi_q(\tilde{B}\phi^{-1}(\tilde{B})\cdots\phi^{-k+1}(\tilde{B}))) = \mathrm{rank}(M \cdot \pi_q(\phi^{-k+1}(D)) < r = \mathrm{rank}(\mathrm{lc}_q(B)).$$

If $k-1$ is still positive then we can repeat this process on the matrix B and the polynomial q until we arrive at $k = 1$. Then we have that

$$\pi_q(q^nB) = \begin{pmatrix} \pi_q(\frac{1}{\phi(q)})I_s & 0_{s,d-s} \\ 0_{d-s,s} & I_{d-s} \end{pmatrix} \cdot \begin{pmatrix} 0_s & M_{1,2} \\ 0_{d-s} & M_{2,2} \end{pmatrix},$$

whose rank is less than r. □

The proof of Proposition 3.18 suggests that Algorithm 2 can be easily adapted to minimize the rank of the leading matrix of a ϕ-minimal pole. In particular, a T can be computed such that $\mathrm{ord}_p(T[A]_\phi) \geq \mathrm{ord}_p(A)$ for $p \in C[z]$. It is to note that rank reduction for a pole in A via Algorithm 2 comes at the potential cost of an increase in order of a pole of A^*, as the next example shows.

Example 3.19. Consider the system with

$$A = \begin{pmatrix} z(z+1) & 0 & 0 \\ 0 & \frac{z+1}{z} & 0 \\ 0 & 0 & \frac{1}{z} \end{pmatrix}, \qquad A^* = \begin{pmatrix} \frac{1}{z(z-1)} & 0 & 0 \\ 0 & \frac{z-1}{z} & 0 \\ 0 & 0 & z-1 \end{pmatrix}.$$

We have $\mathrm{rank}(\mathrm{lc}_z(A)) = 2$ and $\mathrm{ord}_{z-1}(A^*) = -1$, and computing a rank reducing transformation for $[A]_\phi$ via Algorithm 2 gives $T = \mathrm{diag}(z, z, 1)$, which results in

$$T[A]_\phi = \begin{pmatrix} z^2 & 0 & 0 \\ 0 & 1 & 0 \\ 0 & 0 & \frac{1}{z} \end{pmatrix}, \qquad T[A]^*_\phi = \begin{pmatrix} \frac{1}{(z-1)^2} & 0 & 0 \\ 0 & 1 & 1 \\ 0 & 0 & z-1 \end{pmatrix},$$

with $\mathrm{rank}(\mathrm{lc}_z(T[A]_\phi)) = 1$ and $\mathrm{ord}_{z-1}(A^*) = -2$. We note that we merely shifted an already present pole in A^* to the right, as opposed to adding a new factor to the system.

4 APPARENT SINGULARITIES

In this section we establish the connection between the analytical notion of apparent and removable singularities of meromorphic solutions and the algebraic concept desingularization of difference systems. The key observation is the fact that the factorial relation (5) provides a sufficient condition for a singularity to be removable..

Proposition 4.1. *Let $\zeta \in \mathcal{P}_r(A)$ be a pole of A of order $\nu \geq 1$ such that $\zeta - j \notin P_r(A)$ for all positive integers j. Let $\tilde{A} = (z-\zeta)^\nu A$, so that $\tilde{A}(\zeta) \neq 0$. If ζ is a removable r-singularity of $[A]_\phi$, then there exists a positive integer k such that*

$$\tilde{A}(\zeta)A(\zeta-1)\cdots A(\zeta-k) = 0.$$

In particular, the matrix $A(\zeta - j)$ is singular for some non-negative integer j.

Proof. Using a result due to Ramis [3, 14, 20], one can easily prove that for any complex number η with $-\operatorname{Re}\eta$ large enough, there exist a meromorphic fundamental matrix solution $F(z)$ which is holomorphic for $-\operatorname{Re} z$ large enough and satisfies $F(\eta) = I_d$. Choose a positive integer k such that $-\operatorname{Re}(\zeta-k)$ is large enough and take a fundamental matrix solution $F(z)$ as above with $F(\zeta-k) = I_d$. Then one can write

$$F(z+1) = A(z)A(z-1)A(z-2)\cdots A(z-k)F(z-k),$$

and hence

$$(z-\zeta)^\nu F(z+1) = (z-\zeta)^\nu A(z)A(z-1)A(z-2)\cdots A(z-k)F(z-k).$$

Taking the limit as z goes to ζ, we get that

$$0 = \tilde{A}(\zeta)A(\zeta-1)A(\zeta-2)\cdots A(\zeta-k).$$ □

Corollary 4.2. *Let $\zeta \in P_r(A)$ such that there is a ϕ-minimal q with $q(\zeta) = 0$. If ζ is a removable singularity of $[A]_\phi$, then $[A]_\phi$ is desingularizable at q.*

Proof. Let $n := -\operatorname{ord}_q(A)$. We can apply Proposition 3.15 to reduce the multiplicity of q in $\operatorname{den}(A)$ from n to $n-1$. If $n > 1$, q is still ϕ-minimal and ζ still removable, and we can repeat the process until $[A]_\phi$ is desingularized at q. □

Proposition 4.1 and Corollary 4.2 imply that a singularity is apparent if and only if all congruent poles are removable and therefore desingularizable.

5 CONCLUSION AND FUTURE WORK

In this paper we presented two algorithms to desingularize linear first order difference systems and we explored the notions of apparent and removable singularities. These topics have already been studied in the context of difference operators, where usually the solution space of a given operator is increased as a side effect of the desingularization process. An interesting starting point for further research is to investigate the relation of desingularization on a system level and on an operator level in regard to this extension of the solution space.

Concerning pseudo linear systems, we will continue our work in several directions. We aim to establish a clear connection between removable singularities of a system $[A]_\phi$ and the removable singularities of $[A^*]_\phi^{-1}$, as well as the role of removable singularities for extending numerical sequences. Furthermore, studying desingularization at non-ϕ-minimal poles is a promising approach for identifying poles that only appear in some components of fundamental solutions. We are currently also investigating how to characterize poles in solutions that do not propagate to infinitely many congruent points via gauge transformations.

Regarding complexity, it would be desirable to conduct a thorough complexity analysis of desingularization algorithms. Finally, as was shown in [10, 16], removable singularities of operators can negatively impact the running time of some algorithms and it is interesting to investigate whether similar effects occur for linear systems.

Acknowledgements. We would like to thank the reviewers for their very careful reading of the draft and their helpful remarks.

REFERENCES

[1] S. A. Abramov, M. A. Barkatou, and M. van Hoeij. Apparent singularities of linear difference equations with polynomial coefficients. *Appl. Algebra Eng., Commun. Comput.*, 17(2):117–133, June 2006.

[2] S. A. Abramov and M. van Hoeij. Desingularization of linear difference operators with polynomial coefficients. In *Proceedings of ISSAC 1999*, pages 269–275, 1999.

[3] M. A. Barkatou. *Contribution à l'étude des équations différentielles et aux différences dans le champ complexe.* PhD thesis, INPG,Grenoble France, 1989.

[4] M. A. Barkatou. Factoring systems of linear functional equations using eigenrings. In *COMPUTER ALGEBRA 2006, Latest Advances in Symbolic Algorithms. Proceedings of the Waterloo Workshop. Ontario, Canada*, 2006.

[5] M. A. Barkatou and G. Chen. Computing the exponential part of a formal fundamental matrix solution of a linear difference system. *J. Difference Eq. Appl.*, 5(3):1–26, 1999.

[6] M. A. Barkatou and G. Chen. Some formal invariants of linear difference systems. *J. Reine Angew Math.*, 533(2):1–23, 2001.

[7] M. A. Barkatou and S. S. Maddah. Removing apparent singularities of systems of linear differential equations with rational function coefficients. In *Proceedings of ISSAC 2015*, pages 53–60, New York, NY, USA, 2015. ACM.

[8] G. D. Birkhoff. Formal theory of irregular linear difference equations. *Acta. Math.*, 54:205–246, 1930.

[9] M. Bronstein and M. Petkovšek. An introduction to pseudo-linear algebra. *Theoretical Computer Science*, 157:3–33, 1996.

[10] S. Chen, M. Jaroschek, M. Kauers, and M. Singer. Desingularization explains order-degree curves for Ore operators. In *Proceedings of ISSAC 2013*, pages 157–164, 2013.

[11] S. Chen, M. Kauers, and M. F. Singer. Desingularization of ore polynomials. *Journal of Symbolic Computation*, 74:617–626, 2016.

[12] The Sage Developers. *SageMath, the Sage Mathematics Software System (Version 8.1)*, 2018. http://www.sagemath.org.

[13] P. Flajolet and R. Sedgewick. *Analytic Combinatorics.* Cambridge University Press, New York, NY, USA, 1 edition, 2009.

[14] G. K. Immink. On the relation between linear difference and differential equations with polynomial coefficients. *Math. Nachr.*, 200:59–76, 1999.

[15] N. Jacobson. Pseudo-linear transformations. *Annals of Mathematics*, 33(2):484–507, 1937.

[16] M. Jaroschek. Improved polynomial remainder sequences for Ore polynomials. *Journal of Symbolic Computation*, 58:64–76, 2013.

[17] M. Jaroschek. *Removable Singularities of Ore Operators.* PhD thesis, RISC, Johannes Kepler University Linz, November 2013.

[18] M. Kauers and P. Paule. *The Concrete Tetrahedron.* Text and Monographs in Symbolic Computation. Springer Wien, 1st edition, 2011.

[19] C. Praagman. Fundamental solutions for meromorphic linear difference equations in the complex plane, and related problems. *Journal für die reine und angewandte Mathematik*, 369:100–109, 1986.

[20] J.-P. Ramis. Etude des solutions méromorphes des équations aux différences linéaires algébriques. manuscript.

[21] H. Tsai. Weyl closure of a linear differential operator. *Journal of Symbolic Computation*, 29(4-5):747–775, 2000.

[22] Y. Zhang. Contraction of Ore ideals with applications. In *Proceedings ISSAC 2016*, pages 413–420, New York, NY, USA, 2016. ACM.

A New Approach for Formal Reduction of Singular Linear Differential Systems Using Eigenrings

Moulay A. Barkatou
Univ. Limoges, CNRS, XLIM, Limoges, France
moulay.barkatou@unilim.fr

Joelle Saade
Univ. Limoges, CNRS, XLIM, Limoges, France
joelle.saade@unilim.fr

Jacques-Arthur Weil
Univ. Limoges, CNRS, XLIM, Limoges, France
weil@unilim.fr

ABSTRACT

We give a new algorithm for the formal reduction of linear differential systems with Laurent series coefficients. We show how to obtain a decomposition of Balser, Jurkat and Lutz using eigenring techniques. We establish structural information on the obtained indecomposable subsystems and retrieve information on their invariants such as ramification. We show why classical algorithms then perform well on these subsystems. We also give precise estimates of the precision on the power series which is required in each step of our algorithm. The algorithm is implemented in Maple. We give examples in [14].

KEYWORDS

Linear Differential Systems; Formal Solutions; Formal Reduction; Formal Invariants; Eigenrings; Decomposition; Factorization.

ACM Reference Format:
Moulay A. Barkatou, Joelle Saade, and Jacques-Arthur Weil. 2018. A New Approach for Formal Reduction of Singular Linear Differential Systems Using Eigenrings. In *ISSAC '18: 2018 ACM International Symposium on Symbolic and Algebraic Computation, July 16–19, 2018, New York, NY, USA.* ACM, New York, NY, USA, 8 pages. https://doi.org/10.1145/3208976.3209016

1 INTRODUCTION

Throughout this paper, we let C be an effective subfield of $\mathbb{C}$ and we suppose, for sake of clarity, that C is algebraically closed. We denote by $C((x))$ the field of formal Laurent series in x with coefficients in C and consider a first-order linear differential system with coefficients in $C((x))$ of size n and Poincaré rank $q > 0$

$$[A] : \frac{dY}{dx} = A(x)Y. \tag{1}$$

We have $A = \frac{1}{x^{q+1}} \sum_{k=0}^{\infty} A_k x^k$ where the matrices A_k are of size n, they have coefficients in C and $A_0 \neq 0$.

As shown in [3], such a system has a formal fundamental solution matrix of the form

$$F(x)G(x) = F(x)\mathrm{diag}(G_1(x), \dots, G_\ell(x)) \tag{2}$$

where $F \in GL_n(C((x)))$ and G is a block-diagonal matrix composed of blocks G_i, each of the form

$$G_i = x^{\Lambda_i} U_i \exp(Q_i). \tag{3}$$

- Q_i is a diagonal matrix of the form
$$Q_i = q_i(\frac{1}{t})I_{m_i} \oplus q_i(\frac{1}{\omega_i t})I_{m_i} \oplus \dots \oplus q_i(\frac{1}{\omega_i{}^{r_i-1}t})I_{m_i}, \tag{4}$$
where $t = x^{\frac{1}{r_i}}$, with r_i minimal, q_i is a polynomial without constant term, ω_i is a primitive r_i-th root of unity and I_{m_i} is the identity matrix;
- Λ_i is an upper-triangular constant matrix
$$\Lambda_i = J_{m_i}(\lambda_i) \oplus \left(J_{m_i}(\lambda_i) + (\frac{1}{r_i})I_{m_i}\right) \oplus \dots \oplus \left(J_{m_i}(\lambda_i) + (\frac{r_i-1}{r_i})I_{m_i}\right) \tag{5}$$
where $J_{m_i}(\lambda_i)$ is an m_i-dimensional Jordan block, with an eigenvalue λ_i, and
- $U_i = \left(\omega_i^{(j-1)(k-1)} I_{m_i}\right)_{j,k=1,\dots,r_i}$ is a generalized Vandermonde.

The q_i's are called *the exponential parts* of the system $[A]$. Note that G_i is determined by $(q_i, \lambda_i, r_i, m_i)$. We call r_i (respectively, m_i) the *ramification index*, (respectively, the *multiplicity*) of q_i in G_i.

In the sequel, we will refer to this result as BJL Theorem. Following the formal classification in [3], we deduce the following theorem, which is a consequence of theorem I in [3].

Theorem 1.1. *For any system $[A]$, there exists $P \in GL_n(C((x)))$ such that the change of variable $Y = PZ$ reduces system $[A]$ to an equivalent block-diagonal system*

$$[A_1(x)] \oplus \dots \oplus [A_\ell(x)] \tag{6}$$

where each block $[A_i]$ is indecomposable over $C((x))$. Moreover, for each i, there exists a matrix permutation P_i such that:

$$P_i[A_i] := P_i^{-1}A_iP_i - P_i^{-1}\frac{dP_i}{dx} = \begin{pmatrix} B_i & \frac{1}{x}I_{r_i} & 0 \\ & \ddots & \frac{1}{x}I_{r_i} \\ 0 & & B_i \end{pmatrix} \tag{7}$$

where $[B_i]$ is irreducible over $C((x))$ of size r_i and is repeated m_i times. Each $[B_i]$ is decomposable in $C((x^{1/r_i}))$. More precisely, let $t := x^{1/r_i}$ and let $[\mathcal{B}_i]$ denote the resulting system over $C((t))$

$$[\mathcal{B}_i] : \quad \frac{dY}{dt} = \mathcal{B}_i Y, \qquad \mathcal{B}_i := r_i t^{r_i-1} B_i(t^{r_i}).$$

Then there exists a transformation S_i in $GL_{r_i}(C((t)))$ such that $S_i[\mathcal{B}_i] := S_i^{-1}\mathcal{B}_iS_i - S_i^{-1}\frac{dS_i}{dt}$ is a diagonal matrix of the form

$$S_i[\mathcal{B}_i] = (W_i(t)) \oplus \dots \oplus \left(W_i(\omega_i{}^{r_i-1}t)\right), \tag{8}$$

where $W_i(t) = \frac{dq_i(t)}{dt} + \frac{\widetilde{\lambda}_i}{r_i t}$ and $\widetilde{\lambda}_i$ differ from λ_i in (5) by an integer. The exponential parts q_i of $[A]$ are found once all W_i are known.

ISSAC '18, July 16–19, 2018, New York, NY, USA

ACM ISBN 978-1-4503-5550-6/18/07...$15.00
https://doi.org/10.1145/3208976.3209016

This theorem guarantees the existence of transformations that will take the system $[A]$ into the normal form described above from which a fundamental matrix of formal solution is straightforwardly derived. *Formal reduction* is the process of finding such transformations. In the present paper, we develop an algorithm which constructs such transformations.
Our approach is to revisit the main steps of theorem 1.1.

- Using a transformation with coefficient in $C((x))$ computed from the eigenring of $[A]$, we perform a first maximal decomposition. This decomposition gives the block-diagonal system as in (6), where each subsystem is indecomposable and has only one type of exponential part (proposition 3.2).
- Using the structure of each indecomposable system (proposition 3.1 and proposition 3.2), we get the multiplicity of the corresponding exponential part, hence its ramification (proposition 3.3).
- With a transformation in $C((x))$, we obtain the irreducible system $[B_i]$ of (7) (proposition 3.5).
- After applying the appropriate ramification to $[B_i]$, we can compute successively the coefficients of its exponential part using at each step the Moser-reduction algorithm [12] or the splitting lemma as in [4].

Moser-reduction algorithm and the splitting lemma (see section 2) are two important tools in the formal reduction process. The first produces, for a given system, an equivalent one with minimal Poincaré rank; the latter allows to decouple a given system, with a leading matrix A_0 having two or more eigenvalues, into subsystems of smaller size each having a leading matrix with a single eigenvalue. The leading coefficients of the exponential parts are given by the nonzero eigenvalues. If the leading matrix is nilpotent and the Poincaré rank is minimal then it is necessary [4] to introduce a ramification ($t = x^{1/s}$) in order to be able to decouple the system again. Different strategies were developed (see for example in [4, 9, 16]) to find a suitable integer s and compute transformations (in the new variable $t = x^{1/s}$) intended to get a system having a leading matrix with several eigenvalues. In [4], the first author proves that it is enough to take s as the denominator of the so-called *Katz invariant* (the "degree" in x of the exponential part) of the system which can be computed by an algorithm described in the same paper. This algorithm suffers from a practical drawback, namely it could introduce unnecessary ramifications during the formal reduction process; this may happen in the case where the input system has exponential parts with different ramification indices. With our new approach, we avoid this kind of drawback by first splitting the system into indecomposable subsystems with different exponential parts for which we are able to compute the minimal ramification index. Furthermore, once we perform this minimal ramification, we know that no further ramification is needed, so that we can proceed as in [4] (using only the splitting lemma and Moser-reduction) to get the corresponding exponential of each subsystem.

Finally, as we work with Laurent series, we will establish estimates for the number of terms of the series which are required for three basic operations in our setting: computing the characteristic polynomial of a Laurent series matrix in the eigenring, computing a basis of kernels of matrices and computing enough terms in an equivalent system to guarantee that we finally find the exponential parts.

2 PRELIMINARIES AND NOTATION

Notation. We denote by $\mathcal{M}_n\,(C((x)))$ the set of $n \times n$ matrices of Laurent series, $\mathrm{GL}_n\,(C((x)))$ the group of invertible matrices and I_n the identity matrix of size n. We denote by $J_m(\lambda)$ the m-dimensional upper triangular Jordan block, with an eigenvalue λ. The *valuation* $\mathrm{val}(a)$ of a nonzero element $a = \sum_i a_i x^i$ in $C((x))$ is defined as the minimal integer i for which $a_i \neq 0$ (with the convention $\mathrm{val}(0) = \infty$). The valuation of a matrix in $\mathcal{M}_n\,(C((x)))$ is the minimal of valuations of its entries.

We use the $\oplus$ notation for block-diagonal matrices $A_1 \oplus \cdots \oplus A_\ell := \mathrm{diag}(A_1, \ldots, A_\ell)$ and for block-diagonal differential systems:

$$[A_1] \oplus \cdots \oplus [A_\ell] := [A_1 \oplus \cdots \oplus A_\ell].$$

2.1 Basic Tools for Reduction

Equivalent System. A *gauge transformation* of a system $[A]$ is a change of basis $Y = PZ$ where $P \in GL_n(C((x)))$. It leads to a new system

$$[B] : Z' = B(x)Z, \ \text{where } B = P[A] := P^{-1}AP - P^{-1}P'.$$

Two systems $[A]$ and $[B]$ are *equivalent over* $C((x))$ (notation $[A] \sim [B]$) if one can be obtained from the other by a gauge transformation.

Decomposition/Factorization. A system $[A]$ of size n is called *decomposable* over $C((x))$ if there exists $P \in GL_n\,(C((x)))$ such that

$$P[A] = [B_{11}] \oplus [B_{22}]$$

where $B_{ii} \in \mathcal{M}_{n_i}(C((x)))$ with $n_i < n$; otherwise, it is called *indecomposable* over $C((x))$. The process of finding such a P and performing the transformation is called *decomposition.*
We say that a system $[A]$ is *reducible* over $C((x))$ if there exists $P \in GL_n\,(C((x)))$ such that

$$P[A] = \begin{pmatrix} B_{11} & B_{12} \\ 0 & B_{22} \end{pmatrix}$$

where $B_{ii} \in \mathcal{M}_{n_i}(C((x)))$ with $n_i < n$ and $B_{12} \in \mathcal{M}_{n_1 \times n_2}(C((x)))$. Otherwise, we say that it is *irreducible* over $C((x))$. The process of finding such a P and performing the transformation is called *factorization.*
For completeness of this paper we will summarize the operations used in the recursive algorithm given in [4]:

The Splitting Lemma. ([16], Chapter IV, p. 52-54) If the leading matrix A_0 of $[A]$ is of the form $A_0 = A_0^{11} \oplus A_0^{22}$ where A_0^{11} and A_0^{22} have no eigenvalues in common, then there exists a matrix P of the form $P = I + P_1 x + P_2 x^2 + \cdots$ (the P_i are constant matrices) which transforms $[A]$ into an equivalent system $\widetilde{A} = P[A]$ where $\widetilde{A}_0 = A_0$ and $\widetilde{A}$ is block-diagonal with the same partition as in A_0.

Moser-Reduction Algorithm. In [12], Moser gave a method now known as *Moser algorithm* [10] which, given a system $[A]$ over $C((x))$, produces an equivalent system $P[A]$ with minimal Poincaré rank. Moreover the transformation P is polynomial over C. For more details we refer the reader to [10].

Shifting the Eigenvalues of A_0. When A_0 has one single eigenvalue $a \in C$, the change of variable

$$Y = (exp^{\int \frac{a}{x^{q+1}} dx})Z,$$

leads to an equivalent system with A_0 nilpotent.

2.2 Eigenring Approach for Decomposition

Definition 2.1 ([7]). The *eigenring* $\mathcal{E}(A)$ of the system $[A]$ is the set of $n \times n$ matrices $T \in \mathcal{M}_n(C((x)))$ satisfying $T' = [A, T] := AT - TA$.

The eigenring $\mathcal{E}(A)$ is a $C-$ vector space of finite dimension at most n^2 and an associative algebra. Therefore, any $T \in \mathcal{E}(A)$ is similar to a constant matrix and it has a characteristic polynomial with coefficients in the field of constants C.

Computing the eigenring of $[A]$ is equivalent to finding all Laurent series solutions of the system $\left[I_n \otimes A - A^t \otimes I_n\right]$ of size n^2. Algorithms for computing such solutions have been presented in [5, 6, 9].

Definition 2.2. Let $T_1, \ldots, T_d$ be a basis of $\mathcal{E}(A)$. A *general element* M *of* $\mathcal{E}(A)$ is a combination $\sum_{i=1}^{d} t_i T_i$ where the t_i are indeterminates.

A *generic element* in $\mathcal{E}(A)$ is an element with maximal number of distinct eigenvalues in C.

The terminology *general element* comes from the fact that M is a general solution to the system $[I \otimes A - A^t \otimes I]$. A generic element is obtained by specializing the indeterminates t_i to random constants $c_i \in C$.

As shown in ([7], p.32), a maximal decomposition of a system $[A]$ can be obtained using a generic element T in $\mathcal{E}(A)$. If P is a matrix such that $P^{-1}.T.P$ is in block-diagonal form (with disjoint spectra), then we have

$$P[A] = [A_1] \oplus \ldots \oplus [A_\ell].$$

The following type of eigenring will be fundamental in the development of our algorithm.

Proposition 2.3. *Let A be a $m \times r$ block-triangular matrix of the form*

$$\begin{pmatrix} B & \frac{1}{x} I_r & 0 \\ & \ddots & \frac{1}{x} I_r \\ 0 & & B \end{pmatrix},$$

where $[B]$ is irreducible over $C((x))$ of size r repeated m times. Then, the eigenring of $[A]$ consists in matrices of the form

$$M = \begin{pmatrix} c_1 I_r & c_2 I_r & \cdots & c_m I_r \\ 0 & \ddots & \ddots & \vdots \\ \vdots & \ddots & \ddots & c_2 I_r \\ 0 & \cdots & 0 & c_1 I_r \end{pmatrix}$$

where $c_i \in C$. In particular, $\dim(\mathcal{E}(A)) = m$.

Proof. Let T be an element in $\mathcal{E}(A)$ partitioned in m^2 blocks of size r:

$$T = \begin{pmatrix} T_{11} & \cdots & T_{1m} \\ \vdots & \ddots & \vdots \\ T_{m1} & \cdots & T_{mm} \end{pmatrix}.$$

By a direct identification in $T' = [T, A] := TA - AT$, we obtain the system of equations:

$$T'_{i,j} = [T_{i,j}, B] + \frac{1}{x} T_{i,j-1} - \frac{1}{x} T_{i+1,j}, \quad 1 \le i, j \le m.$$

As $[B]$ is irreducible, by Schur's lemma, $\dim(\mathcal{E}(B)) = 1$ and, since $T_{m,1} \in \mathcal{E}(B)$, we obtain $T_{m,1} = cI_r$. with $c \in C$. Each equation of the form

$$T'_{i,1} = [T_{i,1}, B] - \frac{1}{x} T_{i+1,1}$$

can be solved by variation of constants. For $i = m - 1$, this implies to find $f(x) \in C((x))$ such that $f'(x) = \frac{c}{x}$. This is possible only if $c = 0$ (so that $T_{m,1} = 0$) and f is constant. Proceeding similarly for all $i = m - 1, m - 2, \ldots, 1$, we obtain that $T_{i+1,1} = 0$. In the same manner, for all equations

$$T'_{m,j} = [T_{m,j}, B] + \frac{1}{x} T_{m,j-1} \quad j = 2, \ldots, m,$$

we have $T_{m,j-1} = 0$.

At this point, we have been solving all equation of the form:

$$\begin{cases} T'_{i,j} & = & [T_{i,j}, B] + \frac{1}{x} T_{i,j-1} \\ T'_{i,j} & = & [T_{i,j}, B] - \frac{1}{x} T_{i+1,j} \\ T'_{m,1} & = & [T'_{m,1}, B] \end{cases}$$

and so far we have:

$$T = \begin{pmatrix} \alpha_1 I_r & T_{1,2} & \cdots & \cdots & T_{1,m} \\ 0 & T_{22} & \cdots & T_{i,j} & \vdots \\ \vdots & \vdots & \ddots & \vdots & \vdots \\ \vdots & T_{m-1,2} & \cdots & T_{m-1,m-1} & T_{m-1,m} \\ 0 & 0 & \cdots & 0 & \alpha_m I_r \end{pmatrix}.$$

Now we consider the equations

$$T'_{i,j} = [T_{i,j}, B] + \frac{1}{x} T_{i,j-1} - \frac{1}{x} T_{i+1,j}.$$

We begin simultaneously by those in the second column and $(m-1)$-th row and we iterate forward from the bottom to the top. Each system

$$T'_{i,j} = [T_{i,j}, B] + \frac{1}{x} T_{i,j-1} - \frac{1}{x} T_{i+1,j}$$

has as solution $T_{i,j} = \alpha_{i,j} I_r$ and imposes the condition $T_{i,j-1} = T_{i+1,j}$.

Thus, it easily follows that

$$\begin{cases} \forall j < i & , & T_{i,j} & = & 0 \\ \forall j \ge i & , & T_{i,j} & = & T_{i+1,j+1}. \end{cases}$$

Finally,

$$T = \begin{pmatrix} c_1 I_r & c_2 I_r & \cdots & c_m I_r \\ 0 & \ddots & \ddots & \vdots \\ \vdots & \ddots & \ddots & c_2 I_r \\ 0 & \cdots & 0 & c_1 I_r \end{pmatrix},$$

and $\dim(\mathcal{E}(A)) = m$. □

3 OUR APPROACH

The main steps of our algorithm for computing the exponential parts can be summarized as follows:

Step 1 Compute a maximal decomposition of $[A]$ using the eigenring: $[A] \sim [\widetilde{A}_1(x)] \oplus \ldots \oplus [\widetilde{A}_\ell(x)]$ (see section 3.2).

Step 2 For each $[\widetilde{A}_i]$ we get the multiplicity m_i and the ramification r_i (see section 3.3).

Step 3 Compute a factorization (proposition 3.5) to get the irreducible system B_i of size r_i containing the r_i conjugate exponential parts (section 3.4).

Step 4 Apply the ramification in B_i and apply a recursive call of splitting lemma and Moser-reduction.

In the following sections we will describe and justify each step.

3.1 The Balser-Jurkat-Lutz Decomposition

We start by sketching a proof of the first part of Theorem 1.1, namely proving that any system $[A]$ is equivalent to a block-diagonal system of the form (6) where each block is indecomposable and having the special structure (7). For this, we first remark, using (2), that $[A]$ is equivalent to the system $F[A]$ which has the matrix G as fundamental solution matrix. As G is the direct sum of ℓ blocks, we have that $[A]$ is equivalent over $C((x))$ to a block diagonal system of the form (6). Now we show that each individual block $[A_i]$ is equivalent to a system of the special form (7).

Proposition 3.1. *Let $[A_i]$ denote the system satisfied by the matrix $G_i = x^{\Lambda_i} U_i \exp(Q_i)$ from* (3), (4) *and* (5). *There exists a permutation matrix P_i, such that*

$$P_i^{-1} A_i P_i = \begin{pmatrix} B_i & \frac{1}{x} I_{r_i} & & 0 \\ & & \ddots & \frac{1}{x} I_{r_i} \\ 0 & & & B_i \end{pmatrix}$$

where $[B_i]$ is irreducible over $C((x))$ of size r_i repeated m_i times.

Proof. For sake of clarity, we drop the index i in the notation (A_i, G_i, U_i, r_i, etc.). In formula (4) of BJL theorem, we have m times $q(\frac{1}{t})$ then m times $q(\frac{1}{\omega t})$, etc. We choose to regroup them differently, namely consecutively into m blocks with $q(\frac{1}{t}), \ldots, q(\frac{1}{\omega^{r-1} t})$ in each block. Let P be the permutation matrix which achieves this. The system $[\widetilde{A}]$, with $\widetilde{A} := P^{-1}AP$, has as fundamental solution the matrix $\widetilde{G} := x^{\widetilde{\Lambda}} \widetilde{U} \exp\left(\widetilde{Q}\right)$ where

$$\widetilde{\Lambda} = \begin{pmatrix} \widetilde{L} & I_r & & 0 \\ & & \ddots & I_r \\ 0 & & & \widetilde{L} \end{pmatrix}, \quad \widetilde{L} = (\lambda) \oplus (\lambda + \frac{1}{r}) \oplus \ldots \oplus (\lambda + \frac{r-1}{r}).$$

By noticing that $\widetilde{\Lambda} = (J_m(0) \otimes I_r + I_m \otimes \widetilde{L})$ we see that

$$\widetilde{G} = x^{J_m(0)} \otimes H$$

where

$$H := x^{\widetilde{L}}\, U_r \operatorname{diag}(e^{q(\frac{1}{t})}, \ldots, e^{q(\frac{1}{\omega^{r-1}t})}).$$

Let $B := \frac{dH}{dx} H^{-1}$. A straightforward computation gives

$$\widetilde{A} = \frac{d\widetilde{G}}{dx} \widetilde{G}^{-1} = (\frac{1}{x} J_m(0) \otimes I_r + I_m \otimes B).$$

We still have to check that B has its coefficients in $C((x))$. For this, we remark that replacing t by ωt in H results in a permutation of its columns. This means that $H(\omega t) = H(t) \cdot C$ where C is a (constant) cyclic permutation matrix. It follows that B is invariant under the map $t \mapsto \omega t$ so that, by Galois theory, $B \in \mathcal{M}_r(C((x)))$. Finally, $[B]$ is irreducible in $C((x))$ because $C((x^{1/r}))$ is the smallest algebraic extension of $C((x))$ which contains the exponential parts of H: the ramification index r is minimal. □

Proposition 3.2. *Let $[A]$ be a system as in* (1). *The following assertions are equivalent:*

(i) $[A]$ is equivalent to a system of the form (7).
(ii) $[A]$ is indecomposable in $C((x))$.
(iii) $[A]$ has a fundamental solution (2) *with one block G_i ($\ell = 1$).*

Proof. The implication "(i) ⇒ (ii)" follows from proposition 2.3. "(ii) ⇒ (iii)" is clear: indeed, if $\ell \geq 2$ then $[A]$ is decomposable by BJL Theorem. Finally, "(iii) ⇒ (i)" is the result of proposition 3.1. □

3.2 First Step: Maximal Decomposition over $C((x))$

From theorem 1.1, we know that there exists $P \in GL_n(C((x)))$ with

$$P[A] = [\widetilde{A}_1] \oplus \ldots \oplus [\widetilde{A}_\ell], \tag{9}$$

where $[\widetilde{A}_i]$ is indecomposable over $C((x))$ containing one exponential part with its conjugates under the ramification $t^{r_i} = x$. Hence, a generic element in the eigenring of $[A]$ will have ℓ distinct eigenvalues. For completeness, we recall the algorithm of [7] giving such a maximal decomposition:

(1) Compute a basis $T_1, \ldots, T_d$ of $\mathcal{E}(A)$. Let T be a generic element, i. e. $T = \left(\sum_{i=0}^{d} c_i T_i\right)$, where c_i are random in C.
(2) Compute the characteristic polynomial $\mathcal{X}_T$ of T and factor it as $\mathcal{X}_T = \prod_{i=1}^{\ell} (\lambda - \lambda_i)^{h_i}$, $\lambda_i \in C$.
(3) For i from 1 to ℓ : compute a basis of $\ker((T - \lambda_i I_n)^{h_i})$. Construct the invertible matrix P having as columns the basis elements of the $\ker((T - \lambda_i I_n)^{h_i})$.
(4) Compute $P[A]$.

We will have $P[A] = [\widetilde{A}_1] \oplus \cdots \oplus [\widetilde{A}_\ell]$ and, by construction, each $[\widetilde{A}_i]$ is indecomposable.

Remark 1. *The matrix P also decomposes a general element M of the eigenring as $P^{-1}MP = \widetilde{M}_1 \oplus \ldots \oplus \widetilde{M}_\ell$, where each $\widetilde{M}_i$ is a general element of the eigenring $\mathcal{E}(\widetilde{A}_i)$. So, decomposing a generic element in the eigenring provides for free a general element for each eigenring of the smaller blocks.*

Remark 2. *To make step (1) deterministic, we could compute the characteristic polynomials of each $\widetilde{M}_i$ in $C(t_1, \ldots, t_d)[\lambda]$ and factor their squarefree parts; T is generic if and only if each of these polynomials has exactly one factor. This is because two factors of χ_M which are coprime over $C(t_1, \ldots, t_d)[\lambda]$ remain coprime when specializing the t_i to random constants $c_i \in C$.*

In the rest of this section, we drop the index i on $[\widetilde{A}_i]$ (respectively $\widetilde{M}_i$) and name it $[\widetilde{A}]$ (respectively $\widetilde{M}$).

3.3 Second Step: Finding Ramifications and Multiplicities

Let $[\widetilde{A}]$ denotes one of the indecomposable blocks $[\widetilde{A}_i]$ in the decomposition (9). Thanks to proposition 3.2, we know that there is exactly one block G in its fundamental solution matrix. The aim of the present section is to compute the ramification r and the multiplicity m associated to this block G. For coherence, we will say that r (respectively m) is the *ramification index* (respectively the *multiplicity*) associated to the system $[\widetilde{A}]$.

Proposition 3.3. *Let $[\widetilde{A}]$ denote an indecomposable block from (9) of ramification r and multiplicity m. Then, $r = \frac{\text{size}(\widetilde{A})}{\dim(\mathcal{E}(\widetilde{A}))}$.*

Proof. We have seen in proposition 3.2 that an indecomposable system $[\widetilde{A}]$ is equivalent over $C((x))$ to a system of the form:

$$\begin{pmatrix} B & \frac{1}{x}I_r & 0 \\ & \ddots & \frac{1}{x}I_r \\ 0 & & B \end{pmatrix}$$

where B is irreducible over $C((x))$ of size r and repeated m times. It results that $size(\widetilde{A}) = mr$. Moreover, by proposition 2.3, we have $\dim(\mathcal{E}(\widetilde{A})) = m$. It results that $r = \frac{\text{size}(\widetilde{A})}{\dim(\mathcal{E}(\widetilde{A}))}$. □

3.4 Third step : Block Triangular Form

Now we will proceed to compute the irreducible system B from equation (7) in theorem 1.1 so that we will later introduce the ramification for the smallest possible system.

By remark 1, the decomposition process has given us a general element $\widetilde{M}$ of the eigenring $\mathcal{E}(\widetilde{A})$. Specializing $\widetilde{M}$ to a random element, we obtain a generic element T of $\mathcal{E}(\widetilde{A})$. As $[\widetilde{A}]$ is indecomposable over $C((x))$, T has only one eigenvalue $\widetilde{\lambda} \in C$ (see section 3.2). So, its characteristic polynomial is of the form $\chi_T(\lambda) = (\lambda - \widetilde{\lambda})^{mr}$.

Corollary 3.4. *Let $[\widetilde{A}]$ denote an indecomposable block of multiplicity m and ramification r. Let T denote a generic element of $\mathcal{E}(\widetilde{A})$. The minimal polynomial of T is $(\lambda - \widetilde{\lambda})^m$, $\widetilde{\lambda} \in C$.*

Proof. This follows from the shape of M in proposition 2.3. □

Remark 3. *Once we have the characteristic polynomial, the minimal polynomial comes for free because m is given by the dimension of the eigenring.*

Proposition 3.5. *Let $\widetilde{A}$ be an indecomposable system from decomposition (9) with ramification r and multiplicity m. We can construct a transformation $P \in GL_n(C((x)))$ such that*

$$P[\widetilde{A}] := \begin{pmatrix} B & D_1 & \cdots & D_{m-1} \\ 0 & \ddots & \ddots & \vdots \\ \vdots & \ddots & \ddots & D_1 \\ 0 & \cdots & 0 & B \end{pmatrix}.$$

Proof. Let T be a generic element in the eigenring of $[\widetilde{A}]$ as in Corollary 3.4. We have $(T - \widetilde{\lambda}I)^{m-1} \neq 0$. Let $(v_1, \ldots, v_r)$ be r linearly independent vectors such that $(T - \widetilde{\lambda}I)^{m-1}(v_i) \neq 0$. We construct a *Jordan Cycle* of length m by multiplying by $(T - \widetilde{\lambda}I)$ as follows:

$$(v_1, \ldots, v_r) \overset{(T-\widetilde{\lambda}I).}{\longrightarrow} (v_{r+1}, \ldots, v_{2r}) \overset{(T-\widetilde{\lambda}I).}{\longrightarrow} \ldots \overset{(T-\widetilde{\lambda}I).}{\longrightarrow} (0, \ldots, 0)$$

It is easy to verify that the set

$$\{(v_1, \ldots, v_r), ((T - \widetilde{\lambda}I)v_1, \ldots, (T - \widetilde{\lambda}I)v_r), \ldots, ((T - \widetilde{\lambda}I)^{m-1}v_1, \ldots, (T - \widetilde{\lambda}I)^{m-1}v_r)\}$$

is linearly independent. Let P be the transformation having as columns the vectors

$$((T - \widetilde{\lambda}I)^{m-1}v_1, \ldots, (T - \widetilde{\lambda}I)^{m-1}v_r, \ldots, (T - \widetilde{\lambda}I)v_1, \ldots, (T - \widetilde{\lambda}I)v_r, \ldots, v_1, \ldots, v_r).$$

We have

$$S := P^{-1}TP = \begin{pmatrix} \widetilde{\lambda}I_r & I_r & 0 \\ & \ddots & I_r \\ 0 & & \widetilde{\lambda}I_r \end{pmatrix}.$$

The matrix S belongs to the eigenring of $P[\widetilde{A}]$ and is constant. Thus, $P[\widetilde{A}]S - SP[\widetilde{A}] = 0$. Then a simple identification shows that

$$P[\widetilde{A}] = \begin{pmatrix} B & D_1 & \cdots & D_{m-1} \\ 0 & \ddots & \ddots & \vdots \\ \vdots & \ddots & \ddots & D_1 \\ 0 & \cdots & 0 & B \end{pmatrix}. \quad (10)$$

□

3.5 Final step : Computing the Exponential Parts of the Irreducible Subsystem $[B]$

Once we have the smallest possible irreducible system B containing the r conjugate exponential parts stemming from the ramification $t = x^r$, we perform the ramification in B and consider the new system

$$[\mathcal{B}]: \quad \frac{dY}{dt} = \mathcal{B}Y, \qquad \mathcal{B} := rt^{r-1}B(t^r).$$

We know that no further ramification is needed, so we proceed as in [4] using only the splitting lemma, shifting the eigenvalues of B_0 and Moser-reduction to compute the corresponding exponential parts.

3.6 Example: Previous and New Method

We consider the example from [8], the system $[A]$ where

$$A(x) = \frac{1}{x^4}\begin{pmatrix} 0 & 0 & x & 0 \\ 1 & -x^2 & x^2 & -x^2 \\ 0 & 1 & x^2 & 0 \\ x^2 & x^2 & 0 & -x^2 \end{pmatrix}.$$

We first show how algorithm in [4] proceeds to compute exponential parts: we verify that $A(x)$ is Moser-irreducible and the leading matrix A_0 is nilpotent. Then, the Katz invariant is computed from the algorithm given in [4]: $\kappa = 8/3$. Applying the Moser-reduction on the new system where x is substituted by t^3 will lead to a new system where A_0 has four distinct eigenvalues. There are four exponential parts which can be parameterized as

$$x = t^3, \quad q_1(\frac{1}{t}) = -\frac{3}{8t^8} - \frac{1}{4t^4}, \quad q_2(\frac{1}{t}) = \frac{1}{t^3}.$$

We see that the exponential part q_2 involves no ramification and the algorithm was not able to compute it without introducing the ramification.
We now use the new approach. For clarity of exposition, we will just show few terms of the power series. For more details about precise precision used in computation, see example Version1-0 in [14] and section 5. We first compute a generic element T in the eigenring of $[A]$:

$$T = \begin{bmatrix} -10+O(x^5) & O(x^4) & O(x^4) & 5x^2+O(x^5) \\ O(x^8) & -10+O(x^7) & O(x^7) & O(x^5) \\ O(x^6) & O(x^5) & -10+O(x^5) & O(x^3) \\ O(x^3) & -5x^2+O(x^5) & -5x^2+O(x^5) & -5+O(x^5) \end{bmatrix}$$

Its characteristic polynomial is

$$\chi_T(\lambda) = (\lambda + 5)(\lambda + 10)^3$$

We construct a transformation P using Smith normal form (see section 5.2):

$$P = \begin{bmatrix} 0 & 0 & 1 & x^2+O(x^5) \\ 1 & 0 & 0 & O(x^5) \\ 0 & 1 & 0 & O(x^3) \\ x^2+O(x^5) & x^2+O(x^5) & O(x^3) & 1 \end{bmatrix}$$

It decomposes $[A]$ into two subsystems:

$$A_1 := \begin{bmatrix} -x^{-2}-1+O(x^3) & x^{-2}-1+O(x^3) & x^{-4}+3x+2x^2+O(x^3) \\ x^{-4}+O(x^{16}) & x^{-2}+O(x^{18}) & O(x^{20}) \\ O(x^{19}) & x^{-3}+O(x^{17}) & O(x^{19}) \end{bmatrix}$$

and

$$A_2 := \left[-x^{-2}+1+O(x^3) \right]$$

The subsystem A_2 is 1-dimensional, the exponential part is the integration of the singular part:

$$x = t, \quad q_2(\frac{1}{t}) = \frac{1}{t}.$$

The dimension of the eigenring of A_1 is 1. Thus, it is irreducible of ramification $r = 3$. We apply the ramification and Moser-reduction. Then we get the new leading term:

$$\begin{bmatrix} 0 & 0 & 3 \\ 3 & 0 & 0 \\ 0 & 3 & 0 \end{bmatrix}$$

We apply splitting lemma and get as parameterization of the ramified exponential parts:

$$x = t^3, \quad q_1(\frac{1}{t}) = -\frac{3}{8t^8} - \frac{1}{4t^4}.$$

As expected, we see that our algorithm starts by splitting the system into two subsystems (here of dimensions 1 and 3) before introducing any ramification. The ramification is introduced only when needed.

4 WHEN C IS NOT ALGEBRAICALLY CLOSED

In practice, we work with a non-algebraically closed coefficient field C. Our algorithm as described above may involve algebraic extensions for two reasons: first, to express the coefficients of the exponential parts (see example Version1-1 or V1-3 in [14]) and, secondly, to perform intermediate computations, even if the result does not involve them (example V1-2 in [14]).

For a generic element T in $\mathcal{E}(A)$, we factor its characteristic polynomial $\mathcal{X}_T$ over C so that $\mathcal{X}_T = \prod_{i=1}^{\tilde{\ell}} f_i(\lambda)^{h_i}$, where $f_i(\lambda)$ is irreducible in $C[\lambda]$. Then we follow the steps of section 3.2 by considering the factors $f_i(T)^{h_i}$ instead of $(T - \lambda_i)^{h_i}$. We obtain a block diagonal system

$$[A] \sim [A_1] \oplus \ldots \oplus [A_{\tilde{\ell}}] \tag{11}$$

where $[A_i]$ are systems with coefficients in $C((x))$. The $[A_i]$ may still be decomposable as we will see by studying further eigenring properties in this non-algebraically closed case.

For example, if $[A]$ has n copies of an exponential parts w in $x^{-1}C[x^{-1}]$ (i.e. $[A] \sim [w(x)I_n]$), then $\mathcal{E}(A) = \mathcal{M}_n(C)$, it has dimension n^2 and the characteristic polynomial of a general element $\sum_{i=1}^{n^2} t_i T_i$ of $\mathcal{E}(A)$ is an irreducible polynomial of degree n.

Lemma 4.1. *Assume that $[A]$ has exactly n conjugate exponential parts in $x^{-1}F[x^{-1}]$, where F is a minimal algebraic extension of C containing all their coefficients. Then, dim($\mathcal{E}(A)$) = n and the characteristic polynomial of a generic element is irreducible over C.*

Proof. By assumptions, $[A]$ is irreducible over $C((x))$ but decomposes over $\overline{C}((x))$ as a direct sum of 1-dimensional systems which are pairwise non-equivalent. Hence, $(t_1) \oplus \cdots \oplus (t_n)$ is a general element of $\mathcal{E}(A)$ in $F((x))$ and $\dim_C(\mathcal{E}(A)) = \dim_{\overline{C}}(\mathcal{E}(A)) = n$. Let M be a general element of $\mathcal{E}(A)$ and χ_M be its characteristic polynomial. Then χ_M splits as a product of n different factors of degree one over F. If χ_M factored as a product over C, then A would decompose as a sum of two systems over $C((x))$, a contradiction □

Lemma 4.2. *Assume that $[A]$ is equivalent to a direct sum of μ copies of a system $\widetilde{A}$. Then, $\dim(\mathcal{E}(A)) = \mu^2 \times \dim(\mathcal{E}(\widetilde{A}))$ and the characteristic polynomial of a general element $\sum_{i=1}^{\dim(\mathcal{E}(A))} t_i T_i$ of $\mathcal{E}(A)$ has an irreducible factor whose degree is a multiple of μ.*

Proof. $[A] \sim [I_\mu \otimes \widetilde{A}]$ so $\mathcal{E}(A) = \mathcal{M}_\mu(C) \otimes \mathcal{E}(\widetilde{A})$. The characteristic polynomial of a general element of $\mathcal{E}(A)$ has as roots the products of eigenvalues of a general element of $\mathcal{M}_\mu(C)$ by the eigenvalues of a general element of $\mathcal{E}(\widetilde{A})$. It follows that we have an irreducible factor of degree a multiple of μ. □

Combining with proposition 2.3, we obtain:

Proposition 4.3. *Let $[A]$ be a system of dimension n. Let T be a generic element in the eigenring $\mathcal{E}([A])$. Its characteristic polynomial is a power $f(\lambda)^h$ of an irreducible polynomial $f \in C[\lambda]$ if and only if there exist integers r, m, μ and d such that T is an element of*

$$\mathcal{M}_\mu(C) \otimes (t_1 \oplus \ldots \oplus t_d) \otimes \begin{pmatrix} c_1 I_r & c_2 I_r & \cdots & c_m I_r \\ 0 & \ddots & \ddots & \vdots \\ \vdots & \ddots & \ddots & c_2 I_r \\ 0 & \cdots & 0 & c_1 I_r \end{pmatrix} \tag{12}$$

where t_i and c_i are in C.
It then follows that $dim(\mathcal{E}(A)) = \mu^2 \times d \times m$ and $n = m \times r \times \mu \times d$. Furthermore, $\deg(f) = d \times \mu$ and $h = m \times r$.

Proof. Assume that $\chi_T = f(\lambda)^h$, with $f \in C[\lambda]$ irreducible. Then $[A]$ must be a direct sum of μ ($\mu \geq 1$) pairwise equivalent indecomposable systems over $C((x))$: otherwise, χ_T would have two coprime factors, see [7]. Thus we can suppose that $[A]$ is equivalent to $[I_\mu \otimes \widetilde{A}]$ with $[\widetilde{A}]$ indecomposable over $C((x))$. From lemma 4.1, if $[\widetilde{A}]$ has an exponential part with coefficients in an algebraic extension of C of degree d, then it contains all the d conjugates and we have $[\widetilde{A}] \sim [B_1] \oplus \ldots \oplus [B_d]$ over $\overline{C}((x))$ where each $[B_i]$ has coefficients in $\overline{C}((x))$ and are pairwise non-equivalent. Moreover, each $[B_i]$ has the structure described in 3.1 and there corresponds two integers: the size m of the Jordan block and the ramification r. Conversely, when T is an element of (12), proving that χ_T is a power of an irreducible polynomial is like the proof of lemma 4.2. Finally, the dimension results follow from the previous lemma. The degree of f comes from the structure $\mathcal{M}_\mu(C) \otimes (t_1 \oplus \ldots \oplus t_d)$ and the exponent h comes from the rest. □

This proposition shows that, by decomposing using irreducible factors of χ_M in $C[\lambda]$, we still obtain blocks with "one kind" of exponential part, modulo algebraic extension and a ramification.

In contrast to the situation over $\overline{C}((x))$, we cannot obtain the ramification r directly from the dimension of the eigenring. However, as h is a multiple of the ramification, we may decompose in $C((x^{1/h}))$. The algorithm now proceeds like in the algebraically closed case of the previous section.

Remark 4. *We may obtain the actual ramification at an extra cost. If we compute the* minimalpolynomial *of a generic element of $[A]$, we will be able to decompose using the exact ramification r instead of ramifying with $h = m \times r$. In fact, under the hypotheses of proposition 4.3 and by an analogue of proposition 3.4, the minimal polynomial of a generic element of $[A]$ is an m-th power of an irreducible polynomial of degree $\mu \times d$. Then, once we have m (from the minimal polynomial) and h (from the characteristic polynomial) we are able to compute the ramification $r = \frac{h}{m}$.*

5 PRECISION ESTIMATES FOR POWER SERIES

In this section, we explain how we deal with series in our implementation. We will show how to select truncated systems which contain enough informations. In fact, the exponential part Q of the formal fundamental solution matrix is determined by the coefficients $A_0, A_1, \ldots, A_{nq-1}$ of the system $[A]$ ([2], [11]). One can consider from the beginning the truncated system up to order nq. We will denote a truncated matrix of series by $M^{<k>}$ with $M^{<k>} = x^{val(M)}(M_0 + \cdots + x^k M_k)$. We say that M is known up to precision k and we have $M = M^{<k>} + O(x^{val(M)+k+1})$.

5.1 Computing the Characteristic Polynomial

Starting with a truncated system $[A^{<nq>}]$, we will compute the characteristic polynomial of a generic element T in the eigenring of $[A]$. We study how many terms of T are required in order to compute its characteristic polynomial exactly.
We use a lemma from [4].

Lemma 5.1 (lemma 3, p. 10 in [4]). *Let M and H be n-dimensional matrices with coefficients in $C((x))$ with $val(H) > val(M)$. Put $\alpha = max(0, -val(M))$ and define the coefficients $a_i \in C((x))$ by*

$$a_{n-1}\lambda^{n-1} + a_{n-2}\lambda^{n-2} + \ldots + a_0 := det(\lambda I_n - M) - det(\lambda I_n - M + H)$$

Then: $val(a_{n-i}) \geq \alpha(1-i) + val(H) \quad i = 1, \ldots, n$.

Proposition 5.2. *Let $T \in \mathcal{M}_n(C((x)))$ be a generic element in $\mathcal{E}(A)$. Set $\alpha := \max(0, -val(T))$. Then, it is sufficient to consider the first $\alpha n + 1$ terms in T in order to compute its characteristic polynomial.*

Proof. Let $T \in \mathcal{M}_n(C((x)))$ be a generic element in $\mathcal{E}(A)$. Let $\chi_T(\lambda)$ denote its characteristic polynomial. From section 2.2, we know that $\chi_T(\lambda) \in C[\lambda]$. If $val(T) \geq 0$, it follows that $\chi_T = \chi_{T_0}$; as $\alpha = 0$ in this case, the result is proved. If $val(T) < 0$, we have $\alpha = -val(T) > 0$. Given an integer k, let $H := T - T^{<k>}$. We have $val(H) = val(T) + k + 1 = -\alpha + k + 1$. Define a_i as in lemma 5.1. We then have $val(a_{n-i}) \geq \alpha(1-i) - \alpha + k + 1 = -i\alpha + k + 1$. If we choose $k = n\alpha$, we have $val(a_{n-i}) \geq 1$ for all i. As $\chi_T(\lambda) \in C[\lambda]$, this certifies that the term of degree 0 (in x) of $\chi_{T^{<k>}}$ is χ_T. □

5.2 Computing a Basis of Kernel Spaces

After computing the characteristic polynomial of a generic element T of the eigenring of $[A^{<nq>}]$, we need to compute a basis of the kernel of $(T - \lambda I_n)^h$ or $f(T)^h$ (see section 3.2 or section 4).
We address the following problem: Given a matrix $M \in \mathcal{M}_n(C((x)))$, how to compute a basis $\mathcal{B} = \{v_1, \ldots, v_d\}$ of $\ker(M)$ with a given precision k. This means that we want to compute $v_1^{<k>}, \ldots, v_d^{<k>}$.

Let's first note the following fact: if $M \in \mathcal{M}_n(C((x)))$ and some $v \in \ker M$ is an element of the kernel of M with non negative valuation then, for any precision $k \geq 0$, we have $M^{<k>}v^{<k>} = O(x^{k+\text{val}(M)+1})$.

Now, to answer our problem, we will use the *approximate Smith normal form* as introduced in [15].

Definition 5.3 ([15], Definition 1.3.4). Let $M \in \mathcal{M}_n(C((x)))$ be known up to precision k. We call an *approximate Smith Decomposition* of M a factorization

$$M = U\Delta V$$

where U and $V \in GL_n(C[[x]])$ are known up to precision k and $\Delta \in \mathcal{M}_n(C((x)))$ such that $\Delta = \Delta_0 + O(x^{k+\text{val}(M)+1})$, where Δ_0 a diagonal matrix:

$$\Delta_0 = \text{diag}\{x^{a_1}, \ldots, x^{a_s}, 0, \ldots, 0\}.$$

One can find in [15] (algorithm 1.3.5) an algorithm which given a matrix M with coefficients in $C((x))$ known up to precision k produces an *approximate Smith Normal Form* Δ and two unimodular matrices U,V known up to precision k such that $M = U\Delta V$. Note that a slight modification of that algorithm allows to compute also V^{-1} and U^{-1} up to precision k.

As

$$MV^{-1} = U\Delta = U\Delta_0 + O(x^{k+\text{val}(M)+1})$$

we see that the $n-s$ last columns, $v_{n-s+1}, \ldots, v_n$ of V^{-1} satisfy

$$M^{<k>}v_j^{<k>} = O(x^{k+1+\text{val}(M)}).$$

5.3 Precision on $P[A]$

As explained above, the gauge transformation $P \in \mathcal{M}_n(C[[x]])$ that allows to reduce our system $[A]$ to a direct sum of indecomposable subsystems (Step 1 of the algorithm) is constructed by computing bases of kernels of elements of $\mathcal{E}(A)$. Thus P can be chosen of valuation 0 and be computed at any precision k (as described in the previous section). Once P is obtained, we need to compute $P[A]$ with a sufficient precision N to obtain the exact exponential parts of $[A]$. We know that we should take $N \geq -\mathrm{val}(P[A]) \times n$. As $\mathrm{val}(P[A]) \geq \mathrm{val}(P^{-1}) + \mathrm{val}(A)$ it is enough to take $N := (-\mathrm{val}(P^{-1}) - \mathrm{val}(A)) \times n$. The problem now is how to determine a sufficient precision k for P in order to find $P[A]$ up to order N.

Since $\mathrm{val}(P^{-1})$ appears in the definition of the bound N, the first problem is to find first a sufficient precision k for P which allows to compute the valuation of P^{-1}. We state this problem as follows: how to choose the precision k in P such that $\det(P^{<k>}) \neq 0$ and $\mathrm{val}({P^{<k>}}^{-1}) = \mathrm{val}(P^{-1})$. This problem has been studied in [1].

Proposition 5.4 (proposition 3 in [1]). *If $\widetilde{P}$ is a non-singular polynomial matrix of degree k such that $\deg(\widetilde{P}) + \mathrm{val}(\widetilde{P}^{-1}) \geq 0$ then for any $Q \in \mathcal{M}_n(C[[x]])$, the matrix $(\widetilde{P} + x^{k+1}Q)$ is non-singular and the Laurent series expansions of $(\widetilde{P} + x^{k+1}Q)^{-1}$ and $\widetilde{P}^{-1}$ coincide up to order $\deg(\widetilde{P}) + 2\,\mathrm{val}(\widetilde{P}^{-1})$.*

From this we derive the following method to compute the valuation of the inverse of a an invertible matrix of series $P \in \mathcal{M}_n(C[[x]])$: we compute P with a precision k such that $\det(P^{<k>}) \neq 0$ and increase k while $\mathrm{val}({P^{<k>}}^{-1}) + k < 0$. We deduce $\mathrm{val}(P^{-1}) = \mathrm{val}({P^{<k>}}^{-1})$.

At this stage we know $N = -n(\mathrm{val}(P^{-1}) + \mathrm{val}(A))$. Now we need to determine the number of terms to take in A, P and P^{-1} in order to get $P[A]^{<N>}$. They can be found in this classical lemma.

Lemma 5.5 ([11], ([13], Lemma 5.1)). *Let $A \in \mathcal{M}_n(C((x)))$ and $P \in \mathcal{M}_n(C[[x]])$ with $\det(P) \neq 0$ and let $B := P[A] = P^{-1}AP - P^{-1}P'$. Then, the coefficient B_j of the transformed system depends on the coefficients :*

(1) A_i for all $i \leq j - \mathrm{val}(P^{-1})$.
(2) P_i for all $i \leq j - (\mathrm{val}(A) + \mathrm{val}(P^{-1}))$.
(3) $(P^{-1})_i$ for all $i \leq j - \mathrm{val}(A)$.

We may summarize the above discussion as follows.

Proposition 5.6. *In order to obtain all required terms in P and P^{-1} for the computation of $P[A]$ up to order N, it is sufficient to compute P up to order $N - 2\,\mathrm{val}(P^{-1}) - \mathrm{val}(A)$.*

5.4 Effect on the Implementation

Let $[A]$ be an n−dimensional system of the form (1) with Poincaré rank q. Starting with a truncated system $[A^{<nq>}]$, we begin by computing an element T in the eigenring of $[A^{<nq>}]$ up to a low precision k (for example we take $k = 1$) and find the valuation of T. Let $\alpha := max(0, -val(T))$. In order to obtain the characteristic polynomial of T, we compute T up to precision αn. We can now start the decomposition step: computing a transformation P with precision $k := \alpha n$ using approximate Smith normal form. We now have to determine the valuation of P^{-1}. We increase the precision k on P until the conditions $\det(P^{<k>}) \neq 0$ and $k + \mathrm{val}({P^{<k>}}^{-1}) \geq 0$ hold. Then, $\mathrm{val}({P^{<k>}}^{-1})$ gives us the valuation of P^{-1}. Now we put $N := -n(val(P^{-1}) + \mathrm{val}(A))$; we compute P up to precision $N - \mathrm{val}(A) - 2\,\mathrm{val}(P^{-1})$ and consider terms in A, P and P^{-1} as described in lemma 5.5 in order to compute $P[A]$ for sufficient precision N.

6 CONCLUSION

We have elaborated on BJL results and decomposition techniques to establish a method of formal reduction which first "separates" exponential parts before computing them. This sheds new light on reduction techniques. The method will not always be better than previous methods such as [4] or [13]. In forthcoming work, we will establish its complexity to give more precise elements of comparison with other reduction techniques. We will also expand on the specifics of the computation of power series elements of the eigenring. The algorithm is implemented in Maple. The reader may consult [14] for examples illustrating the method and its current implementation.

REFERENCES

[1] S. Abramov and M. Barkatou. 2018. On strongly non-singular polynomial matrices. In *Advances in Computer Algebra: Proceedings of the Waterloo Workshop in Computer Algebra (Proceedings in Mathematics & Statistics)*, C. Schneider and E. (eds.) Zima (Eds.), Vol. 226. Springer.

[2] D. Babbitt and V. Varadarajan. 1983. Formal reduction theory of meromorphic differential equations: a group theoretic view. *Pacific J. Math.* 109, 1 (1983), 1–80.

[3] W. Balser, W. B. Jurkat, and D. A. Lutz. 1979. A general theory of invariants for meromorphic differential equations. I. Formal invariants. *Funkcial. Ekvac.* 22, 2 (1979), 197–221. http://www.math.kobe-u.ac.jp/~fe/xml/mr0556577.xml

[4] M. A. Barkatou. 1997. An algorithm to compute the exponential part of a formal fundamental matrix solution of a linear differential system. *Applicable Algebra in Engineering, Communication and Computing* 8, 1 (1997), 1–23. https://doi.org/10.1007/s002000050048

[5] M. A. Barkatou. 1999. On rational solutions of systems of linear differential equations. *J. Symbolic Comput.* 28, 4-5 (1999), 547–567. https://doi.org/10.1006/jsco.1999.0314 Differential algebra and differential equations.

[6] M. A. Barkatou. 1999. Rational solutions of matrix difference equations: the problem of equivalence and factorization. In *Proceedings of the 1999 International Symposium on Symbolic and Algebraic Computation (Vancouver, BC)*. ACM, New York, 277–282. https://doi.org/10.1145/309831.309956

[7] Moulay A. Barkatou. 2007. Factoring systems of linear functional equations using eigenrings. In *Computer algebra 2006*. World Sci. Publ., Hackensack, NJ, 22–42. https://doi.org/10.1142/9789812778857_0003

[8] M. A. Barkatou. 2010. Symbolic methods for solving systems of linear ordinary differential equations. Part II. *Tutorial at the International Symposium on Symbolic and Algebraic Computation, ACM Press* (July 2010), 7–8.

[9] M. A. Barkatou and E. Pflügel. 1999. An algorithm computing the regular formal solutions of a system of linear differential equations. *J. Symbolic Comput.* 28, 4-5 (1999), 569–587. https://doi.org/10.1006/jsco.1999.0315 Differential algebra and differential equations.

[10] M. A. Barkatou and E. Pflügel. 2009. On the Moser- and super-reduction algorithms of systems of linear differential equations and their complexity. *J. Symbolic Comput.* 44, 8 (2009), 1017–1036. https://doi.org/10.1016/j.jsc.2009.01.002

[11] D. A. Lutz and R. Schäfke. 1985. On the identification and stability of formal invariants for singular differential equations. *Linear Algebra Appl.* 72 (1985), 1–46. https://doi.org/10.1016/0024-3795(85)90140-5

[12] J. Moser. 1959/1960. The order of a singularity in Fuchs' theory. *Math. Z* 72 (1959/1960), 379–398. https://doi.org/10.1007/BF01162962

[13] Eckhard Pflügel. 2000. Effective formal reduction of linear differential systems. *Appl. Algebra Engrg. Comm. Comput.* 10, 2 (2000), 153–187. https://doi.org/10.1007/s002000050002

[14] Joelle Saadé. 2018. Examples of Formal Reduction via Eigenrings. http://www.unilim.fr/pages_perso/joelle.saade/FormalReductionViaEigenring/

[15] T. Vaccon. 2015. *Précision p-adique*. Ph.D. Dissertation. Université Rennes 1.

[16] W. Wasow. 1965. *Asymptotic expansions for ordinary differential equations*. Interscience Publishers John Wiley & Sons, Inc., New York-London-Sydney. ix+362 pages.

On the Maximal Number of Real Embeddings of Spatial Minimally Rigid Graphs

Evangelos Bartzos
Department of Informatics and Telecommunications,
National Kapodistrian University of Athens, and
ATHENA Research Center, Maroussi, Greece
vbartzos@di.uoa.gr

Ioannis Z. Emiris
Department of Informatics and Telecommunications,
National Kapodistrian University of Athens, and
ATHENA Research Center, Maroussi, Greece
emiris@di.uoa.gr

Jan Legerský
Research Institute for Symbolic Computation,
Johannes Kepler University Linz, Austria
jan.legersky@risc.jku.at

Elias Tsigaridas
Sorbonne Université, CNRS, INRIA, Laboratoire
d'Informatique de Paris 6 (LIP6), Équipe PolSys,
4 place Jussieu, 75252 Paris Cedex 05, France
elias.tsigaridas@inria.fr

ABSTRACT

The number of embeddings of minimally rigid graphs in $\mathbb{R}^D$ is (by definition) finite, modulo rigid transformations, for every generic choice of edge lengths. Even though various approaches have been proposed to compute it, the gap between upper and lower bounds is still enormous. Specific values and its asymptotic behavior are major and fascinating open problems in rigidity theory.

Our work considers the maximal number of real embeddings of minimally rigid graphs in $\mathbb{R}^3$. We modify a commonly used parametric semi-algebraic formulation that exploits the Cayley-Menger determinant to minimize the *a priori* number of complex embeddings, where the parameters correspond to edge lengths. To cope with the huge dimension of the parameter space and find specializations of the parameters that maximize the number of real embeddings, we introduce a method based on coupler curves that makes the sampling feasible for spatial minimally rigid graphs.

Our methodology results in the first full classification of the number of real embeddings of graphs with 7 vertices in $\mathbb{R}^3$, which was the smallest open case. Building on this and certain 8-vertex graphs, we improve the previously known general lower bound on the maximum number of real embeddings in $\mathbb{R}^3$.

ACM Reference Format:

Evangelos Bartzos, Ioannis Z. Emiris, Jan Legerský, and Elias Tsigaridas. 2018. On the Maximal Number of Real Embeddings of Spatial Minimally Rigid Graphs. In *ISSAC '18: 2018 ACM International Symposium on Symbolic and Algebraic Computation, July 16–19, 2018, New York, NY, USA.* ACM, New York, NY, USA, 8 pages. https://doi.org/10.1145/3208976.3208994

ISSAC '18, July 16–19, 2018, New York, NY, USA

ACM ISBN 978-1-4503-5550-6/18/07...$15.00
https://doi.org/10.1145/3208976.3208994

1 INTRODUCTION

Rigid graph theory is a very active area of research with many applications in robotics [13, 31, 32], structural bioinformatics [11, 21], sensor network localization [33] and architecture [12].

A graph embedding in $\mathbb{R}^D$, equipped with the standard euclidean norm, is a function that maps the vertices of a graph G to $\mathbb{R}^D$. Let V_G, resp. E_G, denote the set of vertices, resp. edges, of G. We are interested in embeddings that are compatible with edge lengths, namely, if two vertices are connected by an edge, then the distance between them equals a given length for this edge. A graph G is *generically rigid* if all embeddings compatible with generic edge lengths are not continuously deformable. If any edge removal results in a non-rigid mechanism, then the graph is *minimally rigid*. For $D = 2$ these graphs are called *Laman graphs*. For $D = 3$, following [15], we call these graphs *Geiringer graphs* to honor Hilda Pollaczek-Geiringer who worked on rigid graphs in $\mathbb{R}^2$ and $\mathbb{R}^3$ many years before Laman [24, 25].

For a graph G, let $r_D(G, \mathbf{d})$ be the number of embeddings in $\mathbb{R}^D$ that are compatible with edge lengths $\mathbf{d} = (d_e)_{e \in E_G} \in \mathbb{R}_+^{|E_G|}$ modulo rigid motions, and let $r_D(G)$ be the maximum of $r_D(G, \mathbf{d})$ over all $\mathbf{d}$ such that $r_D(G, \mathbf{d})$ is finite. To indicate the maximum number of real embeddings over all graphs with n vertices, we write $r_D(n)$. In this setting, an important question is to find all the possible real embeddings of graphs with k (some constant) number of vertices. This can be used to enumerate and classify conformations of proteins, molecules [11, 21] and robotic mechanisms, e.g., [8, 32]. Furthermore, precise bounds for $r_D(G)$ or $r_D(k)$ are of great importance, since gluing many copies of G together yields lower bounds for $r_D(n)$, for $n \geq k$, e.g., [5, 15].

A natural approach to bound $r_D(G)$ is to use an algebraic formulation to express the embeddings as solutions of a polynomial system. The number of its complex solutions bounds the number of complex embeddings, $c_D(G)$, which bounds $r_D(G)$.

For $D = 2$, there is a recent algorithm [6] to solve the problem of complex embeddings, $c_2(G)$, of minimally rigid graphs in $\mathbb{C}^2$, for any given graph G. Besides this graph-specific approach, using determinantal varieties [4, 5] we can estimate asymptotic bounds, see also [9, 28]; this approach also gives results for $D = 3$. Complex bounds for certain cases of Laman graphs are also given in [18]. For graphs with a constant number of vertices, we know that $r_2(6) = 24$, where the proof technique uses the coupler curve of the Desargues graph [5], and $r_2(7) = 56$, proved by delicate stochastic methods [10]. The second bound yields the best known lower bound for Laman graphs, which is $r_2(n) \geq 2.3003^n$.

For $D = 3$, the problem is much more difficult than in the planar case. One of the reasons is that, unlike the planar case, we lack a combinatorial characterization of minimally rigid (Geiringer) graphs in $\mathbb{R}^3$. The existence of such a characterization is a major open problem in rigid graph theory. The algebraic formulation considers the squared distance between two points, not as a metric, but as the sum of squares of the coordinates. Then, for every edge $v_i v_j$, we have the equation

$$d_{ij}^2 = (x_i - x_j)^2 + (y_i - y_j)^2 + (z_i - z_j)^2 ,$$

where x_i, y_i, z_i are, in general complex, coordinates of a vertex v_i and d_{ij} is the length of the edge $v_i v_j$. If we use the Bézout bound to bound the number of the complex roots of the polynomial system, then the upper bound for $c_3(n)$ is $O(2^{3n})$, which is a very loose bound. Hence, a more sophisticated approach is needed. Nevertheless, this formulation has been successfully used to obtain upper bounds of $r_3(k)$ via mixed volume computation of sparse polynomial systems for 1-skeleta of simplicial polyhedra (a subset of spatial rigid graphs) with $k \leq 10$ vertices [9]. The best known lower bound is $r_3(n) \geq 2.51984^n$ [9]. We improve it to 2.6553^n.

As our goal is to estimate the number of real embeddings, we are interested in the number of real solutions of the corresponding polynomial systems. If we consider the edge lengths as parameters, then we are searching for specializations of the parameters that maximize the number of real solutions of the system and, if possible, to match the number of complex solutions. However, the number of parameters is very big even for graphs with a small number of vertices. Even more, it is an open question in real algebraic geometry to determine if the number of real solutions of a given algebraic system is the same as the number of complex ones up to its parameters. While there are some upper bounds for the number of real positive roots [27], they are generally worse than mixed volume in the case of rigid embeddings. In addition, sparse polynomials have also been used to obtain lower bounds of the number of real positive roots of polynomial systems, see [1, 2] and references therein. Therefore, we need a delicate method to sample in an efficient way the parameter space and maximize the number of real solutions that correspond to embeddings.

For graphs with a given number of vertices, we have a complete classification for all graphs with $n \leq 6$ vertices. Moreover, for the case of the cyclohexane we know the tight bound of $r_3(6) = 16$ embeddings [11]. Let us also mention that for certain applied cases there are ad hoc methods. For example, the maximal number of real embeddings of Stewart platforms was computed [8] using a combination of Newton-Raphson and the steepest descent method.

Our contribution. We extend existing results about the number of the spatial embeddings of minimally rigid graphs. We construct all minimally rigid graphs up to 8 vertices and we classify them according to the last Henneberg step. Then, we model our problem algebraically using two different approaches. Using the algebraic formulation, we compute upper bounds for the number of complex embeddings of all graphs with 7 and 8 vertices. Then, we introduce a method, inspired by coupler curves, to search efficiently for edge lengths that increase the number of real embeddings. We provide an open-source implementation of our method in Python [19], which uses PHCpack [30] for solving polynomial systems. To the best of our knowledge there is no other similar technique, let alone an open-source implementation. Based on our formulation and software, we performed extensive experiments that resulted in a complete classification and tight bounds for the real embeddings for all 7-vertex Geiringer graphs, which was the smallest open case. Moreover, we extend our computations to certain 8-vertex graphs. Even though the computations do not provide a full classification of real embeddings, they are enough to improve the currently known lower bound on the number of embeddings in n, namely $r_3(n) \geq 2.6553^n$.

Organization. The rest of the paper is organized as follows. In Section 2 we present the equations and inequalities of our modeling. In Section 3, we introduce a method for parametric searching for edge lengths inspired by coupler curves. In Section 4, we present $r_3(G)$ for all G with 7 vertices and we establish a new lower bounds on the maximum number of real embeddings. Finally, in Section 5 we conclude and present some open questions.

2 PRELIMINARIES & ALGEBRAIC MODELING

First, we present some general results about rigidity in $\mathbb{R}^3$ and then two algebraic formulations of the problem of graph embeddings. The first, in Section 2.2, is based on 0-dimensional varieties of sphere equations. The second, in Section 2.3, exploits determinantal varieties of Cayley-Menger matrices and inequalities.

2.1 Rigidity in $\mathbb{R}^3$

The first step is the construction of all minimally rigid graphs up to isomorphism for a given number of vertices. The combinatorial characterization of minimally rigid graphs in dimension 3 is a major open problem. It is well known that $|E_G| = 3|V_G| - 6$, and $|E_H| \leq 3|V_H| - 6$ for every subgraph H of G, but this condition is not sufficient for rigidity [26].

It is known that adding a new vertex to a Geiringer graph together with adding and removing certain edges yields another Geiringer graph. These operations are called *Henneberg steps* [29]. Henneberg step I (H1) adds a vertex of degree 3, connecting it with 3 vertices in the original graph. Henneberg step II (H2) deletes an edge from the original graph, a new vertex is connected to the vertices of the deleted edge and to two other vertices of the graph, see Figure 1. For these two steps, the opposite implication also works: If the resulting graph is Geiringer, the original one is Geiringer too. Since the necessary condition for the number of edges guarantees that all Geiringer graphs with ≤ 12 vertices do not have all vertices of degree greater or equal to 5, H1 and H2 are sufficient to construct all Geiringer graphs with ≤ 12 vertices.

There are two additional steps, the so-called X-replacement and double V-replacement (H3x and H3v). They extend rigid graphs in $\mathbb{R}^3$ with a vertex of degree 5, see Figure 1. Every minimally rigid graph in $\mathbb{R}^3$ can be constructed by a sequence of steps H1, H2, H3x or H3v starting from a tetrahedron. On the other hand, it is not proven whether these moves construct only rigid graphs [26]

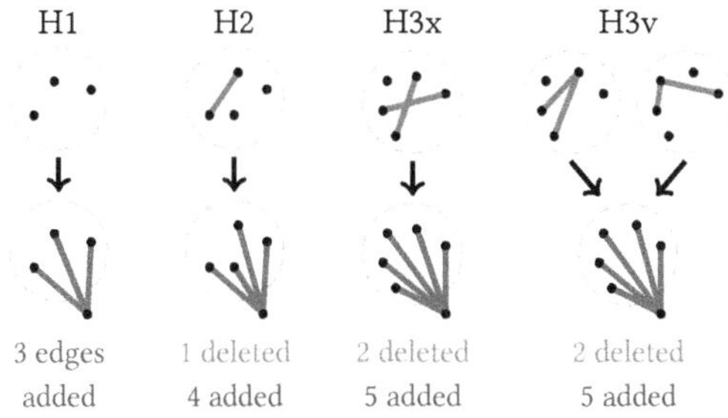

Figure 1: Henneberg steps in $\mathbb{R}^3$

(for dimension 4 there is a counterexample such that 4-dimensional variant of H3x gives a non-rigid graph [22]).

2.2 Equations of spheres

DEFINITION 1. *If $G = (V_G, E_G)$ is a graph with edge lengths $\mathbf{d} = (d_e)_{e\in E_G} \in \mathbb{R}_+^{|E_G|}$ and $v_1, v_2, v_3 \in V_G$ are such that $v_1v_2, v_2v_3, v_1v_3 \in E_G$, then $S(G, \mathbf{d}, v_1v_2v_3) \subset (\mathbb{C}\times\mathbb{C}\times\mathbb{C})^{|V_G|}$ denotes the zero set of the following equations*

$$(x_{v_1}, y_{v_1}, z_{v_1}) = (0,0,0),\ (x_{v_2}, y_{v_2}, z_{v_2}) = (0, d_{v_1v_2}, 0),$$
$$(x_{v_3}, y_{v_3}, z_{v_3}) = (x_3, y_3, 0),\ x_v^2 + y_v^2 + z_v^2 = s_v\ \forall v \in V_G,$$
$$s_u + s_v - 2(x_ux_v + y_uy_v + z_uz_v) = d_{uv}^2\ \forall uv \in E_G,$$

where x_3, y_3 are such that $x_3 \geq 0$, $x_3^2 + y_3^2 = d_{v_1v_3}^2$ and $x_3^2 + (y_3 - d_{v_1v_2})^2 = d_{v_2v_3}^2$. We denote the real solutions $S(G, \mathbf{d}, v_1v_2v_3) \cap (\mathbb{R}\times\mathbb{R}\times\mathbb{R})^{|V_G|}$ by $S_\mathbb{R}(G, \mathbf{d}, v_1v_2v_3)$.

The first 3 equations remove rotations and translations. The distances of vertices from the origin are expressed by new (nonzero) variables to avoid roots at toric infinity which prohibit mixed volume from being tight [9, 28]. The other equations are distances between embedded points.

Notice that $r_3(G, \mathbf{d}) = |S_\mathbb{R}(G, \mathbf{d}, v_1v_2v_3)|$. If $\mathbf{d}$ is generic, then $c_3(G, \mathbf{d}) = |S(G, \mathbf{d}, v_1v_2v_3)| = c_3(G)$ since the number of complex embeddings is a generic property. The mixed volume of the system depends on the choice of the fixed triangle. Hence, all possible choices must be tested for some graphs in order to get the best possible bound.

2.3 Distance geometry

Distance geometry is the study of the properties of points given only the distances between them. A basic tool is the squared distance matrix, extended by a row and a column of ones (except for the diagonal), known as Cayley-Menger matrix [3, Chapter IV, Section 40]:

$$CM = \begin{pmatrix} 0 & 1 & 1 & \cdots & 1 \\ 1 & 0 & d_{12}^2 & \cdots & d_{1n}^2 \\ 1 & d_{12}^2 & 0 & \ddots & \cdots \\ \cdots & \cdots & \ddots & \ddots & \cdots \\ 1 & d_{1n}^2 & d_{2n}^2 & \cdots & 0 \end{pmatrix},$$

where d_{ij} is the distance between point i and j. The points with such distances are embeddable in $\mathbb{R}^D$ if and only if

- $\operatorname{rank}(CM) = D + 2$ and
- $(-1)^k \det(CM') \geq 0$, for every submatrix CM' with size $k + 1 \leq D + 2$ that includes the extending row and column.

The distances among all n points correspond to edge lengths of the complete graph with n vertices. Hence, assuming that lengths of non-edges of our graph G correspond to variables, the first condition gives rise to determinantal equations. This condition suffices for embeddings in $\mathbb{C}^D$. The systems of these equations are overconstrained (for example 21 equations in 6 variables for $n = 7$ and 56 equations in 10 variables for $n = 8$). The second embedding condition can be interpreted by geometrical constraints on the lengths. For $k = 2$ this means simply that a length should be positive. For $k = 3$ the resulting inequality is the triangular one, while for $k = 4$ we obtain *tetrangular inequalities*. The latter can be seen as a generalization of the triangular ones, since they state that the area of no triangle is bigger than the sum of the other three in a tetrahedron.

Although the systems of equations are overconstrained, a square subsystem can be found. The question is if these subsystems can give us information for the whole mechanism. In [17], the authors present an idea relating Cayley-Menger subsystems with *globally rigid* graphs. They are a certain class of graphs consisting of mechanisms with unique realizations up to rigid motions and reflections. If extending G by the edges corresponding to the variables of the square subsystem yields a globally rigid graph, then the number of solutions of the reduced system gives an upper bound for the whole system. Since the reflections are factored out by the distance system, the number of solutions is $c_3(G)/2$. We check global rigidity using stress matrices derived from rigidity matroids [14].

It is easy to find square subsystems from the determinantal equations. The question is what is the smallest number of variables needed to establish an upper bound and if this subsystem captures all solutions of the whole graph. The following lemma provides an estimate of the number of variables.

LEMMA 1. *For every minimally rigid graph G in dimension 3, there is at least one extended graph $H = G\cup\{e_1, e_2, .., e_k\}$, with $k = |V_G| - 4$ and $e_i \notin E_G$, which is globally rigid in $\mathbb{C}^3$.*

PROOF. The only 5-vertex minimally rigid graph is obtained by applying an H1 step to the tetrahedron. If we extend this graph with the only non-existing edge, we obtain the complete graph in 5 vertices, so the lemma holds. Let the lemma hold for all graphs with n or less vertices. For every graph obtained by an H2 step, the lemma holds since H2 preserves global rigidity [7].

Let a graph G_{n+1} be constructed by an H1 move applied to an n-vertex graph G_n, whose extended globally rigid graph is H_n. Without loss of generality, this move connects a new vertex v_{n+1} with the vertices v_1, v_2, v_3. Let u be a neighbour of v_1 in G_{n+1} such that $v_2 \neq u \neq v_3$. The edge uv_1 exists also in G_n and H_n. If we set $H'_{n+1} = (H_n \cup \{v_1v_{n+1}, v_2v_{n+1}, v_3v_{n+1}, uv_{n+1}\}) - \{v_1u\}$, then H'_{n+1} is globally rigid, because it is constructed from H_n by an H2 step. Hence, $H_{n+1} = H'_{n+1} \cup \{uv_{n+1}\}$ is also globally rigid, proving the statement in the case of H1 steps.

As for H3 steps, both H3x and H3v can be seen as an H2 step followed by an edge deletion. Extending the graph with the second deleted edge preserves global rigidity. □

We can extend this result to minimally rigid graphs in arbitrary dimension constructed by appropriate generalizations of Henneberg steps H1, H2 or H3. As we mentioned, the lemma gives only an estimate for the smallest number of variables. It guarantees neither that such subsystem exists in every Cayley-Menger matrix of a minimally rigid graph (in fact we have found graphs with 8 or more vertices with no such a subsystem), nor that the solutions of the subsystem totally define the whole system. On the other hand, if such a subsystem exists, it can definitely give an upper bound.

An example is the 7-vertex graph G_{48} with the maximal number of embeddings ($r_3(G_{48}) = 48 = r_3(7)$, see Section 4). The labeling of the vertices is in Figure 2. There are 5 different square systems in 3 variables that completely define the mechanism. We can choose one of them involving only x_1, x_2, x_3:

$$CM_{G_{48}} = \begin{pmatrix} 0 & 1 & 1 & 1 & 1 & 1 & 1 & 1 \\ 1 & 0 & d_{12}^2 & d_{13}^2 & d_{14}^2 & d_{15}^2 & d_{16}^2 & x_1 \\ 1 & d_{21}^2 & 0 & d_{23}^2 & x_2 & x_3 & d_{26}^2 & d_{27}^2 \\ 1 & d_{31}^2 & d_{32}^2 & 0 & d_{34}^2 & x_4 & x_5 & d_{37}^2 \\ 1 & d_{41}^2 & x_2 & d_{43}^2 & 0 & d_{45}^2 & x_6 & d_{47}^2 \\ 1 & d_{51}^2 & x_3 & x_4 & d_{54}^2 & 0 & d_{56}^2 & d_{57}^2 \\ 1 & d_{61}^2 & d_{62}^2 & x_5 & x_6 & d_{65}^2 & 0 & d_{67}^2 \\ 1 & x_1 & d_{72}^2 & d_{73}^2 & d_{74}^2 & d_{75}^2 & d_{76}^2 & 0 \end{pmatrix}.$$

One advantage of this approach is that we have much less equations compared with the sphere equations approach. In this example, we need a system of only 3 equations for the distance system, while 16 equations are required otherwise. Additionally, every solution of the distance system corresponds to two reflected embeddings. Hence, polynomial homotopy solvers are much faster in this case.

We can also apply algebraic elimination to reformulate this determinantal variety. We noticed that even the graph extended only with the edge v_1v_7 corresponding to the variables x_1 is globally rigid. This led us to compute the resultant of the square 3x3 system for x_1, which can be obtained by repeated Sylvester resultants, Macaulay resultant and sparse resultant method with the same result. In order to specify the realizations, we also need the set of inequalities. There are 35 triangular inequalities and the same number of tetrangular inequalities for the whole set of variables. Since we need to embed only one new edge, we are restricted to find the inequalities for x_1. There are ten inequalities that include only x_1 (5 triangular and 5 tetrangular).

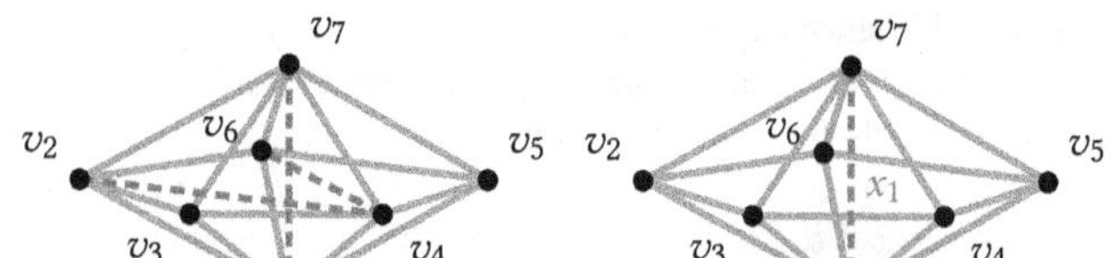

Figure 2: The graph G_{48} (grey edges). There are submatrices of $CM_{G_{48}}$ that involve only variables corresponding to the 3 red dashed edges of the left graph. The graph G_{48} extended by the edge v_1v_7 (that corresponds to the variable x_1) is globally rigid.

On the other hand, we detected graphs for which the subsystems do not fully describe the determinantal variety, since the number of solutions of the whole (overconstrained) system is smaller than this of the (square) subsystem for some generic choices of lengths. We conclude that the drawback of the method is that there is not a 1-1 correspondence between subsystems and global rigidity. Despite this fact, they seem better candidates for tight upper bound mixed volume computations.

3 INCREASING THE NUMBER OF REAL EMBEDDINGS

To improve $r_3(G)$ bounds, our first goal was to prove that $r_3(G_{48}) = c_3(G_{48})$. Initially we used methods already applied to increase the number of real solutions of a given polynomial system. We present a short overview of this approach.

Stochastic methods. A first idea was to use stochastic sampling. Generic configurations of G_{48} embeddings in $\mathbb{R}^3$ were perturbed following the sampling methods presented in [10]. Applying this approach, it was straightforward to find configurations with $r_3(G_{48}, \mathbf{d})$ being equal to 16, 20 or 24. Our best result was $r_3(G_{48}, \mathbf{d}) = 32$.

Parametric searching with CAD method. `Maple`'s subpackage `RootFinding [Parametric]` implements Cylindrical Algebraic Decomposition principles for semi-algebraic sets [20]. This implementation could not work for the system of sphere equations, but was efficient using the semi-algebraic distance system. The algorithm can separate variables and parameters for every equation and give as output a decomposition of the space of parameters up to the number of solutions. In our case, it was possible to use only one parameter due to computational constraints, so all the other distances were fixed (our Maple worksheet is available at [19]).

It was again straightforward to find 24 embeddings even from totally random conformations. To get more we needed to exploit the symmetry of G_{48}, constructing non-generic flexible frameworks. Perturbing the lengths by a small quantity, $r_3(G_{48}, \mathbf{d})$ was again finite. Afterwards, we considered multiple edge lengths as linear combinations of the same parameter. Eventually, applying parameter searching, we were able to find lengths $\bar{\mathbf{d}}$ such that $r_3(G_{48}, \bar{\mathbf{d}}) = 28$:

$$\begin{aligned} \bar{d}_{12} &= 1.99993774567597, & \bar{d}_{27} &= 10.5360917228793, \\ \bar{d}_{13} &= 1.99476987780024, & \bar{d}_{37} &= 10.5363171636461, \\ \bar{d}_{14} &= 2.00343646098439, & \bar{d}_{47} &= 10.5357233031495, \\ \bar{d}_{15} &= 2.00289249524296, & \bar{d}_{57} &= 10.5362736599978, \\ \bar{d}_{16} &= 2.00013424746814, & \bar{d}_{67} &= 10.5364788463527, \\ \bar{d}_{23} &= 0.99961432208948, & \bar{d}_{34} &= 1.00368644488060, \\ \bar{d}_{45} &= 1.00153014850485, & \bar{d}_{56} &= 0.99572361653574, \\ \bar{d}_{26} &= 1.00198771097407 \end{aligned} \tag{1}$$

While this result was lower than the one achieved by stochastic searching, it had some promising properties (variables are taken from the determinantal variety of $CM_{G_{48}}$). Namely, all the solutions for x_1, x_2, x_3 are real, for x_1 even positive, and the x_1 solutions which are not embeddable are very close to the intervals imposed by the triangular and tetrangular inequalities.

Gradient Descent. An algorithm that increases step by step the number of real embeddings is proposed in [8]. This method is based on gradient descent optimization, minimizing the imaginary part of solutions, while forcing existing real roots to remain real via a semidefinite relation.

We applied it to the G_{48} sphere equations and a variant of it for distance equations starting from the optimal configurations found with the two previous approaches. In the first iterations the results were encouraging, but finally we could not generate more real embeddings.

The previous results motivated us to search other ways to achieve our first goal. Inspired by coupler curve visualization, we introduce an iterative procedure that modifies edge lengths so that the number of real embeddings might increase. In particular, it allows to find edge lengths to prove that $r_3(G) = c_3(G)$ for G_{48} and also other 7-vertex graphs G. At each iteration, only lengths of 4 edges in a specific subgraph are changed. One can be changed freely, whereas the other 3 are related. For this two-parametric family, we search values with the maximal number of embeddings globally.

3.1 Coupler curve

For a minimally rigid graph G, removing an edge uc yields a framework $H = (V_G, E_G \setminus uc)$ with one degree of freedom. If we fix a triangle containing u in order to avoid rotations and translations of H, then the vertex c draws the so called *coupler curve* under all possible motions of H. This idea was already used in [5] for obtaining 24 real embeddings of Desargues (3-prism) graph in $\mathbb{R}^2$. A modification into $\mathbb{R}^3$ is straightforward – the number of embeddings of G corresponds to the number of intersection of the coupler curve of c of the graph H with a sphere centered at u with radius d_{uc}. The following definition recalls the concept of coupler curve more precisely.

Definition 2. *Let H be a graph with edge lengths $\mathbf{d} = (d_e)_{e \in E_H}$ and $v_1, v_2, v_3 \in V_H$ be such that $v_1v_2, v_2v_3, v_1v_3 \in E_H$. If the set $S_\mathbb{R}(H, \mathbf{d}, v_1v_2v_3)$ is one dimensional and $c \in V_H$, then the set*

$$C_{c,\mathbf{d}} = \{(x_c, y_c, z_c) : ((x_v, y_v, z_v))_{v \in V_H} \in S_\mathbb{R}(H, \mathbf{d}, v_1v_2v_3)\}$$

is called a coupler curve *of c* w.r.t. the fixed triangle $v_1v_2v_3$.

Obviously, for given lengths $\mathbf{d}$ of the graph H, we may vary the length d_{uc} of the removed edge uc so that the number of intersections of the coupler curve $C_{c,\mathbf{d}}$ with the sphere centered at u with radius d_{uc}, i.e., the number of embeddings of G, is maximal. The following lemma enables us to move also the center of the sphere within a certain one-parameter family without changing the coupler curve.

Lemma 2. *Let G be a minimally rigid graph and let u, v, w, p, c be vertices of G such that $pv, vw \in E$ and the neighbours of u in G are v, w, p and c. Let $C_{c,\mathbf{d}}$ be the coupler curve of c of the graph $H = (V_G, E_G \setminus \{uc\})$ with edge lengths $\mathbf{d} = (d_e)_{e \in E_H}$ w.r.t. the fixed triangle vuw. Let z_p be the altitude of p in the triangle uvp with lengths given by $\mathbf{d}$. The set $\{y_p : ((x_{v'}, y_{v'}, z_{v'}))_{v' \in V_H} \in S_\mathbb{R}(H, \mathbf{d}, vuw)\}$ has only one element y_p'. If the parametric edge lengths $\mathbf{d}'(t)$ are given by*

$$d'_{uw}(t) = ||(x_w, y_w - t, 0)||, \quad d'_{up}(t) = ||(0, y_p' - t, z_p)||,$$
$$d'_{uv}(t) = t, \text{ and } d'_e(t) = d_e \text{ for all } e \in E_H \setminus \{uv, uw, up\},$$

then the coupler curve $C_{c,\mathbf{d}'(t)}$ of c w.r.t. the fixed triangle vuw is the same for all $t \in \mathbb{R}_+$, namely, it is $C_{c,\mathbf{d}}$. Moreover, if $cw \in E_G$, then $C_{c,\mathbf{d}'(t)}$ is a spherical curve.

Proof. Within this proof, all coupler curves are w.r.t. the triangle vuw. The situation is illustrated by Figure 3. Since G is minimally rigid, removing the edge uc yields a graph H such that $S_\mathbb{R}(H, \mathbf{d}, vuw)$ is one dimensional for a generic choice of $\mathbf{d}$. The set $\{y_p : ((x_{v'}, y_{v'}, z_{v'}))_{v' \in V_H} \in S_\mathbb{R}(H, \mathbf{d}, vuw)\}$ has indeed only one element, since the coupler curve $C_{p,\mathbf{d}}$ of p is a circle whose axis of symmetry is the y-axis. The parametric edge lengths $\mathbf{d}'(t)$ are such that the position of v and w is the same for all t. Moreover, the coupler curve $C_{p,\mathbf{d}'(t)}$ of p is independent on t. Hence, the coupler curve $C_{c,\mathbf{d}'(t)}$ is independent on t, because the only vertices adjacent to u in H are p, v and w, i.e., the position of u does not influence positions of the other vertices. □

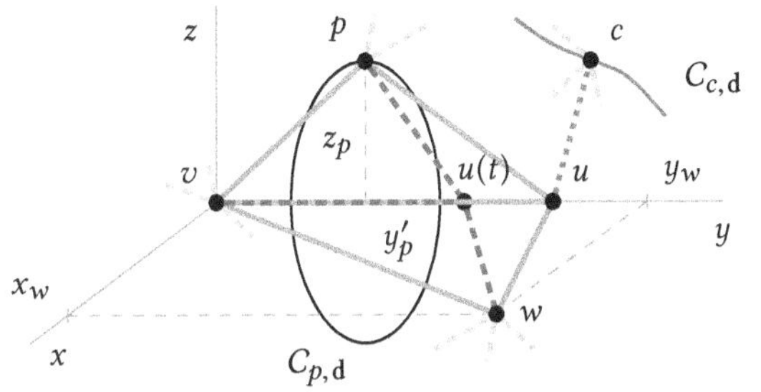

Figure 3: Since the lengths of up and uw are changed accordingly to the length of uv (blued dashed edges), the coupler curves $C_{p,\mathbf{d}'(t)}$ and $C_{c,\mathbf{d}'(t)}$ are independent on t. The red dashed edge uc is removed from G.

Thus, for every subgraph of G given by vertices u, v, w, p, c such that $pv, vw \in E$ and the neighbours of u in G are v, w, p and c, we have a two-parametric family of lengths $\mathbf{d}(t, r)$ such that the coupler curve $C_{c,\mathbf{d}(t,r)}$ w.r.t. the fixed triangle vuw is the same for all t and r, where the parameter t determines lengths of uv, uw and up, and the parameter r represents the length of uc. Within this family, we look for values of t and r that maximize the number of embeddings.

We illustrate the method on the example of G_{48}. Let $\bar{\mathbf{d}}$ be edge lengths given by (1). We developed a program [19] that plots (using `Matplotlib` [16]) the coupler curve of the vertex v_6 of G with the edge v_2v_6 removed w.r.t. the fixed triangle $v_1v_2v_3$. Figure 4 is created by this program. There are 28 embeddings for $\bar{\mathbf{d}}$, but we can find position and radius of the sphere corresponding to the removed edge v_2v_6 such that there are 32 embeddings by using Lemma 2 for the subgraph $(u, v, w, p, c) = (v_2, v_3, v_1, v_7, v_6)$. This is obtained by setting

$$d_{12} = 4.0534, \quad d_{27} = 11.1069, \quad d_{26} = 3.8545, \quad d_{23} = 4.0519. \quad (2)$$

3.2 Sampling

Although edge lengths of G_{48} with 48 real embeddings can be obtained by manual application of Lemma 2 based on plots of coupler curves, we also implemented a program [19] that searches for a good position and radius of the sphere by sampling the parameters. The method and its implementation work also for minimally rigid graphs other than G_{48}.

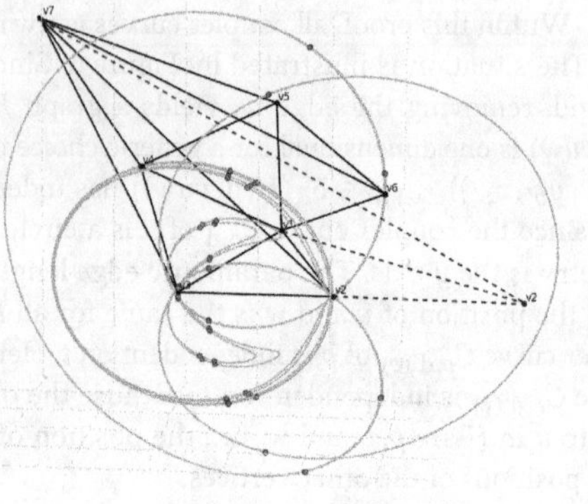

Figure 4: Coupler curve $C_{v_6,\bar{d}}$ of G_{48} with the edge v_2v_6 removed. The 28 red points are intersections of $C_{v_6,\bar{d}}$ with the sphere centered at v_2 with edge lengths $\bar{d}$, whereas the 32 green ones are for edge lengths given by equation (2) (illustrated by blue dashed lines).

We assume that the edge cw is present for a suitable subgraph (actually, this is the case for all suitable subgraphs of G_{48}). Thus, the coupler curve is spherical and the intersections of the coupler curve with the sphere representing the removed edge uc lies on the intersection of these two spheres, which is a circle. Hence, instead of sampling t and r, we sample circles on the sphere containing the coupler curve.

Since the sphere of the coupler curve is centered at w and the intersecting sphere has center at u, the center of the intersection circle is on the line uw and the plane of the circle is perpendicular to this line. Hence, the circle is determined by the angle $\varphi \in (-\pi/2, \pi/2)$ between the altitude of w in the triangle uvw and the line uw, and by the angle $\theta \in (0, \pi)$ between uw and cw, see Figure 5. Thus, we sample φ and θ in their intervals, compute t and r from their values and select edge lengths with the highest number of real embeddings. The algebraic systems are solved by polynomial homotopy continuation using the Python package phcpy [30]. In phcpy, one can specify a starting system with the set of its solutions instead of letting the program to construct it. Since the parameters change only slightly during the sampling, tracking the solutions of a new system from the solutions of the previous one is significantly faster than solving from scratch.

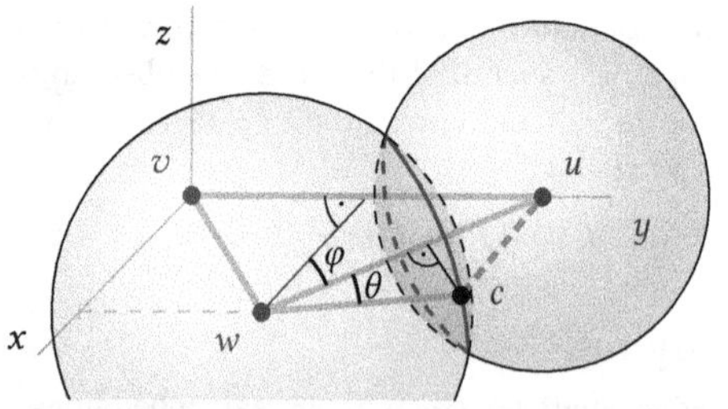

Figure 5: For fixed position of v and w, the angle φ determines the position of u, since u lies on the y-axis. If also the length of cw is given, then θ determines the length of uc. The intersection circle is blue.

3.3 More subgraphs suitable for sampling

Usually, one iteration of the sampling produces many edge lengths with the same number of real embeddings. If this number is not the desired one, then we need to pick starting edge lengths for the next iteration with a different subgraph suitable for sampling. Our heuristic choice is based on clustering of pairs (φ, θ) using the function `DBSCAN` from the `sklearn` Python package [23]. From each cluster, we pick the center of gravity as (φ, θ) for the output lengths, or the pair (φ, θ) closest to this center if the edge lengths corresponding to the center have less real embeddings.

We tested two approaches in sampling for subgraphs:

(1) *Tree search* – we apply the procedure using all suitable subgraphs for given starting lengths and then we do the same recursively for all outputs whose number of embeddings increased until the required number is reached (or there are no increments). We trace the state tree depth-first.

(2) *Linear search* – we order all suitable subgraphs and an output from the procedure applied to starting lengths with the first subgraph is used as input for the procedure with the second subgraph, etc. There is also branching because of multiple clusters – we test all of them in depth-first way.

4 CLASSIFICATION AND LOWER BOUNDS

Henneberg steps may result in isomorphic graphs either constructed by the same H-step or by another one. We recall that no H3x or H3v step is needed for 7 and 8-vertex graphs. We classify each graph up to isomorphism by the sequence of Henneberg steps needed for its construction. We use a certain hierarchy for this classification: on the one hand there are graphs that can be constructed by an H1 move in the last step, while for the others H2 is needed. This process is important, since H1 steps trivially double the number of real embeddings as the new vertex lies in the intersection of 3 spheres. This means that the number of embeddings for H1 graphs is already known, assuming that we know the number for the parent graph. Our `MATLAB` and `SageMath` implementations, which verify each other, were used to apply Henneberg steps and remove isomorphisms (see [19]). This is not a computationally difficult task for $n = 7$ or 8. We remark that this is also done in [15] up to 10 vertices.

The first estimate of $c_3(G)$ is the mixed volume of the algebraic systems. Let f be a square polynomial system in m variables. The convex hull of the exponents vector of each polynomial is its Newton polytope. The mixed volume of the polytope bounds the number of solutions and is tight generically in $(\mathbb{C}^*)^m$. We computed the mixed volume for both sphere and distance equations. We solved the systems for random edge lengths and checked whether the mixed volume bound was tight in all cases. Finally, we used the method in Section 3 to find parameters maximizing the number of real embeddings.

4.1 7-vertex graphs

For $n = 6$, there are three H1 graphs and one obtained with an H2 step – the cyclohexane G_{16}. The number of real embeddings of the H1 graphs is 8, while it is known that $r_3(G_{16}) = 16$ [11]. One can also obtain lengths $\mathbf{d}$ such that $r_3(G_{16}, \mathbf{d}) = 16$ by our method within a few tries with random starting lengths.

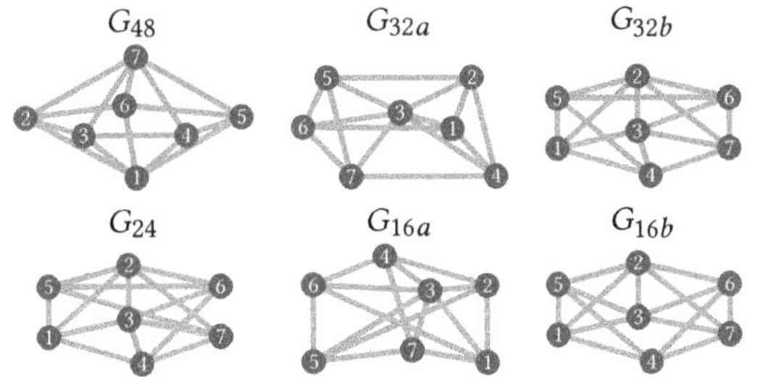

Figure 6: All 7-vertex graphs constructed only by an H2 move in the last step.

Using Henneberg steps, we tackle the case $n = 7$. There are 18 graphs constructed using a sequence of only H1 steps, while two are obtained if we apply H1 to G_{16}. Hence, the number of real embeddings is 16, resp. 32, by the doubling argument. Moreover, there are 6 graphs obtained by H2 on a 6-vertex graph, see Figure 6. See [19] for the full list.

The results (mixed volume for both systems, numbers of complex and real embeddings) for these 6 graphs are in Table 1. These results give a full classification of the embeddings of all 7-vertex minimally rigid graphs in $\mathbb{R}^3$. We present edge lengths for all these graphs proving that all embeddings can be real, i.e., $r_3(G) = c_3(G)$.

Graph	G_{48}	G_{32a}	G_{32b}	G_{24}	G_{16a}	G_{16b}
MV sphere eq.	48	32	32	32	32	32
MV dist. subsyst.	48	32	32	24	24	16
$c_3(G)$	48	32	32	24	16	16
$r_3(G)$	48	32	32	24	16	16

Table 1: Mixed volume (MV) and number of solutions for 7-vertex graphs constructed only by H2 in the last step.

There are 20 subgraphs of G_{48} given by vertices (u, v, w, p, c) satisfying the assumption in Lemma 2, that is, they are suitable for the sampling procedure. Using tree search approach, we obtained $\mathbf{d}$ such that $r_3(G_{48}, \mathbf{d}) = 48$ in only 3 steps (starting from $\bar{\mathbf{d}}$ and using subgraphs $(v_5, v_6, v_1, v_7, v_4)$, $(v_4, v_3, v_1, v_7, v_5)$ and $(v_3, v_2, v_1, v_7, v_4)$):

$d_{12} = 1.9999,$	$d_{16} = 2.0001,$	$d_{45} = 7.0744,$	$d_{47} = 11.8471,$
$d_{13} = 1.9342,$	$d_{26} = 1.0020,$	$d_{56} = 4.4449,$	$d_{57} = 11.2396,$
$d_{14} = 5.7963,$	$d_{23} = 0.5500,$	$d_{27} = 10.5361,$	$d_{67} = 10.5365\,.$
$d_{15} = 4.4024,$	$d_{34} = 5.4247,$	$d_{37} = 10.5245,$	

For other graphs constructed only by an H2 move in the last step we used various starting lengths, we just list the edge lengths that give the appropriate maximal number of real embeddings:

G_{16a} :	$d_{13} = 5.75,$	$d_{56} = 7.90,$	$d_{16} = 8.48,$
$d_{37} = 5.91,$	$d_{25} = 7.15,$	$d_{35} = 5.09,$	$d_{12} = 4.36,$
$d_{46} = 8.78,$	$d_{57} = 10.22,$	$d_{36} = 7.06,$	$d_{17} = 3.77,$
$d_{47} = 7.19,$	$d_{23} = 3.81,$	$d_{34} = 3.23,$	$d_{24} = 6.05\,.$
G_{16b} :	$d_{47} = 4.46,$	$d_{26} = 7.47,$	$d_{45} = 7.72,$
$d_{14} = 6.51,$	$d_{13} = 3.53,$	$d_{23} = 7.69,$	$d_{37} = 5.76,$
$d_{25} = 9.48,$	$d_{35} = 6.10,$	$d_{12} = 4.62,$	$d_{67} = 3.09,$
$d_{27} = 5.90,$	$d_{46} = 7.07,$	$d_{15} = 5.69,$	$d_{36} = 6.43\,.$

G_{24} :	$d_{47} = 5.65,$	$d_{26} = 5.70,$	$d_{56} = 4.70,$
$d_{14} = 8.33,$	$d_{13} = 4.77,$	$d_{23} = 10.31,$	$d_{37} = 7.10,$
$d_{25} = 9.32,$	$d_{12} = 11.05,$	$d_{46} = 6.49,$	$d_{57} = 5.77,$
$d_{27} = 6.00,$	$d_{15} = 9.40,$	$d_{36} = 8.57,$	$d_{34} = 7.64\,.$
G_{32a} :	$d_{13} = 6.27,$	$d_{56} = 9.23,$	$d_{14} = 8.06,$
$d_{23} = 8.83,$	$d_{37} = 5.62,$	$d_{25} = 9.74,$	$d_{35} = 5.60,$
$d_{12} = 10.95,$	$d_{67} = 9.28,$	$d_{57} = 7.88,$	$d_{36} = 8.26,$
$d_{47} = 8.74,$	$d_{16} = 11.56,$	$d_{34} = 6.11,$	$d_{24} = 8.95\,.$
G_{32b} :	$d_{47} = 85.49,$	$d_{26} = 7.11,$	$d_{56} = 22.08,$
$d_{14} = 87.33,$	$d_{13} = 10.81,$	$d_{23} = 4.47,$	$d_{37} = 7.10,$
$d_{25} = 20.70,$	$d_{12} = 11.06,$	$d_{67} = 9.29,$	$d_{15} = 21.49,$
$d_{27} = 7.68,$	$d_{45} = 78.53,$	$d_{36} = 7.53,$	$d_{34} = 84.17\,.$

4.2 8-vertex graphs

We repeated our methods for $n = 8$. There are 311 graphs that can be constructed by an H1 step (hence, $r_3(G)$ is known by H1 doubling argument), while 63 require an H2 step. So we computed only the complex bounds of the latter: 58 of them have 96 complex embeddings or less, one has 112 complex embeddings, 3 have 128 complex embeddings and there is a unique graph G_{160} with 160 complex embeddings.

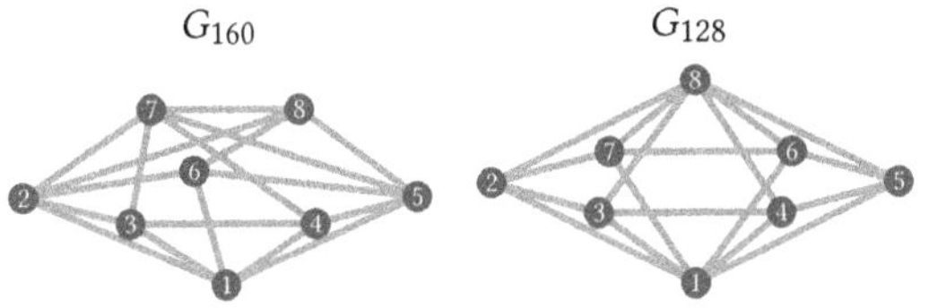

Figure 7: G_{160} has the maximal number of complex embeddings (160). We proved that $r_3(G_{128}) = 128$.

We were interested in improving the lower bound established previously. No graph with less than 128 embeddings could improve the bound obtained by G_{48}. Thus, we applied the technique to maximize real embeddings on two different 8-vertex graphs: G_{160} and G_{128}, see Figure 7. Both can be constructed by H2 step from G_{48}, and the structure of G_{128} is similar to G_{48}. Therefore, we use some lengths of G_{48} with many embeddings for the common edges for the starting lengths. The following edge lengths of G_{128} with 128 real embeddings were found by the algorithm:

$d_{12} = 8.7093,$	$d_{17} = 2.1185,$	$d_{68} = 10.5532,$	$d_{56} = 0.7536,$
$d_{13} = 10.3433,$	$d_{28} = 13.5773,$	$d_{78} = 10.5509,$	$d_{67} = 1.5449,$
$d_{14} = 1.9373,$	$d_{38} = 14.6173,$	$d_{23} = 13.5267,$	$d_{27} = 9.2728\,.$
$d_{15} = 1.9379,$	$d_{48} = 10.5237,$	$d_{34} = 10.1636,$	
$d_{16} = 2.0691,$	$d_{58} = 10.5237,$	$d_{45} = 0.0634,$	

For G_{160} we have obtained lengths for 132 real embeddings:

$d_{12} = 1.999,$	$d_{23} = 1.426,$	$d_{37} = 10.447,$	$d_{58} = 4.279,$
$d_{13} = 1.568,$	$d_{26} = 0.879,$	$d_{45} = 7.278,$	$d_{68} = 0.398,$
$d_{14} = 6.611,$	$d_{27} = 10.536,$	$d_{47} = 11.993,$	$d_{78} = 10.474\,.$
$d_{15} = 4.402,$	$d_{28} = 0.847,,$	$d_{56} = 4.321,$	
$d_{16} = 1.994,$	$d_{34} = 6.494,$	$d_{57} = 11.239,$	

More values for edge lengths of the presented graphs with various number of embeddings are available in [19]. We remark that it takes only few seconds to construct all Geiringer graphs up to 8 vertices and compute their mixed volumes. Complex embeddings computation takes approximately 1 second for one 7-vertex graph and 4 seconds for an 8-vertex graph. Although we take advantage of tracking solutions in our implementation of the sampling method (which speeds up the computation significantly), the time of sampling for G_{160} takes about 8 hours using 8 cores (this time strongly depends on the starting lengths). In order to get the lengths with 132 embeddings, we tested about 200 different starting conformations.

4.3 Lower bounds

To compute a lower bound on the maximum number of embeddings for rigid graphs in the space with n vertices, we use as a building block a rigid graph G with low $|V_G|$, but high $r_3(G)$. To do so, we need the following theorem from [15]:

THEOREM 1. *Let G be a rigid graph, with a rigid subgraph H. We construct a rigid graph using k copies of G, where all the copies have the subgraph H in common. The new graph is rigid, has $n = |V_H| + k(|V_G| - |V_H|)$ vertices, and the number of its real embeddings is at least*

$$2^{(n-|V_H|) \mod (|V_G|-|V_H|)} \cdot r_3(H) \cdot \left(\frac{r_3(G)}{r_3(H)}\right)^{\left\lfloor \frac{n-|V_H|}{|V_G|-|V_H|} \right\rfloor}.$$

If we use G_{160} as G and one of its triangle subgraphs as H, then we obtain the following lower bound.

COROLLARY 1. *The maximum number of real embeddings of rigid graphs in $\mathbb{R}^3$ with n vertices is bounded from below by*

$$2^{(n-3) \mod 5}\, 132^{\lfloor (n-3)/5 \rfloor}.$$

The bound asymptotically behaves as 2.6553^n.

The previous lower bound was 2.51984^n [9], whereas using G_{48} as G gives 2.6321^n. It would be tempting to use as H a tetrahedron, say T, for which it holds $r_3(T) = 2$. Such a choice of a subgraph would have further improved the lower bound as the denominator of the exponent would have been smaller. Unfortunately, G_{48}, G_{128}, and G_{160} do not contain a tetrahedron as a subgraph.

5 CONCLUSION

By exploiting the (semi-)algebraic modeling of the embeddings of minimally rigid spatial graphs we present new classification results and a novel method to maximize $r_3(G)$. The latter led to improved lower bounds. Finding better asymptotic bounds is always an open question. A first step should be to find out the exact value of $r_3(G_{160})$. Furthermore, computations using our method for $n \geq 9$ may also give better results in this direction. Another direction is to find an efficient variant of our sampling method for other dimensions. Finally, subsystems of the determinantal varieties may improve the upper bounds for $c_3(G)$.

Acknowledgments. This work is part of the project ARCADES that has received funding from the European Union's Horizon 2020 research and innovation programme under the Marie Skłodowska-Curie grant agreement No 675789. ET is partially supported by ANR JCJC GALOP (ANR-17-CE40-0009) and the PGMO grant GAMMA.

REFERENCES

[1] F. Bihan, J. M. Rojast, and F. Sottile. 2008. On the sharpness of fewnomial bounds and the number of components of fewnomial hypersurfaces. In *Algorithms in algebraic geometry*. Springer, 15–20.

[2] F. Bihan and P.-J. Spaenlehauer. 2016. Sparse Polynomial Systems with many Positive Solutions from Bipartite Simplicial Complexes. *arXiv:1510.05622* (2016).

[3] L. M. Blumenthal. 1970. *Theory and Applications of Distance Geometry*. Chelsea Publishing Company, New York.

[4] C. S. Borcea. 2002. Point configurations and Cayley-Menger Varieties. *arXiv:math/0207110* (2002).

[5] C. S. Borcea and I. Streinu. 2004. The Number of Embeddings of Minimally Rigid Graphs. *Discrete & Computational Geometry 2* (2004), 287–303.

[6] J. Capco, M. Gallet, G. Grasegger, C. Koutschan, N. Lubbes, and J. Schicho. 2018. The Number of Realizations of a Laman Graph. *SIAM Journal on Applied Algebra and Geometry* 2, 1 (2018), 94–125. https://doi.org/10.1137/17M1118312

[7] R. Connelly. 2005. Generic global rigidity. *Discrete Comput. Geom. 33* 549–563.

[8] P. Dietmaier. 1998. The Stewart-Gough platform of general geometry can have 40 real postures. *Advances in Robot Kinematics: Analysis and Control* (1998), 1–10.

[9] I.Z. Emiris, E. Tsigaridas, and A. Varvitsiotis. 2013. Mixed volume and distance geometry techniques for counting Euclidean embeddings of rigid graphs. *Distance Geometry: Theory, Methods and Applications", edited by A. Mucherino, C. Lavor, L. Liberti and N. Maculan* (2013), 23–45.

[10] I. Z. Emiris and G. Moroz. 2011. The assembly modes of rigid 11-bar linkages. *IFToMM 2011 World Congress, Jun 2011, Guanajuato, Mexico* (2011).

[11] I. Z. Emiris and B. Mourrain. 1999. Computer Algebra Methods for Studying and Computing Molecular Conformations. *Algorithmica 25* (1999), 372–402.

[12] D.G. Emmerich. 1988. *Structures Tendues et Autotendantes*. Ecole d'Architecture de Paris la Villette.

[13] J.C. Faugere and D. Lazard. 1995. The combinatorial classes of parallel manipulators. *Mechanism & Machine Theory 30(6)* (1995), 765–776.

[14] S. Gortler, A. Healy, and D. Thurston. 2010. Characterizing generic global rigidity. *Am. J. Math. 132(4)* (2010), 897–939.

[15] G. Grasegger, C. Koutschan, and E. Tsigaridas. 2018. Lower Bounds on the Number of Realizations of Rigid Graphs. *Experimental Mathematics* (2018), 1–12.

[16] J. D. Hunter. 2007. Matplotlib: A 2D graphics environment. *Computing In Science & Engineering* 9, 3 (2007), 90–95. https://doi.org/10.1109/MCSE.2007.55

[17] B. Jackson and J.C. Owen. 2017. Equivalent Realisations of Rigid Graphs. *10th Japanese-Hungarian Symposium on Discrete Mathematics and Its Applications* (2017), 283–289.

[18] B. Jackson and J.C. Owen. 2018. Equivalent realisations of a rigid graph. *Discrete Applied Mathematics* (2018). https://doi.org/10.1016/j.dam.2017.12.009

[19] J. Legerský and E. Bartzos. 2018. Spatial graph embeddings and coupler curves – source code and results. (2018). https://doi.org/10.5281/zenodo.1244042

[20] S. Liang, J. Gerhard, D. J. Jeffrey, and G. Moroz. 2009. A Package for Solving Parametric Polynomial Systems. *ACM Comm. Comput. Algebra* 43, 3, 61 – 72.

[21] L. Liberti, B. Masson, J. Lee, C. Lavor, and A. Mucherino. 2014. On the number of realizations of certain Henneberg graphs arising in protein conformation. *Discrete Applied Mathematics, 165* (2014), 213–232.

[22] H. Maehara. 1991. On Graver's Conjecture Concerning the Rigidity Problem of Graphs. *Discrete Comput Geom 6* (1991), 339–342.

[23] F. Pedregosa, G. Varoquaux, A. Gramfort, V. Michel, B. Thirion, O. Grisel, M. Blondel, P. Prettenhofer, R. Weiss, V. Dubourg, J. Vanderplas, A. Passos, D. Cournapeau, M. Brucher, M. Perrot, and E. Duchesnay. 2011. Scikit-learn: Machine Learning in Python. *Journal of Machine Learning Research* 12 (2011), 2825–2830.

[24] H. Pollaczek-Geiringer. 1927. Über die Gliederung ebener Fachwerke. *Zeitschrift für Angewandte Mathematik und Mechanik (ZAMM)* 7, 1, 58–72.

[25] H. Pollaczek-Geiringer. 1932. Zur Gliederungstheorie räumlicher Fachwerke. *Zeitschrift für Angewandte Mathematik und Mechanik (ZAMM)* 12, 6, 369–376.

[26] B. Schulze and W. Whiteley. 2017. *Rigidity and scene analysis*. CRC Press LLC, Chapter 61, 1593–1632.

[27] F. Sottile. 2003. Enumerative real algebraic geometry. In *Algorithmic and Quantitative Real Algebraic Geometry, DIMACS Series in Discrete Mathematics and Theoretical Computer Science, Volume 60, AMS*. 139–180.

[28] R. Steffens and T. Theobald. 2010. Mixed volume techniques for embeddings of Laman graphs. *Computational Geometry 43* (2010), 84–93.

[29] T.-S. Tay and W. Whiteley. 1985. Generating isostatic frameworks. *Topologie Structurale* (1985), 21–69.

[30] J. Verschelde. 2014. Modernizing PHCpack through phcpy. In *Proceedings of the 6th European Conference on Python in Science (EuroSciPy 2013)*. 71–76.

[31] D. Walter and M. L. Husty. 2007. On a 9-bar linkage, its possible configurations and conditions for paradoxical mobility. *IFToMM World Congress, Besançon, France*.

[32] D. Zelazo, A. Franchi, F. Allgöwer, H. H. Bülthoff, and P.R. Giordano. 2012. Rigidity Maintenance Control for Multi-Robot Systems. *Robotics: Science and Systems, Sydney, Australia* (2012).

[33] Z. Zhu, A.M.-C. So, and Y. Ye. 2010. Universal rigidity and edge sparsification for sensor network localization. *SIAM Journal on Optimization, 20(6)*, 3059–3081.

Bilinear Systems with Two Supports: Koszul Resultant Matrices, Eigenvalues, and Eigenvectors

Matías R. Bender*
matias.bender@inria.fr

Jean-Charles Faugère*
jean-charles.faugere@inria.fr

Angelos Mantzaflaris
angelos.mantzaflaris@oeaw.ac.at
Johann Radon Institute for Computational and Applied Mathematics (RICAM), Austrian Academy of Sciences, Linz, Austria

Elias Tsigaridas*
elias.tsigaridas@inria.fr
*Sorbonne Université, CNRS, INRIA, Laboratoire d'Informatique de Paris 6, LIP6, Équipe PolSys
F-75005, Paris, France

ABSTRACT

A fundamental problem in computational algebraic geometry is the computation of the resultant. A central question is when and how to compute it as the determinant of a matrix whose elements are the coefficients of the input polynomials up-to sign. This problem is well understood for unmixed multihomogeneous systems, that is for systems consisting of multihomogeneous polynomials with the same support. However, little is known for mixed systems, that is for systems consisting of polynomials with different supports.

We consider the computation of the multihomogeneous resultant of bilinear systems involving two different supports. We present a constructive approach that expresses the resultant as the exact determinant of a *Koszul resultant matrix*, that is a matrix constructed from maps in the Koszul complex. We exploit the resultant matrix to propose an algorithm to solve such systems. In the process we extend the classical eigenvalues and eigenvectors criterion to a more general setting. Our extension of the eigenvalues criterion applies to a general class of matrices, including the Sylvester-type and the Koszul-type ones.

CCS CONCEPTS

• **Computing methodologies → Symbolic calculus algorithms**;

KEYWORDS

Resultant; Sparse Resultant; Determinantal formula; Bilinear system; Mixed Multihomogeneous system; Polynomial solving

ACM Reference Format:
Matías R. Bender*, Jean-Charles Faugère*, Angelos Mantzaflaris, and Elias Tsigaridas*. 2018. Bilinear Systems with Two Supports: Koszul Resultant Matrices, Eigenvalues, and Eigenvectors . In *ISSAC '18: 2018 ACM International Symposium on Symbolic and Algebraic Computation, July 16–19, 2018, New York, NY, USA*. ACM, New York, NY, USA, 8 pages. https://doi.org/10.1145/3208976.3209011

ISSAC '18, July 16–19, 2018, New York, NY, USA

ACM ISBN 978-1-4503-5550-6/18/07...$15.00
https://doi.org/10.1145/3208976.3209011

1 INTRODUCTION

The resultant is a central object in elimination theory and computational algebraic geometry. We use it to decide when an overdetermined polynomial system has a solution and to solve well-defined (square) systems. Moreover, it is one of the few tools that take into account the sparsity of supports of the polynomials.

Usually, we compute the resultant as a quotient of determinants of two matrices [9, 10, 23, 29]. If we can compute the resultant as a determinant of only one matrix whose non-zero entries are forms evaluated at the coefficients of the input polynomials, then we have a *determinantal formula*. Among these cases, the best we can hope for is to have linear forms. In general, determinantal formulas do not exist and it is an open problem to decide when they do.

The matrices appearing in the computation of resultants have a strong structure and we can classify them according to it. For a system $(f_0, \dots, f_n)$, a *Sylvester-type formula* is a matrix that represents a map $(g_0, \dots, g_n) \mapsto \sum_i g_i f_i$. It extends the classical Sylvester matrix and it corresponds to the last map of the Koszul complex of $(f_0, \dots, f_n)$. Another kind of formula is the *Koszul-type formula* that involves the other maps of the Koszul complex. We call the matrices related to this formula *Koszul resultant matrices* [4, 30]. For both formulas, the elements of the matrices are linear polynomials in the coefficients of $(f_0, \dots, f_n)$. Other important resultant matrices include *Bézout-* and *Dixon-type*; we refer to [17] and references therein for details. We consider *Koszul-type determinantal formulas* for mixed multihomogeneous bilinear systems with two supports.

A well-known tool to derive determinantal formulas [4, 11, 15, 16, 30, 37] is the Weyman complex [35], a generalization of the Koszul complex. For an introduction we refer to [36, Sec. 9.2] and [21, Sec. 2.5.C, Sec. 3.4.E]. We follow this approach.

For *unmixed* multihomogeneous systems, that is systems where all the polynomial share the same support, determinantal formulas are well studied, e.g., [5, 10, 11, 25, 33, 36, 37]. On the other hand, when we consider polynomials with different supports, that is *mixed systems*, little is known about determinantal formulas; with the exception of scaled multihomogeneous systems [15], that is when the supports are scaled copies of one of them, and the bivariate tensor-product case [4, 30].

The resultant is also a tool to solve 0-dimensional square polynomial systems $(f_1, \dots, f_n)$. There are different variants, for example by hiding a variable, or using the u-resultant; we refer to [7, Chp. 3] for a general introduction. When a *Sylvester-type formula* is available, we can use the corresponding resultant matrix to obtain the matrix of the multiplication map of a polynomial f_0 in $\mathbb{K}[\boldsymbol{x}]/\langle f_1, \ldots, f_n \rangle$. Then, we can solve the system by computing the eigenvalues and eigenvectors of the latter matrix, e.g., [1, 14]. The eigenvalues correspond to the evaluation of f_0 at every zero of the system. From the eigenvectors we can recover the coordinates of the zeros. To our knowledge similar techniques involving matrices coming from Koszul-type formulas do not exist up to now.

We consider mixed bilinear polynomial systems. On the one hand, this is simplest case of mixed multihomogeneous systems where no resultant formula was known. On the other hand, bilinear, and their generalization multilinear, polynomial systems are common in applications, for example in cryptography [19, 24] and game theory [13]. We refer to [20], see also [32], for computing the roots of unmixed multilinear systems by means of Gröbner bases, and to [16] by using resultants. We refer to [2] for a Gröbner bases approach to solve square mixed multihomogeneous systems.

Our contribution. We introduce a new algorithm to solve square mixed multihomogeneous systems consisting of bilinear polynomials with two different supports. It relies on eigenvalues and eigenvectors computations. Following classic resultant techniques we add a polynomial, f_0, to make the system overdetermined. The polynomial f_0 must be trilinear, as this is simplest one that can separate the roots. Then, we introduce a determinantal formula for the resultant of this overdetermined system. This is the first determinantal formula for a mixed multilinear polynomial system. Using Weyman's complex, we derive a *Koszul-type* formula and compute the resultant as the determinant of a *Koszul resultant matrix.*

We present a general extension of the eigenvalue criterion that works for a general class of formulas (see Def. 4.1), which include the Koszul-type and Sylvester-type formulas as special cases. We consider a square matrix M whose determinant is a multiple of the resultant of a system $(f_0, \ldots, f_n)$. If there is a monomial $\boldsymbol{x}^\sigma$ in f_0 such that we can partition M as $\left[\begin{smallmatrix} M_{1,1} & M_{1,2} \\ M_{2,1} & M_{2,2} \end{smallmatrix}\right]$ where $M_{1,1}$ is invertible, the coefficient of the monomial $\boldsymbol{x}^\sigma$ in f_0 appears solely in the diagonal of $M_{2,2}$ and this diagonal contains only this coefficient, then the evaluations of $\frac{f_0(\boldsymbol{x})}{\boldsymbol{x}^\sigma}$ at the solutions of $(f_1, \ldots, f_n)$, that is $\{\frac{f_0(\boldsymbol{x})}{\boldsymbol{x}^\sigma}|_{\boldsymbol{x}=\alpha} : (\forall i > 0) f_i(\alpha) = 0, \boldsymbol{x}^\sigma|_{\boldsymbol{x}=\alpha} \neq 0\}$, are eigenvalues of the Schur complement of $M_{2,2}$, that is $M_{2,2} - M_{2,1} \cdot M_{1,1}^{-1} \cdot M_{1,2}$.

We extend the eigenvector criteria for these mixed bilinear systems. When M is our *Koszul resultant matrix*, we show how to recover the coordinates of the solutions from the eigenvectors of the Schur complement of $M_{2,2}$. This approach works for systems whose solutions have no multiplicities.

Algorithm 1 summarizes our strategy to solve square 0-dimensional 2-bilinear systems whose solutions have no multiplicities.

2 PRELIMINARIES

Consider $n_x, n_y, n_z \in \mathbb{N}$ and let $\mathcal{P} := \mathbb{P}^{n_x} \times \mathbb{P}^{n_y} \times \mathbb{P}^{n_z}$ be a multiprojective space over an algebraic closed field $\mathbb{K}$ of characteristic 0. Consider $\boldsymbol{x} := \{x_0, \ldots, x_{n_x}\}, \boldsymbol{y} := \{y_0, \ldots, y_{n_y}\}, \boldsymbol{z} := \{z_0, \ldots, z_{n_z}\}$ and let $S_x(d_x) := \mathbb{K}[\boldsymbol{x}]_{d_x}$, $S_y(d_y) := \mathbb{K}[\boldsymbol{y}]_{d_y}$, and $S_z(d_z) := \mathbb{K}[\boldsymbol{z}]_{d_z}$ be the spaces of homogeneous polynomials in variables $\boldsymbol{x}$, $\boldsymbol{y}$ and $\boldsymbol{z}$ and degrees d_x, d_y and d_z, respectively. Let $S(d_x, d_y, d_z) := S_x(d_x) \otimes S_y(d_y) \otimes S_z(d_z)$ be the multihomogeneous polynomials in $\boldsymbol{x}$, $\boldsymbol{y}$, and $\boldsymbol{z}$ of degrees d_x, d_y, and d_z, respectively. We say that the polynomials in $S(d_x, d_y, d_z)$ have multidegree $\boldsymbol{d} := (d_x, d_y, d_z) \in \mathbb{N}_0^3$. To avoid

---

Algorithm 1 `Solve2Bilinear`$((\bar{f}_1, \ldots, \bar{f}_n))$

Input: $(\bar{f}_1, \ldots, \bar{f}_k)$ is a square 2-bilinear system such that $V_{\mathcal{P}}(\bar{f}_1, \ldots, \bar{f}_k)$ is finite and has no multiplicities.

1: $A \leftarrow$ Random linear change of coordinates preserving the structure.

2: $(f_1, \ldots, f_n) \leftarrow (\bar{f}_1 \circ A, \ldots, \bar{f}_n \circ A)$. (Thm. 4.7)

3: $f_0 \leftarrow$ Random trilinear polynomial in $S(1, 1, 1)$.

4: $\left[\begin{smallmatrix} M_{1,1} & M_{1,2} \\ M_{2,1} & M_{2,2} \end{smallmatrix}\right] \leftarrow \Big\{$ Matrix corresponding to $\delta_1((f_0, \ldots, f_n), \boldsymbol{m})$, split wrt the monomial $\boldsymbol{w}^\theta$. (Def. 4.1)

5: $\left\{\left(\frac{f_0}{\boldsymbol{w}^\theta}(\alpha), \bar{v}_\alpha\right)\right\}_\alpha \leftarrow \Big\{$ Set of pairs Eigenvalue-Eigenvector of the Schur complement of $M_{2,2}$. (Thm. 4.2)

6: **for all** $\left(\frac{f_0}{\boldsymbol{w}^\theta}(\alpha), \bar{v}_\alpha\right) \in \left\{\left(\frac{f_0}{\boldsymbol{w}^\theta}(\alpha), \bar{v}_\alpha\right)\right\}_\alpha$ **do**

7: Extract the coordinates α_x, α_y from $\rho_\alpha(\widehat{\boldsymbol{\lambda}_\alpha})$ by recovering it from $\left[\begin{smallmatrix} M_{1,1}^{-1} \cdot M_{2,1} \\ I \end{smallmatrix}\right] \cdot \bar{v}$. (Thm. 4.13)

8: Let $\alpha_z \in \mathbb{P}^{n_z}$ be the unique solution to the linear system given by $\{f_1(\alpha_x, \alpha_y, \boldsymbol{z}) = 0, \ldots, f_n(\alpha_x, \alpha_y, \boldsymbol{z}) = 0\}$, over $\mathbb{K}[\boldsymbol{z}]$.

9: Recover the solution of the system $(\bar{f}_1, \ldots, \bar{f}_n)$, as $A((\alpha_x, \alpha_y, \alpha_z))$.

---

the repetition of the various definitions for x, y, and z, we consider $t \in \{x, y, z\}$. The dual space of $S_t(d_t)$ is $S_t(d_t)^*$. For $\sigma_t \in \mathbb{N}_0^{n_t+1}$, we define $\boldsymbol{t}^{\sigma_t} := \prod_{i=0}^{n_t} t_i^{\sigma_{t,i}}$. Then $\mathcal{A}(d_t) := \{\sigma_t : \boldsymbol{t}^{\sigma_t} \in S_t(d_t)\}$ is the set of the exponents of all the monomials of degree d_t in $\boldsymbol{t}$ and $\mathcal{A}(\boldsymbol{d}) := \mathcal{A}(d_x) \times \mathcal{A}(d_y) \times \mathcal{A}(d_z)$ is the set of all the exponents of the monomials of multidegree $\boldsymbol{d}$. If $\boldsymbol{\sigma} = (\sigma_x, \sigma_y, \sigma_z) \in \mathcal{A}(\boldsymbol{d})$, then $\boldsymbol{w}^{\boldsymbol{\sigma}} := \boldsymbol{x}^{\sigma_x} \boldsymbol{y}^{\sigma_y} \boldsymbol{z}^{\sigma_z}$. Let $n := n_x + n_y + n_z$. For multidegrees $\boldsymbol{d} = (\boldsymbol{d}_0, \ldots, \boldsymbol{d}_n) \in (\mathbb{N}_0^3)^{n+1}$, we consider square multihomogeneous polynomial system

$$\boldsymbol{f} := (f_1, \ldots, f_n) \in S(\boldsymbol{d}_1) \times \cdots \times S(\boldsymbol{d}_n) \ . \tag{1}$$

Let $V_{\mathcal{P}}(\boldsymbol{f})$ be the set of solutions of $\boldsymbol{f}$ over $\mathcal{P}$. The multihomogeneous Bézout bound (MHB) [34] bounds the number of isolated solutions of $\boldsymbol{f}$ over $\mathcal{P}$ [3, 26, 27]. The bound is attained for any *generic* square system $\boldsymbol{f}$. It is the mixed volume of the polytopes $\mathcal{A}(\boldsymbol{d}_1), \ldots, \mathcal{A}(\boldsymbol{d}_n)$ [7, Chp. 7] and appears as the coefficient of the monomial $\prod_{t \in \{x,y,z\}} X_t^{n_t}$ in $\prod_{j=1}^n \sum_{t \in \{x,y,z\}} \boldsymbol{d}_{j,t} X_t$ [31].

In the sequel we consider overdetermined systems which we construct by adding an $f_0 \in S(\boldsymbol{d}_0)$ to $\boldsymbol{f}$, that is,

$$\boldsymbol{f}_0 := (f_0, f_1, \ldots, f_n) \in S(\boldsymbol{d}_0) \times \cdots \times S(\boldsymbol{d}_n) \ . \tag{2}$$

Typically, we will consider $\boldsymbol{d}_0 = (1, 1, 1)$, as we would like f_0 to be as simple as possible while still depending on all the variables.

2.1 Multihomogeneous sparse resultant

The multihomogeneous sparse resultant of $\boldsymbol{f}_0$ is a polynomial in the coefficients of the polynomials in $\boldsymbol{f}_0$, which vanishes if and only if the system has a solution over $\mathcal{P}$. Following [7], for fixed $\boldsymbol{d}_0 \ldots \boldsymbol{d}_n \in \mathbb{N}_0^3$, we introduce a set of variables $\boldsymbol{u}_i := \{u_{i,\sigma}\}_{\sigma \in \mathcal{A}(\boldsymbol{d}_i)}$, for $0 \leq i \leq n$, and $\boldsymbol{u} := \{\boldsymbol{u}_0, \ldots, \boldsymbol{u}_n\}$. Given $P \in \mathbb{K}[\boldsymbol{u}]$, we let $P(\boldsymbol{f}_0)$ denote the value obtained by replacing each variable $u_{i,\sigma}$ with the coefficient of the monomial $\boldsymbol{w}^\sigma$ in the polynomial f_i of $\boldsymbol{f}_0$. In this way we obtain polynomials over the coefficients of a polynomial system. The "universal" system $F_{\boldsymbol{d}_0,\ldots,\boldsymbol{d}_n} \in \mathbb{K}[\boldsymbol{u}_0][\boldsymbol{x}, \boldsymbol{y}, \boldsymbol{z}] \times \cdots \times \mathbb{K}[\boldsymbol{u}_n][\boldsymbol{x}, \boldsymbol{y}, \boldsymbol{z}]$ is

$$F_{\boldsymbol{d}_0,\ldots,\boldsymbol{d}_n} := \Big(\sum_{\sigma \in \mathcal{A}(\boldsymbol{d}_0)} u_{0,\sigma} \boldsymbol{w}^\sigma, \ \ldots, \ \sum_{\sigma \in \mathcal{A}(\boldsymbol{d}_n)} u_{n,\sigma} \boldsymbol{w}^\sigma \Big). \tag{3}$$

Here the variables of $\boldsymbol{u}$ parametrize the systems described by polynomials in $S(\boldsymbol{d}_0) \times \cdots \times S(\boldsymbol{d}_n)$ over $\mathbb{K}^{\#\mathcal{A}(\boldsymbol{d}_0)} \times \cdots \times \mathbb{K}^{\#\mathcal{A}(\boldsymbol{d}_n)}$.

Consider the set of all tuples of $n+1$ multihomogeneous polynomials together with their common solutions over $\mathcal{P}$, $\{(f_0,\dots,f_n,\alpha)\in S(\boldsymbol{d}_0)\times\cdots\times S(\boldsymbol{d}_n)\times\mathcal{P} : (\forall 0\le i\le n)\, f_i(\alpha)=0\}$. The projection of this set on $S(\boldsymbol{d}_0)\times\cdots\times S(\boldsymbol{d}_n)$ is the set of overdetermined systems with common solutions in $\mathcal{P}$, $\{(f_0,\dots,f_n)\in S(\boldsymbol{d}_0)\times\cdots\times S(\boldsymbol{d}_n) : V_{\mathcal{P}}(f_0,\dots,f_n)\neq\emptyset\}$. By the Projective Extension Theorem [6, Chp. 8 Sec. 5], this projection is a closed set under the Zariski topology and it forms an irreducible hypersurface over the vector space $S(\boldsymbol{d}_0)\times\cdots\times S(\boldsymbol{d}_n)$ [21, Chp. 8]. More formally, there is an irreducible polynomial $\mathrm{Res}_{\mathcal{P}}(\boldsymbol{d}_0,\dots,\boldsymbol{d}_n)\in\mathbb{Z}[\boldsymbol{u}]$ such that for all the systems $\boldsymbol{f_0}\in S(\boldsymbol{d}_0)\times\cdots\times S(\boldsymbol{d}_n)$, $V_{\mathcal{P}}(\boldsymbol{f_0})\neq\emptyset$ if and only if $\mathrm{Res}_{\mathcal{P}}(\boldsymbol{d}_0,\dots,\boldsymbol{d}_n)(\boldsymbol{f_0})=0$. This polynomial is the sparse resultant over $\mathcal{P}$ for multihomogeneous systems of multidegrees $(\boldsymbol{d}_0,\dots,\boldsymbol{d}_n)$.

The resultant $\mathrm{Res}_{\mathcal{P}}(\boldsymbol{d}_0,\dots,\boldsymbol{d}_n)$ is itself a multihomogeneous polynomial, homogeneous in each block of variables $\boldsymbol{u}_i$. For each i, its degree with respect to $\boldsymbol{u}_i$ is $\mathrm{MHB}(\boldsymbol{d}_0,\dots,\boldsymbol{d}_{i-1},\boldsymbol{d}_{i+1},\dots,\boldsymbol{d}_n)$.

2.2 2-bilinear systems

A square *2-bilinear system* of type $(n_x,n_y,n_z\ ;\ r,s)$ is a bilinear system $\boldsymbol{f}:=(f_1,\dots,f_n)$ with two different supports, namely $f_1,\dots,f_r\in S(1,1,0)$ and $f_{r+1},\dots,f_n\in S(1,0,1)$, such that $n=r+s$, $n_y\le r$ and $n_z\le s$. It holds $\mathrm{MHB}(\boldsymbol{f})=\binom{r}{n_y}\binom{n-r}{n_z}$.

EXAMPLE 2.1. *The following (Eq. (4)) is a square 2-bilinear system of type* $(1,1,1\ ;\ 2,1)$ *and has two solutions over* $\mathcal{P}$, *namely* $\alpha_1:=(1{:}1\ ;\ 1{:}1\ ;\ 1{:}1)$ *and* $\alpha_2:=(1{:}3\ ;\ 1{:}2\ ;\ 1{:}3)$.

$$\begin{cases} f_1 := 7x_0y_0 - 8x_0y_1 - x_1y_0 + 2x_1y_1 \\ f_2 := -5x_0y_0 + 7x_0y_1 - x_1y_0 - x_1y_1 \\ f_3 := -6x_0z_0 + 9x_0z_1 - x_1z_0 - 2x_1z_1 \end{cases} . \tag{4}$$

Consider the trilinear $f_0\in S(1,1,1)$. We refer to the systems $\boldsymbol{f_0}:=(f_0,f_1,\dots,f_n)$ as overdetermined 2-bilinear systems. We can also consider f_0 in $S(1,1,0)$, $S(1,0,1)$, $S(1,0,0)$, $S(0,1,0)$ and $S(0,0,1)$. We work with a trilinear f_0 because in the other cases it is not always possible to separate all the solutions of $V_{\mathcal{P}}(\boldsymbol{f})$.

EXAMPLE 2.2 (CONT.). *Consider the overdetermined 2-bilinear system* $\boldsymbol{f_0}:=(f_0,f_1,f_2,f_3)$, *where*

$$\begin{aligned} f_0 &:= 3\,x_0y_0z_0 - x_0y_0z_1 - 4\,x_0y_1z_0 + 2\,x_0y_1z_1 \\ &\quad + x_1y_0z_0 + 2\,x_1y_0z_1 + 2\,x_1y_1z_0 - 2\,x_1y_1z_1. \end{aligned}$$

In the following, we use $\boldsymbol{F}^{(2)}$ to denote the "universal" system of overdetermined 2-bilinear systems (see Sec. 2.1). Similarly, we use $\mathrm{Res}^{(2)}_{\mathcal{P}}$, for the resultant of the "universal" system $\boldsymbol{F}^{(2)}$.

LEMMA 2.3. *Let* $\mathrm{MHB}(\boldsymbol{f})=\binom{r}{n_y}\binom{s}{n_z}$. *The degree of* $\mathrm{Res}^{(2)}_{\mathcal{P}}$ *is*

$$\mu := (n_x+1)\,\mathrm{MHB}(\boldsymbol{f})\,\frac{r\cdot s - n_y\cdot n_z + r + s + 1}{(r-n_y+1)(s-n_z+1)} . \tag{5}$$

3 DETERMINANTAL FORMULAS FOR 2-BILINEAR SYSTEMS

A complex $K_\bullet$ is a sequence of modules $\{K_v\}_{v\in\mathbb{Z}}$ together with homomorphisms $\delta_v : K_v \to K_{v-1}$, such that $(\forall v\in\mathbb{Z})\ \mathrm{Im}(\delta_v)\subseteq\mathrm{Ker}(\delta_{v-1})$, i.e., $\delta_v\circ\delta_{v-1}=0$. We say that the complex is exact if $(\forall v\in\mathbb{Z})\ \mathrm{Im}(\delta_v)=\mathrm{Ker}(\delta_{v-1})$. A complex is bounded when there are two constants a and b such that for every $v<a$ or $b<v$, it holds $K_v=0$. If all the K_v are finite dimensional free-modules, then we can choose a basis of them and we can represent the maps δ_v using matrices. Under certain assumptions (see [21, App. A]) given a bounded complex of finite dimensional free-modules we can define its determinant. It is the quotient of minors of the matrices of δ_v and it is not zero if and only if the complex is exact. If there are only two non-zero modules of the same dimensions in the complex (that is all the other modules are the zero module), the determinant of the complex reduces to the determinant of the (matrix of the) map between these modules.

The Weyman Complex [35–37] of a multihomogeneous system $\boldsymbol{f}$ is a bounded complex that is exact if and only if the sparse resultant of the system $\boldsymbol{f}$ does not vanish [36, Thm. 9.1.2]. The determinant of the complex is a power of the resultant [36, Prop. 9.1.3]. When all the multidegrees are bigger than zero, the determinant of this complex is a non-zero constant multiple of the sparse resultant [21, Thm. 3.4.11]. If the Weyman Complex only involves two non-zero modules, the resultant of the corresponding system is the determinant of the map between these modules, and it has a determinantal formula.

Let $\boldsymbol{f_0}:=(f_0,f_1,\dots,f_n)$ be an overdetermined 2-bilinear system. Consider $E:=\mathbb{K}^{n+1}$ and its canonical basis $e_0,\dots,e_n$. Given a set $I\subset\{0,\dots,n\}$, we define $\boldsymbol{e}_I := e_{I_1}\wedge\cdots\wedge e_{I_{\#I}}$ as the exterior product of the elements $e_{I_1},\dots,e_{I_{\#I}}$. As the exterior product is antisymmetric, that is $e_i\wedge e_j=-e_j\wedge e_i$, when we write $e_{I_1}\wedge\cdots\wedge e_{I_{\#I}}$ we assume that $(\forall i)\ I_i<I_{i+1}$. Let $\bigwedge_{a,b,c} E$ be the vector space over $\mathbb{K}$ generated by $\{\boldsymbol{e}_{K\cup I\cup J} : K\subset\{0\}, I\subset\{1,\dots,r\}, J\subset\{r+1,\dots,n\}, \#I=a, \#J=b, \#K=c\}$.

For a *degree vector* $\boldsymbol{m}\in\mathbb{Z}^3$, the Weyman complex is $K_\bullet(\boldsymbol{f_0},\boldsymbol{m})$. Each module of the complex is $K_v(\boldsymbol{m}) := \bigoplus_{p=0}^{n+1} K_{v,p}(\boldsymbol{m})$, where

$$K_{v,p}(\boldsymbol{m}) := \bigoplus_{\substack{a+b+c=p\\ 0\le a\le r\\ 0\le b\le s\\ 0\le c\le 1}} H^{p-v}_{\mathcal{P}}(\boldsymbol{m}-(p,p-b,p-a))\otimes\bigwedge_{a,b,c}E,$$

and $H^q_{\mathcal{P}}(\boldsymbol{m}')$ is the q-th cohomology of $\mathcal{P}$ with coefficients in the sheaf $\mathcal{O}(\boldsymbol{m}')$, and the space of global sections is $H^0_{\mathcal{P}}(\boldsymbol{m}')$ [22]. Note that the terms $K_{v,p}(\boldsymbol{m})$ do not depend on $\boldsymbol{f_0}$ [37, Prop. 2.1]. Since $\mathcal{P}$ is a product of projective spaces, by Künneth's formula

$$H^{p-v}_{\mathcal{P}}\left(m'_x,m'_y,m'_z\right)\cong\bigotimes_{t\in\{x,y,z\}} H^{j_t}_{\mathbb{P}^{n_t}}(m'_t), \tag{6}$$

where $j_x+j_y+j_z=p-v$. By Serre's duality [22, Ch.III,Thm. 5.1] we have the identifications:

PROPOSITION 3.1. *For each* $t\in\{x,y,z\}$, $m'_t\in\mathbb{Z}$, *it holds (1)* $H^0_{\mathbb{P}^{n_t}}(m'_t)\cong S_t(m'_t)$ *if* $m'_t\ge 0$, *(2)* $H^{n_t}_{\mathbb{P}^{n_t}}(m'_t)\cong S_t(-m'_t-1-n_t)^*$ *if* $m'_t<n_t$, *where "∗" denotes the dual space, and (3)* $H^q_{\mathbb{P}^{n_t}}(m'_t)\cong 0$, *of all other values of* q *and* m_t.

As a corollary from Eq. (6), for each $t\in\{x,y,z\}$, $j_t\in\{0,n_t\}$. Moreover, we can identify dual complexes.

PROPOSITION 3.2 ([36, THM. 5.1.4]). *Let* $\boldsymbol{m}$ *and* $\boldsymbol{m}'$ *be degree vectors such that* $\boldsymbol{m}+\boldsymbol{m}'=(n_y+n_z, n_x+n_z-s, n_x+n_y-r)$. *Then,* $K_v(\boldsymbol{m})\cong K_{1-v}(\boldsymbol{m}')^*$ *for all* $v\in\mathbb{Z}$ *and* $K_\bullet(\boldsymbol{f_0},\boldsymbol{m})$ *is dual to* $K_\bullet(\boldsymbol{f_0},\boldsymbol{m}')$.

3.1 Degree vectors and determinantal formulas

If $K_1(\boldsymbol{m})$, $K_0(\boldsymbol{m})$ are the only non-zero modules in the Weyman complex $K_\bullet(f_0, \boldsymbol{m})$, then the determinant of the complex is the determinant of the map, between them, $\delta_1(f_0, \boldsymbol{m})$. In this case, we have a determinantal formula for the resultant. In the following, when it is clear from the context, we write δ_1 instead of $\delta_1(f_0, \boldsymbol{m})$.

THEOREM 3.3. *Let f_0 be a 2-bilinear overdetermined system of type $(n_x, n_y, n_z; r, s)$, with $f_0 \in S(1,1,1)$. The degree vectors (1) $(n_y - 1, -1, n_x + n_y - r + 1)$, (2) $(n_z + 1, n_x + n_z - s + 1, -1)$, (3) $(n_z - 1, n_x + n_z - s + 1, -1)$, (4) $(n_y + 1, -1, n_x + n_y - r + 1)$ lead to determinantal Weyman complexes for $\operatorname{Res}^{(2)}_{\mathcal{P}}(f_0)$.*

OBSERVATION 3.4. *The four degree vectors of Thm. 3.3 provide a single matrix formula. Vector 1 (resp. 2) is obtained from 3 (resp. 4) by exchanging the variables $\boldsymbol{y}$ and $\boldsymbol{z}$. By Prop. 3.2, we can see that 1,2 and 3, 4 are dual pairs, yielding the same matrix transposed.*

PROOF. We consider only the first degree vector $\boldsymbol{m} := (n_y - 1, -1, n_x + n_y - r + 1)$. By Obs.3.4, the other cases are similar.

First, we show that the complex has only two non-zero terms. Since $K_v(\boldsymbol{m}) := \bigoplus_{p=0}^{n+1} K_{v,p}(\boldsymbol{m})$, and in view of Eq. (6), for each $K_{v,p}(\boldsymbol{m})$, we have to consider sums $\sum_{t\in\{x,y,z\}} j_t = p - v$. By Prop. 3.1, if $j_t \notin \{0, n_t\}$, then $K_{v,p} = 0$. The remaining cases are summarized in the following table and their analysis follows.

j_x	j_y	j_z	Case
0	0	0	(1)
n_x	0	0	(1)

j_x	j_y	j_z	Case
0	0	n_z	(1)
n_x	0	n_z	(1)

j_x	j_y	j_z	Case
0	n_y	n_z	(2)
n_x	n_y	n_z	(2)

j_x	j_y	j_z	Case
0	n_y	0	(3)
n_x	n_y	0	(4)

Case 1: $j_y = 0$. The second term in the tensor product of $K_{v,p}$ is $H^0_{\mathbb{P}^{n_y}}(-1 - a - c) \cong S_y(-1 - a - c)$, by Prop. 3.1. As $a, c \geq 0$, $S_y(-1 - a - c) = 0$. Hence, $K_{v,p} = 0$.
Case 2: $j_z = n_z$. The third term in the tensor product of $K_{v,p}$ is $H^{n_z}_{\mathbb{P}^{n_z}}(n_x + n_y - r + 1 - b - c) \cong S_z(-(n_x + n_y + n_z) + r - 2 + b + c)^*$, by Prop. 3.1. As $n_x + n_y + n_z = r + s$, $-(n_x + n_y + n_z) + r - 2 + b + c = -s - 2 + b + c < 0$ because $b \leq s$ and $c \leq 1$. Hence, $H^{n_z}_{\mathbb{P}^{n_z}}(n_x + n_y - r + 1 - b - c) = 0$ and so $K_{v,p} = 0$.
Case 3: $j_x = 0, j_y = n_y$. As $j_y = n_y$, the second term in the tensor product $K_{v,p}$ is $H^{n_y}_{\mathbb{P}^{n_y}}(-1 - a - c) \cong S_y(a + c - n_y)^*$, by Prop. 3.1. This module is not zero iff $a + c \geq n_y$. Consider the first term in the tensor product, $H^0_{\mathbb{P}^{n_x}}(n_y - 1 - p) \cong S_x(n_y - 1 - p)$. If $a + c \geq n_y$, as $p = a + b + c$, then $n_y - 1 - p \leq -1 - b < 0$. Hence, either $H^{n_y}_{\mathbb{P}^{n_y}}(-1 - a - c) = 0$ or $H^0_{\mathbb{P}^{n_x}}(n_y - 1 - p) = 0$, and so $K_{v,p} = 0$.
Case 4: $j_x = 0, j_y = n_y, j_z = 0$. The first term in the tensor product $K_{v,p}$ is $H^{n_x}_{\mathbb{P}^{n_x}}(n_y - 1 - p) \cong S_x(-n_x - n_y + p) = S_x(v)$, as $p - v = j_x + j_y + j_z = n_x + n_y$. Hence, $H^{n_x}_{\mathbb{P}^{n_x}}(n_y - 1 - p) \neq 0$ iff $v \geq 0$. As $j_z = 0$ the third term in the tensor product of $K_{v,p}$ is $H^0_{\mathbb{P}^{n_z}}(n_x + n_y - r + 1 - b - c) \cong S_z(n_x + n_y - r + 1 - b - c)$. This term is not zero iff $n_x + n_y - r + 1 \geq b + c$. Moreover, as $p = a + b + c$, $v = a + b + c - n_x - n_y$. Then, if $H^0_{\mathbb{P}^{n_z}}(n_x + n_y - r + 1 - b - c) \neq 0$, then $v \leq a - r + 1$. By definition $a \leq r$, so $v \leq 1$.

We deduce that all other modules apart from $K_{1,n_x+n_y+1}(\boldsymbol{m})$ and $K_{0,n_x+n_y}(\boldsymbol{m})$ are equal to zero. Hence, by [36, Prop. 9.1.3] the determinant of (a matrix expressing) δ_1 is a power [1] of $\operatorname{Res}^{(2)}_{\mathcal{P}}(f_0)$.

[1]The exponent is known to be one for any very ample supports [21], i.e. $(\forall i, j)\ \boldsymbol{d}_{i,j} > 0$. However, due to the zero degrees, 2-bilinear supports are ample but not very ample.

To conclude, it suffices to show that the exponent is equal to one. Due to the form $\delta_1 : K_{1,q+1}(\boldsymbol{m}) \to K_{0,q}(\boldsymbol{m})$, the elements in a matrix that represents δ_1 have degree $(q+1) - q = 1$ as polynomials in $\mathbb{K}[\boldsymbol{u}]$ [36, Prop. 5.2.4]. Therefore, the exponent is one iff the degree of the resultant is equal to the dimension of the matrix of

$$K_\bullet(f_0, \boldsymbol{m}) : 0 \to K_{1,n_x+n_y+1}(\boldsymbol{m}) \xrightarrow{\delta_1} K_{0,n_x+n_y}(\boldsymbol{m}) \to 0\,.$$

We analyze the possible values for (a, b, c) to compute the dimension. Following **Case 4**, if $H^0_{\mathbb{P}^{n_z}}(n_x + n_y - r + 1 - b - c) \neq 0$, then the possible values for a are $v + r - 1 \leq a \leq r$, for $v \in \{0, 1\}$. As $b = p - a - c$, and $0 \leq c \leq 1$, we enumerate all the options for (a, b, c) and write our modules as

$$\begin{aligned} K_1 = K_{1,n_x+n_y+1} &\cong L_{1,1} \oplus L_{1,2} \\ &= \Big(S_x(1)^* \otimes S_y(r - n_y)^* \otimes S_z(0) \otimes \bigwedge_{r,s-n_z+1,0} E\Big) \oplus \\ &\quad \Big(S_x(1)^* \otimes S_y(r - n_y + 1)^* \otimes S_z(0) \otimes \bigwedge_{r,s-n_z,1} E\Big). \end{aligned} \tag{7}$$

$$\begin{aligned} K_0 = K_{0,n_x+n_y} &\cong L_{0,1} \oplus L_{0,2} \oplus L_{0,3} \oplus L_{0,4} \\ &= \Big(S_x(0)^* \otimes S_y(r - n_y - 1)^* \otimes S_z(0) \otimes \bigwedge_{r-1,s-n_z+1,0} E\Big) \oplus \\ &\quad \Big(S_x(0)^* \otimes S_y(r - n_y)^* \otimes S_z(1) \otimes \bigwedge_{r,s-n_z,0} E\Big) \oplus \\ &\quad \Big(S_x(0)^* \otimes S_y(r - n_y)^* \otimes S_z(0) \otimes \bigwedge_{r-1,s-n_z,1} E\Big) \oplus \\ &\quad \Big(S_x(0)^* \otimes S_y(r - n_y + 1)^* \otimes S_z(1) \otimes \bigwedge_{r,s-n_z-1,1} E\Big). \end{aligned} \tag{8}$$

To compute their dimensions we notice that $\dim\left(\bigwedge_{a,b,c} E\right) = \binom{r}{a}\binom{s}{b}$, and we recall that $\dim S_t(q) = \dim S_t(q)^* = \binom{n_t+q}{q}$. The calculation leads to $\dim(K_1) = \dim(K_0) = \mu$, see Eq. (5). □

The four degree vectors of Thm. 3.3 are not the only ones that lead to determinantal formulas. We are interested in them because, experimentally, there are no Sylvester-type formulas and only these degree vectors lead to Koszul-type formulas [16, 30].

3.2 Construction of the map $\delta_1(f_0, \boldsymbol{m})$

Following [36, Sec. 5.5], we construct the map $\delta_1(f_0, \boldsymbol{m}) : K_1(\boldsymbol{m}) \to K_0(\boldsymbol{m})$. By Obs. 3.4, we only consider $\boldsymbol{m} = (n_y - 1, -1, n_x + n_y - r + 1)$.

In the proof of Thm. 3.3 we saw that the map $\delta_1(F^{(2)}, \boldsymbol{m})$ has linear coefficients in $\mathbb{K}[\boldsymbol{u}]$. As it is a linear map between free modules, it is enough to define it over a basis of K_0 and K_1.

First we introduce some notation. Let $t \in \{x, y, z\}$. For each $\sigma_t \in \mathcal{A}(d)$, $d \in \mathbb{N}_0$, consider $\boldsymbol{\partial t}^{\sigma_t} \in S_t(d)^*$ such that $\boldsymbol{\partial t}^{\sigma_t}(\sum c_{\theta_t} \boldsymbol{t}^{\theta_t}) = c_{\sigma_t}$. The set $\{\boldsymbol{\partial t}^{\sigma_t} : \sigma_t \in \mathcal{A}(d)\}$ forms a basis of $S_t(d)^*$. The map $\star_t : \mathbb{K}[\boldsymbol{t}] \times \mathbb{K}[\boldsymbol{t}]^* \to \mathbb{K}[\boldsymbol{t}]^*$, acts as $(\boldsymbol{t}^{\theta_t}, \boldsymbol{\partial t}^{\sigma_t}) \mapsto \boldsymbol{t}^{\theta_t} \star_t \boldsymbol{\partial t}^{\sigma_t}$, where

$$\boldsymbol{t}^{\theta_t} \star_t \boldsymbol{\partial t}^{\sigma_t} = \begin{cases} \boldsymbol{\partial t}^{\sigma_t - \theta_t} & \text{if } (\forall i,\ 0 \leq i \leq n_t)\ \sigma_{t,i} \geq \theta_{t,i} \\ 0 & \text{otherwise} \end{cases}. \tag{9}$$

This map is graded, that is, for each $(d, \bar{d}) \in \mathbb{Z}^2$, it maps the elements in $S_t(d) \times S_t(\bar{d})^*$ to $S_t(\bar{d} - d)^*$. We will denote the map by "$\star$" when the variable is clear from the context. We define the graded map ψ,

$$\begin{aligned} \psi : (\mathbb{K}[\boldsymbol{x}]^* \otimes \mathbb{K}[\boldsymbol{y}]^* \otimes \mathbb{K}[\boldsymbol{z}]) \times (\mathbb{K}[\boldsymbol{x}] \otimes \mathbb{K}[\boldsymbol{y}] \otimes \mathbb{K}[\boldsymbol{z}]) \\ \to (\mathbb{K}[\boldsymbol{x}]^* \otimes \mathbb{K}[\boldsymbol{y}]^* \otimes \mathbb{K}[\boldsymbol{z}]) \end{aligned} \tag{10}$$

$$\psi(\partial x^{\sigma_x} \otimes \partial y^{\sigma_y} \otimes z^{\sigma_z}, x^{\theta_x} \otimes y^{\theta_y} \otimes z^{\theta_z}) := (x^{\theta_x} \star \partial x^{\sigma_x}) \otimes (y^{\theta_y} \star \partial y^{\sigma_y}) \otimes (z^{\theta_z+\sigma_z})$$

As $\delta_1(\boldsymbol{f_0}, \boldsymbol{m}) : K_1 \longrightarrow K_0$ is linear and $K_1 \cong L_{1,1} \oplus L_{1,2}$, we define the map over a basis of $L_{1,1}$ and $L_{1,2}$. For each $\boldsymbol{\ell} \in S_x(1)^* \otimes S_y(r - n_y)^* \otimes S_z(0)$ and $\boldsymbol{e}_I \in \bigwedge_{r,s-n_z+1,0} E$, we consider $\boldsymbol{\ell} \otimes \boldsymbol{e}_I \in L_{1,1}$ and

$$\delta_1(f_0, \boldsymbol{m})(\boldsymbol{\ell} \otimes \boldsymbol{e}_I) := \sum_{i=1}^{n_x+n_y+1} (-1)^{i-1} \psi(\boldsymbol{\ell}, f_{I_i}) \otimes \boldsymbol{e}_{I \setminus \{I_i\}} \in L_{0,1} \oplus L_{0,2}.$$

For each $\boldsymbol{\ell} \in S_x(1)^* \otimes S_y(r - n_y + 1)^* \otimes S_z(0)$ and $\boldsymbol{e}_J \in \bigwedge_{r,s-n_z,1} E$, we consider $\boldsymbol{\ell} \otimes \boldsymbol{e}_J \in L_{1,2}$ and

$$\delta_1(f_0, \boldsymbol{m})(\boldsymbol{\ell} \otimes \boldsymbol{e}_J) := \sum_{i=1}^{n_x+n_y+1} (-1)^{i-1} \psi(\boldsymbol{\ell}, f_{J_i}) \otimes \boldsymbol{e}_{J \setminus \{J_i\}} \in L_{0,2} \oplus L_{0,3} \oplus L_{0,4}.$$

The map $\delta_1(\boldsymbol{f_0}, \boldsymbol{m})$ corresponds to a Koszul-type formula, involving multiplication and dual multiplication maps. The matrix that represents this map is a Koszul resultant matrix [4, 30].

Example 3.5 (Cont.). *In this case,* $\boldsymbol{m} = (0, -1, 1)$. *We consider the following monomial basis,*

	Basis of K_1 *(Columns)*		*Basis of* K_0 *(Rows)*
(A)	$\partial x_0 \partial y_1^2 \boldsymbol{e}_{\{0,1,2\}}$	(I)	$\boldsymbol{e}_{\{1,3\}}$
(B)	$\partial x_1 \partial y_0^2 \boldsymbol{e}_{\{0,1,2\}}$	(II)	$\boldsymbol{e}_{\{2,3\}}$
(C)	$\partial x_1 \partial y_1^2 \boldsymbol{e}_{\{0,1,2\}}$	(III)	$\partial y_0 \boldsymbol{e}_{\{0,1\}}$
(D)	$\partial x_0 \partial y_0 \boldsymbol{e}_{\{1,2,3\}}$	(IV)	$\partial y_1 \boldsymbol{e}_{\{0,1\}}$
(E)	$\partial x_0 \partial y_1 \boldsymbol{e}_{\{1,2,3\}}$	(V)	$\partial y_0 \boldsymbol{e}_{\{0,2\}}$
(F)	$\partial x_1 \partial y_0 \boldsymbol{e}_{\{1,2,3\}}$	(VI)	$\partial y_1 \boldsymbol{e}_{\{0,2\}}$
(G)	$\partial x_1 \partial y_1 \boldsymbol{e}_{\{1,2,3\}}$	(VII)	$\partial y_0 z_1 \boldsymbol{e}_{\{1,2\}}$
(H)	$\partial x_0 \partial y_0 \partial y_1 \boldsymbol{e}_{\{0,1,2\}}$	(VIII)	$\partial y_1 z_1 \boldsymbol{e}_{\{1,2\}}$
(I)	$\partial x_0 \partial y_0^2 \boldsymbol{e}_{\{0,1,2\}}$	(IX)	$\partial y_0 z_0 \boldsymbol{e}_{\{1,2\}}$
(J)	$\partial x_1 \partial y_0 \partial y_1 \boldsymbol{e}_{\{0,1,2\}}$	(X)	$\partial y_1 z_0 \boldsymbol{e}_{\{1,2\}}$

The following matrix represents $\delta_1(\boldsymbol{f_0}, \boldsymbol{m})$ *wrt the basis above.*

	(A)	(B)	(C)	(D)	(E)	(F)	(G)	(H)	(I)	(J)
(I)	0	0	0	5	−7	1	1	0	0	0
(II)	0	0	0	7	−8	−1	2	0	0	0
(III)	0	−1	0	0	0	0	0	−1	−5	7
(IV)	7	0	−1	0	0	0	0	−1	0	−5
(V)	0	1	0	0	0	0	0	−2	−7	8
(VI)	8	0	−2	0	0	0	0	1	0	−7
(VII)	0	2	0	9	0	−2	0	−2	−1	2
(VIII)	2	0	−2	0	9	0	−2	2	0	−1
(IX)	0	1	0	−6	0	−1	0	2	3	−4
(X)	−4	0	2	0	−6	0	−1	1	0	3

The 2×2 *splitting illustrated above will be used in the next section.*

4 SOLVING 2-BILINEAR SYSTEMS

Consider a 0-dimensional system $f_1, \dots, f_n \in \mathbb{K}[\boldsymbol{x}]$. A common strategy for solving is to work over $\mathbb{K}[\boldsymbol{x}]/\langle f_1, \dots, f_n \rangle$, which is a finite a dimensional vector space over $\mathbb{K}$. We fix a monomial basis, choose $f_0 \in \mathbb{K}[\boldsymbol{x}]$, and compute the matrix that represents the multiplication by f_0 in the quotient ring. Its eigenvalues are the evaluations of f_0 at the solutions. For a suitable basis, from the eigenvectors we can recover the coordinates of all the solutions [7, 8, 12]. To compute these matrices we can use the Sylvester-type formulas [1, 7, 14]. We extend these techniques to a general family of matrices, that includes the Koszul resultant matrix (Sec. 3.2).

4.1 Eigenvalues criteria

In this section we assume fixed multidegrees $\boldsymbol{d}_0, \dots, \boldsymbol{d}_n$.

Definition 4.1 (property Π_θ). *Given* $\theta \in \mathcal{A}(\boldsymbol{d}_0)$ *and a matrix* $M := \begin{bmatrix} M_{1,1} & M_{1,2} \\ M_{2,1} & M_{2,2} \end{bmatrix} \in \mathbb{K}[\boldsymbol{u}]^{\mathcal{K} \times \mathcal{K}}$ *(Sec. 2.1), we say that* M *has the property* $\Pi_\theta(\boldsymbol{d}_0, \dots, \boldsymbol{d}_n)$*, or simply* Π_θ*, when:*

- $Res_{\mathcal{P}}(\boldsymbol{d}_0, \dots, \boldsymbol{d}_n)$ *divides* $\det(M)$*,*
- *the submatrix* $M_{2,2}$ *is square and its diagonal entries equal to* $u_{0,\boldsymbol{\theta}}$*, and*
- *the coefficient* $u_{0,\boldsymbol{\theta}}$ *does not appear anywhere in* M *expect from the diagonal of* $M_{2,2}$*.*

For a system $\boldsymbol{f_0}$, Eq. (2), let $M(\boldsymbol{f_0})$ be the specialization of M at $\boldsymbol{f_0}$ (see Sec. 2.1). If $M_{1,1}(\boldsymbol{f_0})$ is invertible, then the Schur complement of $M_{2,2}(\boldsymbol{f_0})$ is $M_{2,2}(\boldsymbol{f_0}) - M_{2,1}(\boldsymbol{f_0}) \cdot (M_{1,1}(\boldsymbol{f_0}))^{-1} \cdot M_{1,2}(\boldsymbol{f_0})$. To simplify, we write $(M_{2,2} - M_{2,1} \cdot M_{1,1}^{-1} \cdot M_{1,2})(\boldsymbol{f_0})$.

Theorem 4.2. *Consider* $\theta \in \mathcal{A}(\boldsymbol{d}_0)$ *and a matrix* $M \in \mathbb{K}[\boldsymbol{u}]^{\mathcal{K} \times \mathcal{K}}$ *such that* Π_θ *holds (Def. 4.1). Assume a system* $\boldsymbol{f_0}$*, Eq.(2), such that the specialization* $M_{1,1}(\boldsymbol{f_0})$ *is non-singular. Then, for all* $\alpha \in V_{\mathcal{P}}(\boldsymbol{f})$ *such that* $\boldsymbol{w}^{\boldsymbol{\theta}}(\alpha) \neq 0$, $\frac{f_0}{\boldsymbol{w}^{\boldsymbol{\theta}}}(\alpha)$ *is an eigenvalue of the Schur complement of* $M_{2,2}(\boldsymbol{f_0})$.

Proof. The idea of the proof is as follows: For each $\alpha \in V_{\mathcal{P}}(\boldsymbol{f})$, Eq. (1), we consider a system $\boldsymbol{g_0}$, slightly different from $\boldsymbol{f_0}$, with α as a solution. We study the matrices $M(\boldsymbol{f_0})$ and $M(\boldsymbol{g_0})$ and from the kernel of $M(\boldsymbol{g_0})$ we construct an eigenvector for the Schur complement of $M_{2,2}(\boldsymbol{f_0})$ corresponding to an eigenvalue equal to $\frac{f_0}{\boldsymbol{w}^{\boldsymbol{\theta}}}(\alpha)$.

Let $\alpha \in V_{\mathcal{P}}(\boldsymbol{f})$ such that $\boldsymbol{w}^{\boldsymbol{\theta}}(\alpha) \neq 0$. Consider the polynomial $g_0 := f_0 - \frac{f_0}{\boldsymbol{w}^{\boldsymbol{\theta}}}(\alpha) \cdot \boldsymbol{w}^{\boldsymbol{\theta}}$ and a new system $\boldsymbol{g_0} := (g_0, f_1, \dots, f_n)$. The coefficients of the polynomials g_0 and f_0 are the same, with exception of the coefficient of the monomial $\boldsymbol{w}^{\boldsymbol{\theta}}$, so the specializations $u_{i,\sigma}(\boldsymbol{f_0})$ and $u_{i,\sigma}(\boldsymbol{g_0})$ (Sec. 2.1) differ if and only if $i = 0$ and $\boldsymbol{\sigma} = \boldsymbol{\theta}$. Hence, as Π_θ holds, $u_{0,\boldsymbol{\theta}}$ does not appear in $M_{1,1}$, $M_{2,1}$, and $M_{1,2}$, and $M_{1,1}(\boldsymbol{g_0}) = M_{1,1}(\boldsymbol{f_0})$, $M_{1,2}(\boldsymbol{g_0}) = M_{1,2}(\boldsymbol{f_0})$, and $M_{2,1}(\boldsymbol{g_0}) = M_{2,1}(\boldsymbol{f_0})$. The specialization of $u_{0,\boldsymbol{\theta}}$ is a ring homomorphism, so $u_{0,\boldsymbol{\theta}}(\boldsymbol{g_0}) = u_{0,\boldsymbol{\theta}}(\boldsymbol{f_0}) - \frac{f_0}{\boldsymbol{w}^{\boldsymbol{\theta}}}(\alpha)$. By Π_θ, $u_{0,\boldsymbol{\theta}}$ only appears in the diagonal of $M_{2,2}$. Hence, $M_{2,2}(\boldsymbol{g_0}) = M_{2,2}(\boldsymbol{f_0}) - \frac{f_0}{\boldsymbol{w}^{\boldsymbol{\theta}}}(\alpha) \cdot I$, where I is the identity matrix. Therefore,

$$M(\boldsymbol{g_0}) = \begin{bmatrix} M_{1,1} & M_{1,2} \\ M_{2,1} & M_{2,2} \end{bmatrix}(\boldsymbol{f_0}) - \frac{f_0}{\boldsymbol{w}^{\boldsymbol{\theta}}}(\alpha) \cdot \begin{bmatrix} 0 & 0 \\ 0 & I \end{bmatrix}.$$

By construction $g_0(\alpha) = 0$, $\alpha \in V_{\mathcal{P}}(\boldsymbol{f})$, thus $\alpha \in V_{\mathcal{P}}(\boldsymbol{g_0})$, and so $\mathrm{Res}_{\mathcal{P}}(\boldsymbol{g_0})$ vanishes. By property Π_θ, $\det(M)$ is a multiple of $\mathrm{Res}_{\mathcal{P}}(\boldsymbol{d}_0, \dots, \boldsymbol{d}_n)$, hence $M(\boldsymbol{g_0})$ is singular. Let $v \in \ker(M(\boldsymbol{g_0}))$, then

$$M(\boldsymbol{g_0}) \cdot v = 0 \iff \begin{bmatrix} M_{1,1} & M_{1,2} \\ M_{2,1} & M_{2,2} \end{bmatrix}(\boldsymbol{f_0}) \cdot v = \frac{f_0}{\boldsymbol{w}^{\boldsymbol{\theta}}}(\alpha) \cdot \begin{bmatrix} 0 & 0 \\ 0 & I \end{bmatrix} \cdot v \;.$$

Multiplying this equality by the non-singular matrix related to the Schur complement of $M_{2,2}(\boldsymbol{f_0})$, $\begin{bmatrix} I & 0 \\ -M_{2,1} \cdot M_{1,1}^{-1} & I \end{bmatrix}(\boldsymbol{f_0})$, we obtain

$$\begin{bmatrix} M_{1,1} & M_{1,2} \\ 0 & (M_{2,2} - M_{2,1} \cdot M_{1,1}^{-1} \cdot M_{1,2}) \end{bmatrix}(\boldsymbol{f_0}) \cdot v = \frac{f_0}{\boldsymbol{w}^{\boldsymbol{\theta}}}(\alpha) \cdot \begin{bmatrix} 0 & 0 \\ 0 & I \end{bmatrix} \cdot v \;.$$

Consider the lower part of the matrices in the previous identity,

$$\left[\, 0 \;\middle|\; M_{2,2} - M_{2,1} \cdot M_{1,1}^{-1} \cdot M_{1,2} \,\right](\boldsymbol{f_0}) \cdot v = \frac{f_0}{\boldsymbol{w}^{\boldsymbol{\theta}}}(\alpha) \cdot \left[\, 0 \;\middle|\; I \,\right] \cdot v$$

and let $\bar{v} := \left[\begin{array}{c|c} 0 & I \end{array}\right] \cdot v$ be a truncation of the vector v. Then,

$$(M_{2,2} - M_{2,1} \cdot M_{1,1}^{-1} \cdot M_{1,2})(f_0) \cdot \bar{v} = \frac{f_0}{w^{\theta}}(\alpha) \cdot \bar{v} \ .$$

This equality proves that $\frac{f_0}{w^\theta}(\alpha)$ is an eigenvalue of the Schur complement of $M_{2,2}(f_0)$ with eigenvector $\bar{v}$. □

Let $f \in S(d_1) \times \cdots \times S(d_n)$, Eq. (1), be a square system. Consider $f_0 \in S(d_0)$ and $\theta \in \mathcal{A}(d_0)$. We say that the rational function $\frac{f_0}{w^\theta}$ separates the zeros of the system, if for all $\alpha \in V_{\mathcal{P}}(f)$, $w^\theta(\alpha) \neq 0$ and for all $\alpha, \alpha' \in V_{\mathcal{P}}(f_1, \ldots, f_n)$, $\frac{f_0}{w^\theta}(\alpha) = \frac{f_0}{w^\theta}(\alpha') \iff \alpha = \alpha'$.

Corollary 4.3. *Under the assumptions of Thm. 4.2, if the row dimension of $M_{2,2}$ is $\mathsf{MHB}(d_1, \ldots, d_n)$, $\frac{f_0}{w^\theta}$ separates the zeros of $(f_1, \ldots, f_n)$ and there are $\mathsf{MHB}(d_1, \ldots, d_n)$ different solutions for this subsystem (over $\mathcal{P}$), then the Schur complement of $M_{2,2}(f_0)$ is diagonizable with eigenvalues $\frac{f_0}{w^\theta}(\alpha)$, for $\alpha \in V_{\mathcal{P}}(f_1, \ldots, f_n)$.*

Proof. As a consequence of Thm. 4.2, for each $\alpha \in V_{\mathcal{P}}(f)$ we have an eigenvalue $\frac{f_0}{w^\theta}(\alpha)$ for the Schur complement of $M_{2,2}(f_0)$. As $\frac{f_0}{w^\theta}$ separates these zeros, all the eigenvalues are different. Hence, we have as many different eigenvalues as the dimension of the matrix, so the matrix is diagonalizable. □

Note that, as the MHB bounds the number of isolated solutions counting multiplicities, we can not use Thm. 4.3 when we have a square system f such that its solutions over $\mathcal{P}$ have multiplicities.

Lemma 4.4. *Under the assumptions of Thm. 4.2, assume that $\mathrm{Res}_{\mathcal{P}}(f_0) \neq 0$ and $\det(M) = q \cdot \mathrm{Res}_{\mathcal{P}}(d_0, \ldots, d_n)$, where q is a non-zero constant in $\mathbb{K}$. If λ is an eigenvalue of the Schur complement of $M_{2,2}(f_0)$, then there is $\alpha \in V_{\mathcal{P}}(f)$ such that $\lambda = \frac{f_0}{w^\theta}(\alpha)$.*

Proof. Consider the system $g_0 := ((f_0 - \lambda \cdot w^\theta), f_1, \ldots, f_n)$. As the matrix of the Schur complement in the proof of 4.2 is invertible, we extend $\bar{v}$ to $v = \left[\begin{smallmatrix} M_{1,1}^{-1} \cdot M_{2,1} \\ I \end{smallmatrix}\right](f_0)\,\bar{v}$, and reverse the argument in this proof to show that $M(g_0)$ is singular. As the determinant of M is a non-zero constant multiple of the resultant, we deduce that $Res_{\mathcal{P}}(g_0)$ is zero. Let $\alpha \in V_{\mathcal{P}}(g_0)$, then $\alpha \subset V_{\mathcal{P}}(f)$ and $(f_0 - \lambda \cdot w^\theta)(\alpha) = 0$, equivalently, $f_0(\alpha) = \lambda \cdot w^\theta(\alpha)$. As we assumed that $\mathrm{Res}_{\mathcal{P}}(f_0) \neq 0$, then $f_0(\alpha) \neq 0$ and so $\frac{f_0}{w^\theta}(\alpha) = \lambda$. □

Proposition 4.5. *Under the assumptions of Thm. 4.2, assume $\det(M) = q \cdot \mathrm{Res}_{\mathcal{P}}(d_0, \ldots, d_n)$, where q is a non-zero constant in $\mathbb{K}$, and that the (row) dimension of $M_{2,2}$ is $\mathsf{MHB}(d_1, \ldots, d_n)$. Then for any system $f_0 := (f_0, \ldots, f_n)$, $V_{\mathcal{P}}(w^\theta, f_1, \ldots, f_n) = \emptyset$ if and only if $M_{1,1}(f_0)$ is non-singular.*

Proof. Consider the determinant of M. As it is a multiple of the resultant (Sec. 2.1) and the resultant is a multihomogeneous polynomial of degree $\mathsf{MHB}(d_1, \ldots, d_n)$ with respect to u_0, we can write $\det(M) = P(u) \cdot u_{0,\theta}^{\mathsf{MHB}(d_1,\ldots,d_n)} + Q(u)$, where $P(u) \in \mathbb{K}[u]$ does not involve the variables in u_0 and $Q(u) \in \mathbb{K}[u]$ is a polynomial such that none of its monomials are multiple of $u_{0,\theta}^{\mathsf{MHB}(d_1,\ldots,d_n)}$. As Π_θ holds, $u_{0,\theta}$ only appears in the diagonal of $M_{2,2}$. Consider the expansion by minors of $\det(M)$. If the (row) dimension of $M_{2,2}$ is $\mathsf{MHB}(d_1, \ldots, d_n)$, then $P(u) = \pm \det(M_{1,1})$. The polynomial $P(u)$ is a constant multiple of the cofactor of $u_{0,\theta}^{\mathsf{MHB}(d_1,\ldots,d_n)}$ in the resultant $\mathrm{Res}_{\mathcal{P}}(d_0, \ldots, d_n)$.

By construction, $Q(u)$ is a homogeneous polynomial with respect to the variables u_0 of degree $\mathsf{MHB}(d_1, \ldots, d_n)$. As $u_{0,\theta}^{\mathsf{MHB}(d_1,\ldots,d_n)}$ does not divide any monomial in $Q(u)$, each monomial involves a variables of u_0 different to $u_{0,\theta}$. Hence, for any system f_0, we have $Q(w^\theta, f_1, \ldots, f_n) = 0$. By construction, the polynomial $P(u)$ does not involve any of the variables of u_0. Therefore $\det(M_{1,1})(f_0) = \det(M_{1,1})(w^\theta, f_1, \ldots, f_n)$. Therefore, for any system f_0, $q \cdot \mathrm{Res}_{\mathcal{P}}(d_0, \ldots, d_n)(w^\theta, f_1, \ldots, f_n) = \det(M)(w^\theta, f_1 \ldots f_n) = \pm \det(M_{1,1})(w^\theta, f_1 \ldots f_n) = \pm \det(M_{1,1})(f_0)$. The determinant of M is a non-zero constant multiple of the resultant, hence $\det(M_{1,1})(f_0) \neq 0$ if and only if the system $(w^\theta, f_1, \ldots, f_n)$ has no solutions over $\mathcal{P}$, i.e., $V_{\mathcal{P}}(w^\theta, f_1, \ldots, f_n) = \emptyset$. □

If the square system $f = (f_1, \ldots, f_n)$ has no solutions at infinity in $\mathcal{P}$, that is all the coordinates of the solutions are not zero, then the evaluation of the solutions of f at any monomial in $S(d_0)$ is not zero. Hence, for any $w^\theta \in S(d_0)$, $V_{\mathcal{P}}(w^\theta, f_1, \ldots, f_n) = \emptyset$. By Prop. 4.5, $M_{1,1}(f_0, f_1, \ldots, f_n)$ is invertible. To avoid solutions at infinity, in the 0-dimensional multihomogeneous case, we perform a generic linear change of coordinates that preserves the multihomogeneous structure. We state the following corollary without proof.

Corollary 4.6. *Consider a square multihomogeneous system $f \in S(d_1) \times \cdots \times S(d_n)$ with finite $V_{\mathcal{P}}(f)$. Choose $\theta \in \mathcal{A}(d_0)$ and let M be a resultant matrix for $\mathrm{Res}_{\mathcal{P}}(d_0, \ldots, d_n)$, such that Π_θ holds. Consider any $f_0 \in S(d_0)$. Then, for a generic linear change of coordinates A, preserving the multihomogeneous structure, the matrix $M_{1,1}(f_0, f_1 \circ A, \ldots, f_n \circ A)$ is invertible.*

We can use Thm. 4.2 to solve the 2-bilinear systems.

Theorem 4.7. *Assume a 2-bilinear system $f_1, \ldots, f_n$ of type $(n_x, n_y, n_z; r, t)$, such that $V_{\mathcal{P}}(f_1, \ldots, f_n)$ is finite. Choose $\theta \in \mathcal{A}(d_0)$ and consider the M be the matrix of $\delta_1(F^{(2)}, m)$ (Sec. 3.2) for the "universal" system $F^{(2)}$ rearranged with respect to the monomial w^θ. Choose $f_0 \in S(1,1,1)$. Then, after applying a generic linear change of coordinates A, preserving the multihomogeneous structure, the eigenvalues of the Schur complement of $M_{2,2}(f_0, f_1 \circ A, \ldots, f_n \circ A)$ are the evaluations of $\frac{f_0}{w^\theta}$ over $V_{\mathcal{P}}(f_1 \circ A, \ldots, f_n \circ A)$.*

Proof. We only need to check if the Koszul resultant matrix has the property Π_θ. The entries of our matrix are the variables of u up to sign. Note that if $u_{i,\sigma} \in u$ appears in an entry, then it does not appear in the other entries in the same row, or column. Hence, we can rearrange the matrix in such a way that the coefficient $u_{0,\theta}$ only appears in the diagonal of $M_{2,2}$. As the determinant of the system is a constant multiple of the resultant, the dimension of $M_{2,2}$ the degree of u_0 in the determinant, which equals the MHB. □

Example 4.8 (Cont.). *In the previous example (Ex. 3.5), we choose $\theta = ((1,0),(1,0),(1,0)) \in \mathcal{A}(1,1,1)$ and partition the matrix as $\left[\begin{smallmatrix} M_{1,1} & M_{1,2} \\ M_{2,1} & M_{2,2} \end{smallmatrix}\right]$. If we consider the Schur complement, we get $\left[\begin{smallmatrix} 5 & -2 \\ 4 & -1 \end{smallmatrix}\right]$. The characteristic polynomial of this matrix is $X^2 - 4X + 3$, whose roots are $\frac{f_0}{w^\theta}(\alpha_1) = 3$ and $\frac{f_0}{w^\theta}(\alpha_2) = 1$.*

4.2 Eigenvectors for 2-bilinear systems

We fix $\theta \in \mathcal{A}(d_0)$. We consider the degree vector $m = (n_y - 1, -1, n_x + n_y - r + 1)$ and the determinantal formula M for the map $\delta_1(F^{(2)}, m)$ (Sec. 3.2). We study the right eigenvectors of the Schur complement of $M_{2,2}$ to recover the coordinates of all the solutions of a 2-bilinear system f of type $(n_x, n_y, n_z; r, s)$ (Sec. 2.2). We assume that the number of different solutions is $\#V_{\mathcal{P}}(f) = \mathsf{MHB}(f)$.

We augment f to f_0 by adding a trilinear polynomial f_0, which we specify in the sequel. We study the right eigenvalues of the Schur complement of $M_{2,2}(f_0)$. We reduce the analysis of the kernel of $\delta_1(f_0, m)$ to the analysis of a map in a strand of the Koszul complex of a system with common solutions.

Let $\alpha = (\alpha_x, \alpha_y, \alpha_z) \in \mathcal{P}$, and without loss of generality assume that $\alpha_{t,0} \neq 0$, for $t \in \{x, y, z\}$. First, we study the kernel of $\delta_1(f_0, m)$, when the overdetermined system f_0 *has* common solutions. We relate this kernel to the eigenvectors, as we did in the proof of thm. 4.2. For each variable $t \in \{x, y, z\}$, consider the dual form

$$\mathbb{1}^t_\alpha(d_t) := \sum_{\theta_t \in \mathcal{A}(d_t)} \frac{t^{\theta_t}}{t_0^{d_t}}(\alpha_t)\, \partial t^\theta \in S_t(d_t)^*$$

for $d_t \geq 0$. If $d_t < 0$, then we take $\mathbb{1}^t_\alpha(d_t) := 0$.

Observation 4.9. *For each variable $t \in \{x, y, z\}$, given a polynomial $g_t \in S_t(\bar{d}_t)$, such that $\bar{d}_t \leq d_t$, then operator $\star_t$, Eq. (9), acts over g_t and $\mathbb{1}^t_\alpha(d_t)$ as the evaluation of $\frac{g_t}{t_0^{d_t}}$ at α, that is*

$$g_t \star_t \mathbb{1}^t_\alpha(d_t) = \frac{g_t}{t_0^{d_t}}(\alpha_t) \cdot \mathbb{1}^t_\alpha(d_t - \bar{d}_t).$$

To simplify notation, given $f \in S(d_x, d_y, d_z)$ and $(\alpha_x, \alpha_y, \alpha_z) \in \mathcal{P}$, we denote by $f(\alpha_x, \alpha_y) \in S_z(d_z)$ the partial evaluation of $\frac{f}{x_0^{d_x} y_0^{d_y}}$ at $x = \alpha_x$ and $y = \alpha_y$. This evaluation is well-defined because the numerator and denominator share the same degrees w.r.t. x and y.

Lemma 4.10. *Consider $d = (d_x, d_y, d_z)$, $\bar{d} = (\bar{d}_x, \bar{d}_y, \bar{d}_z)$. Let $f \in S(\bar{d})$ and $g_z \in S_z(d_z)$. If $d_x \geq \bar{d}_x$ and $d_y \geq \bar{d}_y$, then the map ψ (Eq. (10)) acts over $\mathbb{1}^x_\alpha(d_x) \otimes \mathbb{1}^y_\alpha(d_y) \otimes g_z$ and f, as the multiplication of g_z and $f(\alpha_x, \alpha_y)$, that is*

$$\psi(\mathbb{1}^x_\alpha(d_x) \otimes \mathbb{1}^y_\alpha(d_y) \otimes g_z, f) = \mathbb{1}^x_\alpha(d_x - \bar{d}_x) \otimes \mathbb{1}^y_\alpha(d_y - \bar{d}_y) \otimes (g_z \cdot f(\alpha_x, \alpha_y)).$$

Let $\omega^{(1)} := \{I : e_I \in \bigwedge_{r, s-n_z+1, 0} E\}$ and $\omega^{(2)} := \{J : e_J \in \bigwedge_{r, s-n_z, 1} E\}$. Let $\rho_\alpha : \mathbb{K}^{\#\omega^{(1)}} \times \mathbb{K}^{\#\omega^{(2)}} \to L_{1,1} \oplus L_{1,2}$, Eq. (7),

$$\rho_\alpha(\lambda^{(1)}, \lambda^{(2)}) := \sum_{I \in \omega^{(1)}} \lambda^{(1)}_I \cdot \left(\mathbb{1}^x_\alpha(1) \otimes \mathbb{1}^y_\alpha(r - n_y) \otimes 1 \otimes e_I\right) + \sum_{J \in \omega^{(2)}} \lambda^{(2)}_J \cdot \left(\mathbb{1}^x_\alpha(1) \otimes \mathbb{1}^y_\alpha(r - n_y + 1) \otimes 1 \otimes e_J\right)$$

As $\#\omega^{(1)} + \#\omega^{(2)} = \binom{s+1}{s-n_z+1}$, we write $\rho_\alpha : \mathbb{K}^{\binom{s+1}{s-n_z+1}} \to K_1$.

Lemma 4.11. *The linear map $\delta_1(f_0, m) \circ \rho_\alpha : \mathbb{K}^{\binom{s+1}{s-n_z+1}} \to K_0$ is equivalent to the $(s - n_z + 1)$-th map of the Koszul complex of the following system, consisting of $s + 1$ linear polynomials in z,*

$$f_z := \left(f_0(\alpha_x, \alpha_y), f_{r+1}(\alpha_x, \alpha_y), \ldots, f_n(\alpha_x, \alpha_y)\right), \tag{11}$$

restricted to its 0-graded part, i.e. the strand of the Koszul complex such that its $(s - n_z + 1)$-th module is isomorphic to $\mathbb{K}^{\binom{s+1}{s-n_z+1}}$.

If f_0 has a solution $(\alpha_x, \alpha_y, \alpha_z) \in V_{\mathcal{P}}(f_0)$, then, α_z is a solution of the linear system f_z, that is $\alpha_z \in V_{\mathcal{P}}(f_z)$. As f_z is an overdetermined system, the Koszul complex f_z is not exact [28, Thm. XXI.4.6].

Lemma 4.12. *Let f_0 be an overdetermined 2-bilinear system. If $\alpha \in V_{\mathcal{P}}(f_0)$, then there is a non-zero $\widehat{\lambda}_\alpha \in \mathbb{K}^{\binom{s+1}{s-n_z+1}}$ such that $\delta_1(f_0, m) \circ \rho_\alpha(\widehat{\lambda}_\alpha) = 0$.*

Proof. Following Lem. 4.11, if we compose $\delta_1(f, m)$ and ρ_α, then we obtain a map which is similar to the 0-graded part of the $(s - n_z + 1)$-th map of the Koszul complex of the $s + 1$ linear polynomials in z, f_z, Eq. (11). As the linear system f_z has a solution α_z, at most n_z of its polynomials are linearly independent. Hence, the Koszul complex of f_z is isomorphic to a Koszul complex $K(\widetilde{f}_1, \ldots, \widetilde{f}_{n_z}, 0, \ldots, 0)$ of a system of $s+1$ linear polynomials, where $(s + 1 - n_z)$ of them are equal to zero [28, Lem. XXI.4.2]. The $(s + 1 - n_z)$-th map of $K(\widetilde{f}_1, \ldots, \widetilde{f}_{n_z}, 0, \ldots, 0)$ maps $e_{n_z+1} \wedge \ldots \wedge e_{s+1-n_z}$ to zero. Hence, its 0-graded part has a non-trivial kernel, and so there is a non-zero $\widehat{\lambda}_\alpha \in \mathbb{K}^{\binom{s}{s-n_z+1}}$ such that $\delta_1(f, m) \circ \rho_\alpha(\widehat{\lambda}_\alpha) = 0$. □

Theorem 4.13. *Let $f = (f_1, \ldots, f_n)$ be a square 2-bilinear system of type $(n_x, n_y, n_z; r, s)$, such that it has $\binom{r}{n_y} \cdot \binom{s}{n_z}$ different solutions over $\mathcal{P}$. Consider $\theta \in \mathcal{A}(1, 1, 1)$ such that*

$$\mathrm{Res}^{(2)}_{\mathcal{P}}(w^\theta, f_1, \ldots, f_n) \neq 0$$

and $f_0 \in S(1, 1, 1)$ such that $\frac{f_0}{w^\theta}$ separates the elements in $V_{\mathcal{P}}(f)$. Let $m := (n_y - 1, -1, n_x + n_y - r + 1)$ and $M \in \mathbb{K}[u]^{\mathcal{K} \times \mathcal{K}}$ related to $\delta_1(F^{(2)}, m)$ for the overdetermined 2-bilinear "universal" system (Thm. 3.3). Then, the Schur complement of $M_{2,2}(f_0)$ is diagonalizable, each eigenvalue is $\frac{f_0}{w^\theta}(\alpha)$, for $\alpha \in V_{\mathcal{P}}(f_1, \ldots, f_n)$, and we can extend the eigenvector $\bar{v}_\alpha$ related to α to $v_\alpha := \left[\begin{smallmatrix} M_{1,1}^{-1} \cdot M_{2,1} \\ I \end{smallmatrix}\right](f_0) \cdot \bar{v}_\alpha$ such that v_α is the element $\rho_\alpha(\widehat{\lambda}_\alpha)$, for some $\widehat{\lambda}_\alpha \in \mathbb{K}^{\binom{s+1}{s-n_z+1}}$.

Proof. By Cor. 4.3, the Schur complex of $M_{2,2}(f_0)$ is diagonalizable and every eigenvalues is different. For each $\alpha \in V_{\mathcal{P}}(f)$, consider the eigenvalue $\frac{f_0}{w^\theta}(\alpha)$, related eigenvector $\bar{v}_\alpha$, and the system $g_\alpha := (f_0 - \frac{f_0}{w^\theta}(\alpha), f_1, \ldots, f_n)$. By Lem. 4.12, there is a $\lambda_\alpha \in \mathbb{K}$ such that $\delta_1(g_\alpha, m) \circ \rho(\lambda_\alpha) = 0$. Hence, there is a w_α, representing $\rho(\lambda_\alpha) = 0$, in the kernel of $M(g_\alpha)$. Following the proof of Thm. 4.2, each element in the kernel of the Schur complement of $M_{2,2}(g_\alpha)$ is related to an eigenvector of the Schur complement of $M_{2,2}(f_0)$ with corresponding eigenvalue $\frac{f_0}{w^\theta}(\alpha)$. As for each eigenvalue we have only one eigenvector, then the dimension of this kernel is 1. Hence, the truncation of w_α, $\bar{w}_\alpha := (0|I) \cdot w_\alpha$, is a multiple of $\bar{v}_\alpha$, where 0 is the zero matrix of appropriate dimension.

As $M_{1,1}(g_\alpha)$ is invertible and $M(g_\alpha) \cdot w_\alpha = 0$, it holds that $\left[\begin{smallmatrix} M_{1,1}^{-1} \cdot M_{2,1} \\ I \end{smallmatrix}\right](g_\alpha)\bar{w}_\alpha = w_\alpha$. As $\left[\begin{smallmatrix} M_{1,1}^{-1} \cdot M_{2,1} \\ I \end{smallmatrix}\right](g_\alpha)$ does not involve $u_{0,\theta}$, then $\left[\begin{smallmatrix} M_{1,1}^{-1} \cdot M_{2,1} \\ I \end{smallmatrix}\right](g_\alpha) = \left[\begin{smallmatrix} M_{1,1}^{-1} \cdot M_{2,1} \\ I \end{smallmatrix}\right](f_0)$. Therefore, we conclude that, as $\bar{v}_\alpha$ is a multiple of $\bar{w}_\alpha$, then $v_\alpha = \left[\begin{smallmatrix} M_{1,1}^{-1} \cdot M_{2,1} \\ I \end{smallmatrix}\right](f_0) \cdot \bar{v}_\alpha$ is a multiple of w_α. □

In the following example we use Thm. 4.13 to recover α_2.

EXAMPLE 4.14 (CONT.). *The eigenvalue of* $\frac{f_0}{w^\theta}(\alpha_2) = 1$ *is* $\bar{v}_{\alpha_2} := (1,2)^\top$. *By extending* $\bar{v}_{\alpha_2}$, *we get*

$$v_{\alpha_2} := \left[\begin{smallmatrix} M_{1,1}^{-1} \cdot M_{2,1} \\ I \end{smallmatrix}\right](f_0) \cdot \left(\begin{smallmatrix} 1 \\ 2 \end{smallmatrix}\right) = (4,3,12,1,2,3,6,6,1,2)^\top$$

which represents $\rho_{\alpha_2}(1,1) =$

$$\left(\boldsymbol{\partial x}^{(1,0)} + 3\,\boldsymbol{\partial x}^{(0,1)}\right) \otimes \left(\boldsymbol{\partial y}^{(2,0)} + 2\,\boldsymbol{\partial y}^{(1,1)} + 4\,\boldsymbol{\partial y}^{(0,2)}\right) \otimes 1 \otimes \boldsymbol{e}_{\{0,1,2\}}$$
$$+ \left(\boldsymbol{\partial x}^{(1,0)} + 3\,\boldsymbol{\partial x}^{(0,1)}\right) \otimes \left(\boldsymbol{\partial y}^{(1,0)} + 2\,\boldsymbol{\partial y}^{(0,1)}\right) \otimes 1 \otimes \boldsymbol{e}_{\{1,2,3\}}$$

Hence, $\mathbb{1}^x_{\alpha_2}(1) = \left(1\,\boldsymbol{\partial x}^{(1,0)} + 3\,\boldsymbol{\partial x}^{(0,1)}\right)$, *and so* $\alpha_{2,x} = (1:3) \in \mathbb{P}^1$. *Also,* $\mathbb{1}^y_{\alpha_2}(1) = \left(1\,\boldsymbol{\partial y}^{(1,0)} + 2\,\boldsymbol{\partial y}^{(0,1)}\right)$, *and then* $\alpha_{2,y} = (1:2) \in \mathbb{P}^1$. *We note that* $\mathbb{1}^y_{\alpha_2}(2) = \left(1 \cdot 1 \cdot \boldsymbol{\partial y}^{(2,0)} + 1 \cdot 2 \cdot \boldsymbol{\partial y}^{(1,1)} + 2 \cdot 2 \cdot \boldsymbol{\partial y}^{(0,2)}\right)$.

We can recover $\alpha_{2,z}$ *as the solution of* $f(\alpha_{2,x}, \alpha_{2,y}, z) = 0$,

$$\begin{cases} f_1(\alpha_{2,x}, \alpha_{2,y}, z) = f_2(\alpha_{2,x}, \alpha_{2,y}, z) = 0 \\ f_3(\alpha_{2,x}, \alpha_{2,y}, z) = -9\,z_0 + 3\,z_1 \end{cases}$$

Hence, $\alpha_{2,z} = (1:3) \in \mathbb{P}^1$ *and so* $\alpha_2 = (1{:}3\,;\ 1{:}2\,;\ 1{:}3) \in \mathcal{P}$.

5 SIZE OF MATRICES AND FGb

As there are no tight bounds for the complexity of Gröbner basis algorithms for solving 2-bilinear systems, we compare against our algorithms experimentally in Table 1. We consider the state-of-the-art Gröbner basis implementation, FGb [18]. For each set of parameters, we consider a random square 2-bilinear system and we dehomogenize the system to compute its Gröbner basis. We compared the ratio between the size of the maximal matrix appearing in the Gröbner basis computation and the size of our Koszul resultant matrix, for all the cases $n \leq 15$. For reasons of space we only present some indicative examples for $n = 12$. The rest of the cases can be found in http://www-polsys.lip6.fr/~bender/2bilinear/. The results are promising and motivate the study of the structure Koszul resultant matrix to develop algorithms for faster linear algebra with such matrices.

Table 1: Matrix sizes and ratios of Koszul matrix and FGb.

n_x	n_y	n_z	r	s	Size δ_1	Size FGb	Ratio
2	6	4	7	5	630 × 630	1769 × 1158	5.1 ~
10	1	1	10	2	352 × 352	709 × 422	2.4 ~
5	5	2	9	3	6804 × 6804	8941 × 8390	1.6 ~
4	4	4	6	6	4125 × 4125	5436 × 4262	1.3 ~
5	5	2	6	6	2106 × 2106	2007 × 1164	1/1.9 ~
6	3	3	6	6	7000 × 7000	4708 × 3801	1/2.7 ~
6	4	2	5	7	2450 × 2450	1773 × 1125	1/3 ~

ACKNOWLEDGMENTS

We thank Laurent Busé and Carlos D'Andrea for helpful discussions and references, and the anonymous reviewers for the comments and suggestions. The authors are partially supported by ANR JCJC GALOP (ANR-17-CE40-0009) and the PGMO grant GAMMA.

REFERENCES

[1] W. Auzinger and H. J. Stetter. 1988. An elimination algorithm for the computation of all zeros of a system of multivariate polynomial equations. In *Numerical Mathematics Singapore 1988*. Springer, 11–30.
[2] M. R. Bender, J.-C. Faugère, and E. Tsigaridas. 2018. Towards Mixed Gröbner Basis Algorithms: the Multihomogeneous and Sparse Case. In *Proc. ACM ISSAC*. ACM, ACM.
[3] D. N. Bernshtein. 1975. The number of roots of a system of equations. *Functional Analysis and its applications* 9, 3 (1975), 183–185.
[4] L. Busé, A. Mantzaflaris, and E. Tsigaridas. 2017. Matrix formulae for Resultants and Discriminants of Bivariate Tensor-product Polynomials. (Dec. 2017). https://hal.inria.fr/hal-01654263
[5] A. D. Chtcherba and D. Kapur. 2000. Conditions for exact resultants using the Dixon formulation. In *Proc. ACM ISSAC*. 62–70.
[6] D. Cox, J. Little, and D. O'shea. 1992. *Ideals, varieties, and algorithms*. Springer.
[7] D. Cox, J. Little, and D. O'Shea. 2006. *Using algebraic geometry*. Springer.
[8] D. A. Cox. 2005. Solving equations via algebras. In *Solving polynomial equations*. Springer, Chapter 2, 63–123.
[9] C. D'Andrea. 2002. Macaulay style formulas for sparse resultants. *Trans. Amer. Math. Soc.* 354, 7 (2002), 2595–2629.
[10] C. D'Andrea and A. Dickenstein. 2001. Explicit formulas for the multivariate resultant. *Journal of Pure and Applied Algebra* 164, 1 (2001), 59–86.
[11] A. Dickenstein and I. Z. Emiris. 2003. Multihomogeneous resultant formulae by means of complexes. *Journal of Symbolic Computation* 36, 3 (2003), 317–342.
[12] M. Elkadi and B. Mourrain. 2007. *Introduction à la résolution des systèmes polynomiaux*. Vol. 59. Springer Science & Business Media.
[13] I. Emiris and R. Vidunas. 2014. Root counts of semi-mixed systems, and an application to counting Nash equilibria. In *Proc. ACM ISSAC*. 154–161.
[14] I. Z. Emiris. 1996. On the complexity of sparse elimination. *Journal of Complexity* 12, 2 (1996), 134–166.
[15] I. Z. Emiris and A. Mantzaflaris. 2012. Multihomogeneous resultant formulae for systems with scaled support. *J. of Symbolic Computation* 47, 7 (2012), 820–842.
[16] I. Z. Emiris, A. Mantzaflaris, and E. Tsigaridas. 2016. On the bit complexity of solving bilinear polynomial systems. In *Proc. ACM ISSAC*. ACM, 215–222.
[17] I. Z. Emiris and B. Mourrain. 1999. Matrices in Elimination Theory. *Journal of Symbolic Computation* 28, 1 (1999), 3 – 44.
[18] J.-C. Faugère. 2010. FGb: A Library for Computing Gröbner Bases. In *Mathematical Software - ICMS 2010 (Lecture Notes in Computer Science)*, Vol. 6327. Springer Berlin / Heidelberg, Berlin, Heidelberg, 84–87.
[19] J.-C. Faugere, F. Levy-Dit-Vehel, and L. Perret. 2008. Cryptanalysis of minrank. In *Advances in Cryptology*. Springer, 280–296.
[20] J.-C. Faugère, M. Safey El Din, and P.-J. Spaenlehauer. 2011. Gröbner bases of bihomogeneous ideals generated by polynomials of bidegree (1,1): Algorithms and complexity. *Journal of Symbolic Computation* 46 (2011), 406–437. Issue 4.
[21] I. M. Gelfand, M. Kapranov, and A. Zelevinsky. 2008. *Discriminants, resultants, and multidimensional determinants*. Springer Science & Business Media.
[22] R. Hartshorne. 1977. *Algebraic Geometry*. Springer, New York.
[23] J.-P. Jouanolou. 1997. Formes d'inertie et résultant: un formulaire. *Advances in mathematics* 126, 2 (1997), 119–250.
[24] A. Joux. 2014. A new index calculus algorithm with complexity $L(1/4 + o(1))$ in small characteristic. In *SAC 2013*. Springer, 355–379.
[25] D. Kapur and T. Saxena. 1997. Extraneous factors in the Dixon resultant formulation. In *Proc. ACM ISSAC*. 141–148.
[26] A. G. Khovanskii. 1978. Newton polyhedra and the genus of complete intersections. *Functional Analysis and its applications* 12, 1 (1978), 38–46.
[27] A. G. Kushnirenko. 1976. Newton polytopes and the Bezout theorem. *Functional analysis and its applications* 10, 3 (1976), 233–235.
[28] S. Lang. 2002. Algebra. *Graduate Texts in Mathematics* 3, 211 (2002).
[29] F. Macaulay. 1902. Some formulae in elimination. *Proceedings of the London Mathematical Society* 1, 1 (1902), 3–27.
[30] A. Mantzaflaris and E. Tsigaridas. 2017. Resultants and Discriminants for Bivariate Tensor-product Polynomials. In *Proc. ACM ISSAC*.
[31] A. Morgan and A. Sommese. 1987. A homotopy for solving general polynomial systems that respects m-homogeneous structures. *Appl. Math. Comput.* 24, 2 (1987), 101–113.
[32] P.-J. Spaenlehauer. 2012. *Solving multi-homogeneous and determinantal systems: algorithms, complexity, applications*. Ph.D. Dissertation. UPMC.
[33] B. Sturmfels and A. Zelevinsky. 1994. Multigraded resultants of Sylvester type. *Journal of Algebra* 163, 1 (1994), 115–127.
[34] B. Van der Waerden. 1978. On varieties in multiple-projective spaces. In *Indagationes Mathematicae (Proceedings)*, Vol. 81. Elsevier, 303–312.
[35] J. Weyman. 1994. Calculating discriminants by higher direct images. *Trans. Amer. Math. Soc.* 343, 1 (Jan. 1994), 367–389.
[36] J. Weyman. 2003. *Cohomology of vector bundles and syzygies*. Vol. 149. Cambridge University Press.
[37] J. Weyman and A. Zelevinsky. 1994. Multigraded formulae for multigraded resultants. *J. Algebr. Geom* 3, 4 (1994), 569–597.

Towards Mixed Gröbner Basis Algorithms: the Multihomogeneous and Sparse Case

Matías R. Bender
Jean-Charles Faugère
Elias Tsigaridas
FirstName.LastName@inria.fr
Sorbonne Université, CNRS, INRIA, Laboratoire d'Informatique de Paris 6, LIP6, Équipe PolSys, France

ABSTRACT

One of the biggest open problems in computational algebra is the design of efficient algorithms for Gröbner basis computations that take into account the sparsity of the input polynomials. We can perform such computations in the case of unmixed polynomial systems, that is systems with polynomials having the same support, using the approach of Faugère, Spaenlehauer, and Svartz [ISSAC'14]. We present two algorithms for sparse Gröbner bases computations for mixed systems. The first one computes with mixed sparse systems and exploits the supports of the polynomials. Under regularity assumptions, it performs no reductions to zero. For mixed, square, and 0-dimensional multihomogeneous polynomial systems, we present a dedicated, and potentially more efficient, algorithm that exploits different algebraic properties that performs no reduction to zero. We give an explicit bound for the maximal degree appearing in the computations.

CCS CONCEPTS

• **Mathematics of computing → Gröbner bases and other special bases;**

KEYWORDS

Mixed Sparse Gröbner Basis; Multihomogeneous Polynomial System; Sparse Polynomial System; Toric variety

ACM Reference Format:

Matías R. Bender, Jean-Charles Faugère, and Elias Tsigaridas. 2018. Towards Mixed Gröbner Basis Algorithms: the Multihomogeneous and Sparse Case. In *ISSAC '18: 2018 ACM International Symposium on Symbolic and Algebraic Computation, July 16–19, 2018, New York, NY, USA.* ACM, New York, NY, USA, 8 pages. https://doi.org/10.1145/3208976.3209018

1 INTRODUCTION

Gröbner bases are in the heart of many algebraic algorithms. One of the most important applications is to solve 0-dimensional polynomial systems. A common strategy is, first to compute a Gröbner basis in some order, usually degree lexicographic, deduce from it multiplication maps in the corresponding quotient ring, and finally recover the lexicographic order using FGLM [21].

Toric geometry [12] studies the geometric and algebraic properties of varieties given by the image of monomial maps and systems of *sparse* polynomial equations; that is systems with polynomials having monomials from a restrictive set. Sparse resultant [23], that generalizes the classical multivariate resultant, extends these ideas in (sparse) elimination theory. There are a lot of algorithms to compute the sparse resultant and to solve sparse systems, for example see [13, 18, 34]. For the related problem of fewnomial systems see [4]. Numerical continuation methods can also benefit from sparsity [29], as well as other symbolic algorithms [24, 27].

Recently Faugère et al. [22] introduced the first algorithm to solve *unmixed* sparse systems, that is systems of sparse polynomials that have the same monomials, using Gröbner basis that exploits sparsity. Their idea is to consider the polytopal algebra associated to the supports of the input polynomials. Roughly speaking, the polytopal algebra is like the standard polynomial algebra, where the variables are the monomials in the supports of the input polynomials. They compute a Gröbner basis of the ideal generated by the polynomials, in the polytopal algebra, by introducing a matrix F5-like algorithm [15, 19]. They homogenize the polynomials and compute a Gröbner basis degree by degree. By dehomogenizing the computed basis, they recover a Gröbner basis of the original ideal. In the 0-dimensional case, they apply a FGLM-like algorithm [21] to obtain a lexicographical Gröbner basis. If the homogenized polynomials form a regular sequence over the polytopal algebra, then the algorithm performs no reductions to zero. When the system is also 0-dimensional, they bound the complexity using the Castelnuovo-Mumford regularity. In this case, taking advantage of the sparsity led to large speed-ups. Hence, our goal is to extend [22] to *mixed* sparse polynomial systems, i.e. systems where the polynomials *do not* have necessarily the same monomials.

The Castelnuovo-Mumford regularity is a fundamental invariant in algebraic geometry, related to the maximal degrees appearing in the minimal resolutions and the vanishing of the local cohomology. It is related to the complexity of computing Gröbner basis [2, 9]. The extension of this regularity in the context of toric varieties is known as multigraded Castelnuovo-Mumford regularity [6, 30, 31].

The multihomogeneous systems form an important subclass of mixed sparse systems as they are ubiquitous in applications. Their properties are well understood, for example, the degree (number of solutions) of the system [37], the arithmetic Nullstellensätze [14], and the (multigraded) Castelnuovo-Mumford regularity [1, 5, 6, 25, 33]. We can solve these systems using general purpose algorithms based on resultants [18] and in some cases benefit

ISSAC '18, July 16–19, 2018, New York, NY, USA

ACM ISBN 978-1-4503-5550-6/18/07...$15.00
https://doi.org/10.1145/3208976.3209018

from the existence of determinantal formulas [35, 38], or we can use homotopy methods [17, 26]. For unmixed bilinear systems, we compute a Gröbner basis [20] with no reductions to zero. Using determinantal formulas we can solve mixed bilinear systems with two supports using eigenvalues/eigenvectors [3]. In the unmixed case, [22] presents bounds for the complexity of computing a sparse Gröbner basis. Our goal is to present a potentially more efficient algorithm and bounds for square mixed multihomogeneous systems.

Our contribution. We present two algorithms to solve 0-dimensional mixed sparse polynomial systems based on Gröbner basis computations. Both of them, under assumptions, compute with no reductions to zero, thus they avoid useless computations.

The first algorithm (Alg. 3.1) takes as input a mixed sparse system and computes a *sparse Gröbner basis* (Def. 3.3). This is a basis for the corresponding ideal over a polytopal algebra and has similar properties to the usual Gröbner basis. Using this basis, we compute normal forms by a modified division algorithm (Lem. 3.4). The orders for the monomials that we consider take into account the supports of the polynomials and they *are not* necessarily monomial orders (Sec. 2.4). We prove that for any of these orders and any ideal there is a finite sparse Gröbner basis (Corollaries 3.11 and 3.13) that we compute with a matrix F5-like algorithm, that we call M^2. Moreover, we introduce a *sparse F5 criterion* to avoid useless computations. Under regularity assumptions, we avoid every reduction to zero (Lem. 3.19). When the ideal is 0-dimensional, we can use a sparse Gröbner basis to compute a Gröbner basis for unmixed systems introduced in [22] using FGLM.

Our second algorithm, $\mathsf{M_3H}$, takes as input a 0-dimensional square multihomogeneous mixed system, that has no solutions at infinity. It outputs a monomial basis and the multiplication map of every affine variable. Both lie in the quotient ring of the dehomogenization of the (input) ideal. Using the multigraded Castelnuovo-Mumford regularity, we present an algorithm (Alg. 4.1) that avoids all reductions to zero (Cor. 4.8). Over $\mathbb{P}^{n_1}\times\cdots\times\mathbb{P}^{n_r}$, if the input polynomials have multidegrees $\boldsymbol{d}_1,\ldots,\boldsymbol{d}_{(n_1+\cdots+n_r)} \in \mathbb{N}^r$, then the dimension of the biggest matrix appearing in the computations is the number of monomials of multidegree $\sum_{i=1}^{n_1+\cdots+n_r} \boldsymbol{d}_i + (1,\ldots,1) - (n_1,\ldots,n_r)$. This bounds the maximal degree of the polynomials appearing in the computations and generalizes the classical Macaulay bound [28], which we recover for $r = 1$. Using the multiplication matrices, we can recover the usual Gröbner basis for the dehomogenized ideal via FGLM.

2 PRELIMINARIES

Let $\mathbb{K}$ be a field of characteristic 0, $\boldsymbol{y} := (y_0,\ldots,y_m)$, and $\mathbb{K}[\boldsymbol{y}] := \mathbb{K}[y_0,\ldots,y_m]$. For $\alpha \in \mathbb{N}^{m+1}$, let $\boldsymbol{y}^\alpha := \prod_{i=0}^m y_i^{\alpha_i}$. Let $\bar{0} := (0\ldots0)$.

2.1 Semigroup Algebra

An affine semigroup S is a finitely-generated additive subsemigroup of $\mathbb{Z}^n$, for some $n \in \mathbb{N}$, such that it contains $0 \in \mathbb{Z}^n$. The semigroup algebra $\mathbb{K}[S]$ is the $\mathbb{K}$-algebra generated by $\{\boldsymbol{X}^s, s \in S\}$, where $\boldsymbol{X}^s \cdot \boldsymbol{X}^t = \boldsymbol{X}^{s+t}$. The set of monomials of $\mathbb{K}[S]$ is $\{\boldsymbol{X}^s, s \in S\}$.

Let $\{a_0, a_1,\ldots,a_m\}$ be a set of generators of $S \subset \mathbb{Z}^n$. Let $e_0\ldots e_m$ be the canonical basis of $\mathbb{Z}^{m+1}$. Consider the homomorphism $\rho : \mathbb{Z}^{m+1} \to S$ that sends e_i to a_i, for $0 \le i \le m$. Then, $\mathbb{K}[S]$ is isomorphic to the quotient ring $\mathbb{K}[\boldsymbol{y}]/T$, where T is the lattice ideal $T := \langle \boldsymbol{y}^u - \boldsymbol{y}^v | u, v \in \mathbb{N}^{m+1}, \rho(u-v) = 0\rangle$ [32, Thm 7.3]. Moreover, the ideal T is prime and $\mathbb{K}[S]$ is an integral domain [32, Thm 7.4].

An affine semigroup S is pointed if it does not contain non-zero invertible elements, that is for all $s, t \in S\setminus\{\bar{0}\}$, $s+t \neq 0$ [32, Def 7.8]. As in [22], we consider only pointed affine semigroups.

Let $M_1,\ldots,M_k \subset \mathbb{R}^n$ be polytopes containing 0. We consider two different semigroups associated to them. First, we consider the affine semigroup $(S_{M_1,\ldots,M_k}, `+')$ generated by the elements in $\cup_{i=1}^k(M_i \cap \mathbb{Z}^n)$ with the addition over $\mathbb{Z}^n$. Second, we consider the affine semigroup $(S^h_{M_1,\ldots,M_k}, `+')$, generated by the elements in $\cup_{i=1}^k\{(s, e_i) : s \in M_i \cap \mathbb{Z}^n\}$, with the addition over $\mathbb{Z}^{n+k}$, where $e_1,\ldots,e_k$ is the standard basis of $\mathbb{R}^k$.

2.2 Sparse degree and homogenization

Given a monomial $\boldsymbol{X}^{(s,d)} \in \mathbb{K}[S^h_{M_1,\ldots,M_k}]$, we define its *degree* as $\deg(\boldsymbol{X}^{(s,d)}) := d \in \mathbb{N}^k$. With this grading, the semigroup algebra $\mathbb{K}[S^h_{M_1,\ldots,M_k}]$ is multigraded by $\mathbb{N}^k$ and generated, as a $\mathbb{K}$-algebra, by the elements of degrees $e_1,\ldots,e_k$, so it is multihomogeneous. For each $d \in \mathbb{N}^k$, let $\mathbb{K}[S^h_{M_1,\ldots,M_k}]_d$ be the vector space of the multihomogeneous polynomials in $\mathbb{K}[S^h_{M_1,\ldots,M_k}]$ of degree $d \in \mathbb{N}^k$.

We define the dehomogenization of $\boldsymbol{X}^{(s,d)}$ as the epimorphism that takes $\boldsymbol{X}^{(s,d)} \in \mathbb{K}[S^h_{M_1\ldots M_k}]$ to $\chi(\boldsymbol{X}^{(s,d)}) = \boldsymbol{X}^s \in \mathbb{K}[S_{M_1\ldots M_k}]$. For an ideal I^h, $\chi(I^h)$ means that we apply χ to the elements of I^h.

Remark 2.1. *For an ideal I^h, for every $f \in I^h \cap \mathbb{K}[S^h_{M_1,\ldots,M_k}]_d$, and $D \ge d$, component-wise, there is $f' \in I^h \cap \mathbb{K}[S^h_{M_1,\ldots,M_k}]_D$ such that $\chi(f) = \chi(f') \in \chi(I^h)$.*

When we work only with one polytope M, that is $k = 1$, we define the *affine degree* of $\boldsymbol{X}^s \in \mathbb{K}[S_M]$, $\delta^A(\boldsymbol{X}^s)$, as the smallest $d \in \mathbb{N}$ such that $\boldsymbol{X}^{(s,d)} \in \mathbb{K}[S^h_M]$. We extend this definition to the affine polynomials in $\mathbb{K}[S_M]$ as the maximal affine degree of each monomial. That is, for $f := \sum_{s\in S_M} c_s\boldsymbol{X}^s \in \mathbb{K}[S_M]$, the affine degree of f is $\delta^A(f) := \max_{s\in S_M}(\delta^A(\boldsymbol{X}^s) : c_s \neq 0)$. Let $\mathbb{K}[S_M]_{\le d}$ be the set of all polynomials in $\mathbb{K}[S_M]$ of degree at most d. The map $\chi^{-1} : \mathbb{K}[S_M] \to \mathbb{K}[S^h_M]$ defines the homogenization of $f := \sum_{s\in S_M} c_s\boldsymbol{X}^s \in \mathbb{K}[S_M]$, where $\chi^{-1}(f) := \sum_{s\in S_M} c_s\boldsymbol{X}^{(s,\delta^A(f))} \in \mathbb{K}[S^h_M]$. Note that this map is not a homomorphism. For an ideal I, $\chi^{-1}(I)$ is the homogeneous ideal generated by applying χ^{-1} to every element of I.

Finally, given a polynomial $f \in \mathbb{K}[S^h_M]$ we define its *sparse degree* as $\delta(f) := \delta^A(\chi(f))$. Note that, the degree is always bigger or equal to the sparse degree. Even though we use the name sparse degree, it does not give a graded structure to the $\mathbb{K}$-algebra $\mathbb{K}[S^h_M]$.

2.3 Mixed systems and Regularity

Consider polytopes $M_1,\ldots,M_k$ and a polynomial system $(f_1\ldots f_k)$ such that $f_i \in \mathbb{K}[S^h_{M_1,\ldots,M_k}]_{e_i}$. We say the system is *regular* if $f_1,\ldots,f_k$ form a regular sequence over $\mathbb{K}[S^h_{M_1,\ldots,M_k}]$. Similarly, $(\chi(f_1)\ldots\chi(f_k))$, that is the dehomogenization of $(f_1,\ldots,f_k)$, is *regular* if $(\chi(f_1)\ldots\chi(f_k))$ form a regular sequence over $\mathbb{K}[S_{M_1\ldots M_k}]$.

When all the polytopes are the same these definitions *match* the definition of regularity for unmixed systems [22]. When every polytope is a n-simplex, these definitions are related to the standard definition of regularity [16, Chp. 17].

Like in the (standard) homogeneous case, the order of the polynomials does not affect the regularity of the system $(f_1. \dots, f_k)$. In addition, the dehomogenization preserves the regularity property.

Lemma 2.2. *Consider $f_i \in \mathbb{K}[S^h_{M_1,\dots,M_k}]_{e_i}$ and σ a permutation of $\{1,\dots,k\}$. If $f_1,\dots,f_k$ is a regular sequence over $\mathbb{K}[S^h_{M_1,\dots,M_k}]$, then $(\chi(f_{\sigma_1}),\dots,\chi(f_{\sigma_k}))$ is a regular sequence over $\mathbb{K}[S_{M_1,\dots,M_k}]$.*

Proof. If $f_1,\dots,f_k$ is a regular sequence, then any permutation of them it is regular [7, §9, Cor. 2]. Hence, we just have to prove that $\chi(f_1),\dots,\chi(f_k)$ is a regular sequence. For $w \leq k$, consider a polynomial $\bar{g}_w \in \mathbb{K}[S_{M_1,\dots,M_k}]$ such that $\bar{g}_w \cdot \chi(f_w) \in \langle \chi(f_1),\dots,\chi(f_{w-1})\rangle$. Then, there are polynomials $\bar{g}_1,\dots,\bar{g}_{w-1} \in \mathbb{K}[S_{M_1,\dots,M_k}]$ such that $\sum_{i=1}^{w} \bar{g}_i \chi(f_i) = 0$. As χ is an epimorphism, for each $\bar{g}_i$, there is $g_i \in \mathbb{K}[S^h_{M_1,\dots,M_k}]$ multihomogeneous such that $\chi(g_i) = \bar{g}_i$. Consider a vector D, such that $\forall i,j,\ D - \deg(f_i) \geq \deg(g_j)$. Then, by Rem. 2.1, there are multihomogeneous polynomials $g'_i \in \mathbb{K}[S^h_{M_1,\dots,M_k}]_{D-\deg(f_i)}$, such that $\chi(g'_i) = \bar{g}_i$. Note that, χ restricted to $\mathbb{K}[S^h_{M_1,\dots,M_k}]_D$ is injective. Hence $\chi(\sum_{i=1}^{w} g'_i f_i) = \sum_{i=1}^{w} \bar{g}_i \chi(f_i) = 0$ implies $\sum_{i=1}^{w} g'_i f_i = 0$. As $f_1,\dots,f_w$ is a regular sequence, $g'_w \in \langle f_1,\dots,f_{w-1}\rangle$ and $\bar{g}_w \in \langle \chi(f_1),\dots,\chi(f_{w-1})\rangle$. □

The proof of existence of regular systems is beyond the scope of this paper. Nevertheless, we can report that we have performed several experiments with many different sparse mixed systems, taking generic coefficients, and all them were regular.

2.4 Orders for Monomials

As in the standard case, a monomial order $<$ for $\mathbb{K}[S]$ is a well-order compatible with the multiplication on $\mathbb{K}[S]$, that is $\forall s \in S, s \neq 0 \implies X^0 < X^s$ and $\forall s,r,t \in S, X^s < X^r \implies X^{s+t} < X^{r+t}$. These orders exist on $\mathbb{K}[S]$ if and only if S is pointed, [22, Def 3.1].

Given any well-order $<$ for $\mathbb{K}[S_M]$, we can extend it to a well-order $<_h$, the grading of $<$, for $\mathbb{K}[S^h_M]$ as follows:

$$X^{(s,d)} < X^{(r,d')} \iff \begin{cases} d < d' \\ d = d' \wedge X^s < X^r \end{cases} \tag{1}$$

If $<$ is a monomial order, then $<_h$ is a monomial order too.

Given an ideal $I \subset \mathbb{K}[S_M]$, a common issue is to study the vector space $I \cap \mathbb{K}[S_M]_{\leq d}$, i.e. the elements of I of degree smaller or equal to d. This information allow us, for example, to compute the Hilbert Series of the affine ideal. It is also important for computational reasons. For example, to maintain the invariants in the signature-based Gröbner basis algorithms, as the F5 algorithm [15, 19].

In our setting, to compute a basis of $I \cap \mathbb{K}[S_M]_{\leq d}$, we have to work with an order for the monomials in $\mathbb{K}[S_M]$ that takes into account the sparse degree. This order, $\prec$, is such that for any $X^s, X^r \in \mathbb{K}[S_M]$, $\delta^A(X^s) < \delta^A(X^r) \implies X^s \prec X^r$. Unfortunately, for most of the polytopal algebras $\mathbb{K}[S_M]$, *there is no monomial order* with this property. Therefore, we are forced to work with well-orders that are not monomial orders.

Example 2.3. *Consider the semigroup generated by $M := \{[0,0],[1,0],[0,1],[1,1]\} \subset \mathbb{N}^2$. Consider a monomial order $<$ for $\mathbb{K}[S_M]$. Without loss of generality, assume $X^{[1,0]} < X^{[0,1]}$. Then, $X^{[2,0]} < X^{[1,1]} < X^{[0,2]}$. But, $\delta^A(X^{[2,0]}) = 2$ and $\delta^A(X^{[1,1]}) = 1$. So, no monomial order on $\mathbb{K}[S_M]$ takes into account the sparse degree.*

Given a monomial order $<_M$ for $\mathbb{K}[S_M]$, we define the *sparse order* $\prec$ for $\mathbb{K}[S_M]$ as follows.

$$X^s \prec X^r \iff \begin{cases} \delta^A(X^s) < \delta^A(X^r) \\ \delta^A(X^s) = \delta^A(X^r) \wedge X^s <_M X^r \end{cases} \tag{2}$$

Let $\prec_h$ be the grading of the sparse order of $\mathbb{K}[S^h_M]$ (Eq. 1). We call this order the *graded sparse order.*

Remark 2.4. *By definition, these two orders are the same for monomials of the same degree. That is,*

$$\forall X^{(s,d)}, X^{(r,d)} \in \mathbb{K}[S^h_M],\ X^{(s,d)} \prec_h X^{(r,d)} \iff X^s \prec X^r .$$

Usually, this order is not compatible with the multiplication. But,

Lemma 2.5. *If $X^s \prec X^t$ and $\delta^A(X^r) + \delta^A(X^t) = \delta^A(X^t \cdot X^r)$, then $X^s \cdot X^r \prec X^t \cdot X^r$.*

Proof. Note that δ^A satisfies the triangular inequality, $\delta^A(X^{s+r}) \leq \delta^A(X^s) + \delta^A(X^r)$. As $X^s \prec X^t$, $\delta^A(X^s) \leq \delta^A(X^t)$. By assumption, $\delta^A(X^t) + \delta^A(X^r) = \delta^A(X^{t+r})$. So, $\delta^A(X^{s+r}) \leq \delta^A(X^s) + \delta^A(X^r) \leq \delta^A(X^t) + \delta^A(X^r) \leq \delta^A(X^{t+r})$. Hence, either $\delta^A(X^{s+r}) < \delta^A(X^{t+r})$ or the sparse degree is the same. In the second case, we conclude $\delta^A(X^s) = \delta^A(X^t)$, and so $X^s <_M X^t$. As $<_M$ is a monomial order, $X^{s+r} <_M X^{t+r}$. Hence, $X^s \cdot X^r \prec X^t \cdot X^r$. □

We extend this property to the homogeneous case.

Corollary 2.6. *If $X^{(s,d_s)} \prec X^{(t,d_t)}$ and $\delta(X^{(r,d_r)}) + \delta(X^{(t,d_t)}) = \delta(X^{(r,d_r)} \cdot X^{(t,d_t)})$, then $X^{(s,d_s)} \cdot X^{(r,d_r)} \prec X^{(t,d_t)} \cdot X^{(r,d_r)}$.*

3 SPARSE GRÖBNER BASIS (sGB)

We want to define and compute Gröbner bases in $\mathbb{K}[S_M]$ and $\mathbb{K}[S^h_M]$ with respect to a (graded) sparse order. As these orders are not compatible with the multiplication, not all the standard definitions of Gröbner basis are equivalent. For example, the set of leading monomials of an ideal in $\mathbb{K}[S_M]$ does not necessarily form an ideal. We say that a set of generators G of an ideal $I \subset \mathbb{K}[S_M]$ is a sparse Gröbner basis with respect to an order $\prec$, if for each $f \in I$, there is a $g \in G$ such that $\mathsf{LM}_\prec(g)$ divides $\mathsf{LM}_\prec(f)$. Similarly for $\mathbb{K}[S^h_M]$.

This definition has a drawback: The multivariate polynomial division algorithm might not terminate. This can happen when $\mathsf{LM}_\prec(f) = X^t \cdot \mathsf{LM}_\prec(g)$ and $\mathsf{LM}_\prec(f) \prec \mathsf{LM}_\prec(X^t \cdot g)$. Then, the reduction step "increases" the leading monomial, so that the algorithm does not necessarily terminates. We can construct examples where we have a periodic sequence of reductions. To avoid this problem, we redefine the division relation.

Definition 3.1 (Division relation). *For any $X^{(s,d_s)}, X^{(r,d_r)} \in \mathbb{K}[S^h_M]$, we say that $X^{(s,d_s)}$ divides $X^{(r,d_r)}$, and write $X^{(s,d_s)} || X^{(r,d_r)}$, if there is a $X^{(t,d_t)} \in \mathbb{K}[S^h_M]$ such that $X^{(s,d_s)} \cdot X^{(t,d_t)} = X^{(r,d_r)}$ and $\delta(X^{(s,d_s)}) + \delta(X^{(t,d_t)}) = \delta(X^{(r,d_r)})$. Similarly, for $X^s, X^r \in \mathbb{K}[S_M]$, we say that X^s divides X^r, and write $X^s || X^r$, if $\chi^{-1}(X^s) || \chi^{-1}(X^r)$.*

Remark 3.2. *If $LM_{\prec_h}(f) || X^{(s,d_s)}$, then there is a $X^{(t,d_t)} \in \mathbb{K}[S^h_M]$ such that $X^{(s,d_s)} = X^{(t,d_t)} \cdot LM_{\prec_h}(f) = LM_{\prec_h}(X^{(t,d_t)} \cdot f)$, by Lem. 2.5. Similarly over $\mathbb{K}[S_M]$.*

We define the sparse Gröbner bases (sGB) as follows.

Definition 3.3 (sparse Gröbner bases). *Given a (graded) sparse order $<$, see Eq. (2), and an ideal $I \subset \mathbb{K}[S_M]$, respectively $I \subset \mathbb{K}[S_M^h]$, a set $sGB(I) \subset I$ is a sparse Gröbner basis (sGB) if it generates I and for any $f \in I$ there is some $g \in sGB(I)$ such that $\mathsf{LM}_<(g) || \mathsf{LM}_<(f)$.*

With this definition, each step in the division algorithm reduces the leading monomial (Rem. 3.2), and so the division algorithm always terminates, see e.g. [10, Thm. 2.3.3,Prop. 2.6.1].

Lemma 3.4. *Let $f \in \mathbb{K}[S_M]$ and G be a set of polynomials in $\mathbb{K}[S_M]$. Using our definition of division relation (Def. 3.1), the multivariate division algorithm [10, Thm. 2.3.3] for the division of f by G, with respect to the order $<$, terminates. Moreover, if G is a sGB of an ideal I with respect to $<$ and $f \equiv f' \mod I$, then the remainder division algorithm for f and f' is the same and unique for any sGB.*

Our next goal is to prove that for every ideal and sparse order, there is a finite sGB. A priori, this is not clear from the Noetherian property of $\mathbb{K}$ as $\mathsf{LM}_<(I)$ is not an ideal. Our strategy is to prove that over $\mathbb{K}[S_M^h]$ there is always a finite sparse Gröbner basis, and then extend this result to $\mathbb{K}[S_M]$. We show that this sGB is related to a standard Gröbner basis over some Noetherian ring, so it is finite.

3.1 Finiteness of sparse Gröbner Bases

Homogeneous case. Let $<_M$ be a monomial order for $\mathbb{K}[S_M]$ and $<$ the sparse order related to $<_M$, Eq. (2). Consider $<_h$ the graded sparse order related to $<$ over $\mathbb{K}[S_M^h]$, Eq. (1).

Consider the lattice ideal T from Sec. 2.1. This ideal T is homogeneous and the algebra $\mathbb{K}[S_M^h]$ is isomorphic to $\mathbb{K}[\boldsymbol{y}]/T$ as a graded algebra. Let $\widetilde{\psi} : \mathbb{K}[\boldsymbol{y}]/T \to \mathbb{K}[S_M^h]$ and $\widetilde{\phi} : \mathbb{K}[S_M^h] \to \mathbb{K}[\boldsymbol{y}]/T$ be the isomorphisms related to $\mathbb{K}[S_M^h] \cong \mathbb{K}[\boldsymbol{y}]/T$, such that they are inverse of each other and $\widetilde{\psi}(\boldsymbol{X}^{(0,1)}) = y_0$. We extend $\widetilde{\psi}$ to $\psi : \mathbb{K}[\boldsymbol{y}] \to \mathbb{K}[S_M^h]$, where $\psi(\boldsymbol{y}^\alpha)$ is the image, under $\widetilde{\psi}$, of $\boldsymbol{y}^\alpha$ modulo T. The map ψ is a 0-graded epimorphism.

For $\boldsymbol{y}^\alpha \in \mathbb{K}[\boldsymbol{y}]$, let $\deg(\boldsymbol{y}^\alpha, y_0)$ be the degree of $\boldsymbol{y}^\alpha$ with respect to y_0 and $\deg(\boldsymbol{y}^\alpha)$ be the total degree. Given a (standard) monomial order $\widetilde{<}$ for $\mathbb{K}[\boldsymbol{y}]$, consider the graded monomial order $<_y$ for $\mathbb{K}[\boldsymbol{y}]$ defined as follows,

$$\boldsymbol{y}^a <_y \boldsymbol{y}^b \iff \begin{cases} \deg(\boldsymbol{y}^a) < \deg(\boldsymbol{y}^b) & \\ \deg(\boldsymbol{y}^a) = \deg(\boldsymbol{y}^b) & \wedge \quad \deg(\boldsymbol{y}^a, y_0) > \deg(\boldsymbol{y}^b, y_0) \\ \deg(\boldsymbol{y}^a) = \deg(\boldsymbol{y}^b) & \wedge \quad \deg(\boldsymbol{y}^a, y_0) = \deg(\boldsymbol{y}^b, y_0) \quad \wedge \\ & \quad\ \psi(\boldsymbol{y}^a) <_M \psi(\boldsymbol{y}^b) \\ \deg(\boldsymbol{y}^a) = \deg(\boldsymbol{y}^b) & \wedge \quad \deg(\boldsymbol{y}^a, y_0) = \deg(\boldsymbol{y}^b, y_0) \quad \wedge \\ & \quad\ \psi(\boldsymbol{y}^a) = \psi(\boldsymbol{y}^b) \quad \wedge \quad \boldsymbol{y}^a \widetilde{<} \boldsymbol{y}^b \end{cases} \tag{3}$$

This order is a monomial order, because it is a total order, $\boldsymbol{y}^0$ is the unique smallest monomial (it is the only one of degree 0), and it is compatible with the multiplication (every case is compatible).

For each $f \in \mathbb{K}[\boldsymbol{y}]$, we define η as the normal form (the remainder of the division algorithm) of f with respect to the ideal T and the monomial order $<_y$. Recall that $\eta = \eta \circ \eta$ and $\mathsf{coker}(\eta) \cong \mathbb{K}[\boldsymbol{y}]/T$. We notice that for each poset in $\mathbb{K}[\boldsymbol{y}]/T$, η assigns the same normal form to all the elements that it contains. Therefore, we abuse notation, and we also use η to denote the map $\mathbb{K}[\boldsymbol{y}]/T \to \mathbb{K}[\boldsymbol{y}]$ that maps each poset to this unique normal form. As T is homogeneous, η is a 0-graded map. We extend $\widetilde{\phi}$ to $\phi : \mathbb{K}[S_M^h] \to \mathbb{K}[\boldsymbol{y}]$ as $\phi := \eta \circ \widetilde{\phi}$. This map is 0-graded and linear, but not a homomorphism. It holds $\psi \circ \phi = Id$ and $\phi \circ \psi = \eta$.

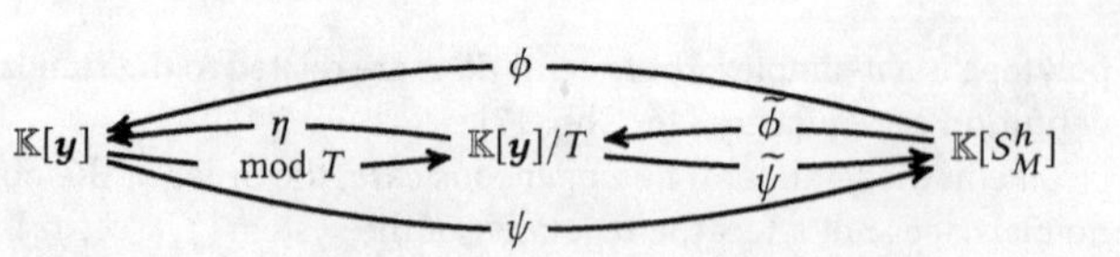

Theorem 3.5. *Let $I^h \subset \mathbb{K}[S_M^h]$ be a homogeneous ideal and consider the homogeneous ideal $J^h := \langle \phi(I^h) + T \rangle \subset \mathbb{K}[\boldsymbol{y}]$. If the Gröbner base of J^h with respect to $<_y$ is $GB_{<_y}(J^h)$, then $\psi(GB_{<_y}(J^h))$ is a sparse Gröbner base of I^h with respect to $<_h$.*

To prove the theorem we need the following lemmas.

Lemma 3.6. *For all $\boldsymbol{y}^\alpha \in \mathbb{K}[\boldsymbol{y}]$, $\deg(\eta(\boldsymbol{y}^\alpha), y_0) = \deg(\boldsymbol{y}^\alpha) - \delta(\psi(\boldsymbol{y}^\alpha))$.*

Proof. Let $\boldsymbol{X}^{(s,d)} := \psi(\boldsymbol{y}^\alpha)$ and $\bar{d} = \delta(\boldsymbol{X}^{(s,d)})$. Note that $d = \deg(\boldsymbol{y}^\alpha)$, because ψ is 0-graded. We can write $\psi(\boldsymbol{y}^\alpha) = \chi^{-1}(\boldsymbol{X}^s) \cdot \boldsymbol{X}^{(0,d-\bar{d})}$. Recall that $\phi \circ \psi = \eta$. Applying ϕ to the previous equality we get, $\eta(\boldsymbol{y}^\alpha) = \eta(\bar{\phi}(\chi^{-1}(\boldsymbol{X}^s)) \cdot \bar{\phi}(\boldsymbol{X}^{(0,d-\bar{d})})) = \eta(\bar{\phi}(\chi^{-1}(\boldsymbol{X}^s)) \cdot y_0^{d-\bar{d}})$. Note that the order $>_y$ acts as the degree reverse lexicographical with respect to y_0, hence $\eta(\bar{\phi}(\chi^{-1}(\boldsymbol{X}^s)) \cdot y_0^{d-\bar{d}}) = \phi(\chi^{-1}(\boldsymbol{X}^s)) \cdot y_0^{d-\bar{d}}$. If y_0 divides $\phi(\chi^{-1}(\boldsymbol{X}^s))$, then there is a monomial $\boldsymbol{y}^\beta$ such that $y_0 \cdot \boldsymbol{y}^\beta = \phi(\chi^{-1}(\boldsymbol{X}^s))$, and so, $\psi(y_0 \cdot \boldsymbol{y}^\beta) = \psi(\phi(\chi^{-1}(\boldsymbol{X}^s)))$. As $\psi \circ \phi = Id$ and ψ is a 0-graded epimorphism, then $\boldsymbol{X}^{(0,1)} \cdot \psi(\boldsymbol{y}^\beta) = \chi^{-1}(\boldsymbol{X}^s)$, but this is not possible by definition of homogenization (Sec. 2.2). Hence, $\deg(\phi(\chi^{-1}(\boldsymbol{X}^s)), y_0) = 0$ and $\deg(\eta(\boldsymbol{y}^\alpha), y_0) = 0 + d - \bar{d}$. □

Corollary 3.7. *For all $\boldsymbol{X}^{(s,d)} \in \mathbb{K}[S_M^h]$, it holds $\delta(\boldsymbol{X}^{(s,d)}) = d - \deg(\phi(\boldsymbol{X}^{(s,d)}), y_0)$.*

As ψ and ϕ are 0-graded maps, by Lem. 3.6 and Cor. 3.7, they preserve the order.

Corollary 3.8. *$\eta(y^\alpha) <_y \eta(y^\beta) \implies \psi(y^\alpha) <_h \psi(y^\beta)$.*

Lemma 3.9. *$\boldsymbol{y}^\alpha | \phi(\boldsymbol{X}^{(s,d)}) \implies \psi(\boldsymbol{y}^\alpha) || \boldsymbol{X}^{(s,d)}$.*

Proof. Let $\boldsymbol{y}^\beta$ such that $\boldsymbol{y}^\alpha \cdot \boldsymbol{y}^\beta = \phi(\boldsymbol{X}^{(s,d)})$, so $\psi(\boldsymbol{y}^\alpha) \cdot \psi(\boldsymbol{y}^\beta) = \boldsymbol{X}^{(s,d)}$. As η is a normal form, $\eta(\phi(\boldsymbol{X}^{(s,d)})) = \phi(\boldsymbol{X}^{(s,d)})$ and then, $\eta(\boldsymbol{y}^\alpha) = \boldsymbol{y}^\alpha$ and $\eta(\boldsymbol{y}^\beta) = \boldsymbol{y}^\beta$. Hence, by Cor. 3.7, $\delta(\psi(\boldsymbol{y}^\alpha \cdot \boldsymbol{y}^\beta)) = \deg(\boldsymbol{y}^\alpha \cdot \boldsymbol{y}^\beta) - \deg(\eta(\boldsymbol{y}^\alpha \cdot \boldsymbol{y}^\beta), y_0) = \deg(\boldsymbol{y}^\alpha) - \deg(\eta(\boldsymbol{y}^\alpha), y_0) + \deg(\boldsymbol{y}^\beta) - \deg(\eta(\boldsymbol{y}^\beta), y_0) = \delta(\psi(\boldsymbol{y}^\alpha)) + \delta(\psi(\boldsymbol{y}^\beta))$, by Lem. 3.6. □

Corollary 3.10. *For all $f \in \mathbb{K}[S_M^h]$, for all $g \in \mathbb{K}[\boldsymbol{y}]$, it holds $\mathsf{LM}_{<_y}(\eta(g)) | \mathsf{LM}_{<_y}(\phi(f)) \implies \mathsf{LM}_{<_h}(\psi(g)) || \mathsf{LM}_{<_h}(f)$.*

Proof. By Cor. 3.8, $\psi(\mathsf{LM}_{<_y}(\eta(g))) = \mathsf{LM}_{<_h}(\psi(g))$ and $\psi(\mathsf{LM}_{<_y}(\phi(f))) = \mathsf{LM}_{<_y}(\psi(\phi(f))) = \mathsf{LM}_{<_h}(f)$. The proof follows from Lem. 3.9. □

Proof of Thm. 3.5. Consider $f \in I^h$, then $\phi(f) \in J^h$. Hence, there are $g_1, \ldots, g_k \in GB_{<_y}(J^h)$ and $p_1, \ldots, p_k \in \mathbb{K}[\boldsymbol{y}]$ such that $\phi(f) = \sum_{i=1}^k p_i \cdot g_i$. As $\psi \circ \phi = Id$ and ψ is an epimorphism such that $\psi(T) = 0$, then $\psi(\phi(f)) = f = \sum_{i=1}^k \psi(p_i) \cdot \psi(g_i)$ and $\psi(g_i), \ldots, \psi(g_k) \in I^h$. Hence, $\psi(GB_{<_y}(J^h))$ generates I^h.

The set $GB_{<_y}(J^h)$ is a Gröbner basis, then there is a $g \in GB_{<_y}(J^h)$ such that $\mathsf{LM}_{<_y}(g) | \mathsf{LM}_{<_y}(\phi(f))$. As $\phi(f) = \eta(\phi(f))$, $\eta(\mathsf{LM}_{<_y}(\phi(f))) = \mathsf{LM}_{<_y}(\phi(f))$ and $\eta(\mathsf{LM}_{<_y}(g)) = \mathsf{LM}_{<_y}(g)$. As η is a normal form wrt $<_y$, $\eta(\mathsf{LM}_{<_y}(g)) = \mathsf{LM}_{<_y}(\eta(g))$. By Cor. 3.10, $\mathsf{LM}_{<_h}(\psi(g)) || \mathsf{LM}_{<_h}(f)$. Hence, $\psi(GB_{<_y}(J^h))$ is a sGB for I^h with respect to $<_h$. □

Corollary 3.11. *Given an ideal $I^h \subset \mathbb{K}[S_M^h]$ and a graded sparse order $<_h$, its sGB with respect to this order is finite.*

Proof. In Thm. 3.5 we construct $sGB_{<_h}(I^h)$ from a (standard) Gröbner basis of an ideal of $\mathbb{K}[\boldsymbol{y}]$, finite as $\mathbb{K}[\boldsymbol{y}]$ is Noetherian. □

Non-homogeneous case. Let $<$ be a sparse order for $\mathbb{K}[S_M]$.

Lemma 3.12. *Let $I^h \subset \mathbb{K}[S_M^h]$ be a homogeneous ideal. Let $<_h$ be the graded sparse order for $\mathbb{K}[S_M^h]$ related to $<$. Then, $\chi(sGB_{<_h}(I^h))$ is a sparse Gröbner Basis for $\chi(I^h)$ with respect to $<$.*

Proof. The set $\chi(sGB_{<_h}(I^h))$ generates $\chi(I^h)$. Note that for homogeneous polynomials, $\mathsf{LM}_{<_h}$ commutes with the dehomogenization, that is for any homogeneous polynomial $g \in \mathbb{K}[S_M^h]$, $\mathsf{LM}_<(\chi(g)) = \chi(\mathsf{LM}_{<_h}(g))$. Consider $\bar{f} \in \chi(I^h)$, then there is an $f \in I^h$ such that $f = \chi(\bar{f})$. In addition, there is $g \in sGB_{<_h}(I^h)$ such that $\mathsf{LM}_{<_h}(g)||\mathsf{LM}_{<_h}(f)$. Let $\boldsymbol{X}^{(s,d)} \in \mathbb{K}[S_M^h]$ such that $\mathsf{LM}_{<_h}(g) \cdot \boldsymbol{X}^{(s,d)} = \mathsf{LM}_{<_h}(f)$ and $\delta(\mathsf{LM}_{<_h}(g)) + \delta(\boldsymbol{X}^{(s,d)}) = \delta(\mathsf{LM}_{<_h}(f))$. The sparse degree δ is independent of the homogeneous degree, so $\delta(\chi(\mathsf{LM}_{<_h}(g))) + \delta(\boldsymbol{X}^s) = \delta(\chi(\mathsf{LM}_{<_h}(f)))$. Hence, $\delta(\mathsf{LM}_<(\chi(g))) + \delta(\boldsymbol{X}^s) = \delta(\mathsf{LM}_<(\bar{f}))$ and $\mathsf{LM}_<(\chi(g)) \cdot \boldsymbol{X}^s = \mathsf{LM}_<(\bar{f})$, so $\mathsf{LM}_<(\chi(g))||\mathsf{LM}_<(\bar{f})$ and $\chi(sGB_{<_h}(I^h))$ is a sGB of $\chi(I^h)$ wrt $<$. □

Corollary 3.13. *The sGB of $I \subset \mathbb{K}[S_M]$ with respect to $<$ is finite.*

Proof. For $\chi^{-1}(I)$, the homogenization of I, $\chi(\chi^{-1}(I)) = I$. So by Lem. 3.12 $\chi(sGB_<(\chi^{-1}(I)))$ is a sGB of I and is finite by Cor. 3.11. □

3.2 Computing sparse Gröbner Bases

Homogeneous case. To compute a sGB of a homogeneous ideal $I^h := \langle f_1, \ldots, f_k \rangle$ with respect to $<_h$, we introduce the D-sparse Gröbner bases [28, Sec. III.B]. A D-sparse Gröbner basis of I^h is a finite set of polynomials $\mathcal{J}^h \subset I^h$ such that for each $f \in I^h$ with $\deg(f) \leq D$, it holds $f \in \langle \mathcal{J}^h \rangle$ and there is a $g \in \mathcal{J}^h$ such that $\mathsf{LM}_{<_h}(g)||\mathsf{LM}_{<_h}(f)$. For big enough D, for example equal to the maximal degree in the polynomials in $sGB_{<_h}(I^h)$, a D-sparse Gröbner basis is a sparse Gröbner basis. The *witness degree* of I^h is the minimal D such that a D-sparse Gröbner basis is a sGB. We compute D-sparse Gröbner bases by using linear algebra.

Definition 3.14. *A Macaulay matrix $\mathcal{M}$ is a matrix whose columns are indexed by monomials in $\mathbb{K}[S_M^h]$ and the rows by polynomials in $\mathbb{K}[S_M^h]$. The set of monomials that index the columns contain all the monomial in the supports of the polynomials of the rows. For a monomial m in a polynomial f, the entry in the matrix indexed by (m, f) is the coefficient of the monomial m in f. We define $\mathsf{Columns}(\mathcal{M})$ as the sequence of the monomials of $\mathcal{M}$ in the order that they index the columns. We define $\mathsf{Rows}(\mathcal{M})$ as the set of* non-zero *polynomials that index the rows of $\mathcal{M}$.*

If we apply a row operation to a Macaulay matrix, we obtain a new Macaulay matrix, where we replace one of the polynomials (that is one of the rows) by linear combinations of some of them. We say that we have a *reduction to zero*, if after we perform a row operation, the resulting row is zero. As observed by Lazard [28], if we sort the columns in decreasing order by $<_h$, we can compute a Gröbner basis using Gaussian elimination. The proof of the following lemma follows from [28].

Lemma 3.15. *Consider the ideal $I^h := \langle f_1, \ldots, f_k \rangle \subset \mathbb{K}[S_M^h]$. Let $\mathcal{M}_D$ be the Macaulay matrix whose columns are all the monomials in $\mathbb{K}[S_M^h]_D$ sorted in decreasing order by $<_h$, and the rows are all the products of the form $\boldsymbol{X}^{(s, D - \deg(f_i))} \cdot f_i \in \mathbb{K}[S_M^h]_D$. Let $\widetilde{\mathcal{M}_D}$ be the matrix obtained by applying Gaussian elimination to $\mathcal{M}_D$ to obtain a reduced row echelon form. Then, the polynomials in $\bigcup_{i=1}^{D} \mathsf{Rows}(\widetilde{\mathcal{M}_i})$ form a D-sparse Gröbner basis. Moreover, if we only consider the set of polynomials whose leading monomial can not be divided by the leading monomial of a polynomial obtained in smaller degree, that is*

$$\bigcup_{i=1}^{D} \{f \in \mathsf{Rows}(\widetilde{\mathcal{M}_i}) : (\nexists g \in \bigcup_{j=1}^{i-1} \mathsf{Rows}(\widetilde{\mathcal{M}_j}))\ \mathsf{LM}_{<_h}(g)||\mathsf{LM}_{<_h}(f)\},$$

then this subset is a D-sparse Gröbner basis too.

Non-homogeneous case. Given an ideal $I := \langle \bar{f}_1 \ldots \bar{f}_r \rangle \subset \mathbb{K}[S_M]$, we homogenize the polynomials and use Lem. 3.15 to compute a sparse Gröbner basis with respect to $<_h$. By Lem. 3.12, if we dehomogenize the computed basis, we obtain a sparse Gröbner basis with respect to $<$ of I. Instead of homogenizing all polynomials $\bar{f}_i$ simultaneously, we consider an iterative approach, which, under regularity assumptions, involves only full-rank matrices, and hence avoids all reductions to zero. The following lemma allows us to compute a sparse Gröbner basis in the homogeneous case, from the non-homogeneous one.

Lemma 3.16. *If G is a sGB of I with respect to $<$, then $G^h := \chi^{-1}(G)$ is a sGB of $\langle \chi^{-1}(I) \rangle$ with respect to $<_h$.*

Proof. First note that the homogenization commutes with the leading monomial, that is $\forall \bar{g} \in \mathbb{K}[S_M], \mathsf{LM}_{<_h}(\chi^{-1}(\bar{g})) = \chi^{-1}(\mathsf{LM}_<(\bar{g}))$. Let $f \in \langle \chi^{-1}(I) \rangle$. We can write f as $\boldsymbol{X}^{(0, \deg(f) - \delta(f))} \cdot \chi^{-1}(\chi(f))$. Consider $\bar{g} \in G$ such that $\mathsf{LM}_<(\bar{g})||\mathsf{LM}_<(\chi(f))$. By definition (Def. 3.1), $\chi^{-1}(\mathsf{LM}_<(\bar{g}))||\chi^{-1}(\mathsf{LM}_<(\chi(f)))$, and by commutativity, it holds that $\mathsf{LM}_{<_h}(\chi^{-1}(\bar{g}))||\mathsf{LM}_{<_h}(\chi^{-1}(\chi(f))$. The sparse degree and the leading monomials with respect to $<_h$ are invariants under the multiplication by $\boldsymbol{X}^{(0,1)}$. Hence, $\mathsf{LM}_{<_h}(\chi^{-1}(\bar{g}))||\mathsf{LM}_{<_h}(f)$. To conclude, we have to prove that G^h is a basis of $\langle \chi^{-1}(I) \rangle$. As for each $f \in \chi^{-1}(I)$ there is a $\bar{g} \in G$ such that $\mathsf{LM}_{<_h}(\chi^{-1}(\bar{g}))||\mathsf{LM}_{<_h}(f)$. Thus, the remainder of the division algorithm (Lem. 3.4) is zero, and so we obtain a representation of f in the basis $\chi^{-1}(G)$. □

Corollary 3.17. *Let $I \subset \mathbb{K}[S_M]$ be an (non-homogeneous) ideal and consider the (non-homogeneous) polynomial $\bar{f} \in \mathbb{K}[S_M]$. Let G be a (non-homogeneous) sGB of I wrt $<$ and $G_{\bar{f}}^h$ be a (homogeneous) sGB of $\langle \chi^{-1}(G) + \chi^{-1}(\bar{f}) \rangle$ wrt $<_h$. Then, $\chi(G_{\bar{f}}^h)$ is a (non-homogeneous) sGB of $\langle I + \bar{f} \rangle$ wrt $<$.*

Cor. 3.17 supports an iterative algorithm to compute a sGB of I. For each $i \leq n$, let $I_i := \langle \bar{f}_1, \ldots, \bar{f}_i \rangle$ and $G_i := sGB_<(I_i)$. Consider $I_i^h := \langle \chi^{-1}(G_{i-1}) + \chi^{-1}(\bar{f}_i) \rangle$. By Cor. 3.17, we can consider G_i as $\chi(sGB_{<_h}(I_i^h))$. To compute $sGB_{<_h}(I_i^h)$ we use Def. 3.14.

Many rows of the Macaulay matrices reduces to zero during the Gaussian elimination procedure. We can adapt the F5 criterion [15, 19] to identify these rows and avoid them.

Lemma 3.18. *Let G be a sGB of the homogeneous ideal I^h wrt $<_h$. Let $\mathcal{N} \subset \mathbb{K}[S_M^h]_D$ be the set of monomials of degree D such that for* *each of them there is a polynomial in G whose leading term divides it, that is* $\mathcal{N} = \left\{X^{(s,D)} \in \mathbb{K}[S^h_M]_D : \exists g \in G \text{ s.t. } \mathsf{LM}_{<_h}(g) || X^{(s,D)}\right\}$. *To each* $X^{(s,D)} \in \mathcal{N}$ *associate only one polynomial* $g \in G$, *such that* $\mathsf{LM}_{<_h}(g)||X^{(s,D)}$. *Let* $\mathcal{R}$ *be the set formed by the polynomials* $\frac{X^{(s,D)}}{\mathsf{LM}_{<_h}(g)} \cdot g$ *where* g *is the polynomial associated to* $X^{(s,D)} \in \mathcal{N}$.

Consider the Macaulay matrix $\mathcal{M}'_D$ *with columns indexed by the monomials in* $\mathbb{K}[S^h_M]_D$ *in decreasing order w.r.t.* $<_h$ *and rows indexed by* $\mathcal{R}$. *Let* $\widetilde{\mathcal{M}'_d}$ *be the Macaulay matrix obtained after applying Gaussian elimination to* $\mathcal{M}'_d$ *to obtain a reduced row echelon form. Then,* $\mathsf{Rows}(\widetilde{\mathcal{M}'_D}) = \mathsf{Rows}(\widetilde{\mathcal{M}_D})$, *where* $\widetilde{\mathcal{M}_d}$ *is the Macaulay matrix of Lem. 3.15 with respect to* G^h. *Moreover, the matrix* M'_D *is full-rank and in row echelon form.*

Lemma 3.19 (Sparse F5 criterion). *Let* G^h *be a sparse Gröbner basis of the homogeneous ideal* I^h *wrt* $<_h$ *and let* $\mathcal{M}'_D$ *be the Macaulay matrix of Lem. 3.18 of degree D. Let* $d \in \mathbb{N}$ *and consider the set* $\mathfrak{b} = \{X^{(s,D-d)} \in \mathbb{K}[S^h_M]_{D-d} : \nexists g \in G^h \text{ s.t. } \mathsf{LM}_{<_h}(g)||X^{(s,D-d)}\}$. *Let* $f \in \mathbb{K}[S^h_M]_d$; *consider the Macaulay matrix* $\mathcal{M}^*_D$ *obtained after appending to* $\mathcal{M}'_D$ *rows indexed by* $\{X^{(s,D-d)} \cdot f : X^{(s,D-d)} \in \mathfrak{b}\}$.

Let $\widetilde{\mathcal{M}^*_D}$ *be the matrix obtained after applying Gaussian elimination to* $\mathcal{M}^*_D$. *Then,* $\mathsf{Rows}(\widetilde{\mathcal{M}^*_D}) = \mathsf{Rows}(\widetilde{\mathcal{M}_D})$, *where* $\widetilde{\mathcal{M}_D}$ *is the Macaulay matrix of Lem. 3.15 for the ideal* $\langle G^h, f\rangle$. *Moreover, if* f *is not a zero-divisor in* $\mathbb{K}[S^h_M]/I^h$, *then* $\mathcal{M}^*_D$ *is full-rank.*

Lemma 3.20. *If* $\bar{f}_1, \ldots, \bar{f}_k \in \mathbb{K}[S_M]$ *is a regular sequence, then for each* $i \leq k$, $\chi^{-1}(\bar{f}_i)$ *is not a zero-divisor of* $\mathbb{K}[S^h_M]/\chi^{-1}(\langle \bar{f}_1, \ldots, \bar{f}_{i-1}\rangle)$.

Proof. If $\chi^{-1}(\bar{f}_i)$ is a zero-divisor of $\mathbb{K}[S^h_M]/\chi^{-1}(\langle \bar{f}_1, \ldots, \bar{f}_{i-1}\rangle)$, there is a $g \in \mathbb{K}[S^h_M]$ such that $g \notin \chi^{-1}(\langle \bar{f}_1, \ldots, \bar{f}_{i-1}\rangle)$ and $g \cdot \chi^{-1}(\bar{f}_i) \in \chi^{-1}(\langle \bar{f}_1, \ldots, \bar{f}_{i-1}\rangle)$. By definition of the homogenization of an ideal, $\chi(g) \notin \langle \bar{f}_1, \ldots, \bar{f}_{i-1}\rangle$ but, as χ is a homomorphism, $\chi(g) \cdot \bar{f}_i \in \langle \bar{f}_1, \ldots, \bar{f}_{i-1}\rangle$. So, $\bar{f}_1, \ldots, \bar{f}_i$ is not a regular sequence. □

Hence, given the witness degrees of each I^h_i, we have the algorithm Alg. 3.1 to compute iteratively a sparse Gröbner basis.

As in the standard case, we can define the reduced sGB and adapt [10, Prop. 2.7.6] to prove their finiteness and uniqueness.

Algorithm 3.1 M^2: Mixed sparse Matrix-F5 with respect to $<$

Input: $\bar{f}_1, \ldots, \bar{f}_k \in \mathbb{K}[S_M]$ and $d^{wit}_1, \ldots, d^{wit}_k$ such that d^{wit}_i is the witness degree of I^h_i.
for $i = 1$ to k **do**
  $G_i \leftarrow \emptyset$
  for $d = 1$ to d^{wit}_i **do**
    $\mathcal{M}^i_d \leftarrow$ Macaulay matrix with columns indexed by the monomials in $\mathbb{K}[S^h_M]_d$ in decreasing order by $<_h$
    for $X^{(s,d)} \in \mathbb{K}[S^h_M]_d$ **do**
      if $\exists g \in G^h_{i-1} : \mathsf{LM}_{<_h}(g)||X^{(s,d)}$ **then**
        Add to $\mathcal{M}^i_d$ the polynomial $\frac{X^{(s,d)}}{\mathsf{LM}_{<_h}(g)} \cdot g$
    for $X^{(s,d-\delta^A(\bar{f}_i))} \in \mathbb{K}[S^h_M]_{d-\delta^A(\bar{f}_i)}$ **do**
      if $\nexists g \in G^h_{i-1}$ such that $\mathsf{LM}_{<_h}(g)||\mathsf{LM}_{<_h}(\chi^{-1}(\bar{f}_i))$ **then**
        Add to $\mathcal{M}^i_d$ the polynomial $X^{(s,d-\delta^A(\bar{f}_i))} \cdot \chi^{-1}(\bar{f}_i)$
    $\widetilde{\mathcal{M}^i_d} \leftarrow$ Gaussian elimination of $\mathcal{M}^i_d$
    $G_i \leftarrow G_i \cup \{\bar{h} \in \chi(\mathsf{Rows}(\widetilde{\mathcal{M}^i_d})) : \nexists \bar{g} \in G_i \wedge \mathsf{LM}_<(\bar{g})||\mathsf{LM}_<(\bar{h})\}$
  $G^h_i \leftarrow \chi^{-1}(G_i)$
return G_k

4 MULTIHOMOGENEOUS SYSTEMS

We consider an algorithm for solving 0-dimensional square multihomogeneous systems with no solutions at infinity.

Notation. Let $n_1, \ldots n_r \in \mathbb{N}$, $N := \sum_i n_i$, and $\boldsymbol{n} := (n_1 \ldots n_r) \in \mathbb{N}^r$. For $1 \leq i \leq r$, let $\boldsymbol{x_i}$ be the set of variables $\{x_{i,0}, \ldots, x_{i,n_i}\}$. Let $\mathbb{K}[\boldsymbol{x}] := \bigotimes_{i=1}^r \mathbb{K}[\boldsymbol{x_i}]$ be the multihomogeneous $\mathbb{K}$-algebra multigraded by $\mathbb{Z}^r$, such that for all $\boldsymbol{d} := (d_1, \ldots, d_r) \in \mathbb{Z}^r$, we have $\mathbb{K}[\boldsymbol{x}]_{\boldsymbol{d}} := \bigotimes_{i=1}^r \mathbb{K}[\boldsymbol{x_i}]_{d_i}$. Given a $\mathbb{K}[\boldsymbol{x}]$-module M, we consider $[\mathrm{M}]_{\boldsymbol{d}}$ as the graded part of M of multidegree $\boldsymbol{d}$. Given two multidegrees $\boldsymbol{d}$ and $\bar{\boldsymbol{d}}$, we say that $\boldsymbol{d} \geq \bar{\boldsymbol{d}}$ if the inequality holds componentwise. We consider the multiprojective space $\mathcal{P} := \mathbb{P}^{n_1} \times \cdots \times \mathbb{P}^{n_r}$.

Let $\bar{1} = (1, \ldots, 1) \in \mathbb{Z}^r$ be the multidegree corresponding to multilinear polynomials in $\mathbb{K}[\boldsymbol{x}]$. Let $B = \cap_{i=1}^r \langle x_{i,0}, \ldots, x_{i,n_i}\rangle$ be the ideal generated by all the polynomials in $\mathbb{K}[\boldsymbol{x}]_{\bar{1}}$.

Consider multihomogeneous polynomials $f_1, \ldots, f_k \in \mathbb{K}[\boldsymbol{x}]$ and denote their multidegrees by $\deg(f_1), \ldots, \deg(f_k) \in \mathbb{N}^r$. Let $V_{\mathcal{P}}(f_1, \ldots, f_k)$ be the zero set of $f_1, \ldots, f_k$ over $\mathcal{P}$. If the dimension of $V_{\mathcal{P}}(f_1, \ldots, f_k)$ over $\mathcal{P}$ is $N - k$, then the polynomials $f_1, \ldots, f_k$ form a regular sequence at each point of $\mathbb{P}^1 \times \cdots \times \mathbb{P}^r$. That is, for each prime ideal $\mathfrak{p}$, such that $\mathfrak{p} \not\subset B$, $(f_1, \ldots, f_k)$ form a regular sequence over $\mathbb{K}[\boldsymbol{x}]_{\mathfrak{p}}$, the localization of $\mathbb{K}[\boldsymbol{x}]$ at $\mathfrak{p}$. In this case, we say that $(f_1, \ldots, f_k)$ is a *regular sequence outside B*. This kind of sequence is related to the filter regular sequence [36, Sec. 2] and the sequence of "almost" nonzero divisors [30, Sec. 3], [33, Sec. 2].

Let $\mathcal{K}_\bullet(f_1, \ldots, f_k ; \mathbb{K}[\boldsymbol{x}])$ be the Koszul complex of $f_1, \ldots, f_k$ over $\mathbb{K}[\boldsymbol{x}]$. Let $H_i(\mathcal{K}_\bullet(f_1, \ldots, f_k ; \mathbb{K}[\boldsymbol{x}]))$ be the i-th Koszul homology module. We also write this homology module as H^k_i.

Let $x_h := \prod_{i=1}^r x_{i,0} \in \mathbb{K}[\boldsymbol{x}]_{\bar{1}}$. We say that a multihomogeneous system $(f_1, \ldots, f_N)$ has *no solutions* at infinity if the system $(f_1, \ldots, f_N, x_h)$ has no solutions over $\mathcal{P}$. We dehomogenize a multihomogeneous polynomial by replacing each variable $x_{i,0}$ with 1. Let $\mathbb{K}[\bar{\boldsymbol{x}}]$ be the $\mathbb{K}$-algebra obtained by the dehomogenization of $\mathbb{K}[\boldsymbol{x}]$. Given $f \in \mathbb{K}[\boldsymbol{x}]$, we consider $\bar{f} \in \mathbb{K}[\bar{\boldsymbol{x}}]$, its dehomogenization.

4.1 Multigraded regularity

Based on Maclagan and Smith [30, 31], Botbol and Chardin [6] define the multigraded Castelnuovo-Mumford regularity over $\mathbb{K}[\boldsymbol{x}]$ in terms of the vanishing of the *local cohomology* modules with respect to B. For an introduction to local cohomology, we refer to [8]. In the following we present some results from [5, Chp. 6], that we need in our setting, see also [1].

Given a module M, $H^j_B(\mathrm{M})$ is the j-th local cohomology module at B and $\mathrm{sp}(\mathrm{M}) := \{\boldsymbol{d} \in \mathbb{Z}^r : [\mathrm{M}]_{\boldsymbol{d}} \neq 0\}$ is the set of multidegrees where the module is not zero.

Consider $\alpha \subset \{1, \ldots, r\}$. We define the Q_α as the convex region of $\mathbb{R}^r$ given by the vectors $(v_1, \ldots, v_r) \in \mathbb{R}^r$ so that for every $i \leq r$,

$$\begin{cases} v_i \leq -n_i - 1 & \text{, if } i \in \alpha \\ v_i \geq 0 & \text{, otherwise.} \end{cases}$$

Consider the multiset $\Sigma_i^k := \{\sum_{j\in I} \deg(f_j) : I \subset \{1 \ldots k\}, \#I = i\}$ containing the sums of the degrees of i (different) polynomials from the set $\{f_1, \ldots, f_k\}$. Given $v \in \mathbb{R}^r$, the displacement of Q_α by v is $Q_\alpha + v := \{w \in \mathbb{R}^r : w - v \in Q_\alpha\}$. Let $N_\alpha := \sum_{i\in\alpha} n_i$.

Proposition 4.1 ([5, Remark 6.4.10], [1, Cor. 4.3]). *If $(f_1, \ldots, f_k)$ form a regular sequence outside B, for every i, j,*

$$\mathsf{sp}(H_B^i(H_j^k)) \subset \bigcup_{\substack{\alpha\subset\{1,\ldots,k\}\\ N_\alpha+1+j-i\le k\\ \alpha\neq\emptyset}} \bigcup_{v\in\Sigma^k_{N_\alpha+1+j-i}} Q_\alpha + v. \quad (4)$$

Proposition 4.2. *If $(f_1, \ldots, f_k)$ form a regular sequence outside B, then for $j > 0$, it holds $H_B^0(H_j^k) = H_j^k$.*

The proposition follows from considering the spectral sequence of the double complex given by the Koszul complex and the Čech complex of $f_1, \ldots, f_k$ over B, when $f_1, \ldots, f_k$ is a regular sequence outside B, [1, Sec. 4].

Corollary 4.3 (Multihomogeneous Macaulay bound). *Let $f_1, \ldots, f_{N+1}$ be regular sequence outside B and $\boldsymbol{D_k} := \left(\sum_{i=1}^k \deg(f_i)\right) - \boldsymbol{n}$. If $\boldsymbol{d} \ge \boldsymbol{D_k}$, then $\forall i, j, k$, $[H_B^j(H_i^k)]_{\boldsymbol{d}} = 0$.*

Proof. We use Prop. 4.1. Fix i and j in Eq. (4), and consider $\alpha \subset \{1, \ldots, k\}$ such that $N_\alpha + 1 + j - i \le k$, $\#\alpha \neq \emptyset$, and $v \in \Sigma^k_{N_\alpha+1+j-i}$. If $t \in \alpha$, then the t-th coordinate of any element in $Q_\alpha + v$ has to be $\le -n_t - 1 + v_t$, where v_t is the t-th coordinate of v. As all the multidegrees $\deg(f_1), \ldots, \deg(f_k)$ are non-negative, $v_t \le \sum_{i=1}^k deg(f_i)_t$. So, $-n_t - 1 + v_t < -n_t + \sum_{i=1}^k deg(f_i)_t = (\boldsymbol{D_k})_t \le \boldsymbol{d}_t$. Hence, $\boldsymbol{d} \notin Q_\alpha + v$. By Prop. 4.1, $[H_B^0(H_i^k)]_{\boldsymbol{d}} = 0$. □

The bound $\boldsymbol{D_k}$ is not tight, e.g. see [1, Sec. 4.4].

Like with homogeneous polynomials, we define the multigraded Hilbert function, HF, of a $\mathbb{K}$-module M as the function that maps the multidegrees $\boldsymbol{d} \in \mathbb{Z}^r$ to $HF(\mathrm{M}, \boldsymbol{d}) = \dim_{\mathbb{K}}([\mathrm{M}]_{\boldsymbol{d}})$. When $\boldsymbol{d}$ is, component-wise, big enough, then $HF(\mathrm{M}, \boldsymbol{d})$ equals a polynomial $P_{\mathrm{M}} \in \mathbb{Q}[y_1, \ldots, y_r]$ evaluated at $\boldsymbol{d}$ [31, Prop. 2.8]; the Hilbert polynomial. If all the local cohomologies of M at a multidegree $\boldsymbol{d}$ vanish, that is for all i, $[H_B^i(\mathrm{M})]_{\boldsymbol{d}} = 0$, then, for this $\boldsymbol{d}$, the Hilbert function and polynomial agree, $HF(\mathrm{M}, \boldsymbol{d}) = P_{\mathrm{M}}(\boldsymbol{d})$ [31, Prop. 2.14].

Corollary 4.4. *Let $\boldsymbol{d} \ge D_K$, component-wise. If $k = N$, then the dimension of $[\mathbb{K}[\boldsymbol{x}]/\langle f_1, \ldots, f_N\rangle]_{\boldsymbol{d}}$ is the number of solutions, counting multiplicities, of the system $(f_1, \ldots, f_N)$ over $\mathcal{P}$. When $k = N + 1$, $\mathbb{K}[\boldsymbol{x}]_{\boldsymbol{d}} = [\langle f_1, \ldots, f_{N+1}\rangle]_{\boldsymbol{d}}$.*

4.2 Computing graded parts of the ideals

Let $(f_1, \ldots, f_k)$ be multihomogeneous system over $\mathcal{P}$. Alg. 4.1 computes a set of generators of the vector space $[\langle f_1, \ldots, f_k\rangle]_{\boldsymbol{d}}$. Moreover, if $(f_1, \ldots, f_k)$ form a regular sequence outside B, and $\boldsymbol{d} \ge \boldsymbol{D_k}$, then it performs no reduction to zero.

Theorem 4.5. *Let $(f_1, \ldots, f_k)$ be a multihomogeneous system. Alg. 4.1 computes a matrix such that the polynomials in its rows form a set of generators of the vector space $[\langle f_1, \ldots, f_k\rangle]_{\boldsymbol{d}}$, $\forall \boldsymbol{d} \in \mathbb{Z}^r$.*

We omit the proof as it is similar to Lemmata 3.18 and 3.19.

Remark 4.6. *Following the definition of the Koszul complex, $[H_i^k]_{\boldsymbol{d}} = 0$ implies that, given any syzygy $\sum_i g_i \cdot f_i = 0$ such that $deg(g_i f_i) = \boldsymbol{d}$, then $\forall j$, $g_j \in [\langle f_1, \ldots, f_{j-1}, f_{j+1}, \ldots, f_k\rangle]_{\boldsymbol{d}-\deg(f_j)}$.*

Algorithm 4.1 $\mathsf{M_3H}(\{f_1, \ldots, f_k\}, \boldsymbol{d}, <)$

Input: $f_1, \ldots, f_k \in \mathbb{K}[\boldsymbol{x}]$, degree $\boldsymbol{d}$ and $<$ a monomial order
$\mathfrak{L} \leftarrow \emptyset$.
if $k = 1$ **then**
  $\mathcal{M}_{\boldsymbol{d}}^k \leftarrow$ Macaulay matrix with columns indexed by the monomials in $\mathbb{K}[\boldsymbol{x}]_{\boldsymbol{d}}$ in decreasing order wrt $<$
else
  $\mathcal{M}_{\boldsymbol{d}}^k \leftarrow \mathsf{M_3H}(\{f_1, \ldots, f_{k-1}\}, \boldsymbol{d}, <)$
  $\mathfrak{L} \leftarrow$ Leading monomials of the Gaussian elimination of $\mathsf{M_3H}(\{f_1, \ldots, f_{k-1}\}, \boldsymbol{d} - \deg(f_k), <)$
for $\boldsymbol{x}^\beta \in \mathbb{K}[\boldsymbol{x}]_{\boldsymbol{d}-\deg(f_k)}$ **do**
  if $\boldsymbol{x}^\beta \notin \mathfrak{L}$ **then**
    Add to $\mathcal{M}_{\boldsymbol{d}}^k$ the polynomial $\boldsymbol{x}^\beta \cdot f_k$
return $\mathcal{M}_{\boldsymbol{d}}^k$

Lemma 4.7. *If $[H_1^k]_{\boldsymbol{d}} = 0$, then every polynomial $\boldsymbol{x}^\beta \cdot f_k$ in $\mathcal{M}_{\boldsymbol{d}}^k$ is linear independent to the (polynomials corresponding to) other rows.*

Proof. If there is a polynomial of the form $\boldsymbol{x}^\beta \cdot f_k$ in $\mathcal{M}_{\boldsymbol{d}}^k$ that is linearly dependent with the other rows of the matrix, then there is a syzygy of the system $(f_1, \ldots, f_k)$ involving f_k. That is, there are multihomogeneous polynomials $g_1, \ldots, g_k$ so that $\sum_i g_i f_i = 0$, for every $\boldsymbol{x}^\sigma$ in the support of g_i it holds $\boldsymbol{x}^\sigma \cdot f_i \in \mathsf{Rows}(\mathcal{M}_{\boldsymbol{d}}^k)$, and $\boldsymbol{x}^\beta$ belongs to the support of g_k. As H_1^k vanishes at degree $\boldsymbol{d}$, by Rem. 4.6, $g_k \in [\langle f_1, \ldots, f_k\rangle]_{\boldsymbol{d}-\deg(f_k)}$. But, by construction, $LM(g_k) \cdot f_k$ does not belong to $\mathsf{Rows}(\mathcal{M}_{\boldsymbol{d}}^k)$. Hence, this syzygy can not be formed with the rows of $\mathcal{M}_{\boldsymbol{d}}^k$. □

Corollary 4.8. *If $(f_1, \ldots, f_k)$ is a regular sequence outside B, then for $\boldsymbol{d} \ge \boldsymbol{D_k}$, all the matrices appearing in Alg. 4.1 are full-rank.*

Proof. We proceed by induction on k. When $k = 1$, the ideal is principal and so the theorem holds. In step k, note that $\boldsymbol{d} \ge \boldsymbol{D_k}$ implies $\boldsymbol{d} \ge \boldsymbol{d} - deg(f_k) \ge \boldsymbol{D_k} - \deg(f_k) = \boldsymbol{D_{k-1}}$. Hence, we have no reduction to zero in the recursive calls. As $\boldsymbol{d} \ge \boldsymbol{D_k}$, by Prop. 4.2, $H_B^0(H_i^k) = H_i^k$, and by Cor. 4.3, $[H_i^k]_{\boldsymbol{d}} = 0$. Hence, by Lem. 4.7, $\mathcal{M}_{\boldsymbol{d}}^k$ has not reduction to zero involving $\boldsymbol{x}^\beta \cdot f_k$. As, by induction, $\mathsf{M_3H}(\{f_1, \ldots, f_{k-1}\}, \boldsymbol{d}, <)$ is full-rank, $\mathcal{M}_{\boldsymbol{d}}^k$ is full-rank. □

4.3 Solving zero-dimensional systems

Our solving strategy is to dehomogenize the system and to compute the multiplication maps for the affine variables. Then we can apply FGLM to compute a Gröbner basis or compute the eigenvalues/eigenvectors of the multiplication maps.

Let $(f_1, \ldots, f_N)$ be a 0-dimensional system over $\mathcal{P}$ with no solutions at infinity. If we do not know if the system has no solutions at infinity, we can ensure it by performing a generic linear change of coordinates preserving the multihomogeneous structure, e.g. see [11, Pg. 121]. We use Alg. 4.1 to construct a monomial basis and the multiplication maps over $\mathbb{K}[\bar{x}]/\langle \bar{f}_1, \ldots, \bar{f}_N\rangle$. Following Alg. 4.1, let $\mathfrak{L}$ be the set of leading monomials of the polynomials in $[\langle f_1, \ldots, f_N\rangle]_{\boldsymbol{D_N}}$, with respect to $<$. Let $\mathfrak{b}$ be a list of monomials in $\mathbb{K}[\boldsymbol{x}]_{\boldsymbol{D_k}}$ not in $\mathfrak{L}$, sorted by $<$. Consider $\boldsymbol{D_{N+1}} := \boldsymbol{D_N} + \bar{1}$.

DEFINITION 4.9. *For a multilinear polynomial* $f_0 \in \mathbb{K}[x]_{\bar{1}}$, *let* $\widetilde{\mathcal{M}}^{f_0}$ *be the Macaulay matrix that we obtain after we permute the columns of* $\mathsf{M_3H}(\{f_1,\ldots,f_N,f_0\},\boldsymbol{D_{N+1}},<)$ *so that the columns indexed by the monomials* $\{x_h \cdot x^\beta : x^\beta \in \mathfrak{b}\}$ *are the last ones. Let* $\widetilde{\mathcal{M}}^{f_0}$ *be* $\left[\begin{smallmatrix} M^{f_0}_{1,1} & M^{f_0}_{1,2} \\ M^{f_0}_{2,1} & M^{f_0}_{2,2} \end{smallmatrix}\right]$, *where the monomials indexing the columns of* $\left[\begin{smallmatrix} M^{f_0}_{1,2} \\ M^{f_0}_{2,2} \end{smallmatrix}\right]$ *are the monomials in* $\{x_h \cdot x^\beta : x^\beta \in \mathfrak{b}\}$, *and the polynomials in the rows of* $\left[\begin{smallmatrix} M^{f_0}_{2,1} & M^{f_0}_{2,2} \end{smallmatrix}\right]$ *are of the form* $\{x^\beta \cdot f_0 : x^\beta \in \mathfrak{b}\}$.

Observe that, the matrix $\left[\begin{smallmatrix} M^{f_0}_{1,1} & M^{f_0}_{1,2} \end{smallmatrix}\right]$ is a permutation of $\mathsf{M_3H}(\{f_1,\ldots,f_N\},\boldsymbol{D_{N+1}},<)$, and the polynomials in its rows do not involve f_0, so we can forget the superscripts.

REMARK 4.10. *By Cor. 4.4, if* $(f_1,\ldots,f_N)$ *is 0-dimensional, and* f_0 *does not vanish on* $V_{\mathcal{P}}(f_1,\ldots,f_N)$, *then* $\widetilde{\mathcal{M}}^{f_0}$ *is invertible.*

THEOREM 4.11. *Let* $\bar{\mathfrak{b}}$ *be the dehomogenization of the monomials in* $\mathfrak{b}$. *If the system* $f_1,\ldots,f_n$ *has no solutions at infinity, then* $\bar{\mathfrak{b}}$ *forms a monomial basis for* $\mathbb{K}[\bar{x}]/\langle \bar{f}_1,\ldots,\bar{f}_N\rangle$.

PROOF. The set $\bar{\mathfrak{b}}$ is a monomial basis if its elements are linear independent on $\mathbb{K}[\bar{x}]/\langle \bar{f}_1,\ldots,\bar{f}_N\rangle$ and generate this quotient ring. By Cor. 4.4, the dimension of the quotient ring, as a vector space, is the same as the number of elements in $\bar{\mathfrak{b}}$, so we only need to prove the linear independence of the elements in $\bar{\mathfrak{b}}$. Assume that there is a linear combination $\bar{p} := \sum_i c_i \bar{\mathfrak{b}}_i$ congruent to 0 in $\mathbb{K}[\bar{x}]/\langle \bar{f}_1,\ldots,\bar{f}_N\rangle$. Then, similarly to Rem. 2.1, there is a $\omega \in \mathbb{N}$, such that $(x_h)^\omega \cdot p \in \langle f_1,\ldots,f_N\rangle$, where $p := \sum_i c_i \mathfrak{b}_i$. By Rem. 4.10, as the system has no solutions at infinity, $\widetilde{\mathcal{M}}^{x_h}$ is invertible. The rows of $\widetilde{\mathcal{M}}^{x_h}$ contain the set $\{x_h \cdot \mathfrak{b}_i\}_i$, so we can form $x_h \cdot p$ by taking a linear combination of them. As the matrix is full-rank, this row is independent from the polynomials in $[\langle f_1,\ldots,f_N\rangle]_{\boldsymbol{D_{N+1}}}$ (Thm. 4.5), and then $x_h \cdot p \notin [\langle f_1,\ldots,f_N\rangle]_{\boldsymbol{D_{N+1}}}$. Hence, $\omega > 1$. The multidegree of $(x_h)^\omega \cdot p$ is $\boldsymbol{D_N} + \omega \cdot \bar{1}$. As $\omega > 1$, $\boldsymbol{D_N} + \omega \cdot \bar{1} \geq \boldsymbol{D_{N+1}}$. By Cor. 4.3, $[H_1(\mathcal{K}_\bullet(f_1,\ldots,f_N,x_h\,;\,\mathbb{K}[x]))]_{\boldsymbol{D_N}+\omega\cdot\bar{1}} = 0$. Then, by Rem. 4.6, $(x_h)^{\omega-1} \cdot p \in \langle f_1,\ldots,f_N\rangle$. But, assuming minimality of ω, $(x_h)^{\omega-1} \cdot p \notin \langle f_1,\ldots,f_N\rangle$. So, $\bar{p}$ does not exist. □

REMARK 4.12. *If the system* $(f_1,\ldots,f_N,x_h)$ *has no solutions over* $\mathcal{P}$, *by Rem. 4.10, the matrix* M^{x_h} *is invertible. As* $M^{x_h}_{2,1}$ *is zero, and* $M^{x_h}_{2,2}$ *is the identity, the matrix* M^{x_h} *is invertible.*

DEFINITION 4.13. *When* $(f_1 \ldots f_N)$ *has no solutions at infinity, we define* $(M^{f_0}_{2,2})^c := M^{f_0}_{2,2} - M^{f_0}_{2,1} \cdot M^{-1}_{1,1} \cdot M_{1,2}$, *the* Schur complement *of* $M^{f_0}_{2,2}$.

THEOREM 4.14. *If the system* $(f_1,\ldots,f_N)$ *has no solutions at infinity, then the matrix* $(M^{f_0}_{2,2})^c$ *is the multiplication map of* $\bar{f}_0$ *over* $\mathbb{K}[\bar{x}]/\langle \bar{f}_1,\ldots,\bar{f}_N\rangle$, *with respect to the basis* $\bar{\mathfrak{b}}$.

PROOF. By Thm. 4.11, $\bar{\mathfrak{b}}$ is a monomial basis of $\mathbb{K}[\bar{x}]/\langle \bar{f}_1,\ldots,\bar{f}_N\rangle$. Hence, for every i, $\mathfrak{b}_i \cdot f_0 \equiv x_h \sum_j (M^{f_0}_{2,2})^c_{i,j} \mathfrak{b}_j \mod \langle f_1,\ldots,f_N\rangle$. If we dehomogenize, $\bar{\mathfrak{b}}_i \cdot \bar{f}_0 \equiv \sum_j (M^{f_0}_{2,2})^c_{i,j} \bar{\mathfrak{b}}_j \mod \langle \bar{f}_1,\ldots,\bar{f}_N\rangle$. □

ACKNOWLEDGMENTS

We thank Laurent Busé, Marc Chardin, and Joaquín Rodrigues Jacinto for the helpful discussions and references. We thanks the anonymous reviewers for their detailed comments and suggestions. The authors are partially supported by ANR JCJC GALOP (ANR-17-CE40-0009) and the PGMO grant GAMMA.

REFERENCES

[1] A. Awane, A. Chkiriba, and M. Goze. 2005. Formes d'inertie et complexe de Koszul associés à des polynômes plurihomogenes. *Revista Matematica Complutense* 18, 1 (2005), 243–260.

[2] D. Bayer and D. Mumford. 1993. What can be computed in algebraic geometry?. In *Proc. Comp. Alg. Geom. and Commut. Algebra*. Cambridge Univ. Press, 1–48.

[3] M. R. Bender, J.-C. Faugère, A. Mantzaflaris, and E. Tsigaridas. 2018. Bilinear systems with two supports: Koszul resultant matrices, eigenvalues, and eigenvectors. In *Proc. ACM ISSAC*. ACM, ACM.

[4] F. Bihan and F. Sottile. 2011. Fewnomial bounds for completely mixed polynomial systems. *Advances in Geometry* 11, 3 (2011), 541–556.

[5] N. Botbol. 2011. *Implicitization of rational maps*. Ph.D. Dissertation. UPMC.

[6] N. Botbol and M. Chardin. 2017. Castelnuovo Mumford regularity with respect to multigraded ideals. *Journal of Algebra* 474 (March 2017), 361–392.

[7] N. Bourbaki. 2007. *Algèbre: chapitre 10. Algèbre homologique*. Vol. 9. Springer.

[8] M. P. Brodmann and R. Y. Sharp. 2013. *Local Cohomology: An Algebraic Introduction with Geometric Applications*. Cambridge University Press.

[9] M. Chardin. 2007. Some results and questions on Castelnuovo-Mumford regularity. *Lecture Notes in Pure and Applied Mathematics* 254 (2007), 1.

[10] D. Cox, J. Little, and D. O'shea. 1992. *Ideals, varieties, and algorithms*. Springer.

[11] D. Cox, J. Little, and D. O'shea. 2006. *Using algebraic geometry*. Springer.

[12] D. Cox, J. Little, and H. Schenck. 2011. *Toric varieties*. AMS.

[13] C. D'Andrea. 2002. Macaulay style formulas for sparse resultants. *Trans. Amer. Math. Soc.* 354, 7 (2002), 2595–2629.

[14] C. D'Andrea, T. Krick, and M. Sombra. 2013. Heights of varieties in multiprojective spaces and arithmetic Nullstellensatze. *Annales Scientifiques de l'École Normale Supérieure* 46 (2013), 549–627.

[15] C. Eder and J.-C. Faugère. 2017. A survey on signature-based algorithms for computing Gröbner bases. *Journal of Symbolic Computation* 80 (2017), 719 – 784.

[16] D. Eisenbud. 2013. *Commutative Algebra: with a view toward algebraic geometry*. Vol. 150. Springer.

[17] M. S. El Din and É. Schost. 2017. Bit complexity for multi-homogeneous polynomial system solving - Application to polynomial minimization. *Journal of Symbolic Computation* (2017).

[18] I. Z. Emiris. 1996. On the complexity of sparse elimination. *Journal of Complexity* 12, 2 (1996), 134–166.

[19] J. C. Faugère. 2002. A New Efficient Algorithm for Computing Gröbner Bases Without Reduction to Zero (F5). In *Proc. ACM ISSAC*. ACM, 75–83.

[20] J.-C. Faugère, M. S. El Din, and P.-J. Spaenlehauer. 2011. Gröbner bases of bihomogeneous ideals generated by polynomials of bidegree (1, 1): Algorithms and complexity. *Journal of Symbolic Computation* 46, 4 (2011), 406–437.

[21] J.-C. Faugère, P. Gianni, D. Lazard, and T. Mora. 1993. Efficient computation of zero-dimensional Gröbner bases by change of ordering. *Journal of Symbolic Computation* 16, 4 (1993), 329–344.

[22] J.-C. Faugère, P.-J. Spaenlehauer, and J. Svartz. 2014. Sparse Gröbner bases: the unmixed case. In *Proc. ACM ISSAC*. ACM, 178–185.

[23] I. M. Gelfand, M. Kapranov, and A. Zelevinsky. 2008. *Discriminants, resultants, and multidimensional determinants*. Springer.

[24] M. Giusti, G. Lecerf, and B. Salvy. 2001. A Gröbner free alternative for polynomial system solving. *Journal of complexity* 17, 1 (2001), 154–211.

[25] H. T. Hà and A. Van Tuyl. 2004. The regularity of points in multi-projective spaces. *Journal of Pure and Applied Algebra* 187, 1-3 (March 2004), 153–167.

[26] J. D. Hauenstein and J. I. Rodriguez. 2015. Multiprojective witness sets and a trace test. *arXiv preprint arXiv:1507.07069* (2015).

[27] M. I. Herrero, G. Jeronimo, and J. Sabia. 2013. Affine solution sets of sparse polynomial systems. *Journal of Symbolic Computation* 51 (2013), 34–54.

[28] D. Lazard. 1983. Gröbner-Bases, Gaussian Elimination and Resolution of Systems of Algebraic Equations. In *Proc. EUROCAL*. Springer-Verlag, 146–156.

[29] T.-Y. Li. 1997. Numerical solution of multivariate polynomial systems by homotopy continuation methods. *Acta numerica* 6 (1997), 399–436.

[30] D. Maclagan and G. G. Smith. 2004. Multigraded Castelnuovo-Mumford Regularity. *J. Reine Angew. Math.* 2004, 571 (Jan. 2004).

[31] D. Maclagan and G. G. Smith. 2005. Uniform bounds on multigraded regularity. *J. Algebraic Geom.* 14 (2005), 137–164. arXiv preprint math/0305215.

[32] E. Miller and B. Sturmfels. 2004. *Combinatorial commutative algebra*. Springer.

[33] J. Sidman and A. Van Tuyl. 2006. Multigraded regularity: syzygies and fat points. *Beiträge Algebra Geom* 47, 1 (2006), 67–87.

[34] B. Sturmfels. 1994. On the Newton polytope of the resultant. *Journal of Algebraic Combinatorics* 3, 2 (1994), 207–236.

[35] B. Sturmfels and A. Zelevinsky. 1994. Multigraded resultants of Sylvester type. *Journal of Algebra* 163, 1 (1994), 115–127.

[36] N. Trung. 1998. The Castelnuovo regularity of the Rees algebra and the associated graded ring. *Trans. Amer. Math. Soc.* 350, 7 (1998), 2813–2832.

[37] B. Van der Waerden. 1978. On varieties in multiple-projective spaces. In *Indagationes Mathematicae (Proceedings)*, Vol. 81. Elsevier, 303–312.

[38] J. Weyman and A. Zelevinsky. 1994. Multigraded formulae for multigraded resultants. *J. Algebr. Geom* 3, 4 (1994), 569–597.

A Polynomial-Division-Based Algorithm for Computing Linear Recurrence Relations

Jérémy Berthomieu
Sorbonne Université, CNRS, INRIA,
Laboratoire d'Informatique de Paris 6, LIP6, Équipe PolSys
F-75005, Paris, France
jeremy.berthomieu@lip6.fr

Jean-Charles Faugère
Sorbonne Université, CNRS, INRIA,
Laboratoire d'Informatique de Paris 6, LIP6, Équipe PolSys
F-75005, Paris, France
jean-charles.faugere@inria.fr

ABSTRACT

Sparse polynomial interpolation, sparse linear system solving or modular rational reconstruction are fundamental problems in Computer Algebra. They come down to computing linear recurrence relations of a sequence with the Berlekamp–Massey algorithm. Likewise, sparse multivariate polynomial interpolation and multidimensional cyclic code decoding require guessing linear recurrence relations of a multivariate sequence.

Several algorithms solve this problem. The so-called Berlekamp–Massey–Sakata algorithm (1988) uses polynomial additions and shifts by a monomial. The Scalar-FGLM algorithm (2015) relies on linear algebra operations on a multi-Hankel matrix, a multivariate generalization of a Hankel matrix. The Artinian Gorenstein border basis algorithm (2017) uses a Gram-Schmidt process.

We propose a new algorithm for computing the Gröbner basis of the ideal of relations of a sequence based solely on multivariate polynomial arithmetic. This algorithm allows us to both revisit the Berlekamp–Massey–Sakata algorithm through the use of polynomial divisions and to completely revise the Scalar-FGLM algorithm without linear algebra operations.

A key observation in the design of this algorithm is to work on the mirror of the truncated generating series allowing us to use polynomial arithmetic modulo a monomial ideal. It appears to have some similarities with Padé approximants of this mirror polynomial.

Finally, we give a partial solution to the transformation of this algorithm into an adaptive one.

CCS CONCEPTS

• **Comput. method. → Symbolic calculus algorithms**;

KEYWORDS

Gröbner bases; linear recursive sequences; Berlekamp–Massey–Sakata; extended Euclidean algorithm; Padé approximants

ACM Reference Format:

Jérémy Berthomieu and Jean-Charles Faugère. 2018. A Polynomial-Division-Based Algorithm for Computing Linear Recurrence Relations. In *ISSAC '18: 2018 ACM International Symposium on Symbolic and Algebraic Computation, July 16–19, 2018, New York, NY, USA.* ACM, New York, NY, USA, 8 pages. https://doi.org/10.1145/3208976.3209017

ISSAC '18, July 16–19, 2018, New York, NY, USA

ACM ISBN 978-1-4503-5550-6/18/07...$15.00
https://doi.org/10.1145/3208976.3209017

1 INTRODUCTION

The Berlekamp–Massey algorithm (BM), introduced by Berlekamp in 1968 [2] and Massey in 1969 [22] is a fundamental algorithm in Coding Theory [8, 19] and Computer Algebra. It allows one to perform efficiently sparse polynomial interpolation, sparse linear system solving or modular rational reconstruction.

In 1988, Sakata extended the BM algorithm to dimension n. This algorithm, known as the Berlekamp–Massey–Sakata algorithm (BMS) [24–26], can be used to compute a Gröbner basis of the zero-dimensional ideal of the relations satisfied by a sequence. Analogously to dimension 1, the BMS algorithm allows one to decode cyclic code in dimension $n > 1$, an extension of Reed–Solomon's codes. Furthermore, the latest versions of the Sparse-FGLM [15, 16] algorithm rely heavily on the efficiency of the BMS algorithm to compute the change of ordering of a Gröbner basis.

1.1 Related Work

In dimension 1, it is well known that the BM algorithm can be seen in a matrix form requiring to solve a linear Hankel system of size D, the order of the recurrence, see [20] or the Levinson–Durbin method [21, 27]. If we let $\mathsf{M}(D)$ be a cost function for multiplying two polynomials of degree D, for instance $\mathsf{M}(D) \in O(D \log D \log\log D)$ [11, 12], then solving a linear Hankel system of size D comes down to performing a truncated extended Euclidean algorithm called on two polynomials of degree D [7, 10, 14]. More precisely, it can be done in $O(\mathsf{M}(D) \log D)$ operations.

In [3, 4], the authors present the Scalar-FGLM algorithm, extending the matrix version of the BM algorithm for multidimensional sequences. It consists in computing the relations of the sequence through the computation of a maximal full-rank matrix of a *multi-Hankel* matrix, a multivariate generalization of a Hankel matrix. Then, it returns the minimal Gröbner basis $\mathcal{G}$ of the ideal of relations satisfied by the sequence. These notions are recalled in Section 2. If we denote by S the staircase defined by $\mathcal{G}$ and T the input set of monomials containing $S \cup \mathcal{G}$, then the complexity of the Scalar-FGLM algorithm is $O((\# T)^{\omega})$, where $2 \leq \omega \leq 3$ is the linear algebra exponent. However, we do not know how to exploit the multi-Hankel structure to improve this complexity.

The Artinian Gorenstein border bases algorithm (AGbb) was presented in [23] for computing a border basis $\mathcal{B}$ of the ideal of relations. It extends the algorithm of [3] using polynomial arithmetic allowing it to reach the better complexity $O((\# S + \# \mathcal{B}) \cdot \# S \cdot \# T)$ with the above notation.

Another viewpoint is that computing linear recurrence relations can be seen as computing Padé approximants of a truncation of the generating series $\sum_{i_1,\ldots,i_n\geq 0} w_{i_1,\ldots,i_n} x_1^{i_1}\cdots x_n^{i_n}$. In [17], the authors extend the extended Euclidean algorithm for computing multivariate Padé approximants. Given a polynomial P and an ideal B, find polynomials F and C such that $P = \frac{F}{C} \bmod B$, where the leading monomials of F and C satisfy some constraints.

It is also worth noticing that we now know that both the BMS and the SCALAR-FGLM algorithms are not equivalent [5], i.e. it is not possible to tweak one algorithm to mimic the behavior of the other. However, if the input sequence is linear recurrent and sufficiently many sequence terms are visited, then both algorithms compute a Gröbner basis of the zero-dimensional ideal of relations.

1.2 Contributions

In all the paper, we assume that the input sets of the SCALAR-FGLM algorithm are the sets of all the monomials less than a given monomial. In order to improve the complexity of the algorithm, we will use polynomial arithmetic in all the operations. Even though they are not equivalent, this reduces the gap between the BMS and the SCALAR-FGLM algorithms and provides a unified presentation.

In Section 3, we present the BM, the BMS and the SCALAR-FGLM algorithms in a unified polynomial viewpoint. Using the mirror of the truncated generating series is a key ingredient letting us perform the computations modulo a specific monomial ideal B: a vector in the kernel of a multi-Hankel matrix is a polynomial C such that

$$\mathrm{LM}(F) = \mathrm{LM}(P\,C \bmod B) \prec t_C, \tag{1}$$

where P is the mirror of the truncated generating series, LM denotes the leading monomial and t_C is a monomial associated to C.

One interpretation of this is the computation of multivariate Padé approximants $\frac{F}{C}$ of P modulo B with different constraints than in [17] since we require that $\mathrm{LM}(C)$ is in a given set of terms and $\mathrm{LM}(F)$ satisfies equation (1).

This polynomial point of view allows us to design the POLYNOMIAL SCALAR-FGLM algorithm (Algorithm 4.4) in Section 4 based on multivariate polynomial divisions. It computes polynomials whose product with P modulo B must satisfy equation (1). If they do not, by polynomial divisions, we make new ones until finding minimal polynomials satisfying this constraint. It is worth noticing that in dimension 1, we recover the truncated extended Euclidean algorithm applied to the mirror polynomial of the generated series of the input sequence, truncated in degree D, and x^{D+1}. All the examples are available on [6].

Our main result is Theorem 4.7, a simplified version of which is

THEOREM 1.1. *Let* $\mathbf{w}$ *be a sequence,* $\prec$ *be a total degree monomial ordering and* a *be a monomial. Let us assume that the Gröbner basis* $\mathcal{G}$ *of the ideal of relations of* $\mathbf{w}$ *for* $\prec$ *and its staircase* S *satisfy* $a \succeq \max(S \cup \mathrm{LM}(\mathcal{G}))$ *and for all* $g \preceq a$, $s = \max_{\sigma\preceq a}\{\sigma,\ \sigma g \preceq a\}$, *we have* $\max(S) \preceq s$. *Then, the* POLYNOMIAL SCALAR-FGLM *algorithm terminates and computes a Gröbner basis of the ideal of relations of* $\mathbf{w}$ *for* $\prec$ *in* $O\big(\#S\,(\#S + \#\mathcal{G})\,\#\{\sigma, \sigma \preceq a\}\big)$ *operations in the base field.*

In applications such as the SPARSE-FGLM one [16], sequence queries are costly. In [3], an adaptive variant of the SCALAR-FGLM algorithm was designed aiming to minimize the number of sequence queries to recover the relations. In Section 5, we show how we can partially transform the ADAPTIVE SCALAR-FGLM algorithm of [3] into an algorithm using polynomial arithmetic. One of the main issues to do so is that now, the monomial ideal B is not fixed: it will grow as the algorithm progresses.

Finally, in Section 6, we compare the POLYNOMIAL SCALAR-FGLM algorithm with our implementations of the BMS, the SCALAR-FGLM and the AGBB algorithms. Our algorithm performs always fewer arithmetic operations than the others starting from a certain size. Even for an example family favorable towards the BMS algorithm, our algorithm performs better.

Although we have compared the numbers of arithmetic operations, it would be beneficial to have an efficient implementation. This would be the first step into designing a similar efficient algorithm for computing linear recurrence relations with polynomial coefficients, extending the Beckermann–Labahn algorithm [1] for computing multivariate Hermite–Padé approximants.

2 NOTATION

We give a brief description of classical notation used in the paper.

2.1 Sequences and relations

For $n \geq 1$, we let $\mathbf{i} = (i_1,\ldots,i_n) \in \mathbb{N}^n$ and for $\mathbf{x} = (x_1,\ldots,x_n)$, we write $\mathbf{x}^{\mathbf{i}} = x_1^{i_1}\cdots x_n^{i_n}$.

Definition 2.1. Let $\mathbb{K}$ be a field, $\mathcal{K} \subseteq \mathbb{N}^n$ be finite and $f = \sum_{\mathbf{k}\in\mathcal{K}} \gamma_{\mathbf{k}} \mathbf{x}^{\mathbf{k}} \in \mathbb{K}[\mathbf{x}]$. We let $[f]_{\mathbf{w}}$, or $[f]$, be the linear combination $\sum_{\mathbf{k}\in\mathcal{K}} \gamma_{\mathbf{k}} w_{\mathbf{k}}$. If for all $\mathbf{i} \in \mathbb{N}^n$, $\left[\mathbf{x}^{\mathbf{i}} f\right] = 0$, then we say that f is the *polynomial of the relation induced by* $\gamma = (\gamma_{\mathbf{k}})_{\mathbf{k}\in\mathcal{K}} \in \mathbb{K}^{\#\mathcal{K}}$.

The main benefit of the [ ] notation resides in the immediate fact that for all index $\mathbf{i}$, its *shift by* $\mathbf{x}^{\mathbf{i}}$ is $\left[\mathbf{x}^{\mathbf{i}} f\right] = \sum_{\mathbf{k}\in\mathcal{K}} \gamma_{\mathbf{k}} w_{\mathbf{k}+\mathbf{i}}$.

Example 2.2. Let $\mathbf{b} = \left(\binom{i}{j}\right)_{(i,j)\in\mathbb{N}^2}$ be the sequence of the binomial coefficients. Then, the Pascal's rule is associated to $x\,y - y - 1$:

$\forall (i,j) \in \mathbb{N}^2$, $[x^i\, y^j\, (x\,y - y - 1)] = \mathbf{b}_{i+1,j+1} - \mathbf{b}_{i,j+1} - \mathbf{b}_{i,j} = 0$.

Definition 2.3 ([18, 24]). Let $\mathbf{w} = (w_{\mathbf{i}})_{\mathbf{i}\in\mathbb{N}^n}$ be an n-dimensional sequence with coefficients in $\mathbb{K}$. The sequence $\mathbf{w}$ is *linear recurrent* if from a nonzero finite number of initial terms $\{w_{\mathbf{i}},\ \mathbf{i} \in S\}$, and a finite number of relations, without any contradiction, one can compute any term of the sequence.

Equivalently, $\mathbf{w}$ is linear recurrent if $\{f,\ \forall\, m \in \mathbb{K}[\mathbf{x}], [m\,f] = 0\}$, its ideal of relations, is *zero-dimensional.*

As the input parameters of the algorithms are the first terms of a sequence, a *table* shall denote a finite subset of terms of a sequence.

2.2 Gröbner bases

Let $\mathcal{T} = \{\mathbf{x}^{\mathbf{i}},\ \mathbf{i} \in \mathbb{N}^n\}$ be the set of all monomials in $\mathbb{K}[\mathbf{x}]$. A monomial ordering $\prec$ on $\mathbb{K}[\mathbf{x}]$ is an order relation satisfying the following three classical properties:

(1) for all $m \in \mathcal{T}$, $1 \preceq m$;
(2) for all $m, m', s \in \mathcal{T}$, $m \prec m' \Rightarrow m\,s \prec m'\,s$;
(3) every subset of $\mathcal{T}$ has a least element for $\prec$.

For a monomial ordering $\prec$ on $\mathbb{K}[\mathbf{x}]$, the *leading monomial* of f, denoted $\mathrm{LM}(f)$, is the greatest monomial in the support of f for $\prec$. The *leading coefficient* of f, denoted $\mathrm{LC}(f)$, is the nonzero coefficient of $\mathrm{LM}(f)$. The *leading term* of f, $\mathrm{LT}(f)$, is defined as $\mathrm{LT}(f) = \mathrm{LC}(f)\ \mathrm{LM}(f)$. For an ideal I, we denote $\mathrm{LM}(I) = \{\mathrm{LM}(f),\ f \in I\}$.

We recall briefly the definition of a Gröbner basis and a staircase.

Definition 2.4. Let I be a nonzero ideal of $\mathbb{K}[\mathbf{x}]$ and let $\prec$ be a monomial ordering. A set $\mathcal{G} \subseteq I$ is a *Gröbner basis* of I if for all $f \in I$, there exists $g \in \mathcal{G}$ such that $\mathrm{LM}(g) | \mathrm{LM}(f)$.

A Gröbner basis $\mathcal{G}$ of I is *minimal* if for any $g \in \mathcal{G}$, $\langle \mathcal{G} \setminus \{g\} \rangle \neq I$.

Furthermore, $\mathcal{G}$ is *reduced* if for any $g, g' \in \mathcal{G}$, $g \neq g'$ and any monomial $m \in \operatorname{supp} g'$, $\mathrm{LM}(g) \nmid m$.

The *staircase* of $\mathcal{G}$ is defined as $S = \mathrm{Staircase}(\mathcal{G}) = \{s \in \mathcal{T},\ \forall g \in \mathcal{G}, \mathrm{LM}(g) \nmid s\}$. It is also the canonical basis of $\mathbb{K}[\mathbf{x}]/I$.

Gröbner basis theory allows us to choose any monomial ordering, among which, we mainly use the

- **LEX$(x_n \prec \cdots \prec x_1)$ ordering** which satisfies $\mathbf{x}^{\mathbf{i}} \prec \mathbf{x}^{\mathbf{i}'}$ if and only if there exists k, $1 \le k \le n$ such that for all $\ell < k$, $i_\ell = i'_\ell$ and $i_k < i'_k$, see [13, Chapter 2, Definition 3];
- **DRL$(x_n \prec \cdots \prec x_1)$ ordering** which satisfies $\mathbf{x}^{\mathbf{i}} \prec \mathbf{x}^{\mathbf{i}'}$ if and only if $i_1 + \cdots + i_n < i'_1 + \cdots + i'_n$ or $i_1 + \cdots + i_n = i'_1 + \cdots + i'_n$ and there exists k, $2 \le k \le n$ such that for all $\ell > k$, $i_\ell = i'_\ell$ and $i_k > i'_k$, see [13, Chapter 2, Definition 6].

However, in the BMS algorithm, we need to be able to enumerate all the monomials up to a bound monomial. This forces the user to take an ordering $\prec$ such that for all $M \in \mathcal{T}$, the set $\mathcal{T}_{\preceq a} = \{m \preceq a,\ m \in \mathcal{T}\}$ is finite. Such an ordering $\prec$ makes $(\mathbb{N}^n, \prec)$ isomorphic to $(\mathbb{N}, <)$. Hence, for a monomial m, it makes sense to speak about the previous (resp. next) monomial m^- (resp. m^+) for $\prec$. The DRL ordering is an example for an ordering on which every term other than 1 has an immediate predecessor.

This request excludes for instance the LEX ordering, and more generally any elimination ordering. In other words, only weighted degree ordering, or *weight ordering*, should be used.

Now that a monomial ordering is defined, we can say that a relation given by a polynomial $f \in \mathbb{K}[\mathbf{x}]$ *fails when shifted by* s if for all monomials $\sigma \prec s$, $[\sigma f] = 0$ but $[s f] \neq 0$, see also [25, 26].

2.3 Multi-Hankel matrices

A matrix $H \in \mathbb{K}^{m \times n}$ is *Hankel*, if there exists a sequence $\mathbf{w} = (w_i)_{i \in \mathbb{N}}$ such that for all $(i, i') \in \{1, \ldots, m\} \times \{1, \ldots, n\}$, the coefficient $h_{i,i'}$ lying on the ith row and i'th column of H satisfies $h_{i,i'} = w_{i+i'}$.

In a multivariate setting, we can extend this notion to *multi-Hankel* matrices. For two sets of monomials U and T, we let $H_{U,T}$ be the multi-Hankel matrix with rows (resp. columns) indexed with U (resp. T) so that the coefficient of $H_{U,T}$ lying on the row labeled with $\mathbf{x}^{\mathbf{i}} \in U$ and column labeled with $\mathbf{x}^{\mathbf{i}'} \in T$ is $w_{\mathbf{i}+\mathbf{i}'}$.

Example 2.5. Let $\mathbf{w} = (w_{i,j})_{(i,j) \in \mathbb{N}^2}$ be a sequence.

(1) For $U = \{1, y, y^2, x, x\,y, x\,y^2\}$ and $T = \{1, y, x, x\,y, x^2, x^2\,y\}$,

$$H_{U,T} = \begin{array}{c} \\ 1 \\ y \\ y^2 \\ x \\ x\,y \\ x\,y^2 \end{array} \begin{array}{c} \begin{array}{cc|cc|cc} 1 & y & x & x\,y & x^2 & x^2\,y \end{array} \\ \left(\begin{array}{cc|cc|cc} w_{0,0} & w_{0,1} & w_{1,0} & w_{1,1} & w_{2,0} & w_{2,1} \\ w_{0,1} & w_{0,2} & w_{1,1} & w_{1,2} & w_{2,1} & w_{2,2} \\ w_{0,2} & w_{0,3} & w_{1,2} & w_{1,3} & w_{2,2} & w_{2,3} \\ \hline w_{1,0} & w_{1,1} & w_{2,0} & w_{2,1} & w_{3,0} & w_{3,1} \\ w_{1,1} & w_{1,2} & w_{2,1} & w_{2,2} & w_{3,1} & w_{3,2} \\ w_{1,2} & w_{1,3} & w_{2,2} & w_{2,3} & w_{3,2} & w_{3,3} \end{array}\right) \end{array}$$

is a 2×3-*block-Hankel* matrix with 3×2-Hankel blocks.

(2) For $T = \{1, y, x, y^2, x\,y, x^2\}$,

$$H_{T,T} = \begin{array}{c} \\ 1 \\ y \\ x \\ y^2 \\ x\,y \\ x^2 \end{array} \begin{array}{c} \begin{array}{cccccc} 1 & y & x & y^2 & x\,y & x^2 \end{array} \\ \begin{pmatrix} w_{0,0} & w_{0,1} & w_{1,0} & w_{0,2} & w_{1,1} & w_{2,0} \\ w_{0,1} & w_{0,2} & w_{1,1} & w_{0,3} & w_{1,2} & w_{2,1} \\ w_{1,0} & w_{1,1} & w_{2,0} & w_{1,2} & w_{2,1} & w_{3,0} \\ w_{0,2} & w_{0,3} & w_{1,2} & w_{0,4} & w_{1,3} & w_{2,2} \\ w_{1,1} & w_{1,2} & w_{2,1} & w_{1,3} & w_{2,2} & w_{3,3} \\ w_{2,0} & w_{2,1} & w_{3,0} & w_{2,2} & w_{3,1} & w_{4,0} \end{pmatrix} \end{array}$$

is a multi-Hankel, yet not block-Hankel, matrix.

2.4 Polynomials associated to multi-Hankel matrices

For two sets of terms T and U, we let $T + U$ denote their Minkowsky sum, i.e. $T + U = \{t\,u,\ t \in T, u \in U\}$, and $2\,T = T + T$.

For a set of terms T, we let $M = \mathrm{LCM}(T)$. We let P_T be the mirror polynomial of the truncated generating series of a sequence $\mathbf{w}$, i.e.

$$P_T = \sum_{t \in T} [t] \, \frac{M}{t}.$$

Example 2.6. Let $\mathbf{w} = (w_{i,j})_{(i,j) \in \mathbb{N}^2}$ be a sequence and $T = \{1, y, x, y^2\}$, then $M = x\,y^2$ and $P_T = [1]\,x\,y^2 + [y]\,x\,y + [x]\,y^2 + [y^2]\,x = w_{0,0}\,x\,y^2 + w_{0,1}\,x\,y + w_{1,0}\,y^2 + w_{0,2}\,x$.

In this paper, we will mostly deal with polynomials P_{T+U} as there is a strong connection between $H_{U,T}$ and P_{T+U}.

Finally, letting $M = \mathrm{LCM}(T + U) = x_1^{D_1} \cdots x_n^{D_n}$ and B be the monomial ideal $\left(x_1^{D_1+1}, \ldots, x_n^{D_n+1}\right)$, we will use pairs of multivariate polynomials $R_m = [F_m, C_m]$ where $\mathrm{LM}(C_m) = m$ and $F_m = P_{T+U}\,C_m \bmod B$.

3 FROM MATRICES TO POLYNOMIALS

Before detailing the unified polynomial viewpoint, we recall the linear algebra viewpoint of the BM, the BMS and the SCALAR-FGLM algorithms.

3.1 The BM algorithm

Let $\mathbf{w} = (w_i)_{i \in \mathbb{N}}$ be a one-dimensional table. Classically, when calling the BM algorithm, one does not know in advance the order of the output relation. Therefore, from a matrix viewpoint, one wants to compute the greatest collection of vectors

$$\begin{pmatrix} \gamma_1 \\ \vdots \\ \gamma_{x^{d-1}} \\ 1 \\ 0 \\ 0 \\ \vdots \\ 0 \end{pmatrix}, \begin{pmatrix} 0 \\ \gamma_1 \\ \vdots \\ \gamma_{x^{d-1}} \\ 1 \\ 0 \\ \vdots \\ 0 \end{pmatrix}, \ldots, \begin{pmatrix} 0 \\ 0 \\ \vdots \\ 0 \\ \gamma_1 \\ \vdots \\ \gamma_{x^{d-1}} \\ 1 \end{pmatrix}$$

in the kernel of $H_{\{1\},\{1,\ldots,x^D\}} = \begin{array}{c} \\ 1 \end{array} \begin{array}{c} \begin{array}{ccc} 1 & \cdots & x^D \end{array} \\ \begin{pmatrix} w_0 & \cdots & w_D \end{pmatrix} \end{array}$, that is $\gamma_1, \ldots, \gamma_{x^{d-1}}$ such that the relation $[C_{x^d}] = w_d + \sum_{k=0}^{d-1} \gamma_{x^k}\,w_k$ and its shifts, $[x\,C_{x^d}], \ldots, [x^{D-d}\,C_{x^d}]$, are all 0. Equivalently, we look for the least d such that $H_{\mathcal{T}_{\le x^{D-d}}, \mathcal{T}_{\le x^d}} \begin{pmatrix} \gamma_1 \\ \vdots \\ \gamma_{x^{d-1}} \\ 1 \end{pmatrix} = 0$.

This Hankel matrix-vector product can be extended into

$$\begin{pmatrix} w_0 & \cdots & w_{d-1} & w_d \\ w_1 & \cdots & w_d & w_{d+1} \\ \vdots & & \vdots & \vdots \\ w_{D-d} & \cdots & w_{D-1} & w_D \\ w_{D-d+1} & \cdots & w_D & 0 \\ \vdots & \iddots & \iddots & \vdots \\ w_D & 0 & \cdots & 0 \end{pmatrix} \begin{pmatrix} \gamma_1 \\ \vdots \\ \gamma_{x^{d-1}} \\ 1 \end{pmatrix} = \begin{pmatrix} 0 \\ 0 \\ \vdots \\ 0 \\ f_{x^{d-1}} \\ \vdots \\ f_1 \end{pmatrix}, \qquad (2)$$

representing the product of polynomials $P_{\mathcal{T}_{\leq x^D}} = \sum_{i=0}^{D} w_i\, x^{D-i}$ and $C_{x^d} = x^d + \sum_{k=0}^{d-1} \gamma_{x^k}\, x^k$ modulo $B = x^{D+1}$. The requirement for C_{x^d} to encode a valid relation is now that $\mathrm{LM}(F_{x^d}) \prec x^d$ with $F_{x^d} = P_{\mathcal{T}_{\leq x^D}}\, C_{x^d} \bmod B$.

This viewpoint gave rise to the following version of the BM algorithm: Start with $R_B = [F_B, C_B] = [B, 0]$ and $B = x^{D+1}$, and $R_1 = [F_1, C_1] = [P_{\mathcal{T}_{\leq x^D}}, 1]$. Compute Q the quotient of the Euclidean division of $F_B = B$ by F_1 and then compute $R_{\mathrm{LT}(Q)} = R_B - Q\, R_1 = [F_B - Q\, F_1, C_B - Q\, C_1] = [F_{\mathrm{LT}(Q)}, C_{\mathrm{LT}(Q)}]$. Repeat with R_1 and $R_{\mathrm{LT}(Q)}$ until reaching a pair $R_{x^d} = [P_{\mathcal{T}_{\leq x^D}}\, C_{x^d} \bmod B, C_{x^d}] = [F_{x^d}, C_{x^d}]$ with $\mathrm{LM}(C_{x^d}) = x^d$ and $\mathrm{LM}(F_{x^d}) \prec x^d$. This is in fact the extended Euclidean algorithm called on $B = x^{D+1}$ and F_1 without any computation of the Bézout's cofactors of x^{D+1}.

Example 3.1. Let us consider the Fibonacci table $\mathbf{F} = (F_i)_{i \in \mathbb{N}}$ with $F_0 = F_1 = 1$ and assume $D = 5$ so that we have $B = x^6$, $R_B = [B, 0]$ and $R_1 = [x^5 + x^4 + 2\,x^3 + 3\,x^2 + 5\,x + 8, 1]$. As we can see $R_1 = [F_1, C_1]$ with $\mathrm{LM}(C_1) = 1$ and $\mathrm{LM}(F_1) = x^5 \succeq 1$.

The first step of the extended Euclidean algorithm yields $R_x = [x^4 + x^3 + 2\,x^2 + 3\,x - 8, x - 1] = [F_x, C_x]$ with $\mathrm{LM}(C_x) = x$ and $\mathrm{LM}(F_x) = x^4 \succeq x$.

Then, the second step yields $R_{x^2} = [-13\,x - 8, x^2 - x - 1] = [F_{x^2}, C_{x^2}]$ with $\mathrm{LM}(C_{x^2}) = x^2$ and $\mathrm{LM}(F_{x^2}) = x \prec x^2$ so C_{x^2} is a valid relation. We return C_{x^2}.

Remark 3.2. The BM algorithm always returns a relation. If no pair $R_{x^\delta} = [F_{x^\delta}, C_{x^\delta}]$ satisfies the requirements, then it will return a pair R_{x^d} with $\mathrm{LM}(C_{x^d}) \succ x^D$. From a matrix viewpoint, it returns an element of the kernel of the empty matrix $H_{\emptyset, \mathcal{T}_{\leq x^d}}$.

3.2 Multidimensional extension

For a multidimensional table $\mathbf{w} = (w_{\mathbf{i}})_{\mathbf{i} \in \mathbb{N}^n}$, the BMS algorithm extends the BM algorithm by computing vectors in the kernel of a multi-Hankel matrix $H_{\{1\}, \mathcal{T}_{\leq a}} = \begin{array}{c} \\ 1 \end{array} \!\!\begin{array}{c} \begin{array}{ccc} 1 & \cdots & a \end{array} \\ \begin{pmatrix} [1] & \cdots & [a] \end{pmatrix} \end{array}$ corresponding to having relations $[C_g] = 0$, with $\mathrm{LM}(C_g) = g$ minimal for $|$ and for all t such that $t\, g \preceq a$, $[t\, C_g] = 0$ as well. This also comes down to finding the least (for the partial order $|$) monomials $g_1, \ldots, g_r \preceq a$ such that $\dim \ker H_{\mathcal{T}_{\leq s_k}, \mathcal{T}_{\leq g_k}} > 0$ with s_k the greatest monomial such that $s_k\, g_k \preceq a$ for all k, $1 \leq k \leq r$.

Remark 3.3. As for the BM algorithm, the BMS algorithm will always return a relation C_g with $\mathrm{LM}(C_g) = g$ a pure power in each variable. Therefore, it can return C_g with $g \succ a$, corresponding to a vector in the kernel of the empty matrix $H_{\emptyset, \mathcal{T}_{\leq g}}$.

The Scalar-FGLM algorithm corresponds to computing vectors in the kernel of a more general multi-Hankel matrix $H_{U,T}$, with T and U two ordered sets of monomials, corresponding also to relations $[C_g] = 0$ with $\mathrm{LM}(C_g) = g$, such that for all $t \in \mathcal{T}$, if $t\, g \in T$, then $[t\, C_g] = 0$, i.e. the vectors corresponding to $t\, C_g$ are also in the kernel of $H_{U,T}$. We now consider that both sets of terms T and U satisfy $T = \mathcal{T}_{\leq a}$ and $U = \mathcal{T}_{\leq b}$. This allows us to encompass both the BMS algorithm and the Scalar-FGLM algorithm.

The multi-Hankel matrix-vector product

$$\begin{array}{c} \\ 1 \\ \vdots \\ b^- \\ b \end{array} \!\! \begin{array}{c} \begin{array}{cccc} 1 & \cdots & a^- & a \end{array} \\ \begin{pmatrix} [1] & \cdots & [a^-] & [a] \\ \vdots & & \vdots & \vdots \\ [b^-] & \cdots & [a^-\, b^-] & [a\, b^-] \\ [b] & \cdots & [a^-\, b] & [a\, b] \end{pmatrix} \end{array} \begin{pmatrix} \gamma_1 \\ \vdots \\ \gamma_{g^-} \\ 1 \\ 0 \\ \vdots \\ 0 \end{pmatrix} = \begin{pmatrix} 0 \\ \vdots \\ 0 \\ 0 \end{pmatrix} \qquad (3)$$

can be extended in the same way as in equation (2) with rows up to monomial $a\, b$ and any table term $[t\, u]$ set to zero whenever $t\, u \succ a\, b$. This extension corresponds to the product of $P_{T+U} = \sum_{\tau \in (T+U)} [\tau]\, \frac{M}{\tau}$, where $M = x_1^{D_1} \cdots x_n^{D_n} = \mathrm{LCM}(T + U)$, and $C_g = g + \sum_{t \prec g} \gamma_t\, t$, with $g \preceq a$, modulo $B = (x_1^{D_1+1}, \ldots, x_n^{D_n+1})$. In that case, equation (3) is equivalent to asking that the coefficients of monomials $\frac{M}{u}$ of $F_g = P_{T+U}\, C_g \bmod B$ are all zero for $u \preceq b$, i.e. $\mathrm{LM}(F_g) \prec \frac{M}{b}$. Thus, we are aiming for a Padé approximant of P_{T+U} of the form $\frac{F_g}{C_g}$ with $\mathrm{LM}(F_g) \prec \frac{M}{b}$ and $\mathrm{LM}(C_g) = g$, see also [17].

The Scalar-FGLM algorithm requires to compute the kernel of $H_{\mathcal{T}_{\leq b}, \mathcal{T}_{\leq a}}$ as relations $[C_g] = 0$ such that $[t\, C_g] = 0$, for any $t \in \mathcal{T}$ such that $t\, g \in T$. Therefore, it comes down to finding $|$-minimal pairs $R_g = [F_g, C_g] = [P_{\mathcal{T}_{\leq b}, \mathcal{T}_{\leq a}}\, C_g \bmod B, C_g]$ with $g = \mathrm{LM}(C_g) \preceq a$ and a condition on $\mathrm{LM}(F_g)$ so that C_g represents a vector in the kernel of $H_{\mathcal{T}_{\leq s}, \mathcal{T}_{\leq g}}$ with s as large as possible. It is clear that this matrix should only have table terms $[\tau]$ that also appear in $H_{\mathcal{T}_{\leq b}, \mathcal{T}_{\leq a}}$, i.e. $\tau \in (T + U)$ and that s should be the greatest monomial as such. Hence,

$$s = \max_{\sigma \in \mathcal{T}} \left\{\sigma,\ \{\sigma\} + \mathcal{T}_{\leq g} \subseteq (T + U)\right\}. \qquad (4)$$

We can now deduce that

Proposition 3.4. *A pair $R_g = [F_g, C_g] = [P_{\mathcal{T}_{\leq a} + \mathcal{T}_{\leq b}}\, C_g \bmod B, C_g]$ corresponds to a kernel vector of the multi-Hankel matrix $H_{\mathcal{T}_{\leq b}, \mathcal{T}_{\leq a}}$ if and only if $\mathrm{LM}(F_g) \prec \frac{M}{s}$, where $M = \mathrm{LCM}(\mathcal{T}_{\leq a} + \mathcal{T}_{\leq b})$ and s is defined as in equation (4): $s = \max_{\sigma \in \mathcal{T}} \left\{\sigma,\ \{\sigma\} + \mathcal{T}_{\leq g} \subseteq (\mathcal{T}_{\leq a} + \mathcal{T}_{\leq b})\right\}$.*

Remark 3.5. Taking $s = \max_{\sigma \in \mathcal{T}} \{\sigma,\ \sigma\, g \preceq a\, b\}$ is not sufficient as proved by the following example. Let $\prec$ be the $\mathrm{DRL}(y \prec x)$ monomial ordering and $T = U = \mathcal{T}_{\leq x\, y}$. If $g = y^2$, then $x^2 = \max_{\sigma \in \mathcal{T}} \{\sigma,\ \sigma\, g \preceq (x\, y)^2\}$. But $H_{\mathcal{T}_{\leq x^2}, \mathcal{T}_{\leq y^2}}$ has the table term $[x^3]$, which is not in $H_{\mathcal{T}_{\leq x\, y}, \mathcal{T}_{\leq x\, y}}$.

4 A DIVISION-BASED ALGORITHM

The goal is now to design an algorithm based on polynomial division to determine all the C_g for $|$ minimal g such that $\mathrm{LM}(F_c) = \mathrm{LM}(P_{T+U}\, C_g \bmod B)$ is small enough.

We start with two sets of terms $T = \mathcal{T}_{\leq a}$ and $U = \mathcal{T}_{\leq b}$ so that $M = x_1^{D_1} \cdots x_n^{D_n} = \mathrm{LCM}(T + U)$. We initialize $B = (B_1, \ldots, B_n) =$

$\left(x_1^{D_1+1}, \ldots, x_n^{D_n+1}\right)$, $R_{B_1} = [B_1, 0], \ldots, R_{B_n} = [B_n, 0]$ and $R_1 = [P_{T+U}, 1]$.

For any $R_g = [F_g, C_g] = [P_{T+U}\, C_g \bmod B, C_g]$, by Proposition 3.4, C_g is a valid relation if $g \in T$ and $\text{LM}(F_g) \prec \frac{M}{s}$ with $s = \max_{\sigma \in \mathcal{T}}\{\sigma, \{\sigma\} + \mathcal{T}_{\preceq g} \subseteq (T+U)\}$. To go along with the fact that the BMS algorithm always returns a relation C_g with $g = \text{LM}(C_g)$ a pure power of a variable, if $g \notin T$, then C_g will automatically be considered a valid relation as well.

From a failing relation C_m, two pieces of information can be retrieved: m and $\frac{M}{\text{LM}(F_m)}$ (Sakata's fail [26]) are in the staircase of the Gröbner basis of relations. Thus, each time a built relation is not valid, we update the staircase of the ideal of relations. At each step, we know the staircase S and equivalently the set $\mathcal{H} = \min_{|}\{h \in \mathcal{T} \setminus S\}$ which are the leading terms of the candidate relations.

For $h \in \mathcal{H}$, we now want to build R_h with the least $\text{LM}(F_h)$.

INSTRUCTION 4.1. *Pick a failing pair $R_m = [F_m, C_m]$ with $h = q\,m$.*

(1) *if there exists another failing pair $R_{m'} = [F_{m'}, C_{m'}]$ such that $\text{LM}(F_{m'}) = q\,\text{LM}(F_m)$, then compute R_h as the* normal form *of $R_{m'}$ wrt. the list $[R_m, R_{B_1}, \ldots, R_{B_n}, R_{t_1}, \ldots, R_{t_n}]$ where $C_{t_1}, \ldots, C_{t_r}$ are failing relations and $\text{LM}(F_{t_1}) \succ \cdots \succ \text{LM}(F_{t_r})$. To do so, compute first $Q_m, Q_{B_1}, \ldots, Q_{B_n}, Q_{t_1}, \ldots, Q_{t_r}$ the quotients of the division of $F_{m'}$ by the list of polynomials $[F_m, B_1, \ldots, B_n, F_{t_1}, \ldots, F_{t_r}]$ and then return $R_h = R_{m'} - Q_m R_m - Q_{B_1} R_{B_1} - \cdots - Q_{B_n} R_{B_n} - Q_{t_1} R_{t_1} - \cdots - Q_{t_r} R_{t_r}$.*
(2) *otherwise, compute R_h as the normal form of $q\,R_m$ wrt. to the list $[R_{B_1}, \ldots, R_{B_n}, R_{t_1}, \ldots, R_{t_n}]$.*

Remark 4.2. If $q\,\text{LM}(F_m)$ is in the ideal spanned by B, then case 2 of Instruction 4.1 is equivalent to computing the normal form of $[q\,\text{LM}(F_m), 0]$ wrt. $[R_m, R_{B_1}, \ldots, R_{B_n}, R_{t_1}, \ldots, R_{t_r}]$. In fact, at the start, $R_1 = [P_{T+U}, 1]$ fails when shifted by a monomial $s = x_1^{i_1} \cdots x_n^{i_n}$ and we have to make new pairs $R_{x_1^{i_1+1}}, \ldots, R_{x_n^{i_n+1}}$. Since $\text{LM}(P_{T+U}) = \frac{M}{s}$, then these pairs can be computed as the normal forms of $[x_k^{i_k+1} \frac{M}{s}, 0] = [B_k, 0]\, M'$, with $M' \in \mathcal{T}$, wrt. the ordered list $[R_1, R_{B_1}, \ldots, R_{B_n}]$. In dimension 1, this comes down to reducing $[x_1^{D_1+1}, 0] = [B_1, 0] = R_{B_1}$ wrt. $[R_1, R_{B_1}]$, and thus R_1 only. This is indeed the first step of the extended Euclidean algorithm called on B_1 and F_1 as described in Section 3.1.

Example 4.3 (See [6]). Let $\mathbf{b} = \left(\binom{i}{j}\right)_{(i,j)\in\mathbb{N}^2}$ be the binomial table, $\prec$ be the $\text{DRL}(y \prec x)$ monomial ordering and $T = \mathcal{T}_{\preceq x^3}$ and $U = \{1\}$ be sets of terms. We have $T = T+U$ and $M = \text{LCM}(T) = x^3 y^3$ so that $P_T = x^3 y^3 + x^2 y^3 + x^2 y^2 + x y^3 + 2 x y^2 + y^3$, $R_1 = [P_T, 1] = [F_1, C_1]$ and $R_{B_1} = [x^4, 0]$, $R_{B_2} = [y^4, 0]$.

- As $\text{LM}(F_1) = \text{LM}(P_T) = x^3 y^3 = \frac{M}{1}$, then the relation C_1 fails when shifting by 1 so that 1 is in the staircase. Thus $\mathcal{H} = \{y, x\}$. We create R_y by computing the normal form of $[y\,\text{LM}(F_1), 0] = [x^3 y^4, 0]$ wrt. $[R_1, R_{B_1}, R_{B_2}]$ and get $R_y = [F_y, C_y] = [x^2 y^3 + 2 x y^3, y]$. Likewise $R_x = [F_x, C_x] = [x^3 y^2 + x^2 y^2 - 2 x y^2 - y^3, x - 1]$.
- As $\text{LM}(F_y) = x^2 y^3 = \frac{M}{x}$, then the relation C_y fails when shifting by x so that y and x are both in the staircase. Thus $\mathcal{H} = \{y^2, x\,y, x^2\}$. We create
  - $R_{y^2} = [0, y^2]$ by computing the normal form of $[y\,\text{LM}(F_y), 0] = [x^2 y^4, 0]$ wrt. $[R_y, R_{B_1}, R_{B_2}, R_1, R_x]$;
  - $R_{x\,y} = [-x^2 y^2 - 3 x y^3 - 2 x y^2 - y^3, x y - y - 1]$ by computing the normal form of R_1 wrt. $[R_y, R_{B_1}, R_{B_2}, R_x]$;
  - $R_{x^2} = [-3 x^2 y^2 - x y^3 + 2 x y^2 + y^3, x^2 - 2x + 1]$ by computing the normal form of $[x\,\text{LM}(F_x), 0] = [x^4 y^2, 0]$ wrt. $[R_x, R_{B_1}, R_{B_2}, R_1, R_y]$.
- There is no need to test R_x since we know x is in the staircase.
- As $F_{y^2} = 0$, then the relation is necessarily valid.
- As $\text{LM}(F_{x\,y}) = x^2 y^2 = \frac{M}{x\,y}$, then the relation $C_{x\,y}$ might fail when shifting by $x\,y$ or greater. As it can only be tested up to a shift $s = \max_{\sigma \in \mathcal{T}} = \{\sigma, \sigma x y \preceq x^3\} = x$, then it actually succeeds.
- Likewise, as $\text{LM}(F_{x^2}) = x^2 y^2 = \frac{M}{x\,y}$, then the relation C_{x^2} can only be tested up to a shift $s = \max_{\sigma\in\mathcal{T}} = \{\sigma, \sigma x^2 \preceq x^3\} = x$, then it succeeds.

We return $C_{y^2} = y^2$, $C_{x\,y} = x\,y - y - 1$ and $C_{x^2} = x^2 - 2x + 1$.

The algorithm is the following Algorithm 4.4. It uses functions

NormalForm$(R_m, [R_{B_1}, \ldots, R_{B_n}, R_{t_1}, \ldots, R_{t_r}])$, for computing the normal form of $[F_m, C_m]$ wrt. to the list $R_{B_1}, \ldots, R_{B_n}, R_{t_1}, \ldots, R_{t_r}$ with $\text{LM}(F_{t_1}) \succ \cdots \succ \text{LM}(F_{t_r})$;

Stabilize(S), for computing the true staircase containing S, i.e. all the divisors of terms in S;

Border(S), for computing the least terms for | outside of S.

Algorithm 4.4: POLYNOMIAL SCALAR-FGLM

Input: A table $\mathbf{w} = (w_i)_{i\in\mathbb{N}^n}$ with coefficients in $\mathbb{K}$, a monomial ordering $\prec$ and two monomials a and b.

Output: A set G of relations generating the ideal of relations.

```
T := {t ∈ 𝒯, t ⪯ a}, U := {u ∈ 𝒯, u ⪯ b}.
M := LCM(T) LCM(U).
For i from 1 to n do R_{B_i} := [x_i^{1+deg_{x_i} M}, 0].   // pairs on the edge
P := Σ_{τ∈(T+U)} [τ] M/τ.          // the mirror of the truncated generating series
R := {[P, 1]}.   // set of pairs [F_m, C_m] = [P · C_m mod B, C_m] to be tested
R' := ∅.                                          // set of failing pairs
G := ∅, S := ∅.              // the future Gröbner basis and staircase
While R ≠ ∅ do
    R_m = [F_m, C_m] := first element of R and remove it from R.
    If m ∉ T or LM(F_m) is as in Proposition 3.4 then     // good relation
        G := G ∪ {C_m}.
    Else                                                  // bad relation
        R' := R' ∪ {R_m}.
        For all r ∈ R do                       // reduce next pairs with it
            r := NormalForm(r, [R_{B_1}, ..., R_{B_r}, R_m]).
        S := Stabilize(S ∪ {m, M/LM(F_m)}).
        H := Border(S).
        For all h ∈ H do                           // compute new pairs
            If there is no relation C_h ∈ G or no pair R_h ∈ R then
                Make a new pair R_h = [F_h, C_h] following
                Instruction 4.1 and add it to R.
Return G.
```

Remark 4.5. Like the BMS algorithm, this algorithm creates new potential relations by making polynomial combinations of failing relations. As a consequence, at each step of the main loop, the potential relations, i.e. elements of R, are not necessarily interreduced. Either we can interreduce the final Gröbner basis before returning it at the last line of the algorithm, or when C_g is added to the set G we can update all the current relations by removing multiples of $[F_g, C_g]$ and likewise, reduce by $[F_g, C_g]$, any subsequent pair $[F_m, C_m]$.

Example 4.6 (See [6]). We give the trace of the Polynomial Scalar-FGLM algorithm with the slight modification above called on the table $\mathbf{w} = ((2\,i+1)+(2\,j-1)\,(-1)^{i+j})_{(i,j)\in\mathbb{N}^2}$, the stopping monomials 1 and y^5 and the monomial ordering $\text{DRL}(y \prec x)$.

We set $T := \mathcal{T}_{\le y^5}, U := \{1\}, M := x^4\,y^5$ and $P = 4\,x^3\,y^5+4\,x^4\,y^3+4\,x^3\,y^4+4\,x^2\,y^5-4\,x^4\,y^2+4\,x^2\,y^4+8\,x\,y^5+8\,x^4\,y+8\,x^3\,y^2+8\,x^2\,y^3+8\,x\,y^4+8\,y^5-8\,x^4$, $R_{B_1} := [x^5, 0], R_{B_2} := [y^6, 0], R = [[P, 1]]$.

Pair $R_1 = [F_1, C_1] = [P, 1]$, $R := \emptyset$ and since $1 \in T$ but $\text{LM}(F_1) = x^3\,y^5 \succeq \frac{M}{s} = x^4$, then

- $R' := \{R_1\}, S := \{1, x\}$ and $H := \{y, x^2\}$.
- We make new pairs added to R:
  - $R_y = [F_y, C_y] :=$ NormalForm($[y\ \text{LM}(F_1), 0], [R_1, R_{B_1}, R_{B_2}]$) which can be normalized into $R_y, = [4\,x^4\,y^4 - \cdots, y-1]$;
  - $R_{x^2} = [F_{x^2}, C_{x^2}] :=$ NormalForm($[x^2\ \text{LM}(F_1), 0], [R_1, R_{B_1}, R_{B_2}]$) which can be normalized into $R_{x^2} = [4\,x^4\,y^3 - \cdots, x^2 - x - 1]$.

Pair $R_y = [F_y, C_y]$, $R := \{R_{x^2}\}$ and since $y \in T$ but $\text{LM}(F_y) = x^4\,y^4 \succeq \frac{M}{s} = x^4\,y$, then

- $R' := \{R_1, R_y\}, S := \{1, y, x\}$ and $H := \{y^2, x\,y, x^2\}$.
- We make new pairs added to R:
  - As $y\ \text{LM}(F_y) = x^4\,y^5 \notin \langle x^5, y^6\rangle$ and $\text{LM}(F_1) \neq y\ \text{LM}(F_y)$, we can only set $R_{y^2} = [F_{y^2}, C_{y^2}] :=$ NormalForm($y\,R_y$, $[R_{B_1}, R_{B_2}, R_1, R_y]$) which can be normalized into $R_{y^2} = [-4\,x^4\,y^3 - \cdots, y^2 - x + 2\,y - 1]$;
  - $R_{x\,y} = [F_{x\,y}, C_{x\,y}] :=$ NormalForm($[x\ \text{LM}(F_y), 0], [R_y, R_{B_1}, R_{B_2}, R_1]$) which can be normalized into $R_{x\,y} = [4\,x^4\,y^2 - \cdots, x\,y - x + y - 1]$.
  - Nothing is done for x^2 since R_{x^2} already exists.

Pair $R_{y^2} = [F_{y^2}, C_{y^2}]$, $R := \{R_{x\,y}, R_{x^2}\}$ and since $y^2 \in T$ but $\text{LM}(F_{y^2}) = x^4\,y^3 \succeq \frac{M}{s} = x^4\,y^2$, then

- As $\text{LM}(F_{x^2}) \succeq \text{LM}(F_{y^2})$, we reduce it and obtain $R_{x^2} := [-8\,x^2\,y^4 - \cdots, x^2 + y^2 - 2\,x + 2\,y - 2]$.
- $R' := \{R_1, R_y, R_{y^2}\}, S := \{1, y, x, y^2\}$ and $H := \{x\,y, x^2, y^3\}$.
- We make new pairs added to R:
  - $R_{x\,y}$ and R_{x^2} already exist so we do nothing for them.
  - Since $\text{LM}(F_y) = y\ \text{LM}(F_{y^2})$, we can set $R_{y^3} = [F_{y^3}, C_{y^3}] :=$ NormalForm($R_y, [R_{y^2}, R_{B_1}, R_{B_2}, R_y, R_1]$) which can be normalized into $R_{y^3} = [4\,x^3\,y^4 - \cdots, y^3 - x\,y + y^2 + x - 2\,y]$.

Pair $R_{x\,y} = [F_{x\,y}, C_{x\,y}]$, $R := \{R_{x^2}, R_{y^3}\}$ and since $x\,y \in T$ and $\text{LM}(F_{x\,y}) = x^4\,y^2 \prec \frac{M}{s} = x^2\,y^5$, then

- $G := \{x\,y - x + y - 1\}$.
- As $C_{y^3} = y^3 - x\,y + y^2 + x - 2\,y$ has a term in $x\,y$, we update $R_{y^3} := R_{y^3} + R_{x\,y} = [4\,x^3\,y^4 - \cdots, y^3 + y^2 - y - 1]$.

Pair $R_{x^2} = [F_{x^2}, C_{x^2}]$, $R := \{R_{y^3}\}$ and since $x^2 \in T$ and $\text{LM}(F_{x^2}) = x^2\,y^4 \prec \frac{M}{s} = x^2\,y^5$, then

- $G := \{x\,y - x + y - 1, x^2 + y^2 - 2\,x + 2\,y - 2\}$.

Pair $R_{y^3} = [F_{y^3}, C_{y^3}]$, $R := \emptyset$ and since $y^3 \in T$ and $\text{LM}(F_{y^3}) = x^3\,y^4 \prec \frac{M}{s} = x^4\,y^3$, then

- $G := \{x\,y - x + y - 1, x^2 + y^2 - 2\,x + 2\,y - 2, y^3 + y^2 - y - 1\}$.

We return G.

Theorem 4.7. *Let a table $\mathbf{w}$, a monomial ordering $\prec$ and two monomials a and b be the input of the Polynomial Scalar-FGLM algorithm. Let us assume that the Gröbner basis $\mathcal{G}$ of the ideal of relations of $\mathbf{w}$ for $\prec$ and its staircase S satisfy $a \succeq \max(S \cup \text{LM}(\mathcal{G}))$ and for all $g \preceq a$, $s = \max_{\sigma\in\mathcal{T}}\{\sigma, \{\sigma\} + \mathcal{T}_{\preceq g} \subseteq (\mathcal{T}_{\preceq a} + \mathcal{T}_{\preceq b})\}$, we have $\max(S) \preceq s$.*

Then, the Polynomial Scalar-FGLM algorithm terminates and computes a Gröbner basis of the ideal of relations of $\mathbf{w}$ for $\prec$ in $O\big(\#S\,(\#S + \#\mathcal{G})\,\#\,(\mathcal{T}_{\preceq a} + \mathcal{T}_{\preceq b})\big)$ operations in the base field.

Proof. The proof is mainly based on the termination and validity of the BMS algorithm. For any monomial $m \in \mathcal{T}_{\preceq a}$, we denote by $C_m^\star$ the last (and therefore one with the largest fail) relation made by the BMS algorithm starting with m, if there is any.

Starting with $R_1 = [F_1, C_1] = [P_{\mathcal{T}_{\preceq a}+\mathcal{T}_{\preceq b}}, 1]$, $\text{LM}(F_1)$ yields exactly the fail of relation $C_1 = C_1^\star$ so that, as in the BMS algorithm, we know the leading monomials of the potential next relations.

Let us assume now that for any monomial $\mu \prec h$, the pair $R_\mu = [F_\mu, C_\mu]$ made by the Polynomial Scalar-FGLM algorithm is equivalent to $C_\mu^\star$, that is either both C_μ and $C_\mu^\star$ fail when shifting by exactly the same monomial or they both succeed on $\mathcal{T}_{\preceq a} + \mathcal{T}_{\preceq b}$.

Since C_μ and $C_\mu^\star$ are equivalent, the current discovered staircase by the BMS and the Polynomial Scalar-FGLM algorithms are the same. Thus either h is a leading monomial of a relation to be built by both algorithms or it is not. Without loss of generality, we can assume it is. There exists a monomial m such that $m|h$ and $R_m = [F_m, C_m]$ and $C_m^\star$ have been made. In the BMS algorithm, the relation $C_h^\star$ is obtained as $\frac{h}{m}\,C_m^\star - \sum_{\mu\prec h} q_\mu^\star\,C_\mu^\star$ while in the Polynomial Scalar-FGLM algorithm, C_h is made as $\frac{h}{m}\,C_m - \sum_{\mu\prec h} q_\mu\,C_\mu$. In each computation, $q_\mu^\star$ and q_μ are chosen so that $C_m^\star$ and C_m have the largest fail (or equivalently F_m has the least leading monomial), hence $C_m^\star$ and C_m are equivalent. For $h \in S$, the potential relation C_h made by the algorithm must fail when shifted by a monomial in S. Thus, there exist σ_1, σ_2 such that $\sigma_1\,\sigma_2 \in S$, $\sigma_1\,h \preceq a$, $\sigma_2 \preceq b$ and the column labeled with $\sigma_1\,h$ of the matrix $H_{\mathcal{T}_{\preceq b},\mathcal{T}_{\preceq a}}$ is independent from the previous ones. For $g \in \text{LM}(\mathcal{G})$, by Section 3.2, the relation C_g has been tested with a shift $s = \max_{\sigma\in\mathcal{T}}\{\sigma, \{\sigma\} + \mathcal{T}_{\preceq g} \subseteq (\mathcal{T}_{\preceq a} + \mathcal{T}_{\preceq b}) \subseteq \mathcal{T}_{\preceq a\,b}\}$. The theorem hypothesis is exactly that the full staircase is included in the set of tested shifts, hence we can ensure that C_g corresponds to a kernel vector of $H_{S,S\cup\{g\}}$ with the last coordinate equal to 1.

Concerning the complexity of the algorithm. Since $\mathcal{T}_{\preceq a}$ and $\mathcal{T}_{\preceq b}$ are stable by division, so is $\mathcal{T}_{\preceq a} + \mathcal{T}_{\preceq b}$. Let us recall that the support of $P_{\mathcal{T}_{\preceq a}+\mathcal{T}_{\preceq b}}$ is $\left\{\frac{M}{\tau}, \tau \in (\mathcal{T}_{\preceq a} + \mathcal{T}_{\preceq b})\right\}$, $M = \text{LCM}(\mathcal{T}_{\preceq a} + \mathcal{T}_{\preceq b})$. Since each F_m satisfies $F_m = P_{\mathcal{T}_{\preceq a}+\mathcal{T}_{\preceq b}}\,C_m \bmod B$, then the monomials in the support of F_m are multiples of the monomials in the support of $P_{\mathcal{T}_{\preceq a}+\mathcal{T}_{\preceq b}}$ and thus are included in the support of $P_{\mathcal{T}_{\preceq a}+\mathcal{T}_{\preceq b}}$. Each pair $R_m = [F_m, C_m]$ for $m \in S \cup \text{LM}(\mathcal{G})$ must be reduced by all the previous ones lying in the staircase in at most $\# S \# (\mathcal{T}_{\leq a} + \mathcal{T}_{\leq b})$ operations. Reducing the relations to obtain a minimal Gröbner basis can be done in $O(\# S \# \mathcal{G} \# (\mathcal{T}_{\leq a} + \mathcal{T}_{\leq b}))$ operations, hence this part is not the bottleneck of the algorithm. □

5 AN ADAPTIVE VARIANT

In this section, due to space limitation, we only give some ideas to design an adaptive version of the POLYNOMIAL SCALAR-FGLM.

In general, the BMS, the SCALAR-FGLM and thus the POLYNOMIAL SCALAR-FGLM algorithms are efficient when the staircase of the Gröbner basis of the ideal of relations is closer to a simplex than to a line. Indeed, for the $\mathrm{DRL}(x_n \prec \cdots \prec x_1)$ ordering, whether the Gröbner basis is $\{x_n, \ldots, x_2, x_1^d\}$ or all the monomials of degree d: $\{x_n^d, x_{n-1}\, x_n^{d-1}, \ldots, x_1\, x_n^{d-1}, \ldots, x_1^d\}$, the BMS algorithm requires to visit all the monomials up to $x_1^{2\,d-1}$ making the algorithm costly in the former case compared to the size of the staircase.

The ADAPTIVE SCALAR-FGLM algorithm [3] was designed to take into account the shape of the Gröbner basis gradually as it is discovered. The idea is to start from S, the empty set, and a list of monomial to visit in increasing order. At step m, the first monomial of that list, if $H_{S\cup\{m\},S\cup\{m\}}$ has a greater rank than $H_{S,S}$, then m is added to S and removed from the list. Otherwise, a relation C_m is found and any multiple of m is removed from the list. For instance, in the line staircase with Gröbner basis $\{x_n, \ldots, x_2, x_1^d\}$, it computes the rank of matrices $H_{\{1\},\{1\}}, H_{\{1,x_n\},\{1,x_n\}}, \ldots, H_{\{1,x_2\},\{1,x_2\}}, H_{\{1,x_1\},\{1,x_1\}}, H_{\{1,x_1,x_1^2\},\{1,x_1,x_1^2\}}, \ldots, H_{\{1,x_1,\ldots,x_1^d\},\{1,x_1,\ldots,x_1^d\}}$. It thus requires merely $2\,(n+d) - 1$ table terms instead of $\binom{n+2\,d-1}{n}$.

The main issue with the POLYNOMIAL SCALAR-FGLM algorithm in this context is that it is based on polynomials from matrices with columns set $\mathcal{T}_{\leq a}$ and rows set $\mathcal{T}_{\leq b}$.

The idea of the adaptive variant of the POLYNOMIAL SCALAR-FGLM algorithm is to replace the linear algebra arithmetic with matrices $H_{S\cup\{m\},S\cup\{m\}}$ by polynomial arithmetic like in Sections 2.4 and 3.2. At each step, we have the polynomial $P_{2\,S}$, a monomial ideal $B_{2\,S}$, determined as in Section 3.2 and pairs $R_{2\,S,t} = [F_{2\,S,t}, C_t] = [P_{2\,S}\, C_t \bmod B_{2\,S}, C_t]$. At the next step, we compute $P_{2\,(S\cup\{m\})}$ from $P_{2\,S}$ by shifting it by $\frac{\mathrm{LCM}(S\cup\{m\})}{\mathrm{LCM}(S)}$ and adding the missing terms, update $B_{2\,S}$ into $B_{2\,(S\cup\{m\})}$ and likewise update each $R_{2\,(S\cup\{m\}),t}$ by shifting $F_{2\,S,t}$ and adding the missing terms to make $F_{2\,(S\cup\{m\}),t}$. Then, $R_{2\,(S\cup\{m\}),m}$ is initialized as $m\, R_{2\,(S\cup\{m\}),1}$ and then reduced, as in Section 4, by $R_{2\,(S\cup\{m\}),B_1}, \ldots, R_{2\,(S\cup\{m\}),B_n}$, where $B_1, \ldots, B_n \in B_{2\,S}$.

When a relation C_g is found, any multiple of g is removed from the set of potential monomials to add to S. Moreover, we can further reduce a future relation $R_{2\,(S\cup\{m\}),m} = [F_{2\,(S\cup\{m\}),m}, C_m]$ with any pair $[\frac{M}{\mu\, g}, 0]$, $m \succeq \mu\, g$, like we reduce it with $R_{2\,(S\cup\{m\}),B_1}, \ldots, R_{2\,(S\cup\{m\}),B_n}$.

This transformation of the POLYNOMIAL SCALAR-FGLM is only partial as we do not know yet how to initialize $R_{2\,(S\cup\{m\}),m}$ as the quotient of two pairs of polynomials.

6 EXPERIMENTS

In this section, we report on the number of arithmetic operations done by the different algorithms for computing the Gröbner basis of the ideal of relations of some table families. They are counted using naive multiplications. Three families in dimension 2 (Figure 1) and dimension 3 (Figure 2) are tested. For each of them we use the $\mathrm{DRL}(z \prec y \prec x)$ ordering and denote by S the staircase and $\mathrm{LM}(\mathcal{G})$ the set of the leading terms of the Gröbner basis of relations.

Simplex tables: $\mathrm{LM}(\mathcal{G}) = \left\{y^d, x\, y^{d-1}, \ldots, x^d\right\}$ in dimension 2 and $\mathrm{LM}(\mathcal{G}) = \left\{z^d, y\, z^{d-1}, x\, z^{d-1}, \ldots, y^d, x\, y^{d-1}, \ldots, x^d\right\}$ in dimension 3, i.e. all the monomials of degree d.

L-shape tables: $\mathrm{LM}(\mathcal{G}) = \left\{x\, y, y^d, x^d\right\}$ in dimension 2 and $\mathrm{LM}(\mathcal{G}) = \left\{y\, z, x\, z, x\, y, z^d, y^d, x^d\right\}$ in dimension 3.

Rectangle tables: $\mathrm{LM}(\mathcal{G}) = \left\{y^{\lfloor d/2 \rfloor}, x^d\right\}$ in dimension 2 and $\mathrm{LM}(\mathcal{G}) = \left\{z^{\lceil d/3 \rceil}, y^{\lfloor d/2 \rfloor}, x^d\right\}$ dimension 3.

Let $a = \max(S \cup \mathrm{LM}(\mathcal{G}))$. Generically, a relation C_m fails when shifted by m. From [9, Prop. 10], we know that the BMS algorithm recover all the relations when called up to monomial $\max(S)\, \max(S \cup \mathrm{LM}(\mathcal{G}))$. Yet, if $\max(\mathrm{LM}(\mathcal{G})) \succ \max(S)$, then for $g \in \mathrm{LM}(\mathcal{G})$, the relation C_g is not necessarily shifted by g, so we called it with a^2. The SCALAR-FGLM algorithm was called on $U = T = \mathcal{T}_{\leq a}$. The POLYNOMIAL SCALAR-FGLM algorithm was called on $U = \{1\}, T = \mathcal{T}_{\leq a^2}$ and $U = T = \mathcal{T}_{\leq a}$ and we report the higher number of operations. The needed input set of monomials for the ARTINIAN GORENSTEIN BORDER BASES algorithm (AGBB) of [23] to recover the ideal of relations was higher than expected in some situations. It explains the big overhead in Figure 1 in dimension 2:

Simplex tables: The correct border basis is not recovered. In dimension 2, we have to visit all the monomials of degree around $5\,d$ or $6\,d$ to close the staircase. This also yields relations of degree higher than expected. For $d = 8$, we obtained $\mathrm{LM}(\mathcal{B}) = \left\{x^i\, y^{18-i},\ 0 \leq i \leq 18\right\}$.

L-shape tables: The correct border basis is not recovered. In dimension 2, we have to visit all the monomials of degree $5\,d - 10$ to close the staircase. This yields relations of degree higher than expected, though. For $d = 8$, we obtained $\mathrm{LM}(\mathcal{B}) = \left\{x\, y^i, x^i\, y, y^{13}, x^{13},\ 1 \leq i \leq 12\right\}$.

Rectangle tables: The border basis is recovered whenever the algorithm visits all the monomials of degree at most $2\,(d + \lfloor d/2 \rfloor + \lceil d/3 \rceil - 1)$.

The POLYNOMIAL SCALAR-FGLM algorithm performs fewer arithmetic operations than the others, for large d. More precisely, its number of operations appears to be linear in $(\# S)^2 = O(\# S\, (\# S + \# \mathcal{G}))$ in fixed dimension.

Simplex tables: While it seems the SCALAR-FGLM algorithm is the fastest in Figure 2, we can expect that it will not be the case in higher degrees, like in Figure 1. This would confirm the observed speedup in dimension 2 to dimension 3.

L-shape tables: Although the obtained speedups are not negligible, the adaptive variant should allow us to perform even fewer operations. See Section 5.

Rectangle tables: While this family has the best behavior for the BMS algorithm, the POLYNOMIAL SCALAR-FGLM algorithm has an even greater speedup than in the Simplex case.

ACKNOWLEDGMENTS

We thank the anonymous referees for their careful reading and their helpful comments. The authors are partially supported by the PGMO grant GAMMA.

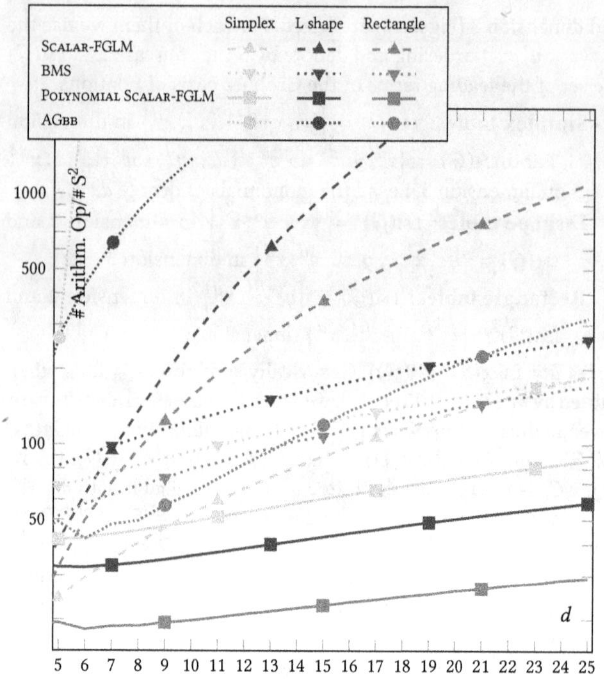

Figure 1: Number of arithmetic operations (2D)

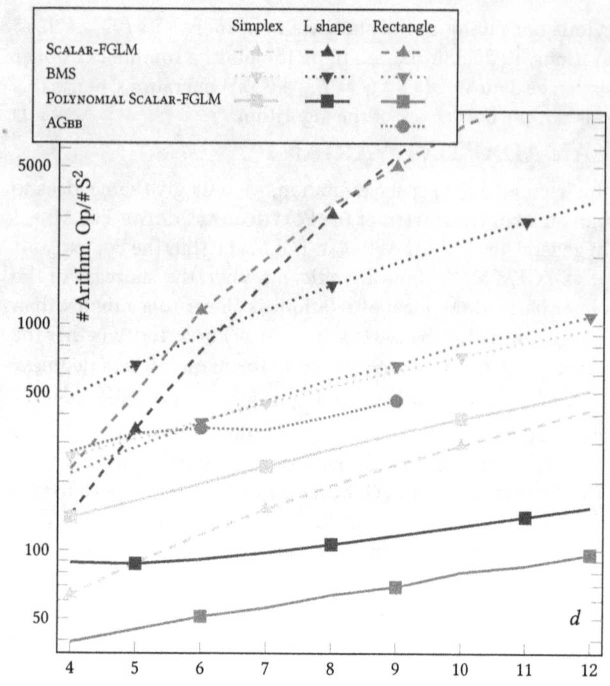

Figure 2: Number of arithmetic operations (3D)

REFERENCES

[1] B. Beckermann and G. Labahn. 1994. A Uniform Approach for the Fast Computation of Matrix-Type Pade Approximants. *SIAM J. Matrix Anal. Appl.* 15, 3 (1994), 804–823. https://doi.org/10.1137/S0895479892230031

[2] E. Berlekamp. 1968. Nonbinary BCH decoding. *IEEE Trans. Inform. Theory* 14, 2 (1968), 242–242. https://doi.org/10.1109/TIT.1968.1054109

[3] J. Berthomieu, B. Boyer, and J.-Ch. Faugère. 2015. Linear Algebra for Computing Gröbner Bases of Linear Recursive Multidimensional Sequences. In *Proceedings of the 2015 ACM on International Symposium on Symbolic and Algebraic Computation (ISSAC '15)*. ACM, New York, NY, USA, 61–68. https://doi.org/10.1145/2755996.2756673

[4] J. Berthomieu, B. Boyer, and J.-Ch. Faugère. 2017. Linear Algebra for Computing Gröbner Bases of Linear Recursive Multidimensional Sequences. *Journal of Symbolic Computation* 83, Supplement C (Nov. 2017), 36–67. https://doi.org/10.1016/j.jsc.2016.11.005 Special issue on the conference ISSAC 2015: Symbolic computation and computer algebra.

[5] J. Berthomieu and J.-Ch. Faugère. 2017. In-depth comparison of the Berlekamp – Massey – Sakata and the Scalar-FGLM algorithms: the non adaptive variants. (May 2017). https://hal.inria.fr/hal-01516708 preprint.

[6] J. Berthomieu and J.-Ch. Faugère. 2018. Experiments. (2018). http://www-polsys.lip6.fr/~berthomieu/ISSAC2018.html

[7] S. R. Blackburn. 1997. Fast rational interpolation, Reed-Solomon decoding, and the linear complexity profiles of sequences. *IEEE Transactions on Information Theory* 43, 2 (1997), 537–548.

[8] R.C. Bose and D.K. Ray-Chaudhuri. 1960. On a class of error correcting binary group codes. *Information and Control* 3, 1 (1960), 68 – 79. https://doi.org/10.1016/S0019-9958(60)90287-4

[9] M. Bras-Amorós and M. E. O'Sullivan. 2006. The Correction Capability of the Berlekamp–Massey–Sakata Algorithm with Majority Voting. *Applicable Algebra in Engineering, Communication and Computing* 17, 5 (2006), 315–335. https://doi.org/10.1007/s00200-006-0015-8

[10] R. P. Brent, F. G. Gustavson, and D. Y.Y. Yun. 1980. Fast solution of Toeplitz systems of equations and computation of Padé approximants. *Journal of Algorithms* 1, 3 (1980), 259 – 295. https://doi.org/10.1016/0196-6774(80)90013-9

[11] D. G. Cantor and E. Kaltofen. 1991. On Fast Multiplication of Polynomials Over Arbitrary Algebras. *Acta Informatica* 28 (1991), 693–701.

[12] J. W. Cooley and J. W. Tukey. 1965. An Algorithm for the Machine Calculation of Complex Fourier Series. *Math. Comp.* 19, 90 (1965), 297–301. http://www.jstor.org/stable/2003354

[13] D. Cox, J. Little, and D. O'Shea. 2015. *Ideals, Varieties, and Algorithms* (fourth ed.). Springer, New York. xvi+646 pages. An introduction to computational algebraic geometry and commutative algebra.

[14] J. Dornstetter. 1987. On the equivalence between Berlekamp's and Euclid's algorithms (Corresp.). *IEEE Transactions on Information Theory* 33, 3 (1987), 428–431. https://doi.org/10.1109/TIT.1987.1057299

[15] J.-Ch. Faugère and Ch. Mou. 2011. Fast Algorithm for Change of Ordering of Zero-dimensional Gröbner Bases with Sparse Multiplication Matrices. In *Proceedings of the 36th International Symposium on Symbolic and Algebraic Computation (ISSAC '11)*. ACM, New York, NY, USA, 115–122. https://doi.org/10.1145/1993886.1993908

[16] J.-Ch. Faugère and Ch. Mou. 2017. Sparse FGLM algorithms. *Journal of Symbolic Computation* 80, 3 (2017), 538 – 569. https://doi.org/10.1016/j.jsc.2016.07.025

[17] P. Fitzpatrick and J. Flynn. 1992. A Gröbner basis technique for Padé approximation. *J. Symbolic Comput.* 13, 2 (1992), 133 – 138. https://doi.org/10.1016/S0747-7171(08)80087-9

[18] P. Fitzpatrick and G.H. Norton. 1990. Finding a basis for the characteristic ideal of an n-dimensional linear recurring sequence. *IEEE Trans. Inform. Theory* 36, 6 (1990), 1480–1487. https://doi.org/10.1109/18.59953

[19] A. Hocquenghem. 1959. Codes correcteurs d'erreurs. *Chiffres* 2 (1959), 147 – 156.

[20] E. Jonckheere and Ch. Ma. 1989. A simple Hankel interpretation of the Berlekamp-Massey algorithm. *Linear Algebra Appl.* 125, 0 (1989), 65 – 76. https://doi.org/10.1016/0024-3795(89)90032-3

[21] N. Levinson. 1947. The Wiener RMS (Root-Mean-Square) error criterion in the filter design and prediction. *J. Math. Phys.* 25 (1947), 261–278.

[22] J. L. Massey. 1969. Shift-register synthesis and BCH decoding. *IEEE Trans. Inform. Theory* IT-15 (1969), 122–127.

[23] Bernard Mourrain. 2017. Fast Algorithm for Border Bases of Artinian Gorenstein Algebras. In *Proceedings of the 2017 ACM on International Symposium on Symbolic and Algebraic Computation (ISSAC '17)*. ACM, New York, NY, USA, 333–340. https://doi.org/10.1145/3087604.3087632

[24] Sh. Sakata. 1988. Finding a minimal set of linear recurring relations capable of generating a given finite two-dimensional array. *J. Symbolic Comput.* 5, 3 (1988), 321–337. https://doi.org/10.1016/S0747-7171(88)80033-6

[25] Sh. Sakata. 1990. Extension of the Berlekamp-Massey Algorithm to N Dimensions. *Inform. and Comput.* 84, 2 (1990), 207–239. https://doi.org/10.1016/0890-5401(90)90039-K

[26] Sh. Sakata. 2009. The BMS Algorithm. In *Gröbner Bases, Coding, and Cryptography*, Massimiliano Sala, Shojiro Sakata, Teo Mora, Carlo Traverso, and Ludovic Perret (Eds.). Springer Berlin Heidelberg, Berlin, Heidelberg, 143–163. https://doi.org/10.1007/978-3-540-93806-4_9

[27] N. Wiener. 1964. *Extrapolation, Interpolation, and Smoothing of Stationary Time Series.* The MIT Press, Cambridge, MA.

Monodromy Solver: Sequential and Parallel

Nathan Bliss
University of Illinois at Chicago
Chicago, Illinois
nbliss2@uic.edu

Timothy Duff
Georgia Institute of Technology
Atlanta, Georgia
tduff3@gatech.edu

Anton Leykin
Georgia Institute of Technology
Atlanta, Georgia
leykin@math.gatech.edu

Jeff Sommars
University of Illinois at Chicago
Chicago, Illinois
sommars1@uic.edu

ABSTRACT

We describe, study, and experiment with an algorithm for finding all solutions of systems of polynomial equations using homotopy continuation and monodromy. This algorithm follows the framework developed in [5] and can operate in the presence of a large number of failures of the homotopy continuation subroutine.

We give special attention to parallelization and probabilistic analysis of a model adapted to parallelization and failures. Apart from theoretical results, we developed a simulator that allows us to run a large number of experiments without recomputing the outcomes of the continuation subroutine.

KEYWORDS

Solving systems of polynomial equations, homotopy continuation, monodromy, probabilistic algorithm, parallel computation.

ACM Reference Format:
Nathan Bliss, Timothy Duff, Anton Leykin, and Jeff Sommars. 2018. Monodromy Solver: Sequential and Parallel. In *ISSAC '18: 2018 ACM International Symposium on Symbolic and Algebraic Computation, July 16–19, 2018, New York, NY, USA.* ACM, New York, NY, USA, 8 pages. https://doi.org/10.1145/3208976.3209007

1 INTRODUCTION

Monodromy Solver (MS) is an algorithmic framework for solving parametric families of polynomial systems. MS relies on numerical homotopy continuation methods [19], which are applicable in a very general setting, and monodromy (Galois group) action, which is specific to polynomial systems. The monodromy technique has been used successfully in *numerical algebraic geometry* (for a good overview, see [21]) mostly for high level tasks: for instance, numerical irreducible decomposition [22] or Galois group computation [9, 15].

Research of TD and AL is supported in part by NSF grant DMS-1719968.

ISSAC '18, July 16–19, 2018, New York, NY, USA

ACM ISBN 978-1-4503-5550-6/18/07...$15.00
https://doi.org/10.1145/3208976.3209007

The MS framework addresses the following basic problem:

> Given a family of polynomial maps F_p, find *all* solutions to $F_p = 0$ for a generic value of p.

Note that, given an ability to construct a complete solution set for a generic value of the parameter, one can find all isolated solutions $F_p = 0$ for an *arbitrary* value of the parameter p by using a coefficient-parameter homotopy [21, §7].

Apart from MS, current methods of polynomial system solving via homotopy continuation include polyhedral approaches [11, 24], total-degree and multihomogeneous-degree homotopies [26], regeneration [10], and various other more specialized methods.

Most methods of homotopy continuation are embarrassingly parallel, in that homotopy paths can be tracked completely independently. Literature on parallelism in relation to homotopy continuation includes [7, 8, 14, 16–18, 20, 25].

While an *atomic task* of MS (one homotopy path track) is independent of another such task, this is only true for the tasks that are *already* scheduled and being processed. The scheduling algorithm, however, follows a probabilistic framework and (at every state when resources free up) attempts to find a task that maximizes the number of solutions known once this task and the current (in progress) tasks are complete. This has to be done using only partial knowledge of the outcome of the current tasks and, hence, implies a *dependence* of the choice of a new candidate task on the current state of the algorithm.

In the context of the framework that allows multiple threads to carry out atomic tasks, we analyze the probabilistic model that results from the assumption of uniform randomness of correspondences induced by edges in an underlying graph (see §2). This is followed by analysis of a model that accounts for failures in the homotopy continuation subroutine.

Last, but not least, we have implemented a simulator for the new algorithm that makes it possible to run fast experiments without rerunning the actual continuation subroutine over and over again. Using this simulator we conduct several computational experiments on both fabricated data using the probability distribution in our model and the data coming from the execution of homotopy continuation algorithms for a family of polynomial systems. This contribution is important for the further development of the MS framework, since our probabilistic assumptions are too simple to completely describe the random behavior in actual computations.

In §2 we give a primer on MS using an example, and then define necessary terminology in §3. The pseudocode for the main algorithm appears in §5. A probabilistic model is analyzed in §4 with a view towards designing a task selection strategy for our algorithm. The study of the threshold for completion depending on the rate of failures is in §6. Finally, in §7, we describe the implementation of the simulator, and use it to showcase the benefits of the new approach via several experiments. A brief conclusion is in §8.

2 MONODROMY SOLVER FRAMEWORK

For a family F_p, the MS approach treats different parameter choices p_i as nodes in a graph, and by tracking along "edges" (i.e. homotopies) between them, seeks to populate the solution set for at least one node. Each of these homotopies is a *coefficient-parameter homotopy*,

$$H(t) = F_{(1+t)p_1+tp_2}, \quad t \in [0,1], \tag{1}$$

which tracks between the parameter choices p_1 and p_2. For generic p, the number of roots of the system is constant, and following loops in the graph permutes the roots. In the case when F_p is linear in p, we may use a *segment homotopy*,

$$H(t) = (1-t)\gamma_1 F_{p_1} + t\gamma_2 F_{p_2}, \quad t \in [0,1], \tag{2}$$

defined for generic $\gamma_1, \gamma_2 \in \mathbb{C}$. This gives us the ability to introduce multiple edges between two nodes, in hope that they would induce distinct maps on the solution sets.

As an example, suppose we want to know the roots of a generic univariate cubic polynomial. Writing it as

$$x^3 + ax^2 + bx + c, \tag{3}$$

we set up a graph for three values $p_1, p_2, p_3 \in \mathbb{C}^3$ of the coefficients. It may help to visualize the family with one parameter: set $a = b = 0$. Then we may just imagine a triangle embedded in the complex plane, i.e., the parameter space of c. This triangle is the *homotopy graph* of Figure 1 that lifts to the *solution graph* above it.

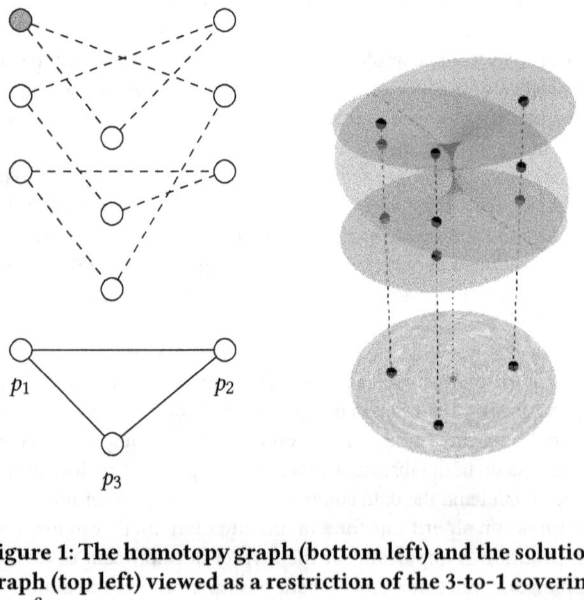

Figure 1: The homotopy graph (bottom left) and the solution graph (top left) viewed as a restriction of the 3-to-1 covering for $x^3 + c = 0$.

Assume that we know one solution (shaded in Figure 1) of F_{p_1}. Now continue this solution along edges of the solution graph. By doing so, we recover *all three* solutions at one of the nodes. As long as the action of the *monodromy group* (see [5] for definition and discussion) is transitive, it is always possible to recover all solutions from one by following along the edges of a graph that is sufficiently large and sufficiently general.

In our very simple example there is always a unique choice for the next edge to track along; in general, this will not be so. The fact that only a subgraph of the solution graph is known at any point of the algorithm complicates the selection of the next (homotopy continuation) atomic task further. Hence, two parts of the MS approach are probabilistic: first, the homotopy graph is created at random; and second, the task selection procedure may either be random or designed to maximize the expectation of some *potential* function (see §4) under a fixed probabilistic model.

It has been shown in [5] that given a simple probabilistic model, the expected number of edges in the solution graph for MS to succeed is *linear* in the number of solutions. This bounds the number of continuation tasks to be carried out and—what seems to be the main reason for the practical success of MS—ties the overall complexity of the approach to the *actual* number of the solutions, and not to some *bound* that may be available a priori for a larger family of systems (e.g., bound of Bézout or Bernstein-Khovanskii-Kouchnirenko).

Note that the Monodromy Solver framework does not specify a stopping criterion. For the discussion of possible stopping criteria see §3.2.2 and §3.2.3 of [5].

3 DEFINITIONS

Let G be a loopless multigraph with vertices $V = V(G)$ and edges $E = E(G)$. Each vertex corresponds to a system F_p specialized at parameters p and is associated with d solutions—we refer to the vertex together with this satellite data as a *node*. Each edge $e \in E$ connecting nodes v_1 and v_2 induces a homotopy that establishes a bijective correspondence between the solutions of the polynomial systems F_{p_1} and F_{p_2}. We assume the following:

Assumption 1. *Edges induce uniformly random correspondences.*

In other words, we assume that all bijective correspondences that could be induced by an edge connecting the solutions of F_{p_1} and F_{p_2} are equally likely. This assumption allows us to simplify the probability calculations and postulate an effective task selection strategy described in §4 especially when tracking multiple paths in parallel. See discussion of randomization in §5.1 of [5].

In general, e will refer to an edge and $\vec{e}$ will refer to a directed edge (a pair of e and a specified direction). A pair $t = (s, \vec{e})$, where $s \in S(v)$ belongs to the solution set $S(v)$ of the polynomial system corresponding to $v = \text{src}(\vec{e})$, represents a candidate for (one) *homotopy path track*, an atomic task that shall be performed by one thread in a parallel algorithm.

We fix the graph $G = (V, E)$ at the initialization stage. At a given *state* $x = (Q, C, A)$ of the algorithm we have the following.

- A collection Q of sets indexed by $v \in V$, where each Q_v is the subset of solutions at v *known* at this state.
- A collection C of sets indexed by $e \in E$. Each $C_e \subset Q_v \times Q_w$ — where v and w are the nodes e connects — is a partial

one-to-one correspondence between subsets of Q_v and Q_w. We denote by π_v and π_w the projections from $Q_v \times Q_w$ to Q_v and Q_w, respectively.
- A set $A = \{t_1, \ldots, t_k\}$ of atomic (homotopy path tracking) tasks currently being processed (using k independent threads).

Given a state $x = (Q, C, A)$ we denote $Q(x) := Q$, $C(x) := C$, and $A(x) := A$. Note that in most states (in our basic framework, in all states but the initial state) one can determine Q from C. We shall call a state x *idle* if $A(x) = \emptyset$.

For an atomic task $t = (s, \vec{e}) \in A$, $\mathrm{src}(t)$ and $\mathrm{dest}(t)$ will refer to the source and destination vertices of $\mathrm{edge}(t) := \vec{e}$.

Prior to running t, it is unknown which solution at $\mathrm{dest}(t)$ will be found. We use the random variable sol_t to denote the outcome of running this task, conditioned on the current state. Likewise, sol_A will denote the random set of solutions known after running the tasks in A. Suppose we know (or can estimate) the solution count for a generic system; refer to this (integer) count as d, the *degree* of the problem. Assumption 1 implies that

$$\Pr(\mathrm{sol}_t \notin Q_{\mathrm{dest}(\vec{e})}) = \frac{d - |Q_{\mathrm{dest}(\vec{e})}|}{d - |C_e|} \tag{4}$$

Define $\mathbf{E}(x)$ to be the expected total number of known solutions at all vertices after running *all* tasks $t \in A$ to completion. That is, if y is the state after the completion, i.e., $A(y) = \emptyset$, then

$$\mathbf{E}(x) = \sum_{v \in V(G)} \mathbf{E}_v(x), \text{ with } \mathbf{E}_v(x) := \mathbb{E}(|Q_v(y)|),$$

where the (new) number of known points $|Q_v(y)|$ is perceived as a random variable with expected value $\mathbb{E}(|Q_v(y)|)$; state transition probabilities are induced by Assumption 1.

4 TASK SELECTION VIA POTENTIAL

We intend to use either $\mathbf{E}(Q, C, A \cup \{t\})$ to define a *potential* function driving our choice of the next task t to append to A once a thread becomes available. The basic update rule is given below:

$$\mathbf{E}_v(Q, C, A \cup \{t\}) = \mathbf{E}_v(Q, C, A) + \Pr(\mathrm{sol}_t \notin \mathrm{sol}_A). \tag{5}$$

This follows by a simple conditioning argument:

$$\begin{aligned}
\mathbf{E}_v(Q, C, A \cup \{t\}) &= \mathbf{E}_v(Q, C, A \cup \{t\} \mid \mathrm{sol}_t \in \mathrm{sol}_A) \Pr(\mathrm{sol}_t \in \mathrm{sol}_A) \\
&\quad + \mathbf{E}_v(Q, C, A \cup \{t\} \mid \mathrm{sol}_t \notin \mathrm{sol}_A) \Pr(\mathrm{sol}_t \notin \mathrm{sol}_A) \\
&= \mathbf{E}_v(Q, C, A) \Pr(\mathrm{sol}_t \in \mathrm{sol}_A) \\
&\quad + \left(1 + \mathbf{E}_v(Q, C, A)\right) \Pr(\mathrm{sol}_t \notin \mathrm{sol}_A) \\
&= \mathbf{E}_v(Q, C, A) + \Pr(\mathrm{sol}_t \notin \mathrm{sol}_A)
\end{aligned}$$

4.1 Potential given no path failures

Since random homotopy paths stay away from the discriminant locus with probability 1, it is natural to seek a "smart" task-selection strategy in the idealized setting when *no failures* in homotopy tracking occur. The following proposition shows that $\mathbf{E}_v(Q, C, A)$ can be computed recursively.

Proposition 4.1. *Let v be a vertex and e an edge incident to v. If t is a candidate path track with* $\mathrm{dest}(t) = v$ *and* $\mathrm{edge}(t) = \vec{e}$, *then*

$$\mathbf{E}_v(Q, C, A \cup \{t\}) = \mathbf{E}_v(Q, C, A) + \frac{d - \mathbf{E}_v(Q, C, A)}{d - |C_e| - \#\{t' \in A : \mathrm{edge}(t') = \vec{e}\}} \tag{6}$$

Thus, if we keep track of these expectations as we go, we may determine the potential of tracking a new thread without recomputing anything else.

Proof. Let X denote the random variable that, conditioned on the idle state $(Q, C, \emptyset)$, counts the total number of solutions at v after completing all tasks in A. Noting equation (5), we have

$$\begin{aligned}
&\Pr(\mathrm{sol}_t \notin \mathrm{sol}_A) = \\
&= \sum_{k \in \mathrm{supp}\, X} \frac{(d-k)}{d - |C_e| - \#\{t' \in A : \mathrm{edge}(t') = \vec{e}\}} \Pr(X = k) \\
&= \frac{d - \mathbf{E}_v(Q, C, A)}{d - |C_e| - \#\{t' \in A : \mathrm{edge}(t') = \vec{e}\}}.
\end{aligned}$$

□

4.2 Potential in the presence of failures

The failure of certain atomic tasks is an inevitable feature of any MS implementation: such failures may occur when paths verge too close to the locus of singular systems, and may be influenced by the aggressiveness of threshold settings in the underlying numerical software as well as various others factors. In anticipation of such failures, we consider the effects of failures in a simple probabilistic model generalizing the results of the previous section.

Assumption 2. *We now assume that the* probability of success *for every atomic task equals a global fixed constant $\alpha \in [0, 1]$ and that formation of edge correspondences and all task failures are mutually independent events.*

Let us emphasize a technical feature of this assumption—if we have $\mathrm{edge}(t) = \mathrm{edge}(t')$ and $\mathrm{dest}(t) = \mathrm{src}(t')$, the tasks t and t' still fail independently. This lack of symmetry should be accounted for in any given state of the algorithm. Thus, we extend our definition of a *state* $x = (Q, C, A, F)$ as follows:

- As before, Q_v denotes the set of solutions known at $v \in V$, each $C_{vw} \subset Q_v \times Q_w$ is a set of *known, successful correspondences*, and A is the set of current tasks.
- Failures are indexed by *directed edges*. For each $\vec{e}$, the set $F_{\vec{e}}$ consists of known solutions $s \in Q_{\mathrm{src}(e)}$ such that the task $(s, \vec{e})$ has completed with a failure. For $\alpha = 1$, we have $F_{\vec{e}}$ empty for all $\vec{e}$ and hence abbreviate $x = (Q, C, A)$.

Proposition 4.2. *With notation as in Proposition 4.1,*

$$\mathbf{E}_v(Q, C, A \cup \{t\}, F) = \mathbf{E}_v(Q, C, A, F) + \alpha \times \frac{\left(d - \mathbf{E}_v(Q, C, A, F)\right)\left(1 - \mathbb{E}\, \frac{\#F_{\mathrm{edge}(t)} + B}{d - \#C_e - \#\{t' \in A | \mathrm{edge}(t') = \vec{e}\} + B}\right)}{d - \#C_e - \#F_{\mathrm{edge}(t)} - \#\{t' \in A \mid \mathrm{edge}(t') = \vec{e}\}}.$$

where B a random variable with a binomial distribution: $B \sim \mathrm{Bin}(\#\{t' \in A : \mathrm{edge}(t') = \vec{e}\}, 1 - \alpha)$.

Proof. Let $u = \mathrm{src}(\mathrm{edge}(t))$. We consider the following set-valued random variables whose state spaces are conditional on the idle state $(Q, C, \emptyset, F)$:

- X is the set of all solutions at v which are known after completing all tasks in A–hence $\mathbb{E}[X] = \mathbb{E}_v(Q, C, A)$.
- Y consists of all solutions at v whose correspondences along $\vec{uv}$ have failed after completing all tasks in A. Thus, the random variable $B := (\#Y - \#F_{\mathrm{edge}(t)})$ has the desired binomial distribution.

Recalling (5), note that task t yields a solution undiscovered by A with probability $\alpha \cdot \Pr(\mathrm{sol}_t \notin \mathrm{sol}_A)$. Moreover, we have

$$\Pr(\mathrm{sol}_t \notin \mathrm{sol}_A) = \frac{d - \mathbb{E}_v(Q, C, A, F) - \mathbb{E}[\#(Y \cap X^c)]}{d - \#C_e - \#F_{\mathrm{edge}(t)} - \#\{t' \in A \mid \mathrm{edge}(t') = \vec{e}\}}$$

Conditional on the event $(X = k, B = j)$, we have that

$$\#Y = \#F_{\mathrm{edge}(t)} + j,$$

but the intersection $Y \cap X^c$ still depends on

$$d - (\#C_e + \#\{t' \in A \mid \mathrm{edge}(t') = \vec{e}\} - j)$$

unknown correspondences. Assumption 1 implies that the conditional distribution may be generated as follows:

1) For each solution at u which is known to fail along $\vec{uv}$ after completing all tasks in A, the corresponding solutions in Y are drawn uniformly without replacement from the $(d - \#C_e - \#\{t' \in A \mid \mathrm{edge}(t') = \vec{e}\} + j)$ solutions at v without correspondences.
2) Declare each solution in $Y \cap X^c$ to be a "success."

Hence the conditional expectation of the number of "successes" is given by the mean of a hypergeometric distribution:

$$\mathbb{E}\left(\#(Y \cap X^c) \mid X = k, B = j\right) = \tag{7}$$

$$\frac{(\#F_{\mathrm{edge}(t)} + j)(d - k)}{d - \#C_e - \#\{t' \in A \mid \mathrm{edge}(t') = \vec{e}\} + j} \tag{8}$$

Averaging over k and then j gives the result. □

In practice, it is also useful to group current tasks together according to their directed edges. This is reflected in the following proposition:

Proposition 4.3. *Let $A \cup A'$ denote the set of tasks, where A' consists of all tasks using the directed edge $\vec{uv}$. Then*

$$\mathbb{E}_v(Q, C, A \cup A', F) = \mathbb{E}_v(Q, C, A, F) + \alpha\, \#A' \left(\frac{d - \mathbb{E}_v(Q, C, A, F)}{d - \#C_e}\right).$$

Proof. Let $A' = \{t_1, \ldots, t_k\}$ and consider the events

$$E_i = \text{“}t_i \text{ finds a solution unknown after completing all tasks in } A\text{.”}$$

Then

$$\begin{aligned}
\mathbb{E}_v(Q, C, A \cup A', F) &= \mathbb{E}_v(Q, C, A, F) + \sum_{i=1}^{k} \Pr(E_i) \\
&= \mathbb{E}_v(Q, C, A, F) + \alpha\, \#A' \Pr(\mathrm{sol}_{t_1} \notin \mathrm{sol}_A) \\
&= \mathbb{E}_v(Q, C, A, F) + \alpha\, \#A' \times \\
&\quad \frac{d - \mathbb{E}_v(Q, C, A, F) - \left(\frac{\#F_{\mathrm{edge}(t)} \cdot (d - \mathbb{E}_v(Q, C, A, F))}{d - \#C_e}\right)}{d - \#C_e - \#F_{\mathrm{edge}(t)}} \\
&= \mathbb{E}_v(Q, C, A, F) + \alpha\, \#A' \times \\
&\quad \left(\frac{d - \mathbb{E}_v(Q, C, A, F)}{d - \#C_e}\right).
\end{aligned}$$

□

5 ALGORITHM

For every edge $\vec{e}$ we have its *potential* $\Delta_{\vec{e}}(x)$ at state $x = (Q, C, A, F)$. The potential guides edge selection in our main algorithm below. Following the study in §4, the natural greedy potential aiming to maximize the expected *total* number of discovered solutions is

$$\Delta^{\mathrm{E}}_{\vec{e}}(x) = \mathrm{E}(Q, C, A \cup \{(s, \vec{e})\}, F) - \mathrm{E}(x).$$

Algorithm 1 (Main algorithm). *The following is executed on all available threads after initializing the state $x = (Q, C, A, F)$.*

while *$\nexists Q_v$ such that $|Q_v| = d$* ***do***
  Pick an edge $\vec{e} = (w, v)$ that maximizes $\Delta_{\vec{e}}(x)$ and such that there is $s \in Q_w \setminus \pi_w C_e$.
  $t \leftarrow (s, \vec{e})$
  Update the state: $x \leftarrow (Q, C, A \cup \{t\}, F)$.
  Update $\Delta(x)$.
  Run homotopy continuation for task t.
  if *the run fails* ***then***
    $F_{\mathrm{edge}(t)} \leftarrow F_{\mathrm{edge}(t)} \cup \{s\}$.
  else
    Update Q_v, C_e, and Δ. {Note that an update is needed only for $\Delta_{\vec{e}'}$ such that $\mathrm{dest}(\vec{e}') = v$.}
  end if
end while

Here are other (heuristic) potential functions we considered: :

$$\begin{aligned}
\Delta^{\mathrm{ord}}_{\vec{e}}(x) &= 1/i, \\
&\quad \text{where } v_i = \mathrm{dest}\,\vec{e} \quad (\text{assuming } i \in \{1, \ldots, N\}) \\
\Delta^{\omega}_{\vec{e}}(x) &= \sum_{v \in V} \omega(v) \left(\mathbb{E}_v(Q, C, A \cup \{(s, \vec{e})\}, F) - \mathbb{E}_v(x)\right), \\
&\quad \text{where weight } \omega(v) \in [0, 1].
\end{aligned}$$

Note Δ^{ord} is designed to bias edge selection towards nodes in their order of appearance. This potential is likely to force the algorithm to complete the solution set of the first node.

The weighted potential Δ^{ω} depends on the design of the weight function. See §7.3 for a family of weight functions that seems to be useful in practice.

In the initial idle state, Δ can be computed and stored and then updated during the computation. Propositions 4.1 and 4.2 allow for an efficient way to do that in both sequential and parallel setting, with or without an assumption of failures.

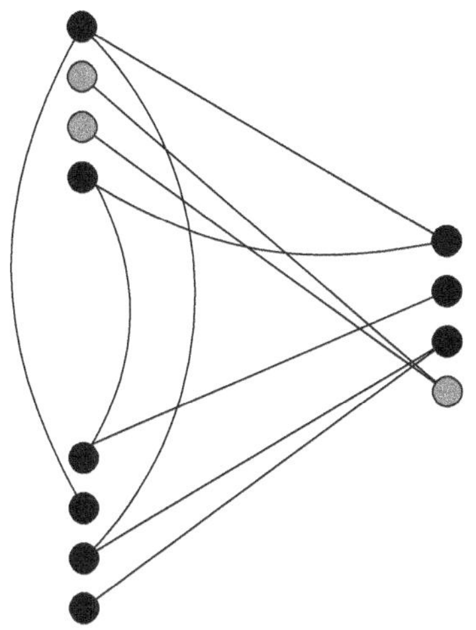

Figure 2: Solution multigraph w/ $N = 3, d = 4, m = 2$.

6 FAILURE RATE AND THRESHOLD

With assumptions 1 and 2, suppose we have a complete multigraph on N nodes with m edges connecting each pair of nodes, d solutions at each node, and tracking success probability α. To each homotopy graph, we associate a *solution (multi)graph* whose vertices are given by all of the solutions at each node and whose edges are the successful correspondences between solutions. One possible instance of this random solution graph is depicted in Figure 2.

Note that the graph in Figure 2 has only 10 edges out of a possible 24. Nevertheless, our algorithm succeeds in completing the bottom node whenever we start from one of the 9 black solutions, which form a large connected component. We see that connectivity of the solution graph is sufficient, but not necessary, for our algorithm to terminate.

In our random solution graph model, define $A := A_{m,N,d}$ to be the event that the algorithm starting at a random node terminates with d solutions. We are interested in the asymptotic behavior of $\Pr(A)$ as $d \to \infty$, with reasonable assumptions on m and N. More precisely, we wish to describe an interval $[a_{m,N,d}, b_{m,N,d}]$ containing a *threshold* for the event A; this means that for $\alpha(m, N, d) = o(a_{m,N,d})$, we have $\Pr(A_{m,N,d}) \to 0$, while $\Pr(A_{m,N,d}) \to 1$ if $\alpha(m, N, D) = \omega(b_{m,N,d})$.

The characterization of thresholds for various properties is a well-studied problem in random graph theory, particularly in the context of the Erdös-Renyi graph model. Our random solution graph does not enjoy the same asymptotic properties as the Edös-Renyi graph—since no two solutions at the same node may be connected, the graph is sparse, even for α near 1. Minding these difficulties, we provide a simple threshold region for the event A in Proposition 6.1—see subsection 7.2 for experimental verification and further discussion.

PROPOSITION 6.1. *With m, N possibly depending on d, we have the following large-d asymptotics:*

i) *If $\alpha(d) = o\left((Nm)^{-1}\right)$ and $N(d) = o\Big(\exp(d)\Big)$, then* $\lim_{d\to\infty} \Pr(A_{m,N,d}) = 0$.

ii) *If $\alpha(d) = \omega(\log d/m)$ and $N(d) = O(\log d)$, then* $\lim_{d\to\infty} \Pr(A_{m,N,d}) = 1$.

We require a simple fact known as the Harris/Kleitman inequality, specialized to our model (cf. [1] pp. 86-87, [2] pp. 39-41):

THEOREM 6.2 (HARRIS/KLEITMAN INEQUALITY). *If $\mathcal{A}$ and $\mathcal{B}$ are events in the random solution graph model which are upward-closed with respect to inclusion,*

$$\Pr(\mathcal{A} \cap \mathcal{B}) \geq \Pr(\mathcal{A}) \times \Pr(\mathcal{B}).$$

In random graph theory, a property which is upward-closed with respect to inclusion is called a *monotone increasing property.* For us, monotone increasing simply means that increasing α does not decrease $\Pr(\mathcal{A})$ or $\Pr(\mathcal{B})$. It is a famous result that every monotone property in the Erdös-Renyi model has a sharp threshold—for a precise statement, see [3].

PROOF OF PROPOSITION 6.1. Consider the following auxiliary events:

- $S := S_{m,N,d,\alpha}$ will denote the event that there exists some node with a successful correspondence at each solution
- $C := C_{m,N,d,\alpha}$ will denote the event that the solution graph is connected

Clearly we have

$$\Pr(C) \leq \Pr(A) \leq \Pr(S) \tag{9}$$

For part i), we may assume WLOG that $\alpha(d) > 0$ for d sufficiently large. Now, simply note that

$$\begin{aligned}\Pr(S) &= 1 - \Pr(\text{ all nodes fail }) \\ &\leq 1 - \prod_{j=1}^{N} \Pr(\text{node } j \text{ fails}) \qquad \text{(Theorem 6.2)} \\ &\leq 1 - \left(1 - (\alpha N m)^d\right)^N.\end{aligned}$$

For $N = O(1)$ as $d \to \infty$, we have

$$(1 - (\alpha N m)^d)^N = (1 - o(1)^d)^N \to 1 \text{ as } d \to \infty.$$

For the regime $\omega(1) = N(d) = o(\exp(d))$, we have

$$(1 - (\alpha N m)^d)^N \sim \exp(-(\alpha N^{1+1/d} m)^d),$$

which is $\omega(1)$ for $\alpha(d) = o(N^{-(1+1/d)}\, m^{-1}) = o((Nm)^{-1})$. In either regime, we have $\Pr(S) \to 0$ as $d \to \infty$.

To bound $\Pr(A)$ from below, let $v_1, \ldots, v_n$ be the nodes of the homotopy graph and G_i denote the subgraph of the solution graph induced by the solutions at nodes v_1 through v_i. By repeated application of Theorem 6.2, we have

$$\begin{aligned}\Pr(C_N) &= \Pr(C_{N-1} \cap \text{ each sol at } v_N \text{ has a nbr in } G_{N-1}) \\ &\geq \Pr(C_{N-1}) \times \Pr(\text{each sol at } v_N \text{ has a nbr in } G_{N-1}) \\ &\geq \prod_{i=1}^{N} \Pr(\text{ all solutions at } v_i \text{ have a nbr in } G_{i-1}) \\ &= \prod_{i=1}^{N} \left(1 - (1-\alpha)^{(N-i)e}\right)^d \\ &\geq \left(1 - \exp(-\alpha m)\right)^{Nd}\end{aligned}$$

Now, setting

$$\alpha(d) = \frac{\log(d) \times \left(1 + \log_d (N + g(d))\right)}{m},$$

with $g(d)$ *any* function such that $g(d) \to \infty$ as $d \to \infty$, we have

$$\Pr(C) \geq (1 - g(d)/(Nd))^{Nd} \sim \exp(-g(d)) \to 1.$$

□

7 EXPERIMENTAL RESULTS

Our simulator enables the study of two types of experiments:

- Experiments analyzing fake solution graph data generated according to Assumptions 1 and 2, and
- experiments based on real parametric systems, for which all data — actual solutions, actual correspondences for edges in the graph, actual timings for each homotopy path that may be tracked — is harvested *before* the experimentation begins.

The simulator (code available at https://github.com/sommars/parallel-monodromy) proceeds in two stages:

- The first stage takes either randomly generated data using Assumption 1, which does not require running homotopy continuation, or collects the data through tracking homotopy paths with existing software.
- The second uses the datafile produced by the first. If several threads are simulated then we assume that there is no communication overhead, which is a close approximation of reality. Indeed, the messages passed around are rather short: a longest one contains coordinates of a newly discovered solution. This cost can be ignored in comparison to the cost of a homotopy continuation task.

Based on observed runs of `PHCpack` [23] and the homotopy tracker of `NumericalAlgebraicGeometry` [13], we chose to model the time taken by each fake path track on the negative binomial distribution with parameters $p = 0.3$, $n = 10$. For clarity and consistency with the results of §6, all simulations have been run using the complete graph configuration described in [5].

7.1 Parallel Performance

To demonstrate the quality of a parallel algorithm, the typical metrics used are *speedup* and *efficiency* (for textbook references, see [12], [27]). For a number of processors p, speedup is defined to be

$$S(p) = \frac{\text{sequential execution time}}{\text{parallel execution time}} \tag{10}$$

while efficiency is defined as

$$E(p) = \frac{S(p)}{p} \times 100\% \tag{11}$$

Ideally one would obtain $S(p) = p$ and $E(p) = 100\%$, which means that all processor resources are constantly in use and no extra work is performed, compared to running the program with a single processor.

We ran two experiments to observe the efficiency of our algorithm, one with simulated data as in (1) and one with observed data as in (2). Table 1 contains efficiency results for the simulated data experiment, while Table 2 has efficiency results for the cyclic-n roots problem.

#Solutions	100	500	1000	5000	10000
1	100%	100%	100%	100%	100%
2	98.87%	98.36%	99.88%	98.61%	99.3%
4	96.71%	96.34%	98.28%	99.75%	100.45%
8	91.92%	95.04%	97.55%	98.7%	100.56%
16	84.65%	92.82%	98.68%	99.24%	99.82%
32	71.39%	87.12%	94.89%	97.8%	100.74%
64	55.04%	78.78%	89.45%	96.7%	99.07%
128	35.95%	65.82%	79.62%	93.68%	97.87%

Table 1: Efficiency for simulated polynomial systems with varied numbers of solutions.

n	5	6	7	8	9	10
1	100%	100%	100%	100%	100%	100%
2	110.48%	98.34%	104.3%	99.41%	99.44%	109.02%
4	107.7%	98.57%	110.79%	103.06%	99.81%	107.62%
8	101.53%	98.23%	108.02%	108.59%	101.02%	106.58%
16	94.88%	91.52%	103.53%	100.53%	101.79%	103.91%
32	76.23%	86.73%	97.72%	100.81%	101.92%	105.54%
64	54.59%	70.47%	93.45%	98.62%	99.92%	102.88%
128	34.38%	52.37%	84%	96.23%	97.81%	102%

Table 2: Efficiency for cyclic-n polynomial systems.

The cyclic n-roots problem is a classic benchmark problem in polynomial system solving, commonly formulated as

$$\begin{cases} x_0 + x_1 + \cdots + x_{n-1} = 0 \\ i = 2, 3, \ldots, n-1 : \sum_{j=0}^{n-1} \prod_{k=j}^{j+i-1} x_{k \bmod n} = 0 \\ x_0 x_1 x_2 \cdots x_{n-1} - 1 = 0. \end{cases} \tag{12}$$

Both Tables 1 and 2 show the same relationships: as the number of threads increases, efficiency slowly decreases, and as the size of the problem increases, efficiency improves. This shows that it is an effective algorithm for running large systems in parallel, though it is unfortunate that for huge numbers of threads that efficiency decreases.

One could be concerned that Algorithm 1 would be slow to start, because initially a single node has a single solution. For small homotopy graphs with large numbers of threads, some threads will by necessity be idle until there are sufficiently many tasks available. Define

$$\%\text{Idle} = \frac{\sum_{i=1}^{p} \text{Idle time}}{\text{Wall time} \times p}. \tag{13}$$

As the number of solutions increases, %Idle approaches zero. It would be possible to make %Idle = 0 through a modification to Algorithm 1. When a thread rests idle waiting for a task to become available, it could define its own edge by picking a random γ and tracking the sole known solution to a different node. In doing this, it has the potential to discover new solutions, but without adding to

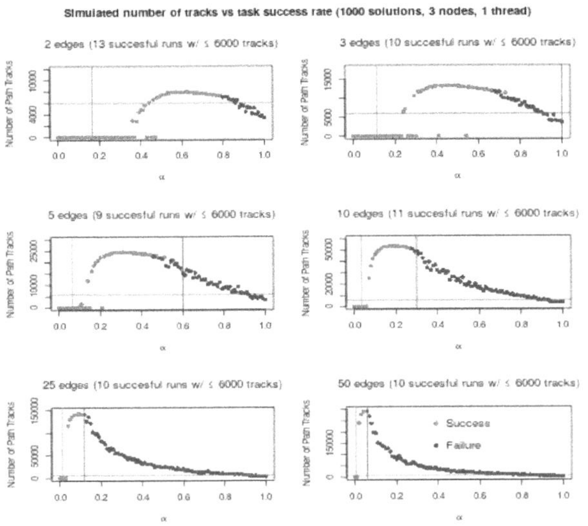

Figure 3: Total number of tracks vs task success rate α for varying edge multiplicities on a 3-node graph with 1000 solutions. The red and blue vertical lines given by $x = 1/3m$ and $x = \log_{10}(d)/m$, respectively, give an approximate window for the failure threshold. To give a sense of scale, a purple horizontal line at $y = 6000$ has been added.

the known set of correspondences. Each thread could do this until it can be assigned a path track as the algorithm prescribes. However, this will provide only a minimal benefit, because the amount of idle time according to a wall clock is low.

7.2 Path Failures

The "probability-one" homotopy in a linear family F_p fails with some nonzero probability. At fixed precision, this probability becomes non-negligible, say, as the degree of the discriminant rises. In practice, the reliability of homotopy continuation may be impacted by more *aggressive path-tracking*. For instance, raising the minimum step-size lowers the number of predictor steps, but there is a risk that errors accumulated may too large to finish continuation. In MS, this risk is spread across its incoming edges. Thus, we are interested in balancing tradeoffs between task reliability and speed.

Assumption 2 gives a simple model for path failures in a practical setting. An important feature of this model is that our simulator assumes a "true correspondence" between the solutions of two connected nodes before declaring that some of these paths fail. Thus, our model of failures ignores the phenomenon of path-jumping (potentially resulting in a 2-1 correspondence between approximate solutions,) or the possibility that some node has a near-singular solution. A logical next step would be to incorporate these possibilities into our model. However, we find that the simple model already sheds some light on the tradeoff previously described.

The plots in figure 3 supplement the results of Section 6. In each panel, the vertical distance equals the theoretical maximum number of tracks for each graph layout. Each run was performed with a single fake thread using the potential potE. These plots illustrate a major strength of using potentials in the presence of failures—even when additional edges are added, the number of path tracks at a *fixed* failure rate is stable (eg. at most 6000 for $\alpha \geq 0.9$.)

The bounds in Proposition 6.1 do not provide a useful upper bound on the threshold of global failure when the number of edges is relatively small (as in the top two plots of Figure 3.) We attempted to determine tighter threshold regions experimentally—see Table 3 for fabricated data and Table 4 for the cyclic n-roots problem.

$d \setminus N$	4	5	6	7	8	9
16	.716	.544	.426	.36	.332	.271
32	.756	.599	.495	.427	.362	.312
64	.771	.62	.537	.47	.391	.366
128	.799	.666	.584	.498	.453	.405
256	.841	.732	.634	.572	.497	.445
512	.873	.752	.674	.598	.536	.49

Table 3: An approximate threshold for the success rate α. N = the number of nodes in the complete graph (with $m = 1$), d = the number of solutions.

$n \setminus N$	5	6	7	8	9
5	.546	.492	.34	.298	.281
6	.605	.516	.416	.344	.316
7	.686	.611	.531	.452	.453
8	.734	.688	.647	.564	.492
9	.818	.733	.672	.629	.556

Table 4: An approximate threshold for the success rate α for the cyclic-n family. N = the number of nodes in the complete graph (with $m = 1$).

7.3 Potential functions and edge selection

We defined potentials Δ^{E}, Δ^{ord}, and Δ^{ω}. The last potential offers a lot of freedom to the user of the method. For instance, we could combine the ideas behind Δ^{E} and Δ^{ord} in Δ^{ω} by setting

$$\omega(v) = (|Q_v|/d)^{\lambda}, \quad \lambda \geq 0, \tag{14}$$

where d is the root count. (It could be replaced with the maximal number of solutions known at any node). Note that if $\lambda = 0$, one gets Δ^{E}; for large λ the effect is similar to that of Δ^{ord} except the nodes are likely to be ordered according to the number of known solutions at any point of the execution.

In the sequential case, [5] shows that edge selection guided by the greedy potential Δ^{E} outperforms several naive choices, among them the random edge selection strategy. According to our experiments this, as we expect, still holds for the parallel setting.

We conducted several experiments with the weight potential Δ^{ω} on graphs with edge multiplicity $m = 1$ for fabricated and cyclic problems of degree up to 10000 with and without failures. The weights described in (14) seem to deliver better (but not necessarily the best) performance as $\lambda \to \infty$. In other words, while a variant of the order potential Δ^{ord} may serve as a good heuristic, there is still some room for improvement for edge selection strategies guiding the MS algorithm.

8 CONCLUSION

The benefits of the Monodromy Solver framework are demonstrated by an implementation in Macaulay2 [4, 6], which outperforms all existing blackbox polynomial system solvers on certain classes of problems. This is reported in §6.4 of the first article devoted to the framework [5].

The present work addressed items 1 (failures) and 3 (parallelization) in the program outlined in §7 of [5]. The experiments conducted with the simulator that we built, albeit not very extensive, shed light on the phenomena arising with the introduction of failures and parallel computation. The results of the experiments and the simulator itself will help to hone the core of the technique as well as construct efficient heuristics for software implementation in the future.

REFERENCES

[1] N. Alon and J. H Spencer. 2004. *The probabilistic method.* John Wiley & Sons.

[2] B. Bollobás and O. Riordan. 2006. *Percolation.* Cambridge University Press.

[3] B. Bollobás and A. G. Thomason. 1987. Threshold functions. *Combinatorica* 7, 1 (01 Mar 1987), 35–38. https://doi.org/10.1007/BF02579198

[4] T. Duff, C. Hill, A. Jensen, K. Lee, A. Leykin, and J. Sommars. [n. d.]. MonodromySolver: a Macaulay2 package for solving polynomial systems via homotopy continuation and monodromy. Available at http://people.math.gatech.edu/~aleykin3/MonodromySolver. ([n. d.]).

[5] T. Duff, C. Hill, A. Jensen, K. Lee, A. Leykin, and J. Sommars. 2018. Solving polynomial systems via homotopy continuation and monodromy. *To appear in IMA Journal of Numerical Analysis* (2018).

[6] D. R. Grayson and M. E. Stillman. [n. d.]. Macaulay2, a software system for research in algebraic geometry. Available at http://www.math.uiuc.edu/Macaulay2/. ([n. d.]).

[7] T. Gunji, S. Kim, K. Fujisawa, and M. Kojima. 2006. PHoMpara – Parallel Implementation of the Polyhedral Homotopy Continuation Method for Polynomial Systems. *Computing* 77, 4 (2006), 387–411. https://doi.org/10.1007/s00607-006-0166-2

[8] S. Harimoto and L.T. Watson. 1989. The Granularity of Homotopy Algorithms for Polynomial Systems of Equations. In *Proceedings of the Third SIAM Conference on Parallel Processing for Scientific Computing.* Society for Industrial and Applied Mathematics, Philadelphia, PA, USA, 115–120. http://dl.acm.org/citation.cfm?id=645818.669226

[9] J.D. Hauenstein, J.I. Rodriguez, and F. Sottile. 2016. Numerical computation of Galois groups. *arXiv preprint arXiv:1605.07806* (2016).

[10] J. Hauenstein, A. Sommese, and C. Wampler. 2011. Regeneration homotopies for solving systems of polynomials. *Math. Comp.* 80, 273 (2011), 345–377.

[11] B. Huber and B. Sturmfels. 1995. A polyhedral method for solving sparse polynomial systems. *Math. Comp.* 64, 212 (1995), 1541–1555.

[12] D.B. Kirk and W.W. Hwu. 2010. *Programming Massively Parallel Processors: A Hands-on Approach* (1st ed.). Morgan Kaufmann Publishers Inc., San Francisco, CA, USA.

[13] A. Leykin. 2011. Numerical algebraic geometry. *The Journal of Software for Algebra and Geometry* 3 (2011), 5–10.

[14] A. Leykin and F. Sottile. 2007. Computing Monodromy via Parallel Homotopy Continuation. In *Proceedings of the 2007 International Workshop on Parallel Symbolic Computation (PASCO '07).* ACM, New York, NY, USA, 97–98. https://doi.org/10.1145/1278177.1278195

[15] A. Leykin and F. Sottile. 2009. Galois groups of Schubert problems via homotopy computation. *Math. Comp.* 78, 267 (2009), 1749–1765.

[16] A. Leykin and J. Verschelde. 2005. Factoring solution sets of polynomial systems in parallel. In *2005 International Conference on Parallel Processing Workshops (ICPPW'05).* 173–180. https://doi.org/10.1109/ICPPW.2005.31

[17] A. Leykin and J. Verschelde. 2009. Decomposing solution sets of polynomial systems: a new parallel monodromy breakup algorithm. *International Journal of Computational Science and Engineering* 4, 2 (2009), 94–101.

[18] A. Leykin, J. Verschelde, and Y. Zhuang. 2006. *Parallel Homotopy Algorithms to Solve Polynomial Systems.* Springer Berlin Heidelberg, Berlin, Heidelberg, 225–234. https://doi.org/10.1007/11832225_22

[19] A. Morgan. 1987. *Solving polynomial systems using continuation for engineering and scientific problems.* Prentice Hall Inc., Englewood Cliffs, NJ. xiv+546 pages.

[20] A.P. Morgan and L.T. Watson. 1989. A globally convergent parallel algorithm for zeros of polynomial systems. *Nonlinear Analysis: Theory, Methods & Applications* 13, 11 (1989), 1339 – 1350. https://doi.org/10.1016/0362-546X(89)90017-5

[21] A.J. Sommese and C.W. Wampler. 2005. *The numerical solution of systems of polynomials.* World Scientific Publishing Co. Pte. Ltd., Hackensack, NJ. xxii+401 pages.

[22] A. J. Sommese, J. Verschelde, and C. W. Wampler. 2001. *Using Monodromy to Decompose Solution Sets of Polynomial Systems into Irreducible Components.* Springer Netherlands, Dordrecht, 297–315. https://doi.org/10.1007/978-94-010-1011-5_16

[23] J. Verschelde. 1999. Algorithm 795: PHCpack: A general-purpose solver for polynomial systems by homotopy continuation. *ACM Trans. Math. Softw.* 25, 2 (1999), 251–276. Available at http://www.math.uic.edu/~jan.

[24] J. Verschelde, P. Verlinden, and R. Cools. 1994. Homotopies Exploiting Newton Polytopes for Solving Sparse Polynomial Systems. *SIAM J. Numer. Anal.* 31, 3 (June 1994), 915–930. https://doi.org/10.1137/0731049

[25] J. Verschelde and Y. Zhuang. 2006. Parallel implementation of the polyhedral homotopy method. In *2006 International Conference on Parallel Processing Workshops (ICPPW'06).* 8 pp.–488. https://doi.org/10.1109/ICPPW.2006.61

[26] C.W. Wampler. 1992. Bezout number calculations for multi-homogeneous polynomial systems. *Appl. Math. Comput.* 51, 2 (1992), 143 – 157. https://doi.org/10.1016/0096-3003(92)90070-H

[27] B. Wilkinson and M. Allen. 2004. *Parallel Programming: Techniques and Applications Using Networked Workstations and Parallel Computers (2nd Edition).* Prentice-Hall, Inc., Upper Saddle River, NJ, USA.

Generalized Hermite Reduction, Creative Telescoping and Definite Integration of D-Finite Functions

Alin Bostan
Inria, France
alin.bostan@inria.fr

Frédéric Chyzak
Inria, France
frederic.chyzak@inria.fr

Pierre Lairez
Inria, France
pierre.lairez@inria.fr

Bruno Salvy*
Inria, France
bruno.salvy@inria.fr

ABSTRACT

Hermite reduction is a classical algorithmic tool in symbolic integration. It is used to decompose a given rational function as a sum of a function with simple poles and the derivative of another rational function. We extend Hermite reduction to arbitrary linear differential operators instead of the pure derivative, and develop efficient algorithms for this reduction. We then apply the generalized Hermite reduction to the computation of linear operators satisfied by single definite integrals of D-finite functions of several continuous or discrete parameters. The resulting algorithm is a generalization of reduction-based methods for creative telescoping.

ACM Reference Format:
Alin Bostan, Frédéric Chyzak, Pierre Lairez, and Bruno Salvy. 2018. Generalized Hermite Reduction, Creative Telescoping and Definite Integration of D-Finite Functions. In *ISSAC '18: 2018 ACM International Symposium on Symbolic and Algebraic Computation, July 16–19, 2018, New York, NY, USA.* ACM, New York, NY, USA, 8 pages. https://doi.org/10.1145/3208976.3208992

1 INTRODUCTION

Ostrogradsky[1] [37] and Hermite [27] showed how to decompose the indefinite integral $\int R$ of a rational function $R \in \mathbb{Q}(x)$ as $U + \int A$, where $U, A \in \mathbb{Q}(x)$, and where A has only simple poles and vanishes at infinity. Their contributions consist in *rational algorithms* to compute A and U, that is algorithms which do not require to manipulate the roots in $\overline{\mathbb{Q}}$ of the denominator of R, but merely its (squarefree) factorization. The rational function A is classically called the *Hermite reduction* of R. In other words, the Hermite reduction of R is a *canonical form* of R modulo the derivatives in $\mathbb{Q}(x)$: it depends $\mathbb{Q}$-linearly on R, it is equal to R modulo the derivatives and it vanishes if and only if $U' = R$ for some $U \in \mathbb{Q}(x)$.

We call *generalized Hermite problem* the analogous question for inhomogeneous linear differential equations of arbitrary order

$$c_r(x)y^{(r)}(x) + \cdots + c_0(x)y(x) = R(x), \tag{1}$$

where R and the c_i are rational functions in $\mathbb{K}(x)$, over some field $\mathbb{K}$ of characteristic zero. In operator notation, given $L = c_r\partial_x^r + \cdots + c_0 \in \mathbb{K}(x)\langle\partial_x\rangle$, the problem is to produce a rational function $[R]$ in $\mathbb{K}(x)$, that depends $\mathbb{K}$-linearly on R, that is equal to R modulo the image $L(\mathbb{K}(x))$ and that vanishes if and only if R is in $L(\mathbb{K}(x))$.

Equations like Eq. (1) occur in relation to *integrating factors*, and ultimately to *creative telescoping*. If L^* denotes the *adjoint* of L, defined as $L^* = \sum_{i=0}^r (-\partial_x)^i c_i(x)$, then for any function f, integration by parts produces Lagrange's identity [29, §5.3]

$$uL(f) - L^*(u)f = \partial_x\left(P_L(f,u)\right), \tag{2}$$

where P_L depends linearly on $f, \dots, f^{(r-1)}, u, \dots, u^{(r-1)}$. It follows that if f is a solution of L, then any $R \in L^*(\mathbb{K}(x))$ is an integrating factor of f, meaning that Rf is a derivative of a $\mathbb{K}(x)$-linear combination of f and its derivatives. The converse holds if L is an operator of minimal order canceling f, see Proposition 4.2.

Contributions

We introduce a *generalized Hermite reduction* to compute such a $[R]$. Classical Hermite reduction addresses the case $L = \partial_x$. The algorithm operates locally at each singularity and it avoids algebraic extensions, similarly to classical Hermite reduction.

Next, we improve Chyzak's algorithm [19] for creative telescoping with the use of generalized Hermite reduction. Recall that creative telescoping is an algorithmic way to compute integrals by repeated differentiation under the integral sign and integration by parts [7]. Chyzak's algorithm repeatedly checks for the existence of a rational solution to equations like (1). A lot of time is spent checking that none exists. The use of generalized Hermite reduction makes the computation incremental and less redundant.

As a simple instance of the creative telescoping problem, let $f(t,x)$ be a function annihilated by a linear differential operator $L \in \mathbb{Q}(t,x)\langle\partial_x\rangle$ in the differentiation with respect to x only, and such that $\partial_t(f) = A(f)$ for another operator A also in $\mathbb{Q}(t,x)\langle\partial_x\rangle$. We look for the minimal relation of the form

$$\lambda_0 f + \cdots + \lambda_s\partial_t^s(f) = \partial_x(G), \tag{3}$$

with $\lambda_0, \dots, \lambda_s \in \mathbb{Q}(t)$ and $G(t,x)$ in the function space spanned by f and its derivatives, with the motive that integrating both sides with respect to x may lead to something useful: on the right-hand side, the integral of the derivative simplifies, often to 0, and on the left-hand side, the integration commutes with the $\lambda_i\partial_t^i$, yielding a differential equation for $\int f(t,x)\,dx$. In Equation (3), the left-hand side is called the *telescoper* and the function $G(t,x)$ the *certificate.*

The new algorithm constructs a sequence of rational functions $R_0, R_1, \dots$ in $\mathbb{Q}(t,x)$ such that $\partial_t^i(f) = R_if + \partial_x(\dots)$. Equation (3) holds if and only if $\lambda_0R_0 + \cdots + \lambda_sR_s$ is an integrating factor of f, which in turn is equivalent to the relation

$$\lambda_0[R_0] + \cdots + \lambda_s[R_s] = 0, \tag{4}$$

*Also with Univ Lyon, Inria, CNRS, ENS de Lyon, Université Claude Bernard Lyon 1, LIP UMR 5668, F-69007 Lyon, France.

[1] Most references in symbolic integration attribute to Ostrogradsky an algorithm to compute U and A based on linear algebra. As a matter of fact, Ostrogradsky introduced before Hermite a polynomial method, based on extended gcds. In passing, he invented an efficient algorithm for squarefree factorization, rediscovered by Yun [47, 48].

ISSAC '18, July 16–19, 2018, New York, NY, USA

ACM ISBN 978-1-4503-5550-6/18/07...$15.00
https://doi.org/10.1145/3208976.3208992

where [ ] is the generalized Hermite reduction with respect to L^*. Starting with $s = 0$, we search for solutions of the equation above and increment s until one is found. Chyzak's algorithm would solve Equation (3) at each iteration mostly from scratch, whereas the new algorithm retains the reduced forms $[R_i]$ from one iteration to the next, computes $[R_s]$ from $[R_{s-1}]$ and solves the straightforward Equation (4). This approach to creative telescoping generalizes to several parameters $t_1, \dots, t_e$ in the integrand and to different kinds of operators acting on them, in the setting of Ore algebras.

The order of the telescopers and even the termination of the creative telescoping process are related to the confinement properties of the generalized Hermite reduction. Assuming that the poles of the rational functions $R_0, R_1, \dots$ all lie in the same finite set, we deduce from a result of Adolphson's an upper bound on the dimension of the subspace spanned by the reductions $[R_i]$, which in turn bounds the order of the minimal telescoper.

Previous work

Extensions of Hermite reduction. Ostrogradsky [37] and Hermite [27] introduced a reduction for rational functions. A century later, it was extended to larger and larger classes of functions: algebraic [43], hypergeometric [3], hyperexponential [22, 26, 10, 11], Fuchsian [16]. Van der Hoeven's preprint [44] considers a reduction w.r.t. the derivation operator on differential modules of finite type, so as to address the general differentially finite case. Our generalized Hermite reduction is inspired by these works. It has the same architecture as several previous ones [10, 16, 11, 44]: local reductions at finite places, followed by a reduction at infinity and the computation of an exceptional set to obtain a canonical form. Our first contribution in the present paper is to open a new direction of generalization, namely by considering reductions with respect to other operators in $\mathbb{K}(x)\langle\partial_x\rangle$ than the derivation operator ∂_x, acting on the space $\mathbb{K}(x)$ of rational functions. An extra benefit of our method is to avoid algebraic extensions of $\mathbb{K}$.

Index theorems. The finite-dimensionality of a function space modulo the image of a differential operator is crucial to the termination of our reduction and creative-telescoping algorithms. This finiteness, and even explicit bounds, are given by *index theorems* for differential equations [35]. Rational versions appeared in work by Monsky [36] related to the finiteness of de Rham cohomology, and by Adolphson [6] in a p-adic context, see also [41, 45], and §3.6.

Creative telescoping by reduction. The use of Hermite-like reductions for computing definite integrals roots in works by Fuchs [25] and Picard [38, 39]. In the realm of creative telescoping, this line of research forms what is called the fourth generation of creative telescoping algorithms. It was first introduced for bivariate rational functions [9], and later extended to the multivariate rational case [12, 32]. For bivariate functions/sequences, the approach was also extended to larger classes: algebraic [15, 14], hyperexponential [10], hypergeometric [13, 28], mixed [11], Fuchsian [16], differentially finite [44]. Our second contribution is the first reduction-based variant, for single integrals, of Chyzak's algorithm [19] for D-finite functions depending on several continuous or discrete parameters.

2 INTRODUCTORY EXAMPLE

2.1 Hermite Reduction

The equation $M(y) = ax^2 + bx + c$, with M defined by

$$M(y) = (x^2 - 1)y'' + (x - 2p(x^2 - 1))y' + (p^2(x^2 - 1) - px - n^2)y,$$

has a rational solution $y \in \mathbb{Q}(n, p, x)$ if and only if $ax^2 + bx + c$ is a multiple of $p^2x^2 - px - n^2 - p^2$. This follows in two steps.

First, a local analysis reveals that if y has a pole at some $\alpha \in \mathbb{C}$, then so does $M(y)$: for any $\alpha \in \mathbb{C} \setminus \{\pm 1\}$ and for any $s > 0$,

$$M\big((x - \alpha)^{-s}\big) = (\alpha^2 - 1)s(s + 1)(x - \alpha)^{-s-2}\,(1 + O(x - \alpha))$$

$$\text{and } M\big((x \pm 1)^{-s}\big) = \pm s(2s + 1)(x \pm 1)^{-s-1}\,(1 + O(x \pm 1))\,.$$

Therefore, if $M(y)$ is a polynomial then y is also a polynomial.

Next, for any $s \geq 0$, $M(x^s) = p^2x^{s+2} + O(x^{s+1})$, as $x \to \infty$. It follows that if $y \in \mathbb{Q}(n, p)[x]$ then $M(y) \in \mathbb{Q}(n, p)[x]$ and $\deg_x M(y) = \deg_x y{+}2$. In particular, every polynomial of degree ≤ 2 in $M(\mathbb{Q}(n, p, x))$ is a multiple of $M(1) = p^2x^2 - px - n^2 - p^2$ over $\mathbb{Q}(n, p)$.

In §3, we define the Hermite reductions w.r.t. M of 1, x and x^2:

$$[1] = 1, \quad [x] = x, \quad \text{and} \quad [x^2] = \frac{x}{p} + \frac{n^2 + p^2}{p^2},$$

showing that $[p^2x^2 - px - n^2 - p^2] = 0$. Similarly, the reduction of any polynomial w.r.t. M is a $\mathbb{Q}(n, p)$-linear combination of 1 and x.

2.2 Creative Telescoping

We consider the classical integral identity [40, §2.18.1, Eq. (10)]

$$\int_{-1}^{1} \frac{e^{-px}T_n(x)}{\sqrt{1 - x^2}}\,\mathrm{d}x = (-1)^n \pi I_n(p),$$

where T_n denotes the nth Chebyshev polynomial of the first kind and I_n the nth modified Bessel function of the first kind. The integrand $F_n(p, x)$ satisfies a system of linear differential and difference equations, easily found from defining equations for $T_n(x)$ and e^{-px}:

$$\frac{\partial F_n}{\partial p} = -xF_n, \quad nF_{n+1} = \frac{\partial}{\partial x}\Big((x^2 - 1)F_n\Big) + (px^2 + (n - 1)x - p)F_n,$$

$$(1 - x^2)\frac{\partial^2 F_n}{\partial x^2} = (2px^2 + 3x - 2p)\frac{\partial F_n}{\partial x} + (p^2x^2 + 3px - n^2 - p^2 + 1)F_n\,.$$

We aim at finding a similar set of linear differential-difference operators in the variables n and p for the integral $\int_{-1}^{1} F_n(p, x)\,\mathrm{d}x$. Note that F_n and all its derivatives w.r.t. x and p and shifts w.r.t. n are $\mathbb{Q}(n, p, x)$-linear combinations of F_n and $\partial F_n/\partial x$.

The *adjoint* of the last equation is $M(y) = 0$, with the operator M of §2.1. The reduction w.r.t. M described above makes the following computation possible. First, F_n is not a derivative (of a $\mathbb{Q}(n, p, x)$-linear combination of F_n and $\partial F_n/\partial x$). Indeed, F_n is a derivative if and only if $1 \in M(\mathbb{Q}(n, p))$. Second, no $\mathbb{Q}(n, p)$-linear relation between F_n and $\partial F_n/\partial p$ is a derivative, because $\partial F_n/\partial p = -xF_n$ and [1] and $[-x]$ are linearly independent over $\mathbb{Q}(n, p)$. Third, the $\mathbb{Q}(n, p)$-linear relation $p^2[x^2] + p[-x] - (n^2 + p^2)[1] = 0$ proves that

$$p^2\frac{\partial^2 F_n}{\partial p^2} + p\frac{\partial F_n}{\partial p} - (n^2 + p^2)F_n = \frac{\partial G}{\partial x} \tag{5}$$

for some $\mathbb{Q}(n, p, x)$-linear combination G of F_n and $\partial F_n/\partial x$. Next, the equation for nF_{n+1} and the equation $[px^2 + (n - 1)x - p] =$

$nx + n^2/p$ show that, for some $\tilde{G}$ as above,

$$F_{n+1} + \frac{\partial F_n}{\partial p} - \frac{n}{p} F_n = \frac{\partial \tilde{G}}{\partial x}. \quad (6)$$

Equations (5) and (6) can then be integrated from −1 to 1. The contour can be deformed so that the right-hand sides vanish (regardless of G and $\tilde{G}$) and the left-hand sides provide the desired operators for the integral. These equations classically define, up to a constant factor, the function $(-1)^n I_n(p)$.

3 GENERALIZED HERMITE REDUCTION

Throughout this section, $M \in \mathbb{K}[x]\langle\partial_x\rangle$ denotes a linear differential operator with polynomial coefficients. We are interested in finding $\mathbb{K}$-linear dependency relations in $\mathbb{K}(x)$ modulo the rational image $M(\mathbb{K}(x))$ by means of a *canonical form with respect to* M.

Definition 3.1. A *canonical form with respect to* M is a $\mathbb{K}$-linear map $[\,] : \mathbb{K}(x) \to \mathbb{K}(x)$ such that for any $R \in \mathbb{K}(x)$:

(i) $[M(R)] = 0$; (ii) $R - [R] \in M(\mathbb{K}(x))$.

Applying $[\,]$ to $R - [R]$ before using (ii) and (i) results in $[[R]] = [R]$.

As can be seen from Eq. (1), computing such canonical forms is tightly related to the computation of rational solutions of linear differential equations. In classical solving algorithms [2,33], bounds on the order of poles of meromorphic solutions are given by indicial equations. Next, in order to factor the computation for different inhomogeneous parts, instead of using a "universal denominator", one could at each singularity identify the polar behaviour of potential meromorphic solutions, so as to reduce rational solving to polynomial solving. This idea is what inspired the reduction algorithm for computing canonical forms in the present section[2].

We begin in §3.1 with a local analysis of $M(\mathbb{K}(x))$. Then we describe in §3.2 a projection map $H : \mathbb{K}(x) \to \mathbb{K}(x)$ that we call *weak Hermite reduction.* It is not quite a canonical form. It misses an *exceptional set* described in §3.3, from which a canonical form is deduced. For simplicity, this is first described in the algebraic closure of the base field $\mathbb{K}$, and in §3.4 we show how to perform the computations in a rational way, i.e., without algebraic extensions.

Finally, in §3.6, we bound the dimension of the quotient $E/M(E)$, for a ring E of rational functions with prescribed poles. This is relevant to getting size and complexity bounds for creative telescoping.

3.1 Local Study

Let $\overline{\mathbb{K}}$ be an algebraic closure of $\mathbb{K}$. For $R \in \overline{\mathbb{K}}(x)$ and $\alpha \in \overline{\mathbb{K}}$, let $R_{(\alpha)}$ denote the *polar part* of R at α. This is the unique polynomial in $(x-\alpha)^{-1}$ with constant term zero such that $R - R_{(\alpha)}$ has no pole at α. Similarly, the *polynomial part* $R_{(\infty)}$ of R is the unique polynomial such that $R - R_{(\infty)}$ vanishes at infinity. By partial fraction decomposition,

$$R = R_{(\infty)} + \sum_{\alpha\in\overline{\mathbb{K}}} R_{(\alpha)}. \quad (7)$$

Let also $\operatorname{ord}_\alpha R$ denote the valuation of R as a Laurent series in $x - \alpha$.

For any $\alpha \in \overline{\mathbb{K}}$, there exists a non-zero polynomial $\operatorname{ind}_\alpha \in \overline{\mathbb{K}}[s]$ and an integer σ_α such that for any $s \in \mathbb{Z}$,

$$M\big((x-\alpha)^{-s}\big) = \operatorname{ind}_\alpha(-s)(x-\alpha)^{-s+\sigma_\alpha}(1+o(1)), \quad \text{as } x \to \alpha. \quad (8)$$

[2]In the case of systems, analogues of indicial equations are more complicated; several alternatives for rational solving exist [1, 8], that resemble the reduction in [44].

The polynomial $\operatorname{ind}_\alpha$ is classically called the *indicial polynomial of* M *at* α [46, 29]; we call the integer σ_α the *shift of* M *at* α. The indicial polynomial and its integer roots give a detailed understanding of the image of M. We similarly define the shift and the indicial polynomial at ∞ by the equation

$$M(x^s) = \operatorname{ind}_\infty(-s)x^{s-\sigma_\infty}(1+o(1)), \quad \text{as } x \to \infty.$$

If $M = \sum_{i=0}^r p_i(x)\partial_x^i$, then

$$\sigma_\alpha = \min_{0\le i\le r} (\operatorname{ord}_\alpha p_i - i) \quad \text{and} \quad \sigma_\infty = \max_{0\le i\le r} (i - \deg p_i).$$

For any $\alpha \in \overline{\mathbb{K}}$ that is not a root of the leading coefficient p_r of M, we have $\operatorname{ind}_\alpha(s) = p_r(\alpha)\cdot s(s-1)\cdots(s-r+1)$ and $\sigma_\alpha = -r$.

3.2 Weak Hermite Reduction

Let $\operatorname{im} M = M(\mathbb{K}(x))$. Let $H_\alpha : \overline{\mathbb{K}}(x) \to \overline{\mathbb{K}}(x)$ be the *local reduction map at* α defined by $H_\alpha(R) = R$ if $\operatorname{ord}_\alpha R \ge 0$ (α is not a pole of R) and by induction on $\operatorname{ord}_\alpha R$,

$$H_\alpha(R) = \begin{cases} H_\alpha\Big(R - \frac{cM((x-\alpha)^{-s-\sigma_\alpha})}{\operatorname{ind}_\alpha(-\sigma_\alpha - s)}\Big) & \text{if } \operatorname{ind}_\alpha(-\sigma_\alpha - s) \neq 0,\\ c(x-\alpha)^{-s} + H_\alpha(R - c(x-\alpha)^{-s}) & \text{otherwise,}\end{cases}$$

where $R = c(x-\alpha)^{-s}(1+o(1))$ as $x \to \alpha$, with $c \in \overline{\mathbb{K}} \setminus \{0\}$ and $s > 0$. The induction is well-founded because in either case of the definition, the argument of H_α in the right-hand side has a valuation at α that is larger than $\operatorname{ord}_\alpha R$. By construction, we check that $R - H_\alpha(R) \in \operatorname{im} M$ for any $R \in \mathbb{K}(x)$.

Similarly, let $H_\infty : \mathbb{K}(x) \to \mathbb{K}(x)$ be the *local reduction map at* ∞ defined by $H_\infty(R) = R$ if $\operatorname{ord}_\infty R > 0$ (that is $R_{(\infty)} = 0$) and by induction on $\operatorname{ord}_\infty(R)$ by

$$H_\infty(R) = \begin{cases} H_\infty\Big(R - \frac{cM(x^{s+\sigma_\infty})}{\operatorname{ind}_\infty(-s-\sigma_\infty)}\Big) & \text{if } \operatorname{ind}_\infty(-s-\sigma_\infty) \neq 0 \text{ and } s+\sigma_\infty \ge 0,\\ cx^s + H_\infty(R - cx^s) & \text{otherwise,}\end{cases}$$

where $R = cx^s(1+o(1))$ as $x \to \infty$. By construction, we check that $R - H_\infty(R) \in \operatorname{im} M$ for any $R \in \mathbb{K}(x)$. The condition $s + \sigma_\infty \ge 0$ ensures that $M(x^{s+\sigma_\infty})$ is a polynomial.

Definition 3.2. The *weak Hermite reduction* is the linear map H, seen either as $H : \mathbb{K}(x) \to \mathbb{K}(x)$ or as $H : \overline{\mathbb{K}}(x) \to \overline{\mathbb{K}}(x)$, and defined by

$$H(R) = H_\infty\Big(R_{(\infty)} + \sum_{\alpha\in\{\text{poles of } R\}} H_\alpha\big(R_{(\alpha)}\big)\Big).$$

Proposition 3.3. *For any* $R \in \mathbb{K}(x)$:

(i) $H(R) = H_\infty \circ H_{\alpha_1} \circ \cdots \circ H_{\alpha_n}(R)$, *where* $\alpha_1, \ldots, \alpha_n \in \overline{\mathbb{K}}$ *are the poles of* R;
(ii) $R - H(R) \in \operatorname{im} M$ *and* $H(M(R)) \in \operatorname{im} M$;
(iii) $H(H(R)) = H(R)$.

Moreover:

(iv) for any $\alpha \in \overline{\mathbb{K}}$ *and for any* $s > 0$,

$$\operatorname{ind}_\alpha(s) \neq 0 \text{ and } \sigma_\alpha - s > 0 \Rightarrow H\big(M((x-\alpha)^{-s})\big) = 0;$$

(v) for any $s \ge 0$, $\operatorname{ind}_\infty(s) \neq 0 \Rightarrow H\big(M(x^s)\big) = 0$.

Proof. By linearity and Equation (7), Property (i) follows from the formulas $H(R_{(\infty)}) = H_\infty(R_{(\infty)})$ and $H(R_{(\alpha)}) = H_\infty(H_\alpha(R_{(\alpha)}))$ derived from the definition of H. The first part of Property (ii) follows from corresponding properties for H_α and H_∞; the second part is a consequence of applying the first to $M(R)$.

As for the idempotence, we observe, first, that every $H(R)$ is a linear combination of some $(x-\alpha)^{-s}$, with $\mathrm{ind}_\alpha(-s-\sigma_\alpha)=0$, and x^s, with $s+\sigma_\infty \geq 0$ and $\mathrm{ind}_\infty(-s-\sigma_\infty)=0$; and second, that H is the identity on such monomials.

As for (iv), the condition $\mathrm{ind}_\alpha(s) \neq 0$ together with (8) imply that $\mathrm{ord}_\alpha M((x-\alpha)^{-s}) = -s-\sigma_\alpha$, and then by definition of H_α,

$$H_\alpha(M((x-\alpha)^{-s})) = H_\alpha(M((x-\alpha)^{-s}) - M((x-\alpha)^{-s})) = 0.$$

The last property is proved similarly. □

3.3 Canonical Form

If H were a canonical form, $H(M(R))$ would be 0 for any $R \in \mathbb{K}(x)$. But this property fails, and more work is required to refine H into a canonical form.

Definition 3.4. The space Exc_M of *exceptional functions* is the $\mathbb{K}$-linear subspace of $\mathbb{K}(x)$ defined by $\mathrm{Exc}_M = H(\mathrm{im}\, M)$.

Lemma 3.5. *For any $R \in \mathbb{K}(x)$, $R \in \mathrm{im}\, M$ if and only if $H(R) \in \mathrm{Exc}_M$.*

Proof. The direct implication is the definition of Exc_M. For the converse, assume $H(R) = H(M(U))$ for some U. As $(R - M(U)) - H(R-M(U)) = M(V)$ for some V by Prop. 3.3 (ii), $R = M(U+V)$. □

The generalized Hermite reduction is not a canonical form, but it is strong enough to ensure that Exc_M is finite-dimensional over $\mathbb{K}$.

Proposition 3.6. *Over $\overline{\mathbb{K}}$, the vector space Exc_M is generated by the finite family*

(a) $H(M((x-\alpha)^{-s}))$ with $\alpha \in \mathrm{Sing}(M)$, $s > 0$ and $\mathrm{ind}_\alpha(-s) = 0$,
(b) $H(M((x-\alpha)^{-s}))$ with $\alpha \in \mathrm{Sing}(M)$, $0 < s \leq \sigma_\alpha$,
(c) $H(M(x^s))$ with $s \geq 0$ and $\mathrm{ind}_\infty(-s) = 0$,

where $\mathrm{Sing}(M) \subset \overline{\mathbb{K}}$ is the set of singularities of M (the zeroes of its leading coefficient).

Proof. The elements $(x-\alpha)^{-s}$ ($\alpha \in \overline{\mathbb{K}}$, $s > 0$) and x^s ($s \geq 0$) form a basis of $\overline{\mathbb{K}}(x)$. In particular, Exc_M, by definition, is generated by the $H((x-\alpha)^{-s})$ and $H(x^s)$. By Proposition 3.3 (iv) and (v), $H(M((x-\alpha)^{-s})) = 0$ when $\mathrm{ind}_\alpha(-s) \neq 0$ and $s < \sigma_\alpha$. Similarly, $H(M(x^s)) = 0$ when $\mathrm{ind}_\infty(-s) \neq 0$. Moreover, any $\alpha \in \overline{\mathbb{K}}$ such that ind_α has a negative root or $\sigma_\alpha > 0$ is a singularity of M. Therefore, the only nonzero generators of Exc_M belong to the set given in the statement. □

Example 3.7. Let $M = x^{10}\partial_x$. We compute $\mathrm{ind}_\alpha(s) = -\alpha^{10}s$ for any $\alpha \in \overline{\mathbb{K}}$ and $\mathrm{ind}_\infty(s) = s$. Moreover $\sigma_\alpha = -1$ for $\alpha \notin \{0, \infty\}$, $\sigma_0 = 9$ and $\sigma_\infty = -9$. It follows that

$$\mathrm{Exc}_M = \mathrm{Vect}\left\{H(M(x^{-9})), \dots, H(M(x^{-1}))\right\} = \mathrm{Vect}\left\{1, x, \dots, x^8\right\}.$$

Lemma 3.8. *Given a finite-dimensional $\mathbb{K}$-linear subspace $W \subset \mathbb{K}(x)$, there is a unique idempotent linear map $\rho_W : \mathbb{K}(x) \to \mathbb{K}(x)$ such that: (i) $W = \ker \rho_W$; (ii) for any $R \in \mathbb{K}(x)$, the degree of the numerator of $\rho_W(R)$ is minimal among all $S \in \mathbb{K}(x)$ with $R - S \in W$.*

The following proof gives an algorithm for computing ρ_W.

Proof. When $W \subset \mathbb{K}[x]$, the value $\rho_W(R)$ is the result of Gaussian elimination applied in the monomial basis to the polynomial part of R with the elements of W.

In the general case, we write $W = Q^{-1}V$, for some subspace $V \subset \mathbb{K}[x]$ and $Q \in \mathbb{K}[x]$, and define $\rho_W(R) = Q^{-1}\rho_V(QR)$. The two properties are easily checked. □

Algorithm 1 Rational weak Hermite reduction.
Input $R \in \mathbb{K}(x)$; M a linear differential operator.
Output The rational weak Hermite reduction of R.

---

function WHermiteRed(R, M)
  if $R = 0$ **then return** 0
  else if R is a polynomial **then**
    write R as cx^s + (lower degree terms)
    if $\mathrm{ind}_\infty(-s-\sigma_\infty) \neq 0$ and $s + \sigma_\infty \geq 0$ **then**
      return WHermiteRed$\left(R - \frac{cM(x^{s+\sigma_\infty})}{\mathrm{ind}_\infty(-s-\sigma_\infty)}, M\right)$
    else return cx^s + WHermiteRed($R - cx^s, M$)
  else
    $P \leftarrow$ an irreducible factor of the denominator of R.
    write R as $\frac{A}{P^sQ}$, with $A, Q \in \mathbb{K}[x]$ and s maximal.
    if $\mathrm{ind}_P(-s-\sigma_P) = 0$ **then**
      $U \leftarrow A/Q \mod P$.
      return U/P^s + WHermiteRed($R - U/P^s, M$)
    else
      $R \leftarrow A/Q/\mathrm{ind}_P(-s-\sigma_P) \mod P$
      return WHermiteRed$\left(R - M(R/P^{s+\sigma_P}), M\right)$

Definition 3.9. The *generalized Hermite reduction with respect to* M is the map $[\,] : \mathbb{K}(x) \to \mathbb{K}(x)$ defined by $[R] = \rho_{\mathrm{Exc}_M}(H(R))$.

Theorem 3.10. *The map $[\,]$ is a canonical form with respect to M.*

Proof. We check the properties of Definition 3.1. Let $R \in \mathbb{K}(x)$. First, $[M(R)] = 0$ because $H(M(R)) \in \mathrm{Exc}_M$ (Lemma 3.5) and then $\rho_{\mathrm{Exc}_M}(H(M(R))) = 0$, by Proposition 3.3 (ii) and the construction of ρ_{Exc_M}. Second, $R - [R] \in \mathrm{im}\, M$ because $R - H(R) \in \mathrm{im}\, M$ (Proposition 3.3) and $H(R) - \rho_{\mathrm{Exc}_M}(H(R)) \in \mathrm{Exc}_M \subset \mathrm{im}\, M$. □

3.4 Rational Generalized Hermite Reduction

In most cases, computing Hermite reduction as it is defined above would require to work with algebraic extensions of the base field. If $P \in \mathbb{K}[x]$ is a monic irreducible polynomial and α a root of P, the reduction can be performed simultaneously at all roots of P without introducing algebraic extensions.

The indicial equation is obtained by considering the leading coefficient of the P-adic expansion of $M(P^{-s})$, see [46, §4.1, p. 107]. More precisely, there is a unique polynomial $\mathrm{ind}_P(s)$ with coefficients in $\mathbb{K}[x]/(P)$ and a unique integer σ_P such that for any $s > 0$,

$$M(P^{-s}) = \mathrm{ind}_P(-s)P^{-s+\sigma_P} + O(P^{-s+\sigma_P+1}),$$

as P-adic expansions. Since P is irreducible, $\mathrm{ind}_P(s)$, for a given s, is either 0 or invertible modulo P. For an irreducible polynomial $P \in \mathbb{K}[x]$, and for $R = UP^{-s} + O(P^{-s+1})$, we define

$$H_P(R) = \begin{cases} UP^{-s} + H_P(R - UP^{-s}) & \text{if } \mathrm{ind}_P(-\sigma_P - s) = 0, \\ H_P\left(R - M(U\, \mathrm{ind}_\alpha(-\sigma_P - s)^{-1}P^{-s-\sigma_P})\right) & \text{otherwise,} \end{cases}$$

where $\mathrm{ind}_\alpha(-\sigma_P - s)^{-1}$ is computed mod P. This is the part of our reduction which most closely resembles the original Hermite reduction, with successive coefficients obtained by modular inversions.

Definition 3.11. The *rational weak Hermite reduction* is the linear map $H_{\mathrm{rat}} : \mathbb{K}(x) \to \mathbb{K}(x)$, defined by

$$H_{\mathrm{rat}}(R) = H_\infty\left(R_{(\infty)} + \sum_P H_P\left(R_{(P)}\right)\right),$$

where the summation runs over the irreducible factors of the denominator of R and $R_{(P)} \in \mathbb{K}[x, P^{-1}]$ denotes the polar part of the P-adic expansion of R.

The maps H and H_{rat} satisfy the same properties, *mutatis mutandis*. In particular, the latter can be used to compute a canonical form in the same way as H. Yet, both reductions are not equal (see also §3.5.1). For example, over $\mathbb{Q}$ with $M = (x^2+1)\partial_x + 10x$, $R = (x^2+1)^{-5}$ and $i^2+1=0$,

$$H(R) = \tfrac{i}{32}\left((x+i)^{-5} - (x-i)^{-5}\right) \quad \text{whereas} \quad H_{\mathrm{rat}}(R) = R.$$

Partial fraction decomposition and actual Hermite reduction can be performed together. This is described in Algorithm 1. Together with the algorithm for the map ρ_{Exc_M}, described in the proof of Lemma 3.8, we obtain an algorithm, denoted CanonicalForm, to compute the map $\rho \circ H_{\mathrm{rat}}$ that is a canonical form modulo M.

3.5 Variants and Improvements

3.5.1 Absolute Hermite reduction. A notion of Hermite reduction that is independent from the base field is obtained by replacing $U \cdot P^{-s}$ with $\frac{\mathrm{d}^{s-1}}{\mathrm{d}x^{s-1}}\frac{U}{P}$ in the definition of H_P. Another benefit of this choice is that it is not necessary that P is irreducible to perform the reduction, but simply that $\mathrm{ind}_P(s)$ is either 0 or invertible. The denominators that appear in the computation can be factored on the fly into factors with the required property: when some $\mathrm{ind}_P(s)$ is neither 0 nor invertible modulo P, a gcd computation gives a non-trivial divisor of P.

3.5.2 Reduction to the polynomial case. The hypothesis that the differential operator M has polynomial coefficients is important for the correctness of Algorithm 1. To compute canonical forms modulo an operator M with rational coefficients, it is sufficient to find a polynomial Q such that MQ has polynomial coefficients and then, to compute canonical forms modulo MQ with the algorithms above. Indeed, the image of $\mathbb{K}(x)$ by MQ and M are the same. The smallest such Q is the gcd of the denominators of the coefficients of the adjoint of M.

3.5.3 Rational factors. The following observation can be used to speed up the computation.

Lemma 3.12. *Let $L, M \in \mathbb{K}[x]\langle\partial_x\rangle$ and A, B in $\mathbb{K}(x)$ such that $MA = BL$. If $[\ ]_L$ is a canonical form w.r.t. L, then $[\ ]_M : R \in \mathbb{K}(x) \mapsto B\,[R/B]_L$ is a canonical form w.r.t. M.*

Proof. We check the properties of Def. 3.1: $[M(y)]_M = B\,[L(A^{-1}y)]_L$ is 0 and $R - [R]_M = B(R/B - [R/B]_L)$ is in $B(\operatorname{im} L) = \operatorname{im} M$. □

Lemma 3.12 may be used with $A = B = \prod_\alpha (x-\alpha)^{m_\alpha}$, where m_α is the smallest negative integer root of the indicial polynomial of M at α, and 0 if none exists. This is mostly useful for equations of order 1, since the corresponding α is not a singularity of the new operator, which becomes smaller. The rational function A plays the role of the *shell* in previous reduction-based algorithms [10, 11].

3.6 Dimension of the Quotient with Fixed Poles

Let $P \in \mathbb{K}[x]$ be a squarefree polynomial and let $E_P = \mathbb{K}\left[x, P^{-1}\right]$. Let $\ker M \subset \mathbb{K}(x)$ be the space of rational solutions of M. Let r be the order of M and d the maximal degree of its coefficients.

Proposition 3.13 (Adolphson [6, Sec. 5, Prop. 1]).

$$\dim_{\mathbb{K}} E_P/M(E_P) = \dim_{\mathbb{K}}(E_P \cap \ker M) - \sigma_\infty - \sum_{P(\alpha)=0} \sigma_\alpha \le (\deg P + 1)\cdot r + d.$$

Sketch of the proof. Let $Z = \{\alpha \in \overline{\mathbb{K}} \mid P(\alpha) = 0\}$. Given $\deg P + 1$ positive integers s_∞ and s_α ($\alpha \in Z$), let $E_P(s)$ denote the subspace of all $R \in E_P$ such that the pole order at α is at most s_α for $\alpha \in Z \cup \{\infty\}$, that is all elements $R \in E_P(s)$ of the form

$$R = \textstyle\sum_{\alpha \in Z} \sum_{s=1}^{s_\alpha} \frac{c_{\alpha,s}}{(x-\alpha)^s} + \sum_{s=0}^{s_\infty} c_{\infty,s} x^s.$$

We choose s_α and s_∞ large enough so that $\ker M \subset E_P(s)$. Let $t_\alpha = s_\alpha - \sigma_\alpha$ ($\alpha \in Z \cup \{\infty\}$). We check $M(E_P(s)) \subseteq E_P(t)$ and that a basis of $E_P(t)/M(E_P(s))$ induces a basis of $E_P/M(E_P)$. The bounds $-\sigma_\alpha \le r$, $-\sigma_\infty \le d$ and $\dim \ker M \le r$ give the inequality. □

4 CREATIVE TELESCOPING

The method of creative telescoping is an approach to the computation of definite sums and integrals of objects characterized by linear functional equations. The notion of linear functional equation is formalized by *Ore algebras*. In this part, we consider the Ore algebra $\mathbb{A} = \mathbb{K}(x)\langle\partial_x, \partial_1, \ldots, \partial_e\rangle$, where ∂_x is the differentiation with respect to x and $\partial_1, \ldots, \partial_e$ are arbitrary Ore operators. In the most typical case, $\mathbb{K} = \mathbb{Q}(t_1, \ldots, t_e)$ and each ∂_i is either the differentiation with respect to t_i or the shift $t_i \mapsto t_i + 1$.

For a given function f in a function space on which $\mathbb{A}$ acts, the annihilating ideal of f is the left ideal $\operatorname{ann} f \subseteq \mathbb{A}$ of all operators that annihilate f. For example, the annihilating ideal in $\mathbb{K}(x)\langle\partial_x\rangle$ of $f = \sin(x)$ is generated by $\partial_x^2 + 1$ because $\sin''(x) = -\sin(x)$.

A left ideal $\mathcal{I}$ is *D-finite* if the quotient $\mathbb{A}/\mathcal{I}$ is a finite-dimensional vector space over $\mathbb{K}(x)$. A function is called *D-finite* if its annihilating ideal is D-finite. We refer to [18, 20, 21] for an introduction to Ore algebras, creative telescoping and their applications.

Given a D-finite function f, the problem of *creative telescoping* is the computation of a generating set of the *telescoping ideal* of f w.r.t. x, or of its residue class in $\mathbb{A}/\operatorname{ann} f$. This is by definition the left ideal $\mathcal{T}_f \subset \mathbb{K}\langle\partial_1, \ldots, \partial_e\rangle$ of all operators T such that $T + \partial_x G \in \operatorname{ann} f$ for some $G \in \mathbb{A}$; equivalently,

$$\mathcal{T}_f = (\operatorname{ann} f + \partial_x \mathbb{A}) \cap \mathbb{K}\langle\partial_1, \ldots, \partial_e\rangle.$$

Example 4.1. In §2.2, we use the Ore algebra $\mathbb{K}(x)\langle\partial_x, \partial_1, \partial_2\rangle$, with $\partial_1 = d/dp$ and $\partial_2 = S_n$ the shift w.r.t. n. The annihilating ideal $\mathcal{I}$ of $F_n(p,x)$ is generated by three operators, one for each functional equation. It is D-finite and the quotient $\mathbb{A}/\mathcal{I}$ has dimension 2, with basis 1 and ∂_x. The telescoping ideal of $F_n(p,x)$ (or, equivalently, of $1 \in \mathbb{A}/\mathcal{I}$) is generated by $p^2\partial_p^2 + p\partial_p - (n^2+p^2)$ and $pS_n + p\partial_p - n$.

4.1 Cyclic Vector

Let $\mathcal{I} \subseteq \mathbb{A}$ be a D-finite ideal and let r be the dimension of $\mathbb{A}/\mathcal{I}$ over $\mathbb{K}(x)$. We denote $L(\gamma)$ the multiplication of an operator $L \in \mathbb{A}$ and a residue class $\gamma \in \mathbb{A}/\mathcal{I}$.

Let $\gamma \in \mathbb{A}/\mathcal{I}$ be a *cyclic vector* with respect to ∂_x. This means that $\Gamma = \{\gamma, \partial_x(\gamma), \ldots, \partial_x^{r-1}(\gamma)\}$ is a basis of $\mathbb{A}/\mathcal{I}$; or, equivalently, that every $f \in \mathbb{A}/\mathcal{I}$ can be written $A_f(\gamma)$ for some $A_f \in \mathbb{K}(x)\langle\partial_x\rangle$.

Let $L \in \mathbb{K}[x]\langle\partial_x\rangle$ be a minimal annihilating operator of γ, that is $L(\gamma) = 0$ and L has order r (because Γ is a basis, there is no non-zero lower order annihilating operator for γ). A cyclic vector always exists when I is D-finite [17, 5]. It plays a role analogous to that of primitive elements for 0-dimensional polynomial systems.

For $1 \leq i \leq e$, we define a $\mathbb{K}$-linear map $\lambda_i : \mathbb{K}(x) \to \mathbb{K}(x)$ as follows. First, we can write $\partial_i(\gamma) = B_i(\gamma)$ for some operator $B_i \in \mathbb{K}(x)\langle\partial_x\rangle$. Next, let σ_i and δ_i be the maps[3] such that $\partial_i R = \sigma_i(R)\partial_i + \delta_i(R)$ for any $R \in \mathbb{K}(x)$. Finally, we define for $R \in \mathbb{K}(x)$

$$\lambda_i(R) = B_i^*(\sigma_i(R)) + \delta_i(R),$$

where $B_i^*(\sigma_i(R)) \in \mathbb{K}(x)$ is the result of applying the adjoint operator B_i^* to $\sigma_i(R)$, not the operator $B_i^*\sigma_i(R)$.

Proposition 4.2. *With the notation above:*

(i) $f = A_f^*(1)\gamma + \partial_x(Q)$, *for some* $Q \in \mathbb{A}/I$.

Moreover, for any $R \in \mathbb{K}(x)$:

(ii) $\partial_i(R\gamma) = \lambda_i(R)\gamma + \partial_x(Q)$, *for some* $Q \in \mathbb{A}/I$.

(iii) $R\gamma \in \partial_x(\mathbb{A}/I)$ *if and only if* $R \in L^*(\mathbb{K}(x))$.

Proof. Using that $f = A_f(\gamma)$, Lagrange's identity (2) shows that $1A_f(\gamma) - A_f^*(1)\gamma = \partial_x(Q)$ for some Q. This gives *(i)*. Similarly, using the commutation rule for ∂_i and the definition of B_i yields *(ii)*. Property *(iii)* is shown by Abramov and van Hoeij [4, Prop. 3]. □

Example 4.3 (Continuing Example 4.1). The element $1 \in \mathbb{A}/I$ is a cyclic vector since $\{1, \partial_x\}$ is a basis of the quotient.

Actual computations are performed using a Gröbner basis of I and linear algebra in the finite-dimensional $\mathbb{K}(x)$-vector space $\mathbb{A}/I$.

4.2 Creative Telescoping by Reduction

We now present our algorithm (Algorithm 2) based on generalized Hermite reduction for the computation of the telescoping ideal $\mathcal{T}_f$ for an element f of some D-finite quotient $\mathbb{A}/I$. The element f is often 1, as in Example 4.1.

In the same way as Chyzak's algorithm [19], ours iterates over monomials in $\partial_1, \dots, \partial_e$ by a strategy reminiscent of the FGLM algorithm [24]. Each iteration finds either a new generator of $\mathbb{K}\langle\partial_1, \dots, \partial_e\rangle/\mathcal{T}_f$ or a new element in $\mathcal{T}_f$. Let [ ] be the generalized Hermite reduction with respect to L^*, the adjoint of the minimal annihilating operator of the cyclic vector γ. Since every visited monomial μ (but the first) can be written $\partial_i\nu$ for a previously visited monomial ν, we define F inductively by the formula $F_\mu = [\lambda_i(F_\nu)]$ and the base case $F_1 = A_f^*(f)$. With Prop. 4.2 and Theorem 3.10, we check that $\mu(f) = F_\mu\gamma + \partial_x(Q_\mu)$, for some $Q_\mu \in \mathbb{A}/I$ and that

$$a_1\mu_1 + \cdots + a_s\mu_s \in \mathcal{T}_f \quad \Leftrightarrow \quad a_1F_{\mu_1} + \cdots + a_sF_{\mu_s} = 0. \qquad (9)$$

Theorem 4.4. *On input I, Algorithm 2 terminates if and only if the telescoping ideal $\mathcal{T}_f$ is D-finite. It outputs a Gröbner basis of $\mathcal{T}_f$ for the grevlex monomial ordering.*

Proof. By construction, when a monomial is added to the set R, it is not a multiple of another monomial in R. By Dickson's lemma [23], this may happen only finitely many times.

The way $\mathcal{L}$ is filled ensures that when a monomial μ is visited, every smaller monomial has been visited or is a multiple of a reducible monomial. This implies, by induction, that Q is the set of all non-reducible monomials that are smaller than μ, when μ is visited.

[3] If ∂_i is the differentiation w.r.t. t_i, then $\sigma_i(R) = R$ and $\delta_i(R) = \partial R/\partial t_i$. If ∂_i is the shift $t_i \mapsto t_i + 1$, then $\sigma_i(R) = R|_{t_i \leftarrow t_i+1}$ and $\delta_i(R) = 0$.

Algorithm 2 Reduction-based creative telescoping algorithm
Input I a D-finite ideal of $\mathbb{A}$ and $f \in \mathbb{A}/I$
Output Generators of the telescoping ideal $\mathcal{T}_f$

```
function CreativeTelescoping(I, f)
  γ ← a cyclic vector of A/I with respect to ∂_x
  L ← the minimal operator annihilating γ
  λ_1, ..., λ_e ← maps as in Prop. 4.2
  F_1 ← CanonicalForm(A_f^*(1), L^*)
  𝓛 ← [1]                  ▷ list of monomials in ∂_1, ..., ∂_e
  G ← {}                   ▷ Gröbner basis being computed
  Q ← {}                   ▷ Generators of the quotient
  R ← {}                   ▷ Set of reducible monomials
  while 𝓛 ≠ ∅ do
    Remove the first element μ of 𝓛
    if μ is a not multiple of an element of R then
      if μ ≠ 1 then
        Pick i such that μ/∂_i ∈ Q
        F_μ ← CanonicalForm(λ_i(F_{μ/∂_i}), L^*)
      if ∃ a K-linear rel. between F_μ and {F_ν | ν ∈ Q} then
        (a_ν)_{ν∈Q} ← coeff. of the relation F_μ = Σ_{ν∈Q} a_ν F_ν
        Add μ − Σ_{ν∈Q} a_ν ν to G; Add μ to R
      else
        Add μ to Q
        for 1 ≤ i ≤ e do Append the monomial ∂_i μ to 𝓛
  return G
```

If $\mathcal{T}_f$ is not D-finite, then there are infinitely many non-reducible monomials and the algorithm does not terminate. Otherwise, the algorithm terminates, since neither Q nor R may grow indefinitely.

To check that G is a Gröbner basis, we note that: $G \subset \mathcal{T}_f$, by the equivalence (9); the leading monomials of the elements of G are the elements of R; and every leading monomial of an element $\mathcal{T}_f$ (that is a reducible monomial) is a multiple of an element of R. □

4.3 Variants and Improvements

4.3.1 Different term order. As stated, Algorithm 2 computes relations by increasing total degree in $(\partial_1, \dots, \partial_e)$. To choose a different term order, it is sufficient to change the selection of the monomial μ at the beginning of the loop and select the smallest one for the given order instead.

4.3.2 Different termination rule. Instead of waiting for the list $\mathcal{L}$ to be empty, one can stop as soon as a relation is found, and then it is the minimal one for the chosen term order. This variant does not require a D-finite ideal to terminate. Another possibility is to stop as soon as the degree of μ is larger than a predefined bound, returning all the relations that exist below this bound.

4.3.3 Certificates. While an important point of the reduction-based approaches to creative telescoping is to avoid the computation of certificates (in contrast with Chyzak's and Koutschan's algorithms that require their computation), it is also possible to modify the algorithm so that it returns a certificate for each element of the basis. Indeed, a certificate of the generalized Hermite reduction of §3 can be propagated through the algorithms.

4.4 D-finiteness of the Telescoping Ideal

In the general case, the telescoping ideal $\mathcal{T}_f$ of a D-finite function f need not be D-finite. However, when the auxiliary operators $\partial_1, \ldots, \partial_e$ are differentiation operators (as opposed to shift operators for example), then $\mathcal{T}_f$ is always D-finite if f is; this is a well-known result in the theory of D-finiteness and holonomy [42]. We give here a new proof of this fact, as a corollary of a more general sufficient condition for general Ore operators.

Definition 4.5. A D-finite function f is *singular* (w.r.t. ∂_x) at $\alpha \in \overline{\mathbb{K}}$ if every nonzero operator $L \in \mathbb{K}(x)\langle\partial_x\rangle$ such that $L(f) = 0$ is singular at α. The *singular set* (w.r.t. ∂_x) of f, denoted $\operatorname{Sing}(f)$, is the set of all singular points of f.

Let $\Theta = \{1, \partial_1, \partial_2, \ldots, \partial_1^2, \partial_1\partial_2, \ldots\}$ be the set of all monomials in the variables $\partial_1, \ldots, \partial_e$.

THEOREM 4.6. *For any D-finite function f, if $\bigcup_{\mu\in\Theta} \operatorname{Sing}(\mu(f))$ is finite, then $\mathcal{T}_f$ is D-finite.*

PROOF. Let γ be a cyclic vector of $\mathbb{A}/\operatorname{ann} f$ w.r.t. ∂_x with minimal annihilating operator $L \in \mathbb{K}(x)\langle\partial_x\rangle$ of order r. For $\mu \in \Theta$, let $A_{\mu(f)} \in \mathbb{K}(x)\langle\partial_x\rangle$ of order $< r$ be such that $\mu(f) = A_{\mu(f)}(\gamma)$, as in §4.1, and let $R_\mu = A^*_{\mu(f)}(1) \in \mathbb{K}(x)$, so that $\mu(f) = R_\mu\gamma + \partial_x(G_\mu)$, for some $G_\mu \in \mathbb{A}/\operatorname{ann} f$. By Proposition 4.2, the $\mathbb{K}$-linear map $\phi : \mathbb{K}\langle\partial_1, \ldots, \partial_n\rangle \to \mathbb{K}(x)$ defined by $\phi(\mu) = R_\mu$ induces an injective map $\mathbb{K}\langle\partial_1, \ldots, \partial_n\rangle/\mathcal{T}_f \to \mathbb{K}(x)/\operatorname{im} L^*$. The telescoping ideal $\mathcal{T}_f$ is D-finite if and only if the image of this map is finite-dimensional. In view of Proposition 3.13, it suffices to show that the poles of all the R_μ lie in a finite subset of $\overline{\mathbb{K}}$. This is obtained by proving that

$$\bigcup_{\mu\in\Theta} \operatorname{poles}(R_\mu) \subseteq \operatorname{Sing}(L) \cup \bigcup_{\mu\in\Theta} \operatorname{Sing}(\mu(f)), \qquad (10)$$

where $\operatorname{Sing}(L)$ is the set of zeroes of the leading coefficient of L.

Indeed, let $\mu \in \Theta$ and $\alpha \in \overline{\mathbb{K}}$ that is not in the right-hand side. We now prove that no coefficient of $A_{\mu(f)}$ has a pole at α, from where it follows that neither has $R_\mu = A^*_{\mu(f)}(1)$. By the hypothesis on α, there exists $M \in \mathbb{K}(x)\langle\partial_x\rangle$ an annihilating operator of $\mu(f)$ regular at α. It satisfies $MA_{\mu(f)}(\gamma) = M(\mu(f)) = 0$ and by minimality of L it follows that $MA_{\mu(f)} = BL$ for some operator B. As a consequence, $0, 1, \ldots, r-1$ are roots of the indicial polynomial of $MA_{\mu(f)}$. Write $A_{\mu(f)} = \sum_{i=0}^{r-1} a_i\partial_x^i$, for some $a_i \in \mathbb{K}(x)$ and let j be the maximal index with $\operatorname{ord}_\alpha a_j = \min_i \operatorname{ord}_\alpha a_i$. Then $j \in \{0, \ldots, r-1\}$ and $\operatorname{ord}_\alpha A_{\mu(f)}\big((x-\alpha)^j\big) = \min_i \operatorname{ord}_\alpha a_i$. Then this last quantity is a zero of the indicial polynomial of M, which implies that it is nonnegative and thus that none of the a_i has a pole at α. □

Recall that for $1 \le i \le e$, the Ore operator ∂_i satisfies a commutation relation $\partial_i a = \sigma_i(a)\partial_i + \delta_i(a)$ for any $a \in \mathbb{K}$, where σ_i is an endomorphism of $\mathbb{K}$ and δ_i is a σ_i-derivation of it. When ∂_i is a differentiation operator, $\sigma_i = \mathrm{id}_{\mathbb{K}}$.

COROLLARY 4.7. *If $\partial_1, \ldots, \partial_e$ are differentiation operators, then $\mathcal{T}_f$ is D-finite for any D-finite function f.*

PROOF. It is sufficient to check that $\operatorname{Sing}(\mu(f)) \subset \operatorname{Sing}(f)$ for any monomial $\mu \in \Theta$ and then conclude by Theorem 4.6.

Integral	(11)	(12)	(13)	(14)	(15)	(16)	(17)
redct	13 s	> 1h	> 1h	1.5 s	1.5 s	165 s	53 s
HF-CT	19 s	253 s	45 s	232 s	516 s	>1h	>1h
HF-FCT	1.9 s*	2.3 s	5.3 s	>1h	2.3 s*	5.4 s	2.2 s*

Table 1 Comparative timings on several instances of creative telescoping. Rows are redct (new algorithm); Koutschan's HolonomicFunctions, using functions `Annihilator` and `CreativeTelescoping` (HF-CT); idem, using `FindCreativeTelescoping` (HF-FCT), a heuristic that does not necessarily find the minimal operators (indicated by *). All examples were run on the same machine, with the latest versions of Maple and Mathematica.

Let $M \in \mathbb{K}[x]\langle\partial_x\rangle$ be an annihilating operator of $g = \mu(f)$ regular at $\alpha \in \overline{\mathbb{K}} \setminus \operatorname{Sing}(f)$. The commutation rules for the differential operators imply that $\partial_i M = M\partial_i + R$, for some $R \in \mathbb{K}[x]\langle\partial_x\rangle$. In particular, we obtain the inhomogeneous differential equation $M(\partial_i(g)) = R(g)$ for $\partial_i(g)$. Since α is neither a singularity of M nor of $R(g)$, it follows that it is not a singularity of $\partial_i(g)$. □

For the case of general Ore operators, we obtain with a similar proof the following result.

COROLLARY 4.8. *For any D-finite function f, if there is a finite set $S \subset \overline{\mathbb{K}}$ such that: (i) $\sigma_i(S) \subseteq S$ for any $1 \le i \le e$ and (ii) $\operatorname{Sing}(f) \subseteq S$, then $\mathcal{T}_f$ is D-finite.*

5 EXPERIMENTS

We present the results of a preliminary Maple implementation called redct[4]. Comparison is done with Koutschan's HolonomicFunctions package [31], the best available code for creative telescoping. Timings are given in Table 1[5].

Koutschan's examples. Koutschan's example session [30] contains 40 integrals on which we tested our code. In most cases, our code compares well with HolonomicFunctions. There are 37 easy cases, all of whose telescopers are found in 3.5 sec. by redct, while 16 sec. are needed by HolonomicFunctions (but that includes certificates). The three other examples are (the nature of the parameters is indicated in the brackets, $C_n^{(\alpha)}$ denotes Gegenbauer polynomials, and J_1, I_1, etc. Bessel functions):

$$\int \frac{2J_{m+n}(2tx)T_{m-n}(x)}{\sqrt{1-x^2}}\,\mathrm{d}x \quad [\text{diff. } t, \text{ shift } n \text{ and } m], \qquad (11)$$

$$\int_0^1 C_n^{(\lambda)}(x)C_m^{(\lambda)}(x)C_\ell^{(\lambda)}(x)(1-x^2)^{\lambda-\frac{1}{2}}\,\mathrm{d}x \quad [\text{shift } n, m, \ell], \qquad (12)$$

$$\int_0^\infty xJ_1(ax)I_1(ax)Y_0(x)K_0(x)\,\mathrm{d}x \quad [\text{diff. } a]. \qquad (13)$$

Longer examples. We mention a few examples, some involving Gegenbauer polynomials [40, 2.21.18.2, 2.21.18.4], that take more time. The advantage of a reduction-based approach becomes visible.

$$\int \frac{n^2+x+1}{n^2+1}\left(\frac{(x+1)^2}{(x-4)(x-3)^2(x^2-5)^3}\right)^n \sqrt{x^2-5}\; e^{\frac{x^3+1}{x(x-3)(x-4)^2}}\,\mathrm{d}x \quad [\text{shift } n], \qquad (14)$$

$$\int C_m^{(\mu)}(x)C_n^{(\nu)}(x)(1-x^2)^{\nu-1/2}\,\mathrm{d}x \quad [\text{shift } n, m, \mu, \nu], \qquad (15)$$

[4] Available with example sessions at https://specfun.inria.fr/chyzak/redct/.

[5] When our code does not terminate, time is spent computing the exceptional set. This seems to be due to apparent singularities of the operators, that become true singularities of their adjoint. Ways of circumventing this issue are under study.

$$\int x^{\ell} C_m^{(\mu)}(x) C_n^{(\nu)}(x)(1-x^2)^{\nu-1/2}\,\mathrm{d}x \quad [\text{shift } \ell, m, n, \mu, \nu], \tag{16}$$

$$\int (x+a)^{\gamma+\lambda-1}(a-x)^{\beta-1} C_m^{(\gamma)}(x/a) C_n^{(\lambda)}(x/a)\,\mathrm{d}x, \quad [\text{diff. } a, \text{shift } n, m, \beta, \gamma, \lambda]. \tag{17}$$

6 CONCLUSION

A closer look at our algorithm reveals several aspects of the complexity of creative telescoping. To simplify the discussion, we restrict to the bivariate case and measure the *arithmetic complexity*, obtained by counting arithmetic operations in $\mathbb{Q}$. We look for bounds in terms of the *input size* (order and degree of the operators at hand).

In this setting, *the complexity of computing $\mathcal{T}_f$ is not bounded polynomially* (whatever the algorithm). Consider for instance, the integral representation of Hermite polynomials

$$H_n(t) = \frac{2^n}{i\sqrt{\pi}} \int_{-i\infty}^{i\infty} (t+x)^n e^{x^2}\,\mathrm{d}x.$$

If one computes a telescoper over $\mathbb{Q}(n, t)$, then our algorithm produces the classical differential equation $y'' + 2ny = 2ty'$. However, if n is a given positive integer then the minimal telescoper is the first-order factor $H_n(t)\partial_t - H_n'(t)$, with coefficients of degree n. Its size *is exponential in the bit size* of the input. Thus, *no algorithm computing the minimal telescoper can run in polynomial complexity.*

However, in the frequent cases like this one where the set S of singularities discussed in Corollary 4.8 is bounded polynomially in terms of the size of the input, then the dimension of the quotient and therefore *the order of the telescopers is bounded polynomially* as a consequence of Adolphson's result (Proposition 3.13). The non-polynomial cost of minimality thus resides only in the degree of the coefficients. Note that in the differential case, polynomial time computation of non-minimal telescopers is also achieved by well-known methods in holonomy theory, e.g., [34, proof of Lemma 3].

In our algorithm, the non-polynomial complexity arises first in the computation of the exceptional set Exc_M and next in the reductions by the elements of this set. Removing this part of the computation and using the weak Hermite reduction yields a weak form of the algorithm that does not find minimal telescopers but runs in polynomial complexity, if the set S has polynomial size.

Acknowledgement. This work was supported in part by FastRelax ANR-14-CE25-0018-01.

REFERENCES

[1] S. A. Abramov. EG-eliminations. *J. Differ. Equations Appl.*, 5(4-5):393–433, 1999.
[2] S. A. Abramov and K. Y. Kvashenko. Fast algorithms for the search of the rational solutions of linear differential equations with polynomial coefficients. In *ISSAC'91*, pages 267–270, 1991.
[3] S. A. Abramov and M. Petkovšek. Minimal decomposition of indefinite hypergeometric sums. In *ISSAC'01*, pages 7–14. ACM, 2001.
[4] S. A. Abramov and M. van Hoeij. Integration of solutions of linear functional equations. *Integral Transform. Spec. Funct.*, 8(1-2):3–12, 1999.
[5] K. Adjamagbo. Sur l'effectivité du lemme du vecteur cyclique. *C. R. Acad. Sci. Paris Sér. I Math.*, 306(13):543–546, 1988.
[6] A. Adolphson. An index theorem for p-adic differential operators. *Trans. Amer. Math. Soc.*, 216:279–293, 1976.
[7] G. Almkvist and D. Zeilberger. The method of differentiating under the integral sign. *J. Symbolic Comput.*, 10(6):571–591, 1990.
[8] M. A. Barkatou. On rational solutions of systems of linear differential equations. *J. Symbolic Comput.*, 28(4-5):547–567, 1999.
[9] A. Bostan, S. Chen, F. Chyzak, and Z. Li. Complexity of creative telescoping for bivariate rational functions. In *ISSAC'10*, pages 203–210. ACM, 2010.
[10] A. Bostan, S. Chen, F. Chyzak, Z. Li, and G. Xin. Hermite reduction and creative telescoping for hyperexponential functions. In *ISSAC'13*, pages 77–84. ACM, 2013.
[11] A. Bostan, L. Dumont, and B. Salvy. Efficient algorithms for mixed creative telescoping. In *ISSAC'16*, pages 127–134. ACM, 2016.
[12] A. Bostan, P. Lairez, and B. Salvy. Creative telescoping for rational functions using the Griffiths-Dwork method. In *ISSAC'13*, pages 93–100. ACM, 2013.
[13] S. Chen, H. Huang, M. Kauers, and Z. Li. A modified Abramov-Petkovšek reduction and creative telescoping for hypergeometric terms. In *ISSAC'15*, pages 117–124. ACM, 2015.
[14] S. Chen, M. Kauers, and C. Koutschan. Reduction-based creative telescoping for algebraic functions. In *ISSAC'16*, pages 175–182. ACM, 2016.
[15] S. Chen, M. Kauers, and M. F. Singer. Telescopers for rational and algebraic functions via residues. In *ISSAC'12*, pages 130–137. ACM, 2012.
[16] S. Chen, M. van Hoeij, M. Kauers, and C. Koutschan. Reduction-based creative telescoping for fuchsian D-finite functions. *J. Symbolic Comput.*, 85:108–127, 2018.
[17] R. C. Churchill and J. J. Kovacic. Cyclic vectors. In *Differential Algebra and Related Topics*, pages 191–218. World Scientific, 2002.
[18] F. Chyzak. *Fonctions holonomes en calcul formel.* PhD Thesis, École polytechnique, 1998.
[19] F. Chyzak. An extension of Zeilberger's fast algorithm to general holonomic functions. *Discrete Math.*, 217(1-3):115–134, 2000.
[20] F. Chyzak. *The ABC of Creative Telescoping — Algorithms, Bounds, Complexity.* Accreditation to supervise research (HDR), École polytechnique, Apr. 2014.
[21] F. Chyzak and B. Salvy. Non-commutative elimination in Ore algebras proves multivariate identities. *J. Symbolic Comput.*, 26(2):187–227, 1998.
[22] J. H. Davenport. The Risch differential equation problem. *SIAM J. Comput.*, 15(4):903–918, 1986.
[23] L. E. Dickson. Finiteness of the Odd Perfect and Primitive Abundant Numbers with n Distinct Prime Factors. *Amer. J. Math.*, 35(4):413–422, 1913.
[24] J. C. Faugère, P. Gianni, D. Lazard, and T. Mora. Efficient computation of zero-dimensional Gröbner bases by change of ordering. *J. Symbolic Comput.*, 16(4):329–344, 1993.
[25] L. Fuchs. Die Periodicitätsmoduln der hyperelliptischen Integrale als Functionen eines Parameters aufgefasst. *J. Reine Angew. Math.*, 71:91–127, 1870.
[26] K. Geddes, H. Le, and Z. Li. Differential rational normal forms and a reduction algorithm for hyperexponential functions. In *ISSAC'04*, pages 183–190, 2004.
[27] C. Hermite. Sur l'intégration des fractions rationnelles. *Ann. Sci. École Norm. Sup. (2)*, 1:215–218, 1872.
[28] H. Huang. New bounds for hypergeometric creative telescoping. In *ISSAC'16*, pages 279–286. ACM, 2016.
[29] E. L. Ince. *Ordinary Differential Equations.* Dover Publications, New York, 1944.
[30] C. Koutschan. Examplesv11.nb. On the HolonomicFunctions web page.
[31] C. Koutschan. *Advanced Applications of the Holonomic Systems Approach.* PhD thesis, RISC-Linz, 2009.
[32] P. Lairez. Computing periods of rational integrals. *Math. Comp.*, 85(300):1719–1752, 2016.
[33] J. Liouville. Second mémoire sur la détermination des intégrales dont la valeur est algébrique. *Journal de l'École polytechnique*, 14:149–193, 1833.
[34] L. Lipshitz. The diagonal of a D-finite power series is D-finite. *J. Algebra*, 113(2):373–378, 1988.
[35] B. Malgrange. Sur les points singuliers des équations différentielles. *Enseignement Math. (2)*, 20:147–176, 1974.
[36] P. Monsky. Finiteness of de Rham cohomology. *Amer. J. Math.*, 94:237–245, 1972.
[37] M. Ostrogradsky. De l'intégration des fractions rationnelles. *Bull. classe phys.-math. Acad. Impériale des Sciences Saint-Pétersbourg*, 4:145–167, 286–300, 1845.
[38] É. Picard. Sur les intégrales doubles de fonctions rationnelles dont tous les résidus sont nuls. *Bull. Sci. Math. (2)*, 26:143–152, 1902.
[39] É. Picard and G. Simart. *Théorie des fonctions algébriques de deux variables indépendantes*, volume I (1897) and II (1906). Gauthier-Villars et fils, 1897.
[40] A. P. Prudnikov, Y. A. Brychkov, and O. I. Marichev. *Integrals and series. Vol. 2.* Gordon & Breach Science Publishers, NY, second edition, 1988. Special functions.
[41] M. S. Rezaoui. Indice polynomial d'une matrice d'opérateurs différentiels. *C. R. Acad. Sci. Paris Sér. I Math.*, 332(6):505–508, 2001.
[42] N. Takayama. An approach to the zero recognition problem by Buchberger algorithm. *Journal of Symbolic Computation*, 14:265–282, 1992.
[43] B. M. Trager. *Integration of Algebraic Functions.* PhD Thesis, MIT, 1984.
[44] J. van der Hoeven. Constructing reductions for creative telescoping, 2017. Technical Report, HAL 01435877, http://hal.archives-ouvertes.fr/hal-01435877/.
[45] M. van der Put and M. Reversat. A local-global problem for linear differential equations. *Pacific J. Math.*, 238(1):171–199, 2008.
[46] M. van der Put and M. F. Singer. *Galois theory of linear differential equations*, volume 328 of *Grundlehren der Mathematischen Wissenschaften.* Springer, 2003.
[47] D. Y. Y. Yun. On square-free decompositions algorithms. In *Proc. 1976 ACM Symposium on Symbolic and Algebraic Computation*, pages 26–35. ACM, 1976.
[48] D. Y. Y. Yun. Fast algorithm for rational function integration. In *Proc. IFIP'77 Congr., Toronto, Ont.*, pages 493–498. North-Holland, 1977.

A Newton-like Validation Method for Chebyshev Approximate Solutions of Linear Ordinary Differential Systems

Florent Bréhard
École Normale Supérieure de Lyon & LAAS-CNRS
Lyon & Toulouse, France
florent.brehard@ens-lyon.fr

ABSTRACT

We provide a new framework for *a posteriori* validation of vector-valued problems with componentwise tight error enclosures, and use it to design a symbolic-numeric Newton-like validation algorithm for Chebyshev approximate solutions of coupled systems of linear ordinary differential equations. More precisely, given a coupled differential system with polynomial coefficients over a compact interval (or continuous coefficients rigorously approximated by polynomials) and componentwise polynomial approximate solutions in Chebyshev basis, the algorithm outputs componentwise rigorous upper bounds for the approximation errors, with respect to the uniform norm over the interval under consideration.

A complexity analysis shows that the number of arithmetic operations needed by this algorithm (in floating-point or interval arithmetics) is proportional to the approximation degree when the differential equation is considered fixed. Finally, we illustrate the efficiency of this fully automated validation method on an example of a coupled Airy-like system.

CCS CONCEPTS

• **Mathematics of computing → Ordinary differential equations; Approximation**; *Interval arithmetic*;

KEYWORDS

Fixed-point validation; Newton's method; D-finite functions

ACM Reference Format:
Florent Bréhard. 2018. A Newton-like Validation Method for Chebyshev Approximate Solutions of Linear Ordinary Differential Systems. In *ISSAC '18: 2018 ACM International Symposium on Symbolic and Algebraic Computation, July 16–19, 2018, New York, NY, USA.* ACM, New York, NY, USA, 8 pages. https://doi.org/10.1145/3208976.3209000

1 INTRODUCTION

Notations. Let p be a positive integer for the ambient space $\mathbb{R}^p$, whose canonical basis is denoted by $(e_1, \dots, e_p)$. For a ring $\mathbb{A}$, $\mathcal{M}_p(\mathbb{A})$ denotes the set of order p square matrices, with $\mathbf{1}$ and $\mathbf{0}$ the identity and zero matrices. The order $\leqslant$ over $\mathbb{R}$ is componentwise extended to a (partial) order over $\mathbb{R}^p$ and $\mathcal{M}_p(\mathbb{R})$: for all $u, v \in \mathbb{R}^p$ (resp. A, B in $\mathcal{M}_p(\mathbb{R})$), $u \leqslant v$ if and only if $u_i \leqslant v_i$ for all $i \in [\![1, p]\!]$ (resp. $A \leqslant B$ iff $A_{ij} \leqslant B_{ij}$ for all $i, j \in [\![1, p]\!]$). The uniform norm of a function f, defined over $[-1, 1]$, is $\|f\|_\infty = \sup_{x \in [-1,1]} |f(x)|$.

General context. Numerical computing with functions is often done via polynomial approximations. For sufficiently smooth functions, defined over a compact interval, truncated Chebyshev series are well-known for their excellent approximation properties, efficient algorithms and software like Chebfun [6, 22]. Broadly speaking, the principle of working with polynomial approximations instead of functions is analogous to using floating-point instead of real numbers. However, some applications such as safety-critical engineering or computer-assisted proofs in mathematics need *effective* and *safe* (rather than *asymptotic*) error enclosures.

Problem statement and contributions. We present a symbolic-numeric *a posteriori* validation algorithm that provides *componentwise* and *tight* error enclosures for Chebyshev approximations to solutions of coupled linear ordinary differential equations (LODEs):

$$Y^{(r)} + A_{r-1}(t) \cdot Y^{(r-1)} + \cdots + A_1(t) \cdot Y' + A_0(t) \cdot Y = G(t), \quad (1)$$

of unknown $Y : [-1, 1] \to \mathbb{R}^p$. Coefficients A_i and G must be continuous functions, given as polynomials with rigorous error bounds. However, for the sake of simplicity, we mainly focus on the polynomial case, and refer to the solutions as *vector-valued D-finite functions.* Although such functions can be seen as vectors of (scalar) D-finite functions, the decoupling of the system followed by a possible desingularization step may produce hard to validate scalar LODEs (see Section 4). Moreover, in the nonpolynomial case, such techniques do not apply.

Using an appropriate integral transform of the linear differential system, we obtain a Volterra integral equation of the second kind with polynomial kernel, whence the following problem statement:

Problem 1.1. *For a given integral equation of unknown* $\Phi : [-1, 1] \to \mathbb{R}^p$*:*

$$\Phi(t) + \int_{-1}^{t} K(t, s) \cdot \Phi(s) ds = \Psi(t),$$

with a p-dimensional polynomial kernel $K(t, s) \in \mathcal{M}_p(\mathbb{R}[t, s])$ *and* $\Psi \in \mathbb{R}[t]^p$*, assuming we are given for each component* $\Phi_i^\star$ *of the exact solution* $\Phi^\star$ *a polynomial approximation* Φ_i° *in Chebyshev basis, compute componentwise error bounds* ε_i*, as tight as desired:*

$$\|\Phi_i^\circ - \Phi_i^\star\|_{\mathcal{U}^1} \leqslant \varepsilon_i, \qquad \textit{for all } i \in [\![1, p]\!].$$

Here, $\|\cdot\|_{\mathcal{U}^1}$ is a norm for absolutely summable Chebyshev series that upper-bounds the $\|\cdot\|_\infty$ norm over $[-1, 1]$ (see Section 3.1).

Fixed-point methods are extensively used in the field of functional analysis and differential equations. They provide iterative approximation schemes, like Picard-Chebyshev which integrates nonlinear dynamical systems arising, for instance, in space flight

ACM ISBN 978-1-4503-5550-6/18/07...$15.00
https://doi.org/10.1145/3208976.3209000

mechanics problems [4, 9]. They also underlie numerous validation methods for function space problems [14, 24].

Many fixed-point validation methods use the Banach fixed-point theorem. Given an equation $x = \mathrm{T} \cdot x$ with T contracting of ratio $\lambda \in (0, 1)$ over a complete metric space, and an approximation x to the exact solution $x^\star$, it provides an error enclosure:

$$\frac{\|x - \mathrm{T} \cdot x\|}{1+\lambda} \leqslant \|x - x^\star\| \leqslant \frac{\|x - \mathrm{T} \cdot x\|}{1-\lambda}. \quad (2)$$

However, in the case we consider, x belongs to a product space, and the classical method consisting in endowing it with a global norm fails to produce componentwise tight error enclosures. This is particularly annoying when the components of the system are of different nature (e.g., position and speed) or magnitude.

Based on a new refinement with lower bounds for the Perov fixed-point theorem (a vector-valued generalization of Banach fixed-point principle), we propose a validation algorithm to solve Problem 1.1. It is a generalization of the validation method presented in [8] to vectorial LODEs, within a new general framework for vector-valued fixed-point validation.

THEOREM 1.2. ***Algorithms 1** and **3** solve together Problem 1.1 by providing componentwise error enclosures, as tight as desired.*

*(i) **Algorithm 1** only depends on the integral equation (not on the provided approximation). It produces and rigorously bounds a Newton-like validation operator and requires $O(p^3 {N_{\mathrm{val}}}^2 d)$ arithmetic operations.*

*(ii) **Algorithm 3** computes the error enclosures for the approximation and runs in linear time with respect to the maximum degree of the approximations Φ_i° and the right-hand sides Ψ_i. More precisely, its complexity is $O(p^2 d^2 N_{\mathrm{app}} + p N_{\mathrm{rhs}} + p^2 N_{\mathrm{val}} \min(\max(N_{\mathrm{app}} + d, N_{\mathrm{rhs}}), N_{\mathrm{val}}))$, where:*

- $N_{\mathrm{app}} = \max_i \deg \Phi_i^\circ$ *and* $N_{\mathrm{rhs}} = \max_i \deg \Psi_i$;
- $d = 1 + \max_{ij} \deg k_{ij}(t, s)$;
- N_{val} *is a truncation index used to rigorously approximate the problem in finite dimension.*

We assume a uniform complexity model, i.e., a unit cost for each arithmetic operation (+, −, ×, /, $\sqrt{}$), with, say, floating-point or interval operands.

The previous complexity estimates still involve a truncation index N_{val}, which is directly related to how tight the desired error enclosures have to be. As detailed in Theorem 3.1, its minimal value ensuring a contracting Newton-like operator is potentially exponential with respect to the magnitude of the coefficients of the integral equation, in the case of stiff LODEs for example. In practice however, this method works efficiently and fully automatically. An open source library implementing this validation method (and its extension to the nonpolynomial case) can be found here [1]. It was also recently used for a space flight dynamics application [3].

Previous work. In this context, applications of the Banach fixed-point theorem include early works [14, 24], where variations of Newton's method perform *a posteriori* validation in function spaces. More recent works developed techniques (e.g., *radii polynomials* [11]) to find a stable neighborhood of an approximation φ over which the Banach fixed-point theorem applies. They have the advantage of dealing with nonlinear problems (examples can be found in [11, 15, 23]). However, the above mentioned methods were not fully automated and little emphasis was put on their algorithmic aspects.

By contrast, [5] is a pioneer work towards effective methods for validation of approximations of D-finite functions in Chebyshev basis. At the cost of a more restricted class of functions, namely, D-finite functions, this article introduces a fully automated algorithm together with complexity estimates, based on a Picard iteration scheme. In line with this work, [8] describes another algorithm based on a Newton-like method in an appropriate function space, which is easily extended to the case of continuous coefficients rigorously approximated by Chebyshev polynomials.

The above mentioned validation techniques are usually transposed to the vectorial case by fixing a norm over the vector-valued function space. However, this does not provide componentwise tight error enclosures. To overcome this limitation, we consider the notion of *vector-valued* (or *generalized*) metric spaces and *generalized contractions* (or *P-contractions*) [12, 18, 21]. The Perov fixed-point theorem [12, 19] is a natural extension of the Banach fixed-point theorem and provides componentwise upper bounds for the approximation error. Several works applied this theorem in various settings, for example [25] for the Newton method or [2, 16, 20] for ODEs with nonlocal conditions. To the best of our knowledge, however, none of these works investigate the existence of lower bounds, nor address validation problems.

Outline. Section 2 introduces a general framework for componentwise fixed-point validation in generalized metric spaces. In Section 3, we design the Newton-like validation algorithm for Chebyshev approximations of vector-valued D-finite functions. Finally, Section 4 details the validation of a two-dimensional highly oscillating system. For completeness, we also provide a comparison with a decoupling technique that boils down to solving scalar LODEs.

2 A FRAMEWORK FOR VECTOR-VALUED VALIDATION PROBLEMS

We address the general problem of componentwise validating an approximation x° to the exact solution $x^\star$ of a fixed-point equation $x = \mathrm{T} \cdot x$. Section 2.1 gives a rigorous definition of "several components and norms" with the notion of generalized metric spaces, leading to the Perov fixed-point theorem. Section 2.2 presents a new result that complements the Perov theorem with lower bounds on the componentwise approximation errors.

A toy example in the plane illustrates the vector-valued validation framework. Consider the trigonometric equation $\sin^3 \vartheta + \cos 3\vartheta = 0$ for $\vartheta \in \mathbb{R}$. By introducing $c = \cos x$ and $s = \sin x$, this is equivalent to finding the roots of the following polynomial system in the plane (c, s):

$$\mathrm{F} \cdot (c, s) = \begin{pmatrix} s^3 + 4c^3 - 3c \\ c^2 + s^2 - 1 \end{pmatrix} = 0. \quad (3)$$

Let $x^\star = (c^\star, s^\star)$ be an exact solution and $x^\circ := (c^\circ, s^\circ) = (0.84, 0.55)$ an approximation of it. In order to validate this solution with respect to a given norm $\|\cdot\|$ on $\mathbb{R}^2$, we define a Newton-like operator $\mathrm{T} \cdot (c, s) = (c, s) - \mathrm{A} \cdot \mathrm{F} \cdot (c, s)$ with $\mathrm{A} := \begin{pmatrix} 0.25 & -0.20 \\ -0.37 & 1.2 \end{pmatrix} \approx (\mathrm{DF}_{x^\circ})^{-1} \in \mathcal{M}_2(\mathbb{R})$ an approximate inverse of the Fréchet derivative DF_{x° of F at x°. Since A is injective, its fixed points are exactly the roots of F. In this example, F is nonlinear, so one must find

[1] http://perso.ens-lyon.fr/florent.brehard

a *stable closed neighborhood* over which T is contracting, for the Banach theorem to apply. It suffices to determine a radius $r > 0$ satisfying the following two conditions:

(i) $\lambda := \sup_{\|x-x^\circ\| \leqslant r} \|1 - \mathbf{A} \cdot \mathrm{DF}_x\| < 1$;
(ii) $\|x^\circ - \mathrm{T} \cdot x^\circ\| + kr \leqslant r$.

If such a radius exists, then by the Banach fixed-point theorem, we have $\|x^\circ - x^\star\| \leqslant \|\mathbf{A} \cdot \mathrm{F} \cdot x\|/(1-\lambda)$. However, such a bound captures a "global" error, which may not be what we expect, if, for example, the two components are of different nature (e.g., position and velocity), or differ by several orders of magnitude.

2.1 Generalized Metric Spaces and Perov Fixed-Point Theorem

Definition 2.1. Let X be a set (resp. E a linear space). A function $d : X \times X \to \mathbb{R}_+^p$ (resp. $\|\cdot\| : E \to \mathbb{R}_+^p$) is a *vector-valued* or *generalized* metric (resp. norm) if for all x, y, z in X or E and $\lambda \in \mathbb{R}$:

- $d(x,y) = 0$ iff $x = y$, *resp.* $\|x\| = 0$ iff $x = 0$;
- $d(x,y) = d(y,x)$, *resp.* $\|\lambda x\| = |\lambda|\|x\|$;
- $d(x,y) \leqslant d(x,z)+d(z,y)$, *resp.* $\|x+y\| \leqslant \|x\| + \|y\|$.

Then (X,d) (resp. $(E, \|\cdot\|)$) is a *vector-valued* or *generalized* metric space (resp. linear space).

A straightforward example is the product of p metric spaces (X_i, d_i), $i \in [\![1,p]\!]$ (resp. p normed linear spaces $(E, \|\cdot\|_i)$) and the vector-valued metric $d(x,y) = (d_1(x_1,y_1), \ldots, d_p(x_p,y_p))$ (resp. the vector-valued norm $\|x\| = (\|x_1\|_1, \ldots, \|x_p\|_p)$).

Remark 2.2. *A vector-valued metric space (respectively a vector-valued normed linear space) can be trivially seen as a metric space (respectively a normed linear space) by taking the maximum of all the components of the vector-valued metric (respectively norm). We therefore recover all the useful topological notions of convergence, limit, neighborhood, completeness, etc.*

In the context of vector-valued metric spaces, the notion of contracting map needs to be generalized. Let $\mathcal{M}_p^{\to 0}(\mathbb{R}) \subseteq \mathcal{M}_p(\mathbb{R})$ denote the *convergent to zero matrices*, that is the matrices M such that $M^k \to 0$ as $k \to \infty$. Equivalently, these are matrices M with spectral radius $\rho(M) < 1$. Then, $\mathcal{M}_p^{\to 0}(\mathbb{R}_+) = \mathcal{M}_p^{\to 0}(\mathbb{R}) \cap \mathcal{M}_p(\mathbb{R}_+)$ denotes those among them with nonnegative coefficients.

Definition 2.3. Let (X,d) be a vector-valued metric space and $\mathrm{T} : X \to X$ an operator.

- T is Λ-Lipschitz for some $\Lambda \in \mathcal{M}_p(\mathbb{R}_+)$ if:
$$d(\mathrm{T} \cdot x, \mathrm{T} \cdot y) \leqslant \Lambda \cdot d(x,y), \qquad \text{for all } x, y \in X.$$
- If moreover Λ is convergent to 0 ($\Lambda \in \mathcal{M}_p^{\to 0}(\mathbb{R}_+)$), then T is said to be a generalized contraction.

Using these definitions, the Perov fixed-point theorem[2] is a generalization of the Banach fixed-point theorem.

Theorem 2.4 (Perov). *Let (X,d) be a complete vector-valued metric space and $\mathrm{T} : X \to X$ a generalized contraction with a Lipschitz matrix $\Lambda \in \mathcal{M}_p^{\to 0}(\mathbb{R}_+)$. Then:*

(i) T admits a unique fixed-point $x^\star \in X$;

(ii) for every $x^\circ \in X$, the iterated sequence defined by $x_0 = x^\circ$ and $x_{n+1} = \mathrm{T} \cdot x_n$ converges to $x^\star$ with the following upper bound on the approximation error:

$$d(x_n, x^\star) \leqslant \Lambda^n \cdot (1-\Lambda)^{-1} \cdot d(x^\circ, \mathrm{T} \cdot x^\circ), \qquad \textit{for all } n \in \mathbb{N}. \quad (4)$$

A proof of this theorem is given in [7, Appendix A.1] or [18].

Perov theorem applied to the toy example. Endowing $\mathbb{R}^2$ with the vector-valued norm $\|(c,s)\| := (|c|, |s|)$ does not change the definition of T. The two conditions needed to apply the Banach fixed-point theorem are adapted to the Perov theorem as follows. Choose a *multi-radius* $r = (r_1, r_2)$ such that

(i) $\Lambda := \left(\sup_{\|x-x^\circ\| \leqslant r} |(\mathrm{DT}_x)_{ij}|\right)_{1 \leqslant i,j \leqslant 2}$ satisfies $\rho(\Lambda) < 1$;
(ii) $\|x^\circ - \mathrm{T} \cdot x^\circ\| + \Lambda \cdot r \leqslant r$.

For $r = (0.005, 0.005)$, one obtains:

$$\Lambda = \begin{pmatrix} 5.81 & 1.31 \\ 5.63 & 3.40 \end{pmatrix} \cdot 10^{-2}, \qquad \rho(\Lambda) = 7.57 \cdot 10^{-2},$$

which satisfies (i) and (ii). Hence, Theorem 2.4 gives:

$$|c^\circ - c^\star| \leqslant 2.90 \cdot 10^{-3}, \qquad |s^\circ - s^\star| \leqslant 3.65 \cdot 10^{-3}.$$

To assess the tightness of these bounds, we provide lower bounds on the componentwise approximation errors.

2.2 Lower Bounds and Error Enclosures

Let $\varepsilon = d(x^\circ, x^\star) \in \mathbb{R}_+^p$ be the vector of unknown errors and $\eta = d(x^\circ, \mathrm{T} \cdot x^\circ) \in \mathbb{R}_+^p$. By the triangle inequality, ε is circumscribed into a polytope of $\mathbb{R}_+^p$:

$$\begin{aligned} (1-\Lambda) \cdot \varepsilon &\leqslant \eta, \\ (1+\Lambda) \cdot \varepsilon &\geqslant \eta, \\ \varepsilon &\geqslant 0. \end{aligned} \quad (5)$$

The first inequality gives the upper bounds $\varepsilon^+ = (1-\Lambda)^{-1} \cdot \eta$, as stated by Theorem 2.4 (with $n = 0$). However, the second one does not directly give the desired lower bounds, say ε^-, because the inverse $(1+\Lambda)^{-1} = \sum_{k \geqslant 0} (-\Lambda)^k$ is not nonnegative in general. It is clear that each ε_i^- is given by the i-th coordinate of some vertex of this polytope. Instead of testing its 2^p vertices, the following theorem identifies the correct one.

Theorem 2.5 (Lower bounds for the Perov theorem). *With the above notations, for each $i \in [\![1,p]\!]$, the lower bound ε_i^- on the i-th component ε_i of the approximation error of x° to $x^\star$ is given by the i-th component of the vertex defined by the intersection of the i-th lower-bound constraint together with all the j-th upper-bound constraints with $j \neq i$ from (5). Formally:*

$$\varepsilon_i \geqslant \varepsilon_i^- \quad \textit{with} \quad \varepsilon_i^- = e_i^T \cdot (1 - D_i \cdot \Lambda)^{-1} \cdot \eta,$$

where D_i is the order p diagonal matrix defined by $(D_i)_{ii} = -1$ and $(D_i)_{jj} = 1$ for $j \neq i$.

Remark 2.6. *Contrary to the one-dimensional case, ε_i^- may be negative (we then round it to 0): the overestimation factor of ε_i^+ provided by Theorem 2.4 is not controlled. A tighter enclosure can be obtained with a more contracting T (see [7, Appendix A.2]).*

[2] Although commonly attributed to Perov [19] (in Russian), the idea of generalizing the Banach fixed-point theorem to generalized norms for investigating the componentwise errors in an iterative process first appeared in Kantorovich's work [12] (in Russian).

Proof of Theorem 2.5. Among the Inequalities (5), take the p upper-bound constraints and replace the i-th one by the corresponding lower-bound constraint. Multiply these $p-1$ upper-bound constraints by -1 to obtain the following system of inequalities:

$$(\Lambda - D_i) \cdot \varepsilon \geqslant -D_i \cdot \eta. \qquad (6)$$

From [7, Lemma A.1], $\Lambda - D_i$ is nonsingular and its inverse has nonnegative coefficients on its i-th row. Hence we can multiply (6) by $(\Lambda - D_i)^{-1}$ and only keep the resulting i-th constraint:

$$\begin{aligned} \varepsilon_i &= e_i^T \cdot (\Lambda - D_i)^{-1} \cdot (\Lambda - D_i) \cdot \varepsilon \\ &\geqslant e_i^T \cdot (\Lambda - D_i)^{-1} \cdot (-D_i) \cdot \eta = e_i^T \cdot (1 - D_i \cdot \Lambda)^{-1} \cdot \eta. \end{aligned}$$

□

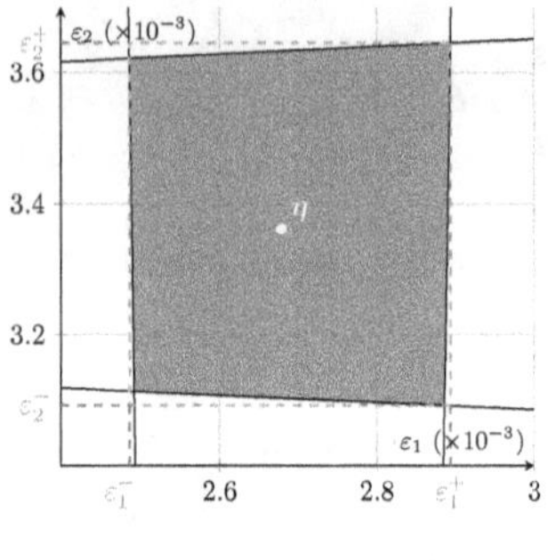

Figure 1: Error polytope for the toy example.

Lower bounds for the toy example. The polytope given by the linear constraints (5) is depicted in Figure 1. The top right vertex corresponds to $(\varepsilon_1^+, \varepsilon_2^+)$. Also, the ε_1^- (resp. ε_2^-) is given by the top left (resp. bottom right) vertex, which is consistent with Theorem 2.5. This gives the following numerical enclosures:

$$\begin{aligned} \varepsilon_1^- &= 2.48 \cdot 10^{-3} \leqslant \varepsilon_1 = |c^\circ - c^\star| \leqslant \varepsilon_1^+ = 2.90 \cdot 10^{-3}, \\ \varepsilon_2^- &= 3.09 \cdot 10^{-3} \leqslant \varepsilon_2 = |s^\circ - s^\star| \leqslant \varepsilon_2^+ = 3.65 \cdot 10^{-3}. \end{aligned} \qquad (7)$$

The tightness of these enclosures is discussed in [7, Appendix A.2]. Roughly speaking, the ratio $\varepsilon_i^+/\varepsilon_i^-$ depends not only on Λ (like in the univariate case), but also on $\eta = d(x^\circ, \mathbf{T} \cdot x^\circ)$.

3 COMPONENTWISE VALIDATION OF CHEBYSHEV APPROXIMATIONS

We present the validation method to solve Problem 1.1. Section 3.1 contains reminders about Chebyshev approximation theory and LODEs. This leads to an efficient approximating procedure (Section 3.2). Section 3.3 presents **Algorithms 1** and **2** to create and bound a Newton-like operator associated to a given vectorial LODE, then **Algorithm 3** to compute componentwise error enclosures for any Chebyshev approximation $(\Phi_i^\circ)_{1 \leqslant i \leqslant p}$.

3.1 Reminders on Chebyshev Approximations

Chebyshev series and $\mathrm{Ч}^1$ space. The Chebyshev family of polynomials is defined by the three-term recurrence $T_{n+2} = 2XT_{n+1} - T_n$ with initial terms $T_0 = 1$ and $T_1 = X$. They satisfy the fundamental trigonometric relation $T_n(\cos\vartheta) = \cos(n\vartheta)$, from which we deduce some of their basic algebraic properties:

$$T_n T_m = \frac{1}{2}(T_{n+m} + T_{|n-m|}), \quad \int T_n = \frac{T_{n+1}}{2(n+1)} - \frac{T_{n-1}}{2(n-1)} = T_n \ (n \geqslant 2), \qquad (8)$$

and that $|T_n(t)| \leqslant 1$ for $x \in [-1, 1]$.

Let $L^2_{\mathrm{Ч}} = L^2(1/\sqrt{1-t^2})$ denote the space of real-valued measurable functions f over $[-1,1]$ such that $\int_{-1}^{1} f(t)^2/\sqrt{1-t^2}\mathrm{d}t < \infty$. The inner product

$$\langle f, g \rangle = \int_{-1}^{1} f(t) g(t)/\sqrt{1-t^2}\mathrm{d}t = \int_0^\pi f(\cos\vartheta) g(\cos\vartheta)\mathrm{d}\vartheta,$$

defines a Hilbert space structure over $L^2_{\mathrm{Ч}}$, for which the Chebyshev polynomials form a complete orthogonal system. To any continuous function f in this space we can associate its Chebyshev coefficients:

$$[f]_n = \begin{cases} \frac{1}{\pi} \int_0^\pi f(\cos\vartheta)\mathrm{d}\vartheta, & \text{if } n = 0, \\ \frac{2}{\pi} \int_0^\pi f(\cos\vartheta)\cos(n\vartheta)\mathrm{d}\vartheta, & \text{if } n > 0. \end{cases}$$

Hence, the truncated Chebyshev series $f^{[N]} = \pi_N \cdot f := \sum_{n=0}^{N} [f]_n T_n$ of f is the orthogonal projection of f onto the finite-dimensional subspace spanned by $T_0, \dots, T_N$. In addition to the $L^2_{\mathrm{Ч}}$ convergence, and analogously to Fourier series, Chebyshev series have excellent approximation properties [6]. For example, if f is of class C^r over $[-1,1]$ with $r \geqslant 1$, then $f^{[N]}$ uniformly converges to f in $O(N^{-r})$, and the convergence is even exponential for analytic functions.

We call $\mathrm{Ч}^1$ the Banach space of continuous functions with absolutely summable Chebyshev series, with norm $\|f\|_{\mathrm{Ч}^1} = \sum_{n \geqslant 0} |[f]_n|$. Note that $\mathrm{Ч}^1$ is analogous to the Wiener algebra $A(\mathbb{T})$ of absolutely convergent Fourier series [13, §I.6]: for $f \in \mathrm{Ч}^1$, we have $\|f\|_{\mathrm{Ч}^1} = \|f(\cos)\|_{A(\mathbb{T})}$. We obtain a Banach algebra structure: $\|fg\|_{\mathrm{Ч}^1} \leqslant \|f\|_{\mathrm{Ч}^1} \|g\|_{\mathrm{Ч}^1}$. Moreover, this norm is a safe overestimation of the uniform norm:

$$\|f\|_{\mathrm{Ч}^1} \geqslant \sup_{-1 \leqslant t \leqslant 1} \sum_{n \geqslant 0} |[f]_n T_n(t)| \geqslant \sup_{-1 \leqslant t \leqslant 1} |f(t)| = \|f\|_\infty.$$

Given an endomorphism $\mathbf{F} : \mathrm{Ч}^1 \to \mathrm{Ч}^1$, the operator norm induced by the $\mathrm{Ч}^1$ norm is given by:

$$\|\mathbf{F}\|_{\mathrm{Ч}^1} = \sup_{\|f\|_{\mathrm{Ч}^1} \leqslant 1} \|\mathbf{F} \cdot f\|_{\mathrm{Ч}^1} = \sup_{n \geqslant 0} \|\mathbf{F} \cdot T_n\|_{\mathrm{Ч}^1}. \qquad (9)$$

This corresponds to the maximum sum of the coefficients in absolute value over all columns of the matrix representation of $\mathbf{F}$.

D-finite equations and integral transforms. We consider a generic p-dimensional order r system of LODEs over the compact interval $[-1, 1]$:

$$Y^{(r)} + A_{r-1}(t) \cdot Y^{(r-1)} + \dots + A_1(t) \cdot Y' + A_0(t) \cdot Y = G(t), \quad (10)$$

of unknown $Y = (Y_1, \dots, Y_p) : [-1,1] \to \mathbb{R}^p$, with polynomial coefficients $A_k = (a_{kij})_{1 \leqslant i,j \leqslant p} \in \mathcal{M}_p(\mathbb{R}[t])$ and right-hand side $G = (G_1, \dots, G_p) \in \mathbb{R}[t]^p$. We also fix initial conditions at -1:

$$Y^{(i)}(-1) = v_i, \qquad v_i \in \mathbb{R}^p, \quad \text{for all } i \in [\![0, r-1]\!]. \qquad (11)$$

Together, (1) and (11) form an *Initial Value Problem* (IVP).

Several barriers arise when working directly on a differential equation (1): the differentiation of Chebyshev polynomials does not admit a compact formula, whence a dense linear system to solve, and, from the theoretical point of view, the space $\mathrm{Ч}^1$ is not stable under differentiation. A common way to circumvent these limitations is to apply an integral transform onto the IVP problem so as to obtain an equivalent *Volterra integral equation of the second kind* over $[-1, 1]$:

$$\Phi + \mathbf{K} \cdot \Phi = \Psi, \quad \text{with} \quad \mathbf{K} \cdot \Phi(t) = \int_{-1}^{t} K(t,s) \cdot \Phi(s)\mathrm{d}s, \qquad (12)$$

with a bivariate polynomial kernel $K = (k_{ij})_{1 \leqslant i,j \leqslant p} \in \mathcal{M}_p(\mathbb{R}[t,s])$ and right-hand side $\Psi = (\Psi_1, \dots, \Psi_p) \in \mathbb{R}[t]^p$. Depending on the integral transform, the unknown function $\Phi = (\Phi_1, \ldots, \Phi_p) : [-1, 1] \to \mathbb{R}^p$ can be either Y or one of its derivatives. For example, [5] acts over Y, whereas [8] considers the last derivative $Y^{(r)}$.

In any case, $\mathbf{K} : \Phi \mapsto \int_{-1}^{t} K(t,s) \cdot \Phi(s)ds$ is a bounded linear operator from $(\text{Ч}^1)^p$ to itself. We may describe it by blocks $\mathbf{K} = (\mathbf{K}_{ij})_{1 \leqslant i,j \leqslant p}$, where each $\mathbf{K}_{ij}$ is a one-dimensional integral operator of kernel $k_{ij}(t,s)$. By decomposing $k_{ij}(t,s)$ in Chebyshev basis with respect to s, we obtain unique polynomials $b_{ijk}(t)$ such that

$$k_{ij}(t,s) = \sum_{k=0}^{\kappa_{ij}} b_{ijk}(t) T_k(s), \quad \mathbf{K}_{ij} \cdot \varphi(t) = \sum_{k=0}^{\kappa_{ij}} b_{ijk}(t) \int_{-1}^{t} T_k(s)\varphi(s)ds.$$

Consequently to the multiplication and integration formulas (8), the (infinite dimensional) matrix representation of $\mathbf{K}_{ij} : \text{Ч}^1 \to \text{Ч}^1$ has a so-called (h_{ij}, d_{ij}) *almost-banded* structure [17], meaning that the nonzero entries are located on the h_{ij} first rows (*horizontal band* with *initial entries*) and the diagonal plus the first d_{ij} upper and lower diagonals (*diagonal band* with *diagonal entries*), with $h_{ij} = \max_{0 \leqslant k \leqslant \kappa_{ij}} \deg b_{ijk}(t)$ and $d_{ij} = 1 + \deg k_{ij}(t,s) = 1 + \max_{0 \leqslant k \leqslant \kappa_{ij}} (k + \deg b_{ijk}(t))$ (see Figure 2(a)).

3.2 Efficient numerical solving

The integral equation (12) is an infinite-dimensional linear system over the Chebyshev coefficients of the unknown function Φ. The *projection method* (also sometimes called *Galerkin method* [10]) consists in truncating for a given index N_{app} and solving the obtained finite-dimensional linear system. In our case, this can be efficiently done by taking advantage of its sparse structure.

Define the N_{app}-th truncation of $\mathbf{K}$ as $\mathbf{K}^{[N_{\text{app}}]} = (\mathbf{K}_{ij}^{[N_{\text{app}}]})_{1 \leqslant i,j \leqslant p}$, where $\Pi_{N_{\text{app}}} \cdot \mathbf{K}_{ij} \cdot \Pi_{N_{\text{app}}}$ (see Figure 2(b)). It is represented by the order $p(N_{\text{app}} + 1)$ square matrix depicted by blocks in Figure 2(c). By permuting the natural basis $\mathcal{B}_{p,N_{\text{app}}}$ of $(\Pi_{N_{\text{app}}} \cdot \text{Ч}^1)^p$ into $\mathcal{B}'_{p,N_{\text{app}}}$:

$$\begin{aligned} \mathcal{B}_{p,N_{\text{app}}} &= (T_0 e_1, \ldots, T_{N_{\text{app}}} e_1, \ldots\ldots, T_0 e_p, \ldots, T_{N_{\text{app}}} e_p), \\ \mathcal{B}'_{p,N_{\text{app}}} &= (T_0 e_1, \ldots, T_0 e_p, \ldots\ldots, T_{N_{\text{app}}} e_1, \ldots, T_{N_{\text{app}}} e_p), \end{aligned} \tag{13}$$

$\mathbf{K}^{[N_{\text{app}}]}$ recovers a (ph, pd) almost-banded structure, where $h = \max_{ij} h_{ij}$ and $d = \max_{ij} d_{ij}$ (see Figure 2(d)).

Hence, solving the approximate problem:

$$\Phi + \mathbf{K}^{[N_{\text{app}}]} \cdot \Phi = \Psi$$

requires $O(p^3 N_{\text{app}} d^2)$ operations, using the algorithm of [17] for solving almost-banded linear systems.

3.3 Validation Procedure

We extend the validation procedure of [8] to the vectorial case. We prove the main Theorem 1.2 in order to solve Problem 1.1 in two steps: (1) a Newton-like validation operator is created and bounded by **Algorithm 1**. This first step is independent of the approximation degree N_{app}. (2) The error enclosure of the given approximation is computed by **Algorithm 3**, following Theorems 2.4 and 2.5.

Newton-like validation operator. Following the idea of Newton's method and similar approaches, Equation (12) is transformed into the fixed-point equation:

$$\mathbf{T} \cdot \Phi = \Phi, \qquad \mathbf{T} \cdot \Phi := \Phi - \mathbf{A} \cdot (\Phi + \mathbf{K} \cdot \Phi - \Psi), \tag{14}$$

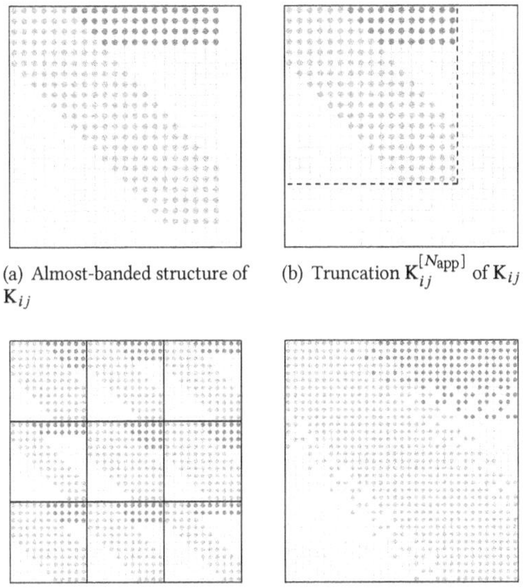

(a) Almost-banded structure of $\mathbf{K}_{ij}$
(b) Truncation $\mathbf{K}_{ij}^{[N_{\text{app}}]}$ of $\mathbf{K}_{ij}$
(c) $\mathbf{K}^{[N_{\text{app}}]}$ in $\mathcal{B}_{p,N_{\text{app}}}$, by blocks ($p = 3$)
(d) $\mathbf{K}^{[N_{\text{app}}]}$ in $\mathcal{B}'_{p,Napp}$ is almost-banded

Figure 2: Almost-banded structure of integral operators

which is equivalent to (12) as soon as $\mathbf{A} : (\text{Ч}^1)^p \to (\text{Ч}^1)^p$ is injective. Moreover, $\mathbf{T}$ is an affine operator of linear part $\mathbf{DT} = \mathbf{1} - \mathbf{A} \cdot (\mathbf{1} + \mathbf{K})$. The main challenge is to efficiently compute $\mathbf{A}$ and bound $\|\mathbf{DT}\|_{(\text{Ч}^1)^p}$. This is handled by **Algorithm 1**. Similarly to numerical solving, $\mathbf{A}$ approximates $(\mathbf{1} + \mathbf{K}^{[N_{\text{val}}]})^{-1}$, for some truncation order N_{val}. Choosing N_{val} is a trade-off between proving $\mathbf{T}$ is contracting (N_{val} must be large enough so that $\|\mathbf{K} - \mathbf{K}^{[N_{\text{val}}]}\|_{(\text{Ч}^1)^p}$ is rigorously proved to be sufficiently small) and efficiency requirements (see [8] for heuristics to find N_{val}).

Once N_{val} is fixed, **Algorithm 1** first computes an approximate inverse A in floating-point (lines 1-4). Since $\mathbf{1} + \mathbf{K}^{[N_{\text{val}}]}$ is almost-banded in $\mathcal{B}'_{p,N_{\text{val}}}$, its numerical inverse can be either computed with the numerically stable algorithm of [17], or approximated by a (ph', pd') almost-banded matrix [8, **Algorithm 5**], in $O(p^3 N_{\text{val}}(h' + d')(h + d))$ operations. The operator $\mathbf{A}$ is defined by extending A to the whole space $(\text{Ч}^1)^p$ by the identity.

Second, **Algorithm 1** bounds a Lipschitz matrix for $\mathbf{T}$, as $\|\mathbf{DT}\|_{(\text{Ч}^1)^p} = (\|(\mathbf{DT})_{ij}\|_{\text{Ч}^1})_{1 \leqslant i,j \leqslant p}$, block by block, using the triangle inequality:

$$\|\mathbf{DT}\|_{\text{Ч}^1} \leqslant \|\mathbf{1} - \mathbf{A} \cdot (\mathbf{1} + \mathbf{K}^{[N_{\text{val}}]})\|_{\text{Ч}^1} + \|\mathbf{A} \cdot (\mathbf{K} - \mathbf{K}^{[N_{\text{val}}]})\|_{\text{Ч}^1}. \tag{15}$$

The first part of (15) is the *approximation error*, measuring how far $\mathbf{A}$ is from the inverse of $\mathbf{1} + \mathbf{K}^{[N_{\text{val}}]}$. This is straightforwardly bounded as Λ^A by **Algorithm 1** (lines 5-9) using $O(p^3 N_{\text{val}}(h' + d')(h + d))$ interval arithmetic operations, and the resulting bound takes into account all sources of errors: rounding errors, sparse approximation, etc. Since only additions and multiplications of matrices are involved, the use of interval arithmetics is not critical. However, if needed, the underlying floating-point precision can be increased.

The second part of (15) is the *truncation error*, because the truncated operator $\mathbf{K}^{[N_{\text{val}}]}$ only approximates $\mathbf{K}$. Let E_{ij} be the (i,j)

block of $\mathbf{E} := \mathbf{A} \cdot (\mathbf{K} - \mathbf{K}^{[N_{\mathrm{val}}]})$:

$$\mathbf{E}_{ij} = \sum_{k=1}^{p} \mathbf{A}_{ik} \cdot (\mathbf{K}_{kj} - \mathbf{K}_{kj}^{[N_{\mathrm{val}}]}). \tag{16}$$

Algorithm 1 (lines 10-16) computes $\Lambda^T \geqslant \|\mathbf{E}\|_{(Ч^1)^p}$ by blocks, with the triangle inequality: each subterm of (16) is rigorously bounded by **Algorithm 2**. This algorithm, detailed below, requires $O((h' + d')(h + d)^2)$ interval arithmetic operations. Hence the computation of Λ^T is in $O(p^3(h' + d')(h + d)^2)$.

Finally, **Algorithm 1** computes $\Lambda = \Lambda^A + \Lambda^T$ and checks that this Lipschitz matrix is convergent to zero, in which case the constructed Newton-like operator $\mathbf{T}$ is contracting. The eigenvalues of Λ can be safely computed with interval arithmetics, for the dimension p is usually small (typically, $p \leqslant 100$).

PROOF OF THEOREM 1.2(I). The detailed description of **Algorithm 1** above proves its correctness, and the given complexity estimates for lines 1-4, 5-9 and 10-16 sum to a global complexity of $O(p^3 N_{\mathrm{val}}(h' + d')(h + d))$ operations. In the worst case, when A is dense ($h' + d' \approx N_{\mathrm{val}}$), we recover the estimate of Theorem 1.2(i). □

Truncation error bounding. From Equation (16), one needs to bound $\|\mathbf{A}_{ik} \cdot (\mathbf{K}_{kj} - \mathbf{K}_{kj}^{[N_{\mathrm{val}}]})\|_{Ч^1}$, where $\mathbf{A}_{ik}$ is the extension to $Ч^1$ of the order $N_{\mathrm{val}} + 1$ matrix A_{ik} by the identity if $i = k$, and zero otherwise. This computation is handled by **Algorithm 2**, which is a modification of [8, **Algorithm 6**], that only treats the case $i = k$.

Specifically, let $\mathbf{K}$ denote here a *one-dimensional* (h, d) almost-banded integral operator, and $\mathbf{A} : Ч^1 \to Ч^1$ the extension of an order $N_{\mathrm{val}} + 1$ matrix A by the identity or zero. We have:

$$\|\mathbf{A} \cdot (\mathbf{K} - \mathbf{K}^{[N_{\mathrm{val}}]})\|_{Ч^1} = \sup_{\ell \geqslant 0} B(\ell), \quad \text{with } B(\ell) = \|\mathbf{A} \cdot (\mathbf{K} - \mathbf{K}^{[N_{\mathrm{val}}]}) \cdot T_\ell\|_{Ч^1}.$$

Indices ℓ are divided into four groups, reflecting how the initial and diagonal coefficients are impacted by the action of $\mathbf{A}$: $[\![0, N_{\mathrm{val}} - d]\!]$, $[\![N_{\mathrm{val}} - d + 1, N_{\mathrm{val}}]\!]$, $[\![N_{\mathrm{val}} + 1, N_{\mathrm{val}} + d]\!]$ and $[\![N_{\mathrm{val}} + d + 1, +\infty]\!]$. The T_ℓ in the first group lie in the kernel. The second and third ones are explicitly computed, yielding bounds $\delta^{(1)}$ and $\delta^{(2)}$ in **Algorithm 2** (lines 1-7 and 8-13). For the infinite last group, $B(\ell)$ is decomposed as $B_I(\ell) + B_D(\ell)$, the contribution of the initial and diagonal coefficients. **Algorithm 2** uses the efficient bounding strategy of [8]. First, it computes the image of $T_{N_{\mathrm{val}}+d+1}$ for the initial and diagonal coefficients (lines 16 and 22). Then, it bounds the difference between the images of $T_{N_{\mathrm{val}}+d+1}$ and the remaining T_ℓ for $\ell > N_{\mathrm{val}} + d + 1$ to finally deduce bounds $\delta^{(3)}$ and $\delta^{(4)}$ (lines 17 and 23).

Error enclosures. Finally, **Algorithm 3** implements the validation procedure of Theorems 2.4 and 2.5 by applying the operator $\mathbf{T}$ to the candidate approximation Φ°, bounding the distance of the resulting polynomial to Φ° and producing componentwise error enclosures to $\Phi^\star$ with respect to the $Ч^1$ norm.

PROOF OF THEOREM 1.2(II). **Algorithm 3** computes $\Phi^\circ - \mathbf{T} \cdot \Phi^\circ = \mathbf{A} \cdot (\Phi^\circ + \mathbf{K} \cdot \Phi^\circ - \Psi)$. Each P_k (line 1) is a polynomial of degree at most $\max(N_{\mathrm{app}} + d, N_{\mathrm{rhs}})$, and computing its Chebyshev coefficients is in $O(pd^2 N_{\mathrm{app}} + N_{\mathrm{rhs}})$. Then, the computation of the coefficients of each $A_{ik} \cdot \pi_{N_{\mathrm{val}}} \cdot P_k$ (line 3) is in $O((h' + d') \deg(\pi_{N_{\mathrm{val}}} \cdot P_k)) = O((h' + d') \min(\max(N_{\mathrm{app}} + d, N_{\mathrm{rhs}}), N_{\mathrm{val}}))$. Finally, the complexity

---

Algorithm 1 Create and bound a Newton-like operator $\mathbf{T}$

Require: A polynomial integral operator $\mathbf{K} = (\mathbf{K}_{ij})_{1 \leqslant i, j \leqslant p}$ given by the $(b_{ijk})_{0 \leqslant k \leqslant \kappa_{ij}}^{1 \leqslant i, j \leqslant p}$, and a truncation order N_{val}.

Ensure: An approximate inverse $\mathbf{A}$ of $1 + \mathbf{K}^{[N_{\mathrm{val}}]}$ and a certified Lipschitz matrix Λ for $1 - \mathbf{A} \cdot (1 + \mathbf{K})$, or fail if N_{val} not large enough.

   ▷ *Compute an approximate inverse matrix A.*

1: $M = (M_{ij})_{1 \leqslant i, j \leqslant p} \leftarrow 1 + \mathbf{K}^{[N_{\mathrm{val}}]}$, by blocks

2: $M' \leftarrow M$ in basis $\mathcal{B}'_{p, N_{\mathrm{val}}}$

3: $A' \leftarrow$ a numerical approximate inverse of M', either dense or almost-banded.

4: $A = (A_{ij})_{1 \leqslant i, j \leqslant p} \leftarrow A'$ in basis $\mathcal{B}_{p, N_{\mathrm{val}}}$, by blocks

   ▷ *Compute the approx error $\Lambda^A = (\lambda_{ij}^A)$ in interval arith.*

5: **for** $i = 1$ **to** p and $j = 1$ **to** p **do**

6:    $C \leftarrow \sum_{1 \leqslant k \leqslant p} A_{ik} \cdot M_{kj}$

7:    **if** $i = j$ **then** $C \leftarrow C - 1_{N_{\mathrm{val}}+1}$

8:    $\lambda_{ij}^A \leftarrow \|C\|_{Ч^1}$

9: **end for**

   ▷ *Compute the trunc error $\Lambda^T = (\lambda_{ij}^T)$ in interval arith.*

10: **for** $i = 1$ **to** p and $j = 1$ **to** p **do**

11:    $\lambda_{ij}^T \leftarrow 0$

12:    **for** $k = 1$ **to** p **do**

13:      $\delta \leftarrow$ **Algorithm 2** on $\mathbf{K}_{jk}, A_{ik}$ and $diag := (i = k)$.

14:      $\lambda_{ij}^T \leftarrow \lambda_{ij}^T + \delta$

15:    **end for**

16: **end for**

   ▷ *Compute Λ and check if $\mathbf{T}$ contracting.*

17: $\Lambda \leftarrow \Lambda^A + \Lambda^T$

18: **if** $\rho(\Lambda) < 1$ **then**

19:    **return** A, Λ

20: **else**

21:    **print** "Fail, Λ is not convergent to 0"

22: **end if**

---

of computing the enclosures (lines 6-7) only depends on p, and is therefore negligible. The overall complexity is:

$$O(p^2 d^2 N_{\mathrm{app}} + p N_{\mathrm{rhs}} + p^2(h' + d') \min(\max(N_{\mathrm{app}} + d, N_{\mathrm{rhs}}), N_{\mathrm{val}})),$$

which gives the estimate of Theorem 1.2(ii) when $h', d' \approx N_{\mathrm{val}}$. □

Estimating N_{val}. The following theorem (proved in [7, Appendix A.3]) provides a worst-case estimate for the minimal value of N_{val}. Although theoretically interesting, this exponential bound is overpessimistic for a wide range of examples.

THEOREM 3.1. *Let $B_{ij} = \sum_{k=0}^{\kappa_{ij}} \|b_{ijk}\|_{Ч^1}$ and $B = (B_{ij})_{1 \leqslant i, j \leqslant p}$. (i) The following bound estimates the minimal possible value for N_{val} making **Algorithm 1** produce a contracting Newton-like operator:*

$$N_{\mathrm{val}} = O\left(d\rho(B)^2 \exp(2\rho(B))\right),$$

*where $\rho(B)$ denotes the spectral radius of B. (ii) For a given approximation Φ° of $\Phi^\star$ and in order that **Algorithm 3** computes error enclosures $[\varepsilon_i^-, \varepsilon_i^+]$ for $\varepsilon_i = \|\Phi_i^\circ - \Phi_i^\star\|_{Ч^1}$ with $\varepsilon_i^+ / \varepsilon_i^- \leqslant \kappa$ (for some $\kappa > 1$), N_{val} for **Algorithm 1** must be at*

Algorithm 2 Bound the truncation error

Require: A polynomial (one-dimensional) integral operator $\mathbf{K}$ given by the $(b_k)_{0 \leqslant k \leqslant \kappa}$, a truncation order N_{val}, a $N_{\text{val}} + 1$ order square matrix A, and a Boolean *diag*.

Ensure: An upper bound δ for $\|\mathbf{A} \cdot (\mathbf{K} - \mathbf{K}^{[N_{\text{val}}]})\|_{Ч^1}$, where $\mathbf{A}$ is the extension of A to the whole space $Ч^1$ by the identity if $diag = true$, and by zero otherwise.

▷ ***All operations are performed in interval arithmetics***

▷ *Compute* $\delta^{(1)} \geqslant \sup_{\ell \in \llbracket N_{\text{val}}-d+1, N_{\text{val}} \rrbracket} B(\ell)$

$\delta^{(1)} \leftarrow 0$
if *diag* **then**
  for $\ell = N_{\text{val}} - d + 1$ **to** N_{val} **do**
    $P \leftarrow (\mathbf{1} - \Pi_{N_{\text{val}}}) \cdot \mathbf{K} \cdot T_\ell$
    if $\|P\|_{Ч^1} > \delta^{(1)}$ **then** $\delta^{(1)} \leftarrow \|P\|_{Ч^1}$
  end for
end if

▷ *Compute* $\delta^{(2)} \geqslant \sup_{\ell \in \llbracket N_{\text{val}}+1, N_{\text{val}}+d \rrbracket} B(\ell)$

$\delta^{(2)} \leftarrow 0$
for $\ell = N_{\text{val}} + 1$ **to** $N_{\text{val}} + d$ **do**
  $P \leftarrow A \cdot \Pi_{N_{\text{val}}} \cdot \mathbf{K} \cdot T_\ell$
  if *diag* **then** $P \leftarrow P + (\mathbf{1} - \Pi_{N_{\text{val}}}) \cdot \mathbf{K} \cdot T_\ell$
  if $\|P\|_{Ч^1} > \delta^{(2)}$ **then** $\delta^{(2)} \leftarrow \|P\|_{Ч^1}$
end for

▷ *Compute* $\delta^{(3)} \geqslant \sup_{\ell \geqslant N_{\text{val}}+d+1} B_D(\ell)$

$\ell_0 \leftarrow N_{\text{val}} + d + 1$ **and** $B \leftarrow \sum_{k=0}^{\kappa} \|b_k\|_{Ч^1}$
if *diag* **then**
  $P \leftarrow (\mathbf{1} - \Pi_{N_{\text{val}}}) \cdot \mathbf{K} \cdot T_{\ell_0}$
  $\delta^{(3)} \leftarrow \|P\|_{Ч^1} + \frac{(\kappa+1)B}{(\ell_0-(\kappa-1))^2}$
else
  $\delta^{(3)} \leftarrow 0$
end if

▷ *Compute* $\delta^{(4)} \geqslant \sup_{\ell \geqslant N_{\text{val}}+d+1} B_I(\ell)$

$B' \leftarrow \sum_{k=0}^{\kappa} \|A \cdot b_k\|_{Ч^1}$
$P \leftarrow A \cdot \Pi_{N_{\text{val}}} \cdot \mathbf{K} \cdot T_{\ell_0}$
$\delta^{(4)} \leftarrow \|P\|_{Ч^1} + \frac{(\kappa+1)^3 B'}{(\ell_0^2-(\kappa+1)^2)^2}$
$\delta \leftarrow \max(\delta^{(1)}, \delta^{(2)}, \delta^{(3)} + \delta^{(4)})$
return δ

least:

$$N_{\text{val}} = O\left(\frac{\nu}{\kappa - 1} d \|B\|_\infty^2 \exp(2\|B\|_\infty)\right),$$

with $\nu = \max_{1 \leqslant i \leqslant p} \|\varepsilon\|_\infty / \varepsilon_i$, $\|\varepsilon\|_\infty = \max_{1 \leqslant i \leqslant p} \varepsilon_i$ *and* $\|B\|_\infty = \max_{1 \leqslant i \leqslant p} \sum_{j=1}^{p} B_{ij}$ *the associated operator norm.*

4 EXAMPLE AND DISCUSSION

Consider the following order 1, two-dimensional system, for $x \in [0, a]$ with $a > 0$, whose solutions (depicted in Figure 3) are highly oscillating functions. Rescale it over $[-1, 1]$ with the change of variable $x = \frac{a}{2}(1 + t)$:

$$\left\{ \begin{array}{l} y_1' = -x^n y_2 \\ y_2' = x^m y_1 \\ y_1(0) = 1, y_2(0) = 0 \end{array} \right. \Rightarrow \left\{ \begin{array}{l} Y_1' = -\left(\frac{a}{2}\right)^{n+1} (1+t)^n Y_2 \\ Y_2' = \left(\frac{a}{2}\right)^{m+1} (1+t)^m Y_1 \\ Y_1(-1) = 1, Y_2(-1) = 0 \end{array} \right. . \tag{17}$$

Algorithm 3 Validate a candidate solution of an integral equation

Require: A polynomial integral operator $\mathbf{K} = (\mathbf{K}_{ij})_{1 \leqslant i,j \leqslant p}$ given by the $(b_{ijk})_{0 \leqslant k \leqslant \kappa_{ij}}^{1 \leqslant i,j \leqslant p}$, a polynomial right-hand side $\Psi = (\Psi_1, \ldots, \Psi_p)$, a truncation order N_{val}, (A, Λ) obtained from **Algorithm 1** with Λ convergent to 0, and a candidate solution $\Phi^\circ = (\Phi_1^\circ, \ldots, \Phi_p^\circ)$.

Ensure: Two vectors of upper and lower bounds ε^+ and ε^- such that $\|\Phi_i^\circ - \Phi_i^\star\|_{Ч^1} \in [\varepsilon_i^-, \varepsilon_i^+]$ for $1 \leqslant i \leqslant p$.

▷ ***All operations are performed in interval arithmetics***

for $k = 1$ **to** p **do** $P_k \leftarrow \Phi_k + \sum_{j=1}^{p} \mathbf{K}_{kj} \cdot \Phi_j^\circ - \Psi_k$
for $i = 1$ **to** p **do**
  $Q_i \leftarrow \sum_{k=1}^{p} A_{ik} \cdot \Pi_{N_{\text{val}}} \cdot P_k + (\mathbf{1} - \Pi_n) \cdot P_i$
  $\eta_i \leftarrow \|Q_i\|_{Ч^1}$
end for
$\varepsilon^+ \leftarrow (1 - \Lambda)^{-1} \cdot \eta$
for $i = 1$ **to** p **do** $\varepsilon_i^- \leftarrow \left((1 - D_i \cdot \Lambda)^{-1} \cdot \eta\right)_i$
return ε^+ and ε^-

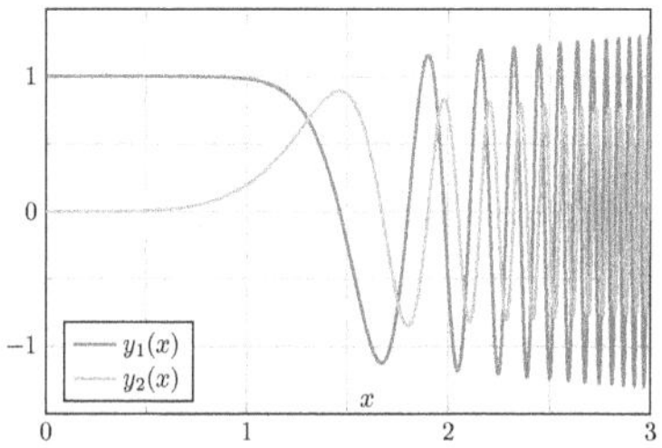

Figure 3: Solution of (17) **with** $n = 5$, $m = 4$ **and** $a = 3$

We give two different integral transforms associated to this equation. The integral transform described in [5] consists in integrating Equation (17) once, resulting into an integral equation for Y with polynomial kernel and right-hand side given by:

$$K(t, s) = \begin{pmatrix} 0 & \left(\frac{a}{2}\right)^{n+1} (1+s)^n \\ -\left(\frac{a}{2}\right)^{m+1} (1+s)^m & 0 \end{pmatrix}, \qquad \Psi(t) = \begin{pmatrix} 1 \\ 0 \end{pmatrix}.$$

$K(t, s)$, which is of degree 0 in t, is decomposed over the Chebyshev basis with respect to s into constant polynomials $b_{001}, b_{101}, \ldots, b_{n01}$ and $b_{010}, b_{110}, \ldots, b_{m10}$.

On the other side, the integral transform used in [8] allows us to validate the derivative $\Phi = Y'$. The polynomial kernel and right-hand side are:

$$K(t, s) = \begin{pmatrix} 0 & \left(\frac{a}{2}\right)^{n+1} (1+t)^n \\ -\left(\frac{a}{2}\right)^{m+1} (1+t)^m & 0 \end{pmatrix}, \qquad \Psi(t) = \begin{pmatrix} \left(\frac{a}{2}\right)^{n+1} (1+t)^n \\ 0 \end{pmatrix}.$$

Now, $K(t, s)$ is of degree 0 with respect to s, giving two polynomials b_{001} and b_{010} of respective degrees n and m.

Let's now focus on the first integral transform, with $n = 5$, $m = 4$, $a = 3$. Using the spectral method explained in Section 3.1 and implemented in our C library, we fix an approximation degree $N_{\text{app}} = 100$ and obtain numerical approximations Y_1° and Y_2°, that must now be validated. The whole implemented procedure automatically computes and bounds for increasing values of N_{val} the Newton-like operator $\mathbf{T}$ associated to the truncated operator $\mathbf{K}^{[N_{\text{val}}]}$. The approximate inverse is computed as an $(2h', 2d')$ almost-banded order

$2(N_{\text{val}}+1)$ matrix. This process stops as soon as the total Lipschitz matrix returned by **Algorithm 1** has a spectral radius less than 1. In case of failure of **Algorithm 1**, the procedure is relaunched with $N_{\text{val}} \leftarrow 2N_{\text{val}}$. For this example, we obtain $N_{\text{val}} = 1664$, $h' = 48$ and $d' = 304$, giving the following Lipschitz matrix:

$$\Lambda = \begin{pmatrix} 9.73 \cdot 10^{-4} & 9.89 \cdot 10^{-2} \\ 3.60 \cdot 10^{-2} & 9.92 \cdot 10^{-2} \end{pmatrix}, \qquad \rho(\Lambda) = 6.06 \cdot 10^{-2}.$$

The last step is performed by **Algorithm 3**. Given the numerical approximations Y_1° and Y_2°, it computes $\eta = \|Y^\circ - \mathbf{T} \cdot Y^\circ\|_{(\mathbb{Y}^1)^2}$ (the examples gives $\eta_1 = 3.20 \cdot 10^{-3}$ and $\eta_2 = 1.91 \cdot 10^{-3}$) and outputs the error enclosures given by Theorems 2.4 and 2.5:

$$\varepsilon_1^- = 2.99 \cdot 10^{-3}, \qquad \varepsilon_1^+ = 3.41 \cdot 10^{-3},$$
$$\varepsilon_2^- = 1.78 \cdot 10^{-3}, \qquad \varepsilon_2^+ = 2.04 \cdot 10^{-3}.$$

This whole process for this example takes about 30 seconds on a modern computer.

Comparison with decoupling/desingularization. In the case of polynomial coefficients, an alternative consists in decoupling the system to obtain p scalar LODEs of order p, at the cost of introducing singularities in the equations. As an example, the first component y_1 in (17) satisfies the following differential equation:

$$xy_1'' - ny_1' + x^{n+m+1}y_1 = 0. \tag{18}$$

This equation is *singular* (its leading coefficient vanishes at 0), so our validation method cannot be used. However, with *desingularization* techniques [1], one obtains a higher order but nonsingular equation, whose set of solutions (strictly) contains the ones of the singular equation. In our example, by differentiating Equation (18) n times and dividing the result by x:

$$y_1^{(n+2)} + \frac{1}{x}\frac{\mathrm{d}^n}{\mathrm{d}x^n}(x^{n+m+1}y_1) = 0. \tag{19}$$

By inverting the roles of n and m, one obtains a similar equation for y_2. Hence, validating the approximation y of (17) can be done with the validation algorithm of [8]. Several caveats must therefore be raised. Applying the integral operator of [8] results into a totally intractable problem, since the minimal value for proving that $\mathbf{T}$ is contracting is far too large (in practice, we stopped at $N_{\text{val}} \simeq 10^6$). This is due to the fact that this transform is used to validate the last derivative $y_1^{(n+2)}$, which increases very rapidly due to the highly oscillating behavior of y_1. On the other hand, the integral transform of [5] yields a far more tractable problem: a truncation order $N_{\text{val}} = 750$ is sufficient for our example. However, Equation (19) is very ill-conditioned because of the factorial terms created by the n differentiations. For instance, with classical double precision (53 bits), the scalar validation procedure is able to produce and bound a contracting Newton-like operator $\mathbf{T}$ (**Algorithm 1**), but **Algorithm 3** outputs an upper bound $\varepsilon_1^+ = 2.57$, which is 3 orders of magnitude larger than what was found with the vector-valued validation method.

The non D-finite case. In the case of nonpolynomial coefficients, there is no general method to decouple and desingularize the system. Moreover, these coefficients may not be known exactly, but only given as polynomial approximations together with rigorous error bounds. We believe that in such a general case, the vector-valued approach presented in this article is essential to approximate and validate the solution. For example, a successful application of our method to a station keeping problem of a satellite is given in [3].

Future extensions include: validated expansions in other orthogonal polynomial bases for LODEs; automation and complexity analysis for some classes of nonlinear ODEs; formally proving this method in a proof assistant.

Heartfelt acknowledgments are extended to Mioara Joldeş and Nicolas Brisebarre for their extraordinary support in the writing of this article, to Bruno Salvy for instructive discussions about D-finite functions, to Bogdan Pasca for his friendly culinary support.

This work was partially funded by the ANR FastRelax project.

REFERENCES

[1] S. A. Abramov, M. A. Barkatou, and M. Van Hoeij. Apparent singularities of linear difference equations with polynomial coefficients. *Appl. Algebra Eng. Commun. Comput.*, 17(2):117–133, 2006.

[2] R. P. Agarwal. Contraction and approximate contraction with an application to multi-point boundary value problems. *J. Comput. Appl. Math.*, 9(4):315–325, 1983.

[3] P. R. Arantes Gilz, F. Bréhard, and C. Gazzino. Validated Semi-Analytical Transition Matrix for Linearized Relative Spacecraft Dynamics via Chebyshev Polynomials. In *2018 Space Flight Mechanics Meeting, AIAA Science and Technology Forum and Exposition*, page 24, 2018.

[4] X. Bai. *Modified Chebyshev-Picard iteration methods for solution of initial value and boundary value problems.* PhD thesis, Texas A&M University, 2010.

[5] A. Benoit, M. Joldeş, and M. Mezzarobba. Rigorous uniform approximation of D-finite functions using Chebyshev expansions. *Math. Comp.*, 86(305):1303–1341, 2017.

[6] J. P. Boyd. *Chebyshev and Fourier spectral methods.* Dover Publications, 2001.

[7] F. Bréhard. A Newton-like Validation Method for Chebyshev Approximate Solutions of Linear Ordinary Differential Systems. Preprint (https://hal.archives-ouvertes.fr/hal-01654396v1), 2018.

[8] F. Bréhard, N. Brisebarre, and M. Joldes. Validated and numerically efficient Chebyshev spectral methods for linear ordinary differential equations. Preprint (https://hal.archives-ouvertes.fr/hal-01526272/), May 2017.

[9] C. Clenshaw and H. Norton. The solution of nonlinear ordinary differential equations in Chebyshev series. *The Computer Journal*, 6(1):88–92, 1963.

[10] D. Gottlieb and S. A. Orszag. *Numerical Analysis of Spectral Methods: Theory and Applications*, volume 26. Siam, 1977.

[11] A. Hungria, J.-P. Lessard, and J. D. Mireles James. Rigorous numerics for analytic solutions of differential equations: the radii polynomial approach. *Math. Comp.*, 85(299):1427–1459, 2016.

[12] L. Kantorovich, B. Vulikh, and A. Pinsker. Functional analysis in partially ordered spaces (in Russian). *Gostekhizdat, Moscow*, 1950.

[13] Y. Katznelson. *An introduction to harmonic analysis.* Cambridge University Press, 2004.

[14] E. W. Kaucher and W. L. Miranker. *Self-validating numerics for function space problems: Computation with guarantees for differential and integral equations*, volume 9. Elsevier, 1984.

[15] J.-P. Lessard and C. Reinhardt. Rigorous numerics for nonlinear differential equations using Chebyshev series. *SIAM J. Numer. Anal.*, 52(1):1–22, 2014.

[16] O. M. Nica-Bolojan. *Fixed point methods for nonlinear differential systems with nonlocal conditions.* PhD thesis, Babes-Bolyai University of Cluj-Napoca, 2013.

[17] S. Olver and A. Townsend. A fast and well-conditioned spectral method. *SIAM Review*, 55(3):462–489, 2013.

[18] J. M. Ortega and W. C. Rheinboldt. *Iterative solution of nonlinear equations in several variables.* SIAM, 1970.

[19] A. I. Perov. On the Cauchy problem for a system of ordinary differential equations. *Približ. Metod. Rešen. Differencial'. Uravnen. Vyp.*, 2:115–134, 1964.

[20] R. Precup. The role of matrices that are convergent to zero in the study of semilinear operator systems. *Math. Comput. Model.*, 49(3):703–708, 2009.

[21] F. Robert. *Étude et utilisation de normes vectorielles en analyse numérique linéaire (in French).* PhD thesis, Université de Grenoble, 1968.

[22] L. N. Trefethen. *Approximation Theory and Approximation Practice.* SIAM, 2013. See http://www.chebfun.org/ATAP/.

[23] J. B. van den Berg and J.-P. Lessard. Rigorous numerics in dynamics. *Notices of the AMS*, 62(9), 2015.

[24] N. Yamamoto. A numerical verification method for solutions of boundary value problems with local uniqueness by Banach's fixed-point theorem. *SIAM J. Numer. Anal.*, 35(5):2004–2013, 1998.

[25] T. Yamamoto. A unified derivation of several error bounds for Newton's process. *J. Comput. Appl. Math.*, 12:179–191, 1985.

Enumeration of Complex Golay Pairs via Programmatic SAT

Curtis Bright
University of Waterloo

Ilias Kotsireas
Wilfrid Laurier University

Albert Heinle
University of Waterloo

Vijay Ganesh
University of Waterloo

ABSTRACT

We provide a complete enumeration of all complex Golay pairs of length up to 25, verifying that complex Golay pairs do not exist in lengths 23 and 25 but do exist in length 24. This independently verifies work done by F. Fiedler in 2013 [11] that confirms the 2002 conjecture of Craigen, Holzmann, and Kharaghani [8] that complex Golay pairs of length 23 don't exist. Our enumeration method relies on the recently proposed SAT+CAS paradigm of combining computer algebra systems with SAT solvers to take advantage of the advances made in the fields of symbolic computation and satisfiability checking. The enumeration proceeds in two stages: First, we use a fine-tuned computer program and functionality from computer algebra systems to construct a list containing all sequences which could appear as the first sequence in a complex Golay pair (up to equivalence). Second, we use a programmatic SAT solver to construct all sequences (if any) that pair off with the sequences constructed in the first stage to form a complex Golay pair.

KEYWORDS

Complex Golay pairs; Boolean satisfiability; SAT solvers; Exhaustive search; Autocorrelation

ACM Reference Format:

Curtis Bright, Ilias Kotsireas, Albert Heinle, and Vijay Ganesh. 2018. Enumeration of Complex Golay Pairs via Programmatic SAT. In *ISSAC '18: 2018 ACM International Symposium on Symbolic and Algebraic Computation, July 16–19, 2018, New York, NY, USA.* ACM, New York, NY, USA, 8 pages. https://doi.org/10.1145/3208976.3209006

1 INTRODUCTION

The sequences which are now referred to *Golay sequences* or *Golay pairs* were first introduced by Marcel Golay in his groundbreaking 1949 paper [18] on multislit spectrometry. He later formally defined them in a 1961 paper [17] where he referred to them as *complementary series*. Since then, Golay pairs and their generalizations have been widely studied for both their elegant theoretical properties and a surprising number of practical applications. For example, they have been applied to radar pulse compression [20], Wi-Fi networks [25], train wheel detection systems [10], optical time domain reflectometry [27], and medical ultrasounds [28]. Golay pairs consist of two sequences and the property that makes them special is, roughly speaking, the fact that one sequence's "correlation" with itself is the inverse of the other sequence's "correlation" with itself; see Definition 2.2 in Section 2 for the formal definition.

Although Golay defined his complementary series over an alphabet of $\{\pm1\}$, later authors have generalized the alphabet to include nonreal roots of unity such as the fourth root of unity $i = \sqrt{-1}$. In this paper, we focus on the case where the alphabet is $\{\pm1, \pm i\}$. In this case the resulting sequence pairs are sometimes referred to as *4-phase* or *quaternary* Golay pairs though we will simply refer to them as *complex* Golay pairs. If a complex Golay pair of length n exists then we say that n is a *complex Golay number.*

Complex Golay pairs have been extensively studied by many authors. They were originally introduced in 1994 by Craigen in order to expand the orders of Hadamard matrices attainable via (ordinary) Golay pairs [7]. In 1994, Holzmann and Kharaghani enumerated all complex Golay pairs up to length 13 [19]. In 2002, Craigen, Holzmann, and Kharaghani enumerated all complex Golay pairs to 19, reported that 21 was not a complex Golay number, and conjectured that 23 was not a complex Golay number [8].

In 2006, Fiedler, Jedwab, and Parker provided a construction which explained the existence of all known complex Golay pairs whose lengths were a power of 2 [12, 13], including complex Golay pairs of length 16 discovered by Li and Chu [23] to not fit into a construction given by Davis and Jedwab [9]. In 2010, Gibson and Jedwab provided a construction which explained the existence of all complex Golay pairs up to length 26 and gave a table that listed the total number of complex Golay pairs up to length 26 [16]. This table was produced by the mathematician Frank Fiedler, who described his enumeration method in a 2013 paper [11] where he also reported that 27 and 28 are not complex Golay numbers.

In this paper we give an enumeration method which can be used to verify the table produced by Fiedler that appears in Gibson and Jedwab's paper; this table contains counts for the total number of complex Golay pairs and the total number of sequences which appear as a member of a complex Golay pair. We implemented our method and obtained counts up to length 25 after about a day of computing on a cluster with 25 cores. The counts we obtain match those in Fiedler's table in each case, increasing the confidence that the enumeration was performed without error. In addition, we also provide counts for the total number of complex Golay pairs up to well-known equivalence operations [19] and explicitly make available the sequences online [6]. To our knowledge, this is the first time that explicit complex Golay pairs (and their counts up to equivalence) have been published for lengths larger than 19. Lastly, we publicly release our code for enumerating complex Golay pairs so that others may verify and reproduce our work; we were not

ISSAC '18, July 16–19, 2018, New York, NY, USA

ACM ISBN 978-1-4503-5550-6/18/07...$15.00
https://doi.org/10.1145/3208976.3209006

able to find any other code for enumerating complex Golay pairs which was publicly available.

Our result is of interest not only because of the verification we provide but also because of the method we use to perform the verification. The method proceeds in two stages. In the first stage, a fine-tuned computer program performs an exhaustive search among all sequences which could possibly appear as the first sequence in a complex Golay pair of a given length (up to an equivalence defined in Section 2). Several filtering theorems which we describe in Section 2 allow us to discard almost all sequences from consideration. To apply these filtering theorems we use functionality from the computer algebra system MAPLE [26] and the mathematical library FFTW [14]. After this filtering is completed we have a list of sequences of a manageable size such that the first sequence of every complex Golay pair of a given length (up to equivalence) appears in the list.

In the second stage, we use the programmatic SAT solver MAPLE-SAT [24] to determine which sequences from the first stage (if any) can be paired up with another sequence to form a complex Golay pair. A SAT instance is constructed from each sequence found in the first stage such that the SAT instance is satisfiable if and only if the sequence is part of a complex Golay pair. Furthermore, in the case that the instance is satisfiable a satisfying assignment determines a sequence which forms the second half of a complex Golay pair.

This method combines both computer algebra and SAT solving and is of interest in its own right because it links the two previously separated fields of symbolic computation and satisfiability checking. Recently there has been interest in combining methods from both fields to solve computational problems as demonstrated by the SC[2] project [1, 2]. Our work fits into this paradigm and to our knowledge is the first application of a SAT solver to search for complex Golay pairs, though previous work exists which uses a SAT solver to search for other types of complementary sequences [3–5, 31].

2 BACKGROUND ON COMPLEX GOLAY PAIRS

In this section we present the background necessary to describe our method for enumerating complex Golay pairs. First, we require some preliminary definitions to define what complex Golay pairs are. Let $\overline{x}$ denote the complex conjugate of x (this is just the multiplicative inverse of x when x is ± 1 or $\pm i$).

Definition 2.1 (cf. [22]). The *nonperiodic autocorrelation function* of a sequence $A = [a_0, \dots, a_{n-1}] \in \mathbb{C}^n$ of length $n \in \mathbb{N}$ is

$$N_A(s) := \sum_{k=0}^{n-s-1} a_k \overline{a_{k+s}}, \qquad s = 0, \dots, n-1.$$

Definition 2.2. A pair of sequences (A, B) with A and B in $\{\pm 1, \pm i\}^n$ are called a *complex Golay pair* if the sum of their nonperiodic autocorrelations is a constant zero for $s \neq 0$, i.e.,

$$N_A(s) + N_B(s) = 0 \qquad \text{for} \qquad s = 1, \dots, n-1.$$

Note that if A and B are in $\{\pm 1, \pm i\}^n$ then $N_A(0) + N_B(0) = 2n$ by the definition of the complex nonperiodic autocorrelation function and the fact that $x\overline{x} = 1$ if x is ± 1 or $\pm i$, explaining why $s \neq 0$ in Definition 2.2.

Example 2.3. $([1, 1, -1], [1, i, 1])$ is a complex Golay pair.

2.1 Equivalence operations

There are certain invertible operations which preserve the property of being a complex Golay pair when applied to a sequence pair (A, B). These are summarized in the following proposition.

PROPOSITION 2.4 (CF. [8]). *Let $([a_0, \dots, a_{n-1}], [b_0, \dots, b_{n-1}])$ be a complex Golay pair. The following are then also complex Golay pairs:*

E1. *(Reversal)* $([a_{n-1}, \dots, a_0], [b_{n-1}, \dots, b_0])$.
E2. *(Conjugate Reverse A)* $([\overline{a_{n-1}}, \dots, \overline{a_0}], [b_0, \dots, b_{n-1}])$.
E3. *(Swap)* $([b_0, \dots, b_{n-1}], [a_0, \dots, a_{n-1}])$.
E4. *(Scale A)* $([ia_0, \dots, ia_{n-1}], [b_0, \dots, b_{n-1}])$.
E5. *(Positional Scaling)* $(i \star A, i \star B)$ *where* $c \star (x_0, \dots, x_{n-1}) := (x_0, cx_1, c^2x_2, \dots, c^{n-1}x_{n-1})$.

Definition 2.5. We call two complex Golay pairs (A, B) and (A', B') *equivalent* if (A', B') can be obtained from (A, B) using the transformations described in Proposition 2.4.

2.2 Useful properties and lemmas

In this subsection we prove some useful properties that complex Golay pairs satisfy and which will be exploited by our method for enumerating complex Golay pairs. The first lemma provides a fundamental relationship that all complex Golay pairs must satisfy. To conveniently state it we use the following definition.

Definition 2.6 (cf. [8]). The *Hall polynomial* of the sequence $A := [a_0, \dots, a_{n-1}]$ is defined to be $h_A(z) := a_0 + a_1 z + \cdots + a_{n-1} z^{n-1} \in \mathbb{C}[z]$.

LEMMA 2.7 (CF. [29]). *Let (A, B) be a complex Golay pair. For every $z \in \mathbb{C}$ with $|z| = 1$, we have*

$$|h_A(z)|^2 + |h_B(z)|^2 = 2n.$$

PROOF. Since $|z| = 1$ we can write $z = e^{i\theta}$ for some $0 \le \theta < 2\pi$. Similar to the fact pointed out in [21], using Euler's identity one can derive the following expansion:

$$|h_A(z)|^2 = N_A(0) + 2\sum_{j=1}^{n-1} \big(\mathrm{Re}(N_A(j))\cos(\theta j) + \mathrm{Im}(N_A(j))\sin(\theta j)\big).$$

Since A and B form a complex Golay pair, by definition one has that $\mathrm{Re}(N_A(j) + N_B(j)) = 0$ and $\mathrm{Im}(N_A(j) + N_B(j)) = 0$ and then

$$|h_A(z)|^2 + |h_B(z)|^2 = N_A(0) + N_B(0) = 2n. \qquad \square$$

This lemma is highly useful as a condition for filtering sequences which could not possibly be part of a complex Golay pair, as explained in the following corollary.

COROLLARY 2.8. *Let $A \in \mathbb{C}^n$, $z \in \mathbb{C}$ with $|z| = 1$, and $|h_A(z)|^2 > 2n$. Then A is not a member of a complex Golay pair.*

PROOF. Suppose the sequence A was a member of a complex Golay pair whose other member was the sequence B. Since $|h_B(z)|^2 \ge 0$, we must have $|h_A(z)|^2 + |h_B(z)|^2 > 2n$, in contradiction to Lemma 2.7. $\square$

In [11], Fiedler derives the following extension of Lemma 2.7. Let A_{even} be identical to A with the entries of odd index replaced by zeros and let A_{odd} be identical to A with the entries of even index replaced by zeros.

Lemma 2.9 (cf. [11]). *Let (A, B) be a complex Golay pair. For every $z \in \mathbb{C}$ with $|z| = 1$, we have*

$$|h_{A_{\text{even}}}(z)|^2 + |h_{A_{\text{odd}}}(z)|^2 + |h_{B_{\text{even}}}(z)|^2 + |h_{B_{\text{odd}}}(z)|^2 = 2n.$$

Proof. The proof proceeds as in the proof of Lemma 2.7, except that one instead obtains that $|h_{A_{\text{even}}}(z)|^2 + |h_{A_{\text{odd}}}(z)|^2$ is equal to

$$N_A(0) + 2 \sum_{\substack{j=1 \\ j \text{ even}}}^{n-1} \big(\text{Re}(N_A(j)) \cos(\theta j) + \text{Im}(N_A(j)) \sin(\theta j)\big). \qquad \square$$

Corollary 2.10. *Let $A \in \mathbb{C}^n$, $z \in \mathbb{C}$ with $|z| = 1$, and $|h_{A'}(z)|^2 > 2n$ where A' is either A_{even} or A_{odd}. Then A is not a member of a complex Golay pair.*

Proof. If either $|h_{A_{\text{even}}}(z)|^2 > 2n$ or $|h_{A_{\text{odd}}}(z)|^2 > 2n$ then the identity in Lemma 2.9 cannot hold. □

The next lemma is useful because it allows us to write $2n$ as the sum of four integer squares. It is stated in [19] using a different notation; we use the notation resum(A) and imsum(A) to represent the real and imaginary parts of the sum of the entries of A. For example, if $A := [1, i, -i, i]$ then resum(A) = imsum$(A) = 1$.

Lemma 2.11 (cf. [19]). *Let (A, B) be a complex Golay sequence pair. Then*

$$\text{resum}(A)^2 + \text{imsum}(A)^2 + \text{resum}(B)^2 + \text{imsum}(B)^2 = 2n.$$

Proof. Using Lemma 2.7 with $z = 1$ we have

$$|\text{resum}(A) + \text{imsum}(A)i|^2 + |\text{resum}(B) + \text{imsum}(B)i|^2 = 2n.$$

Since $|\text{resum}(X) + \text{imsum}(X)i|^2 = \text{resum}(X)^2 + \text{imsum}(X)^2$ the result follows. □

The next lemma provides some normalization conditions which can be used when searching for complex Golay pairs up to equivalence. Since all complex Golay pairs (A', B') which are equivalent to a complex Golay pair (A, B) can easily be generated from (A, B), it suffices to search for complex Golay pairs up to equivalence.

Lemma 2.12 (cf. [11]). *Let (A', B') be a complex Golay pair. Then (A', B') is equivalent to a complex Golay pair (A, B) with $a_0 = a_1 = b_0 = 1$ and $a_2 \in \{\pm1, i\}$.*

Proof. We will transform a given complex Golay sequence pair (A', B') into an equivalent normalized one using the equivalence operations of Proposition 2.4. To start with, let $A := A'$ and $B := B'$.

First, we ensure that $a_0 = 1$. To do this, we apply operation E4 (scale A) enough times until $a_0 = 1$.

Second, we ensure that $a_1 = 1$. To do this, we apply operation E5 (positional scaling) enough times until $a_1 = 1$; note that E5 does not change a_0.

Third, we ensure that $a_2 \neq -i$. If it is, we apply operation E1 (reversal) and E2 (conjugate reverse A) which has the effect of keeping $a_0 = a_1 = 1$ and setting $a_2 = i$.

Last, we ensure that $b_0 = 1$. To do this, we apply operation E3 (swap) and then operation E4 (scale A) enough times so that $a_0 = 1$ and then operation E3 (swap) again. This has the effect of not changing A but setting $b_0 = 1$. □

2.3 Sum-of-squares decomposition types

A consequence of Lemma 2.11 is that every complex Golay pair generates a decomposition of $2n$ into a sum of four integer squares. In fact, it typically generates several decompositions of $2n$ into a sum of four squares. Recall that $i \star A$ denotes positional scaling by i (operation E5) on the sequence A. If (A, B) is a complex Golay pair then applying operation E5 to this pair k times shows that $(i^k \star A, i^k \star B)$ is also a complex Golay pair. By using Lemma 2.11 on these complex Golay pairs one obtains the fact that $2n$ can be decomposed as the sum of four integer squares as

$$\text{resum}(i^k \star A)^2 + \text{imsum}(i^k \star A)^2 + \text{resum}(i^k \star B)^2 + \text{resum}(i^k \star B)^2.$$

For $k > 3$ this produces no new decompositions but in general for $k = 0, 1, 2,$ and 3 this produces four distinct decompositions of $2n$ into a sum of four squares.

With the help of a computer algebra system (CAS) one can enumerate every possible way that $2n$ may be written as a sum of four integer squares. For example, when $n = 23$ one has $0^2+1^2+3^2+6^2 = 2 \cdot 23$ and $1^2 + 2^2 + 4^2 + 5^2 = 2 \cdot 23$ as well as all permutations of the squares and negations of the integers being squared. During the first stage of our enumeration method only the first sequence of a complex Golay pair is known, so at that stage we cannot compute its whole sums-of-squares decomposition. However, it is still possible to filter some sequences from consideration based on analyzing the two known terms in the sums-of-squares decomposition.

For example, say that A is the first sequence in a potential complex Golay pair of length 23 with resum$(A) = 0$ and imsum$(A) = 5$. We can immediately discard A from consideration because there is no way to chose the resum and imsum of B to complete the sums-of-squares decomposition of $2n$, i.e., there are no integer solutions (x, y) of $0^2 + 5^2 + x^2 + y^2 = 2n$.

3 ENUMERATION METHOD

In this section we describe in detail the method we used to perform a complete enumeration of all complex Golay pairs up to length 25. Given a length n our goal is to find all $\{\pm1, \pm i\}$ sequences A and B of length n such that (A, B) is a complex Golay pair.

3.1 Preprocessing: Enumerate possibilities for A_{even} and A_{odd}

The first step of our method uses Fiedler's trick of considering the entries of A of even index separately from the entries of A of odd index. There are approximately $n/2$ nonzero entries in each of A_{even} and A_{odd} and there are four possible values for each nonzero entry. Therefore there are approximately $2 \cdot 4^{n/2} = 2^{n+1}$ possible sequences to check in this step. Additionally, by Lemma 2.12 we may assume the first nonzero entry of both A_{even} and A_{odd} is 1 and that the second nonzero entry of A_{even} is not $-i$, decreasing the number of sequences to check in this step by more than a factor of 4. It is quite feasible to perform a brute-force search through all such sequences when $n \approx 30$.

We apply Corollary 2.10 to every possibility for A_{even} and A_{odd}. There are an infinite number of possible $z \in \mathbb{C}$ with $|z| = 1$, so we do not attempt to apply Corollary 2.10 using all such z. Instead we try a sufficiently large number of z so that in the majority of cases for which a z exists with $|h_{A'}(z)|^2 > 2n$ (where A' is either A_{even}

or A_{odd}) we in fact find such a z. In our implementation we chose to take z to be $e^{2\pi ij/N}$ where $N := 2^{14}$ and $j = 0, \dots, N-1$.

At the conclusion of this step we will have two lists: one list L_{even} of the A_{even} which were not discarded and one list L_{odd} of the A_{odd} which were not discarded.

3.2 Stage 1: Enumerate possibilities for A

We now enumerate all possibilities for A by joining the possibilities for A_{even} with the possibilities for A_{odd}. For each $A_1 \in L_{\text{odd}}$ and $A_2 \in L_{\text{even}}$ we form the sequence A by letting the kth entry of A be either the kth entry of A_1 or A_2 (whichever is nonzero). Thus the entries of A are either ± 1 or $\pm i$ and therefore A is a valid candidate for the first sequence of a complex Golay pair of length n.

At this stage we now use the filtering result of Corollary 2.8 and the sums-of-squares decomposition result of Lemma 2.11 to perform more extensive filtering on the sequences A which we formed above. In detail, our next filtering check proceeds as follows: Let $R_k := \text{resum}(i^k \star A)$ and $I_k := \text{imsum}(i^k \star A)$. By using a Diophantine equation solver we check if the Diophantine equations

$$R_k^2 + I_k^2 + x^2 + y^2 = 2n$$

are solvable in integers (x, y) for $k = 0, 1, 2, 3$. As explained in Section 2.3, if any of these equations have no solutions then A cannot be a member of a complex Golay pair and can be ignored. Secondly, we use Corollary 2.8 with z chosen to be $e^{2\pi ij/N}$ for $j = 0, \dots, N-1$ where $N := 2^7$ (we use a smaller value of N than in the preprocessing step because in this case there are a larger number of sequences which we need to apply the filtering condition on).

If A passes both filtering conditions then we add it to a list L_A and try the next value of A until no more possibilities remain. At the conclusion of this stage we will have a list of sequences L_A which could potentially be a member of a complex Golay pair. By construction, the first member of all complex Golay pairs (up to the equivalence described in Lemma 2.12) of length n will be in L_A.

3.3 Stage 2: Construct the second sequence B from A

In the second stage we take as input the list L_A generated in the first stage, i.e., a list of the sequences A that were not filtered by any of the filtering theorems we applied. For each $A \in L_A$ we attempt to construct a second sequence B such that (A, B) is a complex Golay pair. We do this by generating a SAT instance which encodes the property of (A, B) being a complex Golay pair where the entries of A are known and the entries of B are unknown and encoded using Boolean variables. Because there are four possible values for each entry of B we use two Boolean variables to encode each entry. Although the exact encoding used is arbitrary, we fixed the following encoding in our implementation, where the variables v_{2k} and v_{2k+1} represent b_k, the kth entry of B:

v_{2k}	v_{2k+1}	b_k
F	F	1
F	T	-1
T	F	i
T	T	$-i$

To encode the property that (A, B) is a complex Golay pair in out SAT instance we add the conditions which define (A, B) to be a complex Golay pair, i.e.,

$$N_A(s) + N_B(s) = 0 \quad \text{for} \quad s = 1, \dots, n-1.$$

These equations could be encoded using clauses in conjunctive normal form (for example by constructing logical circuits to perform complex multiplication and addition and then converting those circuits into CNF clauses). However, we found that a much more efficient and convenient method was to use a *programmatic* SAT solver.

The concept of a programmatic SAT solver was first introduced in [15] where a programmatic SAT solver was shown to be more efficient than a standard SAT solver when solving instances derived from RNA folding problems. More recently, a programmatic SAT solver was also shown to be useful when searching for Williamson matrices [5]. Generally, programmatic SAT solvers perform well when there is domain-specific knowledge about the problem being solved that cannot easily be encoded into SAT instances directly but can be used to learn facts about potential solutions which can help guide the solver in its search.

Concretely, a programmatic SAT solver is compiled with a piece of code which encodes a property that a solution of the SAT instance must satisfy. Periodically the SAT solver will run this code while performing its search and if the current partial assignment violates a property that is expressed in the provided code then a conflict clause is generated encoding this fact. The conflict clause is added to the SAT solver's database of learned clauses where it is used to increase the efficiency of the remainder of the search. The reason these clauses can be so useful is because they can encode facts which the SAT solver would have no way of learning otherwise, since the SAT solver has no knowledge of the domain of the problem.

Not only does this paradigm allow the SAT solver to perform its search more efficiently, it also allows instances to be much more expressive. Under this framework SAT instances do not have to consist solely of Boolean formulas in conjunctive normal form (the typical format of SAT instances) but can consist of clauses in conjunctive normal form combined with a piece of code that *programmatically* expresses clauses. This extra expressiveness is also a feature of SMT solvers, though SMT solvers typically require more overhead to use. Additionally, one can compile *instance-specific* programmatic SAT solvers which are tailored to perform searches for a specific class of problems.

For our purposes we use a programmatic SAT solver tailored to search for sequences B that when paired with a given sequence A form a complex Golay pair. Each instance will contain the $2n$ variables $v_0, \dots, v_{2n-1}$ that encode the entries of B as previously specified. In detail, the code given to the SAT solver does the following:

(1) Compute and store the values $N_A(k)$ for $k = 1, \dots, n-1$.
(2) Initialize s to $n-1$. This will be a variable which controls which autocorrelation condition we are currently examining.
(3) Examine the current partial assignment to v_0, v_1, v_{2n-2}, and v_{2n-1}. If all these values have been assigned then we can determine the values of b_0 and b_{n-1}. From these values we compute $N_B(s) = b_0\overline{b_{n-1}}$. If $N_A(s) + N_B(s) \neq 0$ then (A, B) cannot be a complex Golay pair (regardless of the values of $b_1, \dots, b_{n-2}$) and therefore we learn a conflict clause

which says that b_0 and b_{n-1} cannot both be assigned to their current values. More explicitly, if v_k^{cur} represents the literal v_k when v_k is currently assigned to true and the literal $\neg v_k$ when v_k is currently assigned to false we learn the clause

$$\neg(v_0^{\text{cur}} \wedge v_1^{\text{cur}} \wedge v_{2n-2}^{\text{cur}} \wedge v_{2n-1}^{\text{cur}}).$$

(4) Decrement s by 1 and repeat the previous step, computing $N_B(s)$ if the all the b_k which appear in its definition have known values. If $N_A(s) + N_B(s) \neq 0$ then learn a clause preventing the values of b_k which appear in the definition of $N_B(s)$ from being assigned the way that they currently are. Continue to repeat this step until $s = 0$.
(5) If all values of B are assigned but no clauses have been learned then output the complex Golay pair (A, B). If an exhaustive search is desired, learn a clause which prevents the values of B from being assigned the way they currently are; otherwise learn nothing and return control to the SAT solver.

For each A in the list L_A from stage 1 we run a SAT solver with the above programmatic code; the list of all outputs (A, B) in step (5) shown above now form a complete list of complex Golay pairs of length n up to the equivalence given in Lemma 2.12. In fact, since Lemma 2.12 says that we can set $b_0 = 1$ we can assume that both v_0 and v_1 are always set to false. In other words, we can add the two clauses $\neg v_0$ and $\neg v_1$ into our SAT instance without omitting any complex Golay pairs up to equivalence.

3.4 Postprocessing: Enumerating all complex Golay pairs

At the conclusion of the second stage we have obtained a list of complex Golay pairs of length n such that every complex Golay pair of length n is equivalent to some pair in our list. However, because we have not accounted for all the equivalences in Section 2.1 some pairs in our list may be equivalent to each other. In some sense such pairs should not actually be considered distinct, so to count how many distinct complex Golay pairs exist in length n we would like to find and remove pairs which are equivalent from the list. Additionally, to verify the counts given in [16] it is necessary to produce a list which contains *all* complex Golay pairs. We now describe an algorithm which does both, i.e., it produces a list of all complex Golay pairs as well as a list of all inequivalent complex Golay pairs.

In detail, our algorithm performs the following steps:

(1) Initialize Ω_{all} to be the set of complex Golay pairs generated in stage 2. This variable will be a set that will be populated with and eventually contain all complex Golay pairs of length n.
(2) Initialize Ω_{inequiv} to be the empty set. This variable will be a set that will be populated with and eventually contain all inequivalent complex Golay pairs of length n.
(3) For each (A, B) in Ω_{all}:
    (a) If (A, B) is already in Ω_{inequiv} then skip this (A, B) and proceed to the next pair (A, B) in Ω_{all}.
    (b) Initialize Γ to be the set containing (A, B). This variable will be a set that will be populated with and eventually contain all complex Golay pairs equivalent to (A, B).
    (c) For every γ in Γ add $\text{E1}(\gamma), \dots, \text{E5}(\gamma)$ to Γ. Continue to do this until every pair in Γ has been examined and no new pairs are added to Γ.
    (d) Add (A, B) to Ω_{inequiv} and add all pairs in Γ to Ω_{all}.

After running this algorithm listing the members of Ω_{all} gives a list of all complex Golay pairs of length n and listing the members of Ω_{inequiv} gives a list of all inequivalent complex Golay pairs of length n. At this point we can also construct the complete list of sequences which appear in any complex Golay pair of length n. To do this it suffices to add A and B to a new set Ω_{seqs} for each $(A, B) \in \Omega_{\text{all}}$.

3.5 Optimizations

Although the method described will correctly enumerate all complex Golay pairs of a given length n, for the benefit of potential implementors we mention a few optimizations which we found helpful.

In stage 1 we check if Diophantine equations of the form

$$R^2 + I^2 + x^2 + y^2 = 2n \qquad (*)$$

are solvable in integers (x, y) where R and I are given. CAS functions like `PowersRepresentations` in MATHEMATICA or `nsoks` in MAPLE [30] can determine all ways of writing $2n$ as a sum of four integer squares. From this information we construct a Boolean two dimensional array D such that $D_{|R|,|I|}$ is true if and only if $(*)$ has a solution, making the check for solvability a fast lookup. In fact, one need only construct the lookup table for R and I with $R + I \equiv n \pmod 2$ as the following lemma shows.

LEMMA 3.1. *Suppose R and I are the* resum *and* imsum *of a sequence $X \in \{\pm1, \pm i\}^n$. Then $R + I \equiv n \pmod 2$.*

PROOF. Let $\#_c$ denote the number of entries in X with value c. Then

$$R + I = (\#_1 - \#_{-1}) + (\#_i - \#_{-i}) \equiv \#_1 + \#_{-1} + \#_i + \#_{-i} \pmod 2$$

since $-1 \equiv 1 \pmod 2$. The quantity on the right is n since there are n entries in X. □

In stage 1 we check if $|h_A(z)|^2 > 2n$ where $z = e^{2\pi ij/N}$ for $j = 0, \dots, N - 1$ with $N = 2^7$. However, we found that it was more efficient to not check the condition for each j in ascending order (i.e., for each z in ascending complex argument) but to first perform the check on points z with larger spacing between them. In our implementation we first assigned N to be 2^3 and performed the check for odd $j = 1, 3, \dots, N - 1$. Following this we doubled N and again performed the check for odd j, proceeding in this matter until all points z had been checked. (This ignores checking the condition when $z = i^k$ for some k but that is desirable since in those cases $|h_A(i^k)|^2 = \text{resum}(i^k \star A)^2 + \text{imsum}(i^k \star A)^2$ and the sums-of-squares condition is a strictly stronger filtering method.)

In the preprocessing step and stage 1 it is necessary to evaluate the Hall polynomial $h_{A'}$ or h_A at roots of unity $z = e^{2\pi ij/N}$ and determine its squared absolute value. The fastest way we found of doing this used the discrete Fourier transform. For example, let A' be the sequence A_{even}, A_{odd}, or A under consideration but padded with trailing zeros so that A' is of length N. By definition of the discrete Fourier transform we have that

$$\mathrm{DFT}(A') = \left[h_{A'}(e^{2\pi i j/N})\right]_{j=0}^{N-1}.$$

Thus, we determine the values of $|h_{A'}(z)|^2$ by taking the squared absolute values of the entries of DFT(A'). If $|h_{A'}(z)|^2 > 2n$ for some z then by Corollary 2.8 or Corollary 2.10 we can discard A' from consideration. To guard against potential inaccuracies introduced by the algorithms used to compute the DFT we actually ensure that $|h_{A'}(z)|^2 > 2n + \epsilon$ for some tolerance ϵ which is small but larger than the accuracy that the DFT is computed to (e.g., $\epsilon = 10^{-3}$).

In the preprocessing step before setting $N := 2^{14}$ we first set $N := n$ and perform the rest of the step as given. The advantage of first performing the check with a smaller value of N is that the discrete Fourier transform of A' can be computed faster. Although the check with $N = n$ is a less effective filter, it often succeeds and whenever it does it allows us to save time by not performing the more costly longer DFT.

In stage 1 our application of Corollary 2.8 requires computing $|h_A(z)|^2$ where $z = e^{2\pi i j/N}$ for $j = 0, \dots, N-1$. Noting that

$$h_A(z) = h_{A_{\text{even}}}(z) + h_{A_{\text{odd}}}(z)$$

one need only compute $h_{A_{\text{even}}}(z)$ and $h_{A_{\text{odd}}}(z)$ for each each A_{even} and A_{odd} generated in the preprocessing step and once those are known $h_A(z)$ can be found by a simple addition.

In stage 2 one can also include properties that complex Golay sequences must satisfy in the code compiled with the programmatic SAT solver. As an example of this, we state the following proposition which was new to the authors and does not appear to have been previously published.

PROPOSITION 3.2. *Let (A, B) be a complex Golay pair. Then*

$$a_k a_{n-k-1} b_k b_{n-k-1} = \pm 1 \quad \textit{for} \quad k = 0, \dots, n-1.$$

To prove this, we use the following simple lemma.

LEMMA 3.3. *Let $c_k \in \mathbb{Z}_4$ for $k = 0, \dots, n-1$. Then*

$$\sum_{k=0}^{n-1} i^{c_k} = 0 \quad \textit{implies} \quad \sum_{k=0}^{n-1} c_k \equiv 0 \pmod 2.$$

PROOF. Let $\#_c$ denote the number of c_k with value c. Note that the sum on the left implies that $\#_0 = \#_2$ and $\#_1 = \#_3$ because the 1s must cancel with the -1s and the is must cancel with the $-i$s. Then $\sum_{k=0}^{n-1} c_k = \#_1 + 2\#_2 + 3\#_3 \equiv \#_1 + \#_3 \equiv 2\#_1 \equiv 0 \pmod 2$. □

We now prove Proposition 3.2.

PROOF. Let $c_k, d_k \in \mathbb{Z}_4$ be such that $a_k = i^{c_k}$ and $b_k = i^{d_k}$. Using this notation the multiplicative equation from Proposition 3.2 becomes the additive congruence

$$c_k + c_{n-k-1} + d_k + d_{n-k-1} \equiv 0 \pmod 2. \qquad (*)$$

Since (A, B) is a complex Golay pair, the autocorrelation equations give us

$$\sum_{k=0}^{n-s-1} \left(i^{c_k - c_{k+s}} + i^{d_k - d_{k+s}} \right) = 0$$

for $s = 1, \dots, n-1$. Using Lemma 3.3 and the fact that $-1 \equiv 1 \pmod 2$ gives

$$\sum_{k=0}^{n-s-1} (c_k + c_{k+s} + d_k + d_{k+s}) \equiv 0 \pmod 2$$

for $s = 1, \dots, n-1$. With $s = n-1$ one immediately derives $(*)$ for $k = 0$. With $s = n-2$ and $(*)$ for $k = 0$ one derives $(*)$ for $k = 1$. Working inductively in this manner one derives $(*)$ for all k. □

In short, Proposition 3.2 tells us that an even number of a_k, a_{n-k-1}, b_k, and b_{n-k-1} are real for each $k = 0, \dots, n-1$. For example, if exactly one of a_k and a_{n-k-1} is real then exactly one of b_k and b_{n-k-1} must also be real. In this case, using our encoding from Section 3.3 we can add the clauses

$$(v_{2k} \lor v_{2(n-k-1)}) \land (\lnot v_{2k} \lor \lnot v_{2(n-k-1)})$$

to our SAT instance. These clauses say that exactly one of v_{2k} and $v_{2(n-k-1)}$ is true.

	Total CPU Time in hours		
n	Preproc.	Stage 1	Stage 2
17	0.00	0.01	0.06
18	0.01	0.03	0.23
19	0.01	0.07	0.18
20	0.02	0.35	0.43
21	0.04	1.93	1.89
22	0.08	9.58	1.11
23	0.15	42.01	3.02
24	0.32	81.42	5.23
25	0.57	681.31	20.51

Table 1: The time used to run the various stages of our algorithm in lengths $17 \le n \le 25$.

4 RESULTS

In order to provide a verification of the counts from [16] we implemented the enumeration method described in Section 3. The preprocessing step was performed by a C program and used the mathematical library FFTW [14] for computing the values of $h_{A'}(z)$ as described in Section 3.5. Stage 1 was performed by a C++ program, used FFTW for computing the values of $h_A(z)$ and a MAPLE script [30] for determining the solvability of the Diophantine equations given in Section 3.3. Stage 2 was performed by the programmatic SAT solver MAPLESAT [24]. The postprocessing step was performed by a Python script.

We ran our implementation on a cluster of machines running CentOS 7 and using Intel Xeon E5-2683V4 processors running at 2.1 GHz and using at most 300MB of RAM. To parallelize the work in each length n we split L_{odd} into 25 pieces and used 25 cores to complete stages 1 and 2 of the algorithm. Everything in the stages proceeded exactly as before except that in stage 1 the list L_{odd} was 25 times shorter than it would otherwise be, which allowed us to complete the first stages 20.7 times faster and the second stages 23.9 times faster. The timings for the preprocessing step and the two stages of our algorithm are given in Table 1; the timings for the postprocessing step were negligible. The times are given as

n	$\lvert L_{\text{even}}\rvert$	$\lvert L_{\text{odd}}\rvert$	$\lvert L_{\text{A}}\rvert$
1	1	–	1
2	3	1	3
3	3	1	1
4	3	4	3
5	12	4	5
6	12	16	14
7	39	16	12
8	48	64	36
9	153	64	44
10	153	204	120
11	561	252	101
12	645	860	465
13	2121	884	293
14	2463	3284	317
15	8340	3572	1793
16	9087	12116	923
17	31275	12824	3710
18	34560	46080	14353
19	117597	50944	10918
20	130215	173620	26869
21	446052	194004	116612
22	500478	667304	67349
23	1694865	732232	182989
24	1886568	2515424	313878
25	6447090	2727452	1211520

Table 2: The number of sequences A_{even}, A_{odd}, and A that passed the filtering conditions of our algorithm in lengths up to 25.

n	$\lvert\Omega_{\text{seqs}}\rvert$	$\lvert\Omega_{\text{all}}\rvert$	$\lvert\Omega_{\text{inequiv}}\rvert$
1	4	16	1
2	16	64	1
3	16	128	1
4	64	512	2
5	64	512	1
6	256	2048	3
7	0	0	0
8	736	6400	16
9	0	0	0
10	1536	12288	20
11	64	512	1
12	4608	36864	52
13	64	512	1
14	0	0	0
15	0	0	0
16	13312	106496	204
17	0	0	0
18	3072	24576	24
19	0	0	0
20	26880	215040	340
21	0	0	0
22	1024	8192	12
23	0	0	0
24	98304	786432	1056
25	0	0	0

Table 3: The number complex Golay pairs in lengths up to 25. The table counts the number of individual sequences, the number of pairs, and the number of pairs up to equivalence.

the total amount of CPU time used across all 25 cores. Our code is available online as a part of the MATHCHECK project and we have also made available the resulting enumeration of complex Golay pairs [6].

The sizes of the lists L_{even} and L_{odd} computed in the preprocessing step and the size of the list L_{A} computed in stage 1 are given in Table 2 for all lengths in which we completed a search. Without applying any filtering L_{A} would have size 4^n so Table 2 demonstrates the power of the criteria we used to perform filtering; typically far over 99.99% of possible sequences A are filtered from L_{A}. The generated SAT instances had $2n$ variables (encoding the entries $b_0, \dots, b_{n-1}$), 2 unit clauses (encoding $b_0 = 1$), $2\lfloor n/2 \rfloor$ binary clauses (encoding Proposition 3.2), and $n-1$ programmatic clauses (encoding Definition 2.2).

Finally, we provide counts of the total number of complex Golay pairs of length $n \leq 25$ in Table 3. The sizes of Ω_{seqs} and Ω_{all} match those from [16] in all cases and the size of Ω_{inequiv} matches those from [8] for $n \leq 19$ (the largest length they exhaustively solved).

Because [8, 11, 16] do not provide implementations or timings for the enumerations they completed it is not possible for us to compare the efficiency of our algorithm to previous algorithms. However, we note that the results in this paper did not require an exorbitant amount of computing resources. If one has access to 25 modern CPU cores then one can exhaustively enumerate all complex Golay pairs up to length 25 using our software in about a day and we estimate that increasing this to length 26 would take another week. We note that Fiedler's paper [11] enumerates complex Golay pairs to length 28. It is not clear whether this was accomplished using more computing resources or a more efficient algorithm, though we note that the preprocessing and stage 1 of our method is similar to Fiedler's method with some differences in the filtering theorems.

5 FUTURE WORK

Besides increasing the length to which complex Golay pairs have been enumerated there are a number of avenues for improvements which could be made in future work. As one example, we remark that we have not exploited the algebraic structure of complex Golay pairs revealed by Craigen, Holzmann, and Kharaghani [8]. In particular, those authors prove a theorem which implies that if $p \equiv 3 \pmod 4$ is a prime which divides n and A is a member of a complex Golay pair of length n then the polynomial h_A is not irreducible over $\mathbb{F}_p(i)$. Ensuring that this property holds could be added to the filtering conditions which were used in stage 1. In fact, the authors relate the factorization of h_A over $\mathbb{F}_p(i)$ to the factorization of h_B over $\mathbb{F}_p(i)$ for any complex Golay pair (A, B). This factorization could potentially be used to perform stage 2 more efficiently, possibly supplementing or replacing the SAT solver entirely, though it is unclear if such a method would perform better than our method in practice. In any case, it would not be possible to apply their theorem in all lengths (for example when n is a power of 2).

A second possible improvement could be to symbolically determine the value of z with $|z| = 1$ which maximizes $|h_{A'}(z)|^2$ in the preprocessing step. Once this value of z is known then A' can be filtered if $|h_{A'}(z)|^2 > 2n$ and if not then no other value of z needs to be tried. This would save evaluating $h_{A'}(z)$ at the points $z = e^{2\pi ij/N}$ for $j = 0, \ldots, N-1$ and would also increase the number of sequences which get filtered. However, it is unclear if this method would be beneficial in practice due to the overhead of maximizing $|h_{A'}(z)|^2$ subject to $|z| = 1$.

Another possible improvement could be obtained by deriving further properties like Proposition 3.2 that complex Golay pairs must satisfy. We have performed some preliminary searches for such properties; for example, consider the following property which could be viewed as a strengthening of Proposition 3.2:

$$a_k\overline{a_{n-k-1}} = (-1)^{n+1}\overline{b_k\overline{b_{n-k-1}}} \qquad \text{for} \qquad k = 1, \ldots, n-2.$$

An examination of all complex Golay pairs up to length 25 reveals that they all satisfy this property except for a *single* complex Golay pair up to equivalence. The only pair which doesn't satisfy this property is equivalent to

$$\big([1, 1, 1, -1, 1, 1, -1, 1], [1, i, i, -1, 1, -i, -i, -1]\big)$$

and was already singled out in [13] for being special as the only known example of what they call a "cross-over" Golay sequence pair. Since a counterexample exists to this property there is no hope of proving it in general, but perhaps a suitable generalization could be proven.

ACKNOWLEDGEMENTS

This work was made possible by the facilities of the Shared Hierarchical Academic Research Computing Network (SHARCNET) and Compute/Calcul Canada. The authors would also like to thank the anonymous reviewers whose comments improved this article's clarity.

REFERENCES

[1] Erika Ábrahám. 2015. Building bridges between symbolic computation and satisfiability checking. In *Proceedings of the 2015 ACM on International Symposium on Symbolic and Algebraic Computation.* ACM, New York, 1–6.

[2] Erika Ábrahám, John Abbott, Bernd Becker, Anna M. Bigatti, Martin Brain, Bruno Buchberger, Alessandro Cimatti, James H. Davenport, Matthew England, Pascal Fontaine, Stephen Forrest, Alberto Griggio, Daniel Kroening, Werner M. Seiler, and Thomas Sturm. 2016. SC^2: Satisfiability Checking meets Symbolic Computation (Project Paper). In *Intelligent Computer Mathematics: 9th International Conference, CICM 2016, Bialystok, Poland, July 25–29, 2016, Proceedings.* Springer International Publishing, Cham, 28–43. http://www.sc-square.org/.

[3] Curtis Bright. 2017. *Computational Methods for Combinatorial and Number Theoretic Problems.* Ph.D. Dissertation. University of Waterloo.

[4] Curtis Bright, Vijay Ganesh, Albert Heinle, Ilias S. Kotsireas, Saeed Nejati, and Krzysztof Czarnecki. 2016. MATHCHECK2: A SAT+CAS Verifier for Combinatorial Conjectures. In *Computer Algebra in Scientific Computing - 18th International Workshop, CASC 2016, Bucharest, Romania, September 19–23, 2016, Proceedings.* 117–133.

[5] Curtis Bright, Ilias Kotsireas, and Vijay Ganesh. 2018. A SAT+CAS Method for Enumerating Williamson Matrices of Even Order. In *Proceedings of the Thirty-Second AAAI Conference on Artificial Intelligence.*

[6] Curtis Bright, Ilias Kotsireas, Albert Heinle, and Vijay Ganesh. 2018. Complex Golay Pairs via SAT. https://cs.uwaterloo.ca/~cbright/cgpsat/. Complex Golay pairs archived at https://zenodo.org/record/1246337, code available at https://bitbucket.org/cbright/mathcheck2.

[7] R. Craigen. 1994. Complex Golay sequences. *J. Combin. Math. Combin. Comput.* 15 (1994), 161–169.

[8] R. Craigen, W. Holzmann, and H. Kharaghani. 2002. Complex Golay sequences: structure and applications. *Discrete Math.* 252, 1-3 (2002), 73–89.

[9] James A Davis and Jonathan Jedwab. 1999. Peak-to-mean power control in OFDM, Golay complementary sequences, and Reed-Muller codes. *IEEE Transactions on Information Theory* 45, 7 (1999), 2397–2417.

[10] P. G. Donato, J. Urena, M. Mazo, and F. Alvarez. 2004. Train wheel detection without electronic equipment near the rail line. In *IEEE Intelligent Vehicles Symposium, 2004.* 876–880. https://doi.org/10.1109/IVS.2004.1336500

[11] Frank Fiedler. 2013. Small Golay sequences. *Advances in Mathematics of Communications* 7, 4 (2013).

[12] Frank Fiedler, Jonathan Jedwab, and Matthew G Parker. 2008. A Framework for the Construction ofGolay Sequences. *IEEE Transactions on Information Theory* 54, 7 (2008), 3114–3129.

[13] Frank Fiedler, Jonathan Jedwab, and Matthew G Parker. 2008. A multi-dimensional approach to the construction and enumeration of Golay complementary sequences. *Journal of Combinatorial Theory, Series A* 115, 5 (2008), 753–776.

[14] Matteo Frigo and Steven G Johnson. 2005. The design and implementation of FFTW3. *Proc. IEEE* 93, 2 (2005), 216–231.

[15] Vijay Ganesh, Charles W O'Donnell, Mate Soos, Srinivas Devadas, Martin C Rinard, and Armando Solar-Lezama. 2012. Lynx: A programmatic SAT solver for the RNA-folding problem. In *International Conference on Theory and Applications of Satisfiability Testing.* Springer, 143–156.

[16] Richard G Gibson and Jonathan Jedwab. 2011. Quaternary Golay sequence pairs I: Even length. *Designs, Codes and Cryptography* 59, 1-3 (2011), 131–146.

[17] Marcel Golay. 1961. Complementary series. *IRE Transactions on Information Theory* 7, 2 (1961), 82–87.

[18] Marcel J.E. Golay. 1949. Multi-slit spectrometry. *JOSA* 39, 6 (1949), 437–444.

[19] W. H. Holzmann and H. Kharaghani. 1994. A computer search for complex Golay sequences. *Australas. J. Combin.* 10 (1994), 251–258.

[20] Aamir Hussain, Zeashan H. Khan, Azfar Khalid, and Muhammad Iqbal. 2014. *A Comparison of Pulse Compression Techniques for Ranging Applications.* Springer Singapore, Singapore, 169–191. https://doi.org/10.1007/978-981-4585-36-1_5

[21] Hadi Kharaghani and Behruz Tayfeh-Rezaie. 2005. A Hadamard matrix of order 428. *Journal of Combinatorial Designs* 13, 6 (2005), 435–440.

[22] Ilias S Kotsireas. 2013. Algorithms and metaheuristics for combinatorial matrices. In *Handbook of Combinatorial Optimization.* Springer, 283–309.

[23] Ying Li and Wen Bin Chu. 2005. More Golay sequences. *IEEE Transactions on Information Theory* 51, 3 (2005), 1141–1145.

[24] Jia Hui Liang, Pascal Poupart, Krzysztof Czarnecki, and Vijay Ganesh. 2017. An Empirical Study of Branching Heuristics Through the Lens of Global Learning Rate. In *International Conference on Theory and Applications of Satisfiability Testing.* Springer, 119–135.

[25] A. Lomayev, Y.P. Gagiev, A. Maltsev, A. Kasher, M. Genossar, and C. Cordeiro. 2017. Golay sequences for wireless networks. https://www.google.com/patents/US20170324461 US Patent App. 15/280,635.

[26] Michael B. Monagan, Keith O. Geddes, K. Michael Heal, George Labahn, Stefan M. Vorkoetter, James McCarron, and Paul DeMarco. 2005. *Maple 10 Programming Guide.* Maplesoft, Waterloo ON, Canada.

[27] Moshe Nazarathy, Steven A Newton, RP Giffard, DS Moberly, F Sischka, WR Trutna, and S Foster. 1989. Real-time long range complementary correlation optical time domain reflectometer. *Journal of Lightwave Technology* 7, 1 (1989), 24–38.

[28] A Nowicki, W Secomski, J Litniewski, I Trots, and PA Lewin. 2003. On the application of signal compression using Golay's codes sequences in ultrasound diagnostic. *Archives of Acoustics* 28, 4 (2003).

[29] Kenneth G Paterson. 2000. Generalized Reed-Muller codes and power control in OFDM modulation. *IEEE Transactions on Information Theory* 46, 1 (2000), 104–120.

[30] Joe Riel. 2006. nsoks: A MAPLE script for writing n as a sum of k squares. http://www.swmath.org/software/21060.

[31] Edward Zulkoski, Curtis Bright, Albert Heinle, Ilias S. Kotsireas, Krzysztof Czarnecki, and Vijay Ganesh. 2017. Combining SAT Solvers with Computer Algebra Systems to Verify Combinatorial Conjectures. *J. Autom. Reasoning* 58, 3 (2017), 313–339. https://doi.org/10.1007/s10817-016-9396-y

ZpL: a p-adic precision package

Xavier Caruso
CNRS, Université Rennes 1;
xavier.caruso@normalesup.org

David Roe
MIT;
roed@mit.edu

Tristan Vaccon
Université de Limoges;
tristan.vaccon@unilim.fr

ABSTRACT

We present a new package ZpL for the mathematical software system SageMath. It implements a sharp tracking of precision on p-adic numbers, following the theory of ultrametric precision introduced in [4]. The underlying algorithms are mostly based on automatic differentiation techniques. We introduce them, study their complexity and discuss our design choices. We illustrate the benefits of our package (in comparison with previous implementations) with a large sample of examples coming from linear algebra, commutative algebra and differential equations.

CCS CONCEPTS

• **Computing methodologies → Algebraic algorithms**;

KEYWORDS

Algorithms, p-adic precision, Automatic Differentiation

ACM Reference Format:

Xavier Caruso, David Roe, and Tristan Vaccon. 2018. ZpL: a p-adic precision package. In *ISSAC '18: 2018 ACM International Symposium on Symbolic and Algebraic Computation, July 16–19, 2018, New York, NY, USA.* ACM, New York, NY, USA, 8 pages. https://doi.org/10.1145/3208976.3208995

1 INTRODUCTION

When computing with real and p-adic fields, exact results are usually impossible, since most elements have infinite decimal or p-adic expansions. Working with these fields thus requires an analysis of how precision evolves through the sequence of steps involved in carrying out a computation. Such analysis can be carried out automatically by the software, or via theorems specific to a particular application [? ?]. In this paper, we describe a package for computing with p-adic rings and fields [13], based on a series of papers by the same authors [4–7]. The core of the package is a method for tracking precision using p-adic lattices which can yield dramatically more precise results than traditional methods, at the cost of increased runtime and memory usage.

The standard method for handling precision when computing with real numbers is floating point arithmetic, which may also be used in p-adic computation. At a given precision level, a finite set of representable numbers are chosen, and arithmetic operations are defined to give a representable number that is close to the true result [1]. Floating point arithmetic has the benefit of efficient arithmetic operations, but users are responsible for tracking the precision of the results. Numerically unstable algorithms can lead to very inaccurate answers [9].

If provably correct results are desired, interval arithmetic provides an alternative to floating point. Instead of just tracking an approximation to the answer, one also tracks a radius within which the true result lies. This method is commonly used for p-adic computations since the ultrametric property of p-adic fields frequently keeps the radius small. Computations remain fairly efficient with this approach, but numerical instability can still lead to dramatic losses in precision (see §2 for many examples). Tracking the precision of multiple variables concurrently, the set of possible true values associated to an inexact value takes the form of an ellipsoid with axes parallel to the coordinate axes.

For better control of precision, we may allow arbitrary axes. This change would have little utility for real numbers, since such ellipsoids are not preserved by most functions. For p-adic fields, in contrast, differentiable maps with surjective differential will send sufficiently small ellipsoids to other ellipsoids. From an algebraic perspective, these ellipsoids are just cosets of a lattice H inside a p-adic vector space, and the main result of [4] (see also Proposition 3.1 below) describes how the image of such a coset under a map f is given exactly by applying the differential of f to H.

In this paper, we describe an implementation of this idea in SageMath [12]. Rather than attaching a precision to each element, we store the precision of many elements together by tracking a precision module[1] for the whole collection of variables. As variables are created and destroyed, we update a matrix whose rows represent the vectors in the module. Information about the precision of elements is extracted from the matrix as necessary. Concretely, our package provides two new SageMath parents[2], namely ZpLC and ZpLF (and their fraction fields QpLC and QpLF). The acronyms LC and LF stand for "lattice-cap" and "lattice-float" respectively (see §3 for details). Our package has been included in the standard distribution of SageMath since version 8.2.

The article is structured as follows. In §2 we provide a demonstration of the package, showing how it can provide more precise answers than the traditional methods for tracking p-adic precision. In particular, §2.1 describes elementary arithmetic and the SOMOS-4 sequence, §2.2 gives examples from linear algebra, §2.3 examples using polynomials, and §2.4 examples of differential equations. In §3 we give more details on the implementation. §3.1 contains a brief overview on the theory of p-adic precision of [4]. §3.2 is devoted to the implementation of automatic differentiation leading to the

ISSAC '18, July 16–19, 2018, New York, NY, USA

ACM ISBN 978-1-4503-5550-6/18/07...$15.00
https://doi.org/10.1145/3208976.3208995

[1]Throughout the paper, the word "module" has its mathematical meaning: it denotes an additive group endowed with an external product by scalars in $\mathbb{Z}_p$.
[2]Parents in SageMath are the analogues of container objects in computer science. Basically a parent corresponds to an implementation of a concrete mathematical structure, as the ring of p-adic integers.

actual computation of the module that models the precision. In §3.3, we explain how precision on any individual number can be recovered and discuss the validity of our results. The complexity overhead induced by our package is analyzed in §3.4. Finally, §4 contains a discussion of how we see this package fitting into the existing p-adic implementations. While these methods do introduce overhead, they are well suited to exploring precision behavior when designing algorithms, and can provide hints as to when further precision analysis would be useful.

2 SHORT DEMONSTRATION

The first step is to define the parents: the rings of p-adic numbers we will work with.

```
In:  Z2 = ZpXX(2, print_mode='digits')
     Q2 = QpXX(2, print_mode='digits')
```

ZpXX is a generic notation for ZpCR, ZpLC and ZpLF. The first, ZpCR, is the usual constructor for p-adic parents in SageMath. It tracks precision using interval arithmetic. The parents ZpLC and ZpLF provided by our package track precision differently; more details will be provided in Section 3. In the sequel, we will compare the outputs provided by each parent. As the results for ZpLF and ZpLC agree on all examples in this section, we will only give those for ZpLC.

In what follows, random elements in $\mathbb{Z}_p$ are always picked with respect to the Haar measure. Random elements in $\mathbb{Q}_p$ are constructed as a product $p^V \cdot U$ where U is a random element in $\mathbb{Z}_p$ (distributed according to the Haar measure) and V is a random variable taking values in $\mathbb{Z}$ which is independent from U and distributed as follows:

$$\text{Prob}[V{=}0] = \tfrac{1}{5}, \quad \text{Prob}[V{=}v] = \frac{2}{5|v|\cdot(|v|+1)}, \ \forall v \neq 0.$$

This distribution is the default in SageMath, and the function random_element used below picks the same element for each of ZpCR, ZpLC and ZpLF.

2.1 Elementary arithmetic

We begin our tour of the ZpL package with some basic arithmetic. Elements are approximated by giving a valuation and a unit, where the unit is specified modulo a power of p determined by the global lattice precision.

```
In:   x = random_element(Z3, prec=5); x
ZpCR: ...11111
ZpLC: ...11111
```

Multiplication by p (here 3) is a shift on the digits and thus leads to a gain of one digit in absolute precision. In the example below, we observe that when this multiplication is split into several steps, ZpCR does not see the gain of precision while ZpL does.

```
In:   3*x              In:   x + x + x
ZpCR: ...111110        ZpCR:   ...11110
ZpLC: ...111110        ZpLC:  ...111110
```

The same phenomenon occurs for multiplication.

```
In:   x^3              In:   x * x * x
ZpCR: ...010101        ZpCR:   ...10101
ZpLC: ...010101        ZpLC:  ...010101
```

ZpL is also well suited for working with coefficients with unbalanced precision.

```
In:   x = random_element(Z2, prec=10)
      y = random_element(Z2, prec=5)
In:   u, v = x+y, x-y
      u, v
ZpCR: (...10111, ...01111)
ZpLC: (...10111, ...01111)
```

Now, let us compute $u + v$ and compare it with $2x$ (observe that they should be equal).

```
In:   u + v              In:   2*x
ZpCR: ...00110           ZpCR:  ...00110100110
ZpLC: ...00110100110     ZpLC:  ...00110100110
```

Again ZpCR does not output the optimal precision when the computation is split into several steps whereas ZpL does. These basic examples illustrate situations that occur during the execution of many algorithms. As a result, interval arithmetic frequently overestimates the loss of precision. The aim of our package is to reduce this precision loss. In the next subsections, we present a bunch of examples showing the benefit of ZpL in various contexts.

SOMOS 4. A first example is the SOMOS-4 sequence. It is defined by the recurrence:

$$u_{n+4} = \frac{u_{n+1}u_{n+3} + u_{n+2}^2}{u_n}$$

and is known for its high numerical instability (see [4]). Nevertheless, the ZpL package saves precision even when using a generic unstable implementation of the SOMOS iteration.

```
In:   def somos4(u0, u1, u2, u3, n):
          a, b, c, d = u0, u1, u2, u3
          for _ in range(4, n+1):
              a, b, c, d = b, c, d, (b*d + c*c) / a
          return d
In:   u0 = u1 = u2 = Z2(1,15); u3 = Z2(3,15)
      somos4(u0, u1, u2, u3, 18)
ZpCR: ...11
ZpLC: ...100000000000111
In:   somos4(u0, u1, u2, u3, 100)
ZpCR: PrecisionError: cannot divide by something
      indistinguishable from zero.
ZpLC: ...001001001110001
```

2.2 Linear algebra

Many generic algorithms of linear algebra exhibit instability when used with p-adic numbers. Our package ZpL frequently eliminates this instability without having to change either the algorithm or the implementation.

Matrix multiplication. As revealed in [5], a first simple example where instability appears is simply matrix multiplication. This might be surprising because no division occurs in this situation. Observe nevertheless the difference between ZpCR and ZpLC.

```
In:   MS = MatrixSpace(Z2,2)
      M = random_element(MS, prec=5)
      for _ in range(25):
          M *= random_element(MS, prec=5)
      M
ZpCR: [0 0]
      [0 0]
ZpLC: [...100000000000    ...1000000000]
      [   ...010000000     ...00100000]
```

On the aforementioned example, we notice that ZpCR is unable to decide whether the product vanishes or not. Having good estimates on the precision is therefore very important in such situations.

Characteristic polynomials. Characteristic polynomials are notoriously hard to compute [5, 7]. By default, SAGEMATH uses a division-free algorithm over $\mathbb{Q}_p$, this choice is not enough to achieve optimal precision in the QpCR case since negative valuations may appear. We illustrate the different precision behavior in the following example.

```
   In:  M = random_element(MatrixSpace(Q2,3), prec=10)
        M.determinant()
 QpCR:  ...010000010
 QpLC:  ...010000010
   In:  M.charpoly()
 QpCR:  ...00000000000000000001*x^3 +
        ...1001011.011*x^2 + ...0111.01*x + 0
 QpLC:  ...00000000000000000001*x^3 +
        ...1001011.011*x^2 + ...11100111.01*x +
        ...010000010
```

We observe that ZpLC can guarantee 4 more digits on the x coefficient. Moreover, it recovers the correct precision on the constant coefficient (which is the determinant) whereas ZpCR is confused and cannot even certify that it does not vanish.

2.3 Commutative algebra

Our package can be applied to computation with p-adic polynomials.

Euclidean algorithm. A natural example is that of the computation of GCD in the Euclidean ring $\mathbb{Q}_p[X]$, whose stability has been studied in [3]. A naive implementation of the Euclidean algorithm can produce different behavior depending on the type of implementation of the field of p-adic coefficients.

```
   In:  S.<x> = PolynomialRing(Z2)
        P = random_element(S, degree=10, prec=5)
        Q = random_element(S, degree=10, prec=5)
        D = x^5 + random_element(S, degree=4, prec=8); D
 ZpCR:  ...00000000000000000001*x^5 + ...11111010*x^4 +
        ...10000000*x^3 + ...11001111*x^2 +
        ...10000110*x + ...11100010
 ZpLC:  ...00000000000000000001*x^5 + ...11111010*x^4 +
        ...10000000*x^3 + ...11001111*x^2 +
        ...10000110*x + ...11100010
   In:  def euclidean(A,B):
            while B != 0:
                A, B = B, A % B
            return A.monic()
        euclidean(D*P, D*Q)
 ZpCR:  0*x^9 + ...1*x^8 + 0*x^7 + 0*x^6 + 0*x^5 +
        0*x^4 + 0*x^3 + ...1*x^2 + ...10*x + ...10
 ZpLC:  ...00000000000000000001*x^5 + ...11111010*x^4 +
        ...10000000*x^3 + ...11001111*x^2 +
        ...10000110*x + ...11100010
```

With high probability, P and Q are coprime, implying that the gcd of DP and DQ is D. However, we observe that ZpCR output a quite different result. The point is that, in the ZpCR case, Euclidean algorithm stops prematurely because the test `B != 0` fails too early due to the lack of precision.

Gröbner bases. Our package can be applied on complex computations like that of Gröbner bases using generic Gröbner bases algorithms.

```
   In:  R.<x,y,z> = PolynomialRing(Q2, order='invlex')
        F = [ Q2(2,10)*x + Q2(1,10)*z,
              Q2(1,10)*x^2 + Q2(1,10)*y^2 - Q2(2,10)*z^2,
              Q2(4,10)*y^2 + Q2(1,10)*y*z + Q2(8,10)*z^2 ]
   In:  from sage.rings.polynomial.toy_buchberger\
            import buchberger_improved
        g = buchberger_improved(ideal(F))
        g.sort(); g
 QpCR:  [x^3, x*y + ...1100010*x^2,
         y^2 + ...11001*x^2, z + ...0000000010*x]
 QpLC:  [x^3, x*y + ...111100010*x^2,
         y^2 + ...1111111001*x^2, z + ...0000000010*x]
```

As we can see, some loss in precision occurs in the Buchberger algorithm and is avoided thanks to ZpL.

2.4 p-adic differential equations

In [10], the authors studied the computation of isogenies between elliptic curves over finite fields by applying the lattice precision model to p-adic differential equations. Specifically, they considered the equation $y' = g(x) \times h(y)$ with $g, h, y \in \mathbb{Z}_p[\![x]\!]$ such that $g(0) = h(0) = 1$ and $y(0) = 0$.

Their main result was that the intrinsic loss in precision when computing the coefficient x^n of y from g and h was in $\log_p(n)$ even though a naive analysis of the Newton method for solving the equation yields a loss in $\log_p(n)^2$.

We can reach this theoretical loss in precision using ZpL, while ZpCR does not perform as well. We apply N steps of the Newton method for $y' = g \times h(y)$ as described in [10], using a generic `Newton_Iteration_Solver(g,h,N)`.

```
   In:  S.<t> = PowerSeriesRing(Q2, 16)
        h = 1 + t + t^3
        y = t + t^2 * random_element(S, prec=10)
        g = y.derivative() / h(y)
        u = Newton_Iteration_Solver(g, h, 4); u[15]
 QpCR:  ...1101
 QpLC:  ...11011101
```

3 BEHIND THE SCENES

In this section, we explain how our package ZpL works and analyze its performance. The main theoretical result on which our package is based is the ultrametric precision theory developed in [4], which suggests tracking precision *via* lattices and differential computations. For this reason, our approach is very inspired by automatic differentiation techniques [11] and our implementation follows the usual operator overloading strategy. We will introduce two versions of our package, namely ZpLC and ZpLF: this former is safer while the latter is faster.

Remark about the naming. The letter L, which appears in the name of the package, comes from "lattices". The letters C (in ZpLC) and F (in ZpLF) stand for "cap" and "float" respectively.

3.1 The precision Lemma

In [4], we suggest the use of lattices to represent the precision of elements in $\mathbb{Q}_p$-vector spaces. This approach contrasts with the *coordinate-wise method* (of *e.g.* `Zp(5)`) that is traditionally used in SageMath where the precision of an element is specified by giving the precision of each coordinate separately and is updated after each basic operation.

Consider a finite dimensional normed vector space E defined over $\mathbb{Q}_p$. We use the notation $\|\cdot\|_E$ for the norm on E and $B_E^-(r)$ (resp. $B_E(r)$) for the open (resp. closed) ball of radius r centered at the origin. A *lattice* $L \subset E$ is a sub-$\mathbb{Z}_p$-module which generates E over $\mathbb{Q}_p$. Because of ultrametricity, the balls $B_E(r)$ and $B_E^-(r)$ are examples of lattices. Lattices can be thought of as special neighborhoods of 0, and therefore are good candidates to model precision data. Moreover, as revealed in [4], they behave quite well under (strictly) differentiable maps:

Proposition 3.1. *Let E and F be two finite dimensional normed vector spaces over $\mathbb{Q}_p$ and $f : U \to F$ be a function defined on an open subset U of E. We assume that f is differentiable at some point $v_0 \in U$ and that the differential df_{v_0} is surjective. Then, for all $\rho \in (0,1]$, there exists a positive real number δ such that, for all $r \in (0,\delta)$, any lattice H such that $B_E^-(\rho r) \subset H \subset B_E(r)$ satisfies:*

$$f(v_0 + H) = f(v_0) + df_{v_0}(H). \tag{1}$$

This proposition enables the *lattice method* of tracking precision, where the precision of the input is specified as a lattice H and precision is tracked via differentials of the steps within a given algorithm. The equality sign in Eq. (1) shows that this method yields the optimum possible precision. We refer to [4, §4.1] for a more complete exposition.

3.2 Tracking precision

We now explain in more details the internal mechanisms `ZpLC` and `ZpLF` use for tracking precision.

In what follows, it will be convenient to use a notion of discrete time represented by the letter t. Rigorously, it is defined as follows: $t = 0$ when the p-adic ring `ZpLC(...)` or `ZpLF(...)` is created and increases by 1 each time a variable is created, deleted[3] or updated.

Let $\mathcal{V}_t$ be the set of alive variables at time t. Set $E_t = \mathbb{Q}_p^{\mathcal{V}_t}$; it is a finite dimensional vector space over $\mathbb{Q}_p$ which should be thought of as the set of all possible values that can be taken by the variables in $\mathcal{V}_t$. For $\mathsf{v} \in \mathcal{V}_t$, let $e_\mathsf{v} \in E_t$ be the vector whose coordinates all vanish except at position v which takes the value 1. The family $(e_\mathsf{v})_{\mathsf{v}\in\mathcal{V}_t}$ is obviously a basis of E_t; we will refer to it as the *canonical basis*.

3.2.1 The case of `ZpLC`. Following Proposition 3.1, the package `ZpLC` follows the precision by keeping track of a lattice H_t in E_t, which is a global object whose purpose is to model the precision on all the variables in $\mathcal{V}_t$ all together. Concretely, this lattice is represented by a matrix M_t in row-echelon form whose rows form a set of generators. Below, we explain how the matrices M_t are updated each time t increases.

Creating a variable. This happens when we encounter an instruction having one of the two following forms:

[Computation]	`w = f(v_1, ..., v_n)`
[New value]	`w = R(value, prec)`

[3] The deletion can be explicit (through a call to the `del` operator) or implicit (handled by the garbage collector).

In both cases, `w` is the newly created variable. The v_i's stand for already defined variables and f is some n-ary builtin function (in most cases it is just addition, subtraction, multiplication or division). On the contrary, the terms "value" and "prec" refer to user-specified constants or integral values which were computed earlier.

Let us first examine the first construction [Computation]. With our conventions, if t is the time just before the execution of the instruction we are interested in, the v_i's lie in $\mathcal{V}_t$ while w does not. Moreover $\mathcal{V}_{t+1} = \mathcal{V}_t \sqcup \{\mathsf{w}\}$, so that $E_{t+1} = E_t \oplus \mathbb{Q}_p e_\mathsf{w}$. The mapping taking the values of variables at time t to that at time $t+1$ is:

$$\begin{array}{rccc} F: & E_t & \longrightarrow & E_{t+1} \\ & \underline{x} & \mapsto & \underline{x} \oplus f(x_1,\dots,x_n) \end{array}$$

where x_i is the v_i-th coordinate of the vector $\underline{x}$. The Jacobian matrix of F at $\underline{x}$ is easily computed; it is the block matrix $J_{\underline{x}}(F) = \begin{pmatrix} I & L \end{pmatrix}$ where I is the identity matrix of size $\mathrm{Card}\,\mathcal{V}_t$ and L is the column vector whose v-th entry is $\frac{\partial f}{\partial \mathsf{v}}(\underline{x})$ if v is one of the v_i's and 0 otherwise. Therefore, the image of H_t under $dF_{\underline{x}}$ is represented by the matrix $J_{\underline{x}}(F)\cdot M_t = \begin{pmatrix} M_t & C \end{pmatrix}$ where C is the column vector:

$$C = \sum_{i=1}^{n} \frac{\partial f}{\partial \mathsf{v}_i}(\underline{x}) \cdot C_i \tag{2}$$

where C_i is the column vector of M_t corresponding to the variable v_i. Observe that the matrix $J_{\underline{x}}(F)\cdot M_t$ is no longer a square matrix; it has one extra column. This reflects the fact that $\dim E_{t+1} = \dim E_t + 1$. Rephrasing this in a different language, the image of H_t under $dF_{\underline{x}}$ is no longer a lattice in E_{t+1} but is included in an hyperplane, violating our definition of a precision lattice.

The package `ZpLC` tackles this issue by introducing a cap, analogous to adding $O(p^N)$ when creating a p-adic number from an integer. Specifically, we choose an integer N_{t+1} and replace the $\mathbb{Z}_p$-submodule $dF_{\underline{x}}(H_t)$ with the lattice $H_{t+1} = dF_{\underline{x}}(H_t) \oplus p^{N_{t+1}}\mathbb{Z}_p e_\mathsf{w}$. Alternatively, one may introduce the map:

$$\begin{array}{rccc} \tilde{F}: & E_t \oplus \mathbb{Q}_p & \longrightarrow & E_{t+1} \\ & \underline{x} \oplus c & \mapsto & \underline{x} \oplus \big(f(x_1,\dots,x_n) + c\big). \end{array} \tag{3}$$

The lattice H_{t+1} is then the image of $H_t \oplus p^{N_{t+1}}\mathbb{Z}_p$ under $d\tilde{F}_{(\underline{x},\star)}$ for any value of $\star$. In order to carry out this strategy, one must choose N_{t+1}. We do so by associating two constants to each ring: a relative cap RELCAP and an absolute cap ABSCAP. We then set

$$N_{t+1} = \min\big(\text{ABSCAP},\ \text{RELCAP} + v_p(y)\big) \tag{4}$$

with $y = f(x_1,\dots,x_n)$. Larger caps mean that the precision of the final result is less likely to be affected, but require more space. See Remark 3.2 for more details.

In concrete terms, the lattice H_{t+1} is represented by the block matrix:

$$\begin{pmatrix} M_t & C \\ 0 & p^{N_{t+1}} \end{pmatrix}.$$

Performing row operations, we see then that the entries of C can be reduced modulo $p^{N_{t+1}}$ without changing the lattice. In order save space, we perform this reduction and define M_{t+1} by:

$$M_{t+1} = \begin{pmatrix} M_t & C \bmod p^{N_{t+1}} \\ 0 & p^{N_{t+1}} \end{pmatrix}.$$

We observe in particular that M_{t+1} is still in row-echelon form.

Finally, we need to explain which value is set to the newly created variable w. We observe that it cannot be exactly $f(x_1, \ldots, x_n)$ because the latter is *a priori* a p-adic number which cannot be computed exactly. For this reason, we have to truncate it at some finite precision. Again we choose the precision $O(p^{N_{t+1}})$, *i.e.* we define x_{w} as $f(x_1, \ldots, x_n) \bmod p^{N_{t+1}}$. The congruence $\bar{x} \oplus f(x_1, \ldots, x_n) \equiv \bar{x} \oplus x_{\mathrm{w}} \pmod{H_{t+1}}$ (which holds thanks to the extra generator we have added) justifies this choice.

The second construction "w = R(value, prec)" is easier to handle since, roughly speaking, it corresponds to the case $n = 0$. In this situation, keeping in mind the cap, the lattice H_{t+1} is defined by $H_{t+1} = H_t + p^{\min(\mathrm{prec}, N_{t+1})}\mathbb{Z}_p e_{\mathrm{w}}$ for the cap $N_{t+1} = \min\big(\text{ABSCAP}, \text{RELCAP}+v_p(\mathrm{value})\big)$. The corresponding matrix M_{t+1} is then given by:

$$M_{t+1} = \begin{pmatrix} M_t & 0 \\ 0 & p^{\min(\mathrm{prec}, N_{t+1})} \end{pmatrix}.$$

Deleting a variable. Let us now examine the case where a variable w is deleted (or collected by the garbage collector). Just after the deletion, at time $t+1$, we then have $\mathcal{V}_{t+1} = \mathcal{V}_t \backslash \{\mathrm{w}\}$. Thus $E_t = E_{t+1} \oplus \mathbb{Q}_p e_{\mathrm{w}}$. Moreover, the deletion of w is modeled by the canonical projection $f : E_t \to E_{t+1}$. Since f is linear, it is its own differential (at each point) and we set $H_{t+1} = f(H_t)$. A matrix representing H_{t+1} is deduced from M_t by erasing the column corresponding to w. However the matrix we get this way is no longer in row-echelon form. We then need to re-echelonize it.

More precisely, the obtained matrix has this shape:

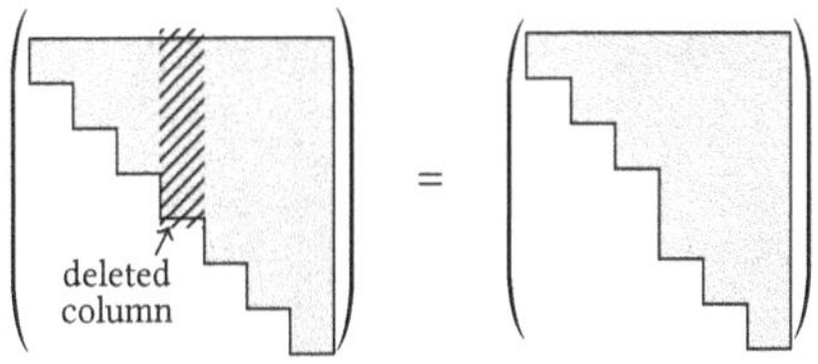

where a cell is colored when it can contain a non-vanishing entry. The top part of the matrix is then already echelonized, so that we only have to re-echelonize the bottom right corner whose size is the distance from the column corresponding to the erased variable to the end. Thanks to the particular shape of the matrix, the echelonization can be performed efficiently: we combine the first rows (of the bottom right part) in order to clear the first unwanted nonzero entry and then proceed recursively.

Updating a variable. Just like for creation, this happens when the program reaches an affectation "w = ..." where the variable w is already defined. This situation reduces to the creation of the temporary variable (the value of the right-hand-size), the deletion of the old variable w and a renaming. It can then be handled using the methods discussed previously.

3.2.2 *The case of* ZpLF. The way the package ZpLF tracks precision is based on similar techniques but differs from ZpLC in that it does not introduce a cap but instead allows H_t to be a sub-$\mathbb{Z}_p$-module of E_t of any codimension. This point of view is nice because it implies smaller objects and consequently leads to faster algorithms. However, it has a huge drawback; indeed, unlike lattices, submodules of E_t of arbitrary codimensions are *not* exact objects, in the sense that they cannot be represented by integral matrices in full generality. Consequently, they cannot be encoded on a computer. We work around this drawback by replacing everywhere exact p-adic numbers by floating point p-adic numbers (at some given relative precision k) [2]. In the floating point model, we approximate all numbers in the disc $p^v(u + O(p^k))$ by a single rational number $p^v u$. Operations on these numbers are then not exact, but instead produce the representative in the correct disc.

The fact that the lattice H_t can now have arbitrary codimension translates to the fact the matrix M_t can be rectangular. Precisely, we will maintain matrices M_t of the shape:

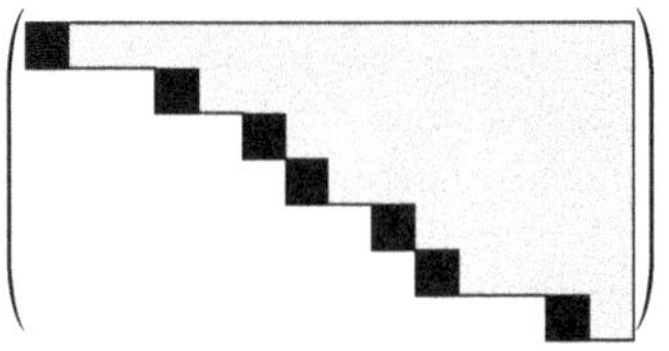
(5)

where only the colored cells may contain a nonzero value and the black cells —the so-called *pivots*— do not vanish. A variable whose corresponding column contains a pivot will be called a *pivot variable at time t*.

Creating a variable. We assume first that the newly created variable is defined through a statement of the form: "w = f(v_1, ..., v_n)". As already explained in the case of ZpLC, this code is modeled by the mathematical mapping:

$$\begin{array}{rccc} F: & E_t & \longrightarrow & E_{t+1} \\ & \underline{x} & \mapsto & \underline{x} \oplus f(x_1, \ldots, x_n). \end{array}$$

Here $\underline{x}$ represents the state of memory at time t, and x_i is the coordinate of $\underline{x}$ corresponding to the variable v_i.

In the ZpLF framework, H_{t+1} is defined as the image of H_t under the differential $dF_{\underline{x}}$. Accordingly, the matrix M_{t+1} is defined as $M_{t+1} = \begin{pmatrix} M_t & C \end{pmatrix}$ where C is the column vector defined by Eq. (2). However, since operations defining M_{t+1} are performed with floating point numbers, the matrix M_{t+1} gives only an approximate basis for H_{t+1}.

If w is created by the code "w = R(value, prec)", we define $H_{t+1} = H_t \oplus p^{\mathrm{prec}}\mathbb{Z}_p e_{\mathrm{w}}$ and consequently:

$$M_{t+1} = \begin{pmatrix} M_t & 0 \\ 0 & p^{\mathrm{prec}} \end{pmatrix}$$

If prec is $+\infty$ (or, equivalently, not specified), we agree that $H_{t+1} = H_t$ and $M_{t+1} = \begin{pmatrix} M_t & 0 \end{pmatrix}$.

Deleting a variable. As for ZpLC, the matrix operation implied by the deletion of the variable w is the deletion of the corresponding column of M_t. If w is not a pivot variable at time t, the matrix M_t keeps the form (5) after erasure; therefore no more treatment is needed in this case.

Otherwise, we re-echelonize the matrix as follows. After the deletion of the column C_{w}, we examine the first column C which was located on the right of C_{w}. Two situations may occur (depending on the fact that C was or was not a pivot column):

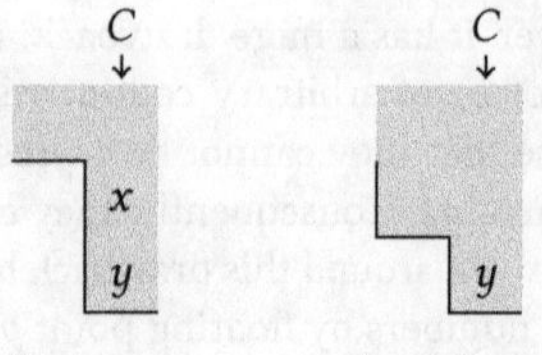

First case Second case

In the first case, we perform row operations in order to replace the pair (x, y) by $(d, 0)$ where d is an element of valuation $\min(v_p(x), v_p(y))$. Observe that y is necessarily nonzero in this case, so that d does not vanish as well. After this operation, we move to the next column and repeat the same process.

The second case is divided into two subcases. First, if y does not vanish, it can serve as a pivot and the obtained matrix has the desired shape. When this occurs, the echelonization stops. On the contrary, if $y = 0$, we just untint the corresponding cell and move to the next column without modifying the matrix.

3.3 Visualizing the precision

Our package implements several methods giving access to the precision structure. In the subsection, we present and discuss the most relevant features in this direction.

Absolute precision of one element. This is the simplest accessible precision datum. It is encapsulated in the notation when an element is printed. For example, the (partial) session:

```
   In:  v = Z2(173,10); v
ZpLC:  ...0010101101
```

indicates that the absolute precision on v is 10 since exactly 10 digits are printed. The method `precision_absolute` provides an easier-to-use access to the absolute precision.

```
   In:  v.precision_absolute()
ZpLC:  10
```

Both ZpLC and ZpLF compute the absolute precision of v (at time t) as the smallest valuation of an entry of the column of M_t corresponding to the variable v. Alternatively, it is the unique integer N for which $\pi_{\mathrm{v}}(H_t) = p^N \mathbb{Z}_p$ where $\pi_{\mathrm{v}} : E_t \to \mathbb{Q}_p$ takes a vector to its v-coordinate. This definition of the absolute precision sounds revelant because, if we believe that the submodule $H_t \subset E_t$ is supposed to encode the precision on the variables in $\mathcal{V}_t$, Proposition 3.1 applied with the mapping π_{v} indicates that a good candidate for the precision on e_{v} is $\pi_{\mathrm{v}}(H_t)$, that is $p^N \mathbb{Z}_p$.

About correctness. We emphasize that the absolute precision computed this way is *not* proved, either for ZpLF or ZpLC. However, in the case of ZpLC, one can be slightly more precise. Let $\mathcal{U}_t$ be the vector space of user-defined variables before time t and U_t be the lattice modeling the precision on them. The pair $(\mathcal{U}_t, U_t)$ is defined inductively as follows: we set $\mathcal{U}_0 = U_0 = 0$ and $\mathcal{U}_{t+1} = \mathcal{U}_t \oplus \mathbb{Q}_p e_{\mathrm{w}}$, $U_{t+1} = U_t \oplus p^{\mathrm{prec}} \mathbb{Z}_p e_{\mathrm{w}}$ when a new variable w is created by "`w = R(value, prec)`"; otherwise, we put $\mathcal{U}_{t+1} = \mathcal{U}_t$ and $U_{t+1} = U_t$. Moreover the values entered by the user defines a vector (with integral coordinates) $\underline{u}_t \in \mathcal{U}_t$.

Similarly, in order to model the caps, we define a pair $(\mathcal{K}_t, K_t)$ by the recurrence $\mathcal{K}_{t+1} = \mathcal{K}_t \oplus \mathbb{Q}_p e_{\mathrm{w}}$, $K_{t+1} = K_t \oplus p^{N_{t+1}} \mathbb{Z}_p e_{\mathrm{w}}$ each time a new variable w is created. Here, the exponent N_{t+1} is the cap defined by Eq. (4). In case of deletion, we put $\mathcal{K}_{t+1} = \mathcal{K}_t$ and $K_{t+1} = K_t$.

Taking the composition of all the functions $\tilde{F}$ (*cf* Eq. (3)) from time 0 to t, we find that the execution of the session until time t is modeled by a mathematical function $\Phi_t : \mathcal{U}_t \oplus \mathcal{K}_t \to E_t$. From the design of ZpLC, we deduce further that there exists a vector $\underline{k}_t \in K_t$ such that:

$$\Phi_t(\underline{u}_t \oplus \underline{k}_t) = \underline{x}_t \quad \text{and} \quad d\Phi_t(U_t \oplus K_t) = H_t$$

where the differential of Φ_t is taken at the point $\underline{u}_t \oplus \underline{k}_t$. Set $\Phi_{t,\mathrm{v}} = \pi_{\mathrm{v}} \circ \Phi_t$; it maps $\underline{u}_t \oplus \underline{k}_t$ to the v-coordinate $x_{t,\mathrm{v}}$ of $\underline{x}_t$ and satisfies $d\Phi_{t,\mathrm{v}}(U_t \oplus K_t) = \pi_{\mathrm{v}}(H_t) = p^N \mathbb{Z}_p$ where N is the value returned by `precision_absolute`. Thus, as soon as the assumptions of Proposition 3.1 are fulfilled, we derive $\Phi_{t,\mathrm{v}}\big((\underline{u}_t + U_t) \oplus (\underline{k}_t + K_t)\big) = x_{t,\mathrm{v}} + p^N \mathbb{Z}_p$. Noting that $k_t \in K_t$, we finally get:

$$\Phi_{t,\mathrm{v}}(\underline{u}_t + U_t) \subset \Phi_{t,\mathrm{v}}\big((\underline{u}_t + U_t) \oplus K_t\big) = x_{t,\mathrm{v}} + p^N \mathbb{Z}_p. \qquad (6)$$

The latter inclusion means that the computed value $x_{t,\mathrm{v}}$ is accurate at precision $O(p^N)$, *i.e.* that the output absolute precision is correct.

Unfortunately, automatically checking the assumptions of Proposition 3.1 in full generality is not straightforward because it requires bounds on higher derivatives. For now, our package does not perform this inspection but we plan to include it in a forthcoming release, along the lines of [4, Proposition 3.12]. Meanwhile, the assumptions can be checked by hand using the results of [3, 4, 10].

Remark 3.2. Assuming that Proposition 3.1 applies, the absolute precision computed as above is optimal if and only if the inclusion of (6) is an equality. Applying again Proposition 3.1 with the restricted mapping $\Phi_{t,\mathrm{v}} : \mathcal{U}_t \to \mathbb{Q}_p$ and the lattice U_t, we find that this happens if and only if $d\Phi_{t,\mathrm{v}}(U_t) = p^N \mathbb{Z}_p$.

Unfortunately, the latter condition cannot be checked on the matrix M_t (because of reductions). However it is possible (and easy) to check whether the weaker condition $d\Phi_{t,\mathrm{v}}(K_t) \subsetneq p^N \mathbb{Z}_p$. This checking is achieved by the method `is_precision_capped` (provided by our package) which returns true if $d\Phi_{t,\mathrm{v}}(K_t) = p^N \mathbb{Z}_p$. As a consequence, when this method answers FALSE, the absolute precision computed by the software is likely optimal.

Precision on a subset of elements. Our package implements the method `precision_lattice` through which we can have access to the joint precision on a set of variables: it outputs a matrix (in echelon form) whose rows generate a lattice representing the precision on the subset of given variables.

When the variables are "independent", the precision lattice is split and the method `precision_lattice` outputs a diagonal matrix:

```
   In:  x = Z2(987,10); y = Z2(21,5)
   In:  # We first retrieve the precision object
        L = Z2.precision()
   In:  L.precision_lattice([x,y])
ZpLC:  [1024    0]
       [   0   32]
```

However, after some computations, the precision matrix evolves and does not remain diagonal in general (though it is always triangular because it is displayed in row-echelon form):

```
    In:  u, v = x+y, x-y
         L.precision_lattice([u,v])
 ZpLC:   [  32 2016]
         [   0 2048]
```

The fact that the precision matrix is no longer diagonal indicates that some well-chosen linear combinations of u and v are known with more digits than u and v themselves. In this particular example, the sum $u + v$ is known at precision $O(2^{11})$ while the (optimal) precision on u and v separately is only $O(2^5)$.

```
    In:  u, v
 ZpLC:   (...10000, ...00110)
    In:  u + v
 ZpLC:   ...11110110110
```

Diffused digits of precision. The phenomenon observed above is formalized by the notion of diffused digits of precision introduced in [5]. We recall briefly its definition.

Definition 3.3. Let E be a $\mathbb{Q}_p$-vector space endowed with a distinguished basis $(e_1, \ldots, e_n)$ and write $\pi_i : E \to \mathbb{Q}_p e_i$ for the projections. Let $H \subset E$ be a lattice. The number of *diffused digits of precision* of H is the length of H_0/H where $H_0 = \pi_1(H) \oplus \cdots \oplus \pi_n(H)$.

If H represents the actual precision on some object, then H_0 is the smallest diagonal lattice containing H. It then corresponds to the maximal *coordinate-wise* precision we can reach on the set of n variables corresponding to the basis $(e_1, \ldots, e_n)$.

The method `diffused_digits` computes the number of diffused digits of precision on a set of variables. Observe:

```
    In:  L.diffused_digits([x,y])
 ZpLC:   0
    In:  L.diffused_digits([u,v])
 ZpLC:   6
```

For the last example, we recall that the relevant precision lattice H is generated by the 2×2 matrix:

$$\begin{pmatrix} 2^5 & 2016 \\ 0 & 2^{11} \end{pmatrix}.$$

The minimal diagonal suplattice H_0 of H is generated by the scalar matrix $2^5 \cdot I_2$ and contains H with index 2^6 in it. This is where the 6 digits of precision come from. There are easily visible here: the sum $u + v$ is known with 11 digits, that is exactly 6 more digits than the summands u and v.

Diffused digits frequently arise in practice. In the context of the matrix multiplication example of §2.2, we get

```
    In:  L.diffused_digits(M.list())
 ZpLC:   11
```

3.4 Complexity

We now discuss the cost of the above operations. In what follows, we shall count operations in $\mathbb{Q}_p$. Although $\mathbb{Q}_p$ is an inexact field, our model of complexity makes sense because the size of the p-adic numbers we manipulate will all have roughly the same size: for ZpLF, it is the precision we use for floating point arithmetic while, for ZpLC, it is the absolute cap which was fixed at the beginning.

It is convenient to introduce a total order on $\mathcal{V}_t$: for $\mathsf{v}, \mathsf{w} \in \mathcal{V}_t$, we say that $\mathsf{v} <_t \mathsf{w}$ if v was created before w. By construction, the columns of the matrix M_t are ordered with respect to $<_t$. We denote by r_t (resp. c_t) the number of rows (resp. columns) of M_t.

Dimension	2	5	10	20	50
Total	35	424	5 539	83 369	3 170 657
Simult.	17	65	225	845	5 101

Computation of characteristic polynomial

Degree	2	5	10	20	50	100
Total	54	130	332	1 036	4 110	10 578
Simult.	18	31	56	106	256	507

Naive Euclidean algorithm

Figure 1: Numbers of involved variables

By construction r_t is also the cardinality of $\mathcal{V}_t$. We have $c_t \leq r_t$ and the equality always holds in the ZpLC case.

For $\mathsf{v} \in \mathcal{V}_t$, we define the *index* of v, denoted by $\mathrm{ind}_t(\mathsf{v})$ as the number of elements of $\mathcal{V}_t$ which are not greater than v. If we sort the elements of $\mathcal{V}_t$ by increasing order, v then appears in $\mathrm{ind}_t(\mathsf{v})$-th position. We also define the *co-index* of v by $\mathrm{coind}_t(\mathsf{v}) = r_t - \mathrm{ind}_t(\mathsf{v})$.

Similarly, for any variable $\mathsf{v} \in \mathcal{V}_t$, we define the *height* (resp. the *co-height*) of v at time t as the number of pivot variables w such that $\mathsf{w} \leq_t \mathsf{v}$ (resp. $\mathsf{w} >_t \mathsf{v}$). We denote it by $\mathrm{hgt}_t(\mathsf{v})$ (resp. by $\mathrm{cohgt}_t(\mathsf{v})$). Clearly $\mathrm{hgt}_t(\mathsf{v}) + \mathrm{cohgt}_t(\mathsf{v}) = c_t$. The height of v is the height of the significant part of the column of M_t which corresponds to v. In the case of ZpLC, all variables are pivot variables and thus $\mathrm{hgt}_t(\mathsf{v}) = \mathrm{ind}_t(\mathsf{v})$ and $\mathrm{cohgt}_t(\mathsf{v}) = \mathrm{coind}_t(\mathsf{v})$ for all v.

Creating a variable. With the notations of §3.2, it is obvious that creating a new variable w requires:

$$O\left(\sum_{i=1}^{n} \mathrm{hgt}_i(\mathsf{v}_i)\right) \subset O(n\, c_t)$$

operations in $\mathbb{Q}_p$. Here, we recall that n is the arity of the operation defining w. In most cases it is 2; thus the above complexity reduces to $O(c_t)$.

In the ZpLF context, c_t counts the number of user-defined variables. It is then expected to be constant (roughly equal to the size of the input) while running a given algorithm.

On the contrary, in the ZpLC context, c_t counts the number of variables which are alive at time t. It is no longer expected to be constant but evolves continuously when the algorithm runs. The tables of Figure 1 show the total number of created variables (which reflects the complexity) together with the maximum number of variables alive at the same time (which reflects the memory usage) while executing two basic computations. The first one is the computation of the characteristic polynomial of a square matrix by the default algorithm used by SageMath for p-adic fields (which is a division-free algorithm of quartic complexity) while the second one is the computation of the gcd of two polynomials using a naive Euclidean algorithm (of quadratic complexity). We can observe that, for both of them, the memory usage is roughly equal to the square root of the complexity.

Deleting a variable. The deletion of the variable w induces the deletion of the corresponding column of M_t, possibly followed

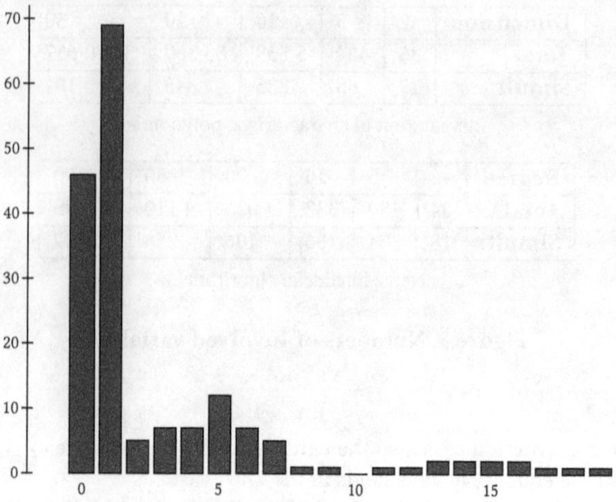

Figure 2: The distribution of $\mathrm{coind}_t(\mathtt{w})$

by a partial row-echelonization. In terms of algebraic complexity, the deletion is free. The cost of the echelonization is within $O(\mathrm{coind}_t(\mathtt{w}) \cdot \mathrm{cohgt}_t(\mathtt{w}))$ operations in $\mathbb{Q}_p$.

In the ZpLF case, we expect that, most of the time, the deleted variables were created after all initial variables were set by the user. This means that we expect $\mathrm{cohgt}_t(\mathtt{w})$ to vanish and so, the corresponding cost to be negligible.

In the ZpLC case, we always have $\mathrm{cohgt}_t(\mathtt{w}) = \mathrm{coind}_t(\mathtt{w})$, so that the cost becomes $O(\mathrm{coind}_t(\mathtt{w})^2)$, which seems high *a priori*. However, the principle of temporal locality [8] asserts that $\mathrm{coind}_t(\mathtt{w})$ tends to be small: destroyed variables are often recently created ones. As a simple example, variables which are local to a small piece of code (*e.g.* a short function or a loop) have a short lifetime. The histogram of Figure 2 shows the distribution of $\mathrm{coind}_t(\mathtt{w})$ while executing the Euclidean algorithm (naive implementation) with two polynomials of degree 7 as input. The bias is evident: most of the time $\mathrm{coind}_t(\mathtt{w}) \leq 1$.

Summary: Impact on complexity. We consider the case of an algorithm with the following characteristics: its complexity is c operations in $\mathbb{Q}_p$ (without any tracking of precision), its memory usage is m elements of $\mathbb{Q}_p$, its input and output have size s_{in} and s_{out} (elements of $\mathbb{Q}_p$) respectively.

In the case of ZpLF, creating a variable has a cost $O(s_{\mathrm{in}})$ whereas deleting a variable is free. Thus when executed with the ZpLF mechanism, the complexity of our algorithm becomes $O(s_{\mathrm{in}}c)$.

In the ZpLC framework, creating a variable has a cost $O(m)$. The case of deletion is more difficult to handle. However, by the temporal locality principle, it seems safe to assume that it is not the bottleneck (which is the case in practice). Therefore, when executed with the ZpLF mechanism, the cost of our algorithm is expected to be roughly $O(mc)$. Going further in speculation, we might estimate the magnitude of m as about $s + \sqrt{c}$ with $s = \max(s_{\mathrm{in}}, s_{\mathrm{out}})$, leading to a complexity of $O(c^{3/2} + sc)$. For quasi-optimal algorithms, the term $sc \simeq c^2$ dominates. However, as soon as the complexity is at least quadratic in s, the dominant term is $c^{3/2}$ and the impact on the complexity is then limited.

4 CONCLUSION

The package ZpL provides powerful tools (based on automatic differentiation) to track precision in the p-adic setting. It frequently outperforms standard interval arithmetic in terms of the precision of the output, as shown in §2. The impact on complexity is controlled but nevertheless non-negligible (see §3.4). For this reason, it is unlikely that a fast algorithm will rely *directly* on the machinery proposed by ZpL, though it might do so for a specific part of a computation. At least for now, bringing together rapidity and stability still requires a substantial human contribution and a careful study of all parameters.

Nevertheless, we believe that ZpL can be extremely helpful to anyone designing a fast and stable p-adic algorithm for a couple of reasons. First, it provides mechanisms to automatically detect which steps of a given algorithm are stable and which ones are not. In this way, it highlights the parts of the algorithm on which the researcher has to concentrate their effort. Second, recall that a classical strategy to improve stability consists of working internally at higher precision. Finding the internal increase in precision that best balances efficiency and accuracy is not an easy task in general. Understanding the diffused precision gives very useful hints in this direction. For example, when there are no diffused digits of precision then the optimal precision completely splits over the variables and there is no need to internally increase the precision. On the contrary, when there are many diffused digits of precision, a large increment is required. Since ZpL gives a direct access to the number of diffused digits of precision, it can be very useful to the designer who is concerned with the balance between efficiency and accuracy.

REFERENCES

[1] *754-2008 - IEEE Std. for Floating-Point Arithmetic.* IEEE, 2008.
[2] Xavier Caruso. Computations with p-adic numbers. pages 1–83, 2017. arxiv:1701.06794.
[3] Xavier Caruso. Numerical stability of euclide algorithm over ultrametric fields. *J. Number Theor. Bordeaux*, 29:503–534, 2017.
[4] Xavier Caruso, David Roe, and Tristan Vaccon. Tracking p-adic precision. *LMS Journal of Computation and Mathematics*, 17(A):274–294, 2014.
[5] Xavier Caruso, David Roe, and Tristan Vaccon. p-Adic Stability In Linear Algebra. In *Proceedings of the 2015 ACM on International Symposium on Symbolic and Algebraic Computation*, ISSAC '15, pages 101–108, New York, NY, USA, 2015. ACM.
[6] Xavier Caruso, David Roe, and Tristan Vaccon. Division and Slope Factorization of p-Adic Polynomials. In *Proceedings of the ACM on International Symposium on Symbolic and Algebraic Computation*, ISSAC '16, pages 159–166, New York, NY, USA, 2016. ACM.
[7] Xavier Caruso, David Roe, and Tristan Vaccon. Characteristic Polynomials of P-adic Matrices. In *Proceedings of the 2017 ACM on International Symposium on Symbolic and Algebraic Computation*, ISSAC '17, pages 389–396, New York, NY, USA, 2017. ACM.
[8] Peter Denning. The locality principle. *Commun. ACM*, 48:19–24, 2005.
[9] Nicholas Higham. *Accuracy and Stability of Numerical Algorithms.* SIAM, Philadelphia, 2nd ed. edition, 2002.
[10] Pierre Lairez and Tristan Vaccon. On p-adic differential equations with separation of variables. In *Proceedings of the ACM on International Symposium on Symbolic and Algebraic Computation, ISSAC 2016, Waterloo, ON, Canada, July 19-22, 2016*, pages 319–323, 2016.
[11] Louis Rall. *Automatic Differentiation: Techniques and Applications*, volume 120 of *Lecture Notes in Computer Science.* Springer, Berlin, 1981.
[12] The Sage Developers. *SageMath, the Sage Mathematics Software System (Version 8.1)*, 2018. http://www.sagemath.org.
[13] Trac #23505: Lattice precision for p-adics. http://trac.sagemath.org/ticket/23505, 2018.

Computing an LLL-reduced Basis of the Orthogonal Lattice

Jingwei Chen
Chongqing Key Lab of Automated Reasoning & Cognition, Chongqing Institute of Green and Intelligent Technology, CAS, Chongqing, China
chenjingwei@cigit.ac.cn

Damien Stehlé
Univ Lyon, ENS de Lyon, CNRS, Inria, Université Claude Bernard Lyon 1, LIP UMR 5668, F-69007 Lyon, France
damien.stehle@ens-lyon.fr

Gilles Villard
Univ Lyon, CNRS, ENS de Lyon, Inria, Université Claude Bernard Lyon 1, LIP UMR 5668, F-69007 Lyon, France
gilles.villard@ens-lyon.fr

ABSTRACT

As a typical application, the Lenstra-Lenstra-Lovász lattice basis reduction algorithm (LLL) is used to compute a reduced basis of the orthogonal lattice for a given integer matrix, via reducing a special kind of lattice bases. With such bases in input, we propose a new technique for bounding from above the number of iterations required by the LLL algorithm. The main technical ingredient is a variant of the classical LLL potential, which could prove useful to understand the behavior of LLL for other families of input bases.

CCS CONCEPTS

• **Computing methodologies → Symbolic and algebraic algorithms**;

KEYWORDS

Lattice basis reduction, LLL, orthogonal lattice, kernel lattice

ACM Reference Format:

Jingwei Chen, Damien Stehlé, and Gilles Villard. 2018. Computing an LLL-reduced Basis of the Orthogonal Lattice. In *ISSAC'18: 2018 ACM International Symposium on Symbolic and Algebraic Computation, July 16–19, 2018, New York, NY, USA.* ACM, New York, NY, USA, 7 pages. https://doi.org/10.1145/3208976.3209013

1 INTRODUCTION

Let $k < n$ be two positive integers. Given a full column rank $n \times k$ integer matrix $\mathbf{A} = (a_{i,j})$, we study the behaviour of the Lenstra-Lenstra-Lovász algorithm [7] for computing a reduced basis for the *orthogonal lattice* of $\mathbf{A}$

$$\mathcal{L}^{\perp}(\mathbf{A}) = \left\{\boldsymbol{m} \in \mathbb{Z}^n : \mathbf{A}^T\boldsymbol{m} = \mathbf{0}\right\} = \mathrm{Ker}(\mathbf{A}^T) \cap \mathbb{Z}^n. \quad (1)$$

The algorithm proceeds by unimodular column transformations from the input matrix $\mathrm{Ext}_K(\mathbf{A}) \in \mathbb{Z}^{(n+k)\times n}$:

$$\mathrm{Ext}_K(\mathbf{A}) := \begin{pmatrix} K\cdot\mathbf{A}^T \\ \mathbf{I}_n \end{pmatrix} = \begin{pmatrix} K\cdot a_{1,1} & K\cdot a_{2,1} & \cdots & K\cdot a_{n,1} \\ \vdots & \vdots & \ddots & \vdots \\ K\cdot a_{1,k} & K\cdot a_{2,k} & \cdots & K\cdot a_{n,k} \\ 1 & 0 & \cdots & 0 \\ 0 & 1 & \cdots & 0 \\ \vdots & \vdots & \ddots & 0 \\ 0 & 0 & \cdots & 1 \end{pmatrix}. \quad (2)$$

where K is a sufficiently large positive integer. The related definitions and the LLL algorithm are given in Section 2. The reader may refer to [11] for a comprehensive review of LLL, and to [14] and [9] concerning the orthogonal lattice.

Usual techniques gives that LLL reduction requires $O(n^2 \log(K \cdot \|\mathbf{A}\|))$ *swaps* (see Step 7 of Algorithm 1) for a basis as in (2), where $\|\mathbf{A}\|$ bounds from above the Euclidean norms of the rows and columns of $\mathbf{A}$. We recall that most known LLL reduction algorithms iteratively perform two types of vector operations: translations and swaps. The motivation for studying bounds on the number of swaps comes from the fact that this number governs known cost analyses of the reduction.

Folklore applications of the reduction of bases as in (2) include, for example, the computation of integer relations between real numbers [1, 3], the computation of minimal polynomials [6] (see also [11]). A main difficulty however, both theoretically and practically, remains to master the *scaling parameter* K that can be very large. Heuristic and practical solutions may for instance rely on a doubling strategy (successive trials with $K = 2, 2^2, 2^4, \ldots$) for finding a suitable scaling. Or an appropriate value for K may be derived from *a priori* bounds such as heights of algebraic numbers [6] and may overestimate the smallest suitable value for actual inputs. Since the usual bound on the number of swaps is linear in $\log K$, the overestimation could be a serious drawback. We show that this may not be always the case.

We consider the reduction of a basis as in (2) for obtaining a basis of the orthogonal lattice (1). We establish a bound on the number of swaps that does not depend on K as soon as K is above a threshold value (as specified in (7)). This threshold depends only on the dimension and invariants of the orthogonal lattice.

Our contribution. The analyses of LLL and many LLL variants bound the number of iterations using the geometric decrease of a potential that is defined using the Gram-Schmidt norms of the basis vectors; see (6). We are going to see that this classical potential does not capture a typical unbalancedness of the Gram-Schmidt

ACM ISBN 978-1-4503-5550-6/18/07…$15.00
https://doi.org/10.1145/3208976.3209013

norms that characterizes bases in (2). Taking into account the latter structure will lead us to a better bound for the number of iterations (see Table 1). Intuitively, as the basis being manipulated becomes reduced, two groups of vectors are formed: some with small Gram-Schmidt norms, and some others with large Gram-Schmidt norms. As soon they are formed, the two groups do not interfere much.

In Section 3 we introduce a new LLL potential function that generalizes the classical one for capturing the previously mentioned unbalancedness. Its geometric decrease during the execution also leads to a bound on the number of iterations (see Theorem 3.3). In Section 4, we specialize the potential to the case of bases as in (2) for computing the orthogonal lattice $\mathcal{L}^{\perp}(\mathbf{A})$. As discussed above, we will see that at some point the number of iterations can be shown to be independent of the scaling parameter K, or, in other words, independent of a further increase of the input size. We note that this new potential is defined for all lattice bases, but it may not always lead to better bounds on the number of LLL iterations.

The extended gcd algorithm in [4] uses a basis as in (2) with $k = 1$. It is shown in [4, Sec. 3, p. 127] that if K is sufficiently large, then the sequence of operations performed by LLL is independent of K. A somewhat similar remark had been made in [13]. We also note that in the analysis of the gradual sub-lattice reduction algorithm of [5], a similar separation of large and small basis vectors was used, also for a better bound on the number of iterations. Our new potential function allows a better understanding of the phenomenon.

We see our potential function for LLL as a new complexity analysis tool that may help further theoretical and practical studies of LLL and its applications. Various approaches exist for computing the orthogonal lattice A, or equivalently an integral kernel basis of $\mathbf{A}^T$. A detailed comparison of the methods remains to be done and would be however outside the scope of this paper that focuses on the properties of the potential. An integral kernel basis may be obtained from a unimodular multiplier for the Hermite normal form of A [19] (see also [18] for the related linear system solution problem), which may be combined as in [15, Ch. 8] and [2] with LLL for minimizing the bit size of the output. A direct application of LLL to $\text{Ext}_K(\mathbf{A})$ is an important alternative solution. We refer to [16] and references therein concerning existing LLL variants.

Future work. Future research directions are to apply this potential to bit complexity studies of the LLL basis reduction [8, 12, 17], especially for specific input bases. Indeed, an interesting problem is to design an algorithm for computing a reduced basis for $\mathcal{L}^{\perp}(\mathbf{A})$ that features a bit complexity bound independent of the scaling parameter, and to compare it to approaches based on the Hermite normal form.

Notations. Throughout the paper, vectors are in column and denoted in bold. For $\boldsymbol{x} \in \mathbb{R}^m$, $\|\boldsymbol{x}\|$ is the Euclidean norm of $\boldsymbol{x}$. Matrices are denoted by upper case letters in bold, such as A, B, etc. For a matrix A, $\mathbf{A}^T$ is the transpose of A, and $\|\mathbf{A}\|$ bounds the Euclidean norms of the columns and rows of A. The base of logarithm is 2.

2 PRELIMINARIES

We give some basic definitions and results that are needed for the rest of the paper. A comprehensive presentation of the LLL algorithm and its applications may be found in [11].

Gram-Schmidt orthogonalization. Let $\boldsymbol{b}_1, \cdots, \boldsymbol{b}_n \in \mathbb{R}^m$ be linearly independent vectors. Their *Gram-Schmidt orthogonalization* $\boldsymbol{b}_1^*, \cdots, \boldsymbol{b}_n^*$ is defined as follows:

$$\boldsymbol{b}_1^* = \boldsymbol{b}_1 \text{ and } \forall i > 1 : \boldsymbol{b}_i^* = \boldsymbol{b}_i - \sum_{j=1}^{i-1} \mu_{i,j} \boldsymbol{b}_j^*,$$

where the $\mu_{i,j} = \frac{\langle \boldsymbol{b}_i, \boldsymbol{b}_j^* \rangle}{\langle \boldsymbol{b}_j^*, \boldsymbol{b}_j^* \rangle}$ for all $i > j$ are called the *Gram-Schmidt coefficients*. We call the $\|\boldsymbol{b}_i^*\|$'s the *Gram-Schmidt norms* of the $\boldsymbol{b}_i$'s.

Lattices. A *lattice* $\Lambda \subseteq \mathbb{R}^m$ is a discrete additive subgroup of $\mathbb{R}^m$. If $(\boldsymbol{b}_i)_{i \le n}$ is a set of generators for Λ, then

$$\Lambda = \mathcal{L}(\boldsymbol{b}_1, \dots, \boldsymbol{b}_n) = \left\{ \sum_{i=1}^{n} z_i \boldsymbol{b}_i : z_i \in \mathbb{Z} \right\}.$$

If the $\boldsymbol{b}_i$'s are linearly independent, then they are said to form a *basis* of Λ. When $n \ge 2$, there exist infinitely many bases for a lattice. Every basis is related by an integral unimodular transformation (a linear transformation with determinant ± 1) to any other. Further, the number of vectors of different bases of a lattice Λ is always the same, and we call this number the *dimension* of the lattice, denoted by $\dim(\Lambda)$. If $\mathbf{B} = (\boldsymbol{b}_1, \dots, \boldsymbol{b}_n) \in \mathbb{R}^{m \times n}$ is a basis for a lattice $\Lambda = \mathcal{L}(\mathbf{B})$, the *determinant* of the lattice is defined as $\det(\Lambda) = \sqrt{\det(\mathbf{B}^T \mathbf{B})}$. It is invariant across all bases of Λ.

Successive minima. For a given lattice Λ, we let $\lambda_1(\Lambda)$ denote the minimum Euclidean norm of vectors in $\Lambda \setminus \{\mathbf{0}\}$. From Minkowski's first theorem, we have $\lambda_1(\Lambda) \le \sqrt{n} \cdot \det(\Lambda)^{1/n}$, where $n = \dim(\Lambda)$. More generally, for all $1 \le i \le n$, we define the i-th *minimum* as

$$\lambda_i(\Lambda) = \min_{\substack{\boldsymbol{v}_1, \cdots, \boldsymbol{v}_i \in \Lambda \\ \text{linearly independent}}} \max_{j \le i} \|\boldsymbol{v}_j\|.$$

Minkowski's second theorem states that $\prod_{i \le n} \lambda_i(\Lambda) \le \sqrt{n}^n \cdot \det(\Lambda)$.

Sublattices. Let $\Lambda \subseteq \mathbb{R}^n$ be a lattice. We say that Λ' is a *sublattice* of Λ if $\Lambda' \subseteq \Lambda$ is a lattice as well. If Λ' is a sublattice of Λ then $\lambda_i(\Lambda) \le \lambda_i(\Lambda')$ for $i \le \dim(\Lambda')$. A sublattice Λ' of $\Lambda \subset \mathbb{R}^n$ is said to be *primitive* if there exists a subspace E of $\mathbb{R}^n$ such that $\Lambda' = \Lambda \cap E$.

Orthogonal lattices. Given a full column rank matrix $\mathbf{A} \in \mathbb{Z}^{n \times k}$, the set $\mathcal{L}^{\perp}(\mathbf{A})$ defined in (1) forms a lattice, called the *orthogonal lattice* of A. We have $\dim(\mathcal{L}^{\perp}(\mathbf{A})) = n - k$. Using $\ker(\mathbf{A}^T)^{\perp} = \text{Im}(A)$ and [14, Cor. p. 328] for primitive lattices we have

$$\det(\mathcal{L}^{\perp}(\mathbf{A})) = \det(\mathbb{Z}^n \cap \ker(\mathbf{A}^T)) = \det(\mathbb{Z}^n \cap \text{Im}(\mathbf{A})),$$

then $\mathcal{L}(\mathbf{A}) \subseteq \mathbb{Z}^n \cap \text{Im}(\mathbf{A})$ and Hadamard's inequality lead to:

$$\det(\mathcal{L}^{\perp}(\mathbf{A})) \le \det(\mathcal{L}(\mathbf{A})) \le \|\mathbf{A}\|^k. \quad (3)$$

LLL-reduced bases. The goal of lattice basis reduction is to find a basis with vectors as short and orthogonal to each other as possible. Among numerous lattice reduction notions, the LLL-reduction [7] is one of the most commonly used. Let $\frac{1}{4} < \delta < 1$. Let $\mathbf{B} = (\boldsymbol{b}_1, \dots, \boldsymbol{b}_n) \in \mathbb{R}^{m \times n}$ be a basis of a lattice Λ. We say that B is *size-reduced* if all Gram-Schmidt coefficients satisfy $|\mu_{ij}| \le \frac{1}{2}$. We say that B satisfies the *Lovász conditions* if for all i we have $\delta \|\boldsymbol{b}_i^*\|^2 \le \|\boldsymbol{b}_{i+1}^*\|^2 + \mu_{i+1,i}^2 \|\boldsymbol{b}_i^*\|^2$. If a basis B is size-reduced and satisfies the Lovász conditions, then we say that B is *LLL-reduced* (with respect to the parameter δ). If a basis $\mathbf{B} = (\boldsymbol{b}_1, \ldots, \boldsymbol{b}_n)$ of Λ is LLL-reduced, then we have:

$$\forall i < n,\ \|\boldsymbol{b}_i^*\|^2 \le \alpha \|\boldsymbol{b}_{i+1}^*\|^2,$$

$$\forall i \le n,\ \|\boldsymbol{b}_i\|^2 \le \alpha^{i-1} \|\boldsymbol{b}_i^*\|^2, \quad (4)$$

$$\forall i \le j \le n,\ \|\boldsymbol{b}_i\| \le \alpha^{\frac{n-1}{2}} \lambda_j(\Lambda), \quad (5)$$

where $\alpha = \frac{4}{4\delta - 1}$. In particular, we have $\|\boldsymbol{b}_1\| \le \alpha^{\frac{n-1}{2}} \lambda_1(\Lambda)$. In this paper, we use the original LLL parameter $\delta = \frac{3}{4}$ and hence $\alpha = 2$.

The LLL algorithm. We now sketch the LLL algorithm. Although there exist many LLL variants in the literature, most of them follow the following structure. Step 7 is called an *LLL swap*.

Algorithm 1 (LLL)

Input: A basis $(\boldsymbol{b}_i)_{i \le n}$ of a lattice $\Lambda \subseteq \mathbb{Z}^n$.
Output: An LLL-reduced basis of Λ.

```
1: i := 2;
2: while i ≤ n do
3:     Size-reduce b_i by b_1, ··· , b_{i−1};
4:     if Lovász condition holds for i then
5:         Set i := i + 1;
6:     else
7:         (LLL swap) Swap b_i and b_{i−1}; set i := max{i − 1, 2};
8:     end if
9: end while
10: Return (b_i)_{i≤n}.
```

To clarify the structure of the algorithm, we omit some details in the above description, e.g., the update of Gram-Schmidt coefficients. From the sketch, we see that we can bound the running-time of LLL by the number of while loop iterations times the cost of each iteration. In fact, most cost bounds for LLL variants proceed via this simple argument. It was showed in [7] that the number of LLL swaps is $O(n^2 \log \|\mathbf{B}\|)$. The following lemma plays a very important role in the analysis of LLL; see [7] for a proof.

Lemma 2.1. *Let* $\mathbf{B}$ *and* $\mathbf{B}'$ *be bases after and before an LLL swap between* $\boldsymbol{b}_i$ *and* $\boldsymbol{b}_{i+1}$. *Then*

$$\begin{array}{rcl} \max\{\|\boldsymbol{b}_i'^*\|, \|\boldsymbol{b}_{i+1}'^*\|\} & \le & \max\{\|\boldsymbol{b}_i^*\|, \|\boldsymbol{b}_{i+1}^*\|\}, \\ \min\{\|\boldsymbol{b}_i'^*\|, \|\boldsymbol{b}_{i+1}'^*\|\} & \ge & \min\{\|\boldsymbol{b}_i^*\|, \|\boldsymbol{b}_{i+1}^*\|\}, \\ \|\boldsymbol{b}_i^*\| \cdot \|\boldsymbol{b}_{i+1}^*\| & = & \|\boldsymbol{b}_i'^*\| \cdot \|\boldsymbol{b}_{i+1}'^*\|, \\ \dfrac{\|\boldsymbol{b}_{i+1}'^*\|}{\|\boldsymbol{b}_{i+1}^*\|} = \dfrac{\|\boldsymbol{b}_i^*\|}{\|\boldsymbol{b}_i'^*\|} & \ge & \dfrac{2}{\sqrt{3}}, \\ \forall j \notin \{i, i+1\} & : & \boldsymbol{b}_j'^* = \boldsymbol{b}_j^*. \end{array}$$

3 A NEW POTENTIAL

In this section, we introduce a variant of the classical LLL potential

$$\Pi(\mathbf{B}) = \sum_{i=1}^{n-1} (n-i) \log \|\boldsymbol{b}_i^*\| \quad (6)$$

of a lattice basis $\mathbf{B}$. The variant we introduce is well-suited for analyzing the number of LLL swaps for the case that both the input and output bases have k large Gram-Schmidt norms and $n-k$ small Gram-Schmidt norms, for some $k < n$. This is for example the case for the input basis as (2); see Section 4.2. The new potential is aimed at accurately measuring the progress made during the LLL execution, for such unbalanced bases.

Definition 3.1. Let $k \le n \le m$ be positive integers and $\mathbf{B} \in \mathbb{R}^{m \times n}$ be full column rank. We let $s_1 < \ldots < s_{n-k}$ be the indices of the $n-k$ smallest Gram-Schmidt norms of $\mathbf{B}$ (using the lexicographical in case there are several $(n-k)$-th smallest Gram-Schmidt norms), and set $S = \{s_i\}_{i \le n-k}$. We let $\ell_1 < \ldots < \ell_k$ be the indices of the other k Gram-Schmidt norms, and set $L = \{\ell_j\}_{j \le k}$. The *k-th LLL potential* of $\mathbf{B}$ is defined as:

$$\Pi_k(\mathbf{B}) = \sum_{j=1}^{k-1} (k-j) \log \|\boldsymbol{b}_{\ell_j}^*\| - \sum_{i=1}^{n-k} i \log \|\boldsymbol{b}_{s_i}^*\| + \sum_{i=1}^{n-k} s_i.$$

Note that for $k = n$, we recover the classical potential Π. The rationale behind Π_k is that in some cases we know that the output basis is made of vectors of very unbalanced Gram-Schmidt norms. As this basis is reduced, this means the first vectors have a small Gram-Schmidt norm, while the last vectors have large Gram-Schmidt norms. During the execution of LLL, such short and large vectors do not interfere much. This is an unusual phenomenon: most often, long vectors are made shorter and short vectors are made longer, so that they are all balanced at the end. But this can happen if the long vectors are rather orthogonal to the short ones. When this is the case, LLL actually runs faster than usual, because it merely "sorts" the short vectors and the long vectors, without making them interact to create shorter vectors. Of course, it can do more intense computations among the short vectors and among the long vectors. Unbalancedness of Gram-Schmidt norms is not captured by the classical potential, but it is with Π_k. In particular, the new potential Π_k allows to not "pay" for the output unbalancedness in the analysis of the number of LLL swaps.

Similarly to the classical potential, the k-th LLL potential monotonically decreases with the number of LLL swaps. More precisely, we have the following

Proposition 3.2. *Let* $\mathbf{B}$ *and* $\mathbf{B}'$ *be the current* n*-dimensional lattice bases before and after an LLL swap. Then for any* $k \le n$, *we have* $\Pi_k(\mathbf{B}) - \Pi_k(\mathbf{B}') \ge \log(2/\sqrt{3})$.

Proof. Recall that S and L are the index sets for the $n-k$ Gram-Schmidt norms and the other k Gram-Schmidt norms for the lattice basis $\mathbf{B}$. We define S' and L' for $\mathbf{B}'$ similarly.

Suppose that this LLL swap occurs between $\boldsymbol{b}_\kappa$ and $\boldsymbol{b}_{\kappa+1}$. Then we must be in one of the following four cases.

Case 1: $\kappa \in S$ and $\kappa + 1 \in S$.

Let $i_0 \le n-k$ such that $\kappa = s_{i_0}$ and $\kappa+1 = s_{i_0+1}$. From Lemma 2.1, we have $S' = S$ and $L' = L$, and hence $\kappa = s'_{i_0}$ and $\kappa + 1 = s'_{i_0+1}$. For the other indices, we have $s'_i = s_i$ (for $i \le n-k$) and $\ell'_j = \ell_j$ (for

$j \leq k$). Then

$$\begin{aligned}\Pi_k(\mathbf{B}) - \Pi_k(\mathbf{B}') &= \sum_{j=1}^{k}(k-j)\log\frac{\|b^*_{\ell_j}\|}{\|b'^*_{\ell'_j}\|} + \sum_{i=1}^{n-k} i\log\frac{\|b'^*_{s'_i}\|}{\|b^*_{s_i}\|} \\ &\quad + \sum_{i=1}^{n-k}(s_i - s'_i) \\ &= i_0\log\frac{\|b'^*_{s'_{i_0}}\|}{\|b^*_{s_{i_0}}\|} + (i_0+1)\log\frac{\|b'^*_{s'_{i_0+1}}\|}{\|b^*_{s_{i_0+1}}\|} \\ &= \log\frac{\|b'^*_{\kappa+1}\|}{\|b^*_{\kappa+1}\|} \geq \log\left(\frac{2}{\sqrt{3}}\right),\end{aligned}$$

where the last inequality follows from Lemma 2.1.

Case 2: $\kappa \in L$ and $\kappa + 1 \in L$.

The treatment of Case 1 can be adapted readily.

Case 3: $\kappa \in L$, $\kappa + 1 \in S$, $S' = S$ and $L' = L$.

Let $j_0 \leq k$ such that $\kappa = \ell_{j_0}$, and $i_0 \leq n-k$ such that $\kappa + 1 = s_{i_0}$. Then we have $\kappa = \ell'_{j_0}$ and $\kappa + 1 = s'_{i_0}$. For the other indices, we have $s'_i = s^{(t)}_i$ (for $i \leq n-k$) and $\ell'_j = \ell^{(t)}_j$ (for $j \leq k$). Thus

$$\begin{aligned}\Pi_k(\mathbf{B}) - \Pi_k(\mathbf{B}') &= \sum_{j=1}^{k}(k-j)\log\frac{\|b^*_{\ell_j}\|}{\|b'^*_{\ell'_j}\|} + \sum_{i=1}^{n-k} i\log\frac{\|b'^*_{s'_i}\|}{\|b^*_{s_i}\|} \\ &\quad + \sum_{i=1}^{n-k}(s_i - s'_i) \\ &= (k-j_0)\log\frac{\|b^*_{\ell_{j_0}}\|}{\|b'^*_{\ell'_{j_0}}\|} + i_0\log\frac{\|b'^*_{s'_{i_0}}\|}{\|b^*_{s_{i_0}}\|} \\ &= (k-j_0+i_0)\log\frac{\|b'^*_{\kappa+1}\|}{\|b^*_{\kappa+1}\|} \geq \log\left(\frac{2}{\sqrt{3}}\right),\end{aligned}$$

where the last inequality follows from Lemma 2.1 and the fact that $k - j_0 + i_0 \geq 1$.

Case 4: $\kappa \in L$, $\kappa+1 \in S$, $S' = S \cup \{\kappa\} \backslash \{\kappa+1\}$ and $L' = L \cup \{\kappa+1\} \backslash \{\kappa\}$.

Let $j_0 \leq k$ such that $\kappa = \ell_{j_0}$, and $i_0 \leq n-k$ such that $\kappa + 1 = s_{i_0}$. Then $\kappa = s'_{i_0}$ and $\kappa + 1 = \ell'_{j_0}$. For other indices, we have $s'_i = s_i$ (for $i \leq n-k$) and $\ell'_j = \ell_j$ (for $j \leq k$). Then

$$\begin{aligned}\Pi_k(\mathbf{B}) - \Pi_k(\mathbf{B}') &= \sum_{j=1}^{k}(k-j)\log\frac{\|b^*_{\ell_j}\|}{\|b'^*_{\ell'_j}\|} + \sum_{i=1}^{n-k} i\log\frac{\|b'^*_{s'_i}\|}{\|b^*_{s_i}\|} \\ &\quad + \sum_{i=1}^{n-k}(s_i - s'_i) \\ &= (k-j_0)\log\frac{\|b^*_{\ell_{j_0}}\|}{\|b'^*_{\ell'_{j_0}}\|} + i_0\log\frac{\|b'^*_{s'_{i_0}}\|}{\|b^*_{s_{i_0}}\|} + 1 \\ &= (k-j_0)\log\frac{\|b^*_{\kappa}\|}{\|b'^*_{\kappa+1}\|} + i_0\log\frac{\|b'^*_{\kappa}\|}{\|b^*_{\kappa+1}\|} + 1 \\ &\geq 1,\end{aligned}$$

where the last inequality follows from Lemma 2.1. The observation that $1 \geq \log(2/\sqrt{3})$ allows to complete the proof. □

With the above property of the k-th LLL potential, we can bound the number of LLL swaps that LLL performs.

Theorem 3.3. *Let $\mathbf{B} \in \mathbb{R}^{m\times n}$ be a full column rank matrix. Let $\mathbf{B}'$ be the basis returned by the LLL algorithm when given $\mathbf{B}$ as input. Then the number of swaps that LLL performs is no greater than*

$$\min_{1\leq k\leq n}\frac{\Pi_k(\mathbf{B}) - \Pi_k(\mathbf{B}')}{\log\left(\frac{2}{\sqrt{3}}\right)}.$$

4 ORTHOGONAL LATTICES

As an application of the k-th LLL potential Π_k, we consider the problem of computing an LLL-reduced basis of an orthogonal lattice. Let $\mathbf{A} \in \mathbb{Z}^{n\times k}$ with $n \geq k$. We aim at computing an LLL-reduced basis of the orthogonal lattice $\mathcal{L}^{\perp}(\mathbf{A})$, by LLL-reducing $\mathrm{Ext}_K(\mathbf{A})$ (as defined in (2)), for a sufficiently large integer K.

In Subsection 4.1, we provide a sufficient condition on the scaling parameter K so that a LLL-reduced basis of $\mathcal{L}^{\perp}(\mathbf{A})$ can be extracted from a LLL-reduced basis of $\mathcal{L}(\mathrm{Ext}_K(\mathbf{A}))$. For such a sufficiently large K, we study the Gram-Schmidt orthogonalizations of the input and output bases of the LLL call to $\mathrm{Ext}_K(\mathbf{A})$ in Subsection 4.2, and we provide a bound on the number of required LLL swaps which is independent of K in Subsection 4.3.

4.1 Correctness

For $n \geq k$, we define $\sigma_{n,k}$ as the map that embeds $\mathbb{R}^n$ into $\mathbb{R}^{n+k}$ by adding 0's in the first k coordinates.

$$\begin{aligned}\sigma_{n,k}: \mathbb{R}^n &\to \mathbb{R}^{n+k} \\ (x_1,\cdots,x_n)^T &\mapsto (\underbrace{0,\cdots,0}_{k},\underbrace{x_1,\cdots,x_n}_{n})^T.\end{aligned}$$

We also define $\delta_{n,k}$ as the map that erases the first k coordinates of a vector in $\mathbb{R}^{n+k}$.

$$\begin{aligned}\delta_{n,k}: \mathbb{R}^{n+k} &\to \mathbb{R}^n \\ (x_1,\cdots,x_k,x_{k+1},\cdots,x_{k+n})^T &\mapsto (x_{k+1},\cdots,x_{k+n})^T.\end{aligned}$$

We extend these functions to matrices in the canonical way. The following proposition is adapted from [9, Theorem 4] (see also [10, Proposition 2.24]). It shows that if K is sufficiently large, then calling the LLL algorithm on $\mathrm{Ext}_K(\mathbf{A})$ provides an LLL-reduced basis of $\mathcal{L}^{\perp}(\mathbf{A})$.

Proposition 4.1. *Let $\mathbf{A} \in \mathbb{Z}^{n\times k}$ be full column rank and $\mathbf{B} = \mathrm{Ext}_K(\mathbf{A})$. If $\mathbf{B}'$ is an LLL-reduced basis of $\mathcal{L}(\mathbf{B})$ and*

$$K > 2^{\frac{n-1}{2}} \cdot \lambda_{n-k}(\mathcal{L}^{\perp}(\mathbf{A})), \tag{7}$$

then $\delta_{n,k}(b'_1),\cdots,\delta_{n,k}(b'_{n-k})$ is an LLL-reduced basis of $\mathcal{L}^{\perp}(\mathbf{A})$.

Proof. As $\mathbf{A} \in \mathbb{Z}^{n\times k}$ is full column rank, we have $\dim(\mathcal{L}^{\perp}(\mathbf{A})) = n-k$. For any basis $\mathbf{C} \in \mathbb{Z}^{n\times(n-k)}$ of $\mathcal{L}^{\perp}(\mathbf{A})$, we have $\sigma_{n,k}(\mathbf{C}) = \mathbf{B}\cdot\mathbf{C}$, and hence the lattice $\sigma_{n,k}(\mathcal{L}^{\perp}(\mathbf{A}))$ is a sublattice of $\mathcal{L}(\mathbf{B})$. This implies that, for all $i \leq n-k$,

$$\lambda_i(\mathcal{L}(\mathbf{B})) \leq \lambda_i(\sigma_{n,k}(\mathcal{L}^{\perp}(\mathbf{A}))) = \lambda_i(\mathcal{L}^{\perp}(\mathbf{A})).$$

It follows from (5) that, for all $i \leq n-k$,

$$\|b'_i\|^2 \leq 2^{n-1}\cdot\lambda^2_{n-k}(\mathcal{L}(\mathbf{B})) \leq 2^{n-1}\cdot\lambda^2_{n-k}(\mathcal{L}^{\perp}(\mathbf{A})). \tag{8}$$

We now assume (by contradiction) that $\delta_{n,k}(b'_i) \notin \mathcal{L}^\perp(A)$ for some $i \le n-k$. Note that

$$b'_i = B \cdot \delta_{n,k}(b'_i) = (K \cdot \delta_{n,k}(b_{i'})^T \cdot A \mid \delta_{n,k}(b'_i)^T)^T.$$

As the subvector $K \cdot \delta_{n,k}(b'_i)^T \cdot A$ is non-zero, and using the assumption on K, we obtain that

$$\|b'_i\|^2 = \|K \cdot \delta_{n,k}(b'_i)^T \cdot A\|^2 + \|\delta_{n,k}(b'_i)\|^2 \ge K^2 > 2^{n-1} \cdot \lambda^2_{n-k}(\mathcal{L}^\perp(A)),$$

which contradicts (8).

From the above, we obtain that $\delta_{n,k}(b'_1), \cdots, \delta_{n,k}(b'_{n-k})$ are linearly independent vectors in $\mathcal{L}^\perp(A)$. They actually form a basis of $\mathcal{L}^\perp(A)$. To see this, consider an arbitrary vector $c \in \mathcal{L}^\perp(A)$. The vector $B \cdot c$ belongs to the real span of $b'_1, \cdots, b'_{n-k}$ and to $\mathcal{L}(B)$. As B' is a basis of $\mathcal{L}(B)$, vector $B \cdot c$ is an integer combination of $b'_1, \cdots, b'_{n-k}$ and vector c is an integer combination of $\delta_{n,k}(b'_1), \cdots, \delta_{n,k}(b'_{n-k})$.

Since B' is LLL-reduced and the first k coordinates of each of $b'_1, \cdots, b'_{n-k}$ are 0, we obtain that $\delta_{n,k}(b'_1), \cdots, \delta_{n,k}(b'_{n-k})$ form an LLL-reduced basis of $\mathcal{L}^\perp(A)$. □

To make this condition on K effective, we use some upper bounds on $\lambda_{n-k}(\mathcal{L}^\perp(A))$. For instance, from Minkowski's second theorem, we have

$$\lambda_{n-k}(\mathcal{L}^\perp(A)) \le (n-k)^{\frac{n-k}{2}} \cdot \det(\mathcal{L}^\perp(A)) \le (n-k)^{\frac{n-k}{2}} \cdot \|A\|^k.$$

Hence

$$K > 2^{\frac{n-1}{2}} \cdot (n-k)^{\frac{n-k}{2}} \cdot \|A\|^k \qquad (9)$$

suffices to guarantee that (7) holds.

The bound in (9) can be very loose. Indeed, in many cases, we expect the minima of $\mathcal{L}^\perp(A)$ to be balanced, and if they are so, then the following bound would suffice

$$K > 2^{\Omega(n)} \cdot \|A\|^{\frac{k}{n-k}}. \qquad (10)$$

For such a scaling paramter K, according to Proposition 4.1, after termination of the LLL call with $\mathrm{Ext}_K(A)$ as its input, the output matrix must be of the following form:

$$\begin{pmatrix} 0 & M \\ C & N \end{pmatrix}, \qquad (11)$$

where the columns of $C \in \mathbb{Z}^{n \times (n-k)}$ form an LLL-reduced basis of the lattice $\mathcal{L}^\perp(A)$. [1]

4.2 On the LLL input and output bases

To bound the number of LLL swaps, we first investigate the matrix $B = \mathrm{Ext}_K(A)$ given as input to the LLL algorithm, and the output matrix B'.

Intuitively, from the shape of B and the fact that A is full rank, there must be k Gram-Schmidt norms of B that are "impacted" by the scaling parameter K, and hence have large magnitude, while other $n-k$ Gram-Schmidt norms of B should be of small magnitude.

On the other hand, recall that B' is of the form (11). Since only the first k coordinates are related to the scaling parameter K, the submatrix C is "independent" of K. Thus, each of $\|b'^*_1\|, \cdots, \|b'^*_{n-k}\|$ should be relatively small (for a sufficiently large K), while each of $\|b'^*_{n-k+1}\|, \cdots, \|b'^*_n\|$ is "impacted" by K, and hence with large magnitude. The following result formalizes this discussion.

Proposition 4.2. *Let $A \in \mathbb{Z}^{n\times k}$ be of full column rank and B' the output basis of LLL with $B = \mathrm{Ext}_K(A)$ as input. If the scaling parameter $K \in \mathbb{Z}$ satisfies (7), then for the output matrix B' we have*

$$\forall i \le n-k, \quad \forall j > n-k, \quad \|b'^*_i\| < \|b'^*_j\|.$$

Proof. From Proposition 4.1, we know that B' is of the form

$$\begin{pmatrix} 0 & * \\ C & * \end{pmatrix},$$

and that the columns of $C \in \mathbb{Z}^{n\times k}$ form an LLL-reduced basis of $\mathcal{L}^\perp(A)$. We thus have, for $i \le n-k$

$$\|b'^*_i\|^2 \le \|b'_i\|^2 = \|c_i\|^2 \le 2^{n-k-1}\lambda^2_{n-k}(\mathcal{L}^\perp(A)).$$

Further, for $n-k < j \le n$, we have

$$\|b'^*_j\|^2 \ge 2^{-k}\|b'^*_{n-k+1}\|^2 \ge 2^{-k}K^2.$$

The choice of K allows to complete the proof. □

We observe again that combining the condition of Proposition 4.2 together with a general purpose bound on $\lambda_{n-k}(\mathcal{L}^\perp(A))$ allows to obtain a sufficient bound on K that can be efficiently derived from A.

Although $\|b^*_{s_i}\|$ is relatively small with respect to K, it can be bounded from below. In fact, we have a more general lower bound:

$$\forall i \le n, \; \|b^*_i\| \ge 1. \qquad (12)$$

This is because that there is a coefficient in b_i which is equal to 1 and 0 for all other b_j's. This lower bound will be helpful in the proof of Theorem 4.3.

4.3 Bounding the number of LLL swaps

Suppose that K is a sufficient large positive integer satisfying (7). Proposition 4.1 guarantees that we can use LLL with $B = \mathrm{Ext}_K(A)$ as input to compute an LLL-reduced basis for $\mathcal{L}^\perp(A)$. We now study the number of LLL swaps performed in this call to the LLL algorithm.

Theorem 4.3. *Let $A \in \mathbb{Z}^{n\times k}$ with a non-zero k-th principal minor, and K an integer satisfying (7). Then, given $B = \mathrm{Ext}_K(A)$ as its input, LLL computes (as a submatrix of the returned basis) an LLL-reduced basis of $\mathcal{L}^\perp(A)$ after at most $O(k^3 + k(n-k)(1+\log\|A\|))$ LLL swaps, where $\|A\|$ is the maximum of the Euclidean norm of all rows and columns of the matrix A.*

Proof. From Proposition 4.1, the LLL algorithm allows to obtain a LLL-reduced basis for $\mathcal{L}^\perp(A)$. We know from Theorem 3.3 that in order to obtain an upper bound on the number of LLL swaps, it suffices to find an upper bound to $\Pi_k(B)$ and a lower bound on $\Pi_k(B')$, where B' is the basis returned by LLL when given B as

[1] In fact, the resulting matrix gives more information than an LLL-reduced basis of $\mathcal{L}^\perp(A)$. For instance, the columns of $\frac{1}{K} \cdot M$ form a basis of the lattice generated by the rows of A.

Table 1: Upper bounds on the number of LLL swaps for different k (K sufficiently large), $\alpha = \log \|\mathbf{A}\|$.

	Classical analysis (9)	Heuristic (10)	New analysis
$k = 1$	$O(n^2 \log n + n\alpha)$	$O(n^2 + n\alpha)$	$O(n\alpha)$
$k = n/2$	$O(n^3 \log n + n^3\alpha)$	$O(n^3 + n^2\alpha)$	$O(n^3 + n^2\alpha)$
$k = n - 1$	$O(n^2\alpha)$	$O(n^2\alpha)$	$O(n^3 + n\alpha)$

input. From (12) we have

$$\begin{aligned}\Pi_k(\mathbf{B}) &= \sum_{j=1}^{k}(k-j)\log\|\boldsymbol{b}^*_{\ell_j}\| - \sum_{i=1}^{n-k} i\log\|\boldsymbol{b}^*_{s_i}\| + \sum_{i=1}^{n-k} s_i \\ &\le \sum_{j=1}^{k}(k-j)\log\|\boldsymbol{b}^*_{\ell_j}\| + \sum_{i=1}^{n-k} s_i \\ &\le \sum_{j=1}^{k}(k-j)\log\|\boldsymbol{b}_{\ell_j}\| + \sum_{i=1}^{n-k}(k+i) \\ &\le (1+\log K + \log\|\mathbf{A}\|)\frac{k(k-1)}{2} + \frac{(n-k)(n+k+1)}{2}.\end{aligned}$$

Thanks to Proposition 4.2, we have

$$\begin{aligned}\Pi_k(\mathbf{B}') &= \sum_{j=1}^{k}(k-j)\log\|\boldsymbol{b}'^*_{\ell'_j}\| - \sum_{i=1}^{n-k} i\log\|\boldsymbol{b}'^*_{s'_i}\| + \sum_{i=1}^{n-k} s'_i \\ &= \sum_{j=1}^{k}(k-j)\log\|\boldsymbol{b}'^*_{n-k+j}\| - \sum_{i=1}^{n-k} i\log\|\boldsymbol{b}'^*_i\| + \sum_{i=1}^{n-k} i.\end{aligned}$$

Since the first k coefficients of $\boldsymbol{b}'^*_i$ are 0 (for $i \le n-k$) and $\mathbf{A}$ is full-rank, we must have $\|\boldsymbol{b}'^*_{n-k+1}\| \ge K$. Further, since $\mathbf{B}'$ is LLL-reduced, combining with (4) we have, for $j \le k$

$$\|\boldsymbol{b}'^*_{n-k+j}\| \ge 2^{\frac{1-j}{2}}\|\boldsymbol{b}'^*_{n-k+1}\| \ge 2^{\frac{1-j}{2}}K \ge 2^{\frac{1-k}{2}}K.$$

We hence obtain

$$\begin{aligned}\Pi_k(\mathbf{B}') &\ge \left(\log K + \frac{1-k}{2}\right)\sum_{j=1}^{k}(k-j) - \sum_{i=1}^{n-k} i\log\|\boldsymbol{b}'^*_i\| \\ &\quad + \frac{(n-k)(n-k+1)}{2} \\ &\ge \frac{k(k-1)}{2}\left(\log K + \frac{1-k}{2}\right) - (n-k)\sum_{i=1}^{n-k}\log\|\boldsymbol{b}'^*_i\| \\ &\quad + \frac{(n-k)(n-k+1)}{2},\end{aligned}$$

where we used the fact that all $\|\mathbf{b}'^*_i\|$'s are ≥ 1. This is true for the $\|\mathbf{b}^*_i\|$'s and LLL cannot make the minimum Gram-Schmidt norm decrease. Using (3), we obtain:

$$\begin{aligned}\Pi_k(\mathbf{B}') &\ge \frac{k(k-1)}{2}\left(\log K + \frac{1-k}{2}\right) - (n-k)k\log\|\mathbf{A}\| \\ &\quad + \frac{(n-k)(n-k+1)}{2}.\end{aligned}$$

Finally, using Theorem 3.3, we obtain that the number of LLL swaps is no greater than

$$\frac{\Pi_k(\mathbf{B}) - \Pi_k(\mathbf{B}')}{\log\left(\frac{2}{\sqrt{3}}\right)} \le \frac{k(n-\frac{k}{2})\log\|\mathbf{A}\| + k^3 + (n-k)k}{\log\left(\frac{2}{\sqrt{3}}\right)},$$

which is of $O(k^3 + k(n-k)(1+\log\|\mathbf{A}\|))$. □

In Table 1 we compare favorably ($k = 1, n/2$) the result of Theorem 4.3 to the bounds on the number of swaps using the classical potential (6) and K fixed from the general threshold (9) or the heuristic one (10). We also consider $k = n-1$. However, in the latter case the problem reduces to linear system solving, and different techniques such as those in [18] should be considered.

With the potential function Π of (6), we have

$$\begin{aligned}\Pi(\mathbf{B}) &\le \log\prod_{i\le n}\left(K^2\|\mathbf{A}\|^2\right)^{\frac{\min(k,i)}{2}} \\ &\le \frac{k(2n-k+1)}{2}\log(K\|\mathbf{A}\|).\end{aligned}$$

The bound on the number of LLL swaps obtained using the classical potential is therefore $O(k(n-k/2)(1+\log K + \log\|\mathbf{A}\|)$. While we see from Theorem 4.3 that the actual number of swaps for computing an LLL-reduced basis for $\mathcal{L}^\perp(\mathbf{A})$ does not grow with K when K is sufficiently large.

ACKNOWLEDGMENTS

Our thanks go to anonymous referees for helpful comments, which make the presentation of the paper better. Jingwei Chen was partially supported by NNSFC (11501540, 11671377, 11771421) and Youth Innovation Promotion Association, CAS. Damien Stehlé was supported by ERC Starting Grant ERC-2013-StG-335086-LATTAC.

REFERENCES

[1] J. Chen, D. Stehlé, and G. Villard. 2013. A new view on HJLS and PSLQ: Sums and projections of lattices. In *Proceedings of ISSAC'13 (June 26-29, 2013, Boston, MA, USA)*. ACM, 149–156.
[2] Z. Chen and A. Storjohann. 2005. A BLAS based C library for exact linear algebra on integer matrices. In *Proceedings of ISSAC'05 (Beijing, China, July 24–27, 2005)*. ACM, 92–99.
[3] J. Håstad, B. Just, J. C. Lagarias, and C. P. Schnorr. 1989. Polynomial time algorithms for finding integer relations among real numbers. *SIAM Journal of Computing* 18, 5 (1989), 859–881. Erratum: SIAM J. Comput., 43(1), 254–254, 2014.
[4] G. Havas, B. S. Majewski, and K. R. Matthews. 1998. Extended GCD and Hermite normal form algorithms via lattice basis reduction. *Experimental Mathematics* 7, 2 (1998), 125–136.
[5] M. van Hoeij and A. Novocin. 2012. Gradual Sub-lattice Reduction and a New Complexity for Factoring Polynomials. *Algorithmica* 63, 3 (2012), 616–633.
[6] R. Kannan, A. K. Lenstra, and L. Lovász. 1984. Polynomial factorization and nonrandomness of bits of algebraic and some transcendental numbers. In *Proceedings of STOC'84 (April 30 - May 2, 1984, Washington, DC, USA)*. ACM, 191–200.
[7] A. K. Lenstra, H. W. Lenstra, and L. Lovász. 1982. Factoring polynomials with rational coefficients. *Mathematische Annalen* 261, 4 (1982), 515–534.

[8] A. Neumaier and D. Stehlé. 2016. Faster LLL-type reduction of lattice bases. In *Proceedings of ISSAC'16 (July 20–22, 2016, Waterloo, Ontario, Canada)*. ACM, 373–380.

[9] P. Nguyen and J. Stern. 1997. Merkle-Hellman revisited: A cryptanalysis of the Qu-Vanstone cryptosystem based on group factorizations. In *Proceedings of CRYPTO'97 (August 17–21, 1997, Santa Barbara, CA, USA)*. LNCS, Vol. 1294. Springer, 198–212.

[10] P. Q. Nguyen. 1999. *La Géométrie des Nombres en Cryptologie*. Ph.D. Dissertation. Université Paris 7, Paris.

[11] P. Q. Nguyen and B. Vallée (Eds.). 2010. *The LLL Algorithm: Survey and Applications*. Springer, Berlin.

[12] A. Novocin, D. Stehlé, and G. Villard. 2011. An LLL-reduction algorithm with quasi-linear time complexity. In *Proceedings of STOC '11 (June 6–8, 2011, San Jose, USA)*. ACM, 403–412.

[13] M. E. Pohst. 1987. A modification of the LLL reduction algorithm. *Journal of Symbolic Computation* 4, 1 (1987), 123–127.

[14] W. M. Schmidt. 1968. Asymptotic formulae for point lattices of bounded determinant and subspaces of bounded height. *Duke Mathematical Journal* 35, 2 (1968), 327–339.

[15] C. C. Sims (Ed.). 1994. *Computation with Finitely Presented Groups*. Cambridge University Press.

[16] D. Stehlé. 2017. Lattice reduction algorithms. In *Proceedings of ISSAC '17 (July 25-28, 2017, Kaiserslautern, Germany)*. ACM, 11–12.

[17] A. Storjohann. 1996. *Faster algorithms for integer lattice basis reduction*. Technical Report 249. ETH, Department of Computer Science, Zürich, Switzerland.

[18] A. Storjohann. 2005. The shifted number system for fast linear algebra on integer matrices. *J. Complexity* 21, 4 (2005), 609–650.

[19] A. Storjohann and G. Labahn. 1996. Asymptotically fast computation of Hermite normal forms of integer matrices. In *Proceedings of ISSAC'96 (July 24-26, 1996, Zurich, Switzerland)*. ACM, 259–266.

Additive Decompositions in Primitive Extensions*

Shaoshi Chen, Hao Du, and Ziming Li
KLMM, Academy of Mathematics and Systems Science, Chinese Academy of Sciences, Beijing 100190, China
School of Mathematical Sciences, University of Chinese Academy of Sciences, Beijing 100049, China
schen@amss.ac.cn,duhao@amss.ac.cn,zmli@mmrc.iss.ac.cn

ABSTRACT

This paper extends the classical Hermite-Ostrogradsky reduction for rational functions to more general functions in primitive extensions of certain types. For an element f in such an extension K, the extended reduction decomposes f as the sum of a derivative in K and another element r such that f has an antiderivative in K if and only if $r = 0$; and f has an elementary antiderivative over K if and only if r is a linear combination of logarithmic derivatives over the constants when K is a logarithmic extension. Moreover, r is minimal in some sense. Additive decompositions may lead to reduction-based creative-telescoping methods for nested logarithmic functions, which are not necessarily D-finite.

KEYWORDS

Additive decompositions, Creative telescoping, Elementary functions, Symbolic integration

ACM Reference Format:
Shaoshi Chen, Hao Du, and Ziming Li. 2018. Additive Decompositions in Primitive Extensions. In *ISSAC '18: 2018 ACM International Symposium on Symbolic and Algebraic Computation, July 16–19, 2018, New York, NY, USA.* ACM, New York, NY, USA, 8 pages. https://doi.org/10.1145/3208976.3208987

1 INTRODUCTION

Symbolic integration, together with its discrete counterpart symbolic summation, nowadays has played a crucial role in building the infrastructure for applying computer algebra tools to solve problems in combinatorics and mathematical physics [17, 18, 30]. The early history of symbolic integration starts from the first tries of developing programs in LISP to evaluate integrals in freshman calculus symbolically in the 1960s. Two representative packages at the time were Slagle's SAINT [31] and Moses's SIN [22], which were both based on integral transformation rules and pattern recognition. The algebraic approach for symbolic integration is initialized by Ritt [28] in terms of differential algebra [16], which eventually leads to the Risch algorithm for the integration of elementary functions [26, 27]. The efficiency of the Risch algorithm is further improved by Rothstein [29], Davenport [13], Trager [32], Bronstein [7, 8] etc. Some standard references on this topic are Bronstein's book [9] and Raab's survey [25] that gives an overview of the Risch algorithm and its recent developments.

The central problem in symbolic integration is whether the integral of a given function can be written in "closed form". Its algebraic formulation is given in terms of differential fields and their extensions [9, 16]. A differential field F is a field together with a derivation $'$ that is an additive map on F satisfying the product rule $(fg)' = f'g + fg'$ for all $f, g \in F$. A given element f in F is said to be *integrable* in F if $f = g'$ for some $g \in F$. The problem of deciding whether a given element is integrable or not in F is called the *integrability problem* in F. For example, if F is the field of rational functions, then for $f = 1/x^2$ we can find $g = -1/x$, while for $f = 1/x$ no suitable g exists in F. When f is not integrable in F, there are several other questions we may ask. One possibility is to ask whether there is a pair (g, r) in $F \times F$ such that $f = g' + r$, where r is minimal in some sense and $r = 0$ if f is integrable. This problem is called the *decomposition problem* in F. Extensive work has been done to solve the integrability and decomposition problems in differential fields of various kinds.

Abel and Liouville pioneered the early work on the integrability problem in the 19th century [28]. In 1833, Liouville provided a first decision procedure for solving the integrability problem on algebraic functions [20]. For an overview of Liouville's work on integration in finite terms, we refer to Lützen's book [21, pp. 351–422]. For other classes of functions, complete algorithms for solving the integrability problem are much more recent: 1) the Risch algorithm [26, 27] in the case of elementary functions was presented in 1969; 2) the Almkvist–Zeilberger algorithm [2] (also known as the differential Gosper algorithm) in the case of hyperexponential functions was given in 1990; 3) Abramov and van Hoeij's algorithm [1] generalized the previous algorithm to the general D-finite functions of arbitrary order in 1997.

The decomposition problem was first considered by Ostrogradsky [23] in 1845 and later by Hermite [15] for rational functions. The idea of Ostrogradsky and Hermite is crucial for algorithmic treatments of the problem, since it avoids the root-finding of polynomials and only uses the extended Euclidean algorithm and squarefree factorization to obtain the additive decomposition of a rational function. This reduction is a basic tool for the integration of rational functions and also plays an important role in the base case of our work. We will refer to this reduction as the *rational reduction* in this paper. The rational reduction has been extended to more general classes of functions including algebraic functions [10, 32], hyperexponential functions [4, 14], multivariate rational functions [5, 19], and more recently including D-finite functions [6, 12, 33]. Blending reductions with creative telescoping [2, 34] leads to the fourth and

*S. Chen and H. Du were supported by the NSFC Grants 11501552, 11688101 and by the Fund of the Youth Innovation Promotion Association, CAS. Z. Li was supported by the NSFC Grant 11771433.

ISSAC '18, July 16–19, 2018, New York, NY, USA

ACM ISBN 978-1-4503-5550-6/18/07...$15.00
https://doi.org/10.1145/3208976.3208987

most recent generation of creative telescoping algorithms, which are called reduction-based algorithms [3–5, 10, 12].

The telescoping problem can also be formulated for elementary functions [11, 24]. Two related problems are how to decide the existence of telescopers for elementary functions and how to compute one if telescopers exist. Reduction algorithms have been shown to be crucial for solving these two problems. This naturally motivates us to design reduction algorithms for elementary functions.

In this paper, we extend the rational reduction to elements in straight and flat towers of primitive extensions (see Definition 3.5). Our extended reductions solve the decomposition problems in such towers without solving any Risch equations (Theorems 4.8 and 5.15), and determine elementary integrability in such towers when primitive extensions are logarithmic (Theorem 6.1).

The remainder of this paper is organized as follows. We present basic notions and terminologies on differential fields, and collect some useful facts about integrability in primitive extensions in Section 2. We define the notions of straight and flat towers, and describe some straightforward reduction processes in Section 3. Additive decompositions in straight and flat towers are given in Sections 4 and 5, respectively. The two decompositions are used to determine elementary integrability in Section 6. Examples are given in Section 7 to illustrate that the decompositions may be useful to study the telescoping problem for elementary functions that are not *D*-finite.

2 PRELIMINARIES

Let $(F, ')$ be a differential field of characteristic zero. An element c of F is called a constant if $c' = 0$. Let C_F denote the set of constants in F, which is a subfield of F. Let (E, D) be a differential field containing F. We say that E is a differential field extension of F if the restriction of D on F is equal to the derivation $'$. The derivation D is also denoted by $'$ when there is no confusion.

Let $(E, ')$ be a differential field extension of F. For $S \subset E$, we use S' to denote the set $\{f' \mid f \in S\}$. If S is a C_E-linear subspace, so is S'. For $a, b \in E$, we write $a \equiv b \mod S$ if $a - b \in S$.

An element z of E is said to be *primitive* over F if $z' \in F$. If z is primitive and transcendental over F with $C_{F(z)} = C_F$, then it is called a *primitive monomial* over F, which is a special instance of Liouvillian monomials according to Definition 5.1.2 in [9].

Let z be a primitive monomial over F in the rest of this section. For $p \in F[z]$, the degree and leading coefficient of p are denoted by $\deg_z(p)$ and $\mathrm{lc}_z(p)$, respectively. By Theorem 5.1.1 in [9], p is squarefree if and only if $\gcd(p, p') = 1$. For $m \in \mathbb{N}$, $F[z]^{(m)}$ stands for $\{p \in F[z] \mid \deg_z(p) < m\}$.

An element $f \in F(z)$ is said to be *z-proper* if the degree of its numerator in z is lower than that of its denominator. In particular, zero is z-proper. It is well-known that f can be uniquely written as the sum of a z-proper element and a polynomial in z. They are called the fractional and polynomial parts of f, and denoted by $\mathrm{fp}_z(f)$ and $\mathrm{pp}_z(f)$, respectively.

An element of $F(z)$ is simple if its denominator is squarefree. By Theorem 5.3.1 in [9], for $f \in F(z)$, there exists a simple element h of $F(z)$ such that $f \equiv h \mod F(z)' + F[z]$. It follows that $f \equiv \mathrm{fp}_z(h) \mod F(z)' + F[z]$, which allows us to focus on simple and z-proper elements. So we say that an element of $F(z)$ is *z-simple* if it is both simple and z-proper. For $f \in F(z)$, Algorithm `HermiteReduce` in [9, page 139] computes a z-simple element g in $F(z)$ such that $f \equiv g \mod F(z)' + F[z]$. This algorithm is fundamental for our additive decompositions in primitive extensions.

Lemma 2.1. *Let $g \in F(z)' + F[z]$. Then $g = 0$ if it is z-simple.*

Proof. Suppose that $g \neq 0$. Since g is z-proper, there exists a nontrivial irreducible polynomial $p \in F[z]$ dividing the denominator of g. Since $g \in F(z)' + F[z]$, there exist $a \in F(z)$ and $b \in F[z]$ such that $g = a' + b$. The order of g at p is equal to -1. But the order of a' at p is either nonnegative or less than -1 by Lemma 4.4.2 (i) in [9], and the order of b at p is nonnegative, a contradiction. ∎

Every element $f \in F(z)$ is congruent to a unique z-simple element g modulo $F(z)' + F[z]$ by Theorem 5.3.1 in [9] and Lemma 2.1. We call g the *Hermitian part* of f with respect to z, denoted by $\mathrm{hp}_z(f)$. The map hp_z is C_F-linear on $F(z)$. Its kernel is $F(z)' + F[z]$. Thus, two elements have the same Hermitian parts if they are congruent modulo $F(z)' + F[z]$. This fact is frequently used later.

Example 2.2. *Let $F = \mathbb{C}(x)$ with $x' = 1$ and $z = \log(x)$. Then z is a primitive monomial over F. By Theorem 5.1.1 in [9], $C_{F(z)} = C_F$. Applying Algorithm* `HermiteReduce`*, we have*

$$f := \frac{z^3 + 2xz^2 + z - x^3 - 1}{z^2 + 2xz + x^2} = \left(\frac{x}{z+x}\right)' - \frac{x^2}{z+x} + z.$$

Then $f \equiv -x^2/(z+x) \mod F(z)' + F[z]$ and $\mathrm{hp}_z(f) = -x^2/(z+x)$.

Now, we collect some basic facts about primitive monomials. They are either straightforward or scattered in [9]. We list them below for the reader's convenience.

Lemma 2.3. *If p belongs to both $F[z]$ and $F(z)'$, then there exists c in C_F such that $\mathrm{lc}_z(p) \equiv cz' \mod F'$.*

Proof. Assume $p = r'$ for some $r \in F(z)$. Then $r \in F[z]$ by Lemma 4.4.2.(i) in [9]. Set $d = \deg_z(p)$ and $\ell = \mathrm{lc}_z(p)$. Then $\deg_z(r) \leq d+1$ by Lemma 5.1.2 in [9]. Assume that $r \equiv az^{d+1} + bz^d \mod F[z]^{(d)}$ for some $a, b \in F$. Then

$$r' \equiv a'z^{d+1} + ((d+1)az' + b')z^d \mod F[z]^{(d)}.$$

Since $p = r'$, we have that $a' = 0$ and $\ell = (d+1)az' + b'$. It follows that $\ell \equiv cz' \mod F'$ with $c = (d+1)a$. ∎

The next lemma will be used to decrease the degree of a polynomial modulo $F(z)'$. Its proof is a straightforward application of integration by parts.

Lemma 2.4. *For all $f \in F$ and $d \in \mathbb{N}$, we have*

$$f'z^d \equiv 0 \mod F(z)' + F[z]^{(d)}.$$

Recall that an element f in F is said to be a *logarithmic derivative in F* if $f = a'/a$ for some nonzero element $a \in F$.

Lemma 2.5. *Let f be a logarithmic derivative in $F(z)$. Then $\mathrm{hp}_z(f)$ is a logarithmic derivative in $F(z)$, and $f = \mathrm{hp}_z(f) + r$, where r is a logarithmic derivative in F.*

Proof. If $f = 0$, then we choose $r = 0$, which equals $1'/1$. Otherwise, there exist two monic polynomials $u, v \in F[z]$ and $w \in F$ such that $f = u'/u - v'/v + w'/w$ by the logarithmic derivative identity on page 104 of [9]. Note that $u'/u - v'/v$ is z-simple by Lemma 5.1.2 in [9] and w'/w is in F. Thus, $\text{hp}_z(f) = u'/u - v'/v$ and $r = w'/w$. ∎

3 PRIMITIVE EXTENSIONS

Let $(K_0, ')$ be a differential field of characteristic zero. Set $C = C_{K_0}$. Consider a tower of differential fields

$$K_0 \subset K_1 \subset \cdots \subset K_n, \tag{3.1}$$

where $K_i = K_{i-1}(t_i)$ for all i with $1 \leq i \leq n$. The tower given in (3.1) is said to be *primitive over* K_0 if t_i is a primitive monomial over K_{i-1} for all i with $1 \leq i \leq n$. The notation introduced in (3.1) will be used in the rest of the paper.

The assumption $C_{K_n} = C$ has a useful consequence.

Lemma 3.1. *Let the tower* (3.1) *be primitive.*

(i) *$t_1', \ldots, t_n'$ are linearly independent over C;*

(ii) *If $K_0 = C(t_0)$ with $t_0' = 1$ and $t_i' \in K_0$ for some i with $1 \leq i \leq n$, then $\text{hp}_{t_0}(t_i')$ is nonzero.*

Proof. (i) If $c_1 t_1' + \cdots + c_n t_n' = 0$ for some $c_1, \ldots, c_n \in C$, then $c_1 t_1 + \cdots + c_n t_n \in C$, which implies that $c_1 = \cdots = c_n = 0$, because $t_1, \ldots, t_n$ are algebraically independent over K_0.

(ii) By the rational reduction, $t_i' = u' + v$ for some $u, v \in K_0$ with v being t_0-simple. Then v is nonzero. For otherwise, $t_i - u$ would be a constant outside C. ∎

The following lemma tells us a way to modify the leading coefficient of a polynomial in $K_{n-1}[t_n]$ via integration by parts and Algorithm HermiteReduce.

Lemma 3.2. *Let the tower* (3.1) *be primitive with $n \geq 1$. Then, for all $\ell \in K_{n-1}$ and $d \in \mathbb{N}$, there exist a t_{n-1}-simple element $g \in K_{n-1}$ and a polynomial $h \in K_{n-2}[t_{n-1}]$ such that*

$$\ell t_n^d \equiv (g + h) t_n^d \mod K_n' + K_{n-1}[t_n]^{(d)}.$$

Proof. By Algorithm HermiteReduce, there are $f, g \in K_{n-1}$ with g being t_{n-1}-simple, and $h \in K_{n-2}[t_{n-1}]$ such that $\ell = f' + g + h$. Then $\ell t_n^d = f' t_n^d + (g+h) t_n^d$. Applying Lemma 2.4 to the term $f' t_n^d$, we prove the lemma. ∎

Let $\prec$ be the purely lexicographic ordering on the set of monomials in $t_1, t_2, \ldots, t_n$ with $t_1 \prec t_2 \prec \ldots \prec t_n$. For $i \in \{0, 1, \ldots, n-1\}$ and $p \in K_i[t_{i+1}, \ldots, t_n]$ with $p \neq 0$, the head monomial of p, denoted by $\text{hm}_i(p)$, is defined to be the highest monomial in $t_{i+1}, \ldots, t_n$ appearing in p with respect to $\prec$. The head coefficient of p, denoted by $\text{hc}_i(p)$, is defined to be the coefficient of $\text{hm}_i(p)$, which belongs to K_i. The head coefficient of zero is set to be zero.

Example 3.3. *Let $\xi = t_1^2 t_2 t_3 + t_2 t_3$. Viewing ξ as an element of $K_0[t_1, t_2, t_3]$, we have $\text{hm}_0(\xi) = t_1^2 t_2 t_3$ and $\text{hc}_0(\xi) = 1$, while, viewing ξ in $K_1[t_2, t_3]$, we have $\text{hm}_1(\xi) = t_2 t_3$ and $\text{hc}_1(\xi) = t_1^2 + 1$.*

The next lemma will be used in Section 5. We present it below because it holds for primitive towers.

Lemma 3.4. *Let $n \geq 1$. For a polynomial $p \in K_{n-1}[t_n]$, there are polynomials $p_i \in K_i[t_{i+1}, \ldots, t_n]$ such that $p \equiv \sum_{i=0}^{n-1} p_i \mod K_n'$, and that $\text{hc}_i(p_i)$ is t_i-simple for all i with $1 \leq i \leq n-1$. Moreover, $\deg_{t_n}(p_i) \leq \deg_{t_n}(p)$ for all i with $0 \leq i \leq n-1$.*

Proof. We proceed by induction on n. If $n = 1$, then it suffices to set $p_0 = p$. Assume that $n > 1$ and that the lemma holds for $n - 1$.

Let $p \in K_{n-1}[t_n]$ and $d = \deg_{t_n}(p)$. By Lemma 3.2,

$$p \equiv (g + h) t_n^d \mod K_n' + K_{n-1}[t_n]^{(d)},$$

where $g \in K_{n-1}$ is t_{n-1}-simple and $h \in K_{n-2}[t_{n-1}]$. By the induction hypothesis, there exist $h_j \in K_j[t_{j+1}, \ldots, t_{n-1}]$ such that $h = \sum_{j=0}^{n-2} h_j + u'$ for some u in K_{n-1} and that $\text{hc}_j(h_j)$ is t_j-simple for all j with $1 \leq j \leq n-2$. Moreover, set $h_{n-1} = g$. By Lemma 2.4,

$$p \equiv \sum_{j=0}^{n-1} h_j t_n^d \mod K_n' + K_{n-1}[t_n]^{(d)}. \tag{3.2}$$

We need to argue inductively on d. If $d = 0$, then it is sufficient to set $p_j = h_j$ for all j with $0 \leq j \leq n-1$, as $K_{n-1}[t_n]^{(0)} = \{0\}$. Assume that $d > 0$ and that the lemma holds for all polynomials in $K_{n-1}[t_n]^{(d)}$. By (3.2) and the induction hypothesis on d, we have

$$p \equiv \sum_{j=0}^{n-1} h_j t_n^d + \sum_{j=0}^{n-1} \tilde{p}_j \mod K_n',$$

where $\tilde{p}_j$ is in $K_j[t_{j+1}, \ldots, t_n]$, $\text{hc}_j(\tilde{p}_j)$ is t_j-simple when $j \geq 1$, and $\deg_{t_n}(\tilde{p}_j) < d$. Set $p_j = h_j t_n^d + \tilde{p}_j$. Then $p \equiv \sum_{j=0}^{n-1} p_j \mod K_n'$. Since $\text{hc}_j(p_j)$ is $\text{hc}_j(h_j)$ if $h_j \neq 0$ and $\text{hc}_j(p_j)$ is $\text{hc}_j(\tilde{p}_j)$ if $h_j = 0$, the requirements on each $\text{hc}_j(p_j)$ with $j \geq 1$ are fulfilled. The induction on d is completed, and so is the induction on n. ∎

Definition 3.5. *Let the tower* (3.1) *be primitive. Then it is said to be* straight *if $\text{hp}_{t_{i-1}}(t_i') \neq 0$ for all i with $2 \leq i \leq n$. The tower is said to be* flat *if $t_i' \in K_0$ for all i with $1 \leq i \leq n$.*

Example 3.6. *Let $K_0 = \mathbb{C}(x)$ with $x' = 1$. Let*

$$\log(x) = \int x^{-1} dx \quad \text{and} \quad \text{Li}(x) = \int \log(x)^{-1} dx.$$

Then the tower $K_0 \subset K_0(\log(x)) \subset K_0(\log(x), \text{Li}(x))$ is straight, while the tower $K_0 \subset K_0(\log(x)) \subset K_0(\log(x), \log(x+1))$ is flat. They contain no new constants by Lemma 5.1.1 in [9].

In this paper, we consider additive decompositions for elements in either straight or flat towers, where $K_0 = C(t_0)$ with $t_0' = 1$.

4 STRAIGHT TOWERS

In this section, we assume that the tower (3.1) is straight and that $K_0 = C(t_0)$ with $t_0' = 1$. The subfield C of constants is denoted by K_{-1} in recursive definitions and induction proofs to be carried out.

Our idea is to reduce a polynomial in $K_{n-1}[t_n]$ to another one of lower degree via integration by parts, whenever it is possible. The notion of t_n-rigid elements describes $r \in K_{n-1}$ such that $r t_n^d$ cannot be congruent to a polynomial of degree lower than d modulo K_n'.

Definition 4.1. *An element $r \in K_{-1}$ is said to be t_0-rigid if $r = 0$. Let $r \in K_{n-1}$, $f = \text{fp}_{t_{n-1}}(r)$ and $p = \text{pp}_{t_{n-1}}(r)$. We say that r is t_n-rigid if f is t_{n-1}-simple, $f \neq c\,\text{hp}_{t_{n-1}}(t_n')$ for any nonzero $c \in C$, and $\text{lc}_{t_{n-1}}(p)$ is t_{n-1}-rigid.*

Zero is t_n-rigid because $\text{hp}_{t_{n-1}}(t_n')$ is nonzero. Furthermore, let r be t_{n-1}-simple. Then $r t_n^d$ cannot be congruent to a polynomial of a lower degree if and only if r is t_n-rigid by Lemma 2.3.

Example 4.2. *Let* $t_0 = x$, $t_1 = \log(x)$ *and* $t_2 = \mathrm{Li}(x)$. *Let*

$$\ell_1 = \frac{1}{x+k_1} \quad \text{and} \quad \ell_2 = \frac{1}{t_1+k_2} + \ell_1 t_1^2 + x t_1 + x^2.$$

Then ℓ_1 *is* t_1*-rigid if* $k_1 \neq 0$ *and* ℓ_2 *is* t_2*-rigid if* $k_1 k_2 \neq 0$.

The next lemma, together with Lemma 2.3, reveals that a nonzero polynomial p in $K_{n-1}[t_n]$ with a t_n-rigid leading coefficient has no antiderivative in K_n.

Lemma 4.3. *Let* $r \in K_{n-1}$ *be* t_n*-rigid. If*

$$r \equiv c t_n' \mod K_{n-1}' \tag{4.1}$$

for some $c \in C$, *then both* r *and* c *are zero.*

Proof. We proceed by induction on n. If $n = 0$, then $r = 0$ by Definition 4.1. Thus, $ct_0' \equiv 0 \mod K_{-1}'$. Consequently, $c = 0$ because $K_{-1}' = \{0\}$ and $t_0' = 1$.

Assume that $n > 0$ and that the lemma holds for $n-1$.

Set $f = \mathrm{fp}_{t_{n-1}}(r)$. Then $f = \mathrm{hp}_{t_{n-1}}(r)$, since f is t_{n-1}-simple by Definition 4.1. Applying the map $\mathrm{hp}_{t_{n-1}}$ to (4.1), we have $f = c\,\mathrm{hp}_{t_{n-1}}(t_n')$ by Lemma 2.1. Hence, $c = 0$ and $f = 0$ by Definition 4.1.

Set $p = \mathrm{pp}_{t_{n-1}}(r)$. Then (4.1) becomes $p \equiv 0 \mod K_{n-1}'$, which, together with Lemma 2.3, implies that $\mathrm{lc}_{t_{n-1}}(p) \equiv \tilde{c} t_{n-1}' \mod K_{n-2}'$ for some $\tilde{c} \in C$. It follows from the induction hypothesis that $\mathrm{lc}_{t_{n-1}}(p)$ is zero, and so is p. Thus, r is zero. ∎

In $K_{n-1}[t_n]$, we define a class of polynomials that have no antiderivatives in K_n.

Definition 4.4. *For* $n \geq 0$, *a polynomial in* $K_{n-1}[t_n]$ *is said to be* t_n-straight *if its leading coefficient is* t_n*-rigid.*

Zero is a t_n-straight polynomial, because its leading coefficient is zero, which is t_n-rigid.

Proposition 4.5. *Let* $p \in K_{n-1}[t_n]$ *be a* t_n*-straight polynomial. Then* $p = 0$ *if* $p \in K_n'$.

Proof. By Lemma 2.3, $\mathrm{lc}_{t_n}(p) \equiv ct_n' \mod K_{n-1}'$ for some $c \in C$. Then $\mathrm{lc}_{t_n}(p) = 0$ by Lemma 4.3. Consequently, $p = 0$. ∎

Next, we reduce a polynomial to a t_n-straight one.

Lemma 4.6. *For* $p \in K_{n-1}[t_n]$, *there exists a* t_n*-straight polynomial* $q \in K_{n-1}[t_n]$ *with* $\deg_{t_n}(q) \leq \deg_{t_n}(p)$ *such that* $p \equiv q \mod K_n'$.

Proof. If $p = 0$, then we choose $q = 0$. Assume that p is nonzero. We proceed by induction on n.

If $n = 0$, then $p \equiv 0 \mod K_0'$, as every element of $K_{-1}[t_0]$ has an antiderivative in the same ring.

Assume that $n > 0$ and that the lemma holds for $n-1$.

Let $p \in K_{n-1}[t_n]$ with degree d and leading coefficient ℓ. We are going to concoct a t_n-rigid element r such that

$$\ell \equiv r \mod K_n'. \tag{4.2}$$

This congruence helps us decrease degrees.

By Algorithm HermiteReduce, there are t_{n-1}-simple elements g, u in K_{n-1} and polynomials h, v in $K_{n-2}[t_{n-1}]$ such that

$$\ell \equiv g + h \mod K_{n-1}' \quad \text{and} \quad t_n' \equiv u + v \mod K_{n-1}'.$$

By the induction hypothesis, for any $c \in C$, $h - cv \equiv \tilde{h}_c \mod K_{n-1}'$, where $\tilde{h}_c$ is a t_{n-1}-straight polynomial in $K_{n-2}[t_{n-1}]$. It follows that $\ell \equiv g - cu + \tilde{h}_c \mod K_n'$. If there exists $\tilde{c} \in C$ such that $g = \tilde{c}u$, then let $r = \tilde{h}_{\tilde{c}}$. Otherwise, let $c = 0$ and $r = g + \tilde{h}_0$. Then $r \in K_{n-1}$ is t_n-rigid and (4.2) holds.

If $d = 0$, then $p = \ell$. By (4.2), we have $p \equiv r \mod K_n'$. Let $q = r$, which is t_n-straight by Definition 4.4.

Assume that $d > 0$ and each polynomial in $K_{n-1}[t_n]^{(d)}$ is congruent to a t_n-straight polynomial modulo K_n'. It follows from (4.2) and Lemma 2.3 that $\ell \equiv r + ct_n' \mod K_{n-1}'$. By Lemma 2.4 and the equality $ct_n' t_n^d = \left(\frac{c}{d+1} t_n^{d+1}\right)'$, we have $p \equiv rt_n^d + \tilde{q} \mod K_n'$ for some $\tilde{q} \in K_{n-1}[t_n]^{(d)}$. If $r \neq 0$, then set $q = rt_n^d + \tilde{q}$. Otherwise, applying the induction hypothesis on d to $\tilde{q}$ yields a t_n-straight polynomial q with $p \equiv q \mod K_n'$. The above reduction clearly implies that $\deg_{t_n}(q) < \deg_{t_n}(p)$. ∎

Example 4.7. *Let us consider* $\int \log(x)\,\mathrm{Li}(x)^2\,dx$. *Set* $t_1 = \log(x)$ *and* $t_2 = \mathrm{Li}(x)$. *Then we reduce the integrand* $t_1 t_2^2$. *We have that* $\mathrm{lc}_{t_2}(t_1 t_2^2) = t_1$. *Since* t_1 *is not* t_2*-rigid,* $t_1 t_2^2$ *can be reduced. In fact,* $t_1 t_2^2 = x' t_1 t_2^2$. *By Lemma 2.4 and a straightforward calculation, we get that* $t_1 t_2^2 \equiv (2x/t_1)t_2 + (x^2/t_1) \mod C(x, t_1, t_2)'$. *Since* $2x/t_1$ *is* t_2*-rigid, we have* $(2x/t_1)t_2 + (x^2/t_1)$ *is* t_2*-straight. Hence,* $t_1 t_2^2$ *has no antiderivative in* $C(x, t_1, t_2)$ *by Proposition 4.5.*

Below is an additive decomposition in a straight tower.

Theorem 4.8. *For* $f \in K_n$, *the following assertions hold.*

(i) *There exist a* t_n*-simple element* $g \in K_n$ *and a* t_n*-straight polynomial* $p \in K_{n-1}[t_n]$ *such that*

$$f \equiv g + p \mod K_n'. \tag{4.3}$$

(ii) $f \in K_n'$ *if and only if both* g *and* p *in (4.3) are zero.*

(iii) *If* $f \equiv \tilde{g} + \tilde{p} \mod K_n'$, *where* $\tilde{g} \in K_n$ *is a* t_n*-simple element and* $\tilde{p} \in K_{n-1}[t_n]$, *then* $g = \tilde{g}$ *and* $\deg_{t_n}(p) \leq \deg_{t_n}(\tilde{p})$.

Proof. (i) By Algorithm HermiteReduce, there exist a t_n-simple element $g \in K_n$ and a polynomial $h \in K_{n-1}[t_n]$ such that

$$f \equiv g + h \mod K_n'.$$

By Lemma 4.6, h can be replaced by a t_n-straight polynomial p.

(ii) Since $f \in K_n'$, the congruence (4.3) becomes $g + p \equiv 0 \mod K_n'$. Applying the map hp_{t_n} to the new congruence, we have that $g = 0$, because $g = \mathrm{hp}_{t_n}(g+p)$. Thus, $p = 0$ by Proposition 4.5.

(iii) Since $g - \tilde{g} \equiv \tilde{p} - p \mod K_n'$, we have $g = \tilde{g}$ by Lemma 2.1. If $\deg_{t_n}(\tilde{p}) < \deg_{t_n}(p)$, then $p - \tilde{p}$ is t_n-straight, because $\mathrm{lc}_{t_n}(p - \tilde{p})$ equals $\mathrm{lc}_{t_n}(p)$. So $p - \tilde{p} = 0$ by Proposition 4.5, a contradiction. ∎

Example 4.9. *Consider the integral*

$$\int \frac{1}{\mathrm{Li}(x)^2} + \log(x)\,\mathrm{Li}(x)^2\,dx.$$

The integrand is equal to $(-\log(x)/\mathrm{Li}(x))' + 1/(x\,\mathrm{Li}(x)) + \log(x)\,\mathrm{Li}(x)^2$ *by Algorithm* HermiteReduce. *Therefore, it has no antiderivative in* $C(x, \log(x), \mathrm{Li}(x))$ *by Theorem 4.8 and Example 4.7.*

5 FLAT TOWERS

In this section, we let the tower (3.1) be flat. The ground field K_0 will be specialized to $C(t_0)$ later in this section. We are not able to fully carry out the same idea as in Section 4, because $\mathrm{hp}_{t_{i-1}}(t_i') = 0$

for all $i = 2, \ldots, n$. This spoils Lemma 4.3 and Proposition 4.5. So we need to study integrability in a flat tower differently.

This section is divided into two parts. First, we extend Lemma 2.4 to the differential ring $K_0[t_1, \ldots, t_n]$. Second, we present a flat counterpart of the results in Section 4.

5.1 Scales

Let us denote $K_0[t_1, \ldots, t_n]$ by R_n. For a monomial ξ in $t_1, \ldots, t_n$, the C-linear subspace $\{p \in R_n \mid p \prec \xi\}$ is denoted by $R_n^{(\xi)}$. The notion of scales is motivated by the following example.

Example 5.1. *Let $n = 2$, and $\xi_0 = 1, \xi_1 = t_1$ and $\xi_2 = t_2$. And let $\ell = t_1' + t_2'$. Using integration by parts, we find three congruences*

$$\ell\xi_0 \equiv 0 \mod K_2', \quad \ell\xi_1 \equiv -t_1' t_2 \mod K_2', \quad \ell\xi_2 \equiv -t_2' t_1 \mod K_2'.$$

The first and third congruences lead to monomials lower than ξ_0 and ξ_2, respectively. But the second one leads to t_2, which is higher than ξ_1. The notion of scales aims to prevent the second congruence from the reduction to be carried out.

Definition 5.2. *For $p \in R_n \setminus K_0$ with $\operatorname{hm}_0(p) = t_1^{e_1} \cdots t_n^{e_n}$, the* scale *of p with respect to n is defined to be s if $e_1 = 0, \ldots, e_{s-1} = 0$ and $e_s > 0$. For $p \in K_0$, the* scale *of p with respect to n is defined to be n. The scale of p with respect to n is denoted by $\operatorname{scale}_n(p)$.*

Example 5.3. *Let $\xi_0 = 1$, $\xi_1 = t_1 t_2$ and $\xi_2 = t_3^2$. Regarding ξ_0, ξ_1 and ξ_2 as elements in R_3, we have that $\operatorname{scale}_3(\xi_0) = 3$, $\operatorname{scale}_3(\xi_1) = 1$ and $\operatorname{scale}_3(\xi_2) = 3$; while, regarding them as elements in R_4, we have that $\operatorname{scale}_4(\xi_0) = 4$, $\operatorname{scale}_4(\xi_1) = 1$ and $\operatorname{scale}_4(\xi_2) = 3$.*

Notably, if $p \in K_0$, then $\operatorname{scale}_n(p) = n$, which varies as n does. On the other hand, $\operatorname{scale}_n(p) = \operatorname{scale}_m(p)$ if $p \in R_m \setminus K_0$ with $m \leq n$.

The next lemma extends Lemma 2.4 and indicates what kind of integration by parts will be used for reduction.

Lemma 5.4. *Let ξ be a monomial in $t_1, \ldots, t_n$. Then the following assertions hold.*

(i) *For all $f \in K_0$, $f'\xi \equiv 0 \mod K_n' + R_n^{(\xi)}$.*
(ii) *Let $s = \operatorname{scale}_n(\xi)$. Then, for all $c_1, \ldots, c_s \in C$,*

$$(c_1 t_1' + \cdots + c_s t_s')\xi \equiv 0 \mod K_n' + R_n^{(\xi)}.$$

Proof. (i) It follows from integration by parts and the fact that ξ' belongs to $R_n^{(\xi)}$.

(ii) Set $L_0 = 0$ and $L_i = \sum_{j=1}^{i} c_j t_j$ for $i = 1, \ldots, n$.

If $\xi = 1$, then $s = n$ and $L_n'\xi \in K_n'$. The assertion clearly holds. Assume that $\xi = t_s^{e_s} \cdots t_n^{e_n}$ with $e_s > 0$. Then $L_s'\xi = L_{s-1}'\xi + c_s t_s'\xi$. Note that $L_{s-1}'\xi$ belongs to $K_n' + R_n^{(\xi)}$ by a direct use of integration by parts. Set $\eta = \xi / t_s^{e_s}$. Then the term $c_s t_s' \xi$ is equal to $\frac{c_s}{e_s+1}\left(t_s^{e_s+1}\right)' \eta$. Integration by parts leads to

$$c_s t_s' \xi \equiv \frac{-c_s}{e_s + 1} t_s^{e_s+1} \eta' \mod K_n'. \tag{5.1}$$

If $\eta = 1$, then $c_s t_s' \xi \in K_n'$ by (5.1). Otherwise, we have $e_j > 0$ for some j with $s < j \leq n$. Then each monomial in $t_s^{e_s+1}\eta'$ is of total degree $\sum_{j=s}^{n} e_j$ and is of degree $e_s + 1$ in t_s. So $t_s^{e_s+1}\eta' \prec \xi$. Consequently, $c_s t_s' \xi \in K_n' + R_n^{(\xi)}$ by (5.1). ∎

In the rest of this section, we let $K_0 = C(t_0)$ with $t_0' = 1$. By Lemma 3.1 (ii), we may further assume that t_i' is nonzero and t_0-simple for all i with $1 \leq i \leq n$.

Definition 5.5. *For every k with $1 \leq k \leq n$, an element of K_0 is said to be* k-rigid *if either it is zero or it is t_0-simple and not a C-linear combination of $t_1', \ldots, t_k'$.*

Proposition 5.6. *For $p \in R_n$, there exists $q \in R_n$ such that $p \equiv q \mod K_n'$ and that $\operatorname{hc}_0(q)$ is s-rigid, where $s = \operatorname{scale}_n(q)$. Moreover, we have $\operatorname{hm}_0(q) \preceq \operatorname{hm}_0(p)$.*

Proof. Set $q = 0$ if $p = 0$. Assume $p \neq 0$ and $\xi = \operatorname{hm}_0(p)$. By the rational reduction, $\operatorname{hc}_0(p) = f' + g$ for some $f, g \in K_0$ with g being t_0-simple. Then $p = f'\xi + g\xi \mod R_n^{(\xi)}$. By Lemma 5.4 (i), $p \equiv g\xi + r \mod K_n'$ for some $r \in R_n^{(\xi)}$. Set $s = \operatorname{scale}_n(\xi)$. If g is nonzero and s-rigid, then set $q = g\xi + r$. Otherwise, $p \equiv \tilde{r} \mod K_n'$ for some $\tilde{r} \in R_n^{(\xi)}$ by Lemma 5.4 (ii). The proposition follows from a direct Noetherian induction on $\operatorname{hm}_0(\tilde{r})$ with respect to $\prec$. ∎

Example 5.7. *Let $K_0 = \mathbb{C}(x)$, $t_1 = \log(x)$, $t_2 = \log(x+1)$ and*

$$p = t_1^2 t_2 + (2/x) t_1 t_2 + ((2/(x+1)) t_1.$$

Then $\operatorname{hc}_0(p) = 1$, which is not 1-rigid. Since $t_1^2 t_2 = x' t_1^2 t_2$, we have that $p = (x t_1^2 t_2)' + q$, where $q = \left(\frac{2}{x} - 2\right) t_1 t_2 - \frac{x}{x+1} t_1^2 + \frac{2}{x+1} t_1$. We can then reduce q further, because $\operatorname{hc}_0(q) = (2t_1 - 2x)'$, which is not 1-rigid either. Repeating this reduction a finite number of times, we see that $\int p\,dx = (x+1)t_1^2 t_2 - 2x t_1 t_2 - x t_1^2 + (2x+2) t_2 + 4x t_1 - 6x$.

5.2 Reduction

A flat analogue of straight polynomials is given below.

Definition 5.8. *A polynomial in $C[t_0]$ is said to be t_0-flat if it is zero. For $n \geq 1$, $p \in K_{n-1}[t_n]$ is called a* t_n-flat *polynomial if there exist $p_i \in K_i[t_{i+1}, \ldots, t_n]$ for all i with $0 \leq i \leq n-1$ such that $p = \sum_{i=0}^{n-1} p_i$, $\operatorname{hc}_i(p_i)$ is t_i-simple for all $i \geq 1$, and $\operatorname{hc}_0(p_0)$ is s-rigid, where $s = \operatorname{scale}_n(p_0)$. The sequence $\{p_i\}_{i=0,1,\ldots,n-1}$ is called a* sequence associated to p.

Example 5.9. *Let $n = 3$ and $t_0 = x$, $t_1 = \log(x)$, $t_2 = \log(x+1)$ and $t_3 = \log(x+2)$. Consider $p \in K_2[t_3]$*

$$p = \underbrace{\frac{1}{t_2} t_3^2}_{p_2} + \underbrace{\frac{1}{t_1} t_2 t_3}_{p_1} + \underbrace{\frac{1}{x+k} t_3^3 + x t_2 t_3}_{p_0},$$

where $k \in \mathbb{Z}$. Obviously, $\operatorname{hc}_2(p_2)$ is t_2-simple and $\operatorname{hc}_1(p_1)$ is t_1-simple. Moreover, $\operatorname{scale}_3(p_0) = 3$ and $\operatorname{hc}_0(p_0)$ is 3-rigid if $k \notin \{0, 1, 2\}$. So p is t_3-flat if $k \notin \{0, 1, 2\}$.

We are going to extend the results in Section 4 to the flat case, based on the following technical lemma.

Lemma 5.10. *Let $n \geq 1$ and p be a t_n-flat polynomial in $K_{n-1}[t_n]$ with $d = \deg_{t_n}(p)$ and $\ell = \operatorname{lc}_{t_n}(p)$. Let $\{p_i\}_{i=0,1,\ldots,n-1}$ be a sequence associated to p, and ℓ_i be the coefficient of t_n^d in p_i. Then*

(i) *$\operatorname{fp}_{t_{n-1}}(\ell)$ is t_{n-1}-simple.*
(ii) *If $\ell_m \neq 0$ for some $m > 0$, then $\ell \notin K_{m-1}[t_m, t_{m+1}, \ldots, t_{n-1}]$.*
(iii) *If $n > 1$, then $\operatorname{pp}_{t_{n-1}}(\ell) - c t_n'$ is t_{n-1}-flat for all $c \in C$.*

Proof. The lemma is trivial if $p = 0$. Assume that p is nonzero. Then $\ell = \sum_{i=0}^{n-1} \ell_i$, $\mathrm{fp}_{t_{n-1}}(\ell) = \ell_{n-1}$ and $\mathrm{pp}_{t_{n-1}}(\ell) = \sum_{i=0}^{n-2} \ell_i$.

(i) Note that $\ell_i = 0$ if $\deg_{t_n}(p_i) < d$, and $\mathrm{hc}_i(\ell_i) = \mathrm{hc}_i(p_i)$ otherwise, because $\prec$ is a purely lexicographic with $t_{i+1} \prec \cdots \prec t_n$. Then $\mathrm{fp}_{t_{n-1}}(\ell)$ is t_{n-1}-simple by Definition 5.8.

(ii) Without loss of generality, assume that $\ell_{n-1} = \cdots = \ell_{m+1} = 0$ and $\ell_m \neq 0$ for some $m > 0$. Then we have $f_m := \mathrm{hc}_m(p_m) \neq 0$. By Definition 5.8, f_m is t_m-simple. So f_m is not in $K_{m-1}[t_m]$, which implies $\ell_m \notin K_{m-1}[t_m, \ldots, t_{n-1}]$. Since $\ell_i \in K_{m-1}[t_m, \ldots, t_{n-1}]$ for all i with $0 \le i \le m-1$, we see that $\ell = \ell_m + \sum_{i=0}^{m-1} \ell_i$ does not belong to $K_{m-1}[t_m, \ldots, t_{n-1}]$ either.

(iii) Assume that $n > 1$. Then

$$\mathrm{pp}_{t_{n-1}}(\ell) - ct_n' = \ell_{n-2} + \cdots + \ell_1 + \tilde{\ell}_0, \tag{5.2}$$

where $\tilde{\ell}_0 = \ell_0 - ct_n'$ and $\mathrm{hc}_i(\ell_i)$ is t_i-simple, $i = 1, \ldots, n-2$.

Set $s = \mathrm{scale}_n(p_0)$ and $\tilde{s} = \mathrm{scale}_{n-1}(\tilde{\ell}_0)$. It suffices to prove that $\mathrm{hc}_0(\tilde{\ell}_0)$ is $\tilde{s}$-rigid by (5.2) and Definition 5.8.

Case 1. $\ell_0 \notin K_0$. Then $s < n$.

$$\mathrm{hm}_0(p_0) = t_s^{e_s} \cdots t_{n-1}^{e_{n-1}} t_n^d \quad \text{and} \quad \mathrm{hm}_0(\ell_0) = t_s^{e_s} \cdots t_{n-1}^{e_{n-1}},$$

where $e_s > 0$. Moreover, $s = \mathrm{scale}_{n-1}(\ell_0)$, $\mathrm{hm}_0(\ell_0) = \mathrm{hm}_0(\tilde{\ell}_0)$ and $\mathrm{hc}_0(p_0) = \mathrm{hc}_0(\ell_0) = \mathrm{hc}_0(\tilde{\ell}_0)$. In particular, $\tilde{s} = s$. Hence, $\mathrm{hc}_0(\tilde{\ell}_0)$ is $\tilde{s}$-rigid, because $\mathrm{hc}_0(p_0)$ is s-rigid.

Case 2. $\ell_0 \in K_0$ with $\ell_0 \neq 0$. Then $\mathrm{hm}_0(p_0) = t_n^d$ and $s = n$. Moreover, $\tilde{s} = n-1$, since $\tilde{\ell}_0 \in K_0$. Note that p is t_n-flat. So $\mathrm{hc}_0(p_0)$ is not a C-linear combination of $\{t_1', \ldots, t_{n-1}', t_n'\}$, and neither is ℓ_0 because $\ell_0 = \mathrm{hc}_0(p_0)$. Consequently, $\tilde{\ell}_0$ is not a C-linear combination of $\{t_1', \ldots, t_{n-1}'\}$, and neither is $\mathrm{hc}_0(\tilde{\ell}_0)$, because $\mathrm{hc}_0(\tilde{\ell}_0) = \tilde{\ell}_0$. Thus, $\mathrm{hc}_0(\tilde{\ell}_0)$ is $(n-1)$-rigid.

Case 3. $\ell_0 = 0$. Then $\tilde{s} = n-1$ and $\mathrm{hc}_0(\tilde{\ell}_0) = \tilde{\ell}_0 = -ct_n'$, which is $\tilde{s}$-rigid by Lemma 3.1 (i). ∎

The next lemma is a flat-analogue of Lemma 4.3

Lemma 5.11. *Let $n \ge 1$ and $p \in K_{n-1}[t_n]$ be t_n-flat. If*

$$\mathrm{lc}_{t_n}(p) \equiv ct_n' \mod K_{n-1}' \tag{5.3}$$

for some $c \in C$, then both p and c are zero.

Proof. If $n = 1$, then the tower $K_0 \subset K_1$ is also straight, and p is t_1-straight by Definition 4.4 and Lemma 3.1 (ii). Both p and c are zero by Lemma 4.3.

Assume $n > 1$ and the lemma holds for $n-1$. Set $\ell = \mathrm{lc}_{t_n}(p)$. Applying the map $\mathrm{hp}_{t_{n-1}}$ to (5.3), we have $\mathrm{hp}_{t_{n-1}}(\ell) = 0$. Then $\mathrm{fp}_{t_{n-1}}(\ell) = 0$ by Lemma 5.10 (i) and Lemma 2.1. Consequently, we have $\ell \in K_{n-2}[t_{n-1}]$. Let $q = \ell - ct_n'$. Then q is t_{n-1}-flat by Lemma 5.10 (iii). On the other hand, $q \in K_{n-1}'$ by (5.3). Then $\mathrm{lc}_{t_{n-1}}(q) \equiv \tilde{c}t_{n-1}' \mod K_{n-2}'$ for some $\tilde{c} \in C$ by Lemma 2.3. So $q = 0$ by the induction hypothesis. Accordingly,

$$\ell = ct_n' \in K_0. \tag{5.4}$$

Let $\{p_i\}_{i=0,1,\ldots,n-1}$ be a sequence associated to p. Let $d = \deg_{t_n}(p)$ and ℓ_0 be the coefficient of t_n^d in p_0. By (5.4) and Lemma 5.10 (ii), we have $\ell = \ell_0$. Then $\ell_0 \in K_0$, which implies that $\mathrm{hm}_0(p_0) = t_n^d$. Therefore, $\mathrm{scale}_n(p_0) = n$. Accordingly, ct_n' is n-rigid by Definition 5.8. It follows form Definition 5.5 that $c = 0$. By (5.4), we conclude that ℓ is zero, and so is p. ∎

The following proposition corresponds to Proposition 4.5.

Proposition 5.12. *Let $n \ge 1$ and p be a t_n-flat polynomial in $K_{n-1}[t_n]$. If $p \in K_n'$, then $p = 0$.*

Proof. Since $p \in K_n'$, we have $\mathrm{lc}_{t_n}(p) \equiv ct_n' \mod K_{n-1}'$ for some $c \in C$ by Lemma 2.3. Then $p = 0$ by Lemma 5.11. ∎

The next lemma corresponds to Lemma 4.6.

Lemma 5.13. *For $p \in K_{n-1}[t_n]$, there exists a t_n-flat polynomial $q \in K_{n-1}[t_n]$ such that $p \equiv q \mod K_n'$. Moreover, $\deg_{t_n}(q)$ is no more than $\deg_{t_n}(p)$.*

Proof. By Lemma 3.4, there exist $p_i \in K_i[t_{i+1}, \ldots, t_n]$ for all i with $0 \le i \le n-1$ such that $p \equiv \sum_{i=0}^{n-1} p_i \mod K_n'$. Moreover, $\mathrm{hc}_i(p_i) \in K_i$ is t_i-simple for all $i \ge 1$, and $\deg_{t_n}(p_i) \le \deg_{t_n}(p)$ for all $i \ge 0$. By Proposition 5.6, there exists an element $r \in R_n$ such that $p_0 \equiv r \mod K_n'$ and that $\mathrm{hc}_0(r)$ is s-rigid, where s equals $\mathrm{scale}_n(r)$. Furthermore, $\mathrm{hm}_0(r) \preceq \mathrm{hm}_0(p_0)$ implies that $\deg_{t_n}(r) \le \deg_{t_n}(p_0)$. Set q to be $\sum_{i=1}^{n-1} p_i + r$. Then q is t_n-flat, $p \equiv q \mod K_n'$, and $\deg_{t_n}(q) \le \deg_{t_n}(p)$. ∎

Example 5.14. *Let p be given in Example 5.9, where we set $k = 1$. By integration by parts, we have*

$$p \equiv p_2 + p_1 + \underbrace{-3t_3't_2t_3^2 + xt_2t_3}_{q_0} \mod K_3'.$$

Then $\mathrm{scale}_3(q_0) = 2$ and $\mathrm{hc}_0(q_0) = -3t_3' = -3/(x+2)$, which is 2-rigid. Hence, $p_2 + p_1 + q_0$ is t_3-flat.

We are ready to present the main result of this section.

Theorem 5.15. *For $f \in K_n$, the following assertions hold.*

(i) *There exist a t_n-simple element $g \in K_n$ and a t_n-flat polynomial $p \in K_{n-1}[t_n]$ such that*

$$f \equiv g + p \mod K_n'. \tag{5.5}$$

(ii) *$f \equiv 0 \mod K_n'$ if and only if both g and p are zero.*

(iii) *If $f \equiv \tilde{g} + \tilde{p} \mod K_n'$, where $\tilde{g} \in K_n$ is t_n-simple and $\tilde{p} \in K_{n-1}[t_n]$, then $g = \tilde{g}$ and $\deg_{t_n}(p) \le \deg_{t_n}(\tilde{p})$.*

Proof. (i) Applying Algorithm `HermiteReduce` to f with respect to t_n, we get a t_n-simple element g of K_n and an element h of $K_{n-1}[t_n]$ such that $f \equiv g + h \mod K_n'$. We can replace h with a t_n-flat polynomial p by Lemma 5.13.

(ii) Assume $f \in K_n'$. Then (5.5) becomes $g + p \equiv 0 \mod K_n'$. Applying the map hp_{t_n} to the above congruence yields $g = 0$ by Lemma 2.1. Thus, $p \equiv 0 \mod K_n'$. Consequently, $p = 0$ by Proposition 5.12.

(iii) Since $(g - \tilde{g}) + (p - \tilde{p}) \equiv 0 \mod K_n'$ and $g - \tilde{g}$ is t_n-simple, we have $g = \tilde{g}$ by Lemma 2.1. So $p - \tilde{p} \equiv 0 \mod K_n'$. By Lemma 2.3, we have $\mathrm{lc}_{t_n}(p - \tilde{p}) \equiv ct_n' \mod K_{n-1}'$ for some $c \in C$. If $\deg_{t_n}(\tilde{p})$ is smaller than $\deg_{t_n}(p)$, then $\mathrm{lc}_{t_n}(p) = \mathrm{lc}_{t_n}(p - \tilde{p}) \equiv ct_n' \mod K_{n-1}'$. By Lemma 5.11, we conclude $p = 0$, a contradiction. ∎

6 ELEMENTARY INTEGRABILITY

Let $(F, ')$ be a differential field. An element $f \in F$ is said to be *elementarily integrable over F* if there exist an elementary extension E of F and an element g of E such that $f = g'$ [9, Definition 5.1.4]. We study elementary integrability of elements in K_n given in (3.1) built up by a straight or flat tower using Theorems 4.8 and 5.15.

Denote by $\mathbb{L}_i$ the C-linear subspace spanned by the logarithmic derivatives in K_i for all i with $0 \le i \le n$.

Theorem 6.1. *Let the tower given in (3.1) be either straight or flat, in which C is algebraically closed, $K_0 = C(t_0)$, $t_0' = 1$ and t_i' belongs to $\mathbb{L}_{i-1}$ for all i with $1 \le i \le n$. Assume that, for $f \in K_n$,*

$$f \equiv g + p \mod K_n', \tag{6.1}$$

where $g \in K_n$ is t_n-simple and $p \in K_{n-1}[t_n]$ is either t_n-straight if (3.1) is straight or t_n-flat if (3.1) is flat. Then f is elementarily integrable over K_n if and only if $g + p \in \mathbb{L}_n$

Proof. Clearly, f is elementarily integrable over K_n if $g+p \in \mathbb{L}_n$.

Conversely, there exists $r \in \mathbb{L}_n$ such that $f \equiv r \mod K_n'$ by Liouville's theorem [9, Theorem 5.5.1]. By (6.1),

$$g + p \equiv r \mod K_n', \tag{6.2}$$

Since hp_{t_n} is C-linear, $r = \mathrm{hp}_{t_n}(r) + \tilde{r}$ for some $\tilde{r} \in \mathbb{L}_{n-1}$ by Lemma 2.5. On the other hand, $\mathrm{hp}_{t_n}(g + p) = g$, as g is t_n-simple. So $g = \mathrm{hp}_{t_n}(r)$ by (6.2) and Lemma 2.1. Hence, $g \in \mathbb{L}_n$ and

$$p \equiv \tilde{r} \mod K_n'. \tag{6.3}$$

Let $d = \deg_{t_n}(p)$ and $\ell = \mathrm{lc}_{t_n}(p)$. If $d > 0$, then $\ell = \mathrm{lc}_{t_n}(p - \tilde{r})$, which, together with (6.3) and Lemma 2.3, implies that $\ell \equiv ct_n'$ mod K_{n-1}' for some $c \in C$. Thus $\ell = 0$ by Lemma 4.3 in the straight case and by Lemma 5.11 in the flat case, a contradiction. So $d = 0$, and, consequently, $\ell = p$.

We show that (6.2) implies $g + p \in \mathbb{L}_n$ by induction. If $n = 0$, then p is zero. The assertion holds. Assume that the assertion holds for $n - 1$. By the equality $\ell = p$, the congruence (6.3) and Lemma 2.3, $\ell \equiv \tilde{r} + ct_n' \mod K_{n-1}'$ for some c in C. It follows that

$$\mathrm{fp}_{t_{n-1}}(\ell) + \mathrm{pp}_{t_{n-1}}(\ell) \equiv \tilde{r} + ct_n' \mod K_{n-1}' \tag{6.4}$$

Note that $\mathrm{fp}_{t_{n-1}}(\ell)$ is t_{n-1}-simple, and that $\mathrm{pp}_{t_{n-1}}(\ell)$ is t_{n-1}-straight (resp. flat) by Definition 4.4 (resp. Lemma 5.10). Moreover, $\tilde{r} + ct_n'$ belongs to $\mathbb{L}_{n-1}$. By (6.4) and the induction hypothesis, we see that ℓ belongs to $\mathbb{L}_{n-1}$, and so does p. Accordingly, $g + p \in \mathbb{L}_n$. ∎

To determine whether an element r of K_n belongs to $\mathbb{L}_n$, we proceed as follows. First, we verify whether $\mathrm{fp}_{t_n}(r)$ is t_n-simple and $\mathrm{pp}_{t_n}(r)$ belongs to K_{n-1}. If so, we check whether the residues of $\mathrm{fp}_{t_n}(r)$ with respect to t_n are constants by the Rothstein–Trager resultants (see Theorem 4.4.3 in [9]). Then we repeat the above steps with $\mathrm{pp}_{t_n}(r)$ recursively.

Example 6.2. *Let K_0, t_1 and t_2 be given in Example 5.7. We compute an additive decomposition for*

$$f = \frac{1}{xt_1} + \frac{1}{xt_2 + t_2} + t_1^2 t_2 + \frac{2}{x} t_1 t_2 + \frac{2}{x+1} t_1 + \frac{1}{x+2}.$$

By Theorem 5.15 and Example 5.7, we have

$$f = a' + \underbrace{\frac{1}{xt_2 + t_2}}_{g} + \underbrace{\frac{1}{xt_1} + \frac{1}{x+2}}_{p},$$

where $a = (x+1)t_1^2 t_2 - 2xt_1t_2 - xt_1^2 + (2x+2)t_2 + 4xt_1 - 6x$. As the Rothstein–Trager resultant of each fraction in $g + p$ has only constant roots, $g + p$ is a C-linear combination of logarithmic derivatives in K_2. So f is elementarily integrable over K_2 by Theorem 6.1. Indeed,

$$\int f\,dx = a + \log(t_2) + \log(t_1) + \log(x+2).$$

7 TELESCOPERS FOR ELEMENTARY FUNCTIONS

The problem of creative telescoping is classically formulated for D-finite functions in terms of linear differential operators [2, 34]. Raab in his thesis [24] has studied the telescoping problem viewed as a special case of the parametric integration problem in differential fields. However, there are no theoretical results concerning the existence of telescopers for elementary functions. To be more precise, let F be a differential field with two derivations D_x and D_y that commute with each other and let F_∂ be the set $\{f \in F \mid \partial(f) = 0\}$ for $\partial \in \{D_x, D_y\}$. For a given element $f \in F$, the telescoping problem asks whether there exists a nonzero linear differential operator $L = \sum_{i=0}^d \ell_i D_x^i$ with $\ell_i \in F_{D_y}$ such that $L(f) = D_y(g)$ for some g in a specific differential extension E of F. We call L a *telescoper* for f and g the corresponding *certificate* for L in E. Usually, we take E to be the field F itself or an elementary extension of F. In contrast to D-finite functions, telescopers may not exist for elementary functions as shown in the following example.

Example 7.1. *Let $F = \mathbb{C}(x, y)$ and $E = F(t_1, t_2)$ be a differential field extension of F with $t_1 = \log(x^2 + y^2)$ and $t_2 = \log(1 + t_1)$. We first show that $f = 1/t_1 \in F(t_1)$ has no telescoper with certificate in any elementary extension of $F(t_1)$. Since t_1 is a primitive monomial over F, we have $F(t_1)_{D_y} = \mathbb{C}(x)$. We claim that for any $i \in \mathbb{N}$, $D_x^i(f)$ can be decomposed as $D_x^i(f) = D_y(g_i) + a_i/t_1$, where $g_i \in F(t_1)$, and $a_i \in F$ satisfies the recurrence relation*

$$a_{i+1} = D_x(a_i) - D_y(xa_i/y) \quad \text{with } a_0 = 1.$$

For $n = 0$, the claim holds by taking $g_0 = 0$. Assume that the claim holds for all $i < k$. Applying the induction hypothesis and Algorithm `HermiteReduce` *to $D_x^k(f)$ yields*

$$D_x^k(f) = D_x(D_x^{k-1}(f)) = D_x\left(D_y(g_{k-1}) + \frac{a_{k-1}}{t_1}\right)$$
$$= D_y\left(D_x(g_{k-1}) + \frac{a_{k-1}x}{yt_1}\right) + \frac{D_x(a_{k-1}) - D_y(\frac{xa_{k-1}}{y})}{t_1}.$$

This completes the induction. A straightforward calculation shows that $a_i = A_i/y^{2i}$ for some $A_i \in \mathbb{C}[x, y] \setminus \{0\}$ with $\deg_y(A_i) < 2i$. Using the notion of residues in [9, page 118], we have

$$\mathrm{residue}_{t_1}\left(\frac{a_i}{t_1}\right) = \frac{a_i}{D_y(t_1)} = \frac{(x^2 + y^2)A_i}{2y^{2i+1}},$$

which is not in $\mathbb{C}(x)$. Then $D_x^i(f)$ is not elementarily integrable over $F(t_1)$ for any $i \in \mathbb{N}$ by the residues criterion in [9, Theorem 5.6.1]. Assume that f has a telescoper $L := \sum_{i=0}^d \ell_i D_x^i$ with $\ell_i \in \mathbb{C}(x)$ not all zero. Then $L(f)$ is elementarily integrable over $F(t_1)$. However,

$$L(f) = D_y\left(\sum_{i=0}^d \ell_i g_i\right) + \frac{\sum_{i=0}^d \ell_i a_i}{t_1}.$$

Since all of the ℓ_i's are in $\mathbb{C}(x)$ and $\gcd(x^2+y^2, y^m) = 1$ for any $m \in \mathbb{N}$, the residue of $\sum_{i=0}^{d} \ell_i a_i / t_1$ is not in $\mathbb{C}(x)$, which implies that $L(f)$ is not elementarily integrable over $F(t_1)$, a contradiction.

We now show that $p = f t_2$ has no telescoper with certificate in any elementary extension of $F(t_1, t_2)$. Since t_2 is also a primitive monomial over $F(t_1)$, we have $E_{D_y} = \mathbb{C}(x)$. Assume that $L := \sum_{i=0}^{d} \ell_i D_x^i$ with $\ell_i \in \mathbb{C}(x)$ not all zero is a telescoper for p. Then $L(p)$ is elementarily integrable over E. By a direct calculation, we get $L(p) = L(f)t_2 + r$ with $r \in F(t_1)$. The elementary integrability of $L(p)$ implies that $L(f) = cD_y(t_2) + D_y(b)$ for some $c \in \mathbb{C}(x)$ and $b \in F(t_1)$ by the formula (5.13) in the proof of Theorem 5.8.1 in [9, page 157]. We claim that $c = 0$. Since $D_x^i(f) = u_i / t_1^{i+1}$ with $u_i \in F[t_1]$ and $\deg_{t_1}(u_i) < i+1$ and $D_y(t_2) = D_y(t_1)/(1+t_1)$, the orders of $D_x^i(f)$ and $D_y(t_2)$ at $1+t_1$ are equal to 0 and 1, respectively. If c is nonzero, the order of $cD_y(t_2)$ at $1+t_1$ is equal to 1, which does not match with that of $L(f) - D_y(b)$ by Lemma 4.4.2 (i) in [9], a contradiction. Then $L(f) = D_y(b)$, i.e., L is a telescoper for f, which contradicts with the first assertion.

The next example shows that additive decompositions in Theorems 4.8 and 5.15 are useful for detecting the existence of telescopers for elementary functions that are not D-finite.

EXAMPLE 7.2. *Let $F = \mathbb{C}(x,y)$ and $E = F(t)$ be a differential field extension of F with $t = \log(x^2+y^2)$. Consider the function $f = t + 1 - \frac{2y}{(x^2+y^2)t^2}$. Since the derivatives $D_x^i(1/t^2) = a_i/t^{i+2}$ with $a_i \in F \setminus \{0\}$ are linearly independent over F, we see that $1/t^2$ is not D-finite over F, and neither is f. Note that f can be decomposed as*

$$f = D_y(1/t) + t + 1.$$

Since $t+1$ is D-finite, it has a telescoper, and so does f.

8 CONCLUSION

In this paper, we developed additive decompositions in straight and flat towers, which enable us to determine in-field integrability and elementary integrability in a straightforward manner. It is natural to ask whether one can develop an additive decomposition in a general primitive tower. Moreover, we plan to investigate about the existence and the construction of telescopers for elementary functions using additive decompositions.

ACKNOWLEDGMENTS

We would like to thank the anonymous reviewers for their constructive and detailed comments.

REFERENCES

[1] S. A. Abramov and M. van Hoeij. A method for the integration of solutions of Ore equations. In *Proc. ISSAC '97*, pp. 172–175, 1997. ACM.

[2] G. Almkvist and D. Zeilberger. The method of differentiating under the integral sign. *J. Symbolic Comput.*, 10:571–591, 1990.

[3] A. Bostan, S. Chen, F. Chyzak, and Z. Li. Complexity of creative telescoping for bivariate rational functions. In *Proc. ISSAC '10*, pp. 203–210, 2010. ACM.

[4] A. Bostan, S. Chen, F. Z. Li, and G. Xin. Hermite reduction and creative telescoping for hyperexponential functions. In *Proc. ISSAC'13*, pp. 77–84, 2013. ACM.

[5] A. Bostan, P. Lairez, and B. Salvy. Creative telescoping for rational functions using the Griffiths-Dwork method. In *Proc. ISSAC'13*, pp. 93–100, 2013. ACM.

[6] A. Bostan, F. Chyzak, P. Lairez, and B. Salvy. Generalized Hermite reduction, creative telescoping and definite integration of differentially finite functions. To appear in *Proc. ISSAC'18*.

[7] M. Bronstein. *Integration of Elementary Functions.* PhD Thesis, University of California, Berkeley, 1987.

[8] M. Bronstein. Integration of elementary functions. *J. Symbolic Comput.*, 9(2):117–173, 1990.

[9] M. Bronstein. *Symbolic Integration I: Transcendental Functions.* Springer-Verlag, Berlin, second edition, 2005.

[10] S. Chen, M. Kauers, and C. Koutschan. Reduction-based creative telescoping for algebraic functions. In *Proc. ISSAC'16*, pp. 175–182, 2016. ACM.

[11] S. Chen and M. Kauers. Some open problems related to creative telescoping. In *J. of Systems Science and Complexity*, pp. 154–172, 2017.

[12] S. Chen, M. van Hoeij, M. Kauers, and C. Koutschan. Reduction-based creative telescoping for fuchsian D-finite functions. *J. Symbolic Comput.*, 85:108 - 127, 2018.

[13] J. H. Davenport. *On the Integration of Algebraic Functions*, volume 102 of *Lecture Notes in Computer Science.* Springer-Verlag, Berlin, 1981.

[14] K. O. Geddes, H. Q. Le, and Z. Li. Differential rational normal forms and a reduction algorithm for hyperexponential functions. In *Proc. ISSAC'04*, pp. 183–190, 2004. ACM.

[15] C. Hermite. Sur l'intégration des fractions rationnelles. *Ann. Sci. École Norm. Sup. (2)*, 1:215–218, 1872.

[16] I. Kaplansky. *An Introduction to Differential Algebra.* Hermann, Paris, 1957.

[17] M. Kauers, C. Koutschan, and D. Zeilberger. Proof of Ira Gessel's lattice path conjecture. *PNAS. USA*, 106(28):11502–11505, 2009.

[18] C. Koutschan, M. Kauers, and D. Zeilberger. Proof of George Andrews's and David Robbins's q-TSPP conjecture. *PNAS. USA*, 108(6):2196–2199, 2011.

[19] P. Lairez. Computing periods of rational integrals. *Math. Comp.*, 85(300):1719–1752, 2016.

[20] J. Liouville. Premier mémoires sur la détermination des intégrales dont la valeur est algébrique. *J. de l'Ecole Polytechnique*, 14:124–148, 1833.

[21] J. Lützen. Joseph Liouville 1809–1882: master of pure and applied mathematics. *Studies in the History of Mathematics and Physical Sciences*, Vol. 15, Springer-Verlag, New York, 1990.

[22] J. Moses. *Symbolic Integration.* PhD Thesis, MIT, 1968.

[23] M. V. Ostrogradskiĭ. De l'intégration des fractions rationnelles. *Bull. de la classe physico-mathématique de l'Acad. Impériale des Sciences de Saint-Pétersbourg*, 4:145–167, 286–300, 1845.

[24] C. G. Raab. *Definite Integration in Differential Fields.* PhD thesis, Johannes Kepler Universitat Linz, Austria, August 2012.

[25] C. G. Raab. Generalization of Risch's algorithm to special functions. In *Computer algebra in quantum field theory*, Texts Monogr. Symbol. Comput., pages 285–304. Springer, Vienna, 2013.

[26] R. H. Risch. The problem of integration in finite terms. *Trans. Amer. Math. Soc.*, 139:167–189, 1969.

[27] R. H. Risch. The solution of the problem of integration in finite terms. *Bull. Amer. Math. Soc.*, 76:605–608, 1970.

[28] J. F. Ritt. *Integration in Finite Terms. Liouville's Theory of Elementary Methods.* Columbia University Press, New York, N. Y., 1948.

[29] M. Rothstein. *Aspects of Symbolic Integration and Simplification of Exponential and Primitive Functions.* PhD Thesis, University of Wisconsin, 1976.

[30] C. Schneider and J. Blümlein, editors. *Computer algebra in quantum field theory: Integration, summation and special functions.* Texts Monogr. Symbol. Comput., Springer, Vienna, 2013.

[31] J. R. Slagle. *A Heuristic Program that Solves Symbolic Integration Problems in Freashman Calculus, Symbolic Automatic Integrator (SAINT).* PhD Thesis, MIT, 1961.

[32] B. M. Trager. *On the Integration of Algebraic Functions.* PhD Thesis, MIT, 1984.

[33] J. van der Hoeven. Constructing reductions for creative telescoping. Preprint, 2017. <hal-01435877v4>

[34] D. Zeilberger. The method of creative telescoping. *J. Symbolic Comput.*, 11(3):195–204, 1991.

A Symplectic Kovacic's Algorithm in Dimension 4

Thierry Combot
University of Burgundy
Dijon, France
thierry.combot@u-bourgogne.fr

Camilo Sanabria
Universidad de los Andes
Bogota, Colombia
c.sanabria135@uniandes.edu.co

ABSTRACT

Let L be a 4th order linear differential operator with coefficients in $\mathbb{K}(z)$, with $\mathbb{K}$ a computable algebraically closed field. The operator L is called symplectic when up to rational gauge transformation, the fundamental matrix of solutions X satisfies $X^tJX = J$ where J is the standard symplectic matrix. It is called projectively symplectic when it is projectively equivalent to a symplectic operator. We design an algorithm to test if L is projectively symplectic. Furthermore, based on Kovacic's algorithm, we design an algorithm that computes Liouvillian solutions of projectively symplectic operators of order 4. Moreover, using Klein's Theorem, algebraic solutions are given as pullbacks of standard hypergeometric equations.

CCS CONCEPTS

• **Mathematics of computing → Mathematical software; Solvers;**

KEYWORDS

Differential Galois theory, Symplectic differential systems, Liouvillian functions, Kovacic's algorithm

ACM Reference Format:

Thierry Combot and Camilo Sanabria. 2018. A Symplectic Kovacic's Algorithm in Dimension 4. In *ISSAC '18: 2018 ACM International Symposium on Symbolic and Algebraic Computation, July 16–19, 2018, New York, NY, USA.* ACM, New York, NY, USA, Article 4, 8 pages. https://doi.org/10.1145/3208976.3209005

1 INTRODUCTION

A solution to a linear ordinary differential equation is called Liouvillian over the base field if it is in a field extension obtained by successively adjoining antiderivative, hyperexponential or algebraic functions. The solutions to a linear ordinary differential equation are all Liouvillian if and only if the connected component of its differential Galois group is solvable. Existing algorithms computing Liouvillian solutions for linear ordinary differential equations with coefficients in $\mathbb{K}(z)$ are Kovacic's algorithm, and more generally the computation of invariant and semi-invariants [9, 15]. For equations of order n, these algorithms require a classification of all algebraic groups in $GL_n(\mathbb{K})$ whose identity components is solvable, a procedure to identify whether the differential Galois group of the equation corresponds to one of these algebraic groups and in such case to which one, and finally an algorithm to effectively compute the solutions. The procedure of identifying the differential Galois group relies on computing the invariants and semi-invariants of the equation (i.e. the rational and hyperexponential solutions to the symmetric powers). The main problem is that, even if the complete list of possible groups is known up to dimension 4, effective calculations of the invariants and semi-invariants is not available because identifying the differential Galois group requires computations of hyperexponential or rational solutions of very high order. Because of this, an effective algorithm for computing Liouvillian solutions has for now been restricted to order 2, the Kovacic algorithm, and order three [14]. This article intends to extend the Galois group computation effectively up to order 4, under the assumption that the equation is symplectic.

In dynamical systems, many physical problems involving conservative forces admit a Hamiltonian formulation, and therefore the conservation of a non-degenerated 2-form, called the symplectic structure. When the system is linearised for analysis of perturbations, the symplectic structure defines a symplectic structure on the linearised system [11]. In the study of the linearised system one often requires the computation of its solutions, and until now solutions can be explicitely computed only in specific cases, namely when the equation splits into equations of order two and the Kovacic algorithm can be used. Now, every symplectic system is even dimensional, however typically symplectic systems do not split into equations of order two, as for $n > 1$, $SP_{2n}(\mathbb{K})$ properly contains $SL_2(\mathbb{K})^n$.

Definition 1. *A matrix $M \in GL_{2n}(\mathbb{K})$ is symplectic if it satisfies $M^tJM = J$ where*

$$J = \begin{pmatrix} 0 & I_n \\ -I_n & 0 \end{pmatrix},$$

is the standard symplectic form. It is projectively symplectic if it satisfies $M^tJM = \lambda J$ for some $\lambda \in \mathbb{K}^*$. The group of symplectic matrices is denoted $SP_{2n}(\mathbb{K})$ and the group of projectively symplectic matrices $PSP_{2n}(\mathbb{K})$.

The Lie algebra of $SP_{2n}(\mathbb{K})$ and $PSP_{2n}(\mathbb{K})$ are respectively

$$\mathfrak{sp}_{2n}(\mathbb{K}) = \{M \in M_{2n}(\mathbb{K}),\ M^tJ + JM = 0\},$$

$$\mathfrak{psp}_{2n}(\mathbb{K}) = \{M \in M_{2n}(\mathbb{K}),\ \exists \lambda \in \mathbb{K},\ M^tJ + JM = \lambda J\}.$$

Let us recall that the Galois group of a linear differential operator L of order n with coefficients in $\mathbb{K}(z)$ is the group of differential automorphisms of the differential field generated by the solutions of L fixing the base field $\mathbb{K}(z)$. This group is always isomorphic to an algebraic subgroup of $GL_n(\mathbb{K})$.

Definition 2. *An operator L of order 2n is symplectic (respectively projectively symplectic) when its Galois group is isomorphic to a subgroup of $SP_{2n}(\mathbb{K})$ (resp. of $PSP_{2n}(\mathbb{K})$).*

ACM ISBN 978-1-4503-5550-6/18/07...$15.00
https://doi.org/10.1145/3208976.3209005

The following Proposition enables an alternative Definition

PROPOSITION 1. *An operator L of order $2n$ is symplectic, respectively projectively symplectic, if and only if there exists an invertible matrix P with entries in $\mathbb{K}(z)$ such that we have respectively*

$$P^{-1}AP + P'P \in \mathfrak{sp}_{2n}(\mathbb{K}(z)), \quad P^{-1}AP + P'P \in \mathfrak{psp}_{2n}(\mathbb{K}(z))$$

where A is the companion matrix associated to L.

PROOF. Writing the linear differential equation $L(f) = 0$ as a linear differential system $X' = AX$ in dimension n, Kolchin-Kovacic Theorem ensures us that if the Galois group of L is contained in a connected algebraic group G, then there exists a gauge transformation such that the linear differential system writes $X' = AX$ with A in the Lie algebra of G [1]. Inversely, the Galois group is invariant by gauge transformation, thus the Galois group of $X' = AX$ equals the Galois group of $X' = (P^{-1}AP + P'P)X$. The Galois group is contained in the Lie algebra generated by the matrix of the system, so here $P^{-1}AP + P'P$, which by assumption is in $\mathfrak{sp}_{2n}(\mathbb{K}(z))$ or $\mathfrak{psp}_{2n}(\mathbb{K}(z))$. And thus the Galois group is in $\mathfrak{sp}_{2n}(\mathbb{C})$ or $\mathfrak{psp}_{2n}(\mathbb{C})$ respectively. □

Linear ordinary differential equations arising from problems in physics with a Hamiltonian formulation are symplectic, however the base field is not always the field of coefficients $\mathbb{K}(z)$. In many cases this is due to algebraic changes of the independent variable, which can introduce algebraic extensions of the base field. In particular, it is possible that the linear system is no longer symplectic, but its Galois group is included in a finite extension of $SP_{2n}(\mathbb{K})$ in $PSP_{2n}(\mathbb{K})$. However these systems are still projectively symplectic (see Proposition 7). Throughout the paper we assume familiarity with the Picard-Vessiot theory and the tensorial constructions of differential modules [13], as well as with the algorithms to factor linear ordinary differential operators [7], to find their rational [3] and hyperexponential solutions [12] over $\mathbb{K}(z)$ or over a quadratic extensions of $\mathbb{K}(z)$ [4].

2 CHECKING SYMPLECTICITY

DEFINITION 3. *Solutions to $X' = AX$ of the form $\exp(\int \lambda)Y$, with λ and the entries of Y in $\mathbb{K}(z)$, are called hyperexponential over $\mathbb{K}(z)$.*

PROPOSITION 2. *Let L be a $2n$-th order operator with coefficients in $\mathbb{K}(z)$ and A its companion matrix. The operator L is symplectic (respectively projectively symplectic) if and only if there exists an invertible antisymmetric matrix W with coefficients in $\mathbb{K}(z)$ such that*

$$A^tW + WA + W' = 0$$

and respectively for projective symplectic a $\lambda \in \mathbb{K}(z)$ such that

$$A^tW + WA + W' + \lambda W = 0. \tag{1}$$

The matrix W will be called a symplectic structure associated to L, and λ its multiplier.

PROOF. Let $X = (x_{i,j})$ be a fundamental matrix of solutions of L. Let V be the vector space over $\mathbb{K}$ generated by the columns of X. Let $G \subseteq GL_{2n}(\mathbb{K})$ be the representation of the Galois group of L associated to X.

Assume first that L is projectively symplectic. Since L is projectively symplectic, we may choose X so that $G \subseteq PSP_{2n}(\mathbb{K})$. Then $\tilde{W} := (X^{-1})^tJX^{-1}$ is an invertible antisymmetric matrix with semi-invariant coefficients. Indeed, for any $g \in G$,

$$(X^{-1})^t(g^{-1})^tJg^{-1}X^{-1} = (X^{-1})^t\lambda_gJX^{-1} = \lambda_g\tilde{W}$$

for some $\lambda_g \in \mathbb{K}$. On the other hand $X^t\tilde{W}X = J$, therefore $A^t\tilde{W} + \tilde{W}' + \tilde{W}A = 0$. The invertible antisymmetric matrix with semi-invariant coefficients $\tilde{W}$ defines a non-degenerate alternating bilinear forms on V, so the coefficients of $\tilde{W}$ form a hyperexponential solution to the exterior square of the dual of the system $X' = AX$ (for, if $\tilde{W} = (\tilde{w}_{i,j})$ and $J = (j_{i,j})$,

$$j_{i,j} = \sum_{k,l=1}^{2n} x_{k,i}\tilde{w}_{k,l}x_{l,j} = \sum_{1=k<l=2n} \tilde{w}_{k,l}(x_{k,i}x_{l,j} - x_{k,j}x_{l,i}).)$$

So there exists $\lambda \in \mathbb{K}(z)$ such that $W = \exp(-\int \lambda(z)dz)\tilde{W} \in \mathbb{K}(z)$ and

$$0 = A^tW + W' + \lambda W + WA.$$

Conversely, assume that there exist an invertible antisymmetric matrix W with coefficients in $\mathbb{K}(z)$ and a $\lambda \in \mathbb{K}(z)$ such that

$$A^tW + WA + W' + \lambda W = 0.$$

Then, if $\tilde{W} = \exp(\int \lambda(z)dz)W$, $X^t\tilde{W}X$ is a matrix with constant coefficients. In particular, for every $g \in G$ we have $g^tX^t\tilde{W}Xg = X^t\tilde{W}X$, so G is isomorphic to a subgroup of $PSP_{2n}(\mathbb{K})$.

The non-projective case corresponds to the case $\lambda = 0$. □

COROLLARY 1. *Let L be a $2n$-th order operator with coefficients in $\mathbb{K}(z)$. If the operator L is symplectic (respectively projectively symplectic) then the exterior square of L has a rational (respectively hyperexponential) solution.*

PROOF. In the proof of proposition 2, we showed that if A is the companion matrix of L, the equation on $\tilde{W}$, $A^t\tilde{W} + \tilde{W}A + \tilde{W}' = 0$, is equivalent to the exterior square of the dual of $X' = AX$. If the system is symplectic (respectively projectively symplectic), the equation $A^tW + WA + W' = 0$ admits a rational (respectively hyperexponential) invertible matrix solution, and thus so does its dual, which is equivalent to the exterior square of L. □

A function is hyperexponential over $\mathbb{K}(z)$ if its logarithmic derivative is in $\mathbb{K}(z)$. The exponential type of f is the equivalence class of f for the equivalence relation

$$f \sim g \Leftrightarrow f/g \in \mathbb{K}(z).$$

DEFINITION 4. *Let L be a $2n$-th order operator with coefficients in $\mathbb{K}(z)$ and A its companion matrix. A non-trivial solution of $A^tW + WA + W' = 0$ which is*

- *hyperexponential is called a projective Poisson structure.*
- *hyperexponential invertible is called a projective symplectic structure.*
- *rational is called a Poisson structure.*
- *rational invertible is called a symplectic structure.*

Note that when W, λ is a solution in the projective case, then $\exp(-\int \lambda(z)dz)W$ is a solution in the non-projective case whenever $\exp\int \lambda(z)dz \notin \mathbb{K}(z)$. In particular we can detect whether the Galois group is a finite extension of $SP_{2n}(\mathbb{K})$.

Proposition 3. *Let L be a $2n$-th order operator with coefficients in $\mathbb{K}(z)$ and A its companion matrix. The Galois group of L is isomorphic to a subgroup of $\mathbb{Z}/p\mathbb{Z} \ltimes SP_{2n}(\mathbb{K})$ if and only if it is projectively symplectic with $\lambda \in \mathbb{K}(z)$ as in Proposition 2 such that*

$$e^{p\int \lambda(z)dz} \in \mathbb{K}(z).$$

Proof. Let L be projectively symplectic. Let $X, W, \tilde{W}$ be defined as in the proof of Proposition 2. Since $\tilde{W}$ is semi-invariant under the action of the Galois group G, for every $\sigma \in G$ there exist $\lambda_\sigma \in \mathbb{K}$ such that $\sigma(\exp \int \lambda(z)dz) = \lambda_\sigma \exp \int \lambda(z)dz$. So $\lambda \in \mathbb{K}(z)$ such that $\exp p \int \lambda(z)dz \in \mathbb{K}(z)$ is equivalent to $\exp(p\int \lambda(z)dz) = \sigma(\exp(p\int \lambda(z)dz)) = \lambda_\sigma^p \exp(p\int\lambda(z)dz)$, or equivalently $\lambda_\sigma^p \in \mathbb{U}_p = \{z \in \mathbb{K}, z^p = 1\}$. Now, if g is the image of σ in the representation of G in $GL_{2n}(\mathbb{K})$ associated to X, we have $g^t J g = \lambda_\sigma J$. Therefore $\exp(p\int\lambda(z)dz) \in \mathbb{K}(z)$ is equivalent to $g \in \mathbb{Z}_p \ltimes SP_{2n}(\mathbb{K})$. □

A symplectic structure is an antisymmetric matrix of dimension $2n$, and thus we can compute its Pfaffian.

Definition 5. *Let $W = (w_{i,j})$ be an antisymmetric matrix of dimension $2n$. The Pfaffian of W is defined by*

$$Pf(W) = \frac{1}{2^n n!}\sum_{\sigma\in S_{2n}} sgn(\sigma)\prod_{i=1}^{n} w_{\sigma(2i-1),\sigma(2i)}.$$

Recall that the square of the Pfaffian is the determinant. From the relation $X^t\tilde{W}X = J$ in the proof of Proposition 2 we get $\mathrm{Pf}(X^t\tilde{W}X) = \mathrm{Pf}(J) = 1$ and thus $\mathrm{Pf}(\tilde{W}) = \det(X)^{-1}$. Hence

$$e^{n\int\lambda(z)dz}\mathrm{Pf}\left(W^{-1}\right) = \det(X).$$

We have $\mathrm{Pf}(W^{-1}) \in \mathbb{K}(z)$ but we cannot deduce the exponential type of $\exp\int\lambda(z)dz$ as n-th roots could appear. In fact

$$\{M \in GL_{2n}(\mathbb{K}),\ \exists\lambda\in\mathbb{U}_n,\ M^tJM = \lambda J\} \subset SL_{2n}(\mathbb{K}).$$

So in particular, even if the Wronskian of the system is a constant and the system is projectively symplectic, the Galois group is either symplectic or a subgroup of $\mathbb{Z}_n \ltimes SP_{2n}(\mathbb{K})$.

Our algorithm to detect symplecticity has two parts. The first part searches for solutions to the exterior square of the dual system. The second part identifies the solutions that define a non-degenerate antisymmetric form and their exponential type.

<u>IsSymplectic</u>
Input: A linear differential operator L of order $2n$ with coefficients in $\mathbb{K}(z)$.
Output: A projective symplectic structure if it exists.

(1) Write down the differential system

$$A^tW + WA + W' = 0. \tag{2}$$

with A the companion matrix of L and W an unknown antisymmetric matrix.

(2) Compute a basis $B = \{\tilde{W}_1, \ldots, \tilde{W}_m\}$ of the hyperexponential solutions of (2), which is equivalent to the exterior square of the dual of $X' = AX$.

(3) For each exponential type of a solution in B, look for linear combinations over $\mathbb{K}$ of the $\tilde{W}_i$'s with the same exponential type, $\tilde{W}_{i_1}, \ldots, \tilde{W}_{i_p}$, such that $\mathrm{Pf}(a_1\tilde{W}_{i_1} + \ldots + a_p\tilde{W}_{i_p}) \neq 0$. If there are none, return []. Else set $\tilde{W} = a_1\tilde{W}_{i_1} + \ldots + a_p\tilde{W}_{i_p}$.

(4) Let $\exp(\int\lambda(z)dz)$ be the exponential type of $\tilde{W}$. Set $W = \exp(-\int\lambda(z)dz)\tilde{W}$

(5) Return $\exp(\int\lambda(z)dz)W(z)$.

Theorem 1. *The algorithm* <u>IsSymplectic</u> *returns a solution if and only if L is projectively symplectic.*

Proof. The solutions W_i form a basis of the projective Poisson structures (step 1). A projective symplectic structure is a hyperexponential solution of (2), and thus is a linear combination of the W_i. As it should be hyperexponential, it can only be a linear combination of W_i of the same type and the invertible condition is equivalent to a non zero Pfaffian (step 2). The symplectic structure and its type is returned (steps 3,4). □

3 A KOVACIC-STYLE ALGORITHM

From now on, we will restrict ourselves to order 4 operators. Let us first classify the possible algebraic groups we will encounter.

3.1 Symplectic groups

Definition 6. *An algebraic subgroup G of $SL_4(\mathbb{K})$ is said to be reducible if it admits a block triangular representation, i.e. if it stabilizes a non-trivial proper subspace of $\mathbb{K}^4$, otherwise it is called irreducible. It is called imprimitive if there exists a decomposition $\mathbb{K}^4 = \oplus_{i=1}^p V_i$, where each V_i is a non-trivial proper subspace, such that G acts permuting the V_i's, i.e.*

$$\forall g \in G, \exists\sigma\in S_p \text{ s.t. } g(V_i) \subset V_{\sigma(i)}, \forall i = 1\ldots p.$$

Otherwise it is called primitive. When G is imprimitive and $p = 4$, G will be called monomial imprimitive.

Proposition 4. *A proper algebraic subgroup of $SP_4(\mathbb{K})$ is up to conjugacy generated by elements of the form*

i) *Upper block triangular matrices with diagonal blocks of size at most 2×2.*
ii) *2×2 block diagonal matrices and anti-diagonal matrices.*

Proof. We recall that a group $G \subsetneq SL_4(\mathbb{K})$ is conjugate to a subgroup of the symplectic group if we can find an antisymmetric invertible matrix $J_0 \in GL_4(\mathbb{K})$ such that

$$g^tJ_0g = J_0, \quad \forall g \in G. \tag{3}$$

We will prove the proposition following the classification of algebraic subgroups of $SL_4(\mathbb{K})$ found in [6], by first examining the irreducible primitive groups, then the irreducible imprimitive non-monomial followed by the irreducible imprimitive monomial and finally the reducible ones.

Let us begin by looking for irreducible primitive groups.

We begin with the 30 finite primitive groups which are listed in [5]. We just have to test the above condition (3) on a generating set of the group. Thus the condition is a set of linear equations in the entries of J_0 and an inequality condition $\mathrm{Pf}(J_0) \neq 0$. We find that none of them is conjugate to a subgroup of $SP_4(\mathbb{K})$.

Now for infinite primitive groups, there are four possibilities with G^0 irreducible, namely $G^0 \simeq SL_4(\mathbb{K}), SP_4(\mathbb{K}), SO_4(\mathbb{K})$ and $SL_2(\mathbb{K})$ in its third symmetric power representation, and the only one satisfying the condition is $SP_4(\mathbb{K})$. We obtain case iii) of the proposition.

The possibilities for infinite primitive groups with G^0 reducible are the groups G with

$$G^0 = \left\{ \begin{pmatrix} A & 0 \\ 0 & A \end{pmatrix}, A \in SL_2(\mathbb{K}) \right\}$$

and $G = HG^0$ where $H = I_2 \otimes T$ and T is a finite subgroup of $SL_2(\mathbb{K})$. The symplectic structures compatible with such G^0 are of the form

$$\begin{pmatrix} 0 & u_1 & 0 & -u_4 \\ -u_1 & 0 & u_4 & 0 \\ 0 & -u_4 & 0 & u_6 \\ u_4 & 0 & -u_6 & 0 \end{pmatrix}$$

Now the possible groups for H are diagonal extensions of order at most 2 of the primitives groups A_4, S_4, A_5. Let us search for 2×2 matrices T of determinant 1 leading to a matrix H compatible with one of the above symplectic structures. If $\det(T) = 1$ and T is not triangular, we find

$$T = \begin{pmatrix} \frac{qt^2 - t^2 w + q + w}{2qt} & -\frac{(q^2-w^2)(t^2-1)}{4qt} \\ -\frac{t^2-1}{qt} & \frac{qt^2+t^2 w + q - w}{2qt} \end{pmatrix}$$

where $q, w \in \mathbb{K}$ are fixed and t is any element in $\mathbb{K}$. These matrices generate either a finite cyclic group if $t \in \mathbb{U}_n$, a group isomorphic to $\mathbb{K}^*$, or when adding a matrix T with $\det(T) = -1$ a degree two extension of these two. So the only finite groups generated by matrices of type T compatible with the symplectic structure are either cyclic or finite dihedral and thus the groups A_4, S_4, A_5 and their diagonal extensions are not possible. Thus this case cannot happen.

Now we consider the irreducible imprimitive non-monomial groups. They exchange two 2-dimensional vector spaces V_1, V_2. On an adapted basis, the group is then generated by 2×2 block diagonal matrices and anti-diagonal matrices. We obtain case ii) of the proposition.

For irreducible imprimitive monomial groups, we need to look for matrices of the form $\mathrm{diag}(a, b, c, d)P$ where P is a permutation matrix of S_4. The permutation group acting on four 1-dimensional vector spaces should be irreducible, and thus can be one of the following groups:

a) $\mathbb{Z}_4 \simeq \langle (1,2,3,4) \rangle$,
b) the Klein group in it standard representation (i.e. generated by $(1,2)(3,4), (1,3)(2,4)$),
c) the dihedral group $D_8 \simeq \langle (1,2,3,4), (1,3) \rangle$,
d) $A_4 = \langle (1,2,3), (1,2)(3,4) \rangle$, and,
e) S_4.

For the Klein group, the group then admits a representation by 2×2 block diagonal and anti-diagonal matrices. For the groups $\mathbb{Z}_4$ and D_8 we can consider the decomposition

$$\{(1,0,0,0), (0,0,1,0)\} \oplus \{(0,1,0,0), (0,0,0,1)\}$$

on which the group either permutes or stabilizes the two 2 dimensional spaces. For these three groups we obtain case ii) of the proposition.

The representation of A_4

$$\left\langle \begin{pmatrix} 0 & 1 & 0 & 0 \\ 0 & 0 & 1 & 0 \\ 1 & 0 & 0 & 0 \\ 0 & 0 & 0 & 1 \end{pmatrix}, \begin{pmatrix} 0 & 1 & 0 & 0 \\ -1 & 0 & 0 & 0 \\ 0 & 0 & 0 & 1 \\ 0 & 0 & -1 & 0 \end{pmatrix} \right\rangle$$

is compatible with the symplectic structure

$$J = \begin{pmatrix} 0 & 1 & -1 & -1 \\ -1 & 0 & 1 & -1 \\ 1 & -1 & 0 & -1 \\ 1 & 1 & 1 & 0 \end{pmatrix}.$$

The subspace V is spanned by

$$v_1 = (-\sqrt{3} - i, i\sqrt{3} - 1, -2 - \sqrt{3} + i, 1 + 2i + i\sqrt{3})^t$$

$$v_2 = (i + i\sqrt{3}, -1 - \sqrt{3}, 1 - i, 1 + i)^t$$

and is stable under this representation. The complex conjugate of V, $\bar{V}$, is also stable by G and $V \oplus \bar{V} = \mathbb{K}^4$. Therefore this group is block diagonalizable with 2×2 blocks. We obtain case i) of the proposition.

The representation of S_4

$$G = \left\langle \begin{pmatrix} 0 & -i & 0 & 0 \\ 0 & 0 & -i & 0 \\ 0 & 0 & 0 & -i \\ i & 0 & 0 & 0 \end{pmatrix}, \begin{pmatrix} 0 & -i & 0 & 0 \\ -i & 0 & 0 & 0 \\ 0 & 0 & -i & 0 \\ 0 & 0 & 0 & i \end{pmatrix} \right\rangle$$

is a degree 2 extension of the previous case, and thus after conjugacy, the group is generated by 2×2 block diagonal matrices and anti-diagonal matrices. We obtain case ii) of the proposition.

The final case, where G is reducible, is treated in [2, Section III.4]) and it corresponds to case i) in the proposition. □

We deduce that if a symplectic L is irreducible but has Liouvillian solutions (case ii) in Proposition 4), then the Galois group is of the form $\mathbb{Z}_2 \ltimes G_1$ with G_1 a proper subgroup of $SL_2(\mathbb{K})$. In particular, in that case L admits a factorization in two operators of order 2 with coefficients in a quadratic extension of $\mathbb{K}(z)$.

3.2 The irreducible solvable case

If L is symplectic irreducible with Liouvillian solutions, we show that the factorization of L in two operators of order 2 with a quadratic extension can be identified using Poisson structures.

Proposition 5. *If the Galois group of a symplectic operator L can be represented as subgroup of $SP_4(\mathbb{K})$ formed by 2×2 block diagonal and anti-diagonal matrices, then L admits two linearly independent rank two Poisson structures with coefficients in a quadratic extension of $\mathbb{K}(z)$.*

Proof. The Galois group of L is isomorphic to $\mathbb{Z}_2 \ltimes G_1$ where G_1 is a subgroup of $SL_2(\mathbb{K})$. Let $X = (x_{i,j})$ be a fundamental matrix of solutions of the companion linear differential system associated to L. Let V be the vector space over $\mathbb{K}$ generated by the columns of X. Since L is symplectic there exits an invertible antisymmetric matrix $W \in GL_4(\mathbb{K}(z))$ such that $X^t W X = J$. Let $K = \mathbb{K}(z)(x_{i,j})$ be the Picard-Vessiot extension of L and $K_1 = K^{G_1}$. We have that K_1 is a quadratic extension of $\mathbb{K}(z)$ and the Galois group of L over K_1 is isomorphic to G_1. Therefore $V = V_1 \oplus V_2$ where V_1 and V_2 are symplectic subspaces invariant under G_1 and there exist 4×4 projection matrices P_1 and P_2 with coefficients in K_1 such that $P_1 + P_2 = I_4$ and the columns of $P_1 X$ and $P_2 X$ span V_1 and V_2 respectively. Define $W_1 = P_1^t W P_1$ and $W_2 = P_2^t W P_2$. The anti-symmetric matrices W_1

and W_2 define two linearly independent rank two Poisson structures with coefficients in a quadratic extension of $\mathbb{K}(z)$. □

Note that the two Poisson structures in the proposition correspond to two conjugate solutions in a quadratic extension of the exterior square of L.

Proposition 6. *The kernel of a Poisson structure W of a symplectic operator L (i.e. the solutions to $WX = 0$) is an invariant vector space.*

Proof. Let $X = (x_{i,j})$ be a fundamental matrix of solutions of L and let V be the vector space over $\mathbb{K}$ generated by the columns of X. The Galois group of L acts on V and it fixes W, for the Poisson structure has coefficients in the ground field. In particular, the Galois group stabilizes the kernel of the Poisson structure. □

Corollary 2.
- i) *If L is symplectic and irreducible, then all projective Poisson structures are projective symplectic structures and their Pfaffians have the same exponential type.*
- ii) *An irreducible symplectic operator L whose Galois group is isomorphic to $\mathbb{Z}_2 \ltimes G_1$, $G_1 \subset SL_2(\mathbb{K})$ admits two linearly independent projective symplectic structures in a quadratic extension of $\mathbb{K}(z)$.*
- iii) *Let L be an irreducible operator admitting a symplectic structure W_1 and a $\mathbb{K}$-linearly independent projective symplectic structure W_2. Then there are two linear combinations of W_1, W_2 that are linearly independent rank two Poisson structures over a quadratic extension of $\mathbb{K}(z)$.*

Proof.
- i) If L admits a projective Poisson structure that is not symplectic, then, after multiplication by a hyperexponential function, we may assume that the Poisson structure has rational coefficients. Now from Proposition 6 it follows that its kernel is a non-trivial invariant vector space of dimension 2, and thus L is reducible. Thus if L is irreducible, then all projective Poisson structure are symplectic structures. Now, since a solution to equation (2) has a Pfaffian equal, up to a constant factor, to the Wronskian of L and the Pfaffian is not zero, they all have the same exponential type (the exponential type of the Wronskian).
- ii) If L is an irreducible symplectic operator with Galois group isomorphic to $\mathbb{Z}_2 \ltimes G_1$ where G_1 is a subgroup of $SL_2(\mathbb{K})$, then from Proposition 5, L admits two linearly independent Poisson structures in a quadratic extension. In particular, it admits two projective Poisson structures and therefore, from i), these are projective symplectic structures.
- iii) Let $W_1, \ldots, W_p$ be a basis of the projective symplectic structures, with W_1 rational. From i) we know all their Pfaffians have the same exponential type, and thus the Pfaffians of $W_2, \ldots, W_p$ are rational. Thus the entries of the W_i belong to a field extension $\mathbb{F} = \mathbb{K}(z, \sqrt{w_2}, \ldots, \sqrt{w_p})$, $w_i \in \mathbb{K}(z)$. So the Galois group $G = \mathrm{Gal}(L/\mathbb{F})$ admits p invariant symplectic structures $J_1, \ldots, J_p$ (obtained by $J_i = X^t W_i X$ where X a fundamental matrix of solutions, see Proposition 2). It also admits Poisson structures which are the linear combinations of the J_i with zero Pfaffian. The space of non invertible Poisson structures stabilized by G is thus of dimension $p-1$. Thus the non invertible Poisson structures over $\mathbb{F}$of L form an algebraic variety over $\mathbb{K}$ of dimension $p-1$. A solution W of (2) in $\mathbb{F}$ can be written as a linear combination of elements in $\sqrt{w_i}M_4(\mathbb{K}(z))$ and $M_4(\mathbb{K}(z))$. From the action of the Galois group on the square roots we see that each of these matrices are themselves solutions of (2), and thus that W is a linear combination of the W_i. Thus the W_i form a basis for the vector space Poisson structures with coefficients in $\mathbb{F}$. Therefore the solutions to the equation

$$\mathrm{Pf}\left(\sum_{i=1}^{p} \lambda_i W_i\right) = 0 \in \mathbb{K}(z) \qquad (4)$$

form an algebraic variety over $\mathbb{K}$ of dimension $p-1$, and so is equivalent to a single equation in $(\lambda_1 : \ldots : \lambda_p) \in \mathbb{P}^{p-1}(\mathbb{K})$. Bézout's theorem implies that this projective variety intersects $\lambda_3 = \cdots = \lambda_p = 0$, and thus that a linear combination of $\mu_1 W_1 + \mu_2 W_2$ gives a rank two Poisson structure. Now if W_2 is rational, then the resulting Poisson structure has coefficients in $\mathbb{K}(z)$, which would mean that L is reducible, contrary to the hypothesis. Thus W_2 is not rational, and its exponential type has a square root. So by Galois action, $\mu_1 W_1 - \mu_2 W_2$ is also a rank two Poisson structure. These are distinct as $\mu_1, \mu_2 \neq 0$, because W_1, W_2 are invertible. □

Example: $G =$

$$\left\langle \begin{pmatrix} \lambda & 0 & 0 & 0 \\ 0 & 1/\lambda & 0 & 0 \\ 0 & 0 & \epsilon\lambda & 0 \\ 0 & 0 & 0 & \epsilon/\lambda \end{pmatrix}, \begin{pmatrix} 0 & 1 & 0 & 0 \\ -1 & 0 & 0 & 0 \\ 0 & 0 & 0 & 1 \\ 0 & 0 & -1 & 0 \end{pmatrix}, \begin{pmatrix} 0 & 0 & 1 & 0 \\ 0 & 0 & 0 & 1 \\ 1 & 0 & 0 & 0 \\ 0 & 1 & 0 & 0 \end{pmatrix} \right\rangle,$$

$\lambda \in \mathbb{K}^*, \epsilon = \pm 1$. This group is irreducible, admits two subgroups of index 2, more precisely generated by removing the third matrix, and restricting $\epsilon = 1$. Each of these subgroups admits two symplectic structures, and the intersection, an index 4 subgroup, admits three symplectic structures.

4 THE ALGORITHM

Note that if L is projectively symplectic, then up to a multiplication of a hyperexponential function, we can ensure that the operator is then symplectic. Indeed, using the notation in the proof of Proposition 2, if $X^t \exp(\int \lambda(z)dz) WX = J$, then for $Y = \exp(\frac{1}{2}\int \lambda(z)dz)X$, we have $Y^t W Y = J$.

We know that if L has Liouvillian solutions, then we can always obtain a factorization with operators of order 2, either over the base field or in quadratic extension of it. To obtain an explicit expression of the Liouvillian solutions, we apply the Kovacic algorithm to the order two factors: More precisely the Ulmer-van Hoeij-Weil version of Kovacic algorithm [8, 15]. Indeed, the important property of it is that it only uses the computation of rational solutions of symmetric powers, which will be here much easier than the computation of hyperexponential solutions for an operator with non-rational coefficients.

<u>SymplecticKovacic</u>

Input: A symplectic linear differential operator $L = \partial^4 + a(z)\partial^3 + b(z)\partial^2 + c(z)\partial + d(z) \in \mathbb{K}(z)[\partial]$.

Output: A basis of the vector space of Liouvillian solutions of L.

(1) Factorize L in $\mathbb{K}(z)[\partial]$ [7].

(2) If $L = L_1L_2L_3L_4$ with L_i of order 1 for $i = 1,2,3,4$ solve by variation of constant and return the solutions.
(3) If there is a single factor $\tilde{L}$ of order 2, then $L = L_1L_2L_3$ where $\tilde{L} = L_i$ for some $i \in \{1,2,3\}$ and the other two factors are of order 1. Apply Kovacic algorithm to $\tilde{L}$ [15].
  (a) If $\tilde{L}$ is solvable, then solve L by variation of constants.
  (b) If $\tilde{L}$ is not solvable, compute hyperexponential solutions of L [12].
    (i) If there is one, then $L = ML_0$ where M is of order 3 and L_0 is of order 1. Compute hyperexponential solution of M [12].
      (A) If there is one, then $L = NM_0L_0$ where N is of order 2 and M_0 is of order 1. Solve M_0L_0 by variation of constants and return their solutions.
      (B) If there are no hyperexponential solutions to M, return a solution of L_0.
    (ii) If there are no hyperexponential solutions to L, return [].
(4) If there are two factors of order 2, $L = L_1L_2$, apply Kovacic's algorithm [15] to each of them
  (a) If L_1 is not solvable, return the Liouvillian solutions of L_2.
  (b) If L_1 and L_2 are solvable compute the solution through variation of constants
  (c) If L_1 is solvable but L_2 is not, compute an LCLM factorization of L [7]. If it has two factors, solve them by Kovacic algorithm and return the Liouvillian solutions. Else return [].
(5) Else L is irreducible. Compute linearly independent projective Poisson structures of L
  (a) If there are less than 2, return [].
  (b) Else denote two projective Poisson structures by W_1,W_2, such that W_1 has rational coefficients and W_2 has coefficients in a quadratic extension. Let $w(z) \in \mathbb{K}(z)$ be such that the coefficients of W_2 are in $\mathbb{K}(z, \sqrt{w(z)})$.
    (i) Solve $\mathrm{Pf}(W_1 + \lambda W_2) = 0$, and compute the two conjugate kernels V_1, V_2 with coefficients in $\mathbb{K}(z, \sqrt{w(z)})$ of $W_1 + \lambda W_2$ for the two solutions λ.
    (ii) Compute the companion linear differential system associated to L restricted to V_1: given a basis v_1, v_2 of V_1 find $a_{ij} \in \mathbb{K}(z, \sqrt{w(z)})$ such that $v_j' = -\sum_i a_{ij}v_i$ (cf. Proposition 6). Use a cyclic vector to compute an operator $\tilde{L}$ of order two with coefficients in $\mathbb{K}(z, \sqrt{w(z)})$.
      (A) If the symmetric square of $\tilde{L}$ has non-trivial solutions in $\mathbb{K}(z, \sqrt{w(z)})$, compute two linearly independent Liouvillian solutions to $\tilde{L}$ [15] of the form

$$e^{\int \sqrt{\alpha(z)+\sqrt{w(z)}\beta(z)dz}}.$$

      (B) Else, if for some $i \in \{6,8,12\}$ the i-th symmetric power of $\tilde{L}$ has non-trivial solutions in $\mathbb{K}(z, \sqrt{w(z)})$, use van Hoeij-Weil algorithm [8] to compute a basis of solutions to $\tilde{L}$ of the form

$$e^{\int \alpha(z)+\sqrt{w(z)}\beta(z)dz}F(p(z) + \sqrt{w(z)}r(z))$$

      where F is a solution of a standard equation (cf. [8]).
      (C) Else $\tilde{L}$ is not solvable.

Return the Liouvillian solutions to $\tilde{L}$ obtained in ii. together with their conjugates under $\sqrt{w(z)} \to -\sqrt{w(z)}$.

Theorem 2. *The algorithm* SymplecticKovacic *returns the vector space of Liouvillian solutions of L.*

Proof. According to Proposition 4 the possible factorizations of L are for factors with orders:
i) 1, 1, 1, 1, ii) 1, 1, 2, iii) 1, 2, 1, iv) 2, 1, 1, v) 2, 2, vi) 4.

The first step tests whether we are in one of the first five cases.

The second step deals with case i), where we can obtain a basis of the space of Liouvillian solutions, which has dimension 4, by using variation of constants.

The third step tests whether we are in cases ii), iii) or iv). If the order 2 factor $\tilde{L}$ is solvable, we can obtain a basis of the space of Liouvillian solutions, which has dimension 4, by using variation of constants after finding Liouvillian solutions to the factor of second order. If $\tilde{L}$ is not solvable, step 3(b) test whether we are in case iv), in which case the space of Liouvillian solutions has dimension two, and a basis can be obtain by variation of constants, or in case iii), in which case the space of Liouvillian solutions has dimension one, and a basis can is obtain by computing hyperexponential solutions to L. If we are not in either of these two cases, the only possible factorization of L is of the form case ii) and there are no Liouvillian solutions, for the order two factor $\tilde{L}$ is not solvable.

The fourth step addresses the case v). If only the right factor is solvable, then the space of Liouvillian solution has dimension two and using Kovacic algorithm one can find a basis of it. If each factor is solvable, then the space of Liouvillian solution has dimension four and using variation of constants one can find a basis of it, after using Kovacic algorithm on both factors. If only the left factor is solvable, then step 4(c) tests whether the Galois group has a representation 2×2 block diagonal. In which case the space of Liouvillian solution has dimension two, as one of the two factors of the LCLM factorization is solvable.

The fifth step deals with the irreducible case, which is case iv). According to Corollary 2 ii), L is not solvable if L does not admit at least two linearly independent projective Poisson structures over a quadratic extension of $\mathbb{K}(z)$. Step 5(a) rules this case out. When there are two linearly independent projective Poisson structures in a quadratic extension, Corollary 2 iii), implies that a linear combination of them will produce two non-trivial and non-invertible Poisson structures. These Poisson structures are obtained in Step 5(b)i. Their kernels are two invariant vector spaces V_1, V_2 of solutions of L. None of these kernels V_1 and V_2 is rational, or else L would possess an invariant vector space of dimension 2, and thus would factorize. Therefore V_1 and V_2 are conjugate by an automorphism of a quadratic extension. In particular the solutions in V_1 are Liouvillian if and only if the solutions in V_2 are Liouvillian. Step 5(b)ii computes the operator L restricted to V_1, tests using Kovacic algorithm whether this restriction is solvable, and in this case computes its Liouvillian solutions. The solutions of V_2 when they are Liouvillian can be obtained by taking the conjugates of the Liouvillian solutions in V_1. □

5 IMPLEMENTATION AND EXAMPLES

The complexity of computing rational solutions of a linear differential operator depends not only on the degree and order of the operator, but also on the local exponents at the singularities [3]. The same applies to operator factorization [7], and therefore also to our work. Because of this, we do not aim at obtaining low complexity in terms of the degree, order and height of the coefficients. The objective is rather to obtain a workable algorithm on reasonable examples rather than on cases of worst possible complexity. The most expensive part is in the last three steps where finite groups are tested and so our algorithm was designed to optimize this part.

- The factorization in a quadratic extension allows to compute symmetric powers of an order 2 operator instead of 4
- The finite Galois groups are tested using invariants instead of semi-invariants. Even if using semi-invariants would allow lower order operators, the search for hyperexponential solutions over a quadratic extension is equivalent to searching for hyperexponential solutions of an operator of order 14, which is too expensive.
- The rational solutions in $\mathbb{K}(z, \sqrt{w(z)})$ are searched by first constructing a linear differential system, which is cheap, and secondly by constructing a universal denominator for each of the two unknowns by computing possible local exponents at the singularities. The rational solutions are then finally obtained using linear algebra.

We present a table of examples obtained by considering the annihilator of $f(\sqrt{z})$ where f is a solution of $f'' + (z^{2n+1} + z + 1)f = 0$. This produces a symplectic operator of order 4, which is bi-projectively symplectic as the Galois group will be a subgroup of $\mathbb{Z}_2 \ltimes SL_2(\mathbb{K})$. This also ensures that the algorithm does not use early termination paths to avoid the last steps. The computations were done on a Macbook pro 2013 2.8 Ghz.

n	0	1	2	3	4
degree	3	7	11	15	19
time	2.4 s	5 s	9.2s	37.5 s	5757s

We present now the solutions of several symplectic operators with finite Galois groups. The pullbacks are obtained using the formulas in [8], where the pullback functions are in a quadratic extension.

A D_8 example. We consider the LCLM of the following operator with its conjugate

$$Dz^2 + \frac{3(20z + 37\sqrt{z} + 21}{256z^2(\sqrt{z}+1)^2}.$$

The solutions are found in $1.7s$:

$$\sqrt{z}(1 \pm \sqrt{z})^{\frac{1}{4}} e^{\frac{1}{16}\int \frac{1}{z\sqrt{1\pm\sqrt{z}}}dz}, \sqrt{z}(1 \pm \sqrt{z})^{\frac{1}{4}} e^{-\frac{1}{16}\int \frac{1}{z\sqrt{1\pm\sqrt{z}}}dz}$$

An A_5 example. We consider the LCLM of the following operator with its conjugate

$$Dz^2 + \frac{1}{2z}Dz + \frac{739z^{3/2} + 864z^2 + 611\sqrt{z} - 314z + 800}{14400z^2(z-1)^2}.$$

The solutions are found in $12.4s$

$$\sqrt[12]{\frac{z^2P(z)(\sqrt{z}-1)^2}{(5589\sqrt{z}-800)^3}}\,\mathcal{L}\left(-\frac{1}{6}, 5, \sqrt{99\frac{(27945z - 19967\sqrt{z} + 1600)^2}{(5589\sqrt{z}-800)^3(1-\sqrt{z})}}\right)$$

together with the conjugates $\sqrt{z} \mapsto -\sqrt{z}$, where $\mathcal{L}$ a basis a solutions of the Legendre differential equation (whose solutions can also be written in terms of the hypergeometric function) and

$$P = 251894530944z^2 - 360031369239z^{3/2} + 134021894211z - 17568425600\sqrt{z} + 765440000$$

An A_4 example. We consider the LCLM of the following operator with its conjugate

$$Dz^2 + \frac{108z^2 + 648z^{3/2} + 1505z + 1498\sqrt{z} + 560}{576(\sqrt{z}+1)^2z^2(2+\sqrt{z})^2}.$$

The solutions are found in $17s$

$$\left(\frac{(189z^2 + 810z^{\frac{3}{2}} + 1118z + 526\sqrt{z} + 20)^{24}z^{10}}{P(z)Q(z)^{14}(2+\sqrt{z})^6(\sqrt{z}+1)^6}\right)^{\frac{1}{24}} {}_2F_1\left(\frac{13}{24}, \frac{25}{24}, \frac{5}{4}, \frac{P(z)/45}{(z+3\sqrt{z}+2)^2Q(z)^2}\right)$$

with

$$P = 67191201z^6 + 863886870z^{11/2} + 4900709061z^5 + 16136882532z^{9/2} + 34114858452z^4 + 48314544768z^{7/2} + 46335734636z^3 + 29648385408z^{5/2} + 12093966336z^2 + 2856633184z^{3/2} + 318081360z + 10315200\sqrt{z} + 104000$$

$$Q = 945z^2 + 3240z^{3/2} + 3354z + 1052\sqrt{z} + 20$$

An S_4 example. We consider the LCLM of the following operator with its conjugate

$$Dz^2 + \frac{4z^{9/2} + 4z^{3/2} + 4z + 3}{16z^2}$$

The solutions are found in $9.3s$

$$((\sqrt{z}+1)^3z^{7/2}(252z + 311\sqrt{z} + 63)^{-3}(144027072z^3 + 534597840z^{5/2} + 774164272z^2 + 550356683z^{3/2} + 198862573z + 34349049\sqrt{z} + 2250423))^{1/8}$$

$$\mathcal{L}\left(-\frac{1}{4}, \frac{1}{3}, \sqrt{-\frac{28(1512z^{3/2} + 2815z + 1496\sqrt{z} + 189)^2}{5(252z + 311\sqrt{z} + 63)^3}}\right)$$

An application in Hamiltonian systems. We consider the potential

$$V = q_1q_2^2 + q_1q_2q_3 + q_1q_3^2 + q_1^2 + q_2^2 + q_3^2.$$

This potential admits a particular solution along the line $q_2 = q_3 = 0$. The variational equation is given by

$$\begin{pmatrix} \ddot{X} \\ \ddot{Y} \\ \ddot{Z} \end{pmatrix} = \begin{pmatrix} -2 & 0 & 0 \\ 0 & -2q_1(t) - 2 & -q_1(t) \\ 0 & -q_1(t) & -2q_1(t) - 2 \end{pmatrix} \begin{pmatrix} X \\ Y \\ Z \end{pmatrix}$$

Now making a time change by denoting $q_1(t) = z$, we obtain in the lower right 2×2 invariant block

$$(1-z^2)\begin{pmatrix} \ddot{Y} \\ \ddot{Z} \end{pmatrix} - z\begin{pmatrix} \dot{Y} \\ \dot{Z} \end{pmatrix} + \begin{pmatrix} 2(z+1) & z \\ z & 2(z+1) \end{pmatrix}\begin{pmatrix} Y \\ Z \end{pmatrix} = 0$$

Applying cyclic vector on $Y(z)$ we obtain the following order 4 operator $L =$

$$Dz^4 + \frac{2(2z^2+1)}{z(z^2-1)}Dz^3 - \frac{4z^5 + 2z^4 - 4z^3 - 3z^2 - 2}{z^2(z^2-1)^2}Dz^2 - \frac{4(z^2 - z + 1)}{(z^2-1)(z-1)z}Dz + \frac{3z^4 + 8z^3 + 2z^2 + 4}{z^2(z^2-1)^2}$$

This operator admits 2 linearly independent projective symplectic structures of same type:

$$\frac{(z^2-1)^{3/2}}{z^2}\begin{pmatrix} 0 & -4\frac{z}{z-1} & \frac{2z^2+1}{z^2-1} & z \\ 4\frac{z}{z-1} & 0 & -z & 0 \\ -\frac{2z^2+1}{z^2-1} & z & 0 & 0 \\ -z & 0 & 0 & 0 \end{pmatrix},$$

$$\frac{(z^2-1)^{3/2}}{z^2}\begin{pmatrix} 0 & -\frac{3z^2-2}{z^2-1} & -6\frac{z}{z^2-1} & -2 \\ \frac{3z^2-2}{z^2-1} & 0 & \frac{4z^2-1}{z^2-1} & z \\ 6\frac{z}{z^2-1} & -\frac{4z^2-1}{z^2-1} & 0 & z^2-1 \\ 2 & -z & -z^2+1 & 0 \end{pmatrix}$$

It is not symplectic despite coming from a Hamiltonian system due to the algebraic change of variable. Indeed the base field we should consider here contains $\sqrt{1-z^2}$, but as it does not appear in the coefficients, we "forget it" in the computations. This adds a finite extension on the Galois group as the base field becomes smaller, but it has no consequences on the Liouvillian solvability of it. Actually algebraic changes of variable never pose a problem to our algorithm, as the resulting operator will always have a Galois group in $PSP_4(\mathbb{K})$.

Proposition 7. *The algebraic subgroups of* $GL_4(\mathbb{K})$ *which are finite extensions of* $SP_4(\mathbb{K})$ *are of the form*

$$\{M \in M_{2n}(\mathbb{K}),\ \exists \lambda \in \mathbb{U}_p,\ M^t JM = \lambda J\} \subset PSP_4(\mathbb{K})$$

where $\mathbb{U}_p$ *is the set of* p*-roots of unity.*

Proof. Using the classification of [6], we look for algebraic group whose identity components are $SP_4(\mathbb{K})$. In $SL_4(\mathbb{K})$ these groups are diagonal extensions of $SP_4(\mathbb{K})$ with an additional generator of the form ωI_4 with $\omega^4 = 1$. The group $GL_4(\mathbb{K})$ is itself a diagonal extension of $SL_4(\mathbb{K})$ and thus finite extensions of $SP_4(\mathbb{K})$ in $GL_4(\mathbb{K})$ are obtained by adding a generator of the form ωI_4 where ω is a root of unity. □

Applying the algorithm SymplecticKovacic returns [], meaning that there are no Liouvillian solutions, and thus that the potential is not integrable [10]. Still, the existence of two symplectic structures of the same exponential type allows us to build two linearly independent Poisson structures, and thus implies that the operator is the LCLM of two operators of order 2:

$$Dz^2 + \frac{zDz}{z^2-1} - \frac{3z+2}{z^2-1},\ Dz^2 + \frac{zDz}{z^2-1} - \frac{z+2}{z^2-1}.$$

Conclusion. We produced an algorithm for computing Liouvillian solutions of symplectic operators of order 4 whose execution time is manageable on reasonable examples. The key point is that the symplectic group admits far fewer primitive/imprimitive finite groups than $SL_4(\mathbb{K})$, allowing the identification of solvable Galois groups to be much faster. In particular, this allows us to study irreducible order 4 operators which were before intractable. One of the applications is the study of variational equations in Hamiltonians with 3 degrees of freedom, which was impossible before as generally the variational equation has its Galois group in $PSP_4(\mathbb{K})$ and so it does not necessarily decouple into smaller order operators. Possible future enhancements include early termination by exponent analysis, optimization of the universal denominator, using the Poisson structures to speed up the factorization in reducible cases, optimization of the pullback expressions for the finite case representation, minimization of iterated integrals in the representation of the solutions, and a better handling of quadratic extensions. The code is available at http://combot.perso.math.cnrs.fr/software.html.

REFERENCES

[1] Ainhoa Aparicio-Monforte, Elie Compoint, and Jacques-Arthur Weil. 2013. A characterization of reduced forms of linear differential systems. *J. Pure Appl. Algebra* 217, 8 (2013), 1504–1516. https://doi.org/10.1016/j.jpaa.2012.11.007

[2] Michèle Audin. 2001. *Les systèmes hamiltoniens et leur intégrabilité.* Cours Spécialisés [Specialized Courses], Vol. 8. Société Mathématique de France, Paris; EDP Sciences, Les Ulis. viii+170 pages.

[3] Moulay A. Barkatou. 1999. On rational solutions of systems of linear differential equations. *J. Symbolic Comput.* 28, 4-5 (1999), 547–567. https://doi.org/10.1006/jsco.1999.0314 Differential algebra and differential equations.

[4] Reinhold Burger, George Labahn, and Mark van Hoeij. 2004. Closed form solutions of linear ODEs having elliptic function coefficients. In *ISSAC 2004.* ACM, New York, 58–64. https://doi.org/10.1145/1005285.1005296

[5] Amihay Hanany and Yang-Hui He. 2001. A monograph on the classification of the discrete subgroups of SU(4). *J. High Energy Phys.* 2 (2001), Paper 27, 12. https://doi.org/10.1088/1126-6708/2001/02/027

[6] Julia Hartmann. 2002. Invariants and differential Galois groups in degree four. In *Differential Galois theory (Bpolhkedlewo, 2001).* Banach Center Publ., Vol. 58. Polish Acad. Sci. Inst. Math., Warsaw, 79–87. https://doi.org/10.4064/bc58-0-7

[7] Mark van Hoeij. 1997. Factorization of differential operators with rational functions coefficients. *J. Symbolic Comput.* 24, 5 (1997), 537–561. https://doi.org/10.1006/jsco.1997.0151

[8] Mark van Hoeij and Jacques-Arthur Weil. 2005. Solving second order linear differential equations with Klein's theorem. In *Proceedings of the 2005 International Symposium on Symbolic and Algebraic Computation (Beijing, China).* ACM, New York, 340–347. https://doi.org/10.1145/1073884.1073931

[9] Jerald J. Kovacic. 1986. An algorithm for solving second order linear homogeneous differential equations. *J. Symbolic Comput.* 2, 1 (1986), 3–43. https://doi.org/10.1016/S0747-7171(86)80010-4

[10] Juan J. Morales Ruiz. 1999. *Differential Galois theory and non-integrability of Hamiltonian systems.* Birkhäuser/Springer, Basel. xiv+167 pages. https://doi.org/10.1007/978-3-0348-8718-2 [2013] reprint of the 1999 edition [MR1713573].

[11] Juan J. Morales-Ruiz and Jean Pierre Ramis. 1999. Galoisian obstructions to integrability of Hamiltonian systems: statements and examples. In *Hamiltonian systems with three or more degrees of freedom (S'Agaró, 1995).* NATO Adv. Sci. Inst. Ser. C Math. Phys. Sci., Vol. 533. Kluwer Acad. Publ., Dordrecht, 509–513.

[12] E. Pflügel. 1997. An algorithm for computing exponential solutions of first order linear differential systems. In *Proceedings of the 1997 International Symposium on Symbolic and Algebraic Computation (Kihei, HI).* ACM, New York, 164–171. https://doi.org/10.1145/258726.258773

[13] Marius van der Put and Michael F. Singer. 2003. *Galois theory of linear differential equations.* Berlin ; New York : Springer, c2003.

[14] Michael F. Singer and Felix Ulmer. 1993. Liouvillian and algebraic solutions of second and third order linear differential equations. *J. Symbolic Comput.* 16, 1 (1993), 37–73. https://doi.org/10.1006/jsco.1993.1033

[15] Felix Ulmer and Jacques-Arthur Weil. 1996. Note on Kovacic's algorithm. *J. Symbolic Comput.* 22, 2 (1996), 179–200. https://doi.org/10.1006/jsco.1996.0047

Symmetric Indefinite Triangular Factorization Revealing the Rank Profile Matrix*

Jean-Guillaume Dumas
Université Grenoble Alpes
Laboratoire Jean Kuntzmann, CNRS, UMR 5224
38058 Grenoble, CEDEX 9, France
Jean-Guillaume.Dumas@univ-grenoble-alpes.fr

Clément Pernet
Université Grenoble Alpes
Laboratoire Jean Kuntzmann, CNRS, UMR 5224
38058 Grenoble, CEDEX 9, France
Clement.Pernet@univ-grenoble-alpes.fr

ABSTRACT

We present a novel recursive algorithm for reducing a symmetric matrix to a triangular factorization which reveals the rank profile matrix. That is, the algorithm computes a factorization $\mathbf{P}^T\mathbf{A}\mathbf{P} = \mathbf{L}\mathbf{D}\mathbf{L}^T$ where $\mathbf{P}$ is a permutation matrix, $\mathbf{L}$ is lower triangular with a unit diagonal and $\mathbf{D}$ is symmetric block diagonal with 1×1 and 2×2 antidiagonal blocks. This algorithm requires $O(n^2r^{\omega-2})$ arithmetic operations, with n the dimension of the matrix, r its rank and ω an admissible exponent for matrix multiplication. Furthermore, experimental results demonstrate that our algorithm has very good performance: its computational speed matches that of its numerical counterpart and is twice as fast as the unsymmetric exact Gaussian factorization. By adapting the pivoting strategy developed in the unsymmetric case, we show how to recover the rank profile matrix from the permutation matrix and the support of the block-diagonal matrix. We also note that there is an obstruction in characteristic 2 for revealing the rank profile matrix, which requires to relax the shape of the block diagonal by allowing the 2-dimensional blocks to have a non-zero bottom-right coefficient. This relaxed decomposition can then be transformed into a standard $\mathbf{P}\mathbf{L}\mathbf{D}\mathbf{L}^T\mathbf{P}^T$ decomposition at a negligible cost.

ACM Reference Format:

Jean-Guillaume Dumas and Clément Pernet. 2018. Symmetric Indefinite Triangular Factorization Revealing the Rank Profile Matrix. In *ISSAC '18: 2018 ACM International Symposium on Symbolic and Algebraic Computation, July 16–19, 2018, New York, NY, USA.* ACM, New York, NY, USA, 8 pages. https://doi.org/10.1145/3208976.3209019

1 INTRODUCTION

Computing a triangular factorization of a symmetric matrix is a commonly used routine to solve symmetric linear systems, or to compute the signature of symmetric bilinear forms. Besides the fact that it is expected to save half of the arithmetic cost of a standard (non-symmetric) Gaussian elimination, it can also recover invariants, such as the signature, specific to symmetric matrices, and thus, e.g., be used to certify positive or negative definiteness or semidefiniteness [13, Corollary 1].

*This work is partly funded by the OpenDreamKit Horizon 2020 European Research Infrastructures project (#676541).

ACM ISBN 978-1-4503-5550-6/18/07...$15.00
https://doi.org/10.1145/3208976.3209019

It is a fundamental computation in numerical linear algebra, and is therefore most often presented in the setting of real matrices. When the matrix is positive definite, the Cholesky factorization can be defined: $\mathbf{A} = \mathbf{L}\mathbf{L}^T$, where $\mathbf{L}$ is lower triangular for which square roots of diagonal elements have to be extracted. Alternatively, gathering the diagonal elements in a central diagonal matrix yields the LDLT factorization $\mathbf{A} = \mathbf{L}\mathbf{D}\mathbf{L}^T$ which no longer requires square roots. Similarly as for the LU decomposition, it is only defined for matrices with generic rank profile, i.e. having their $r = \text{rank}(\mathbf{A})$ first leading principal minors non-zero. For arbitrary matrices, symmetric permutations may lead to the former situations: $\mathbf{P}\mathbf{A}\mathbf{P}^T = \mathbf{L}\mathbf{D}\mathbf{L}^T$. However, this is unfortunately not always the case. For instance there is no permutation $\mathbf{P}$ such that $\mathbf{P}^T\begin{bmatrix}0&1\\1&0\end{bmatrix}\mathbf{P}$ has an LDLT factorization with a diagonal $\mathbf{D}$. This led to a series of generalizations where the matrix $\mathbf{D}$ was replaced first by a tridiagonal symmetric matrix by Parlett and Reid [14], improved by Aasen [1], achieving half the arithmetic cost of Gaussian elimination. Bunch and Kaufman then replaced this tridiagonal matrix by a block diagonal composed of 1 or 2-dimensional antidiagonal blocks to obtain an *indefinite triangular factorization*.

Pivoting. In numerical linear algebra, the choice of the permutation matrix is mainly driven by the need to ensure a good numerical quality of the decomposition. Bunch and Parlett [6] use a full pivoting technique, requiring a cubic number of tests. Bunch and Kaufman's pivoting strategy, implemented in LAPACK, uses a partial pivoting requiring only a quadratic number of tests.

In the context of exact linear algebra, for instance when computing over a finite field, numerical stability is no longer an issue. However, the computation of echelon forms and rank profiles, central in many applications, impose further constraints on the pivoting. A characterization of the requirements for the pivoting strategy is given in [10, 11] so that a PLUQ decomposition can reveal these rank profiles and echelon forms in the non-symmetric case. In particular, it is shown that pivot selection minimizing the lexicographic order on the coordinate of the pivot, combined with row and column rotations to move the pivot to the diagonal, enable the computation of the rank profile matrix, an invariant from which all rank profile information or the row and the column echelon form can be recovered.

Recursive algorithms. As in numerical linear algebra, we try to gather arithmetic operations in level 3 BLAS operations (matrix multiplication based), for it delivers the best computation throughput. Numerical software often use tiled implementations, especially when the pivoting is more constrained by the symmetry [12, 16], or in order to define communication avoiding variants [4]. In exact linear algebra sub-cubic matrix multiplication, such as Strassen's algorithm, can be extensively used with no numerical instability issues. This led to the design of recursive algorithms, which was proven successful in the unsymmetric case, including for shared memory parallel computations [9].

Contribution. The contribution here is to propose a recursive algorithm producing a symmetric factorization PLDLTPT over any field, from which the rank profile matrix of the input can be recovered. This algorithm is a recursive variant of Bunch and Kaufman's algorithm [5] where the pivoting strategy has been replaced by the one developed previously by the authors in the unsymmetric case [11]. Compared to the recursive adaptation of Aasen's algorithm in [15], our algorithm leads to a similar data partitioning but does not suffer from an arithmetic overhead with respect to Aasen's algorithm. Our algorithm has time complexity $O(n^2r^{\omega-2})$ where ω is an admissible exponent for matrix multiplication and r is the rank of the input matrix of dimension n. With $\omega = 3$, the leading constant in the time complexity is 1/3, matching that of the best alternative algorithms based on cubic time linear algebra.

In Section 2 we show that in characteristic two the rank profile matrix can not always be revealed by a symmetric factorization with antidiagonal blocks: sometimes antitriangular blocks are also required. Then we recall in Section 3 the main required level 3 linear algebra subroutines. In Section 4 we present the main recursive algorithm. An alternative iterative Crout variant is presented in Section 5 to be used as a base case in the recursion. We finally show, in Section 6, experiments of the resulting implementation over a finite field. They demonstrate the efficiency of cascading the recursive algorithm with the base case variant, especially with matrices involving a lot of pivoting. They finally confirm a speed-up by a factor of about 2 compared to the state of the art unsymmetric Gaussian elimination.

2 THE SYMMETRIC RANK PROFILE MATRIX

2.1 The pivoting matrix

Theorem 1 recalls the definition of the rank profile matrix (RPM).

THEOREM 1 ([10]). *Let $A \in \mathbb{F}^{m\times n}$. There exists a unique $m \times n$ $\{0,1\}$-matrix $\mathcal{R}_A$ with r 1's in rook placement of which every leading sub-matrix has the same rank as the corresponding leading sub-matrix of A. This matrix is called the* rank profile matrix of A.

LEMMA 1. *A symmetric matrix has a symmetric rank profile matrix.*

PROOF. Otherwise, the rank of some leading submatrix of A and the same leading submatrix of A^T would be different which is absurd. □

Also, any symmetric matrix has a triangular decomposition $A = PLDL^TP^T$ where L is unit lower triangular, P is a permutation matrix and D is block diagonal, formed by 1-dimensional scalar blocks or 2-dimensional antidiagonal blocks of the form $\begin{bmatrix} 0 & x \\ x & 0 \end{bmatrix}$. We further define the support matrix of such a block diagonal matrix as the localization of the non-zero elements:

DEFINITION 1. *The* support matrix *of a block diagonal matrix D, formed by 1-dimensional scalar blocks or 2-dimensional blocks of the form $\begin{bmatrix} 0 & x \\ x & 0 \end{bmatrix}$ is the block diagonal $\{0,1\}$-matrix Ψ_D such that $D = \Psi_D\overline{D}$, with $\overline{D}$ a diagonal matrix.*

DEFINITION 2. *The* pivoting matrix *of a* $PLDL^TP^T$ *decomposition is the matrix $\Pi = P\Psi_DP^T$.*

DEFINITION 3. *A* $PLDL^TP^T$ *decomposition is said to* reveal the rank profile matrix *of a symmetric matrix A if its pivoting matrix equals the rank profile matrix of A.*

2.2 Antitriangular blocks in characteristic two

In zero or odd characteristic, we show next that one can always find such a PLDLTPT decomposition revealing the rank profile matrix. In characteristic two, however, this is not always possible.

LEMMA 2. *In characteristic 2, there is no symmetric indefinite elimination revealing the rank profile matrix of* $A = \begin{bmatrix} 0 & 1 \\ 1 & 1 \end{bmatrix}$.

PROOF. Let J be the 2×2 anti-diagonal identity matrix. This is also the rank profile matrix of A. Now, we let $L = \begin{bmatrix} 1 & 0 \\ x & 1 \end{bmatrix}, \overline{D} = \begin{bmatrix} y & 0 \\ 0 & z \end{bmatrix}$. As the permutation matrices involved, P and Ψ_D, can only be either the identity matrix or J, there are then four cases:

(1) $A = L{\cdot}\overline{D}{\cdot}L^T = \begin{bmatrix} y & xy \\ xy & x^2y+z \end{bmatrix}$, but $y = 0$ and $\text{rank}(\overline{D}) = \text{rank}(A) = 2$ are incompatible.

(2) $A = J{\cdot}L{\cdot}\overline{D}{\cdot}L^T{\cdot}J^T = \begin{bmatrix} x^2y+z & xy \\ xy & y \end{bmatrix}$, but $I = J{\cdot}I{\cdot}J \neq J = \mathcal{R}_A$.

(3) $A = L{\cdot}\overline{D}{\cdot}J{\cdot}L^T = \begin{bmatrix} 0 & y \\ z & xy+xz \end{bmatrix}$, but we need $y = z$ for the symmetry and then $2xy = 0 \neq 1$ in characteristic 2.

(4) $A = J{\cdot}L{\cdot}\overline{D}{\cdot}J{\cdot}L^T{\cdot}J^T = \begin{bmatrix} xy+xz & z \\ y & 0 \end{bmatrix}$ but the bottom right coefficient of A is non zero.

□

However, one can generalize the PLDLTPT decomposition to a block diagonal matrix D having 2-dimensional blocks of the form $\begin{bmatrix} 0 & c \\ c & d \end{bmatrix}$ (lower antitriangular). Then the notion of support matrix can be generalized: for such a block diagonal matrix D, Ψ_D is the block diagonal $\{0,1\}$ matrix such that $D = \Psi_D\overline{D}$, with $\overline{D}$ an upper triangular bidiagonal matrix (or equivalently such that $D = \overline{D}\Psi_D$, with $\overline{D}$ lower triangular bidiagonal). For instance $\begin{bmatrix} 0 & c \\ c & d \end{bmatrix} = \begin{bmatrix} 0 & 1 \\ 1 & 0 \end{bmatrix}\begin{bmatrix} c & d \\ 0 & c \end{bmatrix} = \begin{bmatrix} c & 0 \\ d & c \end{bmatrix}\begin{bmatrix} 0 & 1 \\ 1 & 0 \end{bmatrix}$.

With these generalized definitions, we show in Section 4, that there exists RPM-revealing PLDLTPT decompositions.

2.3 Antitriangular decomposition

Then, such a generalized decomposition can always be further reduced to a strict PLDLTPT decomposition by eliminating each of the antitriangular blocks. For this, the observation is that in characteristic two, a symmetric lower antitriangular 2×2 block is invariant under any symmetric triangular transformation: $\begin{bmatrix} 1 & \\ x & 1 \end{bmatrix}\begin{bmatrix} & c \\ c & d \end{bmatrix}\begin{bmatrix} 1 & x \\ & 1 \end{bmatrix} = \begin{bmatrix} & c \\ c & 2cx+d \end{bmatrix} \equiv \begin{bmatrix} & c \\ c & d \end{bmatrix} \mod 2 = \begin{bmatrix} & 1 \\ 1 & \end{bmatrix}\begin{bmatrix} & c \\ c & d \end{bmatrix}\begin{bmatrix} 1 & \\ & 1 \end{bmatrix}$. Thus for each

2×2 block in a tridiagonal decomposition, the corresponding 2×2 diagonal block in L can be replaced by $\mathbf{I}_2$, via a multiplication by $\begin{bmatrix} 1 & \\ -x & 1 \end{bmatrix}$.

Further, we have that: $\begin{bmatrix} & c \\ c & d \end{bmatrix} = \mathbf{J} \begin{bmatrix} 1 & \\ c/d & 1 \end{bmatrix} \begin{bmatrix} d & \\ & -c^2/d \end{bmatrix} \begin{bmatrix} 1 & c/d \\ & 1 \end{bmatrix} \mathbf{J}$. Now J commutes with the identity $\mathbf{I}_2$ matrix. Therefore we have that: $\begin{bmatrix} 1 & \\ x & 1 \end{bmatrix} \begin{bmatrix} 1 & \\ -x & 1 \end{bmatrix} \mathbf{J} \begin{bmatrix} 1 & \\ c/d & 1 \end{bmatrix} = \mathbf{J} \begin{bmatrix} 1 & \\ x & 1 \end{bmatrix} \begin{bmatrix} 1 & \\ -x & 1 \end{bmatrix} \begin{bmatrix} 1 & \\ c/d & 1 \end{bmatrix}$.

Thus, to eliminate the antitriangular blocks, create a triangular matrix $\mathbf{L}_J$ that starts as the identity and where its $i, i+1$ blocks corresponding to a $\begin{bmatrix} 1 & \\ x & 1 \end{bmatrix}$ block in L is a $\begin{bmatrix} 1 & \\ c/d-x & 1 \end{bmatrix}$ block (associated to an antitriangular $\begin{bmatrix} & c \\ c & d \end{bmatrix}$ block, with $d \neq 0$, in D). Then replace the triangular matrix L by $\tilde{\mathbf{L}} = \mathbf{L} \cdot \mathbf{L}_J$. Also, modify the diagonal matrix D, to $\tilde{\mathbf{D}}$ such that the $\begin{bmatrix} & c \\ c & d \end{bmatrix}$ blocks of D are replaced by $\begin{bmatrix} d & \\ & -c^2/d \end{bmatrix}$ blocks in $\tilde{\mathbf{D}}$. Finally, create a permutation matrix $\mathbf{P}_J$, starting from the identity matrix, where each identity block at position $i, i+1$ corresponding to an antitriangular block in D is replaced by J. Then $\tilde{\mathbf{P}} = \mathbf{P} \cdot \mathbf{P}_J$.

From this we have now a symmetric PLDLTPT factorization, $\mathbf{A} = \tilde{\mathbf{P}} \tilde{\mathbf{L}} \tilde{\mathbf{D}} \tilde{\mathbf{L}}^T \tilde{\mathbf{P}}^T$, with purely 1×1 and 2×2 antidiagonal blocks in $\tilde{\mathbf{D}}$ (but then a direct access to the rank profile matrix, $\mathbf{P} \Psi_{\mathbf{D}} \mathbf{P}^T$, might not be possible from $\tilde{\mathbf{P}}$ and $\tilde{\mathbf{D}}$).

In the following we present some building blocks and then algorithms computing an RPM-revealing symmetric indefinite triangular factorization.

3 BUILDING BLOCKS

We recall here some of the standard algorithms from the BLAS3 [7] and LAPACK [2] interfaces and generalization thereof [3], which will be used to define the main block recursive symmetric elimination.

- **gemm** (C, A, B): general matrix multiplication. Computes $\mathbf{C} \leftarrow \mathbf{C} - \mathbf{AB}$.
- **trmm** (U, B): multiply a triangular and a rectangular matrix in-place. Computes $\mathbf{B} \leftarrow \mathbf{UB}$ where B is $m \times n$ and U is upper or lower triangular.
- **trmm** (C, U, B): multiply a triangular and a rectangular matrix. Computes $\mathbf{C} \leftarrow \mathbf{C} - \mathbf{UB}$ where B and C are $m \times n$ and U is upper or lower triangular. This is an adaptation of the BLAS3 `trmm` to leave the B operand unchanged.
- **trsm** (U, B): solve a triangular system with matrix right hand-side. Computes $\mathbf{B} \leftarrow \mathbf{U}^{-1}\mathbf{B}$ where B is $m \times n$ and U is upper or lower triangular.
- **syrdk** (C, A, D): symmetric rank k update with diagonal scaling. Computes the upper or lower triangular part of the symmetric matrix $\mathbf{C} \leftarrow \mathbf{C} - \mathbf{ADA}^T$ where A is $n \times k$ and D is diagonal or block diagonal.
- **syrd2k** (C, A, D, B): symmetric rank $2k$ update with diagonal scaling. Computes the upper or lower triangular part of the symmetric matrix $\mathbf{C} \leftarrow \mathbf{C} - \mathbf{ADB}^T - \mathbf{BDA}^T$ where A and B are $n \times k$, and D is diagonal or block diagonal.

In addition, we use **scal** for multiplication by a diagonal matrix, **dadd** for matrix addition and diagonal scaling, and we need to introduce the **trssyr2k** routine solving Problem 1:

Problem 1. *Let $\mathbb{F}$ be a field of characteristic different than 2. Given a symmetric matrix $\mathbf{C} \in \mathbb{F}^{n \times n}$ and a unit upper triangular matrix $\mathbf{U} \in \mathbb{F}^{n \times n}$, find an upper triangular matrix $X \in \mathbb{F}^{n \times n}$ such that $\mathbf{X}^T\mathbf{U} + \mathbf{U}^T\mathbf{X} = \mathbf{C}$.*

In characteristic 2, the diagonal of $X^T\mathbf{U} + \mathbf{U}^T X$ is always zero for any matrix X and U, hence Problem 1 has no solution as soon as C has a non-zero diagonal element.

However in characteristic zero or odd, Algorithm 1 presents a recursive implementation of this routine, and is in the same time a constructive proof of the existence of such a solution. Note that it performs a division by 2 in line 2, and therefore requires that the base field does not have characteristic two.

Algorithm 1 `trssyr2k` (U, C)

Require: U, $n \times n$ full-rank upper triangular
Require: C, $n \times n$, symmetric
Ensure: $\mathbf{C} \leftarrow \mathbf{X}$, $n \times n$ upper triangular, s.t. $\mathbf{X}^T\mathbf{U} + \mathbf{U}^T\mathbf{X} = \mathbf{C}$

1: **if** $m = 1$ **then**
2:     **return** $\mathbf{C}_{1,1} \leftarrow \frac{1}{2}\mathbf{C}_{1,1} \cdot \mathbf{U}_{1,1}^{-1}$;
3: **end if**
4: Split $\mathbf{C} = \begin{bmatrix} \mathbf{C}_1 & \mathbf{C}_2 \\ \mathbf{C}_2^T & \mathbf{C}_3 \end{bmatrix}$, $\mathbf{U} = \begin{bmatrix} \mathbf{U}_1 & \mathbf{U}_2 \\ & \mathbf{U}_3 \end{bmatrix}$, $\mathbf{C}_1$ and $\mathbf{U}_1$ are $\lfloor \frac{n}{2} \rfloor \times \lfloor \frac{n}{2} \rfloor$
5: Find $\mathbf{X}_1$ s.t. $\mathbf{X}_1^T\mathbf{U}_1 + \mathbf{U}_1^T\mathbf{X}_1 = \mathbf{C}_1$ {`trssyr2k` $(\mathbf{U}_1, \mathbf{C}_1)$}
6: $\mathbf{D}_2 \leftarrow \mathbf{C}_2 - \mathbf{X}_1^T\mathbf{U}_2$ {`trmm` $(\mathbf{X}_1^T, \mathbf{U}_2)$}
7: $\mathbf{X}_2 \leftarrow \mathbf{U}_1^{-T}\mathbf{D}_2$ {`trsm` $(\mathbf{U}_1^T, \mathbf{D}_2)$}
8: $\mathbf{D}_3 \leftarrow \mathbf{C}_3 - (\mathbf{X}_2^T\mathbf{U}_2 + \mathbf{U}_2^T\mathbf{X}_2)$ {`syrd2k` $(\mathbf{X}_2, \mathbf{U}_2)$}
9: Find $\mathbf{X}_3$ s.t. $\mathbf{X}_3^T\mathbf{U}_3 + \mathbf{U}_3^T\mathbf{X}_3 = \mathbf{D}_3$ {`trssyr2k` $(\mathbf{U}_3, \mathbf{D}_3)$}

Remark 1. *Note that algorithm 1 computes the solution X in place on the symmetric storage of C: by induction $\mathbf{X}_1$ and $\mathbf{X}_3$ overwrite $\mathbf{C}_1$ and $\mathbf{C}_3$, and $\mathbf{X}_2$ overwrites $\mathbf{C}_2$ according to the specifications of the generalized `trmm` routine.*

Lemma 3. *Algorithm `trssyr2k` is correct and runs in $O(n^\omega)$ arithmetic operations.*

Proof. Using the notations of Algorithm 1, let $\mathbf{X} = \begin{bmatrix} \mathbf{X}_1 & \mathbf{X}_2 \\ & \mathbf{X}_3 \end{bmatrix}$. Then expanding $\mathbf{X}^T\mathbf{U} + \mathbf{U}^T\mathbf{X}$ gives

$$\begin{bmatrix} \mathbf{X}_1^T\mathbf{U}_1 + \mathbf{U}_1^T\mathbf{X}_1 & \mathbf{X}_1^T\mathbf{U}_2 + \mathbf{U}_1^T\mathbf{X}_2 \\ (\mathbf{X}_1^T\mathbf{U}_2 + \mathbf{U}_1^T\mathbf{X}_2)^T & \mathbf{X}_2^T\mathbf{U}_2 + \mathbf{U}_2^T\mathbf{X}_2 + \mathbf{X}_3^T\mathbf{U}_3 + \mathbf{U}_3^T\mathbf{X}_3 \end{bmatrix}$$
$$= \begin{bmatrix} \mathbf{C}_1 & \mathbf{C}_2 \\ \mathbf{C}_2^T & \mathbf{C}_3 - \mathbf{D}_3 + \mathbf{X}_3^T\mathbf{U}_3 + \mathbf{U}_3^T\mathbf{X}_3 \end{bmatrix} = \mathbf{C}.$$

which proves the correction by induction. The arithmetic cost satisfies a recurrence of the form $T(n) = 2T(n/2) + Cn^\omega$ and is therefore $T(n) = O(n^\omega)$. □

4 A BLOCK RECURSIVE ALGORITHM

4.1 Sketch of the recursive algorithm

The design of a block recursive PLDLTPT algorithm is based on the generalization of the 2×2 case into a block 2×2 block algorithm. While scalars could be either 0 or invertible, the difficulty in elimination algorithms, is that a submatrix could be rank deficient but non-zero. We start here an overview of the recursive algorithm by considering that the leading principal block is either all zero or invertible. We will later give the general presentation of the algorithm where its rank could be arbitrary.

Let $M \in \mathbb{F}^{(m+n)\times(m+n)}$ be the symmetric matrix to be factorized. Consider its block decomposition $M = \begin{bmatrix} A & B \\ B^T & C \end{bmatrix}$ where $A \in \mathbb{F}^{m\times m}$ and $C \in \mathbb{F}^{n\times n}$ are also symmetric.

If A is full rank, then a recursive call will produce $A = PLDL^TP^T$, and M can thus be decomposed as:

$$M = \begin{bmatrix} P & 0 \\ 0 & I \end{bmatrix} \begin{bmatrix} L & 0 \\ G & I \end{bmatrix} \begin{bmatrix} D & 0 \\ 0 & Z \end{bmatrix} \begin{bmatrix} L^T & G^T \\ 0 & I \end{bmatrix} \begin{bmatrix} P^T & 0 \\ 0 & I \end{bmatrix},$$

where G is such that $PLDG^T = B$ and $Z = C - GDG^T$. Thus G can be computed as the transpose of $D^{-1}L^{-1}P^{-1}B$ which can be obtained by a call to trsm, some permutations and a diagonal scaling. Then Z is computed by a call to syrdk. A second recursive call will then decompose Z and lead to the final factorization of M.

Now if A is the zero matrix, one is reduced to factorize the matrix $M = \left[\begin{smallmatrix} 0 & B \\ B^T & C \end{smallmatrix}\right]$. In order to recover the rank profile matrix, one has to first look for pivots in B before considering the block C. Therefore diagonal pivoting is not an option here. Then the matrix B, which we assume has full rank for the moment, can be decomposed in a *PLDUQ* factorization (P and Q are permutation matrices, L and U are respectively unit lower and unit upper triangular, D is diagonal). We then need to distinguish two cases depending on whether the field characteristic is two or not.

4.1.1 Zero or odd characteristic case. If the characteristic is zero or odd, M can thus be decomposed as:

$$M = \begin{bmatrix} P & 0 \\ 0 & Q^T \end{bmatrix} \begin{bmatrix} L & 0 \\ G & U^T \end{bmatrix} \begin{bmatrix} 0 & D \\ D & 0 \end{bmatrix} \begin{bmatrix} L^T & G^T \\ 0 & U \end{bmatrix} \begin{bmatrix} P^T & 0 \\ 0 & Q \end{bmatrix},$$

where G is such that $Q^T(GDU+U^TDG^T)Q = C$. To compute G, one can first permute C to get $C' = QCQ^T$ (which remains symmetric) and then use a call to trssyr2k.

4.1.2 Characteristic two case. In characteristic two, the equation $GDU+U^TDG^T = QCQ^T$ in unknown G has in general no solution (as soon as C has a non-zero diagonal element).

However, one can still relax Problem 1 and allow the elimination to leave a diagonal of elements not zeroed out. Following Lemma 2, the idea is then to decompose M into a block tridiagonal form:

$$M = \begin{bmatrix} P & 0 \\ 0 & Q^T \end{bmatrix} \begin{bmatrix} L & 0 \\ G & U^T \end{bmatrix} \begin{bmatrix} 0 & D \\ D & \Delta \end{bmatrix} \begin{bmatrix} L^T & G^T \\ 0 & U \end{bmatrix} \begin{bmatrix} P^T & 0 \\ 0 & Q \end{bmatrix},$$

where Δ is a diagonal matrix and now G is such that $Q^T(GDU + U^TDG^T + U^T\Delta U)Q = C$. Therefore Δ can be chosen such that the diagonal of $C'' = QCQ^T - U^T\Delta U = C' - U^T\Delta U$ is zero. As U is unit upper triangular, a simple pass over its coefficients is sufficient to find such a Δ: let $\Delta_{ii} = C'_{ii} - \sum_{j=1}^{i-1}\Delta_{jj}U^2_{j,i}$. The algorithm is thus to permute C to get C'; then compute Δ with the recursive relation above and update $C'' = C' - U^T\Delta U$ with a syrdk. C'' remains symmetric but with a zero diagonal and now trssyr2k can be applied.

4.2 The actual recursive algorithm

4.2.1 First phase: recursive elimination. In the general case, the leading matrices are not full rank, and we have to consider intermediate steps. For the symmetric matrix $M \in \mathbb{F}^{(m+n)\times(m+n)}$ of Section 4.1, its leading principal block $A \in \mathbb{F}^{m\times m}$ has rank $r \le m$. Thus its actual recursive decomposition is of the form:

$$A = P_1 \begin{bmatrix} L_1 \\ M_1 \end{bmatrix} D_1 \begin{bmatrix} L_1^T & M_1^T \end{bmatrix} P_1^T,$$

where $L_1 \in \mathbb{F}^{r\times r}$ is full rank unit lower triangular, $D_1 \in \mathbb{F}^{r\times r}$ is block diagonal with 1 or 2-dimensional diagonal blocks, and $M_1 \in \mathbb{F}^{(m-r)\times r}$. Therefore, forgetting briefly the permutations, the decomposition of M becomes:

$$M = \begin{bmatrix} L_1 & 0 & 0 \\ M_1 & I & 0 \\ G & 0 & I \end{bmatrix} \begin{bmatrix} D_1 & 0 & 0 \\ 0 & 0 & Y \\ 0 & Y^T & Z \end{bmatrix} \begin{bmatrix} L_1^T & M_1^T & G^T \\ 0 & I & 0 \\ 0 & 0 & I \end{bmatrix},$$

where Y is such that $B = \begin{bmatrix} L_1 \\ M_1 \end{bmatrix} D_1 G^T + \begin{bmatrix} 0 \\ Y \end{bmatrix}$.

From this point on, there remains to factorize the submatrix $\left[\begin{smallmatrix} 0 & Y \\ Y^T & Z \end{smallmatrix}\right]$. This will be carried out by the algorithm described in the next section, working on a matrix with a zero leading principal submatrix. Supposing for now that this is possible, Algorithm 2 summarizes the whole procedure.

Algorithm 2 Recursive symmetric indefinite elimination

Require: $A \in \mathbb{F}^{m\times m}$ and $C \in \mathbb{F}^{n\times n}$ both symmetric, $B \in \mathbb{F}^{m\times n}$.
Ensure: P permutation, L unit lower triangular, D block diagonal, s.t. $\left[\begin{smallmatrix} A & B \\ B^T & C \end{smallmatrix}\right] = PLDL^TP^T$.

- Decompose $A = P_1 \begin{bmatrix} L_1 \\ M_1 \end{bmatrix} \begin{bmatrix} D_1 \end{bmatrix} \begin{bmatrix} L_1^T & M_1^T \end{bmatrix} P_1^T$ {Alg. 2}
- let $r = \text{rank}(A)$ s.t. L_1 and D_1 are $r \times r$.
- $B' = P_1^T B$ {perm (P_1^T, B)}
- Split $B' = \begin{bmatrix} B'_1 \\ B'_2 \end{bmatrix}$ where B'_1 is $r \times n$.
- $X \leftarrow L_1^{-1}B'_1$ {trsm (L_1, B'_1)}
- $Y \leftarrow B'_2 - M_1X$ {gemm (B'_2, M_1, X)}
- $G \leftarrow X^TD_1^{-1}$ {scal (X^T, D_1^{-1})}
- $Z \leftarrow C - GD_1G^T$ {syrdk (C, G, D_1)}
- Decompose $\begin{bmatrix} 0 & Y \\ Y^T & Z \end{bmatrix} = P_2L_2D_2L_2^TP_2^T$ {Alg. 3}
- $P \leftarrow \left[\begin{smallmatrix} P_1 & 0 \\ 0 & I_n \end{smallmatrix}\right] \cdot \left[\begin{smallmatrix} I_r & 0 \\ 0 & P_2 \end{smallmatrix}\right]$
- $N_1 \leftarrow P_2^T \begin{bmatrix} M_1 \\ G \end{bmatrix}$ {perm $\left(P_2^T, \begin{bmatrix} M_1 \\ G \end{bmatrix}\right)$}
- $L \leftarrow \begin{bmatrix} L_1 & \\ N_1 & L_2 \end{bmatrix}$
- $D \leftarrow \begin{bmatrix} D_1 & \\ & D_2 \end{bmatrix}$

The correctness of Algorithm 2 is stated in the following Theorem 2 and proven in the remaining of the current Section.

THEOREM 2. *Algorithm 2 correctly computes a symmetric indefinite PLDLTPT factorization revealing the rank profile matrix.*

4.2.2 Second phase: off-diagonal pivoting. Consider $\mathbf{M} = \begin{bmatrix} 0 & \mathbf{B} \\ \mathbf{B}^T & \mathbf{C} \end{bmatrix}$, where $\mathbf{B} \in \mathbb{F}^{m\times n}$, with $m\leq n$, has now an arbitrary rank $r\leq m$. Then its PLDUQ decomposition is of the form

$$\mathbf{B} = \mathbf{P}\begin{bmatrix} \mathbf{L}_1 \\ \mathbf{M}_1 \end{bmatrix}\begin{bmatrix} \mathbf{D}_1 \end{bmatrix}\begin{bmatrix} \mathbf{U}_1 & \mathbf{V}_1 \end{bmatrix}\mathbf{Q},$$

with $\mathbf{D}_1$ diagonal, and $\mathbf{L}_1$ and $\mathbf{U}_1$ unit square triangular matrices, all three of order r. Then consider a conformal block decomposition of $\mathbf{Q}\mathbf{C}\mathbf{Q}^T = \begin{bmatrix} \mathbf{C}_1 & \mathbf{C}_2 \\ \mathbf{C}_2^T & \mathbf{C}_3 \end{bmatrix}$ where $\mathbf{C}_1$ is $r \times r$. It remains to eliminate $\mathbf{C}_1$ and $\mathbf{C}_2$ with the pivots found in B, which leads to the following factorization:

$$\mathbf{M} = \begin{bmatrix} \mathbf{P} & \\ & \mathbf{Q}^T \end{bmatrix}\begin{bmatrix} \mathbf{L}_1 & 0 & 0 \\ \mathbf{M}_1 & 0 & 0 \\ \mathbf{G}_1 & \mathbf{U}_1^T & 0 \\ \mathbf{G}_2 & \mathbf{V}_1^T & \mathbf{I} \end{bmatrix}\begin{bmatrix} 0 & \mathbf{D}_1 & 0 \\ \mathbf{D}_1 & 0 & 0 \\ 0 & 0 & \mathbf{Z} \end{bmatrix}\times \begin{bmatrix} \mathbf{L}_1^T & \mathbf{M}_1^T & \mathbf{G}_1^T & \mathbf{G}_2^T \\ 0 & 0 & \mathbf{U}_1 & \mathbf{V}_1 \\ 0 & 0 & 0 & \mathbf{I} \end{bmatrix}\begin{bmatrix} \mathbf{P}^T & \\ & \mathbf{Q} \end{bmatrix} \tag{1}$$

where $\mathbf{G}_1$ satisfies

$$\mathbf{U}_1^T\mathbf{D}_1\mathbf{G}_1^T + \mathbf{G}_1\mathbf{D}_1\mathbf{U}_1 = \mathbf{C}_1 \tag{2}$$

and $\mathbf{G}_2 = (\mathbf{C}_2^T - \mathbf{V}_1^T\mathbf{D}_1\mathbf{G}_1^T)\mathbf{U}_1^{-1}\mathbf{D}_1^{-1}$ and $\mathbf{Z} = \mathbf{C}_3 - (\mathbf{V}_1^T\mathbf{D}_1\mathbf{G}_2^T + \mathbf{G}_2\mathbf{D}_1\mathbf{V}_1)$.

In order to produce an LDLT decomposition, there still remains to perform permutations to

(1) compact the leading elements of the lower triangular matrix into a $2r \times 2r$ invertible leading triangular submatrix,
(2) make the $\begin{bmatrix} & \mathbf{D}_1 \\ \mathbf{D}_1 & \end{bmatrix}$ matrix block diagonal with 1 or 2-dimensional diagonal blocks.

The permutation matrix

$$\mathbf{P}_c = \begin{bmatrix} \mathbf{I}_r & 0 & 0 & 0 \\ 0 & 0 & \mathbf{I}_{m-r} & 0 \\ 0 & \mathbf{I}_r & 0 & 0 \\ 0 & 0 & 0 & \mathbf{I}_{n-r} \end{bmatrix}, \tag{3}$$

corresponding to a block circular rotation, takes care of condition 1, while preserving precedence in the non-pivot rows. This is a requirement for the factorization to reveal the rank profile matrix [11, Theorem 20]. The decomposition becomes

$$N = \begin{bmatrix} \mathbf{P} & \\ & \mathbf{Q}^T \end{bmatrix}\mathbf{P}_c\begin{bmatrix} \mathbf{L}_1 & 0 & 0 \\ \mathbf{G}_1 & \mathbf{U}_1^T & 0 \\ \mathbf{M}_1 & 0 & 0 \\ \mathbf{G}_2 & \mathbf{V}_1^T & \mathbf{I} \end{bmatrix}\begin{bmatrix} 0 & \mathbf{D}_1 & 0 \\ \mathbf{D}_1 & 0 & 0 \\ 0 & 0 & \mathbf{Z} \end{bmatrix}\times \begin{bmatrix} \mathbf{L}_1^T & \mathbf{G}_1^T & \mathbf{M}_1^T & \mathbf{G}_2^T \\ 0 & \mathbf{U}_1 & 0 & \mathbf{V}_1 \\ 0 & 0 & 0 & \mathbf{I} \end{bmatrix}\mathbf{P}_c^T\begin{bmatrix} \mathbf{P}^T & \\ & \mathbf{Q} \end{bmatrix}. \tag{4}$$

In order to achieve Condition 2, we will transform the matrix $\begin{bmatrix} 0 & \mathbf{D}_1 \\ \mathbf{D}_1 & 0 \end{bmatrix}$ into the block diagonal matrix $\mathrm{Diag}\left(\begin{bmatrix} 0 & d_i \\ d_i & 0 \end{bmatrix}\right)$ where d_i is the ith diagonal element in $\mathbf{D}_1$. To describe the process, we will focus on the matrix

$$\mathbf{M}_2 = \begin{bmatrix} \mathbf{L}_1 & 0 \\ \mathbf{G}_1 & \mathbf{U}_1^T \end{bmatrix}\begin{bmatrix} 0 & \mathbf{D}_1 \\ \mathbf{D}_1 & 0 \end{bmatrix}\begin{bmatrix} \mathbf{L}_1^T & \mathbf{G}_1^T \\ 0 & \mathbf{U}_1 \end{bmatrix} = \overline{\mathbf{L}}\cdot\overline{\Delta}\cdot\overline{\mathbf{L}}^T,$$

and consider a splitting in halves of the matrix $\mathbf{D}_1 = \begin{bmatrix} \mathbf{D}_{11} & \\ & \mathbf{D}_{12} \end{bmatrix}$ where $\mathbf{D}_{11}$ has order r_1 and $\mathbf{D}_{12}$ order r_2. This leads to the conformal decomposition

$$\begin{bmatrix} \mathbf{L}_{11} & 0 & 0 & 0 \\ \mathbf{L}_{12} & \mathbf{L}_{13} & 0 & 0 \\ \mathbf{G}_{11} & \mathbf{G}_{14} & \mathbf{U}_{11}^T & 0 \\ \mathbf{G}_{12} & \mathbf{G}_{13} & \mathbf{U}_{12}^T & \mathbf{U}_{13}^T \end{bmatrix}\begin{bmatrix} 0 & 0 & \mathbf{D}_{11} & 0 \\ 0 & 0 & 0 & \mathbf{D}_{12} \\ \mathbf{D}_{11} & 0 & 0 & 0 \\ 0 & \mathbf{D}_{12} & 0 & 0 \end{bmatrix}\begin{bmatrix} \mathbf{L}_{11}^T & \mathbf{L}_{12}^T & \mathbf{G}_{11}^T & \mathbf{G}_{12}^T \\ 0 & \mathbf{L}_{13}^T & \mathbf{G}_{14}^T & \mathbf{G}_{13}^T \\ 0 & 0 & \mathbf{U}_{11} & \mathbf{U}_{12} \\ 0 & 0 & 0 & \mathbf{U}_{13} \end{bmatrix}$$

Then considering the permutation matrix

$$\mathbf{P}_d = \begin{bmatrix} \mathbf{I}_{r_1} & 0 & 0 & 0 \\ 0 & 0 & \mathbf{I}_{r_2} & 0 \\ 0 & \mathbf{I}_{r_1} & 0 & 0 \\ 0 & 0 & 0 & \mathbf{I}_{r_2} \end{bmatrix},$$

one can form $\mathbf{P}_d^T\overline{\Delta}\mathbf{P}_d = \begin{bmatrix} 0 & \mathbf{D}_{11} & 0 & 0 \\ \mathbf{D}_{11} & 0 & 0 & 0 \\ 0 & 0 & 0 & \mathbf{D}_{12} \\ 0 & 0 & \mathbf{D}_{12} & 0 \end{bmatrix}$ and $\mathbf{P}_d^T\overline{L}\mathbf{P}_d = \begin{bmatrix} \mathbf{L}_{11} & 0 & 0 & 0 \\ \mathbf{G}_{11} & \mathbf{U}_{11}^T & \mathbf{G}_{14} & 0 \\ \mathbf{L}_{12} & 0 & \mathbf{L}_{13} & 0 \\ \mathbf{G}_{12} & \mathbf{U}_{12}^T & \mathbf{G}_{13} & \mathbf{U}_{13}^T \end{bmatrix}$.

Applying this process recursively changes $\overline{\Delta}$ into the desired block diagonal form. Then the transformation of $\overline{\mathbf{L}}$ will remain lower triangular if and only if all $\mathbf{G}_{14}$ matrices are zero: this means that $\mathbf{G}_1$ must be lower triangular in the first place.

Finding $\mathbf{G}_1$ lower triangular satisfying Equation (2), is an instance of Problem 1 for which the routine `trssyr2k` provides a solution.

Note that the actual permutation to transform $\begin{bmatrix} 0 & \mathbf{D}_1 \\ \mathbf{D}_1 & 0 \end{bmatrix}$ into a 2×2-blocks diagonal matrix is a permutation matrix, $\mathbf{P}_i$, resulting from the one by one interleaving of the rows of $[\,\mathbf{I}_r\ 0\,]$ and $[\,0\ \mathbf{I}_r\,]$. If $\mathbf{e}_i = [\,0\ldots0\ 1\ 0\ldots0\,]^T$ is the i-th canonical vector, then:

$$\mathbf{P}_i = \begin{bmatrix} \mathbf{e}_1 & \mathbf{e}_{r+1} & \mathbf{e}_2 & \mathbf{e}_{r+2} & \ldots & \mathbf{e}_r & \mathbf{e}_{2r} \end{bmatrix}. \tag{5}$$

Similarly the triangular factor of the factorization is thus a one by one interleaving of the rows of $[\,\mathbf{L}_1\ 0\,]$ and $[\,\mathbf{G}_1\ \mathbf{U}_1^T\,]$ as well as a one by one interleaving of the columns $\begin{bmatrix} \mathbf{L}_1 \\ \mathbf{G}_1 \end{bmatrix}$ and $\begin{bmatrix} 0 \\ \mathbf{U}_1^T \end{bmatrix}$, which overall remains triangular.

Finally, a call to Algorithm 2 produces a factorization for the remaining Z block and a final block rotation,

$$\begin{bmatrix} \mathbf{I}_{2r} & 0 & 0 \\ 0 & 0 & \mathbf{I}_{m-r} \\ 0 & \mathbf{I}_{n-r} & 0 \end{bmatrix},$$

moves the intermediate zero rows and columns to the bottom right. The full algorithm is presented in details in Algorithm 3 (for zero or odd characteristic, the characteristic two case being presented afterwards in Section 4.3).

4.3 Characteristic two

The case of the characteristic two can be handled similarly, just computing the extra diagonal and updating after the PLDUQ decomposition, as sketched in Section 4.1.2. Indeed, the only issue is the division by 2 in `trssyr2k`, which is removed if the diagonal of $\mathbf{C}_1'$ is zero. Therefore, Algorithm 2 is unchanged, the block diagonal matrix just has lower symmetric antitriangular 2×2 blocks instead of only antidiagonal ones. The only few additional operations appear in Algorithm 3 (lines 4-9, 12, 16 and 21).

Then the tridiagonal form with symmetric antitriangular 2×2 blocks thus obtained by Algorithm 3 can be used to either reveal the rank profile matrix (via computing $\Psi_{\mathbf{D}}$, the support matrix of $\mathbf{D}$, and the pivoting matrix $\mathcal{R} = \mathbf{P}\Psi_{\mathbf{D}}\mathbf{P}^T$) or a PLDLTPT factorization, both at an extra linear cost in the dimension, as shown in Section 2.3.

Algorithm 3 Rank deficient and zero leading principal symmetric elimination

Require: $C \in \mathbb{F}^{n \times n}$ symmetric and $B \in \mathbb{F}^{m \times n}$.

Ensure: P permutation, L unit lower triangular, D block-diagonal, s.t. $\begin{bmatrix} 0 & B \\ B^T & C \end{bmatrix} = PLDL^T P^T$.

Decompose $B = P_B \begin{bmatrix} L_1 \\ M_1 \end{bmatrix} \begin{bmatrix} D_1 \end{bmatrix} \begin{bmatrix} U_1 & V_1 \end{bmatrix} Q$ {PLDUQ}

let $r = \text{rank}(B)$ s.t. L_1, D_1 and U_1 are $r \times r$.

$C' \leftarrow QCQ^T = \begin{bmatrix} C'_1 & C'_2 \\ C'^T_2 & C'_3 \end{bmatrix}$ where C'_1 is $r \times r$ {perm}

if characteristic($\mathbb{F}$) = 2 **then**

  for $i = 1$ **to** r **do**

    $\Delta_{ii} = (C'_1)_{ii} - \sum_{j=1}^{i-1} \Delta_{jj} (U_1)^2_{j,i}$

  end for

  $C'_1 \leftarrow C'_1 - U_1^T \Delta U_1$ {syrdk (C'_1, U_1, Δ)}

end if

Find X s.t. $X^T U_1 + U_1^T X = C'_1$ {trssyr2k (U_1, C'_1)}

$G_1 \leftarrow X^T D_1^{-1}$ {scal (X^T, D_1^{-1})}

if characteristic($\mathbb{F}$) = 2 **then** $X \leftarrow X + \Delta U_1$ **end if** {dadd (X, Δ, U_1)}

$C''_2 \leftarrow C'_2 - X^T V_1$ {trmm (X^T, V_1)}

$Y \leftarrow U_1^{-T} C''_2$ {trsm (U_1^T, C''_2)}

$Z \leftarrow C'_3 - (Y^T V_1 + V_1^T Y)$ {syrd2k (C'_3, Y, V_1)}

if characteristic($\mathbb{F}$) = 2 **then** $Z \leftarrow Z - (V_1^T \Delta V_1)$ **end if** {syrdk (Z, V_1, Δ)}

$G_2 \leftarrow Y^T D_1^{-1}$ {scal (Y^T, D_1^{-1})}

Decompose $Z = P_3 L_3 D_3 L_3^T P_3^T$ {Alg. 2}

$P \leftarrow \begin{bmatrix} P_B & 0 \\ 0 & Q^T \end{bmatrix} \begin{bmatrix} P_c & 0 \\ 0 & I_{n-r} \end{bmatrix} \begin{bmatrix} P_i & 0 \\ 0 & I_{m+n-2r} \end{bmatrix} \begin{bmatrix} I_{m+r} & 0 \\ 0 & P_3 \end{bmatrix} \begin{bmatrix} I_{2r} & 0 & 0 \\ 0 & 0 & I_{m-r} \\ 0 & I_{n-r} & 0 \end{bmatrix}$ {With P_c from (3), and P_i from (5)}

$L \leftarrow \left[\begin{array}{c|c} P_i^T \begin{bmatrix} L_1 & \\ G_1 & U_1^T \end{bmatrix} P_i & \\ \hline \begin{bmatrix} G_2 & V_1^T \\ M_1 & 0 \end{bmatrix} P_i & \begin{matrix} L_3 \\ 0 \end{matrix} \end{array}\right]$

if characteristic($\mathbb{F}$) = 2 **then** $D \leftarrow \left[\begin{array}{c|c} P_i^T \begin{bmatrix} 0 & D_1 \\ D_1 & \Delta \end{bmatrix} P_i & \\ \hline & D_3 \end{array}\right]$ **else** $D \leftarrow \left[\begin{array}{c|c} P_i^T \begin{bmatrix} 0 & D_1 \\ D_1 & 0 \end{bmatrix} P_i & \\ \hline & D_3 \end{array}\right]$ **end if**

5 BASE CASE ITERATIVE VARIANT

The recursion of Algorithm 2 should not be performed all the way to a dimension 1 in practice. For implementations over a finite field, it would induce an unnecessary large number of modular reductions and a significant amount of data movement for the permutations. Instead, we propose in Algorithm 4 an iterative algorithm computing a PLDLTPT revealing the rank profile matrix to be used as a base case in the recursion.

This iterative algorithm has the following features:

(1) it uses a pivot search minimizing the lexicographic order (following the characterization in [11]): if the diagonal element of the current row is 0, the pivot is chosen as the first non-zero element of the row, unless the row is all zero, in which case, it is searched in the following row;
(2) the pivot is permuted with cyclic shifts on the row and columns, so as to leave the precedence in the remaining rows and columns unchanged.
(3) the update of the unprocessed part in the matrix is delayed following the scheme of a Crout elimination schedule [8]. It does not only improve efficiency thanks to a better data locality, but it also reduces the amount of modular reductions, over a finite field, as shown for the unsymmetric case in [9].

We denote by $\rho_{i,n}$ the cyclic shift permutation of order n moving element i to the first position: $\rho_{i,n} = (i, 0, 1, \ldots, i-1, i+1, \ldots n-1)$. Indices are 0 based, index ranges are excluding their upper bound. For instance, $A_{i,0..r}$ denotes the r first elements of the $i+1$st row of A, and $A_{0..r,0..r}$ is the 0-dimensional matrix when $r = 0$.

6 EXPERIMENTS

We now report on experiments of an implementation of these algorithms in the FFLAS-FFPACK library [17], dedicated to dense linear algebra over finite fields. We used the version committed under the reference e12a998 of the master branch. It was compiled with gcc-5.4 and was linked with the numerical library OpenBLAS-0.2.18. Experiments are run on a single core of an Intel Haswell i5-4690, @3.5GHz. Computation speed is normalized as *effective Gfops*, an estimate of the number of field operations that an algorithm with classic matrix arithmetic would perform per second, divided by the computation time. For a matrix of order n and rank r, we defined this as:

$$\text{Effective Gfops} = (r^3/3 + n^2 r - r^2 n)/(10^9 \times \text{time}).$$

Algorithm 4 SYTRF Crout iterative base case

Require: $A \in \mathbb{F}^{n \times n}$ symmetric
Ensure: P, a permutation, L, unit lower triangular and D, block diagonal, such that $A = PLDL^TP^T$

Denote $W = A$ {the working matrix}
$r \leftarrow 0$; $D \leftarrow 0$
for $i = 0..n$ **do**
  Here $W = \begin{bmatrix} L & & & \\ M & 0 & 0 & \\ N & 0 & A_{i..n,i} & A_{i..n,i+1..n} \end{bmatrix}$ with $L \in \mathbb{F}^{r \times r}$
  $v \leftarrow N_{0,0..r} \times D^{-1}_{0..r,0..r}$
  $c \leftarrow A_{i..n,i} - N \times v^T$
  if $c = 0$ **then** Loop to next iteration **end if**
  Let j be the smallest index such that $x = c_j \neq 0$
  Denote $c = \begin{bmatrix} 0 & x & k \end{bmatrix}^T$
  if $j = 0$ **then**
    $\begin{bmatrix} M \\ N \end{bmatrix} \leftarrow \rho_{j,n-r} \times \begin{bmatrix} M \\ N \end{bmatrix}$
    $W_{r..n,r} \leftarrow x^{-1} \times \rho_{j,n-r} \times \begin{bmatrix} 0 \\ c \end{bmatrix}$
    $P \leftarrow P \times \rho^T_{j,n-r}$; $D_{r,r} \leftarrow x$; $r \leftarrow r + 1$
  else
    $w \leftarrow N_{j,0..r} \times D^{-1}_{0..r,0..r}$
    $d \leftarrow A_{i..n,j+i} - N \times w^T (= \begin{bmatrix} 0 & x & g & y & h \end{bmatrix}^T)$
    Here $W = \begin{bmatrix} L & & & & & \\ M & 0 & 0 & 0 & 0 & 0 \\ & 0 & 0 & 0 & x & k^T \\ N & 0 & 0 & F & g & J^T \\ & 0 & x & g^T & y & h^T \\ & 0 & k & J & h & * \end{bmatrix}$
    if characteristic($\mathbb{F}$) = 2 **then**
      $y' \leftarrow 0$; $h' \leftarrow h - yx^{-1}k$
      $D_{r..r+2,r..r+2} \leftarrow \begin{bmatrix} 0 & x \\ x & y \end{bmatrix}$
    else
      $y' \leftarrow y/2$; $h' \leftarrow h - y'x^{-1}k$
      $D_{r..r+2,r..r+2} \leftarrow \begin{bmatrix} 0 & x \\ x & 0 \end{bmatrix}$
    end if
    Perform cyclic symmetric row and column rotations to bring W to the form $W = \left[\begin{array}{c|ccc|ccc} L & & & & & & \\ n' & 1 & & & & & \\ & x^{-1}y' & 1 & & & & \\ \hline M & 0 & 0 & & 0 & 0 & 0 \\ N' & x^{-1}g & 0 & & 0 & F & J^T \\ & x^{-1}h' & x^{-1}k & & 0 & J & * \end{array}\right]$
    Update P accordingly
    $r \leftarrow r + 2$
  end if
end for

All experiments are over the 23-bit finite field $\mathbb{Z}/8388593\mathbb{Z}$ (timings with other primes of similar size are similar).

Figures 1 and 2 compare the computation speed of the pure recursive algorithm, the base case algorithm and a cascade of these two, with a threshold set to its optimum value from experiments on this machine. Remark that the pure recursive variant performs rather well with generic rank profile matrices, while matrices with uniformly random rank profile matrix make this variant very slow, due to an excessive amount of pivoting. As expected, the base case Crout variant speeds up these instances for small dimensions, but then its performance stagnates on large dimensions, due to poor cache efficiency. Lastly the cascade algorithm combines the benefits of the two variants and therefore performs best in all settings. We here used a threshold $n = 128$ for the experiments with random RPM matrices, but of only $n = 48$ for generic rank profile matrices, since the recursive variant becomes competitive much earlier. In most cases, the rank profile structure of given matrices is unknown a priori, making the setting of this threshold speculative. One could instead implement an introspective strategy, updating the threshold from experimenting with running instances.

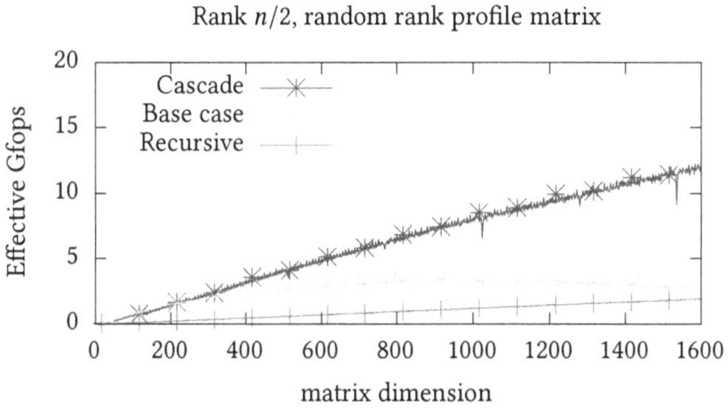

Figure 1: RPM revealing PLDLTPT: base case, pure recursive and cascading variants. Matrices with rank half the dimension and random RPM.

Table 1 compares the computation time of the finite field symmetric decomposition algorithm with several other routines: the unsymmetric elimination over a finite field (running the PLUQ algorithm of [11]) and the numerical elimination routines in double precision of LAPACK [2] provided by OpenBLAS: `dgetrf` (LU decomposition), and 3 variants of `dsytrf` [18] (symmetric LDLT decomposition with pivoting). These experiments first confirm a speed-up factor of about 2 between the symmetric and unsymmetric case over a finite field, which is the expected gain, looking at the constant in the time complexity. Note that on large instances, the PLUQ elimination performs better with random RPM instances than generic rank profiles, contrarily to the LDLT routine. This is due to the lesser amount of arithmetic operations when the RPM is random (some intermediate sub-matrices being rank deficient). On the other hand, these matrices generate more off-diagonal pivots, which cause more pivoting in LDLT than in PLUQ, explaining the slowdown for the symmetric case. On small dimensions, the numercial routines perform best as the quadratic modular reductions is penalizing the routines over a finite field. However, this is compensated by use of Strassen's algorithm, making our implementation outperform LAPACK's best `dsytrf` for larger dimension, even when the rank profile is not generic.

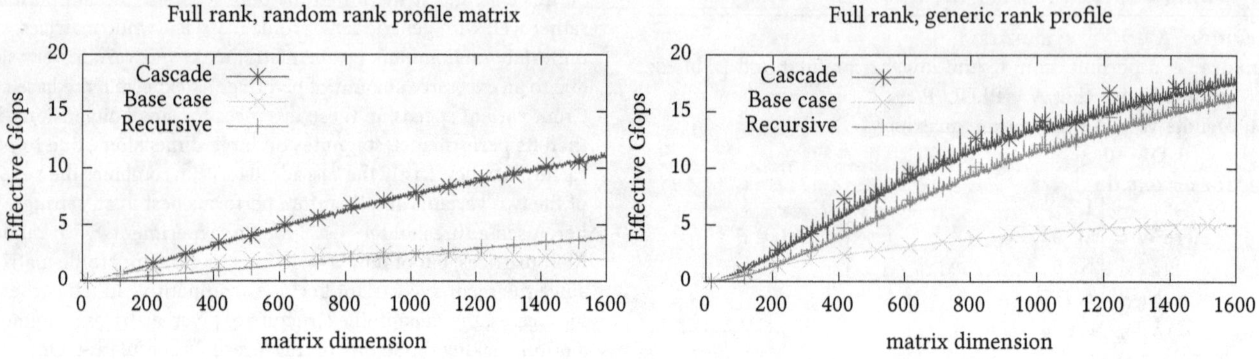

Figure 2: RPM revealing PLDLTPT. Matrices with full rank and random RPM (left) or generic rank profile (right).

n	Gen. rank prof. $r = n$				Gen. rank prof. $r = n$		Random RPM $r = n$		Random RPM $r = n/2$	
	dgetrf	dsytrf	dsytrf_rk	dsytrf_aa	PLUQ	LDLT	PLUQ	LDLT	PLUQ	LDLT
100	1.17e-04	1.31e-04	1.37e-04	9.21e-05	4.64e-04	3.23e-04	5.59e-04	5.22e-04	3.20e-04	3.80e-04
200	3.73e-04	4.39e-04	5.51e-04	4.48e-04	1.87e-03	8.80e-04	2.58e-03	1.59e-03	1.58e-03	1.33e-03
500	3.31e-03	3.78e-03	4.88e-03	3.87e-03	1.73e-02	5.21e-03	2.83e-02	9.85e-03	1.88e-02	7.92e-03
1000	2.19e-02	2.09e-02	2.58e-02	2.05e-02	8.84e-02	2.30e-02	9.95e-02	4.01e-02	6.27e-02	3.18e-02
2000	0.145	0.127	0.154	0.127	0.438	0.127	0.490	0.191	0.274	0.150
5000	2.005	1.604	1.871	1.598	3.904	1.591	3.849	1.744	2.431	1.294
10000	14.948	11.981	13.396	12.008	24.115	10.904	23.985	11.209	14.775	7.894

Table 1: Comparing computation time (s) of numerical routines with the symmetric (LDLT) and unsymmetric (PLUQ) triangular decompositions. Matrices with rank r, generic rank profile or rank profile matrix uniformly random.

ACKNOWLEDGMENT

We thank the referees for their valuable feedback and pointing out the recent work of [18].

REFERENCES

[1] J. O. Aasen. On the reduction of a symmetric matrix to tridiagonal form. *BIT Numerical Mathematics*, 11(3):233–242, Sep 1971. doi:10.1007/BF01931804.

[2] E. Anderson, Z. Bai, C. Bischof, L. S. Blackford, J. Demmel, J. Dongarra, J. Du Croz, A. Greenbaum, S. Hammarling, A. McKenney, et al. *LAPACK Users' guide*. SIAM, 1999. URL: http://www.netlib.org/lapack/lug/lapack_lug.html.

[3] M. Baboulin, D. Becker, and J. Dongarra. A Parallel Tiled Solver for Dense Symmetric Indefinite Systems on Multicore Architectures. In *IEEE 26th International Parallel & Distributed Processing Symposium (IPDPS)*, pages 14–24. IEEE, May 2012. doi:10.1109/IPDPS.2012.12.

[4] G. Ballard, D. Becker, J. Demmel, J. Dongarra, A. Druinsky, I. Peled, O. Schwartz, S. Toledo, and I. Yamazaki. Communication-Avoiding Symmetric-Indefinite Factorization. *SIAM Journal on Matrix Analysis and Applications*, 35(4):1364–1406, Jan. 2014. doi:10.1137/130929060.

[5] J. R. Bunch and L. Kaufman. Some stable methods for calculating inertia and solving symmetric linear systems. *Mathematics of Computation*, 31(137):163–179, 1977. doi:10.2307/2005787.

[6] J. R. Bunch and B. N. Parlett. Direct methods for solving symmetric indefinite systems of linear equations. *SIAM Journal on Numerical Analysis*, 8(4):639–655, Dec. 1971. doi:10.1137/0708060.

[7] J. J. Dongarra, J. Du Croz, S. Hammarling, and I. S. Duff. A Set of Level 3 Basic Linear Algebra Subprograms. *ACM TOMS*, 16(1):1–17, Mar. 1990. doi:10.1145/77626.79170.

[8] J. J. Dongarra, L. S. Duff, D. C. Sorensen, and H. A. V. Vorst. *Numerical Linear Algebra for High Performance Computers*. SIAM, 1998.

[9] J.-G. Dumas, T. Gautier, C. Pernet, J.-L. Roch, and Z. Sultan. Recursion based parallelization of exact dense linear algebra routines for gaussian elimination. *Parallel Computing*, 57:235 – 249, 2016. doi:10.1016/j.parco.2015.10.003.

[10] J.-G. Dumas, C. Pernet, and Z. Sultan. Computing the rank profile matrix. In *Proceedings of the 2015 ACM on International Symposium on Symbolic and Algebraic Computation*, ISSAC '15, pages 149–156, New York, NY, USA, 2015. ACM. doi:10.1145/2755996.2756682.

[11] J.-G. Dumas, C. Pernet, and Z. Sultan. Fast computation of the rank profile matrix and the generalized Bruhat decomposition. *Journal of Symbolic Computation*, 83:187–210, Nov.–Dec. 2017. doi:10.1016/j.jsc.2016.11.011.

[12] E. Elmroth, F. G. Gustavson, I. Jonsson, and B. Kågström. Recursive blocked algorithms and hybrid data structures for dense matrix library software. *SIAM Review*, 46(1):3–45, 2004. doi:10.1137/S0036144503428693.

[13] E. L. Kaltofen, M. Nehring, and B. D. Saunders. Quadratic-time certificates in linear algebra. In A. Leykin, editor, *ISSAC'2011, Proceedings of the 2011 ACM International Symposium on Symbolic and Algebraic Computation, San Jose, California, USA*, pages 171–176. ACM Press, New York, June 2011. doi:10.1145/1993886.1993915.

[14] B. Parlett and J. K. Reid. On the solution of a system of linear equations whose matrix is symmetric but not definite. *BIT*, 10(3):386–397, 1970. doi:10.1007/BF01934207.

[15] M. Rozložník, G. Shklarski, and S. Toledo. Partitioned triangular tridiagonalization. *ACM Trans. Math. Softw.*, 37(4):38:1–38:16, Feb. 2011. doi:10.1145/1916461.1916462.

[16] G. Shklarski and S. Toledo. Blocked and recursive algorithms for triangular tridiagonalization. 2007. URL: http://www.cs.tau.ac.il/~stoledo/Bib/Pubs/ShklarskiToledo-Aasen.pdf.

[17] The FFLAS-FFPACK group. *FFLAS-FFPACK: Finite Field Linear Algebra Subroutines / Package*, 2018. v2.3.2. https://github.com/linbox-team/fflas-ffpack.

[18] I. Yamazaki and J. Dongarra. Aasen's symmetric indefinite linear solvers in LAPACK. Technical Report 294, LAPACK Working Note, Dec. 2017. URL: http://www.netlib.org/lapack/lawnspdf/lawn294.pdf.

Computing Nearby Non-trivial Smith Forms

Mark Giesbrecht
Cheriton School of Computer Science
University of Waterloo
mwg@uwaterloo.ca

Joseph Haraldson
Cheriton School of Computer Science
University of Waterloo
jharalds@uwaterloo.ca

George Labahn
Cheriton School of Computer Science
University of Waterloo
glabahn@uwaterloo.ca

ABSTRACT

We consider the problem of computing the nearest matrix polynomial with a non-trivial Smith Normal Form. We show that computing the Smith form of a matrix polynomial is amenable to numeric computation as an optimization problem. Furthermore, we describe an effective optimization technique to find a nearby matrix polynomial with a non-trivial Smith form. The results are later generalized to include the computation of a matrix polynomial having a maximum specified number of ones in the Smith Form (i.e., with a maximum specified McCoy rank).

We discuss the geometry and existence of solutions and how our results can used for a backwards error analysis. We develop an optimization-based approach and demonstrate an iterative numerical method for computing a nearby matrix polynomial with the desired spectral properties. We also describe the implementation of our algorithms and demonstrate the robustness with examples in `Maple`.

ACM Reference Format:

Mark Giesbrecht, Joseph Haraldson, and George Labahn. 2018. Computing Nearby Non-trivial Smith Forms. In *ISSAC '18: 2018 ACM International Symposium on Symbolic and Algebraic Computation, July 16–19, 2018, New York, NY, USA.* ACM, New York, NY, USA, 8 pages. https://doi.org/10.1145/3208976.3209024

1 INTRODUCTION

Matrix polynomials appear in many areas of computational algebra, control systems theory, differential equations and mechanics. The algebra of matrix polynomials is typically described assuming that the coefficients are from the field of real or complex numbers. However, in some applications, coefficients can come from measured data or contain some amount of uncertainty. As such, arithmetic may contain numerical errors and algorithms are prone to numerical instability.

One problem of computational importance is finding the Smith Normal Form (SNF, or simply Smith form) of a matrix polynomial. Given $\mathcal{A} \in \mathbb{R}[t]^{n\times n}$, the Smith form $\mathcal{S}$ of $\mathcal{A}$ is a matrix polynomial

$$\mathcal{S} = \begin{pmatrix} s_1 & & & \\ & s_2 & & \\ & & \ddots & \\ & & & s_n \end{pmatrix} \in \mathbb{R}[t]^{n\times n},$$

where $s_1, \ldots, s_n$ are monic and $s_i \mid s_{i+1}$ for $1 \le i < n$, such that there exist unimodular $\mathcal{U}, \mathcal{V} \in \mathbb{R}[t]^{n\times n}$ (i.e., with determinants in $\mathbb{R}^*$) with $\mathcal{S} = \mathcal{U}\mathcal{A}\mathcal{V}$. The Smith form always exists and is unique though the matrices $\mathcal{U}$, $\mathcal{V}$ are not unique [14, 18]. The diagonal entries $s_1, \ldots, s_n$ are referred to as the *invariant factors* of $\mathcal{A}$.

The Smith form is important as it reveals the structure of the polynomial lattice of rows and columns, as well as the effects of localizing at individual eigenvalues. That is, it characterizes how the rank decreases as the variable t is set to various eigenvalues. The form is closely related to the more general *Smith-McMillan form* for matrices of rational functions, a form that reveals the structure of eigenvalues at infinity.

In an exact setting, computing the Smith form has been well studied and very efficient procedures are available (see [19] and the references therein). However, in the case that coefficients contain uncertainties, the problem is much less understood. Numerical methods to compute the Smith form of a matrix polynomial typically rely on linearization and orthogonal transformations [3, 6, 24] to infer the Smith form of a nearby matrix polynomial via the Jordan blocks in the Kronecker canonical form (see [18]). These linearization techniques are backwards stable, and for many problems this is sufficient to ensure that the computed solutions are computationally useful when a problem is continuous. However, the eigenvalues of a matrix polynomial are not necessarily continuous functions of the coefficients of the matrix polynomial, and backwards stability is not always sufficient to ensure computed solutions are useful in the presence of discontinuities. These methods are also unstructured in the sense that the computed non-trivial Smith form may not be the Smith form of a matrix polynomial with a prescribed coefficient structure. In extreme instances, the unstructured backwards error can be arbitrarily small, while the structured distance to an interesting Smith form is relatively large. This is often seen in problems with prescribed sparsity patterns or zero-coefficients. Numerical methods can also fail to compute meaningful results on some problems due to uncertainties. Examples of such problems include nearly rank deficient matrix polynomials, repeated eigenvalues or eigenvalues that are close together and other ill-posed instances. The above issues are largely resolved by our optimization-based approach, though at a somewhat higher computational cost.

ISSAC '18, July 16–19, 2018, New York, NY, USA

ACM ISBN 978-1-4503-5550-6/18/07...$15.00
https://doi.org/10.1145/3208976.3209024

The invariant factors $s_1, \ldots, s_n$ of a matrix $A \in \mathbb{R}[t]^{n\times n}$ can also be defined via the *determinantal divisors* $\delta_1, \ldots, \delta_n \in \mathbb{R}[t]$, where

$$\delta_i = \mathrm{GCD}\{\text{all } i \times i \text{ minors of } \mathcal{A}\} \in \mathbb{R}[t].$$

Then $s_1 = \delta_1$ and $s_i = \delta_i/\delta_{i-1}$ for $2 \le i \le n$ (and $\delta_n = \det(\mathcal{A})$). In the case of 2×2 matrix polynomials, computing the nearest non-trivial Smith form is thus equivalent to finding the nearest matrix polynomial whose polynomial entries have a non-trivial GCD. This points to a significant difficulty: approximate GCD problems can have infima that are *unattainable*. That is, there are co-prime polynomials with nearby polynomials with a non-trivial GCD at distances arbitrarily approaching an infimum, while at the infimum itself the GCD is trivial (see, e.g., [11]). This issue extends to Smith forms as is seen in the following example.

Example 1.1. Let $f = t^2 - 2t + 1$ and $g = t^2 + 2t + 2$. We first seek $\widetilde{f}, \widetilde{g} \in \mathbb{R}[t]$ of degree at most 2 such that $\gcd(\widetilde{f}, \widetilde{g}) = \gamma t + 1$ at minimal distance $\|f - \widetilde{f}\|_2^2 + \|g - \widetilde{g}\|_2^2$ for some $\gamma \in \mathbb{R}$. Using the approach of Karmarkar & Lakshman [20] it is shown [16, Example 3.3.6] that this distance is $(5\gamma^4 - 4\gamma^3 + 14\gamma^2 + 2)/(\gamma^4 + \gamma^2 + 1)$. This distance has an infimum of 2 at $\gamma = 0$. However, at $\gamma = 0$ we have $\gcd(\widetilde{f}, \widetilde{g}) = 1$ even though $\deg \gcd(\widetilde{f}, \widetilde{g}) > 0$ for all $\gamma \ne 0$.

Now consider the matrix $\mathcal{A} = \mathrm{diag}(f, g) \in \mathbb{R}[t]^{2\times 2}$. For $\mathcal{A}$ to have a non-trivial Smith form we must perturb f, g such that they have a non-trivial GCD, and thus any such perturbation must be at a distance of at least 2. However, the perturbation of distance precisely 2 has a trivial Smith form. There is clearly no merit to perturbing the off-diagonal entries of $\mathcal{A}$.

Our work indirectly involves measuring the sensitivity to the eigenvalues of $\mathcal{A}$ and the determinant of $\mathcal{A}$. Thus we differ from most sensitivity and perturbation analysis [1, 23] since we also study how perturbations affect the invariant factors, instead of the roots of the determinant. Additionally our theory is able to support the instance of $\mathcal{A}$ being rank deficient and having degree exceeding one. One may also approach the problem geometrically in the context of manifolds [7, 8]. We do not consider the manifold approach directly since it does not yield numerical algorithms.

We address two fundamental questions in this paper: (1) what does it mean for a matrix polynomial $\mathcal{A}$ to have a non-trivial Smith form numerically and (2) how far is $\mathcal{A}$ from another matrix polynomial with an interesting or non-trivial Smith form?

We formulate the answers to these questions as solutions to continuous optimization problems. The main contributions of this paper are deciding when $\mathcal{A}$ has an interesting Smith form, providing bounds on a "radius of triviality" around $\mathcal{A}$ and a structured stability analysis on iterative methods to compute a structured matrix polynomial with desired spectral properties.

The remainder of the paper is organized as follows. In Section 2 we give the notation and terminology along with some needed background used in our work. Section 3 discusses the approximate Smith form computation as an optimization problem and provide some new bounds on the distance to non-triviality. We present an optimization algorithm in Section 4 with local stability properties and rapid local convergence to compute a nearby matrix polynomial with a non-trivial Smith form and discuss implementation details. A method to compute a matrix polynomial with a prescribed lower bound on the number of ones is discussed in Section 5. The paper ends with a discussion of our implementation and examples.

2 PRELIMINARIES

In this section we explore the topology of the approximate Smith normal form and discuss basic results concerning the notion of both *attainable* and *unattainable* solutions.

We make extensive use of the following terminology and definitions. A matrix polynomial $\mathcal{A} \in \mathbb{R}[t]^{n\times n}$ is an $n \times n$ matrix whose entries consist of polynomials of degree at most d. Alternatively, we may express matrix polynomials as $\mathcal{A} = \sum_{1\le j\le d} A_j t^j$ where $A_j \in \mathbb{R}^{n\times n}$. The *degree* of a matrix polynomial d is defined to be the degree of the highest-order non-zero entry of $\mathcal{A}$, or the largest index j such that $A_j \ne 0$. We say that $\mathcal{A}$ has *full rank* or is *regular* if $\det(\mathcal{A}) \not\equiv 0$ and that $\mathcal{A}$ is *unimodular* if $\det(\mathcal{A}) \in \mathbb{R}\backslash\{0\}$. The *(finite) eigenvalues* are the roots of $\det(A) \in \mathbb{R}[t]$.

We define the norm of a polynomial $a \in \mathbb{R}[t]$ as $\|a\| = \|a\|_2 = \|(a_0, a_1, \ldots, a_d, 0, \ldots, 0)\|_2$ and for matrix polynomials we define $\|\mathcal{A}\| = \|\mathcal{A}\|_F = \sqrt{\sum_{i,j} \|\mathcal{A}_{i,j}\|_2^2}$. Our choice of norm is a distributed coefficient norm, sometimes known as the Frobenius norm.

Definition 2.1 (SVD [15]). The Singular Value Decomposition (SVD) of $A \in \mathbb{R}^{n\times n}$ is given by $U^T \Sigma V$, where $U, V \in \mathbb{R}^{n\times n}$ satisfy $U^T U = I$, $V^T V = I$ and $\Sigma = \mathrm{diag}(\sigma_1, \ldots, \sigma_n)$ is a diagonal matrix with non-negative entries of the singular values of A in descending order. The distance to the nearest (unstructured) matrix of rank $m < n$ is $\sigma_{m+1}(A)$.

For scalar matrices we frequently write $\|\cdot\|_2$ for the largest singular value, and $\sigma_{\min}(\cdot)$ for the smallest singular value.

Definition 2.2 (Affine/Linear Structure). A matrix polynomial $\mathcal{A} \in \mathbb{R}[t]^{n\times n}\backslash\{0\}$ of degree at most d has a *linear structure* from the set $\mathcal{K}$ if $\mathcal{A} \in \mathrm{span}(\mathcal{K})$ as a vector space over $\mathbb{R}$, where

$$\mathcal{K} = \{C_{0,0}, \ldots, C_{0,k}, tC_{1,0}, \ldots, tC_{1,l}, \ldots, t^d C_{d,0}, \ldots, t^d C_{d,k}\},$$

with $C_{l,j} \in \mathbb{R}^{n\times n}$ and the vectors in $\mathcal{K}$ are linearly independent. If $\mathcal{A} = \mathcal{C}_0 + \mathcal{C}_1$ where $\mathcal{C}_0 \in \mathbb{R}[t]^{n\times n}\backslash\{0\}$ and $\mathcal{C}_1 \in \mathrm{span}(\mathcal{K})$, then the structure is said to be *affine*.

Examples of matrix polynomials with a linear structure include symmetric matrices, matrices with prescribed zero coefficients, prescribed zero entries, tri-diagonal matrices and several other classes. Affinely structured matrix polynomials include monic matrix polynomials, matrix polynomials with prescribed constant coefficients and banded matrix polynomials are a few of many possible. In this paper we are mainly concerned with preserving the zero structure of a matrix polynomial, that is we do not change zero-coefficients or increase the degree of entries.

The *rank* of a matrix polynomial is the maximum number of linearly independent rows or columns as a vector space over $\mathbb{R}(t)$. This is the rank of the matrix $\mathcal{A}(\omega)$ for any $\omega \in \mathbb{C}$ except when ω is an eigenvalue of $\mathcal{A}(t)$. The McCoy rank of $\mathcal{A}$ is $\min_{\omega\in\mathbb{C}}\{\mathrm{rank}\, \mathcal{A}(\omega)\}$, which is the lowest rank when $\mathcal{A}$ is evaluated at an eigenvalues. The McCoy rank is also the number of ones in the Smith form, or equivalently, if $\mathcal{A}$ has m non-trivial invariant factors, then the McCoy rank of $\mathcal{A}$ is $n - m$. The matrix polynomial $\mathcal{A}$ is said to have a *non-trivial Smith form* if the McCoy rank is at most $n - 2$, or equivalently, has two or more invariant factors of positive degree.

Problem 2.3 (Approximate SNF and Low McCoy Rank). *Given a matrix polynomial $\mathcal{A} \in \mathbb{R}[t]^{n\times n}$, find the distance to a non-trivial SNF and, if possible, a matrix polynomial $\widehat{\mathcal{A}} \in \mathbb{R}[t]^{n\times n}$ of prescribed coefficient structure that has a prescribed McCoy rank of $n-m$ for $m \geq 2$ such that $\|\mathcal{A} - \widehat{\mathcal{A}}\|$ is minimized under $\|\cdot\|$. If such $\widehat{\mathcal{A}}$ exists, then the Smith form of $\widehat{\mathcal{A}}$ is the approximate Smith form of A if $m = 2$ and a lower McCoy rank approximation if $m > 2$.*

As described in Section 1, it is possible that the distance to a non-trivial SNF is not attainable. That is, there is a solution that is approached asymptotically, but where the Smith form is trivial at the infimum. Fortunately, in most instances of interest, solutions will generally be attainable, and we will later discuss how to identify and compute unattainable solutions. This problem admits the nearest rank deficient matrix polynomial as a special case (see [12, 13]). However the computational challenges are fundamentally different for non-trivial instances.

2.1 Basic Results

In this subsection we review some basic results needed to analyze the topology of the approximate Smith form problem. We introduce the notion of a generalized Sylvester matrix, drawing on the theory of resultants.

Definition 2.4. The *adjoint* of a matrix polynomial is the $n \times n$ matrix $\mathrm{Adj}(\mathcal{A})$ that satisfies $\mathrm{Adj}(\mathcal{A})\mathcal{A} = \mathcal{A}\,\mathrm{Adj}(\mathcal{A}) = \det(\mathcal{A})I$. The entries of $\mathrm{Adj}(\mathcal{A})$ are the $(n-1)\times(n-1)$ minors of $\mathcal{A}$ up to a multiple of ± 1.

As $s_n = \delta_n/\delta_{n-1}$ it follows that $\mathcal{A}$ has a non-trivial Smith form if and only if the GCD of all entries of the adjoint is non-trivial, that is, $\deg\gcd(\mathrm{Adj}(\mathcal{A})) \geq 1$. In order to obtain bounds on the distance to a matrix having a non-trivial Smith form, we consider an approximate GCD problem of the form

$$\min\left\{\|\Delta\mathcal{A}\| \text{ such that } \deg\gcd\left\{\mathrm{Adj}\left(\mathcal{A}+\Delta\mathcal{A}\right)_{ij}\right\} \geq 1\right\}.$$

If this was a classical approximate GCD problem, then the use of Sylvester-like matrices would be sufficient. However, in our problem the degrees of the entries of the adjoint may change under perturbations. In order to perform an analysis, we need to study a family of generalized Sylvester matrices that allow higher-degree zero coefficients to be perturbed.

For $a = \sum_{i=0}^{d} a_i t^i \in \mathbb{R}[t]$ of degree at-most d, we define the rth *convolution matrix* of a as

$$\phi_r(a) = \begin{pmatrix} a_0 & \cdots & a_d & & \\ & \ddots & & \ddots & \\ & & a_0 & \cdots & a_d \end{pmatrix} \in \mathbb{R}^{r\times(r+d)}.$$

Let $\mathbf{f} = (f_1,\ldots,f_k) \in \mathbb{R}[t]$ be a vector of polynomials with degrees $\mathbf{d} = (d_1,\ldots,d_k)$ ordered as $d_j \leq d_{j+1}$ for $1 \leq j \neq k-1$ (with $\deg 0 = -\infty$). Set $d = d_1$ and $r = \max(d_2,\ldots,d_k)$ and suppose that for each $2 \leq i \leq k$ f_i is viewed as a polynomial of degree at most r. Then we define the *generalized Sylvester matrix* of f as

$$\mathrm{Syl}(\mathbf{f}) = \mathrm{Syl}_{\mathbf{d}}(\mathbf{f}) = \begin{pmatrix} \phi_r(f_1) \\ \phi_d(f_2) \\ \vdots \\ \phi_d(f_k) \end{pmatrix} \in \mathbb{R}^{(r+(k-1)d)\times(r+d)}.$$

Some authors [10, 25] refer to such a matrix as an expanded Sylvester matrix or generalized resultant matrix. The generalized Sylvester matrix has many useful properties pertaining to the Bézout coefficients. However we are only concerned with the well known result that $\gcd(\mathbf{f}) = 1$ if and only if $\mathrm{Syl}_{\mathbf{d}}(\mathbf{f})$ has full rank.

It will be useful to treat a polynomial of degree d as one of larger degree. This can be accomplished by constructing a similar matrix and padding rows and columns with zero entries. The generalized Sylvester matrix of degree at most $\mathbf{d}' \geq \mathbf{d}$ of $\mathbf{f}$ is defined analogously as $\mathrm{Syl}_{\mathbf{d}'}(\mathbf{f})$, taking d to be the largest degree entry and r to be the largest degree of the remaining entries of $\mathbf{d}'$. Note that $r = d$ is possible and typical. If $\mathbf{f}$ has a non-trivial GCD (possibly unattainable) under a perturbation structure $\Delta\mathbf{f}$, then it is necessary that $\mathrm{Syl}_{\mathbf{d}'}(\mathbf{f})$ is rank deficient, and often this will be sufficient.

If we view the entries of $\mathbf{f}$ of polynomials of degree $\mathbf{d}'$ and $\mathbf{d}_i' > \mathbf{d}_i$ for all i, then the entries of $\mathbf{f}$ has an unattainable GCD of distance zero, typically of the form $1 + \varepsilon t \sim t + \varepsilon^{-1}$. In other words, the underlying approximate GCD problem is ill-posed.

Lemma 2.5. *If* $\max(\mathbf{d}) = \max(\mathbf{d}')$ *then the kernels of* $\mathrm{Syl}_{\mathbf{d}}(\mathbf{f})$ *and* $\mathrm{Syl}_{\mathbf{d}'}(\mathbf{f})$ *have the same dimension.*

Proof. Let d and r be the largest and second largest entries of $\mathbf{d}$ and r' be the second largest entry of $\mathbf{d}'$. The result follows from [25] by considering the case of $r' = d$. □

This lemma characterizes the (generic) case when elements of maximal degree of $\mathbf{f}$ do not change under perturbations, then the generalized Sylvester matrix still meaningfully encodes GCD information. However, it is possible that $\mathrm{Syl}_{\mathbf{d}}(\mathbf{f})$ has full rank and $\mathrm{Syl}_{\mathbf{d}'}(\mathbf{f})$ is rank deficient but the distance to a non-trivial gcd is not zero. This can occur when $\mathbf{d}_j = \mathbf{d}_j'$ for some j and $\mathbf{d}' \geq \mathbf{d}$.

Definition 2.6. The *degree d reversal* of an $f \in \mathbb{R}[t]$ of degree at most d is defined as $\mathrm{rev}_d(f) = t^d f(t^{-1})$. For a vector of polynomials $\mathbf{f} \in \mathbb{R}[t]^{\ell}$ of degrees at most $\mathbf{d} = (d_1,\ldots,d_\ell)$ the *degree* $\mathbf{d}$ *reversal* of $\mathbf{f}$ is the vector $\mathrm{rev}_{\mathbf{d}}(\mathbf{f}) = (\mathrm{rev}_{d_1}(f_1),\ldots,\mathrm{rev}_{d_\ell}(f_\ell))$.

The following lemma enables us to determine if unattainable solutions are occurring in an approximate GCD problem with an arbitrary (possibly non-linear) structure on the coefficients.

Lemma 2.7. *Let* $\mathbf{f}$ *be a vector of non-zero polynomials of degree at most d. Suppose that* $\mathrm{Syl}_{\mathbf{d}}(\mathbf{f})$ *has full rank and* $\mathrm{Syl}_{\mathbf{d}'}(\mathbf{f})$ *is rank deficient, where the perturbations* $\Delta\mathbf{f}$ *have degrees at most* $\mathbf{d}'$ *and the entries of* $\mathbf{f}$ *have degrees* $\mathbf{d}$. *Then* $\mathbf{f}$ *has an unattainable non-trivial GCD of distance zero under the perturbation structure* $\Delta\mathbf{f}$ *if and only if* $\mathrm{Syl}(\mathrm{rev}_{\mathbf{d}'}(\mathbf{f}))$ *is rank deficient.*

Proof. First suppose that $\mathrm{Syl}(\mathrm{rev}_{\mathbf{d}'}(\mathbf{f}))$ has full rank. Then $\gcd(\mathrm{rev}_{\mathbf{d}'}(\mathbf{f})) = 1$, but $\mathrm{rev}_{\mathbf{d}}(\gcd(\mathbf{f})) = \gcd(\mathrm{rev}_{\mathbf{d}}(\mathbf{f})) = \gcd(\mathrm{rev}_{\mathbf{d}'}(\mathbf{f}))$. Hence $\mathbf{f}$ does not have an unattainable non-trivial GCD. Conversely, suppose that $\mathrm{Syl}(\mathrm{rev}_{\mathbf{d}'}(\mathbf{f}))$ is rank deficient. Then, t is a factor of $\gcd(\mathrm{rev}_{\mathbf{d}'}(\mathbf{f}))$ but t is not a factor of $\gcd(\mathrm{rev}_{\mathbf{d}}(\mathbf{f}))$. Accordingly, all non-zero entries of $\mathbf{f}+\Delta\mathbf{f}$ may increase in degree and so the distance of $\mathbf{f}$ having a non-trivial GCD is zero, and so is unattainable. □

If the generalized Sylvester matrix of $\mathbf{f}$ has full rank, but the generalized Sylvester matrix that encodes the perturbations $\mathbf{f}+\Delta\mathbf{f}$ is rank deficient, then either there is an unattainable solution, or the generalized Sylvester matrix is rank deficient due to over-padding with zeros. Lemma 2.7 provides a reliable way to detect this over padding.

Definition 2.8. We say that $\mathcal{A}$ has an *unattainable non-trivial Smith form* if $\gcd(\mathrm{Adj}(\mathcal{A})) = 1$ and $\gcd(\mathrm{Adj}(\mathcal{A} + \Delta\mathcal{A})) \neq 1$ for an infinitesimal perturbation $\Delta\mathcal{A}$ of prescribed affine structure.

Example 2.9. Let $\mathcal{A} = \begin{pmatrix} t & t-1 \\ t+1 & t \end{pmatrix}$. Then the 4×4 matrix polynomial $\mathcal{C} = \begin{pmatrix} \mathcal{A} & \\ & \mathcal{A} \end{pmatrix}$ has an unattainable non-trivial Smith form if all perturbations to $\mathcal{A}$ are support or degree preserving (preserve zero entries or do not increase the degree of each entry), both linear structures. Note that $\mathcal{C}$ and $\mathcal{A}$ are both unimodular. However small perturbations to the non-zero coefficients of $\mathcal{A}$ make $\mathcal{A} + \Delta\mathcal{A}$ non-unimodular.

These examples are non-generic. Generically the degree of the adjoint will be $(n-1)d$ and will remain unchanged locally under perturbations to the coefficients. We can formulate computing the distance to the nearest matrix polynomial with a non-trivial Smith form under a prescribed perturbation structure as finding the nearest rank deficient generalized Sylvester matrix of the adjoint or the $\mathbf{d}'$ reversal of the adjoint.

3 WHEN DOES A NUMERICAL MATRIX POLYNOMIAL HAVE A TRIVIAL SNF?

In this section we consider the question of determining if a matrix polynomial has a non-trivial SNF, or rather how much do the coefficients need to be perturbed to have a non-trivial SNF. We provide a lower bound on the quantity by analyzing the distance to a reduced rank generalized Sylvester matrix.

3.1 Nearest Rank Deficient Structured Generalized Sylvester Matrix

Suppose that $\mathcal{A} \in \mathbb{R}[t]^{n\times n}$ of degree at most d has a trivial Smith form and does not have an unattainable non-trivial Smith form. Then one method to compute a lower bound on the distance the entries of $\mathcal{A}$ need to be perturbed to have an attainable or unattainable non-trivial Smith form is to solve

$$\inf \|\Delta\mathcal{A}\| \text{ such that } \begin{cases} \mathrm{rank}(\mathrm{Syl}_{\mathbf{d}'}(\mathrm{Adj}(\mathcal{A} + \Delta\mathcal{A}))) < e, \\ e = \mathrm{rank}(\mathrm{Syl}_{\mathbf{d}'}(\mathrm{Adj}(\mathcal{A}))). \end{cases} \tag{3.1}$$

Here $\mathbf{d}'$ is the vector of the largest possible degrees each entry of $\mathrm{Adj}(\mathcal{A} + \Delta\mathcal{A})$ and $\Delta\mathcal{A}$ has in a prescribed linear or affine perturbation structure.

It is sufficient to compute $\max(\mathbf{d}')$, and this quantity will generically be $(n-1)d$. For non-generic instances we require the computation of $\mathbf{d}'$. This optimization problem is non-convex, but multi-linear in each coefficient of $\Delta\mathcal{A}$.

We do not attempt to solve this problem directly via numerical techniques, since it enforces a necessary condition that is often sufficient. Instead we use it to develop a theory of solutions which can be exploited by faster and more robust numerical methods.

Lemma 3.1. *Let* $\mathbf{f}$ *be a vector of polynomials with degrees* $\mathbf{d}$ *and admissible perturbations* $\Delta\mathbf{f}$ *of degrees* $\mathbf{d}'$ *where* $\max(\mathbf{d}) \le \max(\mathbf{d}')$. *Then the family of generalized Sylvester matrices* $\mathrm{Syl}_{\mathbf{d}'}(\mathbf{f})$ *of rank at least* e *form an open set under the perturbations* $\Delta\mathbf{f}$.

Proof. By the degree assumption on $\Delta\mathbf{f}$ we have that for an infinitesimal $\Delta\mathbf{f}$ that $\mathrm{Syl}_{\mathbf{d}'}(\mathbf{f})$ and $\mathrm{Syl}_{\mathbf{d}'}(\Delta\mathbf{f})$ have the same dimension. Accordingly, let us suppose that $\mathrm{Syl}_{\mathbf{d}'}(\mathbf{f})$ has rank at least e. Then it must have rank at least e in an open-neighborhood around it. In particular, when $\|\mathrm{Syl}_{\mathbf{d}'}(\Delta\mathbf{f})\|_2 < \sigma_e(\mathrm{Syl}_{\mathbf{d}'}(\mathbf{f}))$ then $\mathrm{rank}\,\mathrm{Syl}_{\mathbf{d}'}(\mathbf{f} + \Delta\mathbf{f}) \ge \mathrm{rank}\,\mathrm{Syl}_{\mathbf{d}'}(\mathbf{f})$ and the result follows. □

Theorem 3.2. *The optimization problem* (3.1) *has an attainable global minimum under linear perturbation structures.*

Proof. Let $\mathcal{S}$ be the set of all rank at most $e-1$ generalized Sylvester matrices of prescribed shape by $\mathbf{d}'$ and $\mathrm{Adj}(\mathcal{A})$. Lemma 3.1 implies that $\mathcal{S}$ is topologically closed.

Let $\mathcal{R} = \{\mathrm{Syl}_{\mathbf{d}'}(\mathrm{Adj}(C))$ such that $\|C\| \le \|\mathcal{A}\|\}$, where the generalized Sylvester matrices are padded with zeros to have the appropriate dimension if required. Since $\Delta\mathcal{A}$ has a linear perturbation structure, a feasible point is always $C = -\mathcal{A}$. By inspection $\mathcal{R}$ is seen to be a non-empty set that is bounded and closed.

The functional $\|\cdot\|$ is continuous over the non-empty closed and bounded set $\mathcal{S} \cap \mathcal{R}$. Let $\mathcal{B} \in \mathcal{S} \cap \mathcal{R}$. By Weierstrass's theorem $\|\mathcal{A} - B\|$ has an attainable global minimum over $\mathcal{S} \cap \mathcal{R}$. □

Note that if a feasible point exists under an affine perturbation structure, then a solution to the optimization problem exists as well. What this result says is that computing the distance to non-triviality is generally a well-posed problem, even though computing a matrix polynomial of minimum distance may be ill-posed. The same results also hold when working over the $\mathbf{d}'$ reversed coefficients.

3.2 Bounds on the Distance to non-triviality

Suppose that $\mathcal{A} \in \mathbb{R}[t]^{n\times n}$, of degree at most d, has a trivial Smith form and does not have an unattainable non-trivial Smith form. This section provides some basic bounds on the distance coefficients of $\mathcal{A}$ need to be perturbed to have a non-trivial Smith form.

If we consider the mapping $\mathrm{Adj}(\cdot)$ as a vector-valued function from $\mathbb{R}^{n^2(d+1)} \to \mathbb{R}^{n^2((n-1)d+1)}$ (with some coordinates possibly fixed to zero), then we note that the mapping is locally Lipschitz. More precisely, there exists $c > 0$ such that

$$\|\mathrm{Adj}(\mathcal{A}) - \mathrm{Adj}(\mathcal{A} + \Delta\mathcal{A})\| \le c\|\Delta\mathcal{A}\|.$$

The quantity c can be bounded above by the (scalar) Jacobian matrix $\nabla\,\mathrm{Adj}(\cdot)$ evaluated at $\mathcal{A}$. A local upper bound for c is approximately $\|\nabla\,\mathrm{Adj}(\mathcal{A})\|_2$.

The entries of $\nabla\,\mathrm{Adj}(\mathcal{A})$ consist of the coefficients of the $(n-2)\times(n-2)$ minors of $\mathcal{A}$. This follows because $\mathrm{Adj}(\cdot)$ is a multi-linear vector mapping and the derivative of each entry is a coefficient of the leading coefficient with respect to the variable of differentiation. The size of each minor can be bounded above by Hadamard's inequality. As such, we have the sequence of bounds

$$\|\nabla\,\mathrm{Adj}(\mathcal{A})\|_2 \le n\sqrt{d+1}\|\nabla\,\mathrm{Adj}(\mathcal{A})\|_\infty \le n^3(d+1)^{3/2}\|\mathcal{A}\|_\infty^n n^{n/2},$$

where $\|\mathcal{A}\|_\infty$ is understood to be a vector norm and $\|\nabla\,\mathrm{Adj}(\mathcal{A})\|_\infty$ is understood to be a matrix norm. The bound in question can be used in conjunction with the SVD to obtain a lower bound on the distance to a matrix polynomial with a non-trivial Smith form.

THEOREM 3.3. *Suppose that* $\mathbf{d}' = (\gamma, \gamma \ldots, \gamma)$ *and* $\mathrm{Syl}_{\mathbf{d}'}(\mathrm{Adj}(\mathcal{A}))$ *has rank e. Then a lower bound on the distance to non-triviality is*

$$\frac{1}{\gamma \|\nabla \mathrm{Adj}(\mathcal{A})\|_F} \sigma_e(\mathrm{Syl}_{\mathbf{d}'}(\mathrm{Adj}(\mathcal{A}))).$$

PROOF. We note that for polynomials $\mathbf{f}$ with degrees $\mathbf{d}'$ that $\|\mathrm{Syl}_{\mathbf{d}'}(\mathbf{f})\| = \gamma\|\mathbf{f}\|$. Accordingly, if $\Delta\mathcal{A}$ is a minimal perturbation to non-triviality, then

$$\begin{aligned}\frac{1}{\gamma}\sigma_e(\mathrm{Syl}_{\mathbf{d}'}(\mathrm{Adj}(\mathcal{A}))) &\leq \| \mathrm{Adj}(\mathcal{A}) - \mathrm{Adj}(\mathcal{A} + \Delta\mathcal{A})\|_F \\ &\leq \|\nabla \mathrm{Adj}(\mathcal{A})\|_F \|\Delta\mathcal{A}\|_F,\end{aligned}$$

and the theorem follows by a simple rearrangement. □

If $\mathbf{d}'$ has different entries, then $r\|\mathbf{f}\| \leq \|\mathrm{Syl}_{\mathbf{d}'}(\mathbf{f})\| \leq \gamma\|\mathbf{f}\|$, where γ and r are the largest and second-largest entries of $\mathbf{d}'$. The lower bound provided can also be improved using the Karmakar-Lakshman distance [20] in lieu of the smallest singular value of the generalized Sylvester matrix, the $\mathbf{d}'$ reversal of the adjoint or other approximate GCD lower bounds [2].

4 APPROXIMATE SNF VIA OPTIMIZATION

In this section we formulate the approximate Smith form problem as the solution to a continuous constrained optimization problem. We assume that the solutions in question are attainable and develop a method with rapid local convergence. As the problem is non-convex, our convergence analysis will be local.

4.1 Constrained Optimization Formulation

An equivalent statement to $\mathcal{A}$ having a non-trivial attainable Smith form is that $\mathrm{Adj}(\mathcal{A}) = f^*h$ where f^* is a vector (matrix) of scalar polynomials and h is a divisor of $\gcd(\mathrm{Adj}(\mathcal{A}))$. This directly leads to the following optimization problem.

$$\min \|\Delta\mathcal{A}\|_F^2 \text{ where } \begin{cases}\mathrm{Adj}(\mathcal{A} + \Delta\mathcal{A}) = f^*h & f^* \in \mathbb{R}[t]^{n\times n}, h \in \mathbb{R}[t] \\ \mathcal{N}_h \mathrm{vec}(h) = 1 & \mathcal{N}_h \in \mathbb{R}^{1\times(\deg h+1)}.\end{cases} \tag{4.1}$$

This is a multi-linearly structured approximate GCD problem, which is a non-convex optimization problem. Instead of finding a rank deficient Sylvester matrix, we directly enforce that the entries of $\mathrm{Adj}(\mathcal{A})$ have a non-trivial GCD. The normalization requirement that $\mathcal{N}_h\mathrm{vec}(h) = 1$ is chosen to force h to have a non-zero degree, so that h is not a scalar. One useful normalization is to define $\mathcal{N}_h$ such that $\mathrm{lcoeff}(h) = 1$, that is, assume the degree of the approximate GCD is known and make it monic. Of course, other valid normalizations also exist.

Since we are working over $\mathbb{R}[t]$, there will always be a quadratic, linear or zero factor of attainable solutions. If we ignore the zero solution for now, then we can assume generically that $\deg h = 1$ or $\deg h = 2$. We note that if $h = 0$ then the approximate SNF of $\mathcal{A}$ is rank deficient and computing approximate SNF reduces to the nearest rank at-most $n - 1$ or $n - 2$ matrix polynomial problems, both of which are well-understood [12, 13]. Accordingly, for the remainder of the paper we will suppose that $h \neq 0$ is monic and that the degree is prescribed. The case of $h = 0$ is mentioned here for completeness but is not considered further.

4.2 Lagrange Multipliers and Optimality Conditions

In order to solve our problem we will employ the method of Lagrange multipliers. The Lagrangian is defined as

$$L = \|\Delta\mathcal{A}\|_F^2 + \lambda^T \begin{pmatrix}\mathrm{vec}(\mathrm{Adj}(\mathcal{A} + \Delta\mathcal{A}) - f^*h) \\ \mathcal{N}_h\mathrm{vec}(h) - 1\end{pmatrix},$$

where $\mathrm{vec}(\cdot)$ stacks a matrix polynomial by columns into a column vector, and λ is a vector of Lagrange multipliers.

A necessary first-order condition (KKT condition, see [4]) for a tuple $z^* = z^*(\Delta\mathcal{A}, f^*, h, \lambda)$ to be a regular (attainable) minimizer is that the gradient of L vanishes, that is,

$$\nabla L(z^*) = 0. \tag{4.2}$$

Let J be the Jacobian matrix of the constraints defined as

$$J = \nabla_{\Delta\mathcal{A}, f^*, h}\left(\mathrm{vec}(\mathrm{Adj}(\mathcal{A} + \Delta\mathcal{A}) - f^*h)\right).$$

The second-order sufficiency condition for optimality at a local minimizer z^* is that

$$\ker(J(z^*))^T \nabla_{xx}^2 L(z^*) \ker(J(z^*)) \succ 0, \tag{4.3}$$

or that the Hessian with respect to $x = x(\Delta\mathcal{A}, f^*, h)$ is positive definite over the kernel of the Jacobian of the constraints. The vector x corresponds to the variables in the affine structure of $\Delta\mathcal{A}$, f^*, and h. If (4.2) and (4.3) both hold, then z^* is necessarily a local minimizer of (4.1). Of course, it is also necessary that $\ker(J(z^*))^T \nabla_{xx}^2 L(z^*) \ker(J(z^*)) \succeq 0$ at a minimizer, which is the second-order necessary condition. Our strategy for computing a local solution is to solve $\nabla L = 0$ by a Newton-like method.

4.3 An Implementation with Local Quadratic Convergence

A problem with Newton type methods is that when the Hessian is rank deficient or ill-conditioned, the Newton step becomes ill-defined or the rate of convergence degrades. The proposed formulation of our problem can encounter a rank deficient Hessian. Despite this we are still able to obtain a method with rapid local convergence under a very weak normalization assumption.

In order to obtain rapid convergence we make use of the Levenberg-Marquart (LM) algorithm. If $H = \nabla^2 L$, then the LM iteration is defined as repeatedly solving for $z^{(k+1)} = z^{(k)} + \Delta z^{(k)}$ by

$$(H^TH + \mu_k I)\Delta z^{(k)} = -H^T\nabla L(z^{(k)}) \text{ where } z = \begin{pmatrix}x \\ \lambda\end{pmatrix} \in \mathbb{R}^\ell,$$

for some $\ell > 0$ and using $\|\nabla L\|_2$ as a merit function. The speed of convergence depends on the choice of $\mu_k > 0$.

Fukushima and Yamashita [26] show that, under a local-error bound condition, a system of non-linear equations $g(z) = 0$ approximated by LM will converge quadratically to a solution with a suitable initial guess.

Essentially, what this says is that to obtain rapid convergence it is sufficient for regularity (J having full rank) to hold or second-order sufficiency, but it is not necessary to satisfy both. The advantage of LM over other quasi-Newton methods is that this method is globalized* in exchange for an extra matrix multiplication, as H^TH+

*Here "globalized" means that the method will converge to a stationary point of the merit function, not a local extrema of the problem.

$\mu_k I$ is always positive definite, and hence always a descent direction for the merit function. We make the choice of $\mu_k \approx \|g(z)\|_2$ based on the results of Fan and Yuan [9].

Definition 4.1 (Local Error Bound). Let Z^* be the set of all solutions to $g(z) = 0$ and X be a subset of $\mathbb{R}^\ell$ such that $X \cap Z^* \neq \emptyset$. We say that $\|g(z)\|$ provides a local error bound on $g(z) = 0$ if there exists a positive constant c such that $c \cdot \operatorname{dist}(z, Z^*) \leq \|g(z)\|$ for all $z \in X$, where $\operatorname{dist}(\cdot)$ is the distance between a point and a set.

THEOREM 4.2. *If the second-order sufficiency condition* (4.3) *holds at an attainable solution to* (4.1), *then the local error-bound property holds.*

Note that this result applies to all equality constrained optimization problems, and not just our specific problem.

PROOF. Let $z = z(x, \lambda)$ and define $g(z) = \nabla L(z)$. First suppose that both the second-order sufficiency condition (4.3) and first-order necessary condition (4.2) hold at the point z^*. We can write the first-order expansion

$$g(z^* + \Delta z) = H(z^*)(\Delta z) + O(\|\Delta z\|_2^2) \approx H(z^*)(\Delta z),$$

noting that $g(z^*) = 0$. Next, we note that $g(x + \Delta x, \lambda + \Delta\lambda) = g(x + \Delta x, \lambda) + g(x, \lambda + \Delta\lambda)$, since g is linear in λ. It is useful to observe that

$$H(z^*) = \begin{pmatrix} H_{xx}(z^*) & J^T(z^*) \\ J(z^*) & \end{pmatrix}.$$

If $\Delta x = 0$ then the error-bound from Hoffman [17] applies and we have that there exists $c_{hof} > 0$ such that $c_{hof}\|\Delta\lambda\| \leq \|g(x, \lambda + \Delta\lambda)\|$. If $\Delta x \neq 0$ then $\left\|\begin{pmatrix} H_{xx}(z^*) \\ J(z^*) \end{pmatrix} \Delta x\right\| \approx \|g(x + \Delta x, \lambda)\|$ and (4.3) implies that $H(z^*)(\Delta z) = 0 \implies \Delta x = 0$, so

$$\sigma_{\min}\begin{pmatrix} H_{xx}(z^*) \\ J(z^*) \end{pmatrix} \|\Delta x\| \leq \|g(x + \Delta x, \lambda)\|.$$

Thus,

$$\min\left\{\sigma_{\min}\left(H_{xx}(z^*) \quad J^T(z^*)\right), c_{hof}\right\} \|\Delta z\| \leq \|g(z^* + \Delta z)\|. \quad \square$$

THEOREM 4.3. *The second-order sufficiency condition holds at minimal solutions with Lagrange multipliers of minimal norm if h is of maximal degree, monic and the minimal structured perturbation $\|\Delta\mathcal{A}^*\|$ is sufficiently small.*

PROOF. The Hessian of L with respect to $x = x(\Delta A, f^*, h)$ is

$$\nabla^2_{xx} L = H_{xx} = \begin{pmatrix} F + 2I & & \\ & & E \\ & E^T & \end{pmatrix},$$

where F is a square matrix with zero diagonal whose entries are a multi-linear polynomial in λ and $\Delta\mathcal{A}$ and E^T is a symmetric matrix whose entries are homogeneous linear functions in λ.

If $\Delta\mathcal{A}^* = 0$ then $\lambda^* = 0$ and hence both $E = 0$ and $F = 0$. Accordingly, if $y \in \ker(H_{xx}) \cap \ker(J)$ then $y = \begin{pmatrix} 0 & y_2 & y_3 \end{pmatrix}^T$. Note that

$$J = \begin{pmatrix} * & \mathcal{C}_{f^*} & \mathcal{C}_h \\ & \mathcal{N}_h & \end{pmatrix},$$

where $*$ are blocks corresponding to differentiating with respect to variables in $\Delta\mathcal{A}$ and the blocks $\mathcal{C}_{f^*}$ and $\mathcal{C}_h$ are block convolution and convolution matrices that respectively correspond to multiplication by f^* and h. The block $\mathcal{N}_h$ contains a normalization vector.

$Jy = 0$ implies that there exists a vector of polynomials v and a polynomial u with the same degrees as f^* and h such that $f^*u + vh = 0$ and $\mathcal{N}_h \operatorname{vec}(u) = 0$.

We have that h is a factor of both f^*u and vh. Since $\gcd(f^*, h) = 1$ it must be that h is a factor of u. It follows that $\deg u = \deg h$, so there exists some $\alpha \neq 0$ such that $\alpha u = h$. Since h is monic, we have that $\mathcal{N}_h \operatorname{vec}(h) = 1$ but $\mathcal{N}_h u = 0$, which implies that $\alpha = 0$, and so $u = 0$. We have that $vh = 0$ and so $v = 0$. Hence $\ker(J) \cap \ker(H_{xx}) = 0$ and second-order sufficiency holds when $\|\Delta\mathcal{A}^*\| = 0$.

If $\|\Delta\mathcal{A}^*\|$ is sufficiently small, then $\|F\|$ will be sufficiently small so that $F + 2I$ has full rank. Accordingly, we have that

$$\ker\begin{pmatrix} F + 2I & & \\ & 0 & E \\ & E^T & 0 \end{pmatrix} \subseteq \ker\begin{pmatrix} 2I & & \\ & 0 & \\ & & 0 \end{pmatrix}. \quad \square$$

We remark that the techniques in the proof are very similar to those of [27] and [11] to show that a Jacobian matrix appearing in approximate GCD computations of two polynomials has full rank.

The implication of the local-error bound property holding is that one can reasonably approximate when quadratic convergence occurs by estimating $\sigma_{\min}\left(\left(H_{xx} \quad J^T\right)\right)$ and c_{hof}. In particular, these quantities act as a structured condition number on the system. A structured backwards-error analysis of existing techniques can be performed using these quantities. Additionally, it is somewhat generic that $F + 2I$ has full rank, hence the local error-bound will hold for most instances of the approximate SNF problem with an attainable solution.

It is also important to note that we did not explicitly use the adjoint matrix. Indeed the result remains valid if we replace the adjoint with minors of prescribed dimension. Likewise, if $\mathcal{A}$ is an ill-posed instance of lower McCoy rank or approximate SNF without an attainable global minimum, then optimizing over a reversal of each entry of $(\operatorname{Adj}(\mathcal{A} + \Delta\mathcal{A}))$ would yield a non-trivial answer and the same stability properties would hold. Thus, poorly posed-problems also remain poorly posed if slightly perturbed.

COROLLARY 4.4. *The LM algorithm for solving $\nabla L = 0$ has quadratic convergence under the assumptions of Theorem 4.2 and using $\mu_k = \|\nabla(L(z^k))\|_2$.*

PROOF. The quantity ∇L is a multivariate polynomial, hence it is locally Lipschitz. Second-order sufficiency holds, thus we have the local error bound property is satisfied. The method converges rapidly with a suitable initial guess. $\square$

These results can also be generalized to form a low McCoy rank approximation. In the next section we discuss a technique that possibly forgoes rapid local convergence, but has a polynomial per iteration cost to compute a low McCoy rank approximation.

4.4 Computational Challenges & Initial Guesses

The most glaring problem in deriving a fast iterative algorithm is that the matrix $\operatorname{Adj}(\mathcal{A} + \Delta\mathcal{A})$ has exponentially many coefficients as a multivariate polynomial in $\Delta\mathcal{A}$. This means computing the adjoint matrix symbolically as an ansatz is not feasible. In order to solve (4.2) we instead approximate the derivatives of the coefficients of the adjoint numerically, which our implementation does asymptotically faster than inverting the Hessian. A detailed discussion of this is left as a future paper.

To compute an initial guess, we can use $\Delta\mathcal{A}_{init} = 0$ and take f^* and h to be a reasonable approximation to an approximate GCD of $\mathrm{Adj}(\mathcal{A})$, which will often be valid as per Theorem 4.2. In the next section we will discuss more sophisticated techniques.

5 LOWER MCCOY RANK APPROXIMATION

In this section we describe how to perform a lower McCoy rank approximation of a matrix polynomial via linearization theory.

Another way to formulate $\mathcal{A}$ having a non-trivial SNF is to solve

$$\min \|\Delta\mathcal{A}\| \text{ such that } (\mathcal{A}(\omega) + \Delta\mathcal{A}(\omega))B = 0 \text{ and } B^*B = I_2,$$

for $B \in \mathbb{C}^{n\times n}$ and $\omega \in \mathbb{C}$. The method is unstable if ω is reasonably large, since the largest terms appearing are of the size $\|\mathcal{A}\|_\infty|\omega|^d$. To remedy this, if we assume that the solution is a full-rank matrix polynomial, we can use linearization theory. If there is no full-rank solution one can simply take a lower-rank approximation [13] and extracts a square pencil of full rank. Alternatively, one may forgo the linearization and work directly with a problem that is more poorly conditioned. We assume for the rest of this section that the solutions to the low McCoy rank problem have full rank.

We can encode the eigenstructure and SNF of $\mathcal{A}$ as a linear pencil of the form $\mathcal{P} \in \mathbb{R}[t]^{nd\times nd}$, defined as

$$\mathcal{P} = \begin{pmatrix} I & & \\ & \ddots & \\ & & A_d \end{pmatrix} t - \begin{pmatrix} & I & & \\ & & \ddots & \\ -A_0 & -A_1 & \cdots & -A_{d-1} \end{pmatrix}.$$

This particular linearization encodes the SNF of $\mathcal{A}$, as $\mathrm{SNF}(\mathcal{P}) = \mathrm{diag}(I, I, \ldots, I, \mathrm{SNF}(\mathcal{A}))$. It follows that $\mathcal{A}$ has a non-trivial SNF if and only if $\mathcal{P}$ has a non-trivial SNF. If we preserve the affine structure of $\mathcal{P}$ and only perturb blocks corresponding to $\mathcal{A}$, then the reduction to a linear pencil will be sufficient. Other linearizations are possible as well. The pencil is generally better behaved numerically since the largest entry is proportional to $\|\mathcal{A}\|_\infty|\omega|$ (it is no longer exponential in ω).

5.1 Low McCoy Rank via Optimization

The theory of low McCoy rank approximations is an immediate generalization of the previous sections if exponentially many more minors were used in the underlying computation.

We formulate the following real optimization problem for $\omega \in \mathbb{C}$.

$$\min \|\Delta\mathcal{A}\|_F^2 \text{ such that } \begin{cases} \Re((\mathcal{P} + \Delta\mathcal{P})(\omega)B) = 0 \\ \Im((\mathcal{P} + \Delta\mathcal{P})(\omega)B) = 0 \\ \Re(B^*B) = I_m \\ \Im(B^*B) = 0, \end{cases} \tag{5.1}$$

where $n-m$ is the desired McCoy rank. The instance of $\Im(\omega_{opt}) = 0$ corresponds to $t - \omega_{opt}$ as an invariant factor of order m, while $\Im(\omega_{opt}) \neq 0$ corresponds to the real irreducible quadratic $(t - \omega_{opt})(t - \overline{\omega_{opt}})$.

In order to approach the problem using the method of Lagrange multipliers we define the Lagrangian as

$$L = \|\Delta\mathcal{A}\|_F^2 + \lambda^T \begin{pmatrix} \Re((\mathcal{P} + \Delta\mathcal{P})(\omega)B) \\ \Im((\mathcal{P} + \Delta\mathcal{P})(\omega)B) \\ \Re(B^*B) - I \\ \Im(B^*B) \end{pmatrix},$$

and proceed to solve $\nabla L = 0$. In our implementation we again make use of the LM method, although given the relatively cheap gradient cost, a first-order method will often be sufficient and faster. The problem is tri-linear, and structurally similar to affinely structured low rank approximation.

5.2 Computing an Initial Guess

In order to compute an initial guess we exploit the tri-linearity of the problem. First we approximate the determinant of $\mathcal{A}$ and consider initial guesses where $\sigma_{n-m}(\mathcal{A}(\omega_{init}))$ is reasonably small. The zeros and local extrema of $\det(\mathcal{A})$ are suitable candidates. B_{init} can be approximated from the smallest m singular vectors of $\mathcal{A}(\omega_{init})$. One can take $\Delta\mathcal{A}_{init} = 0$ or solve a linear least squares problem using B_{init} and ω_{init} as initial guesses.

5.3 Convergence & Prescribed Spectral Structure

The linearization may converge to a solution where the invariant factors are reducible quadratics or degree larger than two. Accordingly, the rate of convergence will be linear with a first-order method and super-linear (but not always quadratic) with reasonable quasi-Newton methods. To obtain a prescribed spectral structure one simply adds constraints of the form (5.1) in conjunction with a "staircase form" constraint [24] to force invariant factors to be repeated or have higher degree.

5.4 About Global Optimization Methods

The discussed problems are NP hard to solve exactly and to approximate with coefficients from $\mathbb{Q}$. This follows because affinely structured low rank approximation [5, 22] is a special case. If we consider a matrix polynomial of degree zero, then this is a scalar matrix with an affine structure. The approximate SNF will be a matrix of rank at most $n-2$, and finding the nearest affinely structured singular matrix is NP hard.

Despite the problem being intractable in the worst case, not all instances are necessarily hard. The formulation (5.1) is multi-linear and polynomial, hence amenable to the sum of squares hierarchy. Lasserre's sum of squares hierarchy [21] is a global framework for polynomial optimization that asymptotically approximates a lower bound. Accordingly, if $\|\omega_{opt}\|$ is bounded, then sum of squares techniques should yield insight into the problem.

6 IMPLEMENTATION AND EXAMPLES

We implemented our methods in `Maple 2016` We use the variant of Levenberg-Marquardt discussed in Section 4 in all instances to solve the first-order necessary condition. All computations are done using hardware precision and measured in floating point operations, or flops. The input size of our problem is measured in the dimension and degree of $\mathcal{A}$, which are n and d respectively. The cost of most quasi-Newton methods is roughly proportional to inverting the Hessian matrix, which is $O(\ell^3)$, where ℓ is the number of variables in the problem.

The method of Section 4 requires approximately $O((n^3d)^3) = O(n^9d^3)$ flops per iteration in an asymptotically optimal implementation with cubic matrix inversion, which is the cost of inverting the Hessian. Computing the Hessian costs roughly $O(n^3d^2 \times (n^2)^2) = O(n^7d^2)$ flops using a blocking procedure, assuming the adjoint computation runs in time $O(n^3d^2)$. There are $O(n^3d)$ Lagrange multipliers since the adjoint has degree at most $(n-1)d$.

The method of Section 5 has a Hessian matrix of size $O(n^2d^2) \times O(n^2d^2)$ in the case of a rank zero McCoy rank approximation. Accordingly, the per iteration cost is roughly $O(n^6d^6)$ flops. Given the lack of expensive adjoint computation, a first-order method will typically require $O(n^2d^2)$ flops per iteration (ignoring the initial setup cost), with local linear convergence.

Example 6.1 (Nearest Interesting SNF). Consider the matrix polynomial $\mathcal{A}$ with a trivial SNF

$$\begin{pmatrix} t^2+.1t+1 & 0 & .3t-.1 & 0 \\ 0 & .9t^2+.2t+1.3 & 0 & .1 \\ .2t & 0 & t^2+1.32+.03t^3 & 0 \\ 0 & .1t^2+1.2 & 0 & .89t^2+.89 \end{pmatrix}$$

of the form $\mathrm{diag}(1,\ldots,1,\det(\mathcal{A}))$.

If we prescribe the perturbations to leave zero coefficients unchanged, then using the methods of Section 4 and Section 5 we compute a local minimizer $\mathcal{A}+\Delta\mathcal{A}_{opt}$ of

$$\begin{pmatrix} 1.0619t^2+.018349t+.94098 & 0 & .27477t-.077901 & 0 \\ 0 & .90268t^2+.22581t+1.2955 & 0 & .058333 \\ .13670t & 0 & .027758t^3+.97840t^2+1.3422 & 0 \\ 0 & .10285t^2+1.1977 & 0 & .84057t^2+.93694 \end{pmatrix},$$

with $\|\Delta\mathcal{A}_{opt}\| \approx .164813183138322$. The SNF of $\mathcal{A}+\Delta\mathcal{A}_{opt}$ is approximately

$$\mathrm{diag}(1,1,s1,s1(t^5+35.388t^4+6.4540t^3+99.542t^2+5.6777t+70.015)),$$

where $s_1 \approx t^2 + 0.0632934647739423t + 0.960572576466186$. s_1 corresponds to $\omega_{opt} \approx -0.0316467323869714 - 0.979576980535687i$.

The method discussed in Section 4 converges to approximately 14 decimal points of accuracy[†] after 69 iterations and the method of Section 5 converges to the same precision after approximately 34 iterations. The initial guess in both instances was $\Delta\mathcal{A}_{init} = 0$. The initial guesses of f^* and h were computed by an approximate GCD routine. For the initial guess of ω we chose a root or local extrema of $\det(\mathcal{A})$ that minimized the second-smallest singular value of $\mathcal{A}(\omega)$, one of which is $\omega_{init} \approx -.12793 - 1.0223i$.

Example 6.2 (Lowest McCoy Rank Approximation). With $\mathcal{A}$ as in the previous example, consider the 0-McCoy rank approximation problem with the same prescribed perturbation structure.

We compute a local minimizer $\mathcal{A}+\Delta\mathcal{A}_{opt}$ to be approximately

$$\begin{pmatrix} .80863t^2+1.1362 & 0 & 0 & 0 \\ 0 & .91673t^2+1.2881 & 0 & 0 \\ 0 & 0 & .95980t^2+1.3486 & 0 \\ 0 & .60052t^2+.84378 & 0 & .71968t^2+1.0112 \end{pmatrix},$$

with $\|\Delta\mathcal{A}_{opt}\| \approx .824645447014665$ after 34 iterations to 14 decimal points of accuracy. We compute $\omega_{opt} \approx -1.18536618732372i$ which corresponds to the single invariant factor $s_1 \approx t^2 + 1.4051$. The SNF of $\mathcal{A}+\Delta\mathcal{A}_{opt}$ is of the form (s_1, s_1, s_1, s_1).

[†] $\nabla L = 0$ is solved to 14 digits of accuracy; the extracted quantities are accurate to approximately the same amount.

7 FUTURE DIRECTIONS

We will continue our research towards a more complete theoretical understanding of computing the nearest matrix polynomial with prescribed finite and infinite spectral structure (or determining non-existence thereof). We also plan to investigate formulating the Smith-McMillan form as an optimization problem and determine if similar existence and stability results can be derived. A detailed exploration of computing the adjoint matrix in a numerically robust manner and corresponding error analysis will also be made.

REFERENCES

[1] S. Ahmad and R. Alam. 2009. Pseudospectra, critical points and multiple eigenvalues of matrix polynomials. *Linear Algebra Appl.* 430, 4 (2009), 1171–1195.
[2] B. Beckermann and G. Labahn. 1998. When are two numerical polynomials relatively prime? *J. Symb. Comp.* 26 (1998), 677–689.
[3] Th. Beelen and P. Van Dooren. 1988. An improved algorithm for the computation of Kronecker's canonical form of a singular pencil. *Linear Algebra Appl.* 105 (1988), 9–65.
[4] D. Bertsekas. 1999. *Nonlinear programming.* Athena Scientific, USA.
[5] R. P. Braatz, P. M. Young, J. C. Doyle, and Manfred M. 1994. Computational complexity of /spl mu/ calculation. *IEEE Trans. Automat. Control* 39, 5 (1994), 1000–1002.
[6] J. W. Demmel and A. Edelman. 1995. The dimension of matrices (matrix pencils) with given Jordan (Kronecker) canonical forms. *Linear Algebra Appl.* 230 (1995), 61–87.
[7] A. Edelman, E. Elmroth, and B. Kågström. 1997. A geometric approach to perturbation theory of matrices and matrix pencils. Part I: Versal deformations. *SIAM J. Matrix Anal. Appl.* 18, 3 (1997), 653–692.
[8] A. Edelman, E. Elmroth, and B. Kågström. 1999. A geometric approach to perturbation theory of matrices and matrix pencils. Part II: A stratification-enhanced staircase algorithm. *SIAM J. Matrix Anal. Appl.* 20, 3 (1999), 667–699.
[9] J-Y. Fan and Y-X. Yuan. 2005. On the quadratic convergence of the Levenberg-Marquardt method without nonsingularity assumption. *Computing* 74, 1 (2005), 23–39.
[10] S. Fatouros and N. Karcanias. 2003. Resultant properties of gcd of many polynomials and a factorization representation of gcd. *Internat. J. Control* 76, 16 (2003), 1666–1683.
[11] M. Giesbrecht, J. Haraldson, and E. Kaltofen. 2016. Computing Approximate Greatest Common Right Divisors of Differential Polynomials. (2016). Submitted.
[12] M. Giesbrecht, J. Haraldson, and G. Labahn. 2017. Computing the Nearest Rank-Deficient Matrix Polynomial. In *Proc. ACM on International Symposium on Symbolic and Algebraic Computation (ISSAC'17).* 181–188.
[13] M. Giesbrecht, J. Haraldson, and G. Labahn. 2017. Lower Rank Approximations of Matrix Polynomials. *J. of Symbolic Computation* (2017). Submitted.
[14] I. Gohberg, P. Lancaster, and L. Rodman. 2009. *Matrix polynomials.* SIAM, USA.
[15] G. Golub and C. Van Loan. 2013. *Matrix Computations* (4 ed.). Johns Hopkins University Press, USA.
[16] J. Haraldson. 2015. *Computing Approximate GCRDs of Differential Polynomials.* Master's thesis. University of Waterloo.
[17] A. J. Hoffman. 1952. On Approximate Solutions of Systems of Linear Inequalities. *J. Res. Nat. Bur. Standards* 49, 4 (1952).
[18] T. Kailath. 1980. *Linear systems.* Vol. 156. Prentice-Hall, USA.
[19] E. Kaltofen and A. Storjohann. 2015. The complexity of computational problems in exact linear algebra. In *Encyclopedia of Applied and Computational Mathematics.* Springer, Germany, 227–233.
[20] N. Karmarkar and Y. N. Lakshman. 1996. Approximate Polynomial Greatest Common Divisors and Nearest Singular Polynomials. In *Proc. International Symposium on Symbolic and Algebraic Computation (ISSAC'96).* ACM Press, Zurich, Switzerland, 35–39.
[21] J-B. Lasserre. 2001. Global optimization with polynomials and the problem of moments. *SIAM Journal on Optimization* 11, 3 (2001), 796–817.
[22] S. Poljak and J. Rohn. 1993. Checking robust nonsingularity is NP-hard. *Mathematics of Control, Signals, and Systems (MCSS)* 6, 1 (1993), 1–9.
[23] G. Stewart. 1994. Perturbation theory for rectangular matrix pencils. *Linear algebra and its applications* 208 (1994), 297–301.
[24] P. Van Dooren and P. Dewilde. 1983. The eigenstructure of an arbitrary polynomial matrix: computational aspects. *Linear Algebra Appl.* 50 (1983), 545–579.
[25] A. Vardulakis and P. Stoyle. 1978. Generalized resultant theorem. *IMA Journal of Applied Mathematics* 22, 3 (1978), 331–335.
[26] N. Yamashita and M. Fukushima. 2001. On the rate of convergence of the Levenberg-Marquardt method. In *Topics Num. Analysis.* Springer, 239–249.
[27] Z. Zeng and B. H. Dayton. 2004. The Approximate GCD of Inexact Polynomials. In *Proc. International Symposium on Symbolic and Algebraic Computation (ISSAC'04).* Santander, Spain, 320–327.

Certification of Minimal Approximant Bases

Pascal Giorgi
LIRMM, Université de Montpellier, CNRS
Montpellier, France
pascal.giorgi@lirmm.fr

Vincent Neiger
Univ. Limoges, CNRS, XLIM, UMR 7252
F-87000 Limoges, France
vincent.neiger@unilim.fr

ABSTRACT

For a given computational problem, a certificate is a piece of data that one (the *prover*) attaches to the output with the aim of allowing efficient verification (by the *verifier*) that this output is correct. Here, we consider the minimal approximant basis problem, for which the fastest known algorithms output a polynomial matrix of dimensions $m \times m$ and average degree D/m using $O\tilde{~}(m^\omega \frac{D}{m})$ field operations. We propose a certificate which, for typical instances of the problem, is computed by the prover using $O(m^\omega \frac{D}{m})$ additional field operations and allows verification of the approximant basis by a Monte Carlo algorithm with cost bound $O(m^\omega + mD)$.

Besides theoretical interest, our motivation also comes from the fact that approximant bases arise in most of the fastest known algorithms for linear algebra over the univariate polynomials; thus, this work may help in designing certificates for other polynomial matrix computations. Furthermore, cryptographic challenges such as breaking records for discrete logarithm computations or for integer factorization rely in particular on computing minimal approximant bases for large instances: certificates can then be used to provide reliable computation on outsourced and error-prone clusters.

KEYWORDS

Certification; minimal approximant basis; order basis; polynomial matrix; truncated product.

ACM Reference Format:
Pascal Giorgi and Vincent Neiger. 2018. Certification of Minimal Approximant Bases. In *ISSAC '18: 2018 ACM International Symposium on Symbolic and Algebraic Computation, July 16–19, 2018, New York, NY, USA.* ACM, New York, NY, USA, 8 pages. https://doi.org/10.1145/3208976.3208991

1 INTRODUCTION

Context. For a given tuple $\mathbf{d} = (d_1, \ldots, d_n) \in \mathbb{Z}^n_{>0}$ called *order*, we consider an $m \times n$ matrix $\mathbf{F}$ of formal power series with the column j truncated at order d_j. Formally, we let $\mathbf{F} \in \mathbb{K}[X]^{m\times n}$ be a matrix over the univariate polynomials over a field $\mathbb{K}$, such that the column j of $\mathbf{F}$ has degree less than d_j. Then, we consider the classical notion of minimal approximant bases for $\mathbf{F}$ [1, 27]. An approximant is a polynomial row vector $\mathbf{p} \in \mathbb{K}[X]^{1\times m}$ such that

$$\mathbf{pF} = \mathbf{0} \bmod \mathbf{X^d}, \quad \text{where } \mathbf{X^d} = \mathrm{diag}(X^{d_1}, \ldots, X^{d_n}); \tag{1}$$

here $\mathbf{pF} = \mathbf{0} \bmod \mathbf{X^d}$ means that $\mathbf{pF} = \mathbf{qX^d}$ for some $\mathbf{q} \in \mathbb{K}[X]^{1\times n}$. The set of all approximants forms a (free) $\mathbb{K}[X]$-module of rank m, $\mathcal{A}_\mathbf{d}(\mathbf{F}) = \{\mathbf{p} \in \mathbb{K}[X]^{1\times m} \mid \mathbf{pF} = \mathbf{0} \bmod \mathbf{X^d}\}$. A basis of this module is called an *approximant basis* (or sometimes an *order basis* or a *σ-basis*); it is a nonsingular matrix in $\mathbb{K}[X]^{m\times m}$ whose rows are approximants in $\mathcal{A}_\mathbf{d}(\mathbf{F})$ and generate $\mathcal{A}_\mathbf{d}(\mathbf{F})$.

The design of fast algorithms for computing approximant bases has been studied throughout the last three decades [1, 14, 15, 26–28]. Furthermore, these algorithms compute *minimal* bases, with respect to some degree measure specified by a shift $\mathbf{s} \in \mathbb{Z}^m$. The best known cost bound is $O\tilde{~}(m^{\omega-1}D)$ operations in $\mathbb{K}$ [15] where D is the sum $D = |\mathbf{d}| = d_1 + \cdots + d_n$. Throughout the paper, our complexity estimates will fit the algebraic RAM model counting only operations in $\mathbb{K}$, and we will use $O(n^\omega)$ to refer to the complexity of the multiplication of two $m \times m$ matrices, where $\omega < 2.373$ [4, 21].

Here, we are interested in the following question:

> *How to efficiently certify that some approximant basis algorithm indeed returns an $\mathbf{s}$-minimal basis of $\mathcal{A}_\mathbf{d}(\mathbf{F})$?*

Since all known fast approximant basis algorithms are deterministic, it might seem that a posteriori certification is pointless. In fact, it is an essential tool in the context of unreliable computations that arise when one delegates the processing to outsourced servers or to some large infrastructure that may be error-prone. In such a situation, and maybe before concluding a commercial contract to which this computing power is attached, one wants to ensure that he will be able to guarantee the correctness of the result of these computations. Of course, to be worthwhile, the verification procedure must be significantly faster than the original computation.

Resorting to such computing power is indeed necessary in the case of large instances of approximant bases, which are a key tool within challenging computations that try to tackle the hardness of some cryptographic protocols, for instance those based on the discrete logarithm problem (e.g. El Gamal) or integer factorization (e.g. RSA). The computation of a discrete logarithm over a 768-bit prime field, presented in [20], required to compute an approximant basis that served as input for a larger computation which took a total time of 355 core years on a 4096-cores cluster. The approximant basis computation itself took 1 core year. In this context, it is of great interest to be able to guarantee the correctness of the approximant basis before launching the most time-consuming step.

Linear algebra operations are good candidates for designing fast verification algorithms since they often have a cost related to matrix multiplication while their input only uses quadratic space. The first example one may think of is linear system solving. Indeed, given a solution vector $\mathbf{x} \in \mathbb{K}^n$ to a system $\mathbf{Ax} = \mathbf{b}$ defined by $\mathbf{A} \in \mathbb{K}^{n\times n}$ and $\mathbf{b} \in \mathbb{K}^n$, one can directly verify the correctness by checking the equations at a cost of $O(n^2)$ operations in $\mathbb{K}$. Comparatively, solving the system with the fastest known algorithm costs $O(n^\omega)$.

ISSAC '18, July 16–19, 2018, New York, NY, USA

ACM ISBN 978-1-4503-5550-6/18/07...$15.00
https://doi.org/10.1145/3208976.3208991

Another famous result, due to Freivalds [11], gives a method to verify a matrix product. Given matrices $\mathbf{A}, \mathbf{B}, \mathbf{C} \in \mathbb{K}^{n\times n}$, the idea is to check $\mathbf{uC} = (\mathbf{uA})\mathbf{B}$ for a random row vector $\mathbf{u} \in \{0,1\}^{1\times n}$, rather than $\mathbf{C} = \mathbf{AB}$. This verification algorithm costs $O(n^2)$ and is *false-biased one-sided* Monte-Carlo (it is always correct when it answers "false"); the probability of error can be made arbitrarily small by picking several random vectors.

In some cases, one may require an additional piece of data to be produced together with the output in order to prove the correctness of the result. For example, Farkas' lemma [10] certifies the infeasibility of a linear program thanks to an extra vector. Although the verification is deterministic in this example, the design of certificates that are verified by probabilistic algorithms opened a line of work for faster certification methods in linear algebra [7, 8, 17, 18].

In this context, one of the main challenges is to design *optimal* certificates, that is, ones which are verifiable in linear time. Furthermore, the time and space needed for the certificate must remain negligible. In this work, we seek such an optimal certificate for the problem of computing shifted minimal approximant bases.

Here, an instance is given by the input $(\mathbf{d}, \mathbf{F}, \mathbf{s})$ which is of size $O(mD)$: each column j of $\mathbf{F}$ contains at most md_j elements of $\mathbb{K}$, and the order sums to $d_1 + \cdots + d_n = |\mathbf{d}| = D$. We neglect the size of the shift $\mathbf{s}$, since one may always assume that it is nonnegative and such that $\max(\mathbf{s}) < mD$ (see [15, App. A]). Thus, ideally one would like to have a certificate which can be verified in time $O(mD)$.

In this paper, we provide a non-interactive certification protocol which uses the input $(\mathbf{d}, \mathbf{F}, \mathbf{s})$, the output $\mathbf{P}$, and a certificate which is a constant matrix $\mathbf{C} \in \mathbb{K}^{m\times n}$. We design a Monte-Carlo verification algorithm with cost bound $O(mD + m^{\omega-1}(m+n))$; this is optimal as soon as D is large compared to m and n (e.g. when $D > m^2 + mn$), which is most often the case of interest. We also show that the certificate $\mathbf{C}$ can be computed in $O(m^{\omega-1}D)$ operations in $\mathbb{K}$, which is faster than known approximant basis algorithms.

Degrees and size of approximant bases. For $\mathbf{P} \in \mathbb{K}[X]^{m\times m}$, we denote the row degree of $\mathbf{P}$ as $\mathrm{rdeg}(\mathbf{P}) = (r_1, \ldots, r_m)$ where $r_i = \deg(\mathbf{P}_{i,*})$ is the degree of the row i of $\mathbf{P}$ for $1 \le i \le m$. The column degree $\mathrm{cdeg}(\mathbf{P})$ is defined similarly. More generally, we will consider row degrees shifted by some additive column weights: for a shift $\mathbf{s} = (s_1, \ldots, s_m) \in \mathbb{Z}^m$ the $\mathbf{s}$-row degree of $\mathbf{P}$ is $\mathrm{rdeg}_\mathbf{s}(\mathbf{P}) = (r_1, \ldots, r_m)$ where $r_i = \max(\deg(\mathbf{P}_{i,1}) + s_1, \ldots, \deg(\mathbf{P}_{i,m}) + s_m)$.

We use $|\cdot|$ to denote the sum of integer tuples: for example $|\mathrm{rdeg}_\mathbf{s}(\mathbf{P})|$ is the sum of the $\mathbf{s}$-row degree of $\mathbf{P}$ (note that this sum might contain negative terms). The comparison of integer tuples is entrywise: $\mathrm{cdeg}(\mathbf{F}) < \mathbf{d}$ means that the column j of $\mathbf{F}$ has degree less than d_j, for $1 \le j \le n$. When adding a constant to a tuple, say for example $\mathbf{s} - 1$, this stands for the tuple $(s_1 - 1, \ldots, s_m - 1)$.

In existing approximant basis algorithms, the output bases may take different forms: essentially, they can be $\mathbf{s}$-minimal (also called $\mathbf{s}$-reduced [27]), $\mathbf{s}$-weak Popov [23], or $\mathbf{s}$-Popov [3]. For formal definitions and for motivating the use of shifts, we direct the reader to these references and to those above about approximant basis algorithms; here the precise form of the basis will not play an important role. What is however at the core of the efficiency of our algorithms is the impact of these forms on the degrees in the basis.

In what follows, by *size* of a matrix we mean the number of field elements used for its dense representation. For a given matrix $\mathbf{P} = [p_{ij}] \in \mathbb{K}[X]^{m\times m}$, we define the quantity

$$\mathrm{Size}(\mathbf{P}) = m^2 + \textstyle\sum_{1\le i,j\le m} \max(0, \deg(p_{ij})).$$

In the next paragraph, we discuss degree bounds on $\mathbf{P}$ when it is the output of any of the approximant basis algorithms mentioned above; note that these bounds all imply that $\mathbf{P}$ has size in $O(mD)$.

There is no general degree bound for approximant bases: any unimodular matrix is a basis of $\mathcal{A}_\mathbf{d}(\mathbf{0}) = \mathbb{K}[X]^{1\times m}$. Still, a basis $\mathbf{P}$ of $\mathcal{A}_\mathbf{d}(\mathbf{F})$ always satisfies $\deg(\det(\mathbf{P})) \le D$. Now, for an $\mathbf{s}$-minimal $\mathbf{P}$, we have $|\mathrm{rdeg}(\mathbf{P})| \in O(D)$ as soon as $|\mathbf{s} - \min(\mathbf{s})| \in O(D)$ [27, Thm. 4.1], and it was shown in [28] that $\mathbf{P}$ has size in $O(mD)$ if $|\max(\mathbf{s}) - \mathbf{s}| \in O(D)$. Yet, without such assumptions on the shift, there are $\mathbf{s}$-minimal bases whose size is in $\Theta(m^2 D)$ [15, App. B], ruling out the feasibility of finding them in time $O\tilde{~}(m^{\omega-1}D)$. In this case, the fastest known algorithms return the more constrained $\mathbf{s}$-Popov basis $\mathbf{P}$, for which $|\mathrm{cdeg}(\mathbf{P})| \le D$ holds independently of $\mathbf{s}$.

Problem and contribution. Certifying that a matrix $\mathbf{P}$ is an $\mathbf{s}$-minimal approximant basis for a given instance $(\mathbf{d}, \mathbf{F}, \mathbf{s})$ boils down to the following three properties of $\mathbf{P}$:

(1) *Minimal:* $\mathbf{P}$ is in $\mathbf{s}$-reduced form. By definition, this amounts to testing the invertibility of the so-called $\mathbf{s}$-leading matrix of $\mathbf{P}$ (see Step **1** of Algorithm 1 for the construction of this matrix), which can be done using $O(m^\omega)$ operations in $\mathbb{K}$.

(2) *Approximant:* the rows of $\mathbf{P}$ are approximants. That is, we should check that $\mathbf{PF} = \mathbf{0} \bmod \mathbf{X^d}$. The difficulty is to avoid computing the full truncated product $\mathbf{PF} \bmod \mathbf{X^d}$, since this costs $O\tilde{~}(m^{\omega-1}D)$. In Section 3, we give a probabilistic algorithm which verifies more generally $\mathbf{PF} = \mathbf{G} \bmod \mathbf{X^d}$ using $O(\mathrm{Size}(\mathbf{P}) + mD)$ operations, without requiring a certificate.

(3) *Basis:* the rows of $\mathbf{P}$ generate the approximant module[1]. For this, we prove that it suffices to verify first that $\det(\mathbf{P})$ is of the form cX^δ for some $c \in \mathbb{K} \setminus \{0\}$ and where $\delta = |\mathrm{rdeg}(\mathbf{P})|$, and second that some constant $m \times (m+n)$ matrix has full rank; this matrix involves $\mathbf{P}(0)$ and the coefficient $\mathbf{C}$ of degree 0 of $\mathbf{PFX^{-d}}$. In Section 2, we show that $\mathbf{C}$ can serve as a certificate, and that a probabilistic algorithm can assess its correctness at a suitable cost.

Our (non-interactive) certification protocol is as follows. Given $(\mathbf{d}, \mathbf{F}, \mathbf{s})$, the *Prover* computes a matrix $\mathbf{P}$, supposedly an $\mathbf{s}$-minimal basis of $\mathcal{A}_\mathbf{d}(\mathbf{F})$, along with a constant matrix $\mathbf{C} \in \mathbb{K}^{m\times n}$, supposedly the coefficient of degree 0 of the product $\mathbf{PFX^{-d}}$. Then, the *Prover* communicates these results to the *Verifier* who must solve Problem 1 within a cost asymptotically better than $O\tilde{~}(m^{\omega-1}D)$.

The main result in this paper is an efficient solution to Problem 1.

Theorem 1.1. *There is a Monte-Carlo algorithm which solves Problem 1 using $O(mD + m^{\omega-1}(m+n))$ operations in $\mathbb{K}$, assuming* $\mathrm{Size}(\mathbf{P}) \in O(mD)$. *It chooses $m+2$ elements uniformly and independently at random from a finite subset $S \subset \mathbb{K}$. If S has cardinality at least $2(D+1)$, then the probability that a* True *answer is incorrect is less than $1/2$, while a* False *answer is always correct.*

A detailed cost bound showing the constant factors is described in Proposition 2.5. If $\mathrm{Size}(\mathbf{P}) \in O(mD)$, then the size of the input of

[1] This is not implied by (1) and (2): for $d = \max(\mathbf{d})$, then $X^d\mathbf{I}_m$ is $\mathbf{s}$-reduced and $X^d\mathbf{I}_m\mathbf{F} = \mathbf{0} \bmod \mathbf{X^d}$ holds; yet, $X^d\mathbf{I}_m$ is not a basis of $\mathcal{A}_\mathbf{d}(\mathbf{F})$ for most $(\mathbf{F}, \mathbf{d})$.

Problem 1: APPROXIMANT BASIS CERTIFICATION
Input:

- order $\mathbf{d} \in \mathbb{Z}^n_{>0}$,
- matrix $\mathbf{F} \in \mathbb{K}[X]^{m\times n}$ with $\mathrm{cdeg}(\mathbf{F}) < \mathbf{d}$,
- shift $\mathbf{s} \in \mathbb{Z}^m$,
- matrix $\mathbf{P} \in \mathbb{K}[X]^{m\times m}$,
- certificate matrix $\mathbf{C} \in \mathbb{K}^{m\times n}$.

Output: True if $\mathbf{P}$ is an $\mathbf{s}$-minimal basis of $\mathcal{A}_{\mathbf{d}}(\mathbf{F})$ and $\mathbf{C}$ is the coefficient of degree 0 of $\mathbf{PFX}^{-\mathbf{d}}$, otherwise *False*.

Problem 1 is in $O(mD)$; the cost bound above is therefore optimal (up to constant factors) as soon as $m^{\omega-2}(m+n) \in O(D)$.

If $\mathbb{K}$ is a small finite field, there may be no subset $S \subset \mathbb{K}$ of cardinality $\#S \geq 2(D+1)$. Then, our approach still works by performing the probabilistic part of the computation over a sufficiently large extension of $\mathbb{K}$. Note that an extension of degree about $1+\lceil \log_2(D)\rceil$ would be suitable; this would increase our complexity estimates by a factor logarithmic in D, which remains acceptable in our context.

Our second result is the efficient computation of the certificate.

THEOREM 1.2. *Let $\mathbf{d} \in \mathbb{Z}^n_{>0}$, let $\mathbf{F} \in \mathbb{K}[X]^{m\times n}$ with $\mathrm{cdeg}(\mathbf{F}) < \mathbf{d}$ and $m \in O(D)$, and let $\mathbf{P} \in \mathbb{K}[X]^{m\times m}$. If $|\mathrm{rdeg}(\mathbf{P})| \in O(D)$ or $|\mathrm{cdeg}(\mathbf{P})| \in O(D)$, there is a deterministic algorithm which computes the coefficient of degree 0 of $\mathbf{PFX}^{-\mathbf{d}}$ using $O(m^{\omega-1}D)$ operations in $\mathbb{K}$ if $m \geq n$ and $O(m^{\omega-1}D\log(n/m))$ operations in $\mathbb{K}$ if $m < n$.*

Note that the assumption $m \in O(D)$ in this theorem is commonly made in approximant basis algorithms, since when $D \leq m$ most entries of a minimal approximant basis have degree in $O(1)$ and the algorithms then rely on methods from dense $\mathbb{K}$-linear algebra.

2 CERTIFYING APPROXIMANT BASES

Here, we present our certification algorithm. Its properties, given in Proposition 2.5, prove Theorem 1.1. One of its core components is the verification of truncated polynomial matrix products; the details of this are in Section 3 and are taken for granted here.

First, we show the basic properties behind the correctness of this algorithm, which are summarized in the following result.

THEOREM 2.1. *Let $\mathbf{d} \in \mathbb{Z}^n_{>0}$, let $\mathbf{F} \in \mathbb{K}[X]^{m\times n}$, and let $\mathbf{s} \in \mathbb{Z}^m$. A matrix $\mathbf{P} \in \mathbb{K}[X]^{m\times m}$ is an $\mathbf{s}$-minimal basis of $\mathcal{A}_{\mathbf{d}}(\mathbf{F})$ if and only if the following properties are all satisfied:*

(i) $\mathbf{P}$ *is* $\mathbf{s}$*-reduced;*
(ii) $\det(\mathbf{P})$ *is a nonzero monomial in* $\mathbb{K}[X]$*;*
(iii) the rows of $\mathbf{P}$ *are in* $\mathcal{A}_{\mathbf{d}}(\mathbf{F})$*, that is,* $\mathbf{PF} = \mathbf{0} \bmod \mathbf{X}^{\mathbf{d}}$*;*
(iv) $[\mathbf{P}(0) \;\; \mathbf{C}] \in \mathbb{K}^{m\times(m+n)}$ *has full rank, where* $\mathbf{C}$ *is the coefficient of degree 0 of* $\mathbf{PFX}^{-\mathbf{d}}$.

We remark that having both $\mathbf{PF} = \mathbf{0} \bmod \mathbf{X}^{\mathbf{d}}$ and $\mathbf{C}$ the constant coefficient of $\mathbf{PFX}^{-\mathbf{d}}$ is equivalent to the single truncated identity $\mathbf{PF} = \mathbf{CX}^{\mathbf{d}} \bmod \mathbf{X}^{\mathbf{t}}$, where $\mathbf{t} = (d_1+1,\ldots,d_n+1)$.

As mentioned above, the details of the certification of the latter identity is deferred to Section 3, where we present more generally the certification for truncated products of the form $\mathbf{PF} = \mathbf{G} \bmod \mathbf{X}^{\mathbf{t}}$.

Concerning Item (ii), the fact that the determinant of any basis of $\mathcal{A}_{\mathbf{d}}(\mathbf{F})$ must divide X^D, where $D = |\mathbf{d}|$, is well-known; we refer to [2, Sec. 2] for a more general result.

The combination of Items (i) and (iii) describes the set of matrices $\mathbf{P} \in \mathbb{K}[X]^{m\times m}$ which are $\mathbf{s}$-reduced and whose rows are in $\mathcal{A}_{\mathbf{d}}(\mathbf{F})$. For $\mathbf{P}$ to be an $\mathbf{s}$-minimal basis of $\mathcal{A}_{\mathbf{d}}(\mathbf{F})$, its rows should further form a generating set for $\mathcal{A}_{\mathbf{d}}(\mathbf{F})$; thus, our goal here is to prove that this property is realized by the combination of Items (ii) and (iv).

For this, we will rely on a link between approximant bases and kernel bases, given in Lemma 2.3. We recall that, for a given matrix $\mathbf{M} \in \mathbb{K}[X]^{\mu\times\nu}$ of rank r,

- a *kernel basis* for $\mathbf{M}$ is a matrix in $\mathbb{K}[X]^{(\mu-r)\times\mu}$ whose rows form a basis of the left kernel $\{\mathbf{p} \in \mathbb{K}[X]^{1\times\mu} \mid \mathbf{pM} = \mathbf{0}\}$,
- a *column basis* for $\mathbf{M}$ is a matrix in $\mathbb{K}[X]^{\mu\times r}$ whose columns form a basis of the column space $\{\mathbf{Mp}, \mathbf{p} \in \mathbb{K}[X]^{\nu\times 1}\}$.

In particular, by definition, a kernel basis has full row rank and a column basis has full column rank. The next result states that the column space of a kernel basis is the whole space (that is, the space spanned by the identity matrix).

LEMMA 2.2. *Let $\mathbf{M} \in \mathbb{K}[X]^{\mu\times\nu}$ and let $\mathbf{B} \in \mathbb{K}[X]^{k\times\mu}$ be a kernel basis for $\mathbf{M}$. Then, any column basis for $\mathbf{B}$ is unimodular. Equivalently, $\mathbf{BU} = \mathbf{I}_k$ for some $\mathbf{U} \in \mathbb{K}[X]^{\mu\times k}$.*

PROOF. Let $\mathbf{S} \in \mathbb{K}[X]^{k\times k}$ be a column basis for $\mathbf{B}$. By definition, $\mathbf{B} = \mathbf{S}\hat{\mathbf{B}}$ for some $\hat{\mathbf{B}} \in \mathbb{K}[X]^{k\times\mu}$. Then $\mathbf{0} = \mathbf{BM} = \mathbf{S}\hat{\mathbf{B}}\mathbf{M}$, hence $\hat{\mathbf{B}}\mathbf{M} = \mathbf{0}$ since $\mathbf{S}$ is nonsingular. Thus, $\mathbf{B}$ being a kernel basis for $\mathbf{M}$, we have $\hat{\mathbf{B}} = \mathbf{TB}$ for some $\mathbf{T} \in \mathbb{K}[X]^{k\times k}$. We obtain $(\mathbf{ST} - \mathbf{I}_k)\mathbf{B} = \mathbf{0}$, hence $\mathbf{ST} = \mathbf{I}_k$ since $\mathbf{B}$ has full row rank. Thus, $\mathbf{S}$ is unimodular. □

This arises for example in the computation of column bases and unimodular completions in [29, 30]; the previous lemma can also be derived from these references, and in particular from [29, Lem. 3.1].

Here, we will use the property of Lemma 2.2 for a specific kernel basis, built from an approximant basis as follows.

LEMMA 2.3. *Let $\mathbf{d} \in \mathbb{Z}^n_{>0}$, $\mathbf{F} \in \mathbb{K}[X]^{m\times n}$, and $\mathbf{P} \in \mathbb{K}[X]^{m\times m}$. Then, $\mathbf{P}$ is a basis of $\mathcal{A}_{\mathbf{d}}(\mathbf{F})$ if and only if there exists $\mathbf{Q} \in \mathbb{K}[X]^{m\times n}$ such that $[\mathbf{P} \;\; \mathbf{Q}]$ is a kernel basis for $[\mathbf{F}^{\mathsf{T}} \;\; -\mathbf{X}^{\mathbf{d}}]^{\mathsf{T}}$. If this is the case, then we have $\mathbf{Q} = \mathbf{PFX}^{-\mathbf{d}}$ and there exist $\mathbf{V} \in \mathbb{K}[X]^{m\times m}$ and $\mathbf{W} \in \mathbb{K}[X]^{n\times m}$ such that $\mathbf{PV} + \mathbf{QW} = \mathbf{I}_m$.*

PROOF. The equivalence is straightforward; a detailed proof can be found in [24, Lem. 8.2]. If $[\mathbf{P} \;\; \mathbf{Q}]$ is a kernel basis for $[\mathbf{F}^{\mathsf{T}} \;\; -\mathbf{X}^{\mathbf{d}}]^{\mathsf{T}}$, then we have $\mathbf{PF} = \mathbf{QX}^{\mathbf{d}}$, hence the explicit formula for $\mathbf{Q}$. Besides, the last claim is a direct consequence of Lemma 2.2. □

This leads us to the following result, which forms the main ingredient that was missing in order to prove Theorem 2.1.

LEMMA 2.4. *Let $\mathbf{d} \in \mathbb{Z}^n_{>0}$ and let $\mathbf{F} \in \mathbb{K}[X]^{m\times n}$. Let $\mathbf{P} \in \mathbb{K}[X]^{m\times m}$ be such that $\mathbf{PF} = \mathbf{0} \bmod \mathbf{X}^{\mathbf{d}}$ and $\det(\mathbf{P})$ is a nonzero monomial, and let $\mathbf{C} \in \mathbb{K}^{m\times(m+n)}$ be the constant coefficient of $\mathbf{PFX}^{-\mathbf{d}}$. Then, $\mathbf{P}$ is a basis of $\mathcal{A}_{\mathbf{d}}(\mathbf{F})$ if and only if $[\mathbf{P}(0) \;\; \mathbf{C}] \in \mathbb{K}^{m\times(m+n)}$ has full rank.*

PROOF. First, assume that $\mathbf{P}$ is a basis of $\mathcal{A}_{\mathbf{d}}(\mathbf{F})$. Then, defining $\mathbf{Q} = \mathbf{PFX}^{-\mathbf{d}} \in \mathbb{K}[X]^{m\times n}$, Lemma 2.3 implies that $\mathbf{PV} + \mathbf{QW} = \mathbf{I}_m$ for some $\mathbf{V} \in \mathbb{K}[X]^{m\times m}$ and $\mathbf{W} \in \mathbb{K}[X]^{n\times m}$. Since $\mathbf{Q}(0) = \mathbf{C}$, this yields $\mathbf{P}(0)\mathbf{V}(0) + \mathbf{CW}(0) = \mathbf{I}_m$, and thus $[\mathbf{P}(0) \;\; \mathbf{C}]$ has full rank.

Now, assume that $\mathbf{P}$ is not a basis of $\mathcal{A}_{\mathbf{d}}(\mathbf{F})$. If $\mathbf{P}$ has rank $< m$, then $[\mathbf{P}(0) \;\; \mathbf{C}]$ has rank $< m$ as well. If $\mathbf{P}$ is nonsingular, $\mathbf{P} = \mathbf{UA}$ for some basis $\mathbf{A}$ of $\mathcal{A}_{\mathbf{d}}(\mathbf{F})$ and some $\mathbf{U} \in \mathbb{K}[X]^{m\times m}$ which is nonsingular but not unimodular. Then, $\det(\mathbf{U})$ is a nonconstant divisor of the nonzero monomial $\det(\mathbf{P})$; hence $\det(\mathbf{U})(0) = 0 = \det(\mathbf{U}(0))$, and thus $\mathbf{U}(0)$ has rank $< m$. Since $[\mathbf{P}\ \ \mathbf{Q}] = \mathbf{U}[\mathbf{A}\ \ \mathbf{AFX}^{-\mathbf{d}}]$, it directly follows that $[\mathbf{P}(0)\ \ \mathbf{C}]$ has rank $< m$. □

Proof of Theorem 2.1. If $\mathbf{P}$ is an $\mathbf{s}$-minimal basis of $\mathcal{A}_{\mathbf{d}}(\mathbf{F})$, then by definition Items (i) and (iii) are satisfied. Since the rows of $X^{\max(\mathbf{d})}\mathbf{I}_m$ are in $\mathcal{A}_{\mathbf{d}}(\mathbf{F})$ and $\mathbf{P}$ is a basis, the matrix $X^{\max(\mathbf{d})}\mathbf{I}_m$ is a left multiple of $\mathbf{P}$ and therefore the determinant of $\mathbf{P}$ divides $X^{m\max(\mathbf{d})}$: it is a nonzero monomial. Then, according to Lemma 2.4, $[\mathbf{P}(0)\ \ \mathbf{C}]$ has full rank. Conversely, if Items (ii) to (iv) are satisfied, then Lemma 2.4 states that $\mathbf{P}$ is a basis of $\mathcal{A}_{\mathbf{d}}(\mathbf{F})$; thus if furthermore Item (i) is satisfied then $\mathbf{P}$ is an $\mathbf{s}$-minimal basis of $\mathcal{A}_{\mathbf{d}}(\mathbf{F})$. □

Algorithm 1: CertifApproxBasis
Input:
- order $\mathbf{d} = (d_1, \ldots, d_n) \in \mathbb{Z}^n_{>0}$,
- matrix $\mathbf{F} \in \mathbb{K}[X]^{m\times n}$ with $\text{cdeg}(\mathbf{F}) < \mathbf{d}$,
- shift $\mathbf{s} = (s_1, \ldots, s_m) \in \mathbb{Z}^m$,
- matrix $\mathbf{P} \in \mathbb{K}[X]^{m\times m}$,
- certificate matrix $\mathbf{C} \in \mathbb{K}^{m\times n}$.

Output: *True* if $\mathbf{P}$ is an $\mathbf{s}$-minimal basis of $\mathcal{A}_{\mathbf{d}}(\mathbf{F})$ and $\mathbf{C}$ is the constant term of $\mathbf{PFX}^{-\mathbf{d}}$, otherwise *True* or *False*.

1. /* P not in s-reduced form ⇒ False */
   $\mathbf{L} \leftarrow$ the matrix in $\mathbb{K}^{m\times m}$ whose entry i,j is the coefficient of degree $\text{rdeg}_{\mathbf{s}}(\mathbf{P}_{i,*}) - s_j$ of the entry i,j of $\mathbf{P}$
   If $\mathbf{L}$ is not invertible *then return False*
2. /* rank([P(0) C]) not full rank ⇒ False */
   If $\text{rank}([\mathbf{P}(0)\ \ \mathbf{C}]) < m$ *then return False*
3. /* det(P) not a nonzero monomial ⇒ False */
   $S \leftarrow$ a finite subset of $\mathbb{K}$
   $\Delta \leftarrow |\text{rdeg}_{\mathbf{s}}(\mathbf{P})| - |\mathbf{s}|$
   $\alpha \leftarrow$ chosen uniformly at random from S
   If $\det(\mathbf{P}(\alpha)) \neq \det(\mathbf{P}(1))\alpha^\Delta$ *then return False*
4. /* certify truncated product $\mathbf{PF} = \mathbf{CX^d} \bmod \mathbf{X^t}$ */
   $\mathbf{t} \leftarrow (d_1 + 1, \ldots, d_n + 1)$
   Return VerifTruncMatProd($\mathbf{t}, \mathbf{P}, \mathbf{F}, \mathbf{CX^d}$)

In order to provide a sharp estimate of the cost of Algorithm 1, we recall the best known cost bound with constant factors of the LQUP factorization of an $m \times n$ matrix over $\mathbb{K}$, which we use for computing ranks and determinants. Assuming $m \leq n$, we have:

$$C(m,n) = \left(\left\lceil \frac{n}{m} \right\rceil \frac{1}{2^{\omega-1}-2} - \frac{1}{2^\omega - 2}\right) MM(m)$$

operations in $\mathbb{K}$ [6, Lem. 5.1], where $MM(m)$ is the cost for the multiplication of $m \times m$ matrices over $\mathbb{K}$.

Proposition 2.5. *Algorithm 1 uses at most*

$$\begin{aligned} &5\text{Size}(\mathbf{P}) + 2m(D + \max(\mathbf{d})) + 3C(m,m) + C(m, m+n) \\ &\qquad + (4m+1)n + 4\log_2(Dd_1 \cdots d_n) \\ &\in O(\text{Size}(\mathbf{P}) + mD + m^{\omega-1}(m+n)) \end{aligned}$$

operations in $\mathbb{K}$, *where* $D = |\mathbf{d}|$. *It is a false-biased Monte Carlo algorithm. If* $\mathbf{P}$ *is not an* $\mathbf{s}$*-minimal basis of* $\mathcal{A}_{\mathbf{d}}(\mathbf{F})$*, then the probability that it outputs* True *is less than* $\frac{D+1}{\#S}$, *where* S *is the finite subset of* $\mathbb{K}$ *from which random field elements are drawn.*

Proof. By definition, $\mathbf{P}$ is $\mathbf{s}$-reduced if and only if its $\mathbf{s}$-leading matrix $\mathbf{L}$ computed at Step **1** is invertible. Thus, Step **1** correctly tests the property in Item (i) of Theorem 2.1. It uses at most $C(m,m)$ operations in $\mathbb{K}$. Furthermore, Step **2** correctly tests the first part of Item (iv) of Theorem 2.1 and uses at most $C(m, m+n)$ operations.

Step **3** performs a false-biased Monte Carlo verification of Item (ii) of Theorem 2.1. Indeed, since $\mathbf{P}$ is $\mathbf{s}$-reduced (otherwise the algorithm would have exited at Step **1**), we know from [16, Sec. 6.3.2] that $\deg(\det(\mathbf{P})) = \Delta = |\text{rdeg}_{\mathbf{s}}(\mathbf{P})| - |\mathbf{s}|$. Thus, $\det(\mathbf{P})$ is a nonzero monomial if and only if $\det(\mathbf{P}) = \det(\mathbf{P}(1))X^\Delta$. Step **3** tests the latter equality by evaluation at a random point α. The algorithm only returns *False* if $\det(\mathbf{P}(\alpha)) \neq \det(\mathbf{P}(1))\alpha^\Delta$, in which case $\det(\mathbf{P})$ is indeed not a nonzero monomial. Furthermore, if we have $\det(\mathbf{P}) \neq \det(\mathbf{P}(1))X^\Delta$, then the probability that the algorithm fails to detect this, meaning that $\det(\mathbf{P}(\alpha)) = \det(\mathbf{P}(1))\alpha^\Delta$, is at most $\frac{\Delta}{\#S}$. Since $\Delta \leq D$ according to [27, Thm. 4.1], this is also at most $\frac{D}{\#S} < \frac{D+1}{\#S}$.

The evaluations $\mathbf{P}(\alpha)$ and $\mathbf{P}(1)$ are computed using respectively at most $2(\text{Size}(\mathbf{P}) - m^2)$ operations and at most $\text{Size}(\mathbf{P}) - m^2$ additions. Then, computing the two determinants $\det(\mathbf{P}(\alpha))$ and $\det(\mathbf{P}(1))$ uses at most $2C(m,m) + 2m$ operations. Finally, computing $\det(\mathbf{P}(1))\alpha^\Delta$ uses at most $2\log_2(\Delta) + 1 \leq 2\log_2(D) + 1$ operations.

Summing the cost bounds for the first three steps gives

$$\begin{aligned} &3(\text{Size}(\mathbf{P}) - m^2) + 3C(m,m) + C(m, m+n) + 2m + 2\log_2(D) + 1 \\ &\leq 3\text{Size}(\mathbf{P}) + 3C(m,m) + C(m, m+n) + 2\log_2(D). \qquad (2) \end{aligned}$$

Step **4** tests the identity $\mathbf{PF} = \mathbf{CX^d} \bmod \mathbf{X^t}$, which corresponds to both Item (iii) of Theorem 2.1 and the second part of Item (iv). Proposition 3.2 ensures that:

- If the call to VerifTruncMatProd returns *False*, we have $\mathbf{PF} \neq \mathbf{CX^d} \bmod \mathbf{X^t}$, and Algorithm 1 correctly returns *False*.
- If $\mathbf{PF} \neq \mathbf{CX^d} \bmod \mathbf{X^t}$ holds, the probability that Algorithm 1 fails to detect this (that is, the call at Step **4** returns *True*) is less than $\frac{\max(\mathbf{d})+1}{\#S}$.

A cost bound for Step **4** is given in Proposition 3.2, with a minor improvement for the present case given in Remark 3.3. Summing it with the bound in Eq. (2) gives a cost bound for Algorithm 1, which is bounded from above by that in the proposition.

Thanks to Theorem 2.1, the above considerations show that when the algorithm returns *False*, then $\mathbf{P}$ is indeed not an $\mathbf{s}$-minimal basis of $\mathcal{A}_{\mathbf{d}}(\mathbf{F})$. On the other hand, if $\mathbf{P}$ is not an $\mathbf{s}$-minimal basis of $\mathcal{A}_{\mathbf{d}}(\mathbf{F})$, the algorithm returns *True* if and only if one of the probabilistic verifications in Steps **3** and **4** take the wrong decision. According to the probabilities given above, this may happen with probability less than $\max(\frac{D+1}{\#S}, \frac{\max(\mathbf{d})+1}{\#S}) = \frac{D+1}{\#S}$. □

3 VERIFYING A TRUNCATED PRODUCT

In this section, we focus on the verification of truncated products of polynomial matrices, and we give the corresponding algorithm VerifTruncMatProd used in Algorithm 1.

Given a truncation order $\mathbf{t}$ and polynomial matrices $\mathbf{P}, \mathbf{F}, \mathbf{G}$, our goal is to verify that $\mathbf{PF} = \mathbf{G} \bmod \mathbf{X^t}$ holds with good probability. Without loss of generality, we assume that the columns of $\mathbf{F}$ and $\mathbf{G}$ are already truncated with respect to the order $\mathbf{t}$, that is, $\text{cdeg}(\mathbf{F}) < \mathbf{t}$

and $\operatorname{cdeg}(\mathbf{G}) < \mathbf{t}$. Similarly, we assume that $\mathbf{P}$ is truncated with respect to $\delta = \max(\mathbf{t})$, that is, $\deg(\mathbf{P}) < \delta$.

Problem 2: TRUNCATED MATRIX PRODUCT VERIFICATION
Input:
- truncation order $\mathbf{t} \in \mathbb{Z}^n_{>0}$,
- matrix $\mathbf{P} \in \mathbb{K}[X]^{m\times m}$ with $\deg(\mathbf{P}) < \max(\mathbf{t})$,
- matrix $\mathbf{F} \in \mathbb{K}[X]^{m\times n}$ with $\operatorname{cdeg}(\mathbf{F}) < \mathbf{t}$,
- matrix $\mathbf{G} \in \mathbb{K}[X]^{m\times n}$ with $\operatorname{cdeg}(\mathbf{G}) < \mathbf{t}$.

Output: True if $\mathbf{PF} = \mathbf{G} \bmod \mathbf{X^t}$, otherwise *False*.

Obviously, our aim is to obtain a verification algorithm which has a significantly better cost than the straightforward approach which computes the truncated product $\mathbf{PF} \bmod \mathbf{X^t}$ and compares it with the matrix $\mathbf{G}$. To take an example: if we have $n \in O(m)$ as well as $|\operatorname{rdeg}(\mathbf{P})| \in O(|\mathbf{t}|)$ or $|\operatorname{cdeg}(\mathbf{P})| \in O(|\mathbf{t}|)$, as commonly happens in approximant basis computations, then this truncated product $\mathbf{PF} \bmod \mathbf{X^t}$ can be computed using $O\tilde{~}(m^{\omega-1}|\mathbf{t}|)$ operations in $\mathbb{K}$.

For verifying the non-truncated product $\mathbf{PF} = \mathbf{G}$, the classical approach would be to use evaluation at a random point, following ideas from [5, 25, 32]. However, evaluation does not behave well with regards to truncation. A similar issue was tackled in [13] for the verification of the middle product and the short products of univariate polynomials. The algorithm of [13] can be adapted to work with polynomial matrices by writing them as univariate polynomials with matrix coefficents; for example, $\mathbf{P}$ is a polynomial $\mathbf{P} = \sum_{0\le i<\delta} \mathbf{P}_i X^i$ with coefficients $\mathbf{P}_i \in \mathbb{K}^{m\times m}$. While this leads to a verification of $\mathbf{PF} = \mathbf{G} \bmod \mathbf{X^t}$ with a good probability of success, it has a cost which is close to that of computing $\mathbf{PF} \bmod \mathbf{X^t}$.

To lower down the cost, we will combine the evaluation of truncated products from [13] with Freivalds' technique [11]. The latter consists in left-multiplying the matrices by some random vector $\mathbf{u} \in \mathbb{K}^{1\times m}$, and rather checking whether $\mathbf{uPF} = \mathbf{uG} \bmod \mathbf{X^t}$; this effectively reduces the row dimension of the manipulated matrices, leading to faster computations. Furthermore, this does not harm the probability of success of the verification, as we detail now.

In what follows, given a matrix $\mathbf{A} \in \mathbb{K}[X]^{m\times n}$ and an order $\mathbf{t} \in \mathbb{Z}^n_{>0}$, we write $\mathbf{A} \operatorname{rem} \mathbf{X^t}$ for the (unique) matrix $\mathbf{B} \in \mathbb{K}[X]^{m\times n}$ such that $\mathbf{B} = \mathbf{A} \bmod \mathbf{X^t}$ and $\operatorname{cdeg}(\mathbf{B}) < \mathbf{t}$. For simplicity, we will often write $\mathbf{A}_1\mathbf{A}_2 \operatorname{rem} \mathbf{X^t}$ to actually mean $(\mathbf{A}_1\mathbf{A}_2) \operatorname{rem} \mathbf{X^t}$.

LEMMA 3.1. *Let S be a finite subset of $\mathbb{K}$. Let $\mathbf{u} \in \mathbb{K}^{1\times m}$ with entries chosen uniformly and independently at random from S, and let $\alpha \in \mathbb{K}$ be chosen uniformly at random from S. Assuming $\mathbf{PF} \neq \mathbf{G} \bmod \mathbf{X^t}$, the probability that $(\mathbf{uPF} \operatorname{rem} \mathbf{X^t})(\alpha) = \mathbf{uG}(\alpha)$ is less than $\frac{\max(\mathbf{t})}{\#S}$.*

PROOF. Let $\mathbf{A} = (\mathbf{PF} - \mathbf{G}) \operatorname{rem} \mathbf{X^t}$. By assumption, there exists a pair (i, j) such that the entry (i, j) of $\mathbf{A}$ is nonzero. Since this entry is a polynomial in $\mathbb{K}[X]$ of degree less than $\delta = \max(\mathbf{t})$, the probability that α is a root of this entry is at most $\frac{\delta-1}{\#S}$. As a consequence, we have $\mathbf{A}(\alpha) \neq \mathbf{0} \in \mathbb{K}^{m\times n}$ with probability at least $1-\frac{\delta-1}{\#S}$. In this case, $\mathbf{uA}(\alpha) = \mathbf{0}$ occurs with probability at most $\frac{1}{\#S}$ (see [22, Sec. 7.1]). Thus, altogether the probability that $\mathbf{uA}(\alpha) = \mathbf{0}$ is bounded from above by $\frac{\delta-1}{\#S} + \left(1 - \frac{\delta-1}{\#S}\right)\frac{1}{\#S} < \frac{\delta}{\#S}$, which concludes the proof. □

We deduce an approach to verify the truncated product: compute $\mathbf{uA}(\alpha) = ((\mathbf{uPF} - \mathbf{uG}) \operatorname{rem} \mathbf{X^t})(\alpha)$ and check whether it is zero or nonzero. The remaining difficulty is to compute $\mathbf{uA}(\alpha)$ efficiently: we will see that this can be done in $O(\operatorname{Size}(\mathbf{P}) + m|\mathbf{t}|)$ operations.

For this, we use a strategy similar to that in [13, Lem. 4.1] and essentially based on the following formula for the truncated product. Consider a positive integer $t \le \delta$ and a vector $\mathbf{f} \in \mathbb{K}[X]^{m\times 1}$ of degree less than t; one may think of $\mathbf{f}$ as a column $\mathbf{F}_{*,j}$ of $\mathbf{F}$ and of t as the corresponding order t_j. Writing $\mathbf{f} = \sum_{0\le k<t} \mathbf{f}_k X^k$ with $\mathbf{f}_k \in \mathbb{K}^{m\times 1}$ and $\mathbf{uP} = \sum_{0\le k<\delta} \mathbf{p}_k X^k$ with $\mathbf{p}_k \in \mathbb{K}^{1\times m}$, we have

$$\mathbf{uPf} \operatorname{rem} X^t = \sum_{k=0}^{t-1}\left(\sum_{i=0}^{t-1-k} \mathbf{p}_i X^i\right)\mathbf{f}_k X^k = X^{t-1}\sum_{k=0}^{t-1}\left(\sum_{i=0}^{t-1-k} \mathbf{p}_{t-1-k-i} X^{-i}\right)\mathbf{f}_k.$$

Thus, the evaluation can be expressed as

$$(\mathbf{uPf} \operatorname{rem} X^t)(\alpha) = \alpha^{t-1}\sum_{k=0}^{t-1} \mathbf{c}_{t-1-k}\mathbf{f}_k, \qquad (3)$$

where we define, for $0 \le k < \delta$,

$$\mathbf{c}_k = (\mathbf{uP} \operatorname{rem} X^{k+1})(\alpha^{-1}) = \sum_{i=0}^{k} \mathbf{p}_{k-i}\alpha^{-i} \in \mathbb{K}^{1\times m}. \qquad (4)$$

These identities give an algorithm to compute the truncated product evaluation $(\mathbf{uPf} \operatorname{rem} X^t)(\alpha)$, which we sketch as follows:
- apply Horner's method to the reversal of $\mathbf{uP} \operatorname{rem} X^t$ at the point α^{-1}, storing the intermediate results which are exactly the t vectors $\mathbf{c}_0, \ldots, \mathbf{c}_{t-1}$;
- compute the scalar products $\lambda_k = \mathbf{c}_{t-1-k}\mathbf{f}_k$ for $0 \le k < t$;
- compute α^{t-1} and then $\alpha^{t-1}\sum_{0\le k<t}\lambda_k$.

The last step gives the desired evaluation according to Eq. (3). In our case, this will be applied to each column $\mathbf{f} = \mathbf{F}_{*,j}$ for $1 \le j \le n$. We will perform the first item only once to obtain the δ vectors $\mathbf{c}_0, \ldots, \mathbf{c}_{\delta-1}$, since they do not depend on $\mathbf{f}$.

PROPOSITION 3.2. *Algorithm 2 uses at most*

$$2\operatorname{Size}(\mathbf{P}) + (6m+1)|\mathbf{t}| + 2n\log_2(\delta) \in O(\operatorname{Size}(\mathbf{P}) + m|\mathbf{t}| + n\log_2(\delta))$$

operations in $\mathbb{K}$, where $\delta \le |\mathbf{t}|$ is the largest of the truncation orders. It is a false-biased Monte Carlo algorithm. If $\mathbf{PF} \neq \mathbf{G} \bmod \mathbf{X^t}$, the probability that it outputs True *is less than $\frac{\delta}{\#S}$, where S is the finite subset of $\mathbb{K}$ from which random field elements are drawn.*

PROOF. The discussion above shows that this algorithm correctly computes $[e_j]_{1\le j\le n} = \mathbf{uG}(\alpha)$ and $[e'_j]_{1\le j\le n} = (\mathbf{uPF} \operatorname{rem} \mathbf{X^t})(\alpha)$. If it returns *False*, then there is at least one j for which $e'_j \neq e_j$, thus we must have $\mathbf{uPF} \operatorname{rem} \mathbf{X^t} \neq \mathbf{uG}$ and therefore $\mathbf{PF} \neq \mathbf{G} \bmod \mathbf{X^t}$. Besides, the algorithm correctly returns *True* if $\mathbf{PF} = \mathbf{G} \bmod \mathbf{X^t}$.

The analysis of the probability of failure (the algorithm returns *True* while $\mathbf{PF} \neq \mathbf{G} \bmod \mathbf{X^t}$) is a direct consequence of Lemma 3.1.

Step **2** uses at most $2\operatorname{Size}(\mathbf{P}) + (2m-1)|\mathbf{t}|$ operations in $\mathbb{K}$. The Horner evaluations at Steps **3** and **4** require at most $2(|\mathbf{t}| - n)$ and at most $1 + 2m(\delta - 1)$ operations, respectively. Now, we consider the j-th iteration of the loop at Step **5**. The scalar products $(\lambda_k)_{0\le k<t_j}$ are computed using at most $(2m-1)t_j$ operations; the sum and multiplication by α^{t_j-1} giving e'_j use at most $t_j + 2\log_2(t_j - 1)$ operations. Summing over $1 \le j \le n$, this gives a total of at most

Algorithm 2: VerifTruncMatProd
Input:
- truncation order $\mathbf{t} = (t_1, \dots, t_n) \in \mathbb{Z}^n_{>0}$,
- matrix $\mathbf{P} \in \mathbb{K}[X]^{m \times m}$ such that $\deg(\mathbf{P}) < \delta = \max(\mathbf{t})$,
- matrix $\mathbf{F} = [f_{ij}] \in \mathbb{K}[X]^{m \times n}$ with $\mathrm{cdeg}(\mathbf{F}) < \mathbf{t}$,
- matrix $\mathbf{G} \in \mathbb{K}[X]^{m \times n}$ with $\mathrm{cdeg}(\mathbf{G}) < \mathbf{t}$.

Output: True if $\mathbf{PF} = \mathbf{G} \bmod \mathbf{X^t}$, otherwise *True* or *False*.

1. `/* Main objects for verification */`
   $S \leftarrow$ a finite subset of $\mathbb{K}$
   $\alpha \leftarrow$ element of $\mathbb{K}$ chosen uniformly at random from S
   $\mathbf{u} \leftarrow$ vector in $\mathbb{K}^{1 \times m}$ with entries chosen uniformly and independently at random from S
2. `/* Freivalds: row dimension becomes 1 */`
   $\mathbf{p} \leftarrow \mathbf{uP}$ `//` in $\mathbb{K}[X]^{1 \times m}$, degree $< \delta$
   $\mathbf{g} \leftarrow \mathbf{uG}$ `//` in $\mathbb{K}[X]^{1 \times n}$, $\mathrm{cdeg}(\mathbf{g}) < \mathbf{t}$
3. `/* Evaluation of right-hand side:` $\mathbf{uG}(\alpha)$ `*/`
   write $\mathbf{g} = [g_1 \; \cdots \; g_n]$ with $g_j \in \mathbb{K}[X]$ of degree $< t_j$
   For j from 1 *to n:*
   $e_j \leftarrow g_j(\alpha)$
4. `/* Truncated evaluations` $\mathbf{c}_0, \dots, \mathbf{c}_{\delta-1}$ `*/`
   write $\mathbf{p} = \sum_{0 \le k < \delta} \mathbf{p}_k X^k$ with $\mathbf{p}_k \in \mathbb{K}^{1 \times m}$
   $\mathbf{c}_0 \leftarrow \mathbf{p}_0$
   For k from 1 *to* $\delta - 1$:
   $\mathbf{c}_k \leftarrow \mathbf{p}_k + \alpha^{-1} \mathbf{c}_{k-1}$
5. `/* Evaluation of left-hand side:` $(\mathbf{uPF} \operatorname{rem} \mathbf{X^t})(\alpha)$ `*/`
   For j from 1 *to n:* `// process column` $\mathbf{F}_{*,j}$
   write $\mathbf{F}_{*,j} = \sum_{0 \le k < t_j} \mathbf{f}_k X^k$
   $(\lambda_k)_{0 \le k < t_j} \leftarrow (\mathbf{c}_{t_j - 1 - k} \cdot \mathbf{f}_k)_{0 \le k < t_j}$
   $e'_j \leftarrow \alpha^{t_j - 1} \sum_{0 \le k < t_j} \lambda_k$
6. *If* $e_j \neq e'_j$ for some $j \in \{1, \dots, n\}$ *then return False*
   Else return True

$2m|\mathbf{t}| + 2\log_2((t_1 - 1) \cdots (t_n - 1))$ operations for Step **5**. Finally, Step **6** uses at most n comparisons of two field elements. Summing these bounds for each step yields the cost bound

$$2\mathrm{Size}(\mathbf{P}) + (4m+1)|\mathbf{t}| + 2m(\delta - 1) - n + 2\log_2((t_1 - 1) \cdots (t_n - 1)), \quad (5)$$

which is at most the quantity in the proposition. □

In the certification of approximant bases, we want to verify a truncated matrix product in the specific case where each entry in the column j of $\mathbf{G}$ is simply zero or a monomial of degree $t_j - 1$. Then, a slightly better cost bound can be given, as follows.

Remark 3.3. Assume that $\mathbf{t} = (d_1 + 1, \dots, d_n + 1)$ and $\mathbf{G} = \mathbf{CX^d}$, for some $\mathbf{d} = (d_1, \dots, d_n) \in \mathbb{Z}^n_{>0}$ and some constant $\mathbf{C} \in \mathbb{K}^{m \times n}$. Then, the computation of $\mathbf{uG}$ at Step **2** uses at most $(2m - 1)n$ operations in $\mathbb{K}$. Besides, since the polynomial g_j at Step **3** is either zero or a monomial of degree d_j, its evaluation e_j is computed using at most $2\log_2(d_j) + 1$ operations via repeated squaring [12, Sec. 4.3]. Thus, Step **3** uses at most $2\log_2(d_1 \cdots d_n) + n$ operations. As a result, defining $D = |\mathbf{d}|$, the cost bound in Eq. (5) is lowered to

$$\begin{aligned} &2\mathrm{Size}(\mathbf{P}) + 2m(|\mathbf{t}| + \delta - 1 + n) + n + 4\log_2(d_1 \cdots d_n) + 1 \\ &= 2\mathrm{Size}(\mathbf{P}) + 2m(D + \max(\mathbf{d}) + 2n) + n + 4\log_2(d_1 \cdots d_n) + 1. \quad □ \end{aligned}$$

4 COMPUTING THE CERTIFICATE

4.1 Context

In this section, we show how to efficiently compute the certificate $\mathbf{C} \in \mathbb{K}^{m \times n}$, which is the term of degree 0 of the product $\mathbf{PFX^{-d}}$, whose entries are Laurent polynomials (they are in $\mathbb{K}[X]$ if and only if the rows of $\mathbf{P}$ are approximants). Equivalently, the column $\mathbf{C}_{*,j}$ is the term of degree d_j of the column j of $\mathbf{PF}$, where $\mathbf{d} = (d_1, \dots, d_n)$.

We recall the notation $D = d_1 + \cdots + d_n$. Note that, without loss of generality, we may truncate $\mathbf{P}$ so that $\deg(\mathbf{P}) \le \max(\mathbf{d})$.

For example, suppose that the dimensions and the order are balanced: $m = n$ and $\mathbf{d} = (D/m, \dots, D/m)$. Then, $\mathbf{C} \in \mathbb{K}^{m \times m}$ is the coefficient of degree D/m of the product $\mathbf{PF}$, where $\mathbf{P}$ and $\mathbf{F}$ are $m \times m$ matrices over $\mathbb{K}[X]$. Thus $\mathbf{C}$ can be computed using D/m multiplications of $m \times m$ matrices over $\mathbb{K}$, at a total cost $O(m^{\omega-1}D)$.

Going back to the general case, the main obstacle to obtain similar efficiency is that both the degrees in $\mathbf{P}$ and the order $\mathbf{d}$ (hence the degrees in $\mathbf{F}$) may be unbalanced. Still, we have $\mathrm{cdeg}(\mathbf{F}) < \mathbf{d}$ with sum $|\mathbf{d}| = D$ and, as stated in the introduction, we may assume that either $|\mathrm{rdeg}(\mathbf{P})| \in O(D)$ or $|\mathrm{cdeg}(\mathbf{P})| \le D$ holds. In this context, both $\mathbf{F}$ and $\mathbf{P}$ are represented by $O(mD)$ field elements.

We will generalize the method above for the balanced case to this general situation with unbalanced degrees, achieving the same cost $O(m^{\omega-1}D)$. As a result, computing the certificate $\mathbf{C}$ has negligible cost compared to the fastest known approximant basis algorithms. Indeed, the latter are in $O\tilde{~}(m^{\omega-1}D)$, involving logarithmic factors in D coming both from polynomial arithmetic and from divide and conquer approaches. We refer the reader to [28, Thm. 5.3] and [15, Thm. 1.4] for more details on these logarithmic factors.

We first remark that $\mathbf{C}$ can be computed by naive linear algebra using $O(m^2D)$ operations. Indeed, writing $\mathrm{rdeg}(\mathbf{P}) = (r_1, \dots, r_m)$, we have the following explicit formula for each entry in $\mathbf{C}$:

$$\mathbf{C}_{i,j} = \sum_{k=1}^{\min(r_i, d_j)} \mathbf{P}_{i,*,k} \, \mathbf{F}_{*,j,d_j - k},$$

where $\mathbf{P}_{i,*,k}$ is the coefficient of degree k of the row i of $\mathbf{P}$ and similar notation is used for $\mathbf{F}$. Then, since $\min(r_i, d_j) \le d_j$, the column $\mathbf{C}_{*,j}$ is computed via md_j scalar products of length m, using $O(m^2 d_j)$ operations. Summing this for $1 \le j \le n$ yields $O(m^2 D)$.

This approach considers each column of $\mathbf{F}$ separately, allowing us to truncate at precision $d_j + 1$ for the column j and thus to rule out the issue of the unbalancedness of the degrees in $\mathbf{P}$. However, this also prevents us from incorporating fast matrix multiplication. In our efficient method, we avoid considering columns or rows separately, while still managing to handle the unbalancedness of the degrees in both $\mathbf{P}$ and $\mathbf{F}$. Our approach bears similarities with algorithms for polynomial matrix multiplication with unbalanced degrees (see for example [31, Sec. 3.6]).

4.2 Sparsity and degree structure

Below, we first detail our method assuming $|\mathrm{rdeg}(\mathbf{P})| \in O(D)$*; until further notice,* $\gamma \ge 1$ *is a real number such that* $|\mathrm{rdeg}(\mathbf{P})| \le \gamma D$.

To simplify the exposition, we start by replacing the tuple $\mathbf{d}$ by the uniform bound $d = \max(\mathbf{d})$. To achieve this, we consider the matrix $\mathbf{H} = \mathbf{FX}^{d - \mathbf{d}}$, where $d - \mathbf{d}$ stands for $(d - d_1, \dots, d - d_n)$: then, $\mathbf{C}$ is the coefficient of degree d in $\mathbf{PH}$.

Since $\text{cdeg}(\mathbf{F}) < \mathbf{d}$, we have $\deg(\mathbf{H}) < d$. The fact that $\mathbf{F}$ has column degree less than $\mathbf{d}$ translates into the fact that $\mathbf{H}$ has column valuation at least $d - \mathbf{d}$ (and degree less than d); like $\mathbf{F}$, this matrix $\mathbf{H}$ is represented by mD field elements. Recalling the assumption $\deg(\mathbf{P}) \leq d$, we can write $\mathbf{P} = \sum_{k=0}^{d} \mathbf{P}_k X^k$ and $\mathbf{H} = \sum_{k=0}^{d} \mathbf{H}_k X^k$, where $\mathbf{P}_k \in \mathbb{K}^{m\times m}$ and $\mathbf{H}_k \in \mathbb{K}^{m\times n}$ for all k (note that $\mathbf{H}_d = \mathbf{0}$). Then, our goal is to compute the matrix

$$\mathbf{C} = \sum_{k=1}^{d} \mathbf{P}_k \mathbf{H}_{d-k}. \tag{6}$$

The essential remark to design an efficient algorithm is that each matrix $\mathbf{P}_k$ has only few nonzero rows when k becomes large, and each matrix $\mathbf{H}_{d-k}$ has only few nonzero columns when k becomes large. To state this formally, we define two sets of indices, for the rows of degree at least k in $\mathbf{P}$ and for the orders at least k in $\mathbf{d}$:

$$\mathcal{R}_k = \{i \in \{1,\ldots,m\} \mid \text{rdeg}(\mathbf{P}_{i,*}) \geq k\},$$
$$\mathcal{D}_k = \{j \in \{1,\ldots,n\} \mid d_j \geq k\}.$$

The latter corresponds to the set of indices of columns of $\mathbf{F}$ which are allowed to have degree $\geq k-1$ or, equivalently, to the set of indices of columns of $\mathbf{H}$ which are allowed to have valuation $\leq d-k$.

Lemma 4.1. *For a given $k \in \{1,\ldots,d\}$: if $i \notin \mathcal{R}_k$, then the row i of $\mathbf{P}_k$ is zero; if $j \notin \mathcal{D}_k$, then the column j of $\mathbf{H}_{d-k}$ is zero. In particular, $\mathbf{P}_k$ has at most $\#\mathcal{R}_k \leq \gamma D/k$ nonzero rows and $\mathbf{H}_{d-k}$ has at most $\#\mathcal{D}_k \leq D/k$ nonzero columns.*

Proof. The row i of $\mathbf{P}_k$ is the coefficient of degree k of the row i of $\mathbf{P}$. If it is nonzero, we must have $i \in \mathcal{R}_k$. Similarly, the column j of $\mathbf{H}_{d-k}$ is the coefficient of degree $d-k$ of the column j of $\mathbf{H} = \mathbf{F}\mathbf{X}^{d-\mathbf{d}}$. If it is nonzero, we must have $d-k \geq d-d_j$, hence $k \in \mathcal{D}_k$.

The upper bounds on the cardinalities of $\mathcal{R}_k$ and $\mathcal{D}_k$ follow by construction of these sets: we have $k \cdot \#\mathcal{D}_k \leq |\mathbf{d}| = D$, and also $k \cdot \#\mathcal{R}_k \leq |\text{rdeg}(\mathbf{P})|$ with $|\text{rdeg}(\mathbf{P})| \leq \gamma D$ by assumption. □

4.3 Algorithm and cost bound

Following Lemma 4.1, in the computation of $\mathbf{C}$ based on Eq. (6) we may restrict our view of $\mathbf{P}_k$ to its submatrix with rows in $\mathcal{R}_k$, and our view of $\mathbf{H}_k$ to its submatrix with columns in $\mathcal{D}_k$. For example, if $k > \gamma D/m$ and $k > D/n$, the matrices in the product $\mathbf{P}_k\mathbf{H}_k$ have dimensions at most $\lfloor \gamma D/k \rfloor \times m$ and $m \times \lfloor D/k \rfloor$. These remarks on the structure and sparsity of $\mathbf{P}_k$ and $\mathbf{H}_k$ lead us to Algorithm 3.

Proposition 4.2. *Algorithm 3 is correct. Assuming that $m \in O(D)$ and $|\text{rdeg}(\mathbf{P})| \in O(D)$, where $D = |\mathbf{d}|$, it uses $O(m^{\omega-1}D)$ operations in $\mathbb{K}$ if $n \leq m$ and $O(m^{\omega-1}D\log(n/m))$ operations in $\mathbb{K}$ if $n > m$.*

Proof. For the correctness, note that for all j the coefficient of degree $d_j - k$ of $\mathbf{F}_{*,j}$ is the coefficient of degree $d-k$ of $\mathbf{H}_{*,j}$. Thus, using notation from Section 4.2, the matrix $\mathbf{B}$ at the iteration k of the loop is exactly the submatrix of $\mathbf{H}_{d-k}$ of its columns in $\mathcal{D}_k$. Therefore, the loop in Algorithm 3 simply applies Eq. (6), discarding from $\mathbf{P}_k$ and $\mathbf{F}_{d-k}$ rows and columns which are known to be zero.

Now, we estimate the cost of updating $\mathbf{C}$ at each iteration of the loop. Precisely, the main task is to compute $\mathbf{AB}$, where the matrices $\mathbf{A}$ and $\mathbf{B}$ have dimensions $\#\mathcal{R} \times m$ and $m \times t$. Then, adding this product to the submatrix $\mathbf{C}_{\mathcal{R},\mathcal{D}}$ only costs $\#\mathcal{R} \cdot t$ additions in $\mathbb{K}$.

Algorithm 3: CertificateComp
Input:
- order $\mathbf{d} \in \mathbb{Z}_{>0}^n$,
- matrix $\mathbf{F} \in \mathbb{K}[X]^{m\times n}$ such that $\text{cdeg}(\mathbf{F}) < \mathbf{d}$,
- matrix $\mathbf{P} \in \mathbb{K}[X]^{m\times m}$ such that $\deg(\mathbf{P}) \leq \max(\mathbf{d})$.

Output: the coefficient $\mathbf{C} \in \mathbb{K}^{m\times n}$ of degree 0 of $\mathbf{P}\mathbf{F}\mathbf{X}^{-\mathbf{d}}$.

1. $(r_1,\ldots,r_m) \leftarrow \text{rdeg}(\mathbf{P})$
2. $\mathbf{C} \leftarrow \mathbf{0} \in \mathbb{K}^{m\times n}$
3. *For k from 1 to* $\max(\mathbf{d})$:
   $\mathcal{R} \leftarrow \{i \in \{1,\ldots,m\} \mid r_i \geq k\}$
   $\mathcal{D} = \{c_1,\ldots,c_t\} \leftarrow \{j \in \{1,\ldots,n\} \mid d_j \geq k\}$
   $\mathbf{A} \in \mathbb{K}^{\#\mathcal{R}\times m} \leftarrow$ coefficient of degree k of $\mathbf{P}_{\mathcal{R},*}$
   $\mathbf{B} \in \mathbb{K}^{m\times t} \leftarrow$ for all $1 \leq j \leq t$, $\mathbf{B}_{*,j}$ is the coefficient of degree $d_j - k$ of $\mathbf{F}_{*,c_j}$
   $\mathbf{C}_{\mathcal{R},\mathcal{D}} \leftarrow \mathbf{C}_{\mathcal{R},\mathcal{D}} + \mathbf{AB}$
4. *Return* $\mathbf{C}$

Consider $\gamma = \lceil |\text{rdeg}(\mathbf{P})|/D \rceil \geq 1$ (indeed, if $|\text{rdeg}(\mathbf{P})| = 0$, then $\mathbf{P}$ is constant and $\mathbf{C} = \mathbf{0}$). By Lemma 4.1, at the iteration k we have $\#\mathcal{R} \leq \min(m, \gamma D/k)$ and $t = \#\mathcal{D} \leq \min(n, D/k)$. We separate the cases $n \leq m$ and $n > m$, and we use the bound $\lceil \gamma D/m \rceil \in O(D/m)$, which comes from our assumptions $m \in O(D)$ and $\gamma \in O(1)$.

First, suppose $n \leq m$. At the iterations $k < \lceil \gamma D/m \rceil$ the matrices $\mathbf{A}$ and $\mathbf{B}$ both have dimensions at most $m \times m$, hence their product can be computed in $O(m^\omega)$ operations. These iterations have a total cost of $O(m^\omega \lceil \gamma D/m \rceil) \subseteq O(m^{\omega-1}D)$. At the iterations $k \geq \lceil \gamma D/m \rceil$, $\mathbf{A}$ and $\mathbf{B}$ have dimensions at most $(\gamma D/k) \times m$ and $m \times (D/k)$, with $D/k \leq \gamma D/k \leq m$; computing their product costs $O((D/k)^{\omega-1}m) \subseteq O(mD^{\omega-1}k^{1-\omega})$. Thus, the total cost for these iterations is in

$$O\left(mD^{\omega-1} \sum_{k=\lceil \gamma D/m \rceil}^{\max(\mathbf{d})} k^{1-\omega}\right)$$
$$\subseteq O\left(mD^{\omega-1}(\lceil \gamma D/m \rceil)^{2-\omega} \textstyle\sum_{i=0}^{+\infty} 2^{i(2-\omega)}\right) \subseteq O(m^{\omega-1}D).$$

For the first inclusion, we apply Lemma 4.3 with $\mu = \lceil \gamma D/m \rceil$, $\nu = \max(\mathbf{d})$, and $\theta = 1 - \omega$. For the second, the sum is finite since $2^{2-\omega} < 1$. Hence Algorithm 3 costs $O(m^{\omega-1}D)$ in the case $n \leq m$.

Now, suppose $n > m$. At the iterations $k < \lceil D/n \rceil$, $\mathbf{A}$ and $\mathbf{B}$ have dimensions at most $m \times m$ and $m \times n$, hence their product can be computed in $O(m^{\omega-1}n)$. The total cost is in $O(m^{\omega-1}D)$ since there are $\lceil D/n \rceil - 1 < D/n$ iterations (with $n \leq D$ by definition). For the iterations $k \geq \lceil \gamma D/m \rceil$, we repeat the analysis done above for the same values of k: these iterations cost $O(m^{\omega-1}D)$ here as well.

Finally, for the iterations $\lceil D/n \rceil \leq k < \lceil \gamma D/m \rceil$, $\mathbf{A}$ and $\mathbf{B}$ have dimensions at most $m \times m$ and $m \times (D/k)$, with $D/k \leq n$. Thus the product $\mathbf{AB}$ can be computed in $O(m^\omega + m^{\omega-1}D/k)$ operations. Summing the term m^ω over these $O(D/m)$ iterations yields the cost $O(m^{\omega-1}D)$. Summing the other term gives the cost $O(m^{\omega-1}D\log(n/m))$ since, by the last claim of Lemma 4.3, we have

$$\sum_{k=\lceil D/n \rceil}^{\lceil \gamma D/m \rceil - 1} k^{-1} \leq 1 + \left\lfloor \log_2\left(\frac{\lceil \gamma D/m \rceil - 1}{\lceil D/n \rceil}\right)\right\rfloor \leq 1 + \log_2(\gamma n/m).$$

Adding the costs of the three considered sets of iterations, we obtain the announced cost for Algorithm 3 in the case $n > m$ as well. □

Lemma 4.3. *Given integers $0 < \mu < \nu$ and a real number $\theta \le 0$,*

$$\sum_{k=\mu}^{\nu} k^{\theta} \le \mu^{\theta+1} \sum_{i=0}^{\ell-1} 2^{i(\theta+1)}$$

holds, where $\ell = \lfloor \log_2(\nu/\mu) \rfloor + 1$. In particular, $\sum_{k=\mu}^{\nu} k^{-1} \le \ell$.

Proof. Note that ℓ is chosen such that $2^{\ell}\mu - 1 \ge \nu$. Then, the upper bound is obtained by splitting the sum as follows:

$$\sum_{k=\mu}^{\nu} k^{\theta} \le \sum_{i=0}^{\ell-1} \sum_{k=2^i\mu}^{2^{i+1}\mu-1} k^{\theta} \le \sum_{i=0}^{\ell-1} \sum_{k=2^i\mu}^{2^{i+1}\mu-1} (2^i\mu)^{\theta} = \sum_{i=0}^{\ell-1} (2^i\mu)^{\theta+1},$$

where the second inequality comes from the fact that $x \mapsto x^{\theta}$ is decreasing on the positive real numbers. □

Finally, we describe minor changes in Algorithm 3 to deal with the case of small average *column* degree $\mathrm{cdeg}(\mathbf{P}) \in O(D)$; precisely, we replace the assumption $|\mathrm{rdeg}(\mathbf{P})| \le \gamma D$ by $|\mathrm{cdeg}(\mathbf{P})| \le \gamma D$. Then, instead of the set $\mathcal{R}_k$ used above, we rather define

$$\mathcal{C}_k = \{j \in \{1, \ldots, m\} \mid \mathrm{cdeg}(\mathbf{P}_{*,j}) \ge k\}.$$

Then we have the following lemma, analogous to Lemma 4.1.

Lemma 4.4. *For $k \in \{1, \ldots, m\}$ and $j \notin \mathcal{C}_k$, the column j of $\mathbf{P}_k$ is zero. In particular, $\mathbf{P}_k$ has at most $\#\mathcal{C}_k \le \gamma D/k$ nonzero columns.*

Thus, we can modify Algorithm 3 to take into account the column degree of $\mathbf{P}$ instead of its row degree. This essentially amounts to redefining the matrices $\mathbf{A}$ and $\mathbf{B}$ in the loop as follows:

- $\mathbf{A} \in \mathbb{K}^{m \times \#\mathcal{C}_k}$ is the coefficient of degree k of $\mathbf{P}_{*,\mathcal{C}_k}$.
- $\mathbf{B} \in \mathbb{K}^{\#\mathcal{C}_k \times t}$ is such that for all $i \in \mathcal{C}_k$ and $1 \le j \le t$, $\mathbf{B}_{i,j}$ is the coefficient of degree $d_j - k$ of $\mathbf{F}_{i,c_j}$

These modifications have obviously no impact on the correctness. Furthermore, it is easily verified that the same cost bound holds since we obtain a similar matrix multiplication cost at each iteration.

5 PERSPECTIVES

As noted in the introduction, our certificate is almost optimal since we can verify it at a cost $O(mD + m^{\omega-1}(m+n))$ while the input size is mD. One should notice that the extra term $O(m^{\omega-1}(m+n))$ corresponds to certifying problems of linear algebra over $\mathbb{K}$, namely the rank and the determinant. These could actually be dealt with in $O(m(m+n))$ operations using interactive certificates built upon the results in [7, 9, 18], thus yielding an optimal certificate. Still, for practical applications, our simpler certification should already be significantly faster than the approximant basis computation, since the constants involved in the cost are small as we have observed in our estimates above. We plan to confirm this for the approximant bases implementations in the LinBox library.

Finally, our verification protocol needs $(m+2)\log_2(\#S)$ random bits, yielding a probability of failure less than $\frac{D+1}{\#S}$. The majority of these bits is required by Algorithm 2 when choosing m random elements for the vector $\mathbf{u}$. As proposed in [19], it may be worthwhile to pick a single random value ζ and to use $\mathbf{u} = [1 \ \zeta \ \cdots \ \zeta^{m-1}]$. In the case where $\max(\mathbf{d}) < D/2$, this choice would not affect the probability of failure while decreasing the number of random bits to $3\log_2(\#S)$. In particular, at the price of the same number of bits as we currently use in our algorithm, we could run our verification $(m+2)/3$ times and decrease the probability of failure to $(\frac{D+1}{\#S})^{\frac{m+2}{3}}$.

REFERENCES

[1] B. Beckermann and G. Labahn. 1994. A Uniform Approach for the Fast Computation of Matrix-Type Padé Approximants. *SIAM J. Matrix Anal. Appl.* 15, 3 (1994), 804–823.

[2] B. Beckermann and G. Labahn. 1997. Recursiveness in matrix rational interpolation problems. *J. Comput. Appl. Math.* 77, 1–2 (1997), 5–34.

[3] B. Beckermann, G. Labahn, and G. Villard. 1999. Shifted Normal Forms of Polynomial Matrices. In *ISSAC'99*. ACM, 189–196.

[4] D. Coppersmith and S. Winograd. 1990. Matrix multiplication via arithmetic progressions. *J. Symbolic Comput.* 9, 3 (1990), 251–280.

[5] R. A. DeMillo and R. J. Lipton. 1978. A Probabilistic Remark on Algebraic Program Testing. *Inform. Process. Lett.* 7, 4 (1978), 193–195.

[6] J.-G. Dumas, P. Giorgi, and C. Pernet. 2008. Dense Linear Algebra over Word-Size Prime Fields: The FFLAS and FFPACK Packages. *ACM Trans. Math. Softw.* 35, 3, Article 19 (2008), 42 pages.

[7] J.-G. Dumas and E. Kaltofen. 2014. Essentially Optimal Interactive Certificates in Linear Algebra. In *ISSAC'14*. ACM, 146–153.

[8] J-G. Dumas, E. Kaltofen, E. Thomé, and G. Villard. 2016. Linear Time Interactive Certificates for the Minimal Polynomial and the Determinant of a Sparse Matrix. In *ISSAC'16*. ACM, 199–206.

[9] J.-G. Dumas, D. Lucas, and C. Pernet. 2017. Certificates for Triangular Equivalence and Rank Profiles. In *ISSAC'17*. ACM, 133–140.

[10] Julius Farkas. 1902. Theorie der einfachen Ungleichungen. *J. Reine Angew. Math.* 124 (1902), 1–27. http://eudml.org/doc/149129

[11] R. Freivalds. 1979. Fast probabilistic algorithms. In *Mathematical Foundations of Computer Science*, Vol. 74. Springer Berlin Heidelberg, 57–69.

[12] J. von zur Gathen and J. Gerhard. 2013. *Modern Computer Algebra (third edition)*. Cambridge University Press.

[13] P. Giorgi. 2017. Certification of Polynomial Middle Product. (2017). Available at https://hal-lirmm.ccsd.cnrs.fr/lirmm-015384532 (accessed in May 2018).

[14] P. Giorgi, C.-P. Jeannerod, and G. Villard. 2003. On the complexity of polynomial matrix computations. In *ISSAC'03*. ACM, 135–142.

[15] C.-P. Jeannerod, V. Neiger, É. Schost, and G. Villard. 2016. Fast computation of minimal interpolation bases in Popov form for arbitrary shifts. In *ISSAC'16*. ACM, 295–302.

[16] T. Kailath. 1980. *Linear Systems*. Prentice-Hall.

[17] E. Kaltofen, B. Li, Z. Yang, and L. Zhi. 2012. Exact certification in global polynomial optimization via sums-of-squares of rational functions with rational coefficients. *J. Symbolic Comput.* 47, 1 (2012), 1–15.

[18] E. Kaltofen, M. Nehring, and B. D. Saunders. 2011. Quadratic-time Certificates in Linear Algebra. In *ISSAC'11*. ACM, 171–176.

[19] T. Kimbrel and R. K. Sinha. 1993. A probabilistic algorithm for verifying matrix products using $O(n^2)$ time and $\log_2(n) + O(1)$ random bits. *Inform. Process. Lett.* 45, 2 (1993), 107–110.

[20] T. Kleinjung, C. Diem, A. K. Lenstra, C. Priplata, and C. Stahlke. 2017. Computation of a 768-Bit Prime Field Discrete Logarithm. In *Eurocrypt 2017*. Springer International Publishing, 185–201.

[21] F. Le Gall. 2014. Powers of Tensors and Fast Matrix Multiplication. In *ISSAC'14*. ACM, 296–303.

[22] R. Motwani and P. Raghavan. 1995. *Randomized Algorithms*. Cambridge University Press, New York, NY, USA.

[23] T. Mulders and A. Storjohann. 2003. On lattice reduction for polynomial matrices. *J. Symbolic Comput.* 35 (2003), 377–401. Issue 4.

[24] V. Neiger. 2016. *Bases of relations in one or several variables: fast algorithms and applications*. Ph.D. Dissertation. École Normale Supérieure de Lyon.

[25] J. T. Schwartz. 1980. Fast Probabilistic Algorithms for Verification of Polynomial Identities. *J. ACM* 27, 4 (1980), 701–717.

[26] A. Storjohann. 2006. Notes on computing minimal approximant bases. In *Challenges in Symbolic Computation Software (Dagstuhl Seminar Proceedings)*.

[27] M. Van Barel and A. Bultheel. 1992. A general module theoretic framework for vector M-Padé and matrix rational interpolation. *Numer. Algorithms* 3 (1992), 451–462.

[28] W. Zhou and G. Labahn. 2012. Efficient Algorithms for Order Basis Computation. *J. Symbolic Comput.* 47, 7 (2012), 793–819.

[29] W. Zhou and G. Labahn. 2013. Computing Column Bases of Polynomial Matrices. In *ISSAC'13*. ACM, 379–386.

[30] W. Zhou and G. Labahn. 2014. Unimodular Completion of Polynomial Matrices. In *ISSAC'14*. ACM, 413–420.

[31] W. Zhou, G. Labahn, and A. Storjohann. 2012. Computing Minimal Nullspace Bases. In *ISSAC'12*. ACM, 366–373.

[32] R. Zippel. 1979. Probabilistic algorithms for sparse polynomials. In *EUROSAM'79 (LNCS)*, Vol. 72. Springer, 216–226.

Computing Free Distances of Idempotent Convolutional Codes*

José Gómez-Torrecillas
University of Granada
Granada, Spain
gomezj@ugr.es

F. J. Lobillo
University of Granada
Granada, Spain
jlobillo@ugr.es

Gabriel Navarro
University of Granada
Granada, Spain
gnavarro@ugr.es

ABSTRACT

We show that, for cyclic convolutional codes, it is possible to compute a sequence of positive integers, called cyclic column distances, which presents a more regular behavior than the classical column distances sequence. We then design an algorithm for the computation of the free distance based on the calculation of this cyclic column distances sequence.

CCS CONCEPTS

• **Mathematics of computing → Coding theory**; • **Computing methodologies** → *Algebraic algorithms*;

KEYWORDS

Cyclic convolutional code, Free distance, Brouwer-Zimmermann algorithm

ACM Reference Format:
José Gómez-Torrecillas, F. J. Lobillo, and Gabriel Navarro. 2018. Computing Free Distances of Idempotent Convolutional Codes. In *ISSAC '18: 2018 ACM International Symposium on Symbolic and Algebraic Computation, July 16–19, 2018, New York, NY, USA*. ACM, New York, NY, USA, 8 pages. https://doi.org/10.1145/3208976.3208985

1 INTRODUCTION

The free distance $\mathrm{d_{free}}$ of a convolutional code was introduced as a useful tool for sequential decoding [2], and it became one of its most relevant parameters ([14], [13]). Its computation is not, in general, an easy task. A method to calculate the free distance is based on the computation of terms of the sequences of column distances and row distances until they meet (see [13, Ch. 3]). More precisely, from a given basic generator matrix of the code, one computes sequences of positive integers $\{d_l^c\}_{l\geq 0}$ and $\{d_l^r\}_{l\geq 0}$ such that

$$d_l^c \leq d_{l+1}^c \leq \mathrm{d_{free}} \leq d_{l+1}^r \leq d_l^r$$

for all $l \geq 0$, and $\lim_{l\to\infty} d_l^c = \mathrm{d_{free}} = \lim_{l\to\infty} d_l^r$. Thus, there must be some index l such that $d_l^c = d_l^r = \mathrm{d_{free}}$. These column and row distance sequences seem to have few further regularities for a general convolutional code. In this paper we prove that, for convolutional codes endowed with suitable cyclic structures, it is possible to compute a sequence of positive integers $\{\delta_l^c\}_{l\geq 0}$ such that

$$\delta_l^c \leq \delta_{l+1}^c \leq \mathrm{d_{free}}$$

for all $l \geq 0$, and $\lim_{l\to\infty} \delta_l^c = \mathrm{d_{free}}$. In addition, adapted as it is to the cyclic structure of the code, this sequence presents a more regular behavior than the classical column distance. In order to describe this regularity, let us say that the role of the polynomial generator matrix of the code will be played in our setting by a non commutative polynomial in the variable z that represents the delay operator with coefficients in some finite (commutative or not) algebra A over a finite field $\mathbb{F}$. Details of the construction, which has its roots in [16] and [17], are given in Section 3. The degree m of such a generator polynomial leads to a remarkable property of the column distances sequence: we prove (Theorem 3.12) that, if l is an index such that $\delta_l^c = \delta_{l+m}^c$, then $\delta_l^c = \mathrm{d_{free}}$. We present an algoritm based on this property (see Algorithm 3). It computes terms of the sequence of cyclic column distances, and it stops when it gets m repeated terms. Each of the column distances is computed as the minimum weight of a block code presented as the set theoretical difference $V \setminus W$, where V is a linear code and W is a nonzero vector subspace of V. To compute them, we present two algorithms. The first one (Algorithm 1) is an adaptation of the general procedure for computing the Hamming minimum distance of a linear code from a parity check matrix, and it should be used if $\mathbb{F}$ is large. The second algorithm for this task adjusts the Brouwer-Zimmermann algorithm to this setting (see Algorithm 2).

2 CONVOLUTIONAL CODES AND THEIR DISTANCES: AN OUTLINE

Let $\mathbb{F}$ be a finite field. In this paper, some results and terminology from [13] will be used, well understood that they are still valid when the binary field used there is replaced by $\mathbb{F}$. Indeed, convolutional codes are modeled over an arbitrary finite field in fundamental references like [5], [16], [17], or [19].

Let $k \leq n$ be positive integers. Recall from [13, Chapter 2] that a *rate k/n convolutional transducer G* transforms *information sequences* $\mathbf{u} = (\mathbf{u}_i)_{i\in\mathbb{Z}}$ ($\mathbf{u}_i \in \mathbb{F}^k$) into *code sequences* $\mathbf{v} = (\mathbf{v}_i)_{i\in\mathbb{Z}}$ ($\mathbf{v}_i \in \mathbb{F}^n$).

The map G is subject to some requirements. First, both the information sequence and the code sequence start at some finite time. This allows to represent them as $\mathbf{u} = \sum_{i=i_0}^{\infty} \mathbf{u}_i t^i \in \mathbb{F}^k((z))$, $\mathbf{v} = \sum_{j=j_0}^{\infty} \mathbf{v}_j t^j \in \mathbb{F}^n((z))$, for some $i_0, j_0 \in \mathbb{Z}$. Here, $\mathbb{F}^k((z))$ denotes the set of all Laurent series in the variable z with coefficients in $\mathbb{F}^k$. The obvious bijection $\mathbb{F}^k((z)) \cong \mathbb{F}((z))^k$ shows how to consider $\mathbb{F}^k((z))$ as a vector space of dimension k over the field of Laurent series $\mathbb{F}((z))$. Obviously, the same considerations apply for the code

*Produces the permission block, and copyright information

ISSAC '18, July 16–19, 2018, New York, NY, USA

ACM ISBN 978-1-4503-5550-6/18/07...$15.00
https://doi.org/10.1145/3208976.3208985

sequences. Then it is assumed that

$$v = uG,$$

where G is a $k \times n$ full rank matrix with entries in the rational function field $\mathbb{F}(z)$, which is a subfield of $\mathbb{F}((z))$.

A *rate k/n convolutional code* over $\mathbb{F}$ is then defined as the image of a convolutional transducer, that is, a k–dimensional vector subspace $\mathcal{D}$ of $\mathbb{F}^n((z))$ which has a basis whose vectors belong to $\mathbb{F}(z)^n$. The matrix G is known as a *generator matrix* of the code, whenever its rational entries belong to the formal power series ring $\mathbb{F}[[z]]$ (that is, their denominators, in an irreducible representation as fractions of polynomials, are delay free, in the terminology of [13, Chapter 2]). The convolutional code $\mathcal{D}$ is uniquely determined by the row space of G in $\mathbb{F}(z)^n$. In other words, a rate k/n convolutional code could be have been equivalently defined as a k–dimensional vector subspace of $\mathbb{F}(z)^n$. Taking this remark, besides some basic facts on finitely generated modules over principal ideal domains, into account, we get the following module-theoretical and coordinate-free refined version of [5, Theorem 3].

Proposition 2.1. *Let $k \leq n$. The map $\mathcal{D} \mapsto \mathcal{D} \cap \mathbb{F}^n[z]$ establishes a bijection between the set of all convolutional codes of rate k/n and the set of all $\mathbb{F}[z]$–submodules of $\mathbb{F}^n[z]$ of rank k that are direct summands of $\mathbb{F}^n[z]$.*

By stacking the (row) vectors of a basis of $\mathcal{D} \cap \mathbb{F}^n[z]$ as an $\mathbb{F}[z]$–module, we get a matrix with polynomial entries called a *basic generator matrix of the code.* Therefore, $\mathcal{D} \cap \mathbb{F}^n[z]$ is a delay free and observable code in the sense of [18]. As a consequence, any convolutional code $\mathcal{D}$ determines (and it is detemined by) a unique delay free observable code.

Let $C = \mathcal{D} \cap \mathbb{F}^n[z]$, where $\mathcal{D}$ is a rate k/n convolutional code. The Hamming weight $\mathrm{w_H}$ on $\mathbb{F}^n$ can be extended to any polynomial with vector coefficients $f = \sum_i z^i f_i \in \mathbb{F}^n[z]$ as

$$\mathrm{w_H}(f) = \textstyle\sum_i \mathrm{w_H}(f_i).$$

The free distance of C is defined as

$$\mathrm{d_{free}}(C) = \min\{\mathrm{w_H}(f) : f \in C, f \neq 0\},$$

and it coincides with the free distance of $\mathcal{D}$, as defined in [13, Ch. 3], since C is a direct summand of $\mathbb{F}^n[z]$ (see also the last paragraph of page 357 in [3]). It follows as well (see e.g. [6, Proposition 2.2]) that there exists $f \in C$ with $f_0 \neq 0$ such that $\mathrm{d_{free}}(C) = \mathrm{w_H}(f)$. One way to compute the free distance of a convolutional code consists in the calculation of the classical column and row distance sequences until they coincide. We recall the definition and some properties of these sequences.

For each $f = \sum_i z^i f_i \in \mathbb{F}^n[z]$, the truncated polynomial at degree j is

$$f_{[0,j]} = \textstyle\sum_{i=0}^{j} z^i f_i.$$

The *jth column distance* of C is defined as

$$d_j^c = \min\left\{\mathrm{w_H}(f_{[0,j]}) : f \in C, f_0 \neq 0\right\}.$$

In fact, as observed in the proof of [13, Theorem 3.1], this definition matches with the column distance of any (rational) generator matrix G of $\mathcal{D}$ such that $G(0)$ has full rank (e.g. when G is a basic generator matrix).

The *jth row distance* of C (or of $\mathcal{D}$) with respect to a basic generator matrix $G = \sum_{i=0}^m z^i G_i$, of degree m is defined as

$$d_j^r = \min\{\mathrm{w_H}(f) : f \in C, f \neq 0, \deg(f) \leq j + m\}.$$

This definition depends on the degree m of G as a polynomial in z with matrix coefficients. See [13, p. 114] or [12, Theorem 14.4.6] for more details.

Row and column distances help to compute the free distance, since, for every index j,

$$d_j^c \leq d_{j+1}^c \leq \mathrm{d_{free}}(C) \leq d_{j+1}^r \leq d_j^r,$$

and $d_s^c = \mathrm{d_{free}}(C) = d_s^r$ for s big enough (see [13, Ch. 3]).

The degree m of G should play some role in row and column distance sequences. In fact, each vector in the information sequence interacts only with the $m + 1$ coefficients of G. This leads to the following natural question:

Does the equality $d_j^c = d_{j+m}^c$ for some $j \geq 0$ imply $d_j^c = \mathrm{d_{free}}(C)$?

The answer is no, as the following example shows.

Example 2.2. Let C be the rate $2/4$ code generated by the basic matrix

$$G = \begin{pmatrix} z^4+z^2+1 & z^3+z^2+z+1 & z^4+z^3 & z^3+z^2+z \\ z^4+z^3+1 & z^3 & z^3+z+1 & 1 \end{pmatrix}.$$

With the aid of the computer software SageMath [20], we have computed the column distances, whose values are written in the following table:

j	0	1	2	3	4	5	6	7	8	9	10	11
d_j^c	2	3	4	5	5	6	6	6	6	6	6	7

So $d_5^c = d_{10}^c = 6$, but $\mathrm{d_{free}}(C) \geq 7$. Actually, $\mathrm{d_{free}}(C) = 8$.

3 COLUMN DISTANCES ADAPTED TO CYCLIC STRUCTURES ON CONVOLUTIONAL CODES.

Let $\mathbb{F}[z]$ denote the polynomial ring in the variable z with coefficients in a finite field $\mathbb{F}$. It follows from Proposition 2.1, and the subsequent discussion on free, row and column distances in Section 2, that we may safely define convolutional codes as follows.

Definition 3.1. Let $k \leq n$ be positive integers. A *rate k/n convolutional code over $\mathbb{F}$* is an $\mathbb{F}[z]$–submodule C of $\mathbb{F}^n[z]$ of rank k such that $\mathbb{F}^n[z] = C \oplus C'$ for some $\mathbb{F}[z]$–submodule $C' \subseteq \mathbb{F}^n[z]$.

Various cyclic structures on convolutional codes have been modeled by using a skew polynomial ring with coefficients in a finite algebra as sentence-ambient algebra [4, 6, 8, 11, 15–17]. We briefly recall this construction. Let A be an $\mathbb{F}$–algebra (associative with unit) of finite dimension n over $\mathbb{F}$, and $\sigma : A \to A$ an $\mathbb{F}$–algebra automorphism. The right skew polynomial ring $A[z;\sigma]$ consists of all polynomials in z with coefficients in A written on the right, whose multiplication is skewed according to the rule $az = z\sigma(a)$ for all $a \in A$. Clearly, since $\mathbb{F}$ is a subalgebra of A, $\mathbb{F}[z]$ is a commutative subring of the non-commutative ring $A[z;\sigma]$. However, $\mathbb{F}[z]$ is not contained in the center of $A[z;\sigma]$, unless σ is the identity map.

Consider $A[z;\sigma]$ as an $\mathbb{F}[z]$–module by defining the action of $f(z) \in \mathbb{F}[z]$ on $g(z) \in A[z;\sigma]$ as the non-commutative product $f(z)g(z)$. Every $\mathbb{F}$–basis $\{b_0, \ldots, b_{n-1}\}$ of A becomes a basis of

$A[z;\sigma]$ as an $\mathbb{F}[z]$-module, and the corresponding isomorphism of vector spaces

$$\mathfrak{v} : A \longrightarrow \mathbb{F}^n$$

extends to an isomorphism of $\mathbb{F}[z]$-modules

$$\mathfrak{v} : A[z;\sigma] \longrightarrow \mathbb{F}^n[z]$$

with inverse

$$\mathfrak{p} : \mathbb{F}^n[z] \longrightarrow A[z;\sigma].$$

At this level of generality, cyclic structures on convolutional codes were introduced in [15] under the name of left ideal convolutional codes. Thus, a convolutional code $C \subseteq \mathbb{F}^n[z]$ is said to be a *left ideal convolutional code* if $\mathfrak{p}(C)$ is a left ideal of $A[z;\sigma]$. Left ideal convolutional codes are often generated, as left ideals, by idempotent elements of $A[z;\sigma]$. This is the case when A is a semisimple commutative algebra [15, Theorem 3.5] and, more generally, when the ring extension $\mathbb{F}[z] \subseteq A[z;\sigma]$ is a separable ring extension [11, Corollary 7]. Moreover, the idempotent generator of each left ideal convolutional code can be, in this case, explicitly computed (see [11, Algorithm 1]). We are interested in the consequences for the cyclic convolutional code of being generated by an idempotent, so we find useful to introduce the following definition.

Definition 3.2. Let $R = A[z;\sigma]$, and fix a basis $\{b_0, b_1, \dots, b_{n-1}\}$ of A over $\mathbb{F}$. A convolutional code $C \subsetneq \mathbb{F}^n[z]$ is said to be an *idempotent convolutional code (ICC)* if there exists an idempotent $\epsilon = \epsilon^2 \in A[z;\sigma]$ such that $\mathfrak{p}(C) = R\epsilon$. By a slight abuse of language, we will simply say that C is generated by ϵ, and we write $C = R\epsilon$.

Many examples, as well as algorithms for their construction, of idempotent convolutional codes (also called split ideal codes in [8]) are given in [8], [11], [10], [7].

We will consider on A a weight function w, that is, a map $\mathrm{w} : A \longrightarrow \mathbb{N}$ such that

(1) $\mathrm{w}(a+b) \leq \mathrm{w}(a) + \mathrm{w}(b)$,
(2) $\mathrm{w}(-a) = \mathrm{w}(a)$,
(3) $\mathrm{w}(a) = 0$ is and only if $a = 0$.

Such a weight function allows to define a distance function $\mathrm{d} : A \times A \longrightarrow \mathbb{N}$ by $\mathrm{d}(a,b) = \mathrm{w}(a-b)$. We extend the weight function to any cartesian product A^l by defining $\mathrm{w} : A^l \longrightarrow \mathbb{N}$ as

$$\mathrm{w}(a_0, \dots, a_{l-1}) = \mathrm{w}(a_0) + \cdots + \mathrm{w}(a_{l-1}).$$

The minimum weight of a subset $S \subseteq A^l$ is defined as usual, namely,

$$\mathrm{d}(S) = \min\{\mathrm{w}(u) : 0 \neq u \in S\},$$

whenever S contains some non zero vector.

The weight function is also extended to $\mathrm{w} : R \longrightarrow \mathbb{N}$ by setting

$$\mathrm{w}\left(\textstyle\sum_i z^i a_i\right) = \textstyle\sum_i \mathrm{w}(a_i),$$

which leads to the definition of the *free distance* of a convolutional code C as

$$\mathrm{d}_{\mathrm{free}}(C) = \min\{\mathrm{w}(f) : f \in C, f \neq 0\}. \quad (1)$$

Remark 3.3. If we consider on A the weight function w that comes from the Hamming weight $\mathrm{w_H}$ in $\mathbb{F}^n$, namely,

$$\mathrm{w} : A \longrightarrow \mathbb{N}, \qquad a \mapsto \mathrm{w}(a) = \mathrm{w_H}(\mathfrak{v}(a)),$$

then (1) is the usual free distance of the convolutional code C. Obviously, w depends on the choice of the basis $\{b_0, b_1, \dots, b_{n-1}\}$ of A over $\mathbb{F}$.

Let $C = R\epsilon$ an ICC generated by an idempotent $\epsilon \neq 0, 1$ of R. Let m be the degree of ϵ in z. Write

$$e = 1 - \epsilon = \sum_{i=0}^{m} z^i e_i,$$

which is also a non trivial idempotent of degree m of R. Then

$$C = \mathrm{Ann}_R^{\ell}(e) = \{g \in R : ge = 0\}. \quad (2)$$

The idempotent ϵ is called an *idempotent generator* of $C = R\epsilon$, and $e = 1 - \epsilon$ is called a *parity check idempotent.*

Consider the following infinite matrix with coefficients in A:

$$E = \begin{pmatrix} e_0 & \sigma^{-1}(e_1) & \sigma^{-2}(e_2) & \cdots & \cdots & \cdots \\ & \sigma^{-1}(e_0) & \sigma^{-2}(e_1) & \sigma^{-3}(e_2) & \cdots & \cdots \\ & & \sigma^{-2}(e_0) & \sigma^{-3}(e_1) & \sigma^{-4}(e_2) & \cdots \\ & & \ddots & \ddots & \ddots & \ddots \end{pmatrix}.$$

If we adopt the convention that $e_i = 0$ for $i < 0$ and $i > m$, then the matrix E can be written as

$$E = \left(\sigma^{-j}(e_{j-i})\right)_{0 \leq i, 0 \leq j}.$$

Next, we introduce and study an increasing sequence of distances bounded from above by the free distance, which will be reached by them in somewhat more controllable way than the classical sequence of column distances.

Let E_l^c be the square submatrix of E consisting in the first $l+1$ rows and columns, that is

$$E_l^c = \left(\sigma^{-j}(e_{j-i})\right)_{0 \leq i, j \leq l}, \quad (3)$$

and let E_l^r be the submatrix of E consisting in the first $l+1$ rows and $m+l+1$ columns, that is

$$E_l^r = \left(\sigma^{-j}(e_{j-i})\right)_{0 \leq i \leq l, 0 \leq j \leq m+l}. \quad (4)$$

The matrices E_l^c and E_l^r follow the patterns described below:

$$E_{l+1}^c = \left(\begin{array}{c|c} E_l^c & \begin{matrix} \sigma^{-(l+1)}(e_{l+1}) \\ \vdots \\ \sigma^{-(l+1)}(e_1) \end{matrix} \\ \hline 0 & \sigma^{-(l+1)}(e_0) \end{array}\right), \quad (5)$$

$$E_{l+1}^r = \left(\begin{array}{c|c} E_l^r & 0 \\ \hline \cdots\ \sigma^{-(l+1)}(e_0)\ \cdots\ \sigma^{-(l+m)}(e_{m-1}) & \sigma^{-(l+m+1)}(e_m) \end{array}\right), \quad (6)$$

$$E_l^r = \left(\begin{array}{c|c} E_l^c & \mathrm{L} \end{array} \right) \quad (7)$$

and

$$E_{l+m}^c = \left(\begin{array}{c} E_l^r \\ \hline \begin{array}{c|c} 0 & \mathrm{U} \end{array} \end{array}\right), \quad (8)$$

where L and U are suitable lower and upper triangular blocks respectively.

Lemma 3.4. *Let $h = \sum_{i=0}^{l} z^i h_i \in R$. Then $h \in C$ if and only if $(\sigma^{-0}(h_0), \dots, \sigma^{-l}(h_l))E_l^r = 0$.*

Proof. The coefficient of degree k of he is $\sum_{i+j=k}\sigma^j(h_i)e_j$. Since σ is an algebra automorphism,

$$\sigma^{-k}\left(\sum_{i+j=k}\sigma^j(h_i)e_j\right) = \sum_{i+j=k}\sigma^{-i}(h_i)\sigma^{-k}(e_j) = \sum_{i+j=k} f_i\sigma^{-k}(e_j),$$

which is $(f_0,\ldots,f_l)$ multiplied by the kth column of E_l^r. Hence the lemma follows from (2). □

The following is a key point in our approach.

Proposition 3.5. *For all $l \geq 0$, E_l^c in an idempotent matrix.*

Proof. The arithmetic of R says that

$$e^2 = \sum_{k\geq 0} z^k\left(\sum_{i+j=k}\sigma^j(e_i)e_j\right).$$

The idempotency of e implies that, for all $k \geq 0$,

$$e_k = \sum_{i+j=k}\sigma^j(e_i)e_j = \sum_{j=0}^{k}\sigma^j(e_{k-j})e_j. \tag{9}$$

Let us write

$$\left(E_l^c\right)^2 = (m_{ij})_{0\leq i,j\leq l}.$$

Then

$$\begin{aligned} m_{ij} &= \sum_{h=0}^{l}\sigma^{-h}(e_{h-i})\sigma^{-j}(e_{j-h}) \\ &= \sigma^{-j}\left(\sum_{h=0}^{l}\sigma^{j-h}(e_{h-i})e_{j-h}\right) \\ &= \sigma^{-j}\left(\sum_{h=i}^{l}\sigma^{j-h}(e_{h-i})e_{j-h}\right) \\ &= \sigma^{-j}\left(\sum_{k=j-l}^{j-i}\sigma^{k}(e_{j-i-k})e_{k}\right) \text{ where } k = j-h \\ &= \sigma^{-j}\left(\sum_{k=0}^{j-i}\sigma^{k}(e_{j-i-k})e_{k}\right) \\ &= \sigma^{-j}(e_{j-i}) \text{ by (9).} \end{aligned}$$

So, by (3), $(E_l^c)^2 = E_l^c$. □

For all l, let

$$K_l = \{(a_0,\ldots,a_l) \in \ker(\cdot E_l^c) : a_0 \neq 0\} \subseteq A^{l+1}. \tag{10}$$

As a consequence of (5), we have that $(f_0,\ldots,f_l,f_{l+1}) \in K_{l+1}$ implies $(f_0,\ldots,f_l) \in K_l$. There is a somehow reciprocal result.

Lemma 3.6. *Let $(f_0,\ldots,f_l) \in K_l$ and let*

$$f_{l+1} = -\sum_{i=0}^{l} f_i\sigma^{-(l+1)}(e_{l+1-i}).$$

Then

$$(f_0,\ldots,f_l,f_{l+1}) \in K_{l+1}.$$

As a consequence, $K_l \neq \emptyset$ for all $l \geq 0$.

Proof. By (5) and Proposition 3.5, we have

$$\begin{pmatrix}\sigma^{-(l+1)}(e_{l+1})\\ \vdots \\ \sigma^{-(l+1)}(e_1)\end{pmatrix} = E_l^c\begin{pmatrix}\sigma^{-(l+1)}(e_{l+1})\\ \vdots \\ \sigma^{-(l+1)}(e_1)\end{pmatrix} + \begin{pmatrix}\sigma^{-(l+1)}(e_{l+1})\\ \vdots \\ \sigma^{-(l+1)}(e_1)\end{pmatrix}\sigma^{-(l+1)}(e_0).$$

Hence, since $(f_0,\ldots,f_l) \in K_l$, we have

$$\begin{aligned} &(f_0,\ldots,f_l)\begin{pmatrix}\sigma^{-(l+1)}(e_{l+1})\\ \vdots \\ \sigma^{-(l+1)}(e_1)\end{pmatrix}(1-\sigma^{-(l+1)}(e_0)) \\ &= (f_0,\ldots,f_l)E_l^c\begin{pmatrix}\sigma^{-(l+1)}(e_{l+1})\\ \vdots \\ \sigma^{-(l+1)}(e_1)\end{pmatrix}(1-\sigma^{-(l+1)}(e_0)) \\ &\quad + (f_0,\ldots,f_l)\begin{pmatrix}\sigma^{-(l+1)}(e_{l+1})\\ \vdots \\ \sigma^{-(l+1)}(e_1)\end{pmatrix}\sigma^{-(l+1)}(e_0)(1-\sigma^{-(l+1)}(e_0)) \\ &= 0, \end{aligned}$$

because $\sigma^{-(l+1)}(e_0)$ is idempotent. So

$$\begin{aligned} (f_0,\ldots,f_l)\begin{pmatrix}\sigma^{-(l+1)}(e_{l+1})\\ \vdots \\ \sigma^{-(l+1)}(e_1)\end{pmatrix} &= (f_0,\ldots,f_l)\begin{pmatrix}\sigma^{-(l+1)}(e_{l+1})\\ \vdots \\ \sigma^{-(l+1)}(e_1)\end{pmatrix}\sigma^{-(l+1)}(e_0) \\ &= \sum_{i=0}^{l} f_i\sigma^{-(l+1)}(e_{l+1-i})\sigma^{-(l+1)}(e_0), \end{aligned}$$

that is,

$$\left(f_0,\ldots,f_l \middle| -\sum_{i=0}^{l} f_i\sigma^{-(l+1)}(e_{l+1-i})\right)\begin{pmatrix}\sigma^{-(l+1)}(e_{l+1})\\ \vdots \\ \sigma^{-(l+1)}(e_1)\\ \hline \sigma^{-(l+1)}(e_0)\end{pmatrix} = 0.$$

Therefore, $\left(f_0,\ldots,f_l,-\sum_{i=0}^{l} f_i\sigma^{-(l+1)}(e_{l+1-i})\right) \in K_{l+1}$ by (5).

To prove that $K_l \neq \emptyset$ for every $l \geq 0$, it suffices to argue that $K_0 \neq \emptyset$, that is, $e_0 \neq 1$. By (9), if $e_0 = 1$ then

$$e_1 = \sigma^{-1}(e_0)e_1 + e_1e_0 = e_1 + e_1,$$

so $e_1 = 0$. Iterating this process we get $e_i = 0$ for all $i > 0$, i.e. $e = 1$. But we have assumed $e \neq 1$, so $e_0 \neq 1$. □

Definition 3.7. Let $l \geq 0$. The lth cyclic column distance of $C = \mathrm{Ann}_R^{\ell}(e)$ is defined as

$$\delta_l^c = \mathrm{d}(K_l) = \min\{\mathrm{w}(a_0,\ldots,a_l) : (a_0,\ldots,a_l) \in K_l\}.$$

We say that the algebra automorphism σ of A is an *isometry* if $\mathrm{w}(\sigma(a)) = \mathrm{w}(a)$ for all $a \in A$.

Example 3.8. If A is a full matrix algebra over $\mathbb{F}$, then every automorphism σ is an isometry with respect to the rank on A used as metric.

Proposition 3.9. *For all $l \geq 0$, $\delta_l^c \leq \delta_{l+1}^c$. Moreover, if σ is an isometry, then $\delta_l^c \leq \mathrm{d}_{\mathrm{free}}(C)$.*

Proof. Let $(f_0,\ldots,f_l,f_{l+1}) \in K_{l+1}$ such that

$$\delta_{l+1}^c = \mathrm{w}(f_0,\ldots,f_l,f_{l+1}).$$

By (5), it follows that $(f_0,\ldots,f_l) \in K_l$, therefore

$$\delta_l^c \leq \mathrm{w}(f_0,\ldots,f_l) \leq \mathrm{w}(f_0,\ldots,f_l,f_{l+1}) = \delta_{l+1}^c.$$

Let $h = \sum_{i=0}^{t} z^i h_i \in C$ with $h_0 \neq 0$ such that $\mathrm{d}_{\mathrm{free}}(C) = \mathrm{w}(h)$. We may take t such that $t + m \geq l$, by adding suitable zero monomials. Let $f_i = \sigma^{-i}(h_i)$. Since $h \in C$, it follows that

$$(f_0, \ldots, f_t)E_t^r = 0$$

by Lemma 3.4. Hence

$$(f_0, \ldots, f_t, 0, \overset{m}{\ldots}, 0)E_{t+m}^c = 0$$

because

$$E_{t+m}^c = \left(\begin{array}{c|c} \multicolumn{2}{c}{E_t^r} \\ \hline 0 & \mathrm{U} \end{array}\right)$$

by (8). Therefore,

$$\begin{aligned} \delta_l^c &\leq \delta_{t+m}^c \leq \mathrm{w}(f_0, \ldots, f_t, 0, \overset{m}{\ldots}, 0) \\ &= \mathrm{w}(f_0, \ldots, f_t) = \mathrm{w}(h) = \mathrm{d}_{\mathrm{free}}(C), \end{aligned}$$

where, in the penultimate equality, we used that σ is an isometry. □

Remark 3.10. By using the matrices E_l^r instead of E_l^c, cyclic row distance can be defined as $\delta_l^r = \mathrm{d}\left(\ker(\cdot E_l^r)\right)$. By Lemma 3.4, it follows that $(a_0, \ldots, a_l) \in \ker(\cdot E_l^r)$ if and only if $\sum_{i=0}^{l} z^i \sigma^i(a_i) \in C$, so, if σ is an isometry for the weight function defined from the Hamming weight according to Remark 3.3 and $l \geq m$, then $\delta_l^r = d_{l-m}^r$.

In order to prove the main result of this section, we need the following lemma.

Lemma 3.11. *Let $l, j \geq 0$ such that $\delta_l^c = \delta_{l+j}^c$. If $(f_0, \ldots, f_{l+j}) \in K_{l+j}$ is such that $\delta_{l+j}^c = \mathrm{w}(f_0, \ldots, f_{l+j})$, then $(f_0, \ldots, f_l) \in K_l$, $(f_{l+1}, \ldots, f_{l+j}) = (0, \ldots, 0)$ and $\delta_l^c = \mathrm{w}(f_0, \ldots, f_l)$.*

Proof. Since

$$E_{l+j}^c = \left(\begin{array}{c|c} E_l^c & \mathrm{L} \\ \hline 0 & \mathrm{U} \end{array}\right),$$

it follows that $(f_0, \ldots, f_l) \in K_l$. Then

$$\delta_{l+j}^c = \delta_l^c \leq \mathrm{w}(f_0, \ldots, f_l) \leq \mathrm{w}(f_0, \ldots, f_l, f_{l+1}, \ldots, f_{l+j}) = \delta_{l+j}^c,$$

so we conclude that

$$\delta_l^c = \mathrm{w}(f_0, \ldots, f_l) \text{ and } (f_{l+1}, \ldots, f_{l+j}) = (0, \ldots, 0)$$

because

$$\mathrm{w}(f_0, \ldots, f_l, f_{l+1}, \ldots, f_{l+j}) = \mathrm{w}(f_0, \ldots, f_l) + \mathrm{w}(f_{l+1}, \ldots, f_{l+j}).$$

□

Theorem 3.12. *Assume that σ is an isometry. If $\delta_l^c = \delta_{l+m}^c$ for some l, then $\delta_l^c = \mathrm{d}_{\mathrm{free}}(C)$.*

Proof. By Lemma 3.11 there exists $(f_0, \ldots, f_l) \in K_l$ such that $(f_0, \ldots, f_l, 0, \ldots, 0) \in K_{l+m}$ and $\delta_l^c = \mathrm{w}(f_0, \ldots, f_l) = \delta_{l+m}^c$. Let $h_i = \sigma^i(f_i)$ for all $0 \leq i \leq l$, and $h = \sum_i z^i h_i$. Then

$$(f_0, \ldots, f_l, 0, \ldots, 0)E_{l+m}^c = 0,$$

which implies, by (8), that $(f_0, \ldots, f_l)E_l^r = 0$. Hence, $h \in C$, by Lemma 3.4, because $f_i = \sigma^{-i}(h_i)$ for all $0 \leq i \leq l$. Therefore

$$\mathrm{d}_{\mathrm{free}}(C) \leq \mathrm{w}(h) = \mathrm{w}(f_0, \ldots, f_l) = \delta_l^c,$$

and, by Proposition 3.9, $\mathrm{d}_{\mathrm{free}}(C) = \delta_l^c$. □

Corollary 3.13. *If σ is an isometry, then the free distance is reached by the sequence $\{\delta_l^c\}_{l \geq 0}$.*

Let us finally compare cyclic column distances with the classical column distances when σ is an isometry and w is defined from the Hamming weight as in Remark 3.3

Proposition 3.14. *Assume σ is an isometry and* w *is defined as in Remark 3.3. For all $j \geq 0$, $\delta_j^c \leq d_j^c$.*

Proof. Let $j \geq 0$. Let $h = \sum_{i=0}^{l} z^i h_i \in C$ with $h_0 \neq 0$. We may assume that $l \geq j$ by adding zeros if needed. By Lemma 3.4,

$$(\sigma^{-0}(h_0), \ldots, \sigma^{-l}(h_l))E_l^r = 0.$$

By (6), (8) and (7)

$$E_l^r = \left(\begin{array}{c|c} \multicolumn{2}{c}{E_j^r} \\ \hline \mathrm{U} & \mathrm{L} \end{array}\right) = \left(\begin{array}{c|c|c} E_j^c & \mathrm{L} & 0 \\ \hline 0 & \mathrm{U} & \mathrm{L} \end{array}\right).$$

Hence

$$(\sigma^{-0}(h_0), \ldots, \sigma^{-j}(h_j))E_j^c = 0,$$

and there is an injective map

$$\begin{aligned} \{h_{[0,j]} : h \in C, h_0 \neq 0\} &\hookrightarrow K_j \\ \textstyle\sum_{i=0}^{j} z^i h_i &\mapsto (\sigma^{-0}(h_0), \ldots, \sigma^{-j}(h_j)) \end{aligned}$$

Since σ is an isometry, $\mathrm{w}(h_{[0,j]}) = \sum_{i=0}^{j} \mathrm{w}(\sigma^{-i}(h_i))$, hence $\delta_j^c \leq d_j^c$. □

4 COMPUTING CYCLIC COLUMN DISTANCES

Theorem 3.12 opens the possibility of designing an algorithm for the computation of the free distance of an idempotent convolutional code C based in the calculation of the cyclic column distances sequence. Each term δ_l^c of this sequence is the minimum weight of $K_l \subseteq A^{l+1}$, which is of the form

$$K_l = N_l \setminus P_l, \tag{11}$$

where

$$N_l = \ker(\cdot E_l^c) \text{ and } P_l = \{(a_0, a_1, \ldots, a_l) \in N_l : a_0 = 0\}. \tag{12}$$

We will discuss how to compute δ_l^c when the weight function d on A comes from the Hamming weight according to Remark 3.3. So, we fix a basis $B = \{b_0, \ldots, b_{n-1}\}$ of our $\mathbb{F}$-algebra A, and the corresponding coordinate isomorphism of vector spaces

$$\mathfrak{v} : A \to \mathbb{F}^n.$$

The right regular representation of A maps each $b \in A$ onto the $\mathbb{F}$-linear endomorphism

$$\rho_b : A \to A, \quad [a \mapsto \rho_b(a) = ab].$$

Taking coordinates with respect to B, we get an injective homomorphism of $\mathbb{F}$-algebras

$$\mathfrak{m} : A \to \mathcal{M}_n(\mathbb{F}),$$

where the matrix $\mathfrak{m}(b)$ is determined, for each $b \in A$ by the condition

$$\mathfrak{v}(\rho_b(a)) = \mathfrak{v}(ab) = \mathfrak{v}(a)\mathfrak{m}(b), \text{ for all } a \in A.$$

These maps extend component wise to an $\mathbb{F}$-linear isomorphism

$$\begin{aligned} \mathfrak{v} : A^{l+1} &\to \mathbb{F}^{(l+1)n} \\ (f_0, \ldots, f_l) &\mapsto \mathfrak{v}(f_0, \ldots, f_l) = (\mathfrak{v}(f_0), \ldots, \mathfrak{v}(f_l)) \end{aligned}$$

and an injective homomorphism of $\mathbb{F}$-algebras

$$\mathfrak{m} : \mathcal{M}_{l+1\times l+1}(A) \to \mathcal{M}_{(l+1)n\times(l+1)n}(\mathbb{F})$$
$$M = (m_{ij}) \mapsto \mathfrak{m}(M) = (\mathfrak{m}(m_{ij})),$$

in such a way that

$$\mathfrak{v}((f_0,\ldots,f_l)M) = \mathfrak{v}(f_0,\ldots,f_l)\mathfrak{m}(M). \qquad (13)$$

Note that, for every $S \subseteq \mathbb{F}^{l+1}$,

$$\mathrm{d}(S) = \mathrm{d}(\mathfrak{v}(S)).$$

In particular, it follows from (13), that

$$\delta_l^c = \mathrm{d}(\{v \in \ker(\cdot\mathfrak{m}(E_l^c)) : v_{[0,n-1]} \neq 0\}). \qquad (14)$$

Here, in analogy with our notation for polynomials, we denote $v_{[0,n]} = (v_0,\ldots,v_n) \in \mathbb{F}^{n+1}$ for any vector $v \in \mathbb{F}^N$ with $n+1 \leq N$.

It follows from (14) that cyclic column distances are distances of some non linear block codes over $\mathbb{F}$. For linear codes, a widely used method for small fields is the Brouwer-Zimmermann algorithm, see e.g. [1, §1.8]. For large fields, the well known characterization of the minimum distance in terms of the linear dependence of the rows of a parity check matrix, [12, Corollary 1.4.14], should work better. However there is not a general efficient deterministic way to compute the minimum weight of a non linear code, all the known methods use some exhaustive search. Even in the linear block case, the computation of the minimum distance is an NP-hard problem, see [21].

We are going to give two ways to compute the cyclic column distances. The first one, Algorithm 1, is an adaptation of the computation of the Hamming distance via parity check matrices. In order to describe it, we need some notation. For each pair of integers $a \leq b$, we denote $[a,b] = \{c \in \mathbb{Z} : a \leq c \leq b\}$. Given a matrix $M \in \mathcal{M}_{s\times t}(\mathbb{F})$ and a subset $J \subseteq [0,s-1]$, we denote by $M[J]$ the submatrix of M formed by the rows labeled by J. The cardinality of J is denoted by $|J|$. For each vector $v \in \mathbb{F}^s$, its support is $\mathrm{supp}(v) = \{i \in [0,s-1] : v_i \neq 0\}$. We write $I = [0,n-1]$, and $I^c = [n,s-1]$. The rank of a matrix M is denoted by $\mathrm{rk}\,M$.

Let H be a matrix with s rows and $n \leq s$. Let

$$C = \{v \in \ker(\cdot H) \; : \; v_{[0,n-1]} \neq 0\} \subseteq \mathbb{F}^s$$

and

$$\mathcal{J} = \{J \subseteq [0,s-1] : \mathrm{rk}\,H[J] < |J| \text{ and } \mathrm{rk}\,H[J\cap I^c] = |J \cap I^c|\}.$$

Lemma 4.1. *For each $v \in C$ there exists $v' \in C$ such that $\mathrm{supp}(v') \subseteq \mathrm{supp}(v)$ and $\mathrm{supp}(v') \in \mathcal{J}$. Reciprocally, for each $J \in \mathcal{J}$, there exists $v \in C$ such that $\mathrm{supp}(v) \subseteq J$.*

Proof. Straightforward. □

The correctness of Algorithm 1 follows from the following

Proposition 4.2. *With the previous notation, assume C is non empty. Then $\{|J| : J \in \mathcal{J}\} = [\mathrm{d}(C), n + \mathrm{rk}\,H[I^c]]$.*

Proof. Since C is non empty, $\{|J| : J \in \mathcal{J}\} \neq \emptyset$ by Lemma 4.1. Let $J \in \mathcal{J}$ and write $d = |J|$. Clearly $d \leq n + \mathrm{rk}\,H[I^c]$. Assume $d < n + \mathrm{rk}\,H[I^c]$. If $\mathrm{rk}\,H[J\cap I^c] < \mathrm{rk}\,H[I^c]$, then there exists $j \in I^c \setminus J$ such that $\mathrm{rk}\,H[(J\cup\{j\})\cap I^c] = |(J\cup\{j\})\cap I^c|$, so $J\cup\{j\} \in \mathcal{J}$; else, $|J \cap I| < n$ and there exists $i \in I \setminus J$, which implies that $J \cup \{i\} \in \mathcal{J}$. We have proved that $d+1 \in \{|J| : J \in \mathcal{J}\}$.

Let $J_0 \in \mathcal{J}$ such that $|J_0| = \min\{|J| : J \in \mathcal{J}\}$. By Lemma 4.1, there exists $u \in C$ such that $\mathrm{supp}(u) \subseteq J_0$, so $\mathrm{d}(C) \leq \mathrm{w}(u) \leq |J_0|$. Let $v \in C$ such that $\mathrm{w}(v) = \mathrm{d}(C)$. By Lemma 4.1, $\mathrm{supp}(v) \in \mathcal{J}$. Therefore $|J_0| \leq |\mathrm{supp}(v)| = \mathrm{w}(v) = \mathrm{d}(C)$. □

Algorithm 1 Minimum distance from parity check

Input: A matrix H with s rows and $n \leq s$.
Output: $\mathrm{d}(C)$, where $C = \{v \in \ker(\cdot H) \mid v_{[0,n-1]} \neq 0\}$.

$d \leftarrow n + \mathrm{rk}(H[I^c])$
continue $\leftarrow$ **true**
while *continue* **do**
  continue $\leftarrow$ **false**
  for all $J \subseteq \{0,\ldots,s-1\}$ with $|J| = d$ **do**
    if $\mathrm{rk}(H[J]) < d$ and $\mathrm{rk}\,H[J\cap I^c] = |J \cap I^c|$ **then**
      $d \leftarrow d - 1$
      continue $\leftarrow$ **true**
return $d + 1$

Alternatively, following a suggestion of Prof. Alfred Wassermann, we may adapt the well known Brouwer-Zimmermann algorithm, in order to calculate the cyclic column distances. Let $V \subseteq W \subseteq \mathbb{F}^s$ be two vector subspaces and let $C = W \setminus V$. Our purpose is to compute $\mathrm{d}(C)$, which covers the computation of the cyclic column distances. Let $k = \dim W$ and $r = \dim V$. Without loss of generality we can assume that W is generated by the rows of a matrix

$$G = \left(\frac{G_1}{G_2}\right)$$

where $G_1 \in \mathcal{M}_{(k-r)\times s}(\mathbb{F})$, $G_2 \in \mathcal{M}_{r\times s}(\mathbb{F})$ and the rows of G_2 generate V. Hence

$$C = \{vG : v_{[0,k-r-1]} \neq 0\}.$$

Up to a suitable permutation of the columns, which is an isometry, we may apply the first part of the Brouwer-Zimmermann algorithm, as presented in [1, §1.8]. We thus obtain t matrices Γ_j such that $\Gamma_j = A_jG$, where A_j is a $k\times k$ non-singular matrix, for any $j = 1,\ldots,t$. The matrix Γ_j has the form

$$\Gamma_j = \left(\; L_j \; \middle| \; \begin{array}{c|c} I_{k_j} & L_j' \\ \hline 0 & 0 \end{array} \right),$$

and the columns where the identity matrix is placed are disjoint for any other matrix Γ_d with $d \neq j$. In particular, the maximum Hamming weight for a vector in W is $\sum_{j=1}^{t} k_j$.

Define the subsets $C_i = \{v\Gamma_j \in C : \mathrm{w}(v) \leq i\}$. Since $\Gamma_i = A_iG$,

$$C_i = \{v\Gamma_j \in W : \mathrm{w}(v) \leq i \text{ and } (vA_j)_{[0,k-r-1]} \neq 0\}.$$

Hence,

$$C_1 \subseteq C_2 \subseteq \cdots \subseteq C_{k-1} \subseteq C_k = C.$$

If we set $\overline{d}_i = \mathrm{d}(C_i)$, we find then that

$$\overline{d}_1 \geq \overline{d}_2 \geq \cdots \geq \overline{d}_{k-1} \geq \overline{d}_k = \mathrm{d}(C).$$

In order to compute an increasing sequence of lower bounds of the distance of C, we may make use the one provided by the Brouwer-Zimmermann algorithm. Indeed, following this algorithm, let

$$\widehat{C}_i = \{v\Gamma_j \in W : \mathrm{w}(v) \leq i\},$$

$\widehat{d}_i = \mathrm{d}(\widehat{C}_i)$ and $\underline{d}_i = \sum_{j=1}^{t}(i+1)-(k-k_j)$. Hence $\mathrm{d}(W\backslash\widehat{C}_i) \geq \underline{d}_i$ for any $i = 1, \ldots, k$, and there exists a minimal i_0 such that $\widehat{d}_{i_0} \leq \underline{d}_{i_0}$. Consequently, $\mathrm{d}(C) = \widehat{d}_{i_0}$. Now,

$$\begin{aligned} W\backslash\widehat{C}_i \supseteq C\backslash\widehat{C}_i &= C\backslash(C_i\backslash V) = C\backslash(C_i \cap V^c) \\ &= C \cap (C_i \cap V^c)^c = C \cap (C_i^c \cup V) \\ &= (C \cap C_i^c) \cup (C \cap V) = C \cap C_i^c = C\backslash C_i, \end{aligned}$$

so $\mathrm{d}(C\backslash C_i) \geq \mathrm{d}(W\backslash\widehat{C}_i) \geq \underline{d}_i$ for any $i = 1, \ldots, k$. Finally, since $\underline{d}_k = t + \sum_{j=1}^{t} k_j = \max\{\mathrm{w}(c) \mid c \in W\}$, there exists a minimal j_0 such that

$$\mathrm{d}(C_i) = \overline{d}_{j_0} \leq \underline{d}_{j_0} \leq \mathrm{d}(C\backslash C_i),$$

and thus $\mathrm{d}(C) = \overline{d}_{j_0}$.

In order to implement this version of the Brower-Zimmermann algorithm to the computation of δ_l^c, it is convenient to present the set K_l, expressed according to (11) and (12), via a generator matrix. To this end, write $F_l^c = I - E_l^c$, which is an idempotent matrix. Here, I denotes a suitable identity matrix. Therefore, $N_l = \mathrm{im}(\cdot F_l^c)$. Indeed, if we pick $a \in A^{l+1}$, then $a \in N_l$ if, and only if, $aF_l^c = a$. On the other hand,

$$E_l^c = \left(\begin{array}{c|c} e_0 & e_{>0} \\ \hline 0 & \sigma^{-1}(E_{l-1}^c) \end{array}\right),$$

where $e_{>0} = (\sigma^{-1}(e_1), \sigma^{-2}(e_2), \ldots)$. Setting $\epsilon_0 = 1 - e_0$ and $\epsilon_{>0} = -e_{>0}$, we get

$$F_l^c = \left(\begin{array}{c|c} \epsilon_0 & \epsilon_{>0} \\ \hline 0 & \sigma^{-1}(F_{l-1}^c) \end{array}\right).$$

Therefore, if we write $a = (a_0|a_{>0}) \in A \times A^l$, then $a \in N_l$ if and only if $a_0 = a_0\epsilon_0$ and $a_{>0} = a_0\epsilon_{>0} + a_{>0}\sigma^{-1}(F_{l-1}^c)$. We thus get that $a \in P_l$ if, and only if, $a = (0|a_{>0})$ with $a_{>0} = a_{>0}\sigma^{-1}(F_{l-1}^c)$. Hence, $P_l = \{(0|b) \in A \times A^l : b \in \mathrm{im}(\cdot\sigma^{-1}(F_{l-1}^c)\}$.

The discussion above ensures the correction of Algorithm 2. By Row(M) we mean the row space of a matrix M.

Finally, we apply these algorithms to some examples of idempotent convolutional codes.

Example 4.3. Let $\mathbb{F} = \mathbb{F}_2(a)$ be the field with 4 elements. Consider the left skew polynomial ring[1] $\mathbb{F}[x;\tau]$, where τ is the Frobenius automorphism, and the quotient algebra $A = \mathbb{F}[x;\tau]/\langle x^2 - 1\rangle$. Since the order of τ is 2, A is isomorphic to the matrix ring $\mathcal{M}_2(\mathbb{F}_2)$, see [9]. Let $R = A[z]$ be the ring of standard polynomials over the algebra A, and consider $e = e_0 + ze_1$, where $e_0 = ax + a$ and $e_1 = x + 1$. It is easy to check that e is idempotent in R, so $C = \mathfrak{v}(R(1-e))$ is an ICC in the sense of Definition 3.2. Observe that

$$\mathfrak{m}(E_0^c) = \begin{pmatrix} a & a \\ a+1 & a+1 \end{pmatrix},$$

so, clearly, $\delta_0^c = 2$. In order to compute δ_1^c, following Algorithm 2, F_1^c is extended to

$$\mathfrak{m}(F_1^c) = \left(\begin{array}{cccc} a+1 & a & 1 & 1 \\ a+1 & a & 1 & 1 \\ \hline 0 & 0 & a+1 & a \\ 0 & 0 & a+1 & a \end{array}\right).$$

[1] i.e. the coefficients are written on the left and the multiplication is based on the rule $xa = \tau(a)x$.

Algorithm 2 Cyclic column distance calculation

Input: The matrix E_j^c, where $j \geq 1$, and $n = \dim_{\mathbb{F}} A$.
Output: The cyclic column distance δ_j^c.

$F_{j-1}^c \leftarrow I - E_{j-1}^c$.
$F_j^c \leftarrow I - E_j^c$.
$a_1, \ldots, a_r \leftarrow$ basis of $\mathrm{Row}(\mathfrak{m}((0|\sigma^{-1}(F_{j-1}^c)))$.
$b_1, \ldots, b_{k-r} \leftarrow$ extension to a basis of $\mathrm{Row}(\mathfrak{m}(F_j^c))$.
$G \leftarrow$ matrix with rows formed by $b_1, \ldots, b_{k-r}, a_1, \ldots, a_r$.
Apply Brouwer-Zimmermann algorithm to G and compute matrices Γ_i, where $\Gamma_i = A_iG$ with A_i non-singular, for any $i = 1, \ldots, m$.
$C_0 \leftarrow 0$
$i \leftarrow 0, \underline{d} \leftarrow 0, \overline{d} \leftarrow \infty$
while $\underline{d} < \overline{d}$ **do**
  $i \leftarrow i + 1$
  $C_i \leftarrow C_{i-1} \cup \bigcup_{j=1}^{m}\{v\Gamma_j \in W \mid \mathrm{w}(v) = i, (vA_i)_{[0,k-r-1]} \neq 0\}$
  $\overline{d} \leftarrow \mathrm{d}(C_i)$
  $\underline{d} \leftarrow \sum_{\substack{j=1 \\ k-k_j \leq i}}^{m} (i+1) - (k-k_j)$
return $\overline{d}$

Algorithm 3 Free distance calculation

Input: A parity check idempotent $e = \sum_{i=0}^{m} z^i e_i$ of an idempotent convolutional code C.
Output: $\mathrm{d}(C)$.

$rep \leftarrow 0, j \leftarrow 0$
while $rep < m$ **do**
  Compute matrix E_j^c
  $\delta_j^c \leftarrow$ Output of Algorithm 1 or Algorithm 2 for E_j^c.
  if $j > 0$ and $\delta_j^c = \delta_{j-1}^c$ **then**
    $rep \leftarrow rep + 1$
  else
    $rep \leftarrow 0$
  $j \leftarrow j + 1$
return δ_j^c

The last two rows generate the vector space P_1 described above, hence, computing its row reduced echelon form, we get a basis of P_1. Concretely, this basis is $\{(0, 0, 1, a+1)\}$. Now, we extend it to a basis of N_1 by adding the first (or the second) row. So we construct

$$G = \begin{pmatrix} a+1 & a & 1 & 1 \\ 0 & 0 & 1 & a+1 \end{pmatrix}.$$

Applying the Brouwer-Zimmermann algorithm we find that $\Gamma_1 = A_1G$ and $\Gamma_2 = A_2G$, where

$$\Gamma_1 = \begin{pmatrix} 1 & a+1 & 0 & a+1 \\ 0 & 0 & 1 & a+1 \end{pmatrix}, \quad A_1 = \begin{pmatrix} a & a \\ 0 & 1 \end{pmatrix},$$

$$\Gamma_2 = \begin{pmatrix} a & 1 & a & 0 \\ 0 & 0 & a & 1 \end{pmatrix}, \quad A_2 = \begin{pmatrix} a+1 & 1 \\ 0 & a \end{pmatrix}.$$

Moreover, $k_1 = 2$ and $k_2 = 2$. An exhaustive search provides that $\overline{d}_1 = 3$ whilst $\underline{d}_1 = 4$. Therefore $\delta_1^c = 3$.

Similarly, we may compute a basis of N_2 by considering

$$\left(\begin{array}{ccc|ccc} a+1 & a & 1 & 1 & 0 & 0 \\ \hline 0 & 0 & 1 & a+1 & 0 & a+1 \\ 0 & 0 & 0 & 0 & 1 & a+1 \end{array}\right).$$

In this case, $\Gamma_1 = A_1 G$ and $\Gamma_2 = A_2 G$, where

$$\Gamma_1 = \begin{pmatrix} 1 & a+1 & 0 & a+1 & 0 & 1 \\ 0 & 0 & 1 & a+1 & 0 & a+1 \\ 0 & 0 & 0 & 0 & 1 & a+1 \end{pmatrix}, \quad A_1 = \begin{pmatrix} a & a & 0 \\ 0 & 1 & 0 \\ 0 & 0 & 1 \end{pmatrix},$$

$$\Gamma_2 = \begin{pmatrix} a & 1 & a & 0 & 1 & 0 \\ 0 & 0 & a & 1 & a & 0 \\ 0 & 0 & 0 & 0 & a & 1 \end{pmatrix}, \quad A_2 = \begin{pmatrix} a+1 & 1 & 1 \\ 0 & a & a \\ 0 & 0 & a \end{pmatrix}.$$

which yields that $\delta_2^c = 4$. Finally, Algorithm 2 outputs that $\delta_3^c = 4$, so, by Theorem 3.12, the free distance $\mathrm{d}_{\mathrm{free}}(C) = 4$.

Example 4.4. Let $\mathbb{F} = \mathbb{F}_2(a)$ be the field with 2^5 elements, where $a^5+a^2+1 = 0$. Consider the left skew polynomial ring $\mathbb{F}[x;\tau]$, where τ is the Frobenius automorphism, and the quotient algebra $A = \mathbb{F}[x;\tau]/\langle x^5 - 1\rangle$. Let $R = A[z]$ be the ring of standard polynomials over the algebra A, and consider $e = e_0 + ze_1$, where

$$e_0 = a^{28} + a^{21}x + a^{11}x^2 + a^{22}x^3 + a^{13}x^4$$
$$e_1 = a^{14} + a^{28}x + a^{25}x^2 + a^{19}x^3 + a^7x^4.$$

It is easy to check that e is idempotent in R, so $C = \mathfrak{v}(R(1-e))$ is an ICC in the sense of Definition 3.2. With the aid of [20], we have applied Algorithms 3 and 1 or 2 getting the following sequence of cyclic distances:

j	0	1	2	3
δ_j^c	5	9	10	10

Hence $\mathrm{d}_{\mathrm{free}}(C) = \delta_2^c = \delta_3^c = 10$. Observe that, in order to compute δ_3^c, it is needed to work with E_3^c, a 20×20 matrix over $\mathbb{F}_{2^5}$.

Our last example is a convolutional code modeled on a Piret algebra, that is, the sentence-ambient algebra is one example of the rings originally considered in [16].

Example 4.5. Let $\mathbb{F} = \mathbb{F}_2$ and $A = \mathbb{F}[x]/\langle x^7 - 1\rangle$. Let $\sigma : A \to A$ defined by $\sigma(x) = x^3$. It is easy to check that σ is indeed an algebra map, with inverse $\sigma^{-1}(x) = x^5$. Let $R = A[z;\sigma]$,

$$\epsilon = z^5\left(x^4+x^3+x^2+1\right) + z\left(x^5+x^2+x+1\right) + x^4+x^2+x+1$$

and

$$e = 1-\epsilon = z^5\left(x^4+x^3+x^2+1\right)+z\left(x^5+x^2+x+1\right)+x^4+x^2+x,$$

which are the idempotent generator and the parity check idempotent of the ICC $C = R\epsilon$. We have applied Algorithm 3 getting the following sequence of cyclic distances:

j	0	1	2	3	4	5	6	7	8	9	10	11
δ_j^c	4	6	8	8	8	10	12	12	12	12	12	12

Hence $\mathrm{d}_{\mathrm{free}}(C) = \delta_6^c = \delta_{11}^c = 12$.

ACKNOWLEDGMENTS

Research partially supported by grant MTM2016-78364-P from Agencia Estatal de Investigación (AEI) and from Fondo Europeo de Desarrollo Regional (FEDER). The authors would like to thank Alfred Wassermann his suggestion of adapting the Brouwer—Zimmermann algorithm in order to compute the distance of a difference set of vector spaces.

REFERENCES

[1] A. Betten, M. Braun, H. Fripertinger, A. Kerber, A. Kohnert, and A. Wassermann. 2006. *Error-Correcting Linear Codes.* Algorithms and Computation in Mathematics, Vol. 18. Springer.
[2] D. J. Costello Jr. 1969. A construction technique for random-error-correcting convolutional codes. *IEEE Transactions on Information Theory* 15, 5 (September 1969), 631–636. https://doi.org/10.1109/TIT.1969.1054337
[3] D. J. Costello Jr. 1974. Free distance bounds for convolutional codes. *IEEE Transactions on Information Theory* 20, 3 (1974), 356–365. https://doi.org/10.1109/TIT.1974.1055223
[4] S. Estrada, J. R. García-Rozas, J. Peralta, and E. Sánchez-García. 2008. Group convolutional codes. *Advances in Mathematics of Communications* 2, 1 (2008), 83–94. https://doi.org/10.3934/amc.2008.2.83
[5] G. D. Forney Jr. 1970. Convolutional codes I: Algebraic structure. *IEEE Transactions on Information Theory* 16, 6 (1970), 720–738. https://doi.org/10.1109/TIT.1970.1054541
[6] H. Gluesing-Luerssen and W. Schmale. 2004. On Cyclic Convolutional Codes. *Acta Applicandae Mathematicae* 82, 2 (2004), 183–237. https://doi.org/10.1023/B:ACAP.0000027534.61242.09
[7] J. Gómez-Torrecillas, F. J. Lobillo, and G. Navarro. 2015. Separable Automorphisms on Matrix Algebras over Finite Field Extensions: Applications to Ideal Codes.. In *Proceedings of the 2015 ACM on International Symposium on Symbolic and Algebraic Computation (ISSAC '15).* ACM, New York, NY, USA, 189–195. https://doi.org/10.1145/2755996.2756671
[8] J. Gómez-Torrecillas, F. J. Lobillo, and G. Navarro. 2016. Convolutional codes with a matrix-algebra word ambient. *Advances in Mathematics of Communications* 10, 1 (2016), 29–43.
[9] J. Gómez-Torrecillas, F. J. Lobillo, and G. Navarro. 2016. A New Perspective of Cyclicity in Convolutional Codes. *IEEE Transactions on Information Theory* 62, 5 (2016), 2702 – 2706. https://doi.org/10.1109/TIT.2016.2538264
[10] J. Gómez-Torrecillas, F. J. Lobillo, and G. Navarro. 2017. Computing separability elements for the sentence-ambient algebra of split ideal codes. *Journal of Symbolic Computation* 83 (2017), 211–227.
[11] J. Gómez-Torrecillas, F. J. Lobillo, and G. Navarro. 2017. Ideal codes over separable ring extensions. *IEEE Transactions on Information Theory* 63, 5 (May 2017), 2796 – 2813. https://doi.org/10.1109/TIT.2017.2682856
[12] W. C. Huffman and V. Pless. 2010. *Fundamentals of Error-Correcting Codes.* Cambridge University Press.
[13] R. Johannesson and K. Sh. Zigangirov. 1999. *Fundamentals of Convolutional Coding.* Wiley-IEEE Press. http://eu.wiley.com/WileyCDA/WileyTitle/productCd-0780334833,miniSiteCd-IEEE2.html
[14] S. Lin and D. J. Costello Jr. 2004. *Error Control Coding, Second Edition.* Prentice-Hall, Inc., Upper Saddle River, NJ, USA.
[15] S. R. López-Permouth and S. Szabo. 2013. Convolutional codes with additional algebraic structure. *Journal of Pure and Applied Algebra* 217, 5 (2013), 958 – 972. https://doi.org/10.1016/j.jpaa.2012.09.017
[16] P. Piret. 1976. Structure and constructions of cyclic convolutional codes. *IEEE Transactions on Information Theory* 22, 2 (1976), 147–155. https://doi.org/10.1109/TIT.1976.1055531
[17] C. Roos. 1979. On the Structure of Convolutional and Cyclic Convolutional Codes. *IEEE Transactions on Information Theory* IT-25, 6 (1979), 676–683.
[18] J. Rosenthal, J. M. Schumacher, and E. V. York. 1996. On behaviors and convolutional codes. *IEEE Transactions on Information Theory* 42, 6 (1996), 1881–1891.
[19] J. Rosenthal and R. Smarandache. 1999. Maximum distance separable convolutional codes. *Applicable Algebra in Engeneering, Communication and Computing* 10, 1 (1999), 15–32.
[20] The Sage Developers. 2017. *SageMath, the Sage Mathematics Software System (Version 7.4).* http://www.sagemath.org/
[21] A. Vardy. 1997. The Intractability of Computing the Minimum Distance of a Code. *IEEE Transactions on Information Theory* 46, 6 (1997), 1757 – 1766. https://doi.org/10.1109/18.641542

Effective Computation of Generalized Spectral Sequences

Andrea Guidolin
Politecnico di Torino
Torino, Italy
andrea.guidolin@polito.it

Ana Romero*
University of La Rioja
Logroño, Spain
ana.romero@unirioja.es

ABSTRACT

In this paper, we present some algorithms and programs for computing generalized spectral sequences, a useful tool in Computational Algebraic Topology which provides topological information on spaces with generalized filtrations over a poset. Our programs have been implemented as a new module for the Kenzo system and solve the classical problems of spectral sequences which are differential maps and extensions. Moreover, combined with the use of effective homology and discrete vector fields, the programs make it possible to compute generalized spectral sequences of big spaces, sometimes of infinite type.

CCS CONCEPTS

• **Computing methodologies → Computer algebra systems; Algebraic algorithms**; • **Mathematics of computing** → *Mathematical software*;

KEYWORDS

Symbolic Computation, Constructive Algebraic Topology, Generalized spectral sequences, Effective homology, Discrete vector fields.

ACM Reference Format:

Andrea Guidolin and Ana Romero. 2018. Effective Computation of Generalized Spectral Sequences. In *Proceedings of 2018 ACM International Symposium on Symbolic and Algebraic Computation (ISSAC '18)*. ACM, New York, NY, USA, 8 pages. https://doi.org/10.1145/3208976.3208984

1 INTRODUCTION

Spectral sequences are a useful tool in Algebraic Topology providing information on homology groups by successive approximations from the homology of appropriate associated complexes. More concretely, a spectral sequence is a family of "pages" $\{E^r_{p,q}, d^r\}$ of differential bigraded modules, each page being made of the homology groups of the preceding one. Spectral sequences were introduced in 1946 by Jean Leray [11] and have been used in many different contexts to determine homology or homotopy groups of interesting spaces (see for example [2, 5, 22]). However, as John McCleary expressed in his famous book [14], "*knowledge of $E^r_{*,*}$ and d^r determines $E^{r+1}_{*,*}$ but not d^{r+1}. If we think of a spectral sequence as a black box, then the input is a differential bigraded module, usually $E^1_{*,*}$, and, with each turn of the handle, the machine computes a successive homology according to a sequence of differentials. If some differential is unknown, then some other (any other) principle is needed to proceed.*" In general spectral sequences can be algorithmically determined when they are related with objects of finite type (see for instance [1] and [6]). However, when the initial object is not of finite type, the higher differentials of the spectral sequence are mathematically defined but their definition is not constructive, i.e., the differentials are not computable with the usually provided information.

A particular case of spectral sequences arises from a filtered chain complex, that is a sequence of chain subcomplexes (indexed over the integer numbers $\mathbb{Z}$) $\ldots \subseteq F_{p-1}C_* \subseteq F_pC_* \subseteq F_{p+1}C_* \subseteq \ldots$ of a chain complex C_*. The spectral sequence produces then a sequence of groups which, in a suitable sense, "converges" to the homology groups of C_*. Although in this case a formal expression for the different groups $E^r_{p,q}$ (as quotients of some subgroups of the filtered complex) is known [14], this expression is not always sufficient to compute the $E^r_{p,q}$'s (and the implementations in [1] and [6] are not valid) when the initial filtered complex is not of finite type, a frequent situation.

Spectral sequences have been recently generalized by Benjamin Matschke [13] to a much broader perspective. The most innovative aspect of his remarkable construction is that it applies to filtrations indexed over any partially ordered set (poset), rather than being limited to filtrations indexed over the set $\mathbb{Z}$ of integer numbers. Furthermore, the collection of groups produced by his generalized construction, which he calls a *spectral system*, is larger than in the classical scenario, as more parameters are taken into account. The main motivation for the introduction of this generalized construction is to describe a mathematical object general enough to unify several spectral sequences which usually one would apply in succession; in this respect, the paper [13] includes several interesting examples which generalize the classical spectral sequences of Serre [22], Eilenberg-Moore [5] and Adams-Novikov [15]. In similar situations, spectral systems are more versatile than successive spectral sequences: if a chain complex C_* is suitably filtered over a poset, one usually has a wider range of possible ways to construct collections of groups which "converge" to the homology groups of C_*. Since a generalized spectral sequence reveals information not only on the homology of C_*, but also on the role played by the generalized filtration, its computation is particularly relevant; however, as in the case of spectral sequences associated with a linear filtration, no algorithm is provided computing the different components when the initial spaces are not of finite type.

*Partially supported by Ministerio de Economía, Industria y Competitividad, Spain, project MTM2017-88804-P.

ISSAC '18, July 16–19, 2018, New York, NY, USA

ACM ISBN 978-1-4503-5550-6/18/07...$15.00
https://doi.org/10.1145/3208976.3208984

In this work we present some algorithms and programs for computing generalized spectral sequences by using the method of *effective homology* [19], that the second author also used in [16] for computing spectral sequences in the linear case. Moreover, we explain how the programs can be enhanced with the use of discrete vector fields [18], and we describe some applications of our algorithms. The programs have been implemented as a new module for the Computer Algebra system Kenzo [4] and are available at http://www.unirioja.es/cu/anromero/research2.html.

2 PRELIMINARIES

2.1 Generalized spectral sequences

Generalized spectral sequences are a construction that extends the classical definition of spectral sequence [14] to the case of filtrations indexed over a poset.

Definition 2.1. A filtration of a chain complex C_* over a poset $(I, \leq)$, briefly called an I-filtration, is a collection of subcomplexes $F = (F_iC_*)_{i\in I}$ such that

$$i \leq j \text{ in } I \quad \Longrightarrow \quad F_iC_* \subseteq F_jC_*.$$

We will often denote the chain subcomplexes simply as F_i, forgetting about the grading of homology, when we are only interested in the filtration index i.

Now, recall that for classical spectral sequences, which arise from a $\mathbb{Z}$-filtration $(F_p)_{p\in\mathbb{Z}}$, we have the formula (see [12]):

$$E^r_{p,q} = \frac{Z^r_{p,q} + F_{p-1}C_{p+q}}{d(Z^{r-1}_{p+r-1,q-r+2}) + F_{p-1}C_{p+q}}, \tag{1}$$

where $Z^r_{p,q} = \{a \in F_pC_{p+q} : d(a) \in F_{p-r}C_{p+q-1}\}$. This formula can be rewritten as

$$E^r_{p,q} = \frac{F_p \cap d^{-1}(F_{p-r})}{d(F_{p+r-1}) + F_{p-1}}, \tag{2}$$

where for simplicity we do not denote the grading of homology. To be precise, as in (2) the denominator is not necessarily a subgroup of the numerator, the formula has to be interpreted keeping in mind that *by convention* we denote A/B meaning $A/(B \cap A) \cong (A + B)/B$. The interest of this formula is that in (2) we can easily observe the interplay of 4 filtration indexes: p and $p - r$ (in the numerator), $p + r - 1$ and $p - 1$ (in the denominator).

In [13], this formula was imitated and generalized to the case of I-filtrations by defining, for every 4-tuple of indexes $z \leq s \leq p \leq b \in I$, the term

$$S[z, s, p, b] = \frac{F_p \cap d^{-1}(F_z)}{d(F_b) + F_s} \equiv \frac{F_p \cap d^{-1}(F_z) + F_s}{F_p \cap d(F_b) + F_s}. \tag{3}$$

The collection of all such terms is called a *generalized spectral sequence* or a *spectral system* for the I-filtration $(F_i)_{i\in I}$.

Generalized spectral sequences are in many aspects similar to classical ones. For example, the next result extends what in the classical case is the way of obtaining terms of the page $r + 1$ by taking homology at page r:

Proposition 2.2 ([13]). *Given an I-filtration $(F_i)_{i\in I}$ for a chain complex C_* and three 4-tuples of indexes satisfying the condition*

$$z_1 \leq s_1 \leq p_1 = z_2 \leq b_1 = s_2 \leq p_2 = z_3 \leq b_2 = s_3 \leq p_3 \leq b_3,$$

the differential of the chain complex C_* induces differentials d_3, d_2 between the terms

$$S[z_3, s_3, p_3, b_3] \xrightarrow{d_3} S[z_2, s_2, p_2, b_2] \xrightarrow{d_2} S[z_1, s_1, p_1, b_1]$$

and by taking homology we obtain

$$\frac{\ker d_2}{\operatorname{Im} d_3} = S[s_1, s_2, p_2, p_3].$$

The paper [13] includes some examples of generalized spectral sequences associated with *interesting* objects. For example, the generalized Serre spectral sequence is defined by means of a tower of fibrations (and generalizes the classical Serre spectral sequence of a fibration [22]). However, the definitions in [13] are formal and the paper does not include a method to compute the spectral systems. In particular, let us remark that the formula (3) can only be directly determined when the initial chain complex is of finite type.

2.2 Effective homology

The effective homology method, introduced in [21] and explained in depth in [19] and [20], is a technique which can be used to determine homology of complicated spaces. We present now the main definitions and ideas of this method.

Definition 2.3. A *reduction* $\rho \equiv (D_* \Rightarrow C_*)$ between two chain complexes D_* and C_* is a triple (f, g, h) where: (a) The components f and g are chain complex morphisms $f : D_* \to C_*$ and $g : C_* \to D_*$; (b) The component h is a homotopy operator $h : D_* \to D_{*+1}$ (a graded group homomorphism of degree +1); (c) The following relations must be satisfied: (1) $fg = \mathrm{id}_{C_*}$; (2) $gf + d_{D_*}h + hd_{D_*} = \mathrm{id}_{D_*}$; (3) $fh = 0$; (4) $hg = 0$; (5) $hh = 0$.

Remark 1. *These relations express that D_* is the direct sum of C_* and a contractible (acyclic) complex. This decomposition is simply $D_* = \ker f \oplus \operatorname{Im} g$, with $\operatorname{Im} g \cong C_*$ and $H_n(\ker f) = 0$ for all n. In particular, this implies that the graded homology groups $H_*(D_*)$ and $H_*(C_*)$ are canonically isomorphic.*

Definition 2.4. A *(strong chain) equivalence* $\varepsilon \equiv (C_* \Longleftrightarrow E_*)$ between two complexes C_* and E_* is a triple (D_*, ρ, ρ') where D_* is a chain complex and ρ and ρ' are reductions from D_* over C_* and E_* respectively: $C_* \overset{\rho}{\Leftarrow} D_* \overset{\rho'}{\Rightarrow} E_*$.

Definition 2.5. An *effective* chain complex C_* is a free chain complex (i.e., a chain complex consisting of free $\mathbb{Z}$-modules) where each group C_n is finitely generated, and there is an algorithm that returns a $\mathbb{Z}$-base β_n in each degree n (for details, see [19]).

The homology groups of an effective chain complex C_* can easily be determined by means of some diagonalization algorithms on matrices (see [9]).

Definition 2.6. An *object with effective homology* is a triple (X, EC_*, ε) where X is an object (e.g. a simplicial set, a topological space) possessing a canonically associated free chain complex $C_*(X)$, EC_* is an effective chain complex and ε is an equivalence between $C_*(X)$ and EC_*, $C_*(X) \overset{\varepsilon}{\Longleftrightarrow} EC_*$.

Remark 2. *It is important to understand that in general the EC_* component of an object with effective homology is not made of the homology groups of X; this component EC_* is a free $\mathbb{Z}$-chain complex of* *finite type, in general with a non-null differential, allowing to compute the homology groups of X; the justification is the equivalence ε.*

The notion of object with effective homology makes it possible in this way to compute homology groups of complicated spaces by using effective complexes and computing their homology groups, which can be easily obtained through some elementary algorithms on matrices. The method is based on the following idea: given some topological spaces $X_1, \ldots, X_n$, a topological constructor Φ produces a new topological space X. If effective homology versions of the spaces $X_1, \ldots, X_n$ are known, then an effective homology version of the space X can also be built, and this version allows us to compute the homology groups of X, even if it is not of finite type. This method has been implemented in the system Kenzo [4], a Common Lisp 16,000 lines program devoted to Symbolic Computation in Algebraic Topology, which has made it possible to determine homology and homotopy groups of complicated spaces and has obtained some results (for example homology groups of iterated loop spaces of a loop space modified by a cell attachment, components of complex Postnikov towers, see [20] for details) which were not known before.

2.3 Discrete vector fields

The notion of discrete vector field (DVF) is due to Robin Forman ([7]); it is an essential component of the so-called discrete Morse theory. This notion is usually described and used in combinatorial topology, but a purely algebraic version can also be given as follows. See [18] for more details.

Definition 2.7. Let $C_* = (C_n, d_n)_{n\in\mathbb{Z}}$ be a free chain complex with distinguished $\mathbb{Z}$-basis $\beta_n \subset C_n$. A *discrete vector field* V on C_* is a collection of pairs $V = \{(\sigma_k; \tau_k)\}_{k\in K}$ satisfying the conditions:

- Every σ_k is some element of some β_n, in which case $\tau_k \in \beta_{n+1}$. The degree n depends on k and in general is not constant.
- Every component σ_k is a *regular face* of the corresponding τ_k (that is, the coefficient of σ_k in $d\tau_k$ is $+1$ or -1).
- Each generator (*cell*) of C_* appears at most one time in V.

It is not required all the cells of C_* appear in the vector field V. In particular, the void vector field is allowed. Moreover, we do not assume the distinguished bases β_n are finite, the chain groups C_n are not necessarily of finite type. The vector field V could also be not finite.

Definition 2.8. A cell $\sigma \in \beta_n$ which does not appear in the discrete vector field V is called a *critical n-cell.*

Definition 2.9. Given a discrete vector field V, a *V-path π of degree n and length m* is a sequence $\pi = \{(\sigma_{k_j}; \tau_{k_j})\}_{0\le j<m}$ satisfying:

- Every pair $(\sigma_{k_j}; \tau_{k_j})$ is a component of V and τ_{k_j} is an n-cell.
- For every $0 < j < m$, the component σ_{k_j} is a *face* of $\tau_{k_{j-1}}$ (that is, the coefficient of σ_{k_j} in $d\tau_{k_{j-1}}$ is non-null), not necessarily regular but different from $\sigma_{k_{j-1}}$.

The V-path is said *starting from* σ_{k_0}.

Definition 2.10. A discrete vector field V is *admissible* if for every $n \in \mathbb{Z}$, a function $\lambda_n : \beta_n \to \mathbb{N}$ is provided satisfying the following property: every V-path starting from $\sigma \in \beta_n$ has a length bounded by $\lambda_n(\sigma)$.

The admissibility property is necessary to exclude infinite paths and loops, and is used to ensure the homotopy type of the corresponding *reduced* chain complex (where only the critical cells are considered) is the same as the initial one. This result is due to Robin Forman [7, Section 8], and can be extended to complexes not necessarily of finite type as follows.

THEOREM 2.11. *([18])[Vector-Field Reduction Theorem] Let $C_* = (C_n, d_n, \beta_n)_{n\in\mathbb{Z}}$ be a free chain complex and $V = \{(\sigma_k; \tau_k)\}_{k\in K}$ be an admissible discrete vector field on C_*. Then the vector field V defines a canonical reduction $\rho = (f, g, h) : (C_n, d_n) \Rightarrow (C_n^c, d_n')$ where $C_n^c = \mathbb{Z}[\beta_n^c]$ is the free $\mathbb{Z}$-module generated by the critical n-cells and d_n' is an appropriate differential canonically deduced from C_* and V.*

See [18] for the definitions of the maps d_n', f, g and h.

Thanks to Theorem 2.11 and the explicit isomorphism $H_n(C_*) \cong H_n(C_*^c)$ deduced from the reduction $\rho : C_* \Rightarrow C_*^c$, one can compute the homology groups of the big (possibly infinite) chain complex C_* by means of the homology groups of C_*^c (whenever C_*^c is of finite type). In [18], this result is used to produce, for example, the effective homology of twisted cartesian products and Eilenberg-MacLane spaces.

Discrete vector fields have been also implemented in the Kenzo system, making it possible to *reduce* the size of chain complexes before computing homology.

3 EFFECTIVE ALGORITHMS FOR COMPUTING GENERALIZED SPECTRAL SEQUENCES

In this section, we present some new algorithms for the computation of generalized spectral sequences. Our algorithms make use of the effective homology method and of discrete vector fields, and have been implemented in the Kenzo system (as it will be explained in Section 4).

Let us begin by considering a chain complex C_* of finite type, with a generalized filtration over a poset $(I, \le)$. Furthermore, let us suppose that C_* is equipped with a distinguished (finite) $\mathbb{Z}$-basis. In this case, all the subgroups which appear in the term $S[z, s, p, b]$ of the associated generalized spectral sequence given by the formula

$$S[z, s, p, b] = \frac{F_p \cap d^{-1}(F_z) + F_s}{F_p \cap d(F_b) + F_s}, \tag{4}$$

can be determined and expressed as matrices containing as columns the generators of the groups. In particular, a matrix D_n^b representing $d(F_b)$ is given by a *submatrix* of the differential matrix $D_n : C_n \to C_{n-1}$ corresponding to the columns of the generators of C_n which are in F_b; $F_p \cap d(F_b)$ is computed as the kernel of a new submatrix of D_n^b given in this case by the rows of generators which are in $F_b - F_p$. Then the corresponding quotient can be computed by means of diagonalization algorithms of matrices in a similar way to the algorithm used to compute homology groups by means of the Smith Normal Form technique (see [9]). The result is a *basis-divisors* description of the group $S[z, s, p, b]$, that is to say, a list of combinations $(c_1, \ldots, c_{\alpha+k})$ which generate the group, as well as the list of non-negative integers $(b_1, \ldots, b_k, 0, \overset{\alpha}{\ldots}, 0)$ (such that each b_j divides b_{j+1}) that contains the torsion coefficients and α

0's corresponding to the free factor. The list of *divisors* can be seen as the list of the coefficients of the elements that appear in the denominator with regard to the list of combinations that generate the group. We obtain in this way the following algorithm:

ALGORITHM 1.
Input:

- *an effective chain complex* $C_* = (C_n, d_n)_{n\in\mathbb{N}}$,
- *a generalized filtration for* C_* *over a poset* $(I, \leq)$,
- *elements* z, s, p, b *in* I *such that* $z \leq s \leq p \leq b$.

Output: a basis-divisors representation of the group $S[z, s, p, b]$.

For the computation of the differential maps $d : S[z_2, s_2, p_2, b_2] \to S[z_1, s_1, p_1, b_1]$, we compute first the basis-divisors representation of both $S[z_2, s_2, p_2, b_2] \equiv S_2$ and $S[z_1, s_1, p_1, b_1] \equiv S_1$ by means of Algorithm 1. Let us suppose that S_2 is generated by a list of combinations $(c_1, \ldots, c_t)$ with divisors $(b_1, \ldots, b_t) = (b_1, \ldots, b_k, 0, \overset{\alpha}{\ldots}, 0)$ (where $t = k + \alpha$). Similarly, S_1 is generated by $(c'_1, \ldots, c'_{t'})$, with divisors $(b'_1, \ldots, b'_{t'}) = (b'_1, \ldots, b'_{k'}, 0, \overset{\alpha'}{\ldots}, 0)$.

Let a be a class of S_2, given by means of its coefficients $(\lambda_1, \ldots, \lambda_t)$ (with $\lambda_i \in \mathbb{Z}$) with respect to the set of generators $(c_1, \ldots, c_t)$. Then, we consider the element $x = \sum_{i=1}^{t} \lambda_i c_i \in a$. To apply the differential map d to the class $a = [x]$, we compute an element $z \in a = [x]$ such that $z \in F_p \cap d^{-1}(F_z)$, in other words, we build the *projection* of $x \in F_p \cap d^{-1}(F_z) + F_s$ over the factor $F_p \cap d^{-1}(F_z)$. Then, we apply the differential map d to the element $z \in F_p \cap d^{-1}(F_z)$, we compute the coefficients of $d(z)$ with respect to the set of generators $(c'_1, \ldots, c'_{t'})$, and we reduce them considering the corresponding divisors $(b'_1, \ldots, b'_{t'})$. We obtain in this way the following algorithm:

ALGORITHM 2.
Input:

- *an effective chain complex* $C_* = (C_n, d_n)_{n\in\mathbb{N}}$,
- *a generalized filtration for* C_* *over a poset* $(I, \leq)$,
- *elements* $z_1, s_1, p_1, b_1, z_2, s_2, p_2, b_2$ *in* I *such that* $z_1 \leq s_1 \leq p_1 = z_2 \leq b_1 = s_2 \leq p_2 \leq b_2$,
- *a class* $a \in S[z_2, s_2, p_2, b_2]$, *given by means of the coefficients* $(\lambda_1, \ldots, \lambda_t)$ *with respect to the basis* $(c_1, \ldots, c_t)$ *of the group* $S[z_2, s_2, p_2, b_2]$ *determined by Algorithm 1.*

Output: the coefficients of the class $d(a) \in S[z_1, s_1, p_1, b_1]$ *with respect to the basis* $(c'_1, \ldots, c'_{t'})$ *computed by means of Algorithm 1.*

Let us consider now a chain complex C_* which is not effective, so that for some $m \in \mathbb{N}$ the group of m-chains C_m can have an infinite number of generators. Therefore, the subgroups which appear in the formula (4) cannot be determined and Algorithms 1 and 2 for computing the different groups and differentials of the generalized spectral sequence cannot be applied.

Let us suppose that C_* is a chain complex with effective homology $C_* \overset{\rho_1}{\Leftarrow} D_* \overset{\rho_2}{\Rightarrow} EC_*$ where $\rho_1 = (f_1, g_1, h_1)$ and $\rho_2 = (f_2, g_2, h_2)$. The object C_* can be implemented by using functional programming and the equivalence $C_* \Leftarrow D_* \Rightarrow EC_*$ is constructed automatically by Kenzo following the ideas of the effective homology method explained in Section 2.2. Let us suppose also that the chain complexes D_* and EC_* are also filtered over the poset I. Let us show now that under certain conditions the generalized spectral sequences of the three complexes are isomorphic and in this way it is possible to compute the spectral system of C_* by applying Algorithms 1 and 2 to the effective chain complex EC_*. The proofs of the following new results can be found in [8].

THEOREM 3.1. *Let* $\rho = (f, g, h) : C_* \Rightarrow D_*$ *be a reduction between the* I*-filtered chain complexes* (C_*, F) *and* (D_*, F'), *and suppose that* f *and* g *are compatible with the filtrations, that is, for all indexes* $i \in I$ *one has* $f(F_i) \subseteq F'_i$ *and* $g(F'_i) \subseteq F_i$. *Then, given four indexes* $z \leq s \leq p \leq b$ *in* I, *the map* f *induces an isomorphism*

$$f^{z,s,p,b} : S[z, s, p, b] \to S'[z, s, p, b]$$

whenever the homotopy $h : C_* \to C_{*+1}$ *satisfies the conditions* $h(F_z) \subseteq F_s$ *and* $h(F_p) \subseteq F_b$.

COROLLARY 3.2. *Let* $\rho = (f, g, h) : C_* \Rightarrow D_*$ *be a reduction between the* I*-filtered chain complexes* (C_*, F) *and* (D_*, F'), *and suppose that the maps* f, g, h *are compatible with the filtrations. Then the map* f *induces isomorphisms*

$$f^{z,s,p,b} : S[z, s, p, b] \to S'[z, s, p, b]$$

for any 4-tuple of indexes $z \leq s \leq p \leq b$ *in* I.

These results allow one to obtain the following algorithms.

ALGORITHM 3.
Input:

- *a chain complex* $C_* = (C_n, d_n)_{n\in\mathbb{N}}$ *with effective homology* $C_* \overset{\rho_1}{\Leftarrow} D_* \overset{\rho_2}{\Rightarrow} EC_*$,
- I*-filtrations for* C_*, D_* *and* EC_* *such that all the maps involved in the reductions* ρ_1 *and* ρ_2 *are compatible with the filtrations,*
- *elements* z, s, p, b *in* I *such that* $z \leq s \leq p \leq b$.

Output: a basis-divisors representation of the group $S[z, s, p, b]$ *of the spectral system associated with the filtered chain complex* (C_*, F).

ALGORITHM 4.
Input:

- *a chain complex* $C_* = (C_n, d_n)_{n\in\mathbb{N}}$ *with effective homology* $C_* \overset{\rho_1}{\Leftarrow} D_* \overset{\rho_2}{\Rightarrow} EC_*$,
- I*-filtrations for* C_*, D_* *and* EC_* *such that all the maps involved in the reductions* ρ_1 *and* ρ_2 *are compatible with the filtrations,*
- *elements* $z_1, s_1, p_1, b_1, z_2, s_2, p_2, b_2$ *in* I *such that* $z_1 \leq s_1 \leq p_1 = z_2 \leq b_1 = s_2 \leq p_2 \leq b_2$,
- *a class* $a \in S[z_2, s_2, p_2, b_2]$, *given by means of the coefficients* $(\lambda_1, \ldots, \lambda_t)$ *with respect to the basis* $(c_1, \ldots, c_t)$ *of the group* $S[z_2, s_2, p_2, b_2]$ *determined by Algorithm 3.*

Output: the coefficients of the class $d(a) \in S[z_1, s_1, p_1, b_1]$ *with respect to the basis* $(c'_1, \ldots, c'_{t'})$ *computed by means of Algorithm 3.*

Sometimes, given a chain complex which is effective, it can be so big that Algorithms 1 and 2 have efficiency problems and the computation of the associated generalized spectral sequence cannot be done in a reasonable time. For that reason, we are interested in using discrete vector fields to produce a smaller chain complex, which is also effective, in such a way that the associated generalized spectral sequences are isomorphic and then we can compute the spectral system of the (big) initial complex by means of the one of the small chain complex. To this aim, we suppose that generalized filtrations defined on a free chain complex $C_* = (C_n, d_n, \beta_n)_{n\in\mathbb{Z}}$ are compatible with *faces* (see Definition 2.9) and we introduce the following definitions.

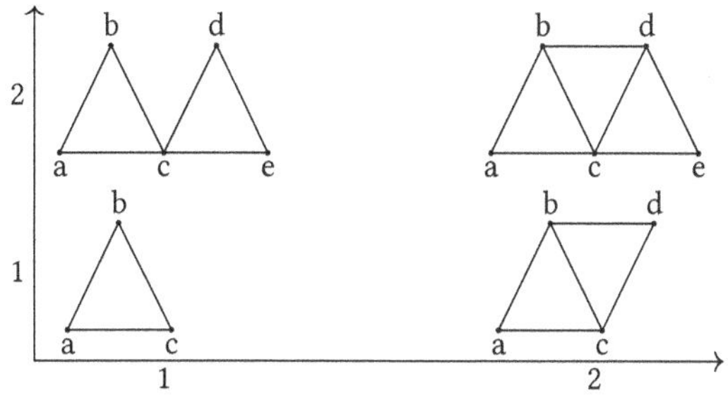

Figure 1: Small chain complex filtered over $\mathbb{Z}^2$.

Definition 3.3. Let $C_* = (C_n, d_n, \beta_n)_{n\in\mathbb{Z}}$ be a free chain complex with a generalized filtration F over a poset $(I, \leq)$ and a discrete vector field $V = \{(\sigma_k; \tau_k)\}_{k\in K}$ on C_*, we say that σ_k and τ_k *appear together* in the filtration if $\sigma_k \in F_i \iff \tau_k \in F_i$, for all $i \in I$.

The previous definition could also be extended to any two generators of C_*, $\sigma \in \beta_n$ and $\sigma' \in \beta_{n'}$.

Definition 3.4. Let $C_* = (C_n, d_n, \beta_n)_{n\in\mathbb{Z}}$ be a free chain complex with a generalized filtration F over a poset $(I, \leq)$ and $\sigma \in \beta_n$ a generator of C_*. We define the *generalized filtration index* of σ, denoted GenFlin(σ), as the set of all indexes $i \in I$ such that $\sigma \in F_i - \bigcup_{t<i} F_t$.

Let us mention that it is not difficult to state suitable hypotheses on the poset I under which Definition 3.3 of two generators appearing together is equivalent to requiring that they have the same generalized filtration index. For example, this equivalence holds for all non-negative filtrations over $\mathbb{Z}^m$. ($\mathbb{Z}^m$ is seen as a poset, endowed with the coordinate-wise partial order $\leq$).

For instance, let us consider the chain complex with a (non-negative) generalized filtration over $\mathbb{Z}^2$ corresponding to the simplicial sets of Figure 1, which shows, associated with each one of the points $(1, 1), (1, 2), (2, 1), (2, 2) \in \mathbb{Z}^2$, a simplicial set constituted by 0-simplices (points $a, b, c, \ldots$) and 1-simplices (edges $ab, ac, \ldots$). The generalized filtration index of the generators a, b and ab is GenFlin(a) = GenFlin(b) = GenFlin(ab) = $\{(1, 1)\}$. One can also observe that GenFlin(d) = $\{(1, 2), (2, 1)\}$ and GenFlin(ce) = $\{(1, 2)\}$. Then, a vector (a, ab) can be considered such that a and ab appear together in the filtration. However, in the vector (c, ce) the generators c and ce do not appear together in the filtration since $c \in F_{(1,1)}$ but $ce \notin F_{(1,1)}$.

Definition 3.5. Let $C_* = (C_n, d_n, \beta_n)_{n\in\mathbb{Z}}$ be a free chain complex with a generalized filtration F over a poset $(I, \leq)$ and $V = \{(\sigma_k; \tau_k)\}_{k\in K}$ be an admissible discrete vector field on C_*. We say that V is compatible with the I-filtration if, for every $k \in K$, σ_k and τ_k appear together in the filtration F.

For instance, in Figure 1 any vector field containing the vector (c, ce) is not compatible with F.

In order to use discrete vector fields to compute generalized spectral sequences of big chain complexes we have proved the following theorem. The proof can be found in [8].

Theorem 3.6. *Let $C_* = (C_n, d_n, \beta_n)_{n\in\mathbb{Z}}$ be a free chain complex with a generalized filtration over a poset $(I, \leq)$ and $V = \{(\sigma_k; \tau_k)\}_{k\in K}$ be an admissible discrete vector field on C_* which is compatible with the filtration. Then (the three maps of the) the canonical reduction $\rho = (f, g, h) : (C_n, d_n) \Rightarrow (C_n^c, d_n')$ described in Theorem 2.11 is compatible with the filtration and therefore the generalized spectral sequences associated with (C_n, d_n) and (C_n^c, d_n') are isomorphic for every indexes z, s, p, b in I such that $z \leq s \leq p \leq b$.*

This result allows one to determine the generalized spectral sequence associated with a big chain complex by defining a discrete vector field producing a smaller chain complex (with isomorphic spectral system). The reader can guess that now the problem is: how can we determine an admissible discrete vector field for a given chain complex C_* which is compatible with the given generalized filtration?

In [18, Ch. 5], an algorithm was presented for computing an admissible maximal[1] discrete vector field for a digital image. The idea of this algorithm is to consider the differential map for some degree n (which is given by an integer matrix M); the entries $M_{i,j}$ which are equal to $+1$ or -1 correspond to pairs (σ, τ) of generators $\sigma = g_i \in \beta_{n-1}$ and $\tau = g_j' \in \beta_n$ which are possible vectors. The difficult part of the algorithm consists in choosing the correct $M_{i,j}$'s such that one obtains a discrete vector field which is admissible (see [18, Ch. 5] for details).

Algorithm 5. *[18]*
Input: A matrix $M \in Mat_{r,s}(\mathbb{Z})$, representing a differential map (for some degree n) of a chain complex C_*.
Output: A maximal admissible discrete vector field V for C_*.

Applying this algorithm to the differential map of C_* of some degree n, one obtains a discrete vector field $V = \{(\sigma_k; \tau_k)\}_{k\in K}$ for C_*, with all $\sigma_k \in \beta_{n-1}, \tau_k \in \beta_n$. Then, applying Theorem 2.11, a reduction $C_* \Rightarrow D_*$ is obtained where D_* is frequently significantly smaller than C_*. The process can be iterated for D_* and a different degree producing again a reduction to a smaller chain complex.

Now, we have modified Algorithm 5 in such a way that we obtain a discrete vector field which is compatible with the generalized filtration over a poset $(I, \leq)$ (and then the generalized spectral sequences of the initial chain complex and the critical one are isomorphic). This can be done by applying separately Algorithm 5 to some *submatrices* corresponding to the rows and columns of the elements which appear together in the filtration (or, equivalently, have the same generalized filtration index).

Given a chain complex of finite type $C_* = (C_n, d_n, \beta_n)_{n\in\mathbb{Z}}$, a degree n and a bounded I-filtration, we consider the (finite) list of generators β_n and we compute the set of all the generalized filtration indexes $L_n = \{\text{GenFlin}(\sigma) | \sigma \in \beta_n\} \subset I$ (which is finite and satisfies card$(L_n) \leq$ card(β_n)). Then, for each $P \in L$ ($P \subset I$) we determine the submatrix of the differential matrix with rows and columns corresponding to elements with generalized filtration index equal to P and we apply Algorithm 5. We obtain so a list of vectors (σ_k, τ_k), with $\sigma_k \in \beta_{n-1}, \tau_k \in \beta_n$ and such that all σ_k and τ_k appear together in the filtration. Repeating the process for all the generalized filtration indexes in L_n and concatenating the results we obtain a discrete vector field which is compatible with the filtration. We obtain in this way the following algorithm, which

[1] A discrete vector field V is said to be *maximal* if it is not possible to add a new vector $(\sigma; \tau)$ to V such that the new vector field $V' := V \cup \{(\sigma; \tau)\}$ is admissible.

is a generalization of the one presented in [17] (where the second author obtained a discrete vector field that is compatible with a linear filtration, and then it could be used for computing persistent homology).

ALGORITHM 6.
Input:

- *an effective chain complex* $C_* = (C_n, d_n)_{n\in\mathbb{N}}$,
- *a generalized filtration for* C_* *over a poset* $(I, \leq)$,
- *a degree* n.

Output: A maximal admissible discrete vector field $V = \{(\sigma_k; \tau_k)\}_{k\in K}$ *for* C_*, *with* $\sigma_k \in \beta_{n-1}, \tau_k \in \beta_n$, *which is compatible with the filtration.*

Applying now Theorem 3.6, a reduction $\rho : C_* \Rightarrow D_*$ is obtained which is compatible with the generalized filtration. Then the process can be repeated for D_* and a different degree n'. Finally we obtain the following algorithm.

ALGORITHM 7.
Input:

- *an effective chain complex* $C_* = (C_n, d_n)_{n\in\mathbb{N}}$,
- *a generalized filtration* F *for* C_* *over a poset* $(I, \leq)$.

Output:

- *A chain complex* EC_*,
- *An* I*-filtration* F' *for* EC_* *(induced by* F*).*
- *A reduction* $\rho : C_* \Rightarrow EC_*$ *compatible with the filtrations, where* EC_* *is effective and (usually) smaller than* C_*.

4 IMPLEMENTATION AND DIDACTIC EXAMPLES

The algorithms presented in Section 3 have been implemented as a new module for the Kenzo system to compute generalized spectral sequences of chain complexes filtered over a poset $(I, \leq)$. The module consists of 2500 lines of Common Lisp code containing new definitions and functions which make it possible to determine the groups $S[z, s, p, b]$ and also the corresponding differential maps (for every level). The programs are available at http://www.unirioja.es/cu/anromero/research2.html.

The new programs work in a similar way to the previous module of spectral sequences explained in [16]: if a (generalized filtered) chain complex is effective, then the groups and differential maps can be directly computed by means of Algorithms 1 and 2; otherwise, the effective homology is used to determine the generalized spectral sequence by means of that of the associated effective chain complex using Algorithms 3 and 4. Moreover, we have enhanced the module with the use of discrete vector fields so that we can *reduce* the size of effective chain complexes before computing the generalized spectral sequence by applying Algorithm 7.

First of all, we have defined two new classes PARTIALLY-ORDERED-SET and GENERALIZED-FILTERED-CHAIN-COMPLEX. In both cases, functional programming plays an important role and makes it possible to work with infinite objects. The definition of the class PARTIALLY-ORDERED-SET is:[2]

[2]Several Lisp technical components without any interest here have been omitted.

```
(DEFCLASS PARTIALLY-ORDERED-SET ()
  ((pocmpr :type (function (element element)
          '(member :less :equal :greater :undefined))))
```

The relevant slot is pocmpr, a function which inputs two elements of the poset and says if the first one is less, equal or greater than the second one or if they are not comparable. As said before, in this way we can implement posets with an infinite number of elements, such as for example $\mathbb{Z}^2$:

```
> (setf z2 (z2))
[K1 Partially-Ordered-Set]
> (pocmpr z2 '(1 2) '(2 2))
:LESS
> (pocmpr z2 '(1 2) '(2 1))
:UNDEFINED
```

The class GENERALIZED-FILTERED-CHAIN-COMPLEX inherits from the Kenzo class CHAIN-COMPLEX and it includes two new slots:

```
(DEFCLASS GENERALIZED-FILTERED-CHAIN-COMPLEX (chain-complex)
  ((pos :type partially-ordered-set )
   (gen-flin :type (function (generator)
                 list-of-filtration-indexes))))
```

The first slot pos is the poset over which the generalized filtration is defined. The second one, gen-flin, is a function which inputs a generator of the chain complex and returns a list of elements of pos, the *generalized filtration index* (as explained in Definition 3.4).

The function for computing the associated generalized spectral sequence is gen-spsq-group, which works as follows. We consider as a didactical example the small chain complex of Figure 1.

```
> (gen-spsq-group K '(1 1) '(1 2) '(2 2) '(2 2) 1)
Generalized spectral sequence S[(1 1),(1 2),(2 2),(2 2)]_{1}
Component Z
> (gen-spsq-group K '(1 1) '(1 1) '(2 2) '(2 2) 1)
Generalized spectral sequence S[(1 1),(1 1),(2 2),(2 2)]_{1}
Component Z
Component Z
```

To clarify the meaning of these computations we can observe for example that, using the definition of generalized spectral sequences, the second group we computed can be seen as the relative homology group $H_1(F_{(2,2)}/F_{(1,1)})$.

It is also possible to determine the generators of these groups by means of the function gen-spsq-gnrts. For example, the group $S[(1, 1), (1, 1), (2, 2), (2, 2)]$ is generated by the combinations $-1 * bd + 1 * cd$ and $1 * cd - 1 * ce + 1 * de$.

```
> (gen-spsq-gnrts K '(1 1) '(1 1) '(2 2) '(2 2) 1)
(
-------------------------------------------{CMBN 1}
<-1 * BD>
<1 * CD>
-------------------------------------------------
-------------------------------------------{CMBN 1}
<1 * CD>
<-1 * CE>
<1 * DE>
-------------------------------------------------
)
```

Finally, as explained in Section 3, we can also compute the differential maps $d : S_2 \equiv S[z_2, s_2, p_2, b_2] \rightarrow S_1 \equiv S[z_1, s_1, p_1, b_1]$. To this aim we must introduce a class a of S_2, given by a list of coefficients $(\lambda_1, \ldots, \lambda_t)$ in $\mathbb{Z}$ with respect to the set of generators of S_2. For instance, the differential map $d : S[(1,1),(1,2),(2,2),(2,2)] \cong \mathbb{Z} \to S[(0,1),(0,1),(2,2),(2,2)] \cong \mathbb{Z}$ is the null morphism:

```
> (gen-spsq-dffr K '(1 1) '(1 2) '(2 2) '(2 2)
            '(0 1) '(0 1) '(2 2) '(2 2) 1 '(1))
(0)
```

In the previous example, since the chain complex is *small* (we have only 5 generators of degree 0 and 7 of degree 1), the computations of the spectral system groups and differential maps have been done directly by means of diagonalization algorithms on matrices as explained for Algorithms 1 and 2. Now, let us consider a *bigger* chain complex such as the one corresponding to the digital image shown in Figure 2, filtered again over $\mathbb{Z}^2$. For details and examples on how a digital image yields a chain complex we refer the reader to [17].

Figure 2: Digital image filtered over $\mathbb{Z}^2$.

In this case the chain complex has 203 vertices, 408 edges and 208 triangles. Even if the chain complex is not very big, it is convenient to use discrete vector fields to *reduce* it and construct a smaller one by means of Algorithm 7. This is done directly by Kenzo such that the reduction is stored as part of the slot `efhm` containing the effective homology of the initial chain complex. The effective chain complex determined by Algorithm 7 has in this case 21 vertices, 23 edges and 5 triangles.

```
> (efhm K2)
[K155 Homotopy-Equivalence K123 <= K123 => K141]
> (setf efK2 (rbcc (efhm K2)))
[K141 Generalized-Filtered-Chain-Complex]
> (length (basis efK2 0))
21
> (length (basis efK2 1))
23
> (length (basis efK2 2))
5
```

The computation of the groups and differential maps of the generalized spectral sequence is done now in a more efficient way by means of Algorithms 3 and 4 (even if the initial chain complex is already of finite type).

```
> (gen-spsq-group K2 '(1 1) '(1 1) '(4 4) '(4 4) 1)
Generalized spectral sequence S[(1 1),(1 1),(4 4),(4 4)]_{1}
Component Z
Component Z
Component Z
Component Z
Component Z
Component Z
Component Z
```

5 APPLICATIONS

5.1 Multidimensional persistence

Generalized spectral sequences over $\mathbb{Z}^m$ are closely connected with multidimensional persistence, a generalization of persistent homology. Persistent homology [10] is a technique in topological data analysis designed to study, using homology, the evolution of topological features across a filtration, and to summarize it in the form of topological invariants. If the filtration is constructed from some data set, the topological invariants represent a topological summary of the data which is informative, easily computable and robust. In its original form, persistent homology deals with $\mathbb{Z}$-filtrations $F = (F_p)_{p\in\mathbb{Z}}$ and produces as invariant the collection of *persistent Betti numbers*

$$\beta_n^{s,t} \equiv \operatorname{rank} \operatorname{Im}(f_n^{s,t} : H_n(F_s) \to H_n(F_t)),$$

for all n and $s \le t$ (where $f_n^{s,t}$ is the map induced by the inclusion $F_s \subseteq F_t$). As the filtration index $p \in \mathbb{Z}$ typically comes from filtering the data with respect to one chosen parameter, considering m different parameters produces a $\mathbb{Z}^m$-filtration $F = (F_P)_{P\in\mathbb{Z}^m}$. Multidimensional persistence [3] studies the topological invariants which can be used to capture the topological information of $\mathbb{Z}^m$-filtrations. In this case, it has been proven [3] that there is no hope to produce a *complete* discrete invariant (like the persistent Betti numbers in the 1-dimensional case), capable to always discriminate between non-isomorphic structures. Nonetheless, some informative invariants can be considered, among which the most used is the *rank invariant*, a direct generalization of persistent Betti numbers given by the collection,

$$\beta_n^{S,T} \equiv \operatorname{rank} \operatorname{Im}(H_n(F_S) \to H_n(F_T)),$$

for all n and $S \le T$ in $\mathbb{Z}^m$.

It can be proven (see the preprint [8]) that the generalized spectral sequence arising from a $\mathbb{Z}^m$-filtration carries the same amount of topological information as the rank invariant: the rank of each term of the spectral sequence can be computed knowing the rank invariant, and vice versa.

In [13] the poset $D(\mathbb{Z}^m)$ of the *downsets* of $\mathbb{Z}^m$ is employed to gain more options in the construction of generalized spectral sequences. A downset of $\mathbb{Z}^m$ is a subset $A \subseteq \mathbb{Z}^m$ such that if $Q \le P$ in $\mathbb{Z}^m$ and $P \in A$, then $Q \in A$; the poset $D(\mathbb{Z}^m)$ is the collection of all downsets of $\mathbb{Z}^m$, endowed with the partial order given by inclusion $\subseteq$. Filtering data with respect to m parameters produces in a natural way also a $D(\mathbb{Z}^m)$-filtration. We have observed that considering filtration indexes in $D(\mathbb{Z}^m)$ allows to produce a more accurate topological summary than the rank invariant; the ranks of the terms of the generalized spectral sequence over $D(\mathbb{Z}^m)$ can therefore be considered as an invariant associated with a filtration which allows to discriminate between a larger number of topological features. Clearly, the cost of this increased level of accuracy is paid in terms of efficiency of the computations. Even if the discrete vector field method presented in Section 3 allows to considerably speed up computations, in many cases the computation of the whole generalized spectral sequence over $D(\mathbb{Z}^m)$ appears to be infeasible. A stimulating challenge (and a theme for future research) is to identify a subset of indexes in $D(\mathbb{Z}^m)$ which allows to extract sufficient information at reasonable computational costs.

5.2 Generalized Serre spectral sequence

The Serre spectral sequence [22] associated with a fibration $G \hookrightarrow E \rightarrow B$ can be used to compute the homology groups of the total space E from the homologies of the base B and the fiber G. More concretely, the *first* page of this spectral sequence, in this case E^2, is defined as

$$E^2_{p,q} \cong H_p(B; H_q(G))$$

that can be computed when the homology groups of B and G are known. Then, in particular cases, if all the differential maps can be deduced and no problems are found at abutment, the homology groups of E can be determined. However, it is worth remarking that this formula is not an algorithm for computing the homology groups of E that can be applied in all situations.

In [13], the Serre spectral sequence is generalized to the case of a tower of m fibrations

$$\begin{array}{ccccc} E_0 & \longrightarrow \cdots \longrightarrow & E_{m-1} & \longrightarrow & B \\ \uparrow & & \uparrow & & \\ G_0 & & G_{m-1} & & \end{array} \tag{5}$$

In that case, the analogue of the page E^2 can be defined in terms of the homology groups of the base B and the fiber spaces $G_0, \ldots, G_{m-1}$ as the collection of abelian groups

$$H_{p_m}(B; H_{p_{m-1}}(G_{m-1}; \ldots H_{p_1}(G_1; H_{p_0}(G_0)))),$$

with $P = (p_1, \ldots, p_m) \in \mathbb{Z}^m$ and $p_0 = n - p_1 - \cdots - p_m$, and under good conditions this spectral sequence converges to the homology groups of the total space E_0. As in the classical case, this formula provides a description of the first page of the spectral sequence but it is not an algorithm producing the homology of E_0 in all situations.

The spectral sequence of the tower of fibrations (5) is defined by means of a generalized filtration over the poset $D(\mathbb{Z}^m)$ (see [13] for details), so that our algorithms and programs presented in Sections 3 and 4 can be applied. If the spaces $B, G_0, \ldots, G_{m-1}$ have effective homology and the fibrations don't have torsion (that is to say, each space E_k is isomorphic to a cartesian product $E_k \cong G_k \times E_{k+1}$), then the effective homology of the total space E_0 is compatible with the generalized filtrations and then we can compute the generalized spectral sequence even if the spaces $B, G_0, \ldots, G_{m-1}$ are not of finite type. If the fibrations are twisted our results cannot be directly applied and new algorithms must be developed.

6 CONCLUSIONS AND FURTHER WORK

In this work we have developed a set of algorithms and programs for computing spectral systems, a useful tool in Algebraic Topology defined by Benjamin Matschke in [13] which generalizes the classical notion of spectral sequence. The algorithms are based on the methods of effective homology and discrete vector fields and make it possible to determine the spectral system of some spaces of infinite type, solving the problems of spectral sequences associated with linear filtrations which are differential maps and extensions at abutment. The programs have been implemented as a new module for the Kenzo system.

A particular application of our programs is the computation of the generalized Serre spectral sequence associated with a tower of fibrations, which generalizes the classical Serre spectral sequence of a fibration $G \hookrightarrow E \rightarrow B$. For the moment we can only consider particular cases where the spaces are of finite type or with effective homology and such that the fibrations don't have torsion (that is to say, each total space in the tower is isomorphic to a cartesian product of the corresponding base and fiber). As further work, other situations must be considered. On the other hand, the paper [13] includes generalizations of other examples of spectral sequences such as those of Eilenberg-Moore [5] and Adams-Novikov [15]. In those cases, appropriate generalized filtrations should be defined and we should study their compatibility with the corresponding effective homologies to see if our programs can also be applied.

Other interesting continuation of this work would be considering chain complexes of arbitrary finitely presented $\mathbb{Z}$-modules instead of free $\mathbb{Z}$-modules, where the Smith Normal Form algorithm for computing homology groups cannot be directly applied and other alternatives should be determined. Moreover, the functoriality of generalized spectral sequences could be studied as a further work.

REFERENCES

[1] M. Barakat. 2009. Spectral Filtrations via Generalized Morphisms. (2009). Preprint. https://arxiv.org/abs/0904.0240.

[2] A. K. Bousfield and D. M. Kan. 1972. The homotopy spectral sequence of a space with coefficients in a ring. *Topology* 11 (1972), 79–106.

[3] G. Carlsson and A. Zomorodian. 2009. The theory of multidimensional persistence. *Discrete & Computational Geometry* 42, 1 (2009), 71–93.

[4] X. Dousson, J. Rubio, F. Sergeraert, and Y. Siret. 1999. The Kenzo program. (1999). http://www-fourier.ujf-grenoble.fr/~sergerar/Kenzo/.

[5] S. Eilenberg and J. C. Moore. 1965. Homology and fibrations, I: Coalgebras, cotensor product and its derived functors. *Commentarii Mathematici Helvetici* 40 (1965), 199–236.

[6] G. Ellis and P. Smith. 2011. Computing group cohomology rings from the Lyndon-Hochschild-Serre spectral sequence. *Journal of Symbolic Computation* 46, 4 (2011), 360–370.

[7] R. Forman. 1998. Morse theory for cell complexes. *Advances in Mathematics* 134 (1998), 90–145.

[8] A. Guidolin and A. Romero. 2018. Effective homology for generalized spectral sequences. (2018). Preprint. www.unirioja.es/cu/anromero/efhm_genss.pdf.

[9] T. Kaczynski, K. Mischaikow, and M. Mrozek. 2004. *Computational Homology*. Applied Mathematical Sciences, Vol. 157. Springer.

[10] M. Kerber. 2016. Persistent Homology - State of the art and challenges. *Internationale mathematische Nachrichten = International mathematical news* 231 (4 2016), 15–33.

[11] J. Leray. 1946. Structure de l'anneau d'homologie d'une représentation. *Comptes Rendus des Séances de l'Academie des Sciences de Paris* 222 (1946), 1419–1422.

[12] S. Maclane. 1963. *Homology*. Berlin.

[13] B. Matschke. 2013. Successive Spectral Sequences. (2013). Preprint. http://arxiv.org/abs/1308.3187v1.

[14] J. McCleary. 1985. *User's guide to spectral sequences*. Publish or Perish.

[15] S Novikov. 1967. Methods of algebraic topology from the point of view of cobordism theory. *Izvestiya Akademii Nauk SSSR. Seriya Matematicheskaya* 31 (1967), 855–951.

[16] A. Romero, J. Rubio, and F. Sergeraert. 2006. Computing Spectral Sequences. *Journal of Symbolic Computation* 41, 10 (2006), 1059–1079.

[17] A. Romero, J. Rubio, and F. Sergeraert. 2016. Effective homology of filtered digital images. *Pattern Recognition Letters* 83 (2016), 23–31.

[18] A. Romero and F. Sergeraert. 2010. Discrete Vector Fields and fundamental Algebraic Topology. (2010). Preprint. http://arxiv.org/abs/1005.5685v1.

[19] J. Rubio and F. Sergeraert. 2002. Constructive Algebraic Topology. *Bulletin des Sciences Mathématiques* 126, 5 (2002), 389–412.

[20] J. Rubio and F. Sergeraert. 2006. Constructive Homological Algebra and Applications. (2006). Preprint. http://arxiv.org/abs/1208.3816.

[21] F. Sergeraert. 1994. The computability problem in Algebraic Topology. *Advances in Mathematics* 104, 1 (1994), 1–29.

[22] J. P. Serre. 1951. Homologie singulière des espaces fibrés. *Annals of Mathematics* 54, 3 (1951), 425–505.

Exact Algorithms for Semidefinite Programs with Degenerate Feasible Set

Didier Henrion
CNRS LAAS - Université de Toulouse
Faculty of Elect. Engin., CTU, Prague
France and Czech Republic
henrion@laas.fr

Simone Naldi
Univ. Limoges, XLIM, UMR 7252
F-87000 Limoges
France
simone.naldi@unilim.fr

Mohab Safey El Din
Sorbonne Université, CNRS, INRIA,
Laboratoire d'Informatique de Paris 6,
LIP6, Équipe PolSys
4 place Jussieu
F-75252, Paris Cedex 05, France
mohab.safey@lip6.fr

ABSTRACT

Let $A_0, \ldots, A_n$ be $m \times m$ symmetric matrices with entries in $\mathbb{Q}$, and let $A(x)$ be the linear pencil $A_0 + x_1A_1 + \cdots + x_nA_n$, where $x = (x_1, \ldots, x_n)$ are unknowns. The linear matrix inequality (LMI) $A(x) \succeq 0$ defines the subset of $\mathbb{R}^n$, called spectrahedron, containing all points x such that $A(x)$ has non-negative eigenvalues. The minimization of linear functions over spectrahedra is called semidefinite programming (SDP). Such problems appear frequently in control theory and real algebra, especially in the context of nonnegativity certificates for multivariate polynomials based on sums of squares.

Numerical software for solving SDP are mostly based on the interior point method, assuming some non-degeneracy properties such as the existence of interior points in the admissible set. In this paper, we design an exact algorithm based on symbolic homotopy for solving semidefinite programs without assumptions on the feasible set, and we analyze its complexity. Because of the exactness of the output, it cannot compete with numerical routines in practice but we prove that solving such problems can be done in polynomial time if either n or m is fixed.

KEYWORDS

Semidefinite programming, Polynomial optimization, Exact computation, Homotopy

ACM Reference format:
Didier Henrion, Simone Naldi, and Mohab Safey El Din. 2018. Exact Algorithms for Semidefinite Programs with Degenerate Feasible Set. In *Proceedings of 2018 ACM International Symposium on Symbolic and Algebraic Computation, New York, NY, USA, July 16–19, 2018 (ISSAC '18)*, 8 pages.
https://doi.org/10.1145/3208976.3209022

1 INTRODUCTION

Let $x = (x_1, \ldots, x_n)$ be variables, and $A_0, A_1, \ldots, A_n$ $m \times m$ symmetric matrices with entries in the field $\mathbb{Q}$ of rational numbers. The goal of this article is to design algorithms for solving the semidefinite programming (SDP) problem

$$\inf \ell(x) \quad \text{s.t.} \quad x \in \mathscr{S}(A) \tag{1.1}$$

where $\ell(x) = \ell_1x_1 + \cdots + \ell_nx_n$ is a linear function and $\mathscr{S}(A)$ is the solution set in $\mathbb{R}^n$ of the linear matrix inequality (LMI)

$$A(x) := A_0 + x_1A_1 + \cdots + x_nA_n \succeq 0. \tag{1.2}$$

In the previous formula, the constraint $A(x) \succeq 0$ means that $A(x)$ is positive semidefinite, that is, that all its eigenvalues are non-negative. The set $\mathscr{S}(A)$, called *spectrahedron*, is a convex and basic semi-algebraic, as affine section of the cone of positive semidefinite matrices.

Linear matrix inequalities and semidefinite programs appear frequently in several applied domains, *e.g.* for stability queries in control theory [11]. They also appear as a central object in convex algebraic geometry and real algebra for computing certificates of non-negativity based on sums of squares [8, 9] following the technique popularized notably by the seminal work of Lasserre [21] and Parrilo [25]. Since the LMI $A(x) \succeq 0$ defines the feasible set of SDP, LMI is also known as the SDP feasibility problem.

Even though SDP can be solved in polynomial time to a fixed accuracy via the ellipsoid algorithm, the complexity status of this problem in the Turing or in the real numbers model is still an open question in computer science (see [2, 26]). On the other hand, very few algebraic methods that can represent an alternative to classical approaches from optimization theory have been developed.

In this paper, we aim at designing a symbolic algorithm for solving the SDP in (1.1), without any assumption on the feasible set $\mathscr{S}(A)$, but with genericity assumptions on the objective function ℓ. It returns an algebraic representation of a feasible solution.

1.1 State of the art

Numerical methods have been developed for solving SDP problems, the most efficient of which are based on the interior point method [23]. This amounts to constructing an algebraic primal-dual curve called *central path*, whose points (x_μ, y_μ) are solutions to the quadratic semi-algebraic problems

$$A(x)Y(y) = \mu\,\mathbb{I}_m \qquad A(x) \succeq 0 \qquad Y(y) \succeq 0. \tag{1.3}$$

Above, $Y(y)$ must be read as a square matrix lying in a space of matrices dual to that of $A(x)$. For small but positive μ, when the LMI has strictly feasible solutions, the points x_μ lie in the interior of $\mathscr{S}(A)$, and converge to a boundary point for $\mu \to 0^+$. Moreover,

Mohab Safey El Din is supported by the ANR grant ANR-17-CE40-0009 Galop and the PGMO grant Gamma.

ISSAC '18, July 16–19, 2018, New York, NY, USA

ACM ISBN 978-1-4503-5550-6/18/07...$15.00
https://doi.org/10.1145/3208976.3209022

barrier logarithmic functions have been extended from the classical setup of linear programming to the semidefinite cone, and can be used to solve (1.1) when $\mathscr{S}(A)$ has interior points.

By the way, there are several obstacles to interior-point strategies. First, $\mathscr{S}(A)$ has empty interior in several situations, for instance when $\mathscr{S}(A)$ consists of sums-of-squares certificates of a polynomial with rational coefficients that does not admit rational certificates, see [33] for a class of such examples. Moreover, as proved in [15], when classical assumptions on the given SDP fail to be satisfied, for instance in absence of strict complementarity, the central path might fail to converge to the optimal face. Finally, even in presence of interior points, it is hard to estimate the degree of the central path (that represents a complexity measure for path-following methods) in practical situations and explicit examples of central paths with exponential curvature have been computed [1].

The several existing variants of the interior-point algorithm are implemented in software running in finite precision, to cite a few SeDuMi [35], SDPT3 [36] and MOSEK [3]. The expected running time is essentially polynomial in $n, m, \log(\eta^{-1})$ (where η is the precision) and in the bit-length of the input [4, Ch.1,Sec.1.4]. Whereas these numerical routines run quite efficiently on huge instances, they may fail on degenerate situations, even on medium or small size problems. This has motivated for instance the development of floating point libraries for SDP working in extended precision [20].

Symbolic computation has been used in the context of SDP to tackle several related problems. First, it should be observed that $\mathscr{S}(A)$ is a semi-algebraic set in $\mathbb{R}^n$ defined by sign conditions on the coefficients of the characteristic polynomial $t \mapsto det(t\,\mathbb{I}_m - A(x))$. Hence, classical real root finding algorithms for semi-algebraic sets such as [5–7, 28] can be used to solve SDP exactly. Using such algorithms leads to solve SDP in time $m^{O(n)}$. Algorithms for solving diophantine problems on linear matrix inequalities have been developed in [14, 32].

More recently, algorithms for solving exactly *generic* LMI [17, 18] and *generic* rank-constrained SDP [22] have been designed, with runtime polynomial in n (the number of variables, or equivalently the dimension of the affine section defining $\mathscr{S}(A)$) if m (the size of the matrix) is fixed. Because of the high degrees needed to encode the output [24], they cannot compete with numerical software but on small size problems offer a nice complement to these techniques in situations where numerical issues are encountered. In both cases, genericity assumptions on the input are required. This means that for some special problems (lying in some Zariski closed subset of the space spanned by the entries of matrices A_i), these algorithms cannot be applied.

1.2 Outline of the main contributions

In this paper, we remove the genericity assumptions on the feasible set $\mathscr{S}_A$ of the input SDP that were required in our previous work [17], and we show that optimization of generic linear functions over $\mathscr{S}_A$ can be performed without significant extra cost from the complexity viewpoint.

Our precise contributions are as follows.

- We design an algorithm for solving the SDP in (1.1) without any assumption on the defining matrix $A(x)$, with genericity assumptions on the objective function;
- we prove that this algorithm uses a number of arithmetic operations which is polynomial in n when m is fixed, and viceversa;
- we report on examples showing the behaviour of the algorithm on small-size but degenerate instances.

The main tool is the construction of a homotopy acting on the matrix representation $A(x)$ rather than on the classical complementarity conditions as in (1.3). This allows to preserve the LMI structure along the perturbation.

We use similar techniques from real algebraic geometry as those in [17], based on transversality theory [12], to prove genericity properties of the perturbed systems. We also investigate closedness properties of linear maps restricted to semi-algebraic sets in a more general setting in Section 2, generalizing similar statements for real algebraic sets in [16, 29].

1.3 General notation

For a matrix of polynomials $f \in \mathbb{R}[x]^{s\times t}$ in $x = (x_1, \ldots, x_n)$, we denote by $Z(f)$ the complex algebraic set defined by the entries of f. If $f \in \mathbb{R}[x]^s$, the Jacobian matrix of f is denoted by $Df := \left(\frac{\partial f_i}{\partial x_j}\right)_{ij}$. A set $S \subset \mathbb{R}^n$ defined by sign conditions on a finite list of polynomials is called a basic semi-algebraic set, and a finite union of such sets is called a semi-algebraic set.

Let $\mathbb{S}_m(\mathbb{Q})$ be the space of $m \times m$ symmetric matrices with entries in $\mathbb{Q}$, and $\mathbb{S}_m^+(\mathbb{Q})$ the cone of positive semidefinite matrices in $\mathbb{S}_m(\mathbb{Q})$. Let $A(x) = A_0 + \sum_{i=1}^n x_i A_i$, with $A_i \in \mathbb{S}_m(\mathbb{Q})$. One can associate to $A(x)$ the hierarchy of algebraic sets

$$\mathcal{D}_r(A) = \{x \in \mathbb{R}^n \,:\, \operatorname{rank} A(x) \leq r\}, \quad r = 1, \ldots, m-1$$

defined by the minors of $A(x)$ of a fixed size. The set $\mathcal{D}_r$ is called a determinantal variety. We recall the definition of incidence variety in the context of semidefinite programming, introduced by the authors in [17]. For $r \in \{1, \ldots, m-1\}$, let $Y = Y(y)$ be a $m \times (m-r)$ matrix of unknowns $y_{i,j}$. Let $\iota \subset \{1, \ldots, m\}$ be a subset of cardinality $m - r$, and Y_ι the submatrix of Y corresponding to lines in ι. The *incidence variety* for $\mathcal{D}_r(A)$ is the algebraic set

$$\mathcal{V}_{r,\iota}(A) = \{(x, y) \in \mathbb{C}^n \times \mathbb{C}^{m(m-r)} \,:\, A(x)Y(y) = 0, Y_\iota = \mathbb{I}_{m-r}\}.$$

We have defined previously the spectrahedron $\mathscr{S}(A) = \{x \in \mathbb{R}^n : A(x) \succeq 0\}$, associated to $A(x)$.

Let $B \in \mathbb{S}_m(\mathbb{Q})$ and $\varepsilon \in [0, 1]$. In this paper, we consider a 1-parameter family of linear matrices

$$A(x) + \varepsilon B = (A_0 + \varepsilon B) + \sum x_i A_i$$

perturbing $A(x)$ in direction B.

2 PRELIMINARIES

In this section, we prove some results of topological nature on spectrahedra and their deformations. Before doing that, we need to recall basics about infinitesimals and Puiseux series rings. More details can be found in [7].

An infinitesimal ε is a positive element which is transcendental over $\mathbb{R}$ and smaller than any positive real number. The Puiseux series field $\mathbb{R}\langle\varepsilon\rangle = \{\sum_{i\geq i_0} a_i \varepsilon^{i/q} \mid i_0 \in \mathbb{Z}, q \in \mathbb{N} - \{0\}\}$ is a real closed one [10, Ex.1.2.3]. An element $z = \sum_{i\geq i_0} a_i \varepsilon^{i/q}$ is bounded over $\mathbb{R}$ if $i_0 \geq 0$. In that case, one says that its limit when ε tends to 0 is a_0

and we write it $\lim_\varepsilon z$. The $\lim_\varepsilon$ operator is a ring homomorphism between $\mathbb{R}\langle\varepsilon\rangle$ and $\mathbb{R}$. We extend it over $\mathbb{R}\langle\varepsilon\rangle^n$ coordinatewise. Also given a subset $Q \subset \mathbb{R}\langle\varepsilon\rangle^n$, we denote by $\lim_\varepsilon Q$ the subset of $\mathbb{R}^n$ of points which are the images by $\lim_\varepsilon$ of bounded elements in Q.

Given a semi-algebraic set $S \subset \mathbb{R}^n$ defined by a semi-algebraic formula with coefficients in $\mathbb{R}$, we denote by $\mathrm{ext}(S, \mathbb{R}\langle\varepsilon\rangle)$ the solution set of that formula in $\mathbb{R}\langle\varepsilon\rangle^n$.

For a linear pencil $A(x) = A_0 + x_1A_1 + \cdots + x_nA_n$ of $m \times m$ symmetric linear matrices and a $m \times m$ positive definite matrix B, we consider the spectrahedron $\mathscr{S}(A + \varepsilon B)$ in $\mathbb{R}\langle\varepsilon\rangle$. Our first result relates $\mathscr{S}(A) \subset \mathbb{R}^n$ with $\mathscr{S}(A + \varepsilon B) \subset \mathbb{R}\langle\varepsilon\rangle^n$.

Lemma 2.1. *Using the above notation, $\mathscr{S}(A)$ is included in (the interior of) $\mathscr{S}(A + \varepsilon B)$.*

Proof. If $\mathscr{S}(A) = \emptyset$, there is nothing to prove. Let $x^* \in \mathscr{S}(A)$. By definition of positive semi-definiteness, for any vector $v \in \mathbb{R}^m$, $v^tA(x^*)v \geq 0$. Since ε is a positive infinitesimal and B is positive definite, we deduce that for any vector $v \in \mathbb{R}^m \setminus \{0\}$, $0 < v^tA(x^*)v + v^t\varepsilon Bv = v^t(A(x^*) + \varepsilon B)v$. We deduce that $A + \varepsilon B$ is positive definite at x^*, hence x^* is in (the interior of) $\mathscr{S}(A + \varepsilon B)$, as requested. □

Further, we identify the set of linear forms $\ell = \ell_1x_1 + \cdots + \ell_nx_n$ with $\mathbb{C}^n$, the linear form ℓ being identified to the point $\ell_1, \ldots, \ell_n$. By a slight abuse of notation we also denote by ℓ the map $x \mapsto \ell(x)$.

Lemma 2.2. *Let $\mathbf{R}$ be a real closed field, $\mathbf{C}$ be an algebraic closure of $\mathbf{R}$ and $S \subset \mathbf{R}^n$ be a closed semi-algebraic set. There exists a non-empty Zariski open set $\mathscr{L}(S) \subset \mathbf{C}^n$ such that for $\ell \in \mathscr{L}(S) \cap \mathbf{R}^n$, $\ell(S)$ is closed for the Euclidean topology.*

Proof. Our proof is by induction on the dimension of S. When S has dimension 0, the statement is immediate.

We let now $d \in \mathbb{N} \setminus \{0\}$, assume that the statement holds for semi-algebraic sets of dimension less than d and that S has dimension d. By [10, Th.2.3.6], it can be partitioned as a finite union of closed semi-algebraically connected semi-algebraic manifolds $S_1, \ldots, S_N$. Note that each S_i is still semi-algebraic. We establish below that there exist non-empty Zariski open sets $\mathscr{L}(S_i) \subset \mathbf{C}^n$ such that for $\ell \in \mathscr{L}(S_i) \cap \mathbf{R}^n$, $\ell(S_i)$ is closed for the Euclidean topology. Taking the intersections of those finitely many non-empty Zariski open set is then enough to define $\mathscr{L}(S)$.

Let $1 \leq i \leq N$. If the dimension of S_i is less than d, we apply the induction assumption and we are done. Assume now that S_i has dimension d. Let $V \subset \mathbf{C}^n$ be the Zariski closure of S_i and C be the semi-algebraically connected component of $V \cap \mathbf{R}^n$ which contains S_i. By [? , Prop.17], there exists a non-empty Zariski open set $\Lambda_{1,i} \subset \mathbf{C}^n$ such that for $\ell \in \Lambda_{1,i} \cap \mathbf{R}^n$, $\ell(C)$ is closed.

By definition of C and using [10, Ch.2.8], C has dimension d, as S_i. We denote by $T_i \subset \mathbf{R}^n$ the boundary of S_i. Observe that it is a closed semi-algebraic set of dimension less than d [10, Ch.2.8]. Using the induction assumption, we deduce that there exists a non-empty Zariski open set $\Lambda_{2,i} \subset \mathbf{C}^n$ such that for $\ell \in \Lambda_{2,i} \cap \mathbf{R}^n$, $\ell(T_i)$ is closed. We claim that one can define $\mathscr{L}(S_i)$ as the intersection $\Lambda_{1,i} \cap \Lambda_{2,i}$, i.e. for $\ell \in \mathscr{L}(S_i) \cap \mathbf{R}^n$, $\ell(S_i)$ is closed.

Indeed, assume that the boundary of $\ell(S_i)$ is not empty (otherwise there is nothing to prove) and take a in this boundary. Without loss of generality, assume also that for all $x \in S_i$, $\ell(x) \geq a$. We need to prove that $a \in S_i$.

Assume first that for all $\eta > 0$, $\ell^{-1}([a, a + \eta])$ has a non-empty intersection with T_i. Since $\ell(T_i)$ is closed by construction, we deduce that there exists $x \in T_i$ such that $\ell(x) = a$. Since S_i is closed by construction and T_i is its boundary, we deduce that $x \in S_i$ and then that $a \in \ell(S_i)$.

Assume now that for some $\eta > 0$, $\ell^{-1}([a, a + \eta])$ has an empty intersection with T_i. Then, we deduce that $\ell^{-1}([a, a + \eta]) \cap S_i = \ell^{-1}([a, a + \eta]) \cap C$. Besides, since $\ell(C)$ is closed, there exists $x \in C$ such that $\ell(x) = a$. Because, $\ell^{-1}([a, a+\eta]) \cap S_i = \ell^{-1}([a, a+\eta]) \cap C$, we deduce that $x \in S_i$ which ends the proof. □

Lemma 2.3. *Let $A(x)$ be as above and let B be a positive definite $m \times m$ matrix. There exists a non-empty Zariski open set $\mathscr{O}_1 \subset \mathbb{C}^n$ such that for $\ell \in \mathscr{O}_1 \cap \mathbb{R}^n$ the following holds:*

- *$\ell(\mathscr{S}(A))$ is closed for the Euclidean topology*
- *$\ell(\mathscr{S}(A + \varepsilon B))$ is closed for the Euclidean topology.*

Proof. If $\mathscr{S}(A) = \emptyset$, there is nothing to prove. Since $\mathscr{S}(A) \subset \mathbb{R}^n$ is a closed semi-algebraic set, one can apply Lemma 2.2 and deduce that there exists a non-empty Zariski open set $\mathscr{O}_1' \subset \mathbb{C}^n$ such that for $\ell \in \mathscr{O}_1' \cap \mathbb{R}^n$, $\ell(\mathscr{S}(A))$ is closed for the Euclidean topology.

The spectrahedron $\mathscr{S}(A + \varepsilon B) \subset \mathbb{R}\langle\varepsilon\rangle^n$ is also a closed semi-algebraic set. Applying Lemma 2.2 with $\mathbf{R} = \mathbb{R}\langle\varepsilon\rangle$, one deduces that there exists a non-empty Zariski open set $\mathscr{O}_\varepsilon'' \subset \mathbb{C}\langle\varepsilon\rangle^n$ such that for $\ell \in \mathscr{O}_\varepsilon'' \cap \mathbb{R}\langle\varepsilon\rangle^n$, $\ell(\mathscr{S}(A + \varepsilon B))$ is closed for the Euclidean topology. Since any non-empty Zariski open set $\mathscr{O}_\varepsilon'' \subset \mathbb{C}\langle\varepsilon\rangle^n$ contains a non-empty Zariski open set of $\mathbb{C}^n$, we pick one such set, denoted by $\mathscr{O}_1''$ and take finally $\mathscr{O}_1 = \mathscr{O}_1' \cap \mathscr{O}_1''$. □

Lemma 2.4. *Let ℓ in $\mathscr{O}_1 \cap \mathbb{R}^n$ where $\mathscr{O}_1$ is the non-empty Zariski open set defined in Lemma 2.3.*

Assume that there exists $x^* \in \mathscr{S}(A)$ such that $\ell(x^*)$ lies in the boundary of $\ell(\mathscr{S}(A))$. Then, there exists $x_\varepsilon^* \in \mathscr{S}(A + \varepsilon B)$ such that $\ell(x_\varepsilon^*)$ lies in the boundary of $\ell(\mathscr{S}(A + \varepsilon B))$ and $\lim_\varepsilon x_\varepsilon^* = x^*$.

Viceversa, if $x_\varepsilon^* \in \mathscr{S}(A + \varepsilon B)$ lies in the boundary of $\ell(\mathscr{S}(A + \varepsilon B))$, and $\mathscr{S}(A) \neq \emptyset$, then $\ell(\lim_\varepsilon x_\varepsilon^*)$ lies in the boundary of $\ell(\mathscr{S}(A))$.

Proof. Fix $r \in \mathbb{R}$ positive and let $B(x^*, r)$ be the ball centered at x^* of radius r. Further we abuse notation by denoting $\mathrm{ext}(\mathscr{S}(A), \mathbb{R}\langle\varepsilon\rangle)$ by $\mathscr{S}(A)$.

Recall that $\mathscr{S}(A)$ is contained in $\mathscr{S}(A + \varepsilon B)$ (Lemma 2.1) and observe that $\mathscr{S}(A + \varepsilon B)$ is infinitesimally close to $\mathscr{S}(A)$ (because of the continuity of the eigenvalues of $A(x) + \varepsilon B$ when x ranges over $\mathscr{S}(A + \varepsilon B)$).

This implies that there exists ρ_ε in the boundary of $\ell(\mathscr{S}(A + \varepsilon B) \cap \mathrm{ext}(B(x^*, r)))$ and which is infintesimally close $\ell(x^*)$. Since $\mathscr{S}(A + \varepsilon B) \cap \mathrm{ext}(B(x^*, r)$ is closed and bounded, $\ell(\mathscr{S}(A + \varepsilon B) \cap \mathrm{ext}(B(x^*, r))$ is closed for the Euclidean topology. Then, there exists $x_\varepsilon^* \in \mathscr{S}(A + \varepsilon B) \cap \mathrm{ext}(B(x^*, r)$ such that $\ell(x_\varepsilon^*) = \rho_\varepsilon$. Since this is true for any $r \in \mathbb{R}$ positive, we deduce the equality $\lim_\varepsilon x_\varepsilon^* = x^*$.

Viceversa, suppose that $x_\varepsilon^* \in \mathscr{S}(A + \varepsilon B)$ is such that $\ell(x_\varepsilon^*)$ lies in the boundary of $\ell(\mathscr{S}(A + \varepsilon B))$. Hence $\ell(x_\varepsilon^*)$ minimizes ℓ on $\mathscr{S}(A + \varepsilon B)$. Let $y \in \mathscr{S}(A)$. From Lemma 2.1, we know that $y \in \mathscr{S}(A + \varepsilon B)$. Since orders are preserved under limit, and by the continuity of ℓ, we get that

$$\ell(x^*) = \ell(\lim_\varepsilon x_\varepsilon^*) = \lim_\varepsilon \ell(x_\varepsilon^*) \leq \lim_\varepsilon \ell(y) = \ell(y).$$

By the arbitrarity of y we deduce that x^* minimizes ℓ on $\mathscr{S}(A)$, hence $\ell(x^*)$ lies in the boundary of $\ell(\mathscr{S}(A))$. □

3 HOMOTOPY FOR SEMIDEFINITE SYSTEMS

We consider the original linear matrix inequality $A(x) \succeq 0$ and its solution set $\mathscr{S}(A)$. In this section, we prove that one gets regularity properties under the the deformation of $\mathscr{S}(A)$ described in the previous sections.

3.1 Regularity of perturbed incidence varieties

Let $B \in \mathbb{S}_m(\mathbb{Q})$ and $\varepsilon \in [0, 1]$. We say that $A + \varepsilon B$ is *regular* if, for every $r = 1, \ldots, m$ and $\iota \subset \{1, \ldots, m\}$ with $\sharp\iota = m - r$, the algebraic set $\mathcal{V}_{r,\iota}(A + \varepsilon B)$ is smooth and equidimensional, of co-dimension $m(m-r) + \binom{m-r+1}{2}$ in $\mathbb{C}^{n+m(m-r)}$.

The following proposition states that such a property holds almost everywhere if the perturbation follows a generic direction.

Proposition 3.1. *There exists a non-empty Zariski open set $\mathscr{B}_1 \subset \mathbb{S}_m(\mathbb{C})$ such that, for all $r \in \{0, \ldots, m\}$, $\iota \subset \{1, \ldots, m\}$ with $\sharp\iota = m - r$, and for $B \in \mathscr{B}_1 \cap \mathbb{S}_m(\mathbb{Q})$, the following holds. For every $\varepsilon \in (0, 1]$, out of a finite set, the matrix $A + \varepsilon B$ is regular.*

Proof. We suppose w.l.o.g. that r is fixed and $\iota = \{1, \ldots, m - r\}$. Let $\mathfrak{B}$ be an unknown $m \times m$ symmetric matrix. For $\varepsilon \in (0, 1]$, we get a matrix $A + \varepsilon\mathfrak{B} = A(x) + \varepsilon\mathfrak{B}$, which is bilinear in the two groups of variables $x, \mathfrak{B}$. Let $f^{(\varepsilon)} = f^{(\varepsilon)}(x, y, \mathfrak{B})$ be the polynomial system given by the (i, j)–entries of $(A + \varepsilon\mathfrak{B})Y$ with $i \geq j$, and by all entries of $Y_\iota - \mathbb{I}_{m-r}$. By [17, Lemma 3.2], $Z(f^{(\varepsilon)}) = Z((A + \varepsilon\mathfrak{B})Y, Y_\iota - \mathbb{I}_{m-r})$, and remark that $\sharp f^{(\varepsilon)} = m(m-r) + \binom{m-r+1}{2}$.

We now proceed with a transversality argument. Consider the map (with abuse of notation)

$$\begin{array}{rccc} f^{(1)}: & \mathbb{C}^n \times \mathbb{C}^{m(m-r)} \times \mathbb{C}^{\binom{m+1}{2}} & \longrightarrow & \mathbb{C}^{m(m-r)+\binom{m-r+1}{2}} \\ & (x, y, \mathfrak{B}) & \longmapsto & f^{(1)}(x, y, \mathfrak{B}). \end{array}$$

We claim that 0 is a regular value of the map $f^{(1)}$ (the claim is proved in the last paragraph). This implies by Thom's Weak Transversality [30, Prop. B.3] that there is a Zariski open set $\mathscr{B}_{r,\iota} \subset \mathbb{S}_m(\mathbb{C})$ such that, if $B \in \mathscr{B}_{r,\iota}$, then 0 is a regular value of the section map $(x, y) \mapsto f^{(1)}(x, y, B)$.

We define $\mathscr{B}_1 := \cap_r \cap_\iota \mathscr{B}_{r,\iota}$, which is a finite intersection of Zariski open sets, hence Zariski open. Now, for a fixed $B \in \mathscr{B}_1$, consider the line tB, $t \in \mathbb{R}$, in $\mathbb{S}_m(\mathbb{C})$. Let $F_1 \in \mathbb{C}[\mathfrak{B}]$ be the generator of the ideal of all polynomials vanishing over the algebraic hypersurface $\mathbb{S}_m(\mathbb{C}) \setminus \mathscr{B}_1$. Then, since $B \in \mathscr{B}_1$ by construction, $t \mapsto F_1(tB)$ does not vanish identically, hence it vanishes exactly $\deg F_1$ many times (counting multiplicities). We deduce that, $\varepsilon B \in \mathscr{B}_1$ except for finitely many values of ε. We conclude that for all r and ι, $\mathcal{V}_{r,\iota}(A + \varepsilon B)$ is smooth and equidimensional of co-dimension $\sharp f^{(\varepsilon)} = m(m-r) + \binom{m-r+1}{2}$, for $\varepsilon \in (0, 1]$ except for finitely many values.

We prove now our claim. It follows by argument similar to the proof of [17, Prop.3.4]. Consider the derivatives of polynomials in $f^{(1)}(x, y, \mathfrak{B})$ with respect to the (i, j)–entries of $\mathfrak{B}$, with either $i \leq m - r$ or $j \leq m - r$, and those with respect to $y_{i,j}$ with $i \in \iota$. It is straightforward to check that this gives a maximal submatrix of the jacobian matrix $Df^{(1)}$ whose determinant is non-zero, proving that 0 is actually a regular value of $f^{(1)}$. □

3.2 Critical points on perturbed LMI

Let $B \in \mathbb{S}_m(\mathbb{Q})$ and let $A + \varepsilon B$ be the perturbed linear pencil defined above. For a fixed $\varepsilon < 1$, we consider the stratification of the hypersurface $Z(\det(A + \varepsilon B))$ given by the varieties $\mathcal{D}_r(A + \varepsilon B)$ of multiple rank defects of $A + \varepsilon B$, and their lifted incident sets $\mathcal{V}_{r,\iota}(A + \varepsilon B)$.

For $r < m$ and $\iota \subset \{1, \ldots, m\}$ with $\sharp\iota = m - r$, let $c := m(m-r) + \binom{m-r+1}{2}$. We recall from the proof of Proposition 3.1 that $f^{(\varepsilon)} \in \mathbb{R}[x, y]^c$ consists of the (i, j)–entries of $A^{(\varepsilon)}Y$ with $i \geq j$, and by all entries of $Y_\iota - \mathbb{I}_{m-r}$. We define the *Lagrange system* $\mathrm{Lag}_{r,\iota}(A + \varepsilon B)$ as follows:

$$\begin{aligned} f_i^{(\varepsilon)}(x, y) &= 0, \quad i = 1, \ldots, c \\ \sum_{i=1}^{c} z_i \nabla f_i^{(\varepsilon)}(x, y) &= \begin{pmatrix} \ell \\ 0 \end{pmatrix} \end{aligned} \tag{3.1}$$

where $\ell : \mathbb{R}^n \to \mathbb{R}$ is linear. As in Section 2, we abuse the notation of ℓ, and identifying it with the vector $(\ell_1, \ldots, \ell_n) \in \mathbb{R}^n$ giving $\ell(x) = \ell_1 x_1 + \cdots + \ell_n x_n$, hence $\ell = \nabla\ell$.

The set $Z(f^{(\varepsilon)}) = \mathcal{V}_{r,\iota}(A + \varepsilon B)$ is smooth for generic B thanks to Proposition 3.1. Hence a solution (x^*, y^*, z^*) of system (3.1) is a critical point (x^*, y^*) of the restriction of ℓ to $\mathcal{V}_{r,\iota}(A+\varepsilon B)$, equipped with a Lagrange multiplier $z^* \in \mathbb{C}^c$. Such a solution is called *of rank r* if rank $(A(x^*) + \varepsilon B) = r$.

Proposition 3.2. *There are two non-empty Zariski-open sets $\mathscr{B}_2 \subset \mathbb{S}_m(\mathbb{C})$ and $\mathscr{L}_2 \subset \mathbb{C}^n$ such that, for $B \in \mathscr{B}_2 \cap \mathbb{S}_m(\mathbb{Q})$, $\ell \in \mathscr{L}_2 \cap \mathbb{Q}^n$, and $\varepsilon \in (0, 1]$ out of a finite set, the following holds. Suppose that ℓ has a minimizer or maximizer x_ε^* on $\mathscr{S}(A + \varepsilon B)$. The projection on the x–space of the union, for $\iota \subset \{1, \ldots, m\}$, $\sharp\iota = m - r$, of the solution sets of rank r of system (3.1), is finite and contains x_ε^*.*

Proof. Let $r \leq m-1$ and $\iota \subset \{1, \ldots, m\}$. Recall by [22, Th. 4] that a minimizer or a maximizer x^* for the SDP $\inf\{\ell(x) : A(x)+\varepsilon B \succeq 0\}$, with rank $(A(x^*)+\varepsilon B) = r$, is a critical point of the restriction of ℓ to $\mathcal{D}_r(A + \varepsilon B)$. Moreover, [22, Lem. 2] implies that such critical points can be computed as projection on the x–space, of the critical points of the restriction of ℓ to $\mathcal{V}_{r,\iota}(A + \varepsilon B)$, for some ι (here we mean the extension $(x, y) \mapsto \ell(x)$ of ℓ to the (x, y)–space). Thus we only need to prove the finiteness of solutions of rank r of system (3.1), for a generic perturbation matrix B and a generic linear function ℓ, *uniformly* on ε.

We denote by $g^{(\varepsilon)} = z^T Df^{(\varepsilon)} - (\ell, 0)^T$ (the polynomials in the second row of (3.1)). The system $(f^{(\varepsilon)}, g^{(\varepsilon)})$ is square, for a fixed ϵ. Consider the polynomial map $(f^{(1)}, g^{(1)})$ sending $(x, y, \mathfrak{B}, z, \mathfrak{l})$ to $(f^{(1)}(x, y, \mathfrak{B}), g^{(1)}(x, y, \mathfrak{B}, z, \mathfrak{l}))$, where $\mathfrak{B}$ and $\mathfrak{l}$ are variables for B and ℓ, of the right size. As in the proof of Proposition 3.1, for generic B the rank of $Df^{(1)}$ is maximal. Hence, following *mutatis mutandis* the proof of [22, Prop.3], we conclude that the jacobian matrix of $(f^{(1)}, g^{(1)})$ has full rank at every point in $Z(f^{(1)}, g^{(1)})$ of rank r. Hence there exist non-empty Zariski open sets $\mathscr{B}_{r,\iota} \subset \mathbb{S}_m(\mathbb{C})$, $\mathscr{L}_{r,\iota} \subset \mathbb{C}^n$ such that if $(B, \ell) \in \mathscr{B}_{r,\iota} \times \mathscr{L}_{r,\iota}$ then system (3.1) has finitely many solutions of rank r, for $\varepsilon = 1$. We define $\mathscr{B}_2 := \cap_r \cap_\iota \mathscr{B}_{r,\iota}$ and $\mathscr{L}_2 := \cap_r \cap_\iota \mathscr{L}_{r,\iota}$ and we conclude the same disregarding r and ι.

Let $F_2 \in \mathbb{C}[\mathfrak{B}, \mathfrak{l}]$ be the generator of the ideal of all polynomials vanishing over $(\mathbb{S}_m(\mathbb{C})\times\mathbb{C}^n) \setminus (\mathscr{B}_2 \times \mathscr{L}_2)$. Then $F_2(B, \ell) \neq 0$, which implies that $t \mapsto F_2(tB, \ell)$ has finitely many roots, hence $(\varepsilon B, \ell) \in (\mathscr{B}_2 \times \mathscr{L}_2)$ almost everywhere in $(0, 1]$. We conclude the proof by defining the claimed finite set as the union of (1) the set of roots of F_2 and (2) the finite set constructed in Proposition 3.1. □

Note that the transversality techniques used in the proofs of Propositions 3.1 and 3.2 are non-constructive. Indeed they prove the existence of the *discriminants* $F_1 \in \mathbb{C}[\mathfrak{B}]$ and $F_2 \in \mathbb{C}[\mathfrak{B}, \mathfrak{l}]$, but do not construct them effectively. If we knew F_1, F_2 one could use separation bounds for real roots of univariate polynomials (*e.g.* [19]) to get upper bounds for the minimum of the finite sets.

3.3 The degree of the homotopy curve

We consider the Lagrange system (3.1), $r < m$ and $\iota \subset \{1, \dots, m\}$ with $\sharp\iota = m - r$. For a given homotopy parameter $\varepsilon \in (0, 1)$ out of the union of the finite sets defined in Propositions 3.1 and 3.2, the system has finitely many solutions of rank r. When ε converges to 0, these solutions draw a (possibly reducible) semi-algebraic curve. This can also be seen as a semi-algebraic subset of dimension 1 in $\mathbb{R}\langle\varepsilon\rangle^n$. We denote this curve by $C_{r,\iota}$.

Contrarily to the classical homotopy based on the central path, whose points lie in the interior of the feasible set, we have constructed homotopy curves containing optimal solutions of given rank of perturbed semidefinite programs. This allows to derive degree bounds that depend on this rank.

Proposition 3.3. *Let r, ι be fixed, let $C_{r,\iota}$ be the curve of solutions or rank r of the Lagrange system (3.1), for positive small enough ε, and $Zar(C_{r,\iota})$ be its complex Zariski closure. Then*

$$\deg Zar(C_{r,\iota}) \leq (1 + 2r(m-r)) \cdot \theta_1$$

where

$$\theta_1 = \sum_k \binom{c}{n-k}\binom{n}{c+k-r(m-r)}\binom{r(m-r)}{k} \qquad (3.2)$$

Proof. We first compute a polynomial system equivalent to (3.1). We make the substitution $Y_\iota = \mathbb{I}_{m-r}$ that eliminates variables $\{y_{i,j} : i \in \iota\}$ in the vector $f^{(\varepsilon)}$ defining the incidence variety $\mathcal{V}_{r,\iota}(A + \varepsilon B)$, hence we suppose $f^{(\varepsilon)} \in \mathbb{Q}[\varepsilon, x, \overline{y}]^c$, with $c = m(m-r) - \binom{m-r}{2} = \frac{(m-r)(m+r+1)}{2}$ and $\overline{y} = \{y_{i,j} : i \notin \iota\}$. (Indeed, $\binom{m-r}{2}$ is the number of redundancies eliminated by [17, Lemma 3.2] recalled in the proof of Proposition 3.1.) Above we have intentionally abused of the notation of $f^{(\varepsilon)}$ and c. Next, the new polynomials f_i do not depend on $y \setminus \overline{y}$. Hence, defining $g := \sum_{i=1}^c z_i \nabla f_i^{(\varepsilon)}(x, \overline{y}) - (\nabla\ell, 0)^T \in \mathbb{Q}[\varepsilon, x, \overline{y}, z]$, with $z = (z_1, \dots, z_c)$, one has $\sharp g = \sharp x + \sharp\overline{y} = n + r(m-r)$.

We conclude that the Lagrange system (3.1) is given after reduction by the entries of $f^{(\varepsilon)}$ and g, that are multilinear in the three groups of variables $\xi := (\varepsilon, x), \overline{y}$ and z. The multidegree with respect to $(\xi, \overline{y}, z)$ is respectively

- $\mathrm{mdeg}_{(\xi,\overline{y},z)}(f_i^{(\varepsilon)}) = (1, 1, 0)$, for $i = 1, \dots, c$
- $\mathrm{mdeg}_{(\xi,\overline{y},z)}(g_i) = (0, 1, 1)$, for $i = 1, \dots, n$
- $\mathrm{mdeg}_{(\xi,\overline{y},z)}(g_{n+j}) = (1, 0, 1)$, for $j = 1, \dots, r(m-r)$

We compute below a multilinear Bézout bound of deg $\mathrm{Zar}(C_{r,\iota})$ (see [30, App.H.1]). This is given by the sum of the coefficients of the polynomial

$$P = (s_1 + s_2)^c (s_2 + s_3)^n (s_1 + s_3)^{r(m-r)}$$

modulo the monomial ideal $I = \langle s_1^{n+2}, s_2^{r(m-r)+1}, s_3^{c+1}\rangle$. Since the maximal admissible power modulo I of s_1 (resp. of s_2, s_3) is $n + 1$ (resp. $r(m-r), c$) and since P is homogeneous of degree $c+n+r(m-r)$ we get

$$P \equiv \theta_1 s_1^n s_2^{r(m-r)} s_3^c + \theta_2 s_1^{n+1} s_2^{r(m-r)-1} s_3^c + \theta_3 s_1^{n+1} s_2^{r(m-r)} s_3^{c-1}$$

modulo I, where $\theta_i = \theta_i(m, n, r)$ are the corresponding coefficiens in the expansion of P, hence the bound is $\theta_1+\theta_2+\theta_3$. Just by expanding P and by solving a linear system over $\mathbb{Z}$ one gets the expression in (3.2), within the range $0 \leq k \leq \min\{n - c + r(m-r), r(m-r)\}$. A similar formula holds for θ_2 where $n - k + 1$ substitutes $n - k$ in the first binomial coefficient. We deduce that

$$\theta_2 \leq \max_k \left\{\frac{c-n+k}{n-k+1}\right\} \theta_1 \leq r(m-r)\theta_1.$$

Moreover the expression of θ_3 equals that of θ_2 except for the second binomial coefficient which is smaller, hence $\theta_3 \leq \theta_2 \leq r(m-r)\theta_1$, and we conclude. □

Recall that the algorithm in [17] solves LMI under genericity properties that cannot be assumed in the context of this paper. It avoids the use of homotopy. We expect that in degenerate situations the degree of the homotopy curve will exceed that of the univariate representation computed in the regular case. We prove that this degree gap is controlled, namely, that the extra factor is linear in n and in the rank-corank coefficient $r(m-r)$.

Proposition 3.4. *Let $\theta = \theta(m, n, r)$ be the bound computed in [17, Prop.5.1]. For all r and ι as above, $\deg Zar(C_{r,\iota}) \leq (1 + 2r(m-r))n\theta$.*

Proof. Let θ_1 be the expression in (3.2). We prove that $\theta_1 \leq n\theta$ and we conclude. Indeed, let $\theta = \sum_k a_k$ and $\theta_1 = \sum_k b_k$. Then

$$\frac{b_k}{a_k} = \frac{n}{c+k-r(m-r)}$$

that does not exceed n for all k. Hence $\theta_1 \leq \sum_k n a_k = n\theta$. □

4 ALGORITHM

4.1 Description

This section contains the formal description of a homotopy-based algorithm for solving the semidefinite program in (1.1), called DegenerateSDP.

We first define the data structures we use to represent algebraic sets of dimension 0 and 1 during the algorithm. A *zero-dimensional parametrization* of a finite set $W \subset \mathbb{C}^n$ is a vector $Q = (q_0, q_1, \dots, q_n, q) \in \mathbb{Q}[t]^{n+2}$ such that q_0, q are coprime and

$$W = \left\{a \in \mathbb{C}^n : a_i = q_i(t)/q_0(t), q(t) = 0, \exists t \in \mathbb{R}\right\}.$$

Similarly a *one-dimensional parametrization* of a curve $C \subset \mathbb{C}^n$ is a vector $Q = (q_0, q_1, \dots, q_n, q) \in \mathbb{Q}[t, u]^{n+2}$ with q_0, q coprime and

$$C = \left\{a \in \mathbb{C}^n : a_i = q_i(t, u)/q_0(t, u), q(t, u) = 0, \exists t, u \in \mathbb{R}\right\}.$$

Abusing notation we denote by $Z(Q)$ the sets in the right part of the previous equalities. If Q is a list of parametrizations, $Z(Q)$ denotes the union of $Z(Q_i)$ for Q_i in Q, and every $x^* \in Z(Q)$ is encoded by $(Q, [a_*, b_*])$, where $a_*, b_* \in \mathbb{Q}$ and $[a_*, b_*]$ is a separating interval for the root that corresponds to x^*. These representations for finite sets and curves are standard in real algebraic geometry, and are called parametrizations in the sequel. By convention, ( ) is a parametrization for $\emptyset$.

We also define the following subroutines manipulating this kind of representations:

- ODP. With input a polynomial system $f = (f_1, \ldots, f_s)$ defining a one-dimensional algebraic set $Z(f)$, and a set of variables x, it returns a one-dimensional parametrization of the projection of $Z(f)$ on the x–space.
- CUT. Given a one-dimensional parametrization Q of the zero set $Z(f) \subset \mathbb{C}^{n+1}$ of polynomials $f_1, \ldots, f_s \in \mathbb{Q}[\varepsilon, x]$, it returns a zero-dimensional parametrization of the projection on the x–space of the limit of $Z(f)$ for $\varepsilon \to 0^+$.
- UNION. Given two parametrizations Q_1, Q_2, it returns a parametrization Q such that $Z(Q) = Z(Q_1) \cup Z(Q_2)$.

The input of DegenerateSDP is the $m \times m$ n–variate symmetric linear matrix $A(x)$ defining the spectrahedron $\mathscr{S}(A)$, and a linear form ℓ. The output is a list $Q = [Q_1, \ldots, Q_{m-1}]$ of zero-dimensional parametrizations containing a solution x^* to the original LMI (with the corresponding interval $[a_*, b_*]$ of rational numbers), or ( ), which means that the original SDP (1.1) is either infeasible ($\mathscr{S}(A) = \emptyset$) or that the infimum in (1.1) equals $-\infty$.

Below we describe each step of the algorithm.

```
1:  procedure DegenerateSDP(A, ℓ)
2:      Generate B ∈ S_m(Q)
3:      Q ← [ ]
4:      for r = 1, ..., m − 1 do
5:          Q_r ← (1)
6:          for ι ⊂ {1, ..., m} with ♯ι = m − r do
7:              L ← Lag_{r,ι}(A + εB)
8:              Q_{r,ι} ← ODP(L, x)
9:              Q_r ← UNION(Q_r, Q_{r,ι})
10:         Q ← [Q, CUT(Q_r)]
11:     if S(A) ∩ Z(Q) = ∅ then return ( )
12:     return (Q, [a_*, b_*])
```

Note that ε in the previous formal description is treated as variable, so that the polynomials in L at step 7 define a curve. Remark that all solutions satisfy $\det A(x) = 0$ hence $\operatorname{rank} A(x) \le m - 1$.

We show in Theorem 4.1 that DegenerateSDP is correct and computes solutions to the original linear matrix inequality as limits of perturbed solutions. We use the results of Sections 2 and 3 and refer to the notation of Zariski open sets constructed in Lemma 2.3 and 2.4, and in Proposition 3.1 and 3.2.

Theorem 4.1. *Let A be a $m \times m$ n–variate symmetric linear matrix. Let $B \in \mathscr{B}_1 \cap \mathscr{B}_2 \cap \mathbb{S}^+_m(\mathbb{Q})$, and $\ell \in \mathscr{L}_1 \cap \mathscr{L}_2 \cap \mathbb{Q}^n$.*

(A) *If $A(x^*) = 0$ for some $x^* \in \mathbb{R}^n$, then x^* is a minimizer in (1.1) or ℓ is unbounded from below on $\mathscr{S}_A$.*

(B) *Otherwise, Q = DegenerateSDP(A, ℓ) fulfils the following condition. If $x^* \in \mathscr{S}(A)$ is a minimizer in (1.1) then $x^* \in \mathscr{S}(A) \cap Z(Q)$. Viceversa, if $\mathscr{S}(A) \neq \emptyset$, and ℓ is not unbounded from below on $\mathscr{S}(A)$, then $\mathscr{S}(A) \cap Z(Q)$ contains a minimizer in (1.1).*

Proof. First, suppose that $A(x^*) = 0$ for some $x^* \in \mathbb{R}^n$. Then $A_0 = -\sum_i x^*_i A_i$, hence $A(x) = (x_1 - x^*_1)A_1 + \cdots + (x_n - x^*_n)A_n$. We deduce that $\mathscr{S}_A$ is the image under the translation $x \mapsto x + x^*$ of a cone, that is: either $\mathscr{S}_A = \{x^*\}$, in which case $\ell \equiv \ell(x^*)$ on $\mathscr{S}_A$, and x^* is a minimizer for (1.1), or $\mathscr{S}_A$ is an unbounded convex cone with origin in x^*. In the second case, since ℓ is linear, either its infimum on $\mathscr{S}_A$ is attained at the origin x^*, or its maximum is attained in x^* and ℓ is unbounded from below on $\mathscr{S}_A$.

We prove the first sentence in (B). Assume that $x^* \in \mathscr{S}(A)$ is a minimizer in (1.1). Then $\ell(x^*)$ lies in the boundary of $\ell(\mathscr{S}(A))$. By Lemma 2.4, we get that there exists $x^*_\varepsilon \in \mathscr{S}(A + \varepsilon B)$ such that $\ell(x^*_\varepsilon)$ lies in the boundary of $\ell(\mathscr{S}(A + \varepsilon B))$ and $\lim_\varepsilon x^*_\varepsilon = x^*$. Hence for $\varepsilon > 0$, x^*_ε is a minimizer of ℓ on $\ell(\mathscr{S}(A + \varepsilon B)) \subset \mathbb{R}^n$. By Proposition 3.2, there exists $r \in \{1, \ldots, m-1\}$, $\iota \subset \{1, \ldots, m\}$ with $\sharp\iota = m - r$, y^*_ε and z^*_ε, such that $(x^*_\varepsilon, y^*_\varepsilon, z^*_\varepsilon)$ is a solution of the Lagrange system $\mathrm{Lag}_{r,\iota}(A + \varepsilon B)$. We deduce that for $\varepsilon > 0$, x^*_ε is parametrized by the one-dimensinal parametrization $Q_{r,\iota} = \mathrm{ODP}(L)$ computed at step 8 of DegenerateSDP, hence by Q_r. We deduce that Q parametrizes the limit $x^* = \lim_\varepsilon x^*_\varepsilon$, that is $x^* \in \mathscr{S}(A) \cap Z(Q)$.

We finally come to the second sentence in (B). Since ℓ is not unbounded on $\mathscr{S}(A)$, and $\mathscr{S}(A) \neq 0$, then the same holds for ℓ on $\mathscr{S}(A + \varepsilon B)$. By Lemma 2.3, $\ell(\mathscr{S}(A))$ and $\ell(\mathscr{S}(A + \varepsilon B))$ are closed intervals. We deduce that the boundary of $\ell(\mathscr{S}(A + \varepsilon B))$ is non-empty. Let x^*_ε be such that $\ell(x^*_\varepsilon)$ lies in the boundary of $\ell(\mathscr{S}(A + \varepsilon B))$. Since $\mathscr{S}(A) \neq \emptyset$, by 2.4 $x^* := \lim_\varepsilon x^*_\varepsilon \in \mathscr{S}(A) \cap Z(Q)$ is such that $\ell(x^*)$ lies in the boundary of $\ell(\mathscr{S}(A))$, hence a minimizer of the SDP in (1.1). □

To conclude, we make explicit the following fact that follows from Theorem 4.1. Recall that a generic linear form over a non-empty convex set is either unbounded from below ($\inf \ell = -\infty$) or its infimum is attained. Theorem 4.1 implies that if ℓ is a generic linear form, then $\mathscr{S}(A) \cap Z(Q) = \emptyset$ if and only if $\mathscr{S}(A) = \emptyset$ or ℓ is unbounded from below on $\mathscr{S}(A)$. We conclude that up to genericity assumptions on the linear form, the algorithm is correct, since it returns a non-empty rational parametrization if and only if problem (1.1) has a feasible solution.

4.2 Complexity analysis

This section contains a rigourous analysis of the arithmetic complexity of DegenerateSDP. Let us first give an overview of the algorithms that are used to perform the subroutines in DegenerateSDP.

The computation of a one-dimensional parametrization of the homotopy curve $\mathrm{Zar}(C_{r,\iota})$ at step 8, that is the routine ODP, is done in two steps. First, we instantiate the system $\mathrm{Lag}_{r,\iota}(A + \varepsilon B)$ to a generic $\varepsilon = \bar{\varepsilon}$. By Proposition 3.2 we deduce that the obtained system is zero-dimensional. We use [31] to compute a zero-dimensional rational parametrization of this system.

The second steps consists in *lifting* the parameter ε and in computing a *parametric geometric resolution* of $\mathrm{Lag}_{r,\iota}(A + \varepsilon B)$ with the algorithm in [34], that is, a parametric analogue of [13]. In our context, there is only one parameter, that is ε.

The routine CUT can be performed via the algorithm in [27] and, finally, the cost of the routine UNION is given in [30, Lem.G.3].

To keep notations simple, let $L = (L_1, \ldots, L_N) \in \mathbb{Q}[\varepsilon, t_1, \ldots, t_N]$ be the polynomials defining the Lagrange system (3.1), in the reduced form as in the proof of Proposition (3.3). Hence $N = c + n + r(m-r)$, where $c = (m-r)(m+r+1)/2$. The complex algebraic set $\mathrm{Zar}(C_{r,\iota}) = Z(L)$ is a curve whose degree is bounded by Proposition 3.3.

THEOREM 4.2. *Let L and N be as above. Under the assumptions of Theorem 4.1, the output Q = DEGENERATESDP(A, ℓ) is returned within*

$$\widetilde{O}\left(n \sum_r \binom{m}{r} r(m-r) N^4 \theta^2\right)$$

arithmetic operations over $\mathbb{Q}$, where $\widetilde{O}(T) = O(T \log^a(T))$ for some a and $\theta \le \binom{m^2+n}{n}^3$.

PROOF. Let $\bar{\varepsilon} \in (0,1)$ be generic, and let $\bar{L}$ be equal to the system L where ε is instantiated to $\bar{\varepsilon}$. Let θ be the value computed in [17, Prop.5.1], that bound the number of solution of $\bar{L} = 0$ in $\mathbb{C}^N$. By the same proposition one gets

$$\theta \le \binom{c+n}{n}^3 \le \binom{m(m-r)+n}{n}^3,$$

from which the claimed bound uniform in r.

Let $\bar{L}' = (\bar{L}'_1, \ldots, \bar{L}'_N)$ be a polynomial vector of lenght N such that $\bar{L}'_i$ has the same multilinear structure as $\bar{L}_i$, for $i = 1, \ldots, N$. Let $H(T, t_1, \ldots, t_N) = T\bar{L} + (1-T)\bar{L}'$. By [31, Prop.5], the complexity of computing a univariate representation of $Z(\bar{L})$ is in $\widetilde{O}(N^3\theta\theta')$ where $\theta' = \deg, Z(H)$. By [17, Lem.5.4], $\theta' \in O(N \min\{n, c\}\theta)$. Hence the complexity of the first step of ODP is in

$$\widetilde{O}(\min\{n, c\} N^4 \theta^2).$$

Next, let $\pi : \mathbb{C}^{N+1} \to \mathbb{C}$ be the projection $(\varepsilon, t_1, \ldots, t_N) \mapsto \varepsilon$. By [17, Prop.5.1], a generic fiber of π has degree bounded by θ. Proposition 3.4 implies that $\deg \mathrm{Zar}(C_{r,\iota})$ is bounded above by $(1 + 2r(m-r))\, n\theta$. We apply the bound in [34, Cor.1], and we get a complexity in

$$\widetilde{O}\left(nr(m-r)N^4\theta^2\right),$$

for the parametric resolution step in ODP. By [31, Lem.13], the complexity of CUT is in $\widetilde{O}\left(N^3\theta\theta'\right)$, hence in

$$\widetilde{O}\left(\min\{n, c\} N^4 \theta^2\right).$$

The complexity of UNION is in $\widetilde{O}(N\theta^2)$ at each step, by [30, Lem.G.3]. This shows that the most expensive step is the lifting step.

The previous complexity bounds depend on r, and hold for all $r = 1, \ldots, m$, and for all index subsets $\iota \subset \{1, \ldots, m\}$. We conclude by summing up with weight $\binom{m}{r}$, the number of subsets $\iota \subset \{1, \ldots, m\}$ of cardinality $m - r$. □

We note that N can be bounded above by $n + 2m^2$ uniformly in r. The complexity of DEGENERATESDP given by Theorem 4.2 is polynomial in n when m is fixed. Moreover, for a generic perturbation matrix B, [17, Lem.3.1] allows to deduce the inequality $n \ge \binom{m-r+1}{2}$: this implies that when n is fixed, then m is bounded above and hence the complexity is still polynomial.

5 EXAMPLE

In this final section we develop a degenerate example in low dimension, showing how our algorithm works from a geometric viewpoint.

Consider the 2×2 semidefinite representation of a point $(p_1, p_2) \in \mathbb{R}^2$:

$$\left\{(x_1, x_2) \in \mathbb{R}^2 : A(x) := \begin{pmatrix} p_1 - x_1 & x_2 - p_2 \\ x_2 - p_2 & x_1 - p_1 \end{pmatrix} \succeq 0\right\} = \{(p_1, p_2)\}.$$

The interior of $\mathscr{S}(A) := \{(p_1, p_2)\}$ in $\mathbb{R}^2$ is empty, and moreover $\mathscr{S}(A)$, corresponding to the intersection of the 2-dimensional linear space of matrices in the pencil $A(x)$ with the the 3-dimensional cone of 2×2 symmetric matrices, has co-dimension 2 in $\mathbb{R}^2$.

We first construct the incidence varieties $\mathcal{V}_{r,\iota}(A)$. For $r = 0$, the incidence variety is smooth, but for $r = 1$ and $\iota = \{1\}$, this is the following algebraic curve in $\mathbb{C}^3$

$$\mathcal{V}_{1,\{1\}} = Z((x_2 - p_2)y + p_1 - x_1, (x_1 - p_1)y + x_2 - p_2)$$

having two complex singularities lifting (p_1, p_2), precisely at $(p_1, p_2, \pm \mathrm{i})$, with $\mathrm{i}^2 = -1$.

According to Proposition 3.1, we can desingularize the varieties $\mathcal{V}_{r,\iota}(A)$ by applying a sufficiently generic homotopy

$$A + \varepsilon B = \begin{pmatrix} p_1 - x_1 & x_2 - p_2 \\ x_2 - p_2 & x_1 - p_1 \end{pmatrix} + \varepsilon \begin{pmatrix} b_{11} & b_{12} \\ b_{12} & b_{22} \end{pmatrix}$$

perturbing the constant term of A. The set $\mathcal{V}_{r,\iota}(A + \varepsilon B)$ is smooth and equidimensional for generic B, and the expected number of critical points of the restriction of a generic linear function $\ell(x_1, x_2) = \ell_1 x_1 + \ell_2 x_2$ is finite for each ε.

In Figure 1 we plot the semi-algebraic curve of solutions to the perturbed systems for a fixed linear objective function. Eliminating variables y and z from the Lagrange system $\mathrm{Lag}_{r,\iota}(A + \varepsilon B)$, one gets a one-dimensional complex curve, representing the Zariski closure of the red curves in Figure 1.

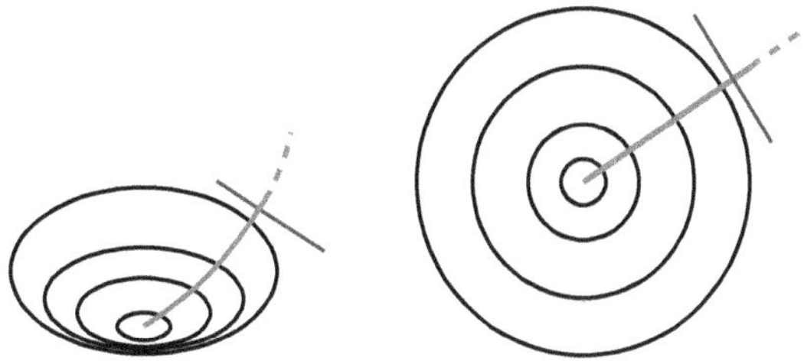

Figure 1: Homotopy curves in red and linear objective function in blue, for generic B (left) and for $B = \mathbb{I}_2$ (right)

For the special choice $B = \mathbb{I}_2$, the real trace of the homotopy curve is the line orthogonal to ℓ, that is parallel to the zero set of $\ell^\perp(x_1, x_2) = \ell_2 x_1 - \ell_1 x_2$ and passing through (p_1, p_2), while if B is drawn randomly the homotopy curve has degree 2. For instance, for $(p_1, p_2) = (1, 1)$, the homotopy curve constructed by DEGENERATESDP is given by the equality

$$2241769\, x_1^2 + 115046296\, x_1 x_2 + 65669911\, x_2^2 - 119529834\, x_1 - 246386118\, x_2 + 182957976 = 0$$

where $\ell(x_1, x_2) = 88x_1 - 94x_2$ is the objective function, and with perturbation matrix

$$B = \begin{pmatrix} 80 & -68 \\ -68 & 109 \end{pmatrix}.$$

We finally remark that, even if the choice $B = \mathbb{I}_2$ exhibits a degenerate behaviour in the sense described above, from the point of view of the homotopy constructed in this work $B = \mathbb{I}_2$ exhibits a generic behaviour: one can check by hand that the incidence variety $\mathcal{V}_{r,\iota}(A + \varepsilon\mathbb{I}_2)$ is singular if and only if $\varepsilon = 0$. Indeed, $\mathcal{V}_{r,\iota}(A + \varepsilon\mathbb{I}_2)$ is defined by the vanishing of $f^{(\varepsilon)} = (\varepsilon - x_1 + x_2 y, x_2 + \varepsilon y + x_1 y)$, and the 2×2 minors of $Df^{(\varepsilon)}$ combined with $f^{(\varepsilon)} = 0$ imply that $y = \pm i$ and $0 = x_2 = \varepsilon - x_1 = \varepsilon + x_1$ hence $x_1 = x_2 = \varepsilon = 0$.

REFERENCES

[1] X. Allamigeon, P. Benchimol, S. Gaubert, and M. Joswig. 2014. Long and winding central paths. *arXiv preprint arXiv:1405.4161* (2014).

[2] X. Allamigeon, S. Gaubert, and M. Skomra. 2016. Solving generic nonarchimedean semidefinite programs using stochastic game algorithms. *Proceedings of ISSAC 2016, Waterloo, Canada* (2016).

[3] E.D. Andersen and K.D. Andersen. 2013. MOSEK: High performance software for large-scale LP, QP, SOCP, SDP and MIP. __, *March* (2013).

[4] M.F. Anjos and J-B. Lasserre. 2012. Introduction to semidefinite, conic and polynomial optimization. In *Handbook on semidefinite, conic and polynomial optimization*. Springer, 1–22.

[5] B. Bank, M. Giusti, J. Heintz, and M. Safey El Din. 2014. Intrinsic complexity estimates in polynomial optimization. *Journal of Complexity* 0 (2014), –. https://doi.org/10.1016/j.jco.2014.02.005

[6] S. Basu, R. Pollack, and M-F. Roy. 1998. A new algorithm to find a point in every cell defined by a family of polynomials. In *Quantifier elimination and cylindrical algebraic decomposition*. Springer-Verlag.

[7] S. Basu, R. Pollack, and M-F. Roy. 2006. *Algorithms in real algebraic geometry* (second ed.). Algorithms and Computation in Mathematics, Vol. 10. Springer-Verlag.

[8] G. Blekherman. 2012. Nonnegative polynomials and sums of squares. *Journal of the American Mathematical Society* 25, 3 (2012), 617–635.

[9] G. Blekherman, P.A. Parrilo, and R.R. Thomas. 2013. *Semidefinite optimization and convex algebraic geometry*. Vol. 13. Siam.

[10] J. Bochnak, M. Coste, and M-F. Roy. 1998. *Real algebraic geometry*. Ergebnisse der Mathematik und ihrer Grenzgebiete, Vol. 36. Springer-Verlag.

[11] S. Boyd, L. El Ghaoui, E. Feron, and V. Balakrishnan. 1994. *Linear matrix inequalities in system and control theory*. Vol. 15. Siam.

[12] M. Demazure. 2013. *Bifurcations and catastrophes: geometry of solutions to nonlinear problems*. Springer Science & Business Media.

[13] M. Giusti, G. Lecerf, and B. Salvy. 2001. A Gröbner-free alternative for polynomial system solving. *Journal of Complexity* 17, 1 (2001), 154–211.

[14] Q. Guo, M. Safey El Din, and L. Zhi. 2013. Computing rational solutions of linear matrix inequalities. In *ISSAC'13*. 197–204.

[15] M. Halická, E. de Klerk, and C. Roos. 2002. On the convergence of the central path in semidefinite optimization. *SIAM Journal on Optimization* 12, 4 (2002), 1090–1099.

[16] D. Henrion, S. Naldi, and M. Safey El Din. 2015. Real root finding for determinants of linear matrices. *Journal of Symbolic Computation* 74 (2015), 205–238. https://doi.org/S0747717115000607

[17] D. Henrion, S. Naldi, and M. Safey El Din. 2016. Exact algorithms for linear matrix inequalities. *SIAM J. Optim.* 26, 4 (2016), 2512–2539.

[18] D. Henrion, S. Naldi, and M. Safey El Din. 2017. SPECTRA: a Maple library for solving linear matrix inequalities in exact arithmetic. *Optimization Methods and Software* (2017).

[19] A. Herman, H. Hong, and E. Tsigaridas. 2017. Improving Root Separation Bounds. *Journal of Symbolic Computation* (2017). https://hal.inria.fr/hal-01456686 (to appear).

[20] M. Joldes, J-M. Muller, and V. Popescu. 2017. Implementation and performance evaluation of an extended precision floating-point arithmetic library for high-accuracy semidefinite programming. *ARITH 2017, London, UK, July 24-26 2017* (2017).

[21] J-B. Lasserre. 2001. Global optimization with polynomials and the problem of moments. *SIAM J. Optim.* 11, 3 (2001), 796–817. https://doi.org/10.1137/S1052623400366802

[22] S. Naldi. 2016. Solving rank-constrained semidefinite programs in exact arithmetic. *Proceedings of the International Symposium on Symbolic and Algebraic Computation, ISSAC* 20-22-July-2016 (2016), 357–364.

[23] Y. Nesterov and A. Nemirovsky. 1994. *Interior-point polynomial algorithms in convex programming*. Studies in Applied Mathematics, Vol. 13. SIAM, Philadelphia.

[24] J. Nie, K. Ranestad, and B. Sturmfels. 2010. The algebraic degree of semidefinite programming. *Mathematical Programming* 122, 2 (2010), 379–405. https://doi.org/10.1007/s10107-008-0253-6

[25] P. Parrilo. 2003. Semidefinite programming relaxations for semialgebraic problems. *Mathematical Programming Ser.B* 96, 2 (2003), 293–320.

[26] M. Ramana. 1997. An exact duality theory for semidefinite programming and its complexity implications. *Mathematical Programming* 77, 1 (1997), 129–162.

[27] F. Rouillier, M-F. Roy, and M. Safey El Din. 2000. Finding at least one point in each connected component of a real algebraic set defined by a single equation. *J. Complexity* 16, 4 (2000), 716–750. http://dx.doi.org/10.1006/jcom.2000.0563

[28] M. Safey El Din. 2007. Testing sign conditions on a multivariate polynomial and applications. *Mathematics in Computer Science* 1, 1 (2007), 177–207. https://doi.org/10.1007/s11786-007-0003-9

[29] M. Safey El Din and É. Schost. 2003. Polar Varieties and Computation of one Point in each Connected Component of a Smooth Real Algebraic Set. In *ISSAC'03*. ACM, 224–231.

[30] M. Safey El Din and E. Schost. 2017. A nearly optimal algorithm for deciding connectivity queries in smooth and bounded real algebraic sets. *J. ACM* 63, 48 (2017). Issue 6.

[31] M. Safey El Din and É. Schost. 2018. Bit complexity for multi-homogeneous polynomial system solving - Application to polynomial minimization. *Journal of Symbolic Computation* 87 (2018), 176 - 206. https://doi.org/10.1016/j.jsc.2017.08.001

[32] M. Safey El Din and L. Zhi. 2010. Computing Rational Points in Convex Semialgebraic Sets and Sum of Squares Decompositions. *SIAM Journal on Optimization* 20, 6 (2010), 2876–2889.

[33] C. Scheiderer. 2016. Sums of squares of polynomials with rational coefficients. *Journal of the European Mathematical Society* 18, 7 (2016), 1495–1513.

[34] É. Schost. 2003. Computing parametric geometric resolutions. *Applicable Algebra in Engineering, Communication and Computing* 13, 5 (2003), 349–393.

[35] J. F. Sturm. 1999. Using SeDuMi 1.02, a MATLAB toolbox for optimization over symmetric cones. *Optim. Methods Softw.* 11/12, 1-4 (1999), 625–653. http://dx.doi.org/10.1080/10556789908805766

[36] K-C. Toh, M.J. Todd, and R. Tütüncü. 1999. SDPT3 - a MATLAB software package for semidefinite programming, version 1.3. *Optimization methods and software* 11, 1-4 (1999), 545–581.

Fast Reduction of Bivariate Polynomials with Respect to Sufficiently Regular Gröbner Bases

Joris van der Hoeven
Robin Larrieu
Laboratoire d'informatique de l'École polytechnique
LIX, UMR 7161 CNRS
Campus de l'École polytechnique
1, rue Honoré d'Estienne d'Orves
Bâtiment Alan Turing, CS35003
91120 Palaiseau, France
vdhoeven@lix.polytechnique.fr
larrieu@lix.polytechnique.fr

ABSTRACT

Let G be the reduced Gröbner basis of a zero-dimensional ideal $I \subseteq \mathbb{K}[X, Y]$ of bivariate polynomials over an effective field $\mathbb{K}$. Modulo suitable regularity assumptions on G and suitable precomputations as a function of G, we prove the existence of a quasi-optimal algorithm for the reduction of polynomials in $\mathbb{K}[X, Y]$ with respect to G. Applications include fast algorithms for multiplication in the quotient algebra $\mathbb{A} = \mathbb{K}[X, Y]/I$ and for conversions due to changes of the term ordering.

ACM Reference format:
Joris van der Hoeven and Robin Larrieu. 2018. Fast Reduction of Bivariate Polynomials with Respect to Sufficiently Regular Gröbner Bases. In *Proceedings of 2018 ACM International Symposium on Symbolic and Algebraic Computation, New York, NY, USA, July 16–19, 2018 (ISSAC'18),* 8 pages.
DOI: https://doi.org/10.1145/3208976.3209003

1 INTRODUCTION

Let $\mathbb{K}$ be an effective field and consider an algebra $\mathbb{A}$ defined as $\mathbb{A} = \mathbb{K}[X_1, \ldots, X_r]/I$, where I is a finitely generated ideal. For actual computations in $\mathbb{A}$, we have three main tasks:

- **T1** define a non-ambiguous representation for elements in $\mathbb{A}$;
- **T2** design a multiplication algorithm for $\mathbb{A}$;
- **T3** show how to convert between different representations for elements in $\mathbb{A}$.

Fast polynomial arithmetic based on FFT-multiplication allows for a quasi-optimal solution in the univariate case. However, reduction modulo an ideal of multivariate polynomials is non-trivial.

The most common approach for computations modulo ideals of polynomials is based on Gröbner bases. This immediately solves the first task, using the fact that any polynomial admits a unique normal form modulo a given Gröbner basis [4]. The second task is solved by reducing the product of two polynomials modulo the Gröbner basis. Finally, given a Gröbner basis with respect to a first term ordering, one may use the FGLM algorithm [9] to compute a reduced Gröbner basis with respect to a second term ordering; algorithms for the corresponding conversions are obtained as a by-product.

There is an abundant literature on efficient algorithms for the computation of Gröbner bases; see for example [7–9] and references therein. Although the worst case complexity is known to be very bad [23], polynomial complexity bounds (for the number of operations in $\mathbb{K}$ in terms of the expected output size) exist for many important cases of interest. For example, for fixed r, and using naive linear algebra on Macaulay matrices, one may show [14, 15, 22] that a sufficiently regular system of r equations of degree δ can be solved in time $O(\delta^{\omega r})$. Here $\omega < 2.3728639$ is the exponent of matrix multiplication [11]. For such a system, the Bezout bound δ^r for the number D of solutions is reached, so the running time $O(D^\omega)$ is polynomial in the expected output size D. The implicit dependency of this bound on r can be improved by using the "matrix-F5" variant [2] of Faugère's F5 algorithm [8].

The F5 algorithm and all other currently known fast algorithms for Gröbner basis computations rely on linear algebra. At this point, one may wonder whether there is an intrinsic reason for this fact, or whether fast FFT-based arithmetic might be used to accelerate Gröbner basis computations. Instead of directly addressing this difficult problem, one may investigate whether such accelerations are possible for simpler problems in this area. One good candidate for such a problem is the reduction of a polynomial P with respect to a fixed reduced Gröbner basis $G = (G_0, \ldots, G_n)$. In that case, the algebra $\mathbb{A}$ is given once and for all, so it becomes a matter of precomputation to obtain G and any other data that could be useful for efficient reductions modulo G.

One step in this direction was made in [21]. Using relaxed multiplication [19], it was shown that the reduction of P with respect to G can be computed in quasi-linear time in terms of the size of the equation $P = Q_0G_0 + \cdots + Q_nG_n + R$. However, even in the case of bivariate polynomials, this is not necessarily optimal. In order to see the reason for this, consider $\mathbb{A} = \mathbb{K}[X, Y]/I$, where I is an ideal generated by two generic polynomials of total degree δ. Then $\dim_{\mathbb{K}} \mathbb{A} = \delta^2$, but the Gröbner basis for I with respect the usual

ISSAC'18, July 16-19, 2018, New York, NY, USA

ACM ISBN: 978-1-4503-5550-6/18/07...$15.00
DOI: https://doi.org/10.1145/3208976.3209003

total degree ordering contains $\delta + 1$ polynomials with $\Theta(\delta^2)$ coefficients. This means that we need $\Theta(\delta^3)$ space, merely to write down G. One crucial prerequisite for even faster algorithms is therefore to design a terser representation for Gröbner bases.

The main aim of this paper is to show that it is actually possible to perform polynomial reductions in quasi-linear time in some very specific cases. For simplicity, we will restrict our attention to bivariate polynomials and to ideals that satisfy suitable regularity conditions. Because of all these precautions, we do not expect our algorithms to be very useful for practical purposes, but rather regard our work as a "proof of concept" that quasi-linear complexities are not deemed impossible to achieve in this context.

More precisely, with $\mathbb{A} = \mathbb{K}[X, Y]/I$ as above, our main results are as follows. We first introduce the concept of a "vanilla Gröbner basis" that captures the regularity assumptions that are needed for our algorithms. Modulo potentially expensive precomputations, we then present a more compact description of such a Gröbner basis G that holds all necessary information in $\tilde{O}(\delta^2)$ space. We next give an algorithm for reducing a bivariate polynomial of total degree d with respect to G in quasi-linear time $\tilde{O}(d^2 + \delta^2)$. In particular, multiplication in $\mathbb{A}$ can be done in time $\tilde{O}(\delta^2)$, which is intrinsically quasi-optimal. We also present an algorithm to convert between normal forms with respect to vanilla Gröbner bases for different monomial orderings. This algorithm is based on a Gröbner walk [6] with at most $O(\log \delta)$ intermediate monomial orderings; its complexity $\tilde{O}(\delta^2)$ is again quasi-optimal.

It is instructive to compare these complexity bounds with the complexities of naive algorithms that are commonly implemented in computer algebra systems. For multiplications in $\mathbb{A}$, one may precompute the $O(\delta^2) \times O(\delta^2)$ matrix that allows us to obtain the reduction of a product of two normal forms using a matrix-vector product of cost $O(\delta^4)$. Since the product of two normal forms can be computed in quasi-linear time $\tilde{O}(\delta^2)$, it follows that multiplications in $\mathbb{A}$ take time $O(\delta^4)$. Similarly, changes of monomial orderings lead to $\delta^2 \times \delta^2$-matrices for representing the corresponding base changes. Naive conversions can then be performed in time $O(\delta^4)$.

As a final remark, we notice that geometric methods provide an alternative to Gröbner basis techniques for the resolution of polynomial systems and computations in quotient algebras $\mathbb{A}$. Examples include the Kronecker solver [16] and Rouillier's RUR [25]. Such algorithms are often faster from a complexity point of view, but essentially only work for bases that correspond to lexicographical orders in the Gröbner basis setting. A similar remark applies to the elimination method by Auzinger-Stetter [1].

Notations and terminology: We assume that the reader is familiar with the theory of Gröbner basis and refer to [3, 12] for basic expositions. We denote the set of *monomials* in r variables by $\mathcal{M} := X_1^{\mathbb{N}} \cdots X_r^{\mathbb{N}} = \{X_1^{i_1} \cdots X_r^{i_r} : i_1, \ldots, i_r \in \mathbb{N}\}$. A *monomial ordering* $\prec$ on $\mathcal{M}$ is a total ordering that is compatible with multiplication. Given a polynomial in r variables $P = \sum_{M \in \mathcal{M}} P_M M \in \mathbb{K}[X_1, \ldots, X_r]$, its *support* $\operatorname{supp} P$ is the set of monomials $M \in \mathcal{M}$ with $P_M \neq 0$. If $P \neq 0$, then $\operatorname{supp} P$ admits a maximal element for $\prec$ that is called its *leading monomial* and that we denote by $\operatorname{lm}(P)$. If $M \in \operatorname{supp} P$, then we say that $P_M M$ is a *term* in P. Given a tuple $A = (A_0, \ldots, A_n)$ of polynomials in $\mathbb{K}[X_1, \ldots, X_r]$, we say that P is *reduced* with respect to A if $\operatorname{supp} P$ contains no monomial that is a multiple of the leading monomial of one of the A_i.

Unless stated otherwise, we will always work in the bivariate setting when $r = 2$, and use X and Y as our main indeterminates instead of X_1 and X_2. In particular, $\mathcal{M} := X^{\mathbb{N}} Y^{\mathbb{N}} = \{X^a Y^b a, b \in \mathbb{N}\}$.

Acknowledgments: We thank the anonymous referees for their detailed comments and suggestions. We are aware that an example would be helpful for the intuition, unfortunately we were not able to give one because of the space constraints. Moreover, the reader should notice that a meaningful example cannot have a very small degree (say, at least 10), and that our setting requires non-structured dense polynomials, so that writing them down explicitly would hardly be readable.

2 VANILLA GRÖBNER BASES

Consider a zero-dimensional ideal I of $\mathbb{K}[X, Y]$ with Gröbner basis $G = (G_0, \ldots, G_n)$ with respect to a given monomial ordering $\prec$. We define the *degree* D of I to be the dimension of the quotient $\mathbb{K}[X, Y]/I$ as a $\mathbb{K}$-vector space. Our algorithms will only work for a special class of Gröbner bases with suitable regularity properties. For a generic ideal in the space of all zero-dimensional ideals with fixed degree D, we expect that these properties are always satisfied, although we have not proved this yet. For the time being, we define a *vanilla Gröbner basis* to be the Gröbner basis of an ideal of this type.

2.1 Monomial orderings

General monomial orderings that are suitable for Gröbner basis computations have been classified in [24]. For the purpose of this paper, it is convenient to restrict our attention to a specific type of bivariate monomial ordering that will allow us to explicitly describe certain Gröbner stairs and to explicitly compute certain dimensions.

Definition 2.1. Let $k \in \mathbb{N} \setminus \{0\}$. We define the ***k*-degree** of a monomial $X^a Y^b$ with $a, b \in \mathbb{N}$ by

$$\deg_k(X^a Y^b) = a + kb.$$

We define the ***k*-order** to be the monomial order $\prec_k$ such that

$$X^a Y^b \prec_k X^u Y^v \Leftrightarrow \begin{cases} \text{either} & a + kb < u + kv \\ \text{or} & a + kb = u + kv \text{ and } a < u \end{cases}$$

The k-order $\prec_k$ is also known as the weighed degree lexicographic order for the weight vector $(1, k)$. Similarly, $\prec_1$ corresponds to the usual total degree order.

2.2 Vanilla Gröbner stairs

Consider a zero-dimensional ideal I of $\mathbb{K}[X, Y]$ of degree D with Gröbner basis $G = (G_0, \ldots, G_n)$ with respect to $\prec_k$. Let $\mathcal{N}_G$ be the set of monomials $X^a Y^b$ that are in normal form with respect to G. In other words, $\mathcal{N}_G$ corresponds to the set of D monomials "under the Gröbner stairs". For a sufficiently generic ideal of degree D, we expect $\mathcal{N}_G$ to consist exactly of the smallest D elements of $\mathcal{M}$ with respect to $\prec_k$.

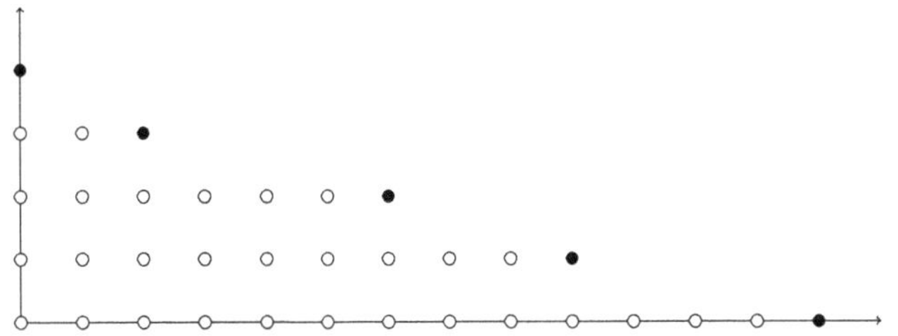

Figure 1: A vanilla Gröbner stairs with respect to $<_4$ ($D = 30, n = 4, q = 1, r = 2$).

Definition 2.2. We say that the leading monomials of G form a **vanilla Gröbner stairs** if $\mathcal{N}_G$ coincides with the set $\mathcal{M}_{k,D}$ of the D smallest elements of $\mathcal{M}$ for $<_k$.

Figure 1 shows an example of a Gröbner basis whose leading monomials form a vanilla Gröbner stairs. We observe that the stair admits almost constant slope k. In fact, the set $\mathcal{M}_{k,D}$ can be described explicitly:

Proposition 2.3. *Let I be an ideal of degree D with Gröbner basis G for $<_k$ with $k \geqslant 2$. Assume that the leading monomials of G form a vanilla Gröbner stairs and define*

$$\begin{aligned} n &:= \left\lceil \frac{\sqrt{8D/k+1}-1}{2} \right\rceil, \\ u &:= D - k\frac{n(n-1)}{2}, \\ q &:= u \operatorname{quo} n, \\ r &:= u \operatorname{rem} n. \end{aligned}$$

Then G has $n+1$ elements $G_0, \ldots, G_n$ and for $0 \leqslant i \leqslant n$, the leading monomial of G_i (denoted by M_i) can be expressed in terms of n, k, q, r. Assuming the basis elements are ordered such that the M_i's have increasing degree in the variable X, we have:

- $M_0 = Y^n$.
- *For all $i \in \{1, \ldots, r\}$, $M_i = X^{q+k(i-1)+1}Y^{n-i}$.*
- *For all $i \in \{r+1, \ldots, n\}$, $M_i = X^{q+k(i-1)}Y^{n-i}$.*

Proof. With this expression of M_i, we first notice that this sequence $M_0, \ldots, M_n$ can indeed be the leading monomials for a reduced Gröbner basis, that is M_i does not divide M_j for any $i \neq j$. This is clear for $(i, j) \neq (1, 0)$, so let us prove that M_1 does not divide M_0. We have $D = kn'(n'+1)/2$ with $n' := \left(\sqrt{8D/k+1}-1\right)/2$, so that

$$\frac{kn(n-1)}{2} < D \leqslant \frac{kn(n+1)}{2}.$$

In particular, this implies $u > 0$, whence $q > 0$ or $r > 0$. Remains to prove that the sequence $M_0, \ldots, M_n$ form a vanilla Gröbner stairs (for a degree D ideal) as claimed. Indeed, there are D monomials under the stairs $M_0, \ldots, M_n$ (i.e. in normal form w.r.t. G), and we notice that a monomial M is under the stairs if and only if $M <_k M_{r+1}$. □

Corollary 2.4. *Let $G = (G_0, \ldots, G_n)$ be as above, and let M_i be the leading monomial of G_i for $0 \leqslant i \leqslant n$. With q, r as in Proposition 2.3, the k-degree of M_i is given by*

$$\deg_k M_i = \begin{cases} kn & \text{if } i = 0 \\ k(n-1)+q+1 & \text{if } 0 < i \leqslant r \\ k(n-1)+q & \text{if } r < i \leqslant n \end{cases}.$$

In particular, for all $i \in \{1, \ldots, n\}$, we have

$$\deg_k M_i \leqslant \deg_k M_{i-1}, \text{ and } \deg_k M_1 - 1 \leqslant \deg_k M_i \leqslant \deg_k M_1.$$

Remark 1. The results of Proposition 2.3 and Corollary 2.4 remain valid for $<_1$ with some precautions: if $r \geqslant 1$, one has to leave out G_r since M_r is divisible by M_{r+1} with the given formulas. Then G consists of n elements $G_0, \ldots, G_{r-1}, G_{r+1}, \ldots, G_n$.

2.3 Existence of relations

The main reduction algorithm in this paper relies on a rewriting strategy that allows us to rewrite general linear combinations $A_0G_0 + \cdots + A_nG_n$ of elements in the Gröbner basis as linear combinations of fewer elements. In particular, it should be possible to express each G_i as a linear combination of elements in a suitable subset Σ of $\{G_0, \ldots, G_n\}$ (this subset then generates the ideal I), with degrees that can be controlled.

It turns out that such a subset S may need to contain three elements at least, but that $\Sigma := \{G_0, G_1, G_n\}$ generically works. In order to control the degrees in the linear combinations, we may also consider intermediate sets between $\{G_0, G_1, G_n\}$ and the full set $\{G_0, \ldots, G_n\}$, such as $\Sigma_\ell := \{G_0, G_1, G_\ell, G_{2\ell}, \ldots, G_{\lfloor n/\ell \rfloor \ell}, G_n\}$ for various integer "step lengths" $\ell \geqslant 2$. This leads us to the following definition:

Definition 2.5. Let $\ell \geqslant 1$ be an integer and consider the set of indices

$$I_\ell := \{0, 1, n\} \cup \{\ell, 2\ell, \ldots, \lfloor n/\ell \rfloor \ell\}. \quad (1)$$

We say that a family of polynomials $P_0, \ldots, P_n \in \mathbb{K}[X, Y]$ is **retractive** for step length ℓ and k-degree δ if for all $i \in \{0, \ldots, n\}$ we can write

$$P_i = \sum_{j \in I_\ell} A_j P_j$$

for some $(A_j)_{j \in I_\ell} \in \mathbb{K}[X, Y]^{I_\ell}$ with $\deg_k A_j \leqslant \delta$.

Consider a Gröbner basis $G_0, \ldots, G_n$ as in Proposition 2.3 and a linear combination $C = \sum_{j \in I_\ell} A_j G_j$ with $\deg_k A_j \leqslant \delta$ for all $j \in I_\ell$. Making rough estimates, the number of monomials in $\mathcal{M}$ of k-degree $\leqslant d$ is $d^2/(2k)$, whence the number of monomials of k-degree between d and $d+\delta$ is bounded by $(d+\delta)\delta/k$. The set $\mathcal{N}_G = \mathcal{M}_{k,D}$ roughly corresponds to the set of monomials of k-degree at most nk, whence the support of C contains at most $(nk+\delta)\delta/k$ monomials that are *not* in $\mathcal{N}_G$. Notice that such a combination C is uniquely determined by its terms *not* in $\mathcal{N}_G$: if all the terms of $C - C' \in I$ are in $\mathcal{N}_G$, then $C - C' = 0$ by definition of a Gröbner basis.

On the other hand the polynomials A_j with $j \in I_\ell$ are determined by approximately $(n/\ell)\delta^2/(2k)$ coefficients. As soon as $\delta > 2k\ell$, it follows that

$$(n/\ell)\delta^2/(2k) > (nk+\delta)\delta/k,$$

and it becomes likely that non-trivial relations of the type $G_i = \sum_{j \in I_\ell} A_j G_j$ indeed exist. A refined analysis and practical experiments show that the precise threshold is located at

$$\delta \geqslant k(2\ell - 1) - 1,$$

although we have no formal proof of this empirical fact.

2.4 Vanilla Gröbner bases

We are now in a position to describe the class of Gröbner bases with enough regularity for our fast reduction algorithm to work.

Definition 2.6. Let $G = (G_0, \ldots, G_n)$ be the reduced Gröbner basis for an ideal $I \subset \mathbb{K}[X, Y]$ with respect to $\prec_k$. We say that G is a **vanilla Gröbner basis** if

a) the leading monomials of G form a vanilla Gröbner stairs;
b) the family $G_0, \ldots, G_n$ is retractive for step length ℓ and k-degree $k(2\ell - 1) - 1$, for $\ell = 2, \ldots, n$.

It appears that reduced Gröbner bases of sufficiently generic ideals are always of vanilla type, although we have not been able to prove this so far. We even do not know whether vanilla Gröbner bases exist for arbitrary fields $\mathbb{K}$ (with sufficiently many elements) and degrees D. Nevertheless, practical computer experiments on suggest that sufficiently random ideals of degree D admit Gröbner bases of this kind. More precisely, we have checked this for ideals that are generated as follows by two random polynomials:

- for $I = (A(X), Y - B(X))$, where A and B are random univariate polynomials of degrees D and $D - 1$, and for any ordering $\prec_k$;
- for $I = (A, B)$, where A and B are random bivariate polynomials of total degree δ (in this case the degree of the ideal is $D = \delta^2$), and for any ordering $\prec_k$ with $k \geqslant 2$;
- for $I = (A, B)$, where A and B are random bivariate polynomials of degree δ in both variables (in this case the degree of the ideal is $D = 2\delta^2$), and for any ordering $\prec_k$ with $k \geqslant 2$.

The tests were made in $\mathbb{Z}_p$ (with p a 16-bit prime) and for a degree D in the range of a few hundreds.

Remark 2. In each of these cases, the threshold $k(2\ell - 1) - 1$ seems to be sharp. Nevertheless, for our complexity bounds, a threshold of the type $Kk\ell$ would suffice, for any constant $K > 0$.

3 ALGORITHMIC PREREQUISITES

In this section, we quickly review some basic complexities for fundamental operations on polynomials over a field $\mathbb{K}$. Notice that results presented in this section are not specific to the bivariate case. Running times will always be measured in terms of the required number of field operations in $\mathbb{K}$.

3.1 Polynomial multiplication

We denote by $\mathsf{M}(d)$ the cost of multiplying two dense univariate polynomials of degree d in $\mathbb{K}[X]$. Over general fields, one may take [5, 26, 27]

$$\mathsf{M}(d) = O(d \log d \log \log d).$$

In the case of fields of positive characteristic, one may even take $\mathsf{M}(d) = O(d \log d \, 4^{\log^* d})$, where $\log^* d$ denotes the iterated logarithm [17, 18]. We make the customary assumptions that $\mathsf{M}(d)/d$ is increasing and that $\mathsf{M}(2d) = O(\mathsf{M}(d))$, with the usual implications, such as $\mathsf{M}(d)+\mathsf{M}(e) \leqslant \mathsf{M}(d + e)$.

For multivariate polynomials, the cost of multiplication depends on the geometry of the support. The multiplication of dense bivariate "block" polynomials in $\mathbb{K}[X_1, \ldots, X_r]$ of degree $< d_i$ in each variable X_i can be reduced to multiplication of univariate polynomials of degree $< 2^{r-1} d_1 \cdots d_r$ using the well known technique of Kronecker substitution [12]. More generally, for polynomials such that the support of the product is included in an initial segment with d elements, it is possible to compute the product in time $O(\mathsf{M}(d))$. Here an initial segment of $\mathcal{M}$ is a subset $\mathcal{S}$ such that all divisors of any monomial $M \in \mathcal{S}$ are again in $\mathcal{S}$.

For the purpose of this paper, we need to consider dense polynomials P in $\mathbb{K}[X, Y]$ whose supports are contained in sets of the form $\mathcal{S}_{l,h} := \{M \in \mathcal{M} : l \leqslant \deg_k M < h\}$. Modulo the change of variables $X^a Y^b \to T^{a+kb} U^b$, such a polynomial can be rewritten as $P(X, Y) = T^l \tilde{P}(T, U)$, where the support of $\tilde{P}$ is an initial segment with the same size as $\mathcal{S}_{l,h}$. For a product of two polynomials of this type with a support of size d, this means that the product can again be computed in time $O(\mathsf{M}(d))$.

3.2 Relaxed multiplication

For the above polynomial multiplication algorithms, we assume that the input polynomials are entirely given from the outset. In specific settings, the input polynomials may be only partially known at some point, and it can be interesting to anticipate the computation of the partial output. This is particularly true when working with (truncated) formal power series $f = f_0 + f_1 z + \cdots \in \mathbb{K}[[z]]$ instead of polynomials, where it is common that the coefficients are given as a stream.

In this so-called "relaxed (or online) computation model", the coefficient $(fg)_d$ of a product of two series $f, g \in \mathbb{K}[[z]]$ must be output as soon as $f_0, \ldots, f_d$ and $g_0, \ldots, g_d$ are known. This model has the advantage that subsequent coefficients $f_{d+1}, f_{d+2}, \ldots$ and $g_{d+1}, g_{d+2}, \ldots$ are allowed to depend on the result $(fg)_d$. This often allows us to solve equations involving power series f by rewriting them into *recursive equations* of the form $f = \Phi(f)$, with the property that the coefficient $\Phi(f)_{d+1}$ only depends on earlier coefficients $f_0, \ldots, f_d$ for all d. For instance, in order to invert a power series of the form $1 + zg$ with $g \in \mathbb{K}[[z]]$, we may take $\Phi(f) = 1 - zfg$. Similarly, if $\mathbb{K}$ has characteristic zero, then the exponential of a power series $g \in \mathbb{K}[[z]]$ with $g_0 = 0$ can be computed by taking $\Phi(f) = 1 + \int f g'$.

From a complexity point of view, let $\mathsf{R}(d)$ denote the cost of the relaxed multiplication of two polynomials of degree $< d$. The relaxed model prevents us from directly using fast "zealous" multiplication algorithms from the previous section that are typically based on FFT-multiplication. Fortunately, it was shown in [10, 19] that

$$\mathsf{R}(d) = O(\mathsf{M}(d) \log d). \tag{2}$$

This relaxed multiplication algorithm admits the advantage that it may use any zealous multiplication as a black box. Through the direct use of FFT-based techniques, the following bound has also been established in [20]:

$$\mathsf{R}(d) = d \log d e^{O\left(\sqrt{\log \log d}\right)}.$$

In the sequel, we will only use a suitable multivariate generalization of the algorithm from [10, 19], so we will always assume that $\mathsf{R}(d)$ is of the form (2). In particular, we have $\mathsf{R}(d) + \mathsf{R}(e) \leqslant \mathsf{R}(d+e)$.

3.3 Polynomial reduction

Let us now consider a Gröbner basis of an ideal in $\mathbb{K}[X_1, \ldots, X_r]$, or, more generally, an auto-reduced tuple $A = (A_0, \ldots, A_n)$ of polynomials in $\mathbb{K}[X_1, \ldots, X_r]$. Then for any $P \in \mathbb{K}[X_1, \ldots, X_r]$, we may compute a relation

$$P = Q_0 A_0 + \cdots + Q_n A_n + R$$

such that R is reduced with respect to A. We call $(Q_0, \ldots, Q_n, R)$ an *extended reduction* of P with respect to A.

The computation of such an extended reduction is a good example of a problem that can be solved efficiently using relaxed multiplication and recursive equations. For a multivariate polynomial T with dense support of any of the types discussed in section 3.1, let $|T|$ denote a bound for the size of its support. With $\mathsf{R}(d)$ as in (2), it has been shown[1] in [21] that the *quotients* $Q_0, \ldots, Q_n$ and the *remainder* R can be computed in time

$$\mathsf{R}(|Q_0 A_0|) + \cdots + \mathsf{R}(|Q_n A_n|) + O(|R|). \tag{3}$$

This implies in particular that the extended reduction can be computed in quasi-linear time in the size of the equation $P = Q_0 A_0 + \cdots + Q_n A_n + R$. However, as pointed out in the introduction, this equation is in general much larger than the input polynomial P.

Extended reductions $(Q_0, \ldots, Q_n, R)$ are far from being unique (only R is unique, and only if A is a Gröbner basis). The algorithm from [21] for the computation of an extended reduction relies on a *selection strategy* that selects a particular index $i_M \in \mathcal{I}_M := \{i \in \{0, \ldots, n\} : \operatorname{lm}(A_i) \mid M\}$ for every monomial $M \in \mathcal{M}$ such that $\mathcal{I}_M$ is non-empty. The initial formulation [21] used the simplest such strategy by taking $i_M = \min \mathcal{I}_M$, but the complexity bound (3) holds for any selection strategy. Now the total size of all quotients $Q_0, \ldots, Q_n$ may be much larger than the size of P for a general selection strategy. One of the key ingredients of the fast reduction algorithm in this paper is the careful design of a "dichotomic selection strategy" that enables us to control the degrees of the quotients.

Remark 3. The notion of selection strategy is somewhat similar to the concept of *involutive division* introduced for the theory of involutive bases [13], although our definition is more permissive.

4 TERSE REPRESENTATIONS OF VANILLA GRÖBNER BASES

Let $G = (G_0, \ldots, G_n)$ be a vanilla Gröbner basis of some ideal $I \subsetneq \mathbb{K}[X, Y]$ with respect to $\prec_k$ and assume the notations from Proposition 2.3. We recall from the introduction that a major obstruction for the design of reduction algorithms that run in quasi-linear time $\tilde{O}(kn^2 + d^2/k)$ is that it requires space $\Theta(kn^3)$ to explicitly write down the full basis G. The aim of this section is to introduce a suitable "terse representation" that can be stored in space $O(kn^2 \log n)$, but that still contains all necessary information for efficient computations modulo G.

[1]The results from [21] actually apply for more general types of supports, but this will not be needed in this paper.

4.1 Retraction coefficients

For each $\ell \geqslant 1$, let I_ℓ be as in (1). Also, for $\lambda \in \{0, \ldots, \lceil \log_2 n \rceil\}$, let J_λ be a shorthand for I_{2^λ}. Since $G = (G_0, \ldots, G_n)$ is a vanilla Gröbner basis, Definition 2.6 ensures in particular the existence of coefficients $C_{\lambda,i,j} \in \mathbb{K}[X, Y]$ for $\lambda \in \{0, \ldots, \lceil \log_2 n \rceil - 1\}$ and $i \in J_\lambda \setminus J_{\lambda+1}$ and $j \in J_{\lambda+1}$, such that

$$\begin{aligned} G_i &= \sum_{j \in J_{\lambda+1}} C_{\lambda,i,j} G_j, \\ \deg_k C_{\lambda,i,j} &\leqslant k(2^{\lambda+2} - 1) - 1. \end{aligned}$$

We call these $C_{\lambda,i,j}$ the *retraction coefficients* for G. For each given i, λ, the computation of the retraction coefficients $C_{\lambda,i,j}$ reduces to a linear system of size $u \times v$ with $u, v = O(kn2^\lambda)$ (for the image space, consider only the monomials that are *above* the Gröbner stairs), which is easily solved by Gaussian elimination. Notice that the space needed to write the retraction coefficients is much smaller than the Gröbner basis:

Lemma 4.1. *The family of all retraction coefficients for G takes space $O(kn^2 \log n)$.*

Proof. For every ℓ, there are $\lceil n/\ell \rceil + 1$ indices in I_ℓ, and we notice that $I_{2\ell} \subseteq I_\ell$. For any given λ, the retraction coefficients involve at most $n/2^{\lambda+1} + 1$ indices i and $n/2^{\lambda+1} + 2$ indices j, whence at most $n^2/4^{\lambda+1} + 3n/2^{\lambda+1} + 2$ pairs (i, j). Since the support of $C_{\lambda,i,j}$ has size $O(k4^\lambda)$, it follows that all retraction coefficient together require space $O(kn^2 \log n)$. □

We observe that the space needed to write all relations is about the same size as the dimension of the quotient algebra $\mathbb{K}[X, Y]/I$, up to a logarithmic factor.

4.2 Upper truncations

For vanilla Gröbner bases, it is *a priori* possible to recover G from G_0, G_1 and G_n using the retraction coefficients: with $h = \lceil \log_2 n \rceil$, first compute $G_{2^{h-1}}$, next $G_{2^{h-2}}$ and $G_{3 \cdot 2^{h-2}}$, and so on. In order to compute reductions of the form $P = Q_0 G_0 + \cdots + Q_n G_n + R$ efficiently, we will need slightly more information. In particular, we wish to access some of the head terms of the G_i. More precisely, if the quotient Q_i has degree d, then we need to know the terms of G_i with degree at least $\deg G_i - d$ in order to compute the quotient Q_i using a relaxed reduction algorithm.

Definition 4.2. Given a polynomial $P \in \mathbb{K}[X, Y]$, we define its **upper truncation with k-precision p** as the polynomial $P^\#$ such that

- all terms of $P^\#$ of k-degree less than $\deg_k P - p$ are zero;
- all terms of $P^\#$ of k-degree at least $\deg_k P - p$ are equal to the corresponding terms in P.

Notice that this upper truncation $P^{\#}$ can be written using space $O((\deg_k P)p/k)$. For the reduction strategy that we plan to use, we will have

$$\deg_k Q_i < 2k2^{\mathrm{val}_2 i} \tag{4}$$

for all $i = 1, \ldots, n-1$, where $\mathrm{val}_2 i$ denotes the 2-adic valuation of i. This motivates the following definition:

Definition 4.3. Let $G = (G_0, \ldots, G_n)$ be a vanilla Gröbner basis for an ideal $I \subseteq \mathbb{K}[X, Y]$ with respect to $<_k$. The **terse representation** of G consists of the following data:

- the sequence of truncated elements $G_0^{\#}, \ldots, G_n^{\#}$, where
  - $G_i^{\#} := G_i$ for $i \in \{0, 1, n\}$;
  - $G_i^{\#}$ is the upper truncation of G_i at precision $2k2^{\mathrm{val}_2 i}$ for all other i;
- the collection of all retraction coefficients $C_{\lambda,i,j}$ as in section 4.1.

Proposition 4.4. *The terse representation of G fits in space $O(kn^2 \log n)$.*

Proof. The upper truncation $G_i^{\#}$ requires space $O(kn2^{\mathrm{val}_2 i})$ for all $1 < i < n$. For each $\lambda < \log_2 n$, there are at most $n/2^\lambda$ indices i such that $\mathrm{val}_2 i = \lambda$; therefore, $G_2^{\#}, \ldots, G_{n-1}^{\#}$ take $O(kn^2 \log n)$ space. The elements $G_0^{\#}$, $G_1^{\#}$ and $G_n^{\#}$ require $O(kn^2)$ additional space, whereas the coefficients $C_{\lambda,i,j}$ account for $O(kn^2 \log n)$ more space, by Lemma 4.1. □

5 FAST REDUCTION

Let $G = (G_0, \ldots, G_n)$ be a vanilla Gröbner basis for an ideal $I \subseteq \mathbb{K}[X, Y]$ as in the previous section and assume that its terse representation has been precomputed. The goal of this section is to present our main algorithm that computes the extended reduction $P = Q_0G_0 + \cdots + Q_nG_n + R$ of a polynomial $P \in \mathbb{K}[X, Y]/I$ of k-degree d in quasi-linear time $\tilde{O}(kn^2 + d^2/k)$. This is quasi-optimal with respect to the dimension of the quotient algebra $\dim_{\mathbb{K}} \mathbb{K}[X, Y]/I = \Theta(kn^2)$ and the size of the support $|P| = \Theta(d^2/k)$.

The reduction algorithm proceeds in two steps: in a first stage, we compute the quotients $Q_0, \ldots, Q_n$; we next evaluate the remainder $R := P - Q_0G_0 - \cdots - Q_nG_n$ by rewriting the linear combination $Q_0G_0 + \cdots + Q_nG_n$ using fewer and fewer terms.

5.1 Computing the quotients

To compute the quotients, we reduce P as in section 3.3 against the tuple $(A_0, \ldots, A_n) := (G_0^{\#}, \ldots, G_n^{\#})$, in such a way that the degrees of the quotients are bounded as in equation (4). This is done using the algorithm from [21], but with the following *dichotomic selection strategy*. Given a monomial $M \in \mathcal{M}$, we reduce M against A_{i_M}, where $i_M \in \mathcal{I}_M := \{i \in \{0, \ldots, n\} : \mathrm{lm}(A_i) \mid M\}$ is determined as follows:

- if $\mathrm{lm}(A_0)$ divides M, then take $i_M := 0$;
- else if $\mathrm{lm}(A_n)$ divides M, then take $i_M := n$;
- else we take i_M to be the unique element in $\mathcal{I}_M$ with $\mathrm{val}_2 i_M = \max\{\mathrm{val}_2 ii \in \mathcal{I}_M\}$.

This selection strategy is illustrated in Figure 2.

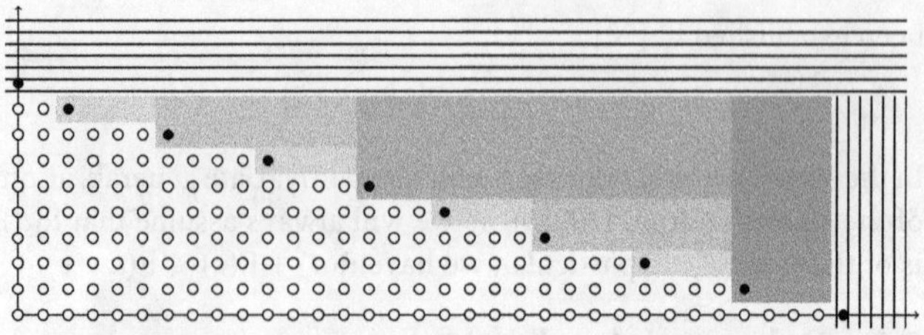

Figure 2: The dichotomic selection strategy: monomials falling in each area are reduced against the corresponding basis element.

Lemma 5.1. *Let $Q_0, \ldots, Q_n$ be the quotients obtained for the reduction of P with respect to $(G_0^{\#}, \ldots, G_n^{\#})$ using the dichotomic selection strategy. Then the bound*

$$\deg_k(Q_i) < 2k2^{\mathrm{val}_2(i)}$$

holds for all $0 < i < n$, so that $|Q_0| + \cdots + |Q_n| = O(kn^2 + d^2/k)$, and the extended reduction $P = Q_0G_0^{\#} + \cdots + Q_nG_n^{\#} + R^{\#}$ can be computed in time

$$O\left(\mathsf{R}(kn^2) \log n + \mathsf{R}(d^2/k)\right).$$

Proof. Let $X^aY^b \in \operatorname{supp} Q_i$ with $0 < i < n$, so that $i = i_M$ for $M = X^aY^b \,\mathrm{lm}(A_i)$, and denote $\ell := 2^{\mathrm{val}_2 i}$. Then we observe that $b < \ell$: if not, then $\mathrm{lm}(A_{i-\ell})$ would divide M, whereas $\mathrm{val}_2(i - \ell) > \mathrm{val}_2 i$. A similar reasoning with $A_{i+\ell}$ (or A_n, whenever $i + \ell > n$) shows that $a < k\ell$. It follows that $\deg_k(X^aY^b) < 2k\ell$.

This also proves that $|Q_i| < 2\ell(2k\ell + 1) = O(k\ell^2)$ and $|Q_iG_i^{\#}| = O(kn\ell)$, for any $0 < i < n$. Since the number of indices $0 < i < n$ with $\ell = 2^{\mathrm{val}_2 i}$ is bounded by n/ℓ, we get

$$|Q_1| + \cdots + |Q_{n-1}| = O(2kn + 4kn + \cdots + 2^{\lfloor \log_2 n \rfloor}kn) = O(kn^2)$$

$$\mathsf{R}(|Q_1G_1^{\#}|) + \cdots + \mathsf{R}(|Q_{n-1}G_{n-1}^{\#}|) = O\left(\mathsf{R}(kn^2) \log n\right).$$

On the other hand, $\deg_k(Q_0G_0^{\#}) \leqslant \deg_k P$ and $\deg_k(Q_nG_n^{\#}) \leqslant \deg_k P$, whence $|Q_0| + |Q_n| = O(d^2/k)$ and $\mathsf{R}(|Q_0G_0^{\#}|) + \mathsf{R}(|Q_nG_n^{\#}|) = O\left(\mathsf{R}(d^2/k)\right)$. We conclude by applying the bound (3) for the complexity of polynomial reduction. □

The next important observation is that the quotients $Q_0, \ldots, Q_n$ obtained in the above way can actually be used as quotients for the extended reduction of P with respect to G:

Proposition 5.2. *Let $Q_0, \ldots, Q_n$ be as in Lemma 5.1 and consider*

$$R := P - Q_0G_0 - \cdots - Q_nG_n.$$

Then R is reduced with respect to G.

Proof. Let $R^{\#} := P - Q_0G_0^{\#} - \cdots - Q_nG_n^{\#}$. By construction, $R^{\#}$ is reduced with respect to $G^{\#} = (G_0^{\#}, \ldots, G_n^{\#})$ and whence with respect to G since $\mathrm{lm}(G_i) = \mathrm{lm}(G_i^{\#})$ for all i. For any $0 < i < n$, we also have $\deg_k(G_i - G_i^{\#}) < \deg_k G_i - 2k2^{\mathrm{val}_2 i}$, whence

$$\deg_k(Q_iG_i - Q_iG_i^{\#}) < \deg_k G_i - 1 \leqslant \min_{0 \leqslant j \leqslant n} \deg_k G_j$$

by Lemma 5.1 and Corollary 2.4. Since $G_0 = G_0^\#$ and $G_n = G_n^\#$, this means that

$$\deg_k(R - R^\#) < \deg_k G_i \text{ for all } 0 \leqslant i \leqslant n.$$

In other words, the polynomials $R^\#$, $R - R^\#$, and therefore R are all reduced with respect to G. □

5.2 Computing the remainder

Once the quotients $Q_0, \ldots, Q_n$ are known, we need to compute the remainder $R := P - Q_0 G_0 - \cdots - Q_n G_n$. We do this by rewriting (or *retracting*) the linear combination $Q_0 G_0 + \cdots + Q_n G_n$ into a linear combination $S_0 G_0 + S_1 G_1 + S_n G_n$ using the following algorithm:

Algorithm 1.
Input: the quotients $Q_0, \ldots, Q_n \in \mathbb{K}[X, Y]$ of the dichotomic extended reduction of P by G
Output: $S_0, S_1, S_n \in \mathbb{K}[X, Y]$ with $Q_0 G_0 + \cdots + Q_n G_n = S_0 G_0 + S_1 G_1 + S_n G_n$

For $j = 0, \ldots, n$, set $Q_{0,j} := Q_j$
For $\lambda = 1, \ldots, \lceil \log_2 n \rceil - 1$ do
  For $j = 0, \ldots, n$ do
    If $1 < j < n$ and $\operatorname{val}_2 j \leqslant \lambda$, then set $Q_{\lambda+1,j} := 0$
    Otherwise, set $Q_{\lambda+1,j} := Q_{\lambda,j} + \sum_{i \in J_\lambda \setminus J_{\lambda+1}} Q_{\lambda,i} C_{\lambda,i,j}$
For $j = 0, 1, n$, define $S_j := Q_{\lceil \log_2 n \rceil, j}$, and return S_0, S_1, S_n

Lemma 5.3. *Algorithm 1 is correct and runs in time* $O\left(\mathsf{M}(kn^2) \log n\right)$.

Proof. By construction, we notice that $Q_{\lambda,j} = 0$ if $1 < j < n$ and $\operatorname{val}_2 j < \lambda$ (that is $j \notin J_\lambda$). Let us now show by induction over λ that

$$Q_{\lambda,0} G_0 + \cdots + Q_{\lambda,n} G_n = Q_0 G_0 + \cdots + Q_n G_n.$$

This is clearly true for $\lambda = 0$. We have

$$\begin{aligned}
\sum_{j \in J_{\lambda+1}} Q_{\lambda+1,j} G_j &= \sum_{j \in J_{\lambda+1}} \left(Q_{\lambda,j} + \sum_{i \in J_\lambda \setminus J_{\lambda+1}} Q_{\lambda,i} C_{\lambda,i,j} \right) G_j \\
&= \sum_{j \in J_{\lambda+1}} Q_{\lambda,j} G_j + \sum_{i \in J_\lambda \setminus J_{\lambda+1}} Q_{\lambda,i} \sum_{j \in J_{\lambda+1}} C_{\lambda,i,j} G_j \\
&= \sum_{j \in J_{\lambda+1}} Q_{\lambda,i} G_i + \sum_{i \in J_\lambda \setminus J_{\lambda+1}} Q_{\lambda,i} G_i \\
&= \sum_{j \in J_\lambda} Q_{\lambda,i} G_i,
\end{aligned}$$

which proves the correctness of Algorithm 1. Again by induction over λ, it is not hard to see that the bound $\deg_k C_{\lambda,i,j} < 4k2^\lambda$ implies

$$\deg_k(Q_{\lambda,i}) \leqslant \max(4k2^\lambda, 2k2^{\operatorname{val}_2(i)}) \text{ for } 1 < i < n. \quad (5)$$

Now, for $i \in J_\lambda \setminus J_{\lambda+1}$ and $j \in J_\lambda$, the product $Q_{\lambda,i} C_{\lambda,i,j}$ is computed in time $O(k4^\lambda)$, and there are $O(n^2/4^\lambda)$ such products (see the proof of Lemma 4.1). Using that $\mathsf{M}(d)/d$ is non-decreasing, we conclude that each step can be computed in time $O(\mathsf{M}(kn^2))$. □

Combining our subalgorithms, we obtain our algorithm for extended reduction.

Algorithm 2.
Input: A tersely represented vanilla Gröbner basis $G = (G_0, \ldots, G_n)$ and $P \in \mathbb{K}[X, Y]$
Output: An extended reduction $(Q_0, \ldots, Q_n, R)$ of P modulo G

Compute the extended reduction $(Q_0, \ldots, Q_n, R^\#)$ with respect to $G^\#$
Compute $S_0, S_1, S_2 \in \mathbb{K}[X, Y]$ as a function of $Q_0, \ldots, Q_n$ using Algorithm 1
Compute $R := P - S_0 G_0^\# - S_1 G_1^\# - S_n G_n^\# = P - S_0 G_0 - S_1 G_1 - S_n G_n$
Return $(Q_0, \ldots, Q_n, R)$.

Theorem 5.4. *Algorithm 2 is correct and runs in time*

$$O\left(\mathsf{R}(kn^2) \log n + \mathsf{R}(d^2/k)\right).$$

Proof. Because of Lemma 5.1, the extended reduction with respect to $G_0^\#, \ldots, G_n^\#$ is computed in time

$$O\left(\mathsf{R}(kn^2) \log n + \mathsf{R}(d^2/k)\right).$$

Proposition 5.2 ensures that the quotients are also valid with respect to $G_0, \ldots, G_n$. The next step is to evaluate the remainder $R := P - Q_0 G_0 - \cdots - Q_n G_n$. The S_i's are computed in time $O\left(\mathsf{M}(kn^2) \log n\right)$ using Lemma 5.3 and we have

$$Q_0 G_0 + \cdots + Q_n G_n = S_0 G_0 + S_1 G_1 + S_n G_n.$$

For $i \in \{0, 1, n\}$, it follows from (5) that $\deg_k(S_i G_i) \leqslant \max(d, 5kn)$. Consequently, the evaluation of R takes time

$$O\left(\mathsf{M}(d^2/k) + \mathsf{M}(kn^2)\right).$$ □

6 APPLICATIONS

6.1 Multiplications in the quotient algebra

Let $G = (G_0, \ldots, G_n)$ be a vanilla Gröbner basis for an ideal $I \subseteq \mathbb{K}[X, Y]$ with respect to $\prec_k$ and assume that we we have precomputed a terse representation for G. Elements in the quotient algebra $\mathbb{A} = \mathbb{K}[X, Y]/I$ can naturally be represented as polynomials in $\mathbb{K}[X, Y]$ that are reduced with respect to G. An immediate application of Theorem 5.4 is a multiplication algorithm for $\mathbb{A}$ that runs in quasi-linear time.

More precisely, with the notations from Proposition 2.3, given two polynomials $P, Q \in \mathbb{K}[X, Y]$ that are reduced with respect to G, we have $\deg_k P \leqslant kn$ and $\deg_k Q \leqslant kn$, whence $\deg_k PQ \leqslant 2kn$ and $|PQ| = O(kn^2) = O(D)$. It follows that PQ can be computed in time $O(\mathsf{M}(D))$, whereas the reduction of PQ with respect to G takes time $O(\mathsf{R}(D) \log D)$. This yields:

Theorem 6.1. *For I as above, multiplication in the quotient algebra $\mathbb{A} = \mathbb{K}[X, Y]/I$ can be performed in time* $O(\mathsf{R}(D) \log D)$.

6.2 Changing the monomial ordering

Let us now assume that our ideal $I \subseteq \mathbb{K}[X, Y]$ admits a vanilla Gröbner basis $G^{[k]}$ with respect to the ordering $\prec_k$ for all k. We will write $\mathbb{A}^{[k]} = K[X, Y]/I$ for the quotient algebra when representing elements using normal forms with respect to $G^{[k]}$. If $k > D = \dim_{\mathbb{K}} \mathbb{A}$, then we notice that $G^{[k]}$ is also a Gröbner basis with respect to the lexicographical monomial ordering $\prec_\infty$. In order to efficiently convert between $\mathbb{A}^{[k]}$ and $\mathbb{A}^{[\ell]}$ with $k < \ell$, we first consider the case when $\ell \leqslant 2k$:

Lemma 6.2. *With the above notations and $k < \ell \leqslant 2k$, assume that we have precomputed terse representations for $G^{[k]}$ and $G^{[\ell]}$. Then back and forth conversions between $\mathbb{A}^{[k]}$ and $\mathbb{A}^{[\ell]}$ can be computed in time $O(\mathsf{R}(D)\log D)$.*

Proof. Assume that $G^{[k]}$ has $n+1$ elements $G_0^{[k]},\ldots,G_n^{[k]}$ and $G^{[\ell]}$ has $m+1$ elements $G_0^{[\ell]},\ldots,G_m^{[\ell]}$. We know from Proposition 2.3 that $kn(n-1) < 2D \leqslant kn(n+1)$ and similarly $\ell(m-1)m < 2D \leqslant \ell m(m+1)$. Now given $P \in \mathbb{K}[X,Y]$ that is reduced with respect to $G^{[k]}$, we have $\deg_k P \leqslant kn$, whence $\deg_\ell P \leqslant \ell n$ and $(\deg_\ell P)^2/\ell \leqslant \ell n^2 \leqslant 2kn^2 = O(D)$. Theorem 5.4 therefore implies that normal form of P w.r.t. $G^{[\ell]}$ can be computed in time

$$O\left(\mathsf{R}(\ell m^2)\log m + \mathsf{R}(D)\right)$$

and we conclude using $\ell m^2 = O(D)$. The proof for the backward conversion is similar. □

For general $k < \ell$, let $a \leqslant b$ be such that $2^{a-1} < k \leqslant 2^a$ and $2^{b-1} < \ell \leqslant 2^b$. Then we may perform conversions between $\mathbb{A}^{[k]}$ and $\mathbb{A}^{[\ell]}$ using a Gröbner walk

$$\mathbb{A}^{[k]} \leftrightarrow \mathbb{A}^{[2^a]} \leftrightarrow \cdots \leftrightarrow \mathbb{A}^{[2^{b-1}]} \leftrightarrow \mathbb{A}^{[\ell]}.$$

All $G^{[k]}$ coincide for $k > D$, so we can assume that $1 \leqslant k < \ell \leqslant D+1$. Then there are at most $\log D$ conversions as above, so that:

Theorem 6.3. *With the above notations and $k < \ell \leqslant D+1$, assume that we have precomputed terse representations for the bases $G^{[k]}, G^{[2^a]}, \ldots, G^{[2^b]}, G^{[\ell]}$. Then back and forth conversions between $\mathbb{A}^{[k]}$ and $\mathbb{A}^{[\ell]}$ can be computed in time $O(\mathsf{R}(D)\log^2 D)$.*

7 CONCLUSION AND PERSPECTIVES

As explained in the introduction, we deliberately chose to present our results in the simplest possible setting. As a future work, it would be interesting to generalize our algorithms. The following two extensions should be rather straightforward:

- The consideration of general monomial orderings, starting with $<_k$ for $k \in \mathbb{Q}^>$.
- Generalizations to polynomials in $r > 2$ variables. We expect no essential problems for fixed r. However, the dependence of the complexity on r is likely to be polynomial in $r!$.

Some of the more challenging problems are as follows:

- Is it true that a "sufficiently generic" zero-dimensional ideal I of fixed degree $D = \dim_{\mathbb{K}} \mathbb{K}[X,Y]/I$ necessarily admits a vanilla Gröbner basis?
- Given a vanilla Gröbner basis, what is the actual complexity of computing its terse representation? Our first analysis suggests a bound $\tilde{O}(D^\omega)$, but we suspect that the computation of the retraction coefficients $C_{\lambda,i,j}$ can be accelerated by using the sygyzies that result from reducing the S-polynomials of basis elements to zero.
- Can our results be generalized to the degenerate case of non-vanilla Gröbner bases G?

On the long run, one might also wonder whether some of the new techniques can be used for the efficient computation of Gröbner bases themselves. For the moment, this seems far beyond reach. Nevertheless, a quasi-optimal algorithm does exist for the particular case of an ideal I generated by two generic polynomials $P, Q \in \mathbb{K}[X,Y]$ of total degree δ, when working with respect to the monomial ordering $<_1$. We intend to report on the details in a forthcoming paper.

REFERENCES

[1] W. Auzinger and H. J. Stetter. An Elimination Algorithm for the Computation of All Zeros of a System of Multivariate Polynomial Equations, *Proceedings of the International Conference on Numerical Mathematics* pages 11-30. Birkhäuser Basel, Basel, 1988.

[2] Magali Bardet, Jean-Charles Faugère, and Bruno Salvy. On the complexity of the F5 Gröbner basis algorithm. *Journal of Symbolic Computation*, pages 1–24, sep 2014.

[3] Thomas Becker and Volker Weispfenning. *Gröbner bases: a computational approach to commutative algebra*, volume 141 of *Graduate Texts in Mathematics*. Springer-Verlag, New York, 1993.

[4] Bruno Buchberger. *Ein Algorithmus zum Auffinden der Basiselemente des Restklassenrings nach einem nulldimensionalen Polynomideal*. PhD thesis, Universitat Innsbruck, Austria, 1965.

[5] David G Cantor and Erich Kaltofen. On fast multiplication of polynomials over arbitrary algebras. *Acta Informatica*, 28(7):693–701, 1991.

[6] Stéphane Collart, Michael Kalkbrener, and Daniel Mall. Converting bases with the gröbner walk. *Journal of Symbolic Computation*, 24(3-4):465–469, 1997.

[7] Jean-Charles Faugère. A new efficient algorithm for computing Gröbner bases (F4). *Journal of Pure and Applied Algebra*, 139(1–3):61–88, 1999.

[8] Jean-Charles Faugère. A new efficient algorithm for computing Gröbner bases without reduction to zero (F5). In *Proceedings of the 2002 international symposium on Symbolic and algebraic computation*, ISSAC '02, pages 75–83. New York, NY, USA, 2002. ACM.

[9] Jean-Charles Faugère, Patrizia Gianni, Daniel Lazard, and Teo Mora. Efficient computation of zero-dimensional Gröbner bases by change of ordering. *Journal of Symbolic Computation*, 16(4):329–344, 1993.

[10] M. J. Fischer and L. J. Stockmeyer. Fast on-line integer multiplication. *Proc. 5th ACM Symposium on Theory of Computing*, 9:67–72, 1974.

[11] F. Le Gall. Powers of tensors and fast matrix multiplication. In *Proc. ISSAC 2014*, pages 296–303. Kobe, Japan, July 23–25 2014.

[12] J. von zur Gathen and J. Gerhard. *Modern Computer Algebra*. Cambridge University Press, 3rd edition, 2013.

[13] Vladimir P. Gerdt and Yuri A. Blinkov. Involutive bases of polynomial ideals. *Mathematics and Computers in Simulation*, 45(5):519–541, 1998.

[14] M. Giusti. Some effectivity problems in polynomial ideal theory. In *Proc. Eurosam '84*, volume 174 of *Lecture Notes in Computer Science*, pages 159–171. Cambridge, 1984. Springer, Berlin.

[15] M. Giusti. A note on the complexity of constructing standard bases. In *Proc. Eurocal '85*, volume 204 of *Lecture Notes in Computer Science*, pages 411–412. Springer-Verlag, 1985.

[16] M. Giusti, G. Lecerf, and B. Salvy. A Gröbner free alternative for polynomial system solving. *Journal of Complexity*, 17(1):154–211, 2001.

[17] D. Harvey and J. van der Hoeven. Faster integer and polynomial multiplication using cyclotomic coefficient rings. Technical Report, ArXiv, 2017. http://arxiv.org/abs/1712.03693.

[18] D. Harvey, J. van der Hoeven, and G. Lecerf. Faster polynomial multiplication over finite fields. *J. ACM*, 63(6), 2017. Article 52.

[19] J. van der Hoeven. Relax, but don't be too lazy. *JSC*, 34:479–542, 2002.

[20] J. van der Hoeven. Faster relaxed multiplication. In *Proc. ISSAC '14*, pages 405–412. Kobe, Japan, July 2014.

[21] J. van der Hoeven. On the complexity of polynomial reduction. In I. Kotsireas and E. Martínez-Moro, editors, *Proc. Applications of Computer Algebra 2015*, volume 198 of *Springer Proceedings in Mathematics and Statistics*, pages 447–458. Cham, 2015. Springer.

[22] D. Lazard. Gröbner bases, Gaussian elimination and resolution of systems of algebraic equations. In J. A. van Hulzen, editor, *Proc. EUROCAL'83*, number 162 in Lect. Notes in Computer Sc., pages 146–156. Springer Berlin Heidelberg, 1983.

[23] Ernst Mayr. Membership in polynomial ideals over Q is exponential space complete. *STACS 89*, pages 400–406, 1989.

[24] L. Robbiano. Term orderings on the polynominal ring. In *European Conference on Computer Algebra (2)*, pages 513–517. 1985.

[25] Fabrice Rouillier. Solving zero-dimensional systems through the rational univariate representation. *Applicable Algebra in Engineering, Communication and Computing*, 9(5):433–461, May 1999.

[26] A. Schönhage. Schnelle Multiplikation von Polynomen über Körpern der Charakteristik 2. *Acta Infor.*, 7:395–398, 1977.

[27] A. Schönhage and V. Strassen. Schnelle Multiplikation großer Zahlen. *Computing*, 7:281–292, 1971.

Constructive Arithmetics in Ore Localizations with Enough Commutativity

Johannes Hoffmann
Lehrstuhl D für Mathematik, RWTH Aachen University
Aachen, Germany
Johannes.Hoffmann@math.rwth-aachen.de

Viktor Levandovskyy
Lehrstuhl D für Mathematik, RWTH Aachen University
Aachen, Germany
Viktor.Levandovskyy@math.rwth-aachen.de

ABSTRACT

We continue the investigations of the constructivity of arithmetics within non-commutative Ore localizations, initiated in our 2017 ISSAC paper, where we have introduced monoidal, geometric and rational types of localizations of domains as objects of our studies. Here we extend this classification to rings with zero divisors and consider Ore sets of the mentioned types which are commutative enough: such a set either belongs to a commutative algebra or it is central or its elements commute pairwise. By using the systematic approach we have developed before, we prove that arithmetic within the localization of a commutative polynomial algebra is constructive and give the necessary algorithms. We also address the important question of computing the local closure of ideals which is also known as the desingularization. We provide algorithms to compute such closures for certain non-commutative rings with respect to Ore sets with enough commutativity.

CCS CONCEPTS

• **Computing methodologies → Algebraic algorithms; Special-purpose algebraic systems;**

KEYWORDS

Ore localization; Noncommutative algebra; Algorithms

ACM Reference Format:
Johannes Hoffmann and Viktor Levandovskyy. 2018. Constructive Arithmetics in Ore Localizations with Enough Commutativity. In *ISSAC '18: 2018 ACM International Symposium on Symbolic and Algebraic Computation, July 16–19, 2018, New York, NY, USA.* ACM, New York, NY, USA, 8 pages. https://doi.org/10.1145/3208976.3209021

INTRODUCTION

In [5] and its extended version [6] we have investigated a constructive approach to arithmetic operations with left and right fractions in Ore localizations of noncommutative domains. We have demonstrated that such operations are based essentially on two algorithms, namely the computation of the kernel of a module homomorphism and the computation of the intersection of a left ideal with a monoid. Especially the latter algorithm is hardly constructive in general, therefore we have introduced a partial classification of types of multiplicative monoids for which the intersection problem can be approached. We recall an extended version of the classification in Definition 1.4.

In this paper we revisit the case of commutative polynomial algebras both on their own and as homomorphic images in a non-commutative ring as either central or pairwise commutative subalgebras. On the one hand we extend our framework to such algebras with zero divisors. On the other hand we also consider the important problem of the computation of the local closure of a submodule with respect to a given denominator set (also known as the desingularization), which is tightly connected with the generalized torsion submodule of a module.

Though some of the algorithms have been known in commutative algebra they are scattered in the existing literature and are often deprived of proofs. We describe the problems in a systematic and self-contained way. In the collection of the algorithms we present, 4, 7 and 8 are new.

The following list summarizes the problems discussed in this paper with references to the corresponding algorithms:

Polynomial algebras: In a polynomial algebra $R = K[\underline{x}]/J$, where J is an ideal in $K[\underline{x}] := K[x_1, \dots, x_n]$, we can compute the intersection of an ideal I in R with a multiplicative subset S of R, if

- $S^{-1}R$ is monoidal and S is finitely generated (Algorithm 4),
- $S^{-1}R$ is geometric (Algorithm 5), or
- $S^{-1}R$ is essential rational (Algorithm 6).

Furthermore, we can decide whether a (multiplicative) submonoid of R contains 0[1] (Algorithm 2).

Commutative rings: In an arbitrary commutative ring R we can compute the closure of an ideal I with respect to a multiplicative set S via Algorithm 7 under the following conditions:

(1) The ideal I is decomposable into primary ideals and such a decomposition is either known or computable.
(2) We can decide whether $Q \cap S = \emptyset$ for any primary ideal Q in R.

G-algebras: In a G-algebra we can compute the closure of an ideal I with a left Ore set S, if

- $S^{-1}R$ is monoidal and S is generated as a monoid by finitely many elements $f_1, \dots, f_k$ that commute pairwise and $Z(A) \cap S$ contains a multiple of $f_1 \cdot \ldots \cdot f_k$ (Remark 5.9), or
- $S^{-1}R$ is central essential rational (Algorithm 8).

1 THE BASICS OF (ORE) LOCALIZATION

All rings are assumed to be associative and unital, but not necessarily commutative.

Definition 1.1. A subset S of a ring R is called

[1] Localizing R at a submonoid S containing 0 yields the trivial localization $S^{-1}R = \{0\}$.

ISSAC '18, July 16–19, 2018, New York, NY, USA

ACM ISBN 978-1-4503-5550-6/18/07...$15.00
https://doi.org/10.1145/3208976.3209021

- a *multiplicative set* if $1 \in S$, $0 \notin S$ and for all $s, t \in S$ we have $s \cdot t \in S$.
- a *left Ore set* if it is a multiplicative set that satisfies the *left Ore condition*: for all $s \in S$ and $r \in R$ there exist $\tilde{s} \in S$ and $\tilde{r} \in R$ such that $\tilde{s}r = \tilde{r}s$.
- a *left denominator set* if it is a left Ore set that is additionally *left reversible*: for all $s \in S$ and $r \in R$ such that $rs = 0$ there exists $\tilde{s} \in S$ satisfying $\tilde{s}r = 0$.

For any subset B of $R \setminus \{0\}$ we can consider the set $[B]$ consisting of all finite products of elements of B where the empty product represents 1. If R is a domain then $[B]$ is always a multiplicative set which is called the *multiplicative closure* of B.

The main goal of localization can be seen from the following axiomatic definition:

Definition 1.2. Let S be a multiplicative subset of a ring R. A ring R_S together with a homomorphism $\varphi : R \to R_S$ is called a *left Ore localization* of R at S if:

(1) For all $s \in S$ the element $\varphi(s)$ is a unit in R_S.
(2) For all $x \in R_S$ there exist $s \in S$ and $r \in R$ such that $x = \varphi(s)^{-1}\varphi(r)$.
(3) We have $\ker(\varphi) = \{r \in R \mid \exists s \in S : sr = 0\}$.

One can show that a left Ore localization of R at S exists if and only if S is a left denominator set. In this case the localization is unique up to isomorphism. The classical construction is given by the following:

Theorem 1.3. *Let S be a left denominator set in a ring R. The relation $\sim$ on $S \times R$, given by*

$$(s_1, r_1) \sim (s_2, r_2) \Leftrightarrow \exists \tilde{s} \in S \exists \tilde{r} \in R : \tilde{s}s_2 = \tilde{r}s_1 \text{ and } \tilde{s}r_2 = \tilde{r}r_1,$$

is an equivalence relation. Now $S^{-1}R := ((S \times R)/\sim, +, \cdot)$ becomes a ring via

$$(s_1, r_1) + (s_2, r_2) := (\tilde{s}s_1, \tilde{s}r_1 + \tilde{r}r_2),$$

where $\tilde{s} \in S$ and $\tilde{r} \in R$ satisfy $\tilde{s}s_1 = \tilde{r}s_2$, and

$$(s_1, r_1) \cdot (s_2, r_2) := (\tilde{s}s_1, \tilde{r}r_2),$$

where $\tilde{s} \in S$ and $\tilde{r} \in R$ satisfy $\tilde{s}r_1 = \tilde{r}s_2$. Together with the structural homomorphism *or* localization homomorphism

$$\rho_{S,R} : R \to S^{-1}R, \quad r \mapsto (1, r),$$

the pair $(S^{-1}R, \rho_{S,R})$ is the left Ore localization of R at S.

The elements of $S^{-1}R$ are called *left fractions* and are denoted again as tuples (s, r) which are identified with their equivalence class modulo $\sim$. The localizations that appear the most in applications are instances of the following three types:

Definition 1.4. Let K be a field and R a K-algebra. Consider the following types of localizations:

Monoidal Let S be a left denominator set in R that is generated as a multiplicative monoid by at most countably many elements. Then $S^{-1}R$ is called a *monoidal localization.*

Geometric Let $n \in \mathbb{N}$, $K[\underline{x}] := K[x_1, \ldots, x_n]$, J an ideal in $K[\underline{x}]$ and $\mathfrak{p}$ a prime ideal in $K[\underline{x}]/J$ such that $S := (K[\underline{x}]/J) \setminus \mathfrak{p}$ is a left denominator set in R. Then $S^{-1}R$ is called a *geometric localization.*

Rational Let T be a K-subalgebra of R such that $S := T \setminus \{0\}$ is a left denominator set in R. Then $S^{-1}R$ is called a *(partial) rational localization.* If R is generated over K by a set of variables $\underline{x} = \{x_1, \ldots, x_n\}$ and T is generated by a subset of $\underline{x}$ we call $S^{-1}R$ an *essential* rational localization.

Definition 1.5. Let S be a left denominator set in a ring R and M a left R-module. Then the *left Ore localization* of M at S is defined as $S^{-1}M := S^{-1}R \otimes_R M$.

Lemma 1.6 (e.g. [16], 7.3). *Let S be a left denominator set in a ring R and M a left R-module. Any element of $S^{-1}M$ can be written in the form $(s, 1) \otimes m$ for some $s \in S$ and $m \in M$.*

Lemma 1.6 allows us to write (s, m) for an element in $S^{-1}M$ in analogy to the notation for elements of $S^{-1}R$.

Alternatively, one can define localization of modules similar to the axiomatic approach in Definition 1.2, prove its uniqueness and give an elementary construction like in Theorem 1.3.

Definition 1.7. Let S be a left denominator set in a ring R and M a left R-module. The *localization map* of M with respect to S is

$$\varepsilon := \varepsilon_{S,R,M} : M \to S^{-1}M, \quad m \mapsto (1, m).$$

It can be shown that ε is a homomorphism of left R-modules with kernel $\{m \in M \mid \exists s \in S : sm = 0\}$.

Definition 1.8. Let S be a left denominator set in a ring R, M a left R-module and P a left R-submodule of M. The *S-closure* or *local closure* with respect to S of P in M is $P^S := \varepsilon_{S,R,M}^{-1}(S^{-1}P)$.

Let S be a left Ore set in a domain R. In our paper [5] we introduced the notion of left saturation closure of S, given by $\mathrm{LSat}(S) := \{r \in R \mid \exists w \in R : wr \in S\}$. We proved that $\mathrm{LSat}(S)$ is a saturated[2] left Ore set in R and that $S^{-1}R$ and $\mathrm{LSat}(S)^{-1}R$ are isomorphic rings via $(s, r) \mapsto (s, r)$, which shows that $\mathrm{LSat}(S)$ is a canonical form of S with respect to the corresponding localization.

To describe the S-closure more directly we introduce a notion of left saturation closure similar to the one for left Ore sets:

Definition 1.9. Let S be a left denominator set in a ring R, M a left R-module and P a left R-submodule of M. The *left saturation closure* of P in M with respect to S is

$$\mathrm{LSat}_S^M(P) := \{m \in M \mid \exists s \in S : sm \in P\}.$$

Note that both notions of left saturation closures are instances of a more general concept which will be explored in a future paper.

Lemma 1.10. *Let S be a left denominator set in a ring R, M a left R-module and P a left R-submodule of M. Then*

$$P^S = \mathrm{LSat}_S^M(P).$$

Proof. Let $\varepsilon := \varepsilon_{S,R,M}$. If $m \in P^S$, then $\varepsilon(m) \in S^{-1}P$, thus there exist $s \in S$ and $p \in P$ such that $(1, m) = \varepsilon(m) = (s, p)$. This implies the existence of $\tilde{s} \in S$ and $\tilde{r} \in R$ such that $\tilde{s} \cdot 1 = \tilde{r}s$ and $\tilde{s}m = \tilde{r}m \in P$, but the last equation implies $m \in \mathrm{LSat}_S^M(P)$. Now let $m \in \mathrm{LSat}_S^M(P)$, then there exists $s \in S$ such that $sm \in P$. But the $\varepsilon(m) = (1, m) = (s, sm) \in S^{-1}P$, thus $m \in \varepsilon^{-1}(S^{-1}P) = P^S$. □

[2] The set S is *saturated* if for all $s, t \in R$ such that $st \in S$ we have $s, t \in S$.

Lemma 1.11. *Let S be a left denominator set in a ring R, M a left R-module and $\{P_j\}_{j\in J}$ a family of left R-submodules of M. Consider their intersection $P := \bigcap_{j\in J} P_j$.*

(a) We have $P^S \subseteq \bigcap_{j\in J} P_j^S$.
(b) If J is finite, then $P^S = \bigcap_{j\in J} P_j^S$.

Proof. (a) Let $m \in P^S$, then there exists $s \in S$ such that $sm \in P = \bigcap_{j\in J} P_j$, thus $sm \in P_j$ and $m \in P_j^S$ for all $j \in J$, which implies $m \in \bigcap_{j\in J} P_j^S$.
(b) Let $m \in \bigcap_{j\in J} P_j^s$, then for all $j \in J$ there exists $s_j \in S$ such that $s_j m \in P_j$. Since J is finite there exists a common left multiple $s \in S$ of the s_j by the left Ore condition, which implies $sm \in P_j$ for all $j \in J$. Therefore, $sm \in \bigcap_{j\in J} P_j = P$ and $m \in P^S$. □

2 ALGORITHMIC TOOLBOX

2.1 Kernels and preimages

Let K be a field and consider the two commutative polynomial rings $K[\underline{x}] := K[x_1, \ldots, x_n]$ and $K[\underline{y}] := K[y_1, \ldots, y_m]$ with the ideals $I = {}_{K[\underline{x}]}\langle h_1, \ldots, h_k\rangle$ and $J = {}_{K[\underline{y}]}\langle g_1, \ldots, g_l\rangle$. Let further $\varphi : K[\underline{x}]/I \to K[\underline{y}]/J$, $x_i \mapsto f_i$ be the ring map induced by elements $f_1, \ldots, f_n \in K[\underline{y}]$. Algorithm 1 outlines a classical Gröbner-driven method for computing $\ker(\varphi)$ (for details see e.g. [4], Section 1.8.10).

Algorithm 1: KernelPolynomialAlgebra

Input: K, I, J, φ as above.
Output: $\ker(\varphi)$.

```
begin
    H := _{K[x,y]}⟨h_1, ..., h_k, g_1, ..., g_l, x_1 − f_1, ..., x_n − f_n⟩;
    compute H' := H ∩ K[x] by eliminating y_1, ..., y_m;
    return H';
end
```

Given a homomorphism of arbitrary rings $\psi : A \to B$ and a two-sided ideal J in B, we have that $\psi^{-1}(J) = \ker(\varphi)$ for the induced homomorphism $\varphi : A \to B/J$. On the other hand the kernel of a homomorphism is the preimage of the zero ideal. Therefore computing kernels and preimages of two-sided ideals is equivalent.[3]

3 INTERSECTION OF IDEALS WITH MULTIPLICATIVE SETS IN COMMUTATIVE POLYNOMIAL ALGEBRAS

The first problem we are interested in solving is the following:

Definition 3.1. Let S be a left denominator set in a ring R and I a left ideal in R. The *intersection problem* is to decide whether $I \cap S = \emptyset$ and to compute an element contained in this intersection when the answer is negative.

In our paper [5] we have shown that this problem is integral to a constructive treatment of the Ore condition in G-algebras which in turn allows us to perform basic arithmetic operations in Ore localizations of G-algebras.

In the commutative setting it is an important ingredient for solving linear systems over commutative localizations [14].

Here we consider commutative polynomial algebras of the form $R := K[\underline{x}]/J$, where J is an ideal in the commutative polynomial ring $K[\underline{x}] := K[x_1, \ldots, x_n]$. Furthermore, let I be an ideal in R and fix some suitable $g_i, h_i \in K[\underline{x}]$ with $J = {}_{K[\underline{x}]}\langle g_1, \ldots, g_l\rangle$ and $I = {}_R\langle h_1 + J, \ldots, h_k + J\rangle$. In the following we give algorithms to solve the intersection problem for $I \cap S$, where S is a multiplicative subset of R belonging to one of the localization types described in Definition 1.4 with some computability restrictions.

3.1 Monoidal

In this subsection we start with the algorithms in commutative rings and later proceed to non-commutative ones.

Suppose we are given a monoid $S \subseteq R$, finitely generated by a set $F = \{f_1+J, \ldots, f_m+J\}$. Then the monoid algebra $K[S] := K[F] \subseteq R$ is a natural subalgebra of R. Moreover, consider $\psi : K[t_1, \ldots, t_m] \to K[\underline{x}]/J$, $t_i \mapsto f_i + J$, then the monoid algebra $K[S]$ is a finitely presented K-algebra which is isomorphic to $K[\underline{t}]/\ker(\psi)$. Since R is commutative, but not necessarily a domain, we have to ensure that $S^{-1}R \neq \{0\}$, which is equivalent to $0 \notin S$. The latter property can be checked with Algorithm 2.

Algorithm 2: ZeroContainedInMonoid

Input: A subset $F = \{f_1 + J, \ldots, f_m + J\} \subseteq R = K[\underline{x}]/J$.
Output: 1, if $0 \in S = [F]$, and 0 otherwise.

```
begin
    let ψ : K[t_1, ..., t_m] → K[x_1, ..., x_n]/J, t_i ↦ f_i + J;
    H := ker(ψ);                                  // preimage ψ^{-1}(0)
    M := H : ⟨t_1 · ... · t_m⟩^∞;
    if 1 ∈ M then
        return 1;
    else
        return 0;
    end
end
```

Proposition 3.2. *Algorithm 2 terminates and is correct.*

Proof. We have $0 \in S$ if and only if there exists $\alpha \in \mathbb{N}_0^m$ such that $f^\alpha = f_1^{\alpha_1} \cdot \ldots \cdot f_m^{\alpha_m} \in J$, which in turn is equivalent to the existence of $\alpha \in \mathbb{N}_0^m$ satisfying $t^\alpha \in \ker(\psi) =: H$. By e. g. [9, 13] an ideal $H \subseteq K[\underline{t}]$ contains a monomial if and only if the ideal $H : \langle t_1 \cdot \ldots \cdot t_m\rangle^\infty$ contains 1. Note that all operations involved are computable: the kernel $\ker(\psi)$ via Algorithm 1 and the saturation $H : \langle t_1 \cdot \ldots \cdot t_m\rangle^\infty$ via [4], Section 1.8.9. □

To solve the intersection problem in the monoidal case, we need to be able to determine the *biggest monomial ideal* contained in an ideal in a commutative polynomial algebra, which can be computed with Algorithm 3.

Proposition 3.3. *Algorithm 3 terminates and is correct.*

[3] This equivalence does not hold for preimages of left ideals, see [11].

Algorithm 3: BiggestMonomialIdeal

Input: An ideal $L + J$ in $R = K[\underline{x}]/J$.
Output: The biggest monomial ideal contained in $L + J$.

begin
  Let $K[\underline{x}, q^{\pm 1}] := K[\underline{x}, q_1, q_1^{-1}, \ldots, q_m, q_m^{-1}]$;
  $\varphi : K[\underline{x}] \to K[\underline{x}, q^{\pm 1}],\ x_i \mapsto q_i x_i$;
  $N := {}_{K[\underline{x}, q^{\pm 1}]}\langle L \rangle \cap K[\underline{x}]$;
  return $(N + J)/J$;
end

Proof. Termination is clear. Consider the Laurent polynomial ring $K[q^{\pm 1}] := K[q_1, q_1^{-1}, \ldots, q_m, q_m^{-1}]$ and a homomorphism of K-algebras $\varphi : K[\underline{x}] \to K[\underline{x}, q^{\pm 1}]$, $x_i \mapsto q_i x_i$. By [9, 13, 15], the biggest monomial ideal contained in $L \subseteq K[\underline{x}]$ is exactly N.

Since for all $m \in K[\underline{x}]$ we have $m + J \in L + J$ if and only if $m \in L$, this is in particular true for monomials. Therefore the biggest monomial ideal of $L + J$ is the biggest monomial ideal of L modulo J. □

Now we have all the tools to consider the general situation.

Proposition 3.4. *Let A be an associative (but not necessarily commutative) unital K-algebra and $F = \{f_1, \ldots, f_m\} \subseteq A$ be a set of* **pairwise commuting elements** *in A. Moreover, let $S \subseteq A$ be the monoid in A generated by F. Then Algorithm 4 correctly computes $I \cap S$. Furthermore its termination depends solely on the termination of the computation of $\psi^{-1}(I)$, which depends on A, I and F.*

Proof. The K-monoid algebra $K[S] = K[f_1, \ldots, f_m] \subseteq A$ is a K-subalgebra of A and there is a natural homomorphism of K-algebras

$$\psi : K[t_1, \ldots, t_m] \to A, t_i \mapsto f_i.$$

Then $K[S] \cong K[t_1, \ldots, t_m]/\ker(\psi)$, hence the monoid algebra $K[S]$ is a finitely presented commutative K-algebra. As soon as the preimage $\psi^{-1}(I) = I \cap K[t_1, \ldots, t_m]$ is computable we are left with the following problem: given an ideal $L \subseteq K[t_1, \ldots, t_m]/J$, compute an intersection of L with the submonoid $[t_1, \ldots, t_m]$, which is solved by Algorithm 3. □

Corollary 3.5. *Consider the situation of Proposition 3.4.*

- *If A is a commutative polynomial algebra, Algorithm 4 terminates for any I and F.*
- *If A is a GR-algebra, an algorithm* NCPreimage *from [11] either returns the preimage or reports that the computability condition[4] is violated.*

3.2 Geometric

Let $\mathfrak{p} = {}_R\langle p_1 + J, \ldots, p_m + J \rangle$ be a prime ideal in R with $p_i \in K[\underline{x}]$ and consider the multiplicative set $S := R \setminus \mathfrak{p}$. The preimage of $\mathfrak{p}$ under the canonical surjection $K[\underline{x}] \to R$ is given by the ideal $\mathfrak{q} := {}_{K[\underline{x}]}\langle p_1, \ldots, p_m, g_1, \ldots, g_l \rangle$. Now there are two possible cases:

[4]The algorithm requires an admissible elimination ordering. It can be obtained from a solution of a certain integer programming problem, while infeasibility of the latter proves that no such ordering exists.

Algorithm 4: NCIdealIntersectionWithMonoid

Input: A left ideal $I \subseteq A$, a generating set (of a monoid S) $F = \{f_1, \ldots, f_m\}$ in the K-algebra A, such that $f_i \in A$ commute pairwise.
Output: $I \cap S$: either $\emptyset$ or a finite set of monomial generators $\{t^\alpha : \alpha \in \mathbb{N}_0^n\} \subseteq [t_1, \ldots, t_m]$.

begin
  $\psi : K[t_1, \ldots, t_m] \to A,\ t_i \mapsto f_i$;
  $L := \psi^{-1}(I) \subseteq K[t_1, \ldots, t_m]$;   // preimage of $I \subseteq A$
  if $\psi(L) = 0$ **then**
    return $\emptyset$;   // since then $\psi^{-1}(I) = \ker(\psi)$
  end
  $R := K[t_1, \ldots, t_m]/\ker(\psi)$;
  $M :=$ BiggestMonomialIdeal(L, R);
  if $M = \{0\}$ **then**
    return $\emptyset$;
  end
  return M;
end

Case 1: $h_i \in \mathfrak{q}$ for all i. Then $h_i + J \in \mathfrak{p}$ for all i and thus $I \subseteq \mathfrak{p}$, which implies $I \cap S = I \cap (R \setminus \mathfrak{p}) = I \setminus \mathfrak{p} = \emptyset$.
Case 2: $h_i \notin \mathfrak{q}$ for some i. Then $h_i + J \notin \mathfrak{p}$ and thus $I \cap S \neq \emptyset$.
Since ideal membership in polynomial rings can be decided with Gröbner basis tools, this observations lead to Algorithm 5, where $\mathrm{NF}(h_i|\mathfrak{q})$ denotes the normal form of h_i with respect to (a Gröbner basis of) the ideal $\mathfrak{q}$.

Algorithm 5: CommutativeGeometricIntersection

Input: Ideals $I, J, \mathfrak{p}$ and the multiplicative set S as above.
Output: An element of $I \cap S$ (if $I \cap S \neq \emptyset$) or 0 (if $I \cap S = \emptyset$).

begin
  let $\mathfrak{q} := {}_{K[\underline{x}]}\langle p_1, \ldots, p_m, g_1, \ldots, g_l \rangle \subseteq K[\underline{x}]$;
  foreach $i \in \{1, \ldots, k\}$ **do**
    if $\mathrm{NF}(h_i|\mathfrak{q}) \neq 0$ **then**
      return $h_i + J$;
    end
  end
  return 0;
end

3.3 Rational

Let $r \in \{1, \ldots, n\}$ and consider $\hat{S} := K[x_1 + J, \ldots, x_r + J]$ as well as $S := \hat{S} \setminus \{0\}$. Let $K[\underline{t}] := K[t_1, \ldots, t_r]$ and define the map $\varphi : K[\underline{t}] \to R$ by $t_i \mapsto x_i$ for $1 \leq i \leq r$.

Lemma 3.6. *In the situation above we have $I \cap S = \emptyset$ if and only if $\varphi^{-1}(I) \subseteq \ker(\varphi)$.*

Proof. Let $I \cap S = \emptyset$, then $I \cap \hat{S} = \{0\}$. Now $\varphi^{-1}(I) \subseteq \ker(\varphi)$ follows directly from $\varphi(\varphi^{-1}(I)) \subseteq I \cap \mathrm{im}(\varphi) = I \cap \hat{S} = \{0\}$.

On the other hand, let $\varphi^{-1}(I) \subseteq \ker(\varphi)$ and choose an element $w \in I \cap \hat{S} = I \cap \mathrm{im}(\varphi)$. Then there exists $v \in K[\underline{t}]$ such that $\varphi(v) =$

$w \in I$ and thus $v \in \varphi^{-1}(I) \subseteq \ker(\varphi)$. This implies $w = \varphi(v) = 0$ and therefore $I \cap \hat{S} = \{0\}$ or, equivalently, $I \cap S = \emptyset$. □

Algorithm 6: CommutativeRationalIntersection

Input: I, J, r, S as above.
Output: An element of $I \cap S$ (if $I \cap S \neq \emptyset$) or 0 (if $I \cap S = \emptyset$).

begin
  let $\varphi : K[\underline{t}] \to K[\underline{x}]/J,\ t_i \mapsto x_i$;
  compute the preimage $\varphi^{-1}(I) = {}_{K[\underline{t}]}\langle w_1, \ldots, w_m \rangle$;
  foreach $i \in \{1, \ldots, m\}$ **do**
    if $\varphi(w_i) \neq 0$ **then**
      return $\varphi(w_i)$;
    end
  end
  return 0;
end

Proposition 3.7. *Algorithm 6 terminates and is correct.*

Proof. Termination is obvious. The preimage $\varphi^{-1}(I)$ can be computed via Algorithm 1. Now we check whether $\varphi^{-1}(I)$ is contained in $\ker(\varphi)$ on the generators w_i. Correctness follows then from Lemma 3.6. □

4 APPLICATION TO LOCAL CLOSURE IN THE COMMUTATIVE SETTING

Recall the following basic concepts of the theory of commutative rings: The *radical* of an ideal I in a commutative ring R is defined as $\sqrt{I} := \{r \in R \mid r^n \in I \text{ for some } n \in \mathbb{N}\}$. A proper ideal I of a commutative ring R is called *primary*, if for all $a, b \in R$ such that $ab \in I$ we have $a \in I$ or $b \in \sqrt{I}$. In a more symmetric view, I is primary if and only if for all $a, b \in R$ with $ab \in I$ we have $a \in I$ or $b \in I$ or ($a \in \sqrt{I}$ and $b \in \sqrt{I}$). An ideal is called *decomposable*, if it can be written as an intersection of finitely many primary ideals.

The goal of this section is to show how to compute the S-closure of an ideal I in a commutative ring R under two assumptions:

(1) We can decide whether $Q \cap S = \emptyset$ for any primary ideal Q in R.
(2) The ideal I is decomposable and we are either given a primary ideal decomposition of I or are able to compute one.[5]

The main ingredient is the following observation, which highlights the differences between primary ideals and arbitrary ideals:

Lemma 4.1. *Let S be a multiplicative set of a commutative ring R.*
(a) If I is an arbitrary ideal in R such that $I \cap S \neq \emptyset$, then $I^S = R$.
(b) If Q is a primary ideal in R such that $Q \cap S = \emptyset$, then $Q^S = Q$.

Proof. Let $w \in I \cap S$, then $w \cdot 1 = w \in I$, thus $1 \in I^S$ and therefore $I^S = R$. On the other hand, let $Q \cap S = \emptyset$ and $r \in Q^S$, then there exists $s \in S$ such that $sr \in Q$. Since Q is primary we have $s \in Q$ or $r \in Q$ or ($s \in \sqrt{Q}$ and $r \in \sqrt{Q}$). But $s \notin \sqrt{Q}$ (and therefore $s \notin Q$), because otherwise $s^n \in Q \cap S = \emptyset$ for some $n \in \mathbb{N}$. Thus the only remaining option is $r \in Q$, which implies $Q^S = Q$. □

[5]Primary decomposition always exists in Noetherian rings. In polynomial algebras it can be computed, see e.g. [4].

Let I be a decomposable ideal with the primary decomposition $I = \bigcap_{i=1}^n Q_i$. Then $I^S = \bigcap_{i=1}^n Q_i^S$ by Lemma 1.11. Combining this with Lemma 4.1 we can compute I^S for any multiplicative set S via Algorithm 7 if we can decide non-emptiness of the intersections $Q_i \cap S$.

Algorithm 7: CommutativeLocalClosureDecomp

Input: A decomposable ideal $I = \bigcap_{i=1}^n Q_i$ and a multiplicative set S in a commutative ring R.
Output: I^S.

begin
  foreach $i \in \{1, \ldots, n\}$ **do**
    if $Q_i \cap S = \emptyset$ **then**
      $\tilde{Q}_i := Q_i$;
    else
      $\tilde{Q}_i := R$;
    end
  end
  return $\tilde{I} := \bigcap_{i=1}^n \tilde{Q}_i$;
end

5 CENTRAL CLOSURE OF SUBMODULES

5.1 Antiblock orderings

Let $n, m \in \mathbb{N}$.

Definition 5.1. A total ordering $\leq$ on $\mathbb{N}_0^n$ with least element 0 is called *admissible* if $\alpha \leq \beta$ implies $\alpha + \gamma \leq \beta + \gamma$ for all $\alpha, \beta, \gamma \in \mathbb{N}_0^n$.

Definition 5.2. Let $\leq_1$ resp. $\leq_2$ be an admissible ordering on $\mathbb{N}_0^n$ resp. $\mathbb{N}_0^m$. The ordering $\leq := (\leq_1, \leq_2)$ on $\mathbb{N}_0^{n+m}$, defined via

$$\alpha \leq \beta \quad :\Leftrightarrow \quad \alpha_2 <_2 \beta_2 \text{ or } (\alpha_2 = \beta_2 \text{ and } \alpha_1 \leq_1 \beta_1),$$

for $\alpha = (\alpha_1, \alpha_2), \beta = (\beta_1, \beta_2) \in \mathbb{N}_0^n \times \mathbb{N}_0^m = \mathbb{N}_0^{n+m}$ is called an *(n, m)-antiblock ordering.*

Definition 5.3. Let $\leq$ be an admissible ordering on $\mathbb{N}_0^n$. The *(ascending) position-over-term ordering* extending $\leq$ is the ordering $\leq^{\text{POT}}$ on $\underline{r} \times \mathbb{N}_0^n$, defined via

$$(i, \alpha) \leq^{\text{POT}} (j, \beta) \quad :\Leftrightarrow \quad i < j \text{ or } (i = j \text{ and } \alpha \leq \beta)$$

for $\alpha, \beta \in \mathbb{N}_0^n$ and $i, j \in \underline{r}$.

Lemma 5.4. *Let $\leq = (\leq_1, \leq_2)$ be an (n, m)-antiblock ordering on $\mathbb{N}_0^{n+m} \cong \mathbb{N}_0^n \times \mathbb{N}_0^m$ and $\preceq := \leq^{\text{POT}}$. Let $(\alpha_1, \alpha_2), (\beta_1, \beta_2) \in \mathbb{N}_0^{n+m}$ and $i, j \in \underline{r}$ such that we have $(i, (\alpha_1, \alpha_2)) \preceq (j, (\beta_1, \beta_2))$, then $(i, \alpha_2) \leq_2^{\text{POT}} (j, \beta_2)$.*

Proof. We have

$$\begin{aligned} & (i, (\alpha_1, \alpha_2)) \preceq (j, (\beta_1, \beta_2)) \\ \Leftrightarrow \quad & (i, (\alpha_1, \alpha_2)) \leq^{\text{POT}} (j, (\beta_1, \beta_2)) \\ \Leftrightarrow \quad & i < j \text{ or } (i = j \text{ and } (\alpha_1, \alpha_2) \leq (\beta_1, \beta_2)) \\ \Rightarrow \quad & i < j \text{ or } (i = j \text{ and } \alpha_2 \leq_2 \beta_2) \\ \Leftrightarrow \quad & (i, \alpha_2) \leq_2^{\text{POT}} (j, \beta_2). \end{aligned}$$

□

5.2 The class of G-algebras

Definition 5.5. For $n \in \mathbb{N}$ and $1 \le i < j \le n$ consider the constants $c_{ij} \in K \setminus \{0\}$ and "polynomials" $d_{ij} \in K[x_1, \dots, x_n]$. Suppose that there exists an admissible ordering $\le$ on $\mathbb{N}_0^n$ such that for any $1 \le i < j \le n$ either $d_{ij} = 0$ or $\operatorname{le}_\le(d_{ij}) < \operatorname{le}_\le(x_i x_j)$, where $\operatorname{le}_\le(f) \in \mathbb{N}_0^n$ denotes the leading exponent of f with respect to $\le$. The K-algebra

$$A := K\langle x_1, \dots, x_n \mid \{x_j x_i = c_{ij} x_i x_j + d_{ij} : 1 \le i < j \le n\}\rangle$$

is called a *G-algebra* if the set $\{x^\alpha \mid \alpha \in \mathbb{N}_0^n\}$ is a K-basis of A.

G-algebras [10, 12] are also known as algebras of solvable type [7, 8] and as PBW algebras [2]. G-algebras are left and right Noetherian domains that occur naturally in various situations and encompass algebras of linear functional operators modeling differential and difference equations like Weyl and shift algebras. We will base our algorithms on the existing Gröbner basis theory for G-algebras which is very close to the commutative case. Details can be found in [10].

5.3 Central saturation

Definition 5.6. For a ring R let $Z(R)$ be the *center* of R. The elements of $Z(R)$ are called *central.*

Definition 5.7. Let R be a ring, $q \in Z(R)$, $k \in \mathbb{N}$ and I a left R-submodule of R^k.

- The *(central) quotient* of I by q is the left R-submodule
$$I : q := \{f \in R^k \mid qf \in I\} = \{f \in R^k \mid fq \in I\}.$$
- The *central saturation* of I by q is the left R-submodule
$$I : q^\infty := \bigcup_{i \in \mathbb{N}_0} (I : q^i) = \{f \in R^k \mid \exists n \in \mathbb{N}_0 : q^n f \in I\}.$$
- The *(central) saturation index* of I by q is
$$\operatorname{Satindex}(I, q) := \min(\{n \in \mathbb{N}_0 \mid (I : q^\infty) = (I : q^n)\} \cup \{\infty\}).$$

These saturations themselves are special cases of left saturation closures, since $I : q = \operatorname{LSat}_{\{q\}}(I)$ and $I : q^\infty = \operatorname{LSat}_{[q]}(I) = I^{[q]}$.

Remark 5.8. In the situation of Definition 5.7, consider the left R-module homomorphism $\phi : R^k \to R^k/I$, $f \mapsto fq + I$. We have

$$\ker(\phi) = \{f \in R^k \mid qf + I = \phi(f) = 0 + I\} = I : q.$$

Thus, if we can compute kernels of such left R-module homomorphisms, we can also compute central quotients. Furthermore, if we can decide equality of left R-modules, then we can also compute the central saturation iteratively, provided the saturation index is finite. The latter is always the case for Noetherian rings.

Remark 5.9. Let $S = [f_1, \dots, f_k]$ be a left Ore set in a G-algebra A, I a left ideal in A and $z \in Z(A) \cap S$. Then $I^{[z]} = \operatorname{LSat}_{[q]}(I) = I : q^\infty$ is computable. Since $[z] \subseteq S$ we have $I^{[z]} \subseteq I^S$. The other inclusion holds if $\operatorname{LSat}(S) = \operatorname{LSat}([z])$, which is equivalent to $f_j \in \operatorname{LSat}([z])$ for all j. A sufficient condition for this is that $f_1, \dots, f_k$ commute pairwise and z is a multiple of $f_1 \cdot \ldots \cdot f_k$. This also includes the special case where $f_1, \dots, f_k \in Z(A)$.

Saturation can be helpful in decomposing ideals:

Lemma 5.10. *Let I be a left ideal in a ring R and $q \in Z(R)$. If $n := \operatorname{Satindex}(I, q) < \infty$, then $I = {}_R\langle I, q^n\rangle \cap (I : q^n)$.*

Proof. Let $J := {}_R\langle I, q^n\rangle \cap (I : q^n)$. Since $I \subseteq {}_R\langle I, q^n\rangle$ and $I \subseteq (I : q^n)$ we clearly have $I \subseteq J$. On the other hand, let $a \in J$, then $q^n a \in I$ (since $a \in (I : q^n)$) and $a = b + rq^n$ for some $b \in I$ and $r \in R$ (since $a \in {}_R\langle I, q^n\rangle$). Now

$$q^{2n} r = q^n r q^n = q^n(a - b) = q^n a - q^n b \in I$$

shows that $r \in (I : q^{2n}) = (I : q^n)$, which implies $rq^n = q^n r \in I$, thus $a = b + rq^n \in I$. □

5.4 The central essential rational closure algorithm

Convention 5.11. In this section let K be a field, $n, m, r \in \mathbb{N}$ and A a G-algebra over K generated by two blocks of variables $\underline{x} = \{x_1, \dots, x_n\}$ and $\underline{y} = \{y_1, \dots, y_m\}$ such that $\underline{x}$ generates a sub-G-algebra B of A with $B \subseteq Z(A)$. Then $S := B \setminus \{0\}$ is a left Ore set in B as well as in A since it is a multiplicative set consisting of central elements. Furthermore, let $\le\, = (\le_1, \le_2)$ be an (n, m)-antiblock ordering satisfying the ordering condition for G-algebras on A and $\le := \le^{\mathrm{POT}}$. Finally, let $\varepsilon := \varepsilon_{S,A,A^r}$, $\rho := \rho_{S,A}$ and $\le_2 = \le_2^{\mathrm{POT}}$.

Remark 5.12.

- We have $\ker(\varepsilon) = \{m \in A^r \mid \exists s \in S : sm = 0\} = \{0\}$ since A is a domain, thus ε is injective.
- Since $B \subseteq Z(A)$ we can identify B with the commutative polynomial ring $K[\underline{x}] = K[x_1, \dots, x_n]$. Then we have $S^{-1}B \cong K(\underline{x})$.
- We can view $S^{-1}A$ as a G-algebra over the field $K(\underline{x})$ in the variables $y_1, \dots, y_m$ with the relations inherited from A, thus the Gröbner basis theory of G-algebras applies.
- The monomials in the module $S^{-1}(A^r) \cong (S^{-1}A)^r$ are of the form $\varepsilon(\underline{y}^\alpha e_i) = \rho(\underline{y}^\alpha)\varepsilon(e_i)$. Let $(s, f) \in S^{-1}A^r$, then (s, f) and $(1, f) = \varepsilon(f)$ have the same leading exponent and the same leading monomial with respect to $\le_2$.

Lemma 5.13. *Let $f \in A^r \setminus \{0\}$ and $\operatorname{le}_\le(f) = (i, (\alpha_1, \alpha_2))$, then $\operatorname{le}_{\le_2}(\varepsilon(f)) = (i, \alpha_2)$.*

Proof. Let

$$\begin{aligned} f &= \sum_{(j,(\beta,\gamma)) \in \underline{r} \times \mathbb{N}_0^{n+m}} c_{(j,(\beta,\gamma))} \underline{x}^\beta \underline{y}^\gamma e_j \\ &= \sum_{(j,\gamma) \in \underline{r} \times \mathbb{N}_0^m} \underbrace{\left(\sum_{\beta \in \mathbb{N}_0^n} c_{(j,(\beta,\gamma))} \underline{x}^\beta \right)}_{=: \tilde{c}_{(j,\gamma)} \in K[\underline{x}]} \underline{y}^\gamma e_j \end{aligned}$$

with $c_{(j,(\beta,\gamma))} \in K$, then $(j, (\beta, \gamma)) \le (i, (\alpha_1, \alpha_2)) = \operatorname{le}_\le(f)$ whenever $c_{(j,(\beta,\gamma))} \neq 0$. Furthermore,

$$\begin{aligned} \varepsilon(f) &= \varepsilon\left(\sum_{(j,\gamma) \in \underline{r} \times \mathbb{N}_0^m} \tilde{c}_{(j,\gamma)} \underline{y}^\gamma e_j \right) = \sum_{(j,\gamma) \in \underline{r} \times \mathbb{N}_0^m} \varepsilon(\tilde{c}_{(j,\gamma)} \underline{y}^\gamma e_j) \\ &= \sum_{(j,\gamma) \in \underline{r} \times \mathbb{N}_0^m} \rho(\tilde{c}_{j,\gamma}) \cdot \varepsilon(\underline{y}^\gamma e_j) \end{aligned}$$

implies that it suffices to show that $(j, \gamma) \leq_2 (i, \alpha_2)$ whenever $\tilde{c}_{(j,\gamma)} \neq 0$. The last condition implies that there is some $\beta \in \mathbb{N}_0^n$ such that $c_{(j,(\beta,\gamma))} \neq 0$. Now $(j, (\beta, \gamma)) \leq (i, (\alpha_1, \alpha_2)) = \text{le}_{\leq}(f)$ implies $(j, \gamma) \leq_2 (i, \alpha_2)$ by Lemma 5.4, thus $\text{le}_{\leq_2}(\varepsilon(f)) = (i, \alpha_2)$. □

PROPOSITION 5.14. *Let I be a left A-submodule of A^r and G a left Gröbner basis of I with respect to $\leq$. Then $\varepsilon(G)$ is a left Gröbner basis of $J := S^{-1}I$ with respect to $\leq_2 = \leq_2^{\text{POT}}$.*

PROOF. Let $z \in J \setminus \{0\}$, then $z = (s, f)$ for some $s \in S$ and $f \in I$. Since G is a left Gröbner basis of I there exists $g \in G$ such that $\text{lm}_{\leq}(g) \mid \text{lm}_{\leq}(f)$. In terms of leading exponents, where $(i, (\alpha_1, \alpha_2)) = \text{le}_{\leq}(g)$ and $(j, (\beta_1, \beta_2)) = \text{le}_{\leq}(f)$, this means $i = j$ and $(\alpha_1, \alpha_2) \leq (\beta_1, \beta_2)$, in particular, we have $\alpha_2 \leq_2 \beta_2$. Since $\text{le}_{\leq_2}(\varepsilon(g)) = (i, \alpha_2)$ and $\text{le}_{\leq}((s, f)) = \text{le}_{\leq_2}(\varepsilon(f)) = (j, \beta_2)$ by the previous Lemma 5.13, we have $\text{lm}_{\leq_2}(\varepsilon(g)) \mid \text{lm}_{\leq_2}(z)$. □

Definition 5.15. Consider a polynomial $f \in K[\underline{x}] \setminus K$. Since $K[\underline{x}]$ is a unique factorization domain, f has a representation as a product of a unit and finitely many irreducible elements. The *square-free part* of f, denoted $\sqrt{f}$, is the product of all unique irreducible elements that occur in this factorization.

Remark 5.16. Algorithm 8 is based on its commutative special case which can be found in [1], Table 8.8, as algorithm EXTCONT.

Algorithm 8: CENTRALESSENTIALRATIONALCLOSURE

Input: A left A-submodule I of A^r.
Output: A left Gröbner basis $G \subseteq A^r$ of I^S with respect to $\leq$.

```
begin
    H := LeftGröbnerBasis(I, ≤);
    h := √(∏_{g∈H} lc_{≤2}(ε(g))) ∈ K[x] \ {0};
    k := Satindex(I, h);
    G := LeftGröbnerBasis(I : h^k, ≤);
    return G;
end
```

In the situation of Algorithm 8 the candidate h is constructed such that for any $g \in H$ there exists $l \in \mathbb{N}$ satisfying $\text{lc}_{\leq_2}(\varepsilon(g)) \mid h^l$.

PROPOSITION 5.17. *Algorithm 8 terminates and is correct.*

PROOF. The saturation index computation is finite since all G-algebras are Noetherian, thus termination of the whole algorithm is ensured. To prove correctness we have to show that $I^S = I : h^k$.

First, let $f \in I : h^k$, then $h^k f \in I$ and $\varepsilon(f) = (1, f) = (h^k, h^k f) \in S^{-1}I$. Thus we have $f \in \varepsilon^{-1}(S^{-1}I) = I^S$, which implies $I : h^k \subseteq I^S$.

For the other inclusion, let $f \in I^S = \varepsilon^{-1}(S^{-1}I)$, then $\varepsilon(f) \in S^{-1}I$. Now $\varepsilon(H)$ is a left Gröbner basis of $S^{-1}I$ with respect to $\leq_2$ by Proposition 5.14. Furthermore, Theorem 1.16 in [10] implies that $\text{LeftNF}(\varepsilon(f)|\varepsilon(H)) = 0$. We now prove $f \in I : h^k$ by an induction on the minimal number $N \in \mathbb{N}$ of steps necessary in the left normal form algorithm[6] to reduce $\varepsilon(f)$ to zero:

Induction base: If $N = 0$, then $\varepsilon(f) = 0$. Since ε is injective we have $f = 0$, which trivially implies $f \in I : h^\infty$.
Induction hypothesis: Assume that for any $\tilde{f} \in I^S$, such that $\varepsilon(\tilde{f})$ can be reduced to zero in $N - 1$ steps by the left normal form algorithm with respect to $\varepsilon(H)$, we have $\tilde{f} \in I : h^k$.
Induction step: Let $f \in I^S$ such that the left normal form algorithm needs at least N steps to reduce $\varepsilon(f)$ to zero with respect to $\varepsilon(H)$. Then there exists $g \in H$ such that $\text{lm}_{\leq_2}(\varepsilon(g)) \mid \text{lm}_{\leq_2}(\varepsilon(f))$. Let $(i_f, \alpha) = \text{le}_{\leq_2}(\varepsilon(f))$ and $(i_g, \beta) = \text{le}_{\leq_2}(\varepsilon(g))$, then $i_g = i_f$ and

$$t := \varepsilon(f) - \frac{\text{lc}_{\leq_2}(\varepsilon(f))}{\text{lc}_{\leq_2}(\varepsilon(\underline{y}^{\alpha-\beta} g))} \rho(\underline{y}^{\alpha-\beta}) \varepsilon(g) \in S^{-1}A^r$$

can be reduced to zero in $N - 1$ steps with respect to $\varepsilon(H)$. Since the relations between the variables in A have the form $y_j y_i = c_{ij} y_i y_j + d_{ij}$ for some $c_{ij} \in K \setminus \{0\}$ and $d_{ij} \in A$ such that $\text{le}_{\leq}(d_{ij}) \prec \text{le}_{\leq}(y_i y_j)$, we have

$$\text{lc}_{\leq_2}(\varepsilon(\underline{y}^{\alpha-\beta} g)) = u \cdot \text{lc}_{\leq_2}(\varepsilon(g))$$

for some $u \in K \setminus \{0\}$, which is just the product of all c_{ij} that occur while bringing $\varepsilon(\underline{y}^{\alpha-\beta} g)$ in standard monomial form, and thus

$$t = \varepsilon(f) - \frac{\text{lc}_{\leq_2}(\varepsilon(f))}{u \, \text{lc}_{\leq_2}(\varepsilon(g))} \rho(\underline{y}^{\alpha-\beta}) \varepsilon(g).$$

Since $\text{lc}_{\leq_2}(\varepsilon(g))$ divides a power of h, there exists $l \in \mathbb{N}$ such that

$$c := \frac{h^l}{u \, \text{lc}_{\leq_2}(\varepsilon(g))} \in K[\underline{x}] \setminus \{0\}$$

and therefore

$$\tilde{f} := h^l f - c \, \text{lc}_{\leq_2}(\varepsilon(f)) \underline{y}^{\alpha-\beta} g \in I^S,$$

since $f \in I^S$ by assumption and $g \in H \subseteq I \subseteq I^S$. Now

$$\begin{aligned} h^l t &= h^l \varepsilon(f) - \frac{h^l}{u \, \text{lc}_{\leq_2}(\varepsilon(g))} \text{lc}_{\leq_2}(\varepsilon(f)) \rho(\underline{y}^{\alpha-\beta}) \varepsilon(g) \\ &= h^l \varepsilon(f) - c \, \text{lc}_{\leq_2}(\varepsilon(f)) \rho(\underline{y}^{\alpha-\beta}) \varepsilon(g) \\ &= \varepsilon(h^l f - c \, \text{lc}_{\leq_2}(\varepsilon(f)) \underline{y}^{\alpha-\beta} g) \\ &= \varepsilon(\tilde{f}), \end{aligned}$$

thus we can apply the induction hypothesis: we have $\tilde{f} \in I^S$ such that $\varepsilon(\tilde{f}) = h^l t$ can be reduced to zero in $N - 1$ steps with respect to $\varepsilon(H)$, since $h^l \in S$ is invertible in $S^{-1}A$ and thus does not change the reducibility of t. This gives us $\tilde{f} \in I : h^k$ or $h^k \tilde{f} \in I$. Now

$$h^{l+k} f = h^k \tilde{f} + h^{l+k} c \, \text{lc}_{\leq_2}(\varepsilon(f)) \underline{y}^{\alpha-\beta} g \in I$$

implies $f \in I : h^{l+k} = I : h^k$, which shows $I^S \subseteq I : h^k$. □

We implemented Algorithm 8 using the computer algebra system SINGULAR:PLURAL[3] and used it on problems coming from e.g. D-module theory:

Example 5.18. In $\mathcal{D}_3[s]$, the third Weyl algebra over the field $K = \mathbb{Q}$ with an additional commutative variable s, we compute the $K[s] \setminus \{0\}$-closure of the left ideal L_1 which is generated by the elements of order 1 in the derivatives

$$x\partial_x + y\partial_y - 5s, xz\partial_z + y\partial_z - xs, y^2z^2\partial_z + y^3\partial_x + x^3\partial_y - y^2zs - x^2\partial_z.$$

The candidate used for saturation is $25s^2 + 25s + 6 = (5s + 2)(5s + 3)$ and the saturation is reached after one step taking barely any time.

[6] As in the commutative case the algorithm is based on constructing S-polynomials, see Algorithm 1.1 in Chapter 2 of [10].

The resulting ideal L is a part of the annihilating ideal I of the special function $((xz+y)(x^4-y^4))^s$. Notably, the factor $5s+2$ is still present among the leading coefficients of generators of L. Moreover, $L_1 \subsetneq L$ shows that I cannot be generated by the elements of order 1 only.

Remark 5.19. Let R be a commutative principal ideal domain and $R[x]$ a polynomial ring with the field of fractions $Q(x)$. Consider a left ideal L in the single Ore extension $Q(x)[\partial;\sigma,\delta]$, then in [17] one finds an algorithm for computing the contraction $Q(x)[\partial;\sigma,\delta]L \cap R[x][\partial;\sigma,\delta]$. We recognize the latter as the $R[x]\setminus\{0\}$-closure of L.

In the setting from Convention 5.11 suppose that A is such a G-algebra over Q that c_{ij} and all the coefficients of d_{ij} are in R, then we define A_R to be an R-algebra subject to the same relations as A.

We can compute the $R[\underline{x}]\setminus\{0\}$-closure of a submodule of A^r in two steps: let $S_1 = Q[\underline{x}]\setminus\{0\}$ and $S_2 = R\setminus\{0\}$. Then one can show that $I^{R[\underline{x}]\setminus\{0\}} = (I^{S_1})^{S_2}$ holds. The left submodule I^{S_1} can be computed with Algorithm 8. Indeed, the same proof as in Algorithm 8 can be applied to the situation of a G-algebra A over Q, a left submodule $I \subseteq A^r$, an algebra A_R over R and $S = S_2 = R\setminus\{0\}$.

Namely, we replace $K[\underline{x}]$ with R and do not need to employ an antiblock ordering. After computing a left Gröbner basis H of I over Q, assume that in H no denominators are present. Now the candidate $h \in R\setminus\{0\}$ and the rest of the algorithm is the same. Also the proof carries almost verbatim with only one modification: since $c := \frac{h^l}{u\,\mathrm{lc}_{\leq_2}(\varepsilon(g))} \in Q\setminus\{0\}$ is a fraction, while $h, u, \mathrm{lc}_{\leq_2}(\varepsilon(g)) \in R$, we just have to replace $\tilde{f}$ with $\hat{f} := u\cdot\tilde{f} \in I^S$. Of course, the computations of the saturation index and the final left Gröbner basis happen over R. A very natural application of the described algorithm is for $R=\mathbb{Z}$.

5.5 Central geometric closure

Consider the setting from Convention 5.11, but we are now interested in computing the closure I^T, where $T := K[\underline{x}]\setminus\mathfrak{p}$ for some prime ideal $\mathfrak{p}$ in $K[\underline{x}]$. By construction we have $I \subseteq I^T \subseteq I^S$ and we can characterize when the second inclusion is in fact an equality:

Lemma 5.20. *We have* $I^T = I^S$ *if and only if* $\mathrm{Ann}_T(I^S/I) \neq \emptyset$[7].

Proof. Let $W \in \{S,T\}$, then I^W is finitely generated by some elements $f_1,\dots,f_k \in A$ and we have that $\mathrm{Ann}_W(I^W/I)$ is nontrivial: since $f_i \in I^W$ there exist $w_i \in W$ such that $w_i f_i \in I$, so $w_1\cdot\ldots\cdot w_k \in \mathrm{Ann}_W(I^W/I)$ due to W being central in A. If $I^S = I^T$ then $\mathrm{Ann}_T(I^S/I) = \mathrm{Ann}_T(I^T/I) \neq \emptyset$. On the other hand, let $t \in \mathrm{Ann}_T(I^S/I)$ and $r \in I^S$, then $tr \in I$ and thus $r \in I^T$, which shows $I^S = I^T$. □

Note that $\mathrm{Ann}_T(I^S/I) \neq \emptyset$ is equivalent to $\mathrm{Ann}_B(I^S/I) \not\subseteq \mathfrak{p}$ and the latter can be checked algorithmically, since I^S is computable via Algorithm 8.

Nevertheless there are situations where neither inclusion is strict:

Example 5.21. Consider $I = {}_A\langle x(x-1)\partial\rangle$, where A is the first Weyl algebra in x and ∂. Then $I^S = {}_A\langle\partial\rangle$ and $I^T = {}_A\langle x\partial\rangle$, if we choose $\mathfrak{p} = {}_{K[x]}\langle x\rangle$, which leads to $I \subsetneq I^T \subsetneq I^S$.

[7] For an A-module I and a subset P of A, $\mathrm{Ann}_P(I) := \{p \in P \mid pI = 0\}$.

Further advances towards an algorithm for computing I^T are the subject of ongoing research.

6 CONCLUSION

We have provided several algorithms for solving the intersection problem and for computing local closure in various settings with respect to Ore sets with enough commutativity. In particular, it follows that arithmetic within the localization of a commutative polynomial algebra is constructive and can be used also in homomorphic images of such algebras inside noncommutative algebras.

Some questions are of further interest. Namely, does there exist an algorithm to compute...

- the closure in the case of geometric localization without invoking primary decomposition?
- the central geometric closure?
- the geometric closure in the Weyl algebra tensored with a commutative polynomial ring?

7 ACKNOWLEDGEMENTS

The authors are grateful to Thomas Kahle (Magdeburg), Gerhard Pfister (Kaiserslautern), Anne Frühbis-Krüger (Hannover) and Jorge Martín-Morales (Zaragoza) for fruitful discussions.

The second author has been supported by Project II.6 of SFB-TRR 195 "Symbolic Tools in Mathematics and their Applications" of the German Research Foundation (DFG).

REFERENCES

[1] Thomas Becker and Volker Weispfenning. 1993. *Gröbner Bases.* Graduate Texts in Mathematics, Vol. 141. Springer-Verlag, New York.
[2] Jose Bueso, Jose Gómez-Torrecillas, and Alain Verschoren. 2003. *Algorithmic methods in non-commutative algebra. Applications to quantum groups.* Kluwer Academic Publishers.
[3] Gert-Martin Greuel, Viktor Levandovskyy, Oleksander Motsak, and Hans Schönemann. 2016. Plural. A Singular 4-1-0 Subsystem for Computations with Noncommutative Polynomial Algebras. Centre for Computer Algebra, TU Kaiserslautern. http://www.singular.uni-kl.de
[4] Gert-Martin Greuel and Gerhard Pfister. 2008. *A SINGULAR Introduction to Commutative Algebra* (2nd ed.). Springer.
[5] Johannes Hoffmann and Viktor Levandovskyy. 2017. A constructive approach to arithmetics in Ore localizations. In *Proc. ISSAC'17.* ACM Press, 197–204.
[6] Johannes Hoffmann and Viktor Levandovskyy. 2017. Constructive Arithmetics in Ore Localizations of Domains. *ArXiv e-prints* (2017). arXiv:math.RA/1712.01773
[7] Abdelilah Kandri-Rody and Volker Weispfenning. 1990. Non-commutative Gröbner bases in algebras of solvable type. *J. Symb. Comp.* 9, 1 (1990), 1–26.
[8] Heinz Kredel. 1993. *Solvable polynomial rings.* Shaker.
[9] Martin Kreuzer and Lorenzo Robbiano. 2005. *Computational commutative algebra 2.* Springer Berlin.
[10] Viktor Levandovskyy. 2005. *Non-commutative Computer algebra for polynomial algebras: Gröbner bases, applications and implementation.* Dissertation. Universität Kaiserslautern. http://kluedo.ub.uni-kl.de/volltexte/2005/1883/
[11] Viktor Levandovskyy. 2006. Intersection of Ideals with Non-commutative Subalgebras. In *Proc. ISSAC'06*, J.-G. Dumas (Ed.). ACM Press, 212–219.
[12] Viktor Levandovskyy and Hans Schönemann. 2003. Plural - a computer algebra system for noncommutative polynomial algebras. In *Proc. ISSAC'03.* ACM Press, 176–183.
[13] Ezra Miller. 2016. *Finding all monomials in a polynomial ideal.* Technical Report. https://arxiv.org/abs/1605.08791
[14] Sebastian Posur. 2017. Linear systems over localizations of rings. *ArXiv e-prints* (2017). arXiv:math.AC/1709.08180
[15] Mutsumi Saito, Bernd Sturmfels, and Nobuki Takayama. 2000. *Gröbner deformations of hypergeometric differential equations.* Algorithms and Computation in Mathematics, Vol. 6. Springer-Verlag, Berlin.
[16] Zoran Škoda. 2006. *Noncommutative localization in noncommutative geometry.* Cambridge University Press, 220–310. http://arxiv.org/abs/math/0403276
[17] Yi Zhang. 2016. Contraction of Ore Ideals with Applications. In *Proc. ISSAC'16.* ACM, New York, NY, USA, 413–420.

Constructive Membership Tests in Some Infinite Matrix Groups

Alexander Hulpke
Colorado State University
Department of Mathematics
Fort Collins, Colorado, USA
hulpke@colostate.edu

ABSTRACT

We describe algorithms and heuristics that allow us to express arbitrary elements of $\mathrm{SL}_n(\mathbb{Z})$ and $\mathrm{Sp}_{2n}(\mathbb{Z})$ as products of generators in particular "standard" generating sets. For elements obtained experimentally as random products, it produces product expressions whose lengths are competitive with the input lengths.

CCS CONCEPTS

• **Computing methodologies** → **Algebraic algorithms**;

KEYWORDS

Linear Groups; Symplectic Group; Factorization; Words

ACM Reference Format:
Alexander Hulpke. 2018. Constructive Membership Tests in Some Infinite Matrix Groups. In *ISSAC '18: 2018 ACM International Symposium on Symbolic and Algebraic Computation, July 16–19, 2018, New York, NY, USA.* ACM, New York, NY, USA, 8 pages. https://doi.org/10.1145/3208976.3208983

1 INTRODUCTION

The constructive membership problem, that is expressing an element g of a group G as a word in a generating set (which might be user-chosen) is one of the fundamental tasks of computational group theory. We call such a word a *factorization* of g (with respect to the chosen generating set). In the case of elementary abelian groups it is simply the well-studied problem of solving a system of linear equations.

Another special case is discrete logarithm, that is expressing an element in a cyclic group as a power of a chosen generator. This is a known, difficult problem [20], thus the best we can hope for are good heuristics rather than a general solution.

We note here that [2] shows that for a large class of groups, including matrix groups, discrete logarithm to be the only obstacle to efficient group order and membership test calculations.

The application to puzzles [8] arguably has the largest visibility for the general public.

In general, factorization underlies much of the functionality for group homomorphisms [15] and is thus at the heart of many group theoretic calculations.

ISSAC '18, July 16–19, 2018, New York, NY, USA

ACM ISBN 978-1-4503-5550-6/18/07...$15.00
https://doi.org/10.1145/3208976.3208983

While for problems such as the Cayley graph for Rubik's cube [14, 18] a shortest word expression is the inherent aim, in most applications the goal is rather to obtain a word expression that is "reasonably short" for practical purposes, but without any guaranteed bound in relation to the optimal length (or even just a straight line program).

For permutation groups, stabilizer chains [21] provide a tool for obtaining such expressions [17]. For finite matrix groups, composition trees and constructive recognition [1] are tools.

The groups we are interested in here will be particular infinite matrix groups over rings of integers, namely $G = \mathrm{SL}_n(\mathbb{Z})$ or $G = \mathrm{Sp}_{2n}(\mathbb{Z})$ with particular generating sets. This is motivated by recent work [6] on finitely generated subgroups of these groups: Given a subgroup $S \leq G$ given by generating matrices, one often would like to determine whether S has finite index in G, in which case S is called *arithmetic*. Calculation in finite images of G allow us [6] to determine the index if it is known to be finite.

Determining *whether* the index is finite, however requires us[1] to verify the index in a finitely presented version of G and thus poses the task to express the generators of S as words in a particularly chosen generating set of G. While methods for word expression exist already for the case of SL, the author has been unable to find such methods for Sp in the literature. The Section 5 below will give an example (taken from [11]) of doing this using the approach presented in this paper.

While these groups clearly exist in arbitrary dimension, the questions and concrete examples studied so far have been of rather limited dimension (≤ 8). One reason for this is that products of elements of infinite matrix groups usually very quickly produce large coefficients, and matrix arithmetic itself becomes a bottleneck. This paper thus is focusing on practically useful methods for small dimensions, even if they scale badly for larger n.

This use of the factorization also indicates that the appropriate measure of success is the length of the resulting words, rather than the time required to obtain such a factorization: The time for the overall calculation will be dominated by the coset enumeration, and shorter words often make success of such an enumeration more likely.

We shall present algorithms that in experiments perform well under this measure, though we cannot give a provable statement about the quality of the word expression obtained. In the case of Sp, furthermore we shall present a heuristic that has worked well

[1] Structural arguments based on the existence of free subgroups show that there cannot be deterministic, bounded-time finite index test. Any method that has a chance of determining the index thus needs to share characteristics of methods for subgroups of finitely presented groups.

for all examples tried, though we cannot prove this statement in general.

2 TWO BASIC ALGORITHMS

We start by fixing notation: We have a group G with a generating sequence $\underline{g} = (g_1, \ldots, g_k)$. The task is to express an arbitrary $e \in G$ as a *word* in $\underline{g}$, that is a product of the elements in $\underline{g}$ and their inverses that equals e. We shall call such a word a *word expression* for e. The smallest number of factors possible in such a word expression for e is called the *word length* of e (with respect to the generating set $\underline{g}$), and such a word is called a *shortest word* for e.

To simplify notation, we shall also assume now that $\underline{g} = \underline{g}^{-1}$ is closed under taking inverses.

The *Cayley graph* Γ of $G = \langle \underline{g} \rangle$ is a digraph with vertex set G and, for $x, y \in G$, an edge (x, y) labeled by g, existent iff $xg = y$. The question for a word of minimal length expressing $e \in G$ thus is the same as that of finding an (undirected) path in Γ of shortest length from 1_G to g.

Standard "shortest path" algorithms for graphs, such as [7] then motivate an exhaustive search that "floods" the Cayley graph vertex by vertex, starting with the identity and stopping once group element e has been reached. The corresponding algorithm for word expression has been known for a long time and is given as algorithm 1:

We use the notation $L[a]$ to get a list element associated to a group element a, this will be implemented though appropriate data structures, such as hashing.

The first stage of this approach can also be considered as an orbit algorithm [12], calculating the (partial) orbit A of 1_G under right multiplication by G. In this form it is easily seen that that it is sufficient not to store full word expressions W, but only the generator labeling the last edge of the shortest path. (In fact, following [4], one can reduce the storage requirement to 2 bits per element by indicating the length of the path modulo 3.)

Fundamentally, this is one of the the only two known approaches that can guarantee[2] to find a shortest word. The other method would be to use a finite, length-based confluent rewriting system for G. (In general we do not have good confluent rewriting systems for arbitrary finite groups, furthermore in the infinite case it is not even known whether such finite systems exist.)

If memory is exhausted, we then can (this is `Stage 2`) use the fact that all elements are invertible and that the Cayley graph looks the same from every vertex to extend the radius by a factor two, before failure: Test whether the ball A (around 1_G) and the ball eA (around e) intersect:

If a word of shortest length is desired, we may not stop at the first word that is found, but must run systematically through all combinations (or run through pairs according to the length of the product).

The storage requirements, which are $O(|A|)$, show that for every group there is a maximal word length that can be tested for. Thus this method can cater only for a finite number of elements in an

[2]E.g. the calculation of the diameter of Rubik's cube [18] ultimately builds on this algorithm

```
Input  : A group G with generating set g and e ∈ G
Output : A word expression in g for e or a memory overflow
         error
Initialize A := {(1_G)};
P := [], P[1_G]:=false ;    // Marker whether an element
  was processed
W := []; W[1_G] := ∅ ;          // Word expressions for
  elements
if e = 1 then
  return ∅;
end
while Memory is not exhausted do
  Let A' = {a ∈ A | P[a] = false};
  foreach a ∈ A' do
    foreach x ∈ g do
      if ax = e then
        return (W[a], x);  // Concatenate words
      end
      else if ax ∉ A then
        add ax to A;
        set W[ax] := (W[a], x);      // Concatenate
         words
        P[ax]:=false;
      end
    end
    Set P[a]:=true;
  end
end
// Stage 2: Word products
foreach a ∈ A do
  if ea ∈ A then
    return (W[ea], W[a^-1]);
  end
end
return Memory exhaustion failure;
```

Algorithm 1: Floodsearch

infinite group. Its use is rather are as "quality control" of the produced word length for other algorithms, or to find explicit word lengths for particular elements.

2.1 Modular reduction

Another algorithm is specific to integral matrix groups: Given $e \in SL_n(\mathbb{Z})$, we find a word expression in a finite congruence image $SL_n(\mathbb{Z}/p\mathbb{Z})$, for example using stabilizer chain methods. Having found such an expression, we then check whether this expression also holds in characteristic zero. Otherwise we consider larger congruence images. The implicit expectation here is that for sufficiently large modulus p no modular reduction happens in evaluating a word expression for e and the calculation modulo p is in fact the same as the calculation in $\mathbb{Z}$. This is decried as algorithm 2.

Despite its simplicity, this method often works well to find short word expressions (as done for example in [5] to find candidates for generic word expression that then are explicitly proven) and

Input : A group $G \leq \mathrm{SL}_n(\mathbb{Z})$ with a generating set $\underline{g}$ and $e \in G$
Output : A word expression in $\underline{g}$ for e or failure
Let $p = 3$;
while $|\mathrm{SL}_n(p)|$ *is not too large* **do**
  Let $\varphi\colon G \longrightarrow \mathrm{SL}_n(p)$ the congruence homomorphism;
  Let $H = \langle\varphi(\underline{g})\rangle$;
  Let w be a word expression for $\varphi(e)$ as a word in $\varphi(\underline{g})$;
  if *w evaluated in $\underline{g}$ equals e* **then**
    return w;
  end
  Increment p to the next prime;
end
return *failure*;

Algorithm 2: Word by congruence image

sometimes works faster (and for longer word lengths) than the previous one. However there is no practical way to determine a priori a small modulus that would guarantee success.

3 NORM BASED METHODS FOR SL

We now consider the special case of $G = \mathrm{SL}_n(\mathbb{Z})$ with generators being elementary matrices. We denote by $t_{i,j}$ the matrix that is the identity with an extra entry one in position i, j and set

$$\underline{g} = \left\{ t_{i,j}^{\pm 1} \mid q \leq i \neq j \leq n \right\}.$$

Then [10] (which is a basic linear algebra argument) shows that $\mathrm{SL}_n(\mathbb{Z}) = \langle\underline{g}\rangle$.

A word in these generators can be considered as performing a sequence of elementary matrix operations, and the inverse of a word expression for $g \in G$ would be a sequence of elementary operations that transform g to the identity, which is also its Hermite Normal Form (HNF). (As the normal form is the identity, the calculation of Hermite Normal Form is effectively the same as that of the Smith Normal Form in this case.)

Calculating Normal Forms of matrices is a classical problem in Computer Algebra [19, 22]. If we perform such a calculation and accumulate the sequence of elementary operations not in transforming matrices, but as words, we obtain a word expression in terms of elementary matrices. We shall call this algorithm 3 the HNF-based algorithm.

Input : A group $G \leq \mathrm{SL}_n(\mathbb{Z})$ with a generating set $\underline{g}$ consisting of elementary matrices, and $e \in G$
Output : A word expression in $\underline{g}$ for e
Calculate the HNF for e and the transforming matrix T such that $Te = 1$. While doing so keep T as a word expression in the elementary matrices $\underline{g}$.;
return T^{-1} ; // Use T^{-1} since T converts e to 1

Algorithm 3: The HNF-based algorithm

An implementation of this algorithm was built on top of the GAP [23] implementation of Hermite Normal Form. For matrices with moderate entries (respectively those who have word length in the generators of not more than 20-30) it produces satisfactory results, but not if examples of longer word length are considered. This is because longer products correlate with larger coefficients. For such matrices the first steps in a normal form calculation are to reduce a row by subtracting the k-th multiple of another row, typically for a large k. Such steps produce an elementary matrix in k-th power and thus makes for very long words. This is corroborated by the examples in section 5.

Note also that this approach only applies if the group is generated by all elementary matrices. It thus is only applicable for SL, not subgroups thereof.

We thus consider further strategies used for calculating normal forms, rather than to utilize the forms themselves.

The starting observation is that matrix multiplication in characteristic zero tends to produce a product that has larger entries than either factor. Reducing the overall size of entries of the matrix thus is expected to be more promising than trying to zero out off-diagonal entries systematically row-by-row and column-by-column.

We shall use the (squared) 2-matrix norm $||M||^2 = \sum_{i,j} m_{i,j}^2$. A smaller norm corresponds to overall smaller entries. In fact, as we know the normal form to be the identity, we use the measure $||M - I||^2$ (I being the identity matrix) in place of $||M||^2$.

We shall denote $||M - I||^2$ from now on as *height*.

The algorithm for factorization now iterates a reduction process for the entries of a matrix $a \in \mathrm{SL}_n(\mathbb{Z})$, as given by algorithm 4: We try to reduce matrix height by forming products with generators. In a greedy algorithm we form products with all generators and choose the one that produces the largest height reduction. If no such generator exists we fall back on the proven HNF-based method.

Input : A group $G \leq \mathrm{SL}_n(\mathbb{Z})$ with generating set $\underline{g}$ (that is assumed, but not required, to contain elementary matrices) and $e \in G$
Output : A word expression in $\underline{g}$ for e or failure
Let $w = \emptyset$, $a := e$;
while $a \neq I$ **do**
  foreach $g_i \in \underline{g}$ **do**
    Calculate $||a \cdot g_i - I||^2$ and $||g_i \cdot a - I||^2$, and find for which g_i and product order the value m is minimal;
  end
  if $m \geq ||a||^2$ **then**
    Factor a with the HNF-based method (algorithm 3), obtaining a word v for a;
    return $v \cdot w^{-1}$;
  end
  Replace a with the product that produced minimal height;
  Replace w by (the corresponding) (w, g_i), respectively (g_i, w);
end
return $w - 1$;

Algorithm 4: Height-based reduction

Applying this algorithm to random elements of $SL_n(\mathbb{Z})$ produces in most cases a significant reduction in the matrix coefficients, but do not reach the identity before having to default to algorithm 3:

For example, let $\underline{g}$ the set of all 4×4 elementary matrices and consider the element

$$a = \begin{pmatrix} 1 & 0 & 1 & -1 \\ 1 & 0 & 0 & 0 \\ 0 & -1 & 2 & 0 \\ 0 & -1 & 0 & 1 \end{pmatrix}.$$

Then $\|a - I\| = 7$, but for no generator $g_i \in \underline{g}$ we get a smaller height.

In such a situation the matrix a typically will have undergone prior reduction and thus have comparatively small coefficients. Thus using the HNF-based algorithm as fall-back is less likely to incur the word length penalty we noted before.

Investigating this example further, we find (using algorithm 1) that a can be written as a product $t_{1,4}^{-1}t_{2,1}t_{3,2}^{-1}t_{1,2}^{-1}t_{2,3}^{-1}t_{4,2}^{-1}$ of length 6. If we calculate the heights of partial products of this word we get $1, 2, 3, 5, 7, 7$ if we take subwords starting from the left, respectively $1, 2, 4, 6, 7, 7$ from the right. The reason for the failure of the height-based approach thus is that the first, as well as the last factor of the product, do not increase the height.

This failure to reduce is the result of small height values and looking at only single generators. If instead we would have considered products of length 2, we would have noticed a jump from 7 to ≤ 6 by multiplying with a product of length 2.

Obviously, one could try also longer products. In an ad-hoc compromise between length and number of products we decided to consider products of length up to 3, as this includes conjugates of generators by other generators.

Let

$$\underline{h} = \underline{g} \cup \underline{g}^2 \cup \underline{g}^3.$$

When the height-based reduction then reaches the stage at which no element of $\underline{g}$ reduces, we repeat the same attempt of height reduction through generators, albeit with $\underline{h}$ in place of $\underline{g}$. To avoid a careless accumulation of longer products, we furthermore weigh the height change achieved by the length of the product expression used.

If use of the generating set $\underline{h}$ achieves a height reduction we change a and w accordingly. If also use of $\underline{h}$ achieved no improvement we pass to the HNF-based algorithm 3. Otherwise the calculation then continues again with reductions by $\underline{g}$.

In experiments with random input (see section 5) we found that the words produced by this approach seemed to be of acceptable length.

The time taken in the examples considered was short enough that we did not look into ways to speed up the calculation, though there are many obvious ways to do so, e.g. by looking at changes locally rather than always processing a whole matrix.

4 THE SYMPLECTIC GROUP

The symplectic group of degree $2n$ is the group of matrices in $SL_{2n}(\mathbb{Z})$ that preserve the bilinear form

$$J = \begin{pmatrix} 0 & I_n \\ -I_n & 0 \end{pmatrix}$$

with I_n denoting an $n \times n$ identity matrix. Thus

$$Sp_{2n}(\mathbb{Z}) = \left(M \in SL_{2n}(\mathbb{Z}) \mid MJM^T = J\right).$$

A presentation for $Sp_{2n}(\mathbb{Z})$ has been calculated by Birman [3], based on prior work by Klingen [13] and unpublished thesis work of Gold [9]. Klingen's results shows that the given elements indeed generate Sp, but is very much non-constructive. It thus does not facilitate an algorithm for decomposition in these generators.

The work in [3] minimally adjusts the generating set of [13] and uses

$$Sp_{2n}(\mathbb{Z}) = \langle Y_i, U_i, Z_j \mid 1 \leq i \leq n, 1 \leq j \leq n-1 \rangle$$

with $Y_i = t_{i,n+i}^{-1}$, $U_i = t_{n+i,i}$ and

$$Z_i = \left(t_{i+1,n+i}/t_{i+1,n+i+1}\right)^{t_{i,i+1}} = \begin{pmatrix} I_n & B_i \\ 0 & I_n \end{pmatrix}$$

with B_i the matrix with submatrix $\begin{pmatrix} -1 & 1 \\ 1 & -1 \end{pmatrix}$ at positions $i, i+1$ along the diagonal (and all other entries zero).

The generators Z_i are not elementary, which does not augur well for simply replicating the approach used for SL. We thus note that by [10] we can generate Sp as well from a generating set consisting of short products of elementary matrices, resulting in a second generating set that overlaps with the previous one:

$$\begin{aligned} Sp_{2n}(\mathbb{Z}) &= \langle \{t_{i,n+j}t_{j,n+i}, t_{n+i,j}t_{n+j,i} \mid 1 \leq i < j \leq s\} \\ &\quad \cup \{t_{i,n+i}, t_{n+i,i} \mid 1 \leq i \leq n\}\rangle. \end{aligned}$$

We however do not have a presentation in this second generating set (though one could produce one through a modified Todd-Coxeter algorithm, albeit at the cost of relator lengths). We simply add these elements as further generators (together with relations that express them as products in the original generating set).

To find the necessary product expressions, we need to express the elements $t_{i,n+j}t_{j,n+i}$ (whose factors lie outside Sp) as product of our chosen (primary) generators for Sp.

In [3] we already find an expression for some of these products: For $i \leq n-1$ we have that

$$\begin{aligned} t_{i,i+1}t_{n+i+1,n+i}^{-1} &= Y_i^{-1}Y_{i+1}^{-1}U_{i+1}^{-1}Y_{i+1}^{-1}Z_iU_{i+1}Y_{i+1} \quad \text{and} \\ t_{i+1,i}t_{n+i,n+i+1}^{-1} &= Y_{i+1}Y_iU_iY_iZ_i^{-1}U_i^{-1}Y_i^{-1} \end{aligned}$$

(Algorithm 1 confirms that these are word expressions of minimal length.)

We similarly used algorithm 1 to suggest short expressions for other products, and obtained for $3 \leq i \leq n$ that:

$$\begin{aligned} t_{i-2,i}t_{n+i-2,n+i}^{-1} &= [Y_{i-1}Z_{i-1}^{-1}U_iY_i, U_{i-1}Y_{i-1}Z_{i-2}^{-1}U_{i-1}^{-1}], \\ &\text{and} \\ t_{i,i-2}t_{n+i,n+i-2}^{-1} &= [Y_{i-1}Z_{i-2}^{-1}U_{i-2}Y_{i-2}, \\ &\qquad U_{i-1}Y_{i-1}Z_{i-1}^{-1}U_{i-1}^{-1}] \end{aligned}$$

with $[a, b] = a^{-1}b^{-1}ab$ denoting the commutator.

These expressions are easily verified in general by considering the images of standard basis vectors under the left hand size products and the right hand side products.

The identity $t_{j,i+j} = [t_{j,i+j-1}, t_{i+j-1,i+j}]$ finally allows us to form all other products $t_{i,j}t^{-1}_{n+j,n+i}$ as commutators of products with smaller index difference.

From now on $\tilde{g}$ shall denote this extended generating set, consisting of the U_i, Y_i, Z_j and products $t_{i,n+j}t_{j,n+i}$, $t_{n+i,j}t_{n+j,i}$ (and inverses thereof).

We experimented with algorithm 4 with this generating set $\tilde{g}$ (of course with the HNF-based method replaced by an error message) on a number of random elements.

The results of these experiments were disappointing: Almost all elements we tried reduced only partially and still left matrices with large entries for which no further reduction process could be found, not even by introducing further short products.

4.1 Decomposing the Symplectic group

Thus a more more guided reduction, adapted to the structure of the symplectic group, is required. We should emphasize however that the following approach is purely heuristic in that we have is no proof of it succeeding in general. In a large number of examples in small dimension, we however also were unable to find a single example in which the approach failed.

We start with a structural observation: The products $t_{i,j}t^{-1}_{n+j,n+i}$ for all $1 \leq i \neq j \leq n$ clearly generate a subgroup

$$S = \left\{ \begin{pmatrix} M & 0 \\ 0 & M^{-1} \end{pmatrix} \mid M \in \mathrm{SL}_n(\mathbb{Z}) \right\} \leq \mathrm{Sp}_{2n}(\mathbb{Z}).$$

such that $S \cong \mathrm{SL}_n(\mathbb{Z})$. The definition of the symplectic group (and the fact that $\mathbb{Z}$ has only two units) shows that for

$$T = \left\{ \begin{pmatrix} \star & 0 \\ 0 & \star \end{pmatrix} \in \mathrm{SL}_{2n}(\mathbb{Z}) \right\}$$

and

$$R = T \cap \mathrm{Sp}_{2n}(\mathbb{Z}) = \left\{ \begin{pmatrix} M & 0 \\ 0 & M^{-1} \end{pmatrix} \in \mathrm{SL}_{2n}(\mathbb{Z}) \right\}$$

we have that $S \leq R$ is of index 2.

This subgroup R lies at the heart of the new approach. If we have an element $e \in R$, we can use multiplication by

$$(Y_1^2 U_1)^2 = \begin{pmatrix} A & 0 \\ 0 & A \end{pmatrix} \text{ with } A = \begin{pmatrix} -1 & & 0 \\ & 1 & \\ 0 & & \ddots & \\ & & & 1 \end{pmatrix}$$

to obtain $e' \in S$. (Of course remembering such an extra factor for the product expression.)

Using algorithm 4 for $\mathrm{SL}_n(\mathbb{Z})$, we then can write the $\{1, \ldots, n\} \times \{1, \ldots, n\}$ minor M of e (respectively e') as a product of elementary matrices in dimension n.

As the generating set $\tilde{g}$ also contains (product expressions for) matrices that act on this minor M as elementary matrices: Let w be an $\mathrm{SL}_n(\mathbb{Z})$ word for M. Evaluating w in the generators $t_{i,j}t^{-1}_{n+j,n+i} \in \tilde{g}$ then gives an expression for e in generators for $\mathrm{Sp}_{2n}(\mathbb{Z})$.

It thus is sufficient to map an element $e \in \mathrm{Sp}_{2n}(\mathbb{Z})$ into R.

An element $a = (a_{i,j}) \in \mathrm{Sp}_{2n}(\mathbb{Z})$ lies in R, if the height function

$$h(a) = \sum_{i=1}^{n} \sum_{j=1}^{n} \left(a^2_{i,n+j} + a^2_{n+i,j} \right)$$

has value zero. This suggests that we can transform $e \in \mathrm{Sp}_{2n}(\mathbb{Z})$ into an element of R by running algorithm 4 with this new height function h (even though it does not have a unique minimal element).

We thus modify the height-based approach of algorithm 4 as follows:

(1) The stopping condition, in the outermost while-loop, is for $h(A) = 0$ rather than $a = I$;
(2) It returns not only the word expression, but also the reduced element a;
(3) the case $m \geq \|a\|$ first uses the above modification of the algorithm that first tries an extended generating set, formed by adding short products in the generators, before triggering an error if this also found no reduction.

Again, experiments with this approach failed, producing matrices that had only a few nonzero entries in the top right and bottom left quadrant with no way to also zero out these remaining entries. The goal to reduce all entries at the same time led to a local, not global, minimum from which escape was not possible.

To avoid such a behavior, we switched to a more localized reduction. Based on the observation that single nonzero entries are hard to clean out if the rest of their row is zero, we switch to an iterated process, reducing row-by-row. That is we define a series of height functions by

$$\begin{aligned} h_0 &= 0 \\ h_i &= h_{i-1} + \sum_{j=n+1}^{2n} a^2_{i,j}, && \text{if } i \leq n \\ h_i &= h_{i-1} + \sum_{j=1}^{n} a^2_{i,j}, && \text{if } i > n. \end{aligned}$$

We then run algorithm 4 to reduce by height function h_1. Afterwards, we reduce further with height function h_2 and so on, up to height function $h_{2n} = h$. If the resulting matrix lies in S, we proceed as described above, producing a word expression for e. We call this approach Algorithm 5.

We note that this improved heuristic succeeded in all examples we tried (i.e found a matrix $a \in S$). We did not encounter a single example in which this approach failed.

It also produced words of acceptable length. Alas, proving these statements as general facts seems to be beyond the capabilities of the author.

What seems to be happening is that the localized heights are willing to accept reduction step that reduce the current row, even if they grow the entries in other places that are not covered by the height.

Contrary to the overall height function h, this approach thus does not forbid a reduction to zero (which might produce a very small height reduction), just because it combines with a growth of larger, not yet reduced, entries of the matrix (note that an entry change m

to $m + 1$ increases the height by roughly $(m+1)^2 - m^2 = 2m + 1$, while a reduction 1 to 0 reduces by 1 only).

5 EXAMPLES

As mentioned in the introduction, our main interest has been to obtain short words for Sp. We thus did not measure run times (which can be heavily biased by setup costs or cleverness in avoiding duplicate calculations of elements) systematically, but rather the quality of words obtained. This was done in a GAP [23] implementation of the algorithms described here, that is part of the author's routines for arithmetic groups, available at www.math.colostate.edu/~hulpke/arithmetic.g.

For a small example, section 7.2 in [16], using Mathematica, computes word expressions for selected elements of $SL_3(\mathbb{Z})$, namely X_0 of length 8 and Y_0 of length 14; algorithm 4 obtained word expressions of length 7 and 13, respectively. Similarly an element X_{-2} is given by a word of length 13 and Z_{-2} by a word of length 16; algorithm 4 calculated expressions of lengths 16 and 10 respectively. The new approach thus performs on par with an existing method.

The next example is the group $G(3,4)$ from [11], already considered in [6]. Using the implementation in GAP we construct a homomorphism from a finitely presented version of $Sp_4(\mathbb{Z})$ to a matrix version, using the extended generating set based on [3]. We also form $G(3,4)$ as a matrix group. We then express (this uses the symplectic method) the group generators as words, and form the subgroup S of the finitely presented $Sp_4(\mathbb{Z})$ that is generated by these words. We finally determine the index $[Sp_4(\mathbb{Z}) : S]$ through a coset enumeration. (This calculation, incidentally, independently verifies that $G(3,4)$ is arithmetic.)

```
gap> hom:=SPNZFP(4);
[ Y1, Y2, U1, U2, Z1 ] ->
[[[1,0,-1,0],[0,1,0,0],[0,0,1,0],[0,0,0,1]], [...]
gap> G34:=HofmannStraatenExample(3,4);
<matrix group with 2 generators>
gap> w:=List(GeneratorsOfGroup(G34),
> x->PreImagesRepresentative(hom,x));
[ U1*(U2^-1*U1*U2^-1)^2*Y1^-1*Y2^-1*U2^-1*Y2^-1
  *Z1*U2*Y2, Y2^-1 ]
gap> S:=Subgroup(Source(hom),w);;
gap> Index(Source(hom),S);
3110400
```

In this example, finding the word expressions (of length 14, respectively 1) takes 0.1 seconds (while the coset enumeration confirming the index takes about 4 minutes).

With algorithm 1, we verified (in 20 minutes) that there is an expression for the first generator of length 12. Using this shorter word did not seem to have a meaningful impact on the time required by the coset enumeration.

The input to all other experiments were matrices obtained as random words, of a preselected length *len*, in the matrix generators of SL, respectively Sp. This produced matrices in the respective group for which an upper bound for the length of a word expression was known. The dimensions considered were chosen for be ≤ 8, as the motivating examples from [6] do not exceed this bound.

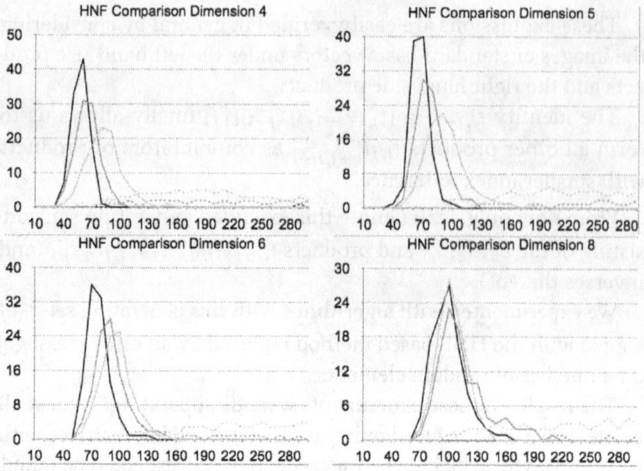

Figure 1: Comparison between HNF-based algorithm 3 and height-based algorithm 4 for SL

We then calculated for each of the matrices a word expression, using the algorithms described in this paper. If an algorithm produced a word of length a for a chosen input length len, we use the scaled ratio $q := 100 \cdot a/len$ as a a measure for the quality of the word expression obtained. The diagrams given indicate a distribution of how often (the ordinate) certain ratios q (the abscissa) occur. (Incidentally, the required runtime is reasonably approximated by this ratio, as the fundamental step in all algorithms is to divide off one generator matrix, building the word in steps of length one.)

The lengths considered were 20 and larger which led to matrices whose entries were frequently in the thousands or more. We therefore did not attempt comparisons with algorithms 1 or 2.

As we only had time for a limited number of trials — we used $20000/len$ matrices of input length len — we discretized the distribution in the following way to produce diagrams that are easily reproduced in print. We grouped the ratios q into intervals of length 10 each, and for each interval calculated the percentage of cases within the experiments for which the obtained ratio fell into this interval. To allow for multiple experiments within one diagram we did plot these results as piecewise linear curves (that somewhat approximate a Gaussian distribution), rather than as bar graphs. So for example in the top-left diagram in figure 1 the continuous black line indicates that about 5% of experiments resulted in a ratio in the interval $[40, 50)$, 32% in the interval $[50, 60)$, 42% in the interval $[60, 70)$ and (this is hard to see) 17% in the interval $[70, 80)$, with the remaining 4% of experiments resulting in ratios outside this range (and too low to really show up in the diagram).

The first series of experiments, given in figure 1, compares the HNF-based algorithm 3 (dashed lines) with the height-based algorithm 4, including the improvements by short products, on matrices in $SL_n(\mathbb{Z})$ (continuous lines). We tested input lengths 20, 50 and 100 with darker colors representing longer input lengths, that is $len = 100$ is black, $len = 50$ is mid-gray and $len = 20$ is light gray. (For a given input length. The *same set* of matrices was used for both algorithms.)

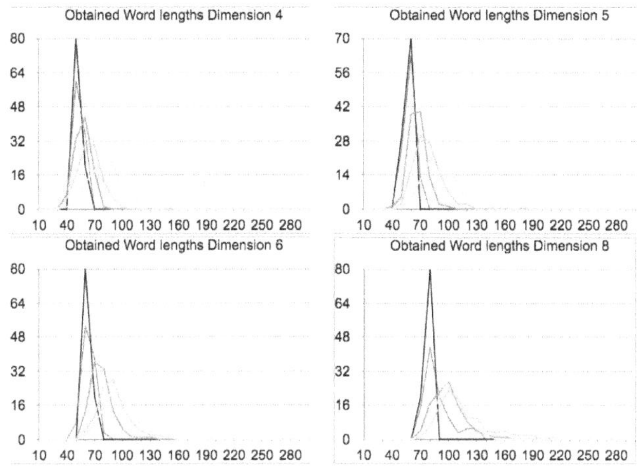

Figure 2: Comparison of obtained word length for SL_n in different dimensions

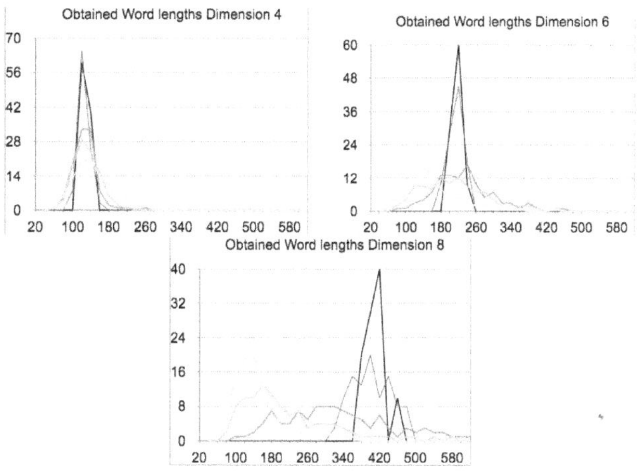

Figure 3: Comparison of obtained word length for Sp_n in different dimensions

One immediately notes from the figures that the height based algorithm produced results that (with some goodwill) can be considered as approximations of a Gaussian distributions, centered not too far off 100.

The pure HNF-based algorithm instead produced a much wider spectrum of results (the curves continue beyond the right edge of the diagram, which is the reason the dashed black curves are practically invisible), with the average length ratio becoming worse with longer word lengths. Concretely, in the case of dimension 4 and input length 100, the HNF-based algorithm produced words whose length ranged between 290 and $8,600,000$ (with an average of $350,000$), making them useless in practice.

We thus conclude (somewhat unsurprisingly, given what is known about integer normal form calculations) that, at similar runtime, algorithm 4 produces significantly shorter words than a systematic HNF calculation.

In the second series of experiments in figure 2 we considered only algorithm 4, but for a broader set of lengths. The input consisted of matrices given by random words of lengths 20, 50, 100, 500 and 2000, with darker colors again representing longer lengths. Again we used $20000/len$ words of length len.

As before we observe curves that approximate a Gaussian distribution, with peaks shifting to the left as the input length increases, and shifting to the right as dimension increases. In the dimension range tested, both changes are small enough to be considered as linear with small constant.

We did not try larger dimensions systematically, as calculations quickly became unreasonably costly.

We note that the seeming improvement in the resulting word lengths for longer input might instead indicate that random words are less likely to be optimally reduced as the length increases.

As for comparison with the optimal word length, this optimal length alas is unknown in the examples (and because of memory limitations cannot be determined for examples with input length 100). Considering the rapid growth observed for small lengths in the number of different elements that can be expressed as words of a particular length, however it seems plausible to have optimal length of the elements considered would differ from the input length by a factor that is logarithmic in the word length rather than linear.

The third series of experiments concerns elements of Sp for various dimensions and lengths, using algorithm 5.

Figure 3 gives the results of these experiments. (Input lengths used and colors are as in the second series.) For each of the random example matrices tested, the approach found a factorization.

In dimension 4 the result is very similar as for SL. With growing dimension the behavior changes: The larger number of generators acting locally on matrices make it more likely that randomly chosen generators commute. If the word length is short one can almost read off the generators involved from the positions of nonzero matrix entries.

Longer words in larger dimensions however show an increased widening of the bell shape and a shift of the peak towards significantly longer words – about 200% for dimension 6 and 400% for dimension 8. This seems to indicate that the approach is feasible for small dimensions (not least for the lack of alternatives) with word lengths not increasing by too much and no observed failure, but that for larger dimensions the ratio to optimal word length gets exponentially worse.

6 CLOSING REMARKS

We have seen practically feasible methods to express elements of $SL_n(\mathbb{Z})$ and $Sp_{2n}(\mathbb{Z})$ (in small dimensions) as products in particular (standard) generating sets.

What is clearly lacking is a proof (and not just experimental evidence) of the approach succeeding in general for Sp, as well as of the produced words being not too worse than the minimal word lengths for the matrices. (The latter seems difficult as the algorithm for SL which is proven to succeed within limited memory – the HNF-based one – produced words of unusable length.) Even without such a proof the heuristic presented will be useful, as long as it produces a result.

The tools motivating our approach were taken from integral matrix normal forms. This raises the question on whether further synergies in either way can be obtained from these problems. A first caveat is that the normal form in the factorization case is always the identity matrix, and that any experiments done here were in tiny dimensions compared with those usually considered for normal forms.

What might be more promising (but we have not investigated) is a relation between word length and size of matrix entries for the transforming matrices for e.g. the Smith Normal Form. We observed that an initial norm-based global reduction of matrix norms produced significantly shorter words. If this can be translated to smaller matrix entries, it would be useful for applications such as the homomorphisms to abelianizations G/G' of finitely presented groups.

7 ACKNOWLEDGMENTS

The author's work has been supported in part by Simons Foundation Collaboration Grants 244502 and 524518 which are gratefully acknowledged. The author also would like to thank the anonymous referees for their helpful remarks.

REFERENCES

[1] Henrik Bäärnhielm, Derek Holt, C. R. Leedham-Green, and E. A. O'Brien. 2015. A practical model for computation with matrix groups. *J. Symbolic Comput.* 68, part 1 (2015), 27–60. https://doi.org/10.1016/j.jsc.2014.08.006

[2] László Babai, Robert Beals, and Ákos Seress. 2009. Polynomial-time Theory of Matrix Groups. In *Proceedings of the 41st Annual ACM Symposium on Theory of Computing, STOC 2009, Bethesda, MD, USA.* ACM Press, 55âĂŞ-64.

[3] Joan S. Birman. 1971. On Siegel's modular group. *Math. Ann.* 191 (1971), 59–68.

[4] Gene Cooperman and Larry Finkelstein. 1992. New methods for using Cayley graphs in interconnection networks. *Discrete Appl. Math.* 37/38 (1992), 95–118.

[5] A. S. Detinko, D. L. Flannery, and A. Hulpke. 2015. Algorithms for arithmetic groups with the congruence subgroup property. *J. Algebra* 421 (2015), 234–259.

[6] A. S. Detinko, D. L. Flannery, and A. Hulpke. 2018. Zariski Density and Computing in Arithmetic Groups. *Math. Comp.* 87, 310 (2018), 967–986. https://doi.org/10.1090/mcom/3236

[7] E. W. Dijkstra. 1959. A note on two problems in connexion with graphs. *Numer. Math.* 1 (1959), 269–271.

[8] Sebastian Egner and Markus Püschel. 1998. Solving puzzles related to permutation groups. In *Proceedings of the 1998 International Symposium on Symbolic and Algebraic Computation,* Oliver Gloor (Ed.). The Association for Computing Machinery, ACM Press, 186–193.

[9] Phillip Gold. 1961. *On the mapping class and symplectic modular group.* Ph.D. Dissertation. New York University.

[10] Alexander J. Hahn and O. Timothy O'Meara. 1989. *The classical groups and K-theory.* Grundlehren der Mathematischen Wissenschaften [Fundamental Principles of Mathematical Sciences], Vol. 291. Springer-Verlag, Berlin.

[11] Jörg Hofmann and Duco van Straten. 2015. Some monodromy groups of finite index in $Sp_4(\mathbb{Z})$. *J. Aust. Math. Soc.* 99, 1 (2015), 48–62.

[12] Derek F. Holt, Bettina Eick, and Eamonn A. O'Brien. 2005. *Handbook of Computational Group Theory.* Chapman & Hall/CRC, Boca Raton, FL.

[13] Helmut Klingen. 1961. Charakterisierung der Siegelschen Modulgruppe durch ein endliches System definierender Relationen. *Math. Ann.* 144 (1961), 64–82.

[14] Daniel Kunkle and Gene Cooperman. 2007. Twenty-six moves suffice for Rubik's cube. In *ISSAC 2007.* ACM, New York, 235–242.

[15] Charles R. Leedham-Green, Cheryl E. Praeger, and Leonard H. Soicher. 1991. Computing with Group Homomorphisms. *J. Symbolic Comput.* 12 (1991), 527–532.

[16] D. D. Long and A. W. Reid. 2011. Small subgroups of SL(3, $\mathbb{Z}$). *Exp. Math.* 20, 4 (2011), 412–425.

[17] Torsten Minkwitz. 1998. An algorithm for solving the factorization problem in permutation groups. *J. Symbolic Comput.* 26, 1 (1998), 89–95.

[18] Tomas Rokicki. 2010. Twenty-Two Moves Suffice for RubikâĂŹs Cube. *The Mathematical Intelligencer* 32 (2010), 33–40. Issue 1.

[19] David Saunders and Zhendong Wan. 2004. Smith normal form of dense integer matrices, fast algorithms into practice. In *ISSAC 2004.* ACM, New York, 274–281. https://doi.org/10.1145/1005285.1005325

[20] René Schoof. 2016. The discrete logarithm problem. In *Open problems in mathematics.* Springer, [Cham], 403–416.

[21] Charles C. Sims. 1970. Computational methods in the study of permutation groups. In *Computational Problems in Abstract Algebra,* John Leech (Ed.). Pergamon press, 169–183.

[22] Arne Storjohann. 1998. Computing Hermite and Smith normal forms of triangular integer matrices. *Linear Algebra Appl.* 282, 1-3 (1998), 25–45.

[23] The GAP Group 2016. *GAP – Groups, Algorithms, and Programming, Version 4.8.6.* The GAP Group, http://www.gap-system.org.

Sparse Polynomial Interpolation With Arbitrary Orthogonal Polynomial Bases

In memory of Bobby F. Caviness (3/24/1940–1/11/2018)

Erdal Imamoglu
Dept. of Math., NCSU
Raleigh, NC, USA

Erich L. Kaltofen
Dept. of Math., NCSU
Raleigh, NC, USA

Zhengfeng Yang
Key Lab Trustworthy Comput.
ECNU, Shanghai, China

ABSTRACT

An algorithm for interpolating a polynomial f from evaluation points whose running time depends on the sparsity t of the polynomial when it is represented as a sum of t Chebyshev Polynomials of the First Kind with non-zero scalar coefficients is given by Lakshman Y. N. and Saunders [SIAM J. Comput., vol. 24, nr. 2 (1995)]; Kaltofen and Lee [JSC, vol. 36, nr. 3–4 (2003)] analyze a randomized early termination version which computes the sparsity t. Those algorithms mirror Prony's algorithm for the standard power basis to the Chebyshev Basis of the First Kind. An alternate algorithm by Arnold's and Kaltofen's [Proc. ISSAC 2015, Sec. 4] uses Prony's original algorithm for standard power terms.

Here we give sparse interpolation algorithms for generalized Chebyshev polynomials, which include the Chebyshev Bases of the Second, Third and Fourth Kind. Our algorithms also reduce to Prony's algorithm. If given on input a bound $B \geq t$ for the sparsity, our new algorithms deterministically recover the sparse representation in the First, Second, Third and Fourth Kind Chebyshev representation from exactly $t + B$ evaluations.

Finally, we generalize our algorithms to bases whose Chebyshev recurrences have parametric scalars. We also show how to compute those parameter values which optimize the sparsity of the representation in the corresponding basis, similar to computing a sparsest shift.

ACM Reference Format:
Erdal Imamoglu, Erich L. Kaltofen, and Zhengfeng Yang. 2018. Sparse Polynomial Interpolation With Arbitrary Orthogonal Polynomial Bases: In memory of Bobby F. Caviness (3/24/1940–1/11/2018). In *ISSAC'18: 2018 ACM Int'l Symposium on Symbolic & Algebraic Computation, July 16–19, 2018, NY, NY, USA.* ACM, New York, NY, USA, 8 pages. https://doi.org/10.1145/3208976.3208999

1. INTRODUCTION

We consider the problem of reconstructing the term degrees and non-zero coefficients of a univariate polynomial f whose evaluation we can obtain at arbitrary values for the variable for a black box for the polynomial. Here f is represented in an orthogonal term basis $P_0(x), P_1(x), P_2(x), \ldots$

$$f(x) = \sum_{j=1}^{t} c_j P_{\delta_j}(x), c_j \in \mathsf{K}, c_j \neq 0, 0 \leq \delta_1 < \delta_2 < \cdots < \delta_t \quad (1)$$

where P_δ are Chebyshev Polynomials of the first, second, or third kind and where K is an arbitrary field of characteristic $\neq 2$. Our algorithms compute the term degrees δ_j and term coefficients c_j, hence perform a sparse polynomial interpolation with one of the Chebyshev bases. The main idea is to reduce the sparse interpolation problem in Chebyshev basis to a sparse interpolation problem in the power basis and apply Prony's algorithm [5, 22] (the 1959 Bose-Chaudhuri-Hocquenghem error correction decoding algorithm) to the latter problem.

As with Prony's algorithm, the sparsity of t need not be given on input. We consider two early termination strategies that determine t: if a bound $B \geq t$ is given on input, we compute t and f deterministically from $t + B$ evaluations. A difficulty is that the constructed Prony problem has sparsity $2t$ and we have to exploit its special structure to reduce the number of evaluations. Our deterministic algorithm can be implemented in $(t + B)^{2+o(1)}$ field operations, degree-t polynomial root finding, and computing t integer logarithms in K. The quadratic exponent is a consequence of the lack of fast main-diagonal Toeplitz solvers with arbitrary look-ahead (cf. [4, 6, 23]). For finite coefficient fields K with a fast discrete logarithm algorithm [20] our algorithm is of bit complexity $((t + B) \log(\deg f))^{O(1)}$. We can also compute t and f by Kaltofen's and Lee's randomized early termination strategy from $2t + 2$ evaluations (see [1, Sec. 4.2]). In order to use soft-linear randomized Toeplitz/Hankel solvers with $t^{1+o(1)}$ arithmetic operations [14] one needs to oversample to $2B$ or $2^{\lceil \log_2(2t+2) \rceil}$ evaluations, respectively.

We now recall the properties of the Chebyshev Polynomials of the First, Second, Third and Fourth Kind. Traditionally, those are n-degree polynomials in x over the field of real numbers denoted by $T_n(x)$ (First Kind), $U_n(x)$ (Second Kind), $V_n(x)$ (Third Kind) and $W_n(x)$ (Fourth Kind). If $P_n(x)$ denotes any of those four polynomials, we have

$$P_0(x) = 1, \quad P_n(x) = 2\,x\,P_{n-1}(x) - P_{n-2}(x) \text{ for } n \geq 2, \quad (2)$$

$P_n = T_n, U_n, V_n, W_n$, and the distinct initializations at $n = 1$,

$$T_1(x) = x, \quad U_1(x) = 2x, \quad V_1(x) = 2x - 1, \quad W_1(x) = 2x + 1. \quad (3)$$

An alternative to (2) is

$$\begin{bmatrix} P_n(x) \\ P_{n+1}(x) \end{bmatrix} = \begin{bmatrix} 0 & 1 \\ -1 & 2x \end{bmatrix}^n \begin{bmatrix} 1 \\ P_1(x) \end{bmatrix} \quad \text{for } n \in \mathbb{Z}. \quad (4)$$

Note that (4) extends the subscript range n to negative integers and by computing the power of 2×2 coefficient matrix gives an algorithm for evaluating all P_n in $O(\log(n))$ scalar operations. All four kinds yield a vector space basis for the ring of polynomials over any field K of characteristic $\neq 2$. From now on, we shall speak of

ISSAC'18, July 16–19, 2018, New York, NY, USA

ACM ISBN 978-1-4503-5550-6/18/07...$15.00
https://doi.org/10.1145/3208976.3208999

Chebyshev-1, Chebyshev-2, Chebyshev-3 and Chebyshev-4 polynomials and bases in reference to first, second, third and fourth kind.

The third and fourth kind polynomials are not as common, because we have $W_n(x) = (-1)^n V_n(-x)$ and $V_n(x) = T_{2n+1}(z)/z$ and $W_n(x) = U_{2n}(z)$ for $z = \sqrt{(x+1)/2}$, that is, the two identities are stated in the algebraic function field $\mathsf{K}(x)[z]/(z^2 - (x+1)/2)$.

There are some well known properties that are the basis of sparse interpolation in Chebyshev-1 Basis.

Fact 1.1. *Let $m, n \in \mathbb{Z}_{\geq 0}$. Then the following hold:*

i. $T_n(T_m(x)) = T_{mn}(x) = T_m(T_n(x))$.

ii. $T_n(\frac{x+\frac{1}{x}}{2}) = \frac{x^n+\frac{1}{x^n}}{2}$ *for all $n \geq 0$.*

Based on Fact 1.1.i, which is that Chebyshev-1 Polynomials commute with respect to composition, Lakshman and Saunders [19] have mirrored Prony's algorithm in order to reconstruct the list of non-zero coefficients c_j and the list of corresponding degrees δ_j from evaluations of

$$f(x)=c_1 T_{\delta_1}(x)+\cdots+c_t T_{\delta_t}(x), c_j\neq 0, 0\leq\delta_1<\delta_2<\cdots<\delta_t \quad (5)$$

at $x = T_0(\beta), T_1(\beta), \ldots$ for a scalar β (see also [1, 9, 18, Sec. 3]). Their reconstruction algorithm is thus a sparse interpolation algorithm in Chebyshev-1 Basis. For sparsity in Chebyshev-2 Polynomials U_n one obstruction is the lack of the commuting property of term substitution. However, performing the substitution given in Fact 1.1.ii, Arnold and Kaltofen [1, Sec. 4] directly reduced the sparse polynomial (5) to a sparse Laurent polynomial in power (standard) basis. More precisely, for f in (5) we have

$$g(y) \stackrel{\text{def}}{=} f((y+\tfrac{1}{y})/2) = \textstyle\sum_{j=1}^{t} \frac{c_j}{2}(y^{\delta_j} + y^{-\delta_j}) \quad (6)$$

and Prony's algorithm can reconstruct the sparse Laurent polynomial g. Here we use the corresponding properties to Fact 1.1.ii for U_n, V_n, W_n, namely,

$$(y-\tfrac{1}{y})\ U_n((y+\tfrac{1}{y})/2) = y^{n+1} - \tfrac{1}{y^{n+1}}, \quad (7)$$

$$(y+\tfrac{1}{y})\ V_n((y^2+\tfrac{1}{y^2})/2) = y^{2n+1} + \tfrac{1}{y^{2n+1}}, \quad (8)$$

$$(y-\tfrac{1}{y})\ W_n((y^2+\tfrac{1}{y^2})/2) = y^{2n+1} - \tfrac{1}{y^{2n+1}}. \quad (9)$$

Note that the multiplicative preconditioner $y \pm 1/y$ is introduced before interpolating the substituted $f((y+\frac{1}{y})/2)$ or $f((y^2+\frac{1}{y^2})/2)$, thus overcoming the long-known obstruction for sparse interpolation with a Chebyshev-2 Basis. Potts and Tasche [21, Equation 4.2] have introduced a corresponding trigonometric multiplier: $\sin(\alpha) \times U_n(\cos(\alpha)) = \sin((n+1)\alpha)$, which with $y = e^{i\alpha}$ is (7). Our substitution does not require the evaluation of a transcendental function and can be realized as an exact algorithm even over a finite field, while the algorithm in [21] uses floating point arithmetic. We think of the polynomial $f(x)$ as a black box polynomial that can be arbitrarily probed. For Kaltofen and Lee [18] randomized sparse interpolation from $2t+2$ values with early termination, an upper bound of $\deg(f)$ is required on input for achieving success probability $\geq 1/2$, for otherwise the polynomials $\prod_j(x-\beta_j)$ and 0 are indistinguishable, where β_j ranges over all possible random choices of evaluation points. For our bases, see Theorem 5.2.

The Lakshman-Saunders [19] method and the Arnold-Kaltofen [1, Sec. 4] substitution (6), which is the approach also here, are related by the substitution $\beta = (\omega + 1/\omega)/2$ for the base points β and ω of the evaluations. That substitution has 2 effects: 1. the arising Toeplitz-plus-Hankel system in Lakshman-Saunders becomes a Toeplitz system; 2. the degrees of the terms are computed as logarithms with integral output values. The Toeplitz matrix allows for the use of the Berlekamp-Massey algorithm. The substitution (6) and (7-9) double the sparsity in the arising Laurent polynomial (an exception is for Chebyshev-1 Basis with $\delta_1 = 0$ when the sparsity is $2t-1$). Luckily, every evaluation $g(\zeta)$ at $\zeta \in \mathsf{K}$, $\zeta \neq \pm 1$, yields a second evaluation $g(1/\zeta) = g(\zeta)$ at $1/\zeta$ for (6,8) and a second evaluation $g(1/\zeta) = -g(\zeta)$ at $1/\zeta$ for (7,9). An exception is $\zeta = \pm 1$, which is a Prony point, and the algorithm in [1, Sec. 4.1] for Chebyshev-1 Basis used one additional evaluation. Here we show that the extra evaluation can be avoided by exploiting additional structure in the arising Prony problem for $g(y)$, thus achieving the optimal number of evaluations for the new substitution method in all cases; see Section 4. The conversion to ω also allows for a discrete logarithm-based computation of all δ_j, even from values of $T_{\delta_j}(\beta)$ as in the original Lakshman-Saunders algorithm; see [11].

Finally, we consider bases given by the recurrence

$$V_0^{[u,v,w]}(x)=1,\ V_1^{[u,v,w]}(x)=ux+w,$$

$$V_n^{[u,v,w]}(x)=vxV_{n-1}^{[u,v,w]}(x)-V_{n-2}^{[u,v,w]}(x) \text{ for } n \geq 2, \quad (10)$$

where $u, v, w \in \mathsf{K}$, $u\neq 0$, $v\neq 0$ and K is a field. Our algorithm here for the Chebyshev-2 basis generalizes and computes the sparse representation with terms from (10); see Section 5. One may also seek for a given polynomial $f \in \mathsf{K}[x]$ those parameters u, v, w which yield the maximum sparsity for the corresponding basis. We show how to compute in polynomial time in $\deg(f)$ the optimal pairs u, v, w; see Section 6. The problem is analogous to computing the sparsest shift [8] in the standard powers of variables basis.

2. CHEBYSHEV-1 BASIS WITH SPARSITY KNOWN ON INPUT

Let K be a field of $\mathrm{char}(\mathsf{K}) \neq 2$. A black box polynomial $f(x) \in \mathsf{K}[x]$ can be written as a t-sparse linear combination of Chebyshev-1 Polynomials $c_1 T_{\delta_1}(x)+\cdots+c_t T_{\delta_t}(x)$, see (5). We seek to determine the coefficients $c_j \in \mathsf{K} \setminus \{0\}$ and the term degrees $\delta_j \in \mathbb{Z}_{\geq 0}$ from evaluations $a_i = f((\omega^i + \omega^{-i})/2)$, $(i = 0, 1, \ldots, 2t-1)$ of the black box for $f(x)$, where $\omega \in \mathsf{K}$, $\omega \neq 0$. The term values ω^{δ_j} of the base point ω are required to be sufficiently distinct, and the δ_j to be recoverable from them. We first assume that we know the sparsity t on input. We also assume that we have a factorization algorithm over K and can compute integral δ from ω^δ.

We define

$$g(y) \stackrel{\text{def}}{=} f(\tfrac{y+y^{-1}}{2}) = \textstyle\sum_{j=1}^{t} \frac{c_j}{2}(y^{\delta_j} + y^{-\delta_j}) \in \mathsf{K}[y, y^{-1}]. \quad (11)$$

The function $g(y)$ is a Laurent polynomial. Let $\omega \in \mathsf{K} \setminus \{0\}$ such that for $i \in \{0, 1, \ldots, 2t-1\}$,

$$a_i \stackrel{\text{def}}{=} g(\omega^i) = f(\tfrac{\omega^i+\omega^{-i}}{2}) = f(T_i(\beta)), \beta \stackrel{\text{def}}{=} \tfrac{\omega+\omega^{-1}}{2}, \quad (12)$$

and for $1\leq i_1<i_2\leq t$, $T_{\delta_{i_1}}(\beta)\neq T_{\delta_{i_2}}(\beta)$ if $\delta_{i_1}\neq\delta_{i_2}$. Note that $a_{-i}=a_i$.

Lemma 2.1. *If $T_{\delta_{i_1}}(\beta) \neq T_{\delta_{i_2}}(\beta)$ for $1 \leq i_1 < i_2 \leq t$, then $\omega^{\delta_{i_1}} \neq \omega^{\delta_{i_2}}$ or $\omega^{\delta_{i_1}} \neq \omega^{-\delta_{i_2}}$.*

Proof. If $T_{\delta_{i_1}}(\beta) \neq T_{\delta_{i_2}}(\beta)$, then $\omega^{\delta_{i_1}} + \omega^{-\delta_{i_1}} \neq \omega^{\delta_{i_2}} + \omega^{-\delta_{i_2}}$. Hence $(\omega^{\delta_{i_1}}\omega^{\delta_{i_2}} - 1)(\omega^{\delta_{i_1}} - \omega^{\delta_{i_2}}) \neq 0$ and so $\omega^{\delta_{i_1}} \neq \omega^{-\delta_{i_2}}$ or $\omega^{\delta_{i_1}} \neq \omega^{\delta_{i_2}}$. □

Lemma 2.2. *Let $1 \leq i_1 < i_2 \leq t$. If the set $\{\omega^{\delta_{i_1}}, \omega^{\delta_{i_2}}, \omega^{-\delta_{i_1}}, \omega^{-\delta_{i_2}}\}$ has at least three elements, then $T_{\delta_{i_1}}(\beta) \neq T_{\delta_{i_2}}(\beta)$.*

Proof. If the set $\{\omega^{\delta_{i_1}}, \omega^{\delta_{i_2}}, \omega^{-\delta_{i_1}}, \omega^{-\delta_{i_2}}\}$ has at least three elements, then "$\omega^{\delta_{i_1}} \neq \omega^{\delta_{i_2}}$ and $\omega^{\delta_{i_1}} \neq \omega^{-\delta_{i_2}}$" and "$\omega^{\delta_{i_1}} \neq \omega^{-\delta_{i_1}}$ or $\omega^{\delta_{i_2}} \neq \omega^{-\delta_{i_2}}$". Then $2T_{\delta_{i_1}}(\beta) = (\omega^{\delta_{i_1}} + \omega^{-\delta_{i_1}}) \neq (\omega^{\delta_{i_2}} + \omega^{-\delta_{i_2}}) = 2T_{\delta_{i_2}}(\beta)$. □

Corollary 2.3. *If the set $\{\omega^{-\delta_t}, \omega^{-\delta_{t-1}}, ..., \omega^{-\delta_1}, \omega^{\delta_1}, ..., \omega^{\delta_{t-1}}, \omega^{\delta_t}\}$ has at least $2t-1$ elements, then $T_{\delta_{i_1}}(\beta) \neq T_{\delta_{i_2}}(\beta)$ for $1 \le i_1 < i_2 \le t$.*

We can interpolate the Laurent polynomial (11) with Prony's algorithm [22] from its $2t$ evaluations $a_0, \ldots, a_{2t-1}$. We query the black box polynomial $f(x)$ to get these evaluations. Since $a_{-i} = a_i$, we actually have $4t-1$ evaluations of $g(y)$: $a_{-2t+1}, \ldots, a_0, \ldots, a_{2t-1}$.

Let α be a symbol for a_{2t}. If $\delta_1 = 0$, then a value for α is not needed for computing the term locator polynomial $\Lambda(z)$ for $g(y)$. The corresponding $2t \times 2t$ matrix $H = [a_{i+j-(2t-1)}]_{i,j=0}^{2t-1}$ will then have been identified by the Berlekamp/Massey algorithm as singular. If $2t = \deg(\Lambda(z))$, then the matrix is identified as non-singular, and $\Lambda(z)$ is computed as a linear form $\Lambda_\alpha(z) = \Lambda^{[0]}(z) + \alpha\Lambda^{[1]}(z)$ from the system

$$\begin{bmatrix} a_{-2t+1} & a_{-2t+2} \ldots a_{-t+1} \ldots & a_{-1} & a_0 \\ a_{-2t+2} & a_{-2t+3} \ldots a_{-t+2} \ldots & a_0 & a_1 \\ \vdots & \vdots \quad \vdots & \vdots & \vdots \\ a_{-1} & a_0 \ \ldots a_{t-2} \ldots & a_{2t-3} & a_{2t-2} \\ a_0 & a_1 \ \ldots a_{t-1} \ldots & a_{2t-2} & a_{2t-1} \end{bmatrix} \begin{bmatrix} 1 \\ \lambda_1 \\ \vdots \\ \lambda_{2t-2} \\ \lambda_{2t-1} \end{bmatrix} = - \begin{bmatrix} a_1 \\ a_2 \\ \vdots \\ a_{2t-1} \\ \alpha \end{bmatrix}. \quad (13)$$

In this case, the term locator polynomial of (11) is

$$\Lambda(z) = \prod_{j=1}^{t}((z - \omega^{\delta_j})(z - \omega^{-\delta_j})) = z^{2t} + \lambda_{2t-1}z^{2t-1} + \cdots + \lambda_1 z + 1$$

and it is a reciprocal polynomial, i.e., $\lambda_{2t-j} = \lambda_j$, ($\lambda_{2t} = \lambda_0 = 1$). We show that (in Theorem 2.5 below), if the set $\{\omega^{-\delta_t}, \omega^{-\delta_{t-1}}, \ldots, \omega^{-\delta_1}, \omega^{\delta_1}, \ldots, \omega^{\delta_{t-1}}, \omega^{\delta_t}\}$ has $2t$ elements, then α is uniquely determined by the symmetry conditions of the coefficients of $\Lambda(z)$. Hence, to determine the δ_j, we do not need to evaluate the black box polynomial $f(x)$ at $T_{2t}(\beta)$ to get a_{2t}.

From the symmetry conditions of the coefficients of $\Lambda(z)$ the system (13) collapses to the following system:

$$\bar{H} \cdot \left[\lambda_t/2 \ \lambda_{t-1} \ldots \lambda_1\right]^{\mathrm{Tr}} = - \left[a_1 + a_{2t-1} \ \ a_2 + a_{2t-2} \ldots 2a_t\right]^{\mathrm{Tr}} \quad (14)$$

where $\bar{H}$ is a "fold" of the coefficient matrix of (13):

$$\bar{H} = \begin{bmatrix} 2a_{t-1} & \cdots & a_1 + a_{2t-3} & a_0 + a_{2t-2} \\ 2a_{t-2} & \cdots & a_0 + a_{2t-4} & a_1 + a_{2t-3} \\ \vdots & & \vdots & \vdots \\ 2a_0 & \cdots & 2a_{t-2} & 2a_{t-1} \end{bmatrix}. \quad (15)$$

We have that $\bar{H}$ is non-singular:

Lemma 2.4. *The matrix $\bar{H}$ in (15) is non-singular.*

Proof. $\bar{H} = J_t \cdot A$ where A is the non-singular matrix in Lemma 3.2 in [1] (for $r = 0$ and $s = 1$) and $J_t \in \mathsf{K}^{t \times t}$ is the exchange matrix (row-reversed identity matrix). Note that by our assumptions on ω the $T_{\delta_j}(\beta)$ are distinct. □

Therefore, we can determine the coefficients $\lambda_1 = \lambda_{2t-1}, \ldots, \lambda_{t-1} = \lambda_{t+1}$, and λ_t of the term locator polynomial $\Lambda(z)$ by solving the folded system (14).

Theorem 2.5. *If the set $\{\omega^{-\delta_t}, \ldots, \omega^{-\delta_1}, \omega^{\delta_1}, \ldots, \omega^{\delta_t}\}$ has $2t$ elements, then α is uniquely determined by the symmetry conditions of the coefficients of the term locator polynomial $\Lambda(z)$ of (11).*

Proof. If there were two values for α, then the folded system (14) of the system (13) would have two different solutions. Since $\bar{H}$ is non-singular, this is impossible. Hence α is unique. □

Therefore, to compute the term locator polynomial $\Lambda(z)$ of (11) we need $2t$ evaluations: $a_0, \ldots, a_{2t-1}$. A root ρ of the term locator polynomial is of the form $\rho = \omega^{\pm\delta_j}$. We can compute the δ_j in (5) from the (possibly discrete) logarithms of the roots of the term locator polynomial as it is commonly done in [2, 7, 10, 16, 18]. After determining the δ_j, ($j = 1, \ldots, t$), we compute the coefficients c_j in (5) by solving the non-singular transposed Vandermonde system

$$\left[\rho_1^i \cdots \rho_t^i \ \rho_t^{-i} \cdots \rho_1^{-i}\right]_{0 \le i \le 2t-1} \cdot \left[c_1 \ldots c_t \ c_t \ldots c_1\right]^{\mathrm{Tr}} = \left[2a_0 \ 2a_1 \ldots 2a_{2t-1}\right]^{\mathrm{Tr}}. \quad (16)$$

Here the ρ_j and ρ_j^{-1}, ($j = 1, \ldots, t$), are the roots of the term locator polynomial $\Lambda(z)$. An $t^{1+o(1)}$-time algorithm is in [17, Sec. 5].

Remark 2.1. If the set $\{\omega^{-\delta_t}, \omega^{-\delta_{t-1}}, ..., \omega^{-\delta_1}, \omega^{\delta_1}, ..., \omega^{\delta_{t-1}}, \omega^{\delta_t}\}$ has $2t-1$ elements, then we can determine the coefficients of the term locator polynomial by solving the system

$$\left[a_{i+j-2t}\right]_{1 \le i,j \le 2t-1} \cdot \left[1 \ \lambda_1 \ldots \lambda_{2t-2}\right]^{\mathrm{Tr}} = - \left[a_1 \ a_2 \ldots a_{2t-1}\right]^{\mathrm{Tr}}$$

(cf. (13)). In this case, for only one δ_j, we have $\omega^{\delta_j} = \omega^{-\delta_j}$. After determining the roots of the term locator polynomial, we can identify that specific δ_j. □

To summarize, we collect the steps of our algorithm as follows:

2.1. Algorithm Sparse Chebyshev-1 Interpolation

Input:
- ▸ A black box polynomial $f(x) \in \mathsf{K}[x]$ where K is a field with $\mathrm{char}(\mathsf{K}) \neq 2$.
- ▸ The sparsity t of $f(x)$.
- ▸ $\omega \in \mathsf{K} \setminus \{0\}$ such that the set of term values $\{\omega^{-\delta_t}, \omega^{-\delta_{t-1}}, \ldots, \omega^{-\delta_1}, \omega^{\delta_1}, \ldots, \omega^{\delta_{t-1}}, \omega^{\delta_t}\}$ has at least $2t$ elements or $2t-1$ elements with $\delta_1 = 0$.
- ▸ A factorization algorithm over K.
- ▸ A integer-valued-logarithm-base-ω algorithm in K.

Output: ▸ The coefficients c_j and the term degrees δ_j such that $f(x) = \sum_{j=1}^{t} c_j T_{\delta_j}(x) \in \mathsf{K}[x]$.

1. *For $0 \le i \le 2t-1$, get the evaluations $a_i = g(\omega^i)$, as in (12), of the Laurent polynomial (11).*
2. *Solve (13) by the Berlekamp/Massey Algorithm to get the coefficients of the term locator polynomial $\Lambda(z)$. Use the symmetry of the term locator polynomial to find the unique α.*
3. *Find all roots of the term locator polynomial. The roots are of the form $\omega^{\pm\delta_j}$. Compute the δ_j from integer logarithms (discrete logarithms if K is a finite field) of the roots of the term locator polynomial.*
4. *Solve the system (16) to get the coefficients c_j.*
5. *Return the δ_j and the c_j.*

3. CHEBYSHEV-2 BASIS WITH SPARSITY KNOWN ON INPUT

Let K be a field of $\mathrm{char}(\mathsf{K}) \neq 2$. We now consider the representation of a black box polynomial $f(x) \in \mathsf{K}[x]$ as a t-sparse linear combination of Chebyshev-2 Polynomials, i.e.,

$$f(x) = c_1 U_{\delta_1}(x) + \cdots + c_t U_{\delta_t}(x) \in \mathsf{K}[x] \quad (17)$$

where $c_j \in \mathsf{K} \setminus \{0\}$ and $\delta_j \in \mathbb{Z}_{\ge 0}$ such that $\delta_1 < \cdots < \delta_t$. Again, we seek to compute the coefficients $c_j \in \mathsf{K} \setminus \{0\}$ and the term degrees $\delta_j \in \mathbb{Z}_{\ge 0}$ from evaluations $f((\omega^i + \omega^{-i})/2)$, ($i = 0, 1, \ldots, 2t-1$) of the black box for $f(x)$, where $\omega \in \mathsf{K}$, $\omega \neq 0$. The term values ω^{δ_j} of the base point ω are required to be sufficiently distinct, and the δ_j to be recoverable from them. Again, we assume that we know the sparsity t.

Our algorithm proceeds as the Chebyshev-1 Algorithm in Section 2 with the following changes: we define

$$g(y) \stackrel{\text{def}}{=} (y - y^{-1}) f(\tfrac{y+y^{-1}}{2}) = \textstyle\sum_{j=1}^{t} \frac{c_j}{2}(y^{\delta_j+1} - y^{-(\delta_j+1)}) \in \mathsf{K}[y, y^{-1}] \quad (18)$$

(see (7)). The function $g(y)$ is a Laurent polynomial. We Prony interpolate for a base point $\omega \in \mathsf{K} \setminus \{0\}$ the values

$$a_0 = 0, a_i = -a_{-i} \stackrel{\text{def}}{=} g(\omega^i) = (\omega - \omega^{-1}) f(\tfrac{\omega^i + \omega^{-i}}{2}), \quad (19)$$

$i \in \{1, \ldots, 2t\}$, and assume that the set of shifted term values $\{\omega^{-(\delta_t+1)}, \omega^{-(\delta_{t-1}+1)}, \ldots, \omega^{-(\delta_1+1)}, \omega^{\delta_1+1}, \ldots, \omega^{\delta_{t-1}+1}, \omega^{\delta_t+1}\}$ has $2t$ or $2t-1$ elements. The difficulties which arose in the Chebyshev-1 case due to $i = 0$ yielding a single evaluation do not occur: $a_0 = 0$ needs no evaluation, and we compute the term locator polynomial from $2t$ black box probes. Algorithm 5.1 below is a generalized variant, which uses randomization to compute t.

4. DETERMINISTIC EARLY TERMINATION WITH A SPARSITY BOUND

We now relax the assumption that on input one has the exact sparsity t, but assume that on input one has an upper bound $B \geq t$ for the sparsity. Our objective is to interpolate with exactly $t + B$ evaluations. Here we assume that the black box for f can be queried as our algorithm proceeds.

Let $a_i = g(\omega^i)$, as in (12), where $g(y)$ is given in (11), and

$$\mathcal{H} = [a_{i+j-(2t+2B+1)}]_{1 \leq i,j \leq 2t+2B}, \quad (20)$$

where $B \geq t$. We will consider non-singular square submatrices of $\mathcal{H}$ in the right upper corner.

Remark 4.1. *The 0×0 matrix is called the* empty matrix. *The empty matrix is considered to be non-singular. In Algorithm 4.1 Step 2b below, if $r = 0$, then $\mathcal{H}_R$ in Step 3 is the empty matrix. In this case $\Lambda(z) = z^0 = 1$.*

4.1. Algorithm Chebyshev-1 Term Locator Polynomial

Input: ▸ A black box polynomial $f(x) \in \mathsf{K}[x]$ where K is a field with $\mathrm{char}(\mathsf{K}) \neq 2$.
▸ An upper bound $B \geq t$ for the sparsity t of $f(x)$.
▸ $\omega \in \mathsf{K} \setminus \{0\}$ such that the set of term values
$$\{\omega^{-\delta_t}, \omega^{-\delta_{t-1}}, \ldots, \omega^{-\delta_1}, \omega^{\delta_1}, \ldots, \omega^{\delta_{t-1}}, \omega^{\delta_t}\} \quad (21)$$
has $2t$ elements or $2t-1$ elements with $\delta_1 = 0$.

Output: ▸ Sparsity t and the term locator polynomial $\Lambda(z)$.

1. *Get the evaluations $a_0, \ldots, a_{B-1}$. If $a_0 = \cdots = a_{B-1} = 0$, then return $t = 0$ and $\Lambda(z) = 1$. Otherwise, proceed to the next step.* Here $a_i = g(w^i)$, as in (12), where $g(y)$ is given in (11). Note that $a_{-i} = a_i$. In Lemma 4.1 below, we prove that $a_0 = \cdots = a_{B-1} = 0$ implies $f(x)$ is identically zero, so $t = 0$ and $\Lambda(z) = z^0 = 1$.
2. *Locate a non-singular leading principal submatrix $\mathcal{H}_{2r-1}$ or $\mathcal{H}_{2r}$ of (20) as follows:*

2a. $r_{old} \leftarrow 0$.

2b. *For r from $r_{old} + 1$ to B do the following:*

2(b)i. *Construct the Hankel matrix* $\mathcal{H}_{2r-1} = \begin{bmatrix} a_{-2r+2} & \cdots & a_0 \\ \vdots & & \vdots \\ a_0 & \cdots & a_{2r-2} \end{bmatrix}$.
If $\mathcal{H}_{2r-1}$ is non-singular, then $r_{old} \leftarrow r$ and break the loop. Otherwise, proceed to the next step.

2(b)ii. *Construct the Hankel matrix* $\mathcal{H}_{2r} = \begin{bmatrix} a_{-2r+1} & \cdots & a_0 \\ \vdots & & \vdots \\ a_0 & \cdots & a_{2r-1} \end{bmatrix}$.
If $\mathcal{H}_{2r}$ is non-singular, then $r_{old} \leftarrow r$ and break the loop. Otherwise, proceed to the next step.
If there is no such non-singular leading principal submatrix, $\mathcal{H}_{2r-1}$ or $\mathcal{H}_{2r}$, then the given bound B is not correct. Note that, if the term values (21) collapse, this algorithm can return a wrong sparsity and a wrong term locator polynomial.

3. *Let $\mathcal{H}_R$ denote the non-singular matrix constructed at the previous step.*

3a. *If the rank of $\mathcal{H}_R$ is odd (the case $R = 2r-1$), then do the following:*

3(a)i. *Solve $\mathcal{H}_R \cdot [\lambda_0 \ldots \lambda_{2r-2}]^{\mathrm{Tr}} = -[a_1 \ldots a_{2r-1}]^{\mathrm{Tr}}$ to compute the linear generator $z^{2r-1} + \lambda_{2r-2}z^{2r-2} + \cdots + \lambda_0$.*

3(a)ii. *For i from 1 to $B - r$ do the following:*
-If $\sum_{k=0}^{2r-2} \lambda_k a_{k-1+i} \neq -a_{2r-2+i}$ then go to Step 2b to locate the next non-singular leading principal submatrix. Otherwise, proceed to the next step.

3(a)iii. *For i from 1 to $B - r + 1$ do the following:*
-If $\sum_{k=0}^{2r-2} \lambda_k a_{k-2r+3-i} \neq -a_{2-i}$ then go to Step 2b to locate the next non-singular leading principal submatrix $\mathcal{H}_R$. Otherwise, proceed to the next step.
At this point, we have found no discrepancies. We prove in Theorem 4.2 below that, in this situation, $t = r$.

3(a)iv. *Return $t = r$ and $\Lambda(z) = z^{2r-1} + \lambda_{2r-2}z^{2r-2} + \cdots + \lambda_0$.*

3b. *If the rank of $\mathcal{H}_R$ is even (the case R=$2r$), then do the following:*

3(b)i. *Compute the linear generator $z^{2r} + \lambda_{2r-1}z^{2r-1} + \cdots + \lambda_0$ of $a_{-2r+1}, \ldots, a_0, \ldots, a_{2r-1}$ as explained in Section 2.*

3(b)ii. *If $\lambda_{2r-1} = \lambda_1, \ldots, \lambda_{r+1} = \lambda_{r-1}$, then proceed to the next step. Otherwise, go to Step 2b to locate the next non-singular leading principal submatrix $\mathcal{H}_R$.*

3(b)iii. *For i from 1 to $B - r$ do the following:*
-(Figure 1) *If $\sum_{k=0}^{2r-1} \lambda_k a_{k-1+i} \neq -a_{2r-1+i}$ then go to Step 2b to locate the next non-singular leading principal submatrix $\mathcal{H}_R$. Otherwise, proceed to the next step.*
At this point, we have found no discrepancies. We prove in Theorem 4.2 below that, in this situation, $t = r$.

3(b)iv. *Return $t = r$ and $\Lambda(z) = z^{2r} + \lambda_{2r-1}z^{2r-1} + \cdots + \lambda_0$.*

Figure 1: Intermediate step in Algorithm 4.1

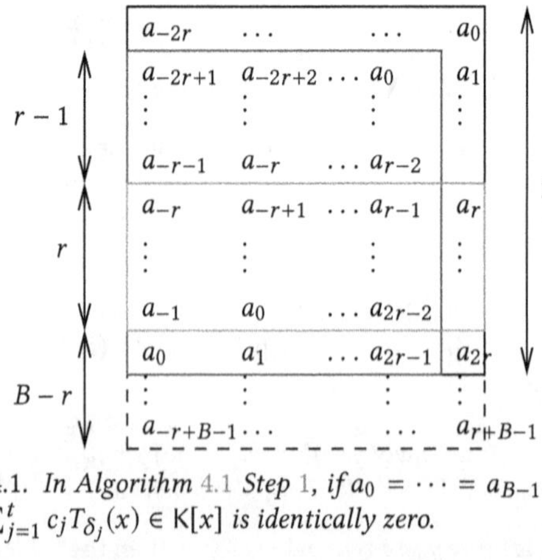

Lemma 4.1. *In Algorithm 4.1 Step 1, if $a_0 = \cdots = a_{B-1} = 0$, then $f(x) = \sum_{j=1}^{t} c_j T_{\delta_j}(x) \in \mathsf{K}[x]$ is identically zero.*

Proof. Let $a_0 = \cdots = a_{B-1} = 0$. Assume that $f(x)$ is a t-sparse non-zero polynomial in the Chebyshev Basis of the first kind. Since

$a_i = a_{-i}$ (from (11)), we have $a_{-(B-1)} = \cdots = a_0 = \cdots = a_{B-1} = 0$. Let $\Lambda(z)$ be the term locator polynomial of the Laurent polynomial $g(y)$ (11). The roots $\rho_1, \ldots, \rho_{2t}$ of $\Lambda(z)$ are of the form $\omega^{\pm\delta_j}$, $(1 \le j \le t)$. Let $\rho_1 = \omega^{-\delta_t}, \ldots, \rho_t = \omega^{-\delta_1}, \rho_{t+1} = \omega^{\delta_1}, \ldots, \rho_{2t} = \omega^{\delta_t}$. From (11) we know $g(y) = f(\frac{y+y^{-1}}{2}) = \sum_{j=1}^{t} \frac{c_j}{2}(y^{\delta_j} + y^{-\delta_j})$. We can find the coefficients $c_1, \ldots, c_t$ of the Laurent polynomial $g(y)$ by solving the following system (cf. (16)):
$[\rho_j^i]_{-(B-1)\le i\le B-1, 1\le j\le 2t} \cdot [c_t \ldots c_1 c_1 \ldots c_t]^{\mathrm{Tr}} = [2a_i]_{-(B-1)\le i \le B-1} = 0$.
From the symmetry conditions of the coefficients of $g(y)$ the above system folds to $\mathcal{R} \cdot [c_1 \ldots c_t]^{\mathrm{Tr}} = [0 \ldots 0]^{\mathrm{Tr}}$ where

$$\mathcal{R} = [\rho_j^{-i} + \rho_j^{i}]_{i=0,1,\ldots B-1,\, j=t,t-1,\ldots,1}.$$

When $B = t$, the determinant of $\mathcal{R}$ factors as

$$\det(\mathcal{R}) = 2/(\rho_1^{t-1} \cdots \rho_t^{t-1}) \cdot \prod_{1\le j<\ell\le t} \Big((\rho_j - \rho_\ell)\cdot(\rho_j\rho_\ell - 1)\Big),$$

which is $\neq 0$ because $\rho_j \neq \rho_\ell$ and $\rho_j \neq \rho_\ell^{-1}$ for $1 \le j < \ell \le t$. Therefore, $c_1 = \cdots = c_t = 0$, contradicting to our assumption. Hence, $f(x)$ is identically zero. □

THEOREM 4.2. *For the largest non-singular matrix $\mathcal{H}_R$ (where $R = 2r$ or $R = 2r - 1$) in Algorithm 4.1, $t = r$.*

PROOF. • Case $R = 2r$: Let $\mathcal{H}_R$ be the largest non-singular matrix in Algorithm 4.1. So, $\mathcal{H}_R$ satisfies the condition in Step 3(b)iii.

- Case $\delta_1 > 0$: If $r < t$, then $\mathcal{H}_R$ would not be the last non-singular matrix in Algorithm 4.1 because $\mathcal{H}_{2t}$ is non-singular. If $r > t$, then the folded matrix $\bar{\mathcal{H}}_R$ (which is very similar to (15)) of $\mathcal{H}_R$, which is needed to compute the linear generator in Step 3(b)i in Section 2, would not be non-singular. So $r = t$.
- Case $\delta_1 = 0$: In this case $\mathcal{H}_R$ would be identified as singular. In this situation $\mathcal{H}_{2r-1}$ might be non-singular. This is the next item in the proof.

• Case $R = 2r - 1$: Let $\mathcal{H}_R$ be the largest non-singular matrix in Algorithm 4.1. So, $\mathcal{H}_R$ satisfies the conditions in Steps 3(a)ii and Step 3(a)iii. If $r < t$, then $\mathcal{H}_R$ would not be the last non-singular matrix in Algorithm 4.1 because $\mathcal{H}_{2t-1}$ is non-singular. If $r > t$, then the conditions Step 3(a)ii and Step 3(a)iii would push the sparsity t beyond the known bound B. So $r = t$. □

THEOREM 4.3. *Algorithm 4.1 requires $t + B$ evaluations.*

PROOF. In Step 1, Algorithm 4.1 looks at B evaluations, namely $a_0, \ldots, a_{B-1}$ (note that $a_{-i} = a_i$). Let $\mathcal{H}_R$ (where $R = 2r$ or $R = 2r - 1$) be the non-singular matrix constructed in Algorithm 4.1 in Step 2. If $R = 2r$, the algorithm uses $2r$ evaluations in Step 3(b)i (in Step 3(a)i when $R = 2r - 1$), namely $a_0, \ldots, a_{2r-1}$. In order to check the linear dependency, it uses $B - r$ evaluations more in Step 3(b)iii (in Step 3(a)iii when $R = 2r - 1$), namely $a_{2r}, \ldots, a_{2r-1+(B-r)}$ $(a_{-2r}, \ldots, a_{2-(B-r+1)}$ when $R = 2r - 1)$. So, the total number of evaluations is $2r + (B - r) = r + B$. Since Algorithm 4.1 terminates when $r = t$, it requires $t + B$ evaluations. □

A difficulty in implementing the algorithm with structured Toeplitz solvers poses Step 2b. By discovering a discrepancy in the column dependency in Steps 3(a)ii, 3(a)iii or 3(b)iii the rank of the $2B\times 2B$ Toeplitz matrix is certified to be larger than the degree R of the current candidate for the term locator polynomial. However, unlike in the Berlekamp-Massey algorithm for Hankel matrices, the dimensions of the new non-singular submatrix can lie beyond the point of the discrepancy. One locates the new non-singular matrix by incremental row elimination of the Schur complements [6, 23], which introduces a running time that is cubic in the distance to the next non-singular Toeplitz submatrix. Alternatively, one could in soft-linear Monte-Carlo time compute the rank of each intermediate Schur complement [14], which yields the $(t+B)^{2+o(1)}$ running time bound cited in the introduction. Note that our matrices can be used to construct symmetric Toeplitz matrices with rational entries that have arbitrary lookahead: for example, the Toeplitz matrix whose first row and first column contain the entries $g_2(2), g_2(2^2), \ldots, g_2(2^{11})$ and whose leading principal submatrices have ranks $1, 2, 2, 2, 2, 2, 4, 6, 8, 10, 11, 11, \ldots$ Here $g_2(x)$ is the symmetric Laurent polynomial $g_2(x) = \frac{32768}{5281339833}(\frac{1}{x^6}+x^6) - \frac{1024}{2540327}(\frac{1}{x^5}+x^5) + \frac{64}{7227}(\frac{1}{x^4}+x^4) - \frac{744}{8687}(\frac{1}{x^3}+x^3) + \frac{62}{153}(\frac{1}{x^2}+x^2) + \frac{254}{189}$. To create that symmetric Toeplitz matrix we started with $g_1(x)=x^{-1}+x$ and then constructed $g_2(x)$ (first with unknown coefficients). Note that $g_1(2^i) = g_2(2^i)$ for $0\le i\le 5$. A worst-case quadratic-time Toeplitz solver that in analogy to the Berlekamp-Massey Hankel solver incrementally steps from non-singular to non-singular leading principal submatrix is not known to us.

Here we would like to mention about our work in progress [11]. In [11], we give an algorithm for computing the Chebyshev term degrees in the original algorithm of Lakshman and Saunders [19] for a very large finite coefficient field $\mathbb{F}_p$; with a method similar to the Silver-Pohlig-Hellman Algorithm [20], one can directly compute the Chebyshev term degree δ from given $\zeta = T_\delta(\beta)$, $\beta = (\omega + 1/\omega)/2 \in \mathbb{F}_p$, without precomputing the order of $\omega \in \mathbb{F}_p, \omega \neq 0$. In [11], we also show that the same strategy applies to the Silver-Pohlig-Hellman [20] discrete logarithm algorithm to compute δ from given $\zeta = \omega^\delta$; one does not need to precompute the order of ω.

The Chebyshev-2 Basis, Chebyshev-3 Basis, and Chebyshev-4 Basis cases can be done in the same way by making use of the properties (7), (8), and (9). Note that in Chebyshev-2 Basis and Chebyshev-4 Basis cases we have a free evaluation: $a_0 = 0$.

5. SPARSE INTERPOLATION WITH PARAMETERIZED RECURSIVE BASES

We now focus on sparse interpolation in more general polynomial bases, which are defined by the recurrence relation (10), namely

$$V_0^{[u,v,w]}(x) = 1, \quad V_1^{[u,v,w]}(x) = u\,x + w,$$
$$V_n^{[u,v,w]}(x) = v\,x\,V_{n-1}^{[u,v,w]}(x) - V_{n-2}^{[u,v,w]}(x) \text{ for } n \ge 2, \qquad (22)$$

where $u, v \in \mathsf{K}\setminus\{0\}$, $w \in \mathsf{K}$ and K is a field. Obviously, Chebyshev-1 through Chebyshev-4 bases are special cases of the above polynomial recurrence bases (22), e.g., $T_n(x) = V_n^{[1,2]}(x) \stackrel{\text{def}}{=} V_n^{[1,2,0]}(x)$, $U_n(x) = V_n^{[2,2]} \stackrel{\text{def}}{=} V_n^{[2,2,0]}(x)$. Note our notation: from now, we omit to write a $w = 0$ in the bracketed superscript. Furthermore, Fact 1.1 can be generalized to the case of the above recurrence bases (22).

FACT 5.1. *Let $u, v \in \mathsf{K}\setminus\{0\}$, $w \in \mathsf{K}$, K is a field, and let $n \in \mathbb{Z}$. Then the following hold: $(x - \frac{1}{x})\, V_n^{[u,v,w]}(\frac{x+\frac{1}{x}}{v}) = \frac{u}{v}\,(x^{n+1} - \frac{1}{x^{n+1}}) + w(x^n - \frac{1}{x^n}) + (\frac{u}{v} - 1)\,(x^{n-1} - \frac{1}{x^{n-1}})$ for all $n \in \mathbb{Z}$.*

REMARK 5.1. If $u = v \neq 0 \in \mathsf{K}$, $w = 0$, Fact 5.1 implies

$$(x - \tfrac{1}{x})\, V_n^{[v,v]}(\tfrac{x+\frac{1}{x}}{v}) = x^{n+1} - \tfrac{1}{x^{n+1}} \text{ for all } n \ge 1. \qquad (23)$$

From $U_n(x) = V_n^{[2,2]}$ we obtain (7). The binomial solutions (8,9) generalize similarly for $u = v$ and $w = \pm 1$. Furthermore, given a recurrence basis $V_n^{[u,v,w]}(x)$, then for each $\sigma \in \mathsf{K} \setminus \{0\}$ and $n \in \mathbb{Z}$ we have $V_n^{[u,v,w]}(x) = V_n^{[\frac{u}{\sigma}, \frac{v}{\sigma}, w]}(\sigma x)$. □

A polynomial $f(x)$ is represented as

$$f(x) = \sum_{j=1}^{t} c_j V_{\delta_j}^{[u,v,w]}(x) \in \mathsf{K}[x], 0 \le \delta_1 < \cdots < \delta_t, \forall j\colon c_j \ne 0. \quad (24)$$

Here we say that $f(x)$ is t-sparse in the recurrence basis (with parameters u, v, w). Suppose a black box of $f(x)$ is given to return the evaluation $f(\omega)$ for any $\omega \in \mathsf{K}$. By performing the substitution in Fact 5.1, we have

$$g(y) = (y - \tfrac{1}{y}) f(\tfrac{y + \frac{1}{y}}{v}) = \sum_{j=1}^{t} c_j \times$$
$$\Big(\tfrac{u}{v}\big(y^{\delta_j+1} - \tfrac{1}{y^{\delta_j+1}}\big) + w\big(y^{\delta_j} - \tfrac{1}{y^{\delta_j}}\big) + \big(\tfrac{u}{v} - 1\big)\big(y^{\delta_j-1} - \tfrac{1}{y^{\delta_j-1}}\big)\Big)$$
$$\stackrel{\text{def}}{=} \sum_{j=1}^{\tau} g_j \big(y^{\gamma_j} - \tfrac{1}{y^{\gamma_j}}\big) \in \mathsf{K}[y, \tfrac{1}{y}], \quad g_j \ne 0 \text{ for all } j, \quad (25)$$

where $1 \le \gamma_1 < \gamma_2 < \cdots < \gamma_\tau$ and 2τ is the sparsity of the Laurent polynomial g in the power basis with $\tau \le 3t$. By (25) the degrees satisfy $\gamma_\tau = \delta_t + 1$. Note that $f(x) = g(z)/(z - \frac{1}{z})$ for $z = (vx \pm (v^2x^2 - 4)^{1/2})/2$.

Now we present an algorithm to interpolate $f(x)$ from the evaluations of the form

$$a_i = -a_{-i} = (\omega^i - \tfrac{1}{\omega^i}) f(\tfrac{\omega^i + \omega^{-i}}{v}) \in \mathsf{K}, \omega \in \mathsf{K}, \omega \ne 0, i = 0, 1, 2, \ldots \quad (26)$$

Let $\rho_j = \omega^{\gamma_j}, j = 1, \ldots, \tau$, and define the term locator polynomial Λ as

$$\Lambda(z) = \prod_{j=1}^{\tau} (z - \rho_j)(z - \tfrac{1}{\rho_j}) = z^{2\tau} + \lambda_{2\tau-1} z^{2\tau-1} + \cdots + \lambda_0 \in \mathsf{K}[z]. \quad (27)$$

Note that (27) is a reciprocal polynomial, that is $\lambda_0 = 1$ and $\lambda_j = \lambda_{2\tau-j}$. Similar to the fact stated before Lemma 4.1 in [1], we have that the sequence of values (26) is linearly generated by the polynomial $\Lambda(z)$, but Λ is the minimal generator only if Λ is squarefree, that is, if the term values are distinct. We can determine τ by early termination as in [1, Section 4.2]. Let

$$\alpha_i = -\alpha_{-i} = g(y^i) = (y^i - \tfrac{1}{y^i}) f(\tfrac{y^i + \frac{1}{y^i}}{v}) \in \mathsf{K}[y, \tfrac{1}{y}], \quad i \in \mathbb{Z},$$

be the evaluations at powers of the variable y for the ω^i. For the evaluations α_i, $-2\tau - 1 \le i \le 2\tau + 1$, we consider the square Hankel matrix

$$\mathcal{H} = \begin{bmatrix} \alpha_{-2\tau-1} & \alpha_{-2\tau} & \cdots & \alpha_{-1} & \alpha_0 \\ \alpha_{-2\tau} & \alpha_{-2\tau+1} & \cdots & \alpha_0 & \alpha_1 \\ \vdots & \vdots & \iddots & \vdots & \vdots \\ \alpha_{-1} & \alpha_0 & \cdots & \alpha_{2\tau-1} & \alpha_{2\tau} \\ \alpha_0 & \alpha_1 & \cdots & \alpha_{2\tau} & \alpha_{2\tau+1} \end{bmatrix} \quad (28)$$

$\in \mathsf{K}[y, y^{-1}]^{(2\tau+2)\times(2\tau+2)}$. As in [1, Theorem 4.3.i], the square submatrices in the right upper corner have the following guaranteed non-singularities.

Theorem 5.2. *Let $\mathcal{H}_i$ be the submatrix of $\mathcal{H}$ formed by the first i rows and the last i columns. Then* $\det(\mathcal{H}_i) \ne 0$ *for* $i = 2, 4, \ldots, 2\tau$, *and* $\det(\mathcal{H}_{2\tau+1}) = \det(\mathcal{H}_{2\tau+2}) = 0$, *where* $\mathcal{H}_{2\tau+2} = \mathcal{H}$ *in* (28).

Proof. The proof of Theorem 4.3.i in [1] is for a Laurent polynomial

$$\sum_{j=1}^{\tau} g_j (y^{\delta_j} + y^{-\delta_j}) \in \mathsf{K}[y, y^{-1}], \quad g_j \ne 0, \quad (29)$$

which is [1, Eq. (16)] with $\tau = t$ and $g_j = c_j/2$. Part i of that Theorem includes $\det(\mathcal{H}_{2\tau}) \ne 0$ for $\delta_1 \ge 1$, which is a property of the degrees γ_j of our terms in (25). The coefficients of our terms in $g(y)$ in (25) are negated for negative term degrees, which is the only difference to (29). Since the proof of Theorem 4.3.i does not use any relation between the coefficients other than they being non-zero (the denominator 2 plays the role of v and could be divided into the coefficient), Part i also holds for the polynomial (25) here.

The singularities of $\mathcal{H}_{2\tau+1}$ and $\mathcal{H}$ follow from the fact that the polynomial $\prod_{j=1}^{\tau}(z - y^{\gamma_j})(z - y^{-\gamma_j})$ is a linear generator for the infinite sequence α_i and its coefficients yield a column relation for $2\tau + 1$ consecutive columns in $\mathcal{H}$. □

Before recovering $f(x)$ in sparse representation in the recurrence basis, we present an early termination algorithm to interpolate the Laurent polynomial $g(y) = (y - 1/y) f((y + 1/y)/v)$ in (25) from the univariate black box polynomial $f(x)$. Suppose ω is selected randomly and uniformly from a sufficiently large finite set of field elements $S \subseteq \mathsf{K} \setminus \{0\}$. For $k = 1, 2, 3, \ldots$ we compute the two new values $a_i = (\omega^i - \omega^{-i}) f((\omega^i + \omega^{-i})/v)$, $i = 2k - 2, 2k - 1$, and the determinants of the $(2k) \times (2k)$ Hankel matrices

$$H_{2k} = \begin{bmatrix} -a_{2k-1} & -a_{2k-2} & \cdots & -a_1 & a_0 \\ -a_{2k-2} & -a_{2k-3} & \cdots & a_0 & a_1 \\ \vdots & \vdots & \iddots & \vdots & \vdots \\ -a_1 & a_0 & \cdots & a_{2k-3} & a_{2k-2} \\ a_0 & a_1 & \cdots & a_{2k-2} & a_{2k-1} \end{bmatrix}, \quad (30)$$

which with $a_{-i} = -a_i$ are the determinants of $\mathcal{H}_{2k}$ in Theorem 5.2 for the evaluation $y = \omega$.

We terminate the loop when $\det(H_{2k}) = 0$, which implies that the number of terms in $g(y)$ is $2k - 2$ with high probability, i.e., $\tau = k - 1$. Suppose now that $k - 1 = \tau$. Then we get the minimal linear generator $\Lambda(z)$ in (27) by solving the following non-singular linear system:

$$H_{2\tau} \cdot \big[\lambda_0\ \lambda_1 \ldots \lambda_{2\tau-1}\big]^{\mathrm{Tr}} = -\big[a_1\ a_2 \ldots a_{2\tau}\big]^{\mathrm{Tr}}. \quad (31)$$

Note that because $\det(H_{2\tau}) \ne 0$ implies $\Lambda(z)$ in (27) must be squarefree (cf. Lemma 4.2 in [1]), and with $\lambda_1 = \lambda_{2\tau-1}, \lambda_2 = \lambda_{2\tau-2}, \ldots$ the system (31) is overdetermined.

Next, we compute all 2τ distinct roots of $\Lambda(z)$, which are ω^{γ_j} and $\omega^{-\gamma_j}$ for $j = 1, \ldots, \tau$. Finally, we compute all the coefficients g_j in (25) by solving a $(2\tau) \times (2\tau)$ non-singular transposed Vandermonde system (32) below. Again, the system (32) is overdetermined. For

$$\big[\rho_1^i \ldots \rho_\tau^i\ \rho_\tau^{-i} \ldots \rho_1^{-i}\big]_{0 \le i \le 2\tau-1} \cdot \big[g_1 \ldots g_\tau\ {-g_\tau} \ldots {-g_1}\big]^{\mathrm{Tr}} = \big[a_0 \ldots a_{2\tau-1}\big]^{\mathrm{Tr}}. \quad (32)$$

the given u, v, the coefficients c_j of $f(x)$ can be obtained by solving a linear system obtained from (25). Given the recurrence basis $V_n^{[u,v,w]}(x)$, for given u, v, w, Algorithm 5.1 below recovers $f(x) = \sum_{j=1}^{t} c_j V_{\delta_j}^{[u,v,w]}(x)$ from the black box.

5.1. Algorithm Sparse Interpolation in a Given Recurrence Basis With Early Termination

Input: ▸ $f(x) \in \mathsf{K}[x]$ input as a black box.
▸ u, v, w: the recursive basis parameters for $V_n^{[u,v,w]}(x)$.

Output: ▸ $f(x) = \sum_{j=1}^{t} c_j V_{\delta_j}^{[u,v,w]}(x)$, where $c_j \ne 0$.

1. *Pick a random element ω from a finite set $S \subseteq \mathsf{K}$.*
2. *Determine the number of terms of $g(y)$.*
   For $i = 1, 2, 3, \ldots$ do
   2a. *Get the evaluations $a_i = (\omega - \frac{1}{\omega}) f(\frac{\omega^i + \omega^{-i}}{v})$ from the black box of $f(x)$, and then construct the Hankel matrix H_{2k} from $a_1, \ldots, a_{2k-1}$.*
   2b. *Check whether H_{2k} is singular. If* $\det(H_{2k}) = 0$, *and then break out of the loop.*
3. *Find the minimal linear generator $\Lambda(z)$ by solving the system* (31).
4. *Compute the roots ρ_j of $\Lambda(z)$, and recover the exponents γ_j of $g(y)$.*

5. *Obtain the coefficients g_j of $g(y)$ by solving the transposed Vandermonde system (32).*
6. *Compute the coefficients c_j of $f(x)$ from (25).*

6. COMPUTING SPARSEST REPRESENTATION

Given a recursive basis $V_n^{[u,v,w]}(x)$ (22), the representation of $f(x)$ in this given basis $V_n^{[u,v,w]}(x)$ is unique. However, different recursive bases, i.e., different u, v, w might change the sparsities of the corresponding representations. For instance,

$$f(x)=\tfrac{1}{2}V_{99}^{[2,2]}=V_1^{[1,2]}(x)+V_3^{[1,2]}(x)+\cdots+V_{97}^{[1,2]}(x)+V_{99}^{[1,2]}(x). \quad (33)$$

(note that we write $V_n^{[u,v]} \overset{\text{def}}{=} V_n^{[u,v,0]}$). Therefore, the sparsity of the representation of $f(x)$ depends on the selected u, v, w of the recursive basis.

In this section, we focus on the choice of the recursive basis such that the representation of $f(x)$ is sparsest, namely, on how to compute u, v, w such that the number of non-zero terms t is minimized in (24). Given a black box of $f(x)$, we first discuss how to recover the Laurent polynomial $g(y)$ in (25) such that the sparsity is optimized over the control variable $v \neq 0$; since the sparsity of (25) is only dependent on the ratio u/v, one may set $u = 1$. Let $g^{[v]}(y) = (y - 1/y)f((y + 1/y)/v)$. The sparsity of $g^{[v]}(y)$ is clearly dependent on the choice of v. For example, if we construct the Laurent polynomials $g^{[v]}(y)$ from $f(x) = \frac{1}{2}V_{99}^{[1,2]}(x)$ by selecting two different $v = 1, 2$, that is,

$$g^{[1]}(y) = (y - \tfrac{1}{y})f(y + \tfrac{1}{y}) = \textstyle\sum_{j=1}^{50} g_{2i}\,(y^{2i} - y^{-2i}),\ g_{2i} \neq 0,$$
$$g^{[2]}(y) = (y - \tfrac{1}{y})f(\tfrac{y+\frac{1}{y}}{2}) = \tfrac{1}{2}y^{100} - \tfrac{1}{2}y^{-100}.$$

It is easy to see that $g^{[1]}(y)$ has 100 non-zero terms, whereas $g^{[2]}(y)$ has 2 non-zero terms.

In this paper, we also strive to minimize the number of evaluations to interpolate $f(x)$. To that end, we determine v such that the number of the non-zero terms in $g^{[v,w]}(y)$ is minimized. Giesbrecht, Kaltofen and Lee [8] introduces the fraction-free Berlekamp/Massey algorithm for computing the sparsest shifts of a given polynomial. This method can be easily adapted for tackling the problem of computing v such that $g^{[v]}(y)$ is sparsest. We now describe a probabilistic algorithm, given in [8], for recovering the sparsest Laurent polynomial $g^{[v]}(y)$ by the combination of the fraction-free Berlekamp/Massey algorithm with a GCD procedure. Let v be an indeterminate, and choose distinct random values $p, q \in S \subseteq \mathsf{K}$. At first two sequences α_i and β_i are constructed as following:

$$\alpha_i = g^{[\frac{1}{v}]}(p^i) = (p^i - \tfrac{1}{p^i})f(vp^i + \tfrac{v}{p^i}) \in \mathsf{K}[v],$$
$$\beta_i = g^{[\frac{1}{v}]}(q^i) = (q^i - \tfrac{1}{q^i})f(vq^i + \tfrac{v}{q^i}) \in \mathsf{K}[v].$$

For $i = 1, 2, \ldots$, the discrepancies $\Delta_i(p) \in \mathsf{K}[v]$ and $\Delta_i(q) \in \mathsf{K}[v]$ are obtained by performing the fraction-free Berlekamp/Massey algorithm on the sequences: α_i and β_i. We terminate the loop when $\Gamma = \gcd(\Delta_i(p), \Delta_i(q))$ has a non-zero root ζ in $\overline{\mathsf{K}}$, the algebraic closure of K. In addition, the fraction-free Berlekamp/Massey algorithm yields the corresponding minimal generators of $(\alpha_i)_{i\geq 0}$ and $(\beta_i)_{i\geq 0}$. In the end, we obtain a sparsest Laurent polynomial $g^{[v^*]}(y)$, with $v^* = 1/\zeta$ by performing Steps 4 and 5 in Algorithm 5.1. The probabilistic analysis can be found in [8].

Given a black box of $f(x)$, the above method can be applied to obtain v^* and the sparsest Laurent polynomial $g^{[v^*]}(y) = (y-1/y) \times f((y + 1/y)/v^*)$. The sparseness of $g^{[v^*]}(y)$ is by Fact 5.1 no more than 6 times the sparsity for the optimal u, v, w values. Note that by (23) the representation of f in the recurrence basis with with $u = v^*$ and $w = 0$ basis has sparsity twice the sparsity of $g^{[v^*]}(y)$ in standard power basis.

Example 6.1. Consider the polynomial $f(x) = 16x^5 - 16x^3 + 3x$, and two representations of $f(x)$ in two different orthogonal bases:

$$f(x) = R_1(x) = -102\, V_1^{[-\frac{1}{2},1]}(x) - 32\, V_5^{[-\frac{1}{2},1]}(x),$$
$$f(x) = R_2(x) = \tfrac{1}{16}\, V_1^{[4,2]}(x) - \tfrac{1}{8}\, V_3^{[4,2]}(x) + \tfrac{1}{4}\, V_5^{[4,2]}(x).$$

For the bases $V^{[-\frac{1}{2},1]}(x)$ and $V^{[4,2]}(x)$, we can get the corresponding Laurent polynomials:

$$g^{[1]}(y)=(y-\tfrac{1}{y})\,f(y+\tfrac{1}{y})=16(y^6-\tfrac{1}{y^6})+48(y^4-\tfrac{1}{y^4})+51(y^2-\tfrac{1}{y^2}),$$
$$g^{[2]}(y)=(y-\tfrac{1}{y})\,f(\tfrac{y+\frac{1}{y}}{2})=\tfrac{1}{2}\,(y^6-\tfrac{1}{y^6}). \quad (34)$$

One can see that the representation $R_1(x)$ is sparser than the representation $R_2(x)$, even though $g^{[1]}(y)$ has more terms by comparison with $g^{[2]}(y)$. Of course, by (34) we must have $f(x) = U_5(x)/2$. □

We do not know an example of a polynomial f where the sparsities in recurrence bases with parameters u, v^*, w, where $v^* \neq 0$ minimizes the sparsity of $g^{[v^*]}(y)$ (25), are larger for all $u \neq 0$ and w than the minimal sparsity that is achieved by a recurrence basis with parameters u', v', w', $u' \neq 0$, $v' \neq 0$ and $v^* \neq v'$. One may compute optimal $u', v', w' \in \overline{\mathsf{K}}$, where $\overline{\mathsf{K}}$ is the algebraic closure of the field K, in time that is polynomial in $\deg(f)$. The algebraic elements u', v', w' are represented in terms of the roots of a polynomial. One computes the coefficients $c_j(u, v, w)$ in (24) for symbolic u, v, w. Because the leading coefficient of $V_\delta^{[u,v,w]}$ is equal $uv^{\delta-1}$, the denominator of the rational function $c_j(u, v, w)$ is a power-term in u, v. We now seek a point $(u', v', w') \in \overline{\mathsf{K}}^3$ that is a zero of a maximum number of the numerator polynomials of $c_j(u, v, w)$. The arising polynomial root finding problem is solvable in polynomial-time in $\deg(f)$. For example, the 0- and 2-dimensional components that zero a maximal number of coefficients are computed via a GCD-free basis computation [3, 13] of the numerator polynomials. Those common factors that occur most often constitute those components. We will analyze the actual complexity of zeroing a maximum number of polynomials in an inconsistent polynomial system elsewhere. The defining equations for the algebraic extensions can be factored lazily by GCDs rather than polynomial factorization (cf. [12]).

Some special cases can be treated by linear algebra. We now present a theorem to show the feasibility of how to select for a given v and $w = 0$ a suitable u in the recurrence basis (22) such that $f(x)$ has the sparsest representation, i.e., how to determine $u \in \overline{\mathsf{K}}, u \neq 0$ for a fixed $v \in \mathsf{K}, v \neq 0$ such that the representation of $f(x)$ in the basis $V_n^{[u,v]}(x) = V_n^{[u,v,0]}(x)$ is the sparsest.

Theorem 6.1. *Let $f(x) = \sum_{j=0}^{d} f_j x^j \in \mathsf{K}[x]$ with $d = \deg(f) \geq 2$, where K is a field, and let $v \in \mathsf{K}, v \neq 0$. For i with $0 \leq i \leq d-2$ define*

$$S_i \overset{\text{def}}{=} \{u \in \overline{\mathsf{K}} \mid f(x) = \textstyle\sum_{j=0}^{d} c_j V_j^{[u,v]}(x) \text{ with } c_i = 0\}. \quad (35)$$

i. *If $d - i \geq 2$ is even, then $|S_i| \leq (d - i)/2$.*

ii. *If $d - i \geq 3$ is odd and $\exists k, 1 \leq k \leq \lfloor (d - i)/2 \rfloor : f_{i+2k} \neq 0$, then $|S_i| \leq \lfloor (d - i)/2 \rfloor$.*

Proof. We first prove Part i. Let $g(y) = (y - \frac{1}{y})f(\frac{y+\frac{1}{y}}{v}) \in \mathsf{K}(y)$. By (25) and we can see that $g(y)$ is of the form

$$g(y) = \textstyle\sum_{j=1}^{d+1} g_j(y^j - y^{-j}), \quad (36)$$

where $g_j \in \mathsf{K}$ for $j = 1, \ldots, d + 1$, and $g_{d+1} \neq 0$. Let $u, c_0, \ldots, c_d$ be parameters, and suppose $p(x, u, c_0, \ldots, c_d) = \sum_{j=0}^{d} c_j V_j^{[u,v]}(x)$. We have from Fact 5.1 that (37) below holds. According to the definition

$$(y - \tfrac{1}{y})p(\tfrac{y+\frac{1}{y}}{v}, u, c_0, \ldots, c_d) = c_d \tfrac{u}{v}(y^{d+1} - y^{-d-1}) + c_{d-1}\tfrac{u}{v}(y^d - y^{-d}) + \Big(\sum_{j=1}^{d-2}(c_j \tfrac{u}{v} + c_{j+2}(\tfrac{u}{v} - 1))(y^{j+1} - y^{-j-1})\Big) + c_2(\tfrac{u}{v} - 1)(y - y^{-1}) + c_0(y - y^{-1}). \quad (37)$$

(35) of S_i, we need find $u, c_0, \ldots, c_u \in \overline{\mathsf{K}}$ that satisfy $c_i = 0$, and the following equation

$$g(y) - (y - \tfrac{1}{y})\,p(\tfrac{y+\frac{1}{y}}{v}, u, c_0, \ldots, c_d) = 0. \quad (38)$$

Since $c_i = 0$ and $d-i$ is even, here we can get the following equations by selecting the coefficients of (38) corresponding to y^{i+1}, y^{i+3}, $\ldots$, y^{d-1}, y^{d+1}:

$$(\tfrac{u}{v} - 1)c_{i+2} - g_{i+1} = 0,\ (\tfrac{u}{v} - 1)c_{i+4} + \tfrac{u}{v}c_{i+2} - g_{i+3} = 0, \ldots,$$
$$(\tfrac{u}{v} - 1)\,c_d + \tfrac{u}{v}\,c_{d-2} - g_{d-1} = 0,\ \tfrac{u}{v}\,c_d - g_{d+1} = 0,$$

whose matrix form is (39) below. The entries of $\Xi^{[i]}$ in (39) are:

$$\Xi^{[i]} \cdot \left[c_{i+2}\ c_{i+4} \ldots c_{d-2}\ c_d\right]^{\mathrm{Tr}} = \left[g_{i+1}\ g_{i+3} \ldots g_{d-1}\ g_{d+1}\right]^{\mathrm{Tr}}. \quad (39)$$

$\xi^{[i]}_{\mu,\nu}{=}u/v{-}1$ if $\mu = \nu$, $\xi^{[i]}_{\mu,\nu}{=}u/v$ if $\mu = \nu{+}1$ and 0 else. The dimension of $\Xi^{[i]}$ in (39) is $(\frac{d-i}{2} + 1) \times \frac{d-i}{2}$.

In the following, two cases will be discussed: $g_{i+1} = 0$ and $g_{i+1}{\neq}0$. We first consider the first case: $g_{i+1} = 0$. We shall investigate the structure of (39). It is easy to check that the above overdetermined linear system is consistent if $u = v$, that implies $v \in S_i$. Now let us consider $u{\neq}v$. The above linear system (39), removing the last equation consists of a square bidiagonal linear system, whose unique solution is expressed as $c_{i+2} = 0$, $c_{i+4} = g_{i+3}/(\frac{u}{v} - 1)$, and so on. Finally, c_d must be of the form $c_d = q_1(u)/(\frac{u}{v} - 1)^l$, where $l = \frac{d-i}{2} - 1$ with $q_1(u) \in \mathsf{K}[u]$ and $\deg(q_1) \le l - 1$. Furthermore c_d must satisfy the last equation in (39), that is,

$$\psi_1(u) \overset{\text{def}}{=} g_{d+1}(\tfrac{u}{v} - 1)^l - \tfrac{u}{v}q_1(u) = 0. \quad (40)$$

Since $g_{d+1}{\neq}0$, $\psi_1(0){\neq}0$ and therefore $\psi_1(u)$ is a nonzero polynomial in $\mathsf{K}[u]$, and $\deg(\psi_1(u)) \le l$. Therefore, for S_i we have the subset relation

$$S_i \subsetneq \{v\} \cup \{\bar{u} \mid \psi_1(\bar{u}) = 0, \psi_1 \in \mathsf{K}[u], \psi_1{\neq}0, \text{ with } \deg(\psi_1(u)) \le (d - i)/2 - 1\}, \quad (41)$$

which implies that $|S_i| \le \frac{d-i}{2}$.

Next, we consider the other case: $g_{i+1}{\neq}0$. A necessary condition that the linear system (39) is consistent is $u{\neq}v$, by the first row. Similarly, one can obtain $c_{i+2}{=}g_{i+1}/(\frac{u}{v}{-}1)$, $c_{i+4}{=}((g_{i+3}{-}g_{i-1})\frac{u}{v}{-}g_{i+3})/(\frac{u}{v}{-}1)^2$, and so on. Finally, c_d is of the form $c_d{=}q_2(u)/(\frac{u}{v}{-}1)^{l+1}$, where $q_2(u){\in}\mathsf{K}[u]$ with $\deg(q_2(u)){\le}l$. By substituting the solution of c_d into the last equation of (39), we have $\psi_2(u) \overset{\text{def}}{=} g_{d+1}(\frac{u}{v}{-}1)^{l+1}{-}\frac{u}{v}q_2(u){=}0$. Likewise, for S_i we have the subset relation

$$S_i \subsetneq \{\bar{u} \mid \psi_2(\bar{u}) = 0, \text{ with } \psi_2(u) \neq 0, \deg(\psi_2(u)) \le \tfrac{d-i}{2}\}, \quad (42)$$

which implies that $|S_i|{\le}\frac{d-i}{2}$.

Because of space constraints, we omit the proof of Part ii. □

Given a polynomial $f(x){=}\sum_{j=0}^{d} f_j x^j$, and i chosen from Part i or Part ii of Theorem 6.1, one is able to compute all $u \in \overline{\mathsf{K}}$ such that $f(x){=}\sum_{j=0}^{d} c_j V_j^{[u,v]}(x)$ with $c_i{=}0$. The second-highest term coefficient c_{d-1}/constant coefficient c_0 is zero/non-zero if and only if g_d/g_1 in (36) is zero/non-zero, independently of the choice of u, v (see (37)). The minimal polynomials for the candidate algebraic number $\bar{u}$ from (41, 42) need not be factored and lazy factorization can be applied (cf. [12]). For each u one can count the number of zero coefficients in (24) and select those with smallest sparsity.

ACKNOWLEDGMENTS

Supported in part by NSF Grants CCF-1421128 and 1717100 (Imamoglu and Kaltofen), and by China National Nat. Sci. Found. Grant 61772203 and Shanghai Nat. Sci. Found. Grant 17ZR1408300 (Yang).

REFERENCES

[1] Andrew Arnold and Erich L. Kaltofen. 2015. Error-Correcting Sparse Interpolation in the Chebyshev Basis. In *ISSAC'15 Proc. 2015 ACM Internat. Symp. Symbolic Algebraic Comput.* ACM, New York, N. Y., 21–28. URL: EKbib/15/ArKa15.pdf.

[2] M. Ben-Or and P. Tiwari. 1988. A deterministic algorithm for sparse multivariate polynomial interpolation. In *Proc. Twentieth Annual ACM Symp. Theory Comput.* ACM Press, New York, N.Y., 301–309.

[3] Daniel J. Bernstein. 2005. Factoring into coprimes in essentially linear time. *J. Algorithms* 54, 1 (2005), 1–30. https://doi.org/10.1016/j.jalgor.2004.04.009

[4] R. P. Brent, F. G. Gustavson, and D. Y. Y. Yun. 1980. Fast solution of Toeplitz systems of equations and computation of Padé approximants. *J. Algorithms* 1 (1980), 259–295.

[5] C. Brezinski. 1991. *History of Continued Fractions and Padé Approximants.* Springer Verlag, Heidelberg, Germany.

[6] T. F. Chan and P. C. Hansen. 1992. A look-ahead Levinson algorithm for general Toeplitz systems. *IEEE Transactions on Signal Processing* 40, 5 (May 1992), 1079–1090. https://doi.org/10.1109/78.134471

[7] S. Garg and É. Schost. 2009. Interpolation of polynomials given by straight-line programs. *Theoretical Computer Science* 410, 27-29 (2009), 2659–2662.

[8] Mark Giesbrecht, Erich Kaltofen, and Wen-shin Lee. 2003. Algorithms for Computing Sparsest Shifts of Polynomials in Power, Chebychev, and Pochhammer Bases. *J. Symb. Comput.* 36, 3–4 (2003), 401–424. URL: EKbib/03/GKL03.pdf.

[9] Mark Giesbrecht, George Labahn, and Wen-shin Lee. 2004. Symbolic-Numeric Sparse Polynomial Interpolation in Chebyshev Basis and Trigonometric Interpolation. In *Proc. Workshop on Computer Algebra in Scientific Computation (CASC).* 195–205. https://cs.uwaterloo.ca/~mwg/files/triginterp.pdf.

[10] Mark Giesbrecht, George Labahn, and Wen-shin Lee. 2006. Symbolic-numeric sparse interpolation of multivariate polynomials. In *ISSAC MMVI Proc. 2006 Internat. Symp. Symbolic Algebraic Comput.*, Jean-Guillaume Dumas (Ed.). ACM Press, New York, N. Y., 116–123. https://doi.org/10.1145/1145768.1145792

[11] E. Imamoglu and E. L. Kaltofen. 2018. On Computing The Degree Of A Chebyshev Polynomial From Its Value. Manuscript. (May 2018). 10 pages.

[12] E. Kaltofen. 1985. Fast parallel absolute irreducibility testing. *J. Symb. Comput.* 1, 1 (1985), 57–67. Misprint corrections: *J. Symbolic Comput.* vol. 9, p. 320 (1989). URL: EKbib/85/Ka85_jsc.pdf.

[13] E. Kaltofen. 1985. Sparse Hensel lifting. In *EUROCAL 85 European Conf. Comput. Algebra Proc. Vol. 2 (Lect. Notes Comput. Sci.)*, B. F. Caviness (Ed.). Springer Verlag, Heidelberg, Germany, 4–17.

[14] E. Kaltofen. 1994. Asymptotically fast solution of Toeplitz-like singular linear systems. In *Proc. 1994 Internat. Symp. Symbolic Algebraic Comput. (ISSAC'94).* ACM Press, New York, N. Y., 297–304. Journal version in [15]. URL: EKbib/94/Ka94_issac.pdf.

[15] E. Kaltofen. 1995. Analysis of Coppersmith's block Wiedemann algorithm for the parallel solution of sparse linear systems. *Math. Comput.* 64, 210 (1995), 777–806. URL: EKbib/95/Ka95_mathcomp.pdf.

[16] Erich L. Kaltofen. 2010. Fifteen years after DSC and WLSS2 What parallel computations I do today [Invited Lecture at PASCO 2010]. In *PASCO'10 Proc. 2010 Internat. Workshop on Parallel Symbolic Comput.*, M. Moreno Maza and Jean-Louis Roch (Eds.). ACM, New York, N. Y., 10–17. URL: EKbib/10/Ka10_pasco.pdf.

[17] E. Kaltofen and Lakshman Yagati. 1988. Improved sparse multivariate polynomial interpolation algorithms. In *Symbolic Algebraic Comput. Internat. Symp. ISSAC '88 Proc. (Lect. Notes Comput. Sci.)*, P. Gianni (Ed.), Vol. 358. Springer Verlag, Heidelberg, Germany, 467–474. URL: EKbib/88/KaLa88.pdf.

[18] Erich Kaltofen and Wen-shin Lee. 2003. Early Termination in Sparse Interpolation Algorithms. *J. Symb. Comput.* 36, 3–4 (2003), 365–400. URL: EKbib/03/KL03.pdf.

[19] Lakshman Y. N. and B. D. Saunders. 1995. Sparse polynomial interpolation in non-standard bases. *SIAM J. Comput.* 24, 2 (1995), 387–397.

[20] C. P. Pohlig and M. E. Hellman. 1978. An improved algorithm for computing logarithms over GF(*p*) and its cryptographic significance. *IEEE Trans. Inf. Theory* IT-24 (1978), 106–110.

[21] D. Potts and M. Tasche. 2014. Sparse polynomial interpolation in Chebyshev bases. *Linear Algebra and Applic.* 441 (2014), 61–87.

[22] R. Prony. III (1795). Essai expérimental et analytique sur les lois de la Dilatabilité de fluides élastiques et sur celles de la Force expansive de la vapeur de l'eau et de la vapeur de l'alkool, à différentes températures. *J. de l'École Polytechnique* 1 (Floréal et Prairial III (1795)), 24–76.

[23] Ali H. Sayed and Thomas Kailath. 1995. A Look-Ahead Block Schur Algorithm for Toeplitz-Like Matrices. *SIAM J. Matrix Anal. Appl.* 16, 2 (1995), 388–414.

Algorithmic Arithmetics with DD-Finite Functions

Antonio Jiménez-Pastor*
DK Computational Mathematics, JKU
Linz, Austria
antonio.jimenez-pastor@dk-compmath.jku.at

Veronika Pillwein
RISC, JKU
Linz, Austria
veronika.pillwein@risc.jku.at

ABSTRACT

Many special functions as well as generating functions of combinatorial sequences that arise in applications are D-finite, i.e., they satisfy a linear differential equation with polynomial coefficients. These functions have been studied for centuries and over the past decades various computer algebra methods have been developed and implemented for D-finite functions. Recently, we have extended this notion to DD-finite functions (functions satisfying linear differential equations with D-finite functions coefficients). Numerous identities for D-finite functions can be proven automatically using closure properties. These closure properties can be shown to hold for DD-finite functions as well. In this paper, we present the algorithmic aspect of these closure properties, discuss issues related to implementation and give several examples.

CCS CONCEPTS

• Mathematics of computing → Generating functions; • Computing methodologies → Symbolic and algebraic algorithms;

KEYWORDS

Holonomic functions, closure properties, algorithms

ACM Reference Format:

Antonio Jiménez-Pastor and Veronika Pillwein. 2018. Algorithmic Arithmetics with DD-Finite Functions. In *ISSAC '18: 2018 ACM International Symposium on Symbolic and Algebraic Computation, July 16–19, 2018, New York, NY, USA.* ACM, New York, NY, USA, 7 pages. https://doi.org/10.1145/3208976.3209009

1 INTRODUCTION

A formal power series $\sum_{n\geq 0} f_n x^n$ is called differentially finite (*D-finite*) or holonomic, if it satisfies a linear differential equation with polynomial coefficients [11, 16, 17]. For these functions, several symbolic algorithms have been developed over the past decades. Among those, there are algorithms for executing closure properties such as addition, multiplication, or algebraic substitution and implementations exist in various computer algebra systems [4, 10, 13]. A key in these algorithms is the finite description of holonomic functions in terms of the polynomial coefficients of a defining differential equation and sufficiently many initial values.

Recently, we have extended the notion of D-finite functions to DD-finite functions [8]: functions satisfying linear differential equations with D-finite functions coefficients. As in the classical case, we work in the setting of formal power series over a field of characteristic zero $K[[x]]$. The objects we consider are of the form $f(x) = \sum_{n\geq 0} f_n x^n$, where we are not concerned with analyticity, but view them as purely algebraic objects. The only evaluation we allow is $f(0) = f_0$.

Van Hoeij [20] has studied formal solutions and factorization of differential operators with power series coefficients. Recently Abramov et al. [1, 2] have investigated linear differential systems with power series coefficients. Since most relevant power series are typically D-finite, these types of problems are in our newly defined class.

DD-finite functions can be represented using essentially the same finite data structure as for D-finite functions. Our main motivation is to be able to extend the scope of symbolic algorithms to a bigger class, starting with such simple examples as $\exp(\exp(x) - 1)$, $\tan(x)$, and Mathieu's functions [5] that are DD-finite, but not D-finite.

We have shown that most of the closure properties for D-finite functions carry over immediately. In these proofs, it becomes apparent that our construction can be iterated and we may as well consider functions defined by linear differential equations with coefficients in some differential subring. Starting from D-finite functions this defines a tower of D^k-finite functions with closure properties holding in every layer. One major aspect discussed in [8] is how many and which initial values are needed to specify a (formal) solution uniquely. Not surprisingly, this is closely related to the zeroes of the leading coefficient of the given defining differential equation.

In this paper, we give an overview of the major closure properties proven in [8]. The focus in this paper is on the algorithmic aspects and we provide several examples. All results presented here have been implemented in the open source software SAGE [18] and the code is free for download [7].

The paper is organized as follows: In section 2, differentially definable functions are introduced. Section 3 recalls the main closure properties that are currently contained in our package and describes the method implemented for the closure properties addition and multiplication. There are several computational issues when working in a differential ring and, in particular, when dealing with functions in a deeper layer of D^k-finite functions, where recursive calls of closure properties are needed. In section 4, we address how these are currently handled in our implementation.

*This research was funded by the Austrian Science Fund (FWF): W1214-N15, project DK15.

ISSAC '18, July 16–19, 2018, New York, NY, USA

ACM ISBN 978-1-4503-5550-6/18/07...$15.00
https://doi.org/10.1145/3208976.3209009

2 DD-FINITE FUNCTIONS

Throughout this paper, we fix the following notation: K denotes a field of characteristic zero, $K[[x]]$ the ring of formal power series over K, ∂ the standard derivation on $K[[x]]$, and $\langle S\rangle_K$ the K-vector space generated by the set S.

Definition 2.1. Let R be a non-trivial differential subring of $K[[x]]$ and $R[\partial]$ the ring of linear differential operators over R. We call $f \in K[[x]]$ *differentially definable over* R if there is a non-zero operator $\mathcal{A} \in R[\partial]$ that annihilates f, i.e., $\mathcal{A}\cdot f = 0$. By $\mathrm{D}(R)$ we denote the set of all $f \in K[[x]]$ that are differentially definable over R. We define the *order of* f *w.r.t.* R as the minimal order of the operators that annihilate f (i.e., the minimal ∂-degree of $\mathcal{A} \in R[\partial]$ such that $\mathcal{A}\cdot f = 0$).

Note that $R \subset R[\partial]$ and hence for non-trivial subrings of $K[[x]]$ the set of differentially definable functions is never empty. Classical D-finite functions are in our notation just $\mathrm{D}(K[x])$. It is well known [11] that $\mathrm{D}(K[x])$ is closed under derivation, addition, and multiplication, i.e., they form a differential subring of $K[[x]]$. Hence the set of *DD-finite functions* can be defined as $\mathrm{D}(\mathrm{D}(K[x]))$.

Example 2.2. $f_0(x) = \exp(x) \in K[[x]]$ is D-finite satisfying $f_0'(x) - f_0(x) = 0$, $f_0(0) = 1$, and so is the constant function $f_1(x) = 1 \in K[[x]]$. Hence $g(x) = \exp(\exp(x) - 1) \in K[[x]]$ is DD-finite as a solution to $f_1(x)g'(x) - f_0(x)g(x) = 0$, $g(0) = 1$. The coefficients in the defining differential equation for $g(x)$ can be represented in turn using their respective defining (in)homogeneous differential equations.

Example 2.3. Mathieu's equation in its standard form is given by [5, 14]

$$w'' + (a - 2q\cos(2x))w = 0, \qquad (1)$$

for some parameters a and q. This differential equation has a pair of fundamental solutions (w_1, w_2) with initial values

$$w_1(0; a, q) = 1,\ w_1'(0; a, q) = 0, \text{ and}$$
$$w_2(0; a, q) = 0,\ w_2'(0; a, q) = 1.$$

$w_1(z; a, q)$ is even and $w_2(z; a, q)$ is odd and both are DD-finite functions. Mathieu functions are related to several problems in applied mathematics and were introduced by Mathieu in the context of vibrating elliptical drumheads [14].

Analogously to D-finite functions, differentially definable functions can be characterized equivalently by an inhomogeneous differential equation or as a finite dimensional vector space.

Theorem 2.4. *Let R be a differential subring of $K[[x]]$, $R[\partial]$ the ring of linear differential operators over R, and $F = Q(R)$ be the field of fractions of R. Let $f \in K[[x]]$. Then the following are equivalent:*

(1) $f \in \mathrm{D}(R)$
(2) $\exists \mathcal{A} \in R[\partial] \setminus \{0\}\ \exists g \in \mathrm{D}(R)\colon \mathcal{A}\cdot f = g$
(3) $\dim\langle f^{(i)} \mid i \in \mathbb{N}\rangle_F < \infty$

Proof. (1)⟹(3): Let $\mathcal{A}$ be a non-zero annihilator of f of order d, say $\mathcal{A} = r_d\partial^d + \dots + r_1\partial + r_0$. Then for any $i \in \mathbb{N}$ we have that there are $r_{i,k} \in R$ s.t.

$$r_d f^{(d+i)} + r_{i,d-1}f^{(d+i-1)} + \dots + r_{i,0}f^{(i)} = 0,$$

with $r_{0,k} = r_k$. Hence any $r_d^{i+1}f^{(d+i)}$ is an R-linear combination of $\{f, f', \dots, f^{(d-1)}\}$ and consequently

$$\dim\langle f^{(i)} \mid i \in \mathbb{N}\rangle_F = d < \infty.$$

(3)⟹(2): Say the dimension of $\langle f^{(i)} \mid i \in \mathbb{N}\rangle$ is $d < \infty$. Then there exist fractions $p_k/q_k \in F$ (not all zero) for $k = 0, \dots, d$ such that,

$$\frac{p_d}{q_d}f^{(d)} + \frac{p_{d-1}}{q_{d-1}}f^{(d-1)} + \dots + \frac{p_0}{q_0}f = 0.$$

Let Q_d be a common multiple of the q_k and let $r_k = \frac{Q_d}{q_k}p_k$. Then $\mathcal{A} = r_d\partial^d + \dots + r_1\partial + r_0$ annihilates f.

(2)⟹(1): Assume that (2) holds. Since $g \in \mathrm{D}(R)$, there exists a non-zero $\mathcal{B} \in \mathrm{D}(R)$ s.t. $\mathcal{B}\cdot g = 0$. Hence $\mathcal{B}\mathcal{A} \in \mathrm{D}(R) \setminus \{0\}$ is an annihilating operator for f. □

3 CLOSURE PROPERTIES

It is well known that D-finite functions satisfy various closure properties [11] and that these closure properties can be executed automatically [4, 10, 13]. In this way identities for holonomic functions can be proven algorithmically [9]. Many of these closure properties can be carried over to differentially definable functions and also the algorithmic aspect can be kept [8]. We recall some of these closure properties and, for the sake of being self-contained, repeat part of the proof.

Theorem 3.1. *Let R be a non-trivial differential subring of $K[[x]]$ (i.e., $R \neq 0$) and $f(x), g(x) \in \mathrm{D}(R)$ with orders d_1 and d_2, respectively, and $r(x) \in R$. Then:*

(1) *$f'(x) \in \mathrm{D}(R)$ with order at most d_1.*
(2) *Any antiderivative of $f(x)$ is in $\mathrm{D}(R)$ with order at most $d_1 + 1$.*
(3) *$f(x) + g(x) \in \mathrm{D}(R)$ with order at most $d_1 + d_2$.*
(4) *$f(x)g(x) \in \mathrm{D}(R)$ with order at most d_1d_2.*
(5) *If $r(0) \neq 0$, then its multiplicative inverse $1/r(x)$ in $K[[x]]$ is in $\mathrm{D}(R)$ with order 1.*

Proof. Given an annihilating operator $\mathcal{A} = r_{d_1}\partial^{d_1} + \dots + r_1\partial + r_0$ with $\mathcal{A}\cdot f = 0$, we have that $r_d\partial^{d_1-1} + \dots + r_1$ annihilates f' if $r_0 = 0$. In the case $r_0 \neq 0$, the operator $(r_0\partial - r_0')\mathcal{A}$ has constant coefficient equal to zero, hence is an annihilating operator for f' of order at most d_1. This yields (1). The annihilating operators for (2) and (5) are immediate.

For the addition of two differentially definable functions let F be the field of fractions of R and given $f \in K[[x]]$ define $V_F(f) = \langle f^{(i)} \mid i \in \mathbb{N}\rangle_F$. By Theorem 2.4 we have that $\dim(V_F(f)) = d_1 < \infty$ and $\dim(V_F(g)) = d_2 < \infty$. Since $V_F(f+g) \subset V_F(f) + V_F(g)$, we have

$$\dim(V_F(f+g)) \leq \dim(V_F(f)) + \dim(V_F(g)) = d_1 + d_2 < \infty.$$

This gives (3) and the closure property (4) follows analogously using the tensor product. □

Because of (1), (3), and (4) in Theorem 3.1, given a differential subring R of $K[[x]]$, $\mathrm{D}(R)$ is again a differential subring of $K[[x]]$. Hence the construction can be iterated with closure properties holding at each level. In this sense, we have that D-finite functions are the same as $\mathrm{D}(K[x])$, DD-finite are $\mathrm{D}^2(K[x])$, and we refer to $\mathrm{D}^k(K[x])$ also as D^k-finite functions.

In order to compute the (DD-finite) annihilating operator of the derivative, antiderivative, or multiplicative inverse it suffices to use a precomputed formula. In this case at most closure properties on the coefficient level need to be applied. We illustrate this with the following example.

Example 3.2. Let us return to Mathieu's function and compute its derivative using the formula shown in the proof of Theorem 3.1. Let $w(x)$ be defined by (1), i.e., the annihilating operator is given by $\mathcal{A} = r_0 + r_2\partial^2$ with $r_2(x) = 1$ and $r_0(x) = a - 2q\cos(2x)$. As stated in the proof, we compute

$$(r_0\partial - r_0') \cdot \mathcal{A} = (r_0\partial^2 - r_0'\partial + r_0^2) \cdot \partial.$$

Hence we have that $w'(x)$ is a solution to

$$\begin{aligned}(a - 2q\cos(2x))y''(x) - 4q\sin(2x)y'(x)\\ +(a - 2q\cos(2x))^2 y(x) = 0.\end{aligned} \tag{2}$$

Note that the coefficient $r_0(x)$ is actually represented in the computer as the D-finite function satisfying

$$y'''(x) + 4y'(x) = 0, \quad y(0) = a - 2q, y'(0) = 0, y''(0) = 8q.$$

Analogously the coefficients in (2) are not given explicitly, but represented in terms of their defining D-finite differential equations plus initial values. These representations are in turn computed using closure properties on the level of D-finite functions.

For computing the closure properties of addition and multiplication of two differentially definable functions, the outline is as follows: given a bound on the order of the resulting operator, we build an ansatz for the homogeneous equation. Equating the coefficients of the basis elements to zero yields a linear system for which a nontrivial element in the nullspace can be computed. For ease of notation, we recall some notions from differential linear algebra.

Definition 3.3. [12, 19] Let (K, ∂) be a differential field of characteristic zero and V a K-vector space. A map $\vec{\partial} : V \to V$ is a *derivation over* V *w.r.t.* ∂ if it satisfies

(1) $\vec{\partial}(v + w) = \vec{\partial}(v) + \vec{\partial}(w)$ for all $v, w \in V$.
(2) $\vec{\partial}(cv) = \partial(c)v + c\vec{\partial}(v)$ for all $c \in K$ and $v \in V$.

Then $(V, \vec{\partial})$ is a *differential vector space over* (K, ∂) and we denote by $\Delta_\partial(V)$ the set of all derivations over V w.r.t. ∂. Given a set of generators Φ, a derivation $\vec{\partial} \in \Delta_\partial(V)$ can be represented by a matrix. This matrix is uniquely defined, if Φ is a basis. Since we do not need uniqueness and later it is computationally simpler to work with a set of generators rather than having to determine a basis, we stick to this more general setting.

Definition 3.4. Let (K, ∂) be a differential field, $(V, \vec{\partial})$ be a differential vector space over (K, ∂), and $\Phi = (\phi_1, ..., \phi_n)$ be a vector of generators of V. We define a *derivation matrix of* $\vec{\partial}$ *w.r.t.* Φ as a matrix $M = (m_{ij})_{i,j=1}^n$ satisfying

$$\vec{\partial}(\phi_j) = m_{1j}\phi_1 + \cdots + m_{nj}\phi_n, \quad \text{for all } j = 1, \ldots, n.$$

In this setting, for any $v = v_1\phi_1 + \cdots + v_n\phi_n \in V$ we have

$$\begin{aligned}\vec{\partial}(v) &= \partial(v_1)\phi_1 + v_1\vec{\partial}(\phi_1) + \cdots + \partial(v_n)\phi_n + v_n\vec{\partial}(\phi_n)\\ &= \sum_{i=1}^n \left(\sum_{j=1}^n m_{ij}v_j + \partial(v_i)\right)\phi_i.\end{aligned}$$

In matrix-vector notation the coefficients in the representation of $\vec{\partial}(v) = \hat{v}_1\phi_1 + \cdots + \hat{v}_n\phi_n$ can thus be computed as

$$\begin{pmatrix}\hat{v}_1\\ \hat{v}_2\\ \vdots\\ \hat{v}_n\end{pmatrix} = M\begin{pmatrix}v_1\\ v_2\\ \vdots\\ v_n\end{pmatrix} + \begin{pmatrix}\partial(v_1)\\ \partial(v_2)\\ \vdots\\ \partial(v_n)\end{pmatrix}.$$

For any set of generators Φ a derivation matrix can be computed and it is unique if Φ is a basis of V.

Let R be a differential subring, F its field of fractions, $f \in \mathrm{D}(R)$ and $V_F(f) = \langle f, f', f'', \ldots\rangle_F$. Then the derivation matrix of ∂ in $V_F(f)$ is the companion matrix of the differential equation defining f.

Lemma 3.5. *Let $f(x) \in \mathrm{D}(R)$ for some differential subring $R \subset K[[x]]$ and $\mathcal{A} = r_d\partial^d + ... + r_0 \in R[\partial]$ be such that $\mathcal{A} \cdot f = 0$. Then the companion matrix*

$$C_f = \begin{pmatrix}0 & \ldots & 0 & -r_0/r_d\\ 1 & \ldots & 0 & -r_1/r_d\\ \vdots & \ddots & \vdots & \vdots\\ 0 & \ldots & 1 & -r_{d-1}/r_d\end{pmatrix}.$$

is a derivation matrix for the standard derivation ∂ over the vector space $V_F(f)$.

Proof. Define the column vectors $\mathbf{v} = (v_i)_{i=0}^{d-1}$ and $\hat{\mathbf{v}} = (\hat{v}_i)_{i=0}^{d-1}$ and let ∂ act component-wise on vectors. Let $g = v_0 f + \cdots + v_{d-1}f^{(d-1)} \in V_F(f)$. Then

$$\begin{aligned}\vec{\partial}g = &\left(\partial(v_0)f + \cdots + \partial(v_{d-1})f^{(d-1)}\right)\\ &+ \left(v_0 f' + \cdots + v_{d-1}f^{(d)}\right),\end{aligned}$$

and $f^{(d)}$ can be expressed in terms of $f, \ldots, f^{(d-1)}$,

$$\begin{aligned}\vec{\partial}g = &\left(\partial(v_0)f - \frac{r_0}{r_d}v_{d-1}\right)f + \left(\partial(v_1) + v_0 - \frac{r_1}{r_d}v_{d-1}\right)f' +\\ &\cdots + \left(\partial(v_{d-1}) + v_{d-2} - \frac{r_{d-1}}{r_d}v_{d-1}\right)f^{(d-1)}.\end{aligned}$$

Thus $\vec{\partial}g = \hat{v}_0 f + \cdots + \hat{v}_{d-1}f^{(d-1)}$ for $\hat{\mathbf{v}} = C_f\mathbf{v} + \partial(\mathbf{v})$. □

In this Lemma and its proof, the multiplicative inverse of the leading coefficient r_d is written explicitely. As the inverse of a D-finite function is in general not D-finite, $1/r_d$ typically cannot be represented by a linear differential equation with coefficients in R. As we detail later in section 4, denominators are handled only symbolically when computing derivatives in $V_F(f)$. In the final result denominators can be cleared and only non-negative powers of the leading coefficient appear.

Given a differentially definable function f of order d, let $\mathbf{f}$ denote the column vector $(f^{(i)})_{i=0}^{d-1}$ and let the derivative act component-wise on the vector. Then for the companion matrix we have that $\partial\mathbf{f} = C_f^T\mathbf{f}$ and for g and $\hat{\mathbf{v}}$ as above, $\vec{\partial}g = \mathbf{f}^T\hat{\mathbf{v}}$.

Next we sketch how to compute addition and multiplication of two DD-finite functions. In either case, we are given a vector of generators $(\phi_0, \dots, \phi_{d-1})$ and seek to compute the coefficient vectors $\mathbf{v}_i = (v_{i,0}, \dots, v_{i,d-1})$ in

$$h^{(i)} = v_{i,0}\phi_0 + \dots + v_{i,d-1}\phi_{d-1},$$

for $i = 0, \dots, d$, where h is either $f + g$ or fg. For this we can use the formula

$$\mathbf{v}_{i+1} = M\mathbf{v}_i + \partial(\mathbf{v}_i), \tag{3}$$

with the derivation matrix M w.r.t. $\{\phi_0, \dots, \phi_{d-1}\}$ and componentwise derivation ∂ on $\mathbf{v}_i$.

Addition. Let $f, g \in D(R)$ of orders d_1 and d_2, respectively, and let $h = f + g$. By Theorem 3.1(3), h is in $D(R)$ of order at most $d = d_1 + d_2$ and $V_F(h)$ is contained in $V_F(f) + V_F(g)$. The set of generators of the latter is the union of the generators of $V_F(f)$ and $V_F(g)$. Now let

$$\mathbf{f} \oplus \mathbf{g} = (f, f', \dots, f^{(d_1-1)}, g, g', \dots, g^{(d_2-1)}).$$

The derivation matrix is given by

$$C_{f+g} = C_f \oplus C_g = \begin{pmatrix} C_f & 0 \\ 0 & C_g \end{pmatrix}.$$

Next we set up an ansatz with unknown coefficients for the differential equation satisfied by h,

$$\alpha_0 h + \dots + \alpha_d h^{(d)} = 0.$$

The derivatives of h can be expressed in terms of the generators $V_F(f) \cup V_F(g)$ using the derivation matrix. The initial vector $\mathbf{v}_0$ has entries 1 at the positions corresponding to f and g and 0 else, i.e.,

$$\mathbf{v}_0^T = (1, 0, \dots, 0, 1, 0, \dots, 0) = \mathbf{e}_{d_1,1} \oplus \mathbf{e}_{d_2,1},$$

where $\mathbf{e}_{d,i}$ denotes the ith unit vector of length d. Equating the coefficients of the generators to zero gives a linear system and any non-trivial element of the right-nullspace gives a defining differential equation for h.

Multiplication. Let $f, g \in D(R)$ of orders d_1 and d_2, respectively, and let $h = fg$. By Theorem 3.1(4), h is in $D(R)$ of order at most $d = d_1 d_2$ and $V_F(h)$ is contained in $V_F(f) \otimes V_F(g)$. The set of generators of the latter is the tensor product of the generators of $V_F(f)$ and $V_F(g)$. Now let

$$\mathbf{f} \otimes \mathbf{g} = (fg, fg', \dots, fg^{(d_2-1)}, f'g, f'g', \dots, f^{(d_1-1)}g, \dots, f^{(d_1-1)}g^{(d_2-1)}).$$

The derivation matrix for the product is given by

$$C_{fg} = C_f \otimes I_{d_2} + I_{d_1} \otimes C_g,$$

where I_n denotes the $n \times n$ identity matrix. Next we set up an ansatz with unknown coefficients for the differential equation satisfied by h,

$$\alpha_0 h + \dots + \alpha_d h^{(d)} = 0.$$

The derivatives of h can be expressed in terms of the generators $V_F(f) \otimes V_F(g)$ using the derivation matrix. The initial vector is given by

$$\mathbf{v}_0^T = (1, 0, \dots, 0) = \mathbf{e}_{d,1} = \mathbf{e}_{d_1,1} \otimes \mathbf{e}_{d_2,1}.$$

Equating the coefficients of the generators to zero gives a linear system and any non-trivial element of the right-nullspace gives a defining differential equation for h.

In either case, initial values need to be computed to define the resulting function uniquely. For this purpose, we consider the formal power series expansions of the given functions. Let $f(x) = \sum_{n \geq 0} f_n x^n \in K[[x]]$ be annihilated by an operator $\mathcal{A} \in R[\partial]$,

$$\mathcal{A} = r_d \partial^d + \dots + r_1 \partial + r_0, \quad \text{with } r_i(x) = \sum_{n \geq 0} r_{i;n} x^n \in R,$$

for some differential subring R of $K[[x]]$. Plugging in the series expansions in the equation $\mathcal{A} \cdot f = 0$, yields a recurrence relation for the coefficients f_n,

$$\sum_{k=0}^{n+d} \left(\sum_{l=\max\{0,k-n\}}^{\min\{d,k\}} k^{\underline{l}} r_{l;n-k+l} \right) f_k = 0, \tag{4}$$

for all $n \in \mathbb{N}$, where $a^{\underline{m}} = a \cdot (a-1) \cdots (a-m+1)$ denotes the falling factorial. Depending on the recurrence coefficients in (4) it can be determined how many and which initial values need to be computed to determine f uniquely. More details can be found in [8].

Example 3.6. Let $f(x) = \exp(\sin(x))$ and $g(x) = \tan(x)$. Both are DD-finite functions with annihilating operators

$$\mathcal{A}_f = \partial - \cos(x) \quad \text{and} \quad \mathcal{A}_g = \cos^2(x)\partial^2 - 2,$$

respectively. Let $h = f + g$. Then h is a DD-finite function of order at most 3. In order to compute a defining differential equation, we first determine the companion matrices

$$C_f = (\cos(x)) \quad \text{and} \quad C_g = \begin{pmatrix} 0 & 2/\cos^2(x) \\ 1 & 0 \end{pmatrix}.$$

With those we build the derivation matrix and construct the system matrix $\mathcal{S}$. After clearing denominators we have

$$\mathcal{S} = \begin{pmatrix} 1 & c & c^2 - s & c^3 - 3sc - c \\ c^3 & 0 & 2c & 4s \\ 0 & c^2 & 0 & 2 \end{pmatrix},$$

where we abbreviate $c = \cos(x)$ and $s = \sin(x)$. The coefficients $(\alpha_0, \alpha_1, \alpha_2, \alpha_3)$ can be computed as element of the right nullspace of $\mathcal{S}$,

$$\begin{aligned} \alpha_0 &= -2c^3 s^2 - 10c^3 s + 4cs^2 - 4c, \\ \alpha_1 &= -2c^4 + 2c^2 s + 4, \\ \alpha_2 &= c^5 s^2 + 3c^5 s - 2cs^2 + 4cs + 2c, \\ \alpha_3 &= c^6 - c^4 s - 2c^2. \end{aligned}$$

In this case none of the coefficients α_i are zero (it is easy to check that $\alpha_3(0) = -1$) and (as expected) three initial values are needed and we obtain for h the representation

$$\alpha_3 h''' + \alpha_2 h'' + \alpha_1 h' + \alpha_0 h = 0, \; h(0) = 1, h'(0) = 3, h''(0) = 1.$$

In this example we simply carried out all computations with the actual coefficient functions, without taking into account any relations between sine and cosine that might help to keep the coefficients small. In the general case, the coefficient functions are given in terms of their defining equations over some differential subring R. This means in particular that this construction may be nested. All operations for the computation of the nullspace can be carried out division free using closure properties of the underlying subring.

These computations quickly become very heavy and it is also difficult to control the size of coefficients or to perform simplifications such as canceling common factors. Hence we treat the coefficient functions as much possible symbolically and execute closure properties only when necessary. But also for these computations, the growth of the coefficients needs be controlled.

In the next section, we describe how our current implementations handles these difficulties.

4 IMPLEMENTATION

For executing the closure properties of addition and multiplication as described in the previous section, all operations need to be carried out in the differential subring R. E.g., for setting up the system matrix $\mathcal{S}$ addition, multiplication, and derivation of elements in R need to be performed. Then finally, the system solving requires again arithmetic operations.

In the case of D-finite functions ($R = K[x]$), these operations can be carried out fast in virtually all available computer algebra systems. However, if we move on to DD-finite functions (or an even deeper layer of D^k-finite functions), addition, multiplication, and derivation of elements in R are recursively computed using closure properties. If directly implemented in this recursive way, the calculations quickly come to a halt because of memory consumption. Every execution of a closure property potentially increases the order of the given recurrence and the size of its coefficients.

Testing the code indicates (as expected) that the major part of computational time is spent for the recursive application of the closure properties. So far, we have not attempted a full complexity analysis, but it seems obvious that this is the bottleneck and further improvement is needed.

We have implemented all algorithms described in this paper in the mathematical software system SAGE [18] in the package dd_functions that is available as a git repository [7]. It also contains a subpackage *tests* with several automated examples to test the correctness and the timings.

In this section we describe how the actual implementation currently handles the closure properties addition and multiplication. (Recall that the others merely require plugging into precomputed formulas.) The two steps are: first constructing the system matrix $\mathcal{S}$ and then computing the nullspace.

In either case (addition or multiplication), we assume to have two given functions $f, g \in \mathrm{D}(R)$, defined by their annihilating operators

$$\mathcal{A}_f = r_n\partial^n + \ldots + r_0 \text{ and } \mathcal{A}_g = s_m\partial^m + \ldots + s_0$$

of orders n and m, respectively. During computations any non-trivial denominator in the companion matrices C_f, C_g (and thus in the derivation matrix M) can only be a product of powers of the leading coefficients r_n, s_m. If at any point in the computations (3) of the coefficient vectors v_i we have a denominator bound $r_n^p s_m^q$, then $r_n^{p+1}s_m^{q+1}$ is a denominator bound for v_{i+1}. At this stage of setting up the system matrix $\mathcal{S}$, the coefficients are kept as indeterminates r_i, s_j and their derivatives are kept as indeterminates $r_k^{(\gamma)}, s_l^{(\delta)}$. No simplifications are attempted and the common denominators are cleared at the end using the (possibly coarse) denominator bound.

At this stage, we have a system matrix $\mathcal{S}$ built from variables $r_i, s_j, r_k^{(\gamma)}, s_l^{(\delta)}$. For computing the nullspace we follow the division-free algorithm described by Bareiss [3]. During these calculations we need to check that we never choose a zero pivot element. To avoid unnecessary execution of closure properties, for this zero testing first it is checked whether the matrix entry evalutes to zero at $x = 0$ (which can be easily computed using the initial values of the coefficients r_i, s_j). Only if this is the case, closure properties on the coefficient ring R are computed. Also when returning the annihilating operator for $h = f + g$ or $h = fg$, the elements of the nullspace have to be given explicitly using the closure properties. For all other computations one may stick to the above set of indeterminates. However, we would like to exploit relations and keep the number of variables low if possible. For this we try to balance the efforts to minimize the number of variables while also keeping the cost of computation low. The two inexpensive means we presently apply after setting up $\mathcal{S}$ are:

Reducing linear relations. After building the system matrix $\mathcal{S}$ we have a list of variables representing $r_i, s_j, r_k^{(\gamma)}$, and $s_l^{(\delta)}$. These coefficient functions in turn are given by defining differential equations plus initial values. From the initial values it is cheap to check pairwise if there are possibly linear relations of the form $Y = cX + d$ among them for some numbers c, d. For each candidate, equality is checked using closure properties in R. For this type of simple identities this is not very costly.

Reducing algebraic relations. This can be done when choosing a new pivot element. At this step closure properties need to be applied in order to verify that we are not computing with a zero pivot. Else, we have found a non-trivial algebraic relation between the variables that we use to reduce the entries in the system.

Every time a new relation is found, it is added to a set of relations that is used to simplify the system using Gröbner basis computations [21]. These algebraic reductions are relevant, because they allow to keep the entries of the system matrix of smaller degree. This way, when closure properties need to be computed recursively, fewer operations are needed. For this reason those relations are also kept during a session of computations in SAGE to be available for different problems. If there is a priori knowledge about algebraic relations between the coefficients, a method is provided to add it directly to the system and improve the performance.

A defining differential equation for h can be obtained from any element in the nullspace. For various reasons one may wish to have an operator of low order. Hence, we compute a normal basis to obtain an appropriate vector in the nullspace [3, 6].

Example 4.1 (Reduction). Let $f(x) \in K[[x]]$ be the DD-finite function defined by

$$f'' + bf' + af = 0, \quad f(0) = 1, \ f'(0) = 0,$$

with D-finite function coefficients a, b given by

$$a' - a = 0, \quad a(0) = 1,$$
$$b''' - 3b'' + 2b' = 0, \quad b(0) = 1, \ b'(0) = -1, \ b''(0) = -3,$$

and $g \in K[[x]]$ the D-finite (and thus also DD-finite) function defined via

$$g'' + g' = 0, \quad g(0) = 1,\ g'(0) = 1.$$

The two companion matrices are given by

$$C_f = \begin{pmatrix} 0 & -a \\ 1 & -b \end{pmatrix}, \quad \text{and} \quad C_g = \begin{pmatrix} 0 & 0 \\ 1 & -1 \end{pmatrix}.$$

With those we build the derivation matrix $M = C_f \oplus C_g$. Starting from the initial vector $\mathbf{v}_0^T = (1, 0, 1, 0)$ the system matrix is computed using (3) to be

$$\begin{pmatrix} 1 & 0 & -a & ab - a' & -ab^2 + 2ab' + a^2 + a'b - a'' \\ 0 & 1 & -b & b^2 - b' - a & -b^3 + 3bb' - 2ba - 2a' - b'' \\ 1 & 0 & 0 & 0 & 0 \\ 0 & 1 & -1 & 1 & -1 \end{pmatrix}.$$

Note that up to this point we did not take into account *any* relations, not even reducing a'' using the defining equation and we formally have the six variables a, a', a'', b, b', b''. Checking for linear relations reveals that $a = a' = a''$ and we are left with four variables x_1, x_2, x_3, x_4 with the interpretations

$$x_1 \leftarrow a,\ x_2 \leftarrow b,\ x_3 \leftarrow b',\ x_4 \leftarrow b''.$$

With these variables the system matrix can be written as

$$\begin{pmatrix} 1 & 0 & -x_1 & x_1(x_2 - 1) & x_1\left(-x_2^2 + x_2 + x_1 + 2x_3 - 1\right) \\ 0 & 1 & -x_2 & x_2^2 - x_1 - x_3 & -x_2^3 + 2x_1x_2 + 3x_3x_2 - 2x_1 - x_4 \\ 1 & 0 & 0 & 0 & 0 \\ 0 & 1 & -1 & 1 & -1 \end{pmatrix}.$$

Next we execute Bareiss' algorithm to compute the nullspace and perform zero-testing at each step. In the first three iterations the pivots are $1, 1, x_1$. In the fourth iteration, the polynomial $x_3x_1 + x_1^2 - 2x_1x_2 + 2x_1$ is checked. Applying (classical) D-finite closure properties shows that this entry corresponds to the function defined by

$$y''' - 6y'' + 11y' - 6y = 0, \quad y(0) = y'(0) = y''(0) = 0.$$

Hence this matrix entry is equal to zero and we found a relation that can be used to reduce the other entries. The next candidate for a pivot in this iteration is $3x_1^2 - 4x_1x_2 + x_1x_4 + 4x_1$. Executing closure properties in this case yields the same differential equation as above, i.e., again a zero entry. At this step we already have found the normal form

$$\begin{pmatrix} 1 & 0 & 0 & 0 & 0 \\ 0 & 1 & 0 & -x_2 + 2 & x_2^2 - 3x_2 - x_3 + 2 \\ 0 & 0 & 1 & -x_2 + 1 & x_2^2 - 3x_2 - x_3 + 3 \\ 0 & 0 & 0 & 0 & 0 \end{pmatrix}.$$

From the generators of the nullspace we choose the smaller order operator

$$\mathcal{A} = \partial^3 + (b - 1)\partial^2 + (b - 2)\partial,$$

and compute that the three initial values $h(0) = 1, h'(0) = 1$, and $h''(0) = -2$ are needed to define $h(x)$ uniquely. In the final step, the representation of the coefficients is computed using again closure properties.

For our concluding example we return to the Mathieu functions introduced above in Example 2.3. We recall the defining differential equation (1),

$$w'' + (a - 2q\cos(2x))w = 0,$$

for some $a, q \in \mathbb{Q}$. In general, this equation does not have a closed form solution. A pair of fundamental solutions is (w_1, w_2) with initial values

$$w_1(0; a, q) = 1,\ w_1'(0; a, q) = 0, \text{ and}$$
$$w_2(0; a, q) = 0,\ w_2'(0; a, q) = 1.$$

For these functions, we have that the Wronskian is constant [5, 14], more precisely,

$$W(x; a, q) := w_1(x; a, q)w_2'(x; a, q) - w_1'(x; a, q)w_2(x; a, q) = 1. \quad (5)$$

Since Mathieu's functions are DD-finite, this statement can be proven using closure properties.

Example 4.2 (Mathieu). The functions w_1, w_2 are solutions to the differential equation $w'' + \alpha_{a,q}w = 0$ with initial values as stated above. As a D-finite function $\alpha_{a,q}$ is defined by the initial value problem:

$$\alpha_{a,q}''' + 4\alpha_{a,q}' = 0,$$
$$\alpha_{a,q}(0) = a - 2q,\ \alpha_{a,q}'(0) = 0, \alpha_{a,q}''(0) = 8q.$$

This we have seen earlier in Example 3.2, where we applied closure properties to compute the derivatives of w_1, w_2 yielding a defining equation (2):

$$\alpha_{a,q}y'' - \alpha_{a,q}'y' + \alpha_{a,q}^2 y = 0.$$

The necessary initial values for the functions w_1', w_2' are

$$w_1'(0) = 0, w_1''(0) = 2q - a, \text{ and } w_2'(0) = 1, w_2''(0) = 0.$$

Both w_1 and w_2 as well as w_1' and w_2' satisfy the same differential equations (with different initial values). Hence, for the computation of the Wronskian, we only need to compute the operator for one of the products $w_1(x)w_2'(x)$ or $w_1'(x)w_2(x)$. The other one satisfies the same differential equation of order at most four. The difference of these products is then also annihilated by this operator and we only need to keep track of the initial values.

We sketch the steps for computing w_1w_2'. The companion matrices are

$$C_{w_1} = \begin{pmatrix} 0 & -\alpha_{a,q} \\ 1 & 0 \end{pmatrix} \quad \text{and} \quad C_{w_2'} = \begin{pmatrix} 0 & -\alpha_{a,q} \\ 1 & \alpha_{a,q}'/\alpha_{a,q} \end{pmatrix}.$$

From those we build the derivation matrix

$$M = C_{w_1} \otimes I_2 + I_2 \otimes C_{w_2'}.$$

Starting from the initial vector $\mathbf{v}_0^T = (1, 0, 0, 0)$ the system matrix $\mathcal{S}$ is computed using (3). It depends on the variables $\alpha_{a,q}, \alpha_{a,q}', \alpha_{a,q}''$ and $\alpha_{a,q}'''$. Checking for linear relations among those using (D-finite) closure properties we find that

$$\alpha_{a,q}'' = -4\alpha_{a,q} + 4a \quad \text{and} \quad \alpha_{a,q}''' = -4\alpha_{a,q}'.$$

Thus we can write the system matrix in the two variables $x_0 \leftarrow \alpha_{a,q}$ and $x_1 \leftarrow \alpha_{a,q}'$ as

$$\begin{pmatrix} 1 & 0 & -2x_0 & -3x_1 & 8x_0^2 + 16x_0 - 16a \\ 0 & x_0 & x_1 & -4x_0^2 - 4x_0 + 4a & -14x_0x_1 - 4x_1 \\ 0 & 1 & 0 & -4x_0 & 10x_1 \\ 0 & 0 & 2x_0 & 3x_1 & -8x_0^2 - 16x_0 + 16a \end{pmatrix}.$$

We perform Bareiss' algorithm with this matrix to compute a normal form. In this example no algebraic relations are found and the smallest generator in the nullspace gives rise to an operator of the form

$$\mathcal{A} = (-3x_1^2 - 8x_0^2 + 8x_0 a)\partial^4 + \beta_3(x_0, x_1)\partial^3 + \beta_2(x_0, x_1)\partial^2 + \beta_1(x_0, x_1)\partial,$$

for some polynomials β_i. The operator $\mathcal{A}$ annihilates $w_1 w_2'$, $w_1' w_2$, and also their difference. At most 4 initial values are needed to define a solution of $\mathcal{A}$, and for the Wronskian they are

$$W(0; a, q) = 1, \qquad W'(0; a, q) = 0,$$
$$W''(0; a, q) = 0, \qquad W'''(0; a, q) = 0.$$

Obviously, we have $\mathcal{A} \cdot 1 = 0$ and the initial values agree. Hence we have completed the proof of (5).

5 CONCLUSION

We have introduced a computable extension of D-finite functions to differentially definable functions. Starting from any differential subring of the formal power series, this construction can be iterated. For these classes of functions essentially the same closure properties hold as for classical D-finite functions. With the example of Mathieu's functions, we have illustrated how the closure properties can be used to prove identities of DD-finite functions.

In this paper, we consider solutions $f(x) = \sum_{n\geq 0} f_n x^n$ in the ring of formal power series and not (necessarily) analytic solutions. For an investigation of the analytic case, one of the main difficulties is the behaviour of the solution depending on a general leading coefficient of the differential equation. As can be seen in [8], even in the formal setting, how many and which initial values are needed to uniquely define a solution, depends on the zeroes of this leading coefficient.

Marc Mezzarobba [15] has developed the package NumGfun for numerical and analytic computation with D-finite functions. With NumGfun, D-finite functions given in terms of a defining linear differential equation, can be evaluated fast to high precision. For well-behaved DD-finite functions, say with a polynomial leading coefficient, we believe that these methods can be extended in a straight-forward manner. This could be one starting point to work with analytic solutions of DD-finite equations.

One of the main reasons to study formal solutions of linear differential equations with polynomial coefficients is that the coefficient sequence $\{f_n\}_{n\geq 0}$ satisfies a linear recurrence with polynomial coefficients [11]. Moreover it is possible to automatically compute this defining recurrence from the differential equation and vice versa. The generating function may be used to prove properties of the coefficient sequence. Also for DD-finite functions, the structure of the coefficient sequences in the formal power series expansion $\sum_{n\geq 0} f_n x^n$ deserves further study. For D-finite functions, closure properties are often used in a combined guess-and-prove approach. Also for DD-finite functions, it would be interesting to have a guessing routine at hand. For this it might be better to start first with guessing at the level of coefficient sequences.

Beyond that, it will be interesting to study analogues of DD-finite functions on the sequence level by defining the equivalent construction extending P-finite sequences (sequences satisfying linear recurrences with polynomial coefficients). The main obstruction here is that in this case we are no longer working with an integral domain. However, in the right algebraic setting, we believe that applicable closure properties of Theorem 3.1 can be carried over analogously. Lastly, a deeper performance study should be done and further improvements of the code are required to cover bigger examples and also include more parameters.

REFERENCES

[1] S.A. Abramov, M. Barkatou, and D.E. Khmelnov. On full rank differential systems with power series coefficients. *J. Symbolic Computation*, 68:120–137, 2015.
[2] S.A. Abramov and D.E. Khmelnov. Regular solutions of linear differential systems with power series coefficients. *Programming and Computer Software*, 40(2):98–106, 2014.
[3] E.H. Bareiss. Sylvester's identity and multistep integer-preserving gaussian elimination. *Mathematics of Computation*, 22:565–578, 1967.
[4] F. Chyzak. Gröbner bases, symbolic summation and symbolic integration. In *Gröbner bases and applications (Linz, 1998)*, volume 251 of *London Math. Soc. Lecture Note Ser.*, pages 32–60. Cambridge Univ. Press, Cambridge, 1998.
[5] *NIST Digital Library of Mathematical Functions.* http://dlmf.nist.gov/, Release 1.0.16 of 2017-09-18. F. W. J. Olver, A. B. Olde Daalhuis, D. W. Lozier, B. I. Schneider, R. F. Boisvert, C. W. Clark, B. R. Miller and B. V. Saunders, eds.
[6] R.A. Horn and C.R. Johnson. *Matrix Analysis.* Cambridge University Press, New York, NY, USA, 1986.
[7] A. Jiménez-Pastor. dd_functions: SAGE package. http://git.risc.jku.at/gitweb/?p=ajpastor/diff_defined_functions.git.
[8] A. Jiménez-Pastor and V. Pillwein. A computable extension for holonomic functions: DD-finite functions. Technical Report 2017-10, DK Computational Mathematics, 12 2017.
[9] M. Kauers. The Holonomic Toolkit. In J. Blümlein and C. Schneider, editors, *Computer Algebra in Quantum Field Theory: Integration, Summation and Special Functions*, pages 119–144. Springer, 2013.
[10] M. Kauers, M. Jaroschek, and F. Johansson. Ore Polynomials in Sage. In Jaime Gutierrez, Josef Schicho, and Martin Weimann, editors, *Computer Algebra and Polynomials*, Lecture Notes in Computer Science, pages 105–125, 2014.
[11] M. Kauers and P. Paule. *The Concrete Tetrahedron: Symbolic Sums, Recurrence Equations, Generating Functions, Asymptotic Estimates.* Springer Publishing Company, Incorporated, 1st edition, 2011.
[12] E.R. Kolchin. *Differential algebra and algebraic groups.* Academic Press New York, 1973.
[13] C. Koutschan. *Advanced Applications of the Holonomic Systems Approach.* PhD thesis, RISC-Linz, Johannes Kepler University, September 2009.
[14] N. W. McLachlan. *Theory and application of Mathieu functions.* Dover Publications, Inc., New York, 1964.
[15] M. Mezzarobba. NumGfun: a package for numerical and analytic computation and D-finite functions. In *ISSAC 2010—Proceedings of the 2010 International Symposium on Symbolic and Algebraic Computation*, pages 139–146. ACM, New York, 2010.
[16] R.P. Stanley. Differentiably finite power series. *European Journal of Combinatorics*, 1(2):175–188, 1980.
[17] R.P. Stanley. *Enumerative Combinatorics*, volume 2. Cambridge University Press, Cambridge, 1999.
[18] W.A. Stein et al. *Sage Mathematics Software (Version 8.1).* The Sage Development Team, 2017. http://www.sagemath.org.
[19] M. van der Put and M.F. Singer. *Galois Theory of Linear Differential Equations.* Grundlehren der mathematischen Wissenschaften. Springer Berlin Heidelberg, 2003.
[20] M. van Hoeij. Formal solutions and factorization of differential operators with power series coefficients. *J. Symbolic Comput.*, 24(1):1–30, 1997.
[21] F. Winkler. *Polynomial Algorithms in Computer Algebra.* Springer-Verlag New York, Inc., Secaucus, NJ, USA, 1996.

An Efficient Algorithm for Computing Parametric Multivariate Polynomial GCD

Deepak Kapur
Department of Computer Science
University of New Mexico
Albuquerque, NM, USA
Kapur@cs.unm.edu

Dong Lu
[1]KLMM, Academy of Mathematics and Systems Science, Chinese Academy of Sciences
Beijing 100190, China
[2]School of Mathematical Sciences, University of Chinese Academy of Sciences
Beijing, China
donglu@amss.ac.cn

Michael Monagan
Department of Mathematics
Simon Fraser University
Burnaby, B.C., V5A 1S6, Canada
mmonagan@cecm.sfu.ca

Yao Sun
SKLOIS, Institute of Information Engineering, Chinese Academy of Sciences
Beijing, China
sunyao@iie.ac.cn

Dingkang Wang
[1]KLMM, Academy of Mathematics and Systems Science, Chinese Academy of Sciences
Beijing 100190, China
[2]School of Mathematical Sciences, University of Chinese Academy of Sciences
Beijing, China
dwang@mmrc.iss.ac.cn

ABSTRACT

A new efficient algorithm for computing a parametric greatest common divisor (GCD) of parametric multivariate polynomials over $k[\bar{u}][\bar{x}]$ is presented. The algorithm is based on a well-known simple insight that the GCD of two multivariate polynomials (non-parametric as well as parametric) can be extracted using the generator of the quotient ideal of a polynomial with respect to the second polynomial. And, further, this generator can be obtained by computing a minimal Gröbner basis of the quotient ideal. The main attraction of this idea is that it generalizes to the parametric case for which a comprehensive Gröbner basis is constructed for the parametric quotient ideal. It is proved that in a minimal comprehensive Gröbner system of a parametric quotient ideal, each branch of specializations corresponds to a principal parametric ideal with a single generator. Using this generator, the parametric GCD of that branch is obtained by division. This algorithm does not need to consider whether parametric polynomials are primitive w.r.t. the main variable. This is in sharp contrast to two algorithms recently proposed by Nagasaka (ISSAC, 2017). The resulting algorithm is not only conceptually simple to understand but is considerably efficient. The proposed algorithm and both of Nagasaka's algorithms have been implemented in Singular (available at http://www.mmrc.iss.ac.cn/~dwang/software.html), and their performance is compared on a number of examples. For more than two polynomials, this process can be repeated by considering pairs of polynomials; the efficiency in that case becomes even more evident.

ACM ISBN 978-1-4503-5550-6/18/07...$15.00
https://doi.org/10.1145/3208976.3208980

CCS CONCEPTS

• **Computing methodologies → Symbolic and algebraic algorithms**; **Algebraic algorithms**;

KEYWORDS

Parametric multivariate polynomial, Parametric GCD, Minimal comprehensive Gröbner system, Quotient ideal

ACM Reference Format:
Deepak Kapur, Dong Lu, Michael Monagan, Yao Sun, and Dingkang Wang. 2018. An Efficient Algorithm for Computing Parametric Multivariate Polynomial GCD. In *ISSAC'18: 2018 ACM International Symposium on Symbolic and Algebraic Computation, July 16–19, 2018, New York, NY, USA*. ACM, New York, NY, USA, 8 pages. https://doi.org/10.1145/3208976.3208980

1 INTRODUCTION

Multivariate polynomial GCD computation is one of the most important operations in computer algebra as it is used in many algorithms and applications. The problem has been extensively investigated and numerous algorithms have been developed to compute the GCD efficiently beyond Euclid's algorithm using division for univariate polynomials and its extension to multivariate polynomials using pseudo-division. Brown's modular GCD algorithm from [3] was the first GCD algorithm that avoided intermediate expression swell. For sparse polynomials Moses and Yun in [14] developed the EZ GCD algorithm which is based on Hensel lifting. Zippel's sparse modular GCD algorithm [21] uses sparse interpolation. It is currently used in Maple, Magma, and Mathematica. We mention also algorithms of Gianni *et al.* [7] and Sasaki *et al.* [18] which compute a GCD from a Gröbner basis. For sparse multivariate polynomials, Sanuki *et al.* [17] utilized Extended Hensel Construction to compute GCD and found that their algorithm to be comparable in performance to Maple's GCD routine.

Using the concept of parametric polynomials, there have also been many publications studying how to compute the GCD of parametric polynomials. Abramov and Kvashenko [1] used the subresultant chain to compute a parametric univariate polynomial GCD. Ayad [2] presented three algorithms based on parametrization of the Gaussian elimination procedure to compute GCD of a finite set of parametric univariate polynomials. At ISSAC 2017, Nagasaka [16] extended the ideas of Gianni and Trager [7] as well as Sasaki *et al.* [18] to polynomials with parameters for computing the GCD of parametric multivariate polynomials. The main tool used in Nagasaka's algorithms is the comprehensive Gröbner system which is the parametric extension of Gröbner basis, introduced by Weispfenning [20] (and independently by [8] as parametric Gröbner basis) and was improved by Suzuki *et al.* [19], Kapur *et al.* [9, 10] and Nabeshima [15]. In Nagasaka's paper, the algorithms to compute the GCD of parametric multivariate polynomials need to consider whether parametric polynomials are primitive w.r.t. x_1 under different parametric constraints. Moreover, he had to construct an ideal that is maximal for any specialization based on extending Gianni and Trager's results [7]. Both of these steps in his algorithms can be extremely time consuming.

This paper presents a new efficient algorithm for the GCD computation of parametric multivariate polynomials. The main idea of the new algorithm comes from computing a minimal Gröbner basis of a non-parametric colon ideal of two polynomials in the nonparametric case. Let k be a field, $k[\vec{x}]$ be the polynomial ring in the variables $\vec{x} = \{x_1, \ldots, x_n\}$. Assume that f and g are two nonzero polynomials in $k[\vec{x}]$. It is easy to see that the minimal Gröbner basis of the quotient ideal $\langle f\rangle : g$ has only one polynomial h. Then, the GCD of f and g is $\frac{f}{h}$. Most importantly, this construction extends to the case of parametric polynomials in which a Gröbner basis computation of the quotient ideal is replaced by comprehensive Gröbner system construction for parametric polynomials. To compute the GCD of more than two parametric polynomials, the above method is repeated much as in the case of computing the GCD of a family of numbers. Compared with Nagasaka's algorithms, the new algorithm has two advantages: there is no need to check whether parametric polynomials are primitive w.r.t. x_1 in each iteration, and further, it is guaranteed that a parametric polynomial f is divisible by the result in the quotient ideal.These merits make the proposed algorithm more efficient.

This paper is organized as follows. In Section 2, we provide background about the GCD and the comprehensive Gröbner computations for parametric multivariate polynomials. Nagasaka's algorithms are reviewed in Section 3. The proposed algorithm is presented in Section 4. To provide intuition and make the presentation simple, we first briefly discuss how the GCD of non-parametric polynomials can be computed using a minimal Gröbner basis of a quotient ideal. This is followed by extending this method to parametric polynomials. The new algorithm is presented. In Section 5, a non-trivial example is given to illustrate the key steps of the proposed algorithm. This is followed by some remarks about computing the GCD of a system of parametric polynomials in Section 6. Experimental data and a comparison with Nagasaka's algorithms are presented in Section 7. We end with some concluding remarks in Section 8.

2 PRELIMINARIES

Let k be a number field, $\bar{k}$ be the algebraic closure of k, $k[\vec{x}]$ be the polynomial ring in the variables $\vec{x} = \{x_1, \ldots, x_n\}$, $k[\vec{u}]$ be the parametric polynomial ring in the parameters $\vec{u} = \{u_1, \ldots, u_m\}$, and $k[\vec{u}][\vec{x}]$ be the polynomial ring over the parameter ring $k[\vec{u}]$ in $\vec{x}$. It is assumed that $\vec{x} \cap \vec{u} = \emptyset$, i.e., $\vec{x}$ and $\vec{u}$ are disjoint sets. In some cases, we abbreviate $\{x_i, x_{i+1}, \ldots, x_n\}$ to $\vec{x}_i$ $(2 \le i \le n)$.

We introduce some notation and definitions for non parametric multivariate polynomials. Two polynomials $f(\vec{x})$, $g(\vec{x}) \in k[\vec{x}]$ are associates if $\exists c \in \bar{k}$ such that $f(\vec{x}) = c\, g(\vec{x})$; we denote this equivalence relation by $f(\vec{x}) \sim g(\vec{x})$. For a polynomial $f \in k[\vec{x}]$, the leading term, leading coefficient, leading monomial and the total degree of f w.r.t. a monomial order $\prec$ are denoted by $\mathrm{lt}(f)$, $\mathrm{lc}(f)$, $\mathrm{lm}(f)$ and $\mathrm{tdeg}(f)$ respectively. We have $\mathrm{lt}(f) = \mathrm{lc}(f) \cdot \mathrm{lm}(f)$. The ideal in $k[\vec{x}]$, generated by $f_1, \ldots, f_s$, is denoted by $\langle f_1, \ldots, f_s\rangle$.

Definition 2.1. Let $f_1, \ldots, f_s \in k[\vec{x}]$. Then $h \in k[\vec{x}]$ is called a **greatest common divisor** (GCD) of $f_1, \ldots, f_s$, denoted $h = \gcd(f_1, \ldots, f_s)$, if

(1) $\forall i$ $(1 \le i \le s)$, h divides f_i and
(2) if g is any polynomial which divides $f_1, \ldots, f_s$, then g divides h.

Particularly, we define $\gcd(f_1, \ldots, f_s) = \gcd(f_2, \ldots, f_s)$ if $f_1 = 0$, and $\gcd(0, 0) = 0$, for convenience.

A GCD of polynomials is defined modulo associates. For any given polynomials $f_1, \ldots, f_s \in k[\vec{x}]$, there exist $\bar{f}_1, \ldots, \bar{f}_s \in$

$k[\vec{x}]$ such that

$$f_i = \gcd(f_1, \ldots, f_s) \cdot \bar{f}_i, \quad (1 \le i \le s)$$

then $\bar{f}_1, \ldots, \bar{f}_s$ are called the **cofactors** of $f_1, \ldots, f_s$.

Definition 2.2. Let $f \in k[\vec{x}]$. f is said to be primitive w.r.t. x_1 if it is primitive as a polynomial in $k[\vec{x}_2][x_1]$, that is, its coefficients in $k[\vec{x}_2]$ are co-prime.

Definition 2.3. Let g be a nonzero multivariate polynomial and I is an ideal in $k[\vec{x}]$. The set

$$I : g = \{f \in k[\vec{x}] : fg \in I\}$$

is called the **quotient ideal** (or **colon ideal**) of I divided by g.

For example, in $k[x_1, x_2, x_3]$ we have $\langle x_1x_3, x_2x_3\rangle : x_3 = \{f \in k[x_1, x_2, x_3] : x_3 f \in \langle x_1x_3, x_2x_3\rangle\} = \{f \in k[x_1, x_2, x_3] : x_3 f = Ax_1x_3 + Bx_2x_3\} = \{f \in k[x_1, x_2, x_3] : f = Ax_1 + Bx_2\} = \langle x_1, x_2\rangle$, where $A, B \in k[x_1, x_2, x_3]$.

Definition 2.4. A **minimal Gröbner basis** for a polynomial ideal $I \subseteq k[\vec{x}]$ is a Gröbner basis G for I such that:

(1) $\mathrm{lc}(p) = 1$ for all $p \in G$;
(2) $\mathrm{lm}(p) \notin \langle \mathrm{lm}(G - \{p\})\rangle$ for all $p \in G$.

Next we introduce some notation and definitions for parametric multivariate polynomials. For a polynomial $g \in k[\vec{u}][\vec{x}]$, the leading term, leading coefficient, leading monomial and total degree of g w.r.t. the monomial order $\prec_{\vec{x}}$ are denoted by $\mathrm{lt}_{\vec{x}}(g)$, $\mathrm{lc}_{\vec{x}}(g)$, $\mathrm{lm}_{\vec{x}}(g)$ and $\mathrm{tdeg}_{\vec{x}}(g)$ respectively. If $g \in k[\vec{x}]$ or $g \in k[\vec{u}][\vec{x}]$, we use $\mathrm{lc}_{x_i}(g)$ to denote the leading coefficient of g w.r.t. x_i.

A **specialization** of $k[\vec{u}]$ is a homomorphism $\sigma : k[\vec{u}] \to \bar{k}$. In this paper, we only consider the specializations induced by the elements in $\bar{k}^m$. That is, for $\vec{a} \in \bar{k}^m$, the induced specialization $\sigma_{\vec{a}}$ is defined as

$$\sigma_{\vec{a}} : \varphi \to \varphi(\vec{a}),$$

where $\varphi \in k[\vec{u}]$. Every specialization σ: $k[\vec{u}] \to \bar{k}$ extends canonically to a specialization σ: $k[\vec{u}][\vec{x}] \to \bar{k}[\vec{x}]$ by applying σ coefficient-wise.

For an ideal $E \subset k[\vec{u}]$, the variety defined by E in $\bar{k}^m$ is denoted by $\mathbf{V}(E) = \{\vec{a} \in \bar{k}^m \mid f(\vec{a}) = 0 \text{ } for \text{ } all \text{ } f \in E\}$. In this paper, an **algebraically constructible set** A always has the form: $A = \mathbf{V}(E) \setminus \mathbf{V}(N)$, where E, N are ideals in $k[\vec{u}]$. It is easy to see that the algebraically constructible set A is not empty by ensuring that at least one $f \in N$ is not in the radical of E. Let $V \subset \bar{k}^m$ be a variety. Let $\mathbf{I}(V) = \{f \in k[\vec{u}] \mid f(\vec{a}) = 0 \text{ } for \text{ } all \text{ } \vec{a} \in V\}$. According to Corollary 3 ([4], page 176), $\mathbf{I}(V)$ is a radical ideal.

For a parametric polynomial system, the comprehensive Gröbner system and minimal comprehensive Gröbner system are given below.

Definition 2.5. Let F be a set in $k[\vec{u}][\vec{x}]$, $A_1, \ldots, A_l$ be algebraically constructible subsets of $\bar{k}^m$, $G_1, \ldots, G_l$ be subsets of $k[\vec{u}][\vec{x}]$, and S be a subset of $\bar{k}^m$ such that $S \subset A_1 \cup \cdots \cup A_l$. A finite set $\mathcal{G} = \{(A_1, G_1), \ldots, (A_l, G_l)\}$ is called a **comprehensive Gröbner system** (CGS) on S for F if $\sigma_{\vec{a}}(G_i)$ is a Gröbner basis for for the ideal $\langle\sigma_{\vec{a}}(F)\rangle \subset \bar{k}[\vec{x}]$ for $\vec{a} \in A_i$ and $i = 1, \ldots, l$. Each (A_i, G_i) is called a branch of $\mathcal{G}$. In particular, if $S = \bar{k}^m$, then $\mathcal{G}$ is called a comprehensive Gröbner system for F.

Definition 2.6. A comprehensive Gröbner system $\mathcal{G} = \{(A_1, G_1), \ldots, (A_l, G_l)\}$ on S for F is said to be **minimal**, if for every $i = 1, \ldots, l$,

(1) $A_i \neq \emptyset$, and furthermore, for each $j = 1, \ldots, l$, $A_i \cap A_j = \emptyset$ whenever $i \neq j$;
(2) $\sigma_{\vec{a}}(G_i)$ is a minimal Gröbner basis for $\langle\sigma_{\vec{a}}(F)\rangle \subset \bar{k}[\vec{x}]$ for $\vec{a} \in A_i$;
(3) for each $g \in G_i$, $\sigma_{\vec{a}}(\mathrm{lc}_{\vec{x}}(g)) \neq 0$ for any $\vec{a} \in A_i$.

Abramov and Kvashenko [1] studied the parametric GCD of univariate polynomials with one parameter. The definition of parametric GCD (one parameter) can be easily extended to the case m ($m \ge 1$).

Definition 2.7. For $F = \{f_1, \ldots, f_s\} \subset k[\vec{u}][\vec{x}]$ and $S \subset \bar{k}^m$, we call $\{(A_1, g_1), \ldots, (A_r, g_r)\}$ a **parametric GCD** of F on S, if for every $i = 1, \ldots, r$, $\sigma_{\vec{a}}(g_i)$ is a GCD of $\sigma_{\vec{a}}(F)$ for any specialization $\vec{a} \in A_i$, where $A_1, \ldots, A_r \subset \bar{k}^m$ are algebraically constructible sets and $S = \cup_{i=1}^r A_i$, $g_1, \ldots, g_r \in k[\vec{u}][\vec{x}]$. If $S = \bar{k}^m$, we simply call it a parametric GCD of F.

3 NAGASAKA'S ALGORITHMS

As stated in the introduction, the GCD of polynomials have been extensively studied in the literature because of the enormous importance of this operation in many symbolic computation algorithms and applications; see [3, 14, 21] for instance. The main issue in the GCD computation is that of intermediate expression swell as analyzed in Knuth vol. 2.

Gianni *et al.* [7] and Sasaki *et al.* [18] studied the GCD of polynomials by computing a Gröbner basis instead of using the Euclidean algorithm. Nagasaka [16] extended their results to polynomials with parameters and proposed two algorithms to compute the parametric GCD of parametric polynomials. In the following, we provide an overview of Nagasaka's algorithms and illustrate their shortcomings; more details about the algorithms can be found in [16].

3.1 Extending Gianni and Trager's Algorithm

Nagasaka extended Proposition 2 in [7] to state:

LEMMA 3.1. *Let $f_1, \ldots, f_s, g \in k[\vec{x}]$ be primitive w.r.t. x_1, J be a maximal ideal in $k[\vec{x}_2]$ such that $\langle f_1, \ldots, f_s, J\rangle \ni 1$ and $\langle \mathrm{lc}_{x_1}(gf_i), J\rangle \ni 1$ for some i. Let G be a Gröbner basis for $\langle gf_1, \ldots, gf_s, J^r\rangle$ w.r.t. any total degree order. Then, the polynomial $\bar{g}$ in G of least total degree is an associate of g if the least total degree of the elements in J^r is larger than* $\mathrm{tdeg}(g)^2$.

Nagasaka further extended Lemma 3.1 to the case of parametric polynomials for which additional conditions on the ideal $J \subset k[\vec{u}][\vec{x}_2]$ for each specialization $\vec{\omega} \in \bar{k}^m$ must be satisfied:

(1) $\sigma_{\vec{\omega}}(f_1), \ldots, \sigma_{\vec{\omega}}(f_s)$ are primitive w.r.t. x_1;

(2) $\sigma_{\vec{\omega}}(J)$ is a maximal ideal in $k[\vec{x}_2]$;
(3) $\langle \mathrm{lc}_{x_1}(\sigma_{\vec{\omega}}(f_i)), \sigma_{\vec{\omega}}(J)\rangle \ni 1$ for some i;
(4) $\langle \bar{f}_1, \ldots, \bar{f}_s, \sigma_{\vec{\omega}}(J)\rangle \ni 1$, where each $\bar{f}_i \in k[\vec{x}]$ is the cofactor of $\sigma_{\vec{\omega}}(f_i)$.

To satisfy these conditions, the parametric space $\bar{k}^m$ needs to be decomposed into branches such that F and each J have the following properties.

Definition 3.2. For the given $F = \{f_1, \ldots, f_s\} \subset k[\vec{u}][\vec{x}]$ with $S \subset \bar{k}^m$ and $J \subset k[\vec{u}][\vec{x}_2]$, we introduce the following.

(1) F is said to be S-**primitive** if for any specialization $\vec{\omega} \in S$, $\sigma_{\vec{\omega}}(f_1), \ldots, \sigma_{\vec{\omega}}(f_s)$ are primitive w.r.t. x_1;
(2) J is said to be S-**maximal** if for any specialization $\vec{\omega} \in S$, $\sigma_{\vec{\omega}}(J)$ is a maximal ideal in $k[\vec{x}_2]$;
(3) F is said to be S-**nonvanishlc** if for any specialization $\vec{\omega} \in S$, $\mathrm{lc}_{x_1}(\sigma_{\vec{\omega}}(f_i)) = \sigma_{\vec{\omega}}(\mathrm{lc}_{x_1}(f_i))$ for each i;
(4) F is said to be S-**nondegenerate** if for any specialization $\vec{\omega} \in S$, $\langle \mathrm{lc}_{x_1}(\sigma_{\vec{\omega}}(f_i)), \sigma_{\vec{\omega}}(J)\rangle \ni 1$ for some i;
(5) J is said to be S-**luckyprime** if for any specialization $\vec{\omega} \in S$, $\langle \bar{f}_1, \ldots, \bar{f}_s, \sigma_{\vec{\omega}}(J)\rangle \ni 1$, where each $\bar{f}_i \in k[\vec{x}]$ is the cofactor of $\sigma_{\vec{\omega}}(f_i)$.

Under these conditions, Nagasaka proposed an algorithm to compute the parametric GCD by combining Lemma 3.1 and Definition 3.2, which we call henceforth, the Nagasaka-GT algorithm.

Step 1: compute the S-primitive part of F w.r.t. x_1;
Step 2: decompose S such that F is S-nonvanishlc;
Step 3: construct a maximal ideal $J \subset k[\vec{x}_2]$ such that F is S-nondegenerate;
Step 4: compute a minimal CGS for $\langle F \cup J^r\rangle$ on S, where r satisfies the degree condition of Lemma 3.1;
Step 5: check whether J is a S-luckyprime, if not, return to the Step 3;
Step 6: obtain the parametric GCD of F.

As the reader will notice, the above conditions are complicated and not easy to appreciate. Further, while implementing the Nagasaka-GT algorithm in Singular, we discovered the following shortcomings. Without any loss of generality, we assume in the following examples that $\vec{u} = \{a, b\}$, $\vec{x} = \{x_1, x_2, x_3\}$ and $S = \mathbb{C}$ and consider the lexicographic order with $x_1 \succ x_2 \succ x_3$.

(1) In Step 1, Nagasaka needs to call this algorithm repeatedly to compute the primitive part of each parametric polynomial. For example, we want to compute the primitive part of $f = (1-a)x_1^3x_2^2 + a(b-1)x_1^3x_2x_3 + (a^2 - a)x_1x_2^2 + (a-b)x_1x_3 + (a-1)x_2^2 + a(b-1)x_2x_3^3 + ax_3$ w.r.t. x_1 on $\mathbb{C}$. We must know the parametric GCD of coefficients of f w.r.t. x_1 on $\mathbb{C}$, i.e., we have to call this algorithm to compute the parametric GCD of f_{11}, f_{12}, f_{13}, where $f_{11} = (1-a)x_2^2 + a(b-1)x_2x_3$, $f_{12} = (a^2-a)x_2^2 + (a-b)x_3$ and $f_{13} = (a-1)x_2^2 + a(b-1)x_2x_3^3 + ax_3$. As the number of variables increases, this becomes more and more tedious, resulting in computational inefficiency.
(2) Step 2 is not necessary. Step 1 has ensured that the leading coefficient of f w.r.t. x_1 is not zero on each branch S_j, i.e, $\mathrm{lc}_{x_1}(\sigma_{\vec{\omega}}(f)) = \sigma_{\vec{\omega}}(\mathrm{lc}_{x_1}(f))$ for any specialization $\vec{\omega} \in S_j$. Therefore, Step 2 can be removed.
(3) If the parameter space S is divided into many small areas, more and more maximal ideals need to be constructed in Step 3. Although Nagasaka proved that a maximal ideal $J \subset k[x_2, x_3]$ which is S-nondegenerate and S-luckyprime can be constructed in a finite number of steps, we do not know how much time it takes to construct so many maximal ideals.
(4) We need to estimate the value of r in Step 4. Since $J = \langle x_2 - c_2, x_3 - c_3\rangle$ and we do not know the polynomial g in Lemma 3.1, we often let $r := \min\{\mathrm{tdeg}_{\vec{x}}(f_i)^2 + 1 \mid f_i \in F\}$. For instance, let $F = \{f_1, f_2\}$, where $f_1 = ax_1^3x_2^2x_3 + (1-b)(x_2^2 + x_3)$, $f_2 = (1-a)x_1^3x_2^2x_3 + b(x_2^2 + x_3)$. Then, $r = 37$. There are two problems: First, it will take more time to compute the minimal CGS of $\langle F \cup J^{37}\rangle$ which sometimes does not terminate. Second, since $c_2, c_3 \in \mathbb{C}$ are chosen randomly, sometimes c_i^{37} is a large integer.

3.2 Extending Sasaki and Suzuki's Algorithm

Sasaki and Suzuki [18] also used a Gröbner basis construction to compute the GCD of polynomials, by improving upon Gianni and Trager's results. They obtained a similar theorem, but did not need to use a maximal ideal J.

THEOREM 3.3. (Theorem 1 in [18]) *Let $f_1, f_2 \in k[\vec{x}]$ be primitive w.r.t. x_1, and G be the Gröbner basis w.r.t. any block order such that $x_1 \succ \vec{x}_2$ for $\langle f_1, f_2\rangle$. Then, there exists a polynomial $h \in k[\vec{x}_2]$ such that $\bar{g} = h \cdot \gcd(f_1, f_2)$, where $\bar{g}$ is the polynomial in G of least degree in x_1.*

Using the insight in Theorem 3.3, Nagasaka proposed a second algorithm (henceforth called, Nagasaka-SS algorithm).

Step 1: compute an S-primitive decomposition;
Step 2: compute a minimal CGS;
Step 3: compute a parametric GCD of coefficients of the candidate factor;
Step 4: compute the primitive part in each branch.

There are similarities between the Nagasaka-SS algorithm and Nagasaka-GT algorithm which are also sources of inefficiency: both need to compute S-primitive decompositions and make recursive calls to compute the parametric GCD of coefficients of polynomials. The Nagasaka-SS algorithm has been observed to be more efficient than the Nagasaka-GT algorithm, since the Nagasaka-SS algorithm does not need to construct many maximal ideals and only needs to compute the minimal CGS of $\langle F\rangle$ rather than $\langle F \cup J^r\rangle$.

4 THE PROPOSED ALGORITHM

We propose a new algorithm for computing the GCD of two parametric multivariate polynomials. To present the key ideas, we first give the algorithm for the non-parametric case and then we extend it to the parametric case. The key idea is well-known: compute the cofactor by computing the quotient ideal of one polynomial with respect to the other polynomial. This quotient ideal is known to be principal and has a single generator which can be computed by a single minimal Gröbner basis computation. This generator, which is the cofactor of the first polynomial, is used to obtain the GCD by dividing the polynomial by its cofactor. For the parametric case, a minimal comprehensive Gröbner system of a module is computed, leading to multiple branches for different specializations; for each branch, the generator is used to obtain the GCD for the associated parametric specializations.

To experimentally compare the proposed algorithm with both of Nagasaka's algorithms, we have implemented them all in Singular on a single platform so that their comparative performance can be fairly analyzed (Section 7).

4.1 GCD for Non-parametric Polynomials

As stated above, there are many well-known algorithms for computing the GCD of multivariate polynomials starting from Euclid's algorithm improved by Collins using reduced polynomial remainder sequences (PRS), Brown and Traub and Brown's subresultant PRS with EZGCD algorithm in MACSYMA for multivariate polynomials in general and Zippel's algorithm based on sparse interpolation which is more efficient for sparse polynomials. There are also algorithms based on Gröbner basis computations. We are, however, interested in algorithms which generalize to parametric polynomial systems. To our knowledge, algorithms based on the Euclidean division algorithm (really pseudo-division in case of multivariate polynomials) and hence, Gröbner bases are most suited to generalize to parametric polynomial systems.

THEOREM 4.1. *Consider two polynomials* $f_1, f_2 \in k[\vec{x}]\setminus\{0\}$ *such that* $f_1 = d \cdot \bar{f}_1$ *and* $f_2 = d \cdot \bar{f}_2$*, where* $d = \gcd(f_1, f_2)$ *and* $\gcd(\bar{f}_1, \bar{f}_2) = 1$*. Then,* $\langle \bar{f}_1 \rangle = \langle f_1 \rangle : f_2$*,* $\langle \bar{f}_2 \rangle = \langle f_2 \rangle : f_1$*.*

Theorem 4.1 implies that $\langle f_1 \rangle : f_2$ is a principal ideal. A minimal Gröbner basis G of $\langle f_1 \rangle : f_2$ w.r.t. a monomial order $\prec$ is $\{g\}$ such that $\gcd(f_1, f_2) = f_1/g$. Depending upon the structure of f_1, f_2 and the degree of their GCD relative to the degrees of f_1, f_2, computing $\langle f_1 \rangle : f_2$ or $\langle f_2 \rangle : f_1$ can have varied performance.

A quotient ideal can be constructed using ideal intersection [4] (pp.183–197) which involves introducing a new variable z to construct a new ideal $J = \langle z f_1, (1-z) f_2 \rangle \subset k[z, \vec{x}]$. Given that the complexity of Gröbner basis computations is heavily influenced by the number of variables and the degrees of the polynomials, we believe that computations over modules are likely to be more efficient (Chapter 5, [5]).

Let $\mathbf{e_1} = (1, 0)$ and $\mathbf{e_2} = (0, 1)$. Then $\{\mathbf{e_1}, \mathbf{e_2}\}$ is a free basis of $(k[\vec{x}])^2$. For any element $\vec{v}$ in $(k[\vec{x}])^2$, it can be expressed as $\vec{v} = h_1 \cdot \mathbf{e_1} + h_2 \cdot \mathbf{e_2}$ where $h_1, h_2 \in k[\vec{x}]$. For any submodule W of $(k[\vec{x}])^2$, we can also compute the Gröbner basis of W. The module case follows the ideal case almost exactly. However, we need to extend the notion of monomial orders to the free module $(k[\vec{x}])^2$. Let $\prec$ be a monomial order on $k[\vec{x}]$, then extend $\prec$ to the $(k[\vec{x}])^2$ in a position over term fashion with $\mathbf{e_2} < \mathbf{e_1}$.

THEOREM 4.2. *Let* f_1, f_2 *be two polynomials in* $k[\vec{x}] \setminus \{0\}$ *and* $\prec$ *be a monomial order on* $k[\vec{x}]$*. Suppose* $W \subset (k[\vec{x}])^2$ *is a* $k[\vec{x}]$*-module generated by* $\{f_1 \cdot \mathbf{e_1}, f_2 \cdot \mathbf{e_1} - \mathbf{e_2}\}$ *and* G *is a* **minimal** *Gröbner basis of* W *w.r.t. an order extended from* $\prec$ *in a position over term fashion with* $\mathbf{e_2} < \mathbf{e_1}$*. Then there exists a unique polynomial* $g \in k[\vec{x}] \setminus \{0\}$ *such that* $g \cdot \mathbf{e_2} \in G$ *and* $\langle g \rangle = \langle f_1 \rangle : f_2$*.*

PROOF. Let $H = \{h \in k[\vec{x}] \mid h \cdot \mathbf{e_2} \in G\}$. We prove $\langle H \rangle = \langle f_1 \rangle : f_2$ below.

We first show $\langle f_1 \rangle : f_2 \subset \langle H \rangle$. For any given polynomial p in $\langle f_1 \rangle : f_2$, there exists a polynomial $q \in k[\vec{x}]$ such that $pf_2 = qf_1$. Then, $p \cdot \mathbf{e_2} = q(f_1 \cdot \mathbf{e_1}) - p(f_2 \cdot \mathbf{e_1} - \mathbf{e_2})$ implies $p \cdot \mathbf{e_2} \in W$. Since G is a minimal Gröbner basis of W, it follows that $p \in \langle H \rangle$.

For the converse, suppose $h \in \langle H \rangle$. Then there exist polynomials $g_1, \ldots, g_s, p_1, \ldots, p_s \in k[\vec{x}]$ such that $h = \sum_{i=1}^{s} (p_i g_i)$ and $g_i \cdot \mathbf{e_2} \in G$ for $1 \le i \le s$. Thus, we have $h \cdot \mathbf{e_2} \in \langle G \rangle$, which implies $h \cdot \mathbf{e_2} = A(f_1 \cdot \mathbf{e_1}) + B(f_2 \cdot \mathbf{e_1} - \mathbf{e_2})$ for some polynomials $A, B \in k[\vec{x}]$. From this equation we can obtain the following equations.

$$\begin{cases} 0 = Af_1 + Bf_2, \\ h = -B. \end{cases}$$

Therefore, we have $h \in \langle f_1 \rangle : f_2$.

In sum, we have $\langle H \rangle = \langle f_1 \rangle : f_2$. By Theorem 4.1, we obtain $\langle \bar{f}_1 \rangle = \langle H \rangle$, where $f_1 = d \cdot \bar{f}_1$, $f_2 = d \cdot \bar{f}_2$, and $d = \gcd(f_1, f_2)$. As f_1 and f_2 are both nonzero by assumption, $\langle H \rangle$ is not empty and is a principal ideal. Besides, G is a Gröbner basis of W, there must exist a polynomial $g \in k[\vec{x}] \setminus \{0\}$ such that $g \cdot \mathbf{e_2} \in G$ and $\mathrm{lm}(g) = \mathrm{lm}(\bar{f}_1)$. Moreover, we have $g = \bar{f}_1$ as G is minimal, because otherwise there should exist another polynomial in G that divides $(g - \bar{f}_1) \cdot \mathbf{e_2}$ and has a smaller leading monomial than $\mathrm{lm}(g)$. □

Theorem 4.1 only discusses the case when f_1 and f_2 are both nonzero polynomials. We can extend the result to more general cases.

COROLLARY 4.3. *Let* f_1, f_2 *be two polynomials in* $k[\vec{x}]$ *and* $\prec$ *be a monomial order on* $k[\vec{x}]$*. Suppose* $W \subset (k[\vec{x}])^2$ *is a* $k[\vec{x}]$*-module generated by* $\{f_1 \cdot \mathbf{e_1}, f_2 \cdot \mathbf{e_1} - \mathbf{e_2}\}$ *and* G *is a* **minimal** *Gröbner basis for* W *w.r.t. an order extended from* $\prec$ *in a position over term fashion with* $\mathbf{e_2} < \mathbf{e_1}$*. Let* $H = \{h \in k[\vec{x}] \mid h \cdot \mathbf{e_2} \in G\}$*. Then*

(1) *If* H *is empty, then* $f_1 = 0$ *and* $f_2 \neq 0$*. In this case,* $\gcd(f_1, f_2) = f_2$*.*
(2) *If* H *is not empty, then* $H = \{g\}$ *and* $\gcd(f_1, f_2) = f_1/g$*.*

PROOF. If $f_1 = 0, f_2 \neq 0$, then H can be checked to be empty. If $f_1 = f_2 = 0$, then $H = \{1\}$. If $f_1 \neq 0$ and $f_2 = 0$, then $H = \{1\}$ and $\gcd(f_1, f_2) = f_1$. In the case of f_1 and f_2 being nonzero, the result follows Theorem 4.2. □

By Corollary 4.3, the GCD of f_1 and f_2 can be obtained from the Gröbner basis G directly without any knowledge of f_1 or f_2 being zero or not.

4.2 GCD for Parametric Polynomials

The nice thing about using quotient ideals for computing the GCD is that Corollary 4.3 generalizes easily to the parametric case.

THEOREM 4.4. *Given $f_1, f_2 \in k[\vec{u}][\vec{x}]$ and an algebraically constructible set $A = \mathbf{V}(E) \setminus \mathbf{V}(N) \subset \bar{k}^m$, let $\mathcal{G} = \{(A_i, G_i)\}_{i=1}^{l}$ be a* **minimal** *comprehensive Gröbner system of the module $W = \langle f_1 \cdot \mathbf{e_1}, f_2 \cdot \mathbf{e_1} - \mathbf{e_2} \rangle$ on A w.r.t. an order extended from $\prec_{\vec{x}}$ in a position over term fashion with $\mathbf{e_2} < \mathbf{e_1}$. For each branch (A_i, G_i) let $H_i = \{h \in k[\vec{u}][\vec{x}] \mid h \cdot \mathbf{e_2} \in G_i\}$. Then we have the following results.*

(1) *If H_i is empty, then $\gcd(\sigma_{\vec{\omega}}(f_1), \sigma_{\vec{\omega}}(f_2)) = \sigma_{\vec{\omega}}(f_2)$ for any $\vec{\omega} \in A_i$.*
(2) *If H_i is not empty, then $H_i = \{g_i\}$ and $\gcd(\sigma_{\vec{\omega}}(f_1), \sigma_{\vec{\omega}}(f_2)) = \frac{\sigma_{\vec{\omega}}(f_1)}{\sigma_{\vec{\omega}}(g_i)}$ for any $\vec{\omega} \in A_i$.*

PROOF. Since $\mathcal{G}$ is a **minimal** comprehensive Gröbner system, in each branch (A_i, G_i), the set $\sigma_{\vec{\omega}}(G_i)$ is a minimal Gröbner basis for any $\vec{\omega} \in A_i$. Besides, there is no polynomial G_i specializes to 0 because the leading coefficients of all polynomials in G_i are nonzero under specialization. □

Note that in Theorem 4.4 (2), the expression $\frac{\sigma_{\vec{\omega}}(f_1)}{\sigma_{\vec{\omega}}(g_i)}$ is a polynomial in $k[\vec{x}]$ for any $\vec{\omega} \in A_i$, but the expression f_1/g_i is not necessarily a polynomial in $k[\vec{u}][\vec{x}]$. However, using pseudo-division of f_1 by g_i since $\mathrm{lc}_{\vec{x}}(g_i)$ is a nonzero polynomial in $k[\vec{u}]$ that does not vanish for any σ in the branch, an associate of $\frac{\sigma_{\vec{\omega}}(f_1)}{\sigma_{\vec{\omega}}(g_i)}$ is computed.

To compute $q \in k[\vec{u}][\vec{x}]$ such that $\sigma_{\vec{\omega}}(q) \sim \sigma_{\vec{\omega}}(f_1/g_i) = \sigma_{\vec{\omega}}(f_1)/\sigma_{\vec{\omega}}(g_i)$, f_1 is multiplied by $\mathrm{lc}_{\vec{x}}(g_i)$ repeatedly during pseudo-division so that

$$(\mathrm{lc}_{\vec{x}}(g_i))^k f_1 = q \cdot g_i + r,$$

and no term in r is divisible by the leading term $\mathrm{lm}_{\vec{x}}(g_i)$.

We use a simple example to illustrate this. Let $f = x^2 - by + b$, $g = ax$ with $q = \mathrm{Quo}(f, g)$ and an algebraically constructible set $A = \mathbf{V}(\langle ab \rangle) \setminus \mathbf{V}(\langle a \rangle)$. Using a lexicographic order on $\vec{x}$, where $\vec{x} = \{x, y\}$ and $x > y$, g pseudo-divides f in $k[\vec{u}][\vec{x}]$, giving $\mathrm{lc}_{\vec{x}}(g) \cdot f = x \cdot g + r$, where $r = -aby + ab$. It is obvious that r is zero on A. Thus $q = x$. Moreover, for any $\vec{\omega} \in A$, $\frac{\sigma_{\vec{\omega}}(f)}{\sigma_{\vec{\omega}}(g)} = \frac{1}{a}x$. Therefore, $\sigma_{\vec{\omega}}(q) \sim \sigma_{\vec{\omega}}(f)/\sigma_{\vec{\omega}}(g)$. This operation is similar to the pseudo-division algorithm in [12, 13].

4.3 The Algorithm

Now, we propose the main algorithm in this paper to compute the parametric GCD of parametric multivariate polynomials. This algorithm is called the **parametric GCD algorithm**.

PROPOSITION 4.5. *The parametric GCD algorithm works correctly.*

PROOF. The proof follows directly from Theorem 4.4. □

Algorithm 1: parametric GCD algorithm

Input : $f_1, f_2 \in k[\vec{u}][\vec{x}]$, a constructible set $A \subset \bar{k}^m$, and two monomial orders $\prec_{\vec{x}}, \prec_{\vec{u}}$.
Output : a comprehensive GCD: $\{(A_j, h_j)\}_{j=1}^{s}$, where $h_i = \gcd(f_1, f_2)$ under any specialization from A_j and $\cup_{j=1}^{s} A_j = A$.

```
begin
    compute a comprehensive Gröbner system
      {(A_i, G_i)}_{i=1}^s for the module ⟨f_1 · e_1, f_2 · e_1 − e_2⟩.
    let i = 1.
    while i ≤ s do
        let H_i = {h ∈ k[u][x] | h · e_2 ∈ G_i}.
        if H_i is empty then
            h_i = f_2 on A_i;
        else
            H_i has exactly one polynomial, say g_i; and
            h_i = Quo(f_1, g_i) on A_i.
        end if
        let i = i + 1.
    end while
    return {(A_j, h_j)}_{j=1}^s.
end
```

In the parametric GCD algorithm, if f_1 (or f_2) vanishes on the constructible set A, we only need to compute a minimal comprehensive Gröbner system $\{(A_j, h_j)\}_{j=1}^{s}$ of f_2 (or f_1), and then the GCD of f_1 and f_2 on each branch A_j is h_j.

We can compute the parametric GCD recursively if the number of polynomials is bigger than two.

5 AN ILLUSTRATIVE EXAMPLE

We illustrate the algorithm with a simple example. Let $f_1, f_2, f_3 \in \mathbb{C}[\vec{u}][\vec{x}]$ be as follows:

$$f_1 = ax^2 + bxy + a^2xz + abx + abyz + b^2y,$$
$$f_2 = ax^2 + bxy + (ab - a)xz - a^2x + (b^2 - b)yz - aby,$$
$$f_3 = ax^2 + bxy + a^2xz + (a^2 - ab)x + abyz + (ab - b^2)y,$$

where $\vec{u} = \{a, b\}$, $\vec{x} = \{x, y, z\}$, $\prec_{\vec{x}}$ and $\prec_{\vec{u}}$ are all lexicographic orders with $z < y < x$ and $b < a$, respectively.

We first compute a minimal CGS $\mathcal{G}_0$ of $\langle f_1 \cdot \mathbf{e_1}, f_2 \cdot \mathbf{e_1} - \mathbf{e_2} \rangle$. There are six branches in $\mathcal{G}_0$. The first branch of $\mathcal{G}_0$ is $(A_1, G_0) = (\mathbf{V}(\langle 0 \rangle) \setminus \mathbf{V}(\langle a^3 - a^2b + a^2 \rangle), \{(x + az + b) \cdot \mathbf{e_2}, ((a^2 - ab + a)xz + (a^2 + ab)x + (ab - b^2 + b)yz + (ab + b^2)y) \cdot \mathbf{e_1} + \mathbf{e_2}, f_1 \cdot \mathbf{e_1}\})$. Then, $H_0 = \{x + az + b \in \mathbb{C}[\vec{u}][\vec{x}] \mid (x + az + b) \cdot \mathbf{e_2} \in G_0\}$ and the GCD of f_1 and f_2 on A_1 is $h_1 = f_1/(x + az + b) = ax + by$. Similarly, the GCDs on other five branches are: $(A_2, h_2) = (\mathbf{V}(\langle a - b + 1 \rangle) \setminus \mathbf{V}(\langle 2b^2 - 3b + 1 \rangle), (b - 1)x + by)$, $(A_3, h_3) = (\mathbf{V}(\langle a, b - 1 \rangle), y)$, $(A_4, h_4) = (\mathbf{V}(\langle 2a + 1, 2b - 1 \rangle) \setminus \mathbf{V}(\langle b - 1 \rangle), -\frac{1}{2}x^2 + \frac{1}{2}xy + \frac{1}{4}xz - \frac{1}{4}x - \frac{1}{4}yz + \frac{1}{4}y)$, $(A_5, h_5) = (\mathbf{V}(\langle a, b \rangle), 0)$, and $(A_6, h_6) = (\mathbf{V}(\langle a \rangle) \setminus \mathbf{V}(\langle ab^3 - ab^2 - b^4 + 2b^3 - b^2 \rangle), by)$.

For A_1, we now compute the GCD of h_1 and f_3. A minimal CGS $\mathcal{G}_1$ of $\langle h_1 \cdot \mathbf{e_1}, f_3 \cdot \mathbf{e_1} - \mathbf{e_2} \rangle$ on A_1 has one branch: $(A_1, G_1) = (\mathbf{V}(\langle 0 \rangle) \setminus \mathbf{V}(\langle a^3 - a^2b + a^2 \rangle), \{\mathbf{e_2}, h_1 \cdot \mathbf{e_1}\})$. Then

$H_1 = \{1\}$ and the GCD of h_1 and f_3 on A_1 is $h_{11} = h_1/1 = ax + by$.

Using GCDs for other branches, compute the GCD of h_2 and f_3 on A_2. A minimal CGS $\mathcal{G}_2$ of $\langle h_2 \cdot \mathbf{e_1}, f_3 \cdot \mathbf{e_1} - \mathbf{e_2}\rangle$ on A_2 has one branch: $(A_2, G_2) = (\mathbf{V}(\langle a - b + 1\rangle) \setminus \mathbf{V}(\langle 2b^2 - 3b + 1\rangle), \{\mathbf{e_2}, h_2 \cdot \mathbf{e_1}\})$. Then $H_2 = \{1\}$ and the GCD of h_2 and f_3 on A_2 is $h_{22} = h_2/1 = (b-1)x + by$.

For the GCD of h_3 and f_3 on A_3: A minimal CGS $\mathcal{G}_3$ of $\langle h_3 \cdot \mathbf{e_1}, f_3 \cdot \mathbf{e_1} - \mathbf{e_2}\rangle$ on A_3, and obtain one branch: $(A_3, G_3) = (\mathbf{V}(\langle a, b-1\rangle), \{\mathbf{e_2}, h_3 \cdot \mathbf{e_1}\})$. $H_3 = \{1\}$ so the GCD of h_3 and f_3 on A_3 is $h_{33} = h_3/1 = y$.

For the GCD of h_4 and f_3 on A_4: A minimal CGS $\mathcal{G}_4$ of $\langle h_4 \cdot \mathbf{e_1}, f_3 \cdot \mathbf{e_1} - \mathbf{e_2}\rangle$ on A_4, has one branch: $(A_4, G_4) = (\mathbf{V}(\langle 2a+1, 2b-1\rangle) \setminus \mathbf{V}(\langle b-1\rangle), \{(2x - z + 1)\mathbf{e_2}, (3x - 3y) \cdot \mathbf{e_1} - 4\mathbf{e_2}\})$. $H_4 = \{2x - z + 1\}$ so the GCD of h_4 and f_3 on A_4 is $h_{44} = h_4/(2x - z + 1) = -x + y$.

For branch A_5, $h_5 = 0$ and f_3 vanishes giving the GCD $h_{55} = 0$.

For the GCD of h_6 and f_3 on A_6: A minimal CGS $\mathcal{G}_6$ of $\langle h_6 \cdot \mathbf{e_1}, f_3 \cdot \mathbf{e_1} - \mathbf{e_2}\rangle$ on A_6 also has a single branch: $(A_6, G_6) = (\mathbf{V}(\langle a\rangle) \setminus \mathbf{V}(\langle ab^3 - ab^2 - b^4 + 2b^3 - b^2\rangle), \{\mathbf{e_2}, h_6 \cdot \mathbf{e_1}\})$. Then $H_6 = \{1\}$ so the GCD of h_6 and f_3 on A_6 is $h_{66} = h_6/1 = by$.

The parametric GCDs of $\{f_1, f_2, f_3\}$ are

$$\begin{cases} (\mathbf{V}(\langle 0\rangle) \setminus \mathbf{V}(\langle a^3 - a^2b + a^2\rangle), ax + by), \\ (\mathbf{V}(\langle a - b + 1\rangle) \setminus \mathbf{V}(\langle 2b^2 - 3b + 1\rangle), (b-1)x + by), \\ (\mathbf{V}(\langle a, b-1\rangle), y), \\ (\mathbf{V}(\langle 2a+1, 2b-1\rangle) \setminus \mathbf{V}(\langle b-1\rangle), -x + y), \\ (\mathbf{V}(\langle a, b\rangle), 0), \\ (\mathbf{V}(\langle a\rangle) \setminus \mathbf{V}(\langle ab^3 - ab^2 - b^4 + 2b^3 - b^2\rangle), by). \end{cases}$$

6 GCD OF A SYSTEM OF POLYNOMIALS

Given a system of parametric polynomials (with more than 2 polynomials), their GCD can also be computed by successively computing the GCD two polynomials at a time. Which two polynomials we choose can make a big difference. We recognize that many heuristics are possible based on the degrees of the polynomials as well as by first considering specializations on which all but one polynomials vanish.

Currently, we compute the GCD of a pair of parametric polynomials whose output is a finite set of constructible sets with the corresponding GCD. For each such branch, the GCD is used to compute its GCD with the next polynomial leading to more branches. The performance of our naive implementation is reasonable because as computations proceed, the degree of intermediate GCDs goes down substantially. Our ultimate goal is to use a single comprehensive Gröbner system computation for this but we have not been able to develop such an algorithm yet.

7 IMPLEMENTATION AND COMPARATIVE PERFORMANCE

The proposed algorithm has been implemented in the computer algebra system *Singular (4-0-3)* [6]. The implementation has been tried on a number of examples including the examples in [16] and it has been compared with implementations of the two algorithms proposed by Nagasaka. The following table compares our implementation with Nagasaka's two algorithms for computing GCD of parametric multivariate polynomials (Nagasaka-GT and Nagasaka-SS) implemented by us in Singular. The parametric polynomials for the examples are given below:

Ex.1: $F_1 = \{ax^3 + (a^3 - a + 1)x^2y + (a^2 + 2)xy^2 + (3a^2 - 3)y^3, ax^3 + (a+1)x^2y + 4xy^2 + 3y^3\}$, $\vec{x} = \{x, y\}$, $\vec{u} = \{a\}$.

Ex.2: $F_2 = \{(x + ay + bz)^3 + c(x + ay + bz) + d, 3(x + ay + bz)^2 + c, 3a(x + ay + bz)^2 + ac, 3b(x + ay + bz)^2 + bc\}$, $\vec{x} = \{x, y, z\}$, $\vec{u} = \{a, b, c, d\}$.

Ex.3: $F_3 = \{axz + (a-1)yz, (a-1)x^2 + axy\}$, $\vec{x} = \{x, y, z\}$, $\vec{u} = \{a\}$.

Ex.4: $F_4 = \{ax^3y^2z + (1-b)(y^2+z), (1-a)x^3y^2z + b(y^2+z)\}$, $\vec{x} = \{x, y, z\}$, $\vec{u} = \{a, b\}$.

Ex.5: $F_5 = \{(1-a)y^2 - bx^2 - cxy, (1-b)x^2 - ay^2 - cxy\}$, $\vec{x} = \{x, y\}$, $\vec{u} = \{a, b, c\}$.

Ex.6: $F_6 = \{ax^2 + bxy + a^2xz + abx + abyz + b^2y, ax^2 + bxy + (ab-a)xz - a^2x + (b^2 - b)yz - aby, ax^2 + bxy + a^2xz + (a^2 - ab)x + abyz + (ab - b^2)y\}$, $\vec{x} = \{x, y, z\}$, $\vec{u} = \{a, b\}$.

Ex.7: $F_7 = \{ax^2y + bx + y^3, ax^2y + bxy + cx, y^2 + bx^2y + cxy\}$, $\vec{x} = \{x, y\}$, $\vec{u} = \{a, b, c\}$.

Ex.8: $F_8 = \{ax^3y + cxz^2, x^2y + 3dy + z, cx^2 + bxy, x^2y^2 + ax^2\}$, $\vec{x} = \{x, y, z\}$, $\vec{u} = \{a, b, c, d\}$.

Ex.9: $F_9 = \{(ax+by)(x+a)(y-b), (aby^2 + b - 1)(bx + ay)(x + b)(y - a), (axy + a^2x - 3a)(ax + by)(x + b), (bx + ay)(ax + by)(ax + b)(by + a)\}$, $\vec{x} = \{x, y\}$, $\vec{u} = \{a, b\}$.

Ex.10: $F_{10} = \{(1-a)x^2y + bx^2 + y^2, ax^2y + (1-b)xy + cx, y^2 + bx^2y + (1-c)xy\}$, $\vec{x} = \{x, y\}$, $\vec{u} = \{a, b, c\}$.

For all these examples, the term orders used on $\vec{u}$ and $\vec{x}$ are lexicographic orders, respectively.

In Table 1, entries labeled **New** are for the proposed algorithm. Timings were obtained on a Core i7-4790 3.60GHz with 4GB Memory running Windows 7. As is evident from Table 1, the proposed algorithm performs better than the Nagasaka's algorithms. Since the proposed algorithm is quite different from Nagasaka's algorithms, it is hard to analyze in theory where the improvements come from. In our opinion, the avoidance of checking primitivity contributes to most of the improvements. For interested readers, more comparative examples can be generated by the codes at: http://www.mmrc.iss.ac.cn/~dwang/software.html.

8 CONCLUDING REMARKS

A new algorithm for computing the parametric GCD has been proposed. Using module comprehensive Göbner system, the parametric GCD of multivariate polynomials can be computed. The experimental data in Table 1 suggests that the proposed algorithm is superior in practice in comparison with both the algorithms proposed by Nagasaka. We think this is because our method does not compute the primitive part of polynomials in different parameter spaces, and our theorem guarantees that a parametric polynomial is divisible by another parametric polynomial on various algebraically constructible sets. Since the computational efficiency of our algorithm depends on the number of branches in a module

Table 1: Timings

Example	Algorithm	Time(sec.)
Ex.1	New	0.640
	Nagasaka-GT	2.062
	Nagasaka-SS	0.809
Ex.2	New	1.023
	Nagasaka-GT	47.210
	Nagasaka-SS	19.680
Ex.3	New	0.836
	Nagasaka-GT	6.730
	Nagasaka-SS	4.125
Ex.4	New	0.597
	Nagasaka-GT	> 1h
	Nagasaka-SS	12.736
Ex.5	New	2.475
	Nagasaka-GT	10.760
	Nagasaka-SS	4.108
Ex.6	New	2.426
	Nagasaka-GT	> 1h
	Nagasaka-SS	21.558
Ex.7	New	6.419
	Nagasaka-GT	> 1h
	Nagasaka-SS	> 1h
Ex.8	New	5.286
	Nagasaka-GT	> 1h
	Nagasaka-SS	37.172
Ex.9	New	15.351
	Nagasaka-GT	> 1h
	Nagasaka-SS	98.744
Ex.10	New	10.011
	Nagasaka-GT	> 1h
	Nagasaka-SS	> 1h

comprehensive Gröbner system, we believe that the proposed algorithm can be further improved by removing inessential polynomials from comprehensive Gröbner system computations as discussed in [11]. This will be further studied in the future along with heuristics to minimize the number of branches to be considered for computing the GCD of a system of polynomials.

ACKNOWLEDGMENTS

This research was supported in part by the National Natural Science Foundation of China under Grant No. 11371356, the CAS Project QYZDJ-SSW-SYS022, the National Science Foundation DMS-1217054, the CAS/SAFEA International Partnership Program for Creative Research Teams, and the Strategy Cooperation Project AQ-1701. The authors would like to thank the anonymous referees for their detailed suggestions on the paper which have made it more readable.

REFERENCES

[1] S.A. Abramov and K.Y. Kvashenko. 1993. On the greatest common divisor of polynomials which depend on a parameter. In *Proceedings of the 1993 ACM International Symposium on Symbolic and Algebraic Computation*. 152–156.

[2] A. Ayad. 2010. Complexity of algorithms for computing greatest common divisors of parametric univariate polynomials. *International Journal of Algebra* 4, 4 (2010), 173–188.

[3] W.S. Brown. 1971. On Euclid's algorithm and the computation of polynomial greatest common divisors. *J. ACM* 18 (1971), 478–504.

[4] D. Cox, J. Little, and D. O'shea. 1992. *Ideals, varieties, and algorithms*. Springer, third edition.

[5] D. Cox, J. Little, and D. O'shea. 2005. *Using algebraic geometry*. Springer, New York, second edition.

[6] W. Decker, G.-M. Greuel, G. Pfister, and H. Schoenemann. 2016. SINGULAR 4.0.3. a computer algebra system for polynomial computations, FB Mathematik der Universitaet, D-67653 Kaiserslautern. https://www.singular.uni-kl.de/.

[7] P. Gianni and B. Trager. 1985. GCDs and factoring multivariate polynomials using Gröbner bases. In *Proceedings of EUROCAL '85, European Conference on Computer Algebra. Lecture Notes in Computer Science, vol 204. Springer, Berlin, Heidelberg*. 409–410.

[8] D. Kapur. 1995. An approach for solving systems of parametric polynomial equations. In *Principles and Practices of Constraint Programming*, Saraswat and Van Hentenryck (Eds.). MIT Press, 217–244.

[9] D. Kapur, Y. Sun, and D.K. Wang. 2010. A new algorithm for computing comprehensive Gröbner systems. In *Proceedings of the 2010 ACM International Symposium on Symbolic and Algebraic Computation*. 29–36.

[10] D. Kapur, Y. Sun, and D.K. Wang. 2013. An efficient algorithm for computing a comprehensive Gröbner system of a parametric polynomial system. *Journal of Symbolic Computation* 49 (2013), 27–44.

[11] D. Kapur and Y. Yang. 2014. An algorithm for computing a minimal comprehensive Gröbner basis of a parametric polynomial system. In *Proceedings of Conference Encuentros de Algebra Comptacionaly Aplicaciones (EACA)*.

[12] A. Montes. 2002. A new algorithm for discussing Gröbner bases with parameters. *Journal of Symbolic Computation* 33, 2 (2002), 183–208.

[13] A. Montes and H. Schoenemann. 2016. grobcov.lib. http://www.singular.uni-kl.de/Manual/latest/sing_900.htm.

[14] J. Moses and D.Y.Y. Yun. 1973. The EZ GCD algorithm. In *Proceedings of ACM'73*. ACM Press, New York, 159–166.

[15] K. Nabeshima. 2012. Stability conditions of monomial bases and comprehensive Gröbner systems. In *Proceedings of the International Conference on Computer Algebra in Scientific Computing*, Vol. 7442. Springer-Verlag, 248–259.

[16] K. Nagasaka. 2017. Parametric greatest common divisors using comprehensive Gröbner systems. In *Proceedings of the 2017 ACM on International Symposium on Symbolic and Algebraic Computation*. 341–348.

[17] M. Sanuki, D. Inaba, and T. Sasaki. 2016. Computation of GCD of sparse multivariate polynomials by extended hensel construction. In *Proceedings of the 2016 IEEE International Symposium on Symbolic and Numeric Algorithms for Scientific Computing*. 34–41.

[18] T. Sasaki and M. Suzuki. 1992. Three new algorithms for multivariate polynomial GCD. *Journal of Symbolic Computation* 13, 4 (1992), 395–411.

[19] A. Suzuki and Y. Sato. 2006. A simple algorithm to compute comprehensive Gröbner bases using Gröbner bases. In *Proceedings of the 2006 ACM International Symposium on Symbolic and Algebraic Computation*. 326–331.

[20] V. Weispfenning. 1992. Comprehensive Gröbner bases. *Journal of Symbolic Computation* 14, 3 (1992), 669–683.

[21] R. Zippel. 1979. Probabilistic algorithms for sparse polynomials. In *Proceedings of EUROSAM'79*. Springer-Verlag, 216–226.

Real Space Sextics and their Tritangents

Avinash Kulkarni
Simon Fraser University
Burnaby, Canada
avi_kulkarni@sfu.ca

Yue Ren
Max Planck Institute MIS Leipzig
Leipzig, Germany
yueren@mis.mpg.de

Mahsa Sayyary Namin
Max Planck Institute MIS Leipzig
Leipzig, Germany
mahsa.sayyary@mis.mpg.de

Bernd Sturmfels
Max Planck Institute MIS Leipzig
Leipzig, Germany
bernd@mis.mpg.de

ABSTRACT

The intersection of a quadric and a cubic surface in 3-space is a canonical curve of genus 4. It has 120 complex tritangent planes. We present algorithms for computing real tritangents, and we study the associated discriminants. We focus on space sextics that arise from del Pezzo surfaces of degree one. Their numbers of planes that are tangent at three real points vary widely; both 0 and 120 are attained. This solves a problem suggested by Arnold Emch in 1928.

ACM Reference Format:
Avinash Kulkarni, Yue Ren, Mahsa Sayyary Namin, and Bernd Sturmfels. 2018. Real Space Sextics and their Tritangents. In *ISSAC '18: 2018 ACM International Symposium on Symbolic and Algebraic Computation, July 16–19, 2018, New York, NY, USA*. ACM, New York, NY, USA, 8 pages. https://doi.org/10.1145/3208976.3208977

1 INTRODUCTION

We present a computational study of canonical curves of genus 4 over the field $\mathbb{R}$ of real numbers. Such a curve C, provided it is smooth and non-hyperelliptic, is the complete intersection in $\mathbb{P}^3$ of a unique surface Q of degree two and a (non-unique) surface K of degree three. Conversely, any smooth complete intersection of a quadric and a cubic in $\mathbb{P}^3$ is a genus 4 curve. The degree of $C = Q \cap K$ is six: any plane in $\mathbb{P}^3$ meets C in six complex points, counting multiplicity. We refer to such a curve C as a *space sextic*.

Any space sextic C has at least 120 complex tritangent planes, one for each odd theta characteristic of C. If the quadric Q is smooth, then these 120 planes are exactly the tritangents [9, Theorem 2.2]. However, if Q is singular, then the curve C has infinitely many tritangents. We can see this as follows. Any plane H tangent to Q contains the singular point of Q, and it is tangent to Q at every point in the line $H \cap Q$. Since the intersection of H and C is contained in Q, the plane H is tangent to C at every point in $C \cap H$.

In what follows we focus on the case when the quadric surface Q containing the space sextic C is singular. We adopt the convention that a *tritangent* of C is one of the 120 complex planes corresponding to the odd theta characteristics of C. A tritangent is *real* if it is defined by a linear form with real coefficients. A real tritangent is *totally real* if it touches the curve C at three distinct real points.

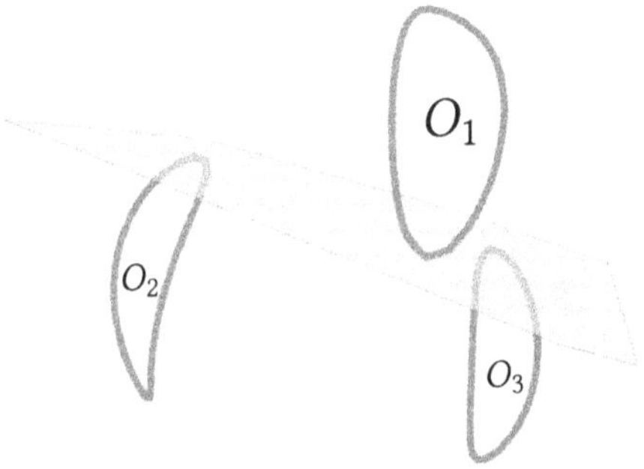

Figure 1: Totally real tritangent of a curve with three ovals. The plane touches O_1 on one side and O_2, O_3 on the other.

A space sextic C has at most five ovals [9, §3], since the maximum number of ovals is the genus of C plus one. By [9, Proposition 3.1], all 120 tritangents of C are real if and only if the number of ovals of C attains this upper bound. A heuristic argument suggests that at least $80 = \binom{5}{3} \times 8$ of the 120 real tritangents are totally real, since eight planes can touch three ovals as in Figure 1. The analogous fact for genus three curves is true: a plane quartic with four ovals has 28 real bitangents, of which at least $24 = \binom{4}{2} \times 4$ are totally real. The situation is more complicated in genus 4, as seen in Figure 2.

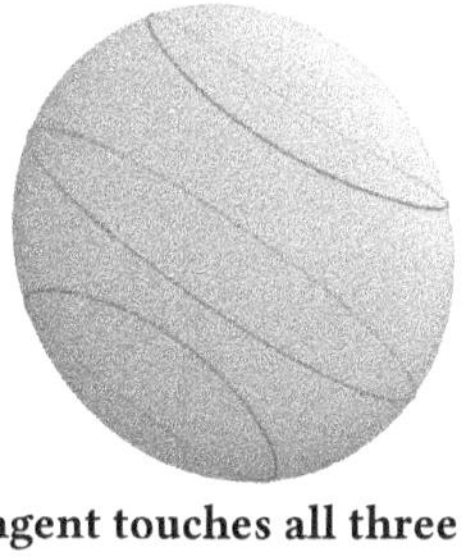

Figure 2: No tritangent touches all three ovals of this curve.

In 1928, Emch [6, §49] asked whether there exists a space sextic with all of its 120 tritangent planes totally real. He exhibited a curve suspected to attain the bound 120. However, ninety years later, Harris and Len [9, Theorem 3.2] showed that only 108 of the

ACM ISBN 978-1-4503-5550-6/18/07...$15.00
https://doi.org/10.1145/3208976.3208977

tritangents of Emch's curve are totally real. In [9, Question 3.3] they reiterated the question whether 120 totally real tritangents are possible. Our Example 2.2 answers that question affirmatively.

THEOREM 1.1. *The number of totally real tritangents of a space sextic with five ovals can be any integer between* 84 *and* 120. *Each of these numbers is realized by an open semialgebraic set of such curves.*

This article is organized as follows. In Section 2 we construct space sextics associated with del Pezzo surfaces of degree one. These curves lie on a singular quadric Q and are obtained by blowing up eight points in the plane. This construction has the advantage of producing 120 rational tritangents when the points are rational. In Section 2 we also prove Theorem 1.1. In Section 3 we extend this construction to real curves obtained from complex configurations in $\mathbb{P}^2$ that are invariant under complex conjugation. Theorem 3.1 summarizes what we know about these special space sextics. In Section 4 we turn to arbitrary space sextics, where Q is now generally smooth, and we show how to compute the 120 tritangents of $C = Q \cap K$ directly from the equations defining Q and K. Section 5 offers a study of the discriminants associated with our polynomial system, and Section 6 sketches some directions for future research. Finally, the scripts used throughout this article are available at [13].

2 EIGHT POINTS IN THE PLANE

We shall employ the classical construction of space sextics from del Pezzo surfaces of degree one. We describe this construction below and direct the reader to [5, §8] or [11, §2] for further details. Any space sextic C that is obtained from this construction is special: the quadric Q that contains C is singular. See also [12], where these curves C are referred to as *uniquely trigonal genus* 4 *curves.*

Fix a configuration $\mathcal{P} = \{P_1, P_2, P_3, P_4, P_5, P_6, P_7, P_8\}$ of eight points in $\mathbb{P}^2_{\mathbb{R}}$. We may assume that $\mathcal{P}$ is sufficiently generic to allow for the choices to be made below. Additionally, genericity of $\mathcal{P}$ ensures that the resulting space sextic C is a smooth curve in $\mathbb{P}^3$. For practical computations we always choose points P_i whose coordinates are in the field $\mathbb{Q}$ of rational numbers. This ensures that each object arising in our computations is defined over $\mathbb{Q}$.

The space of ternary cubics that vanish on $\mathcal{P}$ is two-dimensional. We compute a basis $\{u, v\}$ for that space. The space of ternary sextics that vanish doubly on $\mathcal{P}$ is four-dimensional, and it contains the three-dimensional subspace spanned by $\{u^2, uv, v^2\}$. We augment this to a basis by another sextic w that vanishes to order two on $\mathcal{P}$.

The blow-up of $\mathbb{P}^2$ at the eight points in $\mathcal{P}$ is a *del Pezzo surface* $X_{\mathcal{P}}$ of degree one. Our basis $\{u^2, uv, v^2, w\}$ specifies a rational map $\mathbb{P}^2 \dashrightarrow \mathbb{P}^3$ that is regular outside $\mathcal{P}$ and hence lifts to $X_{\mathcal{P}}$. This map is 2-to-1 and its image is the singular quadric $V(x_0x_2 - x_1^2)$. The ramification locus consists of two connected components, the isolated point $(0:0:0:1)$ and the intersection of the quadric $V(x_0x_2 - x_1^2)$ with a cubic C that is unique modulo $\langle x_0x_2 - x_1^2\rangle$.

Following [11, Example 2.5], we parametrize the singular quadric Q as $\{(1 : t : t^2 : W)\}$. This represents C by a polynomial in two unknowns (t, W) that has Newton polygon $\operatorname{conv}\{(0, 0), (6, 0), (0, 3)\}$:

$$C : t^6+c_1t^5+c_2t^4W+c_3t^4+c_4t^3W+c_5t^2W^2+c_6t^3+c_7t^2W+ \\ c_8tW^2+c_9W^3+c_{10}t^2+c_{11}tW+c_{12}W^2+c_{13}t+c_{14}W+c_{15}. \qquad (1)$$

We derive 120 tritangents of our curve C in $\mathbb{P}^3$ from the 240 exceptional curves on the del Pezzo surface $X_{\mathcal{P}}$ (cf. Lemma 2.1). There is an order two automorphism ι of $X_{\mathcal{P}}$, called the *Bertini involution.* The image of an exceptional curve C_1 under the Bertini involution ι is another exceptional curve $C_2 = \iota(C_1)$. If $\varphi\colon X_{\mathcal{P}} \to V(x_0x_2 - x_1^2)$ is the 2-to-1 covering branched along C, then $\varphi \circ \iota = \varphi$. In particular, $\varphi(C_1) = \varphi(C_2)$. The intersection $C_1 \cap C_2$ consists of three points on $X_{\mathcal{P}}$. Their image under φ is the triple of points at which the tritangent corresponding to $\{C_1, C_2\}$ touches C. We can thus decide whether a tritangent is totally real by checking whether the intersection $C_1 \cap C_2$ in $X_{\mathcal{P}}$ contains one or three real points. This intersection can be carried out in $\mathbb{P}^2$, as we shall explain next.

Recall that $X_{\mathcal{P}}$ is the blow-up of $\mathbb{P}^2$ at $\mathcal{P}$. By blowing down, we may view the eight exceptional fibers of the blow-up as the eight points of $\mathcal{P}$, and we may view the remaining 112 exceptional curves of $X_{\mathcal{P}}$ as (possibly singular) curves in $\mathbb{P}^2$. We can determine the images of the exceptional curves in $\mathbb{P}^2$ from [19, Table 1], as well as how they are matched into pairs $\{C_1, C_2\}$ via the Bertini involution:

- 8: The exceptional fiber at one point P_i matches the sextic vanishing triply at P_i and doubly at the other seven points. The three components of the tangent cone of this sextic determine the three desired points on the branch curve C.
- 28: The line through P_i and P_j matches the quintic vanishing at all eight points and doubly at the six points in $\mathcal{P}\backslash\{P_i, P_j\}$. Their intersection in $\mathbb{P}^2 \setminus \mathcal{P}$ consists of three complex points. Either one or three of them are real (see Figure 3).

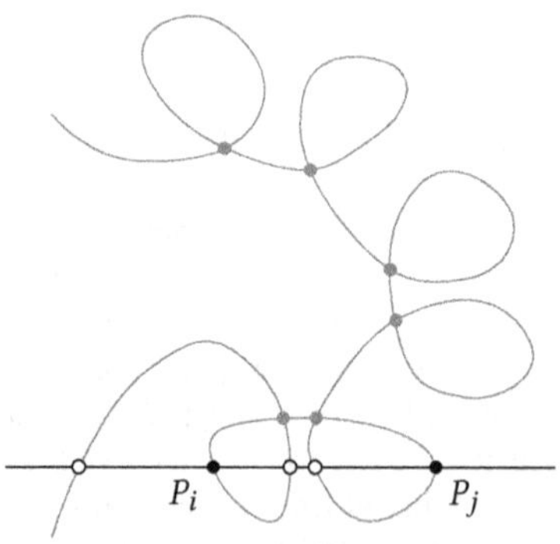

Figure 3: $\mathcal{P}$ determines 28 **lines meeting a rational quintic**

- 56: The conic through $P_{i_1}, \ldots, P_{i_5}$ matches the quartic vanishing at $\mathcal{P}$ and doubly at the three other points. Their intersection in $\mathbb{P}^2 \setminus \mathcal{P}$ consists of three complex points (see Figure 4).
- 56/2: For two points P_i and P_j, the cubic vanishing doubly at P_i, non-vanishing at P_j, and vanishing singly at $\mathcal{P}\backslash\{P_i, P_j\}$ matches the cubic vanishing doubly at P_j, non-vanishing at P_i, and vanishing singly at $\mathcal{P}\backslash\{P_i, P_j\}$. Their intersection in $\mathbb{P}^2\backslash\mathcal{P}$ consists of three points in $\mathbb{P}^2$ (see Figure 5).

The following lemma summarizes the reality issues on the del Pezzo surface $X_{\mathcal{P}}$ that arises from the constructions in $\mathbb{P}^2$ described above.

LEMMA 2.1. *Let $\{C_1, C_2\}$ be a pair of exceptional curves of type 8, 28, 56 or 56/2 contained in the del Pezzo surface $X_{\mathcal{P}}$ Then $\varphi(C_1 \cap C_2)$ spans a tritangent plane of the space sextic C in $\mathbb{P}^3$. That tritangent is totally real if and only if the intersection $C_1 \cap C_2$ is real on $X_{\mathcal{P}}$.*

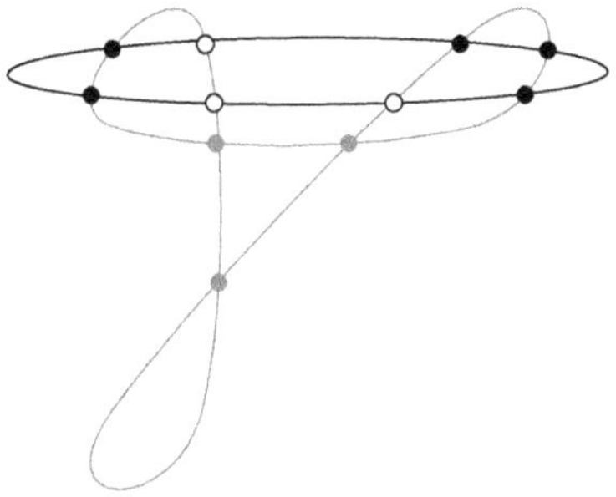

Figure 4: $\mathcal{P}$ determines 56 conics meeting a rational quartic

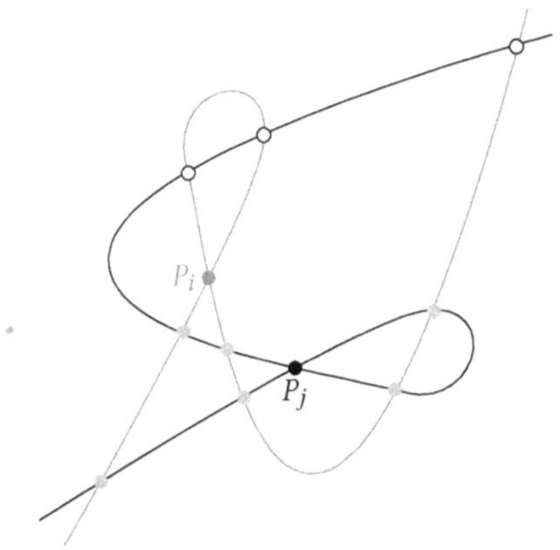

Figure 5: $\mathcal{P}$ determines 56/2 pairs of rational cubics

Proof. Let $-K$ be the anticanonical divisor class of $X_{\mathcal{P}}$. Then $-K$ and $-2K$ are ample but not very ample. The class $-3K$ is very ample, and its linear system embeds $X_{\mathcal{P}}$ into $\mathbb{P}^6$. Consider the sequence of maps $\mathbb{P}^2 \dashrightarrow X_{\mathcal{P}} \to V(x_0x_2 - x_1^2) \subset \mathbb{P}^3$. The first map is the blow-up, which is birational. The second map is the 2-1 morphism φ given by the linear system $|-2K|$. The second map takes the 240 exceptional curves in pairs $\{C_1, C_2\}$ onto the 120 hyperplane sections of $V(x_0x_2 - x_1^2)$ defined by the tritangent planes of C.

The pairs are as indicated above, since their classes add up to $-2K$ by [19, Table 1]. Intersection points of the pairs of curves on $X_{\mathcal{P}}$ become singular points of the intersection curves on $V(x_0x_2 - x_1^2)$, so the planes are tangent at those points. The tritangent being totally real means that these three points have real coordinates. □

In our computations, the del Pezzo surface $X_{\mathcal{P}}$ is represented by $(\mathbb{P}^2, \mathcal{P})$. For each of the triples of points described above, we can compute their images in $V(x_0x_2 - x_1^2) \subset \mathbb{P}^3$ using Gröbner-based elimination. These triples are the contact points of the corresponding tritangent plane of C. We may choose an affine open subset of $V(x_0x_2 - x_1^2)$, isomorphic to $\mathbb{A}^2$, containing these three points. The intersection of a plane in $\mathbb{P}^3$ with the singular quadric Q is represented on this open subset by a plane curve with Newton polygon $\operatorname{conv}\{(0,0), (2,0), (0,1)\}$. We normalize this as follows:

$$\text{tritangent planes:} \qquad t^2 + e_1t + e_2 + e_3W. \tag{2}$$

The upper bound in Theorem 1.1 is attained with Example 2.2.

Example 2.2. Consider the following configuration of eight points:

$$\mathcal{P} = \{ (1{:}0{:}0),\ (0{:}1{:}0),\ (0{:}0{:}1),\ (1{:}1{:}1),\ (10{:}11{:}1), \\ (27{:}2{:}17),\ (-19{:}11{:}-12),\ (-15{:}-19{:}20)\} \subset \mathbb{P}^2_{\mathbb{R}}.$$

The resulting space sextic C in $V(x_0x_2 - x_1^2)$ has 120 totally real tritangents. We prove this by computing the pairs of special curves in $\mathbb{P}^2$ and by computing their triples of intersection points as described above. For each of the $112 = 28 + 56 + 56/2$ pairs of curves as above, we found that all three intersection points are real. We verified that the remaining eight tritangents of C are also totally real by computing the tangent cones of the special sextics in item 8.

We now convert the curve C to the format in (1). From that we can recover the pair (Q, K) defining the canonical model of C, for the independent verification in Example 4.1. We start by computing the cubics u, v. They are minimal generators of the ideal $I := \bigcap_{i=1}^{8} \mathfrak{m}_{P_i}$, where $\mathfrak{m}_{P_i}$ denotes the maximal ideal corresponding to the point P_i:

$$\begin{aligned} u = {} & 7151648400xy^2 - 434820164119x^2z + 354394201544xyz \\ & - 38806821565y^2z + 692107405715xz^2 - 580026269975yz^2, \\ v = {} & 14303296800x^2y - 782195108453x^2z + 613370275528xyz - \\ & 49450554755y^2z + 1245021817105xz^2 - 1041049726225yz^2. \end{aligned}$$

Next, we compute the sextic w. It is the element of lowest degree in $I^{(2)} \setminus I^2$, where $I^{(2)}$ is the *symbolic square* of the ideal I. We find

$$\begin{aligned} w = {} & 17567406364174826186307358196968928 0x^4yz \\ & + 111155154295545647506864393467014 40x^3y^2z \\ & - 445819563363162103552629662552521920x^2y^3z \\ & + 264167833624792096768707005238371200xy^4z \\ & - 200369626564548183654878856379681 07x^4z^2 \\ & - 294913066878605444782558855953184976x^3yz^2 \\ & - 440622710904767923701179945218196 42x^2y^2z^2 \\ & + 755657199632193956412295956477085200xy^3z^2 \\ & - 416363969347671237983809688854251675y^4z^2 \\ & + 329055128149267102548173318886152 30x^3z^3 \\ & + 289931566371655705099858080895789 30x^2yz^3 \\ & + 408084518267021777532269243486778 90xy^2z^3 \\ & - 786825285955642438281852193533136 50y^3z^3 \\ & - 174528373018867309329004510048947 5x^2z^4 \\ & - 523785002916549858130362906690985 0xyz^4 \\ & - 246023791579452575541006631825987 5y^2z^4. \end{aligned}$$

The curve C is defined by the generator of the principal ideal

$$\left(\left(\langle \det J(u, v, w) \rangle + \mathrm{Minors}_{2\times 2} \begin{pmatrix} u^2 & uv & v^2 & w \\ 1 & t & t^2 & W \end{pmatrix} \right) : \langle u, v \rangle^2 \right) \cap \mathbb{Q}[t, W],$$

where $J(u, v, w)$ is the Jacobian matrix of the map $(x, y, z) \mapsto (u, v, w)$. The determinant of $J(u, v, w)$ gives the singular model of the branch curve in $\mathbb{P}^2$ and the 2×2 minors determine its image in the singular quadric in $\mathbb{P}^3$. In our case, the generator of the principal ideal is in the form of (1), and explicitly is given by

$$\begin{aligned} C:\ & 220701798714766542157344369814603731920649470787977748209t^6 \\ & + 5585831392725719195345163470516310362705889042844010328t^5 \\ & + 14175569812724447393500233789877848531491265t^4 W \\ & - 447718078603500717216424896040737869157828321607704039864t^4 \\ & - 86567655386571901223236593151698362962027440t^3 W \\ & + 57114529769698357624742306475t^2 W^2 \\ & + 474302309016648096934423520799618219755274954155075926592t^3 \\ & + 192856342071229007723481356183461213738057680t^2 W \\ & - 194302706043604453258752959400t W^2 - 26371599148125 W^3 \\ & + 2341397816853864817617847981162945070584483528261510775184t^2 \\ & - 183528856281941126263893376861009344326329920t W \\ & + 164969244105921949388612135400 W^2 \\ & - 5390258693970772695117811943833419754488807920338145746560t \\ & + 61550499069700173478724063089387654812308400W \\ & + 3193966974265623365398753846860968247266969720956505401600. \end{aligned}$$

We next compute each of the 120 tritangent planes explicitly, in the format (2). For instance, the tritangent that arises from the line spanned by the points (10:11:1) and (27:2:17) in $\mathcal{P}$ is found to be

$$\begin{aligned} & 345059077005W - 153208173277626716984179949t^2 \\ & + 277165925195542929496239488t - 2613400142391424482367340. \end{aligned}$$

We now have a list of 120 such polynomials. Each of these intersects the curve C in three complex points with multiplicity two in the (t, W)-plane. All of these complex points are found to be real.

Example 2.3. A similar computation verifies that the following configuration of eight points gives 84 totally real tritangents:

$$\mathcal{P} = \{(-12:9:11), (7:-5:-7), (1:3:3), (2:2:-1), (-2:2:1), (1:3:1), (3:3:2), (8:-8:-7)\} \subset \mathbb{P}^2_{\mathbb{R}}.$$

Proof of Theorem 1.1. The 120 tritangent planes arising from the construction above correspond to the odd theta characteristics of C. They are tritangent to C but they do not pass through the singular point $(0:0:0:1)$ of the quadric $V(x_0x_2 - x_1^2)$ in $\mathbb{P}^3$. Each such tritangent is an isolated regular solution to the polynomial equations that define the tritangents of C. These equations are described explicitly as the tritangent ideal in Section 4. We may perturb the equation $x_0x_2 - x_1^2$ to obtain a new curve C'. By the Implicit Function Theorem, for each tritangent H of C there is a nearby tritangent plane H' of C'. Moreover, if the perturbation is sufficiently small and the three points of $C \cap H$ are real and distinct, then $C' \cap H'$ also consists of three distinct real points. Conversely, if two points of $C \cap H$ are distinct and complex conjugate, then two points of $C' \cap H'$ will also be distinct and complex conjugate.

Hence, if our blow-up construction gives m totally real tritangents for some $m \leq 120$ then that same number of real solutions persists throughout some open semialgebraic subset in the space $\mathbb{P}^9_{\mathbb{R}} \times \mathbb{P}^{19}_{\mathbb{R}}$ of pairs (Q, K) of a real quadric and a real cubic in $\mathbb{P}^3$.

Examples 2.3 and 2.2 exhibit configurations with $m = 84$ and $m = 120$. Every integer m between these two values can be realized as well. We verified that assertion computationally, by constructing a configuration $\mathcal{P}$ in $\mathbb{P}^2_{\mathbb{Q}}$ for every integer between 84 and 120. □

Remark 2.4. It may be possible to prove by hand that every integer m between 84 and 120 is realizable. The idea is to connect the two extreme configurations with a general semialgebraic path in $\mathbb{P}^9_{\mathbb{R}} \times \mathbb{P}^{19}_{\mathbb{R}}$. That path crosses the *tritangent discriminant* Δ_2 (cf. Section 5) transversally. At such a crossing point, precisely one of the 120 configurations marked 8, 28, 56 or 56/2 fails to have its three intersection points distinct. This means that the number of real triples changes by exactly one. So, the number of totally real tritangents of the associated space sextic changes by exactly one. This is not yet a proof because the path might cross the discriminant Δ_1.

3 SPACE SEXTICS WITH FEWER OVALS

In Section 2 we started with eight points in the real projective plane $\mathbb{P}^2_{\mathbb{R}}$. Here we generalize by taking a configuration $\mathcal{P}$ in the complex projective plane $\mathbb{P}^2_{\mathbb{C}}$ that is invariant under complex conjugation. This also defines a real curve C in $V(x_0x_2 - x_1^2) \subset \mathbb{P}^3_{\mathbb{R}}$. To be precise, for $s \in \{1, 2, 3, 4, 5\}$, let $\mathcal{P}$ consist of $2s - 2$ real points and $5 - s$ complex conjugate pairs. Such a configuration of eight points defines a real del Pezzo surface $X_{\mathcal{P}}$. Additionally, the map $\mathbb{P}^2 \dashrightarrow \mathbb{P}^3$ and its branch curve C are defined over $\mathbb{R}$. The space sextic C has s ovals and it is not of dividing type when $s \leq 4$. By, [9, Proposition 3.1], the number of real tritangents of C equals 2^{s+2}. For curves which come from the construction in Section 2, we can derive this number by examining how complex conjugation acts on the special curves in $\mathbb{P}^2_{\mathbb{C}}$ we had associated with the point configuration $\mathcal{P}$:

- 8: The exceptional fiber over a point P_i defines a real tritangent if and only if the point P_i itself is real.
- 28: This tritangent is real if and only if the pair $\{P_i, P_j\}$ is real, i.e. either P_i and P_j are both real, or P_j is the conjugate of P_i. Among the 28 pairs, the number of real pairs is thus $\mathbf{4} = 0+4$, $\mathbf{4} = \binom{2}{2} + 3$, $\mathbf{8} = \binom{4}{2} + 2$ and $\mathbf{16} = \binom{6}{2} + 1$ for $s = 1, 2, 3, 4$.
- 56: This tritangent is real if and only if the triple of singular points in the quartic is real. This happens if either the three points are real, or there is one real point and a conjugate pair. Among the 56 triples, the number of real triples is thus $\mathbf{0}$, $\mathbf{6} = 0 + 2 \cdot 3$, $\mathbf{12} = \binom{4}{3} + 4 \cdot 2$, $\mathbf{26} = \binom{6}{3} + 6 \cdot 1$ for $s = 1, 2, 3, 4$.
- 56/2: In this case, the tritangent is real if and only if the two cubics are conjugate, and this happens if and only if the pair $\{P_i, P_j\}$ is real. Hence the count is $\mathbf{4}, \mathbf{4}, \mathbf{8}, \mathbf{16}$, as in the case 28.

For each value of $s \in \{1, 2, 3, 4\}$, if we add up the respective four numbers then we obtain 2^{s+2}. For instance, for $s = 3$, the analysis above shows that $4 + 8 + 12 + 8 = 32$ of the 120 tritangents are real.

We wish to know how many of these 2^{s+2} real tritangents can be totally real, as $\mathcal{P}$ ranges over the various types of real configurations. Our investigations led to the findings summarized in Theorem 3.1.

Theorem 3.1. *The third row in Table 1 lists the ranges of currently known values for the number of totally real tritangents of real space sextics C that are constructed by blowing up eight points in* $\mathbb{P}^2$*:*

s ovals	1	2	3	4	5
real	8	16	32	64	120
totally real	[0, 8]	[1, 15]	[10, 32]	[35, 63]	[84, 120]

Table 1: Real and totally real tritangents of a space sextic C on a singular quadric Q, according to number of ovals of C.

The following examples exhibit some lower and upper bounds.

Example 3.2 (s = 1). Let $\mathcal{P}$ be the following configuration in $\mathbb{P}^2_{\mathbb{C}}$:

$$P_1 = (i : 1 - i : 0), \qquad P_2 = \overline{P_1},$$
$$P_3 = (2 - i : -3 - i : 3 + i), \qquad P_4 = \overline{P_3},$$
$$P_5 = (2 - i : 1 - i : -2 - i), \qquad P_6 = \overline{P_5},$$
$$P_7 = (4i : -i : 4), \qquad P_8 = \overline{P_7}.$$

The curve C consists of only one oval in $\mathbb{P}^3_{\mathbb{R}}$. One checks that **none** of the eight real tritangents of C is totally real, i.e. no plane is tangent to C at three real points. On the other hand, for the following configuration, **all** eight real tritangents are totally real:

$$P_1 = (i : 0 : 1), \qquad P_2 = \overline{P_1},$$
$$P_3 = (1 - 3i : -3 + 2i : 1), \qquad P_4 = \overline{P_3},$$
$$P_5 = (0 : 2 + 3i : -3 - 2i), \qquad P_6 = \overline{P_5},$$
$$P_7 = (4i : -3 + 4i : 1 + i), \qquad P_8 = \overline{P_7}.$$

Example 3.3 (s = 2). We fix the following configuration $\mathcal{P}$ of two real points and three pairs of complex conjugate points in $\mathbb{P}^2$:

$$P_1 = (1 : -2i : 2i), \qquad P_2 = \overline{P_1},$$
$$P_3 = (1 : 3 + 2i : -3i), \qquad P_4 = \overline{P_3},$$
$$P_5 = (1 + 2i : 4 + 2i : -4 + i), \qquad P_6 = \overline{P_5},$$
$$P_7 = (1 : 0 : -1), \qquad P_8 = (0 : 4 : 1).$$

The associated curve C has two ovals. Of its 16 real tritangents, **exactly one** is totally real. By a random search, we found examples where up to 15 of the real tritangents of the curve C are totally real. At present, we have not found any $\mathcal{P}$ where the associated curve has either 0 or 16 totally real tritangents.

Figure 6 shows the empirical distribution we observed for $s = 3$ (left) and $s = 4$ (right). The respective ranges are $[10, 32]$ and $[35, 63]$.

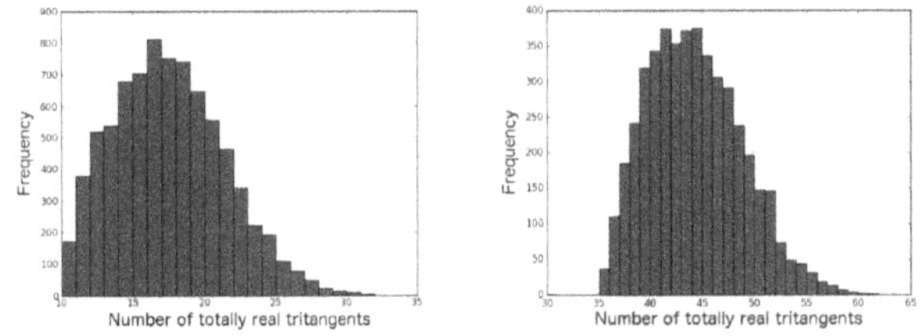

Figure 6: Count of totally real tritangents for $s = 3$ and $s = 4$.

Example 3.4 (s = 3). The following configuration $\mathcal{P}$ gives a space sextic C with three ovals that has 32 totally real tritangents:

$$P_1 = (-204813760 - 55982740i : 452442430 + 319792532i : 1), \ P_2 = \overline{P_1},$$
$$P_3 = (252002303 - 508295920i : 418802957 + 255990940i : 1), \ P_4 = \overline{P_2},$$
$$P_5 = (420794066 : 346448315 : 1), \ P_6 = (64527687 : 183049780 : 1),$$
$$P_7 = (410335352 : 364471450 : -1), \ P_8 = (210806629 : 146613813 : -1).$$

4 SOLVING THE TRITANGENT EQUATIONS

In Sections 2 and 3 we studied space sextics C lying on a singular quadric surface Q. By perturbing these, we obtained generic space sextics with many different numbers of totally real tritangents. However, not all numbers between 0 and 120 were attained by this method. To remedy this, we considered arbitrary space sextics $C = Q \cap K$, defined by a random quadric Q and a random cubic K.

However, we found the problem of computing the tritangents directly from (Q, K) to be quite challenging. We conjecture that all integers between 0 and 120 can be realized by the totally real tritangents of some space sextic. But, at present, some gaps in Table 1 persist.

In what follows we describe our algorithm – and its implementation – for computing the 120 tritangents directly from the homogeneous polynomials of degree two resp. three in x_0, x_1, x_2, x_3 that define the quadric Q resp. the cubic K. We introduce four unknowns u_0, u_1, u_2, u_3 that serve as coordinates on the space $(\mathbb{P}^3)^\vee$ of planes:

$$H \ : \ u_0x_0 + u_1x_1 + u_2x_2 + u_3x_3 \ = \ 0. \tag{3}$$

For generic real values of the u_i, the intersection $Q \cap K \cap H = C \cap H$ consists of six distinct complex points in $\mathbb{P}^3$. We are interested in the special cases when these six points become three double points. We seek to find the *tritangent ideal* $\mathcal{I}_C$, consisting of polynomials in u_0, u_1, u_2, u_3 that vanish at those H that are tritangent planes of C.

We fix the projective space $\mathbb{P}^6$ whose points are the binary sextics

$$f \ = \ a_0t_0^6 + a_1t_0^5t_1 + a_2t_0^4t_1^2 + a_3t_0^3t_1^3 + a_4t_0^2t_1^4 + a_5t_0t_1^5 + a_6t_1^6.$$

Inside that $\mathbb{P}^6$ we consider the threefold of squares of binary cubics:

$$f \ = \ \left(b_0t_0^3 + b_1t_0^2t_1 + b_2t_0t_1^2 + b_3t_1^3\right)^2. \tag{4}$$

The defining prime ideal of that threefold is minimally generated by 45 quartics in $a_0, a_1, a_2, a_3, a_4, a_5, a_6$. This is revealed by the row labeled $\lambda = (2, 2, 2)$ in [15, Table 1]. Computing these 45 quartics is a task of elimination, which we carried out in a preprocessing step.

Consider now a specific instance (Q, K), defining $C = Q \cap K$. We then transform the above 45 quartics in $a_0, \ldots, a_6$ into higher degree equations in $u_0, \ldots, u_3$. This is done by projecting $C \cap H$ onto a line. This gives a univariate polynomial of degree six whose seven coefficients are polynomials of degree 12 in u_0, u_1, u_2, u_3. We replace $a_0, \ldots, a_6$ by these polynomials. Theoretically, it suffices to project onto a single generic line. Practically, we had more success with multiple (possibly degenerate) projections onto the coordinate axes, and gathering the resulting systems of 45 equations each.

To be more precise, fix one of the 12 ordered pairs (x_i, x_j). First, solve the equation (3) for x_i, substitute into the equations of Q and K, and clear denominators. Next, eliminate x_j from the resulting ternary quadric and cubic. The result is a binary sextic f in the two unknowns $\{x_0, x_1, x_2, x_3\} \backslash \{x_i, x_j\}$ whose coefficients $a_0, \ldots, a_6$ are expressions of degree 12 in $u_0, \ldots, u_3$. We substitute these expressions into the 45 quartics precomputed above. This results in 45 polynomials of degree 48 in $u_0, \ldots, u_3$ that lie in the tritangent ideal $\mathcal{I}_C$. Repeating this elimination process for the other 11 pairs (x_i, x_j), we obtain additional polynomials in $\mathcal{I}_C$. Altogether, we have now enough polynomials of degree 48 to generate $\mathcal{I}_C$ on any desired affine open subset in the dual $(\mathbb{P}^3)^\vee$ of planes in $\mathbb{P}^3$. The homogeneous ideal $\mathcal{I}_C$ is radical and it has 120 zeros in $(\mathbb{P}^3)^\vee$.

To compute these zeros, we restrict ourselves to an open chart, say $U = \{u_3 \neq 0\} \simeq \mathbb{C}^3$. The resulting system (with $u_3 = 1$) is grossly over-constrained, with up to 12×45 equations in the three unknowns u_0, u_1, u_2. We compute a lexicographic Gröbner basis, using `fglm` [8], as our ideal is zero-dimensional. For generic instances (Q, K), the lexicographic Gröbner basis has the shape

$$\{ u_1 - p_1(u_3),\ u_2 - p_2(u_3),\ p_3(u_3) \}, \tag{5}$$

where $\deg(p_3) = 120$ and $\deg(p_1) = \deg(p_2) = 119$. For degenerate (Q, K) we proceed with a triangular decomposition.

We implemented this method in MAGMA [1]. The Gröbner basis computation was very hard to carry out. It took several days to finish for Example 4.2. The output had coefficients of size $\sim 10^{680}$.

We applied our implementation to several curves C, some from configurations $\mathcal{P} \subset \mathbb{P}^2_{\mathbb{Q}}$, and some from general instances (Q, K).

The first case is used as a tool for independent verification, e.g. for Example 2.2. Here, p_3 decomposes into linear factors over $\mathbb{Q}$. Each factor yields a rational tritangent, for which we compute the three (double) points in $H \cap C$ symbolically. To check whether one or three are real, we again project onto a line. This yields a univariate rational polynomial of degree 6. We can test whether it is the square of a cubic with positive discriminant. More generally, any non-linear factor with only real roots also allows us to continue our computations symbolically over an algebraic field extension.

In the second case, the univariate polynomial p_3 is typically irreducible over $\mathbb{Q}$, and we solve (5) numerically. We compute all real tritangents H and their intersections $H \cap C$. Based on the resulting numerical data, we decide which H are totally real. Complex zeroes are also counted, to attest that there are indeed 120 solutions. This certifies that the chosen open chart U was indeed generic.

Example 4.1. The polynomial $C(t, W)$ in Example 2.2 translates into a cubic $K(x_0, x_1, x_2, x_3)$ which is unique modulo the quadric $Q = x_0x_2 - x_1^2$. We apply the algorithm above to the instance (Q, K) with $U = \{u_3 \neq 0\}$. The result verifies that all 120 tritangents are rational and totally real. Interestingly, two of the 120 tritangents have a coordinate that is zero. These two special planes are

$$\begin{aligned} 0 = {} & 66672785890792863054280513488716189515\,7u_0 \\ & - 371406861222752391050720128495402169926u_1 \\ & - 1314885999729297115548301\,5u_3 \end{aligned}$$

and

$$\begin{aligned} 0 = {} & 798487890643662871638730874554378847\,2u_1 \\ & - 444610889957505571930558230563361607\,1u_2 \\ & + 106897050552377064523\,95u_3. \end{aligned}$$

Example 4.2. The curve $C = Q \cap K$ in [9, §3] is given by

$$\begin{aligned} Q &= x_0^2 + x_1^2 + x_2^2 - 25x_3^2, \\ K &= \left(x_0 + \sqrt{3}x_3\right)\left(x_0 - \sqrt{3}x_1 - 3x_3\right)\left(x_0 + \sqrt{3}x_1 - 3x_3\right) - 2x_3^3. \end{aligned}$$

It has five ovals, so all tritangents are real. Our computation shows that there are only 108 distinct tritangents. Twelve are solutions of multiplicity two in the ideal I_C, and none of the tritangents are rational. This verifies [9, Theorem 3.2]. Figure 7 shows three tritangents, meeting 3, 2 and 1 ovals of the red curve respectively.

In [9, Question 3.3], Harris and Len asked whether this example can be replaced by one with 120 distinct totally teal tritangents. Our computations in Examples 2.2 and 4.1 establish the affirmative answer. However, we do not yet know whether all integers between 0 and 120 are possible for the number of totally real tritangents.

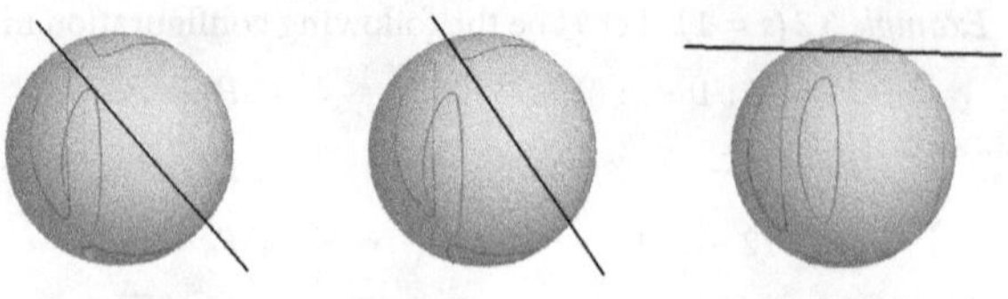

Figure 7: The curve in Example 4.2 has 108 real tritangents

5 DISCRIMINANTS

In this paper we considered two parameter spaces for space sextics. First, there is the space $\mathbb{P}^9_{\mathbb{R}} \times \mathbb{P}^{19}_{\mathbb{R}}$ of pairs (Q, K) consisting of a real quadric and a real cubic in $\mathbb{P}^3$. The regions for which the number of real tritangents remains constant partitions $\mathbb{P}^9_{\mathbb{R}} \times \mathbb{P}^{19}_{\mathbb{R}}$ into open strata. This stratification is refined by regions for which the number of totally real tritangents remains constant. We are interested in the discriminantal hypersurfaces that separate these strata.

Second, there is the space $(\mathbb{P}^2_{\mathbb{R}})^8$ of configurations $\mathcal{P}$ of eight labeled points in the plane. This space works for any fixed value of s in $\{1, 2, 3, 4, 5\}$, representing configurations of $2s - 2$ real points and $5 - s$ complex conjugate pairs. For simplicity of exposition we focus on the fully real case $s = 5$. In any case, the number of real tritangents is fixed, and we care about the open strata in $(\mathbb{P}^2_{\mathbb{R}})^8$ in which the number of totally real tritangents is constant. Again, we seek to describe the discriminantal hypersurface, but now in $(\mathbb{P}^2)^8$.

For $\mathcal{P} \in (\mathbb{P}^2)^8$, denote the associated space sextic by $C_{\mathcal{P}}$. Let Σ denote the locus of configurations in $(\mathbb{P}^2)^8$ which are not in general position. We define the *tritangent discriminant locus* by

$$Y = \overline{\left\{ \mathcal{P} \in (\mathbb{P}^2)^8 \backslash \Sigma : \begin{array}{l} C_{\mathcal{P}} \text{ has a tritangent with contact} \\ \text{order at least 4 at some point} \end{array} \right\}},$$

where the over-line denotes the Zariski closure.

LEMMA 5.1. *Every irreducible component of Y is a hypersurface.*

PROOF. Let $\mathcal{P}_0 \in Y \backslash \Sigma$, and fix local coordinates $\bar{p} = (p_1, \ldots, p_{16})$ for a neighborhood $\mathcal{U}$ of $\mathcal{P}_0 = \bar{p}_0$ in $(\mathbb{P}^2)^8$. The bivariate equation (1) that represents C_0 is the specialization at $\bar{p}_0$ of a general equation

$$C: \quad c(t, W) = t^6 + d_1(\bar{p})t^5 + d_2(\bar{p})t^4W + \cdots + d_{15}(\bar{p}), \tag{6}$$

where the coefficients $d_i(\bar{p})$ are rational functions regular at p_0. Let H_0 be a tritangent plane to C_0 with a contact point of order at least 4. Then H_0 is either the tritangent associated to a point in $\mathcal{P}_0$ or associated to one of the patterns in Figure 3, 4 or 5. Either way, we see that H_0 is obtained by specializing an equation of the form

$$H: \quad h(t, W) = t^2 + e_1(\bar{p})t + e_2(\bar{p}) + e_3(\bar{p})W, \tag{7}$$

where the coefficients $e_i(\bar{p})$ are rational functions regular at $\bar{p}_0$.

The resultant of $c(t, W)$ and $h(t, W)$ with respect to W is a polynomial $f(t)$ of degree 6 whose coefficients are rational functions in $\bar{p}$. Note that H is a tritangent plane to C, so $f = g^2$ as in (4). The roots of the cubic g correspond to the contact points of H with C. In particular, $H_{\bar{p}}$ has a point of contact with $C_{\bar{p}}$ of order at least 4 precisely when the discriminant of g is zero. Since the coefficients of g are rational functions in $\bar{p}$, regular at $\bar{p}_0$, this means that a neighborhood of $\mathcal{P}_0$ in Y has codimension 1 in $\mathcal{U}$. This implies that every irreducible component of Y has codimension 1. □

The following theorem describes these irreducible components:

Theorem 5.2. *The tritangent discriminant locus Y is the union of $120 = 8+28+56+56/2$ irreducible hypersurfaces in $(\mathbb{P}^2)^8$, one for each point in $\mathcal{P}$ and each pattern in Figures 3, 4 and 5. The components of type 8 have total degree 306, namely 54 in the point corresponding to the exceptional curve and 36 in the other seven points. The components of type 28 have total degree 216, namely 18 in each of the two points on the line and 30 for the six on the quintic. The components of type 56 have total degree 162, namely 18 in each of the five points on the conic and 24 for the three on the quartic. The components of type 56/2 have total degree 144, namely 18 in each of the eight points.*

We prove Theorem 5.2 computationally. In order to do so, it is convenient to make the following observation. Let $Y = V(f)$ with f a $\mathbb{Z}^8$-homogeneous polynomial of $\mathbb{Z}^8$-degree $(d_1, \ldots, d_8)$. We scale f so that its coefficients are relatively prime integers. For a prime p, let f_p denote the reduction of f modulo p. If p is large, then

$$Y_p = V(f_p) \subset (\mathbb{P}^2_{\mathbb{F}_p})^8$$

has the same $\mathbb{Z}^8$-degree as Y. We can thus calculate $(d_1, \ldots, d_8)$ by using Gröbner bases over a large finite field $\mathbb{F}_p$.

Let $k = \mathbb{F}_p$ be the field with $p = 10^6 + 3$ elements and k^{al} its algebraic closure. Let $S = \mathbb{P}^1_k$ and let $R = k[a, b]$ be the coordinate ring of S. Let $\mathbb{P}^2_R := \text{Proj}\, R[x, y, z]$ be the projective plane over R. If X is some family, its specialization to $(a : b) \in S$ is denoted $X_{(a:b)}$.

We use the following configuration of eight points in $\mathbb{P}^2_R$:

$$\mathcal{P} = \{ (24 : -23 : 57), (11 : 25 : -27), (-30 : 29 : 79), (14 : -23 : 26), (43 : 92 : 61), (-34 : 81 : 7), (88 : 29 : 69), (a : b : 0) \} \subset \mathbb{P}^2_{\mathbb{R}}.$$

Note $\mathcal{P}$ is in general position for generic a, b. Let $\mathcal{U}$ be the open subset of S parameterizing specializations in general position. The following result concerns generic specializations. We omit the proof.

Proposition 5.3. *There exists a pair of ternary cubics $u, v \in R[x, y, z]$, a ternary sextic $w \in R[x, y, z]$, bivariate polynomials $c, h \in R[t, W]$ as in (6) and (7), and an explicitly computable finite set $X \subset S(k^{\text{al}})$ such that, whenever $(a : b) \in \mathcal{U} \backslash X$, the following hold:*

(a) The specializations $u_{(a:b)}, v_{(a:b)}$ span the space of cubics passing through all eight points in $\mathcal{P}_{(a:b)}$.
(b) The specializations $u^2_{(a:b)}, uv_{(a:b)}, v^2_{(a:b)}, w_{(a:b)}$ span the space of sextics vanishing doubly at each point in $\mathcal{P}_{(a:b)}$.
(c) The specialization $\{c_{(a:b)}(t, W) = 0\}$ is a smooth genus 4 curve $C_{a:b}$ lying on a singular quadric surface.
(d) The specialization $\{h_{(a:b)}(t, W) = 0\}$ is a tritangent plane to $C_{(a:b)}$ where the coefficient of W is nonzero.
(e) For any $(a : b) \in X$, the curve $C_{(a:b)}$ is smooth, genus 4, and none of the tritangent planes have a point of contact order larger than 4.

We now derive Theorem 5.2 from Proposition 5.3. The degree d_8 of Y in the last point P_8 is computed by restricting to the slice

$$\{(24 : -23 : 57)\} \times \{(11 : 25 : -27)\} \times \ldots \times \{(88 : 29 : 69)\} \times \mathbb{P}^2.$$

This restriction of Y is a curve of degree d_8 in $\mathbb{P}^2$. We compute this degree as the number of points in the intersection with the line

$$S = \{(a : b : c) \in \mathbb{P}^2 : c = 0\}.$$

The same argument works also for each irreducible component of Y. These components correspond to the various tritangent patterns, marked 8, 28, 56 and 56/2. We perform this computation for each pattern over $\mathbb{F}_p$, and we obtain the numbers stated in Theorem 5.2.

We now turn to the canonical representation of arbitrary space sextics $C = Q \cap K$, namely by pairs (Q, K) in $\mathbb{P}^9 \times \mathbb{P}^{19}$. We shall identify three irreducible hypersurfaces in $\mathbb{P}^9 \times \mathbb{P}^{19}$ that serve as discriminants for different scenarios of how C can degenerate. For each hypersurface, we shall determine its *bidegree* (α, β). Here α is the degree of its defining polynomial in the coefficients of Q, and β is the degree of its defining polynomial in the coefficients of K.

First, there is the classical discriminant Δ_1, which parametrizes all pairs (Q, K) such the curve $C = Q \cap K$ is singular. This is an irreducible hypersurface in $\mathbb{P}^9 \times \mathbb{P}^{19}$, revisited recently in [2]. The general points of Δ_1 are irreducible curves C of arithmetic genus 4 that have one simple node, so the geometric genus of C is 3. The discriminant Δ_1 specifies the wall to be crossed when the number of real tritangents changes as (Q, K) moves throughout $\mathbb{P}^9_{\mathbb{R}} \times \mathbb{P}^{19}_{\mathbb{R}}$.

Second, there is the wall to be crossed when the number of totally real tritangents changes. The discriminant Δ_2 comprises space sextics with a tritangent H that is degenerate, in the sense that H is tangent at one point and doubly tangent at another point of C. For real pairs (C, H), such a point of double tangency deforms into two contact points of a tritangent H_ϵ at a nearby curve C_ϵ, and this pair is either real or complex conjugate. On the hypersurface in $\mathbb{P}^9 \times \mathbb{P}^{19}$ where Q is singular, the locus Δ_2 is the image of the discriminant with 120 components in Theorem 5.3 under the map that takes a configuration $\mathcal{P} \in (\mathbb{P}^2)^8$ to its associated curve $C_{\mathcal{P}}$.

Our third discriminant Δ_3 parametrizes pairs (Q, K) such that the curve $C = Q \cap K$ has two distinct tritangents that share a common contact point on C. In other words, the curve C has a point whose tangent line is contained in two tritangent planes. The discriminant Δ_3 furnishes an embedded realization of the *common contact locus* that was studied in the dissertation of Emre Sertöz [18, §2.4].

The following theorem was found with the help of Gavril Farkas and Emre Sertöz. The numbers are derived from results in [7, 18].

Theorem 5.4. *The discriminantal loci Δ_1, Δ_2 and Δ_3 are irreducible and reduced hypersurfaces in $\mathbb{P}^9 \times \mathbb{P}^{19}$. Their bidegrees are*

$$\begin{aligned} \text{bidegree}(\Delta_1) &= (33, 34), \\ \text{bidegree}(\Delta_2) &= (744, 592), \\ \text{bidegree}(\Delta_3) &= (8862, 5236). \end{aligned}$$

Proof. Consider the discriminant Δ_1 for curves in $\mathbb{P}^3$ that are intersections of two surfaces of degree d and e. It has bidegree

$$\big(e(3d^2+2de+e^2-8d-4e+6),\ d(3e^2+2de+d^2-8e-4d+6) \big).$$

This can be found in many sources, including [2, Proposition 3]. For $d = 2$ and $e = 3$ we obtain bidegree$(\Delta_1) = (33, 34)$, as desired.

To determine the other two bidegrees, we employ known facts from the enumerative geometry of $\overline{\mathcal{M}}_4$, the moduli space of stable curves of genus 4. The Picard group $\text{Pic}(\overline{\mathcal{M}}_4)$ is generated by four classes $\lambda, \delta_0, \delta_1, \delta_2$. Here λ is the *Hodge class*, and the δ_i are classes of irreducible divisors in the boundary $\overline{\mathcal{M}}_4 \backslash \mathcal{M}_4$. They represent:

δ_0: a genus 3 curve that self-intersects at one point;
δ_1: a genus 1 curve intersects a genus 3 curve at one point;
δ_2: two genus 2 curves intersect at one point.

Our discriminants Δ_i are the inverse images of known irreducible divisors in the moduli space under the rational map $\mathbb{P}^9 \times \mathbb{P}^{19} \dashrightarrow \overline{\mathcal{M}}_4$.

First, Δ_2 is the pull-back of the divisor $D_4 \subset \overline{\mathcal{M}}_4$ of curves with degenerate odd spin structures. It follows from [7, Theorem 0.5] that

$$[D_4] \;=\; 1440\lambda - 152\delta_0 - \alpha\delta_1 - \beta\delta_2 \quad \text{for some } \alpha, \beta \in \mathbb{N}. \quad (8)$$

For any curve $\gamma \subset \overline{\mathcal{M}}_4$, the sum $\sum_{i=0}^{2} \gamma \cdot \delta_i$ counts points on γ whose associated curve is singular. Write h resp. v for the curve γ that represents *line* × *point* resp. *point* × *line* in $\mathbb{P}^9 \times \mathbb{P}^{19}$. We saw

$$(h \cdot \delta_0, v \cdot \delta_0) \;=\; \text{bidegree}(\Delta_1) \;=\; (33, 34).$$

Moreover, it can be shown that

$$h \cdot \lambda = v \cdot \lambda = 4 \qquad \text{and} \qquad h \cdot \delta_i = v \cdot \delta_i = 0 \quad \text{for } i = 1, 2.$$

This implies the assertion about the bidegree of our discriminant:

$$\text{bidegree}(\Delta_2) = (h \cdot [D_4], v \cdot [D_4]) = (1440 \cdot 4 - 152 \cdot 33, 1440 \cdot 4 - 152 \cdot 34).$$

Similarly, Δ_3 is the pull-back of the *common contact divisor* $Q_4 \subset \overline{\mathcal{M}}_4$ studied by Sertöz. It follows from [18, Theorem II.2.43] that

$$[Q_4] \;=\; 32130\lambda - 3626\delta_0 - \alpha\delta_1 - \beta\delta_2 \quad \text{for some } \alpha, \beta \in \mathbb{N}. \quad (9)$$

Replacing (8) with (9) in our argument, we find that bidegree(Δ_3) is

$$(h \cdot [Q_4], v \cdot [Q_4]) \;=\; (32130 \cdot 4 - 3626 \cdot 33,\; 32130 \cdot 4 - 3626 \cdot 34).$$

This completes our derivation of the bidegrees in Theorem 5.4.

The irreducibility of the loci Δ_i is shown by a standard double-projection argument. One marks the relevant special point(s) on C. Then Δ_i becomes a family of linear spaces of fixed dimension. □

6 WHAT NEXT?

In this paper, we initiated the computational study of totally real tritangents of space sextics in $\mathbb{P}^3$. These objects are important in algebraic geometry because they represent odd theta characteristics of canonical curves of genus 4. We developed systematic tools for constructing curves all of whose tritangents are defined over algebraic extensions of $\mathbb{Q}$, and we used this to answer the longstanding question whether the upper bound of 120 totally real tritangent planes can be attained. We argued that computing the tritangents directly from the representation $C = Q \cap K$ is hard, and we characterized the discriminants for these polynomial systems.

This article leads to many natural directions to be explored next. We propose the following eleven specific problems for further study.

(1) Decide whether every integer between 0 and 120 is realizable.

(2) Determine the correct upper and lower bounds in Table 1. In particular, is 84 the lower bound for curves with five ovals?

(3) A smooth quadric Q is either an ellipsoid or a hyperboloid. Degtyarev and Zvonilov [4] characterized the topological types of real space sextics on these surfaces. What are the possible numbers of totally real tritangents for their types?

(4) What does [4] tell us about space sextics on a singular quadric Q? Which types arise on Q, how do they deform to those on a hyperboloid, and what does this imply for tritangents?

(5) Given a space sextic C whose quadric Q is singular, how to best compute a configuration $\mathcal{P} \in (\mathbb{P}^2)^8$ such that $C = C_{\mathcal{P}}$? Our idea is to design an algorithm based on the constructions described in [12, Proposition 4.8 and Remark 4.12].

(6) Lehavi [16] shows that a general space sextic C can be reconstructed from its 120 tritangents. How to do this in practice?

(7) Let $C_{\mathcal{P}}$ be the space sextic of a configuration $\mathcal{P} \in (\mathbb{P}^2)^8$. How to see the ovals of $C_{\mathcal{P}}$ in $\mathbb{P}^2$? For each tritangent as in Figure 3, 4 or 5, how to see the number of ovals it touches?

(8) Design a custom-tailored *homotopy algorithm* for numerically computing the 120 tritangents from the pair (Q, K).

(9) The *tropical limit* of a space sextic has 15 classes of tritangents, each of size eight [9, Theorem 5.2]. This is realized classically by a $K_{3,3}$-*curve*, obtained by taking K as three planes tangent to a smooth quadric Q. How many totally real tritangents are possible in the vicinity of (Q, K) in $\mathbb{P}^9_{\mathbb{R}} \times \mathbb{P}^{19}_{\mathbb{R}}$?

(10) The 28 bitangents of a plane quartic are the off-diagonal entries of a symmetric 8×8-matrix, known as the *bitangent matrix* [3]. How to generalize this to genus 4? Is there such a canonical matrix (or tensor) for the 120 tritangents?

(11) What is maximal number of 2-dimensional faces in the convex hull of a space sextic in $\mathbb{R}^3$? There are at most 120 such facets. In addition, there are infinitely many edges. These form a ruled surface of degree 54, by [17, Theorem 2.1].

Between the initial and the final version of this paper, much progress was made on Question (2) in [10, 14], and Question (11) was answered in [14]: there are at most 8 facets.

REFERENCES

[1] Wieb Bosma, John Cannon, and Catherine Playoust. 1997. The Magma algebra system. I. The user language. *J. Symbolic Comput.* 24, 3-4 (1997), 235–265. Computational algebra and number theory (London, 1993).

[2] Laurent Busé and Ibrahim Nonkané. 2015. Discriminants of complete intersection space curves. In *ISSAC'17—Proceedings of the 2017 ACM International Symposium on Symbolic and Algebraic Computation.* ACM, New York. arXiv:1702.01694

[3] Francesco Dalla Piazza, Alessio Fiorentino, and Riccardo Salvati Manni. 2017. Plane quartics: the universal matrix of bitangents. *Israel J. Math.* 217, 1 (2017), 111–138.

[4] A.I. Degtyarev and V.I. Zvonilov. 1999. Rigid isotopy classification of real algebraic curves of bidegree (3,3) on quadrics. *Mathematical Notes* 66 (1999), 670–674.

[5] Igor V. Dolgachev. 2012. *Classical Algebraic Geometry: A Modern View.* Cambridge University Press. xii+639 pages.

[6] Arnold Emch. 1928. Mathematical models. *Univ. of Illinois Bull.* XXV, 43 (1928), 5–38.

[7] Gavril Farkas and Alessandro Verra. 2014. The geometry of the moduli space of odd spin curves. *Ann. of Math. (2)* 180, 3 (2014), 927–970.

[8] J. C. Faugère, P. Gianni, D. Lazard, and T. Mora. 1993. Efficient computation of zero-dimensional Gröbner bases by change of ordering. *J. Symbolic Comput.* 16, 4 (1993), 329–344.

[9] Corey Harris and Yoav Len. 2018. Tritangent planes to space sextics: the algebraic and tropical stories. In *Combinatorial Algebraic Geometry*, G.G. Smith and B. Sturmfels (Eds.). Fields Inst. Res. Math. Sci., 47–63.

[10] Jonathan Hauenstein, Avinash Kulkarni, Emre Can Sertöz, and Samantha Sherman. 2018. Certifying reality of projections. (2018). arXiv:1804.02707

[11] Avinash Kulkarni. 2016. An explicit family of cubic number fields with large 2-rank of the class group. (2016). arXiv:1610.07668

[12] Avinash Kulkarni. 2017. An arithmetic invariant theory of curves from E_8. (2017). arXiv:1711.08843

[13] Avinash Kulkarni, Mahsa Sayyary, Yue Ren, and Bernd Sturmfels. 2017. Data and scripts for this article. Available at: software.mis.mpg.de. (2017).

[14] Mario Kummer. 2018. Totally real theta characteristics. (2018). arXiv:1802.05297

[15] Hwangrae Lee and Bernd Sturmfels. 2016. Duality of multiple root loci. *J. Algebra* 446 (2016), 499–526.

[16] David Lehavi. 2015. Effective reconstruction of generic genus 4 curves from their theta hyperplanes. *Int. Math. Res. Not. IMRN* 19 (2015), 9472–9485.

[17] Kristian Ranestad and Bernd Sturmfels. 2012. On the convex hull of a space curve. *Advances in Geometry* 12 (2012), 157–178.

[18] Emre Sertöz. 2017. Enumerative Geometry of Double Spin Curves. Doctoral Dissertation, HU Berlin, https://edoc.hu-berlin.de/handle/18452/19134. (2017).

[19] Damiano Testa, Anthony Várilly-Alvarado, and Mauricio Velasco. 2009. Cox rings of degree one del Pezzo surfaces. *Algebra Number Theory* 3, 7 (2009), 729–761.

Bivariate Dimension Polynomials of Non-Reflexive Prime Difference-Differential Ideals. The Case of One Translation

Alexander Levin
The Catholic University of America
Washington, D. C.
levin@cua.edu

ABSTRACT

We use the method of characteristic sets with respect to two term orderings to prove the existence and obtain a method of computation of a bivariate dimension polynomial associated with a non-reflexive difference-differential ideal in the algebra of difference-differential polynomials with several basic derivations and one translation. As a consequence, we obtain a new proof and a method of computation of the dimension polynomial of a non-reflexive prime difference ideal in the algebra of difference polynomials over an ordinary difference field. We also discuss applications of our results to systems of algebraic difference-differential equations.

CCS CONCEPTS

• **Symbolic and Algebraic Manipulation → Algebraic Algorithms**;

KEYWORDS

Difference-differential polynomial, dimension polynomial, reduction, characteristic set

ACM Reference Format:

Alexander Levin. 2018. Bivariate Dimension Polynomials of Non-Reflexive Prime Difference-Differential Ideals. The Case of One Translation. In *ISSAC '18: 2018 ACM International Symposium on Symbolic and Algebraic Computation, July 16–19, 2018, New York, NY, USA.* ACM, New York, NY, USA, 8 pages. https://doi.org/10.1145/3208976.3209008

1 INTRODUCTION

The role of dimension polynomials in differential and difference algebra is similar to the role of Hilbert polynomials in commutative algebra and algebraic geometry. An important feature of such polynomials is that they describe in exact terms the freedom degree of a continuous or discrete dynamic system as well as the number of arbitrary constants in the general solution of a system of partial algebraic differential or difference equations. The notion of a differential dimension polynomial was introduced by E. Kolchin [6] who proved the following fundamental result.

Theorem 1.1. *Let K be a differential field (*Char $K = 0$*), that is, a field considered together with the action of a set $\Delta = \{\delta_1, \dots, \delta_m\}$ of mutually commuting derivations of K into itself. Let Θ denote the free commutative semigroup of all power products of the form $\theta = \delta_1^{k_1} \dots \delta_m^{k_m}$ ($k_i \geq 0$), let* ord $\theta = \sum_{i=1}^{m} k_i$*, and for any $r \geq 0$, let $\Theta(r) = \{\theta \in \Theta \mid ord\, \theta \leq r\}$. Furthermore, let $L = K\langle \eta_1, \dots, \eta_n \rangle_\Delta$ be a differential field extension of K generated by a finite set $\eta = \{\eta_1, \dots, \eta_n\}$. (As a field, $L = K(\{\theta\eta_j \mid \theta \in \Theta, 1 \leq j \leq n\})$.)*

Then there exists a polynomial $\omega_{\eta|K}(t) \in \mathbb{Q}[t]$ such that

(i) *$\omega_{\eta|K}(r) = trdeg_K K(\{\theta\eta_j \mid \theta \in \Theta(r), 1 \leq j \leq n\})$ for all sufficiently large $r \in \mathbb{Z}$;*

(ii) *$\deg \omega_{\eta|K} \leq m$ and $\omega_{\eta|K}(t)$ can be written as $\omega_{\eta|K}(t) = \sum_{i=0}^{m} a_i \binom{t+i}{i}$ where $a_0, \dots, a_m \in \mathbb{Z}$;*

(iii) *$d = \deg \omega_{\eta|K}$, a_m and a_d do not depend on the choice of the system of Δ-generators η of the extension L/K (clearly, $a_d \neq a_m$ if and only if $d < m$, that is $a_m = 0$). Moreover, a_m is equal to the differential transcendence degree of L over K, that is, to the maximal number of elements $\xi_1, \dots, \xi_k \in L$ such that the set $\{\theta\xi_i \mid \theta \in \Theta, 1 \leq i \leq k\}$ is algebraically independent over K.*

The corresponding dimension polynomials of difference and difference-differential field extensions were introduced in [9] and [14]. The importance of these characteristics is determined by at least three factors. First, for a wide class of algebraic differential (respectively, difference or difference-differential) equations, the dimension polynomial of the corresponding field extension expresses the strength of the system of equations in the sense of A. Einstein. In the case of a system of partial differential equations, this concept, introduced in [2] as an important qualitative characteristic of a system, was expressed by a certain differential dimension polynomial in [16]; the corresponding algebraic interpretations of the strength of systems of difference and difference-differential equations were obtained in [8, Sect. 6.4] and [12, Sect. 7.7]. Second, the dimension polynomial associated with a finitely generated differential, difference or difference-differential field extension carries certain birational invariants, that is, numbers that do not change when we switch to another finite system of generators of the extension. These invariants are closely connected with some other important characteristics; for example, one of them is the differential (respectively, difference or difference-differential) transcendence degree of the extension. Finally, properties of dimension polynomials associated with prime differential (respectively, difference or difference-differential) ideals provide a powerful tool in the dimension theory of the corresponding rings (see, for example, [4], [5], [8, Ch.7], and [15]).

In this paper we adjust a generalization of the Ritt-Kolchin method of characteristic sets developed in [13] to the case of (non-inversive) difference-differential polynomials with one translation

ISSAC '18, July 16–19, 2018, New York, NY, USA

ACM ISBN 978-1-4503-5550-6/18/07...$15.00
https://doi.org/10.1145/3208976.3209008

and apply this method to prove the existence and outline a method of computation of a bivariate dimension polynomial associated with a non-reflexive difference-differential polynomial ideal. Our main result (Theorem 4.2) can be viewed as an essential generalization (in the case of one translation) of the existing theorems on bivariate dimension polynomials of difference-differential and difference field extensions, see [10, Theorem 5.4] and [12, Theorems 4.2.16 and 4.2.17]. The latter theorems deal with extensions that arise from factor rings of difference-differential (or difference) polynomial rings by reflexive difference-differential (respectively, difference) prime ideals. Our paper extends these results to the case when the prime ideals are not necessarily reflexive, so the induced translations of the factor rings are not necessarily injective.

We also discuss the relationship between the obtained difference-differential dimension polynomial and the concept of strength of a system of algebraic difference-differential equations in the sense of A. Einstein. Furthermore, as a consequence of our main result, we obtain a new proof and a method of computation of the dimension polynomial of a non-reflexive prime difference ideal in the algebra of difference polynomials over an ordinary difference field. The existence of such a polynomial was first established in [3, Section 4.4], an alternative proof was obtained in [17, Section 5.1]. However, these proofs are not constructive, while our approach leads to an algorithm for computing dimension polynomials.

2 PRELIMINARIES

Throughout the paper $\mathbb{Z}$, $\mathbb{N}$, $\mathbb{Q}$ and $\mathbb{R}$ denote the sets of all integers, all non-negative integers, all rational numbers and all real numbers, respectively. For any positive integer p, we set $\mathbb{N}_p = \{1, \dots, p\}$. By a ring we always mean an associative ring with unity. Every ring homomorphism is unitary (maps unity onto unity), every subring of a ring contains the unity of the ring, and every algebra over a commutative ring is unitary. Every field considered below is supposed to have zero characteristic.

If $B = A_1 \times \dots \times A_k$ is a Cartesian product of k ordered sets with orders $\leq_1, \dots \leq_k$, respectively ($k \in \mathbb{N}$, $k \geq 1$), then by the product order on B we mean a partial order $\leq_P$ such that $(a_1, \dots, a_k) \leq_P (a'_1, \dots, a'_k)$ if and only if $a_i \leq_i a'_i$ for $i = 1, \dots, k$. In particular, if $a = (a_1, \dots, a_k)$, $a' = (a'_1, \dots, a'_k) \in \mathbb{N}^k$, then $a \leq_P a'$ if and only if $a_i \leq a'_i$ for $i = 1, \dots, k$. We write $a <_P a'$ if $a \leq_P a'$ and $a \neq a'$.

The proof of the following statement can be found in [7, Chapter 0, Lemma 15].

Lemma 2.1. *Let A be an infinite subset of $\mathbb{N}^m \times \mathbb{N}_n$ ($m, n \in \mathbb{N}$, $n \geq 1$). Then there exists an infinite sequence of elements of A, strictly increasing relative to the product order, in which every element has the same projection on $\mathbb{N}_n$.*

NUMERICAL POLYNOMIALS OF SUBSETS OF $\mathbb{N}^m \times \mathbb{Z}$

Definition 2.2. A polynomial $f(t_1, \dots, t_p)$ in p variables $t_1, \dots, t_p$ ($p \in \mathbb{N}$, $p \geq 1$) with rational coefficients is called *numerical* if $f(t_1, \dots, t_p) \in \mathbb{Z}$ for all sufficiently large p-tuples $(t_1, \dots, t_p) \in \mathbb{Z}^p$ (that is, there exist integers $s_1, \dots, s_p$ such that $f(r_1, \dots, r_p) \in \mathbb{Z}$ whenever $(r_1, \dots, r_p) \in \mathbb{Z}$ and $r_i \geq s_i$ for all $i = 1, \dots, p$.)

Obviously, every polynomial with integer coefficients is numerical. As an example of a numerical polynomial in p variables with non-integer coefficients ($p \in \mathbb{N}, p \geq 1$) one can consider a polynomial $\prod_{i=1}^{p} \binom{t_i}{m_i}$ where $m_1, \dots, m_p \in \mathbb{N}$. (As usual, $\binom{t}{k}$ ($k \in \mathbb{Z}$, $k \geq 1$) denotes the polynomial $\frac{t(t-1)\dots(t-k+1)}{k!}$ in one variable t, $\binom{t}{0} = 1$, and $\binom{t}{k} = 0$ if $k < 0$.) It can be shown (see [8, Corollary 2.1.5]) that a numerical polynomial $f(t_1, \dots, t_p)$ in p variables can be expressed as a linear combination of products of the form $\binom{t_1 + i_1}{i_1} \dots \binom{t_p + i_p}{i_p}$ with integer coefficients ($i_1, \dots, i_p \in \mathbb{N}$).

In the rest of the section we deal with subsets of $\mathbb{N}^{m+1}$ (m is a positive integer) treated as a Cartesian product $\mathbb{N}^m \times \mathbb{N}$ (so that the last coordinate has a special meaning). If $a = (a_1, \dots, a_{m+1}) \in \mathbb{N}^{m+1}$, we set $\text{ord}_1\, a = \sum_{i=1}^{m} a_i$ and $\text{ord}_2\, a = a_{m+1}$. Furthermore, we treat $\mathbb{N}^{m+1}$ as a partially ordered set with respect to the product order $\leq_P$.

If $A \subseteq \mathbb{N}^{m+1}$, then V_A will denote the set of all elements $v \in \mathbb{N}^{m+1}$ such that there is no $a \in A$ with $a \leq_P v$. Clearly, $v = (v_1, \dots, v_{m+1}) \in V_A$ if and only if for any element $(a_1, \dots, a_{m+1}) \in A$, there exists $i \in \mathbb{N}$, $1 \leq i \leq m+1$, such that $a_i > v_i$. Furthermore, for any $r, s \in \mathbb{N}$, we set

$$A(r, s) = \{x = (x_1, \dots, x_{m+1}) \in A \mid \text{ord}_1\, x \leq r, \text{ord}_2\, x \leq s\}.$$

The following theorem is a direct consequence of the corresponding statement proved in [8, Chapter 2]; it generalizes the well-known Kolchin's result on the univariate numerical polynomials associated with subsets of $\mathbb{N}^m$ (see [7, Chapter 0, Lemma 17]).

Theorem 2.3. *Let A be a subset of $\mathbb{N}^{m+1}$. Then there exists a numerical polynomial $\omega_A(t_1, t_2)$ with the following properties:*

(i) $\omega_A(r, s) = \text{Card}\, V_A(r, s)$ for all sufficiently large $(r, s) \in \mathbb{N}^2$. (As in Definition 2.2, it means that there exist $r_0, s_0 \in \mathbb{N}$ such that the equality holds for all integers $r \geq r_0$, $s \geq s_0$; as usual, Card M *denotes the number of elements of a finite set M).*

(ii) $\deg_{t_1} \omega_A \leq m$ and $\deg_{t_2} \omega_A \leq 1$ (so the total degree $\deg \omega_A$ *of the polynomial does not exceed $m+1$).*

(iii) $\deg\, \omega_A = m+1$ *if and only if $A = \emptyset$. In this case $\omega_A(t_1, t_2) = \binom{t_1+m}{m}(t_2 + 1)$.*

(iv) ω_A is a zero polynomial if and only if $(0, \dots, 0) \in A$.

Definition 2.4. The polynomial $\omega_A(t_1, t_2)$ whose existence is stated by Theorem 2.4 is called the dimension polynomial of the set $A \subseteq \mathbb{N}^{m+1}$ associated with the orders ord_1 and ord_2.

A closed-form formula for $\omega_A(t_1, t_2)$ can be found in [8, Proposition 2.2.11].

BASIC NOTATION AND TERMINOLOGY ON DIFFERENCE-DIFFERENTIAL RINGS AND FIELDS

By a *difference-differential ring* we mean a commutative ring R considered together with finite sets $\Delta = \{\delta_1, \dots, \delta_m\}$ and $\Sigma = \{\sigma_1, \dots, \sigma_n\}$ of derivations and injective endomorphisms of R, respectively, such that any two mappings of the set $\Delta \bigcup \Sigma$ commute. In what follows, we consider a special case when the set Σ consists of a single endomorphism σ called a *translation*. The set $\Delta \bigcup \{\sigma\}$

will be referred to as a *basic set* of the difference-differential ring R, which is also called a Δ-σ-ring. If R is a field, it is called a *difference-differential field* or a Δ-σ-field. We will often use prefix Δ-σ- instead of the adjective "difference-differential".

Let T be the free commutative semigroup generated by the set $\Delta\bigcup\{\sigma\}$, that is, the semigroup of all power products

$$\tau = \delta_1^{k_1}\dots\delta_m^{k_m}\sigma^l \qquad (k_i, l \in \mathbb{N}).$$

The numbers $\text{ord}_\Delta \tau = \sum_{i=1}^{m} k_i$ and $\text{ord}_\sigma \tau = l$ are called the *orders* of τ with respect to Δ and σ, respectively. For every $r, s \in \mathbb{N}$, we set

$$T(r, s) = \{\tau \in T \mid \text{ord}_\Delta \tau \le r,\ \text{ord}_\sigma \tau \le s\}.$$

Furthermore, Θ will denote the subsemigroup of T generated by Δ, so every element $\tau \in T$ can be written as $\tau = \theta\sigma^l$ where $\theta \in \Theta$, $l \in \mathbb{N}$. If $r \in \mathbb{N}$, we set $\Theta(r) = \{\theta \in \Theta \mid \text{ord}_\Delta \theta \le r\}$.

A subring (ideal) R_0 of a Δ-σ-ring R is called a difference-differential (or Δ-σ-) subring of R (respectively, a difference-differential (or Δ-σ-) ideal of R) if R_0 is closed with respect to the action of any operator of $\Delta\bigcup\sigma$. In this case the restriction of a mapping from $\Delta\bigcup\sigma$ on R_0 is denoted by the same symbol. If a prime ideal P of R is closed with respect to the action of $\Delta\bigcup\sigma$, it is called a *prime difference-differential* (or Δ-σ-) *ideal* of R.

If R is a Δ-σ-field and R_0 a subfield of R which is also a Δ-σ-subring of R, then R_0 is said to be a Δ-σ-subfield of R; R, in turn, is called a difference-differential (or Δ-σ-) field extension or a Δ-σ-overfield of R_0. In this case we also say that we have a Δ-σ-field extension R/R_0.

If R is a Δ-σ-ring and $S \subseteq R$, then the intersection of all Δ-σ-ideals of R containing the set S is, obviously, the smallest Δ-σ-ideal of R containing S. This ideal is denoted by $[S]$; as an ideal, it is generated by all elements $\tau\eta$ where $\tau \in T$, $\eta \in S$. (Here and below we frequently write $\tau\eta$ for $\tau(\eta)$ ($\tau \in T$, $\eta \in R$).) If the set S is finite, $S = \{\eta_1, \dots, \eta_p\}$, we say that the Δ-σ-ideal $I = [S]$ is finitely generated (in this case we write $I = [\eta_1, \dots, \eta_p]$) and call $\eta_1, \dots, \eta_p$ difference-differential (or Δ-σ-) generators of I. A Δ-σ-ideal I of a Δ-σ-ring R is called *reflexive* if the inclusion $\sigma^k(a) \in I$ ($k \in \mathbb{N}$, $a \in R$) implies that $a \in I$. For any Δ-σ-ideal I of R, the set $I^* = \{a \in R \mid \sigma^k(a) \in I \text{ for some } k \in \mathbb{N}\}$ is the smallest reflexive Δ-σ-ideal containing I; it is called the *reflexive closure* of I in R.

If K_0 is a Δ-σ-subfield of a Δ-σ-field K and $S \subseteq K$, then the intersection of all Δ-σ-subfields of K containing K_0 and S is the unique Δ-σ-subfield of K containing K_0 and S and contained in every Δ-σ-subfield of K containing K_0 and S. It is denoted by $K_0\langle S\rangle$. If S is finite, $S = \{\eta_1, \dots, \eta_n\}$, then K is said to be a finitely generated Δ-σ-extension of K_0 with the set of Δ-σ-generators $\{\eta_1, \dots, \eta_n\}$. In this case we write $K = K_0\langle\eta_1, \dots, \eta_n\rangle$. As a field, $K_0\langle\eta_1, \dots, \eta_n\rangle$ coincides with the field $K_0(\{\tau\eta_i|\tau \in T, 1 \le i \le n\})$.

Let R and S be two difference-differential rings with the same basic set $\Delta\bigcup\{\sigma\}$, so that elements of Δ and σ act on each of the rings as derivations and an endomorphism, respectively, and every two mapping of the set $\Delta\bigcup\{\sigma\}$ commute. A ring homomorphism $\phi : R \longrightarrow S$ is called a *difference-differential* (or Δ-σ-) *homomorphism* if $\phi(\alpha a) = \alpha\phi(a)$ for any $\alpha \in \Delta\bigcup\{\sigma\}$, $a \in R$. In this case $\text{Ker}\,\phi$ is a reflexive Δ-σ-ideal of R. Furthermore, if J is a reflexive Δ-σ-ideal of Δ-σ-ring R, then the factor ring R/J has a natural structure of a Δ-σ-ring such that the canonical epimorphism $R \to R/J$ is a Δ-σ-homomorphism.

If K is a Δ-σ-field and $Y = \{y_1, \dots, y_n\}$ is a finite set of symbols, then one can consider a countable set of symbols $TY = \{\tau y_j|\tau \in T, 1 \le j \le n\}$ and the polynomial ring $R = K[\{\tau y_j|\tau \in T, 1 \le j \le n\}]$ in the set of indeterminates TY over the field K. This polynomial ring is naturally viewed as a Δ-σ-ring where $\alpha(\tau y_j) = (\alpha\tau)y_j$ for any $\alpha \in \Delta\bigcup\{\sigma\}$, $\tau \in T$, $1 \le j \le n$, and the elements of $\Delta\bigcup\{\sigma\}$ act on the coefficients of the polynomials of R as they act in the field K. The ring R is called the *ring of difference-differential* (or Δ-σ-) *polynomials* in the set of difference-differential (Δ-σ-) indeterminates $y_1, \dots, y_n$ over K. This ring is denoted by $K\{y_1, \dots, y_n\}$ and its elements are called difference-differential (or Δ-σ-) polynomials. If $f \in K\{y_1, \dots, y_n\}$ and $\eta = (\eta_1, \dots, \eta_n)$ is an n-dimensional vector with coordinates in some Δ-σ-overfield of K, then $f(\eta)$ (or $f(\eta_1, \dots, \eta_n)$) denotes the result of the replacement of every entry τy_i in f by $\tau\eta_i$ ($\tau \in T$, $1 \le i \le n$).

A Δ-σ-ideal in the ring $K\{y_1, \dots, y_n\}$ is called *linear* if it is generated (as a Δ-σ-ideal) by homogeneous linear Δ-σ-polynomials (i. e., Δ-σ-polynomials of the form $\sum_{i=1}^{d} a_i\tau_i y_{k_i}$ where $a_i \in K$, $\tau_i \in T$, $1 \le k_i \le n$).

Let R be a Δ-σ-ring and $\mathcal{U}$ a family of elements of some Δ-σ-overring of R. We say that $\mathcal{U}$ is *Δ-σ-algebraically) dependent* over R, if the family $T\mathcal{U} = \{\tau u \mid \tau \in T,\ u \in \mathcal{U}\}$ is algebraically dependent over R (that is, there exist elements $u_1, \dots, u_k \in T\mathcal{U}$ and a nonzero polynomial f in k variables with coefficients in R such that $f(u_1, \dots, u_k) = 0$). Otherwise, the family $\mathcal{U}$ is said to be *Δ-σ-algebraically independent* over R.

If K is a Δ-σ-field and L a Δ-σ-field extension of K, then a set $B \subseteq L$ is said to be a *Δ-σ-transcendence basis* of L over K if B is Δ-σ-algebraically independent over K and every element $a \in L$ is Δ-σ-algebraic over $K\langle B\rangle$ (it means that the set $\{\tau a \mid \tau \in T\}$ is algebraically dependent over the field $K\langle B\rangle$). If L is a finitely generated Δ-σ-field extension of K, then all Δ-σ-transcendence bases of L over K are finite and have the same number of elements (one can easily obtain this result by mimicking the proof of Proposition 4.1.6 of [12]). This number is called the *Δ-σ-transcendence degree* of L over K (or the Δ-σ-transcendence degree of the extension L/K); it is denoted by Δ-σ-tr. $\deg_K L$.

Let K be a Δ-σ-field K and L a finitely generated Δ-σ-extension of K with a set of Δ-σ-generators $\eta = \{\eta_1, \dots, \eta_n\}$, $L = K\langle\eta_1, \dots, \eta_n\rangle$. Then there exists a natural Δ-σ-homomorphism Φ_η of the ring of Δ-σ-polynomials $K\{y_1, \dots, y_n\}$ onto the Δ-σ-subring $K\{\eta_1, \dots, \eta_n\}$ of L such that $\Phi_\eta(a) = a$ for any $a \in K$ and $\Phi_\eta(y_j) = \eta_j$ for $j = 1, \dots, n$. If A is a Δ-σ-polynomial in $K\{y_1, \dots, y_n\}$, then the element $\Phi_\eta(A)$ is called the *value* of A at η and is denoted by $A(\eta)$. Obviously, the kernel P of the Δ-σ-homomorphism Φ_η is a prime reflexive Δ-σ-ideal of $K\{y_1, \dots, y_n\}$. This ideal is called the *defining* ideal of η. If we consider the quotient field Q of the factor ring $K\{y_1, \dots, y_n\}/P$ as a Δ-σ-field (where $\delta(\frac{u}{v}) = \frac{v\delta(u)-u\delta(v)}{v^2}$ and $\sigma(\frac{u}{v}) = \frac{\sigma(u)}{\sigma(v)}$ for any $u, v \in \bar{R}$, $\delta \in \Delta$), then this quotient field is naturally Δ-σ-isomorphic to the field L. The Δ-σ-isomorphism of Q onto L is identical on K and maps the canonical images of the Δ-indeterminates $y_1, \dots, y_n$ in $K\{y_1, \dots, y_n\}/P$ to the elements $\eta_1, \dots, \eta_n$, respectively.

3 REDUCTION OF Δ-σ-POLYNOMIALS. CHARACTERISTIC SETS

Let K be a difference-differential field with a basic set $\Delta \bigcup \{\sigma\}$ ($\Delta = \{\delta_1, \dots, \delta_m\}$ is a set of derivations, σ is an endomorphism of K). Let $R = K\{y_1, \dots, y_n\}$ be the ring of Δ-σ-polynomials in the set of Δ-σ-indeterminates $y_1, \dots, y_n$ over K and let TY denote the set of all elements $\tau y_i \in R$ ($\tau \in T$, $1 \le i \le n$) called *terms*. If $u = \tau y_i \in TY$, then the numbers $\mathrm{ord}_\Delta \tau$ and $\mathrm{ord}_\sigma \tau$ are called the orders of the term u with respect to Δ and σ, respectively.

We will consider two total orders $<_\Delta$ and $<_\sigma$ on the set of all terms TY defined as follows:

If $u = \delta_1^{k_1} \dots \delta_m^{k_m} \sigma^p y_i$ and $v = \delta_1^{l_1} \dots \delta_m^{l_m} \sigma^q y_j$ $(1 \le i, j \le n)$, then $u <_\Delta v$ (respectively, $u <_\sigma v$) if the $(m+3)$-tuple $(\mathrm{ord}_\Delta u, \mathrm{ord}_\sigma u, k_1, \dots, k_m, i)$ is less than the $(m+3)$-tuple $(\mathrm{ord}_\Delta v, \mathrm{ord}_\sigma v, l_1, \dots, l_m, j)$ (respectively, the $(m+3)$-tuple $(\mathrm{ord}_\sigma u, \mathrm{ord}_\Delta u, k_1, \dots, k_m, i)$ is less than the $(m+3)$-tuple $(\mathrm{ord}_\sigma v, \mathrm{ord}_\Delta v, l_1, \dots, l_m, j)$) with respect to the lexicographic order on $\mathbb{N}^{m+3}$. We write $u \le_\Delta v$ if either $u <_\Delta v$ or $u = v$; the relation $\le_\sigma$ is defined in the same way.

An element $\tau \in T$ is said to be divisible by an element $\tau' \in T$ if $\tau = \tau'' \tau'$ for some $\tau'' \in T$. In this case we write $\tau' \mid \tau$ and $\tau'' = \dfrac{\tau}{\tau'}$.

The least common multiple of elements $\tau_1, \dots, \tau_p \in T$, where $\tau_i = \delta_1^{k_{i1}} \dots \delta_m^{k_{im}} \sigma^{l_i}$ $(1 \le i \le p)$ is defined as $\tau = \delta_1^{d_1} \dots \delta_m^{d_m} \sigma^l$ with $d_j = \max\{k_{1j}, \dots, k_{pj}\}$ $(1 \le j \le m)$, $l = \max\{l_1, \dots, l_p\}$; it is denoted by $\mathrm{lcm}\{\tau_1, \dots, \tau_p\}$.

If $u = \tau_1 y_i$, $v = \tau_2 y_j \in TY$, we say that u divides v and write $u \mid v$ if and only if $i = j$ and $\tau_1 \mid \tau_2$. In this case the ratio $\dfrac{v}{u}$ is defined as $\dfrac{\tau_2}{\tau_1}$. If $u_1 = \tau_1 y_i, \dots, u_p = \tau_p y_i$ are terms with the same Δ-σ-indeterminate y_i, then the least common multiple of these terms, denoted by $\mathrm{lcm}(u_1, \dots, u_p)$, is defined as $\mathrm{lcm}(\tau_1, \dots, \tau_p) y_i$.

The following statement is a consequence of Lemma 2.1.

Lemma 3.1. *Let S be any infinite set of terms in $K\{y_1, \dots, y_n\}$. Then there exists an infinite sequence of terms $u_1, u_2, \dots$ in S such that $u_k \mid u_{k+1}$ for every $k = 1, 2, \dots$.*

If $A \in K\{y_1, \dots, y_n\} \setminus K$, then the highest with respect to the orderings $<_\Delta$ and $<_\sigma$ terms that appear in A are called the *Δ-leader* and the *σ-leader* of A; they are denoted by u_A and v_A, respectively. If A is written as a polynomial in one variable v_A, $A = I_d(v_A)^d + I_{d-1}(v_A)^{d-1} + \dots + I_0$ (Δ-σ-polynomials $I_d, I_{d-1}, \dots, I_0$ do not contain v_A), then I_d is called a *leading coefficient* of A; the partial derivative $\partial A / \partial v_A = d I_d (v_A)^{d-1} + (d-1) I_{d-1} (v_A)^{d-2} + \dots + I_1$ is called a *separant* of A. The leading coefficient and the separant of a Δ-σ-polynomial A are denoted by I_A and S_A, respectively.

Definition 3.2. Let A and B be two Δ-σ-polynomials in the ring $K\{y_1, \dots, y_n\}$. We say that A has lower rank than B and write $\mathrm{rk}\,A < \mathrm{rk}\,B$ if either $A \in K$, $B \notin K$, or $(v_A, \deg_{v_A} A, \mathrm{ord}_\Delta u_A)$ is less than $(v_B, \deg_{v_B} B, \mathrm{ord}_\Delta u_B)$ with respect to the lexicographic order (where the terms v_A and v_B are compared with respect to the order $<_\sigma$ and the other coordinates are compared with respect to the natural order on $\mathbb{N}$). If the two vectors are equal (or $A, B \in K$), we say that the Δ-σ-polynomials A and B are of the same rank and write $\mathrm{rk}\,A = \mathrm{rk}\,B$.

Definition 3.3. If $A, B \in K\{y_1, \dots, y_n\}$, then B is said to be **reduced** with respect to A if

(i) B does not contain terms τv_A such that $\mathrm{ord}_\Delta \tau > 0$ and $\mathrm{ord}_\Delta(\tau u_A) \le \mathrm{ord}_\Delta u_B$.

(ii) If B contains a term τv_A where $\mathrm{ord}_\Delta \tau = 0$, then either $\mathrm{ord}_\Delta u_B < \mathrm{ord}_\Delta u_A$ or $\mathrm{ord}_\Delta u_A \le \mathrm{ord}_\Delta u_B$ and $\deg_{\tau v_A} B < \deg_{v_A} A$.

If $B \in K\{y_1, \dots, y_n\}$, then B is said to be reduced with respect to a set $\mathcal{A} \subseteq K\{y_1, \dots, y_n\}$ if B is reduced with respect to every element of $\mathcal{A}$.

Remark 3.4. *It follows from the last definition that a Δ-σ-polynomial B is not reduced with respect to a Δ-σ-polynomial A ($A \notin K$) if either B contains some term τv_A such that $\mathrm{ord}_\Delta \tau > 0$ and $\mathrm{ord}_\Delta(\tau u_A) \le \mathrm{ord}_\Delta u_B$ or B contains $\sigma^i v_A$ for some $i \in \mathbb{N}$ and in this case $\mathrm{ord}_\Delta u_A \le \mathrm{ord}_\Delta u_B$ and $\deg_{v_A} A \le \deg_{\sigma^i v_A} B$.*

Definition 3.5. A set of Δ-σ-polynomials $\mathcal{A}$ in $K\{y_1, \dots, y_n\}$ is called **autoreduced** if $\mathcal{A} \bigcap K = \emptyset$ and every element of $\mathcal{A}$ is reduced with respect to any other element of this set.

Proposition 3.6. *Every autoreduced set of Δ-σ-polynomials in the ring $K\{y_1, \dots, y_n\}$ is finite.*

Proof. Suppose that $\mathcal{A}$ is an infinite autoreduced subset of $K\{y_1, \dots, y_n\}$. Then there is an infinite subset $\mathcal{A}'$ of $\mathcal{A}$ such that all Δ-σ-polynomials in $\mathcal{A}'$ have distinct σ-leaders. Indeed, otherwise there exists an infinite set $\mathcal{A}_1 \subseteq \mathcal{A}$ such that all Δ-σ-polynomials in $\mathcal{A}_1$ have the same σ-leader v. It follows that the infinite set $\{\mathrm{ord}_\Delta u_A \mid A \in \mathcal{A}_1\}$ contains a nondecreasing infinite sequence $\mathrm{ord}_\Delta u_{A_1} \le \mathrm{ord}_\Delta u_{A_2} \le \dots$. Since the sequence $\{\deg_v A_i | i = 1, 2, \dots\}$ cannot be strictly decreasing, there exists two indices i and j such that $i < j$ and $\deg_v A_i \le \deg_v A_j$. We obtain that A_j is not reduced with respect to A_i that contradicts the fact that $\mathcal{A}$ is an autoreduced set.

Thus, we can assume that all leaders of our infinite autoreduced set $\mathcal{A}$ are distinct. By Lemma 3.1, there exists an infinite sequence $B_1, B_2, \dots$ of elements of $\mathcal{A}$ such that $v_{B_i} \mid v_{B_{i+1}}$ for all $i = 1, 2, \dots$. (Also, since the leaders of elements of our sequence are distinct, $\dfrac{v_{B_{i+1}}}{v_{B_i}} \neq 1$.)

Let $k_i = \mathrm{ord}_\sigma v_{B_i}$ and $l_i = \mathrm{ord}_\Delta u_{B_i}$. Since u_{B_i} is the Δ-leader of B_i, $l_i \ge k_i$ $(i = 1, 2, \dots)$, so that the infinite set $\{l_i - k_i \mid i \in \mathbb{N}, i \ge 1\}$ contains a nondecreasing sequence $l_{i_1} - k_{i_1}, l_{i_2} - k_{i_2}, \dots$. Then $\mathrm{ord}_\Delta(\frac{v_{B_{i_2}}}{v_{B_{i_1}}} u_{B_{i_1}}) = k_{i_2} - k_{i_1} + l_{i_1} \le k_{i_2} + l_{i_2} - k_{i_2} = l_{i_2} = \mathrm{ord}_\Delta u_{B_{i_2}}$. It follows that B_{i_2} contains a term $\tau v_{B_{i_1}} = v_{B_{i_2}}$ such that $\mathrm{ord}_\Delta \tau > 0$ and $\mathrm{ord}_\Delta(\tau u_{B_{i_1}}) \le \mathrm{ord}_\Delta u_{B_{i_2}}$. Thus, the Δ-σ-polynomial B_{i_2} is reduced with respect to B_{i_1} that contradicts the fact that $\mathcal{A}$ is an autoreduced set. □

The proof of the following statement is similar to the proof of the reduction theorem for difference-differential polynomials in the case of classical autoreduced sets, see [1].

Proposition 3.7. *Let $\mathcal{A} = \{A_1, \dots, A_p\}$ be an autoreduced set in the ring of Δ-σ-polynomials $K\{y_1, \dots, y_n\}$ and let $B \in K\{y_1, \dots, y_n\}$. Then there exist a Δ-σ-polynomial B_0 and nonnegative integers k_i, l_i*

$(1 \le i \le p)$ such that B_0 is reduced with respect to $\mathcal{A}$, $\mathrm{rk}\, B_0 \le \mathrm{rk}\, B$, and $\prod_{i=1}^{p} I_{A_i}^{k_i} S_{A_i}^{l_i} B \equiv B_0\,(mod[\mathcal{A}])$.

With the notation of the last proposition, we say that the Δ-σ-polynomial B *reduces to* B_0 modulo $\mathcal{A}$.

Throughout the rest of the paper, while considering an autoreduced set $\mathcal{A} = \{A_1, \dots, A_p\}$ in the ring $K\{y_1, \dots, y_n\}$ we always assume that its elements are arranged in order of increasing rank, $rk\, A_1 < \dots < rk\, A_p$.

Definition 3.8. If $\mathcal{A} = \{A_1, \dots, A_p\}$, $\mathcal{B} = \{B_1, \dots, B_q\}$ are two autoreduced sets of Δ-σ-polynomials $K\{y_1, \dots, y_n\}$, we say that $\mathcal{A}$ has lower rank than $\mathcal{B}$ if one of the following two cases holds:

(1) There exists $k \in \mathbb{N}$ such that $k \le \min\{p, q\}$, $\mathrm{rk}\, A_i = \mathrm{rk}\, B_i$ for $i = 1, \dots, k-1$ and $\mathrm{rk}\, A_k < \mathrm{rk}\, B_k$.

(2) $p > q$ and $\mathrm{rk}\, A_i = \mathrm{rk}\, B_i$ for $i = 1, \dots, q$.

If $p = q$ and $\mathrm{rk}\, A_i = \mathrm{rk}\, B_i$ for $i = 1, \dots, p$, then $\mathcal{A}$ is said to have the same rank as $\mathcal{B}$. In this case we write $\mathrm{rk}\, \mathcal{A} = \mathrm{rk}\, \mathcal{B}$.

Repeating the arguments of the proof of the corresponding result for autoreduced sets of differential polynomials (see [7, Chapter I, Proposition 3]) we obtain the following statement.

PROPOSITION 3.9. *In every nonempty family of autoreduced sets of differential polynomials there exists an autoreduced set of lowest rank.*

This statement shows that if J is a Δ-σ-ideal (or even a subset) of the ring of Δ-σ-polynomials $K\{y_1, \dots, y_n\}$, then J contains an autoreduced subset of lowest rank.(Clearly, the set of all autoreduced subsets of J is not empty: if $A \in J$, then $\{A\}$ is an autoreduced subset of J.)

Definition 3.10. If J is a subset (in particular, a Δ-σ-ideal) of the ring of Δ-σ-polynomials $K\{y_1, \dots, y_n\}$, then an autoreduced subset of J of lowest rank is called a **characteristic set** of J.

PROPOSITION 3.11. *Let $\mathcal{A} = \{A_1, \dots, A_p\}$ be a characteristic set of a nonempty subset J of the ring of Δ-σ-polynomials $R = K\{y_1, \dots, y_n\}$. Then an element $B \in J$ is reduced with respect to $\mathcal{A}$ if and only if $B = 0$.*

PROOF. First of all, note that if $B \ne 0$ and $\mathrm{rk}\, B < \mathrm{rk}\, A_1$, then $\{B\}$ is an autoreduced set and $\mathrm{rk}\{B\} < \mathrm{rk}\, \mathcal{A}$ that contradicts the fact that $\mathcal{A}$ is a characteristic set of J. Let $\mathrm{rk}\, B > \mathrm{rk}\, A_1$ and let $A_1, \dots, A_j$ $(1 \le j \le p)$ be all elements of $\mathcal{A}$ whose rank is lower that the rank of B. Then the set $\mathcal{A}' = \{A_1, \dots, A_j, B\}$ is autoreduced. Indeed, the Δ-σ-polynomials $A_1, \dots, A_j$ are reduced with respect to each other and B is reduced with respect to the set $\{A_1, \dots, A_j\}$, since B is reduced with respect to $\mathcal{A}$. Furthermore, each A_i $(1 \le i \le j)$ is reduced with respect to B because $\mathrm{rk}\, A_i < \mathrm{rk}\, B$. By the choice of B, if $j < p$, then $\mathrm{rk}\, B < \mathrm{rk}\, A_{j+1}$, so $\mathrm{rk}\, \mathcal{A}' < \mathrm{rk}\, \mathcal{A}$; if $j = p$, then we still have the inequality $\mathrm{rk}\, \mathcal{A}' < \mathrm{rk}\, \mathcal{A}$ by the second part of Definition 3.8. It follows that $\mathcal{A}$ is not a characteristic set of J, contrary to our assumption. Thus, $B = 0$. □

Definition 3.12. Let $\mathcal{A} = \{A_1, \dots, A_p\}$ be an autoreduced set in the ring $K\{y_1, \dots, y_n\}$ such that all Δ-σ-polynomials A_i $(1 \le i \le p)$ are linear. Then the set $\mathcal{A}$ is said to be coherent if it satisfies the following two conditions.

(i) τA_i reduces to zero modulo $\mathcal{A}$ for any $\tau \in T$, $1 \le i \le p$.

(ii) For every $A_i, A_j \in \mathcal{A}$, $1 \le i < j \le p$, let $w = \mathrm{lcm}\{v_{A_i}, v_{A_j}\}$ and $\tau' = \frac{w}{v_{A_i}}$, $\tau'' = \frac{w}{v_{A_j}}$. Then $(\tau'' I_{A_j})(\tau' A_i) - (\tau' I_{A_i})(\tau'' A_j)$ reduces to zero modulo $\mathcal{A}$.

The proof of the following statement can be obtained by mimicking the proof of the corresponding result for autoreduced sets of difference polynomials, see [8, Theorem 6.5.3].

PROPOSITION 3.13. *Every characteristic set of a linear Δ-σ-ideal in the ring of Δ-σ-polynomials $K\{y_1, \dots, y_n\}$ is a coherent autoreduced set. Conversely, if $\mathcal{A}$ is a coherent autoreduced set in $K\{y_1, \dots, y_n\}$ consisting of linear Δ-σ-polynomials, then $\mathcal{A}$ is a characteristic set of the linear Δ-σ-ideal $[\mathcal{A}]$.*

4 DIMENSION POLYNOMIALS. THE MAIN THEOREM

Let K be a Δ-σ-field (as before $\Delta = \{\delta_1, \dots, \delta_m\}$ is a set of mutually commuting derivations of K and σ is an endomorphism of K that commutes with every δ_i). Let $R = K\{y_1, \dots, y_n\}$ be the ring of Δ-σ-polynomials over K and P a prime Δ-σ-ideal of R. Let P^* denote the reflexive closure of P in R (as we have mentioned, P^* is also a prime Δ-σ-ideal of R) and for every $r, s \in \mathbb{N}$, let $R_{rs} = K[\{\tau y_i \mid \tau \in T(r, s), 1 \le i \le n\}]$. In other words, R_{rs} is a polynomial ring over K in indeterminates τy_i such that $\mathrm{ord}_\Delta \tau \le r$ and $\mathrm{ord}_\sigma \tau \le s$. Let $P_{rs} = P \bigcap R_{rs}$, $P^*_{rs} = P^* \bigcap R_{rs}$, and let L, L^*, L_{rs} and L^*_{rs} denote the quotient fields of the integral domains R/P, R/P^*, R_{rs}/P_{rs} and R_{rs}/P^*_{rs}, respectively. If η_i denotes the canonical image of y_i in R_{rs}/P^*_{rs}, then L^* is a Δ-σ-field extension of K, $L^* = K\langle \eta_1, \dots, \eta_n \rangle$, and $L^*_{rs} = K(\{\tau \eta_i \mid \tau \in T(r, s),\ 1 \le i \le n\})$.

The following statement is an analog of the theorem on the dimension polynomial of an inversive difference-differential field extension proved in [13].

THEOREM 4.1. *With the above notation, there exists a numerical polynomial $\phi_{P^*}(t_1, t_2) \in \mathbb{Q}[t_1, t_2]$ such that*

(i) *$\phi_{P^*}(r, s) = \mathrm{tr.\,deg}_K\, L^*_{rs}$ for all sufficiently large pairs $(r, s) \in \mathbb{N}^2$.*

(ii) *The polynomial $\phi_{P^*}(t_1, t_2)$ is linear with respect to t_2 and $\deg_{t_1} \phi_{P^*} \le m$, so this polynomial can be written as*

$$\phi_{P^*}(t_1, t_2) = \phi^{(1)}_{P^*}(t_1) t_2 + \phi^{(2)}_{P^*}(t_1)$$

where $\phi^{(1)}_{P^*}(t_1)$ and $\phi^{(2)}_{P^*}(t_1)$ are numerical polynomials in one variable that, in turn, can be written as

$$\phi^{(1)}_{P^*}(t_1) = \sum_{i=0}^{m} a_i \binom{t_1 + i}{i} \quad and \quad \phi^{(2)}_{P^*}(t_1) = \sum_{i=0}^{m} b_i \binom{t_1 + i}{i}$$

with $a_i, b_i \in \mathbb{Z}$ $(1 \le i \le m)$. Furthermore, $a_m = \Delta$-σ-$\mathrm{tr.\,deg}_K\, L^*$.

PROOF. Let $\mathcal{A} = \{A_1, \dots, A_p\}$ be a characteristic set of the Δ-σ-ideal P^* and for any $r, s \in \mathbb{N}$, let

$U_{rs} = \{u \in TY \mid \mathrm{ord}_\Delta u \le r$, $\mathrm{ord}_\sigma u \le s$ and either u is not a multiple of any v_{A_i} or u is a multiple of some σ-leader of an element of $\mathcal{A}$ and for every $\tau \in T, A \in \mathcal{A}$ such that $u = \tau v_A$, one has $\mathrm{ord}_\Delta(\tau u_A) > r\}$.

Using our concept of an autoreduced and the arguments of the proof of Theorem 6 in [7, Chapter II], we obtain that the set $U_{rs}(\eta) = \{u(\eta) \mid u \in U_{rs}\}$ is a transcendence basis of L^*_{rs} over K. In order to evaluate the number of elements of U_{rs} (and therefore, tr. $\deg_K L^*_{rs}$), let us consider the sets $U'_{rs} = \{u \in TY \mid \text{ord}_\Delta u \le r, \text{ord}_\sigma u \le s$ and u is not a multiple of any $v_{A_i}\}$ and $U''_{r,s} = \{u \in TY \mid \text{ord}_\Delta u \le r, \text{ord}_\sigma u \le s$ and there exist $A \in \mathcal{A}$ such that $u = \tau v_A$ and $\text{ord}_\Delta(\tau u_A) > r\}$. Clearly, $U'_{rs} \bigcap U''_{r,s} = \emptyset$ and $U_{r,s} = U'_{r,s} \bigcup U''_{r,s}$.

By Theorem 2.3, there exists a numerical polynomial in two variables $\phi^{(1)}(t_1, t_2)$ such that $\phi^{(1)}(r, s) = \text{Card}\, U'_{rs}$ for all sufficiently large $(r, s) \in \mathbb{N}^2$, $\deg_{t_1} \phi^{(1)} \le m$, and $\deg_{t_2} \phi^{(1)} \le 1$. Furthermore, repeating the arguments of the proof of Theorem 4.2 of [11] (considered in the case of one translation) we obtain that there exists a bivariate numerical polynomial $\phi^{(2)}(t_1, t_2)$ such that $\phi^{(2)}(r, s) = \text{Card}\, U''_{rs}$ for all sufficiently large $(r, s) \in \mathbb{N}^2$ and $\phi^{(2)}(t_1, t_2)$ is an alternating sum of bivariate numerical polynomials of subsets of $\mathbb{N}^{m+1}$ described in section 2. Each such a polynomial can be represented in the form (2), so $\deg_{t_1} \phi^{(2)} \le m$ and $\deg_{t_2} \phi^{(2)} \le 1$. Clearly the polynomial $\phi_{P^*}(t_1, t_2) = \phi^{(1)}(t_1, t_2) + \phi^{(2)}(t_1, t_2)$ satisfies all conditions of the theorem. The fact that $a_m = \Delta$-σ-tr. $\deg_K L^*$ can be established in the same way as in the last part of the proof of Theorem 3.1 in [13]. □

Note that in the case when σ is an automorphism of K, the statement of the last theorem was proved in [10] with the use of a theorem on the multivariate dimension polynomial of a difference-differential module and properties of modules of Kähler differentials.

The following theorem is the main result of the paper.

THEOREM 4.2. *With the notation introduced at the beginning of this section, there exists a bivariate numerical polynomial $\psi_P(t_1, t_2)$ such that*

(i) $\psi_P(r, s) = \text{tr.}\deg_K L_{rs}$ *for all sufficiently large pairs* $(r, s) \in \mathbb{N}^2$.

(ii) *The polynomial $\psi_P(t_1, t_2)$ is linear with respect to t_2 and $\deg_{t_1} \psi_P \le m$, so it can be written as*

$$\psi_P(t_1, t_2) = \psi_P^{(1)}(t_1)t_2 + \psi_P^{(2)}(t_1)$$

where $\psi_P^{(1)}(t_1)$ and $\psi_P^{(2)}(t_1)$ are numerical polynomials in one variable.

PROOF. We start with the proof for the case $\Delta = \emptyset$. In this case we will use the above notation and conventions just replacing the prefix Δ-σ- by σ- (and "difference-differential" by "difference"). Let $\mathcal{A} = \{A_1, \dots, A_p\}$ be a characteristic set of the σ-ideal P^* (the reflexive closure of the prime σ-ideal P of the ring of σ-polynomials $R = K\{y_1, \dots, y_n\}$) and let v_j denote the σ-leader of A_j ($j = 1, \dots, p$). Let $\eta_i = y_i + P$ ($1 \le i \le n$), $L = K(\{\sigma^k \eta_i \mid k \in \mathbb{N}, 1 \le i \le n\})$ (the quotient field of R/P) and $L_s = K(\{\sigma^k \eta_i \mid 0 \le k \le s, 1 \le i \le n\})$.

For every $j = 1, \dots, p$, let s_j be the smallest nonnegative integer such that $\sigma^{s_j}(A_j) \in P$. Furthermore, let

$$V = \{u \in TY \mid u \ne \sigma^i v_j \text{ for any } i \in \mathbb{N}, 1 \le j \le p\},$$

$V_r = \{v \in V \mid \text{ord}_\sigma v \le r\}$ ($r \in \mathbb{N}$), $V(\eta) = \{u(\eta) \mid u \in V\}$, $W = \{\sigma^k v_j \mid 1 \le j \le p, 0 \le k \le s_j - 1\}$, and $W(\eta) = \{u(\eta) \mid u \in W\}$.

It is easy to see that the set $V(\eta)$ is algebraically independent over K. Indeed, suppose there exist $v_1, \dots, v_l \in V$ and a polynomial $f(X_1, \dots, X_l)$ in l variables with coefficients in the field K such that $f(v_1(\eta), \dots, v_l(\eta)) = 0$. Then $f(v_1, \dots, v_l) \in P \subseteq P^*$ and $f(v_1, \dots, v_l)$ is reduced with respect to the characteristic set $\mathcal{A}$ (this σ-polynomial does not contain any transforms of the leaders of elements of $\mathcal{A}$). Therefore, $f = 0$, so the set $V(\eta)$ is algebraically independent over K.

Now we notice that every element of the field L is algebraic over its subfield $K(V(\eta) \bigcup W(\eta))$.

Indeed, since $L = K(V(\eta) \bigcup W(\eta) \bigcup \{\sigma^k v_j(\eta) \mid 1 \le j \le p, k \ge s_i\})$, it is sufficient to prove that every element $\sigma^k v_j(\eta)$ with $k \ge s_j$ ($1 \le i \le p$) is algebraic over $K(V(\eta) \bigcup W(\eta))$.

Since $\sigma^{s_j} A_j \in P$, we have $\sigma^{s_j} A_j(\eta) = 0$, hence $\sigma^k A_j(\eta) = 0$ for all $k \ge s_j$. If one writes A_j as a polynomial in v_j,

$$A_j = I_{q_j}^{(j)} v_j^{q_j} + I_{q_j-1}^{(j)} v_j^{q_j-1} + \dots + I_0^{(j)}$$

($I_{q_j}^{(j)}, \dots, I_0^{(j)}$ do not contain v_j) and $k \ge s_j$, then

$$\sigma^k A_j(\eta) = \left(\sigma^k I_{q_j}^{(j)}(\eta)\right) v_j(\eta)^{q_j} + \left(\sigma^k I_{q_j-1}^{(j)}(\eta)\right) v_j(\eta)^{q_j-1} + \dots + \sigma^k I_0^{(j)}(\eta) = 0.$$

Note that $I_{q_j}^{(j)} \notin P^*$, since $I_{q_j}^{(j)}$ is an initial of an element of the characteristic set of P^* and therefore is reduced with respect to this set (by Proposition 3.11, the inclusion $I_{q_j}^{(j)} \in P^*$ would imply $I_{q_j}^{(j)} = 0$). Since the σ-ideal P^* is reflexive, $\sigma^k I_{q_j}^{(j)} \notin P^*$, hence $\sigma^k I_{q_j}^{(j)}(\eta) \ne 0$. It follows that $\sigma^k v_j(\eta)$ is algebraic over the field $K\left(V(\eta) \bigcup W(\eta) \bigcup \{u(\eta) \mid u <_\sigma \sigma^k u_i\}\right)$ (the term ordering $<_\sigma$ was defined at the beginning of section 3). By induction on the well-ordered (with respect to $<_\sigma$) set of terms TY we obtain that all elements $\sigma^k v_j(\eta)$ ($1 \le j \le p, k \in \mathbb{N}$) are algebraic over $K(V(\eta) \bigcup W(\eta))$, so L is algebraic over this field as well.

Let $\{w_1, \dots, w_q\}$ be a maximal subset of W such that the set $\{w_1(\eta), \dots, w_q(\eta)\}$ is algebraically independent over $K(V(\eta))$. Then $V(\eta) \bigcup \{w_1(\eta), \dots, w_q(\eta)\}$ is a transcendence basis of the field L over K. Furthermore, since the set $W(\eta)$ is finite, there exists $r_0 \in \mathbb{N}$ such that

(i) $w_1, \dots, w_q \in R_{r_0}$;
(ii) $r_0 \ge \max\{\text{ord}_\sigma v_j + s_j \mid 1 \le j \le p\}$;
(iii) Every element of $W(\eta)$ is algebraic over the field $K(V_{r_0}(\eta) \bigcup \{w_1(\eta), \dots, w_q(\eta)\})$.

Let $r \ge r_0$, $R_r = K[\{\sigma^k y_i \mid 1 \le i \le n, 0 \le k \le r\}]$, and $P_r = P \bigcap R_r$. Let L_r denote the quotient field of the integral domain R_r/P_r and $\zeta_i^{(r)} = y_i + P_r \in R_r/P_r \subseteq L_r$ ($1 \le i \le n$). Furthermore, let $\zeta^{(r)} = \{\zeta_1^{(1)}, \dots, \zeta_n^{(1)}\}$, and $V_r(\zeta^{(r)}) = \{v(\zeta^{(r)}) \mid v \in V_r\}$. We are going to prove that

$$B_r = V_r(\zeta^{(r)}) \bigcup \{w_1(\zeta^{(r)}), \dots, w_q(\zeta^{(r)})\}$$

is a transcendence basis of L_r over K.

Repeating the arguments of the proof of Theorem 4.1 (applied to $V_r(\zeta^{(r)})$ instead of $V(\eta)$) we obtain that $V_r(\zeta^{(r)})$ is algebraically independent over K. Let us show that the elements $w_1(\zeta^{(r)}), \dots, w_q(\zeta^{(r)})$ are algebraically independent over the field $K(V_r(\zeta^{(r)}))$. Suppose that $g(w_1(\zeta^{(r)}), \dots, w_q(\zeta^{(r)})) = 0$ for some polynomial g in q

indeterminates with coefficients in $K\left(V_r(\zeta^{(r)})\right)$. Then there exist elements $z_1, \dots, z_d \in V_r$ such that all coefficients of f lie in $K(z_1(\zeta^{(r)}), \dots, z_d(\zeta^{(r)}))$. Multiplying f by the common denominator of these coefficients we obtain a nonzero polynomial g in $d+q$ indeterminates such that

$$g(z_1(\zeta^{(r)}), \dots, z_d(\zeta^{(r)}), w_1(\zeta^{(r)}), \dots, w_q(\zeta^{(r)})) = 0,$$

hence $g(z_1, \dots, z_d, w_1, \dots, w_q) \in P_r \subseteq P$.

Considering the image of g under the natural homomorphism $R \to R/P \subseteq L$ we obtain that $g(z_1(\eta), \dots, z_d(\eta), w_1(\eta), \dots, w_q(\eta)) = 0$ where $z_i(\eta) \in K(V(\eta))$, $1 \le i \le d$. Since $V(\eta) \bigcup \{w_1(\eta), \dots, w_q(\eta)\}$ is a transcendence basis of L/K, $g = 0$, a contradiction. Therefore, the elements $w_1(\zeta^{(r)}), \dots, w_q(\zeta^{(r)})$ are algebraically independent over $K\left(V_r(\zeta^{(r)})\right)$, so that the set B_r is algebraically independent over K.

Now let $r \ge r_0$ and let $u = \sigma^l y_i$ where $0 \le l \le r$ $(1 \le i \le n)$. If u is not a transform of any v_k $(1 \le k \le p)$, then $u \in V_r$ and $u(\zeta) \in V_r(\zeta)$.

If $u = \sigma^j v_k$ where $0 \le j \le s_k - 1$ (in this case $\mathrm{ord}_\sigma u < r$), then $u \in W$, hence the element $u(\eta)$ is algebraic over the field $K\left(V_r(\eta) \bigcup \{w_1(\eta), \dots, w_q(\eta)\}\right)$. As above, we obtain the existence of a nonzero polynomial h in $d+q+1$ variables ($d \in \mathbb{N}$) and elements $z_1, \dots, z_d \in V_r$ such that $h(z_1, \dots, z_d, w_1, \dots, w_q, u) \in P_r$. Then $h(z_1(\zeta^{(r)}), \dots, z_d(\zeta^{(r)}), w_1(\zeta^{(r)}), \dots, w_q(\zeta^{(r)}), u(\zeta^{(r)})) = 0$ hence $u(\zeta^{(r)})$ is algebraic over the field $K(B_r)$.

Suppose that $u = \sigma^j v_k$ where $s_k \le j \le r - \mathrm{ord}\, v_k$ $(1 \le k \le p)$. Then $\sigma^j A_k \in P_r$, hence $\sigma^j A_k(\zeta^{(r)}) = 0$. If one writes A_k as a polynomial of v_k,

$$A_k = I_{kd_k} v_k^{d_k} + \dots + I_{k1} v_k + I_{k0}$$

(I_{ij} do not contain v_k and all terms in I_{ij} are lower than v_k with respect to $<_\sigma$), then $\sigma^j I_{kd_k} \notin P^*$, since I_{kd_k} is the initial of an element of a characteristic set of P^* and the ideal P^* is reflexive. Therefore, $\sigma^j I_{kd_k}(\zeta^{(r)}) \neq 0$, so the equality $\sigma^j A_k(\zeta^{(r)}) = 0$ shows that the element $u(\zeta^{(r)}) = \sigma^j v_k(\zeta^{(r)})$ is algebraic over the field $K\left(V_r(\zeta^{(r)}) \bigcup \{v(\zeta^{(r)}) \mid v \in TY,\ v <_\sigma u\}\right)$.

Using the induction on the well-ordered (with respect to the order $<_\sigma$) set TY we obtain that $u(\zeta^{(r)})$ is algebraic over the field $K\left(V_r(\zeta^{(r)}) \bigcup \{\sigma^j v_k(\zeta^{(r)}) \mid 1 \le k \le d,\ 0 \le j \le s_k - 1\}\right)$, which, as we have seen, is algebraic over $K(B_r)$. It follows that $u(\zeta^{(r)})$ is algebraic over $K(B_r)$ for every term u with $\mathrm{ord}_\sigma u \le r$. Therefore, B_r is a transcendence basis of L_r over K.

Now we are going to complete the proof of the theorem considering the case when $\mathrm{Card}\, \Delta = m > 0$. In this case, the field L_{rs} can be treated as the subfield $K(\{\theta\sigma^j\xi_i \mid \theta \in \Theta(r), 0 \le j \le s, 1 \le i \le n\})$ of the differential (Δ-) overfield $K\langle\{\sigma^j\xi_i \mid 0 \le j \le s, 1 \le i \le n\}\rangle_\Delta$ of K. (ξ_i is the canonical image of y_i in R_{rs}/P_{rs}; the index Δ indicates that we consider a differential, not a difference-differential, field extension.)

By the Kolchin's theorem (Theorem 1.1), for any $s \in \mathbb{N}$, there exists a numerical polynomial $\chi_s(t) = \sum_{i=0}^m a_i(s)\binom{t+i}{i}$ in one variable t such that $\chi_s(r) = \mathrm{tr.\,deg}_K L_{rs}$ for all sufficiently large $r \in \mathbb{N}$ and $a_i(s) \in \mathbb{Z}$ $(0 \le i \le m)$.

On the other hand, the first part of the proof (with the use of the finite set of σ-indeterminates $\{\Theta(r)y_i \mid \theta \in \Theta(r),\ 1 \le i \le n\}$ instead of $\{y_1, \dots, y_n\}$) shows that $\mathrm{tr.\,deg}_K L_{rs} = \mathrm{Card}\, V_{rs} + \lambda(r)$ where $V_{rs} = \{u = \tau y_i \in TY \mid \tau \in T(r,s)$ and $u \neq \tau' v_j$ for any $\tau' \in T$, $1 \le j \le p\}$. (v_j denotes the σ-leader of the element A_j of a characteristic set $\mathcal{A} = \{A_1, \dots, A_p\}$ of the reflexive closure P^* of P.) Since the set W in the first part of the proof is finite and depends only on the σ-orders of terms of A_j, $1 \le j \le p$, the number of elements of the corresponding set in the general case depends only on r; we have denoted it by $\lambda(r)$.

By Theorem 2.3, there exist $r_0, s_0 \in \mathbb{N}$ and a bivariate numerical polynomial $\omega(t_1, t_2)$ such that $\omega(r,s) = \mathrm{Card}\, V_{rs}$ for all $r \ge r_0$, $s \ge s_0$, $\deg_{t_1} \omega \le m$ and $\deg_{t_2} \omega \le 1$. Thus, $\mathrm{tr.\,deg}_K L_{rs} = \omega(r,s) + \lambda(r)$ for all $r \ge r_0$, $s \ge s_0$. At the same time, we have seen that $\mathrm{tr.\,deg}_K L_{rs_0} = \chi_{s_0}(r) = \sum_{i=0}^m a_i(s_0)\binom{r+i}{i}$ for all sufficiently large $r \in \mathbb{N}$ ($a_i(s_0) \in \mathbb{Z}$). It follows that $\lambda(r)$ is a polynomial of r for all sufficiently large $r \in \mathbb{N}$, say, for all $r \ge r_1$. Therefore, for any $s \ge s_0$, $r \ge \max\{r_0, r_1\}$, $\mathrm{tr.\,deg}_K L_{rs} = \omega(r,s) + \lambda(r)$ is expressed as a bivariate numerical polynomial in r and s. □

Definition 4.3. The numerical polynomial $\psi_P(t_1, t_2)$ whose existence is established by Theorem 4.2 is called the Δ-σ-dimension polynomial of the Δ-σ-ideal P.

The proof of the last theorem (as well as the proof of Theorem 4.1) shows that the main step in the computation of a Δ-σ-dimension polynomial is the construction of a characteristic set in the sense of section 3. It can be realized by the corresponding generalization of the Ritt-Kolchin algorithm described in [8, Section 5.5], but the development and implementation of such a generalization is the subject of future research.

The following illustrating example uses the notation of the proofs of Theorems 4.1 and 4.2.

Example 4.4. Let K be a difference-differential (Δ-σ-) field with two basic derivations, $\Delta = \{\delta_1, \delta_2\}$, and one basic endomorphism σ. Let $K\{y\}$ be the ring of Δ-σ-polynomials in one Δ-σ-indeterminate y over K and let P be a linear (and therefore prime) Δ-σ-ideal of $K\{y\}$ generated by the Δ-σ-polynomial $A = \sigma^2 y + \sigma\delta_1^2 y + \sigma\delta_2^2 y$ (that is, $P = [A]$). Then $P^* = [B]$, where $B = \sigma y + \delta_1^2 y + \delta_2^2 y$, and Proposition 3.13 shows that $\{B\}$ is a characteristic set of the Δ-σ-ideal P^*. With the notation of the proof of Theorem 4.1, we have $U'_{rs} = \{u \in TY \mid \mathrm{ord}_\Delta u \le r, \mathrm{ord}_\sigma u \le s$ and u is not a multiple of $\sigma y\}$ and $U''_{rs} = \{u \in TY \mid \mathrm{ord}_\Delta u \le r, \mathrm{ord}_\sigma u \le s$ and there is $\tau \in T$ such that $u = \tau(\sigma y)$ and $\mathrm{ord}_\Delta(\tau\delta_1^2) > r\}$. Then

$$\mathrm{Card}\, U'_{rs} = \mathrm{Card}\{\delta_1^i\delta_2^j y \mid i + j \le r\} = \binom{r+2}{2} \text{ and}$$

$$\mathrm{Card}\, U''_{rs} = \mathrm{Card}\{\sigma^i\delta_1^j\delta_2^k y \mid 1 \le i \le s,\ r-2 < j+k \le r\} =$$

$$s\left(\binom{r+2}{2} - \binom{r+2-2}{2}\right) = (2r+1)s.$$

Since $\sigma B \in P$, the proof of Theorem 4.2 shows that if $\psi_P(t_1, t_2)$ is the Δ-σ-dimension polynomial of the Δ-σ-ideal P, then

$$\psi(r,s) = \mathrm{Card}\, U'_{rs} + \mathrm{Card}\, U''_{rs} + \mathrm{Card}\{\sigma\delta_1^i\delta_2^j y \mid i + j \le r - 2\}$$

for all sufficiently large $(r,s) \in \mathbb{N}^2$*. It follows that* $\psi_P(t_1,t_2) = (2t_1+1)t_2 + \binom{t_1+2}{2} + \binom{t_1}{2}$*, that is*

$$\psi_P(t_1,t_2) = (2t_1+1)t_2 + t_1^2 + t_1 + 1.$$

We conclude with a brief discussion of the connection between the Δ-σ-dimension polynomial and the concept of strength of a system of difference-differential equations in the sense of A. Einstein.

Consider a system of difference-differential equations

$$A_i(f_1,\dots,f_n) = 0 \qquad (i=1,\dots,q) \tag{1}$$

with m basic partial derivations and one translation σ over a field K of functions of m real variables $x_1,\dots,x_m$ treated as a difference-differential field with basic set of derivations $\Delta = \{\delta_1,\dots,\delta_m\}$ and one translation σ where $\delta_i = \partial/\partial x_i$ $(1 \le i \le m)$ and $\sigma : f(\overline{x}) \mapsto f(\overline{x}+\overline{h})$ is a shift of the argument $\overline{x} = (x_1,\dots,x_m)$ by some vector $\overline{h}$ in $\mathbb{R}^m$. $(f_1,\dots,f_n$ are unknown functions of $x_1,\dots,x_m)$. We assume that system (3) is algebraic, that is, all $A_i(y_1,\dots,y_n)$ are elements of a ring of Δ-σ-polynomials $K\{y_1,\dots,y_n\}$ over the functional Δ-σ-field K.

Let us consider a sequence of nodes in $\mathbb{R}^m$ that begins at some initial node $\mathcal{P}$ and goes in the direction of the vector $\overline{h}$ with step $|\overline{h}|$. We say that *a node* Q *has* σ*-order* i (with respect to $\mathcal{P}$) if the distance between Q and $\mathcal{P}$ is $i|\overline{h}|$.

Let us consider the values of the unknown functions $f_1,\dots,f_n$ and their partial derivatives of order at most r at the nodes of σ-order at most s (r and s are positive integers). With the notation of section 2, we can say that we consider the values $\tau f_i(\mathcal{P})$ where $\tau \in T$, $\mathrm{ord}_\Delta \tau \le r$ and $\mathrm{ord}_\sigma \tau \le s$.

If $f_1,\dots,f_n$ should not satisfy any system of equations (or any other condition), these values can be chosen arbitrarily. Because of the system (and equations obtained from the equations of the system by partial differentiations and translations in the direction $\overline{h}$, the number of independent values of the functions $f_1,\dots,f_n$ and their partial derivatives whose order does not exceed r at the nodes of σ-order at most s decreases. This number, which is a function of two variables, r and s, is the "measure of strength" of the system in the sense of A. Einstein. We denote it by S_{rs}. Suppose that the Δ-σ-ideal P generated in $K\{y_1,\dots,y_n\}$ by the Δ-σ-polynomials $A_1,\dots,A_q$ is prime (e. g., the polynomials are linear). Then we say that the system of difference-differential equations (1) is prime. In this case, the Δ-σ-dimension polynomial $\psi_P(t_1,t_2)$ has the property that $\psi_P(r,s) = S_{rs}$ for all sufficiently large $(r,s) \in \mathbb{N}^2$, so this dimension polynomial is the measure of strength of the system of difference-differential equations (1) in the sense of A. Einstein.

An important perspective for the use of the obtained results is the computation of dimension polynomials (and therefore the Einstein's strength) of differential equations with delay that arise in applications. Examples of the corresponding computation in the differential and inverse difference cases can be found in [8, Chapters 6 and 9]. Computations of the same kind in the non-inverse case (based on the results of this paper) is a subject for future work.

5 ACKNOWLEDGES

This research was supported by the NSF grant CCF-1714425.

REFERENCES

[1] R. Cohn. A difference-differential basis theorem. *Canadian J. Math.*, 22 (1970), no.6, 1224–1237.
[2] A. Einstein. *The Meaning of Relativity. Appendix II (Generalization of gravitation theory)*, pp. 153–165. Princeton University Press, Princeton, NJ, 1953.
[3] E. Hrushovski. The Elementary Theory of the Frobenius Automorphisms *arXiv:math*/0406514v1, 2004, 1–135. The updated version (2012): http://www.ma.huji.ac.il/ ehud/FROB.pdf
[4] J. L. Johnson. Kähler differentials and differential algebra. *Ann. of Math.*, 89 (2) (1969), 92–98.
[5] J. L. Johnson. A notion on Krull dimension for differential rings. *Comm. Math. Helv.*, 44 (1969), 207–216.
[6] E. R. Kolchin. The notion of dimension in the theory of algebraic differential equations. *Bull. Amer. Math. Soc.*, 70 (1964), 570–573.
[7] E. R. Kolchin. *Differential Algebra and Algebraic Groups.* Academic Press, 1973.
[8] M. V. Kondrateva, A. B. Levin, A. V. Mikhalev, and E. V. Pankratev. *Differential and Difference Dimension Polynomials.* Kluwer Acad. Publ., 1999.
[9] A. B. Levin. Characteristic polynomials of filtered difference modules and difference field extensions. *Russian Mathematical Surveys*, 33 (1978), 165–166.
[10] A. B. Levin. Reduced Gröbner bases, free difference-differential modules and difference-differential dimension polynomials. *J. Symb. Comput.*, 29 (2000), 1–26, 2000.
[11] A. B. Levin. Gröbner bases with respect to several orderings and multivariable dimension polynomials. *J. Symb. Comput.*, 42 (2007), no. 5, 561–578.
[12] A. B. Levin. *Difference Algebra.* Springer, 2008.
[13] A. B. Levin. Multivariate Difference-Differential Polynomials and New Invariants of Difference-Differential Field Extensions. *Proc. of ISSAC*, 2013, 267–274.
[14] A. B. Levin; A. V. Mikhalev. Difference-differential dimension polynomials. *VINITI* (Moscow, Russia), 1988, no. 6848-B88, pp. 1–64.
[15] A. B. Levin; A. V. Mikhalev. Type and Dimension of Finitely Generated G-algebras. *Contemp. Math.*, 184 (1995), 275–280.
[16] A. V. Mikhalev and E. V. Pankratev. Differential dimension polynomial of a system of differential equations. In *Algebra*, pp. 57–67. Moscow State University Press, 1980.
[17] M. Wibmer. Algebraic Difference Equations. Lecture Notes. 2013, https://www.math.upenn.edu/ wibmer/AlgebraicDifferenceEquations.pdf

Frobenius Additive Fast Fourier Transform

Wen-Ding Li
Research Center for Information Technology Innovation, Academia Sinica, Taiwan
thekev@crypto.tw

Ming-Shing Chen
Research Center for Information Technology Innovation, Academia Sinica, Taiwan
mschen@crypto.tw

Po-Chun Kuo
Department of Electrical Engineering, National Taiwan University, Taiwan
kbj@crypto.tw

Chen-Mou Cheng
Graduate School of Engineering, Osaka University, Japan
ccheng@cy2sec.comm.eng.osaka-u.ac.jp

Bo-Yin Yang
Institute of Information Science, Academia Sinica, Taiwan
by@crypto.tw

ABSTRACT

In ISSAC 2017, van der Hoeven and Larrieu showed that evaluating a polynomial $P \in \mathbb{F}_q[x]$ of degree $< n$ at all n-th roots of unity in $\mathbb{F}_{q^d}$ can essentially be computed d times faster than evaluating $Q \in \mathbb{F}_{q^d}[x]$ at all these roots, assuming $\mathbb{F}_{q^d}$ contains a primitive n-th root of unity [18]. Termed the Frobenius FFT, this discovery has a profound impact on polynomial multiplication, especially for multiplying binary polynomials, which finds ample application in coding theory and cryptography. In this paper, we show that the theory of Frobenius FFT beautifully generalizes to a class of additive FFT developed by Cantor and Gao-Mateer [5, 11]. Furthermore, we demonstrate the power of Frobenius additive FFT for $q = 2$: to multiply two binary polynomials whose product is of degree < 256, the new technique requires only 29,005 bit operations, while the best result previously reported was 33,397 [1]. To the best of our knowledge, this is the first time that FFT-based multiplication outperforms Karatsuba and the like at such a low degree in terms of bit-operation count.

CCS CONCEPTS

• **Mathematics of computing → Mathematical software performance; Computations in finite fields;**

KEYWORDS

Fast Fourier Transform, additive FFT, Frobenius FFT, Frobenius additive FFT, polynomial multiplication, finite field, complexity bound, Frobenius automorphism

ACM Reference Format:

Wen-Ding Li, Ming-Shing Chen, Po-Chun Kuo, Chen-Mou Cheng, and Bo-Yin Yang. 2018. Frobenius Additive Fast Fourier Transform. In *ISSAC '18: 2018 ACM International Symposium on Symbolic and Algebraic Computation, July 16–19, 2018, New York, NY, USA.* ACM, New York, NY, USA, 8 pages. https://doi.org/10.1145/3208976.3208998

ACM ISBN 978-1-4503-5550-6/18/07.
https://doi.org/10.1145/3208976.3208998

1 INTRODUCTION

Let $\mathbb{F}_{q^d}$ be the finite field of q^d elements, and let $\xi \in \mathbb{F}_{q^d}$ be a primitive n-th root of unity. Let $\mathbb{F}_{q^d}[x]_{<n}$ denote the set of polynomials in $\mathbb{F}_{q^d}[x]$ with degree $< n$. The (discrete) Fourier transform of a polynomial $P \in \mathbb{F}_{q^d}[x]_{<n}$ is $(P(1), P(\xi), P(\xi^2), \ldots, P(\xi^{n-1}))$, namely, evaluating P at all n-th roots of unity. How to efficiently compute the Fourier transform not only is an important problem in its own right but also finds a wide variety of applications. As a result, there is a long line of research aiming to find what is termed "fast" Fourier tranform, or FFT for short, for various situations.

Arguably, one of the most important applications of FFT over finite fields is fast polynomial multiplication. In particular, the case of $q = 2$ has received a lot of attention from the research communities due to its wide-ranging application, e.g., in coding theory and cryptography. Obviously, here we need to go to an appropriate extension field $\mathbb{F}_{2^d}$ in order to obtain a primitive n-th root of unity for any practically meaningful n. In this case, we can use the well-known Kronecker method to efficiently compute binary polynomial multiplication [12]. Such FFT-based techniques have better asymptotic complexity compared with school-book and Karatsuba algorithms. However, it is a conventional wisdom that FFT may not be suitable for polynomial multiplication of small degrees because of the large hidden constant in the big-O notation [10].

In ISSAC 2017, van der Hoeven and Larrieu showed how to use the Frobenius map $x \mapsto x^q$ to speed up the Fourier transform of $P \in \mathbb{F}_q[x]$ essentially by a factor of d over $Q \in \mathbb{F}_{q^d}[x]$ and hence avoid the factor-of-two loss as in the Kronecker method [18]. However, the Frobenius FFT is complicated, especially when the Cooley-Tukey algorithm is used for a (highly) composite n. One of the reasons behind might be that the Galois group of $\mathbb{F}_{q^n}$ over $\mathbb{F}_q$ is generated by the Frobenius map and isomorphic to a cyclic subgroup of the *multiplicative* group of units of $\mathbb{Z}/n\mathbb{Z}$, whereas the Cooley-Tukey algorithms works by decomposing the *additive* group $\mathbb{Z}/n\mathbb{Z}$. The complicated interplay between these two group structures can bring a lot of headaches to implementers.

Can we hope for a better alignment between the Frobenius map and FFT-style algorithms? In his seminal work, Cantor showed how to evaluate a polynomial on some additive subgroup of size n of a tower of Artin-Schreier extensions of a finite field of characteristic p and gave an $O(n(\log n)^{1+\log_p((p+1)/2)})$ FFT-like algorithm based on polynomial division [5]. Based on Cantor's construction, Gao and Mateer gave a Cooley-Tukey-style algorithm whose complexity is $O(n \lg(n) \lg \lg(n))$ for the specialized case of $n = 2^{2^r}$ [11], using which Chen *et al.* achieved a competitive performance among the state of the art in binary polynomial multiplication algorithms [9]. As will become clear later in this paper, the theory of Frobenius FFT beautifully generalizes to such additive FFT techniques developed by Cantor and Gao-Mateer because the group it works on comes from the same Frobenius map. In the rest of this paper, we shall refer to such a generalization as *the Frobenius additive FFT*, or FAFFT for short, and although we will restrict our discussion to the case of $p = 2$, most of our results can be extended to the case of general p.

We will use binary polynomial multiplication as a vehicle to demonstrate the power of FAFFT, for which we will use the bit-operation—mainly AND and XOR, as we are working in $\mathbb{F}_2$—count as the main measure for computational complexity. Although this may not be the most accurate performance indicator on modern CPUs, it is still a useful metric for complexity estimation, especially for hardware implementation using digital circuits or "bitsliced" software implementation widely used in embedded systems. In such a performance metric, today's most competitive techniques for multiplying binary polynomials of small degrees are almost all based on the Karatsuba algorithm or its generalization to n-way split [1, 6–8, 21]. As we will see, FAFFT techniques can break this monopoly and outperform Karatsuba-like algorithms in multiplying binary polynomials of degree as small as 231. To the best of our knowledge, this is the first time FFT-based techniques are shown to be competitive for multiplying polynomials of such small degrees.

Last but not least, we have released to the general public our software that generates computational procedures for polynomial multiplication:

https://github.com/fast-crypto-lab/Frobenius_AFFT .

The rest of this paper is organized as follows. In Section 2, we will review the theory and some important techniques for additive FFT; then in Section 3, we will develop those for FAFFT. Finally in Section 4, we will show how we can set a few new speed records, both theoretically and in practice, for binary polynomial multiplication using FAFFT.

2 REVIEW OF ADDITIVE FFT

2.1 Cantor's construction

An Artin-Schreier extension of a finite field of characteristic p is a degree-p Galois extension. Let $\mathbb{F}_p$ be the field of p elements, and $\mathbb{F}$ an Artin-Schreier extension field containing $\mathbb{F}_p$. The Artin-Schreier polynomial $\wp(x) = x^p - x$ is a linear map on the vector space $\mathbb{F}$ over $\mathbb{F}_p$. In other words, it is an additive polynomial: $\wp(x + y) = \wp(x) + \wp(y)$. Furthermore, the composition of i additive Artin-Schreier polynomials

$$s_i(x) := \underbrace{(\wp \circ \wp \circ \cdots \circ \wp)}_{i}(x) = \wp^{\circ i}(x)$$

is again a linear map on $\mathbb{F}$ over $\mathbb{F}_p$ and therefore additive. Following Cantor's seminal work [5], we define $s_0(x) := x$ and let W_i be the kernel of s_i as a linear map. Cantor showed that $\mathbb{F}_p = W_1 \subset W_2 \subset \cdots$, $\dim_{\mathbb{F}_p} W_i = i$, $|W_i| = p^i$, and W_i is a field if and only if $i = p^j$ for some positive integer j. Furthermore, $\deg s_i = p^i$, so the roots of s_i are precisely those in W_i, and hence $s_i(x) = \prod_{\omega \in W_i}(x - \omega)$ is exactly the *vanishing polynomial* for the subspace W_i. Last but not least, $s_i(x)$ is sparse, having at most $i + 1$ nonzero coefficients. More precisely, $s_i(x)$ is a linear combination of the monomials $x, x^p, \ldots, x^{p^i}$; in particular, we have the following property.

LEMMA 2.1. *Given a vanishing polynomial $s_i(x)$ as defined above, $s_i(x) = x^{p^i} - x$ if and only if $i = p^j$ and $j \in \mathbb{N} \cup \{0\}$.*

These vanishing polynomials have a nice decomposition:

$$\begin{aligned} s_i(x) &= \prod_{\omega \in W_1} \left(s_{i-1}(x) - \omega\right) \\ &= \prod_{\omega \in W_2} \left(s_{i-2}(x) - \omega\right) \\ &\vdots \\ &= \prod_{\omega \in W_i} \left(x - \omega\right). \end{aligned}$$

Based on this decomposition, Cantor gave an FFT-like algorithm for evaluating $P \in \mathbb{F}[x]$ with $\deg P < n = p^m$ at all $\omega \in W_m$ by iteratively computing the following set of polynomials:

$$\mathcal{A}_m = \left\{P_\omega^{(i)}(x) := P(x) \bmod \left(s_i(x) - \omega\right) : 0 \le i \le m, \omega \in W_{m-i}\right\}. \tag{1}$$

That is, we start from $P_0^{(m)}(x) = P(x)$ and compute $P^{(m-1)}, \ldots$; the constant polynomials $P_\omega^{(0)}\ \forall \omega \in W_m$ are the evaluation results. We note that for any polynomial $P \in \mathbb{F}[x]$, P divides $s(P) = P^p - P$. In particular, for $\omega \in W_{m-i}$, $s_i(x) - \omega$ divides $s(s_i(x) - \omega) = s_{i+1}(x) - s(\omega)$. Therefore, once we have computed $P_{s(\omega)}^{(i+1)}$, we can compute

$$\begin{aligned} P_\omega^{(i)}(x) &= P(x) \bmod \left(s_i(x) - \omega\right) \\ &= \left(P(x) \bmod \left(s_{i+1}(x) - s(\omega)\right)\right) \bmod \left(s_i(x) - \omega\right) \\ &= P_{s(\omega)}^{(i+1)}(x) \bmod \left(s_i(x) - \omega\right). \end{aligned}$$

In this paper, we define the additive fourier transform of P as

$$AFT_n(P) = \left\{P(x) \bmod \left(s_0(x) - \omega\right) : \omega \in W_m\right\} = \{P(\omega) : \omega \in W_m\}$$

2.2 Cantor bases

The complexity of Cantor's algorithm is $O(n(\log n)^{1+\log_p((p+1)/2)})$ for general p and n a power of p. For the case of $p = 2$ and $n = 2^{2^r}$ a power of a power of two, Gao and Mateer showed how to reduce the complexity to $O(n \lg(n) \lg \lg(n))$ via a Cooley-Tukey-style algorithm [11]. From now on, we will restrict our discussion to the special case of $p = 2$; nevertheless, we would like to stress that the theory of Frobenius FFT applies to the general additive FFT techniques developed by Cantor. Before we present more details, we need to introduce a sequence of explicit and computationally useful bases for extension fields given by Cantor [5].

Let $\mathbb{F}_{2^d}$ denote an binary extension field, and let

$$\boldsymbol{v} = (v_0, v_1, \ldots, v_{d-1}).$$

We call $\boldsymbol{v}$ a basis for $\mathbb{F}_{2^d}$ if $v_0, v_1, \ldots, v_{d-1}$ are linearly independent over $\mathbb{F}_2$. Throughout this paper, we often represent an element ω_i

of a binary extension field as

$$\omega_i = i_0 v_0 + i_1 v_1 + \cdots + i_{d-1} v_{d-1},$$

where $i = i_0 + 2i_1 + 2^2 i_2 + \cdots + 2^{d-1} i_{d-1}$, $i_j \in \{0,1\}\ \forall 0 \le j < d$, with the basis elements $v_0, v_1, \ldots, v_{d-1}$ inferred from the context.

Definition 2.2. Given a sequence $u_0, u_1, u_2, \ldots$ of elements from the algebraic closure of $\mathbb{F}_2$ satisfying

$$u_i^2 + u_i = (u_0 u_1 \cdots u_{i-1}) + [\text{a sum of monomials of lower degrees}],$$

where each "monomial of a lower degree" has the form $u_0^{j_0} u_1^{j_1} \cdots u_{i-1}^{j_{i-1}}$ such that $\forall 0 \le k < i, j_k \in \{0,1\}$ and $\exists k, j_k = 0$. For $d = 2^r$, a Cantor basis $\boldsymbol{v}_d = (v_0, \ldots, v_{d-1})$ for $\mathbb{F}_{2^d}$ is given by

$$v_i = u_0^{i_0} u_1^{i_1} \cdots u_{r-1}^{i_{r-1}},$$

where $i = i_0 + 2i_1 + \cdots + 2^{r-1} i^{r-1}$.

If we fix $\mathbb{F}_{2^{2^k}} = \mathbb{F}_2(u_0, u_1, \ldots, u_{k-1})$ for $k = 1, 2, \ldots$, then we have a tower of Artin-Schreier extension fields containing $\mathbb{F}_2$. As a quick example, the following tower of extension fields of $\mathbb{F}_2$ are one such construction:

$$\begin{aligned}
\mathbb{F}_4 &:= \mathbb{F}_2[u_0]/(u_0^2 + u_0 + 1),\\
\mathbb{F}_{16} &:= \mathbb{F}_4[u_1]/(u_1^2 + u_1 + u_0),\\
\mathbb{F}_{256} &:= \mathbb{F}_{16}[u_2]/(u_2^2 + u_2 + u_1 u_0),\\
\mathbb{F}_{65536} &:= \mathbb{F}_{256}[u_3]/(u_3^2 + u_3 + u_2 u_1 u_0),\\
&\ \ \vdots
\end{aligned}$$

In this case, for example, the Cantor basis for $\mathbb{F}_{65536}$ is

$$\boldsymbol{v}_{16} = (1, u_0, u_1, u_0 u_1, u_2, u_0 u_2, u_1 u_2, \ldots, u_0 u_1 u_2 u_3).$$

An important property of a Cantor basis $\boldsymbol{v}_d$ is that, $\forall 0 \le i < d$, the subspace spanned by $(v_0, v_1, \ldots, v_{i-1})$ coincides with the subspace W_i on which $s_i(x)$ vanishes. That is, if we let $W_0 := \{0\}$, then we have

$$W_i = \left\{ \sum_{j=0}^{i-1} a_j v_j : a_j \in \mathbb{F}_2 \right\}.$$

We summarize some essential consequences of this property in the following lemma.

LEMMA 2.3. *Given a Cantor basis $\boldsymbol{v}_d$, $\forall 0 \le j \le k \le d$, we have $v_k \in W_{k+1}$, so*

$$s_j(v_k) \in W_{k-j+1} \setminus W_{k-j}, \text{ or } s_j(v_k) + v_{k-j} \in W_{k-j}.$$

In particular, for $j = 1$, we have $s_1(v_k) + v_{k-1} \in W_{k-1}$, and for $j = k$, $s_k(v_k) + v_0 \in W_0 = \{0\}$, or $s_k(v_k) = 1$.

Before leaving our discussion on finite field arithmetic, let us remark briefly on its computational complexity. Unless stated otherwise, we will use the bit complexity model in this paper. We use $A(d)$ to denote the complexity of adding two elements in $\mathbb{F}_{2^d}$; as usual, $A(d) = O(d)$. Now let $M_q(d)$ denote the complexity of multiplying two polynomials of degree $< d$ over $\mathbb{F}_q$. Currently, the best known bound for M_q is $M_q(d) = O(d \log q \log(d \log q) 8^{\log^*(d \log q)})$, where $\log^*(\cdot)$ is the iterated logarithm function [13]. It is conventional to assume that $M_q(d)/d$ is an increasing function of d. We will denote as $M(d)$ the bit complexity of multiplying two elements in $\mathbb{F}_{2^d}$ represented in a Cantor basis. We can use the modular decomposition technique to convert $\mathbb{F}_{2^d}$ to $\mathbb{F}_2[x]$ [20], so it follows that $M(d) = O(M_2(d))$. As a result, we also assume that $M(d)/d$ is an increasing function in d. Finally, we note that in some cases, Cantor's construction allows for more efficient multiplication. For example, given $\alpha, \beta \in \mathbb{F}_{2^{2^k}} := \mathbb{F}_{2^{2^{k-1}}}[u_{k-1}]/(u_{k-1}^2 + u_{k-1} + \zeta)$, if α happens to be in the (proper) subfield $\mathbb{F}_{2^{2^{k-1}}}$, then multiplying α and β can be computed using only two multiplications in $\mathbb{F}_{2^{2^{k-1}}}$. In this case, the cost of multiplication becomes $2M(2^{k-1})$ rather than $M(2^k)$. As we shall see, we often multiply elements from different extension fields of $\mathbb{F}_2$, so Cantor's trick plays an important role in reducing bit complexity.

2.3 Additive FFT on subgroups of $\mathbb{F}_{2^{2^r}}$

In this section, we come back to the Cooley-Tukey-style algorithm given by Gao and Mateer [11]. Here we will follow the exposition due to Lin, Chung, and Han [15]. In computing the polynomials in $\mathcal{A}_m$ in Eq. (1), one needs to compute remainders of division by polynomials of the form $s_i(x) - \omega$. Thus we can replace division by substitution if we write the dividend polynomials as linear combinations of monomials of the form $\prod s_i^{b_i}$ [15]:

Definition 2.4. Given a (Cantor) basis $\boldsymbol{v}_d$ and its subspace vanishing polynomials $s_0, s_1, \ldots, s_{d-1}$, we define its corresponding *novel polynomial basis* as the polynomials $X_k\ \forall 0 \le k < n = 2^d$, where

$$X_k(x) := \prod (s_i(x))^{b_i} \text{ for } k = \sum_{i=0}^{d-1} 2^i b_i \text{ with } b_i \in \{0,1\}.$$

It is easy to see that, as $\deg s_i = 2^i$, $\deg X_k = k$. Thus, a polynomial $P \in \mathbb{F}_{2^d}[x]$ with $\deg P < n$ can be represented in novel polynomial basis:

$$P(x) = p_0 X_0(x) + p_1 X_1(x) + \cdots + p_{n-1} X_{n-1}(x) \text{ for } p_i \in \mathbb{F}_{2^d}.$$

We note that the notion of a novel polynomial basis can be defined for d not a power of two. However, there is no gain in this case in terms of complexity because conversion from the usual monomial basis to novel polynomial basis has the same complexity $O(n \lg n (\lg n)^2)$ as Cantor's iterative division algorithm. When d is a power of two, on the other hand, both Gao-Mateer and Lin *et al.* gave $O(n \lg n \lg \lg n)$ algorithms for basis conversion; in Algorithm 1, we present the version given by the latter [16]. We also note that for a polynomial that admits coefficients from $\mathbb{F}_2$, we can easily gain a factor of d because addition in $\mathbb{F}_2$ costs $A(1)$ rather than $A(d)$.

Finally, we are ready to define the additive FFT of a polynomial $P \in \mathbb{F}_{2^d}[x]$ with $\deg P < 2^k$ as

$$\mathsf{AFFT}(k, P, \alpha) := \Big(P(\omega_i + \alpha)\Big)_{i=0}^{2^k - 1}.$$

Now if $n_1 = 2^{k-1}$, then

$$\begin{aligned}
P(\omega_i + \alpha) &= P(\omega_{n_1 \cdot i_1 + i_2} + \alpha)\\
&= \sum_{0 \le j_2 < n_1} \sum_{0 \le j_1 < 2} p_{n_1 \cdot j_1 + j_2} X_{n_1 \cdot j_1 + j_2}(\omega_{n_1 \cdot i_1 + i_2} + \alpha)\\
&= \sum_{0 \le j_2 < n_1} \Big(p_{j_2} + s_{k-1}(\omega_{n_1 \cdot i_1 + i_2} + \alpha) \cdot p_{n_1 + j_2}\Big) X_{j_2}(\omega_{n_1 \cdot i_1 + i_2} + \alpha)\\
&= \sum_{0 \le j_2 < n_1} \Big(p_{j_2} + s_{k-1}(\omega_{n_1 \cdot i_1} + \alpha) \cdot p_{n_1 + j_2}\Big) X_{j_2}(\omega_{i_2} + (\alpha + \omega_{n_1 \cdot i_1})).
\end{aligned}$$

```
BasisConversion(f(x)) :
input  : f(x) = f_0 + f_1 x + ... + f_{n-1} x^{n-1}
output : g(X) = g_0 + g_1 X_1(x) + ... + g_{n-1} X_{n-1}(x) = f(x)
if deg f(x) ≤ 1 then return g(X) = f_0 + X_1 f_1 ;
Let k = max{2^i : deg s_{2^i}(x) ≤ deg f(x)} .
Compute h'(y) = h'_0(x) + h'_1(x)y + h'_2(x)y^2 + ··· such that
  h'(s_k(x)) = f(x) and all h'_i(x) has degree < 2^k.
h(Y) ← BasisConversion( h'(y))
// we have h'(y) = h(Y) = h_0(x) + h_1(x)Y_1 + h_2(x)Y_2 + ···
// h'(s_k(x)) = h(X) = h_0(x) + h_1(x)X_{2^k} + h_2(x)X_{2^{k+1}} + ···
g_i(X) ← BasisConversion( h_i(x)) for all h_i(x).
return g_0(X) + g_1(X)X_{2^k} + g_2(X)X_{2^{k+1}} + ···
```

Algorithm 1: Converting from monomial to novel polynomial basis

We can see that the AFFT with input polynomial degree of 2^k-1 can be computed using two AFFT with input polynomial of degree $2^{k-1}-1$ corresponding to $i_1 = 0$ and 1, which leads us to Algorithm 2.

```
AFFT(k, P(x), α) :
input  : P(x) = p_0 X_0(x) + p_1 X_1(x) + ... + p_{2^k-1} X_{2^k-1}(x) , all
           p_i ∈ F_{2^d}
           α ∈ F_{2^d}, k ≤ d
output : (P(ω_0 + α), P(ω_1 + α), ..., P(ω_{2^k-1} + α)) .
if k = 0 then return p_0 ;
// Decompose P(x) = P_0(x) + s_{k-1}(x) · P_1(x).
P_0(x) ← p_0 X_0(x) + p_1 X_1(x) + ... p_{2^{k-1}-1} X_{2^{k-1}-1}(x)
P_1(x) ← p_{2^{k-1}} X_0(x) + p_{2^{k-1}+1} X_1(x) + ... p_{2^k-1} X_{2^{k-1}-1}(x)
Q_0(x) ← P_0(x) + s_{k-1}(α) · P_1(x).
Q_1(x) ← Q_0(x) + s_{k-1}(v_{k-1}) · P_1(x).
return AFFT(k − 1, Q_0(x), α)||AFFT(k − 1, Q_1(x), v_{k-1} + α)
```

Algorithm 2: Addtive FFT in novel polynomial basis [15]

We note that for a Cantor basis, $s_{k-1}(\omega_{n_1}) = s_{k-1}(v_{k-1}) = 1$ from Lemma 2.3. Given $P \in \mathbb{F}_{2^d}[x]$ with $\deg P < n$ represented in monomial basis and $n = 2^m$, its additive Fourier transform $AFT_n(P)$ can be computed as follow. We first perform basis conversion to get p_i such that $P(x) = p_0X_0(x)+p_1X_1(x)+\ldots+p_{2^m-1}X_{2^m-1}(x)$. Then we perform AFFT$(m, P(x), 0)$. Thus, to compute AFT_n(P) using AFFT, the maximum depth of recursion is m, and the algorithm performs total $\frac{1}{2}n$ multiplications and n additions in each depth of recursion. Therefore the cost of the algorithm is $\frac{1}{2}n\lg(n)(M(d)+2A(d))$, where $n = 2^m$ is the number of terms.

3 FROBENIUS ADDITIVE FOURIER TRANSFORM

Let P be a polynomial in $\mathbb{F}_2[x]$ and $\boldsymbol{v}_d$, a Cantor basis for $\mathbb{F}_{2^d}$. Recall that for all $\alpha \in \mathbb{F}_{2^d}$, $P(\phi(\alpha)) = \phi(P(\alpha))$, where ϕ is the Frobenius map that sends x to x^2. The core idea of the Frobenius Fourier transform is to evaluate P at a minimal number of points such that the values of P at other points can be derived through the Frobenius map ϕ when $P \in \mathbb{F}_2[x] \subset \mathbb{F}_{2^d}[x]$. This minimal set of points is called a *cross section* [18]. Formally, given a set $W \subseteq \mathbb{F}_{2^d}$, a subset $\Sigma \subseteq W$ is called a cross section of W if for every $w \in W$, there exists exactly one $\sigma \in \Sigma$ such that $\phi^{\circ j}(\sigma) = w$ for some j. Let $\boldsymbol{v}_d$ denote a basis of $\mathbb{F}_{2^d}$. Given a polynomial $P \in \mathbb{F}_2[x]$ with $\deg P < n = 2^m$, the $AFT_n(P)$ is the evaluation of the points in $W_m = \{\omega_0, \omega_1, \omega_2, \ldots, \omega_{2^m-1}\}$. To perform a Frobenius additive Fourier transform, we partition W_m into disjoint orbits under the action of ϕ. If there exists a subset Σ of W_m that contains exactly one element in each orbit, then Σ is a cross section of W_m, and the Frobenius map allows us to recover $AFT_n(P)$ from the values of P on Σ. We denote

$$\left\{P(\sigma) : \sigma \in \Sigma\right\}$$

the *Frobenius additive Fourier transform* (*FAFT*) of polynomial P. In the rest of this section, we will show how to generalize the theory of Frobenius FFT to additive FFT by explicitly constructing the cross sections.

3.1 Frobenius maps and Cantor bases

We recall that the Frobenius map ϕ on $\mathbb{F}_{2^d}$ generates the (cyclic) Galois group $\mathrm{Gal}(\mathbb{F}_{2^d}/\mathbb{F}_2)$ of order $[\mathbb{F}_{2^d} : \mathbb{F}_2] = d$, which naturally acts on $\mathbb{F}_{2^d}$ by taking $\alpha \in \mathbb{F}_{2^d}$ to $\phi(\alpha)$. The orbit of α under this action is thus

$$\mathrm{Orb}_\alpha = \left\{\sigma(\alpha) : \sigma \in \mathrm{Gal}(\mathbb{F}_{2^d}/\mathbb{F}_2)\right\}.$$

LEMMA 3.1. *Given a Cantor basis $\boldsymbol{v}_d$, $\forall k > 0$, $\forall w \in W_{k+1} \setminus W_k$,*

$$\left|\mathrm{Orb}_w\right| = 2^{\lfloor \lg k \rfloor + 1}.$$

PROOF. Let $\ell = \lfloor \lg k \rfloor$. In this case, $2^\ell \le k < 2^{\ell+1}$, and $v_k = u_\ell u_{\ell-1}^{j_{\ell-1}} \cdots u_0^{j_0}$, $j_i \in \{0,1\} \forall 0 \le i < \ell$. Since $w \in W_{k+1} \setminus W_k$, we can write

$$w = v_k + \alpha = u_\ell u_{\ell-1}^{j_{\ell-1}} \cdots u_0^{j_0} + \alpha$$

for some $\alpha \in W_k$. Obviously the smallest field containing w is $\mathbb{F}_{2^{2^{\ell+1}}} = \mathbb{F}_2(u_0, u_1, \ldots, u_\ell)$, so the stabilizer of w is the subgroup of $\mathrm{Gal}(\mathbb{F}_{2^d}/\mathbb{F}_2)$ generated by $\phi^{2^{\ell+1}}$. It follows immediately from the orbit-stabilizer theorem and Lagrange's theorem that

$$\left|\mathrm{Orb}_w\right| = 2^{\lfloor \lg k \rfloor + 1}.$$

□

Consider the field $\mathbb{F}_{2^d}$ with a Cantor basis $\boldsymbol{v}_d$ for d a power of two. From Lemma 2.3, we have $\phi(v_0) = v_0$, and $\phi(v_i) = s(v_i)+v_i = v_i + v_{i-1} + \alpha$, where $\alpha \in W_{i-1}$ for $i > 0$. Based on this, we can further characterize the orbit of $w \in W_{k+1} \setminus W_k$ using the following lemma.

LEMMA 3.2. *Given a Cantor basis $\boldsymbol{v}_d$, $\forall k > 0$, consider the orbit of $w \in W_{k+1} \setminus W_k$ under the action of $\mathrm{Gal}(\mathbb{F}_{2^d}/\mathbb{F}_2)$. For each $i = 1, 2, 4, \ldots$, let j_i be in $\{0,1\}$, there is precisely one element $w' \in \mathrm{Orb}_w$ such that $w' = v_k + j'_1 v_{k-1} + \cdots + j'_k v_0 \in W_{k+1} \setminus W_k$, $\forall j'_i \in \{0,1\}$, and $j'_i = j_i$ for $i = 1, 2, 4, \ldots, 2^{\lfloor \lg k \rfloor}$.*

PROOF. Let ℓ be a power of two. From Lemma 2.1, we have $\phi^{\circ \ell}(x) = x^{2^\ell} = s_\ell(x)+x$. From Lemma 2.3, we see that $\phi^{\circ \ell}(w)+w = s_\ell(w) \in W_{k-\ell+1} \setminus W_{k-\ell}$. That is, $\phi^{\circ \ell}(w) + w \in v_{k-\ell} + W_{k-\ell}$. In other words, $\phi^{\circ \ell}$ allows us to flip j_ℓ, while $j_1, j_2, \ldots, j_{\ell-1}$ remain the same. E.g., for $\ell = 1$, we see that one of w and $\phi(w)$ has $j'_1 = 0$ and the other has $j'_1 = 1$ for any $w \in W_{k+1} \setminus W_k$. Similarly for $\ell = 2$, one of w and $\phi^{\circ 2}(w)$ has $j'_2 = 0$ and the other has $j'_2 = 1$, while both w and $\phi^{\circ 2}(w)$ have the same j_1'. The same argument holds for $\phi(w)$ and $\phi^{\circ 2}(\phi(w)) = \phi^{\circ 3}(w)$. Thus $w, \phi(w), \phi^{\circ 2}(w), \phi^{\circ 3}(w)$ cover all 4 combinations of j_1 and j_2. Continuing, we see that w and $\phi^{\circ 4}(w)$ have different j_4' but the same j_1' and j_2'. Proceeding thusly, $w, \phi(w), \ldots, \phi^{\circ 2^{\lfloor \lg k \rfloor+1}-1}(w)$ cover all combinations of $j_i' \in \{0,1\}$, for $i = 1, 2, 4, \ldots, 2^{\lfloor \lg k \rfloor}$. Finally, as $|\mathrm{Orb}_w| = 2^{\lfloor \lg k \rfloor+1}$, we see that for each such combination, there is precisely one corresponding element in Orb_w combination due to the pigeonhole principle. □

Now we can explicitly construct a cross section. Let $\Sigma_0 = \{0\}$, and $\forall k > 0$, let

$$\Sigma_k = \left\{ v_{k-1} + j_1 v_{k-2} + \cdots + j_{k-1} v_0 : \begin{array}{l} j_i = 0 \text{ if } i \text{ is a power of } 2, \\ j_i \in \{0,1\} \text{ otherwise.} \end{array} \right\}$$

THEOREM 3.3. *Σ_k is a cross section of $W_k \setminus W_{k-1}$. That is, $\forall k > 0$, $\forall w \in W_k \setminus W_{k-1}$, there exists exactly one $\sigma \in \Sigma_k$ such that $\phi^{\circ j}(\sigma) = w$ for some j.*

PROOF. First, any two elements of Σ_k are in different orbits for any k; this is a corollary of Lemma 3.2. Next, we know that $\forall w \in W_k \setminus W_{k-1}$, $|\mathrm{Orb}_w| = 2^{\lfloor \lg(k-1) \rfloor+1}$, and $\phi^{\circ j}(w) \in W_k \setminus W_{k-1}$, $\forall j$. So each orbit generated by the element in Σ_k has the size $2^{\lfloor \lg(k-1) \rfloor+1}$, and $2^{\lfloor \lg(k-1) \rfloor+1} \cdot |\Sigma_k| = 2^{k-1} = |W_k \setminus W_{k-1}|$. By the pigeonhole principle, each element in $W_k \setminus W_{k-1}$ must be in an orbit generated by exactly one element in Σ_k. □

3.2 Frobenius additive Fast Fourier transform

By Theorem 3.3, a cross section of W_m is

$$\Sigma_0 \cup \Sigma_1 \cup \Sigma_2 \cup \ldots \cup \Sigma_m \ .$$

Given $P(x) \in \mathbb{F}_2[x]$ with $\deg P < n$ represented with novel polynomial basis and Cantor basis $\boldsymbol{v}_d$ of field $\mathbb{F}_{2^d}$ where $n = 2^m$, instead of computing $AFT_n(P) = (P(\omega_0), P(\omega_1), \ldots, P(\omega_{2^m-1}))$, we only need to compute $FAFT_n(P) = \{P(\sigma) : \sigma \in \Sigma_0 \cup \Sigma_1 \cup \Sigma_2 \cup \ldots \cup \Sigma_m\}$ and then use Frobenius map ϕ to get the rest.

Due to the structure of the additive FFT, we can simply "truncate" to those points. In the original additive FFT (Algorithm 2), each FAFFT calls two FAFFT routines recursively. Those two recursive calls correspond to evaluating points in $\alpha + W_{k-1}$ and $\alpha + v_{k-1} + W_{k-1}$. We can omit one of the two calls and only compute on $\alpha + W_{k-1}$, so we will not evaluate the points not in the cross section Σ, as $\Sigma \cap (\alpha + v_{k-1} + W_{k-1}) = \emptyset$. This is how we arrive at Algorithm 3, in which we define $\rho(l)$:

$$\rho(l) = \begin{cases} 1 & \text{if } l = 0, \\ 2^{\lceil \lg l \rceil} & \text{otherwise.} \end{cases}$$

It is easy to see that $\mathtt{FAFFT}(m, 1, P(x), v_m)$ computes $\{P(x) : x \in \Sigma_m\}$ because truncation happens when the v_{m-l-1} component is zero for all points in Σ_m, i.e., l is a power of two. To compute *FAFT*(P), we call $\mathtt{FAFFT}(m, 0, P(x), 0)$.

Figure 1 is a graphical illustration of the $\mathtt{FAFFT}(5, 0, f, 0)$ routine, which computes $FAFT_{32}(f)$ for $f = g_0X_0(x) + g_1X_1(x) + g_2X_2(x) + \ldots + g_{31}X_{31}(x)$. It consists of five layers, each corresponding to one level of recursion in the pseudocode. Each grey box is a "butterfly unit" that performs a multiplication and an addition. A butterfly unit has two inputs $a, b \in \mathbb{F}_{2^d}$. For normal butterfly unit with two output a', b', it performs

$$a' \leftarrow a + b \cdot s_k(\alpha),$$
$$b' \leftarrow a' + b,$$

while the truncated one only outputs a'. In the figure, we denote the $s_k(\alpha)$ in each butterfly unit $c_{i,j}$. Butterflies are also labelled with the value l coressponding to each recursive calls FAFFT. We can see that truncated butterflies happen when l is a power of 2. Initially, the inputs to butterfly units, $g_0, g_1, \ldots, g_{31}$, are all in $\mathbb{F}_2$. But as it goes through the layers, the bit size of the input to the following butterfly unit grows larger, as the multiplicands $c_{i,j}$ may be in extension fields. For example, after the second layer, the lower half of the input are in $\mathbb{F}_{2^2}$ because $c_{3,1}$ are in $(W_2 \setminus W_1) \subset \mathbb{F}_{2^2}$. Then they go through butterfly unit with $c_{2,2} \in (W_3 \setminus W_2) \subset \mathbb{F}_{2^4}$ and finally arrive in $\mathbb{F}_{2^4}$.

$\mathtt{FAFFT}(k, l, P(x), \alpha)$:
input : $k \in \mathbb{N}, l \in \mathbb{N}$,
$P(x) = p_0X_0(x) + p_1X_1(x) + \ldots + p_{2^k-1}X_{2^k-1}(x)$
where $p_i \in \mathbb{F}_{2^{\rho(l)}}$,
$\alpha \in W_{k+l} \setminus W_k$ if $l > 0$, otherwise $\alpha = 0$.
output: $P(\sigma)_{\sigma \in \Sigma}$ where $\Sigma = (\Sigma_0 \cup \Sigma_1 \cup \ldots \cup \Sigma_{k+l}) \cap (\alpha + W_k)$,
if $k = 0$ **then return** p_0 ;
Decompose $P(x) = P_0(x) + s_{k-1}(x) \cdot P_1(x)$.
$Q_0(x) \leftarrow P_0(x) + s_{k-1}(\alpha) \cdot P_1(x)$.
$Q_1(x) \leftarrow Q_0(x) + P_1(x)$.
if $l = 0$ **then**
  return $\mathtt{FAFFT}(k-1, 0, Q_0(x), \alpha) \ ||$
    $\mathtt{FAFFT}(k-1, 1, Q_1(x), v_{k-1} + \alpha)$
else if *l is a power of two* **then**
  return $\mathtt{FAFFT}(k-1, l+1, Q_0(x), \alpha)$
else
  return $\mathtt{FAFFT}(k-1, l+1, Q_0(x), \alpha) \ ||$
    $\mathtt{FAFFT}(k-1, l+1, Q_1(x), v_{k-1} + \alpha)$
end

Algorithm 3: Frobenius Additive FFT in novel polynomial basis.

3.3 Complexity Analysis

In this section, we analyze the complexity of FAFFT in Algorithm 3. Let $F(k, l)$ and $F_A(k, l)$ denote the cost of multiplication and addition to compute $\mathtt{FAFFT}(k, l, P(x), \alpha)$ for $P \in \mathbb{F}_2[x]$ with $\deg P < 2^k$ and $\alpha \in W_{k+l} \setminus W_k$.

First, it is straightforward to verify that for all $\mathtt{FAFFT}(k', l', P'(x), \alpha')$ calls during the recursion:

- $\alpha' \in W_{k'+l'} \setminus W_{k'}$ if $l' > 0$, otherwise $\alpha' = 0$;
- $P'(x) = \sum p_i' X_i(x)$, $p_i' \in \mathbb{F}_{2^{\rho(l')}}$;
- $s_{k-1}(\alpha') \in (W_{l'+1} \setminus W_{l'}) \quad \subset \begin{cases} u_{\lg l'} + \mathbb{F}_{2^{l'}} & \text{if } l' \text{ is a power of two,} \\ \mathbb{F}_{2^{2^{\lceil \lg l' \rceil}}} & \text{otherwise.} \end{cases}$

Then we have $F(k, l)$

$$\leq \begin{cases} F(k-1, l) + F(k-1, l+1) + 2^{k-1}(M(1)) & \text{if } l = 0, \\ F(k-1, l+1) + 2^{k-1}(M(l)) & \text{if } l \text{ is a power of two,} \\ 2 \cdot F(k-1, l+1) + 2^{k-1}(M(2^{\lceil \lg l \rceil})) & \text{otherwise.} \end{cases}$$

Figure 1: Illustration of the butterfly network with $n = 32$. $f(0), f(1) \in \mathbb{F}_2, f(\omega_2) \in \mathbb{F}_{2^2}, f(\omega_4), f(\omega_8), f(\omega_9) \in \mathbb{F}_{2^4}$ and $f(\omega_{16}), f(\omega_{18}) \in \mathbb{F}_{2^8}$

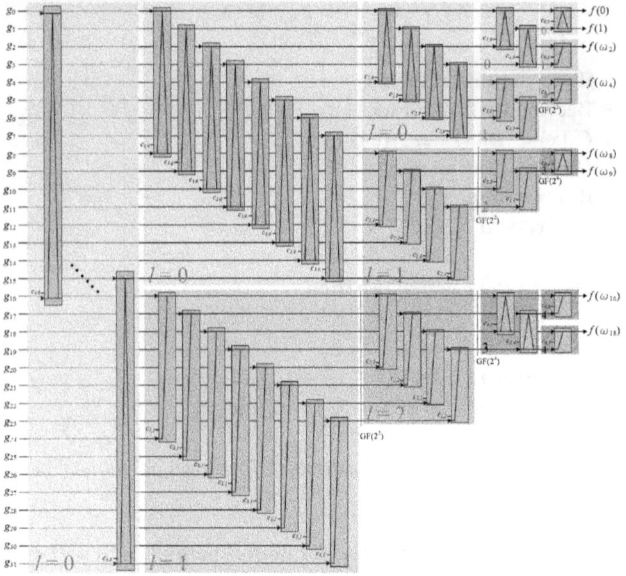

Theorem 3.4. (multiplication complexity) *Given $n = 2^m$, for $m + l \leq d$, d a power of two, we have*

$$F(m, l) \leq \frac{1}{2} n \lg n \frac{M(d)}{d} \rho(l),$$

assuming that $\frac{M(l)}{l}$ is increasing in l.

Proof. We prove by induction. Consider $m = 1$: $F(1, l) = M(l) \leq \frac{M(d)}{d} l$. Assume the statement holds for $m = k - 1$ and for any $l \leq d - m$,

$$F(m, l) \leq \frac{1}{2} 2^m m \frac{M(d)}{d} \rho(l).$$

We then check three cases: first, $m = k$ and $l = 0$:

$$\begin{aligned} F(k, l) &\leq F(k-1, 0) + F(k-1, 1) + 2^{k-1} \cdot M(1) \\ &= \frac{1}{2}(k-1) 2^k \frac{M(d)}{d} + 2^k \cdot M(1) \\ &\leq \frac{1}{2} k 2^k \frac{M(d)}{d}. \end{aligned}$$

Second, $m = k$ and l is a power of two:

$$\begin{aligned} F(k, l) &\leq F(k-1, l+1) + \cdot 2^{k-1} \cdot M(l) \\ &= (k-1) 2^k \frac{M(d)}{d} l + 2^{k-1} \cdot M(l) \\ &\leq \frac{1}{2}(k-1) 2^k \frac{M(d)}{d} l + 2^{k-1} \frac{M(d)}{d} l \\ &= \frac{1}{2} k 2^k \frac{M(d)}{d} l. \end{aligned}$$

Finally, $l > 0$ and is not a power of two:

$$\begin{aligned} F(k, l) &\leq 2 \cdot F(k-1, l+1) + 2^{k-1} \cdot M(2^{\lceil \lg l \rceil}) \\ &= \frac{1}{2}(k-1) 2^k \frac{M(d)}{d} 2^{\lceil \lg l + 1 \rceil} + 2^{k-1} \cdot M(2^{\lceil \lg l \rceil}) \\ &\leq \frac{1}{2}(k-1) 2^k \frac{M(d)}{d} 2^{\lceil \lg l \rceil} + 2^{k-1} \cdot \frac{M(2^{\lceil \lg l \rceil})}{2^{\lceil \lg l \rceil}} 2^{\lceil \lg l \rceil} \\ &\leq \frac{1}{2} k 2^k \frac{M(d)}{d} l. \end{aligned}$$

□

For the cost of addition, it can be proven following the same procedure as above, substituting $M(d)$ with $2A(d)$ and noting that $\frac{A(d)}{d}$ is constant.

Theorem 3.5. (addition complexity) *Given $n = 2^m$, for $m + l \leq d$, d a power of two, we have*

$$F_A(m, l) \leq n \lg n \frac{A(d)}{d} \rho(l).$$

Given $P \in \mathbb{F}_2[x]$ with $\deg P < n$, a power of two, to compute $FAFT_n(P)$, we call FAFFT$(\lg(n), 0, P, 0)$. Thus, the cost to compute $FAFT_n(P)$ is $\frac{1}{2} n \lg(n) \frac{M(d)}{d} + n \lg(n) \frac{A(d)}{d}$. Comparing with the cost of additive FFT $\frac{1}{2}(n \lg(n)(M(d) + 2A(d))$, we indeed gain a speed-up factor of d.

3.4 Inverse Frobenius additive FFT

The inverse Frobenius additive FFT is straightforward because for the butterfly unit with two output, it is easy to find its inverse. However, due to the truncation, it is not obvious how to perform inversion when l is a power of two. Here we show that it is always invertible. In the Algorithm 3, when l is a power of two, it truncates and only computes *FAFT* of $Q_0(x) = P_0(x) + s_{k-1}(\alpha) \cdot P_1(x)$. To be able to invert, we need to recover $P_0(x)$ and $P_1(x)$ from $Q_0(x)$. Note that $s_{k-1}(\alpha) \in (W_{l+1} \setminus W_l) = v_l + W_l$ because $\alpha \in W_{k+l+1} \setminus W_{k+l}$ and Lemma 2.3. Since we use a Cantor basis, c.f. Definition 2.2, $v_l = u_{\lg l}$ when l is a power of two. We can rewrite the equation from the point of $\mathbb{F}_{2^l}[u_{\lg l}][x]$. Let $s_{k-1}(\alpha) = u_{\lg l} + c$ and $c \in \mathbb{F}_{2^l}$,

$$Q_0(x) = R_0(x) + R_1(x) u_{\lg l} = P_0(x) + (c + u_{\lg l}) \cdot P_1(x),$$

where $R_0(x), R_1(x) \in \mathbb{F}_{2^l}[x]$. Then we have

$$\begin{aligned} P_0(x) &= R_0(x) + R_1(x) \cdot c, \\ P_1(x) &= R_1(x). \end{aligned}$$

Thus we can always recover $P_0(x)$ and $P_1(x)$ from $Q(x)$. The full inverse Frobenius additive FFT algorithm is shown in Algorithm 4. It can be shown that the complexity of the inverse FAFFT is also bounded by $\frac{1}{2} n \lg(n) \frac{M(d)+2A(d)}{d}$ following the analysis in the previous section.

4 APPLICATION TO $\mathbb{F}_2[x]$-MULTIPLICATION

In this section, we will show that FAFFT is competitive both theoretically (measured by the number of bit operations involved) and in practice (measured by actual speeds on modern CPUs) when applied to multiplying two polynomials in $\mathbb{F}_2[x]$.

$\texttt{IFAFFT}(k, l, A, \alpha)$:
input : $A = P(\sigma)_{\sigma \in \Sigma}$
where $\Sigma = (\Sigma_0 \cup \Sigma_1 \cup \ldots \cup \Sigma_{k+l}) \cap (\alpha + W_k)$,
$\alpha \in W_{k+l} \setminus W_k$ if $l > 0$, otherwise $\alpha = 0$.
output: $P(x) = p_0 X_0(x) + p_1 X_1(x) + \ldots + p_{2^k-1} X_{2^k-1}(x)$
where $p_i \in \mathbb{F}_{2^{\rho(l)}}$.

if $k = 0$ **then return** the only element in A ;
if $l = 0$ **then**
  Divide the set A to A_0, A_1
  $Q_0(x) \leftarrow \texttt{IFAFFT}(k-1, 0, A_0, \alpha)$
  $Q_1(x) \leftarrow \texttt{IFAFFT}(k-1, 1, A_1, v_{k-1} + \alpha)$
  $P_1(x) \leftarrow (Q_0(x) + Q_1(x))$
  $P_0(x) \leftarrow Q_0(x) + s_{k-1}(\alpha) \cdot P_1(x)$
else if *l is a power of 2* **then**
  $Q(x) \leftarrow \texttt{IFAFFT}(k-1, l+1, A, \alpha)$
  Let $s_{k-1}(\alpha) = c + u_{\lg(l)}$
  Let $Q(x) = R_0(x) + u_{\lg(l)} \cdot R_1(x)$
  $P_0(x) \leftarrow R_0(x) + R_1(x) \cdot c$
  $P_1(x) \leftarrow R_1(x)$
else
  Divide the set A to A_0, A_1
  $Q_0(x) \leftarrow \texttt{IFAFFT}(k-1, l+1, A_0, \alpha)$
  $Q_1(x) \leftarrow \texttt{IFAFFT}(k-1, l+1, A_1, v_{k-1} + \alpha)$
  $P_1(x) \leftarrow Q_0(x) + Q_1(x)$
  $P_0(x) \leftarrow Q_0(x) + s_{k-1}(\alpha) \cdot P_1(x)$
end
return $P_0(x) + P_1(x) \cdot s_{k-1}(x)$

Algorithm 4: Inverse FAFFT in novel polynomial basis

4.1 New speed records in terms of bit-operation count

One of our motivating applications is to multiply binary polynomials, which finds ample application in, e.g., implementation of elliptic-curve cryptography (ECC). For example, Bernstein pointed out that ECC over a binary field can be faster than ECC over a prime field at the same security level [1]. Thus, multiplications of binary polynomials of some specific sizes are of interest to the cryptographic engineering community [1, 6]. The previous speed records in terms of bit-operation count for multiplying two binary polynomials of small degrees, say, < 1000, were set by Bernstein [1] and Cenk-Hasan [6], both of which are based on Karatsuba-like algorithms.

With FAFFT and its inverse, we can now efficiently multiply two polynomials $P, Q \in \mathbb{F}_2[x]$ without Kronecker segmentation. First, we apply forward FAFFT on P and Q; we then pointwise-multiply the results and apply an inverse FAFFT to get the product PQ. To further reduce the bit-operation count, we also eliminate some common subexpressions [17].

Figure 2 shows the comparison against two best results previously known in the literature: Bernstein set a comprehensive set of speed records for polynomials of degree up to 1000 [1], whereas Cenk and Hasan selectively improved some of his results up to 4.5% [6]. Since FAFFT works with polynomials whose size is a power of two, we apply FAFFT to multiplying polynomials of size 256, 512, and 1024; such a small disadvantage apparently did not stop FAFFT from setting new speed records. Specifically, when compared

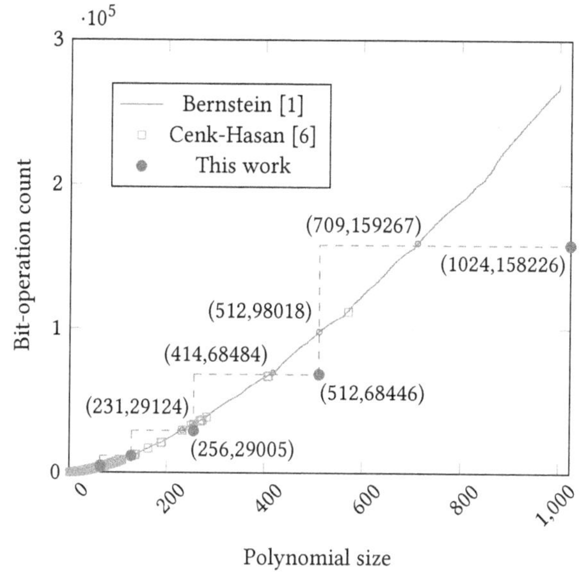

Figure 2: Complexity for multiplication in $\mathbb{F}_2[x]$

against Karatsuba-like algorithms for multiplying polynomials of size 256, 512, and 1000, FAFFT is faster by 19.1%, 29.7%, and 41.1%, respectively. To the best of our knowledge, it is the first time FFT-based method outperforms Karatsuba-like algorithm in such low degree in terms of bit-operation count.

We also try to push the limit by applying FAFFT to multiplying polynomials of size as small as 128, a degree way too small for FFT-based techniques to prevail according to the traditional wisdom. However, we are able to achieve a bit-operation count of 11,556 using FAFFT, which is only slightly worse than 11,466 achieved by Cenk and Hasan [6]. We note that this would not be possible without Frobenius FFT. Using Kronecker segmentation and a highly optimized implementation of additive FFT by [2], one would achieve a bit-operation count of 22,292. As expected, we gain a factor of two speed-up here using FAFFT.

4.2 New speed records on modern CPUs

Now we will show that FAFFT is also competitive in practice when applied to multiplying two polynomials in $\mathbb{F}_2[x]$. On modern CPUs, we can use the carryless multiplication instruction PCLMULQDQ for achieving further speed-up [14]. Similar to van der Hoeven, Larrieu, and Lecerf [19, Prop. 1], here we need a bijection for multiplying polynomials in $\mathbb{F}_2[x]_{<2^{m-1}}$.

Proposition 4.1. *Let $P \in \mathbb{F}_2[x]_{<2^m}$, $7 < m \leq 71$, $57 + m < k \leq 128$ and $S = v_{k-1} + W_{m-7}$ where v_{k-1} and W_{m-7} are defined as in Section 2 w.r.t. $\boldsymbol{v}_{128}$, a Cantor basis for $\mathbb{F}_{2^{128}}$. Then the map $P \in \mathbb{F}_2[x]_{<2^m} \mapsto (P(w))_{w \in S} \in \mathbb{F}_{2^{128}}^{2^{m-7}}$ is a bijection.*

Proof. $\forall w \in S$, $|\mathrm{Orb}_w| = 128$ (Lemma 3.1). Every two points in S are in different orbits (Lemma 3.2). Let $\mathrm{Orb}_S := \cup_{w \in S} \mathrm{Orb}_w$. Then $|\mathrm{Orb}_S| = 128 \cdot |S| = 2^m$. Since $(P(w))_{w \in S}$ determines $(P(w))_{w \in \mathrm{Orb}_S}$ via the Frobenius map, and the latter is P on 2^m points, $(P(w))_{w \in S}$

Table 1: Timing of multiplications in $\mathbb{F}_2[x]_{<n}$ on Intel Skylake Xeon E3-1275 v5 @ 3.60GHz (10^{-3} sec.)

$\log_2(n/64)$	16	17	18	19	20	21	22	23
This work, $\mathbb{F}_{2^{128}}$	9	20	41	88	192	418	889	1865
FDFT [19] [c]	11	24	56	127	239	574	958	2465
ADFT[9]	16	34	74	175	382	817	1734	3666
$\mathbb{F}_{2^{60}}$ [12][b]	22	51	116	217	533	885	2286	5301
gf2x [3] [a]	23	51	111	250	507	1182	2614	6195

[a] Version 1.2. Available from http://gf2x.gforge.inria.fr/
[b] SVN r10663. Available from svn://scm.gforge.inria.fr/svn/mmx
[c] SVN r10681. Available from svn://scm.gforge.inria.fr/svn/mmx

determines P. So $P \in \mathbb{F}_2[x]_{<2^m} \mapsto (P(w))_{w\in S} \in \mathbb{F}_{2^{128}}^{2^{m-7}}$ is bijective. □

To compute $(P(w))_{w\in S}$, we perform $\mathsf{AFFT}(m, P(x), v_{k-1}) = (P(w))_{w\in v_{k-1}+W_m}$. As we only need the points $S = v_{k-1} + W_{m-7}$, we further truncate the first 7 butterfly layers of the AFFT to only evaluate points in S. The composition of these 7 layers can be written as matrix-vector products over $\mathbb{F}_2$. The multiplications in subsequent layers are all in $\mathbb{F}_{2^{128}}$. This lets us use PCLMULQDQ to multiply in $\mathbb{F}_{2^{128}}$ (analogously to [19]).

We report our benchmark on Intel Skylake architecture in Table 1. [3], [12] and [9] use Kronecker segmentation with triadic variants of Schönhage-Strassen, DFT over $\mathbb{F}_{2^{60}}$ and additive FFT over $\mathbb{F}_{2^{256}}$, respectively. Instead of Kronecker segmentation, [19] applied Frobenius FFT to improve [12] by a factor of 2 and achieved the best result. We use the variant of Frobenius additive FFT to improve the result of [9] by about a factor of 2 and outperform [19]. Thus, for polynomial of size n where $\log_2(n/64) = 16, 17, \ldots, 23$, our implementation outperforms the previous best results in the literature.

ACKNOWLEDGMENTS

The authors would like to thank Dr. Tung Chou for his valuable suggestions to improve the article, as well as the anonymous reviewers for their insightful comments and helpful suggestions. The work is supported by the Ministry of Science and Technology, Taiwan, R.O.C. under Grant No. 105-2923-E-001-003-MY3.

REFERENCES

[1] Daniel J. Bernstein. 2009. Batch Binary Edwards. In *Advances in Cryptology - CRYPTO 2009, 29th Annual International Cryptology Conference, Santa Barbara, CA, USA, August 16-20, 2009. Proceedings*. 317–336. https://doi.org/10.1007/978-3-642-03356-8_19

[2] Daniel J. Bernstein and Tung Chou. 2014. Faster Binary-Field Multiplication and Faster Binary-Field MACs. In *Selected Areas in Cryptography - SAC 2014 - 21st International Conference, Montreal, QC, Canada, August 14-15, 2014, Revised Selected Papers (Lecture Notes in Computer Science)*, Antoine Joux and Amr M. Youssef (Eds.), Vol. 8781. Springer, 92–111. https://doi.org/10.1007/978-3-319-13051-4_6

[3] Richard P Brent, Pierrick Gaudry, Emmanuel Thomé, and Paul Zimmermann. 2008. Faster Multiplication in GF (2)(x). *Lecture Notes in Computer Science* 5011 (2008), 153–166.

[4] Michael A. Burr, Chee K. Yap, and Mohab Safey El Din (Eds.). 2017. *Proceedings of the 2017 ACM on International Symposium on Symbolic and Algebraic Computation, ISSAC 2017, Kaiserslautern, Germany, July 25-28, 2017*. ACM. https://doi.org/10.1145/3087604

[5] David G. Cantor. 1989. On Arithmetical Algorithms over Finite Fields. *J. Comb. Theory Ser. A* 50, 2 (March 1989), 285–300. https://doi.org/10.1016/0097-3165(89)90020-4

[6] Murat Cenk and M. Anwar Hasan. 2015. Some new results on binary polynomial multiplication. *J. Cryptographic Engineering* 5, 4 (2015), 289–303. https://doi.org/10.1007/s13389-015-0101-6

[7] Murat Cenk, M. Anwar Hasan, and Christophe Nègre. 2014. Efficient Subquadratic Space Complexity Binary Polynomial Multipliers Based on Block Recombination. *IEEE Trans. Computers* 63, 9 (2014), 2273–2287. https://doi.org/10.1109/TC.2013.105

[8] Murat Cenk, Christophe Nègre, and M. Anwar Hasan. 2013. Improved Three-Way Split Formulas for Binary Polynomial and Toeplitz Matrix Vector Products. *IEEE Trans. Computers* 62, 7 (2013), 1345–1361. https://doi.org/10.1109/TC.2012.96

[9] Ming-Shing Chen, Chen-Mou Cheng, Po-Chun Kuo, Wen-Ding Li, and Bo-Yin Yang. 2017. Faster Multiplication for Long Binary Polynomials. *CoRR* abs/1708.09746 (2017). arXiv:1708.09746 http://arxiv.org/abs/1708.09746

[10] Haining Fan and M. Anwar Hasan. 2015. A Survey of Some Recent Bit-parallel GF (2 N) Multipliers. *Finite Fields Appl.* 32, C (March 2015), 5–43. https://doi.org/10.1016/j.ffa.2014.10.008

[11] Shuhong Gao and Todd Mateer. 2010. Additive Fast Fourier Transforms over Finite Fields. *IEEE Trans. Inf. Theor.* 56, 12 (Dec. 2010), 6265–6272. https://doi.org/10.1109/TIT.2010.2079016

[12] David Harvey, Joris van der Hoeven, and Grégoire Lecerf. 2016. Fast Polynomial Multiplication over $\mathbb{F}_{2^{60}}$. In *Proceedings of the ACM on International Symposium on Symbolic and Algebraic Computation, ISSAC 2016, Waterloo, ON, Canada, July 19-22, 2016*, Sergei A. Abramov, Eugene V. Zima, and Xiao-Shan Gao (Eds.). ACM, 255–262. https://doi.org/10.1145/2930889.2930920

[13] David Harvey, Joris van der Hoeven, and Grégoire Lecerf. 2017. Faster Polynomial Multiplication over Finite Fields. *J. ACM* 63, 6 (2017), 52:1–52:23. https://doi.org/10.1145/3005344

[14] Intel Corp. 2008. Carry-Less Multiplication and Its Usage for Computing The GCM Mode. http://http://software.intel.com/en-us/articles/carry-less-multiplication-and-its-usage-for-computing-the-gcm-mode.

[15] Sian-Jheng Lin, Wei-Ho Chung, and Yunghsiang S. Han. 2014. Novel Polynomial Basis and Its Application to Reed-Solomon Erasure Codes. In *55th IEEE Annual Symposium on Foundations of Computer Science, FOCS 2014, Philadelphia, PA, USA, October 18-21, 2014*. IEEE Computer Society, 316–325. https://doi.org/10.1109/FOCS.2014.41

[16] Sian-Jheng Lin, Tareq Y. Al-Naffouri, and Yunghsiang S. Han. 2016. FFT Algorithm for Binary Extension Finite Fields and Its Application to Reed–Solomon Codes. *IEEE Trans. Inf. Theor.* 62, 10 (Oct. 2016), 5343–5358. https://doi.org/10.1109/TIT.2016.2600417

[17] C. Paar. 1997. Optimized arithmetic for Reed-Solomon encoders. In *Proceedings of IEEE International Symposium on Information Theory*. 250–. https://doi.org/10.1109/ISIT.1997.613165

[18] Joris van der Hoeven and Robin Larrieu. 2017. The Frobenius FFT, See [4], 437–444. https://doi.org/10.1145/3087604.3087633

[19] Joris van der Hoeven, Robin Larrieu, and Grégoire Lecerf. 2017. Implementing Fast Carryless Multiplication. In *Mathematical Aspects of Computer and Information Sciences - 7th International Conference, MACIS 2017, Vienna, Austria, November 15-17, 2017, Proceedings (Lecture Notes in Computer Science)*, Johannes Blömer, Ilias S. Kotsireas, Temur Kutsia, and Dimitris E. Simos (Eds.), Vol. 10693. Springer, 121–136. https://doi.org/10.1007/978-3-319-72453-9_9

[20] Joris van der Hoeven and Grégoire Lecerf. 2017. Composition Modulo Powers of Polynomials, See [4], 445–452. https://doi.org/10.1145/3087604.3087634

[21] Joachim von zur Gathen and Jamshid Shokrollahi. 2005. Efficient FPGA-Based Karatsuba Multipliers for Polynomials over $\mathbb{F}_2$. In *Selected Areas in Cryptography, 12th International Workshop, SAC 2005, Kingston, ON, Canada, August 11-12, 2005, Revised Selected Papers (Lecture Notes in Computer Science)*, Bart Preneel and Stafford E. Tavares (Eds.), Vol. 3897. Springer, 359–369. https://doi.org/10.1007/11693383_25

Extending the GVW Algorithm to Local Ring

Dong Lu
[1]KLMM, Academy of Mathematics and Systems Science, Chinese Academy of Sciences
Beijing 100190, China
[2]School of Mathematical Sciences, University of Chinese Academy of Sciences
Beijing, China
donglu@amss.ac.cn

Dingkang Wang
[1]KLMM, Academy of Mathematics and Systems Science, Chinese Academy of Sciences
Beijing 100190, China
[2]School of Mathematical Sciences, University of Chinese Academy of Sciences
Beijing, China
dwang@mmrc.iss.ac.cn

Fanghui Xiao
[1]KLMM, Academy of Mathematics and Systems Science, Chinese Academy of Sciences
Beijing 100190, China
[2]School of Mathematical Sciences, University of Chinese Academy of Sciences
Beijing, China
xiaofanghui@amss.ac.cn

Jie Zhou
Xihua University
Chengdu, Sichuan, China
jiezhou@amss.ac.cn

ABSTRACT

A new algorithm, which combines the GVW algorithm with the Mora normal form algorithm, is presented to compute the standard bases of ideals in a local ring. Since term orders in local ring are not well-orderings, there may not be a minimal signature in an infinite set, and we can not extend the GVW algorithm from a polynomial ring to a local ring directly. Nevertheless, when given an anti-graded order in R and a term-over-position order in R^m that are compatible, we can construct a special set such that it has a minimal signature, where R, R^m are a local ring and a R-module, respectively. That is, for any given polynomial $v_0 \in R$, the set consisting of signatures of pairs $(\mathbf{u}, v) \in R^m \times R$ has a minimal element, where the leading power products of v and v_0 are equal. In this case, we prove a cover theorem in R, and use three criteria (syzygy criterion, signature criterion and rewrite criterion) to discard useless J-pairs without any reductions. Mora normal form algorithm is also extended to do regular top-reductions in $R^m \times R$, and the correctness and termination of the algorithm are proved. The proposed algorithm has been implemented in the computer algebra system Maple, and experiment results show that most of J-pairs can be discarded by three criteria in the examples.

CCS CONCEPTS

• **Computing methodologies → Symbolic and algebraic algorithms; Algebraic algorithms;**

ACM ISBN 978-1-4503-5550-6/18/07...$15.00
https://doi.org/10.1145/3208976.3208979

KEYWORDS

GVW algorithm, Local ring, Signature, Standard bases

ACM Reference Format:
Dong Lu, Dingkang Wang, Fanghui Xiao, and Jie Zhou. 2018. Extending the GVW Algorithm to Local Ring. In *ISSAC'18: 2018 ACM International Symposium on Symbolic and Algebraic Computation, July 16–19, 2018, New York, NY, USA.* ACM, New York, NY, USA, 8 pages. https://doi.org/10.1145/3208976.3208979

1 INTRODUCTION

The Gröbner bases was first presented by Buchberger in 1965 [3]. It is useful for solving polynomial equations, the ideal membership problem and so on. The original algorithm of computing Gröbner bases was proposed by Buchberger, and it has been implemented in most computer algebra systems. Since then, many researchers have done some works to improve the efficiency of the algorithm, such as Buchberger[4], [5], Faugère [12], Gebauer and Möller [16], Giovini et.al. [18], Mora et.al. [21]. One important improvement is that Lazard pointed out the connection betwwen Gröbner basis and linear algebra [20], which will speed up the reduction step. In Buchberger original algorithm, there are many useless S-polynomials which are reduced to zero. The other improvement is deleting these useless S-polynomials without performing any reduction. In 2002, the notation of "signature" and rewriting rules, which can detect many useless S-polynomials, were proposed by Faugère in the F5 algorithm [13]. After that, several variants of F5 have been presented including Arri and Perry [1], Eder and Perry [9, 10], Hashemi and Ars [2], Sun and Wang [23],[24], Gerdt, Hashemi and M.-Alizadeh [17]. Eder et.al. [11] generalized signature-based Gröbner basis algorithms to Euclidean rings, in particular, the integers. They also shown how signature based computation can be efficiently used as a pre-reduction step for a classical Gröbner basis computation over Euclidean rings. There is by now a large literature on signature-based Gröbner basis computation; see [8] for a comprehensive survey.

Gao et. al. presented a new simple theory for computing Gröbner bases. Based on the theory, they proposed an incremental signature-based algorithm G^2V [14], and an extended version GVW algorithm [15]. The correctness and finite termination of the GVW algorithm have been proved.

In algebraic geometry, many questions are related to the local properties of varieties. Such as given a zero-dimensional ideal I in $k[x_1, \ldots, x_n]$, we want to know the multiplicity of an isolated singular point p in the variety $\mathbb{V}(I) \subset k^n$, or the Milnor and Tjurina numbers of the point. The local ring is useful for solving these questions.

As Gröbner bases in polynomial ring, there is a similar notation called standard bases in local ring. Through computing a standard bases G of the ideal I in local ring, the local properties of original point can be got. For other point p, we only need change the coordinates to translate the point p to the origin.

Given a collection $f_1, \ldots, f_s$ of polynomials which generate the ideal I, we would like to find a standard bases of I in a local ring with respect to some semigroup orders. There are two main algorithms to compute the standard bases of the ideal I in the local ring. One is based on the Lazard's homogeneous idea, and the other one is based on the Mora normal form algorithm. Let f^H be the homogenization of f in $k[t, x_1, \ldots, x_n]$. According to Lazard's idea, we only need to compute a Gröbner basis of $\langle f_1^H, \ldots, f_s^H \rangle$ with respect to some special global semigroup orders, then the dehomogenizations of elements of the Gröbner basis is a standard basis of I in the local ring. The other one is combining the Mora normal form algorithm [22] with Buchberger algorithm to compute the standard basis. The algorithm has been implemented in Singular and REDUCE, but not in Maple or Mathematica. The experience seems to indicate that standard bases computation with Mora's normal form algorithm is more efficient than computations using Lazard's method (quote from [6]).

Since the GVW algorithm is more efficient than the Buchberger algorithm for computing Gröbner bases, it is asked naturally whether the GVW algorithm can be used to compute the standard bases instead of Buchberger algorithm. The answer is yes. In this paper, we will combining the Mora normal form algorithm with GVW algorithm to compute the standard bases in the local ring. What's more, we have implemented the idea in the Maple.

The paper is organized as follows. Some basic notations about local ring, signature, and strong standard basis are introduced in the section 2. In section 3, we present the GVW algorithm in local ring. The correctness and finite termination of the algorithm are proved in this section. An example is given for illustrating our method in the section 4. We conclude this paper in the last section.

2 PRELIMINARIES

In this section, we first review some basic definitions about local ring. The details can refer to [6]. Then we give the definition of strong standard bases in local ring, which is similar to strong Gröbner bases [15] in polynomial ring. Finally, we propose the term orders that we should consider in this paper.

2.1 Local Ring

Let X be the n variables $x_1, \ldots, x_n$; $k[X]$ be the polynomial ring in variables X with coefficients in a field k; $\{X^\alpha : \alpha \in \mathbb{Z}^n_{\geq 0}\}$ be the set of monomials in $k[X]$.

Definition 2.1 (Semigroup Order). An order $>$ on $\mathbb{Z}^n_{\geq 0}$ or, equivalently, on $\{X^\alpha : \alpha \in \mathbb{Z}^n_{\geq 0}\}$, is said to be a *semigroup order* if it satisfies:

(1) $>$ is a total order on $\mathbb{Z}^n_{\geq 0}$;
(2) $>$ is compatible with multiplication of monomials.

As in Definition 2.1, being a total order means that for any $\alpha, \beta \in \mathbb{Z}^n_{\geq 0}$, exactly one of the following is true:

$$X^\alpha > X^\beta, \quad X^\alpha = X^\beta, \quad \text{or } X^\alpha < X^\beta.$$

Compatibility with multiplication means that for any X^γ in $\{X^\alpha : \alpha \in \mathbb{Z}^n_{\geq 0}\}$, if $X^\alpha > X^\beta$, then $X^\alpha X^\gamma > X^\beta X^\gamma$.

For any $\alpha \neq (0, \ldots, 0)$, if $X^\alpha > 1$, the semigroup order is called *global order*; and if $X^\alpha < 1$, it is called *local order*. For example, the lexicographic order is a global order and the antigraded lexicographic order (abbreviated *alex*) is a local order. The definition of *alex* is as follows.

Definition 2.2. Let $\alpha, \beta \in \mathbb{Z}^n_{\geq 0}$. We say $X^\alpha >_{alex} X^\beta$ if $|\alpha| = \sum_{i=1}^n \alpha_i < |\beta| = \sum_{i=1}^n \beta_i$, or if $|\alpha| = |\beta|$ and $X^\alpha >_{lex} X^\beta$.

Let f be a polynomial in $k[X]$, $>$ be a semigroup order on the monomials in $k[X]$, the leading power product, the leading coefficient of f is denoted by $\mathrm{lpp}(f)$, $\mathrm{lc}(f)$ respectively, and the leading term, $\mathrm{lt}(f) = \mathrm{lc}(f)\mathrm{lpp}(f)$. The localization of $k[X]$ with respect to $>$ is defined as follows.

Definition 2.3 (Localization of Ring). Let $>$ be a semigroup order on monomials in $k[X]$, and let $S = \{1 + g : g = 0 \text{ or } \mathrm{lt}(g) < 1\}$. The *localization* of $k[X]$ w.r.t. $>$ is the ring

$$\mathrm{Loc}_>(k[X]) = \{f/(1+g) : f, g \in k[X] \text{ and } 1 + g \in S\}.$$

Notes that, if $>$ is a global order, $\mathrm{Loc}_>(k[X]) = k[X]$. On the other hand, if $>$ is a local order, $\mathrm{Loc}_>(k[X]) = k[X]_{\langle x_1, \ldots, x_n \rangle}$. For briefly, we denote $\mathrm{Loc}_>(k[X])$ by R w.r.t. a local order $>$ in the following.

The semigroup order $>$ on the monomials in $k[X]$ can be naturally extended to R. For any $h = f/(1+g) \in R$, the leading power product, the leading coefficient, and the leading term of h are defined to be same as those of f, that is, $\mathrm{lpp}(h) = \mathrm{lpp}(f)$, $\mathrm{lc}(h) = \mathrm{lc}(f)$, and $\mathrm{lt}(h) = \mathrm{lt}(f)$.

For any $h_1, \ldots, h_m$ in R, an ideal $I \subset R$ generated by them is $I = \langle h_1, \ldots, h_m \rangle = \{\sum_{i=1}^m u_i h_i : \forall u_1, \ldots, u_m \in R\}$. The n-tuple $(u_1, \ldots, u_m)$ is called a *syzygy* of $\{h_1, \ldots, h_m\}$, if $\sum_{i=1}^m u_i h_i = 0$.

Definition 2.4 (Standard basis). Let $>$ be a semigroup order on the monomials in $k[X]$, and I be an ideal in R. A *standard basis* of I is a set $\{g_1, \ldots, g_s\}$ in I such that $\langle \mathrm{lt}(I) \rangle = \langle \mathrm{lt}(g_1), \ldots, \mathrm{lt}(g_s) \rangle$.

Since k is a field, the set $\{g_1, \ldots, g_s\}$ is a standard basis of I if and only if $\langle \mathrm{lpp}(I) \rangle = \langle \mathrm{lpp}(g_1), \ldots, \mathrm{lpp}(g_s) \rangle$. If $>$ is a global order, the standard basis is exactly the Gröbner basis. So the standard bases in R is more extensive than Gröbner bases.

In order to compute a standard basis of $I \subset R$ w.r.t. a local order, we need to develop an extension of the division algorithm in $k[X]$

which will yield information about ideals in R. Since we deal with orders that are not well-orderings, the difficult part is to give a division process that is guaranteed to terminate. We can evade this difficulty with a splendid idea of Mora, and obtain the Mora normal form algorithm in R.

Corollary 2.5 (Mora Normal Form Algorithm). *Let $>$ be a semigroup order on the monomials in $k[X]$, $g \in R$ and $g_1, \ldots, g_s \in k[X]$ be nonzero. Then there is an algorithm for producing polynomials $a_1, \ldots, a_s, h \in R$ such that $g = a_1 g_1 + \cdots + a_s g_s + h$, where $\mathrm{lpp}(a_i)\mathrm{lpp}(g_i) \preceq \mathrm{lpp}(g)$ for all i with $a_i \neq 0$, and either $h = 0$, or $\mathrm{lpp}(h) \preceq \mathrm{lpp}(g)$ and $\mathrm{lpp}(h)$ is not divisible by any of $\mathrm{lpp}(g_1), \ldots, \mathrm{lpp}(g_s)$.*

Remark 1. Based on Mora's research, Greuel and Pfister in [19] obtained a normal form algorithm in R^m, when they studied the standard bases for modules. That is, for any given module order $<'$ in R^m, $\mathbf{u} \in R^m$ and $\mathbf{u}_1, \ldots, \mathbf{u}_s \in (k[X])^m$ are nonzero, then there is an algorithm for producing polynomials $b_1, \ldots, b_s \in R$ and $\mathbf{r} \in R^m$ such that $\mathbf{u} = b_1\mathbf{u}_1 + \cdots + b_s\mathbf{u}_s + \mathbf{r}$, where $\mathrm{lpp}(b_i)\mathrm{lpp}(\mathbf{u}_i) \preceq' \mathrm{lpp}(\mathbf{u})$ for all i with $b_i \neq 0$, and either $\mathbf{r} = \mathbf{0}$, or $\mathrm{lpp}(\mathbf{r})$ is not divisible by any $\mathrm{lpp}(\mathbf{u}_i)$, $i = 1, \ldots, s$.

2.2 Strong Standard Basis

By analogy with the notation of strong Gröbner bases [15] in $(k[X])^m \times k[X]$, we will define the strong standard bases in $R^m \times R$ w.r.t a local order $>$. Cox et.al. [6] proved that every ideal $I \subset k[X]_{\langle x_1, \ldots, x_n \rangle}$ has a generating set consisting of polynomials in $k[X]$. By the above fact, restricting to ideals generated by polynomials in this paper entails loss of generality when we are studying ideals in $R = k[X]_{\langle x_1, \ldots, x_n \rangle}$ for a local order $>$.

In this paper, elements in R^m are denoted by the bold letters $\mathbf{f}, \mathbf{u}$ etc., while elements in R are denoted by the letters v, r etc. Let $\mathbf{f} = (f_1, \ldots, f_m)$ in $(k[X])^m$, we can define a subset in $R^m \times R$:

$$M = \{(\mathbf{u}, v) \in R^m \times R : \mathbf{u} \cdot \mathbf{f} = v, \mathbf{u} \in R^m\},$$

For any $(\mathbf{u}_1, v_1), (\mathbf{u}_2, v_2) \in M$, and $r \in R$, since $r\mathbf{u}_1 \cdot \mathbf{f} + \mathbf{u}_2 \cdot \mathbf{f} = (r\mathbf{u}_1 + \mathbf{u}_2) \cdot \mathbf{f} = rv_1 + v_2$, so $(r\mathbf{u}_1 + \mathbf{u}_2, rv_1 + v_2) \in M$, and M is a R-submodule in $R^m \times R$. It is obvious that M is generated by $(\mathbf{e}_1, f_1), \ldots, (\mathbf{e}_m, f_m)$, where $\mathbf{e}_i$ is the i-th unit vector of R^m, i.e., $(\mathbf{e}_i)_j = \delta_{ij}$, δ_{ij} is the Kronecker delta. We say $X^\alpha \mathbf{e}_i$ *divides* $X^\beta \mathbf{e}_j$ if X^α divides X^β and $i = j$.

Fix any local order $<_1$ in R, and any module order $<_2$ in R^m. For any element $v \in R$, the leading power product, the leading coefficient of v w.r.t. $<_1$ is denoted by $\mathrm{lpp}_{<_1}(v)$, $\mathrm{lc}_{<_1}(v)$ respectively. Similarly, any element $\mathbf{u} \in R^m$, the leading power product, the leading coefficient of $\mathbf{u}$ w.r.t. $<_2$ is denoted by $\mathrm{lpp}_{<_2}(\mathbf{u})$, $\mathrm{lc}_{<_2}(\mathbf{u})$ respectively. For convenient, we denote them by $\mathrm{lpp}(v), \mathrm{lc}(v), \mathrm{lpp}(\mathbf{u}), \mathrm{lc}(\mathbf{u})$ with no confusion. For any $p = (\mathbf{u}, v)$ in M, the $\mathrm{lpp}(\mathbf{u})$ is called the *signature* of p.

We say $<_2$ is *compatible* with $<_1$, if it satisfies that: $X^\alpha <_1 X^\beta$ if and only if $X^\alpha \mathbf{e}_i <_2 X^\beta \mathbf{e}_i$ for all $i = 1 \ldots m$.

Definition 2.6 (Top-reducible). Let $p_1 = (\mathbf{u}_1, v_1)$, $p_2 = (\mathbf{u}_2, v_2)$ be two elements in M. We say p_1 is *top-reducible* by p_2, if it satisfies:

(1) when $v_2 = 0$, $\mathrm{lpp}(\mathbf{u}_2)$ divides $\mathrm{lpp}(\mathbf{u}_1)$; and
(2) when $v_1 v_2 \neq 0$, $\mathrm{lpp}(v_2)$ divides $\mathrm{lpp}(v_1)$ and $t\mathrm{lpp}(\mathbf{u}_2) \preceq_2 \mathrm{lpp}(\mathbf{u}_1)$, where $t = \mathrm{lpp}(v_1)/\mathrm{lpp}(v_2)$.

When $v_1 v_2 \neq 0$, the corresponding one-step top-reduction is

$$\mathrm{OneRed}(p_1, p_2) = p_1 - ctp_2 = (\mathbf{u}_1 - ct\mathbf{u}_2, v_1 - ctv_2),$$

where $c = \mathrm{lc}(v_1)/\mathrm{lc}(v_2)$. Such a top-reduction is called *regular* if $\mathrm{lpp}(\mathbf{u}_1 - ct\mathbf{u}_2) = \mathrm{lpp}(\mathbf{u}_1)$, and *super* otherwise. When v_1 is zero, the corresponding top-reduction is always called *super*. Let G be any set of pairs in $R^m \times R$, we call a pair $(\mathbf{u}, v)$ *eventually super top-reducible* by G if there is a sequence of regular top-reductions by pairs in G that reduce $(\mathbf{u}, v)$ to a pair $(\hat{\mathbf{u}}, \hat{v})$ that is no longer regular top-reducible by G but is super top-reducible by at least one pair in G.

Definition 2.7 (Strong standard bases). Let $G = \{(\mathbf{u}_1, v_1), \ldots, (\mathbf{u}_s, v_s)\}$ be a finite subset of M, where $\mathbf{u}_1, \ldots, \mathbf{u}_s \in (k[X])^m$ and $v_1, \ldots, v_s \in k[X]$. Then G is called a *strong standard basis* for M, if for any nonzero $(\mathbf{u}, v)$ in M, $(\mathbf{u}, v)$ is top-reducible by some element in G.

In Gao et. al. [15], the authors have proved that if $G = \{(\mathbf{u}_1, v_1), \ldots, (\mathbf{u}_s, v_s)\}$ is a strong standard basis for M, then $\{v_i : 1 \leqslant i \leqslant s\}$ is a Gröbner basis for $I = \langle f_1, \ldots, f_m \rangle$ in $k[X]$ w.r.t. a global order. In their proof, they can select a minimal $\mathrm{lpp}(\mathbf{u})$ such that $\mathbf{u} \cdot \mathbf{f} = v$, since the monomials order in $k[X]$ satisfies the well-ordering relation. However, local orders are not well-orderings, and we can not get a minimal $\mathrm{lpp}(\mathbf{u})$. Therefore, we need a new method to solve this problem.

Proposition 2.8. *Let $<_1$ be an arbitrary local order in R and $<_2$ be a module order in R^m. Suppose that $G = \{(\mathbf{u}_1, v_1), \ldots, (\mathbf{u}_s, v_s)\}$ is a strong standard basis for M, then*

(1) *$G_0 = \{\mathbf{u}_i : v_i = 0, 1 \leqslant i \leqslant s\}$ is a standard basis for the syzygy module of $\{f_1, \ldots, f_m\}$, and*
(2) *$G_1 = \{v_i : 1 \leqslant i \leqslant s\}$ is a standard basis for ideal $I = \langle f_1, \ldots, f_m \rangle$ in R.*

Proof. Since the proof of (1) is same as the proposition 2.2 in Gao et. al. [15], we only prove the second assertion.

Without loss of generality, let $G_0 = \{\mathbf{u}_i : v_i = 0, 1 \leqslant i \leqslant k\}$ and $G_1 = \{v_i : k+1 \leqslant i \leqslant s\}$, where $1 \leq k < s$. We select $v \in I$ such that $v \neq 0$. Then there exists $\mathbf{u} \in R^m$ so that $\mathbf{u} \cdot \mathbf{f} = v$. Remark 1 implies that there exist $a_1, \ldots, a_k \in R$ and $\mathbf{h} \in R^m$ such that $\mathbf{u} = a_1\mathbf{u}_1 + \cdots + a_k\mathbf{u}_k + \mathbf{h}$, where $\mathrm{lpp}(a_i)\mathrm{lpp}(\mathbf{u}_i) \preceq_2 \mathrm{lpp}(\mathbf{u})$ for all i with $a_i \neq 0$, and either $\mathbf{h} = \mathbf{0}$, or $\mathbf{h} \notin \langle G_0 \rangle$. It follows from $v \neq 0$ that $\mathbf{h} \neq 0$. Hence, $(\mathbf{u}, v) \in M$ can be top-reducible to $(\mathbf{h}, v)$ by $\{(\mathbf{u}_i, 0) : \mathbf{u}_i \in G_0\}$. Since $(\mathbf{h}, v) \in M$ and $\mathbf{h} \notin \langle G_0 \rangle$, it can be top-reducible by some $(\mathbf{u}_i, v_i) \in G$ with $v_i \in G_1$. So $v_i \neq 0$ and $\mathrm{lpp}(v_i)$ divides $\mathrm{lpp}(v)$. Hence G_1 is a standard basis for I. □

2.3 Term Orders

In the following, we consider a local order $<_1$ in R and a module order $<_2$ in R^m. For any $<_1$, there are many ways that we can extend $<_1$ to $<_2$. For example, we get $<_2$ as follows.

(1) Position Over Term (POT). We say that $X^\beta \mathbf{e}_j <_2 X^\alpha \mathbf{e}_i$ if $j > i$, or if $j = i$ and $X^\beta <_1 X^\alpha$.
(2) Term Over Position (TOP). We say that $X^\beta \mathbf{e}_j <_2 X^\alpha \mathbf{e}_i$ if $X^\beta <_1 X^\alpha$, or if $X^\beta = X^\alpha$ and $j > i$.
(3) $\mathbf{f}$-weighted anti-degree followed by TOP. We say that $X^\beta \mathbf{e}_j <_2 X^\alpha \mathbf{e}_i$ if $\mathrm{tdeg}(X^\beta f_j) > \mathrm{tdeg}(X^\alpha f_i)$, or if $\mathrm{tdeg}(X^\beta f_j) =$

$\text{tdeg}(X^\alpha f_i)$ and $X^\beta \mathbf{e}_j \prec_{TOP} X^\alpha \mathbf{e}_i$, where tdeg is for total degree.

(4) f-weighted $\prec_1$ followed by POT. We say that $X^\beta \mathbf{e}_j \prec_2 X^\alpha \mathbf{e}_i$ if $\text{lpp}(X^\beta f_j) \prec_1 \text{lpp}(X^\alpha f_i)$, or if $\text{lpp}(X^\beta f_j) = \text{lpp}(X^\alpha f_i)$ and $X^\beta \mathbf{e}_j \prec_{POT} X^\alpha \mathbf{e}_i$.

For any $(\mathbf{u}_0, v_0) \in M$, we consider the set

$$L(\text{lpp}(v_0)) = \{\text{lpp}(\mathbf{u}) : (\mathbf{u}, v) \in M \text{ and } \text{lpp}(v) = \text{lpp}(v_0)\}.$$

Note that $L(\text{lpp}(v_0))$ is a nonempty set. But, $L(\text{lpp}(v_0))$ may not have a minimal element. For example, let $\prec_1$ be an anti-graded lex order with $x_2 \prec_1 x_1$ on R, and $\prec_2$ be a POT order with $\mathbf{e}_2 = (0,1) \prec_2 \mathbf{e}_1 = (1,0)$ on R^2, where $R = k[x_1, x_2]_{\langle x_1, x_2 \rangle}$. Consider M generated by $(\mathbf{e}_1, x_1)$ and $(\mathbf{e}_2, x_2)$. Let $p_0 = (\mathbf{u}_0, v_0) = ((x_1, x_1+1), x_1^2 + x_1x_2 + x_2)$, then $p_0 \in M$ and $\text{lpp}(\mathbf{u}_0) = x_1\mathbf{e}_1, \text{lpp}(v_0) = x_2$. We can construct $p_i = (\mathbf{u}_i, v_i) = ((x_1^{1+i}, x_1 + 1), x_1^{2+i} + x_1x_2 + x_2)$, where $i \in \mathbb{Z}_{\geq 1}$. Then $p_i \in M$, $\text{lpp}(v_i) = \text{lpp}(v_0)$ and $L(\text{lpp}(v_0)) \supseteq \{x_1^i \mathbf{e}_1 : i \in \mathbb{Z}_{\geq 1}\}$. Obviously, $L(\text{lpp}(v_0))$ has not a minimal element. Moreover, if G is a subset of M and p_0 is not top-reducible by any pair in G, then p_i is also not top-reducible by any pair in G.

Nevertheless, if $\prec_1$ is an anti-graded order in R and $\prec_2$ is a TOP order in R^m, then we can prove that $L(\text{lpp}(v_0))$ has a minimal element.

Lemma 2.9. *Let $\prec_1$ be an anti-graded order in R, and $\prec_2$ be a TOP order in R^m, where $\prec_2$ is compatible with $\prec_1$. Then for any $(\mathbf{u}_0, v_0) \in M$, $L(\text{lpp}(v_0))$ has a minimal element.*

Proof. Without loss of generality, we suppose $\text{lpp}(f_1)$ is maximal in $\{\text{lpp}(f_1), \ldots, \text{lpp}(f_m)\}$. For any $(\mathbf{u}, v) \in M$ which satisfies $\text{lpp}(v) = \text{lpp}(v_0)$, we have $u_1 f_1 + \cdots + u_m f_m = v$, where $\mathbf{u} = (u_1, \ldots, u_m)$. Let $\text{lpp}(\mathbf{u}) = \text{lpp}(u_i)\mathbf{e}_i$ for some i, where $1 \leq i \leq m$. Since $\prec_2$ is a TOP order in R^m and is compatible with $\prec_1$, $\text{lpp}(u_i) = \max\{\text{lpp}(u_1), \ldots, \text{lpp}(u_m)\}$. It follows from $v = \sum_{j=1}^m u_j f_j$ that there exists some j such that $\text{lpp}(v) = \text{lpp}(v_0) \preceq_1 \text{lpp}(u_j)\text{lpp}(f_j)$, where $1 \leq j \leq m$. Then we have $\text{lpp}(v_0) \preceq_1 \text{lpp}(u_j)\text{lpp}(f_1) \preceq_1 \text{lpp}(u_i)\text{lpp}(f_1)$. Since $\preceq_1$ is an anti-graded order, there are a finite number of $\text{lpp}(u_i)$ for which the inequality $\text{lpp}(v_0) \preceq_1 \text{lpp}(u_i)\text{lpp}(f_1)$ holds. Therefore, $L(\text{lpp}(v_0))$ is a finite set, and has a minimal element. □

Remark 2. If $\prec_2$ is not a TOP order in R^m, then $\text{lpp}(u_i) = \max\{\text{lpp}(u_1), \ldots, \text{lpp}(u_m)\}$ may not hold. Moreover, if $\prec_1$ is not an anti-graded order in R, there may be an infinite number of $\text{lpp}(u_i)$ for which the inequality $\text{lpp}(v_0) \preceq_1 \text{lpp}(u_i)\text{lpp}(f_1)$ holds. In either case, $L(\text{lpp}(v_0))$ may not have a minimal element.

3 THE GVW ALGORITHM IN LOCAL RING

In order to compute the strong standard basis for M, we need to define a concept of J-pair which is similar to S-polynomial in Buchberger's algorithm. Suppose $p_1 = (\mathbf{u}_1, v_1), p_2 = (\mathbf{u}_2, v_2)$ are two pairs in M with $v_1v_2 \neq 0$. Let $t = \text{lcm}(\text{lpp}(v_1), \text{lpp}(v_2))$, $t_1 = t/\text{lpp}(v_1)$, $t_2 = t/\text{lpp}(v_2)$, $c = \text{lc}(v_1)/\text{lc}(v_2)$, and $T = \max\{t_1\text{lpp}(\mathbf{u}_1), t_2\text{lpp}(\mathbf{u}_2)\}$. Without loss of generality, we assume $T = t_1\text{lpp}(\mathbf{u}_1)$. If

$$\text{lpp}(t_1\mathbf{u}_1 - ct_2\mathbf{u}_2) = T,$$

then t_1p_1 is called the *J-pair* of p_1 and p_2, and T is called the *J-signature* of the J-pair. It is obvious that the J-pair t_1p_1 is regular top-reducible by p_2.

We say that a pair $(\mathbf{u}, v) \in M$ is *covered* by $G \subset M$, if there is a pair $(\mathbf{u}_i, v_i) \in G$ such that $\text{lpp}(\mathbf{u}_i)$ divides $\text{lpp}(\mathbf{u})$ and $t\text{lpp}(v_i) \prec_1 \text{lpp}(v)$, where $t = \text{lpp}(\mathbf{u})/\text{lpp}(\mathbf{u}_i)$.

3.1 The Algorithm

The following theorem is the theoretical foundation of the GVW algorithm in local ring.

Theorem 3.1 (Cover Theorem). *Suppose the TOP order $\prec_2$ in R^m is compatible with the anti-graded order $\prec_1$ in R. Let G be a finite subset of M such that, for any term $T \in R^m$, there is a pair $(\mathbf{u}, v) \in G$ and a monomial t such that $T = t\text{lpp}(\mathbf{u})$, where for every pair $(\mathbf{u}, v) \in G$, $\mathbf{u} \in (k[X])^m$ and $v \in k[X]$. Then the following are equivalent:*

(a) *G is a strong standard basis for M;*
(b) *every J-pair of G is eventually super top-reducible by G;*
(c) *every J-pair of G is covered by G.*

Proof. We only prove $(c) \Rightarrow (a)$, other proofs are same as the Theorem 2.4 in Gao et. al. [15]. We prove by contradiction.

Let $W = \{(\mathbf{u}, v) \in M : (\mathbf{u}, v)$ is not top-reducible by any pair in $G\}$. Since $\prec_1$ is a local order in R, we can construct a subset $W_1 \subset W$ such that $W_1 = \{(\mathbf{u}, v) \in W : \text{lpp}(v)$ is maximal$\}$. Then, for any element $(\mathbf{u}, v) \in W_1$, the leading power product of v is equal and maximal in W. Since $\prec_2$ in R^m is compatible with $\prec_1$, according to Lemma 2.9 we can also construct a subset $W_2 \subset W_1$ such that $W_2 = \{(\mathbf{u}, v) \in W_1 : \text{lpp}(\mathbf{u})$ is minimal$\}$. Therefore, we can pick a pair $p_0 = (\mathbf{u}_0, v_0) \in W_2$ such that $\text{lpp}(v_0)$ is maximal in W and $\text{lpp}(\mathbf{u}_0)$ is minimal in W_1. Next, we select a pair $p_1 = (\mathbf{u}_1, v_1)$ from G such that

(*i*) $\text{lpp}(\mathbf{u}_0) = t\text{lpp}(\mathbf{u}_1)$ for some monomial t, and
(*ii*) $t\text{lpp}(v_1)$ is minimal among all $p_1 \in G$ satisfying (*i*).

Then $t(\mathbf{u}_1, v_1)$ is not regular top-reducible by G (this proof can be found in Theorem 2.4, [15]). Consider

$$(\mathbf{u}_*, v_*) := (\mathbf{u}_0, v_0) - ct(\mathbf{u}_1, v_1), \tag{1}$$

where $c = \text{lc}(\mathbf{u}_0)/\text{lc}(\mathbf{u}_1)$ so that $\text{lpp}(\mathbf{u}_*) \prec_2 \text{lpp}(\mathbf{u}_0)$. Note that $\text{lpp}(v_0) \neq t\text{lpp}(v_1)$, since otherwise $(\mathbf{u}_0, v_0)$ would be top-reducible by $p_1 \in G$ contradicting the choice of $(\mathbf{u}_0, v_0)$. Then, we consider the following two cases:

- If $\text{lpp}(v_0) \prec_1 t\text{lpp}(v_1)$, then $\text{lpp}(v_*) = t\text{lpp}(v_1)$. Since every element $(\mathbf{u}, v) \in W$ satisfies that $\text{lpp}(v) \preceq_1 \text{lpp}(v_0)$, we have that $(\mathbf{u}_*, v_*) \notin W$ and it is top-reducible by G. Without loss of generality, we assume that $(\mathbf{u}_*, v_*)$ is top-reducible by $p_2 = (\mathbf{u}_2, v_2) \in G$ with $v_2 \neq 0$. Hence, $\text{lpp}(v_2) \mid t\text{lpp}(v_1)$ and $t_2\text{lpp}(\mathbf{u}_2) \preceq_2 \text{lpp}(\mathbf{u}_*) \prec_2 t\text{lpp}(\mathbf{u}_1)$, $t_2 = t\text{lpp}(v_1)/\text{lpp}(v_2)$. It follows that $t(\mathbf{u}_1, v_1)$ is regular top-reducible by $p_2 \in G$. Since $t(\mathbf{u}_1, v_1)$ is not regular top-reducible by any pair in G, this case impossible.
- If $t\text{lpp}(v_1) \prec_1 \text{lpp}(v_0)$, then $\text{lpp}(v_*) = \text{lpp}(v_0)$. We assert that $(\mathbf{u}_*, v_*) \notin W$. If otherwise, $\text{lpp}(v_*) = \text{lpp}(v_0)$ implies that $(\mathbf{u}_*, v_*) \in W_1$. It follows that $\text{lpp}(\mathbf{u}_*) \succeq_2 \text{lpp}(\mathbf{u}_0)$, which leads to a contradiction. So $(\mathbf{u}_*, v_*) \notin W$ is top-reducible by G. Without loss of generality, we assume that $(\mathbf{u}_*, v_*)$ is top-reducible by $p_3 = (\mathbf{u}_3, v_3) \in G$ with $v_3 \neq 0$. We have $\text{lpp}(v_3) \mid \text{lpp}(v_0)$ and $t_3\text{lpp}(\mathbf{u}_3) \preceq_2 \text{lpp}(\mathbf{u}_*) \prec_2 \text{lpp}(\mathbf{u}_0)$, where $t_3 = \text{lpp}(v_0)/\text{lpp}(v_3)$. Therefore, $(\mathbf{u}_0, v_0)$ is regular

top-reducible by $p_3 \in G$, contradicting the fact that $(\mathbf{u}_0, v_0)$ is not top-reducible by any pair in G.

Therefore such a pair $(\mathbf{u}_0, v_0)$ does not exist in M, so every pair in M is top-reducible by G. This proves $(c) \Rightarrow (a)$. □

REMARK 3. If $L(\text{lpp}(v_0))$ has not a minimal element, then $(\mathbf{u}_*, v_*)$ may not be top-reducible by any pair in G under the case of $t\text{lpp}(v_1) \prec_1 \text{lpp}(v_0)$. If $(\mathbf{u}_*, v_*) \in W$, we need to select another pair $p_4 = (\mathbf{u}_4, v_4)$ from G and repeat the process of equation (1). Since $\prec_2$ is a local order, the process of equation (1) may not terminate, and the above theorem can not be justified.

It follows from Theorem 3.1 that any J-pair that is covered by G can be discarded without performing any reductions. As a consequence, there are three criteria used to discard superfluous J-pairs.

COROLLARY 3.2 (SYZYGY CRITERION). *For any J-pair $(\mathbf{u}, v)$ of G, it can be discarded if* $\text{lpp}(\mathbf{u})$ *is divided by* $\text{lpp}(\mathbf{w})$ *for some* $(\mathbf{w}, 0)$ *in* M.

COROLLARY 3.3 (SIGNATURE CRITERION). *Among all J-pairs with a same signature, only one (with the polynomial part minimal) needs to be stored.*

COROLLARY 3.4 (REWRITE CRITERION). *For any J-pair $(\mathbf{u}, v)$ of G, it can be discarded if $(\mathbf{u}, v)$ is covered by G.*

Before presenting the GVW algorithm in local ring, we need to make some explanations. Since storing and updating vectors $\mathbf{u} \in R^m$ are expensive, we will store $\text{lpp}(\mathbf{u})$ instead of $\mathbf{u}$ in our computation, which does not effect the correctness and termination of the algorithm. That is, for any given set $G' = \{(\mathbf{u}_1, v_1), \ldots, (\mathbf{u}_s, v_s)\} \subset M$, we will use the set $G = \{(\text{lpp}(\mathbf{u}_1), v_1), \ldots, (\text{lpp}(\mathbf{u}_s), v_s)\}$ instead of G' to compute a standard basis of $\langle f_1, \ldots, f_m \rangle \subset R$. Assume that the J-pair of $(\mathbf{u}_i, v_i)$ and $(\mathbf{u}_j, v_j)$ is $(\mathbf{u}, v)$, then the J-pair (T, v) of $(\text{lpp}(\mathbf{u}_i), v_i)$ and $(\text{lpp}(\mathbf{u}_j), v_j)$ is defined as $(\text{lpp}(\mathbf{u}), v)$, where $1 \le i \ne j \le s$. For simplicity, we use $\overline{(T, v)}^G$ to denote the remainder obtained by using G to regular top-reduce (T, v) repeatedly until it is not regular top-reducible, we will prove that this process is terminated within a finite number of steps in Section 3.2.

According to the Theorem 3.1, and the Corollary 3.2, 3.3, 3.4, the GVW algorithm in local ring is presented below.

$\diamond$: The trivial principle syzygies are used to delete the redundant J-pairs.

♣: Only storing the J-pairs whose signatures are not divided by $\{(T, 0) \mid T \in H\}$ and only storing one J-pair for each distinct signature with v-part minimal. (syzygy criterion and signature criterion)

♠: The principle syzygy is stored only when $\text{lpp}(v_j T_0 - v_0 T_j) = \max\{\text{lpp}(v_j T_0), \text{lpp}(v_0 T_j)\}$.

The correctness of the algorithm follows directly from the theorem 3.1. The algorithm can terminate if the regular top-reduction can terminate in the local ring.

3.2 Regular Top-Reduction in Local Ring

Since the local order is not a well-ordering, a sequence of successive one-step regular top-reductions may not terminate.

Algorithm 1: GVW algorithm in local ring

Input : $F = \{f_1, \ldots, f_m\} \subset k[X]$, an anti-graded order $\prec_1$ in R, and a TOP order $\prec_2$ in R^m, where $\prec_2$ is compatible with $\prec_1$.

Output: two sets V and H, where V is the set of a standard basis for $\langle f_1, \ldots, f_m \rangle \subset R$, and H is the set consisting of the leading power products of a standard basis for the syzygy of F.

begin
  Initial:
    $G := \{(\mathbf{e}_1, f_1), \ldots, (\mathbf{e}_m, f_m)\}$;
    $H := \{\text{lpp}(f_i \mathbf{e}_j - f_j \mathbf{e}_i) \mid 1 \leqslant i < j \leqslant m\}^{\diamond}$;
    $JP := \{$J-pairs of $G\}$♣;
  while $JP \neq \emptyset$ **do**
    choose $(T, v) \in JP$, and $JP := JP \setminus \{(T, v)\}$;
    if (T, v) is covered by G **then**
      next;
    else
      $(T_0, v_0) := \overline{(T, v)}^G$;
      if $v_0 = 0$ **then**
        $H := H \cup \{T_0\}$;
        $JP := JP \setminus \{(T', v') \in JP$ satisfies T_0 divides $T'\}$;
      else
        $H := H \cup \{\text{lpp}(v_0 T_j - v_j T_0) \mid (T_j, v_j) \in G\}$♠;
        $JP := JP \cup \{$J-pairs between (T_0, v_0) and $G\}$♣;
        $G := G \cup \{(T_0, v_0)\}$;
      end if
    end if
  end while
  return $V := \{v \mid (T, v) \in G\}$ and H.
end

Example 3.5. Let $p_1 = (\mathbf{u}_1, v_1) = (\mathbf{e}_1, x_1)$, $p_2 = (\mathbf{u}_2, v_2) = (\mathbf{e}_2, x_1 - x_1^2)$, $\prec_1$ is the anti-graded lexicographic order, $\prec_2$ is a TOP order and compatible with $\prec_1$, where $\mathbf{e}_2 \prec_2 \mathbf{e}_1$.

Since $\text{lpp}(v_2) = \text{lpp}(v_1) = x_1$ and $\text{lpp}(\mathbf{u}_2) = \mathbf{e}_2 \prec_2 \text{lpp}(\mathbf{u}_1) = \mathbf{e}_1$, p_1 is regular top-reducible by p_2. Then we have

$$p_3 = (\mathbf{u}_3, v_3) = \text{OneRed}(p_1, p_2) = (\mathbf{e}_1 - \mathbf{e}_2, x_1^2).$$

Similarly, $x_1 \text{lpp}(v_2) = \text{lpp}(v_3)$ and $x_1 \text{lpp}(\mathbf{u}_2) = x_1 \mathbf{e}_2 \prec_2 \text{lpp}(\mathbf{u}_3) = \mathbf{e}_1$ imply that p_3 is still regular top-reducible by p_2:

$$p_4 = \text{OneRed}(p_3, p_2) = (\mathbf{e}_1 - (1 + x_1)\mathbf{e}_2, x_1^3).$$

Continue the regular top-reduction steps, we have:

$p_5 = \text{OneRed}(p_4, p_2) = (\mathbf{e}_1 - (1 + x_1 + x_1^2)\mathbf{e}_2, x_1^4)$;

$p_6 = \text{OneRed}(p_5, p_2) = (\mathbf{e}_1 - (1 + x_1 + x_1^2 + x_1^3)\mathbf{e}_2, x_1^5)$;

$p_7 = \text{OneRed}(p_6, p_2) = (\mathbf{e}_1 - (1 + x_1 + x_1^2 + x_1^3 + x_1^4)\mathbf{e}_2, x_1^6)$;

...

The above example shows that the top-reduction steps may not terminate in the local ring, if we use the usual division algorithm in the polynomial ring [7]. Thanks to the splendid idea of Mora, the termination problem can be solved by the Mora Normal Form Algorithm [6]. The notation écart will be used in the algorithm. Let

$f \in k[X]$, the écart of f is

$$ecart(f) = \deg(f) - \deg(\mathrm{lpp}(f)),$$

where $\deg(f)$ is the total degree of f. For an element $p = (\mathbf{u}, f)$ in $(k[X])^m \times k[X]$, we define the écart of p is equal to $ecart(f)$.

Theorem 3.6. *Assume $\prec_1, \prec_2$ be the semigroup orders on the monomials in the ring $k[X]$ and $(k[X])^m$ respectively, where $\prec_1$ is a local order and $\prec_2$ is compatible with $\prec_1$. Let $p = (\mathbf{u}, f)$ be a J-pair of $G = \{p_1 = (\mathbf{u}_1, f_1), \ldots, p_s = (\mathbf{u}_s, f_s)\} \subset (k[X])^m \times k[X]$ and p is not covered by G. Then there is an algorithm for producing polynomials $h, a_1, \ldots, a_s$ in $k[X]$ and $r = (\mathbf{w}, v)$ in $(k[X])^m \times k[X]$ such that*

$$hp = a_1 p_1 + \cdots + a_s p_s + r, \tag{2}$$

where $\mathrm{lpp}(h) = 1$ (so h is a unit in R), $\mathrm{lpp}(a_i f_i) \preceq_1 \mathrm{lpp}(f)$, $\mathrm{lpp}(a_i \mathbf{u}_i) \preceq_2 \mathrm{lpp}(\mathbf{u})$ for all i with $a_i \neq 0$, $\mathrm{lpp}(\mathbf{w}) = \mathrm{lpp}(\mathbf{u})$, and either $v = 0$ or $\mathrm{lpp}(v)$ is not divisible by any $\mathrm{lpp}(f_i)$. The r is called the remainder of p regular top-reduced by G.

Proof. Since $p = (\mathbf{u}, f)$ is a J-pair of G, there exists a pair $p_i = (\mathbf{u}_i, f_i) \in G$ such that p is regular top-reducible by p_i. Let $r_0 := (\mathbf{w}_0, v_0) = p - c_i^{(0)} t_i^{(0)} p_i$, where $c_i^{(0)} = \mathrm{lc}(f)/\mathrm{lc}(f_i)$ and $t_i^{(0)} = \mathrm{lpp}(f)/\mathrm{lpp}(f_i)$, then $\mathrm{lpp}(v_0) \prec_1 \mathrm{lpp}(f)$ and $\mathrm{lpp}(\mathbf{w}_0) = \mathrm{lpp}(\mathbf{u})$. If r_0 can be expressed as $hr_0 = a_1p_1 + \cdots + a_sp_s + r$, then the equation (2) holds for $(\mathbf{u}, f)$. We give a constructive proof by the following algorithm, which is similar to the algorithm in page 173 of [6].

Input: $r_0 = (\mathbf{w}_0, v_0), p_1 = (\mathbf{u}_1, f_1), \ldots, p_s = (\mathbf{u}_s, f_s)$;
Output: r as statement of theorem 3.6.
Initial: $r := (\mathbf{w}, v)$; $\mathbf{w} := \mathbf{w}_0$; $v := v_0$; $L := \{p_1, \ldots, p_s\}$;
    $M := \{g \in L : r$ is regular top-reducible by $g\}$.
WHILE ($v \neq 0$ AND $M \neq \emptyset$) THEN
  SELECT $g \in M$ with ecart(g) minimal;
  IF ecart(g) > ecart(r) THEN
    $L := L \cup \{r\}$;
  END IF;
  $r :=$ OneRed(r, g);
  IF $v \neq 0$ THEN
    $M := \{g \in L : r$ is regular top-reducible by $g\}$;
  END IF;
END DO.

To prove the correctness, we will prove by induction on $j \geq 0$ that we have identities of the form

$$h_j r_0 = a_1^{(j)} p_1 + \cdots + a_s^{(j)} p_s + r_j, \tag{3}$$

where $\mathrm{lpp}(h_j) = 1$, $\mathrm{lpp}(a_i^{(j)} f_i) \preceq_1 \mathrm{lpp}(v_0)$, $\mathrm{lpp}(a_i^{(j)} \mathbf{u}_i) \preceq_2 \mathrm{lpp}(\mathbf{w}_0)$, and $\mathrm{lpp}(\mathbf{w}_j) = \mathrm{lpp}(\mathbf{w}_0)$. Setting $h_0 = 1$ and $a_i^{(0)} = 0$ for all i shows that everything works for $j = 0$. Now suppose that in the first $l - 1$ steps, the equation (3) is satisfied, where $l \geq 1$. Then we need to prove that $r_l = (\mathbf{w}_l, v_l)$ produced by the l-th pass through the loop satisfies the above conditions.

If $v_{l-1} \neq 0$ and $M_{l-1} \neq \emptyset$, in the step l, there is $g_l = (\mathbf{s}_l, b_l) \in M_{l-1}$ such that r_{l-1} is regular top-reducible by g_l. Then

$$r_l = \mathrm{OneRed}(r_{l-1}, g_l) = r_{l-1} - c_l t_l g_l, \tag{4}$$

where $t_l = \mathrm{lpp}(v_{l-1})/\mathrm{lpp}(b_l)$, $c_l = \mathrm{lc}(v_{l-1})/\mathrm{lc}(b_l)$ and $\mathrm{lpp}(\mathbf{w}_l) = \mathrm{lpp}(\mathbf{w}_{l-1})$. For g_l, there are two cases:

($\star$) $g_l = p_i \in \{p_1, \ldots, p_s\}$;
($\star\star$) $g_l = r_n \in \{r_0, r_1, \ldots, r_{l-2}\}$.

In case ($\star$), substituting $r_{l-1} = c_l t_l p_i + r_l$ to the right-side of equation (3) for $j = l - 1$, we have

$$h_{l-1} r_0 = a_1^{(l-1)} p_1 + \cdots + a_s^{(l-1)} p_s + c_l t_l p_i + r_l.$$

Setting $h_l := h_{l-1}$, $a_i^{(l)} := a_i^{(l-1)} + c_l t_l$ and $a_k^{(l)} := a_k^{(l-1)}$ for $k \in \{1, \ldots, s\} \setminus \{i\}$, the equation (3) holds for $j = l$.

In case ($\star\star$), $g_l = r_n = h_n r_0 - \sum_{i=1}^{s} a_i^{(n)} p_i$ and $\mathrm{lpp}(b_l) \succ_1 \mathrm{lpp}(v_{l-1})$, where $n \in \{0, \ldots, l-2\}$. Substituting g_l to the right-hand side of (4), we have $r_{l-1} = c_l t_l (h_n r_0 - \sum_{i=1}^{s} a_i^{(n)} p_i) + r_l$. Substituting r_{l-1} to the right-hand side of (3) for $j = l - 1$, we have

$$h_{l-1} r_0 = a_1^{(l-1)} p_1 + \cdots + a_s^{(l-1)} p_s + c_l t_l (h_n r_0 - \sum_{i=1}^{s} a_i^{(n)} p_i) + r_l,$$

i.e., $(h_{l-1} - c_l t_l h_n) r_0 = \sum_{i=1}^{s} (a_i^{(l-1)} - c_l t_l a_i^{(n)}) p_i + r_l$. Setting $h_l := h_{l-1} - c_l t_l h_n$ and $a_i^{(l)} := a_i^{(l-1)} - c_l t_l a_i^{(n)}$. $\mathrm{lpp}(b_l) \succ_1 \mathrm{lpp}(v_{l-1})$ implies that $\mathrm{lpp}(c_l t_l) = \mathrm{lpp}(v_{l-1})/\mathrm{lpp}(b_l) \neq 1$. Since $\prec_1$ is a local order, $1 = \mathrm{lpp}(h_{l-1}) \succ_1 \mathrm{lpp}(c_l t_l h_n)$, where $\mathrm{lpp}(h_n) = 1$. Therefore, $\mathrm{lpp}(h_l) = \mathrm{lpp}(h_{l-1} - c_l t_l h_n) = 1$, and the equation (3) also holds for $j = l$.

If the algorithm terminates after N steps, then $h := h_N$, $a_i := a_i^{(N)}$ and $r := r_N$ satisfy the conditions in Theorem 3.6, so the algorithm is correct.

To prove the termination, the order $\prec_1$ extends to a semigroup order $\prec'$ on monomials in $t, x_1, \ldots, x_n$ in the following way. Define $t^a X^\alpha \prec' t^b X^\beta$, if either $a + |\alpha| < b + |\beta|$, or $a + |\alpha| = b + |\beta|$ and $X^\alpha \prec_1 X^\beta$. The order $\prec'$ is a global order. Let f^H denote the homogenization of f with respect to a new variable t. For any $f \in k[X]$, we have $\mathrm{lpp}_{\prec'}(f^H) = t^{ecart(f)} \mathrm{lpp}_{\prec_1}(f)$. For any $r = (\mathbf{w}, v) \in (k[X])^m \times k[X]$, the homogenization of r is defined by $r^H = (t^{ecart(v)} \mathbf{w}, v^H)$. And for any pairs $r_1 = (\mathbf{w}_1, v_1), r_2 = (\mathbf{w}_2, v_2)$, we say that r_1 *divides* r_2 if $\mathrm{lpp}(\mathbf{w}_1) \mid \mathrm{lpp}(\mathbf{w}_2)$ and $\mathrm{lpp}(v_1) \mid \mathrm{lpp}(v_2)$.

Let IniHom(L) $= \{(t^{ecart(v)} \mathrm{lpp}(\mathbf{w}), \mathrm{lpp}_{\prec'}(v^H)) : (\mathbf{w}, v) \in L\}$, we claim that if $r_{l-1} = (\mathbf{w}_{l-1}, v_{l-1})$ is added to the set L_l in the step l, the $(t^{ecart(v_{l-1})} \mathrm{lpp}(\mathbf{w}_{l-1}), \mathrm{lpp}_{\prec'}(v_{l-1}^H))$ is not divisible by any element in IniHom(L_{l-1}). We prove it by contradiction. Assume that $(t^{ecart(v_{l-1})} \mathrm{lpp}(\mathbf{w}_{l-1}), \mathrm{lpp}_{\prec'}(v_{l-1}^H))$ is divisible by some element in IniHom(L_{l-1}), then there exists $g = (\mathbf{s}, b) \in L_{l-1}$ such that

$$\begin{cases} t^{ecart(b)} \mathrm{lpp}(\mathbf{s}) \mid t^{ecart(v_{l-1})} \mathrm{lpp}(\mathbf{w}_{l-1}), \\ \mathrm{lpp}_{\prec'}(b^H) \mid \mathrm{lpp}_{\prec'}(v_{l-1}^H). \end{cases}$$

Therefore, $\mathrm{lpp}(\mathbf{s}) \mid \mathrm{lpp}(\mathbf{w}_{l-1})$, $\mathrm{lpp}(b) \mid \mathrm{lpp}(v_{l-1})$ and $ecart(b) \leqslant ecart(v_{l-1})$. Let $\mathrm{lpp}(v_{l-1}) = X^\alpha \mathrm{lpp}(b)$ and $\mathrm{lpp}(\mathbf{w}_{l-1}) = X^\beta \mathrm{lpp}(\mathbf{s})$. For g, there are two cases:

- $g \in L_{l-1} \backslash G \subset \{r_0, r_1, \ldots, r_{l-2}\}$;
- $g \in G$.

If $g \in L_{l-1} \backslash G$, then $\mathrm{lpp}(\mathbf{s}) = \mathrm{lpp}(\mathbf{w}_{l-1}) = \mathrm{lpp}(\mathbf{w}_0)$ and $\mathrm{lpp}(v_{l-1}) \neq \mathrm{lpp}(b)$. Then $X^\alpha \prec_1 X^\beta$ since $\prec_1$ is a local order, $X^\alpha \neq 1$ and $X^\beta = 1$. We have:

$$\frac{\mathrm{lpp}(v_{l-1})}{\mathrm{lpp}(b)} \mathrm{lpp}(\mathbf{s}) = X^\alpha \mathrm{lpp}(\mathbf{s}) \prec_2 X^\beta \mathrm{lpp}(\mathbf{s}) = \mathrm{lpp}(\mathbf{w}_{l-1}),$$

and $\text{lpp}(b) \mid \text{lpp}(v_{l-1})$, so r_{l-1} is regular top-reducible by g and $g \in M_{l-1}$. But $ecart(g) \leqslant ecart(r_{l-1})$, this contradicts that r_{l-1} is added to L_l only when $ecart(r_{l-1}) < ecart(g')$ for any $g' \in M_{l-1}$.

If $g \in G$ and $X^\alpha \prec_1 X^\beta$, it is contradictory by the same analysis as above. If $g \in G$ and $X^\alpha \succeq_1 X^\beta$, then

$$X^\beta \text{lpp}(b) \preceq_1 X^\alpha \text{lpp}(b) = \text{lpp}(v_{l-1}) \preceq_1 \text{lpp}(v_0) \prec_1 \text{lpp}(f),$$

and $\text{lpp}(\mathbf{s})|\text{lpp}(\mathbf{w}_{l-1}) = \text{lpp}(\mathbf{w}_0) = \text{lpp}(\mathbf{u})$. This contradicts that $p = (\mathbf{u}, f)$ is not cover by G.

Above all, $(t^{ecart(v_{l-1})}\text{lpp}(\mathbf{w}_{l-1}), \text{lpp}_{\succ'}(v_{l-1}^H))$ is not divisible by $\text{IniHom}(L_{l-1})$. Therefore, we have a sequence $r_{j_1}, r_{j_2}, \ldots, r_{j_i}, \ldots \in L$, which corresponds to a sequence

$$\begin{aligned}&(t^{ecart(v_{j_1})}\text{lpp}(\mathbf{w}_{j_1}), \text{lpp}(v_{j_1}^H)), (t^{ecart(v_{j_2})}\text{lpp}(\mathbf{w}_{j_2}),\\ &\text{lpp}(v_{j_2}^H)), \ldots, (t^{ecart(v_{j_i})}\text{lpp}(\mathbf{w}_{j_i}), \text{lpp}(v_{j_i}^H)), \ldots\end{aligned} \tag{5}$$

with no pair divisible by any previous one.

We introduce new variables $\vec{y}_i = (y_{i_0}, y_{i_1}, \ldots, y_{i_n})$. Each pair $(t^a X^\alpha \mathbf{e}_i, t^a X^\beta)$ corresponds to a term $\vec{y}_i^{(a,\alpha)} t^a X^\beta$ in the variables x_i, t, y_{i_j} (this idea is similar to that on Page 4 of the paper [10]), where $i = 1, \ldots, n, j = 0, \ldots, n$. Then the pairs in (5) give us a list of monomials in $x_i, t, y_{i_j}, i = 1, \ldots, n, j = 0, \ldots, n$ with no one divisible by any previous one. Since every polynomial ring over a field is Noetherian, the list of monomials must be finite. So there is some N such that $L_N = L_{N+1} = L_{N+2} = \cdots$. Then the algorithm continues with a fixed set of L. For $m \geqslant N$, since any regular top-reduction of r_m by L_m corresponds to a regular top-reduction of r_m^H by $L_m^H = L_N^H$, the reduction must terminate after finite steps. □

Example 3.7 (Continue Example 3.5). The J-pair of p_1 and p_2 is $p = (\mathbf{u}, v) = (\mathbf{e}_1, x_1)$, which is not covered by p_1 and p_2. We start the division algorithm with $r_0 := p - p_2 = (\mathbf{e}_1 - \mathbf{e}_2, x_1^2)$, and $L_0 = \{p_1, p_2\}$. Since r_0 is regular top-reducible by p_1 and p_2, $M_0 = \{p_1, p_2\}$. In the step 1, p_1 is chosen to reduce r_0 since $ecart(p_1) = 0 < 1 = ecart(p_2)$. $r_1 := OneRed(r_0, p_1) = r_0 - x_1 p_1 = ((1 - x_1)\mathbf{e}_1 - \mathbf{e}_2, 0)$. The division algorithm terminates, and $p = x_1 p_1 + p_2 + ((1 - x_1)\mathbf{e}_1 - \mathbf{e}_2, 0)$.

4 AN ILLUSTRATIVE EXAMPLE

The following is an example to illustrate our algorithm in local ring.

Example 4.1. Let $R = \text{Loc}_{\prec_1}(\mathbb{C}[x_1, x_2, x_3])$, and $I = \langle f_1, f_2, f_3 \rangle = \langle x_1^2 - 5x_2x_3 - 2x_2^2x_3, 2x_1x_2 + 2x_2^3 - x_3^3, -x_1x_2 + x_2x_3^2 \rangle \subset R$, where $\prec_1$ is the anti-graded revlex order with $x_1 \succ_1 x_2 \succ_1 x_3$. Suppose $\prec_2$ is a TOP order in R^3 and compatible with $\prec_1$, where $\mathbf{e}_1 \succ_2 \mathbf{e}_2 \succ_2 \mathbf{e}_3$. Computing a standard basis for I and the leading power products of a standard basis for the syzygy module of $\{f_1, f_2, f_3\}$.

Initial:
$G_0 := \{p_1, p_2, p_3\} = \{(\mathbf{e}_1, f_1), (\mathbf{e}_2, f_2), (\mathbf{e}_3, f_3)\}$;
$H_0 := \{x_1^2\mathbf{e}_2, x_1^2\mathbf{e}_3, x_1x_2\mathbf{e}_2\}$ is the set of the leading power products of principle syzygies $\{\mathbf{e}_1 f_2 - \mathbf{e}_2 f_1, \mathbf{e}_1 f_3 - \mathbf{e}_3 f_1, \mathbf{e}_2 f_3 - \mathbf{e}_3 f_2\}$;
$JP_0 := \{(T_1, v_1), (T_2, v_2), (T_3, v_3)\} = \{(x_1\mathbf{e}_3, x_1 f_3), (x_1\mathbf{e}_2, x_1 f_2), (\mathbf{e}_2, f_2)\}$ is the J-pairs set of G_0.
First cycle:
We select the J-pair (T_1, v_1) from JP_0 and use G_0 to reduce it. By computing, (T_1, v_1) is not covered by G_0. So (T_1, v_1) can be regular top-reducible by G_0 to $p_4 = (T_1, \tilde{v}_1) = (x_1\mathbf{e}_3, -5x_2^2x_3 + x_1x_2x_3^2 - 2x_2^3x_3)$. Since $\tilde{v}_1 \neq 0$, computing the principle syzygies of p_4 with G_0, and adding the leading power product of these syzygies to H_0 (delete any redundant ones), we obtain $H_1 := H_0$. Computing the J-pairs of p_4 with elements in G_0 and getting $JP_1 := \{(T_2, v_2), (T_3, v_3)\}$. Moreover, $G_1 := G_0 \cup \{p_4\}$.
Second cycle:
We select (T_2, v_2) from JP_1 and $JP_2 := \{(T_3, v_3)\}$. (T_2, v_2) can be regular top-reducible by G_1 to $p_5 = (T_2, \tilde{v}_2) = (x_1\mathbf{e}_2, -x_1x_3^3 + 2x_2^3x_3^2 + 2x_2x_3^4)$. According to syzygy criterion and signature criterion, we obtain $H_2 := H_0$, $JP_2 := \{(T_3, v_3)\}$ and $G_2 := G_1 \cup \{p_5\}$.
Third cycle:
We select (T_3, v_3) from JP_2 and $JP_3 := \emptyset$. (T_3, v_3) can be regular top-reducible by G_2 to $p_6 = (T_3, \tilde{v}_3) = (\mathbf{e}_2, 2x_2^3 + 2x_2x_3^2 - x_3^3)$. According to syzygy criterion and signature criterion, we obtain $H_3 := H_0 \cup \{x_2^2x_3\mathbf{e}_2\}$, $JP_3 := \{(T_4, v_4), (T_5, v_5)\}$ and $G_3 := G_2 \cup \{p_6\}$, where $(T_4, v_4) = (x_3\mathbf{e}_2, x_3\tilde{v}_3)$ and $(T_5, v_5) = (x_1\mathbf{e}_2, x_1\tilde{v}_3)$.
Fourth cycle:
We select (T_4, v_4) from JP_3 and $JP_4 := \{(T_5, v_5)\}$. (T_4, v_4) can be regular top-reducible by G_3 to $p_7 = (T_4, \tilde{v}_4) = (x_3\mathbf{e}_2, 2x_2x_3^3 - x_3^4 + \frac{2}{5}x_1x_2^2x_3^2 - \frac{4}{5}x_2^4x_3)$. According to syzygy criterion and signature criterion, we obtain $H_4 := H_3$, $JP_4 := \{(T_6, v_6), (T_7, v_7), (T_5, v_5)\}$ and $G_4 := G_3 \cup \{p_7\}$, where $(T_6, v_6) = (x_2x_3\mathbf{e}_2, x_2\tilde{v}_4)$ and $(T_7, v_7) = (x_1x_3\mathbf{e}_2, x_1\tilde{v}_4)$.
Fifth cycle:
We select (T_6, v_6) from JP_4 and $JP_5 := \{(T_7, v_7), (T_5, v_5)\}$. (T_6, v_6) can be regular top-reducible by G_4 to $p_8 = (T_6, \tilde{v}_6) = (x_2x_3\mathbf{e}_2, (-\frac{1}{2}x_3^5 - \frac{4}{5}x_2^5x_3 + \frac{2}{5}x_1x_2^3x_3^2 - \frac{2}{5}x_2^4x_3^2 + \frac{1}{5}x_1x_2^2x_3^2 - \frac{4}{5}x_2^3x_3^3 + \frac{2}{5}x_1x_2x_3^4)$. According to syzygy criterion and signature criterion, we obtain $H_5 := H_4$, $JP_5 := \{(T_7, v_7), (T_5, v_5)\}$ and $G_5 := G_4 \cup \{p_8\}$.
Sixth cycle:
We select (T_7, v_7) from JP_5 and $JP_6 := \{(T_5, v_5)\}$. By computing, (T_7, v_7) is covered by G_5. According to rewrite criterion, we get $H_6 := H_5$, $JP_6 := \{(T_5, v_5)\}$ and $G_6 := G_5$.
Seventh cycle:
We select (T_5, v_5) from JP_6 and $JP_7 := \emptyset$. By computing, (T_5, v_5) is covered by G_6. According to rewrite criterion, we get $H_7 := H_7$, $JP_7 := \emptyset$ and $G_7 := G_6$.
Output:
Since JP_7 is empty, the algorithm terminates. Therefore, the standard basis of I in R is $\{f_1, f_2, f_3, \tilde{v}_1, \tilde{v}_2, \tilde{v}_3, \tilde{v}_4, \tilde{v}_6\}$, and the leading power products of the standard basis for the syzygy module is $\{x_1^2\mathbf{e}_2, x_1^2\mathbf{e}_3, x_1x_2\mathbf{e}_2, x_2^2x_3\mathbf{e}_2\}$.

It is apparent from the above example that we discard 23 J-pairs by using three criteria, and only do 5 regular top-reductions. In order to illustrate that the three criteria can improve the computational efficiency, we compare our algorithm with a classical Gröbner basis algorithm (non signature-based) [19] that uses standard criteria to discard useless S-polynomials. We randomly generate 10 ideals in $R = \text{Loc}_{\prec_1}(\mathbb{C}[x_1, x_2, x_3, x_4])$, and they are as follows.

- $I_1 = \langle -x_1^3 + x_3^3, -x_1x_3x_4 + x_2^2x_3, x_1^2x_4 - x_3x_4^2, x_2^2x_4 + x_2x_4 \rangle$;
- $I_2 = \langle x_1x_4^2, x_1^3 - x_3^2x_4 - x_4^3, x_1^2x_4 - x_2^2, -x_2^2x_3 - x_1x_2 \rangle$;
- $I_3 = \langle -x_1x_2^2, x_1^2x_3x_4 + x_1x_3, x_2^4 - x_1x_3 + x_4, x_3^4 + x_1x_2^2 + x_1 \rangle$;
- $I_4 = \langle x_1x_2^3 - x_1^2x_4, x_3^4 + x_3^3x_4, -x_3, -x_1^2x_2^2 - x_1x_4^2 - x_2x_4^2 \rangle$;
- $I_5 = \langle x_2x_3x_4 - 3x_2x_4^2 - 4x_2x_3, -4x_1^2x_3x_4 - 4x_2^3, -5x_4^2, -4x_1^2x_4^2 + 2x_3^3x_4 - 3x_1x_2x_4 \rangle$.

- $I_6 = \langle 8x_1^2x_3x_4 - 7x_1x_3^3 + 8x_3x_4, x_1x_2^2 - 6x_1x_3^2 - 7x_4, -5x_2^4 + 2x_1x_2x_4\rangle$;
- $I_7 = \langle 5x_1^2x_2^2 - 3x_1x_2x_3^2 + x_1^2x_2, 3x_2x_3^3 + 2x_3^2x_4^2 + x_3x_4^3, 5x_1^4 - x_1x_2x_3^2 - 7x_2x_4^2\rangle$.
- $I_8 = \langle -6x_4^3 - x_1x_3 + 7x_4^2, -x_2^4 + 4x_1x_2x_3 + 4x_3x_4, 2x_1x_3^2x_4 - 3x_1x_3x_4^2 + 7x_2^2x_4^2\rangle$.
- $I_9 = \langle -x_2^3x_3 + 6x_2^2x_4^2 - 4x_1x_2x_4, 2x_1^3x_4 - 4x_2x_3x_4 + 2x_3, 6x_1x_3^2 + 4x_1x_2^2x_4 + 3x_1x_4^2\rangle$.
- $I_{10} = \langle 3x_1x_4^2 + 7x_2^3 + 4x_2x_3^2, 5x_1x_3 - 10x_1x_4 - 5x_3^2, -8x_1x_2 + 3x_3^2 + 4x_2^2x_4\rangle$.

For all these examples, the term order in R and R^m ($3 \le m \le 4$) is anti-graded revlex order and TOP order, respectively. We implement the two algorithms on the computer algebra system *Maple*, and the codes and examples are available on the web: http://www.mmrc.iss.ac.cn/~dwang/software.html.

Table 1: examples

ideal	signature-based method			classical method		
	J-pairs	discard	ratio	S-polys	discard	ratio
I_1	21	14	67%	28	6	21%
I_2	21	14	67%	21	9	43%
I_3	15	12	80%	15	8	53%
I_4	20	16	80%	21	10	48%
I_5	15	9	60%	15	4	27%
I_6	20	16	80%	21	6	29%
I_7	14	11	79%	15	4	27%
I_8	35	29	83%	28	9	32%
I_9	10	7	70%	15	6	40%
I_{10}	21	17	81%	66	28	43%

The second column and fifth column in Table 1 represents the total number of J-pairs and S-polynomials (abbreviated S-polys) generated during the calculation, respectively. The third column (sixth column) represents the useless J-pairs (useless S-polys) that are discarded. The fourth column (last column) shows the percentage of the number of discarded J-pairs (S-polys) to the number of the total J-pairs (S-polys). Experimental data in Table 1 suggests that the proposed algorithm is superior in practice in comparison with the classical Gröbner basis algorithm.

5 CONCLUDING REMARKS

The paper proposed an efficient algorithm to compute the standard bases in local ring. In the process of extending the GVW algorithm from polynomial ring to local ring, we solved two key problems. First, an infinite set has not a minimal element in local ring. Under the situation that $\prec_1$ is an anti-graded order in $k[X]$ and $\prec_2$ is a TOP order in $(k[X])^m$, we proved that the signature set $L(\text{lpp}(v_0))$ w.r.t. v_0 has a minimal element. Then we generalized the cover theorem to local ring to discard the useless J-pairs. Second, since the general division algorithm may not terminate in local ring, Mora normal form algorithm is used to do regular top-reduction, and the proposed algorithm terminates in finite steps.

Although we only consider the case that $\prec_2$ is a TOP order in $(k[X])^m$, if $\prec_2$ is an f-weighted anti-degree followed by TOP or an f-weighted $\prec_1$ followed by POT, Lemma 2.9 and Theorem 3.1 are also established. Moreover, an alternative method to compute the standard bases is using the Lazard's homogeneous idea. In the future work, we will consider the case of $\prec_1$ is not an anti-graded order in $k[X]$. We hope that the results of this paper will motivate new progress in this research topic.

ACKNOWLEDGMENTS

This research was supported in part by the National Natural Science Foundation of China under Grant No. 11371356 and CAS Project QYZDJ-SSW-SYS022. The authors would like to thank anonymous referees for detailed suggestions on the paper which have made it more readable.

REFERENCES

[1] A. Arri and J. Perry. 2011. The F5 criterion revised. *Journal of Symbolic Computation* 46, 9 (2011), 1017–1029.

[2] G. Ars and A. Hashemi. 2010. Extended F5 criteria. *Journal of Symbolic Computation* 45 (2010), 1330–1340.

[3] B. Buchberger. 1965. *Ein Algorithmus zum Auffinden der Basiselemente des Restklassenrings nach einem nulldimensionalen Polynomideal.* Ph.D. Dissertation.

[4] B. Buchberger. 1979. A criterion for detecting unnecessary reductions in the construction of Gröbner-bases. In *Symbolic and Algebraic Computation.* Springer, 3–21.

[5] B. Buchberger. 1985. Grobner bases: an algorithmic method in polynomial ideal theory. *Multidimensional systems theory* (1985), 184–232.

[6] D. Cox, J. Little, and D. O'shea. 2005. *Using Algebraic Geometry.* Springer.

[7] D. Cox, J. Little, and D. O'shea. 2007. *Ideals, Varieties, and Algorithms: An Introduction to Computational Algebraic Geometry and Commutative Algebra.* Springer.

[8] C. Eder and J.-C. Faugère. 2017. A survey on signature-based Gröbner basis computations. *Journal of Symbolic Computation* 80 (2017), 719–784.

[9] C. Eder and J. Perry. 2010. F5C: a variant of Faugère's F5 algorithm with reduced Gröbner bases. *Journal of Symbolic Computation* 45, 12 (2010), 1442–1458.

[10] C. Eder and J. Perry. 2011. Signature-based algorithms to compute Gröbner bases. In *Proceedings of the 2011 international symposium on Symbolic and algebraic computation.* ACM, 99–106.

[11] C. Eder, G. Pfister, and A. Popescu. 2017. On Signature-based Gröbner bases over Euclidean Rings. In *Proceedings of the 2017 International Symposium on Symbolic and Algebraic Computation.* ACM, 141–148.

[12] J.-C. Faugère. 1999. A new efficient algorithm for computing Gröbner bases (F4). *Journal of pure and applied algebra* 139, 1 (1999), 61–88.

[13] J.-C. Faugère. 2002. A new efficient algorithm for computing Gröbner bases without reduction to zero (F5). In *Proceedings of the 2002 international symposium on Symbolic and algebraic computation.* ACM, 75–83.

[14] S.H. Gao, Y. Guan, and F. Volny IV. 2010. A new incremental algorithm for computing Gröbner bases. In *Proceedings of the 2010 International Symposium on Symbolic and Algebraic Computation.* ACM, 13–19.

[15] S.H. Gao, F. Volny IV, and M.S. Wang. 2016. A new framework for computing Gröbner bases. *Math. Comp.* 85, 297 (2016), 449–465.

[16] R. Gebauer and H.M. Möller. 1986. Buchberger's algorithm and staggered linear bases. In *Proceedings of the 5th ACM symposium on Symbolic and algebraic computation.* ACM, 218–221.

[17] V.-P. Gerdt, A. Hashemi, and B. M.-Alizadeh. 2013. Involutive Bases Algorithm Incorporating F5 Criterion. *Journal of Symbolic Computation* 59 (2013), 1–20.

[18] A. Giovini, T. Mora, G. Niesi, L. Robbiano, and C. Traverso. 1991. "One sugar cube, please" or selection strategies in the Buchberger algorithm. In *Proceedings of the 1991 international symposium on Symbolic and algebraic computation.* ACM, 49–54.

[19] G.M. Greuel and G. Pfister. 2002. *A Singular Introduction to Commutative Algebra.* Springer-Verlag Berlin Heidelberg.

[20] D. Lazard. 1983. Gröbner bases, Gaussian elimination and resolution of systems of algebraic equations. In *Computer algebra.* Springer, 146–156.

[21] H.M. Möller, T. Mora, and C. Traverso. 1992. Gröbner bases computation using syzygies. In *Proceedings of the 1992 international symposium on Symbolic and algebraic computation.* ACM, 320–328.

[22] T. Mora, G. Pfister, and C. Traverso. 1992. An introduction to the tangent cone algorithm. *Issues in non-linear geometry and robotics, CM Hoffman ed* (1992).

[23] Y. Sun and D.K. Wang. 2011. The F5 algorithm in Buchberger's style. *Journal of Systems Science and Complexity* 24, 6 (2011), 1218–1231.

[24] Y. Sun and D.K. Wang. 2011. A generalized criterion for signature related Gröbner basis algorithms. In *Proceedings of the 2011 international symposium on Symbolic and algebraic computation.* ACM, 337–344.

On Exact Polya and Putinar's Representations

Victor Magron
CNRS Verimag, Sorbonne Université, INRIA,
Laboratoire d'Informatique de Paris 6, LIP6, Équipe PolSys
F-75252, Paris Cedex 05, France
victor.magron@polsys.lip6.fr

Mohab Safey El Din
Sorbonne Université, CNRS, INRIA,
Laboratoire d'Informatique de Paris 6, LIP6, Équipe PolSys
F-75252, Paris Cedex 05, France
mohab.safey@lip6.fr

ABSTRACT

We consider the problem of finding exact sums of squares (SOS) decompositions for certain classes of non-negative multivariate polynomials, relying on semidefinite programming (SDP) solvers. We start by providing a hybrid numeric-symbolic algorithm computing exact rational SOS decompositions for polynomials lying in the interior of the SOS cone. It computes an approximate SOS decomposition for a perturbation of the input polynomial with an arbitrary-precision SDP solver. An exact SOS decomposition is obtained thanks to the perturbation terms. We prove that bit complexity estimates on output size and runtime are both polynomial in the degree of the input polynomial and simply exponential in the number of variables. Next, we apply this algorithm to compute exact Polya and Putinar's representations respectively for positive definite forms and positive polynomials over basic compact semi-algebraic sets. We also compare the implementation of our algorithms with existing methods in computer algebra including cylindrical algebraic decomposition and critical point method.

KEYWORDS

Semidefinite programming, sums of squares decomposition, Polya's representation, Putinar's representation, hybrid numeric-symbolic algorithm, real algebraic geometry.

ACM Reference Format:

Victor Magron and Mohab Safey El Din. 2018. On Exact Polya and Putinar's Representations. In *ISSAC '18: 2018 ACM International Symposium on Symbolic and Algebraic Computation, July 16–19, 2018, New York, NY, USA.* ACM, New York, NY, USA, 8 pages. https://doi.org/10.1145/3208976.3208986

1 INTRODUCTION

Let $\mathbb{Q}$ (resp. $\mathbb{R}$) be the field of rational (resp. real) numbers and $X = (X_1, \ldots, X_n)$ be a sequence of variables. We consider the problem of deciding the non-negativity of $f \in \mathbb{Q}[X]$ either over $\mathbb{R}^n$ or over a semi-algebraic set S defined by some constraints $g_1 \geq 0, \ldots, g_m \geq 0$ (with $g_j \in \mathbb{Q}[X]$). Further, d denotes the maximum of the total degrees of these polynomials.

This problem is known to be co-NP hard [10]. The Cylindrical Algebraic Decomposition algorithm [13] allows to solve it in time doubly exponential in n (and polynomial in d). This complexity result has been improved later on, through the so-called critical point method, starting from [17] which culminates with [8] to establish that this decision problem can be solved in time $((m+1)d)^{O(n)}$. These latter ones have been developed to obtain implementations which reflect the complexity gain (see e.g. [3–6, 15, 16, 19, 39, 40]) but still within a singly exponential complexity in n. Besides, these algorithms are "root finding" ones: they try to find a point at which f is negative over the considered domain. When f is positive, they return an empty list without a *certificate* that can be checked *a posteriori*.

To compute certificates of non-negativity, an approach based on *sums of squares* (SOS) decompositions (and their variants) has been popularized by Lasserre [25] and Parillo [32] (see also the survey [26] and references therein). In a nutshell, the idea is as follows. A polynomial f is non-negative over $\mathbb{R}^n$ if it can be written as an SOS $s_1^2 + \cdots + s_r^2$ with $s_i \in \mathbb{R}[X]$ for $1 \leq i \leq r$. Also f is non-negative over the semi-algebraic set S if it can be written as $s_1^2 + \cdots + s_r^2 + \sum_{j=1}^m \sigma_j g_j$ where σ_i is a sum of squares in $\mathbb{R}[X]$ for $1 \leq j \leq m$. It turns out that, thanks to the "Gram matrix method" (see e.g. [12, 25, 32]), computing such decompositions can be reduced to solving Linear Matrix Inequalities (LMI). This boils down to considering a semidefinite programming (SDP) problem. For instance, on input $f \in \mathbb{Q}[X]$ of even degree $d = 2k$, the decomposition $f = s_1^2 + \cdots + s_r^2$ is a by-product of a decomposition of the form $f = v_k^T L^T D L v_k$, where v_k is the vector of all monomials of degree $\leq k$ in $\mathbb{Q}[X]$, L is a lower triangular matrix with non-negative real entries on the diagonal and D is a diagonal matrix with non-negative real entries. The matrices L and D are obtained after computing a symmetric matrix G (the Gram matrix), semidefinite positive, such that $f = v_k^T G v_k$. Such a matrix G is found using solvers for LMIs. Such inequalities can be solved symbolically (see [22]), but the degrees of the algebraic extensions needed to encode exactly the solutions are prohibitive on large examples [30]. Besides, there exist fast numerical solvers for solving LMIs implemented in double precision, e.g. SeDuMi [42], SDPA [43] as well as arbitrary-precision solvers, e.g. SDPA-GMP [29], successfully applied in many contexts, including bounds for kissing numbers [1] or computation of (real) radical ideals [23].

But using uniquely numerical solvers yields "approximate" non-negativity certificates. In our example, the matrices L and D (and consequently the polynomials $s_1, \ldots, s_r$) are not known exactly.

This raises topical questions. The first one is how to let symbolic computation interact with these numerical solvers to get *exact*

Mohab Safey El Din is supported by the ANR grant ANR-17-CE40-0009 Galop and the PGMO grant Gamma. Victor Magron is supported by the LabEx PERSYVAL-Lab and European Research Council under the European Union's Seventh Framework Programme (FP/2007-2013) / ERC Grant Agreement nr. 306595 "STATOR".

Conference ISSAC'18, July 2018, New York, NY, USA

ACM ISBN 978-1-4503-5550-6/18/07...$15.00
https://doi.org/10.1145/3208976.3208986

certificates? Since not all positive polynomials are SOS, what to do when SOS certificates do not exist? Also, given inputs with rational coefficients, can we obtain certificates with rational coefficients? For these questions, we inherit from previous contributions in the univariate case [11, 27] as well as in the multivariate case [24, 33]. Diophantine aspects are considered in [20, 41]. When an SOS decomposition exists with coefficients in a totally real Galois field, [36] provides bounds on the total number of squares. In the univariate (un)-constrained case, the algorithm from [11] computes an exact weighted SOS decomposition for a given positive polynomial $f \in \mathbb{Q}[X]$. The algorithm considers a perturbation of f, performs (complex) root isolation to get an approximate SOS decomposition of f. When the isolation is precise enough, the algorithm relies the perturbation terms to recover an exact rational decomposition. In the multivariate unconstrained case, Parillo and Peyrl designed a rounding-projection algorithm in [33] to compute a weighted rational SOS decompositon of a given polynomial f in the interior of the SOS cone. The algorithm computes an approximate Gram matrix of f, and rounds it to a rational matrix. With sufficient precision digits, the algorithm performs an orthogonal projection to recover an exact Gram matrix of f. The SOS decomposition is then obtained with an exact LDL^T procedure. This approach was significantly extended in [24] to handle rational functions.

Main contributions. This work provides an algorithmic framework to handle (un)-constrained polynomial problems with exact rational weighted SOS decompositions. The first contribution, given in Section 3, is a hybrid numeric-symbolic algorithm, called `intsos`, providing rational SOS decompositions for polynomials lying in the interior of the SOS cone. As for the algorithm from [11], the main idea is to perturbate the input polynomial, then to obtain an approximate Gram matrix of the perturbation by solving an SDP problem, and to recover an exact decomposition with the perturbation terms. In Section 4, we rely on `intsos` to compute decompositions of positive definite forms into SOS of rational functions, based on Polya's representations, yielding a second algorithm, called `Polyasos`. In Section 5, we rely on `intsos` to compute weighted SOS decompositions for polynomials positive over compact semi-algebraic sets, yielding a third algorithm, called `Putinarsos`.

When the input is an n-variate polynomial of degree d with integer coefficients of maximum bit size τ, we prove in Section 3 that Algorithm `intsos` runs in boolean time $\tau^2 d^{O(n)}$ and outputs SOS polynomials of bit size bounded by $\tau d^{O(n)}$. This also yields bit complexity analysis for Algorithm `Polyasos` (see Section 4) and Algorithm `Putinarsos` (see Section 5). To the best of our knowledge, these are the first complexity estimates for the output of algorithms providing exact multivariate SOS decompositions.

The three algorithms are implemented within a Maple library, called `multivsos`. In Section 6, we provide numerical benchmarks to evaluate the performance of `multivsos` against existing methods based on CAD or critical point methods.

2 PRELIMINARIES

Let $\mathbb{Z}$ be the set of integers. For $\alpha = (\alpha_1, \ldots, \alpha_n) \in \mathbb{N}^n$, one has $|\alpha| := \alpha_1 + \cdots + \alpha_n$ and $X^\alpha := X_1^{\alpha_1} \ldots X_n^{\alpha_n}$. For all $k \in \mathbb{N}$, we let $\mathbb{N}_k^n := \{\alpha \in \mathbb{N}^n : |\alpha| \leq k\}$, whose cardinality is the binomial $\binom{n+k}{k}$. A polynomial $f \in \mathbb{R}[X]$ of degree $d = 2k$ is written as $f = \sum_{|\alpha| \leq d} f_\alpha X^\alpha$ and we identify f with its vector of coefficients $\mathbf{f} = (f_\alpha)$ in the basis (X^α), $\alpha \in \mathbb{N}_d^n$. Let $\Sigma[X]$ be the convex cone of sums of squares in $\mathbb{R}[X]$ and $\mathring{\Sigma}[X]$ be the interior of $\Sigma[X]$. We note $\Sigma_\mathbb{Z}(X) := \mathbb{Z}[X] \cap \Sigma[X]$ and $\mathring{\Sigma}_\mathbb{Z}[X] := \mathbb{Z}[X] \cap \mathring{\Sigma}[X]$. For instance, the polynomial $f = 4X_1^4 + 4X_1^3X_2 - 7X_1^2X_2^2 - 2X_1X_2^3 + 10X_2^4 = (2X_1X_2 + X_2^2)^2 + (2X_1^2 + X_1X_2 - 3X_2^2)^2$ belongs to $\Sigma_\mathbb{Z}(X)$.

We rely on the bit complexity model for complexity estimates. The bit size of an integer b is denoted by $\tau(b) := \lfloor \log_2(|b|) \rfloor + 1$ with $\tau(0) := 1$. For $f = \sum_{|\alpha| \leq d} f_\alpha X^\alpha \in \mathbb{Z}[X]$ of degree d, we note $\|f\|_\infty := \max_{|\alpha| \leq d} |f_\alpha|$ and $\tau(f) := \tau(\|f\|_\infty)$ with slight abuse of notation. Given $b \in \mathbb{Z}$ and $c \in \mathbb{Z} \backslash \{0\}$ with $\gcd(b, c) = 1$, we define $\tau(b/c) := \max\{\tau(b), \tau(c)\}$. For two mappings $g, h : \mathbb{N}^l \to \mathbb{R}$, we use the notation "$g(v) = O(h(v))$" to state the existence of $b \in \mathbb{N}$ such that $g(v) \leq bh(v)$, for all $v \in \mathbb{N}^l$.

The *Newton polytope* or *cage* $C(f)$ is the convex hull of the vectors of exponents of monomials that occur in $f \in \mathbb{R}[X]$. For the above example, $C(f) = \{(4, 0), (3, 1), (2, 2), (1, 3), (0, 4)\}$. For a symmetric real matrix G, we note $G \succeq 0$ (resp. $G \succ 0$) when G has only nonnegative (resp. positive) eigenvalues and we say that G is *positive semidefinite* (SDP) (resp. *positive definite*).

With $f \in \mathbb{R}[X]$ of degree $d = 2k$, we consider the SDP program:

$$\inf_{G \succeq 0} \quad \mathrm{Tr}(G B_0) \quad \text{s.t.} \quad \mathrm{Tr}(G B_\gamma) = f_\gamma, \quad \forall \gamma \in \mathbb{N}_d^n, \tag{1}$$

where B_γ has rows (resp. columns) indexed by $\mathbb{N}_k^n$ with (α, β) entry equal to 1 if $\alpha + \beta = \gamma$ and 0 otherwise.

Theorem 2.1. *[25, Theorem 3.2] Let $f \in \mathbb{R}[X]$ of degree $d = 2k$ and global minimum $f^\star := \inf_{\mathbf{x} \in \mathbb{R}^n} f(\mathbf{x})$. Assume that SDP (1) has a feasible solution $G^\star = \sum_{i=1}^r \lambda_i \mathbf{q}_i \mathbf{q}_i^T$, with the $\mathbf{q}_i$ being the eigenvectors of $G^\star$ corresponding to the non-negative eigenvalues λ_i, for all $i = 1, \ldots, r$. Then $f - f^\star = \sum_{i=1}^r \lambda_i q_i^2$.*

For the sake of efficiency, one reduces the size of matrix G indexing its rows and columns by half of $C(f)$:

Theorem 2.2. *[37, Theorem 1] Let $f \in \Sigma[X]$ with $f = \sum_{i=1}^r s_i^2$ and $P := C(f)$. Then for all $i = 1, \ldots, r$, $C(s_i) \subseteq P/2$.*

Given $f \in \mathbb{R}[X]$, Theorem 2.1 states that one can theoretically certify that f lies in $\Sigma[X]$ by solving SDP (1). However, available SDP solvers are typically implemented in finite-precision and require the existence of a strictly feasible solution $G \succ 0$ to converge. This is equivalent for f to lie in $\mathring{\Sigma}[X]$ as stated in [12, Proposition 5.5]:

Theorem 2.3. *Let $f \in \mathbb{Z}[X]$ with $P := C(f)$, $Q := P/2 \cap \mathbb{N}^n$ and v_k be the vector of all monomials with support in Q. Then $f \in \mathring{\Sigma}[X]$ if and only if there exists a positive definite matrix G such that $f = v_k^T G v_k$.*

3 EXACT SOS REPRESENTATIONS

The aim of this section is to state and analyze a hybrid numeric-symbolic algorithm, called `intsos`, computing weighted SOS decompositions of polynomials in $\mathring{\Sigma}_\mathbb{Z}[X]$. This algorithm relies on perturbations of such polynomials.

Proposition 3.1. *Let $f \in \mathring{\Sigma}_\mathbb{Z}[X]$ of degree $d = 2k$, with $\tau = \tau(f)$, $P = C(f)$ and $Q := P/2 \cap \mathbb{N}^n$. Then, there exists $N \in \mathbb{N} - \{0\}$ such that for $\varepsilon := \frac{1}{2^N}$, $f - \varepsilon \sum_{\alpha \in Q} X^{2\alpha} \in \mathring{\Sigma}[X]$, with $N \leq \tau(\varepsilon) \leq \tau d^{O(n)}$.*

Proof. Let v_k be the vector of all monomials X^α, with α in Q. Note that each monomial in v_k has degree $\leq k$ and that $v_k^T v_k = \sum_{\alpha \in Q} X^{2\alpha}$. Since $f \in \mathring{\Sigma}[X]$, there exists by Theorem 2.3 a matrix

$G \succ 0$ such that $f = v_k^T G v_k$, with positive smallest eigenvalue λ. Let us define $N := \lceil \log_2 \frac{1}{\lambda} \rceil + 1$, i.e. the smallest integer such that $\varepsilon = \frac{1}{2^N} \leq \frac{\lambda}{2}$. Then, $\lambda > \varepsilon$ and the matrix $G - \varepsilon I$ has only positive eigenvalues. Hence, one has $f_\varepsilon := f - \varepsilon \sum_{\alpha \in Q} X^{2\alpha} = v_k^T G v_k - \varepsilon v_k^T I v_k = v_k^T (G - \varepsilon I) v_k$, yielding $f_\varepsilon \in \mathring{\Sigma}[X]$. For the second claim, let us consider the set $A := \{e \in \mathbb{R} : \forall \mathbf{x} \in \mathbb{R}^n, f(\mathbf{x}) - e \sum_{\alpha \in Q} \mathbf{x}^{2\alpha} \geq 0\}$. Using [9, Thm 14.16], A is defined by univariate polynomials of degree in $d^{O(n)}$ with coefficients of bit size bounded by $\tau d^{O(n)}$. Hence the bit size of the mimimum absolute value of their non-zero real roots is below bounded by $\tau d^{O(n)}$. □

The following can be found in [2, Lemma 2.1] and [2, Theorem 3.2].

Proposition 3.2. *Let $\tilde{G} \succ 0$ be a matrix with rational entries indexed on $\mathbb{N}_r^n$. Let L be the factor of $\tilde{G}$ computed using Cholesky's decomposition with finite precision δ_c. Then $LL^T = \tilde{G} + E$ where*

$$|E_{\alpha,\beta}| \leq (r+1) 2^{-\delta_c} |\tilde{G}_{\alpha,\alpha} \tilde{G}_{\beta,\beta}|^{\frac{1}{2}} / (1 - (r+1) 2^{-\delta_c}). \quad (2)$$

In addition, if the smallest eigenvalue $\tilde{\lambda}$ of $\tilde{G}$ satisfies the inequality

$$2^{-\delta_c} < \tilde{\lambda} / (r^2 + r + (r-1)\tilde{\lambda}), \quad (3)$$

Cholesky's decomposition returns a rational nonsingular factor L.

3.1 Algorithm intsos

We present our algorithm `intsos` computing exact weighted rational SOS decompositions for polynomials in $\mathring{\Sigma}_{\mathbb{Z}}[X]$.

Algorithm 1 `intsos`

Input: $f \in \mathbb{Z}[X]$, positive $\varepsilon \in \mathbb{Q}$, precision parameters δ, $R \in \mathbb{N}$ for the SDP solver, precision $\delta_c \in \mathbb{N}$ for the Cholesky's decomposition
Output: list `c_list` of numbers in $\mathbb{Q}$ and list `s_list` of polynomials in $\mathbb{Q}[X]$
1: $P := C(f)$, $Q := P/2 \cap \mathbb{N}^n$
2: $t := \sum_{\alpha \in Q} X^{2\alpha}$, $f_\varepsilon := f - \varepsilon t$
3: **while** $f_\varepsilon \notin \mathring{\Sigma}[X]$ **do** $\varepsilon := \frac{\varepsilon}{2}$, $f_\varepsilon := f - \varepsilon t$
4: **done**
5: ok := false
6: **while** not ok **do**
7: $(\tilde{G}, \tilde{\lambda})$:= sdp(f_ε, δ, R)
8: $(s_1, \ldots, s_r)$:= cholesky($\tilde{G}$, $\tilde{\lambda}$, δ_c) ▷ $f_\varepsilon \simeq \sum_{i=1}^r s_i^2$
9: $u := f_\varepsilon - \sum_{i=1}^r s_i^2$
10: `c_list` := $[1, \ldots, 1]$, `s_list` := $[s_1, \ldots, s_r]$
11: **for** $\alpha \in Q$ **do** $\varepsilon_\alpha := \varepsilon$
12: **done**
13: `c_list`, `s_list`, (ε_α) := absorb(u, Q, (ε_α), `c_list`, `s_list`)
14: **if** $\min_{\alpha \in Q} \{\varepsilon_\alpha\} \geq 0$ **then** ok := true
15: **else** $\delta := 2\delta$, $R := 2R$, $\delta_c := 2\delta_c$
16: **end**
17: **done**
18: **for** $\alpha \in Q$ **do** `c_list` := `c_list` $\cup \{\varepsilon_\alpha\}$, `s_list` := `s_list` $\cup \{X^\alpha\}$
19: **done**
20: **return** `c_list`, `s_list`

Algorithm 2 `absorb`

Input: $u \in \mathbb{Q}[X]$, multi-index set Q, lists (ε_α) and `c_list` of numbers in $\mathbb{Q}$, list `s_list` of polynomials in $\mathbb{Q}[X]$
Output: lists (ε_α) and `c_list` of numbers in $\mathbb{Q}$, list `s_list` of polynomials in $\mathbb{Q}[X]$
1: **for** $\gamma \in \operatorname{supp}(u)$ **do**
2: **if** $\gamma \in (2\mathbb{N})^n$ **then** $\alpha := \frac{\gamma}{2}$, $\varepsilon_\alpha := \varepsilon_\alpha + u_\gamma$
3: **else**
4: Find $\alpha, \beta \in Q$ such that $\gamma = \alpha + \beta$
5: $\varepsilon_\alpha := \varepsilon_\alpha - \frac{|u_\gamma|}{2}$, $\varepsilon_\beta := \varepsilon_\beta - \frac{|u_\gamma|}{2}$
6: `c_list` := `c_list` $\cup \{\frac{|u_\gamma|}{2}\}$
7: `s_list` := `s_list` $\cup \{X^\alpha + \operatorname{sgn}(u_\gamma) X^\beta\}$
8: **end**
9: **done**

Given $f \in \mathbb{Z}[X]$ of degree $d = 2k$, one first computes its Newton polytope $P := C(f)$ (see line 1) and $Q := P/2 \cap \mathbb{N}^n$ using standard algorithms such as quickhull [7]. The loop going from line 3 to line 4 finds a positive $\varepsilon \in \mathbb{Q}$ such that the perturbed polynomial $f_\varepsilon := f - \varepsilon \sum_{\alpha \in Q} X^{2\alpha}$ is also in $\mathring{\Sigma}[X]$. This is done thanks to an oracle based on SDP or computer algebra procedures (e.g. CAD or critical points). If $f \in \mathring{\Sigma}_{\mathbb{Z}}[X]$, the existence of ε is ensured as in the proof of Theorem 3.1 if $A := \{e \in \mathbb{R} : \forall \mathbf{x} \in \mathbb{R}^n, f(\mathbf{x}) - e \sum_{\alpha \in Q} \mathbf{x}^{2\alpha} \geq 0\}$ is non empty.

Next, we enter in the loop starting from line 6. Given $f_\varepsilon \in \mathbb{Z}[X]$, positive integers δ and R, the `sdp` function calls an SDP solver and tries to compute a rational approximation $\tilde{G}$ of the Gram matrix associated to f_ε together with a rational approximation $\tilde{\lambda}$ of its smallest eigenvalue. In practice, we use an arbitrary-precision SDP solver implemented with an interior-point method. However, in order to analyse the complexity of the procedure (see Remark 1), we assume that `sdp` relies on the ellipsoid algorithm [18].

Remark 1. *In [14], the authors analyze the complexity of the short step, primal interior point method, used in SDP solvers. Within fixed accuracy, they obtain a polynomial complexity, as for the ellipsoid method, but the exact value of the exponents is not provided.*

SDP problems are solved with this latter algorithm in polynomial-time within a given accuracy δ and a radius bound R on the Frobenius norm of $\tilde{G}$. The first step consists of solving SDP (1) by computing an approximate Gram matrix $\tilde{G} \succeq 2^{-\delta} I$ such that $|\operatorname{Tr}(\tilde{G} B_\gamma) - (f_\varepsilon)_\gamma| = |\sum_{\alpha+\beta=\gamma} \tilde{G}_{\alpha,\beta} - (f_\varepsilon)_\gamma| \leq 2^{-\delta}$ and $\sqrt{\operatorname{Tr}(\tilde{G}^2)} \leq R$. We pick large enough δ and R to obtain $\tilde{G} \succ 0$ and $\tilde{\lambda} > 0$ when $f_\varepsilon \in \mathring{\Sigma}[X]$.

The `cholesky` function computes the approximate Cholesky's decomposition LL^T of $\tilde{G}$ with precision δ_c. In order to guarantee that L will be a rational nonsingular matrix, a preliminary step consists of verifying that the inequality from (3) holds, which happens when δ_c is large enough. Otherwise, `cholesky` selects the smallest δ_c such as (3) holds. Let v_k be the size r vector of all monomials X^α with α belonging to Q. The output is a list of rational polynomials $[s_1, \ldots, s_r]$ such that for all $i = 1, \ldots, r$, s_i is the inner product of the i-th row of L by v_k. By Theorem 2.1, one would have $f_\varepsilon = \sum_{i=1}^r s_i^2$ with $s_i \in \mathbb{R}[X]$ after using exact SDP and Cholesky's decomposition. Here, we have to consider the remainder $u = f - \varepsilon \sum_{\alpha \in Q} X^{2\alpha} - \sum_{i=1}^r s_i^2$, with $s_i \in \mathbb{Q}[X]$.

After these numeric steps, the algorithm starts to perform symbolic computation with the `absorb` subroutine at line 13. The loop from `absorb` is designed to obtain an exact weigthed SOS decomposition of $\varepsilon t + u = \varepsilon \sum_{\alpha \in Q} X^{2\alpha} + \sum_\gamma u_\gamma X^\gamma$, yielding in turn an exact decomposition of f. Each term $u_\gamma X^\gamma$ can be written either $u_\gamma X^{2\alpha}$ or $u_\gamma X^{\alpha+\beta}$, for $\alpha, \beta \in Q$. In the former case (line 2), one has $\varepsilon X^{2\alpha} + u_\gamma X^{2\alpha} = (\varepsilon + u_\gamma) X^{2\alpha}$. In the latter case (line 4), one has $\varepsilon(X^{2\alpha} + X^{2\beta}) + u_\gamma X^{\alpha+\beta} = |u_\gamma|/2 (X^\alpha + \operatorname{sgn}(u_\gamma) X^\beta)^2 + (\varepsilon - |u_\gamma|/2)(X^{2\alpha} + X^{2\beta})$. If the positivity test of line 14 fails, then the coefficients of u are too large and one cannot ensure that $\varepsilon t + u$ is SOS. So we repeat the same procedure after increasing the precision of the SDP solver and Cholesky's decomposition.

In prior work [27], the authors and Schweighofer formalized and analyzed an algorithm called `univsos2`, initially provided in [11].

Given a univariate polynomial $f > 0$ of degree $d = 2k$, this algorithm computes weighted SOS decompositions of f. With $t := \sum_{i=0}^{k} X^{2i}$, the first numeric step of `univsos2` is to find ε such that the perturbed polynomial $f_\varepsilon := f - \varepsilon t > 0$ and to compute its complex roots, yielding an approximate SOS decomposition $s_1^2 + s_2^2$. The second symbolic step is very similar to the loop from line 1 to line 9 in `intsos`: one considers the remainder polynomial $u := f_\varepsilon - s_1^2 - s_2^2$ and tries to computes an exact SOS decomposition of $\varepsilon t + u$. This succeeds for large enough precision of the root isolation procedure. Therefore, `intsos` can be seen as an extension of `univsos2` in the multivariate case by replacing the numeric step of root isolation by SDP and keeping the same symbolic step.

Example 3.3. We apply Algorithm `intsos` on $f = 4X_1^4 + 4X_1^3X_2 - 7X_1^2X_2^2 - 2X_1X_2^3 + 10X_2^4$, with $\varepsilon = 1$, $\delta = R = 60$ and $\delta_c = 10$. Then $Q := C(f)/2 \cap \mathbb{N}^n = \{(2,0),(1,1),(0,2)\}$ (line 1). The loop from line 3 to line 4 ends and we get $f - \varepsilon t = f - (X_1^4 + X_1^2X_2^2 + X_2^2) \in \mathring{\Sigma}[X]$. The `sdp` (line 7) and `cholesky` (line 8) procedures yield $s_1 = 2X_1^2 + X_1X_2 - \frac{8}{3}X_2^2$, $s_2 = \frac{4}{3}X_1X_2 + \frac{3}{2}X_2^2$ and $s_3 = \frac{2}{7}X_2^2$. The remainder polynomial is $u = f - \varepsilon t - s_1^2 - s_2^2 - s_3^2 = -X_1^4 - \frac{1}{9}X_1^2X_2^2 - \frac{2}{3}X_1X_2^3 - \frac{781}{1764}X_2^4$.
At the end of the loop from line 1 to line 9, we obtain $\varepsilon_{(2,0)} = (\varepsilon - X_1^4 = 0$, which is the coefficient of X_1^4 in $\varepsilon t + u$. Then, $\varepsilon(X_1^2X_2^2 + X_2^4) - \frac{2}{3}X_1X_2^3 = \frac{1}{3}(X_1X_2 - X_2^2)^2 + (\varepsilon - \frac{1}{3})(X_1^2X_2^2 + X_2^4)$. In the polynomial $\varepsilon t + u$, the coefficient of $X_1^2X_2^2$ is $\varepsilon_{(1,1)} = \varepsilon - \frac{1}{3} - \frac{1}{9} = \frac{5}{9}$ and the coefficient of X_4^4 is $\varepsilon_{(0,2)} = \varepsilon - \frac{1}{3} - \frac{781}{1764} = \frac{395}{1764}$.
Eventually, we obtain the weighted rational SOS decomposition: $4X_1^4 + 4X_1^3X_2 - 7X_1^2X_2^2 - 2X_1X_2^3 + 10X_2^4 = \frac{1}{3}(X_1X_2 - X_2^2)^2 + \frac{5}{9}(X_1X_2)^2 + \frac{395}{1764}X_2^4 + (2X_1^2 + X_1X_2 - \frac{8}{3}X_2^2)^2 + (\frac{4}{3}X_1X_2 + \frac{3}{2}X_2^2)^2 + (\frac{2}{7}X_2^2)^2)$.

3.2 Correctness and bit size of the output

Let $f \in \mathring{\Sigma}_{\mathbb{Z}}[X]$ of degree $d = 2k$, $\tau := \tau(f)$ and $Q := C(f)/2 \cap \mathbb{N}^n$.

Proposition 3.4. *Let G be a positive definite Gram matrix associated to f and $0 < \epsilon \in \mathbb{Q}$ be such that $f_\varepsilon = f - \varepsilon \sum_{\alpha \in Q} X^{2\alpha} \in \mathring{\Sigma}[X]$. Then, there exist positive integers δ, R such that $G - \varepsilon I$ is a Gram matrix associated to f_ε, satisfies $G - \varepsilon I \succeq 2^{-\delta} I$ and $\sqrt{\mathrm{Tr}\,(G - \varepsilon I^2)} \leq R$. Also, the maximal bit sizes of δ and R are upper bounded by $\tau d^{O(n)}$.*

Proof. Let λ be the smallest eigenvalue of G. By Proposition 3.1, $G \succeq \varepsilon I$ for $\varepsilon = \frac{1}{2^N} \leq \frac{\lambda}{2}$. With $\delta = N + 1$, $2^{-\delta} = \frac{1}{2^{N+1}} \leq \frac{\lambda}{4} < \frac{\lambda}{2}$, yielding $G - \varepsilon \succeq \frac{\lambda}{2} I \succeq 2^{-\delta} I$. As $N \leq \tau d^{O(n)}$, one has $\delta \leq \tau d^{O(n)}$. As in the proof of Proposition 3.1, we consider the largest eigenvalue λ' of the Gram matrix G of f and prove that the set $A' := \{e' \in \mathbb{R} : \forall \mathbf{x} \in \mathbb{R}^n, -f(\mathbf{x}) + e' \sum_{\alpha \in Q} \mathbf{x}^{2\alpha} \geq 0\}$ is not empty. We use again [9, Thm 14.16] to prove that A' contains an interval $]0, \frac{1}{2^N}[$ with $N \leq \tau d^{O(n)}$. This allows in turn to obtain a rational upper bound ε' of λ' with bit size $\tau d^{O(n)}$). The size of G is bounded by $\binom{n+k}{n}$, thus the trace of G^2 is less than $\binom{n+k}{n}\varepsilon'^2$. Using that for all $k \geq 2$, $\binom{n+k}{n} = \frac{(n+k)\cdots(k+1)}{n!} = (1 + \frac{k}{n})(1 + \frac{k}{n-1}) \cdots (1+k) \leq k^{n-1}(1+k) \leq 2k^n \leq d^n$, one has $\sqrt{\mathrm{Tr}\,(G - \varepsilon I)^2} \leq d^{\frac{n}{2}} \varepsilon' = \tau d^{O(n)}$. □

Proposition 3.5. *Let f be as above. When applying Algorithm `intsos` to f, the procedure always terminates and outputs a weighted rational SOS decompositon of f. The maximum bit size of the coefficients involved in this SOS decomposition is upper bounded by $\tau d^{O(n)}$.*

Proof. Let us first consider the loop of Algorithm `intsos` defined from line 3 to line 4. From Proposition 3.1, this loop terminates when $f_\varepsilon \in \mathring{\Sigma}[X]$ for $\varepsilon = \frac{1}{2^N}$ and $N \leq \tau d^{O(n)}$.
When calling the `sdp` function at line 7 to solve SDP (1) with precision parameters δ and R, we compute an approximate Gram matrix $\tilde{G}$ of f_ε such that $\tilde{G} \succeq 2^\delta I$ and $\mathrm{Tr}\,(\tilde{G}^2) \leq R^2$. From Proposition 3.4, this procedure succeeds for large enough values of δ and R of bitisze upper bounded by $\tau d^{O(n)}$. In this case, we obtain a positive rational approximation $\tilde{\lambda} \geq 2^{-\delta}$ of the smallest eigenvalue of $\tilde{G}$.
Then the Cholesky's decomposition of $\tilde{G}$ is computed when calling the `cholesky` function at line 8. The decomposition is guaranteed to succeed by selecting a large enough δ_c such that (3) holds. Let r be the size of $\tilde{G}$ and δ_c be the smallest integer such that $2^{-\delta_c} < \frac{2^{-\delta}}{r^2+r+(r-1)2^{-\delta}}$. Since the function $x \mapsto \frac{x}{r^2+r+(r-1)x}$ is increasing on $[0,\infty)$ and $\tilde{\lambda} \geq 2^{-\delta}$, (3) holds. We obtain an approximate weighted SOS decomposition $\sum_{i=1}^{r} s_i^2$ of f_ε with rational coefficients.
Let us now consider the remainder polynomial $u = f_\varepsilon - \sum_{i=1}^{r} s_i^2$. The second loop of Algorithm `intsos` defined from line 6 to line 17 terminates when for all $\alpha \in Q$, $\varepsilon_\alpha \geq 0$. This condition is fulfilled when for all $\alpha \in Q$, $\varepsilon - \sum_{\beta \in Q} |u_{\alpha+\beta}|/2 + u_\alpha \geq 0$. This latter condition holds when for all $\gamma \in \mathrm{supp}(u)$, $|u_\gamma| \leq \frac{\varepsilon}{r}$.
Next, we show that this happens when the precisions δ of `sdp` and δ_c of `cholesky` are both large enough. From the definition of u, one has for all $\gamma \in \mathrm{supp}(u)$, $u_\gamma = f_\gamma - \varepsilon_\gamma - (\sum_{i=1}^{r} s_i^2)_\gamma$, where $\varepsilon_\gamma = \varepsilon$ when $\gamma \in (2\mathbb{N})^n$ and $\varepsilon_\gamma = 0$ otherwise. The positive definite matrix $\tilde{G}$ computed by the SDP solver is an approximation of an exact Gram matrix of f_ε. At precision δ, one has for all $\gamma \in \mathrm{supp}(f)$, $\tilde{G} \succeq 2^{-\delta} I$ such that $|f_\gamma - \varepsilon_\gamma - \mathrm{Tr}\,(\tilde{G}B_\gamma)| = |f_\gamma - \varepsilon_\gamma - \sum_{\alpha+\beta=\gamma} \tilde{G}_{\alpha,\beta}| \leq 2^{-\delta}$. In addition, it follows from (2) that the approximated Cholesky decomposition LL^T of $\tilde{G}$ performed at precision δ satisfies $LL^T = \tilde{G} + E$ with $|E_{\alpha,\beta}| \leq \frac{(r+1)2^{-\delta_c}}{1-(r+1)2^{-\delta_c}} |\tilde{G}_{\alpha,\alpha} \tilde{G}_{\beta,\beta}|^{\frac{1}{2}}$, for all $\alpha, \beta \in Q$. Moreover, by using Cauchy-Schwartz inequality, one has $\sum_{\alpha \in Q} \tilde{G}_{\alpha,\alpha} = \mathrm{Tr}\,\tilde{G} \leq \sqrt{\mathrm{Tr}\,I}\sqrt{\mathrm{Tr}\,\tilde{G}^2} \leq \sqrt{r}R$. For all $\gamma \in \mathrm{supp}(u)$, this yields $\left|\sum_{\alpha+\beta=\gamma} \tilde{G}_{\alpha,\alpha} \tilde{G}_{\beta,\beta}\right|^{\frac{1}{2}} \leq \sum_{\alpha+\beta=\gamma} \frac{\tilde{G}_{\alpha,\alpha} + \tilde{G}_{\beta,\beta}}{2} \leq \mathrm{Tr}\,\tilde{G} \leq \sqrt{r}R$ (the first inequality is again from Cauchy-Schwartz inequality).
Thus, for all $\gamma \in \mathrm{supp}(u)$, one has $\left|\sum_{\alpha+\beta=\gamma} \tilde{G}_{\alpha,\beta} - (\sum_{i=1}^{r} s_i^2)_\gamma\right| = \left|\sum_{\alpha+\beta=\gamma} \tilde{G}_{\alpha,\beta} - \sum_{\alpha+\beta=\gamma} (LL^T)_{\alpha,\beta}\right| = \left|\sum_{\alpha+\beta=\gamma} E_{\alpha,\beta}\right|$ which is bounded by $\frac{(r+1)2^{-\delta_c}}{1-(r+1)2^{-\delta_c}} \sum_{\alpha+\beta=\gamma} |\tilde{G}_{\alpha,\alpha} \tilde{G}_{\beta,\beta}|^{\frac{1}{2}} \leq \frac{\sqrt{r}(r+1)2^{-\delta_c} R}{1-(r+1)2^{-\delta_c}}$.
Now, let us take the smallest δ such that $2^{-\delta} \leq \frac{\varepsilon}{2r} = \frac{1}{2^{N+1}r}$ as well as the smallest δ_c such that $\frac{\sqrt{r}(r+1)2^{-\delta_c} R}{1-(r+1)2^{-\delta_c}} \leq \frac{\varepsilon}{2r}$, that is $\delta = \lceil N + 1 + \log_2 r \rceil$ and $\delta_c = \lceil \log_2 R + \log_2(r+1) + \log_2(2^{N+1} r \sqrt{r} + 1) \rceil$.
From the previous inequalities, for all $\gamma \in \mathrm{supp}(u)$, it holds that $|u_\gamma| = |f_\gamma - \varepsilon_\gamma - (\sum_{i=1}^{r} s_i^2)_\gamma| \leq |f_\gamma - \varepsilon_\gamma - \sum_{\alpha+\beta=\gamma} \tilde{G}_{\alpha,\beta}| + |\sum_{\alpha+\beta=\gamma} \tilde{G}_{\alpha,\beta} - (\sum_{i=1}^{r} s_i^2)_\gamma| \leq \frac{\varepsilon}{2r} + \frac{\varepsilon}{2r} = \frac{\varepsilon}{r}$. This ensures that Algorithm `intsos` terminates.
Let us note $\Delta(u) := \{(\alpha,\beta) : \alpha + \beta \in \mathrm{supp}(u), \alpha, \beta \in Q, \alpha \neq \beta\}$. When terminating, the first output `c_list` of Algorithm `intsos` is a list of non-negative rational numbers containing the list $[1,\ldots,1]$ of length r, the list $\{\frac{|u_{\alpha+\beta}|}{2} : (\alpha,\beta) \in \Delta(u)\}$ and the list $\{\varepsilon_\alpha : \alpha \in \frac{P}{2}\}$. The second output `s_list` of Algorithm `intsos` is a list of monomials containing the list $[s_1,\ldots,s_r]$, the list $\{X^\alpha + \mathrm{sgn}\,(u_{\alpha+\beta})X^\beta :$

$(\alpha, \beta) \in \Delta(u)\}$ and the list $\{X^\alpha : \alpha \in Q\}$. From the output, we obtain the following weigthed SOS decomposition $f = \sum_{i=1}^r s_i^2 + \sum_{(\alpha,\beta)\in\Delta(u)} \frac{|u_{\alpha+\beta}|}{2}(X^\alpha + \operatorname{sgn}(u_{\alpha+\beta})X^\beta)^2 + \sum_{\alpha\in\frac{P}{2}} \varepsilon_\alpha X^{2\alpha}$.

Now, we bound the bit size of the coefficients. Since $r \leq \binom{n+k}{n} \leq d^n$ and $N \leq \tau d^{O(n)}$, one has $\delta \leq \tau d^{O(n)}$. Similarly, $R, \delta_c \leq \tau d^{O(n)}$. This bounds also the maximal bit size of the coefficients involved in the approximate decomposition $\sum_{i=1}^r s_i^2$ as well the coefficients of u. In the worst case, the coefficient ε_α involved in the exact SOS decomposition is equal to $\varepsilon - \sum_{\beta\in Q} |u_{\alpha+\beta}|/2 + u_\alpha$ for some $\alpha \in Q$. Using again that the cardinal r of Q is less than $\binom{n+k}{n} \leq d^n$, we obtain a maximum bit size upper bounded by $\tau d^{O(n)}$. □

3.3 Bit complexity analysis

Theorem 3.6. *For f as above, there exist $\varepsilon, \delta, R, \delta_c$ of bit sizes $\leq \tau d^{O(n)}$ such that* `intsos`$(f, \varepsilon, \delta, R, \delta_c)$ *runs in boolean time $\tau^2 d^{O(n)}$.*

Proof. We consider ε, δ, R and δ_c as in the proof of Proposition 3.5, so that Algorithm `intsos` only performs a single iteration within the two while loops before terminating. Thus, the bit size of each input parameter is upper bounded by $\tau d^{O(n)}$.

Computing $C(f)$ with the quickhull algorithm runs in boolean time $O(V^2)$ for a polytope with V vertices. In our case $V \leq \binom{n+d}{n} \leq 2d^n$, so that this procedure runs in boolean time $O(d^{2n})$. Next, we investigate the computational cost of the call to `sdp` at line 7. Let us note $n_{\text{sdp}} = r$ (resp. m_{sdp}) the size (resp. number of entries) of $\tilde{G}$. This step consists of solving SDP (1), which is performed in $O(n_{\text{sdp}}^4 \log_2(2^\tau n_{\text{sdp}} R\, 2^\delta))$ iterations of the ellipsoid method, where each iteration requires $O(n_{\text{sdp}}^2(m_{\text{sdp}} + n_{\text{sdp}}))$ arithmetic operations over $\log_2(2^\tau n_{\text{sdp}} R\, 2^\delta)$-bit numbers (see e.g. [18]). Since $m_{\text{sdp}}, n_{\text{sdp}} \leq \binom{n+d}{n} \leq 2d^n$, one has $\log_2(2^\tau n_{\text{sdp}} R\, 2^\delta) \leq \tau d^{O(n)}$, $n_{\text{sdp}}^2(m_{\text{sdp}} + n_{\text{sdp}}) \leq O(\tau d^{3n})$ and $n_{\text{sdp}}^4 \log_2(2^\tau n_{\text{sdp}} R\, 2^\delta) \leq \tau d^{O(n)}$. Overall, the ellipsoid algorithm runs in boolean time $\tau^2 d^{O(n)}$ to compute the approximate Gram matrix $\tilde{G}$. We end with the cost of the call to `cholesky` at line 8. Cholesky's decomposition is performed in $O(n_{\text{sdp}}^3)$ arithmetic operations over δ_c-bit numbers. Since $\delta_c \leq \tau d^{O(n)}$, the function runs in boolean time $\tau d^{O(n)}$. The other elementary arithmetic operations performed while running Algorithm `intsos` have a negligable cost w.r.t. to the `sdp` procedure. □

4 EXACT POLYA'S REPRESENTATIONS

Next, we show how to apply Algorithm `intsos` to decompose positive definite forms into SOS of rational functions.

Let $G_n := \sum_{i=1}^n X_i^2$ and $\mathbb{S}^{n-1} := \{\mathbf{x} \in \mathbb{R}^n : G_n(\mathbf{x}) = 1\}$ be the unit $(n-1)$-sphere. A positive definite form $f \in \mathbb{R}[X]$ is a homogeneous polynomial which is positive over $\mathbb{S}^{n-1}$. For such a form, we set $\varepsilon(f) := \frac{\min_{\mathbf{x}\in\mathbb{S}^{n-1}} f(\mathbf{x})}{\max_{\mathbf{x}\in\mathbb{S}^{n-1}} f(\mathbf{x})}$, which measures how close f is to having a zero in $\mathbb{S}^{n-1}$. While there is no guarantee that $f \in \Sigma[X]$, Reznick proved in [38] that for large enough $D \in \mathbb{N}$, $fG_n^D \in \Sigma[X]$. The proof being based on prior work by Polya [34], such SOS decompositions are called *Polya's representations* and D is called the Polya's degree. Our next result states that for large enough $D \in \mathbb{N}$, $fG_n^D \in \mathring{\Sigma}[X]$.

Lemma 4.1. *Let f be a positive definite form of degree d in $\mathbb{Z}[X]$ and $D \geq \frac{nd(d-1)}{4\log 2\, \varepsilon(f)} - \frac{n+d}{2}$. Then $f\, G_n^{D+1} \in \mathring{\Sigma}[X]$.*

Proof. Let $P := C(f)$, $Q := P/2 \cap \mathbb{N}^n$ and $t := \sum_{\alpha\in Q} X^{2\alpha}$. Since f is a form, then each term $X^{2\alpha}$ has degree d, for all $\alpha \in Q$, thus t is a form. First, we show that for any positive $e < \frac{\min_{\mathbf{x}\in\mathbb{S}^{n-1}} f(\mathbf{x})}{\max_{\mathbf{x}\in\mathbb{S}^{n-1}} t(\mathbf{x})}$, the form $(f - et)$ is positive definite: for any nonzero $\mathbf{x} \in \mathbb{R}^n$, one has $f(\mathbf{x}) - et(\mathbf{x}) = G_n(\mathbf{x})^d [f(\frac{\mathbf{x}}{G_n(\mathbf{x})}) - et(\frac{\mathbf{x}}{G_n(\mathbf{x})})] > 0$ since $(f - et)$ is positive on $\mathbb{S}^{n-1}$. Next, [38, Theorem 3.12] implies that for any positive integer $D_e \geq \underline{D_e} := \frac{nd(d-1)}{4\log 2\, \varepsilon(f-et)} - \frac{n+d}{2}$, one has $(f - et)G_n^{D_e} \in \Sigma[X]$. As in the proof of Proposition 3.1, this yields $f\, G_n^{D_e} \in \mathring{\Sigma}[X]$. Next, with $\underline{D} = \frac{nd(d-1)}{4\log 2\, \varepsilon(f)} - \frac{n+d}{2}$, we prove that there exists $N \in \mathbb{N}$ such that for $e = \frac{\min_{\mathbf{x}\in\mathbb{S}^{n-1}} f(\mathbf{x})}{N \max_{\mathbf{x}\in\mathbb{S}^{n-1}} t(\mathbf{x})}$, $\underline{D_e} \leq \underline{D} + 1$. Since $f\, G_n^{D_e} \in \mathring{\Sigma}[X]$ for all $D_e \geq \underline{D_e}$, this will yield the desired result. For any $\mathbf{x} \in \mathbb{S}^{n-1}$, one has $\min_{\mathbf{x}\in\mathbb{S}^{n-1}} f(\mathbf{x}) - e \max_{\mathbf{x}\in\mathbb{S}^{n-1}} t(\mathbf{x}) \leq f(\mathbf{x}) - et(\mathbf{x}) \leq \max_{\mathbf{x}\in\mathbb{S}^{n-1}} f(\mathbf{x})$. Hence, $\varepsilon(f - et) \geq \frac{\min_{\mathbf{x}\in\mathbb{S}^{n-1}} f(\mathbf{x}) - e\max_{\mathbf{x}\in\mathbb{S}^{n-1}} t(\mathbf{x})}{\max_{\mathbf{x}\in\mathbb{S}^{n-1}} f(\mathbf{x})} = \varepsilon(f)\frac{N-1}{N}$. Therefore, one has $\underline{D_e} \leq \frac{N}{N-1}\frac{nd(d-1)}{4\log 2\, \varepsilon(f)} - \frac{n+d}{2}$, yielding $\underline{D_e} - \underline{D} \leq \frac{1}{N-1}\frac{nd(d-1)}{4\log 2\, \varepsilon(f)}$. By choosing $N := \lfloor \frac{nd(d-1)}{4\log 2\, \varepsilon(f)} - 1 \rfloor$, one ensures that $\underline{D_e} - \underline{D} \leq 1$, which concludes the proof. □

Algorithm `Polyasos` takes as input $f \in \mathbb{Z}[X]$, finds the smallest $D \in \mathbb{N}$ such that $f\, G_n^D \in \mathring{\Sigma}[X]$, thanks to an oracle as in `intsos`. Then, `intsos` is applied on $f\, G_n^D$.

Algorithm 3 `Polyasos`

Input: $f \in \mathbb{Z}[X]$, positive $\varepsilon \in \mathbb{Q}$, precision parameters $\delta, R \in \mathbb{N}$ for the SDP solver, precision $\delta_c \in \mathbb{N}$ for the Cholesky's decomposition
Output: list `c_list` of numbers in $\mathbb{Q}$ and list `s_list` of polynomials in $\mathbb{Q}[X]$
1: $D := 0$
2: **while** $f\, G_n^D \notin \mathring{\Sigma}[X]$ **do** $D := D + 1$
3: **done**
4: **return** `intsos`$(f\, G_n^D, \varepsilon, \delta, R, \delta_c)$

Example 4.2. Let us apply `Polyasos` on the perturbed Motzkin polynomial $f = (1 + 2^{-20})(X_3^6 + X_1^4 X_2^2 + X_1^2 X_2^4) - 3X_1^2 X_2^2 X_3^2$. With $D = 1$, one has $f\, G_n = (X_1^2 + X_2^2 + X_3^2)\, f \in \mathring{\Sigma}[X]$ and `intsos` yields an SOS decomposition of $f\, G_n$ with $\varepsilon = 2^{-20}$, $\delta = R = 60$, $\delta_c = 10$.

Theorem 4.3. *Let $f \in \mathbb{Z}[X]$ be a positive definite form of degree d, coefficients of bit size at most τ. On input f, Algorithm* `Polyasos` *terminates and outputs a weighted SOS decomposition for f. The maximum bit size of its coefficients involved and the boolean running time of the procedure are both upper bounded by $2^{\tau d^{O(n)}}$.*

The proof is available in Section 4 of arxiv:1802.10339.

5 EXACT PUTINAR'S REPRESENTATIONS

We let $f, g_1, \ldots, g_m$ in $\mathbb{Z}[X]$ of degree $\leq d$ and τ be a bound on the bit size of their coefficients. Assume that f is positive over $S := \{\mathbf{x} \in \mathbb{R}^n : g_1(\mathbf{x}) \geq 0, \ldots, g_m(\mathbf{x}) \geq 0\}$ and reaches its infimum with $f^\star := \min_{\mathbf{x}\in S} f(\mathbf{x}) > 0$. With $f = \sum_{|\alpha|\leq d} f_\alpha \mathbf{x}^\alpha$, we set $\|f\| := \max_{|\alpha|\leq d} \frac{f_\alpha \alpha_1! \cdots \alpha_n!}{|\alpha|!}$ and $g_0 := 1$. We consider the quadratic module $Q(S) := \{\sum_{j=0}^m \sigma_j g_j : \sigma_j \in \Sigma[\mathbf{x}]\}$ and, for $D \in \mathbb{N}$, the D-truncated quadratic module $Q_D(S) := \{\sum_{j=0}^m \sigma_j g_j : \sigma_j \in \Sigma[\mathbf{x}],\ \deg(\sigma_j g_j) \leq D\}$ generated by $g_1, \ldots, g_m$. We say that $Q(S)$ is *archimedean* if $N - G_n \in Q(S)$ for some $N \in \mathbb{N}$. We also assume in this section:

Assumption 1. *The set S is a basic compact semi-algebraic set with nonempty interior, included in $[-1, 1]^n$ and $Q(S)$ is archimedean.*

Under Assumption 1, f is positive over S only if $f \in Q_D(S)$ for some $D \in 2\mathbb{N}$ (see [35]). In this case, there exists a *Putinar's representation* $f = \sum_{i=0}^m \sigma_j g_j$ with $\sigma_j \in \Sigma[X]$ for $0 \leq j \leq m$. Let $w_j := \lceil \deg g_j/2 \rceil$, for all $1 \leq j \leq m$. One can certify that $f \in Q_D(S)$ for $D = 2k$ by solving the next SDP with $k \geq \max\{\lceil d/2 \rceil, w_1, \ldots, w_m\}$:

$$\begin{aligned} \inf_{G_0, G_1, \ldots, G_m \succeq 0} \quad & \operatorname{Tr}(G_0 B_0) + \sum_{i=1}^m g_j(0) \operatorname{Tr}(G_j C_{j0}) \\ \text{s.t.} \quad & \operatorname{Tr}(G_0 B_\gamma) + \sum_{j=1}^m \operatorname{Tr}(G_j C_{j\gamma}) = f_\gamma, \quad \forall \gamma \in \mathbb{N}_D^n, \end{aligned} \tag{4}$$

where B_γ is as for SDP (1) and $C_{j\gamma}$ has rows (resp. columns) indexed by $\mathbb{N}_{k-w_j}^n$ with (α, β) entry equal to $\sum_{\alpha+\beta+\delta=\gamma} g_{j\delta}$. SDP (4) is a reformulation of the problem $\sup\{b : f - b \in Q_D(S)\}$, with optimal value denoted by $f_D^\star$. Next result follows from [25, Theorem 4.2].

Theorem 5.1. *We use the notation and assumptions introduced above. For $D \in 2\mathbb{N}$ large enough, one has $0 < f_D^\star \leq f^\star$. In addition, SDP (4) has an optimal solution $(G_0, G_1, \ldots, G_m)$, yielding the following Putinar's representation: $f - f_D^\star = \sum_{i=1}^r \lambda_{i0} q_{i0}^2 + \sum_{i=1}^m g_j \sum_{i=1}^{r_j} \lambda_{ij} q_{ij}^2$ where the vectors of coefficients of the polynomials q_{ij} are the eigenvectors of G_j with respective eigenvalues λ_{ij}, for all $j = 0, \ldots, m$.*

The complexity of Putinar's Positivstellensätz was analyzed in [31]:

Theorem 5.2. *With the notation and assumptions introduced above, there exists a real $\chi_S > 0$ depending on S such that*
(i) for all even $D \geq \chi_S \exp(d^2 n^d \frac{\|f\|}{f^\star})^{\chi_S}$, $f \in Q_D(S)$.
(ii) for all even $D \geq \chi_S \exp(2d^2 n^d)^{\chi_S}$, $0 \leq f^\star - f_D^\star \leq \frac{6d^3 n^{2d} \|f\|}{\chi_S \sqrt{\log \frac{D}{\chi_S}}}$.

In theory, one can certify that f belongs to $Q_D(S)$ for $D = 2k$ large enough, by solving SDP (4). Next, we show how to ensure the existence of a strictly feasible solution for SDP (4) after replacing the initial set of constraints S by $S' := \{\mathbf{x} \in S : 1 - \mathbf{x}^{2\alpha} \geq 0, \forall \alpha \in \mathbb{N}_k^n\}$. We first give a lower bound for $f^\star$ (see arxiv:1802.10339 for a proof).

Proposition 5.3. *With the above notation and assumptions, one has $f^\star \geq 2^{-(\tau+d+d\log_2 n+1)d^{n+1}} d^{-(n+1)d^{n+1}} = 2^{-\tau d^{O(n)}}$.*

Theorem 5.4. *We use the notation and assumptions introduced above. There exists $D \in 2\mathbb{N}$ such that:*
(i) $f \in Q_D(S)$ with the representation $f = f_D^\star + \sum_{j=0}^m \sigma_j g_j$ for $f_D^\star > 0$, $\sigma_j \in \Sigma[X]$ with $\deg(\sigma_j g_j) \leq D$ for all $j = 0, \ldots, m$.
(ii) $f \in Q_D(S')$ with the representation $f = \sum_{j=0}^m \mathring{\sigma}_j g_j + \sum_{|\alpha| \leq k} c_\alpha (1 - X^{2\alpha})$ for $\mathring{\sigma}_j \in \mathring{\Sigma}[X]$ with $\deg(\mathring{\sigma}_j g_j) \leq D$, for all $j = 0, \ldots, m$, and some sequence of positive numbers $(c_\alpha)_{|\alpha| \leq k}$.
(iii) There exists a real $C_S > 0$ depending on S and $\varepsilon = \frac{1}{2^N}$ with positive $N \in \mathbb{N}$ such that $f - \varepsilon \sum_{|\alpha| \leq k} X^{2\alpha} \in Q_D(S')$ and $N \leq 2^{\tau d^{n C_S}}$, where τ is the maximal bit size of the coefficients of $f, g_1, \ldots, g_m$.

Proof. Let χ_S be as in Theorem 5.2 and $D = 2k$ be the smallest integer larger than $\underline{D} := \max\{\chi_S \exp(\frac{12d^3 n^{2d} \|f\|}{f^\star})^{\chi_S}, \chi_S \exp(2d^2 n^d)^{\chi_S}\}$. Theorem 5.2 implies $f \in Q_D(S)$ and $f^\star - f_D^\star \leq \frac{6d^3 n^{2d} \|f\|}{\chi_S \sqrt{\log \frac{D}{\chi_S}}} \leq \frac{f^\star}{2}$.

(i) This yields the representation $f - f_D^\star = \sum_{j=0}^m \sigma_j g_j$, with $f_D^\star \geq \frac{f^\star}{2} > 0$, $\sigma_j \in \Sigma[X]$ and $\deg(\sigma_j g_j) \leq D$ for all $j = 0, \ldots, m$.

(ii) For $1 \leq j \leq m$, let us define $t_j := \sum_{|\alpha| \leq k - w_j} X^{2\alpha}$, $t_0 := \sum_{|\alpha| \leq k} X^{2\alpha}$ and $t := \sum_{j=0}^m t_j g_j$. For a given $\nu > 0$, we use the perturbation polynomial $-\nu t = -\nu \sum_{|\gamma| \leq D} t_\gamma X^\gamma$. For each term $-t_\gamma X^\gamma$, one has $\gamma = \alpha + \beta$ with $\alpha, \beta \in \mathbb{N}_k^n$, thus $-t_\gamma X^\gamma = |t_\gamma|(-1 + \frac{1}{2}(1 - X^{2\alpha}) + \frac{1}{2}(1 - X^{2\beta}) + \frac{1}{2}(X^\alpha - \operatorname{sgn}(t_\gamma) X^\beta)^2)$. As in the proof of Proposition 3.5, let us note $\Delta(t) := \{(\alpha, \beta) : \alpha + \beta \in \operatorname{supp}(t), \alpha, \beta \in \mathbb{N}_k^n, \alpha \neq \beta\}$. Hence, there exist $d_\alpha \geq 0$ for all $\alpha \in \mathbb{N}_k^n$ such that $f = f - \nu t + \nu t = f_D^\star - \sum_{|\gamma| \leq D} \nu |t_\gamma| + \sum_{j=0}^m \sigma_j g_j + \nu t + \sum_{|\alpha| \leq k} d_\alpha (1 - X^{2\alpha}) + \nu \sum_{(\alpha,\beta) \in \Delta(t)} \frac{|t_{\alpha+\beta}|}{2} (X^\alpha - \operatorname{sgn}(t_{\alpha+\beta}) X^\beta)^2$. Since one has not necessarily $d_\alpha > 0$ for all $\alpha \in \mathbb{N}_k^n$, we now explain how to handle the case when $d_\alpha = 0$ for $\alpha \in \mathbb{N}_k^n$. We write $-\sum_{|\gamma| \leq D} \nu |t_\gamma| + \sum_{|\alpha| \leq k} d_\alpha (1 - X^{2\alpha}) = -\sum_{|\gamma| \leq D} \nu |t_\gamma| - \sum_{\alpha : d_\alpha = 0} \nu + \sum_{\alpha : d_\alpha = 0} \nu (1 - X^{2\alpha}) + \sum_{\alpha : d_\alpha = 0} \nu X^{2\alpha} + \sum_{|\alpha| : d_\alpha = 0} d_\alpha (1 - X^{2\alpha}) + \sum_{|\alpha| : d_\alpha > 0} d_\alpha (1 - X^{2\alpha})$. For $\alpha \in \mathbb{N}_k^n$, we define $c_\alpha := \nu$ if $d_\alpha = 0$ and $c_\alpha := d_\alpha$ otherwise, $a := \sum_{|\gamma| \leq D} |t_\gamma| + \sum_{\alpha : d_\alpha = 0} 1$, $\mathring{\sigma}_j := \sigma_j + \nu t_j$, for each $j = 1, \ldots, m$ and $\mathring{\sigma}_0 := f_D^\star - \nu a + \sigma_0 + \nu t_0 + \nu \sum_{(\alpha,\beta) \in \Delta(t)} \frac{|t_{\alpha+\beta}|}{2} (X^\alpha - \operatorname{sgn}(t_{\alpha+\beta}) X^\beta)^2 + \sum_{\alpha : d_\alpha = 0} \nu X^{2\alpha}$. So, there exists a sequence of positive numbers $(c_\alpha)_{|\alpha| \leq k}$ such that $f = \sum_{j=0}^m \mathring{\sigma}_j g_j + \sum_{|\alpha| \leq k} c_\alpha (1 - X^{2\alpha})$. Now, let us select $\nu := \frac{1}{2^M}$ with M being the smallest positive integer such that $0 < \nu \leq \frac{f_D^\star}{2a}$. This implies the existence of a positive definite Gram matrix for $\mathring{\sigma}_0$, thus by Theorem 2.3, $\mathring{\sigma}_0 \in \mathring{\Sigma}[X]$. Similarly, for $1 \leq j \leq m$, $\mathring{\sigma}_j$ belongs to $\mathring{\Sigma}[X]$, which proves the second claim.

(iii) Let $N := M + 1$ and $\varepsilon := \frac{1}{2^N} = \frac{\nu}{2}$. One has $f - \varepsilon \sum_{|\alpha| \leq k} X^{2\alpha} = f - \varepsilon t_0 = \mathring{\sigma}_0 - \varepsilon t_0 + \sum_{j=1}^m \mathring{\sigma}_j g_j + \sum_{|\alpha| \leq k} c_\alpha (1 - X^{2\alpha})$. Thus, $\sigma_0 + (\nu - \varepsilon) t_0 \in \mathring{\Sigma}[X]$. This implies that $\mathring{\sigma}_0 - \varepsilon t_0 \in \mathring{\Sigma}[X]$ and $f - \varepsilon t_0 \in Q_D(S')$. Next, we derive a lower bound of $\frac{f_D^\star}{a}$. Since $t = \sum_{|\alpha| \leq k} X^{2\alpha} + \sum_{j=1}^m g_j \sum_{|\alpha| \leq k - w_j} X^{2\alpha}$, one has $\sum_{|\gamma| \leq D} |t_\gamma| \leq 2^\tau (m+1) \binom{n+D}{n}$. This implies that $a \leq 2^\tau (m+1) \binom{n+D}{n} + \binom{n+k}{k} \leq 2^\tau (m+2) \binom{n+D}{n}$. Recall that $\frac{f^\star}{2} \leq f_D^\star$, implying $\frac{f_D^\star}{a} \geq \frac{f^\star}{2^{\tau+1}(m+2)\binom{n+D}{n}} \geq \frac{1}{(m+2) 2^{\tau d^{O(n)}} D^n}$, where the last inequality follows from Theorem 5.3. Let us now give an upper bound of $\log_2 D$. First, note that for all $\alpha \in \mathbb{N}^n$, $\frac{|\alpha|!}{\alpha_1! \cdots \alpha_n!} \geq 1$, thus $\|f\| \leq 2^\tau$. Since D is the smallest even integer larger than $\underline{D}$, one has $\log_2 D \leq 1 + \log_2 \underline{D} \leq 1 + \log \chi_S + (12 d^3 n^{2d} 2^\tau 2^{\tau d^{O(n)}})^{\chi_S}$. Next, since N is the smallest integer such that $\varepsilon = \frac{1}{2^N} = \frac{\nu}{2} \leq \frac{f_D^\star}{2a}$, it is enough to take $N \leq 1 + \log_2(m+2) + \tau d^{O(n)} + n \log_2 D \leq 2^{\tau d^{n C_S}}$ for some real $C_S > 0$ depending on S, the desired result. □

We can now present Algorithm Putinarsos. For $f \in \mathbb{Z}[X]$ positive over a basic compact semi-algebraic set S satisfying Assumption 1, the first loop outputs the smallest positive integer $D = 2k$ such that $f \in Q_D(S)$. Then the procedure is similar to intsos. As for the first loop of intsos, the loop from line 6 to line 7 allows to obtain a perturbed polynomial $f_\varepsilon \in Q_D(S')$, with $S' := \{\mathbf{x} \in S : 1 - \mathbf{x}^{2\alpha} \geq 0, \forall \alpha \in \mathbb{N}_k^n\}$. Then one solves SDP (4) with the sdp procedure and performs Cholesky's decomposition to obtain an approximate Putinar's representation of $f_\varepsilon = f - \varepsilon t$ and a remainder u. Next, we apply the absorb subroutine as in intsos. The rationale is that with large enough precision parameters for the procedures sdp and cholesky, one finds an exact weighted SOS decomposition of $u + \varepsilon t$, which yields in turn an exact Putinar's representation of f in $Q_D(S')$ with rational coefficients.

Algorithm 4 Putinarsos.

Input: $f \in \mathbb{Z}[X]$, $S := \{x \in \mathbb{R}^n : g_1(x) \geq 0, \ldots, g_m(x) \geq 0\}$ with $g_1, \ldots, g_m \in \mathbb{Z}[X]$, positive $\varepsilon \in \mathbb{Q}$, precision parameters δ, $R \in \mathbb{N}$ for the SDP solver, precision $\delta_c \in \mathbb{N}$ for the Cholesky's decomposition

Output: lists c_list$_0$, ..., c_list$_m$, c_alpha of numbers in $\mathbb{Q}$ and lists s_list$_0$, ..., s_list$_m$ of polynomials in $\mathbb{Q}[X]$

1: $k := \max\{\lceil d/2 \rceil, w_1, \ldots, w_m\}$, $D := 2k$, $g_0 := 1$
2: **while** $f \notin Q_D(S)$ **do** $k := k + 1$, $D := D + 2$
3: **done**
4: $P := \mathbb{N}_D^n$, $Q := \mathbb{N}_k^n$, $S' := \{x \in S : 1 - x^{2\alpha} \geq 0, \forall \alpha \in \mathbb{N}_k^n\}$
5: $t := \sum_{\alpha \in Q} X^{2\alpha}$, $f_\varepsilon := f - \varepsilon t$
6: **while** $f_\varepsilon \notin Q_D(S')$ **do** $\varepsilon := \frac{\varepsilon}{2}$, $f_\varepsilon := f - \varepsilon t$
7: **done**
8: ok := false
9: **while** not ok **do**
10:    $[\tilde{G}_0, \ldots, \tilde{G}_m, \tilde{\lambda}_0, \ldots, \tilde{\lambda}_m, (\tilde{c}_\alpha)_{|\alpha| \leq k}]$, := sdp$(f_\varepsilon, \delta, R, S')$
11:    c_alpha := $(\tilde{c}_\alpha)_{|\alpha| \leq k}$
12:    **for** $j \in \{0, \ldots, m\}$ **do**
13:      $(s_{1j}, \ldots, s_{r_j j}) := $ cholesky$(\tilde{G}_j, \tilde{\lambda}_j, \delta_c)$, $\tilde{\sigma}_j := \sum_{i=1}^{r_j} s_{ij}^2$
14:      c_list$_j := [1, \ldots, 1]$, s_list$_j := [s_{1j}, \ldots, s_{r_j j}]$
15:    **done**
16:    $u := f_\varepsilon - \sum_{j=0}^m \tilde{\sigma}_j g_j - \sum_{|\alpha| \leq k} \tilde{c}_\alpha (1 - X^{2\alpha})$
17:    **for** $\alpha \in Q$ **do** $\varepsilon_\alpha := \varepsilon$
18:    **done**
19:    c_list, s_list, $(\varepsilon_\alpha) := $ absorb$(u, Q, (\varepsilon_\alpha), $ c_list, s_list$)$
20:    **if** $\min_{\alpha \in Q} \{\varepsilon_\alpha\} \geq 0$ **then** ok := true
21:    **else** $\delta := 2\delta$, $R := 2R$, $\delta_c := 2\delta_c$
22:    **end**
23: **done**
24: **for** $\alpha \in Q$ **do**
25:    c_list$_0 := $ c_list$_0 \cup \{\varepsilon_\alpha\}$, s_list$_0 := $ s_list$_0 \cup \{x^\alpha\}$
26: **done**
27: **return** c_list$_0$, ..., c_list$_m$, c_alpha, s_list$_0$, ..., s_list$_m$

Example 5.5. Let us apply Putinarsos to $f = -X_1^2 - 2X_1 X_2 - 2X_2^2 + 6$, $S := \{(x_1, x_2) \in \mathbb{R}^2 : 1 - x_1^2 \geq 0, 1 - x_2^2 \geq 0\}$ and the same precision parameters as in Example 3.3. The first and second loop yield $D = 2$ and $\varepsilon = 1$. After running absorb, we obtain the exact Putinar's representation $f = \frac{23853407}{292204836} + \frac{23}{49} X_1^2 + \frac{130657269}{291009481} X_2^2 + \frac{1}{2442^2} + (X_1 - X_2)^2 + (\frac{X_2}{2437})^2 + (\frac{11}{7})^2 (1 - X_1^2) + (\frac{13}{7})^2 (1 - X_2^2)$.

THEOREM 5.6. *We use the notation and assumptions introduced above. For some $C_S > 0$ depending on S, there exist $\varepsilon, \delta, R, \delta_c$ and $D = 2k$ of bit sizes less than $O(2^{\tau d^{nC_S}})$ for which* Putinarsos$(f, S, \varepsilon, \delta, R, \delta_c)$ *terminates and outputs an exact Putinar's representation with rational coefficients of $f \in Q(S')$, with $S' := \{x \in S : 1 - x^{2\alpha} \geq 0, \forall \alpha \in \mathbb{N}_k^n\}$. The maximum bit size of these coefficients is bounded by $O(2^{\tau d^{nC_S}})$ and the procedure runs in boolean time $O(2^{2^{\tau d^{nC_S}}})$.*

The proof is available in arxiv:1802.10339. The complexity is polynomial in the degree D of the representation, often close in practice to the degrees of the involved polynomials, as shown in Section 6.

6 PRACTICAL EXPERIMENTS

We provide practical performance results for Algorithms intsos, Polyasos and Putinarsos. These are implemented in a library, called multivsos, written in Maple. More details about installation and benchmark execution are given on the two webpages dedicated to univariate[1] and multivariate[2] polynomials. All results were obtained on an Intel Core i7-5600U CPU (2.60 GHz) with 16Gb of RAM. We use the Maple Convex package[3] to compute Newton polytopes.

[1] https://github.com/magronv/univsos
[2] https://github.com/magronv/multivsos
[3] http://www.home.math.uwo.ca/faculty/franz/convex

Our subroutine sdp relies on the arbitrary-precision solver SDPA-GMP [29] and the cholesky procedure is implemented with the function LUDecomposition available within Maple. Most of the time is spent in the sdp procedure for all benchmarks.

In Table 1, we compare the performance of multivsos for nine univariate polynomials being positive over compact intervals. More details about these benchmarks are given in [11, Section 6] and [27, Section 5]. In this case, we use Putinarsos. The main difference is that we use SDP in multivsos instead of complex root isolation in univsos2. The results emphasize that univsos2 performs better and provides more concise SOS certificates, especially for high degrees (see e.g. # 5). For # 3, we were not able to obtain a decomposition within a day of computation, as meant by the symbol − in the corresponding column entries. Large values of d and τ require more precision. The values of ε, δ and δ_c are respectively between 2^{-80} and 2^{-240}, 30 and 100, 200 and 2000.

Next, we compare the performance of multivsos with other tools in Table 2. The two first benchmarks are built from the polynomial $f = (X_1^2 + 1)^2 + (X_2^2 + 1)^2 + 2(X_1 + X_2 + 1)^2 - 268849736/10^8$ from [25, Example 1], with $f_{12} := f^3$ and $f_{20} := f^5$. For these two benchmarks, we apply intsos. We use Polyasos to handle M_{20} (resp. M_{100}), obtained as in Example 4.2 by adding 2^{-20} (resp. 2^{-100}) to the positive coefficients of the Motzkin polynomial and r_i, which is a randomly generated positive definite quartic with i variables. We implemented in Maple the projection and rounding algorithm from [33] also relying on SDP, denoted by RoundProject. For multivsos, the values of ε, δ and δ_c lie between 2^{-100} and 2^{-10}, 60 and 200, 10 and 60. We compare with RAGLib based on critical points and the SamplePoints procedure (abbreviated as CAD) based on CAD, both available in Maple. While these methods outperform the two SDP-based algorithms for examples with $n \leq 3$, they are less efficient for larger examples such as r_6^2 and suffer from a severe computational burden when $n \geq 8$. An additional drawback is that they do not provide non-negativity certificates. However, note that they can solve less restrictive problems, involving positive semidefinite forms or non-negative polynomials. As shown in [24], SDP-based methods may provide exact certificates even in such cases and can be extended to rational functions. The algorithms we developed in this paper are unable to handle such cases. In most cases, multivsos is more efficient than RoundProject and outputs more concise representations. The reason is that multivsos performs approximate Cholesky's decompositions while RoundProject computes exact LDL^T decompositions of Gram matrices obtained after the two steps of rounding and projection. Note that we could not solve the examples of Table 2 with less precision.

Finally, we compare the performance of multivsos (Putinarsos) on positive polynomials on basic compact semi-algebraic sets in Table 3. The first benchmark is from [25, Problem 4.6]. Each benchmark f_i comes from an inequality of the Flyspeck project [21]. The three last benchmarks are from [28]. The maximal degree of the polynomials involved in each system is denoted by d. We emphasize that the degree $D = 2k$ of each Putinar representation obtained in practice with Putinarsos is very close to d, which is in contrast with the theoretical complexity estimates obtained in Section 5. The values of ε, δ and δ_c lie between 2^{-30} and 2^{-10}, 60 and 200, 10 and 30. As for Table 2, RAGLib performs better for problems with $d \leq 3$

Table 1: `multivsos` **vs** `univsos2` **[27] for benchmarks from [11].**

Id	d	τ (bits)	`multivsos`		`univsos2`	
			τ_1 (bits)	t_1 (s)	τ_2 (bits)	t_2 (s)
# 1	13	22 682	387 178	0.84	51 992	0.83
# 3	32	269 958	–	–	580 335	2.64
# 4	22	47 019	1 229 036	2.08	106 797	1.78
# 5	34	117 307	10 271 899	69.3	265 330	5.21
# 6	17	26 438	713 865	1.15	59 926	1.03
# 7	43	67 399	10 360 440	16.3	152 277	11.2
# 8	22	27 581	1 123 152	1.95	63 630	1.86
# 9	20	30 414	896 342	1.54	68 664	1.61
# 10	25	42 749	2 436 703	3.02	98 926	2.76

Table 2: `multivsos` **vs** `RoundProject` **[33] vs** `RAGLib` **vs** `CAD` **(Polya).**

Id	n	d	`multivsos`		`RoundProject`		`RAGLib`	`CAD`
			τ_1 (bits)	t_1 (s)	τ_2 (bits)	t_2 (s)	t_3 (s)	t_4 (s)
f_{12}	2	12	162 861	5.96	5 185 020	6.92	0.15	0.07
f_{20}	2	20	745 419	110.	78 949 497	141.	0.16	0.03
M_{20}	3	8	4 695	0.18	3 996	0.15	0.13	0.05
M_{100}	3	8	17 232	0.35	18 831	0.29	0.15	0.03
r_2	2	4	1 866	0.03	1 031	0.04	0.09	0.01
r_4	4	4	14 571	0.15	47 133	0.25	0.32	–
r_6	6	4	56 890	0.34	475 359	0.54	623.	–
r_8	8	4	157 583	0.96	2 251 511	1.41	–	–
r_{10}	10	4	344 347	2.45	8 374 082	4.59	–	–
r_6^2	6	8	1 283 982	13.8	146 103 466	106.	10.9	–

Table 3: `multivsos` **vs** `RAGLib` **vs** `CAD` **(Putinar).**

Id	n	d	`multivsos`			`RAGLib`	`CAD`
			k	τ_1 (bits)	t_1 (s)	t_2 (s)	t_3 (s)
p_{46}	2	4	3	21 723	0.83	0.15	0.81
f_{260}	6	3	2	114 642	2.72	0.12	–
f_{491}	6	3	2	108 359	9.65	0.01	0.05
f_{752}	6	2	2	10 204	0.26	0.07	–
f_{859}	6	7	4	6 355 724	303.	5896.	–
f_{863}	4	2	1	5 492	0.14	0.01	0.01
f_{884}	4	4	3	300 784	25.1	0.21	–
f_{890}	4	4	2	60 787	0.59	0.08	–
butcher	6	3	2	247 623	1.32	47.2	–
heart	8	4	2	618 847	2.94	0.54	–
magnetism	7	2	1	9 622	0.29	434.	–

and $n \leq 4$. Larger problems (e.g. magnetism, f_{859}) are handled more efficiently with `multivsos` and `CAD` can only solve 3 benchmarks out of 10. We plan to extend the procedure `RoundProject` and the algorithm from [24] to the case of such constrained problems.

REFERENCES

[1] C. Bachoc and F. Vallentin. New upper bounds for kissing numbers from semidefinite programming. *Journal of the AMS*, 21(3):909–924, 2008.

[2] Z. Bai, J. Demmel, and A. McKenney. On Floating Point Errors in Cholesky. Technical report, 1989. (LAPACK Working Note 14).

[3] B. Bank, M. Giusti, J. Heintz, and G.-M. Mbakop. Polar varieties and efficient real elimination. *Mathematische Zeitschrift*, 238(1):115–144, 2001.

[4] B. Bank, M. Giusti, J. Heintz, and L.-M. Pardo. Generalized polar varieties: Geometry and algorithms. *Journal of complexity*, 2005.

[5] B. Bank, M. Giusti, J. Heintz, and M. Safey El Din. Intrinsic complexity estimates in polynomial optimization. *Journal of Complexity*, 30(4):430–443, 2014.

[6] B. Bank, M. Giusti, J. Heintz, M. Safey El Din, and É. Schost. On the geometry of polar varieties. *Applicable Algebra in Engineering, Communication and Computing*, 21(1):33–83, 2010.

[7] C. B. Barber, D. P. Dobkin, and H. Huhdanpaa. The Quickhull Algorithm for Convex Hulls. *ACM Trans. Math. Softw.*, 22(4):469–483, 1996.

[8] S. Basu, R. Pollack, and M.-F. Roy. A new algorithm to find a point in every cell defined by a family of polynomials. In *Quantifier elimination and cylindrical algebraic decomposition*. Springer-Verlag, 1998.

[9] S. Basu, R. Pollack, and M.-F. Roy. *Algorithms in Real Algebraic Geometry (Algorithms and Computation in Mathematics)*. Springer-Verlag New York, Inc., Secaucus, NJ, USA, 2006.

[10] L. Blum, F. Cucker, M. Shub, and S. Smale. *Complexity and real computation*. Springer Science & Business Media, 2012.

[11] S. Chevillard, J. Harrison, M. Joldes, and C. Lauter. Efficient and accurate computation of upper bounds of approximation errors. *Theoretical Computer Science*, 412(16):1523 – 1543, 2011.

[12] M. D. Choi, T. Y. Lam, and B. Reznick. Sums of squares of real polynomials. volume 58 of *Proc. Sympos. Pure Math.*, pages 103–126. Amer. Math. Soc., 1995.

[13] G. E Collins. Quantifier elimination for real closed fields by cylindrical algebraic decompostion. In *ATFL 2nd GI Conf. Kaiserslautern*, pages 134–183, 1975.

[14] E. de Klerk and F. Vallentin. On the Turing Model Complexity of Interior Point Methods for Semidefinite Programming. *SIAM Journal on Optimization*, 26(3):1944–1961, 2016.

[15] A. Greuet and M. Safey El Din. Probabilistic Algorithm for Polynomial Optimization over a Real Algebraic Set. *SIAM Journal on Optimization*, 24(3):1313–1343, 2014.

[16] A. Greuet, F. Guo, M. Safey El Din, and Lihong Zhi. Global optimization of polynomials restricted to a smooth variety using sums of squares. *Journal of Symbolic Computation*, 47(5):503 – 518, 2012.

[17] D. Grigoriev and N. Vorobjov. Solving systems of polynomials inequalities in subexponential time. *Journal of Symbolic Computation*, 5:37–64, 1988.

[18] M. Grötschel, L. Lovász, and A. Schrijver. *Geometric Algorithms and Combinatorial Optimization*, volume 2 of *Algorithms and Combinatorics*. Springer, second corrected edition edition, 1993.

[19] F. Guo, M. Safey El Din, and L. Zhi. Global optimization of polynomials using generalized critical values and sums of squares. In *Proceedings of the 2010 International Symposium on Symbolic and Algebraic Computation*, ISSAC '10, pages 107–114, New York, NY, USA, 2010. ACM.

[20] Q. Guo, M. Safey El Din, and L. Zhi. Computing rational solutions of linear matrix inequalities. In *Proceedings of the 38th International Symposium on Symbolic and Algebraic Computation*, pages 197–204. ACM, 2013.

[21] Thomas C. Hales. The flyspeck project, 2013.

[22] D. Henrion, S. Naldi, and M. Safey El Din. Exact Algorithms for Linear Matrix Inequalities. *SIAM Journal on Optimization*, 26(4):2512–2539, 2016.

[23] J.B. Lasserre, M. Laurent, B. Mourrain, P. Rostalski and P. TréBuchet. Moment Matrices, Border Bases and Real Radical Computation. *J. Symb. Computation.*, 51:63–85, 2013.

[24] E. Kaltofen, B. Li, Z. Yang, and L. Zhi. Exact certification of global optimality of approximate factorizations via rationalizing sums-of-squares with floating point scalars. In *Proceedings of the twenty-first international symposium on Symbolic and algebraic computation*, pages 155–164. ACM, 2008.

[25] J.-B. Lasserre. Global Optimization with Polynomials and the Problem of Moments. *SIAM Journal on Optimization*, 11(3):796–817, 2001.

[26] M. Laurent. *Sums of squares, moment matrices and optimization over polynomials.* Springer, 2009.

[27] V. Magron, M. Safey El Din, and M. Schweighofer. Algorithms for Sums of Squares Decompositions of Non-negative Univariate Polynomials, 2017. Submitted.

[28] C. Muñoz and A. Narkawicz. Formalization of Bernstein Polynomials and Applications to Global Optimization. *J. Aut. Reasoning*, 51(2):151–196, 2013.

[29] M. Nakata. A numerical evaluation of highly accurate multiple-precision arithmetic version of semidefinite programming solver: SDPA-GMP, -QD and -DD. In *CACSD*, pages 29–34, 2010.

[30] J. Nie, K. Ranestad, and B. Sturmfels. The algebraic degree of semidefinite programming. *Mathematical Programming*, 122(2):379–405, 2010.

[31] J. Nie and M. Schweighofer. On the complexity of Putinar's Positivstellensatz. *Journal of Complexity*, 23(1):135 – 150, 2007.

[32] P. A. Parrilo. *Structured Semidefinite Programs and Semialgebraic Geometry Methods in Robustness and Optimization.* PhD thesis, California Inst. Tech., 2000.

[33] H. Peyrl and P.A. Parrilo. Computing sum of squares decompositions with rational coefficients. *Theoretical Computer Science*, 409(2):269–281, 2008.

[34] G. Pólya. Über positive Darstellung von Polynomen. *Naturforsch. Ges.,Zürich*, 73:141–145, 1928.

[35] M. Putinar. Positive polynomials on compact semi-algebraic sets. *Indiana University Mathematics Journal*, 42(3):969–984, 1993.

[36] Ronan Quarez. Tight bounds for rational sums of squares over totally real fields. *Rendiconti del Circolo Matematico di Palermo*, 59(3):377–388, Dec 2010.

[37] B. Reznick. Extremal PSD forms with few terms. *Duke Mathematical Journal*, 45(2):363–374, 1978.

[38] B. Reznick. Uniform denominators in Hilbert's seventeenth problem. *Mathematische Zeitschrift*, 220(1):75–97, Dec 1995.

[39] M. Safey El Din. Testing sign conditions on a multivariate polynomial and applications. *Mathematics in Computer Science*, 1(1):177–207, 2007.

[40] M. Safey El Din and É. Schost. Polar varieties and computation of one point in each connected component of a smooth real algebraic set. In *ISSAC'03*, pages 224–231. ACM, 2003.

[41] M. Safey El Din and L. Zhi. Computing Rational Points in Convex Semialgebraic Sets and Sum of Squares Decompositions. *SIAM J. on Optimization*, 20(6):2876–2889, September 2010.

[42] J. F. Sturm. Using SeDuMi 1.02, a MATLAB toolbox for optimization over symmetric cones, 1998.

[43] M. Yamashita, K. Fujisawa, K. Nakata, M. Nakata, M. Fukuda, K. Kobayashi, and K. Goto. A high-performance software package for semidefinite programs : SDPA7. Technical report, Dept. of Information Sciences, Tokyo Inst. Tech., 2010.

On the Chordality of Polynomial Sets in Triangular Decomposition in Top-Down Style*

Chenqi Mou and Yang Bai
LMIB – School of Mathematics and Systems Science /
Beijing Advanced Innovation Center for Big Data and Brain Computing
Beihang University, Beijing 100191, China
{chenqi.mou,yangbai}@buaa.edu.cn

ABSTRACT

In this paper the chordal graph structures of polynomial sets appearing in triangular decomposition in top-down style are studied when the input polynomial set has a chordal associated graph. We prove that the associated graph of one specific triangular set computed in any algorithm for triangular decomposition in top-down style is a subgraph of the chordal graph of the input polynomial set and that all the polynomial sets, including all the computed triangular sets, appearing in one specific algorithm for triangular decomposition in top-down style (Wang's method) have associated graphs which are subgraphs of the chordal graph of the input polynomial set.

CCS CONCEPTS

• **Computing methodologies → Symbolic and algebraic algorithms**; • **Theory of computation →** *Design and analysis of algorithms*;

KEYWORDS

Chordal graph; triangular decomposition; top-down style; Wang's method

ACM Reference Format:

Chenqi Mou and Yang Bai. 2018. On the Chordality of Polynomial Sets in Triangular Decomposition in Top-Down Style. In *ISSAC '18: 2018 ACM International Symposium on Symbolic and Algebraic Computation, July 16–19, 2018, New York, NY, USA.* ACM, New York, NY, USA, 8 pages. https://doi.org/10.1145/3208976.3208997

1 INTRODUCTION

This paper is inspired by the pioneering work on the connections between chordal graphs and triangular sets [10], where the authors introduced the concept of chordal networks and proposed an algorithm for constructing chordal networks for polynomial sets based on the computation of triangular decomposition. In particular, the authors found that for input polynomial sets with chordal associated graphs, the elimination methods due to Wang become more efficient. It is worth mentioning that the authors also studied the connections between chordal graphs and Gröbner bases and found that the chordal structures of polynomial sets are destroyed in the computation of Gröbner bases [9].

The chordal graph structures have been studied and applied in the prediction of structures of matrices appearing in solving (especially sparse) linear systems. It is shown that the sparsity of the matrices handled by Gaussian elimination can be kept if the associated graph of this input matrix is chordal [18, 23, 25].

Like the Gröbner basis which has been greatly developed in its theory, methods, implementations, and applications [6, 11–13], the triangular set is another powerful algebraic tool in the study on and computation of polynomials symbolically, especially for elimination theory and polynomial system solving [2, 8, 16, 21, 22, 27, 30, 31], with diverse applications [7, 32]. The process of decomposing a polynomial set into finitely many triangular sets or systems (probably with additional properties like being regular or normal, etc.) with associated zero and ideal relationships is called triangular decomposition of the input polynomial set. Triangular decomposition of polynomial sets can be regarded as multivariate generalization of Gaussian elimination for solving linear equations.

The top-down strategy in triangular decomposition means that the variables appearing in the input polynomial set are handled in a strictly decreasing order, and it is a widely-used strategy in the design and implementations of algorithms for triangular decomposition. In particular, most algorithms for triangular decomposition due to Wang are in top-down style [27–29]. A Boolean algorithm for triangular decomposition in top-down style with refinement in the Boolean settings has also been proposed [17]. The fact that elimination in it is performed in a strictly decreasing order makes triangular decomposition in top-down style the closest among all kinds of triangular decomposition to Gaussian elimination, in which the elimination of entries in different columns of the matrix is also performed in a strict order.

In this paper we study the chordal structures of polynomial sets appearing in the algorithms for triangular decomposition in top-down style, in particular the graph structures of the triangular sets computed by such algorithms. This is multivariate generalization of the study on the roles chordal structures play in Gaussian elimination, and it is highly non-trivial in this polynomial (and thus nonlinear) case because of the complicated process of triangular decomposition due to splitting.

With the introduction of associated graphs of polynomial sets in Section 2, we define a polynomial set to be chordal if its associated

*This work was partially supported by the National Natural Science Foundation of China (NSFC 11401018 and 11771034)

ISSAC '18, July 16–19, 2018, New York, NY, USA

ACM ISBN 978-1-4503-5550-6/18/07...$15.00
https://doi.org/10.1145/3208976.3208997

graph is chordal. A chordal graph implies a perfect elimination ordering of the vertices, and we assume that the polynomial set $\mathcal{F}$ to decompose is chordal and that the variables are ordered as one perfect elimination ordering of its chordal associated graph $G(\mathcal{F})$. Under such assumptions, in this paper the graph structures of polynomial sets after reduction with respect to one variable and all the variables in triangular decomposition in top-down style are exploited in Section 3. In particular, it is proved that the associated graph of one specific triangular set computed in an arbitrary algorithm for triangular decomposition in top-down style is a subgraph of $G(\mathcal{F})$. Then in Section 4, for a specific simply-structured algorithm for triangular decomposition in top-down style, namely Wang's method, after reformulation of the underlying structures of its decomposition tree, we prove that each polynomial set appearing in the decomposition process has an associated graph which is a subgraph of $G(\mathcal{F})$, which implies that all the triangular sets computed by Wang's method have associated graphs which are subgraphs of $G(\mathcal{F})$. This paper ends with brief discussions on the applications of graph structures of polynomial sets on expressing the variable sparsity of polynomial sets and potential refined complexity analyses on triangular decomposition in top-down style in Section 5.

2 PRELIMINARIES

Let $\mathbb{K}$ be a field, and $\mathbb{K}[x_1,\ldots,x_n]$ be the multivariate polynomial ring over $\mathbb{K}$ in the variables $x_1,\ldots,x_n$. For the sake of simplicity, we write $(x_1,\ldots,x_n)$ as $\boldsymbol{x}$, $(x_1,\ldots,x_i)$ as $\boldsymbol{x}_i$ for some i $(1 \leq i < n)$, and $\mathbb{K}[x_1,\ldots,x_n]$ as $\mathbb{K}[\boldsymbol{x}]$.

2.1 Polynomial sets and associated graphs

For a polynomial $F \in \mathbb{K}[\boldsymbol{x}]$, define the (variable) *support* of F, denoted by $\operatorname{supp}(F)$, to be the set of variables in $\{x_1,\ldots,x_n\}$ which effectively appear in F. For a polynomial set $\mathcal{F} \subset \mathbb{K}[\boldsymbol{x}]$, $\operatorname{supp}(\mathcal{F}) := \cup_{F\in\mathcal{F}} \operatorname{supp}(F)$.

The *associated graph* $G(\mathcal{F})$ of a polynomial set $\mathcal{F} \subset \mathbb{K}[\boldsymbol{x}]$ is an undirected graph constructed in the following way:

(a) The vertices of $G(\mathcal{F})$ are the variables in $\operatorname{supp}(\mathcal{F})$.
(b) There exists an edge connecting two vertices x_i and x_j in $G(\mathcal{F})$ for $1 \leq i \neq j \leq n$ if there exists one polynomial $F \in \mathcal{F}$ such that $x_i, x_j \in \operatorname{supp}(F)$.

Example 2.1. The associated graphs of

$$\mathcal{P} = \{x_2 + x_1, x_3 + x_1, x_4^2 + x_2, x_4^3 + x_3, x_5 + x_2, x_5 + x_3 + x_2\}$$

$$\mathcal{Q} = \{x_2 + x_1, x_3 + x_1, x_3, x_4^2 + x_2, x_4^3 + x_3, x_5 + x_2\}$$

are shown in Figure 1.

Definition 2.2. Let $G = (V,E)$ be a graph with $V = \{x_1,\ldots,x_n\}$. Then an ordering $x_{i_1} < x_{i_2} < \cdots < x_{i_n}$ of the vertices is called a *perfect elimination ordering* of G if for each $j = i_1,\ldots,i_n$, the restriction of G on the following set

$$X_j = \{x_j\} \cup \{x_k : x_k < x_j \text{ and } (x_k,x_j) \in E\} \quad (1)$$

is a clique. A graph G is said to be *chordal* if there exists a perfect elimination ordering of it.

An equivalent condition for a graph $G = (V,E)$ to be *chordal* is the following: for any cycle C contained in G of four or more

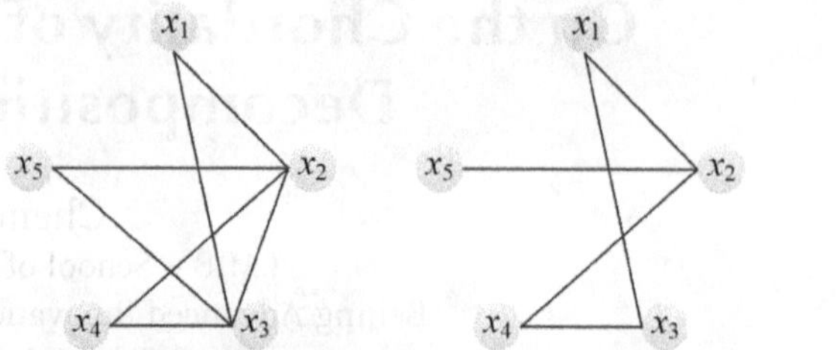

Figure 1: The associated graphs $G(\mathcal{P})$ (left) and $G(\mathcal{Q})$ (right) in Example 2.1

vertices, there is an edge $e \in E \setminus C$ connecting two vertices in C. The edge e in this case is called a *chord* of C. A chordal graph is also called a triangulated one.

Definition 2.3. A polynomial set $\mathcal{F} \subset \mathbb{K}[\boldsymbol{x}]$ is said to be *chordal* if its associated graph $G(\mathcal{F})$ is chordal.

Example 2.4. In Example 2.1 and Figure 1, the associated graph $G(\mathcal{P})$ is chordal by definition and thus $\mathcal{P}$ is chordal, while $G(\mathcal{Q})$ is not.

2.2 Triangular sets and triangular decomposition

Throughout this subsection the variables are ordered as $x_1 < \cdots < x_n$. For an arbitrary polynomial $F \in \mathbb{K}[\boldsymbol{x}]$, the greatest variable appearing in F is called its *leading variable*, denoted by $\operatorname{lv}(F)$. Let $\operatorname{lv}(F) = x_k$. Write $F = Ix_k^d + R$ with $I \in \mathbb{K}[x_1,\ldots,x_{k-1}]$, $R \in \mathbb{K}[x_1,\ldots,x_k]$, and $\deg(R,x_k) < d$. Then the polynomial I and R are called the *initial* and *tail* of F and denoted by $\operatorname{ini}(F)$ and $\operatorname{tail}(F)$ respectively. For two polynomial sets $\mathcal{F},\mathcal{G} \subset \mathbb{K}[\boldsymbol{x}]$, the set of common zeros of $\mathcal{F}$ is denoted by $\mathsf{Z}(\mathcal{F})$, and $\mathsf{Z}(\mathcal{F}/\mathcal{G}) := \mathsf{Z}(\mathcal{F}) \setminus \mathsf{Z}(\prod_{G\in\mathcal{G}} G)$.

Definition 2.5. An ordered set of non-constant polynomials $\mathcal{T} = [T_1,\ldots,T_r] \subset \mathbb{K}[\boldsymbol{x}]$ is called a *triangular set* if $\operatorname{lv}(T_1) < \cdots < \operatorname{lv}(T_r)$. A pair $(\mathcal{T},\mathcal{U})$ with $\mathcal{T},\mathcal{U} \subset \mathbb{K}[\boldsymbol{x}]$ is called a *triangular system* if $\mathcal{T}$ is a triangular set.

Definition 2.6. Let $\mathcal{F} \subset \mathbb{K}[\boldsymbol{x}]$ be a polynomial set. Then a finite number of triangular sets $\mathcal{T}_1,\ldots,\mathcal{T}_r \subset \mathbb{K}[\boldsymbol{x}]$ are called a *decomposition* of $\mathcal{F}$ *into triangular sets* if the zero relationship $\mathsf{Z}(\mathcal{F}) = \cup_{i=1}^{r} \mathsf{Z}(\mathcal{T}_i/\operatorname{ini}(\mathcal{T}_i))$ holds, where $\operatorname{ini}(\mathcal{T}_i) := \{\operatorname{ini}(T) : T \in \mathcal{T}_i\}$.

Definition 2.7. Let $\mathcal{F} \subset \mathbb{K}[\boldsymbol{x}]$ be a polynomial set. Then a finite number of triangular systems $(\mathcal{T}_1,\mathcal{U}_1),\ldots,(\mathcal{T}_r,\mathcal{U}_r)$ are called a *decomposition* of $\mathcal{F}$ *into triangular systems* if the zero relationship $\mathsf{Z}(\mathcal{F}) = \cup_{i=1}^{r} \mathsf{Z}(\mathcal{T}_i/\mathcal{U}_i)$ holds.

As shown in Definitions 2.5, 2.6, and 2.7, triangular systems are generalization of triangular sets. For a triangular system $(\mathcal{T},\mathcal{U})$, $\mathcal{T}$ is a triangular set which represents the equations $\mathcal{T} = 0$ while $\mathcal{U}$ is a polynomial set which represents the inequations $\mathcal{U} \neq 0$.

In general, the process of computing a decomposition of a polynomial set into triangular sets or systems is called *triangular decomposition*. There exist many algorithms for decomposing polynomial sets into triangular sets or systems with different properties. One of the main strategies for designing such algorithms for triangular decomposition is to carry out reduction on polynomials containing the largest (unprocessed) variable until there is only one such polynomial, at the same time producing new polynomials whose leading variables are strictly smaller than the processed variable.

For any polynomial set $\mathcal{P} \subset \mathbb{K}[\boldsymbol{x}]$ and an integer i $(1 \leq i \leq n)$, we denote $\mathcal{P}^{(i)} := \{P \in \mathcal{P} : \mathrm{lv}(P) = x_i\}$. The smallest integer i $(0 \leq i \leq n)$ such that $\#(\mathcal{P}^{(j)}) = 0$ or 1 for each $j = i+1, \ldots, n$ is called the *level* of $\mathcal{P}$ and denoted by level($\mathcal{P}$). Obviously a polynomial set $\mathcal{P}$ containing no constant forms a triangular set if level$(\mathcal{P}) = 0$.

Let $\mathcal{F}$ be a polynomial set in $\mathbb{K}[\boldsymbol{x}]$ and Φ be a set of polynomial sets, initialized with $\{\mathcal{F}\}$. Then an algorithm $\mathcal{A}$ for computing triangular decomposition of $\mathcal{F}$ is said to be in *top-down style* if for each polynomial set $\mathcal{P} \in \Phi$ with level$(\mathcal{P}) = k > 0$, the algorithm $\mathcal{A}$ handles the polynomials in $\mathcal{P}^{(k)}$ to produce finitely many polynomials sets $\mathcal{Q}_1, \ldots, \mathcal{Q}_s$ such that $\mathsf{Z}(\mathcal{P}) = \cup_{i=1}^{s} \mathsf{Z}(\mathcal{Q}_i)$ and for $i = 1, \ldots, s$, $\mathcal{Q}_i^{(j)} = \mathcal{P}^{(j)}$ for $j = k+1, \ldots, n$, $\mathrm{supp}(\mathcal{Q}_i^{(j)}) \subset \mathrm{supp}(\mathcal{P}^{(j)}) \cup \mathrm{supp}(\mathcal{P}^{(k)})$ for $j = 1, \ldots, k$, $\#(\mathcal{Q}_{i_0}^{(k)}) = 1$ for some $\mathcal{Q}_{i_0}$ $(1 \leq i_0 \leq s)$, and the other $\mathcal{Q}_i$ $(i \neq i_0)$ are put into Φ for later computation.

The requirements on $\mathrm{supp}(\mathcal{Q}_i^{(j)})$ for $j = 1, \ldots, k$ are due to the fact that when handling a polynomial set $\mathcal{P} \in \Phi$ with level$(\mathcal{P}) = k$, only the polynomials in $\mathcal{P}^{(k)}$ are reduced in a certain way in algorithms for triangular decomposition in top-down style, producing new polynomials in the variables from $\mathrm{supp}(\mathcal{P}^{(k)})$.

3 CHORDALITY OF POLYNOMIAL SETS IN GENERAL TRIANGULAR DECOMPOSITION IN TOP-DOWN STYLE

In this section, the graph structures of polynomial sets in an arbitrary algorithm for triangular decomposition in top-down style are studied when the input polynomial set is chordal. We start this section with the connections between the associated graphs of a triangular set reduced from a chordal polynomial set and the chordal associated graph of the input polynomial set.

Proposition 3.1. *Let $\mathcal{P} \subset \mathbb{K}[\boldsymbol{x}]$ be a chordal polynomial set with $x_1 < \cdots < x_n$ as one perfect elimination ordering. For $i = 1, \ldots, n$, let $T_i \in \mathbb{K}[\boldsymbol{x}]$ be a polynomial such that $\mathrm{lv}(T_i) = x_i$ and $\mathrm{supp}(T_i) \subset \mathrm{supp}(\mathcal{P}^{(i)})$ (T_i is set null if $\mathcal{P}^{(i)} = \emptyset$). Then $\mathcal{T} = [T_1, \ldots, T_n]$ is a triangular set, and $G(\mathcal{T}) \subset G(\mathcal{P})$. In particular, if $\mathrm{supp}(T_i) = \mathrm{supp}(\mathcal{P}^{(i)})$ for $i = 1, \ldots, n$, then $G(\mathcal{T}) = G(\mathcal{P})$.*

Proof. It is straightforward that $\mathcal{T}$ is a triangular set with $\mathrm{lv}(T_i) = x_i$ if $\mathcal{P}^{(i)} \neq \emptyset$ for $i = 1, \ldots, n$.

For any edge $(x_i, x_j) \in G(\mathcal{T})$, there exists an integer k $(i, j \leq k \leq n)$ such that $x_i, x_j \in \mathrm{supp}(T_k)$. Then $x_i, x_j \in \mathrm{supp}(\mathcal{P}^{(k)})$, and thus $(x_i, x_k) \in G(\mathcal{P})$ and $(x_j, x_k) \in G(\mathcal{P})$. Since $G(\mathcal{P})$ is chordal with $x_1 < \ldots < x_n$ as a perfect elimination ordering and $x_i < x_k$, $x_j < x_k$, we know that $(x_i, x_j) \in G(\mathcal{P})$ by Definition 2.2. This proves the inclusion $G(\mathcal{T}) \subset G(\mathcal{P})$.

In the case when $\mathrm{supp}(T_i) = \mathrm{supp}(\mathcal{P}^{(i)})$ for $i = 1, \ldots, n$, next we show the inclusion $G(\mathcal{T}) \supset G(\mathcal{P})$, which implies the equality $G(\mathcal{T}) = G(\mathcal{P})$. For any $(x_i, x_j) \in G(\mathcal{P})$, there exists an integer k and a polynomial P such that $x_i, x_j \in \mathrm{supp}(P)$ with $P \in \mathcal{P}^{(k)}$. Since $\mathrm{supp}(P) \subseteq \mathrm{supp}(T_k)$, we know that $x_i, x_j \in \mathrm{supp}(T_k)$ and thus $(x_i, x_j) \in G(\mathcal{T})$. □

Example 3.2. Proposition 3.1 does not necessarily hold in general if the polynomial set $\mathcal{P}$ is not chordal. Consider the same $\mathcal{Q}$ as in Example 2.1 whose associated graph $G(\mathcal{Q})$ is not chordal. Let

$$\mathcal{T} = [x_2 + x_1, x_3 + x_1, -x_2x_4 + x_3, x_5 + x_2].$$

Then one can check that for $i = 2, \ldots, 5$, $\mathrm{supp}(\mathcal{T}^{(i)}) = \mathrm{supp}(\mathcal{Q}^{(i)})$, but the associated graph $G(\mathcal{T})$, as shown in Figure 2, is not a subgraph of $G(\mathcal{Q})$.

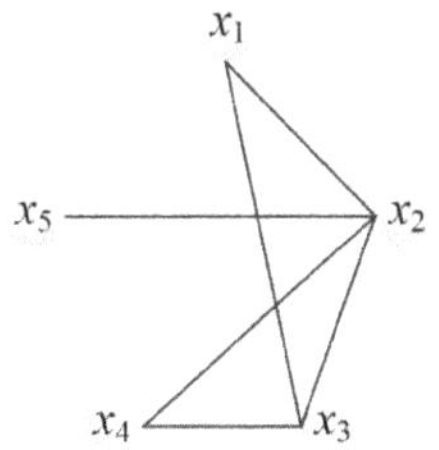

Figure 2: The associated graph $G(\mathcal{T})$ in Example 3.2

The following theorem relates the associated graph of a chordal polynomial set and that of the polynomial set after reduction with respect to one variable.

Theorem 3.3. *Let $\mathcal{P} \subset \mathbb{K}[\boldsymbol{x}]$ be a chordal polynomial set such that $\mathcal{P}^{(n)} \neq \emptyset$ and $x_1 < \ldots < x_n$ is one perfect elimination ordering. Let $T \in \mathbb{K}[\boldsymbol{x}]$ be a polynomial such that $\mathrm{lv}(T) = x_n$ and $\mathrm{supp}(T) \subset \mathrm{supp}(\mathcal{P}^{(n)})$, and $\mathcal{R} \subset \mathbb{K}[\boldsymbol{x}]$ be a polynomial set such that $\mathrm{supp}(\mathcal{R}) \subset \mathrm{supp}(\mathcal{P}^{(n)}) \setminus \{x_n\}$. Then for the polynomial set $\tilde{\mathcal{P}} = \tilde{\mathcal{P}}^{(1)} \cup \cdots \cup \tilde{\mathcal{P}}^{(n-1)} \cup \{T\}$, where $\tilde{\mathcal{P}}^{(k)} = \mathcal{P}^{(k)} \cup \mathcal{R}^{(k)}$ for $k = 1, \ldots, n-1$, we have $G(\tilde{\mathcal{P}}) \subset G(\mathcal{P})$. In particular, if $\mathrm{supp}(T) = \mathrm{supp}(\mathcal{P}^{(n)})$, then $G(\tilde{\mathcal{P}}) = G(\mathcal{P})$.*

Proof. To prove the inclusion $G(\tilde{\mathcal{P}}) \subset G(\mathcal{P})$, it suffices to show that for each edge $(x_i, x_j) \in G(\tilde{\mathcal{P}})$, we have $(x_i, x_j) \in G(\mathcal{P})$. For an arbitrary edge $(x_i, x_j) \in G(\tilde{\mathcal{P}})$, there exists a polynomial $P \in \tilde{\mathcal{P}}$ and an integer k $(i, j \leq k \leq n)$ such that $x_i, x_j \in \mathrm{supp}(P)$ and $P \in \tilde{\mathcal{P}}^{(k)}$.

If $k = n$, then $x_i, x_j \in \mathrm{supp}(T)$, and by $\mathrm{supp}(T) \subset \mathrm{supp}(\mathcal{P}^{(n)})$ we have $x_i, x_j \in \mathrm{supp}(\mathcal{P}^{(n)})$. This implies that $(x_i, x_n), (x_j, x_n) \in G(\mathcal{P}^{(n)}) \subset G(\mathcal{P})$ and by the chordality of $G(\mathcal{P})$ we have $(x_i, x_j) \in G(\mathcal{P})$.

Else if $k < n$, then by $\tilde{\mathcal{P}}^{(k)} = \mathcal{P}^{(k)} \cup \mathcal{R}^{(k)}$ there are two cases for P accordingly: when $P \in \mathcal{P}^{(k)} \subset \mathcal{P}$, clearly $(x_i, x_j) \in G(\mathcal{P})$; when $P \in \mathcal{R}^{(k)}$, we have $x_i, x_j \in \mathrm{supp}(\mathcal{R}^{(k)}) \subset \mathrm{supp}(\mathcal{P}^{(n)})$, and thus $(x_i, x_n), (x_j, x_n) \in G(\mathcal{P}^{(n)}) \subset G(\mathcal{P})$, and the chordality $G(\mathcal{P})$ implies $(x_i, x_j) \in G(\mathcal{P})$.

In particular, if $\mathrm{supp}(T) = \mathrm{supp}(\mathcal{P}^{(n)})$, then by $G(\mathcal{P}^{(k)}) \subset G(\tilde{\mathcal{P}}^{(k)})$ for $k = 1, \ldots, n-1$ and $G(\mathcal{P}^{(n)}) \subset G(T)$, we have $G(\mathcal{P}) \subset G(\tilde{\mathcal{P}})$. This proves the equality $G(\tilde{\mathcal{P}}) = G(\mathcal{P})$. □

Example 3.4. Let $\mathcal{P}$ be the chordal polynomial set as in Example 2.1. Then $\mathcal{P}^{(5)} = \{x_5 + x_2, x_5 + x_3 + x_2\}$. If we take $T = x_5 + x_2$, and $\mathcal{R} = \{\mathrm{prem}(x_5 + x_3 + x_2, x_5 + x_2)\} = \{x_3\}$, then $\tilde{\mathcal{P}}$ equals $\mathcal{Q}$ in Example 2.1, and $G(\tilde{\mathcal{P}})$ is a (strict) subgraph of $G(\mathcal{P})$; If we take $T = x_5 + x_3 + x_2$, and $\mathcal{R} = \{\mathrm{prem}(x_5 + x_2, x_5 + x_3 + x_2)\} = \{-x_3\}$, then $\mathrm{supp}(T) = \mathrm{supp}(\mathcal{P}^{(5)})$ and thus $G(\tilde{\mathcal{P}}) = G(\mathcal{P})$.

Next we introduce some notations to formulate the reduction process in Theorem 3.3. Denote the power set of a set S by 2^S. For an integer i ($1 \le i \le n$), let f_i be a mapping

$$\begin{aligned} f_i : 2^{\mathbb{K}[\boldsymbol{x}_i]\setminus\mathbb{K}[\boldsymbol{x}_{i-1}]} &\to (\mathbb{K}[\boldsymbol{x}_i] \setminus \mathbb{K}[\boldsymbol{x}_{i-1}]) \times 2^{\mathbb{K}[\boldsymbol{x}_{i-1}]} \\ \mathcal{P} &\mapsto (T, \mathcal{R}) \end{aligned} \tag{2}$$

such that $\mathrm{supp}(T) \subset \mathrm{supp}(\mathcal{P})$ and $\mathrm{supp}(\mathcal{R}) \subset \mathrm{supp}(\mathcal{P})$, where $\mathbb{K}[\boldsymbol{x}_0]$ is understood as $\mathbb{K}$. For a polynomial set $\mathcal{P} \subset \mathbb{K}[\boldsymbol{x}]$ and a fixed integer i ($1 \le i \le n$), suppose that $(T_i, \mathcal{R}_i) = f_i(\mathcal{P}^{(i)})$ for some f_i as stated above. For $j = 1, \dots, n$, define the polynomial set

$$\mathrm{red}_i(\mathcal{P}^{(j)}) := \begin{cases} \mathcal{P}^{(j)}, & \text{if } j > i \\ \{T_i\}, & \text{if } j = i \\ \mathcal{P}^{(j)} \cup \mathcal{R}_i^{(j)}, & \text{if } j < i \end{cases}$$

and $\mathrm{red}_i(\mathcal{P}) := \cup_{j=1}^{n} \mathrm{red}_i(\mathcal{P}^{(j)})$. In particular, write

$$\overline{\mathrm{red}_i}(\mathcal{P}) := \mathrm{red}_i(\mathrm{red}_{i+1}(\cdots(\mathrm{red}_n(\mathcal{P}))\cdots)) \tag{3}$$

for simplicity.

Here $\mathrm{red}_i(\cdot)$ denotes the result of reduction with respect to x_i and $\overline{\mathrm{red}_i}(\cdot)$ denotes the result of successive reduction with respect to $x_n, x_{n-1}, \dots, x_i$. Following the above terminologies, Theorem 3.3 can be reformulated as $G(\mathrm{red}_n(\mathcal{P})) \subset G(\mathcal{P})$, and the equality holds if $\mathrm{supp}(T_n) = \mathrm{supp}(\mathcal{P}^{(n)})$.

Proposition 3.5. *Let $\mathcal{P} \subset \mathbb{K}[\boldsymbol{x}]$ be a chordal polynomial set with $x_1 < \cdots < x_n$ as one perfect elimination ordering. For each i ($1 \le i \le n$), suppose that $(T_i, \mathcal{R}_i) = f_i(\overline{\mathrm{red}_{i+1}}(\mathcal{P})^{(i)})$ for some f_i as in* (2) *and* $\mathrm{supp}(T_i) = \mathrm{supp}(\overline{\mathrm{red}_{i+1}}(\mathcal{P})^{(i)})$, *where $\overline{\mathrm{red}_{n+1}}(\mathcal{P})$ is understood as $\mathcal{P}$. Then $G(\overline{\mathrm{red}_1}(\mathcal{P})) = G(\mathcal{P})$.*

Proof. Repeated use of Theorem 3.3 implies

$$G(\mathcal{P}) = G(\mathrm{red}_n(\mathcal{P})) = G(\overline{\mathrm{red}_{n-1}}(\mathcal{P})) = \cdots = G(\overline{\mathrm{red}_1}(\mathcal{P})),$$

and the conclusion follows. □

Note that $\overline{\mathrm{red}_1}(\mathcal{P})$ forms a triangular set after reordering if it does not contain any non-zero constant. Indeed, the reduction process to compute this triangular set is commonly used in algorithms for triangular decomposition in top-down style, and the mapping f_i in (2) is an abstraction of specific reductions used in different kinds of algorithms for triangular decomposition [20]. For example, one specific kind of such reduction is performed by using pseudo-divisions, and in this case $\mathcal{R}$ in (2) consists of pseudo-remainders which do not contain x_i.

Proposition 3.5 holds because after every reduction $G(\overline{\mathrm{red}_i}(\mathcal{P}))$ remains the same as the chordal graph $G(\mathcal{P})$, and thus the hypotheses of Theorem 3.3 remain satisfied. If we loosen the condition $\mathrm{supp}(T_i) = \mathrm{supp}(\overline{\mathrm{red}_{i+1}}(\mathcal{P})^{(i)})$ in Proposition 3.5 to $\mathrm{supp}(T_i) \subset \mathrm{supp}(\overline{\mathrm{red}_{i+1}}(\mathcal{P})^{(i)})$, then in general we will not have

$$G(\overline{\mathrm{red}_1}(\mathcal{P})) \subset \cdots \subset G(\overline{\mathrm{red}_{n-1}}(\mathcal{P})) \subset G(\mathrm{red}_n(\mathcal{P})) \subset G(\mathcal{P}),$$

as shown by the following example (though the last inclusion always holds because $G(\mathcal{P})$ is chordal).

Example 3.6. Let us continue with Example 3.4 with $\mathcal{P}$ and $\mathcal{Q} = \mathrm{red}_5(\mathcal{P})$, where $G(\mathcal{Q}) \subsetneq G(\mathcal{P})$. Take

$$T_4 = \mathrm{prem}(x_4^3 + x_3, x_4^2 + x_2) = -x_2x_4 + x_3,$$

$$\mathcal{R}_4 = \{\mathrm{prem}(x_4^2 + x_2, -x_2x_4 + x_3)\} = \{x_3^2 - x_2^3\},$$

then

$$\mathcal{Q}' := \overline{\mathrm{red}_4}(\mathcal{P}) = \{x_2 + x_1, x_3 + x_1, x_3^2 - x_2^3, x_3, -x_2x_4 + x_3, x_5 + x_2\}.$$

The associated graph $G(\mathcal{Q}')$ is shown below. Note that $G(\mathcal{Q}') \not\subset G(\mathcal{Q})$ but $G(\mathcal{Q}') \subset G(\mathcal{P})$.

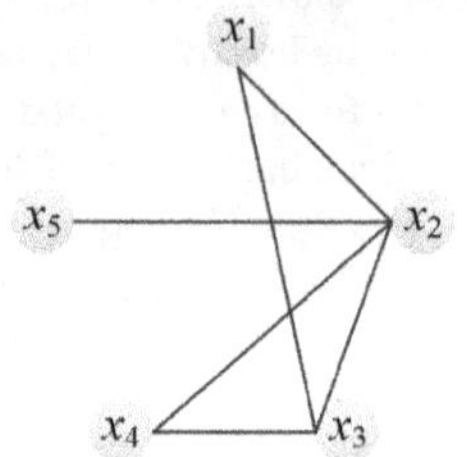

Figure 3: The associated graph $G(\mathcal{Q}')$ in Example 3.6

Despite of this example where successive inclusions of the associated graphs in the reduction chain does not hold, it can be proved that for each $i = n, \dots, 1$, $G(\overline{\mathrm{red}_i}(\mathcal{P}))$ is a subgraph of the original graph $G(\mathcal{P})$.

Lemma 3.7. *Let $\mathcal{P} \subset \mathbb{K}[\boldsymbol{x}]$ be a chordal polynomial set with $x_1 < \cdots < x_n$ as one perfect elimination ordering and $\overline{\mathrm{red}_i}(\mathcal{P})$ be defined in* (3) *for $i = n, \dots, 1$. Then for each $i = n, \dots, 1$ and any two variables x_p and x_q, if there exists an integer k such that $x_p, x_q \in \mathrm{supp}(\overline{\mathrm{red}_i}(\mathcal{P})^{(k)})$, then $(x_p, x_q) \in G(\mathcal{P})$.*

Proof. We induce on the integer i. In the case $i = n$, from the proof of Theorem 3.3 one can easily find that the proposition is true. Now suppose that the proposition holds for $i = j$ ($< n$), and next we prove that it also holds for $i = j - 1$, namely for any x_p and x_q, if there exists k ($\ge p, q$) such that $x_p, x_q \in \mathrm{supp}(\overline{\mathrm{red}_{j-1}}(\mathcal{P})^{(k)})$, then $(x_p, x_q) \in G(\mathcal{P})$.

First by $\overline{\mathrm{red}_{j-1}}(\mathcal{P}) = \mathrm{red}_{j-1}(\overline{\mathrm{red}_j}(\mathcal{P}))$ we know that there exists a polynomial set $\tilde{\mathcal{R}}$ such that

$$\overline{\mathrm{red}_{j-1}}(\mathcal{P})^{(k)} = \overline{\mathrm{red}_j}(\mathcal{P})^{(k)} \cup \tilde{\mathcal{R}}^{(k)}$$

and $\mathrm{supp}(\tilde{\mathcal{R}}) \subset \mathrm{supp}(\overline{\mathrm{red}_j}(\mathcal{P})^{(j-1)}) \setminus \{x_{j-1}\}$.

(a) If $\tilde{\mathcal{R}} = \emptyset$, then $x_p, x_q \in \mathrm{supp}(\overline{\mathrm{red}_j}(\mathcal{P})^{(k)})$, and by the induction assumption we know that $(x_p, x_q) \in G(\mathcal{P})$.

(b) If $\tilde{\mathcal{R}} \neq \emptyset$, then $x_k \in \mathrm{supp}(\tilde{\mathcal{R}}^{(k)}) \subset \mathrm{supp}(\overline{\mathrm{red}_j}(\mathcal{P})^{(j-1)})$. Next we consider the following three cases.

Case (1), $x_p, x_q \in \mathrm{supp}(\overline{\mathrm{red}_j}(\mathcal{P})^{(k)})$: with the same argument as in (a) we know that $(x_p, x_q) \in G(\mathcal{P})$.

Case (2), $x_p, x_q \in \mathrm{supp}(\tilde{\mathcal{R}}^{(k)}) \subset \mathrm{supp}(\overline{\mathrm{red}_j}(\mathcal{P})^{(j-1)})$: by the induction assumption we know that $(x_p, x_q) \in G(\mathcal{P})$.

Case (3), $x_p \in \mathrm{supp}(\overline{\mathrm{red}_j}(\mathcal{P})^{(k)})$ and $x_q \in \mathrm{supp}(\tilde{\mathcal{R}}^{(k)})$: Since $x_p, x_k \in \mathrm{supp}(\overline{\mathrm{red}_j}(\mathcal{P})^{(k)})$, by the induction assumption we have $(x_p, x_k) \in G(\mathcal{P})$; since $x_q, x_k \in \mathrm{supp}(\overline{\mathrm{red}_j}(\mathcal{P})^{(j-1)})$, by the induction assumption we have $(x_q, x_k) \in G(\mathcal{P})$. Then by the chordality of $\mathcal{P}$, $(x_p, x_k) \in G(\mathcal{P})$ and $(x_q, x_k) \in G(\mathcal{P})$ imply that $(x_p, x_q) \in G(\mathcal{P})$.

This ends the proof of this proposition by induction on i. □

THEOREM 3.8. *Let $\mathcal{P} \subset \mathbb{K}[\boldsymbol{x}]$ be a chordal polynomial set with $x_1 < \cdots < x_n$ as one perfect elimination ordering and $\overline{\mathrm{red}}_i(\mathcal{P})$ be defined in (3) for $i = n, \ldots, 1$. Then for each $i = n, \ldots, 1$, $G(\overline{\mathrm{red}}_i(\mathcal{P})) \subset G(\mathcal{P})$.*

PROOF. By the construction of $\overline{\mathrm{red}}_i(\mathcal{P})$, we know that all the vertices of $G(\overline{\mathrm{red}}_i(\mathcal{P}))$ are also vertices of $G(\mathcal{P})$. For each edge $(x_p, x_q) \in G(\overline{\mathrm{red}}_i(\mathcal{P}))$, there exists an integer k ($p, q \leq k \leq n$) and a polynomial P such that $x_p, x_q \in \mathrm{supp}(P)$ and $P \in \overline{\mathrm{red}}_i(\mathcal{P})^{(k)}$. Then by Lemma 3.7, we know that $(x_p, x_q) \in G(\mathcal{P})$, and thus $G(\overline{\mathrm{red}}_i(\mathcal{P})) \subset G(\mathcal{P})$. □

COROLLARY 3.9. *Let $\mathcal{P} \subset \mathbb{K}[\boldsymbol{x}]$ be a chordal polynomial set with $x_1 < \cdots < x_n$ as one perfect elimination ordering and $\overline{\mathrm{red}}_i(\mathcal{P})$ be defined in (3) for $i = n, \ldots, 1$. If $\mathcal{T} := \overline{\mathrm{red}}_1(\mathcal{P})$ does not contain any nonzero constant, then $\mathcal{T}$ forms a triangular set such that $G(\mathcal{T}) \subset G(\mathcal{P})$.*

Corollary 3.9 tells us that under the conditions that the input polynomial set is chordal and the variable ordering is one perfect elimination ordering, the associated graph of one specific triangular set computed in any algorithm for triangular decomposition in top-down style is a subgraph of the associated graph of the input polynomial set. In fact, this triangular set is the "main branch" in the triangular decomposition in the sense that other branches are obtained by adding additional constrains in the splitting in the process of triangular decomposition.

Note that in the case when the input polynomial set $\mathcal{P}$ is not chordal, a process of chordal completion can be carried out on $G(\mathcal{P})$ to generate a chordal graph (in the worst case this chordal completion results in a complete graph which is trivially chordal). After this chordal completion the conditions of Corollary 3.9 will be satisfied.

The chordality of any triangular sets other than the specific one above in a triangular decomposition computed by an algorithm in top-down style is dependent on the splitting strategy in the algorithm. Therefore in the next section we focus on Wang's method, one specific algorithm for triangular decomposition in top-down style, and prove that the associated graphs of all the triangular sets computed by Wang's method are subgraphs of the associated graph of a chordal input polynomial set.

4 CHORDALITY OF POLYNOMIAL SETS COMPUTED BY WANG'S METHOD

A simply-structured algorithm was proposed by Wang for triangular decomposition in top-down style in 1993 [27], which is referred to as Wang's method in the literature (see. e.g., [3]). In this section the chordaility of polynomial sets in the decomposition process of Wang's method is studied.

4.1 Restatement of Wang's method

For the self-containness of this paper, Wang's method for triangular decomposition is outlined in Algorithm 1 below. In this algorithm, the data structure $(\mathcal{P}, \mathcal{Q}, i)$ is used to represent two polynomial sets $\mathcal{P}$ and $\mathcal{Q}$ such that $\#(\mathcal{P}^{(j)}) = 1$ or 0 for $j = i+1, \ldots, n$, and the subroutine pop(Φ) returns an element in Φ and then removes it from Φ.

Algorithm 1: Wang's method for triangular decomposition $\Psi := \mathrm{TriDecWang}(\mathcal{F})$

Input: $\mathcal{F}$, a polynomial set in $\mathbb{K}[\boldsymbol{x}]$
Output: Ψ, a set of finitely many triangular systems which form a triangular decomposition of $\mathcal{F}$

1 $\Phi := \{(\mathcal{F}, \emptyset, n)\}$;
2 **while** $\Phi \neq \emptyset$ **do**
3     $(\mathcal{P}, \mathcal{Q}, i) := \mathrm{pop}(\Phi)$;
4   **if** $i = 0$ **then**
5         $\Psi := \Psi \cup \{(\mathcal{P}, \mathcal{Q})\}$;
6   Break;
7   **while** $\#(\mathcal{P}^{(i)}) > 1$ **do**
8         $T :=$ a polynomial in $\mathcal{P}^{(i)}$ with minimal degree in x_i;
9         $\Phi := \Phi \cup \{(\mathcal{P} \setminus \{T\} \cup \{\mathrm{ini}(T), \mathrm{tail}(T)\}, \mathcal{Q}, i)\}$;
10         $\overline{\mathcal{P}} := \mathcal{P}^{(i)} \setminus \{T\}$;
11         $\mathcal{P} := \mathcal{P} \setminus \overline{\mathcal{P}}$;
12   **for** $P \in \overline{\mathcal{P}}$ **do**
13             $\mathcal{P} := \mathcal{P} \cup \{\mathrm{prem}(P, T)\}$;
14         $\mathcal{Q} := \mathcal{Q} \cup \{\mathrm{ini}(T)\}$;
15     $\Phi := \Phi \cup \{(\mathcal{P}, \mathcal{Q}, i-1)\}$;
16 **for** $(\mathcal{P}, \mathcal{Q}) \in \Psi$ **do**
17   **if** *$\mathcal{P}$ contains a non-zero constant* **then**
18         $\Psi := \Psi \setminus \{(\mathcal{P}, \mathcal{Q})\}$;
19 **return** Ψ;

As shown in Algorithm 1, for each $(\mathcal{P}, \mathcal{Q}, i)$ picked from Φ, if $\mathcal{P}$ is already a triangular set (namely $i = 0$ and $\mathcal{P}$ contains no non-zero constant), then $(\mathcal{P}, \mathcal{Q})$ is included in the output Ψ. Note that $\mathcal{Q}$ is for collecting the inequations $\mathrm{ini}(T) \neq 0$ for T in Line 8 of Algorithm 1 and it does not impose any influence on the graph structures of the triangular sets computed by Wang's method.

The decomposition process in Wang's method (Algorithm 1) applied to $\mathcal{F}$ can be viewed as a binary tree with its root as $(\mathcal{F}, \emptyset, n)$. The nodes of this binary tree are all the tuples $(\mathcal{P}, \mathcal{Q}, i)$ picked from Φ, and each node $(\mathcal{P}, \mathcal{Q}, i)$ has two children $(\mathcal{P}', \mathcal{Q}', i)$ and $(\mathcal{P}'', \mathcal{Q}'', i)$, where

$$\mathcal{P}' := \mathcal{P} \setminus \mathcal{P}^{(i)} \cup \{T\} \cup \{\mathrm{prem}(P, T) : P \in \mathcal{P}^{(i)}\}, \quad \mathcal{Q}' := \mathcal{Q} \cup \{\mathrm{ini}(T)\},$$
$$\mathcal{P}'' := \mathcal{P} \setminus \{T\} \cup \{\mathrm{ini}(T), \mathrm{tail}(T)\}, \qquad \mathcal{Q}'' := \mathcal{Q},$$

with T as a polynomial in $\mathcal{P}^{(i)}$ with minimal degree in x_i. In fact, the left child node corresponds to the case when $\mathrm{ini}(T) \neq 0$ and thus reduction of $\mathcal{P}^{(i)}$ are performed with respect to T; while the right child node corresponds to the case $\mathrm{ini}(T) = 0$, where T is replaced by $\mathrm{ini}(T)$ and $\mathrm{tail}(T)$.

The binary decomposition tree for Wang's method and the splitting at one node are illustrated in Figures 4 and 5 respectively.

4.2 Chordality of polynomial sets in Wang's method

With a chordal polynomial set as input of Wang's method, the relationships between the associated graphs of the polynomial sets

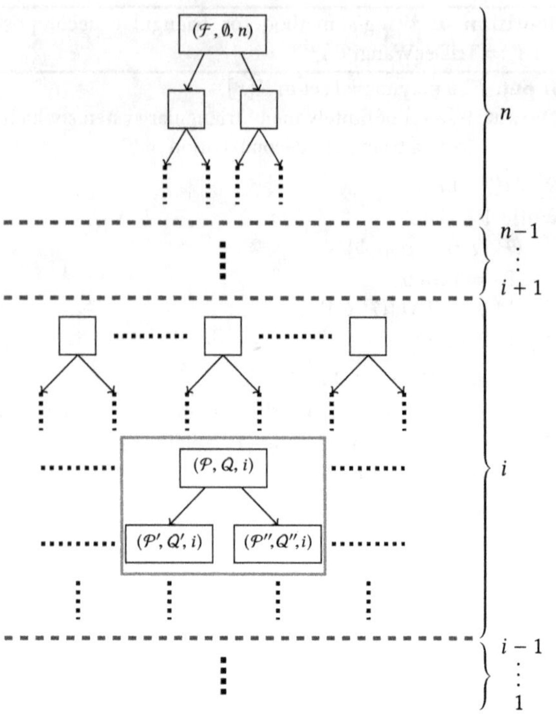

Figure 4: Binary decomposition tree for Wang's method

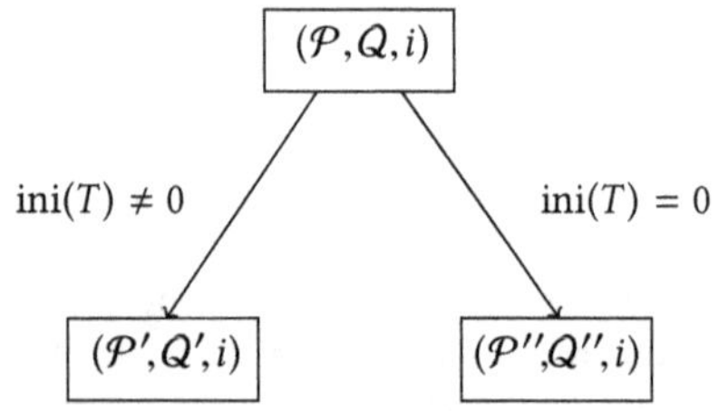

$\mathcal{P}' = \mathcal{P}\setminus\mathcal{P}^{(i)}\cup\{T\}\cup\{\text{prem}(P,T)\colon P\in\mathcal{P}^{(i)}\}$, $\mathcal{Q}' = \mathcal{Q}\cup\{\text{ini}(T)\}$

$\mathcal{P}'' = \mathcal{P}\setminus\{T\}\cup\{\text{ini}(T),\text{tail}(T)\}$, $\mathcal{Q}'' = \mathcal{Q}$

Figure 5: Splitting at one node $(\mathcal{P},\mathcal{Q},i)$ in the binary decomposition tree

in the left nodes and that of the input polynomial set and between the associated graphs of the polynomial sets in the right child nodes and those in the parent nodes are clarified in the following propositions.

Proposition 4.1. *Let $\mathcal{F}\subset\mathbb{K}[\mathbf{x}]$ be a chordal polynomial set with $x_1<\cdots<x_n$ as one perfect elimination ordering and $(\mathcal{P},\mathcal{Q},i)$ be any node in the binary decomposition tree for Wang's method applied to $\mathcal{F}$ such that $G(\mathcal{P})\subset G(\mathcal{F})$, T be a polynomial in $\mathcal{P}$ with minimal degree in x_i. Denote $\mathcal{P}'=\mathcal{P}\setminus\mathcal{P}^{(i)}\cup\{T\}\cup\{\text{prem}(P,T):\ P\in\mathcal{P}^{(i)}\}$. Then $G(\mathcal{P}')\subset G(\mathcal{F})$.*

Proof. Clearly the vertices of $G(\mathcal{P}')$ are also those of $G(\mathcal{P})$ and thus those of $G(\mathcal{F})$, and it suffices to prove that for any edge $(x_p,x_q)\in G(\mathcal{P}')$, we have $(x_p,x_q)\in G(\mathcal{F})$.

Denote $\mathcal{R} := \{\text{prem}(P,T) : P\in\mathcal{P}^{(i)}\setminus\{T\}\}$. Then by definition $\text{supp}(\mathcal{R}^{(\ell)})\subset\text{supp}(\mathcal{P}^{(i)})$ for any $\ell=1,\ldots,i$. Furthermore, the following relationships hold: $\mathcal{P}'^{(\ell)}=\mathcal{P}^{(\ell)}\cup\mathcal{R}^{(\ell)}$ for $\ell=1,\ldots,i-1$ and $\mathcal{P}'^{(i)}=\{T\}\cup\mathcal{R}^{(i)}$. For any edge $(x_p,x_q)\in G(\mathcal{P}')$, there exist an integer k ($p,q\le k\le i$) and a polynomial $P\in\mathcal{P}'^{(k)}$ such that $x_p,x_q\in\text{supp}(P)$.

In the case when $k=i$, we have $(x_p,x_q)\in G(\mathcal{P}'^{(i)})$. Then $x_p,x_q\in\text{supp}(T)\cup\text{supp}(\mathcal{R}^{(i)})\subset\text{supp}(\mathcal{P}^{(i)})$ and thus (x_p,x_i), $(x_q,x_i)\in G(\mathcal{P}^{(i)})\subset G(\mathcal{F})$. By the chordality of $\mathcal{F}$, we have $(x_p,x_q)\in G(\mathcal{F})$.

In the case when $k<i$, we have $(x_p,x_q)\in G(\mathcal{P}'^{(k)})$ with $\mathcal{P}'^{(k)}=\mathcal{P}^{(k)}\cup\mathcal{R}^{(k)}$. If $P\in\mathcal{P}^{(k)}$, then it is obvious that $(x_p,x_q)\in G(\mathcal{P}^{(k)})\subset G(\mathcal{F})$; otherwise if $P\in\mathcal{R}^{(k)}$, then $x_p,x_q\in\text{supp}(R^{(k)})\subset\text{supp}(\mathcal{P}^{i})$ and thus $(x_p,x_i),(x_q,x_i)\in G(\mathcal{P})\subset G(\mathcal{F})$, then by the chordality of $\mathcal{F}$, we have $(x_p,x_q)\in G(\mathcal{F})$. □

Proposition 4.2. *Let $(\mathcal{P},\mathcal{Q},i)$ be any node in the binary decomposition tree for Wang's method and T be a polynomial in $\mathcal{P}^{(i)}$ with minimal degree in x_i. Denote $\mathcal{P}''=\mathcal{P}\setminus\{T\}\cup\{\text{ini}(T),\text{tail}(T)\}$. Then $G(\mathcal{P}'')\subset G(P)$. In particular, if $\text{supp}(\text{tail}(T))=\text{supp}(T)$, then $G(\mathcal{P}'')=G(\mathcal{P})$.*

Proof. Since $\mathcal{P}''$ is constructed by replacing T in $\mathcal{P}$ with $\text{ini}(T)$ and $\text{tail}(T)$, we only need to study the differences between $G(\mathcal{P})$ and $G(\mathcal{P}'')$ caused by this replacement. First, by $\text{supp}(\text{ini}(T))\cup\text{supp}(\text{tail}(T))\subset\text{supp}(T)$ we have $\text{supp}(\mathcal{P}'')\subset\text{supp}(\mathcal{P})$. Second, for any edge (x_p,x_q) in $G(\text{ini}(T))$ or in $G(\text{tail}(T))$, we know that $(x_p,x_q)\in G(T)$, which means that all the edges of $G(\mathcal{P}'')$ are also edges of $G(\mathcal{P})$. Therefore, $G(\mathcal{P}'')\subset G(\mathcal{P})$.

In particular, if $\text{supp}(\text{tail}(T))=\text{supp}(T)$, then $\text{supp}(\text{ini}(T))\cup\text{supp}(\text{tail}(T))=\text{supp}(T)$ and any edge $(x_p,x_q)\in\text{supp}(T)$ is also contained in $G(\text{tail}(T))$, and thus $G(\mathcal{P}'')=G(\mathcal{P})$. □

Example 4.3. Let

$$\mathcal{P}_1=[x_1+x_2,x_1+x_3,x_2+x_3,x_4^3+x_1,x_3x_4^2+x_3+x_4],$$
$$\mathcal{P}_2=[x_1+x_2,x_1+x_3,x_2+x_3,x_4^3+x_1,x_3x_4^2+x_4].$$

Then $G(\mathcal{P}_1)=G(\mathcal{P}_2)$ is shown in Figure 6 below (left). Let $\mathcal{P}_1''$ and $\mathcal{P}_2''$ be constructed from $\mathcal{P}_1$ and $\mathcal{P}_2$ with respect to x_4 respectively. Then $x_3x_4^2+x_3+x_4$ and $x_3x_4^2+x_4$ are chosen as T respectively and

$$\mathcal{P}_1''=[x_1+x_2,x_1+x_3,x_2+x_3,x_3,x_4^3+x_1,x_3+x_4],$$
$$\mathcal{P}_2''=[x_1+x_2,x_1+x_3,x_2+x_3,x_3,x_4^3+x_1,x_4].$$

One may check that $G(\mathcal{P}_1'')=G(\mathcal{P}_1)$ while $G(\mathcal{P}_2'')\neq G(\mathcal{P}_2)$, with $G(\mathcal{P}_2'')$ shown in Figure 6 below (right).

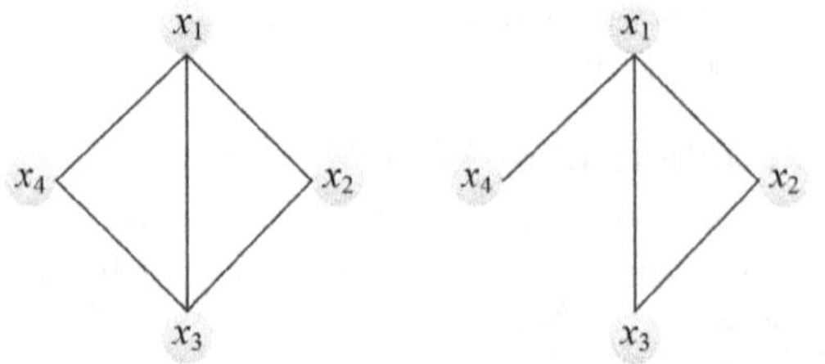

Figure 6: The associated graphs $G(\mathcal{P}_1)=G(\mathcal{P}_2)=G(\mathcal{P}_1'')$ (left) and $G(\mathcal{P}_2'')$ (right) in Example 4.3

Next we prove that with a chordal input polynomial set, the polynomial sets in all the nodes of the decomposition tree of Wang's method, and thus all the computed triangular sets, have associated graphs which are subgraphs of that of the input polynomial set.

Theorem 4.4. *Let $\mathcal{F} \subset \mathbb{K}[\boldsymbol{x}]$ be a chordal polynomial set with $x_1 < \cdots < x_n$ as one perfect elimination ordering and $(\mathcal{P}, \mathcal{Q}, i)$ be any node in the binary decomposition tree for Wang's method applied to $\mathcal{F}$. Then $G(\mathcal{P}) \subset G(\mathcal{F})$.*

Proof. We induce on the depth d of $(\mathcal{P}, \mathcal{Q}, i)$ in the binary decomposition tree. When $d = 1$, then $(\mathcal{P}, \mathcal{Q}, i)$ is a child node of $(\mathcal{F}, \emptyset, n)$, and $G(\mathcal{P}) \subset G(\mathcal{F})$ by Proposition 4.1 if it is a left child node or by Proposition 4.2 otherwise. Now assume that the first polynomial in any node of depth d in the decomposition tree has an associated graph which is a subgraph of $G(\mathcal{F})$. Let $(\mathcal{P}, \mathcal{Q}, i)$ be of depth $d+1$ and $(\tilde{\mathcal{P}}, \tilde{\mathcal{Q}}, i)$ be its parent of depth d in the decomposition. Then $G(\mathcal{P}) \subset G(\mathcal{F})$ by Proposition 4.1 if $(\mathcal{P}, \mathcal{Q}, i)$ is a left child node or $G(\mathcal{P}) \subset G(\tilde{\mathcal{P}}) \subset G(\mathcal{F})$ by Proposition 4.2 otherwise. This ends the inductive proof. □

Corollary 4.5. *Let $\mathcal{F} \subset \mathbb{K}[\boldsymbol{x}]$ be a chordal polynomial set with $x_1 < \cdots < x_n$ as one perfect elimination ordering and $\mathcal{T}_1, \ldots, \mathcal{T}_r$ be the triangular sets computed by Wang's method applied to $\mathcal{F}$. Then $G(\mathcal{T}_i) \subset G(\mathcal{F})$ for $i = 1, \ldots, r$.*

Proof. Straightforward from Theorem 4.4 with the fact that each triangular set $\mathcal{T}_j$ for some i $(1 \leq i \leq r)$ is from a node $(\mathcal{T}_i, \mathcal{Q}_i, 0)$ in the decomposition tree such that $\mathcal{T}_i$ contains no non-zero constant. □

4.3 An illustrative example

Here we illustrate the changes of chordality of polynomial sets computed in the triangular decomposition via Wang's method applied to

$$\mathcal{F} = \{x_2 + x_1 + 2, (x_2+2)x_3 + x_1, (x_3+x_2)x_4 + x_3 - 1, x_4 + x_2\} \quad (4)$$

in $\mathbb{Q}[x_1, x_2, x_3, x_4]$ for the variable ordering $x_1 < x_2 < x_3 < x_4$. The associated graph $G(\mathcal{F})$ is shown in Figure 7, and one can check that $G(\mathcal{F})$ is chordal with $x_1 < x_2 < x_3 < x_4$ as one perfect elimination ordering.

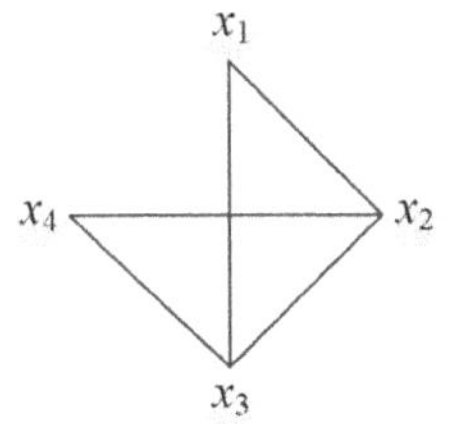

Figure 7: The associated graph $G(\mathcal{F})$ with $\mathcal{F}$ from (4)

First $T = (x_3 + x_2)x_4 + x_3 - 1$ is chosen as the polynomial in $\mathcal{F}^{(4)}$ with minimal degree in x_4, then a new polynomial set $\mathcal{F}' = \{x_2+x_1+2, (x_2+2)x_3+x_1, (x_3+x_2), x_3-1, x_4+x_2\}$, which corresponds to the right child node for the case $\text{ini}(T) = x_3 + x_2 = 0$ in the binary decomposition tree, is added to Φ for further computation. The psuedo division of $x_4 + x_2$ over T results in

$$\mathcal{P} = \{x_2+x_1+2, (x_2+2)x_3+x_1, (x_2-1)x_3+x_2^2+1, (x_3+x_2)x_4+x_3-1\},$$

and thus the left child node is $(\mathcal{P}, \{x_3 + x_2\}, 3)$ in the binary tree.

Next $T' = (x_2+2)x_3+x_1$ is chosen as the polynomial in $\mathcal{P}^{(3)}$ with minimal degree in x_3, then a new polynomial set $\mathcal{F}'' = \{x_1, x_2 + x_1 + 2, x_2 + 2, (x_2 - 1)x_3 + x_2^2 + 1, (x_3 + x_2)x_4 + x_3 - 1\}$ is added to Φ, and the pseudo division of $(x_2 - 1)x_3 + x_2^2 + 1$ over $(x_2 + 2)x_3 + x_1$ results in

$$\mathcal{P}' = \{x_2 + x_1 + 2, x_2^3 + 2x_2^2 - (x_1 - 1)x_2 + x_1 + 2,$$
$$(x_2 + 2)x_3 + x_1, (x_3 + x_2)x_4 + x_3 - 1\}$$

and the left node is $(\mathcal{P}', \{x_x + x_2, x_2 + 2\}, 2)$.

At this step $T'' = x_2 + x_1 + 2$ is chosen as the polynomial in $\mathcal{P}'^{(2)}$ with minimal degree in x_2, then no polynomial set is added to Φ since $\text{ini}(T'') = 1$, and the pseudo-division of $x_2^3 + 2x_2^2 - (x_1 - 1)x_2 + x_1 + 2$ over T'' results in the first triangular set

$$\mathcal{T}_1 = [-x_1^3+x_1^2+14x_1+16, x_2+x_1+2, (x_2+2)x_3+x_1, (x_3+x_2)x_4+x_3-1]. \quad (5)$$

With similar treatments on $\mathcal{F}'$ and $\mathcal{F}''$ in Φ, the other two triangular sets

$$\begin{aligned} \mathcal{T}_2 &= [x_1 + 1, x_2 + 1, x_3 - 1, x_4 + x_2], \\ \mathcal{T}_3 &= [x_1, x_2 + 2, (x_2 - 1)x_3 + x_2^2 + 1, (x_3 + x_2)x_4 + x_3 - 1] \end{aligned} \quad (6)$$

are computed.

The associated graphs of all these three computed triangular sets are shown in Figure 8. One can find that the associated graphs $G(\mathcal{F})$ and $G(\mathcal{T}_1)$ are the same, while $G(\mathcal{T}_2)$ and $G(\mathcal{T}_3)$ are strict subgraphs of $G(\mathcal{F})$.

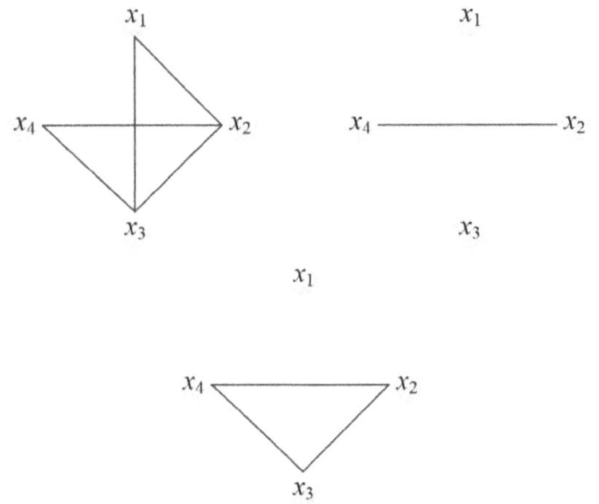

Figure 8: The associated graphs $G(\mathcal{T}_1)$ (top left), $G(\mathcal{T}_2)$ (top right), and $G(\mathcal{T}_3)$ (bottom) with $\mathcal{T}_1$ from (5) and $\mathcal{T}_2, \mathcal{T}_3$ from (6)

5 FURTHER REMARKS ON THE APPLICATIONS

5.1 Variable sparsity of polynomial sets

When referring to a polynomial set $\mathcal{F} \subset \mathbb{K}[\boldsymbol{x}]$ as sparse, one usually means that the percentage of terms effectively appearing in $\mathcal{F}$ in all the possible terms in the variables $x_1, \ldots, x_n$ up to a certain degree is low. This kind of sparsity for polynomial sets is convenient for the computation of Gröbner bases which is essentially based on reduction with respect to terms. In fact, efficient algorithms for computing Gröbner bases for sparse polynomial sets defined in this way have been proposed, implemented, and analyzed [15].

Instead of terms of polynomials, triangular sets focus on the variables of polynomials. As exploited in [10], sparsity of the polynomial sets with respect to their variables are partially reflected in their associated graphs. To make it precise, let $G(\mathcal{F}) = (V, E)$ be the associated graph of a polynomial set $\mathcal{F} = \{F_1, \ldots, F_r\} \subset \mathbb{K}[\boldsymbol{x}]$. Then the *variable sparsity* $s_v(\mathcal{F})$ of $\mathcal{F}$ can be defined as

$$s_v(\mathcal{F}) = |E| / \binom{2}{|V|},$$

where the denominator is the number of edges of a complete graph composed of $|V|$ vertices.

The associated graph $G(\mathcal{F})$ can be extended to a weighted one $G^w(\mathcal{F})$ by associating the number $\#\{F \in \mathcal{F} : x_i, x_j \in \text{supp}(F)\}$ to each edge (x_i, x_j) of $G(\mathcal{F})$. Let $G^w(\mathcal{F}) = (V, E)$, with the weight w_e for each $e \in E$, be the weighted associated graph of $\mathcal{F}$. Then the *weighted variable sparsity* $s_v^w(\mathcal{F})$ of $\mathcal{F}$ can be defined as

$$s_v^w(\mathcal{F}) = \frac{\sum_{e \in E} w_e}{r \cdot \binom{2}{|V|}},$$

where r is the number of polynomials in $\mathcal{F}$.

Chordality and variable sparsity are special structures of polynomial sets, and specialized (and probably more efficient) algorithms for triangular decomposition may be designed for such structured polynomial sets. This is expected to be investigated in our future works.

5.2 Complexity analysis for triangular decomposition in top-down style

In general, due to the complicated behaviors in the decomposition process, the complexity of triangular decomposition is not as clearly known as that of computation of Gröbner bases [4, 5, 14, 19, 24, 26].

For a graph G, another graph G' is called a *chordal completion* if G' is chordal with G as its subgraph. The *treewidth* of a graph G is defined to be the minimum of the sizes of the largest cliques in all the possible chordal completions of G. It has been shown that many NP-complete problems related to graphs can be solved efficiently if the graphs have bounded treewidth [1].

As shown by Theorem 4.4, when the input polynomial set is chordal, the associated graphs of all the polynomial sets in the decomposition process of Wang's method are subgraphs of the chordal associated graph of the input polynomial set. In other words, the input chordal associated graph imposes some kind of upper bound for all the polynomial sets in the decomposition process. Furthermore, the complexity of computing Gröbner bases has been analyzed for polynomial systems by using the treewidth of their associated graphs [9]. These comments lead to the hope of refined complexity analysis of triangular decomposition in top-down style, especially on Wang's method, from the viewpoint of chordal graphs and their treewidth.

Acknowledgements The authors would like to thank Dongming Wang and Diego Cifuentes for discussions on Wang's methods and on chordal graph structures of polynomial sets in triangular decomposition respectively. They also would like to thank the anonymous reviewers for their helpful comments.

REFERENCES

[1] Stefan Arnborg and Andrzej Proskurowski. 1989. Linear time algorithms for NP-hard problems restricted to partial k-trees. *Discrete Appl. Math.* 23, 1 (1989), 11–24.
[2] Philippe Aubry, Daniel Lazard, and Marc Moreno Maza. 1999. On the theories of triangular sets. *J. Symbolic Comput.* 28, 1–2 (1999), 105–124.
[3] Philippe Aubry and Marc Moreno Maza. 1999. Triangular sets for solving polynomial systems: A comparative implementation of four methods. *J. Symbolic Comput.* 28, 1–2 (1999), 125–154.
[4] Magali Bardet, Jean-Charles Faugère, and Bruno Salvy. 2004. On the complexity of Gröbner basis computation of semi-regular overdetermined algebraic equations. In *International Conference on Polynomial System Solving - ICPSS*. 71 –75.
[5] Magali Bardet, Jean-Charles Faugère, Bruno Salvy, and Pierre-Jean Spaenlehauer. 2013. On the complexity of solving quadratic Boolean systems. *J. Complexity* 29, 1 (2013), 53–75.
[6] Bruno Buchberger. 1965. *Ein Algorithmus zum Auffinden der Basiselemente des Restklassenrings nach einem nulldimensionalen Polynomideal.* Ph.D. Dissertation. Universität Innsbruck, Austria.
[7] Fengjuan Chai, Xiao-Shan Gao, and Chunming Yuan. 2008. A characteristic set method for solving Boolean equations and applications in cryptanalysis of stream ciphers. *J. Syst. Sci. Complex.* 21, 2 (2008), 191–208.
[8] Changbo Chen and Marc Moreno Maza. 2012. Algorithms for computing triangular decompositions of polynomial systems. *J. Symbolic Comput.* 47, 6 (2012), 610–642.
[9] Diego Cifuentes and Pablo A Parrilo. 2016. Exploiting chordal structure in polynomial ideals: A Gröbner bases approach. *SIAM J. Discrete Math.* 30, 3 (2016), 1534–1570.
[10] Diego Cifuentes and Pablo A Parrilo. 2017. Chordal networks of polynomial ideals. *SIAM J. Appl. Algebra Geom.* 1, 1 (2017), 73–110.
[11] David A. Cox, John B. Little, and Donal O'Shea. 1998. *Using Algebraic Geometry.* Springer Verlag.
[12] Jean-Charles Faugère. 1999. A new efficient algorithm for computing Gröbner bases (F_4). *J. Pure Appl. Algebra* 139, 1–3 (1999), 61–88.
[13] Jean-Charles Faugère and Antoine Joux. 2003. Algebraic cryptanalysis of hidden field equation (HFE) cryptosystems using Gröbner bases. In *Advances in Cryptology – CRYPTO 2003*, Dan Boneh (Ed.). Springer, 44–60.
[14] Jean-Charles Faugère and Chenqi Mou. 2017. Sparse FGLM algorithms. *J. Symbolic Comput.* 80, 3 (2017), 538–569.
[15] Jean-Charles Faugère, Pierre-Jean Spaenlehauer, and Jules Svartz. 2014. Sparse Gröbner bases: The unmixed case. In *Proceedings of ISSAC 2014*, Katsusuke Nabeshima and Kosaku Nagasaka (Eds.). ACM, 178–185.
[16] Xiao-Shan Gao and Shang-Ching Chou. 1992. Solving parametric algebraic systems. In *Proceedings of ISSAC 1992*, Paul Wang (Ed.). ACM, 335–341.
[17] Xiao-Shan Gao and Zhenyu Huang. 2012. Characteristic set algorithms for equation solving in finite fields. *J. Symbolic Comput.* 47, 6 (2012), 655–679.
[18] John R. Gilbert. 1994. Predicting structure in sparse matrix computations. *SIAM J. Matrix Anal. Appl.* 15, 1 (1994), 62–79.
[19] Zhenyu Huang, Yao Sun, and Dongdai Lin. 2014. On the efficiency of solving Boolean polynomial systems with the characteristic set method. *arXiv preprint arXiv:1405.4596* (2014).
[20] Meng Jin, Xiaoliang Li, and Dongming Wang. 2013. A new algorithmic scheme for computing characteristic sets. *J. Symbolic Comput.* 50 (2013), 431–449.
[21] Michael Kalkbrener. 1993. A generalized Euclidean algorithm for computing triangular representations of algebraic varieties. *J. Symbolic Comput.* 15, 2 (1993), 143–167.
[22] Xiaoliang Li, Chenqi Mou, and Dongming Wang. 2010. Decomposing polynomial sets into simple sets over finite fields: The zero-dimensional case. *Comput. Math. Appl.* 60, 11 (2010), 2983–2997.
[23] Seymour Parter. 1961. The use of linear graphs in Gauss elimination. *SIAM Rev.* 3, 2 (1961), 119–130.
[24] Adrien Poteaux and Éric Schost. 2013. On the complexity of computing with zero-dimensional triangular sets. *J. Symbolic Comput.* 50 (2013), 110–138.
[25] Donald J. Rose. 1970. Triangulated graphs and the elimination process. *J. Math. Anal. Appl.* 32, 3 (1970), 597–609.
[26] Agnes Szanto. 1999. *Computation with Polynomial Systems.* Ph.D. Dissertation. Cornell University, USA.
[27] Dongming Wang. 1993. An elimination method for polynomial systems. *J. Symbolic Comput.* 16, 2 (1993), 83–114.
[28] Dongming Wang. 1998. Decomposing polynomial systems into simple systems. *J. Symbolic Comput.* 25, 3 (1998), 295–314.
[29] Dongming Wang. 2000. Computing triangular systems and regular systems. *J. Symbolic Comput.* 30, 2 (2000), 221–236.
[30] Dongming Wang. 2001. *Elimination Methods.* Springer-Verlag, Wien.
[31] Wen-Tsun Wu. 1986. On zeros of algebraic equations: An application of Ritt principle. *Kexue Tongbao* 31, 1 (1986), 1–5.
[32] Wen-Tsun Wu. 1994. *Mechanical Theorem Proving in Geometries: Basic Principles.* Springer-Verlag, Wien [Translated from the Chinese by X. Jin and D. Wang].

Computing Popov and Hermite Forms of Rectangular Polynomial Matrices

Vincent Neiger*
Univ. Limoges, CNRS, XLIM, UMR 7252
F-87000 Limoges, France
vincent.neiger@unilim.fr

Johan Rosenkilde
Technical University of Denmark
Kgs. Lyngby, Denmark
jsrn@jsrn.dk

Grigory Solomatov
Technical University of Denmark
Kgs. Lyngby, Denmark
grigorys93@gmail.com

ABSTRACT

We consider the computation of two normal forms for matrices over the univariate polynomials: the Popov form and the Hermite form. For matrices which are square and nonsingular, deterministic algorithms with satisfactory cost bounds are known. Here, we present deterministic, fast algorithms for rectangular input matrices. The obtained cost bound for the Popov form matches the previous best known randomized algorithm, while the cost bound for the Hermite form improves on the previous best known ones by a factor which is at least the largest dimension of the input matrix.

KEYWORDS

Polynomial matrix; Reduced form; Popov form; Hermite form.

1 INTRODUCTION

In this paper we deal with (univariate) polynomial matrices, i.e. matrices in $\mathbb{K}[x]^{m\times n}$ where $\mathbb{K}$ is a field admitting exact computation, typically a finite field. Given such an input matrix whose row space is the real object of interest, one may ask for a "better" basis for the row space, that is, another matrix which has the same row space but also has additional useful properties. Two important normal forms for such bases are the Popov form [21] and the Hermite form [11], whose definitions are recalled in this paper. The Popov form has rows which have the minimal possible degrees, while the Hermite form is in echelon form. A classical generalisation is the *shifted* Popov form of a matrix [1], where one incorporates degree weights on the columns: with zero shift this is the Popov form, while under some extremal shift this becomes the Hermite form [2]. We are interested in the efficient computation of these forms, which has been studied extensively along with the computation of the related but non-unique reduced forms [6, 13] and weak Popov forms [16].

Hereafter, complexity estimates count basic arithmetic operations in $\mathbb{K}$ on an algebraic RAM, and asymptotic cost bounds omit factors that are logarithmic in the input parameters, denoted by $O\tilde{~}(\cdot)$. We let $2 \le \omega \le 3$ be an exponent for matrix multiplication: two matrices in $\mathbb{K}^{m\times m}$ can be multiplied in $O(m^\omega)$ operations. As shown in [5], the multiplication of two polynomials in $\mathbb{K}[x]$ of degree at most d can be done in $O\tilde{~}(d)$ operations, and more generally the multiplication of two polynomial matrices in $\mathbb{K}[x]^{m\times m}$ of degree at most d uses $O\tilde{~}(m^\omega d)$ operations.

Consider a square, nonsingular $\mathbf{M} \in \mathbb{K}[x]^{m\times m}$ of degree d. For the computation of a reduced form of $\mathbf{M}$, the complexity $O\tilde{~}(m^\omega d)$ was first achieved by a Las Vegas algorithm of Giorgi et al. [7]. All the subsequent work mentioned in the next paragraph achieved the same cost bound, which was taken as a target: up to logarithmic factors, it is the same as the cost for multiplying two matrices with dimensions and degree similar to those of $\mathbf{M}$.

The approach of [7] was de-randomized by Gupta et al. [9], while Sarkar and Storjohann [23] showed how to compute the Popov form from a reduced form; combining these results gives a deterministic algorithm for the Popov form. Gupta and Storjohann [8, 10] gave a Las Vegas algorithm for the Hermite form; a Las Vegas method for computing the shifted Popov form for any shift was described in [18]. Then, a deterministic Hermite form algorithm was given by Labahn et al. [14], which was one ingredient in a deterministic algorithm due to Neiger and Vu [19] for the arbitrary shift case.

The Popov form algorithms usually exploit the fact that, by definition, this form has degree at most $d = \deg(\mathbf{M})$. While no similarly strong degree bound holds for shifted Popov forms in general (including the Hermite form), these forms still share a remarkable property in the square, nonsingular case: each entry outside the diagonal has degree less than the entry on the diagonal in the same column. These diagonal entries are called *pivots* [13]. Furthermore, their degrees sum to $\deg(\det(\mathbf{M})) \le md$, so that these forms can be represented with $O(m^2 d)$ field elements, just like $\mathbf{M}$. This is especially helpful in the design of fast algorithms since this provides ways to control the degrees of the manipulated matrices.

These degree constraints exist but become weaker in the case of *rectangular* shifted Popov forms, say $m \times n$ with $m < n$. Such a normal form does have m columns containing pivots, whose average degree is at most the degree d of the input matrix $\mathbf{M}$. Yet it also contains $n - m$ columns without pivots, which may all have large degree: up to $\Theta(md)$ in the case of the Hermite form. As a result, a dense representation of the latter form may require $\Omega(m^2(n-m)d)$ field elements, a factor of m larger than for $\mathbf{M}$. Take for example some $\mathbf{U} \in \mathbb{K}[x]^{m\times m}$ of degree d which is unimodular, meaning that $\mathbf{U}^{-1}$ has entries in $\mathbb{K}[x]$. Then, the Hermite form of $[\mathbf{U}\ \ \mathbf{I}_m\ \ \cdots\ \ \mathbf{I}_m]$ is $[\mathbf{I}_m\ \ \mathbf{U}^{-1}\ \ \cdots\ \ \mathbf{U}^{-1}]$, and the entries of $\mathbf{U}^{-1}$ may have degree in $\Omega(md)$. However, the Popov form, having minimal degree, has size in $O(mnd)$, just like $\mathbf{M}$. Thus, unlike in the nonsingular case, one

*Part of the research leading to this work was conducted while Vincent Neiger was with Technical University of Denmark, Kgs. Lyngby, Denmark, with funding from the People Programme (Marie Curie Actions) of the European Union's Seventh Framework Programme (FP7/2007-2013) under REA grant agreement number 609405 (COFUNDPostdocDTU).

ISSAC '18, July 16–19, 2018, New York, NY, USA

ACM ISBN 978-1-4503-5550-6/18/07...$15.00
https://doi.org/10.1145/3208976.3208988

would set different target costs for the computation of Popov and Hermite forms, such as $O\tilde{}(m^{\omega-1}nd)$ for the former and $O\tilde{}(m^{\omega}nd)$ for the latter (note that the exponent affects the small dimension).

For a rectangular matrix $\mathbf{M} \in \mathbb{K}[x]^{m\times n}$, Mulders and Storjohann [16] gave an iterative Popov form algorithm which costs $O(rmnd^2)$, where r is the rank of $\mathbf{M}$. Beckermann et al. [3] obtain the shifted Popov form for any shift by computing a basis of the left kernel of $[\mathbf{M}^\mathsf{T}\ \ \mathbf{I}_n]^\mathsf{T}$. This approach also produces a matrix which transforms $\mathbf{M}$ into its normal form and whose degree can be in $\Omega(md)$: efficient algorithms usually avoid computing this transformation. To find the sought kernel basis, the fastest known method is to compute a shifted Popov approximant basis of the $(m+n)\times n$ matrix above, at an order which depends on the shift. [3] relies on a fraction-free algorithm for the latter computation, and hence lends itself well to cases where $\mathbb{K}$ is not finite. In our context, following this approach with the fastest known approximant basis algorithm [12] yields the cost bounds $O\tilde{}((m+n)^{\omega-1}nmd)$ for the Popov form and $O\tilde{}((m+n)^{\omega-1}n^2md)$ for the Hermite form. For the latter this is the fastest existing algorithm, to the best of our knowledge.

For $\mathbf{M}$ with full rank and $m \le n$, Sarkar [22] showed a Las Vegas algorithm for the Popov form achieving the cost $O\tilde{}(m^{\omega-1}nd)$. This uses random column operations to compress $\mathbf{M}$ into an $m\times m$ matrix, which is then transformed into a reduced form. Applying the same transformation on $\mathbf{M}$ yields a reduced form of $\mathbf{M}$ with high probability, and from there the Popov form can be obtained. Lowering this cost further seems difficult, as indicated in the square case by the reduction from polynomial matrix multiplication to Popov form computation described in [23, Thm. 22].

For a matrix $\mathbf{M} \in \mathbb{K}[x]^{m\times n}$ which is rank-deficient or has $m > n$, the computation of a basis of the row space of $\mathbf{M}$ was handled by Zhou and Labahn [29] with cost $O\tilde{}(m^{\omega-1}(m+n)d)$. Their algorithm is deterministic, and the output basis $\mathbf{B} \in \mathbb{K}[x]^{r\times n}$ has degree at most d. This may be used as a preliminary step: the normal form of $\mathbf{M}$ is also that of $\mathbf{B}$, and the latter has full rank with $r \le n$.

We stress that, from a rectangular matrix $\mathbf{M} \in \mathbb{K}[x]^{m\times n}$, it seems difficult in general to predict which columns of its shifted Popov form will be pivot-free. For this reason, there seems to be no obvious deterministic reduction from the rectangular case to the square case, even when n is only slightly larger than m. Sarkar's algorithm is a Las Vegas reduction, *compressing* the matrix to a nonsingular $m\times m$ matrix; another Las Vegas reduction consists in *completing* the matrix to a nonsingular $n\times n$ matrix (see Section 3).

In the nonsingular case, exploiting information on the pivots has led to algorithmic improvements for normal form algorithms [10, 12, 14, 23]. Following this, we put our effort into two computational tasks: finding the location of the pivots in the normal form (the *pivot support*), and using this knowledge to compute this form.

Our first contribution is to show how to efficiently find the pivot support of $\mathbf{M}$. For this we resort to the so-called saturation of $\mathbf{M}$ computed in a form which reveals the pivot support (Section 4.1), making use of an idea from [28]. While this is only efficient for $n \in O(m)$, using this method repeatedly on well-chosen submatrices of $\mathbf{M}$ with about $2m$ columns allows us to find the pivot support using $O\tilde{}(m^{\omega-1}nd)$ operations for any dimensions $m \le n$ (Section 4.2).

In our second main contribution, we consider the shifted Popov form of $\mathbf{M}$, for any shift. We show that once its pivot support is known, then this form can be computed efficiently (Section 6 and Proposition 6.1). In particular, combining both contributions yields a fast and deterministic Popov form algorithm.

Theorem 1.1. *For a matrix $\mathbf{M} \in \mathbb{K}[x]^{m\times n}$ of degree at most d and with $m \le n$, there is a deterministic algorithm which computes the Popov form of $\mathbf{M}$ using $O\tilde{}(m^{\omega-1}nd)$ operations in $\mathbb{K}$.*

The second contribution may of course be useful in situations where the pivot support is known for some reason. Yet, there are even general cases where it can be computed efficiently, namely when the shift has very unbalanced entries. This is typically the case of the Hermite form, for which the pivot support coincides with the column rank profile of $\mathbf{M}$. The latter can be efficiently obtained via an algorithm due to Zhou [26, Sec. 11], based on the kernel basis algorithm from [30]. This leads us to the next result.

Theorem 1.2. *Let $\mathbf{M} \in \mathbb{K}[x]^{m\times n}$ with full rank and $m < n$. There is a deterministic algorithm which computes the Hermite form of $\mathbf{M}$ using $O\tilde{}(m^{\omega-1}n\delta)$ operations in $\mathbb{K}$, where δ is the minimum of the sum of column degrees of $\mathbf{M}$ and of the sum of row degrees of $\mathbf{M}$.*

Using this quantity δ (see Eq. (6) for a more precise definition), the mentioned cost for the kernel basis approach of [3] becomes $O\tilde{}((m+n)^{\omega-1}n^2\delta)$. Thus, when $n \in O(m)$ the cost in the above theorem already gains a factor n compared to this approach; when n is large compared to m, this factor becomes $n(\frac{n}{m})^{\omega-1}$.

2 PRELIMINARIES

2.1 Basic notation

If $\mathbf{M}$ is an $m\times n$ matrix and $1 \le j \le n$, we denote by $\mathbf{M}_{*,j}$ the jth column of $\mathbf{M}$. If $J \subseteq \{1,\ldots,n\}$ is a set of column indices, $\mathbf{M}_{*,J}$ is the submatrix of $\mathbf{M}$ formed by the columns at the indices in J. We use analogous row-wise notation. Similarly, for a tuple $\boldsymbol{t} \in \mathbb{Z}^n$, then $\boldsymbol{t}_J$ is the subtuple of $\boldsymbol{t}$ formed by the entries at the indices in J.

When adding a constant to an integer tuple, for example $\boldsymbol{t}+1$ for some $\boldsymbol{t} = (t_1,\ldots,t_m) \in \mathbb{Z}^m$, we really mean $(t_1+1,\ldots,t_m+1)$; when comparing a tuple to a constant, for example $\boldsymbol{t} \le 1$, we mean $\max(\boldsymbol{t}) \le 1$. Two tuples of the same length will always be compared entrywise: $\boldsymbol{s} \le \boldsymbol{t}$ stands for $s_i \le t_i$ for all i. We use the notation $\mathrm{amp}(\boldsymbol{t}) = \max(\boldsymbol{t}) - \min(\boldsymbol{t})$, and $|\boldsymbol{t}| = t_1 + \ldots + t_m$ (note that the latter will mostly be used when $\boldsymbol{t}$ has nonnegative entries).

For a given nonnegative integer tuple $\boldsymbol{t} = (t_1,\ldots,t_m) \in \mathbb{Z}^m_{\ge 0}$, we denote by $\mathbf{x}^{\boldsymbol{t}}$ the diagonal matrix with entries $x^{t_1},\ldots,x^{t_m}$.

2.2 Row spaces, kernels, and approximants

For a matrix $\mathbf{M} \in \mathbb{K}[x]^{m\times n}$, its *row space* is the $\mathbb{K}[x]$-module generated by its rows, that is, $\{\boldsymbol{\lambda}\mathbf{M}, \boldsymbol{\lambda} \in \mathbb{K}[x]^{1\times m}\}$. Then, a matrix $\mathbf{B} \in \mathbb{K}[x]^{r\times n}$ is a *row basis* of $\mathbf{M}$ if its rows form a basis of the row space of $\mathbf{M}$, in which case r is the rank of $\mathbf{M}$.

The *left kernel* of $\mathbf{M}$ is the $\mathbb{K}[x]$-module $\{\mathbf{p} \in \mathbb{K}[x]^{1\times m} \mid \mathbf{pM} = \mathbf{0}\}$. A matrix $\mathbf{K} \in \mathbb{K}[x]^{k\times m}$ is a *left kernel basis of* $\mathbf{M}$ if its rows form a basis of this kernel, in which case $k = m - r$. Similarly, a *right* kernel basis of $\mathbf{M}$ is a matrix $\mathbf{K} \in \mathbb{K}[x]^{n\times(n-r)}$ whose *columns* form a basis of the right kernel of $\mathbf{M}$.

Given $\boldsymbol{d} = (d_1,\ldots,d_n) \in \mathbb{Z}^n_{>0}$, the set of *approximants for* $\mathbf{M}$ *at order* $\boldsymbol{d}$ is the $\mathbb{K}[x]$-module of rank m defined as

$$\mathcal{A}_{\boldsymbol{d}}(\mathbf{M}) = \{\mathbf{p} \in \mathbb{K}[x]^{1\times m} \mid \mathbf{pM} = \mathbf{0} \bmod \mathbf{x}^{\boldsymbol{d}}\}.$$

The identity $\mathbf{pM} = \mathbf{0} \bmod \mathbf{x}^{\mathbf{d}}$ means that the jth entry of the vector $\mathbf{pM} \in \mathbb{K}[x]^{1\times n}$ is divisible by x^{d_j}, for all j.

Two $m \times n$ matrices $\mathbf{M}_1$, $\mathbf{M}_2$ have the same row space if and only if they are *unimodularly equivalent*, that is, there is a unimodular matrix $\mathbf{U} \in \mathbb{K}[x]^{m\times m}$ such that $\mathbf{UM}_1 = \mathbf{M}_2$. For $\mathbf{M}_3 \in \mathbb{K}[x]^{r\times n}$ with $r \leq m$, $\mathbf{M}_1$ and $\mathbf{M}_3$ have the same row space exactly when $\mathbf{M}_3$ padded with $m - r$ zero rows is unimodularly equivalent to $\mathbf{M}_1$.

2.3 Row degrees and reduced forms

For a matrix $\mathbf{M} \in \mathbb{K}[x]^{m\times n}$, we denote by $\operatorname{rdeg}(\mathbf{M})$ the tuple of the degrees of its rows, that is, $(\deg(\mathbf{M}_{1,*}), \ldots, \deg(\mathbf{M}_{m,*}))$.

If $\mathbf{M}$ has no zero row, the *(row-wise) leading matrix* of $\mathbf{M}$, denoted by $\operatorname{lm}(\mathbf{M})$, is the matrix in $\mathbb{K}^{m\times n}$ whose entry i, j is equal to the coefficient of degree $\deg(\mathbf{M}_{i,*})$ of the entry i, j of $\mathbf{M}$.

For a matrix $\mathbf{R} \in \mathbb{K}[x]^{m\times n}$ with no zero row and $m \leq n$, we say that $\mathbf{R}$ is *(row) reduced* if $\operatorname{lm}(\mathbf{R})$ has full rank. Thus, here a reduced matrix must have full rank (and no zero row), as in [6]. For more details about reduced matrices, we refer the reader to [3, 6, 13, 25]. In particular, we have the following characterizing properties:

- *Predictable degree property [6] [13, Thm. 6.3-13]:* we have
$$\deg(\boldsymbol{\lambda}\mathbf{R}) = \max\{\deg(\lambda_i) + \operatorname{rdeg}(\mathbf{R}_{i,*}),\ 1 \leq i \leq m\}$$
for any vector $\boldsymbol{\lambda} = [\lambda_i]_i \in \mathbb{K}[x]^{1\times m}$.
- *Minimality of the sum of row degrees [6]:* for any nonsingular matrix $\mathbf{U} \in \mathbb{K}[x]^{m\times m}$, we have $|\operatorname{rdeg}(\mathbf{UR})| \geq |\operatorname{rdeg}(\mathbf{R})|$.
- *Minimality of the tuple of row degrees [26, Sec. 2.7]:* for any nonsingular matrix $\mathbf{U} \in \mathbb{K}[x]^{m\times m}$, we have $\boldsymbol{s} \leq \boldsymbol{t}$ where the tuples $\boldsymbol{s}$ and $\boldsymbol{t}$ are the row degrees of $\mathbf{R}$ and of $\mathbf{UR}$ sorted in nondecreasing order, respectively.

From the last item, it follows that two unimodularly equivalent reduced matrices have the same row degree up to permutation.

For a matrix $\mathbf{M} \in \mathbb{K}[x]^{m\times n}$, we call *reduced form of* $\mathbf{M}$ any reduced matrix $\mathbf{R} \in \mathbb{K}[x]^{r\times n}$ which is a row basis of $\mathbf{M}$. The third item above shows that $\deg(\mathbf{R}) \leq \deg(\mathbf{M})$.

2.4 Pivots and Popov forms

For a nonzero vector $\mathbf{p} = [p_j]_j \in \mathbb{K}[x]^{1\times m}$, the *pivot index* of $\mathbf{p}$ is the largest index j such that $\deg(p_j) = \deg(\mathbf{p})$ [13, Sec. 6.7.2]. In this case we call p_j the *pivot entry* of $\mathbf{p}$. For the zero vector, we define its degree to be $-\infty$ and its pivot index to be 0. Further, the *pivot index* of a matrix $\mathbf{M} \in \mathbb{K}[x]^{m\times n}$ is the tuple $(j_1, \ldots, j_m) \in \mathbb{Z}^m_{\geq 0}$ such that j_i is the pivot index of $\mathbf{M}_{i,*}$. Note that we will only use the word "pivot" in this row-wise sense.

A matrix $\mathbf{P} \in \mathbb{K}[x]^{m\times n}$ is in *weak Popov form* if it has no zero row and the entries of the pivot index of $\mathbf{P}$ are all distinct [16]; a weak Popov form is further called *ordered* if its pivot index is in (strictly) increasing order. A weak Popov matrix is also reduced.

The (ordered) weak Popov form is not canonical: a given row space may have many (ordered) weak Popov forms. The Popov form adds a normalization property, yielding a canonical form; we use the definition from [2, Def. 3.3]:

A matrix $\mathbf{P} \in \mathbb{K}[x]^{m\times n}$ is in *Popov form* if it is in ordered weak Popov form, the corresponding pivot entries are monic, and in each column of $\mathbf{P}$ which contains a (row-wise) pivot the other entries have degree less than this pivot entry.

For a matrix $\mathbf{M} \in \mathbb{K}[x]^{m\times n}$ of rank r, there exists a unique $\mathbf{P} \in \mathbb{K}[x]^{r\times n}$ which is in Popov form and has the same row space as $\mathbf{M}$ [3, Thm. 2.7]. We call $\mathbf{P}$ *the Popov form of* $\mathbf{M}$. For a more detailed treatment of Popov forms, see [2, 3, 13].

For example, consider the unimodularly equivalent matrices
$$\begin{bmatrix} x^2 & x+1 & 2 \\ 2x+2 & 2x & 2 \end{bmatrix} \quad \text{and} \quad \begin{bmatrix} x^2-x-1 & 1 & 1 \\ x+1 & x & 1 \end{bmatrix},$$
defined over $\mathbb{F}_7[x]$; the first one is in weak Popov form and the second one is its Popov form. Note that any deterministic rule for ordering the rows would lead to a canonical form; we use that of [2, 3], while that of [13, 16] sorts the rows by degrees and would consider the second matrix not to be normalized.

Going back to the general case, we denote by $\boldsymbol{\pi}(\mathbf{M}) \in \mathbb{Z}^r_{>0}$ the pivot index of the Popov form of $\mathbf{M}$, called the *pivot support* of $\mathbf{M}$. In most cases, $\boldsymbol{\pi}(\mathbf{M})$ differs from the pivot index of $\mathbf{M}$. We have the following important properties:

- The pivot index of $\mathbf{M}$ is equal to the pivot support $\boldsymbol{\pi}(\mathbf{M})$ if and only if $\mathbf{M}$ is in ordered weak Popov form.
- For any $\boldsymbol{\lambda} \in \mathbb{K}[x]^{1\times m}$ such that $\boldsymbol{\lambda}\mathbf{M} \neq \mathbf{0}$, the pivot index of $\boldsymbol{\lambda}\mathbf{M}$ appears in the pivot support $\boldsymbol{\pi}(\mathbf{M})$; in particular each nonzero entry of the pivot index of $\mathbf{M}$ is in $\boldsymbol{\pi}(\mathbf{M})$.

For the first item, we refer to [3, Sec. 2] (in this reference, the set formed by the entries of the pivot support is called "pivot set" and ordered weak Popov forms are called quasi-Popov forms). The second item is a simple extension of the predictable degree property (see for example [17, Lem. 1.17] for a proof).

2.5 Computational tools

We will rely on the following result from [30, Cor. 4.6 and Thm. 3.4] about the computation of kernel bases in reduced form. Note that a matrix is *column reduced* if its transpose is reduced.

Theorem 2.1 ([30]). *There is an algorithm* MinimalKernelBasis *which, given a matrix* $\mathbf{M} \in \mathbb{K}[x]^{m\times n}$ *with* $m \leq n$*, returns a right kernel basis* $\mathbf{K} \in \mathbb{K}[x]^{m\times(n-r)}$ *of* $\mathbf{M}$ *in column reduced form using*
$$\tilde{O}\left(n^{\omega}\lceil m\deg(\mathbf{M})/n\rceil\right) \subseteq \tilde{O}\left(n^{\omega}\deg(\mathbf{M})\right)$$
operations in $\mathbb{K}$*. Furthermore,* $|\operatorname{cdeg}(\mathbf{K})| \leq r\deg(\mathbf{M})$.

For the computation of normal forms of square, nonsingular matrices, we use the next result ($\boldsymbol{s}$-Popov forms will be introduced in Section 5; Popov forms as above correspond to $\boldsymbol{s} = \mathbf{0}$).

Theorem 2.2 ([19]). *There is an algorithm* NonsingularPopov *which, given a nonsingular matrix* $\mathbf{M} \in \mathbb{K}[x]^{m\times m}$ *and a shift* $\boldsymbol{s} \in \mathbb{Z}^m$*, returns the* $\boldsymbol{s}$*-Popov form of* $\mathbf{M}$ *using*
$$\tilde{O}\left(m^{\omega}\lceil|\operatorname{rdeg}(\mathbf{M})|/m\rceil\right) \subseteq \tilde{O}\left(m^{\omega}\deg(\mathbf{M})\right)$$
operations in $\mathbb{K}$.

This is [19, Thm. 1.3] with a minor modification: we have replaced the so-called generic determinant bound by a larger quantity (the sum of row degrees), since this is sufficient for our needs here.

3 POPOV FORM VIA COMPLETION INTO A SQUARE AND NONSINGULAR MATRIX

We now present a new Las Vegas algorithm for computing the (non-shifted) Popov form $\mathbf{P}$ of a rectangular matrix $\mathbf{M} \in \mathbb{K}[x]^{m\times n}$ with full rank and $m < n$, relying on algorithms for the case of square, nonsingular matrices. In the case $n \in O(m)$, this results in a cost bounded by $O\tilde{~}(m^\omega \deg(\mathbf{M}))$, which has already been obtained by the Las Vegas algorithm of Sarkar [22]; however, the advantage of our approach is that it becomes asymptotically faster if the *average* row degree of $\mathbf{M}$ is significantly smaller than $\deg(\mathbf{M})$.

The idea is to find a matrix $\mathbf{C} \in \mathbb{K}[x]^{(n-m)\times n}$ such that the Popov form of $[\mathbf{M}^\mathsf{T} \;\; \mathbf{C}^\mathsf{T}]^\mathsf{T}$ contains $\mathbf{P}$ as an identifiable subset of its rows. We will show that if $\mathbf{C}$ is drawn randomly of sufficiently high degree, then this is true with high probability.

Definition 3.1. Let $\mathbf{M} \in \mathbb{K}[x]^{m\times n}$ have full rank with $m < n$ and let $\mathbf{P} \in \mathbb{K}[x]^{m\times n}$ be the Popov form of $\mathbf{M}$. A *completion of* $\mathbf{M}$ is any matrix $\mathbf{C} \in \mathbb{K}[x]^{(n-m)\times n}$ such that:

$$\min(\mathrm{rdeg}(\mathbf{C})) > \deg(\mathbf{P}) \text{ and } \begin{bmatrix}\mathbf{P}\\ \mathbf{C}\end{bmatrix} \text{ is row reduced.}$$

The next lemma shows that: 1) if $\mathbf{C}$ is a completion, then $\mathbf{P}$ will appear as a submatrix of the Popov form of $[\mathbf{M}^\mathsf{T} \;\; \mathbf{C}^\mathsf{T}]^\mathsf{T}$; and 2) we can easily check from that Popov form whether $\mathbf{C}$ is a completion or not. The latter is essential for a Las Vegas algorithm.

Lemma 3.2. *Let* $\mathbf{M} \in \mathbb{K}[x]^{m\times n}$ *have full rank with* $m < n$ *with Popov form* $\mathbf{P}$, *and let* $\mathbf{C} \in \mathbb{K}[x]^{(n-m)\times n}$ *be such that* $[\mathbf{M}^\mathsf{T} \;\; \mathbf{C}^\mathsf{T}]^\mathsf{T}$ *has full rank and* $\min(\mathrm{rdeg}(\mathbf{C})) > \deg(\mathbf{P})$. *Then,* $\mathbf{C}$ *is a completion of* $\mathbf{M}$ *if and only if* $\mathrm{rdeg}(\hat{\mathbf{P}})$ *contains a permutation of* $\mathrm{rdeg}(\mathbf{C})$, *where* $\hat{\mathbf{P}}$ *is the Popov form of* $[\mathbf{M}^\mathsf{T} \;\; \mathbf{C}^\mathsf{T}]^\mathsf{T}$. *In this case,* $\mathbf{P}$ *is the submatrix of* $\hat{\mathbf{P}}$ *formed by its rows of degree less than* $\min(\mathrm{rdeg}(\mathbf{C}))$.

Proof. First, we assume that $\mathbf{C}$ is a completion of $\mathbf{M}$. Then $[\mathbf{P}^\mathsf{T} \;\; \mathbf{C}^\mathsf{T}]^\mathsf{T}$ is reduced, and therefore it has the same row degree as its Popov form $\hat{\mathbf{P}}$ up to permutation. Hence, in particular, $\mathrm{rdeg}(\hat{\mathbf{P}})$ contains a permutation of $\mathrm{rdeg}(\mathbf{C})$.

Now, we assume that $\mathrm{rdeg}(\hat{\mathbf{P}})$ contains a permutation of $\mathrm{rdeg}(\mathbf{C})$ and our goal is to show that $[\mathbf{P}^\mathsf{T} \;\; \mathbf{C}^\mathsf{T}]^\mathsf{T}$ is reduced and $\hat{\mathbf{P}}$ contains $\mathbf{P}$ as a submatrix. Let $\hat{\mathbf{P}}_1$ be the submatrix of $\hat{\mathbf{P}}$ of its rows of degree less than $\min(\mathrm{rdeg}(\mathbf{C}))$; and $\hat{\mathbf{P}}_2$ be the submatrix of the remaining rows. By assumption, $\hat{\mathbf{P}}_2$ has at least $n-m$ rows and $\hat{\mathbf{P}}_1$ has at most m rows. Since $\hat{\mathbf{P}}$ is also the Popov form of $[\mathbf{P}^\mathsf{T} \;\; \mathbf{C}^\mathsf{T}]^\mathsf{T}$, there is a unimodular transformation

$$\begin{bmatrix}\mathbf{U}_{11} & \mathbf{U}_{12}\\ \mathbf{U}_{21} & \mathbf{U}_{22}\end{bmatrix}\begin{bmatrix}\hat{\mathbf{P}}_1\\ \hat{\mathbf{P}}_2\end{bmatrix} = \begin{bmatrix}\mathbf{P}\\ \mathbf{C}\end{bmatrix}. \quad (1)$$

By the predictable degree property we obtain $\mathbf{U}_{12} = \mathbf{0}$; thus, since $\mathbf{P}$ has full rank m, then $\hat{\mathbf{P}}_1$ has exactly m rows, and $\mathbf{U}_{11}$ is unimodular. Therefore $\hat{\mathbf{P}}_1 = \mathbf{P}$ since both matrices are in Popov form. As a result, $\mathrm{rdeg}(\hat{\mathbf{P}})$ is a permutation of $(\mathrm{rdeg}(\mathbf{P}), \mathrm{rdeg}(\mathbf{C}))$. □

Lemma 3.3. *Let* $\mathbf{M} \in \mathbb{K}[x]^{m\times n}$ *have full rank with* $m < n$. *Let* $S \subseteq \mathbb{K}$ *be finite of cardinality* q *and let* $\mathbf{L} \in \mathbb{K}^{(n-m)\times n}$ *with entries chosen independently and uniformly at random from* S. *Then* $x^{\deg(\mathbf{M})+1}\mathbf{L}$ *is a completion of* $\mathbf{M}$ *with probability at least* $\prod_{i=1}^{n-m}(1-q^{-i})$ *if* $\mathbb{K}$ *is finite and* $S = \mathbb{K}$, *and at least* $1 - \frac{n-m}{q}$ *otherwise.*

Proof. Let $d = \deg(\mathbf{M})$. We first note that for $x^{d+1}\mathbf{L}$ to be a completion of $\mathbf{M}$, it is enough that the matrix

$$\mathrm{lm}\left(\begin{bmatrix}\mathbf{P}\\ \mathbf{C}\end{bmatrix}\right) = \begin{bmatrix}\mathrm{lm}(\mathbf{P})\\ \mathrm{lm}(\mathbf{C})\end{bmatrix} = \begin{bmatrix}\mathrm{lm}(\mathbf{P})\\ \mathbf{L}\end{bmatrix} \in \mathbb{K}^{n\times n}$$

be invertible. Indeed, this implies first that $[\mathbf{P}^\mathsf{T} \;\; \mathbf{C}^\mathsf{T}]^\mathsf{T}$ is reduced; and second, that $\mathbf{C}$ has no zero row, hence $\mathrm{rdeg}(\mathbf{C}) = (d+1, \ldots, d+1)$ and $\min(\mathrm{rdeg}(\mathbf{C})) = d+1 > \deg(\mathbf{M}) \geq \deg(\mathbf{P})$.

In the case of a finite field $\mathbb{K}$ with q elements, the probability that the above matrix is invertible is $\prod_{i=1}^{n-m}(1-q^{-i})$. If $\mathbb{K}$ is infinite or of cardinality $\geq q$, the Schwartz-Zippel lemma implies that the probability that the above matrix is singular is at most $(n-m)/q$. □

Thus, if $\mathbb{K}$ is infinite, it is sufficient to take S of cardinality at least $2(n-m)$ to ensure that $x^{d+1}\mathbf{L}$ is a completion with probability at least $1/2$. On the other hand, if $\mathbb{K}$ is finite of cardinality q, we have the following bounds on the probability:

$$\prod_{i=1}^{n-m}(1-q^{-i}) > \begin{cases} 0.28 & \text{if } q = 2,\\ 0.55 & \text{if } q = 3,\\ 0.75 & \text{if } q > 5.\end{cases}$$

In Algorithm 1, we first test the nonsingularity of $\mathbf{N} = [\mathbf{M}^\mathsf{T} \;\; \mathbf{C}^\mathsf{T}]^\mathsf{T}$ before computing $\hat{\mathbf{P}}$, since the fastest known Popov form algorithms in the square case do not support singular matrices. Over a field with at least $2n\deg(\mathbf{N})+1$ elements, a simple Monte Carlo test for this is to evaluate the polynomial matrix at a random $\alpha \in \mathbb{K}$ and testing the resulting scalar matrix for nonsingularity; this falsely reports singularity only if $\det(\mathbf{N})$ is divisible by $(x-\alpha)$. Alternatively, a deterministic check is as follows. First, apply the partial linearization of [9, Sec. 6], yielding a matrix $\overline{\mathbf{N}} \in \mathbb{K}[x]^{\overline{n}\times\overline{n}}$ such that $\overline{\mathbf{N}}$ is nonsingular if and only if $\mathbf{N}$ is nonsingular; $\overline{n} \in O(n)$; and $\deg(\overline{\mathbf{N}}) \leq \lceil |\mathrm{rdeg}(\mathbf{N})|/n \rceil$. This does not involve arithmetic operations. Since $\overline{\mathbf{N}}$ is nonsingular if and only if its kernel is trivial, it then remains to compute a kernel basis via the algorithm in [27], using $O\tilde{~}(n^\omega \deg(\overline{\mathbf{N}})) \subseteq O\tilde{~}(n^\omega \lceil |\mathrm{rdeg}(\mathbf{N})|/n \rceil)$ operations in $\mathbb{K}$. Instead of considering the kernel, one could also test the nonsingularity of $\overline{\mathbf{N}}$ using algorithms from [9], as explained in [22, p. 24].

Algorithm 1: RandomCompletionPopov
Input: matrix $\mathbf{M} \in \mathbb{K}[x]^{m\times n}$ with full rank and $m < n$; subset $S \subseteq \mathbb{K}$ of cardinality q.
Output: the Popov form of $\mathbf{M}$, or *failure*.

1. $\mathbf{L} \leftarrow$ matrix in $\mathbb{K}^{(n-m)\times n}$ with entries chosen uniformly and independently at random from S.
2. $\mathbf{C} \leftarrow x^{\deg(\mathbf{M})+1}\mathbf{L}$
3. *If* $[\mathbf{M}^\mathsf{T} \;\; \mathbf{C}^\mathsf{T}]^\mathsf{T}$ is singular *then return failure*
4. $\hat{\mathbf{P}} \leftarrow$ NonsingularPopov($[\mathbf{M}^\mathsf{T} \;\; \mathbf{C}^\mathsf{T}]^\mathsf{T}$)
5. *If* $\mathrm{rdeg}(\hat{\mathbf{P}})$ does not contain a permutation of $\mathrm{rdeg}(\mathbf{C})$ *then return failure*
6. *Return* the submatrix of $\hat{\mathbf{P}}$ formed by its rows of degree less than $\min(\mathrm{rdeg}(\mathbf{C}))$

Proposition 3.4. *Algorithm 1 is correct and the probability that a failure is reported at Step 3 or Step 5 is as indicated in Lemma 3.3. If* NonsingularPopov *is the algorithm of [19], Algorithm 1 uses*

$$\tilde{O}\left(n^\omega \left\lceil \frac{|\mathrm{rdeg}(\mathbf{M})| + (n-m)\deg(\mathbf{M})}{n} \right\rceil\right) \subseteq \tilde{O}\left(n^\omega \deg(\mathbf{M})\right)$$

operations in $\mathbb{K}$.

Indeed, from Theorem 2.2, Step 4 uses $O\tilde{~}(n^\omega \lceil \Delta/n \rceil)$ operations where $\Delta = |\mathrm{rdeg}([\mathbf{M}^\top\ \mathbf{C}^\top]^\top)| = |\mathrm{rdeg}(\mathbf{M})| + (n-m)(\deg(\mathbf{M})+1)$.

While other Popov form algorithms could be used, that of [19] allows us to take into account the average row degree of $\mathbf{M}$. Indeed, if $|\mathrm{rdeg}(\mathbf{M})| \ll m\deg(\mathbf{M})$ and $n - m \ll n$, the cost bound above is asymptotically better than $O\tilde{~}(n^\omega \deg(\mathbf{M}))$.

Remark 1: As we mentioned in Section 2.4, the pivot index of $\mathbf{M}$ is a subset of $\pi(\mathbf{M})$. Therefore, one can let $\mathbf{L}$ be zero at all columns where $\mathbf{M}$ has a pivot, or indices one otherwise knows appear in $\pi(\mathbf{M})$. If $\mathbf{M}$ has uneven degrees (e.g. it has the form $\hat{\mathbf{M}}\mathbf{x}^s$ for some shift s, see Section 5.1), then this can be particularly worthwhile. In the case where for some reason we know $\pi(\mathbf{M})$, then $\mathbf{L}$ can simply be taken such that $\mathbf{L}_{*,\{1,\ldots,n\}\setminus\pi(\mathbf{M})}$ is the identity matrix. In that case, Algorithm 1 becomes deterministic.

4 COMPUTING THE PIVOT SUPPORT

We now consider a matrix $\mathbf{M} \in \mathbb{K}[x]^{m\times n}$ with $m < n$, possibly rank-deficient, and we focus on the computation of its pivot support $\pi(\mathbf{M})$. In Section 4.1, we give a deterministic algorithm which is efficient when $n \in O(m)$. In Section 4.2 we explain how this can be used iteratively to efficiently find the pivot support when $m \ll n$.

4.1 Deterministic pivot support computation via column basis factorization

Our approach stems from the fact (see Lemma 4.2) that $\pi(\mathbf{M})$ is also the pivot support of any basis of the *saturation* of the row space of $\mathbf{M}$ [4, Sec. II.§2.4], defined as

$$\{\boldsymbol{\lambda}\mathbf{M}, \boldsymbol{\lambda} \in \mathbb{K}(x)^{1\times m}\} \cap \mathbb{K}[x]^{1\times m}.$$

This notion of saturation was already used in [28] in order to compute column bases of $\mathbf{M}$ by relying on the following factorization:

Lemma 4.1 ([28, Sec. 3]). *Let $\mathbf{M} \in \mathbb{K}[x]^{m\times n}$ have rank $r \in \mathbb{Z}_{>0}$, let $\mathbf{K} \in \mathbb{K}[x]^{n\times(n-r)}$ be a right kernel basis of $\mathbf{M}$, and let $\mathbf{S} \in \mathbb{K}[x]^{r\times n}$ be a left kernel basis of $\mathbf{K}$. Then, we have $\mathbf{M} = \mathbf{CS}$ for some column basis $\mathbf{C} \in \mathbb{K}[x]^{m\times r}$ of $\mathbf{M}$.*

One can easily verify that the left kernel of $\mathbf{K}$ is precisely the saturation of $\mathbf{M}$, and therefore the matrix $\mathbf{S}$ is a (row) basis of this saturation. Here, we are particularly interested in the following consequence of this result:

Lemma 4.2. *The matrices $\mathbf{M}$ and $\mathbf{S}$ in Lemma 4.1 have the same pivot support, that is, $\pi(\mathbf{M}) = \pi(\mathbf{S})$.*

Proof. Since $\mathbf{M} = \mathbf{CS}$, the row space of $\mathbf{M}$ is contained in that of $\mathbf{S}$. Hence, by the properties at the end of Section 2.4, $\pi(\mathbf{M}) \subseteq \pi(\mathbf{S})$ as sets. But since $\mathbf{M}$ and $\mathbf{S}$ both have rank r, both pivot supports have exactly r different elements, and must be equal. □

We will read off $\pi(\mathbf{S})$ from $\mathbf{S}$ by ensuring that this matrix is in ordered weak Popov form. First, we obtain a column reduced right kernel basis $\mathbf{K}$ of $\mathbf{M}$ using MinimalKernelBasis (see Theorem 2.1). However, the degree profile of $\mathbf{K}$ prevents us from using the same algorithm to compute a left kernel basis $\mathbf{S}$ efficiently, since the average row degree of $\mathbf{K}$ could be as large as $r\deg(\mathbf{M})$. To circumvent this issue, we combine the observations that $\deg(\mathbf{S})$ is bounded and that $\mathbf{K}$ has small average *column* degree to conclude that $\mathbf{S}$ can be efficiently obtained via an approximant basis (see Section 2).

Lemma 4.3. *Let $\mathbf{M} \in \mathbb{K}[x]^{m\times n}$ have rank $r \in \mathbb{Z}_{>0}$ and let $\mathbf{K} \in \mathbb{K}[x]^{n\times(n-r)}$ be a right kernel basis of $\mathbf{M}$. Then, any left kernel basis of $\mathbf{K}$ which is in reduced form must have degree at most $d = \deg(\mathbf{M})$. As a consequence, if $\hat{\mathbf{P}} \in \mathbb{K}[x]^{n\times n}$ is a reduced basis of $\mathcal{A}_{\mathbf{d}}(\mathbf{K})$, where $\mathbf{d} = \mathrm{cdeg}(\mathbf{K}) + d + 1 \in \mathbb{Z}^{n-r}$, then the submatrix $\mathbf{P}$ of $\hat{\mathbf{P}}$ formed by its rows of degree at most d is a reduced left kernel basis of $\mathbf{K}$.*

Proof. Let $\mathbf{S} \in \mathbb{K}[x]^{r\times n}$ be a left kernel basis of $\mathbf{K}$ in reduced form. By Lemma 4.1, $\mathbf{M} = \mathbf{CS}$ for some matrix $\mathbf{C} \in \mathbb{K}[x]^{m\times r}$. Then, the predictable degree property implies that $\deg(\mathbf{S}) \le \deg(\mathbf{CS}) = d$.

For the second claim (which is a particular case of [28, Lem. 4.2]), note that $\mathbf{P}$ is reduced as a subset of the rows of a reduced matrix. Besides, $\mathrm{cdeg}(\mathbf{PK}) < \mathbf{d}$ by construction, hence $\mathbf{PK} = \mathbf{0} \bmod \mathbf{x}^{\mathbf{d}}$ implies $\mathbf{PK} = \mathbf{0}$. It remains to show that $\mathbf{P}$ generates the left kernel of $\mathbf{K}$. Indeed, there exists a basis of this kernel which has degree at most d, and on the other hand any vector of degree at most d in this kernel is in particular in $\mathcal{A}_{\mathbf{d}}(\mathbf{K})$ and therefore is a combination of the rows of $\hat{\mathbf{P}}$; using the predictable degree property, we obtain that this combination only involves rows from the submatrix $\mathbf{P}$. □

If we compute $\hat{\mathbf{P}}$ in ordered weak Popov form, then the submatrix $\mathbf{P}$ is in ordered weak Popov form as well, and therefore $\pi(\mathbf{M})$ can be directly read off from it. The computation of an approximant basis in ordered weak Popov form can be done via the algorithm of [12], which returns one in Popov form.

> *Algorithm 2:* PivotSupportViaFactor
> *Input:* matrix $\mathbf{M} \in \mathbb{K}[x]^{m\times n}$ with $m \le n$.
> *Output:* the pivot support $\pi(\mathbf{M})$ of $\mathbf{M}$.
> 1. *If* $\mathbf{M} = \mathbf{0}$ *then return* the empty tuple $() \in \mathbb{Z}^0_{>0}$
> 2. $\mathbf{K} \in \mathbb{K}[x]^{n\times(n-r)} \leftarrow$ MinimalKernelBasis($\mathbf{M}$)
> 3. $\hat{\mathbf{P}} \in \mathbb{K}[x]^{n\times n} \leftarrow$ ordered weak Popov basis of $\mathcal{A}_{\mathbf{d}}(\mathbf{K})$, with $\mathbf{d} = \mathrm{cdeg}(\mathbf{K}) + (\deg(\mathbf{M})+1) \in \mathbb{Z}^{n-r}$
> 4. $\mathbf{S} \in \mathbb{K}[x]^{r\times n} \leftarrow$ the rows of $\hat{\mathbf{P}}$ of degree at most $\deg(\mathbf{M})$
> 5. *Return* the pivot index of $\mathbf{S}$

Proposition 4.4. *Algorithm 2 is correct and uses $O\tilde{~}(n^\omega \deg(\mathbf{M}))$ operations in $\mathbb{K}$.*

Proof. Note that we compute the rank of $\mathbf{M}$ as r by the indirect assignment at Step 2. Besides, $\mathbf{S}$ is in ordered weak Popov form since it is a submatrix formed by rows of $\hat{\mathbf{P}}$ itself in ordered weak Popov form. This implies that Step 5 indeed returns the pivot support of $\mathbf{S}$. Then, the correctness directly follows from Lemmas 4.2 and 4.3.

By Theorem 2.1, Step 2 costs $O\tilde{~}(n^\omega d)$, where $d = \deg(\mathbf{M})$, and $|\mathrm{cdeg}(\mathbf{K})| \le rd$. Thus, the sum of the approximation order defined at Step 3 is $|\mathbf{d}| = |\mathrm{cdeg}(\mathbf{K})| + (n-r)(d+1) < n(d+1)$. Then, this step uses $O\tilde{~}(n^{\omega-1}|\mathbf{d}|) \subseteq O\tilde{~}(n^\omega d)$ operations [12, Thm. 1.4]. □

Note that in this algorithm we do not require that $\mathbf{M}$ has full rank. The only reason why we assume $m \le n$ is because the cost bound for the computation of a kernel basis at Step 2 is not clear to us in the case $m > n$ (the same assumption is made in [30]).

Here, it seems more difficult to take average degrees into account than in Algorithm 1. While the average degree of the m columns of $\mathbf{M}$ with largest degree could be taken into account by the kernel basis algorithm of [30], it seems that the computation of $\mathbf{S}$ via an approximant basis remains in $O\tilde{~}(n^\omega d)$ nevertheless.

4.2 The case of wide matrices

In this section we will deal with pivots of submatrices $\mathbf{M}_{*,J}$, where $J = \{j_1 < \ldots < j_k\} \subseteq \{1,\ldots,n\}$. To use column indices of $\mathbf{M}_{*,J}$ in $\mathbf{M}$, we introduce for any such J the operator $\phi_J : \{1,\ldots,k\} \to \{1,\ldots,n\}$ satisfying $\phi_J(i) = j_i$. We abuse notation by applying ϕ_J element-wise to tuples, such as in $\phi_J(\pi(\mathbf{M}_{*,J}))$.

The following simple lemma is the crux of the algorithm:

Lemma 4.5. *Let* $\mathbf{M} \in \mathbb{K}[x]^{m\times n}$, *and consider any set of indices* $J \subseteq \{1,\ldots,n\}$. *Then* $(\pi(\mathbf{M}) \cap J) \subseteq \phi_J(\pi(\mathbf{M}_{*,J}))$ *with equality whenever* $\pi(\mathbf{M}) \subseteq J$.

Proof. If a vector $\mathbf{v} \in \mathbb{K}[x]^{1\times n}$ in the row space of $\mathbf{M}$ is such that $\pi(\mathbf{v}) \in J$, then $\pi(\mathbf{v}) = \phi_J(\pi(\mathbf{v}_{*,J}))$. This implies $(\pi(\mathbf{M}) \cap J) \subseteq \phi_J(\pi(\mathbf{M}_{*,J}))$ since the pivot index of any vector in the row space of $\mathbf{M}$ (resp. $\mathbf{M}_{*,J}$) appears in $\pi(\mathbf{M})$ (resp. $\pi(\mathbf{M}_{*,J})$), see Section 2.4. It also immediately implies the equality whenever $\pi(\mathbf{M}) \subseteq J$. □

These properties lead to a fast method for computing the pivot support when $n \gg m$, relying on a black box PivotSupport which efficiently finds the pivot support when $n \in O(m)$: one first considers the $2m$ left columns $\mathbf{M}_{*,\{1,\ldots,2m\}}$ and uses PivotSupport to compute their pivot support π_1. Then, Lemma 4.5 suggests to discard all columns of $\mathbf{M}$ in $\{1,\ldots,2m\} \setminus \pi_1$, thus obtaining a matrix $\mathbf{M}_1$. Then, we repeat the same process to obtain $\mathbf{M}_2, \mathbf{M}_3$, etc.

Algorithm 3: WideMatrixPivotSupport
Input: matrix $\mathbf{M} \in \mathbb{K}[x]^{m\times n}$.
Output: the pivot support $\pi(\mathbf{M})$ of $\mathbf{M}$.
Assumption: the algorithm PivotSupport takes as input $\mathbf{M}$ and returns $\pi(\mathbf{M})$.

1. *If* $n \leq 2m$ *then return* PivotSupport($\mathbf{M}$)
2. $\pi_0 \leftarrow$ PivotSupport($\mathbf{M}_{*,\{1,\ldots,2m\}}$)
3. $\hat{\mathbf{M}} \leftarrow [\mathbf{M}_{*,\pi_0} \quad \mathbf{M}_{*,\{2m+1,\ldots,n\}}]$
4. $[\pi_1 \quad \pi_2] \leftarrow$ WideMatrixPivotSupport($\hat{\mathbf{M}}$), such that $\max(\pi_1) \leq \#\pi_0$ and $\min(\pi_2) > \#\pi_0$.
5. *Return* $[\phi_{\pi_0}(\pi_1) \quad \phi_{\{2m+1,\ldots,n\}}(\pi_2)]$

Proposition 4.6. *Algorithm 3 is correct. It uses at most* $\lceil n/m \rceil$ *calls to* PivotSupport, *each with a* $m \times k$ *submatrix of* $\mathbf{M}$ *as input, where* $k \leq 2m$. *If* $m \leq n$ *and* PivotSupport *is Algorithm 2, then Algorithm 3 uses* $O\tilde{~}(m^{\omega-1} n \deg(\mathbf{M}))$ *operations in* $\mathbb{K}$.

Proof. The correctness follows from Lemma 4.5, and the operation count is obvious. If using Algorithm 2 for PivotSupport, the correctness and cost bound follow from Proposition 4.4. □

5 PRELIMINARIES ON SHIFTED FORMS

5.1 Shifted forms

The notions of reduced and Popov forms presented in Sections 2.3 and 2.4 can be extended by introducing additive integer weights in the degree measure for vectors, following [24, Sec. 3]: a *shift* is a tuple $\boldsymbol{s} = (s_1,\ldots,s_n) \in \mathbb{Z}^n$, and the *shifted degree* of a row vector $\mathbf{p} = [p_1 \cdots p_n] \in \mathbb{K}[x]^{1\times n}$ is

$$\mathrm{rdeg}_{\boldsymbol{s}}(\mathbf{p}) = \max(\deg(p_1) + s_1, \ldots, \deg(p_n) + s_n) = \mathrm{rdeg}(\mathbf{p}\mathbf{x}^{\boldsymbol{s}}),$$

where $\mathbf{x}^{\boldsymbol{s}} = \mathrm{diag}(x^{s_1},\ldots,x^{s_n})$. Note that here $\mathbf{p}\mathbf{x}^{\boldsymbol{s}}$ may be over the ring of Laurent polynomials if $\min(\boldsymbol{s}) < 0$; below, actual computations will always remain over $\mathbb{K}[x]$. Note that with $\boldsymbol{s} = \mathbf{0}$ we recover the notion of degree used in the previous sections.

This leads to shifted reduced forms for cases where one is interested in matrices whose rows minimize the $\boldsymbol{s}$-degree, instead of the usual $\mathbf{0}$-degree. The generalized definitions from Section 2 can be concisely described as follows. For a matrix $\mathbf{M} \in \mathbb{K}[x]^{m\times n}$, its $\boldsymbol{s}$-row degree is $\mathrm{rdeg}_{\boldsymbol{s}}(\mathbf{M}) = \mathrm{rdeg}(\mathbf{M}\mathbf{x}^{\boldsymbol{s}})$. If $\mathbf{M}$ has no zero row, its $\boldsymbol{s}$-leading matrix is $\mathrm{lm}_{\boldsymbol{s}}(\mathbf{M}) = \mathrm{lm}(\mathbf{M}\mathbf{x}^{\boldsymbol{s}})$, and the $\boldsymbol{s}$-pivot index and entries of $\mathbf{M}$ are the pivot index and entries of $\mathbf{M}\mathbf{x}^{\boldsymbol{s}}$. The $\boldsymbol{s}$*-pivot degree* of $\mathbf{M}$ is the tuple of the degrees of its $\boldsymbol{s}$-pivot entries; this is equal to $\mathrm{rdeg}_{\boldsymbol{s}}(\mathbf{M}) - \boldsymbol{s}_J$, where J is the $\boldsymbol{s}$-pivot index of $\mathbf{M}$ and $\boldsymbol{s}_J$ the corresponding subshift.

If $\mathbf{M}$ has no zero row and $m \leq n$, then $\mathbf{M}$ is in $\boldsymbol{s}$-reduced, $\boldsymbol{s}$-(ordered) weak Popov or $\boldsymbol{s}$-Popov form if $\mathbf{M}\mathbf{x}^{\boldsymbol{s}}$ has the respective non-shifted form, whenever $\min(\boldsymbol{s}) \geq 0$. Since adding a constant to all the entries of $\boldsymbol{s}$ simply shifts the $\boldsymbol{s}$-degree of vectors by this constant, this does not change the $\boldsymbol{s}$-leading matrix or the $\boldsymbol{s}$-pivots, and thus does not affect the shifted forms. Therefore we can extend the definitions of these to also cover $\boldsymbol{s}$ with negative entries; one may alternatively assume $\min(\boldsymbol{s}) = 0$ without loss of generality.

The $\boldsymbol{s}$-Popov form $\mathbf{P}$ of a matrix $\mathbf{M} \in \mathbb{K}[x]^{m\times n}$ is the unique row basis of $\mathbf{M}$ which is in $\boldsymbol{s}$-Popov form. The $\boldsymbol{s}$-pivot support of $\mathbf{M}$ is the $\boldsymbol{s}$-pivot index of $\mathbf{P}$ and is denoted by $\pi_{\boldsymbol{s}}(\mathbf{M}) \in \mathbb{Z}^r_{>0}$, where r is the rank of $\mathbf{M}$. For more details on shifted forms, we refer to [3].

Computationally, it is folklore that finding the shifted Popov form easily reduces to the non-shifted case: given a matrix $\mathbf{M} \in \mathbb{K}[x]^{m\times n}$ and a nonnegative shift $\boldsymbol{s} \in \mathbb{Z}^n$, the non-shifted Popov form $\hat{\mathbf{P}}$ of $\mathbf{M}\mathbf{x}^{\boldsymbol{s}}$ has the form $\hat{\mathbf{P}} = \mathbf{P}\mathbf{x}^{\boldsymbol{s}}$, with $\mathbf{P}$ the $\boldsymbol{s}$-Popov form of $\mathbf{M}$. If $m < n$ and the computation of $\hat{\mathbf{P}}$ can be carried out in $O\tilde{~}(m^{\omega-1} n \deg(\mathbf{M}))$ operations, this approach yields $\mathbf{P}$ in $O\tilde{~}(m^{\omega-1} n(\deg(\mathbf{M}) + \mathrm{amp}(\boldsymbol{s})))$. While this cost is satisfactory whenever $\mathrm{amp}(\boldsymbol{s}) \in O(\deg(\mathbf{M}))$, one may hope for improvements especially when $\mathrm{amp}(\boldsymbol{s}) > m\deg(\mathbf{M})$. Indeed, Eq. (5) in Lemma 5.1 shows $\deg(\mathbf{P}) \leq m\deg(\mathbf{M})$, suggesting the target cost $O\tilde{~}(m^{\omega} n \deg(\mathbf{M}))$ for the computation of $\mathbf{P}$.

5.2 Hermite form

A matrix $\mathbf{H} = [h_{i,j}] \in \mathbb{K}[x]^{r\times n}$ with $r \leq n$ is in *Hermite form* [11, 15, 20] if there are indices $1 \leq j_1 < \cdots < j_r \leq n$ such that:

- $h_{i,j} = 0$ for $1 \leq j < j_i$ and $1 \leq i \leq r$,
- h_{i,j_i} is monic (therefore nonzero) for $1 \leq i \leq r$,
- $\deg(h_{i',j_i}) < \deg(h_{i,j_i})$ for $1 \leq i' < i \leq r$.

We call $(j_1,\ldots,j_r)$ the *Hermite pivot index* of $\mathbf{H}$; note that it is precisely the column rank profile of $\mathbf{H}$.

For a matrix $\mathbf{M} \in \mathbb{K}[x]^{m\times n}$, its Hermite form $\mathbf{H} \in \mathbb{K}[x]^{r\times n}$ is the unique row basis of $\mathbf{M}$ which is in Hermite form. We call *Hermite pivot support* of $\mathbf{M}$ the Hermite pivot index of $\mathbf{H}$. Note that this is also the column rank profile of $\mathbf{M}$, since $\mathbf{M}$ is unimodularly equivalent to $\mathbf{H}$ (up to padding $\mathbf{H}$ with zero rows).

For a given $\mathbf{M}$, the Hermite form can be seen as a specific shifted Popov form: defining the shift $\boldsymbol{h} = (nt,\ldots,2t,t)$ for any $t > \deg(\mathbf{H})$, the $\boldsymbol{h}$-Popov form of $\mathbf{M}$ coincides with its Hermite form [3, Lem. 2.6]. Besides, the $\boldsymbol{h}$-pivot index of $\mathbf{H}$ is $(j_1,\ldots,j_r)$; in other words, the Hermite pivot support $\pi_{\boldsymbol{h}}(\mathbf{M})$ is the column rank profile of $\mathbf{M}$.

5.3 Degree bounds for shifted Popov forms

The next result states that the unimodular transformation U between M and its s-Popov form P only depends on the submatrices of M and P formed by the columns in the s-pivot support. It also gives useful degree bounds for the matrices U and P; for a more general study of such bounds, we refer to [3, Sec. 5].

Lemma 5.1. *Let* $\mathbf{M} \in \mathbb{K}[x]^{m\times n}$ *have full rank with* $m \le n$, *let* $\mathbf{s} \in \mathbb{Z}^n$, *let* $\mathbf{P} \in \mathbb{K}[x]^{m\times n}$ *be the* $\mathbf{s}$*-Popov form of* M, *and let* $\boldsymbol{\pi} = \boldsymbol{\pi}_{\mathbf{s}}(\mathbf{M})$ *be the* $\mathbf{s}$*-pivot index of* P. *Then* $\mathbf{M}_{*,\boldsymbol{\pi}} \in \mathbb{K}[x]^{m\times m}$ *is nonsingular,* $\mathbf{P}_{*,\boldsymbol{\pi}}$ *is its* $\mathbf{s}_{\boldsymbol{\pi}}$*-Popov form, and* $\mathbf{U} = \mathbf{P}_{*,\boldsymbol{\pi}}\mathbf{M}_{*,\boldsymbol{\pi}}^{-1} \in \mathbb{K}[x]^{m\times m}$ *is the unique unimodular matrix such that* $\mathbf{UM} = \mathbf{P}$.

Furthermore, we have the following degree bounds:

$$\deg(\mathbf{P}) \le \deg(\mathbf{M}) + \mathrm{amp}(\mathbf{s}), \tag{2}$$

$$\mathrm{cdeg}(\mathbf{U}_{*,i}) \le |\mathrm{rdeg}(\mathbf{M})| - \mathrm{rdeg}(\mathbf{M}_{i,*}) \;\; \textit{for } 1 \le i \le m, \tag{3}$$

$$\deg \mathbf{U} \le |\mathrm{cdeg}(\mathbf{M}_{*,\boldsymbol{\pi}})|, \tag{4}$$

$$\deg(\mathbf{P}) \le \min(|\mathrm{rdeg}(\mathbf{M})|, |\mathrm{cdeg}(\mathbf{M}')|) \le m\deg(\mathbf{M}) \;\; \textit{where } \mathbf{M}' \textit{ is } \mathbf{M} \textit{ with its zero columns removed.} \tag{5}$$

Proof. Let $\hat{\mathbf{P}} = \mathbf{M}_{*,\boldsymbol{\pi}}$, $\hat{\mathbf{M}} = \mathbf{M}_{*,\boldsymbol{\pi}}$, and $\hat{\mathbf{s}} = \mathbf{s}_{\boldsymbol{\pi}}$. Note first that $\hat{\mathbf{P}}$ is nonsingular and in $\hat{\mathbf{s}}$-Popov form. Let $\mathbf{V} \in \mathbb{K}[x]^{m\times m}$ be any unimodular matrix such that $\mathbf{VM} = \mathbf{P}$. Then in particular $\mathbf{V}\hat{\mathbf{M}} = \hat{\mathbf{P}}$, hence $\hat{\mathbf{M}}$ is nonsingular and unimodularly equivalent to $\hat{\mathbf{P}}$, which is therefore the $\hat{\mathbf{s}}$-Popov form of $\hat{\mathbf{M}}$. Besides, we have $\mathbf{V} = \hat{\mathbf{P}}\hat{\mathbf{M}}^{-1} = \mathbf{U}$.

It remains to prove the degree bounds. The first one comes from the minimality of P. Indeed, since P is an $\mathbf{s}$-reduced form of M we have $\max(\mathrm{rdeg}_{\mathbf{s}}(\mathbf{P})) \le \max(\mathrm{rdeg}_{\mathbf{s}}(\mathbf{M}))$; the left-hand side of this inequality is at least $\deg(\mathbf{P}) + \min(\mathbf{s})$ while its right-hand side is at most $\deg(\mathbf{M}) + \max(\mathbf{s})$.

Let $\boldsymbol{\delta} \in \mathbb{Z}^m_{\ge 0}$ be the $\mathbf{s}$-pivot degree of P. Then, $\hat{\mathbf{P}}$ is in $(-\boldsymbol{\delta})$-Popov form with $\mathrm{rdeg}_{-\boldsymbol{\delta}}(\hat{\mathbf{P}}) = \mathbf{0}$ and $\mathrm{cdeg}(\hat{\mathbf{P}}) = \boldsymbol{\delta}$ [12, Lem. 4.1]. Besides, $\hat{\mathbf{P}}$ is column reduced and thus $|\mathrm{cdeg}(\hat{\mathbf{P}})| = \deg(\det(\hat{\mathbf{P}}))$ [13, Sec. 6.3.2], hence $|\boldsymbol{\delta}| = \deg(\det(\hat{\mathbf{M}}))$.

Let $\mathbf{t} = (t_1, \ldots, t_m) = \mathrm{rdeg}(\mathbf{U}^{-1})$. We obtain $\mathrm{rdeg}_{-\boldsymbol{\delta}}(\hat{\mathbf{M}}) = \mathrm{rdeg}_{-\boldsymbol{\delta}}(\mathbf{U}^{-1}\hat{\mathbf{P}}) = \mathrm{rdeg}_{\mathbf{0}}(\mathbf{U}^{-1}) = \mathbf{t}$ by the predictable degree property (with shifts, see e.g. [26, Lem. 2.17]). Now, U being the transpose of the matrix of cofactors of $\mathbf{U}^{-1}$ divided by the constant $\det(\mathbf{U}^{-1}) \in \mathbb{K} \setminus \{0\}$, we obtain $\mathrm{cdeg}(\mathbf{U}_{*,i}) \le |\mathbf{t}| - t_i$ for $1 \le i \le m$. Since $-\boldsymbol{\delta} \le \mathbf{0}$ we have $\mathbf{t} = \mathrm{rdeg}_{-\boldsymbol{\delta}}(\hat{\mathbf{M}}) \le \mathrm{rdeg}(\mathbf{M})$, hence $|\mathbf{t}| - t_i \le |\mathrm{rdeg}(\mathbf{M})| - \mathrm{rdeg}(\mathbf{M}_{i,*})$. This proves (3).

Every entry of the adjugate of $\hat{\mathbf{M}}$ has degree at most $|\mathrm{cdeg}(\hat{\mathbf{M}})|$. Then, $\mathbf{U} = \hat{\mathbf{P}}\hat{\mathbf{M}}^{-1}$ gives $\deg(\mathbf{U}) \le \deg(\hat{\mathbf{P}}) - \deg(\det(\hat{\mathbf{M}})) + |\mathrm{cdeg}(\hat{\mathbf{M}})|$. This yields (4) since $\deg(\hat{\mathbf{P}}) = \max(\boldsymbol{\delta}) \le |\boldsymbol{\delta}| = \deg(\det(\hat{\mathbf{M}}))$.

The second inequality in (5) is implied by $|\mathrm{rdeg}(\mathbf{M})| \le m\deg(\mathbf{M})$. Besides, from $\mathbf{P} = \mathbf{UM} = \sum_{i=1}^{m} \mathbf{U}_{*,i}\mathbf{M}_{i,*}$ we see that (3) implies $\deg(\mathbf{P}) \le |\mathrm{rdeg}(\mathbf{M})|$. For $j \in \boldsymbol{\pi}$ we have $\mathrm{cdeg}(\mathbf{P}_{*,j}) \le |\mathrm{cdeg}(\hat{\mathbf{P}})| = \deg(\det(\hat{\mathbf{M}})) \le |\mathrm{cdeg}(\mathbf{M}')|$. Now, let $j \in \{1, \ldots, n\} \setminus \boldsymbol{\pi}$: if $\mathbf{M}_{*,j} = \mathbf{0}$ then $\mathbf{P}_{*,j} = \mathbf{0}$, and otherwise it follows from (4) that $\mathrm{cdeg}(\mathbf{P}_{*,j}) = \deg(\mathbf{UM}_{*,j}) \le |\mathrm{cdeg}(\hat{\mathbf{M}})| + \mathrm{cdeg}(\mathbf{M}_{*,j}) \le |\mathrm{cdeg}(\mathbf{M}')|$. □

6 SHIFTED POPOV FORM WHEN THE PIVOT SUPPORT IS KNOWN

Now, we focus on computing the $\mathbf{s}$-Popov form P of M when the $\mathbf{s}$-pivot support $\boldsymbol{\pi}_{\mathbf{s}}(\mathbf{M})$ is known; here, M has full rank with $m < n$.

To exploit the knowledge of $\boldsymbol{\pi} = \boldsymbol{\pi}_{\mathbf{s}}(\mathbf{M})$, a first approach follows from Remark 1: use Algorithm 1 with L such that $\mathbf{L}_{*,\{1,\ldots,n\}\setminus\boldsymbol{\pi}}$ is the identity matrix and its other columns are zero. Then, it is easily checked that $\mathbf{C} = \mathbf{L}\mathbf{x}^{\max(\mathrm{rdeg}_{\mathbf{s}}(\mathbf{M}))-\mathbf{s}}$ is a completion of $\hat{\mathbf{M}} = \mathbf{M}\mathbf{x}^{\mathbf{s}}$; hence Algorithm 1 returns the Popov form $\hat{\mathbf{P}} = \mathbf{P}\mathbf{x}^{\mathbf{s}}$ of $\hat{\mathbf{M}}$. This yields P deterministically in $\tilde{O}(n^{\omega}(\deg(\mathbf{M}) + \mathrm{amp}(\mathbf{s})))$ operations.

Both factors in this cost bound are unsatisfactory in some parameter ranges. When $n \gg m$, a sensible improvement would be to replace the matrix dimension factor n^{ω} with one which has the exponent on the smallest dimension, such as $m^{\omega-1}n$. Similarly, when $\mathrm{amp}(\mathbf{s}) \gg m\deg(\mathbf{M})$, a sensible improvement would be to replace the polynomial degree factor $\deg(\mathbf{M}) + \mathrm{amp}(\mathbf{s})$ with one suggested by the bounds on $\deg(\mathbf{P})$ given in Eq. (5) of Lemma 5.1.

We achieve both improvements with our second approach, which works in three steps and is formalised as Algorithm 4. First, we compute the $\mathbf{s}_{\boldsymbol{\pi}}$-Popov form of the submatrix $\mathbf{M}_{*,\boldsymbol{\pi}}$, which can be done efficiently since this submatrix is square and nonsingular. Then, we use polynomial matrix division to obtain the unimodular transformation $\mathbf{U} \in \mathbb{K}[x]^{m\times m}$ such that $\mathbf{M}_{*,\boldsymbol{\pi}_{\mathbf{s}}(\mathbf{M})} = \mathbf{U}\mathbf{P}_{*,\boldsymbol{\pi}_{\mathbf{s}}(\mathbf{M})}$. Lastly, we compute the remaining part of the $\mathbf{s}$-Popov form of M as $\mathbf{U}^{-1}\mathbf{M}_{*,\{1,\ldots,n\}\setminus\boldsymbol{\pi}}$. Note that, even for $\mathbf{s} = \mathbf{0}$, all entries of $\mathbf{U}^{-1}$ may have degree in $\Theta(m\deg(\mathbf{M}))$; we avoid handling such large degrees by computing this product truncated at precision x^{δ}, where δ is a (strict) upper bound on the degree of the $\mathbf{s}$-Popov form P. For example, if $\mathbf{s} = \mathbf{0}$ we can take $\delta = 1 + \deg(\mathbf{M})$.

Algorithm 4: KnownSupportPopov
Input:
- matrix $\mathbf{M} \in \mathbb{K}[x]^{m\times n}$ with full rank and $m < n$,
- shift $\mathbf{s} \in \mathbb{Z}^n$,
- the $\mathbf{s}$-pivot support $\boldsymbol{\pi} = \boldsymbol{\pi}_{\mathbf{s}}(\mathbf{M})$ of M,
- bound $\delta \in \mathbb{Z}_{>0}$ on the degree of the $\mathbf{s}$-Popov form of M.

Default: $\delta = 1 + \min(|\mathrm{rdeg}(\mathbf{M})|, |\mathrm{cdeg}(\mathbf{M}')|, \deg(\mathbf{M}) + \mathrm{amp}(\mathbf{s}))$, where $\mathbf{M}'$ is M with zero columns removed.
Output: the $\mathbf{s}$-Popov form of M.

1. $\mathbf{P} \leftarrow$ zero matrix in $\mathbb{K}[x]^{m\times n}$
2. $\mathbf{P}_{*,\boldsymbol{\pi}} \leftarrow$ NonsingularPopov$(\mathbf{M}_{*,\boldsymbol{\pi}}, \mathbf{s}_{\boldsymbol{\pi}})$
3. $\mathbf{U} \leftarrow \mathbf{M}_{*,\boldsymbol{\pi}}\mathbf{P}_{*,\boldsymbol{\pi}}^{-1} \in \mathbb{K}[x]^{m\times m}$
4. $\delta \leftarrow \min(\delta,\; 1 + \max(\mathrm{rdeg}_{\mathbf{s}_{\boldsymbol{\pi}}}(\mathbf{P}_{*,\boldsymbol{\pi}})) - \min(\mathbf{s}_{(1,\ldots,n)\setminus\boldsymbol{\pi}}))$
5. $\mathbf{P}_{*,\{1,\ldots,n\}\setminus\boldsymbol{\pi}} \leftarrow \mathbf{U}^{-1}\mathbf{M}_{*,\{1,\ldots,n\}\setminus\boldsymbol{\pi}} \bmod x^{\delta}$
6. *Return* P

Proposition 6.1. *Algorithm 4 is correct and uses* $\tilde{O}(m^{\omega-1}n\delta)$ *operations in* $\mathbb{K}$, *where*

$$\delta = 1 + \min(|\mathrm{rdeg}(\mathbf{M})|, |\mathrm{cdeg}(\mathbf{M}')|, \deg(\mathbf{M}) + \mathrm{amp}(\mathbf{s})),$$

and $\mathbf{M}'$ *is* M *with zero columns removed.*

Proof. Let $\mathbf{Q} \in \mathbb{K}[x]^{m\times n}$ be the $\mathbf{s}$-Popov form of M. For correctness we prove that $\mathbf{P} = \mathbf{Q}$. The first part of Lemma 5.1 shows that indeed $\mathbf{Q}_{*,\boldsymbol{\pi}} = \mathbf{P}_{*,\boldsymbol{\pi}}$, and that $\mathbf{U} = \mathbf{M}_{*,\boldsymbol{\pi}}\mathbf{P}_{*,\boldsymbol{\pi}}^{-1} = \mathbf{M}_{*,\boldsymbol{\pi}}\mathbf{Q}_{*,\boldsymbol{\pi}}^{-1}$ computed at Step 3 is the unimodular matrix such that $\mathbf{M} = \mathbf{UQ}$.

The last item of Lemma 5.1 proves that the input default value of δ is more than $\deg(\mathbf{Q})$. Besides, by definition of $\mathbf{s}$-pivots and $\mathbf{s}$-Popov form, the column j of Q has degree at most

$$\max(\mathrm{rdeg}_{\mathbf{s}_{\boldsymbol{\pi}}}(\mathbf{Q}_{*,\boldsymbol{\pi}})) - s_j = \max(\mathrm{rdeg}_{\mathbf{s}_{\boldsymbol{\pi}}}(\mathbf{P}_{*,\boldsymbol{\pi}})) - s_j.$$

It follows that $\delta > \deg(\mathbf{Q}_{*,\{1,\ldots,n\}\setminus\pi})$ holds after Step 4, and thus the submatrix $\mathbf{Q}_{*,\{1,\ldots,n\}\setminus\pi}$ is equal to the truncated product $\mathbf{U}^{-1}\mathbf{M}_{*,\{1,\ldots,n\}\setminus\pi} \bmod x^{\delta}$ computed at Step 5. Hence $\mathbf{Q} = \mathbf{P}$.

Now we explain the cost bound. Step 2 uses $O(m^{\omega}\deg(\mathbf{M}_{*,\pi}))$ operations, by Theorem 2.2. Step 3 has the same cost by Lemma 6.2 below; note that $\mathbf{P}_{*,\pi}$ is in $\mathbf{s}_{\pi}$-Popov form and thus column reduced. This is within the announced bound since

$$O(m^{\omega}\deg(\mathbf{M}_{*,\pi})) \subseteq O(m^{\omega-1}n\deg(\mathbf{M}))$$

and $\deg(\mathbf{M}) \leq \delta$ holds by definition of δ.

Finally, Step 5 costs $O\tilde{~}(m^{\omega-1}n\delta)$ operations in $\mathbb{K}$: since $\mathbf{U}(0) \in \mathbb{K}^{m\times m}$ is invertible, the truncated inverse of $\mathbf{U}$ is computed by Newton iteration in time $O\tilde{~}(m^{\omega}\delta)$; then, the truncated product uses $O\tilde{~}(m^{\omega}\lceil(n-m)/m\rceil\delta)$ operations. □

At Step 3, we compute a product of the form $\mathbf{B}\mathbf{A}^{-1}$, knowing that it has polynomial entries and that $\mathbf{A}$ is column reduced; in particular, $\deg(\mathbf{B}\mathbf{A}^{-1}) \leq \deg(\mathbf{B})$ [19, Lem. 3.1]. Then, it is customary to obtain $\mathbf{B}\mathbf{A}^{-1}$ via a Newton iteration on the "reversed matrices" (see e.g. [22, Chap. 5] and [26, Chap. 10]).

Lemma 6.2. *For a column reduced matrix* $\mathbf{A} \in \mathbb{K}[x]^{m\times m}$ *and a matrix* $\mathbf{B} \in \mathbb{K}[x]^{m\times m}$ *which is a left multiple of* $\mathbf{A}$*, the quotient* $\mathbf{B}\mathbf{A}^{-1}$ *can be computed using* $O\tilde{~}(m^{\omega}\deg(\mathbf{B}))$ *operations in* $\mathbb{K}$.

Proof. We follow Steps 1 and 2 of the algorithm PM-QuoRem from [19], on input $\mathbf{A}$, $\mathbf{B}$, and $d = \deg(\mathbf{B}) + 1$; hence the requirement $\mathrm{cdeg}(\mathbf{B}) < \mathrm{cdeg}(\mathbf{A}) + (d, \ldots, d)$ is satisfied. It is proved in [19, Prop. 3.4] that these steps correctly compute the quotient $\mathbf{B}\mathbf{A}^{-1}$; yet we do a different cost analysis since the assumptions on parameters in [19, Prop. 3.4] might not be satisfied here.

Step 1 of PM-QuoRem computes a type of reversals $\hat{\mathbf{A}}$ and $\hat{\mathbf{B}}$ of the matrices $\mathbf{A}$ and $\mathbf{B}$: this uses no arithmetic operation. These matrices also have dimensions $m \times m$ and the constant coefficient of $\hat{\mathbf{A}}$ is invertible because $\mathbf{A}$ is column reduced. Step 2 computes the truncated product $\hat{\mathbf{B}}\hat{\mathbf{A}}^{-1} \bmod x^{d+1}$, which can be done via Newton iteration in $O\tilde{~}(m^{\omega}d)$ operations in $\mathbb{K}$. □

Since Algorithm 4 works for an arbitrary shift, it allows us in particular to find the Hermite form of $\mathbf{M}$ when its Hermite pivot support is known. It turns out that the latter can be computed efficiently via a column rank profile algorithm from [26].

Proof of Theorem 1.2. Here, the integer δ is defined as

$$\delta = 1 + \min(|\mathrm{rdeg}(\mathbf{M})|, |\mathrm{cdeg}(\mathbf{M}')|), \tag{6}$$

where $\mathbf{M}'$ is $\mathbf{M}$ with zero columns removed.

Let $\boldsymbol{h} = (n\delta, \ldots, 2\delta, \delta)$. By Lemma 5.1, δ is more than the degree of the Hermite form of $\mathbf{M}$; therefore the $\boldsymbol{h}$-Popov form of $\mathbf{M}$ is also its Hermite form (see Section 5.2). Thus, up to the knowledge of the Hermite pivot support $\pi_{\boldsymbol{h}}(\mathbf{M})$ of $\mathbf{M}$, we can compute the Hermite form of $\mathbf{M}$ using $O\tilde{~}(m^{\omega-1}n\delta)$ operations via Algorithm 4.

As mentioned in Section 5.2, $\pi_{\boldsymbol{h}}(\mathbf{M})$ is also the column rank profile of $\mathbf{M}$. It is shown in [26, Sec. 11.2] how to use row basis and kernel basis computations to obtain this rank profile in $O\tilde{~}(m^{\omega-1}n\sigma)$ operations, where $\sigma = \lceil|\mathrm{rdeg}(\mathbf{M})|/m\rceil$ is roughly the average row degree of $\mathbf{M}$. We have $\sigma \leq 1 + |\mathrm{rdeg}(\mathbf{M})|$ by definition, and it is easily verified that $|\mathrm{rdeg}(\mathbf{M})|/m \leq |\mathrm{cdeg}(\mathbf{M}')|$, hence $\sigma \leq \delta$. □

ACKNOWLEDGMENTS

The authors are grateful to Clément Pernet for pointing at the notion of saturation.

REFERENCES

[1] B. Beckermann and G. Labahn. 2000. Fraction-Free Computation of Matrix Rational Interpolants and Matrix GCDs. *SIAM J. Matrix Anal. Appl.* 22, 1 (2000), 114–144.
[2] B. Beckermann, G. Labahn, and G. Villard. 1999. Shifted Normal Forms of Polynomial Matrices. In *ISSAC'99*. ACM, 189–196.
[3] B. Beckermann, G. Labahn, and G. Villard. 2006. Normal forms for general polynomial matrices. *J. Symbolic Comput.* 41, 6 (2006), 708–737.
[4] N. Bourbaki. 1972. *Commutative Algebra.* Hermann.
[5] D. G. Cantor and E. Kaltofen. 1991. On fast multiplication of polynomials over arbitrary algebras. *Acta Inform.* 28, 7 (1991), 693–701.
[6] G. D. Forney, Jr. 1975. Minimal Bases of Rational Vector Spaces, with Applications to Multivariable Linear Systems. *SIAM Journal on Control* 13, 3 (1975), 493–520.
[7] P. Giorgi, C.-P. Jeannerod, and G. Villard. 2003. On the complexity of polynomial matrix computations. In *ISSAC'03*. ACM, 135–142.
[8] S. Gupta. 2011. *Hermite forms of polynomial matrices.* Master's thesis. University of Waterloo, Canada.
[9] S. Gupta, S. Sarkar, A. Storjohann, and J. Valeriote. 2012. Triangular x-basis decompositions and derandomization of linear algebra algorithms over $K[x]$. *J. Symbolic Comput.* 47, 4 (2012), 422–453.
[10] S. Gupta and A. Storjohann. 2011. Computing Hermite Forms of Polynomial Matrices. In *ISSAC'11*. ACM, 155–162.
[11] C. Hermite. 1851. Sur l'introduction des variables continues dans la théorie des nombres. *Journal für die reine und angewandte Mathematik* 41 (1851), 191–216.
[12] C.-P. Jeannerod, V. Neiger, É. Schost, and G. Villard. 2016. Fast computation of minimal interpolation bases in Popov form for arbitrary shifts. In *ISSAC'16*. ACM, 295–302.
[13] T. Kailath. 1980. *Linear Systems.* Prentice-Hall.
[14] G. Labahn, V. Neiger, and W. Zhou. 2017. Fast, deterministic computation of the Hermite normal form and determinant of a polynomial matrix. *J. Complexity* 42 (2017), 44–71.
[15] C. C. MacDuffee. 1933. *The Theory of Matrices.* Springer-Verlag Berlin Heidelberg. https://doi.org/10.1007/978-3-642-99234-6
[16] T. Mulders and A. Storjohann. 2003. On lattice reduction for polynomial matrices. *J. Symbolic Comput.* 35 (2003), 377–401. Issue 4.
[17] V. Neiger. 2016. *Bases of relations in one or several variables: fast algorithms and applications.* Ph.D. Dissertation. École Normale Supérieure de Lyon. https://tel.archives-ouvertes.fr/tel-01431413
[18] V. Neiger. 2016. Fast computation of shifted Popov forms of polynomial matrices via systems of modular polynomial equations. In *ISSAC'16*. ACM, 365–372.
[19] V. Neiger and T. X. Vu. 2017. Computing canonical bases of modules of univariate relations. In *ISSAC'17*. ACM.
[20] M. Newman. 1972. *Integral Matrices.* Number v. 45 in Integral matrices. Academic Press.
[21] V. M. Popov. 1972. Invariant Description of Linear, Time-Invariant Controllable Systems. *SIAM Journal on Control* 10, 2 (1972), 252–264.
[22] S. Sarkar. 2011. *Computing Popov Forms of Polynomial Matrices.* Master's thesis. University of Waterloo, Canada.
[23] S. Sarkar and A. Storjohann. 2011. Normalization of row reduced matrices. In *ISSAC'11*. ACM, 297–304.
[24] M. Van Barel and A. Bultheel. 1992. A general module theoretic framework for vector M-Padé and matrix rational interpolation. *Numer. Algorithms* 3 (1992), 451–462.
[25] W. A. Wolovich. 1974. *Linear Multivariable Systems.* Applied Mathematical Sciences, Vol. 11. Springer-Verlag New-York.
[26] W. Zhou. 2012. *Fast Order Basis and Kernel Basis Computation and Related Problems.* Ph.D. Dissertation. University of Waterloo.
[27] W. Zhou and G. Labahn. 2012. Efficient Algorithms for Order Basis Computation. *J. Symbolic Comput.* 47, 7 (2012), 793–819.
[28] W. Zhou and G. Labahn. 2013. Computing Column Bases of Polynomial Matrices. In *ISSAC'13*. ACM, 379–386.
[29] W. Zhou and G. Labahn. 2014. Unimodular Completion of Polynomial Matrices. In *ISSAC'14*. ACM, 413–420.
[30] W. Zhou, G. Labahn, and A. Storjohann. 2012. Computing Minimal Nullspace Bases. In *ISSAC'12*. ACM, 366–373.

Polynomial Equivalence Problems for Sums of Affine Powers

Ignacio García-Marco
Facultad de Ciencias. Universidad de La Laguna
iggarcia@ull.es

Pascal Koiran
LIP, ENS Lyon. Université de Lyon
pascal.koiran@ens-lyon.fr

Timothée Pecatte
LIP, ENS Lyon. Université de Lyon
timothee.pecatte@ens-lyon.fr

ABSTRACT

A sum of affine powers is an expression of the form

$$f(x_1,\ldots,x_n)=\sum_{i=1}^{s}\alpha_i\ell_i(x_1,\ldots,x_n)^{e_i}$$

where ℓ_i is an affine form. We propose polynomial time black-box algorithms that find the decomposition with the smallest value of s for an input polynomial f. Our algorithms work in situations where s is small enough compared to the number of variables or to the exponents e_i. Although quite simple, this model is a generalization of Waring decomposition. This paper extends previous work on Waring decomposition as well as our work on univariate sums of affine powers (ISSAC'17).

ACM Reference Format:
Ignacio García-Marco, Pascal Koiran, and Timothée Pecatte. 2018. Polynomial Equivalence Problems for Sums of Affine Powers. In *ISSAC '18: 2018 ACM International Symposium on Symbolic and Algebraic Computation, July 16–19, 2018, New York, NY, USA.* ACM, New York, NY, USA, 9 pages. https://doi.org/10.1145/3208976.3208993

1 INTRODUCTION

Let $\mathbb{F}[X]=\mathbb{F}[x_1,\ldots,x_n]$ be a ring of polynomials in n variables over a characteristic 0 field. This paper studies the multivariate version of the Affine Power model, i.e., we study expressions of a polynomial $f\in\mathbb{F}[X]$ as

$$f=\sum_{i=1}^{s}\alpha_i\ell_i^{e_i}, \tag{1}$$

where $e_i\in\mathbb{N}$, $\alpha_i\in\mathbb{F}$ and ℓ_i is a (non constant) affine form for all i. We denote by $\mathrm{AffPow}_{\mathbb{F}}(f)$ (or $\mathrm{AffPow}(f)$ when $\mathbb{F}$ is clear from the context) the minimum value s such that there exists a representation of the previous form with s terms.

The main goal of this work is to design algorithms that reconstruct the optimal representation of polynomials in this model, i.e., algorithms that receive as input $f\in\mathbb{F}[X]$ and compute the exact value $s=\mathrm{AffPow}_{\mathbb{F}}(f)$ and a set of triplets of coefficients, affine forms and exponents $\{(\alpha_i,\ell_i,e_i)\mid 1\le i\le s\}\subseteq\mathbb{F}\times\mathbb{F}[X]\times\mathbb{N}$ such that $f=\sum_{i=1}^{s}\alpha_i\ell_i^{e_i}$.

ISSAC '18, July 16–19, 2018, New York, NY, USA

ACM ISBN 978-1-4503-5550-6/18/07...$15.00
https://doi.org/10.1145/3208976.3208993

The univariate version of this model and several related problems have been extensively studied in [8–10, 14]. These works provide lower bounds, structural results and reconstruction algorithms under certain hypotheses for this model. This paper concerns the reconstruction in the multivariate version of this problem.

Model (1) extends the Waring model, where all the exponents are equal to the degree of the polynomial, i.e., $e_i=\deg(f)$ for all i. For a homogeneous polynomial f of degree d, consider expressions of f of the form:

$$f=\sum_{i=1}^{s}\alpha_i\ell_i^d$$

with $\alpha_i\in\mathbb{F}$ and ℓ_i are linear forms. We denote by $\mathrm{Waring}(f)$ the *Waring rank* of f, which is the minimum value s such that there exists a representation of the previous form with s terms.

Waring rank has been studied by algebraists and geometers since the 19th century. We refer to [11] for the historical background. The algorithmic study of the univariate case is often attributed to Sylvester (see [11, section 1.3]). Most of the subsequent work was devoted to the multivariate version[1] with much of the 20th century work focused on the determination of the Waring rank of generic polynomials [1, 4, 11]. A few recent papers [7, 17] have begun to investigate the Waring rank of specific polynomials such as monomials, sums of coprime monomials, the permanent and the determinant.

Waring decomposition has also been studied from an algorithmic point of view, see e.g. [3, 15, 16, 20]. Since Model (1) is more general than the Waring model, the algorithms we provide here can be adapted to find Waring decompositions.

1.1 Our results

In this work we devise algorithms for finding optimal representations of a polynomial $f\in\mathbb{F}[X]$ in Model (1), provided the value of $\mathrm{AffPow}(f)$ is small compared to the number of variables or to the degree of f.

Let us denote by $\mathrm{EssVar}(f)$ the number of *essential variables* of f. This is roughly speaking the number of variables on which f "truly depends" up to a linear change of variables [5, 15]. A first easy remark is that the value $\mathrm{AffPow}(f)$ is at least equal to $\mathrm{EssVar}(f)$. In Section 3 we investigate when this is an equality and provide an algorithm that decides whether $\mathrm{AffPow}(f)=\mathrm{EssVar}(f)$ and, if so, provides an optimal expression in the model.

In Section 4, we generalise the previous results to characterize by means of an algorithm when a polynomial $f\in\mathbb{F}[X]$ can be written as a sum of univariates after an affine change of coordinates. It is plausible that when this is a case, an optimal expression of f

[1] In the literature, Waring rank is usually defined for homogeneous polynomials.

can be built by putting together the optimal expressions of all the univariate polynomials involved. We believe this is true and we give a proof for $n = 2$. The general case ($n \geq 3$) is left as an open problem.

In Section 5, we focus on the reconstruction problem when $\mathrm{AffPow}(f) \leq \binom{n+1}{2}$. In the main result of this section, we provide a randomized algorithm that works when in the optimal decomposition all the e_i's are ≥ 5 and the coefficients of the ℓ_i's are taken uniformly at random from a finite set. In particular, this provides a new algorithm for computing Waring decompositions of "generic polynomials with $\mathrm{Waring}(f) \leq \binom{n+1}{2}$". For comparison, note that the algorithm from [15] can only find Waring decompositions up to size n, and that the Waring decomposition algorithm from [16] is only interesting when d is relatively large compared to s (see Theorem 5 and Remark 6 in that paper). Our main tool in this section is a "4th order Hessian" inspired from the ordinary Hessian determinant used in [15].

Finally, in Section 6 we propose an algorithm that performs random univariate projections, calls our univariate algorithm for sums of affine powers [9] and reconstructs f from this univariate information.

1.2 Model of computation

Throughout this paper, we will work in the black box model: we assume that our algorithm has access to f only through a "black box" that outputs $f(x_1, \ldots, x_n)$ when queried on an input $(x_1, \ldots, x_n) \in \mathbb{F}^n$.

Our algorithms handle polynomials with coefficients in an arbitrary field $\mathbb{F}$ of characteristic 0. At this level of generality, we need to be able to perform arithmetic operations (additions, multiplications) and equality tests between elements of $\mathbb{F}$. We will additionally assume that we are able to solve polynomial equations in one variable. When we write that an algorithm runs in polynomial time, we mean that the number of such steps and of calls to the black box is polynomial in the input size.

Whenever $\mathbb{F}$ is an algebraically closed field, then we may assume without loss of generality that all the α_i's equal 1 in a expression in Model (1). For the sake of conciseness, we assume this is the case. However, one can restate all the results in this work for a non algebraically closed field by just adding the α_i's.

1.3 Future work

The problem studied in the present paper is far from completely solved: our algorithms rely on assumption on $\mathrm{AffPow}(f)$ being small and, sometimes, on a random choice of the affine forms involved in the optimal expression. It would be very interesting to weaken these assumptions, or even to remove them entirely, even though the recent NP-hardness result of Waring decomposition [21] and the similarity of both problems seems to indicate that it might be hard to do so.

We prove in Proposition 4.9 that whenever a bivariate polynomial $f(x_1, x_2)$ is a sum of two univariate ones $g_1(x_1), g_2(x_2)$, one can construct an optimal expression of f in Model (1) by gathering the (univariate) optimal expressions of f_1 and f_2 and putting together the terms of degree 1. We do not know if this phenomenon is also true for polynomials in more than two variables that can be written as a sum of univariates. Even more generally, we wonder if whenever $f(X) \in \mathbb{F}[X]$ can be expressed as a sum of two polynomials g_1, g_2 in disjoints set of variables, then an optimal expression for f in Model (1) can be built up from the optimal expressions of g_1 and g_2 by just putting together the terms of degree 1. This could be seen as a analog of the Strassen's conjecture for the symmetric tensor rank, which can be stated as follows: the rank is additive on the sum of forms in different set of variable (see [22]). Our result should be compared with [6, Theorem 5.6], where the authors prove the conjecture for homogeneous polynomials in four variables that can be written as a sum of two bivariate ones.

2 PRELIMINARIES

2.1 Essential variables

We say that a polynomial $f \in \mathbb{F}[X]$ *depends on a variable* if it appears in at least one of the monomials of $f(X)$. The *number of essential variables* of a polynomial f, denoted by $\mathrm{EssVar}(f)$, is the least integer $t \in [\![0, n]\!]$ such that there exists an invertible linear transformation $A \in \mathrm{GL}_n(\mathbb{F})$ such that $f(A \cdot X)$ depends on t variables. The number of essential variables of a polynomial is given by the following result due to Carlini [5, Proposition 1].

PROPOSITION 2.1. *For a polynomial $f \in \mathbb{F}[X]$, we have*

$$\mathrm{EssVar}(f) = \dim_{\mathbb{F}} \left\langle \frac{\partial f}{\partial x_i} \mid 1 \leq i \leq n \right\rangle.$$

A first easy observation is that if $f(X) = \sum_{i=1}^{s} \ell_i^{e_i}$ with ℓ_i affine forms and $e_i \in \mathbb{N}$; then $\langle \frac{\partial f}{\partial x_i} \mid 1 \leq i \leq n \rangle \subseteq \langle \ell_i^{e_i - 1} \mid 1 \leq i \leq s \rangle$ and, hence, $\mathrm{EssVar}(f) \leq s$. In particular, $\mathrm{EssVar}(f) \leq \mathrm{AffPow}(f)$.

A polynomial $f \in \mathbb{F}[X]$ is said *regular* if it has n essential variables. From now on we always assume that the input polynomial $f \in \mathbb{F}[X]$ is regular. This can be achieved through a preliminary step consisting of eliminating the redundant variables using a randomized polynomial time algorithm (see, e.g., [16, Lemma 17] and [15, Theorem 4.1]).

2.2 Algorithmic preliminaries

In the rest of this paper, we will design algorithms that work in the "black box" setting: they have access to the input polynomial only through an oracle so that for any point $a \in \mathbb{F}^n$, we can obtain $f(a)$ in a single step by querying this oracle. This very general model is standard for the study of many problems about multivariate polynomials such as, e.g., factorization [12], sparse interpolation [2, 18], sparsest shift [19] or Waring decomposition [13]. In this section, we describe some useful blackbox subroutines that our algorithms will use.

2.2.1 Polynomial Identity Testing. Given a blackbox access to a polynomial $f \in \mathbb{F}[X]$ of degree d, the Schwartz-Zippel lemma ensures that evaluating f at random points yields a randomized polynomial time algorithm that tests whether f is equal to the zero polynomial.

2.2.2 Obtaining the derivatives.

PROPOSITION 2.2. *[16, Proposition 18] Let $f(X) \in \mathbb{F}[X]$ be an n-variate polynomial of degree d. Given blackbox access to f, in time $\mathrm{poly}(dn)$, we obtain blackbox access to any derivative $\frac{\partial f}{\partial x}$ of f.*

2.2.3 Obtaining the homogeneous components. For a polynomial $f(X) \in \mathbb{F}[X]$ we will denote by $[f]_k$ its homogeneous component of degree k. We will also sometimes use the notation $[f]_{\geq k}$ defined as $[f]_{\geq k} := \sum_{i \geq k} [f]_i$.

PROPOSITION 2.3. *[16, Proposition 19] Let $f \in \mathbb{F}[X]$ be a polynomial of degree d. Given blackbox access to f and a point $a \in \mathbb{F}^n$, we can compute $[f]_i(a)$ for each $i \in [0..d]$ in polynomial time.*

2.2.4 Factorization. To factorize a polynomial, we will use the randomized polynomial time algorithm described in [12] which outputs blackbox access to its factors. In order to apply this algorithm, we will assume that we have an effective polynomial factorization algorithm for $\mathbb{F}[x]$. In the following, we will often need to reconstruct the coefficients of a degree 1 factor h from a blackbox access to it. This can be easily done using an additional randomized step in poly(n) time: we evaluate h in $n+2$ random points and then interpolate the coefficients.

3 FROM RECONSTRUCTION TO POLYNOMIAL EQUIVALENCE

Let us first consider $f \in \mathbb{F}[X]$ a regular polynomial such that AffPow$(f) = n$, i.e. there exists a decomposition $f(X) = \sum_{i=1}^n \ell_i^{e_i}$. We construct the matrix A from the linear parts of the ℓ_i's and the vector b from the constant terms. Since f is regular, we have that $A \in \mathrm{GL}_n(\mathbb{F})$. This implies that $f(A^{-1}X - A^{-1}b) = \sum_{i=1}^n x_i^{e_i}$ and motivates the following definitions.

Definition 3.1. [16] We will say that two n-variate polynomials f and g are equivalent, denoted $f \sim g$, if there exists an invertible linear transformation $A \in \mathrm{GL}_n(\mathbb{F})$ such that $f(X) = g(A \cdot X)$. Moreover, we will say that f and g are affine equivalent, denoted $f \equiv g$ if there exists a vector $c \in \mathbb{F}^n$ such that $f(X+c) \sim g$, or similarly if $f = g(A \cdot X + b)$ with $A \in \mathrm{GL}_n(\mathbb{F}), b \in \mathbb{F}^n$.

With these notations, for a regular polynomial f, we have that AffPow$(f) = n$ if and only if $f \equiv g$ where $g = \sum_{i=1}^n x_i^{e_i}$ for some $(e_i) \in \mathbb{N}^n$. This restates the problem of checking whether AffPow$(f) = n$ into a problem of testing affine equivalence. The affine equivalence problem was already investigated in [16]. One major difference of our situation with respect to [16] is that instead of testing affine equivalence to one target polynomial g, we test affine equivalence to a family of polynomials. Another difference is that its author used [16, Theorem 28] as a preliminary step to reduce the affine equivalence problem to an equivalence problem, which cannot be used here since the polynomials we consider are not homogeneous in general. Yet, the techniques used to solve some special cases of the equivalence problem in [15] have been a source of inspiration to design the algorithms of this paper.

3.1 Algorithm overview

Let us fix some notations: unless stated otherwise, f will always denote the input polynomial and g one target polynomial. Whenever $f \equiv g$, we will usually denote by A and b the matrices such that $f(X) = g(A \cdot X + b)$, with $A \in \mathrm{GL}_n(\mathbb{F})$. Moreover, we will define the associated affine and linear forms: $\ell_i = \sum_{j=1}^n A_{i,j} x_j + b_i$ and $[\ell_i] = \ell_i - b_i$. The main tool of the algorithms is the Hessian matrix, whose entries are the second order derivatives of the polynomial.

Definition 3.2. For a polynomial $f \in \mathbb{F}[X]$, the Hessian matrix $H_f \in \mathcal{M}_n(\mathbb{F}[X])$ is defined as

$$(H_f)_{i,j} = \frac{\partial^2 f}{\partial x_i \partial x_j}$$

In the following, the most useful property of the Hessian matrix is how affine transformations change the matrix. This Lemma is an affine analogue of [15, Lemma 5.1] and can be proved similarly.

LEMMA 3.3. *Let $g \in \mathbb{F}[X]$, $A \in \mathcal{M}_n(\mathbb{F})$ be a linear transformation, and $b \in \mathbb{F}^n$. Consider $f(X) = g(A \cdot X + b)$, then,*

$$H_f(X) = A^T \cdot H_g(A \cdot X + b) \cdot A.$$

In particular we have $\det(H_f(X)) = \det(A)^2 \det(H_g(A \cdot X + b))$.

In particular when $f \equiv g$, the matrix A is invertible and hence the determinant of the Hessian matrix of f can be understood by studying an affine transformation of the determinant of the Hessian matrix of g. For instance, when $g = \sum_{i=1}^n x_i^{e_i}$, observe that the matrix H_g is diagonal, and we therefore have

$$\det(H_g(X)) = \prod_{i=1}^n e_i(e_i - 1) x_i^{e_i - 2}.$$

In particular, Lemma 3.3 directly implies the following result.

LEMMA 3.4. *Let f be a regular polynomial such that $f(X) = \sum_{i=1}^n \ell_i(X)^{e_i}$ where $\ell_1, \ldots, \ell_n$ are affine forms and $e_i \geq 2$. Then there exists a nonzero constant $c \in \mathbb{F}$ such that*

$$\det(H_f(X)) = c \cdot \prod_{i=1}^n \ell_i(X)^{e_i - 2}.$$

This results yields a blueprint for an algorithm to find a decomposition of f when AffPow$(f) = n$: factorize $\det(H_f(X))$ to obtain candidates for the affine forms and associated exponents, then try to express f as a linear combination of these affine powers. However, if AffPow$(f) = n$ and one e_i is ≤ 1 then $\det(H_f(X)) = 0$, and if some of the e_i's are equal to 2 then ℓ_i is not a factor of $\det(H_f(X))$. This makes this idea fail on such scenarios. Therefore, in order to have an algorithm that decides whether AffPow$(f) = n$, one also needs to handle the case when some of the (e_i)'s are smaller than 3. In the next section, we start tackling this problem by studying the case where f is a quadratic polynomial.

3.2 Quadratic polynomials

The goal of this subsection is to describe how to obtain an optimal expression in the Affine Powers model for every polynomial of degree 2. In particular, we are going to generalize the following classical result concerning homogeneous polynomials of degree 2.

PROPOSITION 3.5. *Let $f, g \in \mathbb{F}[X]$ be homogeneous quadratic polynomials. Then $f \sim g \Leftrightarrow$ EssVar(f) = EssVar(g).*

As a consequence, for a quadratic homogeneous regular polynomial f, we have AffPow(f) = EssVar$(f) = n$ since $f \sim \sum_{i=1}^n x_i^2$. Now we can proceed with the classification of degree 2 polynomials.

THEOREM 3.6. *Let $f \in \mathbb{F}[X]$ be a polynomial of degree at most 2. Then, there exists a polynomial time algorithm that obtains an expression of f as either*

(a) $\sum_{i=1}^s \ell_i^2$, (b) $\sum_{i=1}^s \ell_i^2 + c$ with $c \in \mathbb{F}^*$, or (c) $\sum_{i=1}^{s-1} \ell_i^2 + \ell_s$, with $r \in [\![0, n]\!]$, and ℓ_i linear forms.

Proof. We propose a greedy algorithm showing how to write f in one of the three forms. We proceed by induction on the number of variables of f. If f has 0 or 1 variables or f has degree one, it is trivial to write f in one of the desired forms. Assume now that f has $n \geq 2$ variables and that f has degree 2. If there exists a variable x such that the monomial x^2 appears in f, then after multiplying f by a constant if necessary, we write $f = x^2 + xt + g$, where t is a linear form in $n-1$ variables and g is a polynomial of degree ≤ 2 in $n-1$ variables. Thus setting $\ell_1 = x + (t/2)$, we have that $f = \ell_1^2 + g - (t^2/4)$ and proceeding by induction on $g - (t^2/4)$ we are done. If for every variable there is no monomial of the form x^2 in f, then we take two variables x, y such that the monomial xy appears in f. After multiplying f by a constant if necessary, we have that $f = xy + xt_1 + yt_2 + g$, where t_1, t_2 are linear forms in $n-2$ variables and g is a polynomial of degree ≤ 2 in $n-2$ variables. So we set $\ell_1 = (x + y + t_1 + t_2)/2$ and $\ell_2 = (x - y - t_1 + t_2)/2$ and we have that $f = \ell_1^2 - \ell_2^2 + g - t_1t_2$ and we proceed by induction on $g - t_1t_2$. We also observe that by construction the linear parts of the affine forms $\ell_1, \dots, \ell_s$ we obtain are linearly independent. Thus, $s = \mathrm{EssVar}(f)$. □

As a consequence we have the following result, which shows that the greedy algorithm of Theorem 3.6 provides an effective method to compute the exact value of AffPow(f) for any degree 2 polynomial f. In particular, it implies that a quadratic polynomial always has an optimal decomposition with exponents at most 2.

Corollary 3.7. *Let $f \in \mathbb{F}[X]$ be a regular polynomial of degree at most 2. Then, AffPow(f) $= n + 1$ if we have $f \equiv \sum_{i=1}^{n} x_i^2 + c$ with $c \in \mathbb{F}^*$; and AffPow(f) $= n$ otherwise.*

Proof. By Theorem 3.6 we know that f is equivalent to

(a) $\sum_{i=1}^{n} x_i^2$, (b) $\sum_{i=1}^{n} x_i^2 + c$ with $c \in \mathbb{F}^*$, or (c) $\sum_{i=1}^{n-1} x_i^2 + x_n$.

Let us prove now that these scenarios are disjoint. First, in (a) or (b) we have that $\det(H_f(X)) \neq 0$, whereas $\det(H_f(X)) = 0$ in (c). For any polynomial g, we denote by $g^h \in \mathbb{F}[X, z]$ its homogenization with respect to a new variable z. In (a) we have that $f^h = \sum_{i=1}^{n} (\ell_i^h)^2$, whereas $f^h = \sum_{i=1}^{n-1} \ell_i^2 + cz^2$ in (b). By Proposition 3.5, in (a) we have that $\mathrm{EssVar}(f^h) = n$ whereas in (b) we have that $\mathrm{EssVar}(f^h) = n+1$; showing the disjointness.

If $f \equiv \sum_{i=1}^{n} x_i^2$ or $f \equiv \sum_{i=1}^{n-1} x_i^2 + x_n$, then AffPow($f$) $\leq n$ and equality holds because AffPow(f) $\geq$ EssVar(f) $= n$. It only remains to consider when $f \equiv \sum_{i=1}^{n} x_i^2 + c$ with $c \in \mathbb{F}^*$. In this case we clearly have that AffPow(f) $\leq n+1$, hence to prove equality we just need to prove that AffPow(f) $\neq n$. Assume for contradiction that $f = \sum_{i=1}^{n} \ell_i^{e_i}$ for some affine forms ℓ_i and some $e_i \in \mathbb{N}$. Since we have neither $f \equiv \sum_{i=1}^{n} x_i^2$ nor $f \equiv \sum_{i=1}^{n-1} x_i^2 + x_n$, there exists some exponent $e_i \geq 3$. By Lemma 3.4, we have that $\det(H_f)$ is a non-constant polynomial or zero, a contradiction.

3.3 Linear terms in an optimal expression

We now investigate the case where $f \equiv g$ with $g = \sum_{i=1}^{n} x_i^{e_i}$ and $\min(e_i) = 1$. Notice first that $e_i = 1$ can only hold for one $i \in [\![1, n]\!]$ since otherwise $\mathrm{EssVar}(f) = \mathrm{EssVar}(g) < n$. Up to renaming the variables, we can therefore write g as $g = \sum_{i=1}^{n-1} x_i^{e_i} + x_n$. We define $h = g - x_n$ and we decompose A along its last line l so that the equality of Lemma 3.3 can be rewritten as

$$H_f(X) = (B^T \; l^T) \cdot \begin{pmatrix} H_h(A \cdot X + b) & 0 \\ 0 & 0 \end{pmatrix} \cdot \begin{pmatrix} B \\ l \end{pmatrix}$$

If we denote by $[H_f]_{k,k}$ the submatrix of H_f obtained by deleting the kth row and the kth column of H_f, and by $[B]_k$ the square submatrix of B obtained by deleting the kth column, then we have:

$$[H_f(X)]_{k,k} = ([B]_k)^T \cdot H_h(A \cdot X + b) \cdot [B]_k$$

Since $A \in \mathrm{GL}_n(\mathbb{F})$, we have $\mathrm{rank}\, B = n - 1$ and therefore there exists $k \in [\![1, n]\!]$ such that $[B]_k \in \mathrm{GL}_{n-1}(\mathbb{F})$. Finally, since $\det(H_h(X)) = \prod_{i=1}^{n-1} e_i(e_i - 1)x_i^{e_i-2}$, we get the following result.

Lemma 3.8. *Let f be a regular polynomial such that $f(X) = \sum_{i=1}^{n-1} \ell_i(X)^{e_i} + \ell_n(X)$ where $\ell_1, \dots, \ell_n$ are affine forms. Then there exists an integer $k \in [\![1, n]\!]$ and a nonzero constant $c \in \mathbb{F}$ such that*

$$\det([H_f(X)]_{k,k}) = c \cdot \prod_{i=1}^{n-1} \ell_i(X)^{e_i-2}$$

3.4 Wrapping up : the algorithm

The goal of this subsection is to design a polynomial-time randomized algorithm that receives as input a blackbox access to a regular polynomial $f \in \mathbb{F}[X]$, and decides whether AffPow(f) $= n$ and, in such a case, provides an optimal expression of f in Model (1).

Theorem 3.9. *There exists a polynomial-time randomized algorithm* `Build1` *that receives as input a blackbox access to a regular polynomial $f \in \mathbb{F}[X]$ and finds an optimal decomposition of f in the Affine Powers model if AffPow(f) $= n$, or rejects otherwise.*

Proof. We obtain blackbox access to $D(X) = \det(H_f(X))$ and distinguish two cases depending on whether it vanishes or not.

Case $D \neq 0$: if D does not split into degree 1 factors, we reject. Otherwise we write $D = c \cdot \prod_{i=1}^{t} \ell_i^{m_i}$ with $c \in \mathbb{F}^*$ and $\ell_1, \dots, \ell_t$ affine forms. If $t > n$, we reject. Consider the $t \times s$ matrix A whose rows are the $[\ell_i]$'s, and the matrix b whose entries are the constant terms. If the system $A \cdot X = -b$ has no solution, we reject. Otherwise, let X_0 be one solution, and consider $h(X) = g(X + X_0)$ so that $(\ell_i(X - X_0))^{m_i+2} = [\ell_i]^{m_i+2}$ is a homogeneous polynomial of degree $m_i + 2 \geq 3$. By Lemma 3.4, these are the only terms of degree ≥ 3 in an expression of f as a combination of n affine powers. Therefore, if $[h]_{\geq 3} \notin \langle [\ell_i]^{m_i+2} \rangle$ (see Section 2.2.3), then we reject. Otherwise, let (α_i) be such that $h = \sum_{i=1}^{t} \alpha_i [\ell_i]^{m_i+2} + [h]_{\leq 2}$. We express $[h]_{\leq 2} = \sum_{i=1}^{r} \beta_i t_i^{e_i}$ as in Theorem 3.6. If $r + t \neq n$, then reject. Otherwise output the optimal expression of $f(X) = g(B^{-1} \cdot X) = h(B^{-1} \cdot X - X_0)$.

Case $D = 0$: for all k such that $\det([H_f(X)]_{k,k}) \neq 0$, we repeat the previous procedure. If no such k exists, or if we reject for all such k, then we reject; otherwise we output the optimal expression.

Correctness of the algorithm is justified by Lemma 3.4 and Lemma 3.8. □

In Sections 4 and 5, we generalize this algorithm in two natural ways: by allowing the affine forms to be repeated, or by allowing more than EssVar(f) different affine forms.

4 REPEATED AFFINE FORMS

In this section, we investigate the case where there exists a decomposition of a regular polynomial f with n different affine forms that can be used possibly several times in the decomposition. Since f is regular, the n affine forms are necessarily linearly independent. In other words, we want to test if $f \equiv g$ with $g = \sum_{i=1}^{n} \sum_{j=1}^{t_i} \alpha_{i,j} x_i^{e_{i,j}}$. In such a scenario, we can write f as a sum of univariate polynomials: $f = \sum_{i=1}^{n} g_i(\ell_i(X))$ with $g_i(x) = \sum_{j=1}^{t_i} \alpha_{i,j} x^{e_{i,j}}$ and ℓ_i an affine form. Conversely, if f can be written in this way, we can obtain a decomposition with n linearly independent affine forms by taking a decomposition for each univariate polynomial g_i. This motivates the study of the following problem of *univariate decomposition*:

Problem 4.1. *Given $f \in \mathbb{F}[X]$, is $f \equiv g$ with $g = \sum_{i=1}^{n} g_i(x_i)$?*

Yet, this problem does not completely capture the problem of finding an optimal decomposition in the AffPow model: indeed, even if a polynomial has a univariate decomposition $f(X) = \sum_{i=1}^{n} g_i(\ell_i(X))$, we have no guarantee that taking an optimal AffPow decomposition for each g_i will yield an optimal decomposition of f in Model (1). In the following, we first study Problem 4.1 on its own, and then solve the bivariate case by proving that indeed an optimal univariate decomposition is optimal in Model (1).

4.1 Decomposing a polynomial as sum of univariates

The goal of this section is to design an algorithm in Theorem 4.4 that receives as input a regular polynomial f and computes a univariate decomposition if there is one. Notice first that Problem 4.1 is equivalent to testing if there exists univariate polynomials $(g_i(x))$ such that $f \sim g_1(x_1) + \cdots + g_n(x_n)$. A more general version of this problem has been already studied in Appendix C of [15] where the following result is proved:

Theorem 4.2. *[15, Theorem C.2] Given an n-variate polynomial $f(X) \in \mathbb{F}[X]$, there exists an algorithm that finds a decomposition of f as $f(A \cdot X) = p(x_1, \dots, x_t) + q(x_{t+1}, \dots, x_n)$, with A invertible, if it exists, in randomized polynomial time provided* $\det(H_f)$ *is a regular polynomial, i.e. it has n essential variables.*

In the following, we will see how to find a univariate decomposition even if the determinant of the Hessian is not regular. The following result both provides the main ideas and justifies the correctness of the algorithm we propose.

Proposition 4.3. *Let $f \in \mathbb{F}[X]$, and let g_i's be univariate polynomials sorted by decreasing degree. Let $d_i := \deg(g_i)$ and $k := \max\{i : d_i \geq 3\}$. Let $\ell_1, \dots, \ell_n$ be linear forms such that $f = \sum_{i=1}^{n} g_i(\ell_i)$. Then,*

$$\det(H_f(X)) = c \cdot \prod_{i=1}^{k} \prod_{j=1}^{d_i - 2} (\ell_i - \alpha_{i,j}),$$

where $c \in \mathbb{F}$, and $\alpha_{i,j}$ are the roots of $g_i''(x)$ for $1 \leq i \leq k$.

Moreover, if $\ell_1, \dots, \ell_n$ are linearly independent, for any solution $X_0 \in \mathbb{F}^n$ to the system $B \cdot X_0 = (\alpha_{1,1}, \dots, \alpha_{k,1})^T$, where B is the $k \times n$ matrix whose rows are the coefficients of the $\ell_1, \dots, \ell_k$, we have that

(a) $[f(X + X_0)]_{\geq 3} = \sum_{i=1}^{k} h_i(\ell_i)$ for some unique $h_i \in \mathbb{F}[x]$, and
(b) EssVar$([f(X + X_0)]_2) = |\{i \mid \deg(g_i) = 2\}|$.

Proof. By Lemma 3.3, $\det(H_f(X)) = (\det(A))^2 \prod_{i=1}^{n} g_i''(\ell_i)$, where A is the matrix whose i-th row corresponds to the coefficients of ℓ_i. It suffices to write $g_i''(x) = c_i \prod_{i=1}^{d_i-2} (x - \alpha_{i,j})$ for all $i \in [\![1, k]\!]$ to get the first part of the result.

We assume now that $\ell_1, \dots, \ell_n$ are linearly independent. To prove (a), we observe that

$$[f(X + X_0)]_{\geq 3} = \sum_{i=1}^{k} [g_i(\ell_i(X + X_0))]_{\geq 3} = \sum_{i=1}^{k} [g_i(\ell_i + \alpha_{i,1})]_{\geq 3};$$

so it suffices to take $h_i(x) := [g_i(x + \alpha_{i,1})]_{\geq 3}$ for $i = 1, \dots, k$. Uniqueness of h_i comes directly from the fact that $\ell_1, \dots, \ell_k$ are linearly independent.

To prove (b) we observe first that $[g_i(x + \alpha_{i,1})]_2 = 0$ because $g_i''(\alpha_{i,1}) = 0$ for $i = 1, \dots k$. Since ℓ_i is a linear form this implies that $[g_i(\ell_i + \alpha_{i,1})]_2 = 0$ for all $i \in [\![1, k]\!]$, and then

$$[f(X + X_0)]_2 = \sum_{d_i = 2} [g_i(\ell_i(X + X_0))]_2 = \sum_{d_i = 2} \gamma_i \ell_i^2,$$

for some $\gamma_i \neq 0$ and, thus, (b) follows from Proposition 3.5. □

Theorem 4.4. *There exists a polynomial-time randomized algorithm that receives as input a blackbox access to a regular polynomial $f \in \mathbb{F}[X]$ and finds a univariate decomposition of f if such a decomposition exists, or rejects otherwise.*

Proof. The algorithm works as follows. We first compute $D(X) = \det(H_f(X))$ and separate two cases.

Case $D \neq 0$: if $D(X)$ does not split into polynomials of degree 1, we reject. Otherwise we take $\ell_1, \dots, \ell_k$ all the non-proportional linear parts of the factors and build the associated $k \times n$ matrix B. If $\text{rank}(B) \neq k$, we reject. Otherwise, we gather the factors to write

$$D(X) = c' \cdot \prod_{i=1}^{k} p_i(\ell_i(X)) \quad \text{with} \quad p_i(x) = \prod_{j=1}^{d_i} (x - \alpha_{ij})$$

where c' are nonzero constants. Now we take X_0 a solution of $B \cdot X_0 = (\alpha_{1,1}, \dots, \alpha_{k,1})^T$ and consider $g(X) = f(X + X_0)$. Let $h_1, \dots, h_k \in \mathbb{F}[x]$ be the only polynomials so that $[g]_{\geq 3} = \sum_{i=1}^{k} h_i(\ell_i)$ (or reject if they do not exist). Then we use the greedy algorithm of Section 3.2 to write $[g]_2$ as $\sum_{i=k+1}^{m} \gamma_i \ell_i^2$ for some new linear forms $\ell_{k+1}, \dots, \ell_m$. If $m \neq n$ or $\ell_1, \dots, \ell_n$ are not linearly independent, we reject. Otherwise, we express $[g]_{\leq 1} = \sum_{i=1}^{n} \delta_i \ell_i + b$ for some $\delta_1, \dots, \delta_n, b \in \mathbb{F}$. Putting all together we have that g can be written as $\sum_{i=1}^{k} (h_i(\ell_i) + \delta_i \ell_i) + \sum_{i=k+1}^{n} \left(\gamma_i \ell_i^2 + \delta_i \ell_i\right) + b$, and we finally get an univariate decomposition of f as $f(X) = \sum_{i=1}^{n} q_i(t_i)$ with

$$q_i(x) := \begin{cases} h_1(x) + \delta_1 x + b & \text{for } i = 1 \\ h_i(x) + \delta_i x & \text{for } i = 2, \dots, k \\ \gamma_i x^2 + \delta_i x & \text{for } i = k+1, \dots, n \end{cases}$$

and $t_i(X) := \ell_i(X - X_0)$ an affine form for all $i \in [\![1, n]\!]$.

Case $D = 0$: this case happens whenever f is equivalent to a sum of univariate polynomials where one of the g_i's is of degree 1. To handle this situation we proceed similarly to Section 3.3. Again we can have at most one g_i of degree 1 since otherwise the number of essential variables of f would not be n. In this case we use the following more general version of Lemma 3.8 which can be proved using similar techniques.

Lemma 4.5. *Let $f(X)$ be a regular polynomial such that $f(X) = \sum_{i=1}^{n-1} g_i(\ell_i(X)) + \ell_n(X)$ where $\ell_1, \dots, \ell_n$ are affine forms, and g_i is a univariate polynomial of degree ≥ 2 for all i. Then there exists an* *integer $k \in [\![1,n]\!]$ and $c \neq 0$ such that*

$$\det([H_f(X)]_{k,k}) = c \cdot \prod_{i=1}^{n-1} g_i''(\ell_i(X))$$

Hence, for all k such that $D_k := \det([H_f(X)]_{k,k}) \neq 0$, we proceed as before with D_k and try to express $[f]_{\geq 2}$ as $[\sum_{i=1}^{n-1} q_i(t_i)]_{\geq 2}$. If we succeed, we set $t_n := f - \sum_{i=1}^{n-1} q_i(t_i)$, $q_n := x$ and output the optimal expression. If there is no k with $D_k \neq 0$, or if we reject for all such k, then we reject. □

4.2 The bivariate case

Let $f \in \mathbb{F}[x_1, x_2]$ be a bivariate polynomial that admits a univariate decomposition $f = f_1(\ell_1) + f_2(\ell_2)$. In this case, we are going to describe how the optimal expression of f can be obtained from the (univariate) optimal expressions of f_1 and f_2, by putting together, if possible, the terms of degree ≤ 1 in one bivariate polynomial. More precisely, write $f_i = \sum_{j=1}^{s_i} \alpha_{i,j}(x_i + a_{i,j})^{e_{i,j}}$, with $s_i := \text{AffPow}(f_i)$ and $e_{i,1} \leq \cdots \leq e_{i,s_i}$. We separate two cases: if there exist optimal expressions of f_1 and f_2 with $e_{1,1} \leq 1$ and $e_{2,1} \leq 1$; we define $\text{UnivAffPow}(f) := s_1 + s_2 - 1$. Otherwise, we define $\text{UnivAffPow}(f) := s_1 + s_2$.

We prove in Proposition 4.9 $\text{AffPow}(f) = \text{UnivAffPow}(f)$. Notice first that every univariate polynomial g of degree d satisfies that $\text{AffPow}(g) \leq r := \lceil \frac{d+1}{2} \rceil$. Moreover, if $\text{AffPow}(g) = r$, then g admits an expression as $\sum_{i=1}^{r} \alpha_i (x + a_i)^{e_i}$ with $d = e_1$ and $e_i - e_{i+1} \geq 2$ for all i and, thus, $e_r \in \{0, 1\}$ (see [8, Proposition 18]).

Lemma 4.6. *Let $f_i \in \mathbb{F}[x_i]$ polynomials of degree d_i for $i = 1, 2$. Then,*

$$\text{UnivAffPow}(f_1 + f_2) \leq \left\lceil \frac{d_1+1}{2} \right\rceil + \left\lceil \frac{d_2+1}{2} \right\rceil - 1.$$

Proof. Let $s_i := \text{AffPow}(f_i)$ for $i = 1, 2$. If $s_i < \lceil \frac{d_i+1}{2} \rceil$ for some i, the result follows directly since $\text{UnivAffPow}(f_1 + f_2) \leq s_1 + s_2$. Otherwise, $s_i = \lceil \frac{d_i+1}{2} \rceil$ for $i = 1, 2$; in this case both f_i can be written in an optimal way that uses a term of degree ≤ 1; hence, $\text{UnivAffPow}(f_1 + f_2) = s_1 + s_2 - 1$, proving the result. □

Lemma 4.7. *Let $s, d \in \mathbb{Z}^+$ and $b \in (\mathbb{F}^*)^s$ such that $b_i \neq b_j$. If*

$$\lambda_1 x_1^d + \lambda_2 x_2^d = \sum_{i=1}^{s} \gamma_i (x_1 + b_i x_2)^d, \tag{2}$$

with $\lambda_1, \lambda_2 \in \mathbb{F}$ and $\gamma_i \in \mathbb{F}$ not all zero, then $s \geq d$. Moreover, if $\lambda_1 = 0$ or $\lambda_2 = 0$ then $s \geq d + 1$; and if $\lambda_1 = \lambda_2 = 0$, then $s \geq d + 2$.

Proof. Consider $c \in \mathbb{F}^*$ different from b_i for all i and the evaluation map φ induced by $x_1 \mapsto -cx$, $x_2 \mapsto x + 1$. Then, $\varphi(x_1 + b_i x_2) = (b_i - c)(x + \frac{b_i}{b_i - c})$. Thus, by applying φ in (2) we get that $\{x^d, (x+1)^d, (x + \frac{b_i}{b_i-c})^d \mid 1 \leq i \leq s\}$ is linearly dependent. Hence, the result follows from the well-known fact that for every $r < d+2$ and $c_1, \ldots, c_r$ different elements of $\mathbb{F}$, then the set $\{(x+c_i)^d \mid 1 \leq i \leq r\}$ is $\mathbb{F}$-linearly independent. □

Lemma 4.8. *Let $f = \sum_{i=1}^{s} \alpha_i (x_1 + b_i x_2 + c_i)^{e_i} \in \mathbb{F}[x_1, x_2]$ be a polynomial of degree ≥ 2, with $\alpha_i, b_i \in \mathbb{F}^*$ for all $i \in [\![1, s]\!]$. If $f = f_1 + f_2$ with $f_i \in \mathbb{F}[x_i]$, then $s \geq \text{UnivAffPow}(f_1 + f_2)$.*

Proof. Let $\ell_i := x_1 + b_i x_2 + c_i$ for $i = 1, \ldots, s$, and $d_j := \deg(f_j)$ for $j = 1, 2$. We know that $s_i := \text{AffPow}(f_i) \leq \lceil (d_i + 1)/2 \rceil$ and we assume that $d_1 \geq d_2$.

For all $e \in \mathbb{N}$, consider $[f]_e$, the homogeneous component of degree e of f. We have:

$$[f_1]_e + [f_2]_e = \sum_{e_i \geq e} \alpha_i [\ell_i^{e_i}]_e \in \langle (x_1 + b_i x_2)^e \mid e_i \geq e \rangle.$$

Case 1: $d_1 > d_2$. We have that $0 \neq [f_1]_{d_1} = \sum_{e_i \geq d_1} \gamma_i (x_1 + b_i x_2)^{d_1}$ with $\gamma_i \in \mathbb{F}$, hence by Lemma 4.7 there are at least $d_1 + 1$ exponents e_i that are $\geq d_1$. So, by Lemma 4.6 we get

$$s \geq d_1 + 1 \geq \left\lceil \frac{d_1+1}{2} \right\rceil + \left\lceil \frac{d_2+1}{2} \right\rceil > \text{UnivAffPow}(f_1 + f_2).$$

Case 2: $d_1 = d_2$. We have that $[f_1]_{d_1} + [f_2]_{d_2} = \sum_{e_i \geq d_1} \gamma_i (x_1 + b_i x_2)^{d_1}$ with $\gamma_i \in \mathbb{F}$, hence by Lemma 4.7 there are at least d_1 exponents bigger than or equal to d_1. So, by Lemma 4.6 we get

$$s \geq |\{i : e_i \geq d_1\}| \geq d_1 \geq 2\left\lceil \frac{d_1+1}{2} \right\rceil - 2 \geq \text{UnivAffPow}(f_1 + f_2) - 1.$$

If one of these inequalities is strict, the result is proved; so assume by contradiction that they are all equalities. In particular, we have that $b_i \neq b_j$ for all $i \neq j$. We claim that $e_i = d_1$ for all i. Otherwise, taking $e := \max(e_i) > d_1$ and observing the homogeneous component of degree e, we get that $0 = \sum_{e_i = e} \alpha_i (x_1 + b_i x_2)^e$; but again by Lemma 4.7, this implies that the number of ℓ_i with $e_i = e$ is at least $e + 2 \geq d_1 + 3 > s$, a contradiction. Hence,

$$f_1 + f_2 = \sum_{i=1}^{s} \alpha_i (x_1 + b_i x_2 + c_i)^{d_1}.$$

Now set $\beta_i \in \mathbb{F}$ the (only) root of the derivative of order $d_1 - 1$ of f_i and consider $g_i(x_i) := f_i(x_i + \beta_i)$. We have that $g_1 + g_2 = \sum_{i=1}^{s} \alpha_i (x_1 + b_i x_2 + c_i')^{d_1}$. Since $[g_1]_{d_1 - 1} = [g_2]_{d_1 - 1} = 0$; the homogeneous component of degree $d_1 - 1$ in this expression is

$$0 = \sum_{i=1}^{s} d_1 \alpha_i c_i' (x_1 + b_i x_2)^{d_1 - 1}.$$

Since $s < d_1 + 2$, Lemma 4.7 yields that $c_i' = 0$ for all i. Since $f_1(x_1 + \beta_1)$, $f_2(x_2 + \beta_2)$ are univariate polynomials, then $f_1(x_1 + \beta_1) + f_2(x_2 + \beta_2) = \gamma_1 x_1^{d_1} + \gamma_2 x_2^{d_2}$. However, this implies that $\text{AffPow}(f_1) = \text{AffPow}(f_2) = 1$ and, then, $1 \geq \text{UnivAffPow}(f) - 1 = d_1 = d_2$, a contradiction. □

As a consequence of Lemma 4.8, we obtain the main result of this subsection:

Proposition 4.9. *Let $f_1 \in \mathbb{F}[x_1]$ and $f_2 \in \mathbb{F}[x_2]$, then*

$$\text{AffPow}(f_1 + f_2) = \text{UnivAffPow}(f_1 + f_2).$$

Proof. It is obvious that $\text{AffPow}(f_1 + f_2) \leq \text{UnivAffPow}(f_1 + f_2)$. Let $s := \text{AffPow}(f_1 + f_2)$ and consider $f_1 + f_2 = \sum_{i=1}^{s} \ell_i^{e_i}$ an optimal expression of $f_1 + f_2$ in Model (1). We write $\ell_i = a_i x_1 + b_i x_2 + c_i$ with $a_i, b_i, c_i \in \mathbb{F}$. Set $g := f_1 + f_2 - \sum_{b_i = 0 \text{ or } c_i = 0} \ell_i^{e_i}$. Clearly, g is a sum of two univariate polynomials and can be written as

$$g = \sum_{\substack{a_i \neq 0 \\ b_i \neq 0}} \ell_i^{e_i} = \sum_{\substack{a_i \neq 0 \\ b_i \neq 0}} a_i^{e_i} \left(x_1 + \frac{b_i}{a_i} x_2 + \frac{c_i}{a_i} \right)^{e_i}.$$

Setting $r := |\{i : a_i \neq 0 \text{ and } b_i \neq 0\}|$, by Lemma 4.8 we have $\text{UnivAffPow}(g) \leq r$. Hence we can rewrite g as $g = \sum_{i=1}^{r'} (\alpha_i x + \beta_i y + \gamma_i)^{d_i}$ with either $\alpha_i = 0$, $\beta_i = 0$ or $d_i = 1$, and $r' \leq r$. As a consequence, $f = \sum_{i=1}^{r'} (\alpha_i x + \beta_i y + \gamma_i)^{d_i} + \sum_{b_i = 0 \text{ or } c_i = 0} \ell_i^{e_i}$ is an expression of f with $s-r+r'$ terms. Since $s-r+r' \leq s$, this shows that $\text{UnivAffPow}(f_1+f_2) \leq s = \text{AffPow}(f_1+f_2)$.

5 ALLOWING MORE AFFINE FORMS

In what follows we investigate the case where the number of affine forms used to express f in Model (1) is greater than the number of essential variables. The most basic such case is when $f \equiv g$ with $g = \sum_{i=1}^{n} x_i^{e_i} + \ell^e$, where ℓ is an affine form and $e \in \mathbb{N}^*$. Let us first see why the algorithm of Section 3 cannot be straightforwardly generalised to recover the optimal expression of f. We set $h := g - \ell^e$ so that we have $H_g = H_h + H_{\ell^e}$ by linearity of differentiation. Notice that $H_{\ell^e} = e^{\underline{2}}\, \ell^{e-2} \beta\beta^T$, where β is the column vector associated to the coefficients of ℓ and $e^{\underline{i}} := e \cdots (e-i+1)$. In order to compute $\det(H_g)$, we use the *matrix determinant lemma*. We therefore have $\det(H_g) = \det(H_h) + e^{\underline{2}}\, \ell^{e-2} \beta^T \operatorname{adj}(H_h)\beta$. Hence, if $f = g(A \cdot X + b)$, Lemma 3.4 implies that

$$\det(H_f) = \det(A)^2 \left(\prod_{i=1}^{n} e_i^{\underline{2}}\, \ell_i(X)^{e_i-2} + e^{\underline{2}}\, \ell(A \cdot X + b)^{e-2}\, P(X) \right)$$

with $P(X) = \sum_{i=1}^{n} \beta_i^2 \left(\prod_{j \neq i} e_j^{\underline{2}}\, \ell_j(X)^{e_i-2} \right) \in \mathbb{F}[X]$. In most cases neither the ℓ_i's nor ℓ are factors of $\det(H_f)$, which makes the (straightforward generalization of) algorithm of Section 3 fail.

The main idea we propose to generalize the algorithm is to consider an extension of the Hessian by looking at higher order derivatives. We will therefore consider the *symmetric 4-th order Hessian* $\overline{H}_f \in \mathcal{M}_{\binom{n+1}{2}}(\mathbb{F}[X])$ whose entries are:

$$\forall a \leq b,\ i \leq j, \quad (\overline{H}_f)_{(a,b),(i,j)} = \frac{\partial^4 f}{\partial x_a \partial x_b \partial x_i \partial x_j}.$$

In this section, we will design a randomized algorithm that can reconstruct a decomposition in Model (1) that uses up to $\binom{n+1}{2}$ distinct affine forms. However, it will not work for all input polynomials of such type. Indeed, it will work whenever all the exponents involved in the optimal expression of f are ≥ 5 and a certain matrix U, which depends on the affine forms involved, is invertible. We will conduct a randomized analysis to show that our method is correct with high probability (over the choice of the input polynomial and of the internal coin tosses of the algorithm). We begin by proving an analogue of Lemma 3.4 for the symmetric 4-th order Hessian.

Proposition 5.1. *Let $n \in \mathbb{N}^*$, $m := \binom{n+1}{2}$ and $f = \sum_{i=1}^{m} \ell_i^{e_i}$, with $\ell_i = \sum_{j=1}^{n} b_{i,j}x_j + b_{i,0}$ affine forms and $e_i \geq 4$ for all i. Let U be the square $m \times m$ matrix with entries $U_{(i,j),k} := b_{k,i}\, b_{k,j}$ for all $1 \leq k \leq m$, $1 \leq i \leq j \leq n$. If $\det(U) \neq 0$, there exists $c \neq 0$ such that*

$$\det(\overline{H}_f(X)) = c \cdot \prod_{i=1}^{m} \ell_i^{e_i-4},$$

Proof. By linearity of the symmetric 4-th order Hessian, we have

$$\overline{H}_f(X) = \sum_{k=1}^{m} \overline{H}_{\ell_k}(X) = \sum_{k=1}^{m} e_k^{\underline{4}}\, \ell_k^{e_k-4} (u_k \cdot u_k^T) = U \cdot D \cdot U^T,$$

where $D = \operatorname{Diag}(e_1^{\underline{4}}\, \ell_1^{e_1-4}, \ldots, e_m^{\underline{4}}\, \ell_m^{e_m-4})$, and u_k is the column vector whose (i,j)-th entry is $b_{k,i}b_{k,j}$ with $1 \leq i \leq j \leq n$. Thus, $\det(\overline{H}_f(X)) = \det(U)^2 \prod_{k=1}^{m} e_k^{\underline{4}}\, \ell_k^{e_k-4}$. □

Now, we are going to prove that if the coefficients of the ℓ_i are chosen uniformly at random, then with a high probability we have $\det(U) \neq 0$. Thus, whenever $e_i \geq 5$ for all i, one can find ℓ_i as a factor of $\det(\overline{H}_f(X))$ of multiplicity $e_i - 4$.

Lemma 5.2. *Let $n \in \mathbb{N}^*$ and $m := \binom{n+1}{2}$, and consider the set of variables $\mathcal{V} := \{y_{(k,l),i} \mid 1 \leq k \leq l \leq n,\ 1 \leq i \leq n\}$. Let U be the $m \times m$ square matrix with entries $U_{(i,j),(k,l)} := y_{(k,l),i}\, y_{(k,l),j}$, where $1 \leq i \leq j \leq n$, $1 \leq k \leq l \leq n$. Then, $\det(U) \in \mathbb{Z}[\mathcal{V}]$ is a nonzero polynomial of degree $2m$.*

Proof. Since all the entries of the matrix are homogeneous polynomials of degree 2, it is clear that $\det(U)$ is either zero or a polynomial of degree $2m$. To prove that $\det(U) \neq 0$ it suffices to exhibit a nonzero evaluation of $\det(U)$. We consider the matrix $\tilde{U}$ given by the evaluation $y_{(k,l),i} \mapsto 1$ if $i \in \{k,l\}$; or $y_{(k,l),i} \mapsto 0$ otherwise. By ordering pairs (i,j) with $i = j$ first, we obtain the following shape

$$\tilde{U} = \begin{array}{c} \\ i=j \\ i<j \end{array} \begin{array}{c} \begin{matrix} k=l & k<l \end{matrix} \\ \left(\begin{matrix} \mathrm{Id}_n & (*) \\ 0 & \mathrm{Id}_{m-n} \end{matrix} \right) \end{array},$$

proving that $\det(\tilde{U}) = 1$ and therefore that $\det(U) \neq 0$. □

Theorem 5.3. *Let $n \geq 2$ and $m := \binom{n+1}{2}$. Let $\ell_i = \sum_{j=1}^{n} b_{i,j}x_j + b_{i,0}$: $1 \leq i \leq m$ whose coefficients $b_{i,j}$ are taken uniformly at random from a finite set S and take $f := \sum_{i=1}^{m} \ell_i^{e_i} \in \mathbb{F}[X]$ with $e_i \geq 4$ for all i. Then, $\det(\overline{H}_f(X)) \neq 0$ with probability at least $1 - \frac{2m}{|S|}$.*

Proof. By Proposition 5.1, it is enough to show that $\det(U) \neq 0$, where U is the matrix defined by $U_{(i,j),k} = b_{k,i}b_{k,j}$. By Schwartz-Zippel lemma and Lemma 5.2, the probability that $\det(U) \neq 0$ is at least $1 - \frac{2m}{|S|}$. □

This theorem suggests a polynomial time algorithm for finding an optimal expression of a polynomial f with high probability when $\text{AffPow}(f) \leq m = \binom{n+1}{2}$, the affine forms in optimal expression of f are chosen at random from a finite set and all the exponents involved are ≥ 5. It is enough to start with $k = m-1$, choose randomly k affine forms $t_1, \ldots, t_k$ with exponents $d_i = 4$ and denote $g := f + \sum_{i=1}^{k} t_i^{d_i}$. If $D := \det(\overline{H}_f(X)) = 0$, we decrease the value of k by one unit and repeat the argument, or we reject if $k = 0$. If $D \neq 0$, we factorize it. If D splits into linear factors $l_1, \ldots, l_{m-k}$ of multiplicities $r_1, \ldots, r_{m-k}$ and $f \in \langle l_i^{r_i+4} \mid 1 \leq i \leq m-k \rangle$, then $\text{AffPow}(f) = m-k$ and we output the optimal expression. Otherwise, we reject.

6 UNIVARIATE PROJECTIONS

We denote by n_e the number of exponents smaller than $e \in \mathbb{N}$, i.e., $n_e = \#\{i : e_i \leq e\}$. The main result of this section is an algorithm that finds the optimal reconstruction under the condition on n_e being small. We will proceed by reduction to the univariate case: we solve n univariate projections of the multivariate problem using algorithms from [9], and then "lift" them to a solution of the multivariate problem.

6.1 Essentially unique optimal expressions

The notion of *essentially equal* expressions was introduced in [16]. We say that $\sum_{i=1}^{s} \ell_i^{e_i} = \sum_{i=1}^{r} t_i^{d_i}$ are essentially equal if $r = s$ and after a permutation $\ell_i^{e_i} = t_i^{d_i}$ for all i. Likewise, we say that f has an *essentially unique* optimal decomposition in Model (1) if any two optimal decompositions of f are essentially equal. The following result extends [9, Corollary 3.14], providing a sufficient condition to have an essentially unique optimal decomposition.

PROPOSITION 6.1. *Let $f = \sum_{i=1}^{s} \ell_i^{e_i} \in \mathbb{F}[X]$, where the ℓ_i are affine forms, and ℓ_i is not proportional to ℓ_j whenever $e_i = e_j$. If $n_e \leq \sqrt{\frac{e+1}{2}}$ for all $e \in \mathbb{N}$, then AffPow$(f) = s$ and the optimal representation of f is essentially unique.*

Proof. Let $r := \text{AffPow}(f) \leq s$ and let $f = \sum_{i=s+1}^{s+r} \ell_i^{e_i}$ be an optimal representation of f. We write $\ell_i = \sum_{j=1}^{n} a_{ij}x_j + a_{i0}$ for all $i \in \{1, \ldots, s+r\}$. Consider $\varphi : \mathbb{F}[X] \to \mathbb{F}[x]$ induced by $x_i \mapsto \omega_i x + \lambda_i$ where $\omega, \lambda \in \mathbb{F}^n$. We denote $\varphi(\ell_i) = b_i x + c_i$ and choose ω and λ (a generic choice would suffice) so that

(1.a) $\varphi(\ell_i)^{e_i} = \varphi(\ell_j)^{e_j}$ if and only if $\ell_i^{e_i} = \ell_j^{e_j}$, and

(1.b) whenever $e_i = e_j$ with $1 \leq i < j \leq s$, then $c_i/b_i \neq c_j/b_j$.

Then,
$$\varphi(f) = \sum_{i=1}^{s} \varphi(\ell_i)^{e_i} = \sum_{i=1}^{s} b_i^{e_i}(x + c_i/b_i)^{e_i} = \sum_{i=s+1}^{s+r} \varphi(\ell_i)^{e_i} = \sum_{i=s+1}^{s+r} b_i^{e_i}(x + c_i/b_i)^{e_i}.$$

We consider the expression $\varphi(f)$ in the univariate Affine Power model. Since (1.b) holds and $n_e \leq \sqrt{\frac{e+1}{2}}$ for all $e \in \mathbb{N}$, by [9, Corollary 3.14] we get that $r = s$ and that both expressions for $\varphi(f)$ are the same. By (1.a) we obtain the result. □

6.2 Projection and recovery

Our goal is to provide an algorithm that, given blackbox access to $f \in \mathbb{F}[X]$, computes $s = \text{AffPow}(f)$ and an optimal expression for f. It is a multivariate analogue of [9, Theorem 4.5] where the condition of "distinct nodes" is replaced by "the ℓ_i's in the decomposition are not proportional". The idea of the algorithm is to perform a random change of coordinates and then project to n univariate problems that we solve using [9, Theorem 4.5]. One minor difficulty is that the univariate algorithms of [9] are presented for polynomials given in dense representation rather than in black box representation, but we can obtain the dense representation of a univariate polynomial by random evaluations and, then, interpolation.

THEOREM 6.2. *Let $f = \sum_{i=1}^{s} \ell_i^{e_i} \in \mathbb{F}[X]$, where the ℓ_i are pairwise non-propoportional linear forms, and $e_i \in \mathbb{N}$. Assume that $n_i \leq (3i/4)^{1/3} - 1$ for all $i \geq 2$. Then, AffPow$(f) = s$ and there is a randomized algorithm* `MultiBuild`(f) *that, given access to a black box for f, computes the set of terms $T(f) = \{\ell_i^{e_i} \mid 1 \leq i \leq s\}$. The algorithm runs in time polynomial in n and d, and works as follows:*

1. *We define $g := \phi(f)$ where ϕ is a random affine change of coordinates ($x_i \mapsto \sum_{j=1}^{n} \lambda_{ij}x_j + \lambda_i$ for all i).*
2. *For each $j \in [\![1, n]\!]$, we set $g_j := \pi_j(g)$ where π_j is induced by $x_k \mapsto 0$ if $k \neq j$ and $x_j \mapsto x$.*
3. *Apply* `Build`(g_j) *from [9, Theorem 4.5] to obtain $s_j := \text{AffPow}(g_j)$ and the triplets $(\beta_{ij}, b_{ij}, e_{ij})$ such that $g_j = \sum_{i=1}^{s_j} \beta_{ij}(x + b_{ij})^{e_{ij}}$.*
4. *We define $P_j := \{(c_{ij}, 1/b_{ij}, e_{ij}) \mid c_{ij} := \beta_{ij} b_{ij}^{e_{ij}},\ 1 \leq i \leq s_i\}$.*
5. *We reorder the elements of $P_2, \ldots, P_n$ so that $c_i := c_{i1} = c_{i2} = \cdots = c_{in}$ and $e_i := e_{i1} = e_{i2} = \cdots = e_{in}$ for all $i \in \{1, \ldots, s_1\}$.*
6. *If $g = \sum_{i=1}^{s} c_i(1 + \sum_{j=1}^{n} x_j/b_{ij})^{e_i}$, we output $f = \phi^{-1}(g)$.*

Or we reject if any of these steps is not feasible.

Proof. We observe that AffPow$(f) = s$ and the optimal representation of f is essentially unique by Proposition 6.1.

With high probability we have that ϕ is invertible and $g = \sum_{i=1}^{s} t_i^{e_i}$ with $t_i = \sum_{j=1}^{n} a_{ij}x_j + a_{i0}$ satisfies that:

(i) $a_{ij} \neq 0$ for all i, j.

(ii) for all $j \neq 0$, then $a_{ij}/a_{i0} \neq a_{i'j}/a_{i'0}$ for all i, i', and

(iii) $a_{i0}^{e_i} \neq a_{i'0}^{e_{i'}}$ for all $i \neq i'$.

In **Step 2**, for all $j \in \{1, \ldots, n\}$ we consider
$$\pi_j(g) = \sum_{i=1}^{s} a_{i0}^{e_i}\left(1 + \frac{a_{ij}}{a_{i0}}x\right)^{e_i} = \sum_{i=1}^{s} a_{ij}^{e_i}\left(x + \frac{a_{i0}}{a_{ij}}\right)^{e_i}.$$

Since $\pi_j(g)$ satisfies the hypotheses of [9, Theorem 4.5], `Build`$(\pi_j(g))$ outputs $\{(a_{ij}^{e_i}, \frac{a_{i0}}{a_{ij}}, e_i) \mid 1 \leq i \leq s\}$. From these values we obtain $P_j = \{(a_{i0}^{e_i}, \frac{a_{ij}}{a_{i0}}, e_i) \mid 1 \leq i \leq s\}$. The uniqueness of the expression of g_j for all j and (iii) guarantee that we recover g in **Step 6**.

REFERENCES

[1] J. Alexander, A. Hirschowitz. Polynomial interpolation in several variables. *Journal of Algebraic Geometry*, 4(2):201–222, 1995.
[2] M. Ben-Or, P. Tiwari. A deterministic algorithm for sparse multivariate polynomial interpolation. In *Proc. 20th annual ACM Symposium on Theory of Computing*, 1988.
[3] J. Brachat, P. Comon, B. Mourrain, E. Tsigaridas. Symmetric tensor decomposition. Linear Algebra and its Applications 433, 11:1851-1872, 2010.
[4] M. C. Brambilla, G. Ottaviani. On the Alexander –Hirschowitz theorem. *Journal of Pure and Applied Algebra*, 212(5):1229–1251, 2008.
[5] E. Carlini. Reducing the number of variables of a polynomial. In *Algebraic geometry and geometric modeling*, Math. Vis., 237–247. Springer, Berlin, 2006.
[6] E. Carlini, M. V. Catalisano, L. Chiantini. Progress on the symmetric Strassen conjecture. *J. Pure Appl. Algebra*, 219(8):3149–3157, 2015.
[7] E. Carlini, M. V. Catalisano, A. V. Geramita. The solution to the Waring problem for monomials and the sum of coprime monomials. *J. of Algebra*, 370:5–14, 2012.
[8] I. García-Marco, P. Koiran. Lower bounds by Birkhoff interpolation. *J. Complexity*, 39:38–50, 2017.
[9] I. García-Marco, P. Koiran, T. Pecatte. Reconstruction algorithms for sums of affine powers. *arXiv preprint arXiv:1607.05420*. Conference version in: *Proceedings of the ISSAC '17*, pages 317–324, 2017.
[10] I. García-Marco, P. Koiran, T. Pecatte. On the linear independence of shifted powers. J. Complexity 45 (2018), 67–82.
[11] A. Iarrobino, V. Kanev. *Power Sums, Gorenstein Algebras, and Determinantal Loci.* Springer, 1999.
[12] E. Kaltofen, B. M. Trager. Computing with polynomials given by black boxes for their evaluations: greatest common divisors, factorization, separation of numerators and denominators. *J. Symbolic Comput.*, 9(3):301–320, 1990.
[13] N. Kayal. An exponential lower bound for the sum of powers of bounded degree polynomials. *Electronic Colloquium on Computational Complexity (ECCC)*, 19, 2012.
[14] N. Kayal, P. Koiran, T. Pecatte, and C. Saha. Lower bounds for sums of powers of low degree univariates. In *Proc. 42nd International Colloquium on Automata, Languages and Programming (ICALP 2015), part I*, LNCS 9134, pages 810–821. Springer, 2015. Available from http://perso.ens-lyon.fr/pascal.koiran.
[15] N. Kayal. Efficient algorithms for some special cases of the polynomial equivalence problem. In *Symposium on Discrete Algorithms (SODA)*. January 2011.
[16] N. Kayal. Affine projections of polynomials. In *Proceedings of the 44th Annual ACM Symposium on Theory of Computing*, pages 643–662. ACM, 2012.
[17] J. M. Landsberg, Z. Teitler. On the ranks and border ranks of symmetric tensors. *Foundations of Computational Mathematics*, 10(3):339–366, 2010.
[18] G. Labahn, M. Giesbrecht, W.-S. Lee. Symbolic-numeric sparse interpolation of multivariate polynomials. *J. Symbolic Computation*, 44(8):943–959, 2009.
[19] W. Lee, M. Giesbrecht, E. Kaltofen. Algorithms for computing sparsest shifts of polynomials in power, chebyshev and pochhammer bases. *J. Symbolic Computation*, 36(3-4):401–424, 2003.
[20] L. Oeding, G. Ottaviani. Eigenvectors of tensors and algorithms for Waring decomposition. *J. of Symbolic Computation*, 54:9–35,2013.
[21] Y. Shitov. How hard is the tensor rank?. CoRR, arXiv:1611.01559, 2016.
[22] V. Strassen. Vermeidung von Divisionen. *J. Reine Angew. Math.*, 264:184–202, 1973.

Irredundant Triangular Decomposition

Gleb Pogudin
Courant Institute of Mathematical Sciences
New York, NY
pogudin@cims.nyu.edu

Agnes Szanto
North Carolina State University
Raleigh, NC
aszanto@ncsu.edu

ABSTRACT

Triangular decomposition is a classic, widely used and well-developed way to represent algebraic varieties with many applications. In particular, there exist

- sharp degree bounds for a single triangular set in terms of intrinsic data of the variety it represents,
- powerful randomized algorithms for computing triangular decompositions using Hensel lifting in the zero-dimensional case and for irreducible varieties.

However, in the general case, most of the algorithms computing triangular decompositions produce embedded components, which makes it impossible to directly apply the intrinsic degree bounds. This, in turn, is an obstacle for efficiently applying Hensel lifting due to the higher degrees of the output polynomials and the lower probability of success.

In this paper, we give an algorithm to compute an irredundant triangular decomposition of an arbitrary algebraic set W defined by a set of polynomials in $\mathbb{C}[x_1, x_2, \ldots, x_n]$. Using this irredundant triangular decomposition, we are able to give intrinsic degree bounds for the polynomials appearing in the triangular sets and apply Hensel lifting techniques. Our decomposition algorithm is randomized, and we analyze the probability of success.

ACM Reference Format:
Gleb Pogudin and Agnes Szanto. 2018. Irredundant Triangular Decomposition. In *ISSAC '18: 2018 ACM International Symposium on Symbolic and Algebraic Computation, July 16–19, 2018, New York, NY, USA.* ACM, New York, NY, USA, 8 pages. https://doi.org/10.1145/3208976.3208996

1 INTRODUCTION

Given a set of polynomials $f_1, \ldots, f_s \in \mathbb{C}[x_1, x_2, \ldots, x_n]$, consider the algebraic set

$$W = \{\mathbf{z} \in \mathbb{C}^n \ : \ f_1(\mathbf{z}) = \cdots = f_s(\mathbf{z}) = 0\}.$$

There are several common representations of algebraic sets that allow one to answer different questions about algebraic sets or perform operations with them efficiently, for example representations via Gröbner bases, geometric resolution, and triangular decomposition. This paper is focused on the latter.

Triangular decomposition is an important tool with many applications, its origins going back to the works of Ritt [20], who introduced the concept of characteristic sets. Several authors, including Wu [27], Lazard [17], Kalkbrener [14], Wang [26], Moreno Maza [19], Schost [22], Chen [4, 5], Dahan et al. [8], have worked on triangular decompositions of algebraic sets, and some of these algorithms are implemented in MAPLE in the package `RegularChains`. There exist sharp degree and height bounds for a single triangular set in terms of intrinsic data of the variety it represents, see for example the sequence of papers [21, 22, 7, 9], these bounds are polynomial in the degree and the height of the variety. There are also powerful randomized algorithms for computing triangular decompositions using Hensel lifting in the zero-dimensional case [8] and for irreducible varieties [21].

On the other hand, most of the algorithms computing triangular decompositions in the general case produce embedded components. We are not aware of any easy way to delete all the embedded components afterward. Moreover, the problem of checking inclusion between two algebraic sets defined by triangular sets is known as the algebraic version of the *Ritt problem* (see [16, p. 190] and [1, p. 44] for the algebraic version) and appears to be hard. Embedded components make it impossible to directly apply the intrinsic degree bounds. The best known degree bounds for the polynomials in a triangular decomposition are essentially $D^{O(n^2)}$ [10, 24, 2] (D is a bound on the total degrees of $f_1, \ldots, f_s$), which is not polynomial in the degree of the algebraic set represented by the triangular decomposition. As we show in the present paper, an irredundant triangular decomposition was needed to apply the intrinsic degree bounds of [7] that are polynomial in the degree of the variety. We note that one could achieve irredundant triangular decompositions by computing the irreducible components of the variety and their Gröbner basis, which would allow one to factor out repeated and embedded components [25, 15]. However, this method is too expensive, for example, they require polynomial factorization and Gröbner basis computation with much higher worst-case degree bounds that we aim in this paper.

We also mention that using random linear changes of the variables one can avoid embedded components and compute an irredundant equidimensional decomposition, as demonstrated in [13, 18]. However, changing the coordinate system destroys the triangular structure in the original variables, and, in particular, does not allow to perform elimination of some of the original variables. We use [13] in the present paper as one of the subroutines, but in a way that our final output does not use coordinate transformations.

As far as we know, irredundant decomposition using triangular sets, without random changes of variables, was not known previously. There are two difficulties:

(1) The first difficulty is to detect common irreducible components among triangular sets of the same dimension but with different sets of *free variables* (see Definition 1), because even in the equidimensional case we may need to compute triangular sets using

ISSAC '18, July 16–19, 2018, New York, NY, USA

ACM ISBN 978-1-4503-5550-6/18/07...$15.00
https://doi.org/10.1145/3208976.3208996

different sets of free variables. As far as we know, there were no previous methods to detect if two such representations have a common irreducible component or not. One of the main results of this paper is a new technique that ensures that triangular sets representing equidimensional components with different sets of free variables have no common irreducible components (see Step 2d of Algorithm 3 and Lemma 5).

(2) The second difficulty is to factor out components that are embedded in higher dimensional irreducible components, similarly as it is stated in the Ritt problem, mentioned above. This problem has only been solved for triangular sets in one and two dimensions [6, 1]. The second result of this paper is that we show how to use the results in [13] and turn their irredundant equidimensional decomposition into an irredundant triangular decomposition. To do that, we use the zero-dimensional *equiprojectable* decomposition of [8] and the lifting techniques of [21].

2 MAIN RESULT

For $T \subset \mathbb{C}[\mathbf{x}]$, $Z(T) \subset \mathbb{C}^n$ denotes the set of common roots of T. For $V \subset \mathbb{C}^n$, $I(V)$ denotes the set of polynomials in $\mathbb{C}[\mathbf{x}]$ vanishing on V. We recall some definitions from [12].

Definition 1. A set of polynomials Δ of the form

$$\Delta = \{g_1(\mathbf{y}, z_1), g_2(\mathbf{y}, z_1, z_2), \dots, g_m(\mathbf{y}, z_1, \dots, z_m)\} \subset \mathbb{C}[\mathbf{x}], \quad (1)$$

where $\mathbf{y} = y_1, \dots, y_d$, $\{x_1, \dots, x_n\} = \{\mathbf{y}, z_1, \dots, z_m\}$, $d + m = n$, and g_i involves z_i for every $1 \leqslant i \leqslant m$ is said to be a *triangular set.*

The variables $\mathbf{y}$ are called *free variables.* For every $1 \leqslant i \leqslant m$, z_i is said to be *the leader* of g_i, and we denote the leading coefficient of g_i, viewed as a univariate polynomial in z_i, by $\mathrm{lc}(g_i)$. Let $I_\Delta := \{\mathrm{lc}(g_k) : k = 1, \dots, m\}$. The ideal generated by Δ in $\mathbb{C}[\mathbf{x}]$ is denoted by (Δ), and the ideal "pseudo-generated" by Δ is the saturated ideal

$$\mathcal{I}(\Delta) := (\Delta) : I_\Delta^\infty.$$

$\mathrm{Rep}(\Delta)$ denotes the affine variety represented by a triangular set Δ, defined as

$$\mathrm{Rep}(\Delta) := Z(\mathcal{I}(\Delta)) = \overline{Z(\Delta) \setminus Z(\prod_k \mathrm{lc}(g_k))} \subset \mathbb{C}^n.$$

Definition 2. The triangular set (1) is called a *regular chain* if

- $\deg_{z_i}(g_j) < \deg_{z_i}(g_i)$ for every $1 \leqslant i < j \leqslant m$;
- $\mathrm{lc}(g_k)$ is not a zero divisor in $\mathbb{C}[\mathbf{y}, z_1, \dots, z_{k-1}]/\mathcal{I}(g_1, \dots, g_{k-1})$ for every $1 \leqslant k \leqslant m$.

The regular chain Δ is called a *square-free regular chain* if it is a regular chain and g_k is a square-free polynomial in z_k over $\mathbb{C}[\mathbf{y}, z_1, \dots, z_{k-1}]/\mathcal{I}(g_1, \dots, g_{k-1})$ for every $1 \leqslant k \leqslant m$.

The main result of the paper is the following.

THEOREM 3. *Let $W = Z(f_1, \dots, f_s)$ for $f_i \in \mathbb{C}[x_1, x_2, \dots, x_n]$ for $i = 1, \dots s$. Assume that the total degree of f_i does not exceed $D \geqslant 2$ for every $1 \leqslant i \leqslant s$. We give a randomized algorithm (Algorithm 3) that computes*

$$\mathrm{T} = \{\Delta_i \ : \ 1 \leqslant i \leqslant N\}$$

such that

(1) Δ_i is a square-free regular chain *for every $1 \leqslant i \leqslant N$;*
(2) None of the irreducible components of $\mathrm{Rep}(\Delta_i)$ *is contained in* $\mathrm{Rep}(\Delta_j)$ *for $i \neq j$;*
(3) $W = \bigcup_{i=1}^{N} \mathrm{Rep}(\Delta_i)$;
(4) For every $1 \leqslant i \leqslant N$ and every $g \in \Delta_i$, the total degree of g with respect to the free variables does not exceed $(\deg W)^2$ and the degree with respect to every other variable does not exceed $\deg W$;
(5) All polynomials appearing in Algorithm 3 have total degrees bounded by

$$\max\left((n+1)D^{n+1}, D^{2n} + D^n\right);$$

(6) Assuming that in Algorithm 3 we make random choices independently and uniformly from a finite subset $\Gamma \subset \mathbb{C}$, the probability that the output of Algorithm 3 is correct is at least

$$1 - \frac{cD^{n^2+n} + (n+1)^4 D^{c'(n+1)}}{|\Gamma|}$$

for some constants c and c'.

Remark 3. One can check that our algorithm uses only gcd computation and linear algebra, so if the input polynomials are over a subfield $k \subset \mathbb{C}$ (for example, $k = \mathbb{Q}$), then the output polynomials will be also over this subfield.

4 THE TOOLBOX

4.1 Notation

Let $\mathbf{x} = (x_1, \dots, x_n)$, and for a subset $S = \{i_1, \dots, i_m\} \subset \{1, \dots, n\}$, denote $\mathbf{x}_S := (x_{i_1}, \dots, x_{i_m})$ with $i_1 < i_2 < \dots < i_m$.

4.2 Equidimensional decomposition

We use the method in [13] to eliminate embedded components in our Main Algorithm. The main idea of [13] to avoid embedded components is to represent each equidimensional part as the intersections of $n+1$ hypersurfaces, each a Chow form with respect to a random coordinate system. Then they use the equations of the higher dimensional parts to factor out lower dimensional embedded components. Algorithm 1 below is the input and output specification of the algorithm in [13].

Algorithm 1 EquiDim($f_1, \dots, f_s$)

Input $f_1, \dots, f_s \in \mathbb{C}[x_1, \dots, x_n]$, defining an algebraic variety $W = Z(f_1, \dots, f_s)$ and a real number $0 < p < 1$.
Output The sets

$$\mathrm{p}_0 = \{p_{0,0}, \dots, p_{0,n}\}, \dots, \mathrm{p}_{n-1} = \{p_{n-1,0}, \dots, p_{n-1,n}\}$$

of polynomials in $\mathbb{C}[x_1, \dots, x_n]$ represented by straight-line programs such that with probability at least p the following holds

- the set $Z(p_{\ell,0}, \dots, p_{\ell,n}) \subset \mathbb{C}^n$ is exactly W_ℓ, that is the union of all irreducible components of W of dimension ℓ, for all $0 \leqslant \ell \leqslant n-1$;
- $\deg p_{\ell,i} \leqslant \deg W_\ell$ for all $0 \leqslant \ell \leqslant n-1$ and $0 \leqslant i \leqslant n$.

4.3 Canny's generalized resultant

Consider polynomials $f_1, \dots, f_{n+1} \in \mathbb{C}[\mathbf{x}, \mathbf{y}]$, where $\mathbf{x} = (x_1, \dots, x_n)$ and $\mathbf{y} = (y_1, \dots, y_m)$. Let $\deg f_i \leqslant D$ for every $1 \leqslant i \leqslant n+1$. By $\pi\colon \mathbb{C}^{m+n} \to \mathbb{C}^m$ we denote the projection of the $(\mathbf{x}, \mathbf{y})$-space onto the y-coordinates. Then the construction of the generalized perturbed resultant proposed in [3] provides a non zero polynomial $\mathrm{PRes}_{\mathbf{x}}(f_1, \ldots, f_{n+1}) \in \mathbb{C}[\mathbf{y}]$ such that

- $\mathrm{PRes}_{\mathbf{x}}(f_1, \ldots, f_{n+1})$ vanishes on $\pi(C)$ for every irreducible component $C \subset Z(f_1, \ldots, f_{n+1})$ with $\overline{\pi(C)} \neq \mathbb{C}^m$;
- $\deg \mathrm{PRes}_{\mathbf{x}}(f_1, \ldots, f_{n+1}) \leqslant (n+1)D^{n+1}$ (this follows from the degree bound for multivariate resultants [11, Proposition 1.1]);
- $\mathrm{PRes}_{\mathbf{x}}(f_1, \ldots, f_{n+1})$ can be computed using one multivariate resultant computation for $n+1$ polynomials of degree at most D.

4.4 Triangular Decomposition over Fraction Fields

A randomized algorithm TriangularZeroDim with the following specifications will be used as a subroutine in Algorithm 3. One possible way to design such an algorithm is based on the equiprojectable triangular decomposition algorithm of [8] and is described in Section 6. There are also other possibilities such as the unmixed procedure from [24].

Algorithm 2 TriangularZeroDim($S, \{h_1, \ldots, h_\ell\}$)

Input
- a proper subset $S := \{i_1, \ldots, i_m\} \subset \{1, \ldots, n\}$ with $i_1 < \ldots < i_m$
- polynomials $h_1, \ldots, h_\ell \in \mathbb{C}[\mathbf{x}]$ with $\ell \geqslant m$ such that
  (1) the ideal I generated by $h_1, \ldots, h_\ell$ in $\mathbb{C}(\mathbf{x}_{\overline{S}})[\mathbf{x}_S]$ is zero dimensional
  (2) the Jacobian of $h_1, \ldots, h_m$ with respect to $\mathbf{x}_S$ is invertible at every solution of I in the algebraic closure $\overline{\mathbb{C}(\mathbf{x}_{\overline{S}})}$

Output Square-free regular chains $\Delta_1, \ldots, \Delta_q \subset \mathbb{C}[\mathbf{x}]$ such that
(1) leaders of Δ_j are $x_{i_1}, \ldots, x_{i_m}$ for every $1 \leqslant j \leqslant q$
(2) $\mathrm{Rep}(\Delta_i)$ and $\mathrm{Rep}(\Delta_j)$ do not have common irreducible components for every $1 \leqslant i < j \leqslant q$
(3) $\bigcap_{i=1}^{q} I(\Delta_i) \cdot \mathbb{C}(\mathbf{x}_{\overline{S}}) = \sqrt{I}$
(4) for every $g \in \Delta_1 \cup \ldots \cup \Delta_q$, the coefficients of g considered as a polynomial in $\mathbf{x}_S$ are coprime.

Note that the algorithm in Section 6 returns triangular sets such that the leading coefficients of their elements belong to $\mathbb{C}[\mathbf{x}_{\overline{S}}]$. This property is not needed in the proof of correctness of Algorithm 3, but we use it to prove our degree bounds.

5 THE MAIN ALGORITHM

See our Main Algorithm, Algorithm 3, below.

Proof of Theorem 3 (1)-(5). Denote by $\{\Delta_1, \ldots, \Delta_N\}$ the output of Algorithm 3. We make the following assumptions on random choices made in Algorithm 3 (the probabilities will be estimated in the proof of (6) in Section 6):

A1 The choice of $\lambda_{i,j}$ in Step 2a satisfies the following property: for every $-1 \leqslant d \leqslant n-1$, $Z(\widetilde{f}_1, \ldots, \widetilde{f}_{n-d})$ and W have the same irreducible components of dimensions larger than d.
A2 The point $\boldsymbol{\alpha}$ in Step 2d is chosen such that $\hat{g}_S(\boldsymbol{\alpha}) \neq 0$ for all $S \subset \{1, \ldots, n\}$.

Proof of (1). The fact that Δ_i is a squarefree regular chain would follow from the specification of TriangularZeroDim if we show that

---

Algorithm 3 Main Algorithm

Input $f_1, \ldots, f_s \in \mathbb{C}[x_1, x_2, \ldots, x_n]$ defining the affine variety $W = Z(f_1, \ldots, f_s)$.
Output Representation of W as a union of varieties defined by square-free regular chains, as described in Theorem 3.

(1) *Compute the equidimensional decomposition.* For every $0 \leqslant d < n$, we call the subroutine EquiDim($f_1, \ldots, f_s$) described in Section 4.2 to compute a set of polynomials
$$\mathbf{p}_d := \{p_{d,0}, \ldots, p_{d,n}\}$$
such that
$$Z(\mathbf{p}_d) = W_d,$$
where W_d is the union of irreducible components of dimension d in W. Let d_0 and d_1 be the minimal and maximal dimensions, respectively.
(2) *Compute a cover by "univariate" triangular sets.*
  (a) *Square the system.* Let
  $$\widetilde{f}_i := \lambda_{i,1} f_1 + \ldots + \lambda_{i,s} f_s \text{ for } 1 \leqslant i \leqslant n - d_0 + 1,$$
  where $\lambda_{i,j}$ is chosen uniformly random from a finite set $\Gamma \subset \mathbb{C}$.
  (b) *Compute projections.* For each $S \subset \{1, \ldots, n\}$ such that $n - d_1 - 1 \leq |S| \leq n - d_0 - 1$, compute Canny's generalized resultants
  $$\hat{g}_S := \mathrm{PRes}_{\mathbf{x}_S}(\widetilde{f}_1, \ldots, \widetilde{f}_m) \in \mathbb{C}[\mathbf{x}_{\overline{S}}] \subset \mathbb{C}[\mathbf{x}],$$
  defined in Section 4.3, where $|S| = m - 1$.
  (c) *Define the cover.* For each $S \subset \{1, \ldots, n\}$ such that $n - d_1 \leq |S| \leq n - d_0$ define
  $$\hat{\nabla}_S := \{\hat{g}_{S_1}, \ldots, \hat{g}_{S_m}\},$$
  where $S = \{i_1, \ldots, i_m\} \subset \{1, \ldots, n\}$ with $i_1 < \ldots < i_m$, and $S_j := S \setminus \{i_j\}$
  (d) *Avoid repetitions.* Choose a random point $\boldsymbol{\alpha} := (\alpha_1, \ldots, \alpha_n) \in \Gamma^n$ such that $\hat{g}_S(\boldsymbol{\alpha}) \neq 0$ for all $S \subset \{1, \ldots, n\}$.
  For every $n - d_1 \leqslant m \leqslant n - d_0$, for every subset $S = \{i_1, \ldots, i_m\} \subset \{1, \ldots, n\}$ with $i_1 < \ldots < i_m$, let
  $$\nabla_S := \{g_{S,1}, \ldots, g_{S,m}\},$$
  where $g_{S,j}$ is the squarefree part of
  $$\hat{g}_{S_j}\left(\alpha_1, \ldots, \alpha_{i_j - 1}, x_{i_j}, \ldots, x_n\right)$$
  for $1 \leqslant j \leqslant m$, considered as a univariate polynomial in x_{i_j}.
(3) *Compute the result.* Return
$$\bigcup_{d=d_0}^{d_1} \bigcup_{\substack{S \subset \{1,\ldots,n\},\\ |S| = n-d}} \mathrm{TriangularZeroDim}(S, \nabla_S \cup \mathbf{p}_d)$$
The subroutine TriangularZeroDim is described in Section 4.4.

---

the input specification of TriangularZeroDim is satisfied. We fix $S \subset \{1, \ldots, n\}$ of cardinality $n - d$. Then the first $n - d$ polynomials in the input of
$$\mathrm{TriangularZeroDim}(S, \nabla_S \cup \mathbf{p}_d)$$
in Step 3 are ∇_S. These polynomials already generate a zero-dimensional ideal in $\mathbb{C}(\mathbf{x}_{\overline{S}})[\mathbf{x}_S]$, so $\nabla_S \cup \mathbf{p}_d$ also do. Since $g_{S,j}$ belongs to $\mathbb{C}[x_{i_j}, \mathbf{x}_{\overline{S}}]$, the Jacobian of ∇_S with respect to $\mathbf{x}_S$ is a diagonal matrix. Moreover, since every $g_{S,j}$ is squarefree, the matrix is invertible at every solution of (∇_S) in $\overline{\mathbb{C}(\mathbf{x}_{\overline{S}})}$.

Proof of (2). Let C be an irreducible component of $\mathrm{Rep}(\Delta_i)$. Below, Lemma 4 implies that C is an irreducible component of W.

Using A1 and Lemma 5, we conclude that C is contained in $\text{Rep}(\Delta_j)$ only for $j = i$. This proves the statement.

Proof of (3). Lemma 4 implies that $\bigcup_{i=1}^{N} \text{Rep}(\Delta_i) \subset W$. Lemma 5 together with A1 imply that $W \subset \bigcup_{i=1}^{N} \text{Rep}(\Delta_i)$.

Proof of (4). Fix $S = \{i_1, \ldots, i_m\}$ with $i_1 < \cdots < i_m$, and consider the coordinate system $\mathbf{x}_S = (x_{i_1}, \ldots, x_{i_m}) =: (z_1, \ldots, z_m)$ and $\mathbf{y} := \mathbf{x}_{\overline{S}}$. First we prove that if V is represented by a square-free regular chain in the fixed coordinate system, then this square-free regular chain representing V is unique, as long as the leading coefficients are in $\mathbb{C}[\mathbf{y}]$ and the coefficients in $\mathbb{C}[\mathbf{y}]$ of each polynomials are relatively prime. This is because for any such square-free regular chain, after dividing by the leading coefficients, we get a reduced Gröbner basis with respect to the lexicographic monomial ordering with $z_1 < \cdots < z_m$ of the ideal generated by $I(V)$ in the ring $\mathbb{C}(\mathbf{y})[\mathbf{z}]$. Since the reduced Gröbner basis of an ideal with a fixed monomial ordering is unique, using the assumption that the coefficients of each polynomial in the regular chain are relatively prime, we get that the square-free regular chain representing V that satisfy the above conditions is unique.

Statement (4) of Theorem 3 follows from the fact that, as described in Section 6, TriangularZeroDim$(S, \nabla_S \cup \mathbf{p}_d)$ returns a set $\{\Delta_a, \ldots, \Delta_b\}$ of square-free regular chains such that the leading terms are in $\mathbb{C}[x_{\overline{S}}]$ and the coefficients of the polynomials in the triangular sets are relatively prime. Moreover, the output of $\{\Delta_a, \ldots, \Delta_b\}$ is an irredundant triangular decomposition of W_S, where W_S is the union of all irreducible components C of W of co-dimension m such that $\mathbf{x}_{\overline{S}}$ is the maximal subset of $\{x_1, \ldots, x_n\}$ among the subsets of free variables for C, with respect to the lexicographic ordering of the variables $x_1, \ldots, x_n$. So for each $i = a, \ldots, b$, $V := \text{Rep}(\Delta_i)$ is a disjoint union of irreducible components of W_S. Finally we note that $\Delta_i = \{g_1, \ldots, g_m\}$ is the unique square-free regular chain representing V with leading coefficients in $\mathbb{C}[\mathbf{y}]$, so we can apply the degree bounds proved in [7, Theorem 2] to get for $k = 1, \ldots, m$

$$\deg_{\mathbf{y}}(g_k) \leq \left(1 + 2\sum_{i \leq k-1} (d_i - 1)\right) \deg(V_k) \leq \deg(W_{S,k})^2 \qquad (2)$$

where $d_i := \deg_{z_i}(g_i)$, and V_k ($W_{S,k}$) is the projection of V (W_S) to the coordinates $(\mathbf{y}, z_1, \ldots, z_k)$. Since $\deg(W_{S,k}) \leqslant \deg(W)$, we get the desired bound for the free variable.

For the non-free variables, we use inequalities

$$\prod_{i=1}^{m} \deg_{z_i} g_i \leqslant \deg W \text{ and } \deg_{\mathbf{z}} g_k \leqslant \sum_{i=1}^{m} \deg_{z_i} g_i - m + 1$$

to deduce $\deg_{\mathbf{z}} g_k \leqslant \deg W$ for $k = 1, \ldots, m$.

Proof of (5). Due to Section 4.2, the degrees of the polynomials appearing in Step 1 of the algorithms do not exceed $\deg W \leqslant D^n$.

The bounds on the degrees of the polynomials in Step 2 of the algorithm are bounded by $(n+1)D^{n+1}$, the bound on the degree of Canny's generalized resultant (see Section 4.3).

As we show in Section 6, we can use Hensel lifting in the $\mathbf{x}_{\overline{S}}$ variables to compute the output of TriangularZeroDim$(S, \nabla_S \cup \mathbf{p}_d)$, thus the $\mathbf{x}_{\overline{S}}$-degrees and $\mathbf{x}_S$-degrees of the polynomials computed in this subroutine do not exceed the bounds D^{2n} and D^n, respectively, stated in (4). □

Lemma 4. *Let C be an irreducible component of $\text{Rep}(\Delta_i)$ for some $1 \leqslant i \leqslant N$. Then C is an irreducible component of W.*

Proof. Since Δ_i belongs to the output of Algorithm 3, Δ_i belongs to

$$\text{TriangularZeroDim}(S, \{g_{S,1}, \ldots, g_{S,m}\} \cup \mathbf{p}_{n-m})$$

for some $S := \{i_1, \ldots, i_m\} \subset \{1, \ldots, n\}$. The specification of TriangularZeroDim implies that

(1) $|\Delta_i| = |S| = m$, so $\dim C = n - m$ by [12, Theorem 4.4];
(2) leaders of Δ_i are $x_{i_1}, \ldots, x_{i_m}$, so $I(C) \cap \mathbb{C}[\mathbf{x}_{\overline{S}}] = 0$ by [12, Proposition 5.8];
(3) the ideal generated by $\mathcal{I}(\Delta_i)$ in $\mathbb{C}(\mathbf{x}_{\overline{S}})[\mathbf{x}_S]$ contains $\mathbf{p}_{n-m}$.

Due to (3), there exists $q_j \in \mathbb{C}[x_{\overline{S}}]$ such that $q_j p_{n-m,j} \in \mathcal{I}(\Delta_i) \subset I(C)$ for every $0 \leqslant j \leqslant n$. Since $I(C)$ is prime and $I(C) \cap \mathbb{C}[x_{\overline{S}}] = 0$ due to (2), $p_{n-m,j} \in I(C)$ for every $0 \leqslant j \leqslant n$. Since $W_{n-m} = Z(\mathbf{p}_{n-m})$, we have $C \subset W_{n-m}$. Moreover, C is an irreducible component of W_{n-m} since $\dim C = n - m$ due to (1). This proves the lemma. □

Lemma 5. *Assume that Assumptions A1 and A2 are satisfied. Then for every irreducible component $C \subset W$, there exists a unique $1 \leqslant i \leqslant N$ such that $C \subset \text{Rep}(\Delta_i)$. Moreover, C is an irreducible component of $\text{Rep}(\Delta_i)$.*

Proof. **Existence.** Let C be an irreducible component of W, $m := \text{codim}\, C$ and $d := n - m$. Consider all subsets $\{j_1, \ldots, j_d\} \subset \{1, \ldots, n\}$ such that the image of $x_{j_1}, \ldots, x_{j_d}$ constitute a transcendence basis of $\mathbb{C}[\mathbf{x}]$ modulo $I(C)$. Among all these sets we find one for which the tuple $(j_1, \ldots, j_d)$ (assuming that $j_1 < j_2 < \ldots < j_d$) is maximal with respect to the lexicographic ordering. By $S := \{i_1, \ldots, i_m\}$ we denote the complement to this subset in $\{1, \ldots, n\}$.

Since $\dim C = d$ and $W \subset Z(\widetilde{f}_1, \ldots, \widetilde{f}_{n-d})$, our assumption that $Z(\widetilde{f}_1, \ldots, \widetilde{f}_{n-d})$ and W have the same irreducible components of dimension larger than d implies that C is a (non-embedded) irreducible component of $Z(\widetilde{f}_1, \ldots, \widetilde{f}_{n-d})$. Since $\dim C = d$, C does not project dominantly on the $\mathbf{x}_{\overline{S} \cup \{i_k\}}$-coordinates for $1 \leqslant k \leqslant m$. Then the property 4.3 of the Canny's resultant implies that $\hat{g}_{S_k}$ (defined in Step 2b with $S_k := S \setminus \{i_k\}$) vanishes on C for every $1 \leqslant k \leqslant m$. Consider $1 \leqslant k \leqslant m$. We will prove that $g_{S,k}$ (defined in Step 2d) vanishes on C. Let

$$B := \{\ell \mid x_\ell \text{ appears in } \hat{g}_{S_k},\ \ell < i_k\}.$$

If $B = \emptyset$, then $g_{S,k} = \hat{g}_{S_k}$ and vanishes on C. Otherwise, we write $\hat{g}_{S_k}$ as $\sum_{i=1}^{M} c_i m_i$, where $m_0, \ldots, m_M$ are distinct monomials in $\mathbf{x}_B$ with $m_0 = 1$ and $c_0, \ldots, c_M$ are polynomials in $\mathbb{C}[\mathbf{x}_{\overline{B}}]$. If all $c_0, \ldots, c_M$ vanish on C, then $g_{S,k}$ vanishes on C. Otherwise, there exists $1 \leqslant t \leqslant M$ such that c_t does not vanish on C. Let x_{j_ℓ} be any variable in m_t, then $\hat{g}_{S_k} = 0$ is a nontrivial algebraic equation for x_{j_ℓ} over $\mathbf{x}_{\overline{S}} \setminus \{x_{j_\ell}\} \cup \{x_{i_k}\}$ modulo $I(C)$. Then, replacing x_{j_ℓ} with x_{i_k}, we obtain a lexicographically larger transcendence basis of $\mathbb{C}[\mathbf{x}]$ modulo $I(C)$. Thus $g_{S,k}$ vanishes on C.

Let $\{\Delta_a, \ldots, \Delta_b\} = \text{TriangularZeroDim}(S, \nabla_S \cup \mathbf{p}_d)$ for some $1 \leqslant a \leqslant b \leqslant N$ with $\nabla_S = \{g_{S,1}, \ldots, g_{S,m}\}$. The specification of TriangularZeroDim together with the fact that $\{g_{S,1}, \ldots, g_{S,m}\} \cup$

$\mathfrak{p}_d \subset I(C)$ imply

$$\bigcap_{i=a}^{b} \mathbb{C}(\mathbf{x}_{\overline{S}})\mathcal{I}(\Delta_i) = \sqrt{I} \subset \mathbb{C}(\mathbf{x}_{\overline{S}})I(C).$$

Since the latter ideal is prime, there exists $a \leqslant c \leqslant b$ such that

$$\mathbb{C}(\mathbf{x}_{\overline{S}})\mathcal{I}(\Delta_c) \subset \mathbb{C}(\mathbf{x}_{\overline{S}})I(C).$$

Since $I(C) \cap \mathbb{C}[\mathbf{x}_{\overline{S}}] = 0$, we have $\mathcal{I}(\Delta_c) \subset I(C)$. Hence $C \subset \mathrm{Rep}(\Delta_c)$. Since $\dim C = \dim \mathrm{Rep}(\Delta_c)$, C is an irreducible component of $\mathrm{Rep}(\Delta_c)$. The existence is proved.

Uniqueness. Assume that $C \subset \mathrm{Rep}(\Delta_{c'})$ for some $c' \neq c$. Consider the following cases

Case 1. $\dim \mathrm{Rep}(\Delta_{c'}) = D > d = \dim C$ Since $\mathrm{Rep}(\Delta_{c'}) \subset W_D$ and C is an irreducible component of W_d by Lemma 4, C cannot be contained in $\mathrm{Rep}(\Delta_{c'})$.

Case 2. $\dim \mathrm{Rep}(\Delta_{c'}) = d = \dim C$ Let

$$\Delta_{c'} \subset \mathrm{TriangularZeroDim}(S', \{g_{S',1}, \ldots, g_{S',m}\} \cup \mathfrak{p}_d)$$

for some $S' = \{i'_1, \ldots, i'_m\} \subset \{1, \ldots, n\}$. Consider an arbitrary $1 \leqslant k \leqslant n$, and define $\overline{S}_k := \overline{S} \cap \{k, \ldots, n\}$. Since $I(C)$ contains $g_{S,1}, \ldots, g_{S,m}$, $\mathbf{x}_{\overline{S}_k}$ is a transcendence basis of $\mathbb{C}[x_k, \ldots, x_n]$ modulo $I(C) \cap \mathbb{C}[x_k, \ldots, x_n]$, since $\mathbf{x}_{\overline{S}_k}$ is clearly algebraically independent modulo $I(C) \cap \mathbb{C}[x_k, \ldots, x_n]$, and for all $j \geq k$ such that $j \in S$ there exists $t \in \{1, \ldots, m\}$ such that $j = i_t$ and by the construction in Step 2d we have $g_{S,t} \in I(C) \cap \mathbb{C}[x_k, \ldots, x_n]$. Analogously, for $\overline{S'}_k := \overline{S'} \cap \{k, \ldots, n\}, \mathbf{x}_{\overline{S'}_k}$ is a transcendence basis of $\mathrm{C}[x_k, \ldots, x_n]$ modulo $I(C) \cap \mathbb{C}[x_k, \ldots, x_n]$. Hence

$$\left|\overline{S} \cap \{k, \ldots, n\}\right| = \left|\overline{S'} \cap \{k, \ldots, n\}\right|$$

for every $1 \leqslant k \leqslant n$. Thus, $S = S'$. Then varieties $\mathrm{Rep}(\Delta_c)$ and $\mathrm{Rep}(\Delta_{c'})$ do not have common irreducible components due to the specification of TriangularZeroDim. □

6 ZERO-DIMENSIONAL TRIANGULAR DECOMPOSITION OVER RATIONAL FUNCTIONS

In this section we describe a slight modification of the zero dimensional equiprojectable triangular decomposition algorithm of [8] that was given over the field $K = \mathbb{Q}$, while here we work over the field $K = \mathbb{C}(\mathbf{y})$ for $\mathbf{y} = y_1, \ldots, y_d$.

6.1 Equiprojectable decomposition

Definition 6 ([8], p. 109). Given $h_1, \ldots, h_\ell \in K[z_1, \ldots, z_m]$ where K is a field (here we use both $K = \mathbb{C}(\mathbf{y})$ and $K = \mathbb{C}$), assume that

$$V = Z(h_1, \ldots, h_\ell) \subset \overline{K}^m$$

is zero-dimensional, where $\overline{K}$ is the algebraic closure of K. Consider $\pi : \overline{K}^n \to \overline{K}^{n-1}$ the projection onto the first $n-1$ coordinates, and for each $x \in V$ let $N(x) := \#\pi^{-1}(\pi(x))$, the number of points in V in the π-fiber of x. Then decompose $V = V_1 \cup \cdots \cup V_d$ such that $V_i := \{x \in V \;:\; N(x) = i\}$ for $i = 1, \ldots d$. Apply this splitting process recursively to each $V_1, \ldots, V_d$, using the fibers of the successive projections $\overline{K}^n \to \overline{K}^i$ onto the first i coordinates, for $i = n-2, \ldots, 1$. Thus we obtain a decomposition of V into pairwise disjoint varieties that are each *equiprojectable*, which form the *equiprojectable decomposition* of V.

The reason we consider the equiprojectable decomposition is because each equiprojectable component of V is representable by a single triangular set with coefficients in K (c.f. [8, Section 2]). We use this fact to ensure that when lifting the equiprojectable components from $\mathbb{C}$ to $\mathbb{C}[[\mathbf{y}]]$ (see below), the resulting triangular sets are reconstructable over $K = \mathbb{C}(\mathbf{y})$.

The main idea for computing an equiprojectable decomposition, encoded by triangular sets, of a zero-dimensional affine variety defined by polynomials $\mathbf{H} = \{h_1, \ldots, h_\ell\} \subset \mathbb{C}(\mathbf{y})[\mathbf{z}]$, is first to specify the variables $\mathbf{y}$ in a random point $\mathbf{y}^* \in \mathbb{C}^d$ such that the equiprojectable decomposition of $Z(\mathbf{H}) \subset \overline{\mathbb{C}(\mathbf{y})}^m$, described by triangular sets in $\mathbb{C}(\mathbf{y})[\mathbf{z}]$, specializes to the equiprojectable decomposition of $Z(\mathbf{H}_{\mathbf{y}=\mathbf{y}^*}) \subset \mathbb{C}^m$. Then we can lift each triangular set in the equiprojectable decomposition of $Z(\mathbf{H}_{\mathbf{y}=\mathbf{y}^*}) \subset \mathbb{C}^m$ to a triangular set in $\mathbb{C}(\mathbf{y})[\mathbf{z}]$ in the equiprojectable decomposition of $Z(\mathbf{H}) \subset \overline{\mathbb{C}(\mathbf{y})}^m$.

To compute the equiprojectable decomposition, encoded by triangular sets, of a zero-dimensional affine variety $Z(\mathbf{H}_{\mathbf{y}=\mathbf{y}^*}) \subset \mathbb{C}^m$, we cite the algorithm outlined in [8, Section 4.]. Namely, they first call the zero-dimensional triangularization algorithm of [19], followed by the Split-and-Merge algorithm of [8, Section 2.].

6.2 Lifting and reconstructing

The lifting algorithm is a (slight extension) of the lifting procedure from [22, Section 4.2]. We will work in the ring $\mathbb{C}[\mathbf{y}, \mathbf{z}]$ with $\mathbf{y} = (y_1, \ldots, y_d)$ and $\mathbf{z} = (z_1, \ldots, z_m)$ with $d + m = n$.

For a single lifting step we restate the specification of [22, Algorithm Lift] as follows:

Algorithm 4 Lift($\mathbf{H}, \mathbf{y}^*, s, \widetilde{\Delta}$)

Input
(1) set of polynomials $\mathbf{H} = \{h_1(\mathbf{y}, \mathbf{z}), \ldots, h_m(\mathbf{y}, \mathbf{z})\} \subset \mathbb{C}[\mathbf{y}, \mathbf{z}]$;
(2) a point $\mathbf{y}^* \in \mathbb{C}^d$;
(3) a nonnegative integer s;
(4) a regular chain $\widetilde{\Delta} = \{\widetilde{g}_1(\mathbf{y}, z_1), \widetilde{g}_2(\mathbf{y}, z_1, z_2), \ldots, \widetilde{g}_m(\mathbf{y}, \mathbf{z})\} \subset \mathbb{C}[\mathbf{y} - \mathbf{y}^*, \mathbf{z}]$ such that
- $\mathrm{lc}(\widetilde{g}_k) = 1$ for $k = 1, \ldots, m$
- $\widetilde{g}_k$ is reduced modulo $\{\widetilde{g}_1, \ldots, \widetilde{g}_{k-1}\}$
- there exists $\Delta = \{g_1(\mathbf{y}, z_1), g_2(\mathbf{y}, z_1, z_2), \ldots, g_m(\mathbf{y}, \mathbf{z})\} \subset \mathbb{C}(\mathbf{y})[\mathbf{z}]$ such that
  - every element of $\mathbf{H}$ can be reduced to zero using Δ
  - $\widetilde{\Delta} \equiv \Delta \pmod{(\mathbf{y} - \mathbf{y}^*)^{2^s}}$
- $\mathrm{jac}_{\mathbf{z}}(\mathbf{H}|_{\mathbf{y}=\mathbf{y}^*})$ is invertible modulo $\widetilde{\Delta}|_{\mathbf{y}=\mathbf{y}^*}$;

Output Regular chain $\widehat{\Delta} = \{\widehat{g}_1(\mathbf{y}, z_1), \ldots, \widehat{g}_m(\mathbf{y}, \mathbf{z})\} \subset \mathbb{C}[\mathbf{y} - \mathbf{y}^*, \mathbf{z}]$ satisfying
- $\mathrm{lc}(\widehat{g}_k) = 1$ for $k = 1, \ldots, m$;
- $\widehat{\Delta} \equiv \Delta \pmod{(\mathbf{y} - \mathbf{y}^*)^{2^{s+1}}}$;

Then one can adapt the general strategy of the main algorithm from [8, p. 113] to generalize the algorithm from [21, p. 584] as shown in Algorithm 5.

In Algorithm 5, we use the subroutine RationalReconstruction described in [22, Section 4.3.1].

The following lemma is an adaptation of the arguments presented in [8, Section 3] for the rational function field case. Since the

Algorithm 5 TriangularZeroDim via Hensel lifting

Input Set of polynomials $\mathrm{H} = \{h_1(\mathrm{y},\mathrm{z}),\ldots,h_\ell(\mathrm{y},\mathrm{z})\} \subset \mathbb{C}[\mathrm{y},\mathrm{z}]$ such that $\mathrm{jac}_\mathrm{z}(\mathrm{H}_0)$ is invertible at every solution of H in $\overline{\mathbb{C}(\mathrm{y})}$, where $\mathrm{H}_0 = \{h_1(\mathrm{y},\mathrm{z}),\ldots,h_m(\mathrm{y},\mathrm{z})\}$.

Output Equiprojectable triangular decomposition of H

(1) Pick coordinates of $\mathrm{y}_1,\mathrm{y}_2 \in \mathbb{C}^d$ randomly from a finite $\Gamma \subset \mathbb{C}$
(2) Compute the equiprojectable decompositions $\widetilde{\Delta}_1,\ldots,\widetilde{\Delta}_N$ and $\overline{\Delta}_1,\ldots,\overline{\Delta}_N$ of $\mathrm{H}|_{\mathrm{y}=\mathrm{y}_1}$ and $\mathrm{H}|_{\mathrm{y}=\mathrm{y}_2}$, respectively
(3) $s = 0$
(4) While not Stop
  (a) $\widetilde{\Delta}_i := \mathrm{Lift}(\mathrm{H}_0,\mathrm{y}_1,s,\widetilde{\Delta}_i)$ for every $1 \leqslant i \leqslant N$
  (b) $s := s + 1$
  (c) $\Delta_i := \mathrm{RationalReconstruction}(\widetilde{\Delta}_i)$ for every $1 \leqslant i \leqslant N$
  (d) if $\{\overline{\Delta}_1,\ldots,\overline{\Delta}_N\} = \{\Delta_1|_{\mathrm{y}=\mathrm{y}_2},\ldots,\Delta_N|_{\mathrm{y}=\mathrm{y}_2}\}$, then Stop := true
(5) Return $\{\Delta_1,\ldots,\Delta_N\}$

bounds in [8, Section 3] were given in terms of heights of rational numbers, we cannot straightforwardly cite those results, so we present the analogous bounds for $\mathbb{C}(\mathrm{y})$.

LEMMA 7. *Assume that* $\mathrm{H} = \{h_1(\mathrm{y},\mathrm{z}),\ldots,h_\ell(\mathrm{y},\mathrm{z})\} \subset \mathbb{C}[\mathrm{y},\mathrm{z}]$ *satisfies the input specifications of Algorithm 5, and assume that* $\deg_{(\mathrm{z},\mathrm{y})}(h_i) \le \mathcal{H}$ *for* $i = 1,\ldots,\ell$. *Denote by P the (finite) number of solutions of* H *in the algebraic closure* $\overline{\mathbb{C}(\mathrm{y})}$ *and by Q the degree of the affine variety* $Z(\mathrm{H})$ *in* $\mathbb{C}^{m+d} = \mathbb{C}^n$. *Then there exists a polynomial* $F \in \mathbb{C}[\mathrm{y}]$ *with*

$$\deg_\mathrm{y}(F) \leqslant 4m^2PQ\mathcal{H}^2$$

with the property that if $F(y^*) \neq 0$ *for* $y^* \in \mathbb{C}^d$ *then the equiprojectable triangular decomposition of* H *specializes to the equiprojectable triangular decomposition of* $\mathrm{H}|_{\mathrm{y}=\mathrm{y}^*}$, *and the Jacobian of* $\mathrm{H}_0|_{\mathrm{y}=\mathrm{y}^*}$ *does not vanish at any of the solutions of* $\mathrm{H}|_{\mathrm{y}=\mathrm{y}^*}$ *in* $\mathbb{C}^m$.

PROOF. Using the notation of [8, Section 3], for $k = 1,\ldots,m$, denote by $u_k = u_{k,1}z_1 + \cdots + u_{k,k}z_k$ ($u_{k,j} \in \mathbb{C}$) a primitive element for the projection of the finite number of solutions of H in the algebraic closure $\overline{\mathbb{C}(\mathrm{y})}$, where the projection is to the $(z_1,\ldots,z_k)$ coordinates. Let $\mu_k \in \mathbb{C}[\mathrm{y}][T]$ be the minimal polynomial of u_k. Furthermore, let $w_1,\ldots,w_m \in \mathbb{C}(\mathrm{y})[T]$ be the parametrization of the solutions of H in $\overline{\mathbb{C}(\mathrm{y})}$ with respect to u_m. Analogously to [8, Lemmas 4-7], we can prove that the 3 hypotheses

H_1: None of the coefficients of $\mu_m, w_1,\ldots,w_m$ vanish at $\mathrm{y} = \mathrm{y}^*$;
H_2: $\mu_k|_{\mathrm{y}=\mathrm{y}^*} \in \mathbb{C}[T]$ is squarefree for $k = 1,\ldots,m$;
H_3: The Jacobian of $\mathrm{H}_0|_{\mathrm{y}=\mathrm{y}^*}$ is not zero at the solutions of $\mathrm{H}|_{\mathrm{y}=\mathrm{y}^*}$;

imply that the equiprojectable triangular decomposition of H specializes to the equiprojectable triangular decomposition of $\mathrm{H}|_{\mathrm{y}=\mathrm{y}^*}$, and the set of solutions of H in $\overline{\mathbb{C}(\mathrm{y})}$ specializes at $\mathrm{y} = \mathrm{y}^*$ to the set of solutions of $\mathrm{H}|_{\mathrm{y}=\mathrm{y}^*}$ in $\mathbb{C}^m$. In [8, Lemma 8] they prove that H_1 and H_2 is satisfied if for $a_k := \mathrm{Res}_T(\mu_k,\mu_k') \in \mathbb{C}[\mathrm{y}]$ we have $a_k(\mathrm{y}^*) \neq 0$ for $k = 1,\ldots,m$. Let $a = a_1 \cdots a_m$. Using that $\deg_T(\mu_k) \le P$ and $\deg_\mathrm{y}(\mu_k) \le Q$ by [22, Theorem 1], we can see that

$$\deg_\mathrm{y}(a) \le m(2P-1)Q.$$

Furthermore, let J^h be the homogenization of the Jacobian of H_0 by adding a homogenizing variable z_0 to $z_1,\ldots,z_m$, and consider $J^h(\mu_m',v_1,\ldots,v_m)$ where $v_k := w_k\mu_m' \mod \mu_m \in \mathbb{C}[\mathrm{y}][T]$ (note that this homogenization step turns the polynomials w_i from having coefficients in $\mathbb{C}(\mathrm{y})$ with higher degree numerators and denominators into polynomials $v_i \in \mathbb{C}[\mathrm{y}][T]$ with y-degrees at most Q, see [22] for more details). In [8, Lemma 9] they prove that H_3 is satisfied if for the Sylvester resultant $b := \mathrm{Res}_T(J^h(\mu_m',v_1,\ldots,v_m),\mu_m) \in \mathbb{C}[\mathrm{y}]$ we have $b(\mathrm{y}^*) \neq 0$. To bound the degree of b first note that

$$\deg_T J^h(\mu_m',v_1,\ldots,v_m) \le mP\mathcal{H}$$

and

$$\deg_\mathrm{y} J^h(\mu_m',v_1,\ldots,v_m) \le mQ\mathcal{H}$$

again by [22, Theorem 1], so

$$\deg_\mathrm{y}(b) \le 2m^2QP\mathcal{H}^2.$$

Putting it all together, for $F = ab$ we get the claimed degree bound. □

Now we are able to prove the last remaining part of our main theorem:

Proof of Theorem 3, (6). Assume that $\deg_\mathrm{x}(f_i) \le D$ for $i = 1,\ldots,s$. In Algorithm 3, we have the following independent random uniform choices from a finite subset Γ of the coefficient field $\mathbb{C}$, and we bound the probability of success using the Schwartz-Zippel lemma [28, 23].

- In Step 1 we call the equidimensional decomposition algorithm of [13] with input $f_1,\ldots,f_s$. In [13, Remark 10] they prove that the probability of success for their algorithm is at least
$$1 - \frac{c_1D^{n^2+n} + D^{c_2(n+1)}}{|\Gamma|}$$
where c_1 and c_2 are constants. They use randomization to obtain linear combinations of the input polynomials, changes of variables and the linear forms for the primitive elements used in each step.
- In Step 2a, we choose at most $n+1$ random linear combinations $\widetilde{f}_1,\ldots,\widetilde{f}_{n+1}$ of the input polynomials $f_1,\ldots,f_s$. The correctness of the algorithm requires the assumption A1 to hold. In [13, Remark 4] they prove that this can be done with a probability of success
$$\prod_{h=1}^{n+1}\left(1 - \frac{D^{h-1}}{|\Gamma|}\right).$$
- In Step 2d we choose $\alpha \in \Gamma^n$ randomly, and we require Assumption A2 to hold. Since $\deg_\mathrm{x}(\hat{g}_S) \leqslant (n+1)D^{n+1}$ (due to the degree bound for a Canny's resultant, see Section 4.3), we have that the probability of success is at least
$$1 - \frac{2^n(n+1)D^{n+1}}{|\Gamma|}$$
- In Step 3 we assume that we use the randomized algorithm described in Algorithm 5 with input $\mathrm{H} = \{h_1,\ldots,h_\ell\}$. We use Lemma 7 to bound the probability of success. We have

$\deg_{\mathbf{x}}(h_i) \leq \mathcal{H} = (n+1)D^{n+1}$, $P, Q \leq \deg W \leq D^n$, $m \leq n$, so we get that the probability of success is at least

$$1 - \frac{(n+1)^4 D^{4(n+1)}}{|\Gamma|}.$$

Since these random choices are independent, the probability of the success is the product of the individual probabilities, thus we get that the probability of the overall success of Algorithm 3 is at least the product of the above four probabilities, which, as long as $D \geq 2$, can be bounded from below by

$$1 - \frac{cD^{n^2+n} + (n+1)^4 D^{c'(n+1)}}{|\Gamma|},$$

for some constants c and c', proving the claim. □

7 EXAMPLES

To keep the presentation simple, in the following examples instead of random choices of numbers we use some choices which satisfy the requirements of the algorithm.

Example 8. This simple example demonstrates how our algorithm avoids repetition of irreducible components when they need different sets of free variables. Let $n = 2$, $s = 1$, and $f_1 = x_1x_2(x_1 + x_2)$. Then

(1) All irreducible components are of dimension one, so $\mathbf{p}_1 = \{f_1\}$ and $d_0 = d_1 = 1$. Note that for a hypersurface, EquiDim from [13] always returns its defining equation.

(2)(a) Since $s = 1$, $\widetilde{f_1} = f_1$.

(b) $n - d_1 - 1 \leqslant |S| \leqslant n - d_0 - 1$ implies $S = \emptyset$. We set

$$\hat{g}_\emptyset = \mathrm{PRes}_\emptyset(f_1) = f_1.$$

(c) We define $\widehat{\nabla}_{S_1} = \widehat{\nabla}_{S_2} = \{\hat{g}_\emptyset\} = \{f_1\}$.

(d) We choose $\boldsymbol{\alpha} = (1, 1)$. Then

$$\nabla_{S_1} := \{f_1\}, \ \ \nabla_{S_2} := \{f_1|_{x_1=1}\} = \{x_2(x_2+1)\}.$$

(3) The output is a union of
- TriangularZeroDim($\{1\}, \{f_1\} \cup \{f_1\}$). Since f_1 alone is already a triangular set over $\mathbb{C}(\mathbf{x}_{\overline{\{1\}}}) = \mathbb{C}(x_2)$, we only have to make its coefficient coprime by division by x_2. Thus, the output is $\{x_1(x_1 + x_2)\}$.
- TriangularZeroDim($\{2\}, \{x_2(x_2+1)\} \cup \{f_1\}$). This is equal to the gcd of $x_2(x_2+1)$ and f_1 as univariate polynomials in x_2, that is x_2.

So, the output is $\{x_1(x_1 + x_2)\}, \{x_2\}$.

Example 9. Here, the algebraic set is the projective twisted cubic space curve (interpreted as the cone over it in $\mathbb{C}^4$). Since this curve is not a complete intersection, leading coefficients of its triangular set vanish on an extraneous projective curve, independently of the coordinate system. The intersection of this extraneous curve with the original twisted cubic will create embedded components that Triangularize in Maple does not factor out. Here we show how our algorithm handles this example. Let $n = 4$, $s = 3$, and

$$(f_1, f_2, f_3) = (x_1x_3 - x_2^2,\ x_2^2 + x_2x_4 - x_3^2,\ x_1(x_2 + x_4) - x_2x_3).$$

Then

(1) The system $f_1 = f_2 = f_3 = 0$ defines an irreducible two-dimensional variety, so $d_0 = d_1 = 2$. The output of [13] is a set of at most 5 polynomials defining this irreducible variety, so we can assume that $\mathbf{p}_2 = \{f_1, f_2, f_3\}$.

(2)(a) One can check that the choice $\widetilde{f_1} = f_1$ and $\widetilde{f_2} = f_2$ satisfies A1.

(b) Since $n - d_0 - 1 = n - d_1 - 1 = 3$, we compute four Canny's resultants, which turn out to be usual resultants in this case

$$\hat{g}_{\{1\}} = x_2^2 + x_2x_4 - x_3^2,$$
$$\hat{g}_{\{2\}} = x_3(x_1x_4^2 - x_1^2x_3 + 2x_1x_3^2 - x_3^3),$$
$$\hat{g}_{\{3\}} = x_2(x_1^2x_4 + x_1^2x_2 - x_2^3),$$
$$\hat{g}_{\{4\}} = x_1x_3 - x_2^2.$$

(c) Using $\hat{g}_{\{1\}}, \ldots, \hat{g}_{\{4\}}$, we can define $\widehat{\nabla}_S$ for every two-element subset $S \subset \{1,2,3,4\}$. In what follows, we will discuss only $S_1 = \{1,2\}$ and $S_2 = \{1,4\}$. Other subsets will yield to the results similar to S_2.

(d) We can set $\boldsymbol{\alpha} = (1,1,1,1)$. Then $g_{S_1,1} = \hat{g}_{\{2\}}$, $g_{S_1,2} = \hat{g}_1$, so $\nabla_{S_1} = \{\hat{g}_{\{2\}}, \hat{g}_{\{1\}}\}$. For S_2 we have $g_{S_2,1} = \hat{g}_{\{4\}}$ and

$$g_{S_2,2} = (x_2^2 + x_2x_4 - x_3^2)|_{x_2=1, x_3=1} = x_4.$$

(3) TrianguarizeZeroDim($S_1, \nabla_{S_1} \cup \{f_1, f_2, f_3\}$) will return a single triangular set

$$\{x_3x_1^2 + x_2x_4 - x_3^2, x_2^2 + x_2x_4 - x_3^2\}.$$

One can see that TrianguarizeZeroDim($S_2, \nabla_{S_2} \cup \{f_1, f_2, f_3\}$) is empty, because

$$f_2 - x_2 g_{S_2,2} = x_2^2 - x_3^2 \in \mathbb{C}[\mathbf{x}_{\overline{S_2}}].$$

Analogously, all other calls of TriangularizeZeroDim will return empty sets.

Although the ideal generated by f_1, f_2, f_3 in this example is prime, Triangularize function for RegularChains library (Maple 2016) returns two additional triangular sets, namely $\{x_1, x_2, x_3\}$ and $\{x_2, x_3, x_4\}$.

Example 10. Our last example demonstrates how Algorithm 3 handles mixed dimensional algebraic sets with embedded components. Let $n = 2$, $s = 2$, and

$$(f_1, f_2) = \left(x_2(x_1 + x_2)(x_1^2 - 2), x_2(x_1 + x_2)(x_2^2 - 2)\right).$$

Then

(1) The system $f_1 = f_2 = 0$ defines a union of two lines and two points, so $d_0 = 0$, $d_1 = 1$, and we assume that [13] returns

$$\mathbf{p}_0 = \{(x_1 - 2x_2)^2 - 2, (x_1 + x_2)^2 - 8, (x_1 + 2x_2)^2 - 18\},$$
$$\mathbf{p}_1 = \{x_2(x_1 + x_2)\}.$$

(2)(a) The choice $\widetilde{f_1} = f_1$ and $\widetilde{f_2} = f_2$ satisfies A1.

(b) We compute

$$\hat{g}_\emptyset = \mathrm{PRes}_\emptyset(f_1) = f_1,$$
$$\hat{g}_{\{1\}} = \mathrm{PRes}_{x_1}(f_1, f_2) = x_2^2(x_2 - 1)(x_2^2 - 2)^3,$$
$$\hat{g}_{\{2\}} = \mathrm{PRes}_{x_2}(f_1, f_2) = 2(x_1 - 1)(x_1^2 + 2x_1 - 2)(x_1^2 - 2)^3,$$

where $\hat{g}_{\{1\}}$ and $\hat{g}_{\{2\}}$ are actually perturbed resultants, because f_1 and f_2 are not coprime.

(c) We set $\widehat{\nabla}_{\{1,2\}} = \{\hat{g}_{\{2\}}, \hat{g}_{\{1\}}\}$, $\widehat{\nabla}_{\{1\}} = \widehat{\nabla}_{\{2\}} = \{\hat{g}_\emptyset\}$.

(d) We chose $\alpha = (1, 1)$. Then $\nabla_{\{1\}} = \widehat{\nabla}_{\{1\}}$,

$$\nabla_{\{2\}} = \{f_1|_{x_1=1}\} = \{-x_2(x_2+1)\},$$

and $\nabla_{\{1,2\}}$ is obtained from $\widehat{\nabla}_{\{1,2\}}$ by taking squarefree parts

$$\nabla_{\{1,2\}} = \{2(x_1-1)(x_1^2+2x_1-2)(x_1^2-2), x_2(x_2-1)(x_2^2-2)\}.$$

(3) The output is a union of

- TriangularZeroDim($\{1,2\}, \nabla_{\{1,2\}} \cup \mathbf{p}_0$). The output is $\{x_1 - x_2, x_2^2 - 2\}$.
- TriangularZeroDim($\{1\}, \nabla_{\{1\}} \cup \mathbf{p}_1$). Since $\nabla_{\{1\}} \cup \mathbf{p}_1$ consists of $x_2(x_1+x_2)(x_1^2-2)$ and $x_2(x_1+x_2)$, the ideal is defined by a single polynomial $x_2(x_1+x_2)$, which is already a triangular set itself. Dividing it by x_2, we make all its coefficients coprime as elements of $\mathbb{C}[x_2]$, so the output will be $\{x_1+x_2\}$.
- TriangularZeroDim($\{2\}, \nabla_{\{2\}} \cup \mathbf{p}_1$). Since $\nabla_{\{2\}} \cup \mathbf{p}_1$ consists of $-x_2(x_2+1)$ and $x_2(x_1+x_2)$, the result will consist of the gcd of these two polynomials as polynomials in x_2, that is x_2 itself. Hence, the output is $\{x_2\}$.

Thus, we obtain three triangular sets

$$\{x_1 - x_2, x_2^2 - 2\}, \{x_1 + x_2\}, \{x_2\}.$$

The output of Triangularize function from RegularChains library (Maple 2016) consists of $\{x_1^2-2, x_2^2-2\}, \{x_1+x_2\}, \{x_2\}$, so it contains embedded components.

8 CONCLUDING REMARKS

In a longer version of this paper we plan to further extend the results of this paper as follows:

- Consider a modification of our algorithms that outputs squarefree regular chains that have degrees essentially bounded by deg W. These triangular sets were studied for example in [7], they are multiples of the ones our algorithm outputs, and have leading coefficients that depend on non-parametric variables.
- Modify the algorithm so that all intermediate degrees are also bounded by intrinsic geometric data of the input.
- Consider algebraic sets defined by polynomials over $\mathbb{Q}$ and bound the height of the coefficients of the polynomials in the triangular sets. Such bit-size estimates were given for a single triangular set in the positive dimensional case in [9].
- Generalize Algorithm 3 to the case when the input system contains inequations.

ACKNOWLEDGEMENTS

Gleb Pogudin was supported by NSF grants CCF-0952591, CCF-1563942, DMS-1413859, by PSC-CUNY grant #60098-00 48, by Queens College Research Enhancement, and by the Austrian Science Fund FWF grant Y464-N18. The authors would like to thank the Department of Mathematics at North Carolina State University and the Symbolic Computation Group for their hospitality during the visit of Gleb Pogudin in 2017, allowing to make progress on this research. The authors are grateful to the referees for the comments which helped to improve the paper.

REFERENCES

[1] P. Alvandi. *Computing Limit Points of Quasi-components of Regular Chains and its Applications.* PhD thesis, The University of Western Ontario, 2017. Electronic Thesis and Dissertation Repository. 4565.

[2] E. Amzallag, G. Pogudin, M. Sun, and N. Thieu Vo. Complexity of triangular representations of algebraic sets. arxiv.org/abs/1609.09824, 2016.

[3] J. Canny. Generalised characteristic polynomials. *Journal of Symbolic Computation*, 9(3):241 – 250, 1990. URL https://doi.org/10.1016/S0747-7171(08)80012-0.

[4] C. Chen. *Solving Polynomial Systems via Triangular Decomposition.* PhD thesis, The University of Western Ontario, 2011.

[5] C. Chen and M. Moreno Maza. Algorithms for computing triangular decomposition of polynomial systems. *J. Symbolic Comput.*, 47(6):610–642, 2012. ISSN 0747-7171. URL https://doi.org/10.1016/j.jsc.2011.12.023.

[6] C. Chen, P. Alvandi, and M. Moreno Maza. Computing the limit points of the quasi-component of a regular chain in dimension one. In *Proceedings of Computer Algebra in Scientific Computing - 15th International Workshop, CASC 2013*, Lecture Notes in Computer Science, volume 8136, pages 30–45. Springer-Verlag, 2013.

[7] X. Dahan and E. Schost. Sharp estimates for triangular sets. In *ISSAC 2004*, pages 103–110. 2004. URL http://dx.doi.org/10.1145/1005285.1005302.

[8] X. Dahan, M. Moreno Maza, E. Schost, W. Wu, and Y. Xie. Lifting techniques for triangular decompositions. In *ISSAC'05*, pages 108–115. ACM, New York, 2005.

[9] X. Dahan, A. Kadri, and E. Schost. Bit-size estimates for triangular sets in positive dimension. *J. Complexity*, 28(1):109–135, 2012. ISSN 0885-064X.

[10] G. Gallo and B. Mishra. Wu-Ritt characteristic sets and their complexity. In *Discrete and computational geometry (New Brunswick, NJ, 1989/1990)*, volume 6 of *DIMACS Ser. Discrete Math. Theoret. Comput. Sci.*, pages 111–136. Amer. Math. Soc., Providence, RI, 1991.

[11] I. M. Gelfand, M. M. Kapranov, and A. V. Zeleveinsky. *Discriminants, Resultants and Multidimensional Determinants.* Brikhäuser Boston, 1994.

[12] E. Hubert. Notes on triangular sets and triangulation-decomposition algorithms I: Polynomial systems. In *Proceedings of the 2nd International Conference on Symbolic and Numerical Scientific Computation*, SNSC'01, pages 1–39, Berlin, Heidelberg, 2003. Springer-Verlag.

[13] G. Jeronimo and J. Sabia. Effective equidimensional decomposition of affine varieties. *Journal of Pure and Applied Algebra*, 169(2):229 – 248, 2002. URL https://doi.org/10.1016/S0022-4049(01)00083-4.

[14] M. Kalkbrener. A generalized Euclidean algorithm for computing triangular representations of algebraic varieties. *J. Symbolic Comput.*, 15(2):143–167, 1993. ISSN 0747-7171. URL https://doi.org/10.1006/jsco.1993.1011.

[15] M. Kalkbrener. Prime decompositions of radicals in polynomial rings. *J. Symbolic Comput.*, 18(4):365–372, 1994. ISSN 0747-7171. URL https://doi.org/10.1006/jsco.1994.1052.

[16] E. R. Kolchin. *Differential algebra and algebraic groups.* Academic Press, New York-London, 1973. Pure and Applied Mathematics, Vol. 54.

[17] D. Lazard. A new method for solving algebraic systems of positive dimension. *Discrete Appl. Math.*, 33(1-3):147–160, 1991. ISSN 0166-218X. URL https://doi.org/10.1016/0166-218X(91)90113-B. Applied algebra, algebraic algorithms, and error-correcting codes (Toulouse, 1989).

[18] G. Lecerf. Computing the equidimensional decomposition of an algebraic closed set by means of lifting fibers. *J. Complexity*, 19(4):564–596, 2003. ISSN 0885-064X.

[19] M. Moreno Maza. On triangular decompositions of algebraic varieties. Presented at the MEGA-2000 conference, Bath, UK, June 2000. URL www.csd.uwo.ca/~moreno/Publications/M3-MEGA-2005.pdf.

[20] J. F. Ritt. *Differential algebra.* Dover Publications, Inc., New York, 1966.

[21] É. Schost. Complexity results for triangular sets. *Journal of Symbolic Computation*, 36(3):555 – 594, 2003. URL https://doi.org/10.1016/S0747-7171(03)00095-6.

[22] É. Schost. Computing parametric geometric resolutions. *Applicable Algebra in Engineering, Communication and Computing*, 13(5):349–393, 2003. URL https://doi.org/10.1007/s00200-002-0109-x.

[23] J. T. Schwartz. Fast probabilistic algorithms for verification of polynomial identities. *J. ACM*, 27(4):701–717, Oct. 1980. ISSN 0004-5411. URL http://doi.acm.org/10.1145/322217.322225.

[24] A. Szanto. *Computation with polynomial systems.* PhD thesis, Cornell University, 1999.

[25] D. M. Wang. Irreducible decomposition of algebraic varieties via characteristic sets and Gröbner bases. *Comput. Aided Geom. Design*, 9(6):471–484, 1992. ISSN 0167-8396. URL https://doi.org/10.1016/0167-8396(92)90045-Q.

[26] D. M. Wang. An elimination method for polynomial systems. *J. Symbolic Comput.*, 16(2):83–114, 1993. ISSN 0747-7171. URL https://doi.org/10.1006/jsco.1993.1035.

[27] W. J. Wu. Basic principles of mechanical theorem proving in elementary geometries. *J. Systems Sci. Math. Sci.*, 4(3):207–235, 1984. ISSN 1000-0577.

[28] R. Zippel. Probabilistic algorithms for sparse polynomials. In *Proceedings of the International Symposium on Symbolic and Algebraic Computation*, EUROSAM '79, pages 216–226, London, UK, UK, 1979. Springer-Verlag. ISBN 3-540-09519-5. URL http://dl.acm.org/citation.cfm?id=646670.698972.

Volume of Alcoved Polyhedra and Mahler Conjecture

María J. de la Puente
Universidad Complutense
Facultad de Mátemáticas
Madrid, Spain
mpuente@ucm.es

Pedro L. Clavería
Universidad de Zaragoza
Zaragoza, Spain
plcv@unizar.es

ABSTRACT

The facet equations of a 3–dimensional alcoved polyhedron $\mathcal{P}$ are only of two types ($x_i = cnst$ and $x_i - x_j = cnst$) and the f–vector of $\mathcal{P}$ is bounded above by $(20, 30, 12)$. In general, $\mathcal{P}$ is a dodecahedron with 20 vertices and 30 edges. We represent an alcoved polyhedron by a real square matrix A of order 4 and we compute the exact volume of $\mathcal{P}$: it is a polynomial expression in the a_{ij}, homogeneous of degree 3 with rational coefficients. Then we compute the volume of the polar $\mathcal{P}^\circ$, when $\mathcal{P}$ is centrally symmetric. Last, we show that Mahler conjecture holds in this case: the product of the volumes of $\mathcal{P}$ and $\mathcal{P}^\circ$ is no less that $4^3/3!$, with equality only for boxes. Our proof reduces to computing a certificate of non–negativeness of a certain polynomial (in 3 variables, of degree 6, non homogeneous) on a certain simplex.

CCS CONCEPTS

• **Computing methodologies → Representation of mathematical objects;**

KEYWORDS

volume, alcoved polyhedron, tropical semiring, idempotent semiring, dioid, normal matrix, idempotent matrix, symmetric matrix, perturbation, Mahler conjecture, polynomial, certificate of non–negativeness.

ACM Reference Format:
María J. de la Puente and Pedro L. Clavería. 2018. Volume of Alcoved Polyhedra and Mahler Conjecture. In *ISSAC '18: 2018 ACM International Symposium on Symbolic and Algebraic Computation, July 16–19, 2018, New York, NY, USA.* ACM, New York, NY, USA, 8 pages. https://doi.org/10.1145/3208976.3208990

1 INTRODUCTION

The theory of polytopes is a meeting point for optimization, convex geometry, lattice geometry and geometry of numbers. There are deep results, computationally difficult problems and open conjectures concerning polytopes, even in three–dimensional space, as the collective book [22] beautifully shows. The computation of the volume is ♯-*P*, as M.E. Dyer and A.M. Frieze (together with Valiant's result on permanents) and, independently, L. Khachiyan showed in the 1980's. The difficulty is present, no matter whether the description is by given the list of vertices or the facet equations. The Mahler conjecture (an easy–to–state question on the product of the volumes of a symmetric polytope and its polar) remains open since 1938, although progress has been reported [11, 12, 16, 24].

Volumes can be used to compute intersection numbers in algebraic geometry. More general than volume is the concept of mixed volume, introduced by H. Minkowski. In the survey paper [8], the authors ask for families of polytopes for which volume and mixed volumes can be computed. We propose alcoved polytopes (as described in this paper) for that role, as well as more general alcoved polytopes (as in [18, 19, 25]). Volumes of matroid polytopes are introduced in [2]. A lack of concrete non–trivial worked examples in these papers is filled in by the present paper.

A frequent problem in *real algebraic geometry* is checking whether a given polynomial is positive on a given semi–algebraic set. This and related questions were studied by D. Hilbert and H. Minkowski. The foundational statement is *Hilbert 17th problem.* An algebraic method to give an answer to such queries is to show a *certificate*, i.e., to express the given polynomial with a formula for which the positiveness is self–evident.

In classical linear algebra one works with matrices. A linear map between finite–dimensional spaces is represented by a matrix, after having fixed bases. Here we do something similar: an alcoved polyhedra is represented by a matrix. Then we develop a *dictionary*: properties of alcoved polyhedra are converted into properties of matrices, and viceversa. Our matrix–based technique has a big potential and could be extended to higher dimensions and to alcoved based on different root systems.

Our main result is the exact volume formula in theorem 4.1. As application, we show that *Mahler conjecture* for alcoved centrally symmetric polyhedra holds true. In this case, the conjecture is equivalent to the following assertion: the polynomial MC displayed in p. 7 is non–negative on a certain simplex $\mathcal{S} \subsetneq \mathbb{R}^3$. We show that this is true, by finding a certificate of non–negativeness of MC over $\mathcal{S}$, i.e., we express MC as a linear combination, with non–negative coefficients, of products of polynomials w_1, w_2, w_3, w_4 such that w_j is non–negative on $\mathcal{S}$, all j. The w_j provide equations for the facets of $\mathcal{S}$.

We work with *normal* matrices operated tropically. We further need to impose *tropical idempotency* on matrices in order to achieve convexity (alcoved polytopes, in our setting). Without idempotency, we do not get one convex set, but a complex of such sets. Among NI matrices, we concentrate on two matrix families: visualized and symmetric. *Visualized matrices* are easy to work with because in them we clearly distinguish *two parts*: a *box matrix* and a *perturbation matrix.* Accordingly, the alcoved polyhedron is simply a *perturbed box*, where we are able to read off the edge–lengths.

ISSAC '18, July 16–19, 2018, New York, NY, USA

ACM ISBN 978-1-4503-5550-6/18/07...$15.00
https://doi.org/10.1145/3208976.3208990

Symmetric matrices are useful because, as our dictionary shows, an alcoved polyhedron is symmetric with respect to the origin if and only if its defining matrix is symmetric.

The oldest known volume formula is Egyptian, found in Problem 14 in the Moscow Mathematical Papyrus (ca. 1850 BC). It expresses the volume of a frustum of a square pyramid. Later, Piero della Francesca (s. XVI) and Carnot (s. XVIII) found polynomial expressions with rational coefficients for the square of the volume of a tetrahedron in terms of the edge–lengths. Both expressions can be rewritten, obtaining the Cayley–Menger determinantal formula.

Our volume formula has the same flavor, for two reasons. First, it is a polynomial formula, with rational coeffcients. Second, any alcoved polyhedron *is a tetrahedron*, in the sense that it is spanned (tropically) by four points.

Tropical mathematics (also called Idempotent mathematics or Max–plus mathematics) is the setting of this paper. There are several books and paper collections on the subject (with grown branches in analysis, geometry, algebra, etc.) For algebra, we refer the reader to [1, 4, 20]. Normal matrices can be traced back to a paper of M. Yoeli in the 1960's (under a different name). Lately, they have been used by Butcovič [4] and thoroughly studied in the thesis [21] (under a different name). Idempotent tropical matrices have been used in [14]. Visualized tropical matrices have been used in [23].

Volumes for non–square classical (i.e., non–tropical) matrices have been introduced in [3].

2 MATRICES WITH TROPICAL OPERATIONS

For $n \in \mathbb{N}$, let $[n]$ denote the set $\{1,2,\ldots,n\}$. Consider the *tropical semiring* (also called *max–plus semiring*) $(\overline{\mathbb{R}},\oplus,\odot)$, where $\overline{\mathbb{R}} := \mathbb{R} \cup \{-\infty\}$ is the extended real numbers and $a \oplus b = \max\{a,b\}$ and $a \odot b = a + b$, $a,b \in \overline{\mathbb{R}}$. The neutral element with respect to *tropical addition* $\oplus$ is $-\infty$, and the neutral element with respect to *tropical multiplication* $\odot$ is 0. Addition is idempotent, because $a \oplus a = \max\{a,a\} = a$, so that $(\overline{\mathbb{R}},\oplus,\odot)$ is an *idempotent semiring* or *dioid.* Let M_n be the set of order n square matrices over $\overline{\mathbb{R}}$. The tropical operations are extended to matrices in the standard way. $(M_n,\oplus,\odot)$ is a semiring. We also add matrices classically, but we *never* multiply them classically. Therefore, we omit the symbol $\odot$ between matrices (for simplicity). For example:

$$A = \begin{bmatrix} 1 & 2 \\ 3 & 4 \end{bmatrix}, \quad B = \begin{bmatrix} -1 & 0 \\ -\infty & 5 \end{bmatrix}, \quad A + B = \begin{bmatrix} 0 & 2 \\ -\infty & 9 \end{bmatrix}$$

$$A \oplus B = \begin{bmatrix} 1 & 2 \\ 3 & 5 \end{bmatrix}, AB = \begin{bmatrix} \max\{0,-\infty\} & \max\{1,7\} \\ \max\{2,-\infty\} & \max\{3,9\} \end{bmatrix} = \begin{bmatrix} 0 & 7 \\ 2 & 9 \end{bmatrix}.$$

Definition 2.1. A matrix $A = [a_{ij}] \in M_n$ is *normal* if $a_{ii} = 0$ and $a_{ij} \leq 0$, all $i,j \in [n]$.

Why normal? The matrix $[a_{ij}] \in M_n$ with $a_{ii} = 0$ and $a_{ij} = -\infty$, for $i \neq j$ is denoted I_n. The all–zero matrix is denoted Z_n.

A normal matrix A satisfies $AZ_n = Z_n = Z_nA$ (but a general matrix does not). A matrix A is normal if and only if $I_n \leq A \leq Z_n$ if and only if $I_n \leq A \leq A^2 \leq A^3 \leq \cdots \leq Z_n$ (since matrix tropical multiplication is monotonic).

In the set M_n^N of normal matrices, notice that I_n is the identity for both tropical addition and multiplication in M_n^N (but not in M_n).

Restricting to work with normal matrices is advantageous and no serious limitation. Indeed, every matrix can be normalized (in a non unique way, using the *Hungarian algorithm* [17]). Normalization consists of a translation and a rearrangement of columns. This is explained below.

Definition 2.2. In M_n,

(1) a matrix $D = [d_{ij}] \in M_n$ is *diagonal* if d_{ii} is real and $d_{ij} = -\infty$, if $i \neq j$. The *inverse* of the diagonal matrix D, denoted D^{-1}, is $[a_{ij}]$ such that $a_{ii} = -d_{ii}$ and $a_{ij} = -\infty$, if $i \neq j$.
(2) For a permutation $\sigma \in S_n$, the permutation matrix $P^\sigma = [a_{ij}]$ is defined by $a_{i\sigma(i)} = 0$, $a_{ij} = -\infty$, otherwise.

Definition 2.3. For a matrix $A \in M_n$, we define

(1) $\mathrm{row}(A,j)$ to be the j–th row of A, and $\mathrm{col}(A,j)$ to be the j–th column of A, all $j \in [n]$,
(2) if $\mathrm{row}(A,n)$ is real, then the *visualization* of A is the matrix $A_0 := AD^{-1}$, where D is the diagonal $D = \mathrm{diag}(\mathrm{row}(A,n))$. Obviously, $\mathrm{row}(A_0,n)$ is all–zero.

Visualization has a meaning. Think of the columns of a matrix $A \in M_n$ as n points in n–dimensional space. Consider n parallel lines passing through these points with directional vector $(1,\ldots,1)$. Intersect these n lines with the hyperplane $\{x_n = 0\}$ and write the coordinates of the resulting points as the columns of a matrix. This matrix is A_0. When the matrix is visualized, we have $A = A_0$.

What do we want to see? The set $\mathrm{span}\,A$ gathers of all tropical linear combinations of columns of $A \in M_n$

$$\mathrm{span}\,A := \{\lambda_1 \,\mathrm{col}(A,1) \oplus \cdots \oplus \lambda_n \,\mathrm{col}(A,n) : \lambda_1,\ldots,\lambda_n \in \overline{\mathbb{R}}\}. \quad (1)$$

Clearly $\mathrm{span}\,A = \mathrm{span}\,A_0$ (because columns of A and A_0 are proportional).

Normality has a geometric meaning: A is normal if and only if

$$\mathrm{col}(A_0,j) \in R_j, \text{ all } j \in [n]. \quad (2)$$

where the regions

$$R_j := \{x \in \mathbb{R}^{n-1} : 0 \leq x_j \text{ and } x_k \leq x_j,\ k \in [n-1]\}, \quad j \in [n-1],$$

$$R_n := \{x \in \mathbb{R}^{n-1} : x_k \leq 0,\ k \in [n-1]\}.$$

provide a closed covering of $\mathbb{R}^{n-1} = \cup_{j=1}^n R_j$ and $\mathbb{R}^{n-1}$ is identified with $\{x_n = 0\}$ inside $\mathbb{R}^n$ (see figure 1).

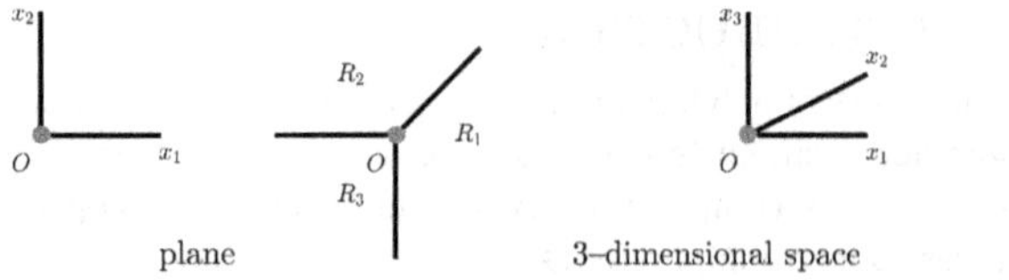

Figure 1: Coordinate axes in the plane (left), closed regions R_1, R_2, R_3 in the plane (center) and coordinate axes in 3–dimensional space (right).

Definition 2.4. A matrix $A \in M_n$ is *visualized* if $A = A_0$.

Definition 2.5. Given matrices $A, D, P^\sigma \in M_n$ with D diagonal and P^σ permutation matrix,

(1) the *translate* of A by D is the matrix DA,
(2) the *conjugate* of A by D is the matrix ${}^DA := DAD^{-1}$,

(3) the matrix AP^{σ} is the result of relabeling the columns of A according to the permutation σ.

In the paragraph prior to definition 2.2, we said that every matrix $M \in M_n$ can be normalized. This means that a there exists a translate DM of M, and a relabeling of columns DMP of DM, such that $A = DMP$ satisfies (2).

Definition 2.6. A matrix $A = [a_{ij}] \in M_n$ is *idempotent* if $A^2 = A$.

Thus, a matrix A is normal idempotent if and only if $I_n \leq A^2 \leq A \leq Z_n$ if and only if

$$a_{ii} = 0 \text{ and } a_{ij} + a_{jk} \leq a_{ik} \leq 0, \text{ all } i,j,k \in [n]. \quad (3)$$

Let M_n^{NI} the set of normal idempotent matrices of order n.

Corollary 2.7. *Any conjugate* ${}^{D}A$ *is normal (resp. idempotent), whenever* A *is.*

A matrix is *symmetric* if $A = A^T$, where A^T is the classical *transposed* matrix. Let M_n^{SNI} the set of symmetric normal idempotent matrices and M_n^{VNI} be the set of visualized normal idempotent matrices. The only symmetric and visualized normal idempotent matrix is the zero matrix Z_n.

In the rest of paper we work with normal idempotent matrices, the reason being that they represent alcoved polyhedra.

3 ALCOVED POLYHEDRA FROM NORMAL IDEMPOTENT MATRICES

In order to study the set span $A \subset \mathbb{R}^n$ defined in (1), it is enough to study its intersection with the hyperplane $\{x_n = 0\}$ (identified with $\mathbb{R}^{n-1}$), because both sets determine each other

$$\mathcal{P}(A) := \operatorname{span} A \cap \{x_n = 0\}. \quad (4)$$

For a general matrix $A \in M_n$, the set $\mathcal{P}(A) \subset \mathbb{R}^{n-1}$ is a polytopal complex of impure dimension no bigger that $n-1$. However, if A is **normal idempotent**, then $\mathcal{P}(A)$ reduces to just one convex polytope and this polytope is **alcoved** (see [5, 6, 13, 15, 18, 19, 23, 25]). In other words, normality and idempotency prevents the existence of lower dimensional parts in $\mathcal{P}(A)$.

Definition 3.1. An **alcoved polytope** in $\mathbb{R}^{n-1}$ is a bounded polytope $\mathcal{P}$ whose facet equations are of type $x_i = cnst$, and $x_i - x_j = cnst$, $i,j \in [n-1]$. A **box** in $\mathbb{R}^{n-1}$ is a bounded polytope $\mathcal{B}$ whose facet equations are of type $x_i = cnst$, $i \in [n-1]$. A **cube** is a box of equal edge–lengths.

Clearly, the property of being alcoved is preserved by translation. The simplest alcoved polytopes are boxes. Every alcoved polytope is a perturbed box, more precisely, it is a **canted box**. The verb to cant means to bevel, to form an oblique surface upon something. We cant edges of boxes, always at an angle of $\pi/4$ radians (45 degrees). To cant an edge in a box means to create a new facet. 45 degrees is the angle determined by the intersecting planes $x_i = cnst$ and $x_i - x_j = cnst$. Note that Assume $n = 4$, so our box is in $\mathbb{R}^3$. Only six edges of a box are cantable: front top, top left, left back, back bottom, bottom right and right front. Note that the cantable edges are arranged in a *cycle*: $\ell_1, \ell_2, \ldots, \ell_6$ (see figure 2).

For each alcoved polytope $\mathcal{P} \subset \mathbb{R}^{n-1}$ we have a *preferred translation*; it is $v_{\mathcal{P}} : \mathbb{R}^{n-1} \to \mathbb{R}^{n-1}$ such that the origin O of $\mathbb{R}^{n-1}$ satisfies $O = \max v_{\mathcal{P}}(\mathcal{P})$. This is easily achieved matrix–wise, as the next lemma shows.

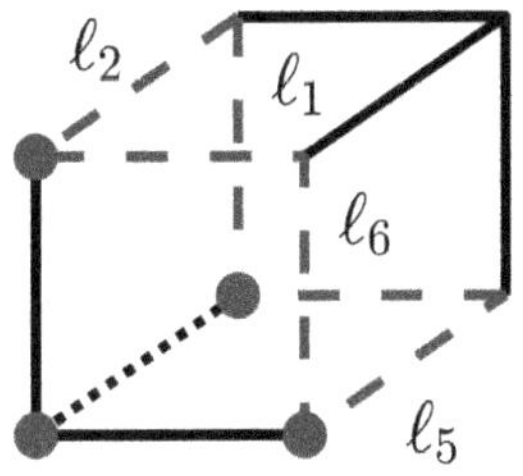

Figure 2: Cantable edges (in dashed blue lines) in a cube make a cycle: ℓ_1 is front top, ℓ_2 is top left, ℓ_3 is left back, ℓ_4 is back bottom, ℓ_5 is bottom right and ℓ_6 is right front. Generators are marked with big blue dots and labeled 1, 2, 3, 4, indicating the column in A_0 each of them is: 1 is bottom right, 2 is bottom back, 3 is top left, 4 is bottom left.

Lemma 3.2. *For* $A \in M_n^{NI}$, *the matrix* A *is visualized if and only if* $O = \max \mathcal{P}(A)$.

Proof. We know that $\mathcal{P}(A)$ is alcoved. Assume $A = A_0$ is NI. By (2) we have $\operatorname{col}(A_0, j) \in R_j \cap R_n$, all j, whence $O \in \mathcal{P}(A)$ and $\mathcal{P}(A)$ is contained in the non–positive octant R_n. Thus $O = \max \mathcal{P}(A)$. The converse is similar. □

Mahler conjecture deals with centrally symmetric bodies. For a centrally symmetric alcoved polytope $\mathcal{P} \subset \mathbb{R}^{n-1}$, a *preferred translation* is $s_{\mathcal{P}} : \mathbb{R}^{n-1} \to \mathbb{R}^{n-1}$ such that O is the center of symmetry of $s_{\mathcal{P}}(\mathcal{P})$. This is easily achieved matrix–wise, as the next lemma shows.

Lemma 3.3 (Lemma 3 in [13]). *For* $A \in M_n^{NI}$, *the matrix* A *is symmetric if and only if* $-\mathcal{P}(A) = \mathcal{P}(A)$ *(i.e.,* O *is the center of symmetry of* $\mathcal{P}(A)$*).*

Example 3.4. Given a column vector $t \in \mathbb{R}^4_{\leq 0}$ with coordinates $(t_1, t_2, t_3, 0)^T$, the following matrix (easily checked to be idempotent) is called **visualized box matrix**

$$VB(t) := \begin{bmatrix} 0 & t_1 & t_1 & t_1 \\ t_2 & 0 & t_2 & t_2 \\ t_3 & t_3 & 0 & t_3 \\ 0 & 0 & 0 & 0 \end{bmatrix} \in M_4^{VNI}. \quad (5)$$

A conjugate of $VB(t)$ is the matrix $SB(t) = {}^{D}VB(t)$, with $D = \operatorname{diag}(-t/2)$). We have $SB(t) = (tt^T)/2 \oplus I_4 = [b_{ij}]$, with $b_{ii} = 0$ and $b_{ij} = (t_i + t_j)/2$, if $i \neq j$. The matrix $SB(t)$ is called **symmetric box matrix** and we easily get

$$SB(t)_0 = \begin{bmatrix} -t_1/2 & t_1/2 & t_1/2 & t_1/2 \\ t_2/2 & -t_2/2 & t_2/2 & t_2/2 \\ t_3/2 & t_3/2 & -t_3/2 & t_3/2 \\ 0 & 0 & 0 & 0 \end{bmatrix}. \quad (6)$$

The polyhedron $\mathcal{P}(SB(t))$ is a box in $\mathbb{R}^3$, centered at O, whose edge–lengths are $|t_1|, |t_2|, |t_3|$. The polyhedron $\mathcal{P}(VB(t))$ is a translate of $\mathcal{P}(SB(t))$, satisfying $O = \max \mathcal{P}(VB(t))$. Note that $\min \mathcal{P}(VB(t))$ is the vector t.

These boxes are cubes if $t_i = t_j$, $i \neq j$.

We will work in $\mathbb{R}^3$, from now on.

Definition 3.5 (Perturbation). For a visualized normal idempotent matrix $V = [v_{ij}] \in M_4^{VNI}$, we write $B := VB(\mathrm{col}(V,4))$ (as in (5)) and $E := B - V$. The matrix E is called **perturbation matrix** of V.

By definition, B is a visualized matrix box. We say that V is the result of **perturbing** B by E. Similarly, we say that $\mathcal{P}(B)$ is the **bounding box** of $\mathcal{P}(V)$ (see figure 3).

Notice that a perturbation matrix E is normal visualized, but not idempotent, in general.

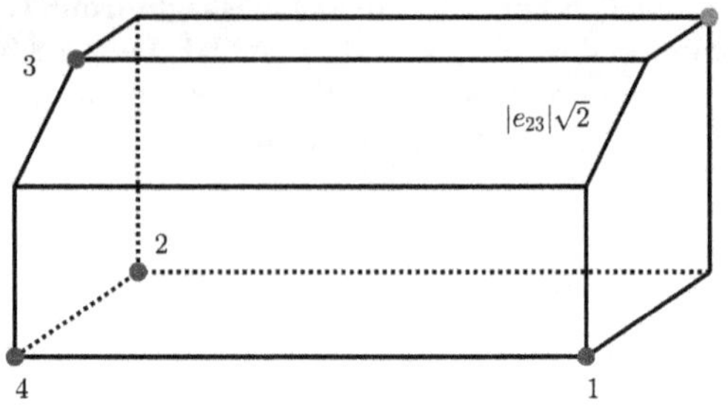

Figure 3: One cant performed on a box. The box is contained in the non-positive orthant R_3. The origin O is marked in red. Generators, i.e., columns of the defining matrix $A = A_0$ are marked in blue big dots and labeled 1,2,3,4. We have $O = \max \mathcal{P}(A)$ with $A = B - E$ and $e_{ij} = 0$ unless $(i,j) = (2,3)$. Notice the edge-length $|e_{23}|\sqrt{2}$.

Definition 3.6 (Cant tuple). For $V = B - E \in M_4^{VNI}$ as in definition 3.5, the **cant tuple** of V is $c = (c_j) \in \mathbb{R}^6_{\leq 0}$, with $c_1 := e_{23}$, $c_2 := e_{13}$, $c_3 := e_{12}$, $c_4 := e_{32}$, $c_5 := e_{31}$ and $c_6 := e_{21}$. Set $m_j := \min\{|c_j|, |c_{j+1}|\}$, $M_j := \max\{|c_j|, |c_{j+1}|\}$, $j \in [6]$ and $c_7 = c_1$. Also set $\ell_i := |v_{i4}|$, $i \in [3]$.

In summary, every alcoved polytope is a perturbed box. A box is rather degenerate (i.e., non-maximal) alcoved polyhedron.

4 VOLUME OF AN ALCOVED POLYHEDRON

In this section we show that the volume of an alcoved convex polyhedron $\mathcal{P}$ is a *cubic homogeneous polynomial in the entries v_{ij} of a defining matrix V for $\mathcal{P}$, with rational coefficients.* Multiplying by 3! we get integral coefficients.

The volume is a *valuation*, i.e., $\mathrm{vol}(\mathcal{P}_1) + \mathrm{vol}(\mathcal{P}_2) = \mathrm{vol}(\mathcal{P}_1 \cup \mathcal{P}_1) + \mathrm{vol}(\mathcal{P}_1 \cap \mathcal{P}_2)$. Further, the volume of $\mathcal{P}$ is preserved under translation, so we can assume that a defining matrix for $\mathcal{P}$ is VNI.

Theorem 4.1. *For $V = [v_{ij}] \in M_4^{VNI}$, take c_j, m_j, M_j, ℓ_j as in definition 3.6. Then the volume of the alcoved polytope $\mathcal{P}(V)$ is*

$$\mathrm{vol}\,\mathcal{P}(V) = \ell_1\ell_2\ell_3 + \sum_{j=1}^{6} \frac{m_j^2 M_j}{2} - \frac{m_j^3}{6} - \frac{c_j^2 \ell_j}{2}. \quad (7)$$

Proof. Write $V = B - E$. The volume of the bounding box is $\ell_1\ell_2\ell_3$. From this box we remove six right prisms $\mathcal{P}_j$, $j \in [6]$. The base of prism $\mathcal{P}_j$ is a right isosceles triangle legged $|c_j|$. The prisms are organized in a cycle. The intersection of two consecutive prisms has been removed twice, so it must be added once. We get

$$\mathrm{vol}\,\mathcal{P}(V) = \mathrm{vol}\,\mathcal{P}(B) - \sum_{j=1}^{6} \mathrm{vol}\,\mathcal{P}_j + \sum_{j \in [6] \mod 6} \mathrm{vol}(\mathcal{P}_j \cap \mathcal{P}_{j+1}). \quad (8)$$

Clearly we have $\mathrm{vol}\,\mathcal{P}_j = \frac{c_j^2 \ell_j}{2}$, where $\ell_i = \ell_{i-3}$, $i = 4,5,6$. In addition, the intersection $\mathcal{P}_j \cap \mathcal{P}_{j+1}$ is a wedge, (i.e., a prism $\mathcal{P}_j$ from which a tetrahedron $\mathcal{T}$ has been removed) (see figures 4 and 5). Thus $\mathrm{vol}(\mathcal{P}_j \cap \mathcal{P}_{j+1}) = \mathrm{vol}\,\mathcal{P}_j - \mathrm{vol}\,\mathcal{T} = \frac{m_j^2 M_j}{2} - \frac{m_j^3}{6}$. □

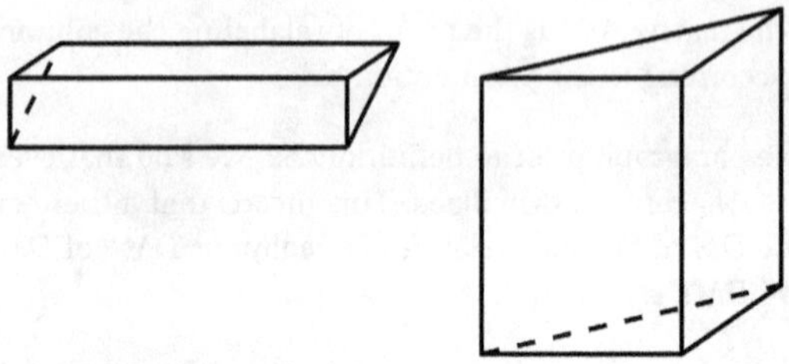

Figure 4: Two prisms $\mathcal{P}_1$ (left) and $\mathcal{P}_6$ (right) to be intersected.

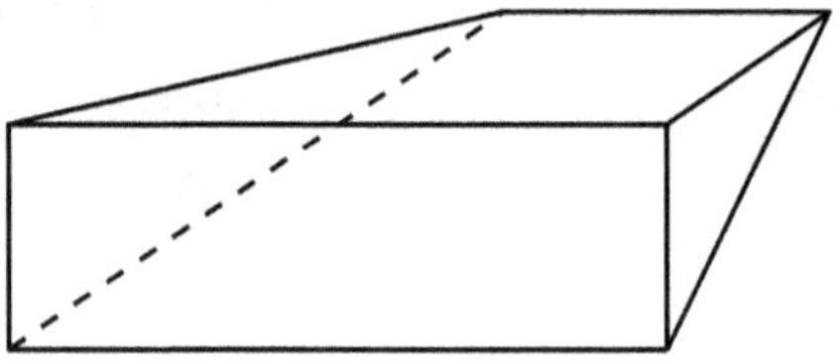

Figure 5: The wedge $\mathcal{P}_6 \cap \mathcal{P}_1$.

After a symmetry of $\mathbb{R}^3$ (i.e., a map preserving distances and angles), each prism $\mathcal{P}_j$ is an alcoved polyhedron. The same holds for the tetrahedron $\mathcal{T}$ appearing in the former proof. Tetrahedra as such have been studied by M. Fiedler, and called *Schläfli simplex* by this author. $\mathcal{T}$ is a right simplex whose tree of legs is a path (see [7]).

Example 4.2. We want to compute the volume of the polyhedron $\mathcal{P}$ defined by the inequalities $-7 \leq x_1 \leq 1$, $-6 \leq x_2 \leq 1$, $-5 \leq x_3 \leq -3$, $-6 \leq x_1 - x_2 \leq 1$, $-8 \leq x_2 - x_3 \leq 3$, $-1 \leq x_3 - x_1 \leq 8$. A defining matrix is $A = \begin{bmatrix} 0 & -6 & -8 & -7 \\ -1 & 0 & -8 & -6 \\ -1 & -3 & 0 & -5 \\ -1 & -2 & -3 & 0 \end{bmatrix}$, which is normal and idempotent. The conjugate matrix of A by $D = \mathrm{diag}(\mathrm{row}(A,4))$ is $V = V_0 = \begin{bmatrix} 0 & -5 & -6 & -8 \\ -2 & 0 & -7 & -8 \\ -3 & -4 & 0 & -8 \\ 0 & 0 & 0 & 0 \end{bmatrix}$ and $\mathcal{P}(V)$ is a translate of $\mathcal{P}$. To V we apply theorem 4.1: we let $V = B - E$ with perturbation matrix $E = \begin{bmatrix} 0 & -3 & -2 & 0 \\ -6 & 0 & -1 & 0 \\ -5 & -4 & 0 & 0 \\ 0 & 0 & 0 & 0 \end{bmatrix}$ and cubic box of edge-length 8. The

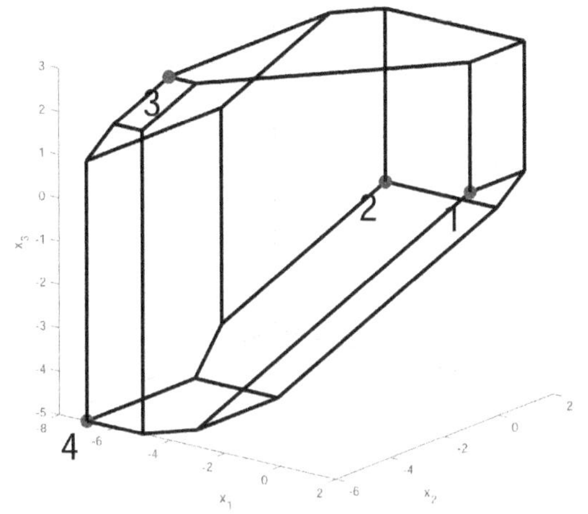

Figure 6: The polyhedron $\mathcal{P}$ in example 4.2. It is a dodecahedron. The generators, i.e., the columns of matrix A_0 are marked with big blue dots and labeled 1,2,3,4.

cant tuple is $c = (-1,-2,-3,-4,-5,-6)$, whence $m = (1,2,3,4,5,1)$, $M = (2,3,4,5,6,6)$, $\ell_j = 8$, so that

$$\sum_{j=1}^{6} \frac{m_j^2 M_j}{2} = \frac{428}{3}, \qquad \sum_{j=1}^{6} \frac{m_j^3}{6} = \frac{113}{3}, \qquad \sum_{j=1}^{6} \frac{c_j^2 \ell_j}{2} = 364$$

giving a total value $\operatorname{vol}\mathcal{P} = \operatorname{vol}\mathcal{P}(V) = 512 + \frac{428}{3} - \frac{113}{3} - 364 = \frac{760}{3}$.

Note that the former polyhedron $\mathcal{P}$ is maximal, i.e., its f-vector is $(f_0, f_1, f_2) = (20, 30, 12)$ (see [5, 6, 13, 15]) and $\mathcal{P}$ is a dodecahedron. For general n, the number f_0 of vertices is bounded above by $\binom{2n-2}{n-1}$, as proved in [6].

5 THE 2-MINORS OF A MATRIX

How do we compute the edge-lengths of the alcoved $\mathcal{P}(A)$ from the entries a_{ij} of A? The answer is easy if the matrix A is VNI: take the $b_{ij} = a_{i4}$ and the e_{ij}, for $A = B - E$, $B = [b_{ij}]$ box matrix, $E = [e_{ij}]$ perturbation matrix (see figure 3). In general, if A is only NI, the first thing we must do is computing the conjugate matrix $V = {}^{D}A$.

In this section we introduce the 2-minors of A and show that the entries of the conjugate matrix V are certain 2-minors of A. The same is true for the perturbation matrix E of V.

Definition 5.1. (1) The **difference** of matrix $\begin{bmatrix} a & b \\ c & d \end{bmatrix}$ is $a + d - b - c$.

(2) The **2-minors of a matrix** $A = [a_{ij}]$ are the differences of the order 2 submatrices of A. If $i, j, k, l \in [n]$, $i < j$ and $k < l$, we write

$$a_{ij;kl} := a_{ik} + a_{jl} - a_{il} - a_{jk}, \quad \text{and} \tag{9}$$

$$a_{ij;kl} = -a_{ji;kl} = -a_{ij;lk} = a_{ji;lk}. \tag{10}$$

If $i = j$ or $k = l$, we write $a_{ij;kl} = 0$.

Straightforward computations yield the following.

Lemma 5.2 (Entries of conjugate matrix). *Let $V = {}^{D}A = [v_{ij}] \in M_4^{VNI}$ be the conjugate of $A = [a_{ij}] \in M_4^{NI}$ by $D = \operatorname{diag}(\operatorname{row}(A, 4))$ and write $V = B - E$, with perturbation matrix $E = [e_{ij}]$. Then*

$$v_{ij} = a_{4i;ij}, \qquad e_{ij} = a_{4i;j4}. \tag{11}$$

6 SYMMETRY

In this section we show that symmetry is transferred from a matrix S to the perturbation matrix E of its conjugate ${}^{D}S$, and conversely.

Lemma 6.1 (Conjugation and symmetry).
(1) *If $S \in M_4^{SNI}$ and $V = {}^{D}S = B - E$ is the conjugate of S by $D = \operatorname{diag}(\operatorname{row}(S, 4))$, then E is symmetric.*
(2) *If $V = B - E \in M_4^{VNI}$ with E symmetric, then ${}^{D}V \in M_4^{SNI}$, with $D = \operatorname{diag}(-v_{14}/2, -v_{24}/2, -v_{34}/2, 0)$.*
(3) *In either case if, in addition, B is a visualized cube matrix, then $s_{ij} = v_{ij}$, for $i, j \in [3]$.*

Proof. From lemma 5.2, $S = S^T$ and equalities (10), we get $e_{ij} = s_{4i;j4} = s_{j4;4i} = s_{4j;i4} = e_{ji}$, whence $E = E^T$, proving item 1.

For the proof of item 2 write $S = {}^{D}V$. We have $s_{ij} = v'_{ij;j4}$ if $j \in [3]$, $s_{i4} = v'_{i4}$, where $V' = [v'_{ij}]$ is an auxiliary matrix such that $v'_{i4} = v_{i4}/2$ and $v'_{ij} = v_{ij}$, otherwise. Then $S = S^T$ follows from $E = E^T$, S idempotent follows from V idempotent and S normal follows from $S = S^T$ and V normal.

Last, if B is a visualized cube matrix, then $v_{i4} = v_{j4}$, for $i, j \in [3]$, whence $s_{ij} = v'_{ij;j4} = v_{ij} + v_{j4}/2 - v_{i4}/2 - v_{jj} = v_{ij}$, proving item 3. □

Corollary 6.2 (Volume formula for V such that $E = E^T$). *If $V = B - E \in M_4^{VNI}$ with symmetric E, then*

$$\operatorname{vol}\mathcal{P}(V) = \ell_1\ell_2\ell_3 + \sum_{j=1}^{3} m_j^2 M_j - \frac{m_j^3}{3} - c_j^2 \ell_j. \tag{12}$$

Proof. We have $c_j = c_{j+3}$, $m_j = m_{j+3}$ and $M_j = M_{j+3}$. □

7 POLARS AND MAHLER CONJECTURE

Let $r \in \mathbb{N}$ and $p_1, p_2, \dots, p_r$ be vectors in $\mathbb{R}^n$. Let $\langle , \rangle$ denote the standard inner product. If $\mathcal{P} = \{x \in \mathbb{R}^n : \langle x, p_k \rangle \le 1, \forall k \in [r]\}$, then the *polar* $\mathcal{P}^\circ$ is defined as $\operatorname{conv}(p_1, p_2, \dots, p_r)$, the *convex hull* of vectors $p_1, p_2, \dots, p_r$; see figure 7. Moreover, if O belongs to the interior of $\mathcal{P}$, then $(\mathcal{P}^\circ)^\circ = \mathcal{P}$.

Let (v_1, v_2, v_3) be the canonical basis in $\mathbb{R}^3$ and let x_1, x_2, x_3 be coordinates in $\mathbb{R}^3$.

We know that a SNI matrix S yields a centrally symmetric alcoved polyhedron $\mathcal{P}(S)$, by lemma 3.3.

Lemma 7.1 (Polar of a centrally symmetric alcoved polyhedron). *If $S = [s_{ij}] \in M_4^{SNI}$ with $s_{ij} < 0$, all $i \neq j$, then*

$$(\mathcal{P}(S))^\circ = \operatorname{conv}\left(\pm\frac{v_i}{s_{i4}}, \pm\frac{v_i - v_j}{s_{ij}} : i, j \in [3], i \neq j\right). \tag{13}$$

Proof. We know that $s_{ij} = s_{ji} \le 0$. The alcoved polyhedron $\mathcal{P}(S)$ is defined by $s_{i4} \le x_i \le -s_{i4}$ and $s_{ij} \le x_i - x_j \le -s_{ij}$, or equivalently,

$$-1 \le \frac{x_i}{s_{i4}} = \left\langle x, \frac{v_i}{s_{i4}} \right\rangle \le 1 \text{ and } -1 \le \frac{x_i - x_j}{s_{ij}} = \left\langle x, \frac{v_i - v_j}{s_{ij}} \right\rangle \le 1,$$

$i, j \in [3]$, $i \neq j$, whence the result follows. □

A normal matrix without zeros outside the diagonal (as in the former lemma) is called *strictly normal.*

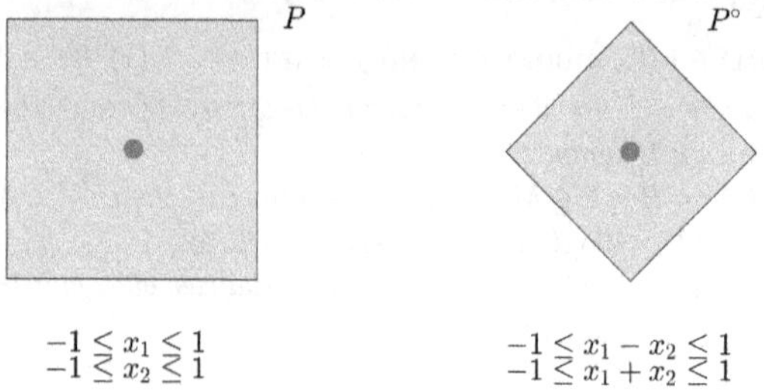

Figure 7: Unit square centered at O and its polar. The origin is marked in red

8 MAHLER CONJECTURE HOLDS FOR ALCOVED POLYHEDRA

The *Mahler volume product* of $\mathcal{P}$ is the product $\operatorname{vol}(\mathcal{P})\operatorname{vol}(\mathcal{P}^\circ)$, by definition. It is well known that Mahler volume product is invariant with respect to affine–linear transformations and homotheties. For a centrally symmetric convex body, the *Mahler conjecture* is

$$\operatorname{vol}(\mathcal{P})\operatorname{vol}(\mathcal{P}^\circ) \ge \frac{4^3}{3!} \tag{14}$$

with equality if and only if $\mathcal{P}$ is a box. It dates back to 1938. A recent survey on the conjecture is [16]; see also [11, 24] and the bibliography therein. A proof of the conjecture in 3–dimensional space is announced in [12].

In this section we show that Mahler conjecture holds true, for centrally symmetric alcoved polyhedra.

First, we compute the volume of the polar of a centrally symmetric alcoved polyhedron $\mathcal{P}$. We write a defining matrix $S \in M_4^{SNI}$ for $\mathcal{P}$ and, if $V = DS$ is a conjugate of S, then $\operatorname{vol}\mathcal{P} = \operatorname{vol}\mathcal{P}(V)$. Now corollary 6.2 applies to V, because the symmetry is transferred from S to $E = B - V$ (by item 1 in lemma 6.1).

It is no restriction to assume that $\mathcal{P}$ is maximal with respect to f–vector. Then the matrix $S \in M_4^{SNI}$ satisfies $s_{ij} \neq 0$, unless $i = j$. By affine invariance of the Mahler volume product, we may assume that the bounding box of $\mathcal{P}$ is the unit cube (of edge–length 2), centered at the origin. Further, we may assume that $-1 \le e_{12} \le e_{13} \le e_{23} \le 0$, without loss of generality. Thus, our matrices are

$$S = \begin{bmatrix} 0 & -2-e_{12} & -2-e_{13} & -1 \\ -2-e_{21} & 0 & -2-e_{23} & -1 \\ -2-e_{31} & -2-e_{31} & 0 & -1 \\ -1 & -1 & -1 & 0 \end{bmatrix} \tag{15}$$

$$V = \begin{bmatrix} 0 & -2-e_{12} & -2-e_{13} & -2 \\ -2-e_{21} & 0 & -2-e_{23} & -2 \\ -2-e_{31} & -2-e_{32} & 0 & -2 \\ 0 & 0 & 0 & 0 \end{bmatrix} \tag{16}$$

with $E = E^T$. For simplicity of notation, we write $x = e_{23}$, $y = e_{13}$ and $z = e_{12}$, with

$$-1 \le z \le y \le x \le 0. \tag{17}$$

The cant sequence is $c = (x, y, z, x, y, z)$ and $m = (|x|, |y|, |x|, |x|, |y|, |x|)$, $M = (|y|, |z|, |z|, |y|, |z|, |z|)$. Using formula (12), we get

$$\operatorname{vol}(\mathcal{P}) = 8 - x^2(y+z) - y^2 z + \frac{1}{3}\left(2x^3 + y^3\right) - 2\left(x^2 + y^2 + z^2\right). \tag{18}$$

Assume $y = x = 0$. We get

$$\operatorname{vol}(\mathcal{P}|_{y=x=0}) = 8 - 2z^2.$$

Indeed, $\mathcal{P}|_{y=x=0}$ is the unit cube Q (of volume 8) canted by the two planes of equations

$$\frac{x_2 - x_1}{2+z} = \pm 1.$$

Since the polar of Q is an octahedron, then the polar of $\mathcal{P}|_{y=x=0}$ is Q° with two additional vertices:

$$\pm\frac{v_2 - v_1}{2+z}.$$

Since both $\mathcal{P}$ and $\mathcal{P}^\circ$ are symmetric, we look at the upper half of these bodies. There, the plane $\frac{x_2 - x_1}{2+z} = 1$ yields a 4–gonal facet in $\mathcal{P}$, whence the vertex $\frac{v_2 - v_1}{2+z}$ yields 4 concurrent facets in $\mathcal{P}^\circ$. The difference between $\mathcal{P}^\circ$ and Q° is that tetrahedra with vertices 0, $\frac{v_2 - v_1}{2+z}$, v_2, $\pm v_3$ and tetrahedra with vertices 0, $\frac{v_2 - v_1}{2+z}$, $-v_1$, $\pm v_3$ have been added (to Q°) and tetrahedra with vertices 0, v_2, $-v_1$, $\pm v_3$ have been removed (from Q°). The volume of any of the added tetrahedra is $\frac{1}{6(2+z)}$ and the volume of any of the removed tetrahedra is $\frac{1}{6}$. So, when passing from Q° to $\mathcal{P}^\circ$, we have a total volume gain of

$$2\left(\frac{4}{6(2+z)} - \frac{2}{6}\right) = \frac{-2z}{3(2+z)}$$

and we get

$$\operatorname{vol}((Q)^\circ) = \frac{4}{3}, \qquad \operatorname{vol}((\mathcal{P}|_{y=x=0})^\circ) = \frac{4}{3} + \frac{-2z}{3(2+z)}.$$

Assume now $x = 0$. From (18), we have

$$\operatorname{vol}(\mathcal{P}|_{x=0}) = 8 - 2z^2 - (2+z)y^2 + \frac{y^3}{3}.$$

Indeed, $\mathcal{P}|_{x=0}$ is the unit cube Q canted by the 4 planes of equations

$$\frac{x_2 - x_1}{2+z} = \pm 1, \qquad \frac{x_3 - x_1}{2+y} = \pm 1. \tag{19}$$

We look at the upper half of $\mathcal{P}$ and $\mathcal{P}^\circ$ and note that two vertices appear in the polar $\mathcal{P}^\circ$

$$\frac{v_2 - v_1}{2+z}, \qquad \frac{v_3 - v_1}{2+y}. \tag{20}$$

The planes (19) yield a 4–gon and an adjacent 5–gon as facets in $\mathcal{P}$. Thus, the vertices (20) yield a 4–pyramid and an adjacent 5–pyramid in $\mathcal{P}^\circ$. Some computations show that

$$\operatorname{vol}((\mathcal{P}|_{x=0})^\circ) = \frac{4}{3} + g(y,z), \qquad g(y,z) := \frac{-3y - 4z - 3yz}{3(2+y)(2+z)}.$$

Note that $g(0,z) = \frac{-2z}{3(2+z)}$ agrees with the case $y = x = 0$ above.

General case: similar computations show that $\mathrm{vol}(\mathcal{P}^\circ) = \frac{4}{3} + h(x,y,z)$ with $h(x,y,z) := \frac{2/3}{(2+x)(2+y)} + \frac{2/3}{(2+y)(2+z)} + \frac{2/3}{(2+z)(2+x)} + \frac{1/3}{2+y} + \frac{2/3}{2+z} - 1$ and $h(0,y,z) = g(y,z)$. We have proved

THEOREM 8.1. *If $\mathcal{P} \subset \mathbb{R}^3$ is the centrally symmetric alcoved polyhedron given by the inequalities $-1 \le x_j \le 1$, $j \in [3]$, $-2-z \le x_1 - x_2 \le 2+z$, $-2-x \le x_2 - x_3 \le 2+x$, $-2-y \le x_3 - x_1 \le 2+y$, then*

$$\mathrm{vol}(\mathcal{P}^\circ) = \frac{1}{3} + \frac{2/3}{(2+x)(2+y)} + \frac{2/3}{(2+y)(2+z)} + \frac{2/3}{(2+z)(2+x)} + \frac{1/3}{2+y} + \frac{2/3}{2+z}. \tag{21}$$

PROOF. $\mathcal{P} = \mathcal{P}(S)$ with $S = \begin{bmatrix} 0 & -2-z & -2-y & -1 \\ -2-z & 0 & -2-x & -1 \\ -2-y & -2-x & 0 & -1 \\ -1 & -1 & -1 & 0 \end{bmatrix}$. □

Using (18) and (21), and clearing denominators, we transform *Mahler conjecture* (14) into the question of whether the below defined polynomial MC is non–negative on the simplex $\mathcal{S}$ given by $-1 \le z \le y \le x \le 0$, where $MC = \sum_{j=1}^{6} MC_j$, with MC_j homogeneous in x, y, z of degree j:

$$\begin{aligned}
MC_6 &= 2x^4yz - 3x^3y^2z - 3x^3yz^2 + xy^4z - 3xy^3z^2, \\
MC_5 &= 8x^4y + 6x^4z - 12x^3y^2 - 23x^3yz - 9x^3z^2 \\
&\quad -6x^2y^2z - 6x^2yz^2 \\
&\quad +4xy^4 - 15xy^3z - 9xy^2z^2 - 6xyz^3 + 2y^4z - 6y^3z^2, \\
MC_4 &= 24x^4 - 40x^3y - 38x^3z - 30x^2y^2 - 66x^2yz \\
&\quad -24x^2z^2 - 12xy^3 - 54xy^2z \\
&\quad -24xyz^2 - 18xz^3 + 10y^4 - 34y^3z - 24y^2z^2 - 12yz^3, \\
MC_3 &= -8x^3 - 156x^2y - 144x^2z - 72xy^2 - 72xyz \\
&\quad -72xz^2 - 28y^3 - 144y^2z - 60yz^2 - 48z^3, \\
MC_2 &= -192x^2 - 96xy - 120xz - 192y^2 - 144yz - 192z^2, \\
MC_1 &= -96x - 144y - 192z.
\end{aligned}$$

In order to answer the question $MC|_{\mathcal{S}} \ge 0$, we consider the polynomials $w_1 = 1+z$, $w_2 = y-z$, $w_3 = x-y$, $w_4 = -x$, which determine the simplex $\mathcal{S}$ and are non-negative on $\mathcal{S}$. We have $x = -w_4$, $y = -w_3 - w_4$, $z = -w_2 - w_3 - w_4$ and the relation

$$1 = w_1 + w_2 + w_3 + w_4. \tag{22}$$

For each $j \in [6]$, we compute $MC_j = 1^{6-j} MC_j = (w_1 + w_2 + w_3 + w_4)^{6-j} MC_j$, a degree 6 polynomial, homogeneous in the w_j's, and we add from 1 to 6, getting the following expression

$$\begin{aligned}
MC = {} & 192w_1^5w_2 + 336w_1^5w_3 + 432w_1^5w_4 + 768w_1^4w_2^2 + 2112w_1^4w_2w_3 \\
& +2472w_1^4w_2w_4 + 1152w_1^4w_3^2 + 2568w_1^4w_3w_4 + 1224w_1^4w_4^2 \\
& +1200w_1^3w_2^3 + 4524w_1^3w_2^2w_3 + 5076w_1^3w_2^2w_4 \\
& +4824w_1^3w_2w_3^2 + 10440w_1^3w_2w_3w_4 + 4992w_1^3w_2w_4^2 \\
& +1528w_1^3w_3^3 + 4896w_1^3w_3^2w_4 + 4740w_1^3w_3w_4^2 + 1380w_1^3w_4^3 \\
& +912w_1^2w_2^4 + 4392w_1^2w_2^3w_3 + 4830w_1^2w_2^3w_4 + 6960w_1^2w_2^2w_3^2 \\
& +14850w_1^2w_2^2w_3w_4 + 7146w_1^2w_2^2w_4^2 + 4442w_1^2w_2w_3^3 \\
& +14034w_1^2w_2w_3^2w_4 + 13656w_1^2w_2w_3w_4^2 + 4050w_1^2w_2w_4^3 \\
& +972w_1^2w_3^4 + 4092w_1^2w_3^3w_4 + 6072w_1^2w_3^2w_4^2 + 3702w_1^2w_3w_4^3 \\
& +774w_1^2w_4^4 + 336w_1w_2^5 + 1980w_1w_2^4w_3 + 2160w_1w_2^4w_4 \\
& +4176w_1w_2^3w_3^2 + 8862w_1w_2^3w_3w_4 + 4302w_1w_2^3w_4^2 \\
& +4030w_1w_2^2w_3^3 + 12657w_1w_2^2w_3^2w_4 + 12414w_1w_2^2w_3w_4^2 \\
& +3744w_1w_2^2w_4^3 + 1790w_1w_2w_3^4 + 7475w_1w_2w_3^3w_4 + 11163w_1w_2w_3^2w_4^2 \\
& +6918w_1w_2w_3w_4^3 + 1482w_1w_2w_4^4 + 292w_1w_3^5 + 1534w_1w_3^4w_4 \\
& +3120w_1w_3^3w_4^2 + 2988w_1w_3^2w_4^3 + 1326w_1w_3w_4^4 + 216w_1w_4^5 \\
& +48w_2^6 + 336w_2^5w_3 + 366w_2^5w_4 + 888w_2^4w_3^2 + 1884w_2^4w_3w_4 \\
& +924w_2^4w_4^2 + 1152w_2^3w_3^3 + 3615w_2^3w_3^2w_4 + 3582w_2^3w_3w_4^2 \\
& +1098w_2^3w_4^3 + 776w_2^2w_3^4 + 3233w_2^2w_3^3w_4 + 4875w_2^2w_3^2w_4^2 \\
& +3072w_2^2w_3w_4^3 + 672w_2^2w_4^4 + 256w_2w_3^5 + 1340w_2w_3^4w_4 \\
& +2752w_2w_3^3w_4^2 + 2682w_2w_3^2w_4^3 + 1218w_2w_3w_4^4 + 204w_2w_4^5 \\
& +32w_3^6 + 204w_3^5w_4 + 540w_3^4w_4^2 + 728w_3^3w_4^3 + 516w_3^2w_4^4 \\
& +180w_3w_4^5 + 24w_4^6.
\end{aligned}$$

This is a certificate of non–negativeness of MC on $\mathcal{S}$, since all the coefficients are non–negative. The only missing term in MC (as a homogeneous polynomial in w_1, w_2, w_3, w_4) is w_1^6. This means that the only real root of MC is given by $w_1 = 1$ and $w_2 = w_3 = w_4 = 0$, equivalently, by $x = y = z = 0$. This shows that *equality is only attained by boxes, among centrally–symmetric alcoved polyhedra.* We have proved *Mahler conjecture* for alcoved polyhedra. The conjecture also holds for limits of centrally symmetric alcoved polyhedra. □

Inspiration came from [9] and 2.24 in [10], for the former proof.

9 SUMMARY, FINAL REMARKS AND FUTURE DEVELOPMENTS

We have computed the volume of alcoved polyhedra and we have verified Mahler conjecture. Geometry tells us that our polyhedron is a perturbed box, more precisely, a canted box. In general, it is a dodecahedron with 20 vertices and 30 edges. Our method is to represent a d–dimensional polytope by a normal idempotent square matrix of order $n = d + 1$. Then, geometric questions about the polytope are answered through matrix computations. We have worked out the case $d = 3$. By a translation of the polyhedron, the vertex having larger coordinates can be moved to the origin. The corresponding matrix is then visualized, in which case the matrix splits as a (classical) sum of a box matrix and a perturbation matrix.

The entries of these two matrices are precisely the edge–lengths of the polyhedron. The volume formula follows from here.

What is specific of our method in dimension 3 is a natural question to ask. The particularities of dimensions $d = 2$ and 3 are various. First, we know the f–vectors of maximal alcoved polytopes, which are $(6,6)$, for $d = 2$, and $(20,30,12)$ for $d = 3$. In other words, we have hexagons, for $d = 2$, and dodecahedra with 20 vertices and 30 facets, for $d = 3$. Second, we know how many cantable faces are there, and how are they organized. Indeed, for $d = 2$, we have two cantable vertices in a rectangle, and for $d = 3$ we have a 3–dimensional box with six (out of a total of 30) cantable edges, $\ell_1, \ell_2, \ldots, \ell_6$, arranged in a topological 1–dimensional sphere or cycle. At the matrix level, the counterpart are the entries e_{ij} of the perturbation matrix, organized in a cycle, renamed $(c_1, c_2, \ldots, c_6)$ and called cant tuple. The cyclic structure is essential for us to obtain formula 4.1.

What do we know for higher dimensions? For $n - 1 = d = 4$ we can prove that $(f_0, f_1, f_2, f_3) = (70, 140, 90, 20)$ is the f–vector of maximal alcoved polytopes (using simplicity and zero Euler characteristic). However, we only know two entries of this vector for $n - 1 = d > 4$, namely, the number of vertices is $f_0 = \binom{2n-2}{n-1}$ and the number of facets is $f_{n-1} = n^2 - n$, in the alcoved case. We also know that maximal alcoved polytopes are simple. Which faces are cantable and how are they arranged?

Another question is whether one can use a similar method to obtain volume formulas for polytopes arising from other root systems. Connections with Ehrhart theory could be sought. We do not have answers yet.

An application of our volume expression is the possibility of producing a formula for mixed volumes, in the alcoved case. We will report this in a subsequent paper.

Our second contribution on the volume product lower bound is a simple proof of Mahler conjecture in a particular case. We are expectant to learn whether the 67 pages long preprint by Iriyeh and Shibata provides a correct proof of the conjecture in 3 dimensions.

ACKNOWLEDGMENTS

The first author has been partially supported by Ministerio de Economía y Competitividad, Proyecto I+D MTM2016–76808–P, www.mat.ucm.es/~cruizb/Investigacion/Proyecto-Web-16.

REFERENCES

[1] M. Akian, R. Bapat, and S. Gaubert. 2007. Max–plus algebra. In *Handbook of linear algebra*, L. Hobgen (Ed.). Chapman and Hall, Chapter 25.
[2] F. Ardila, C. Benedetti, and J. Doker. 2010. Matroid polytopes and their volumes. *Discrete and Computational Geometry* 43, 4 (June 2010), 841–854. arXiv:0810.3947v3(2011)
[3] A. Ben-Israel. 1992. A volume associated with $m \times n$ matrices. *Linear Algebra Appl.* 167 (1992), 87–111.
[4] P. Butkovič. 2010. *Max–plus linear systems: theory and algorithms.* Springer.
[5] M.J. de la Puente. 2013. On tropical Kleene star matrices and alcoved polytopes. *Kybernetika* 49, 6 (2013), 897–010.
[6] M. Develin and B. Sturmfels. 2004. Tropical convexity. *Doc. Math.* 9 (2004), 1–27. Erratum in Doc. Math. **9** (electronic), (2004) 205–206.
[7] M. Fiedler. 2007. Some applications of matrices and graphs in Euclidean Geometry. In *Handbook of linear algebra*, L. Hobgen (Ed.). Chapman and Hall, Chapter 66.
[8] P. Gritzmann and V. Klee. 1994. On the complexity of some basic problems in computational convexity II: Volume and Mixed Volume. In *Polytopes: abstract, convex and computational*, T. Bisztriczky, P. McMullen, R. Schneider, and I. Weiss (Eds.). NATO ASI Series, SeiresC: Mathematical and Physical Sciences, Vol. 440. Kluwer Academic Publishers, 373–466.
[9] D.F. Handelman. 1988. Representing polynomials by positive linear functions on compact convex polyhedra. *Pacific J. Math* 132, 1 (1988), 35–62.
[10] G.H. Hardy, J.E. Littlewood, and G. Pólya. 2010. *Inequalities* (2nd ed.). Cambridge Univ. Press.
[11] M. Henze. 2008. *The Mahler conjecture.* Master's thesis. Fakultat für Mathematik, Institut für Algebra und Geometrie.
[12] H. Iriyeh and M. Shibata. 2017. Symmetric Mahler conjecture for the volume product in the three dimensional case. (Oct. 2017). https://arxiv.org/abs/1706.01749
[13] A. Jiménez and M.J. de la Puente. 2012. Six combinatorial clases of maximal convex tropical polyhedra. (Oct. 2012). https://arxiv.org/abs/1706.01749v2
[14] M. Johnson and M. Kambites. 2014. Idempotent tropical matrices and finite metric spaces. *Advances in Geometry* 14, 2 (2014). https://doi.org/10.1515/advgeom-2013-0034 arXiv: 1203.2480, 2012.
[15] M. Joswig and K. Kulas. 2010. Tropical and ordinary convexity combined. *Advances in Geometry* 10 (2010), 333-352.
[16] E. Makai Jr. 2015. The recent status of the volume product problem. (2015). https://arxiv.org/abs/1507.01473
[17] H.W. Kuhn. 1955. The Hungarian method for the assignment problem. *Naval Research Logistics* 2 (1955), 83–97.
[18] T. Lam and A. Postnikov. 2007. Alcoved polytopes I. *Discrete and Computational Geometry* 38, 3 (2007), 453–478.
[19] T. Lam and A. Postnikov. 2012. Alcoved polytopes II. (2012). arXiv:1202.4015v1
[20] G.L. Litvinov and S.N. Sergeev (Eds.). 2009. *Tropical and Idempotent Mathematics. International workshop tropical -07.* Contemporary Mathematics, Vol. 495. AMS. ISBN: 987-0-8218-4782-4.
[21] A. Miné. 2004. *Domaines numériques abstraits faiblement relationnels.* Ph.D. Dissertation. L'École Polytechnique, Université Paris IX Dauphine.
[22] M. Senechal (Ed.). 2012. *Shaping Space. Exploring Polyhedra in Nature, Art, and the Geometrical Imagination.* Springer.
[23] S. Sergeev, H. Scheneider, and P. Butkovič. 2009. On visualization, subeigenvectors and Kleene stars in max algebra. *Linear Algebra Appl.* 431 (2009), 2395–2406.
[24] T. Tao. 2007. Open question: the Mahler conjecture on convex bodies. (2007). https://terrytao.wordpress.com/2007/03/08/open-problem-the-mahler-conjecture-on-convex-bodies/
[25] A. Werner and J. Yu. 2014. Symmetric alcoved polytopes. *The electronic journal of combinatorics* 21, 1 (2014). arXiv:1201.4378v1(2012)

The Importance of Being Zero*

Tomás Recio
Departamento de Matemáticas,
Universidad de Cantabria
Santander, Spain
tomas.recio@unican.es

J.Rafael Sendra
Dep. de Física y Matemáticas,
Research Group ASYNAC,
Universidad de Alcalá.
Alcalá de Henares, Madrid, Spain
rafael.sendra@uah.es

Carlos Villarino
Dep. de Física y Matemáticas,
Research Group ASYNAC,
Universidad de Alcalá.
Alcalá de Henares, Madrid, Spain
carlos.villarino@uah.es

ABSTRACT

We present a deterministic algorithm for deciding if a polynomial ideal, with coefficients in an algebraically closed field $\mathbb{K}$ of characteristic zero, of which we know just some very limited data, namely: the number n of variables, and some upper bound for the geometric degree of its zero set in $\mathbb{K}^n$, is or not the zero ideal. The algorithm performs just a finite number of decisions to check whether a point is or not in the zero set of the ideal. Moreover, we extend this technique to test, in the same fashion, if the elimination of some variables in the given ideal yields or not the zero ideal. Finally, the role of this technique in the context of automated theorem proving of elementary geometry statements, is presented, with references to recent documents describing the excellent performance of the already existing prototype version, implemented in GeoGebra.

CCS CONCEPTS

• **Computing Methodologies; Symbolic and algebraic manipulation; Algebraic algorithms**;

KEYWORDS

zero-test, polynomial ideals, Schwartz-Zippel Lemma, automated reasoning in geometry, proving by examples, GeoGebra,

ACM Reference Format:

Tomás Recio, J.Rafael Sendra, and Carlos Villarino. 2018. The Importance of Being Zero. In *ISSAC '18: 2018 ACM International Symposium on Symbolic and Algebraic Computation, July 16–19, 2018, New York, NY, USA.* ACM, New York, NY, USA, 7 pages. https://doi.org/10.1145/3208976.3208981

1 INTRODUCTION

Let us suppose we are given, as a query, an ideal $\mathrm{I} \subset \mathbb{K}[x_1, \ldots, x_n]$, with coefficients in an algebraically closed field $\mathbb{K}$ of characteristic zero, of which we know just some very limited data: the number n of variables, and some upper bound for the geometric degree (in the sense of [6], see Definition 2.1 below) of its zero set in $\mathbb{K}^n$, whether the ideal is not zero. Moreover, we have an oracle that allows us to check, given a point in $\mathbb{K}^n$, whether this point is or not in the zero set of I. Our first goal is to present an algorithm to conclude, by just using this protocol, whether I is the identically zero ideal or not.

As a trivial example, suppose that we deal with some unknown ideal $\mathrm{I} \subsetneq \mathbb{K}[x]$, i.e. $n = 1$, and assume that we know that, if the given ideal is not zero, the cardinal of its roots (that is, in the one variable case, the geometric degree) will be bounded by d. Then, choose $d + 1$ different points in $\mathbb{K}$ and, for each of them, check if it is a root of I. If it is so in all cases, it is obvious that we are going beyond the given number of roots bound, so the ideal I must be identically zero. Else, if we have found a point in $\mathbb{K}$ which is not a zero of I, it is also obvious to conclude that I can not be zero.

The problem of detecting, by evaluation on a finite number of instances, whether a polynomial is or not zero, is a classical issue in computer algebra and complexity theory. It is impossible to summarize in a few references the state of the art. We can just mention the classical, purely algebraic, statement bounding the number of the required instances for zero-testing in [24]; the probabilistic approach in the Schwartz-Zippel Lemma [26], [22], with a curious history behind [16] that shows the wide interest of the scientific community concerning this problem; the research on *questor set* related to the BPP (Bounded error Probability Polynomial) time, as in [7], see also [18] and [19] for a historical account, etc.

It must be clarified that in most of these contributions the *rigurous* or *deterministic* approach to zero testing is not the relevant goal, since it is considered both well known (in classical references as [24]) and unpractical, for the involved exponential number of required tests. Instead, their objective is to find some feasible strategies for zero-testing with high probability.

Our contribution here goes in a different direction. First of all, a relative novelty could be the extension of the exact zero-testing protocol, from polynomials to ideals in polynomial rings of several variables (see [5], Section 2, and [17], Section 4, for related results). Let us remark that our goal is to find a kind of universal zero-testing set, i.e. we are looking for a single set to perform the test to all ideals of given bounded degree and embedded in the same polynomial ring.

In Section 2 we have accomplished this goal by introducing the notion of test-sets (playing a similar role to a fixed collection of $d+1$ points on a line, for testing the vanishing of degree d univariate polynomials), proving that this property can be reduced to testing hypersurfaces (Theorem 2.3), that it is kept under bijective affine transformations (Theorem 2.8), and providing a general example of test-sets with minimal cardinality (see Theorem 2.7). Moreover, for technical reasons, we have extended this concept to sets such that any subset of a certain cardinality is also a test-set (what we

*Authors supported by the Spanish Ministerio de Economía y Competitividad , and by the European Regional Development Fund (ERDF), under the Project MTM2017-88796-P.

ISSAC '18, July 16–19, 2018, New York, NY, USA

ACM ISBN 978-1-4503-5550-6/18/07...$15.00
https://doi.org/10.1145/3208976.3208981

have called "disjunctive test-sets", c.f. Definition 2.9). Let us remark that the terminology of "test-sets" comes from the attempts to mechanizing inductive reasonings [15].

But the final goal of our work is not exactly finding zero-test protocols for given ideals of a certain degree. It is something closely related, but more general. Assume we are given a certain ideal $I \subset \mathbb{K}[x_1, \ldots, x_n]$ of which we just know a bound of the degree d of its zero set, and the number of variables n. Then we want to decide if the result of eliminating some variables in the ideal I, say, if $I_r = I \cap \mathbb{K}[x_1, \ldots, x_r]$, yields or not to the zero ideal. And this zero-checking for I_r is to be performed only through a number of tests that, like in the previous situation, will consist in choosing some points $(a_1, \ldots, a_r) \in \mathbb{K}^r$, and then verifying, with an oracle, if they can be (or not) lifted to a point $(a_1, \ldots, a_n)$ in the zero-set defined by I. See Section 3.1 for details, but let us illustrate here both the goal and the method we have developed, through the following example.

Example 1.1. Imagine we are given an ideal I (of whatever dimension) in $\mathbb{K}[x_1, x_2, x_3]$, and we just know that the degree of its zero set is bounded by 2. Then we would like to check if the elimination $I_2 = I \cap \mathbb{K}[x_1, x_2]$ is zero. Roughly speaking, we could argue like this: this elimination variety $\mathbb{V}(I_2)$ is, surely, also of degree bounded by 2, as the degree bound is preserved under affine mappings [6]. And the same happens for the Zariski closure of $\mathbb{V}(I_2)$ minus the projection π of $\mathbb{V}(I)$ over the (x_1, x_2)-plane (c.f. proof of Theorem 3.1 at Section 3).

Then, take 11 points on the plane (what we will call a "disjunctive test-set" for degree two varieties over the plane), arranged in such a way that no subset of six points lies on a conic. Next, consider each one of these 11 points and verify if they can be lifted to a zero of I in $\mathbb{K}^3$, that is, for each of these points (a_1, a_2), check if there is a $a_3 \in \mathbb{K}$ so that $(a_1, a_2, a_3) \in \mathbb{V}(I) \subset \mathbb{K}^3$. Let A be the subset of the 11 points that can be lifted and let B its complementary. Obviously, either the cardinal of A or the cardinal of B must be strictly greater than 5.

Thus, if cardinal of A is 6 or more, we are sure that $\mathbb{V}(I_2)$, since it is either of degree 2 or the whole plane, and it contains A, it must be the whole plane, so I_2 is zero. Assume, on the contrary, that B has cardinal greater than 6. Now we consider the partition of the plane in three different sets of points: those in the projection of $\mathbb{V}(I)$, those in $\mathbb{V}(I_2)$ but not in this projection, those not in $\mathbb{V}(I_2)$.

By definition, B is outside the projection, so it must be included in the union of $\mathbb{V}(I_2) \setminus \pi(\mathbb{V}(I))$ with $\mathbb{K}^2 \setminus \mathbb{V}(I_2)$. Now it happens that not all the points in B can be within $\mathbb{V}(I_2) \setminus \pi(\mathbb{V}(I))$, since it will imply that its Zariski closure, also of degree bounded by 2, is the whole plane. But this Zariski closure must be strictly contained in $\mathbb{V}(I_2)$ (c.f. [2]), which will be impossible in this case.

It follows that B cannot be fully contained in $\mathbb{V}(I_2) \setminus \pi(\mathbb{V}(I))$. Thus there must be points in B that are neither in the 'bad set" (i.e. $\mathbb{V}(I_2) \setminus \pi(\mathbb{V}(I))$), nor in the projection, so outside of $\mathbb{V}(I_2)$, and we conclude that this variety can not be the whole plane, achieving in this way a complete decision protocol.

Thus, in the last Section of this paper we will describe an algorithm for achieving such a test of the nullity of elimination ideals. Although we estimate that the theoretical foundations we have developped are already interesting, we will summarily present, as well, a concrete application of this technique, in the context of automated reasoning for geometry statements. It has been already implemented in the popular dynamic geometry and computer algebra program GeoGebra[1] (see [1] for a condensed presentation of this feature in a prototype version, although without technical details; see also [14], column "Recio").

We expect to be able to present in a near future, to the scientific community, complete results concerning the already promising performance of theorem proving algorithms using this particular approach.

2 TEST-SETS

In this section, we introduce the notion of test-set and we state its main properties. The concept of test-set will depend on two positive integer numbers (d, r). d will denote the degree of the variety to be tested and r the dimension of the affine space where the test set, or the tested variety, is included; or equivalently, r is the number of variables of the polynomial ring.

Definition 2.1. We recall that the geometric degree of an irreducible affine variety $\mathcal{U} \subset \mathbb{K}^k$ is the number of intersections of $\mathcal{U}$ with a generic affine linear variety of codimension $\dim(\mathcal{U})$. When the variety is reducible, the degree is defined as the sum of the degrees of the reducible components; for further details we refer to Def. 1. and Remark 2 in [6].

Definition 2.2. A finite subset $A \subseteq \mathbb{K}^r$ is a (d, r)-test set, with $d > 0$, if no proper variety $\mathcal{W}$ of $\mathbb{K}^r$ of geometric degree less or equal than d contains A.

Let us show a couple of trivial and typical examples of (d, r)-test sets. First example: $d + 1$ different points on a line $\mathbb{K}$ are a $(d, 1)$-test set, since there is no non-zero polynomial in one variable, of degree less or equal than d, with $d + 1$ roots. Another easy one: $r + 1$ points in $\mathbb{K}^r$, affinely independent, are a $(1, r)$-test set, since no hyperplane in $\mathbb{K}^r$ contains them.

Remark. Given a constructible set $C \subseteq \mathbb{K}^r$, let us say it is a *proper* constructible set if its closure $\overline{C}$ is a proper algebraic variety, i.e., if $\overline{C} \neq \mathbb{K}^r$. Then, an equivalent definition for (d, r)-test sets can be stated replacing in the above definition the word "variety" by "constructible set". In fact, it is enough to recall that the degree of a constructible set is, by definition, that of its Zariski closure (see [6]).

The next theorem shows that (d, r)-test set candidates need to be verified just for hypersurfaces, i.e., for single polynomials of degree up to d and r variables.

Theorem 2.3. *Let $A \subseteq \mathbb{K}^r$ and $d \in \mathbb{Z}_{>0}$. Then A is a (d, r)-test set if and only if no hypersurface of $\mathbb{K}^r$, of geometric degree less or equal than d, contains A.*

Proof. Let $A \subseteq \mathbb{K}^r$ be a (d, r)-test set. Then, obviously, no proper hypersurface $\mathcal{W}$ of $\mathbb{K}^r$ defined by a polynomial of degree less or equal than d contains A. Conversely, assume that $A \subseteq \mathbb{K}^r$ is such that no proper hypersurface $\{F = 0\} \subseteq \mathbb{K}^r$ defined by a polynomial $F(x_1, \ldots, x_r)$, of degree less or equal than d, contains A. Then,

[1] http://geogebra.org

given any proper variety $\mathcal{W}$ of $\mathbb{K}^r$, of degree at most d, let us show that it can not contain A. In fact, $\mathcal{W}$ is always contained in a hypersurface of degree bounded by d: consider $\mathcal{W} = \mathcal{W}_1 \cup \cdots \cup \mathcal{W}_m$ be the irreducible decomposition of $\mathcal{W}$. Let $\deg(\mathcal{W}_i) \leq d_i$. Then, $d_1 + \cdots + d_m \leq d$. By [6], Prop. 3, pp. 256, each $\mathcal{W}_i$ can be defined as the zero-set of a finite family of polynomials with degree bounded by d_i. Let $F = f_1 \cdots f_m$, taking each $f_i \neq 0$ in the generator set of $\mathcal{W}_i$. Then it is clear that $\mathcal{W} \subseteq \{F = 0\}$. □

In the next part of the section, we will describe a test-set of minimal cardinality. In the following, for $m_1, m_2 \in \mathbb{Z}_{>0}$, we denote by

$$\mathrm{Supp}(m_1, m_2) \subseteq \mathbb{Z}_{>0}^{m_2}$$

the set of exponents on the support of a generic polynomial of degree m_1 in m_2 variables. We recall that its cardinal is

$$\#(\mathrm{Supp}(m_1, m_2)) = \binom{m_1 + m_2}{m_2}.$$

We start with some technical lemmas

Lemma 2.4. *Let* $\Pi : \mathbb{K}^r \to \mathbb{K}^{r-1}, \Pi(x_1, \ldots, x_r) = (x_2, \ldots, x_r)$. *If* A *is a* (d, r)*-test set then* $\Pi(A)$ *is a* $(d, r-1)$*-test set.*

Proof. Let $\mathcal{W}^*$ be a variety of $\mathbb{K}^{r-1}$ with $\deg(\mathcal{W}^*) \leq d$ and such that $\Pi(A) \subseteq \mathcal{W}^*$. We consider the variety $\mathcal{W} = \mathbb{K} \times \mathcal{W}^* \subseteq \mathbb{K}^r$. We observe that

$$A \subseteq \mathbb{K} \times \Pi(A) \subseteq \mathcal{W} \subseteq \mathbb{K}^r$$

and $\deg(\mathcal{W}) \leq d$. Since A is a (d, r)-test set, $\mathcal{W} = \mathbb{K}^r$. Therefore, $\mathcal{W}^* = \mathbb{K}^{r-1}$. So, one concludes that $\Pi(A)$ is a $(d, r-1)$-test set. □

Lemma 2.5. *Let* $\Pi : \mathbb{N}^r \to \mathbb{N}^{r-1}, \Pi(x_1, \ldots, x_r) = (x_2, \ldots, x_r)$. *Then,* $\Pi(\mathrm{Supp}(d, r)) = \mathrm{Supp}(d, r-1)$

Proof. Let $\overline{u} \in \mathrm{Supp}(d, r-1)$, then $(0, \overline{u}) \in \mathrm{Supp}(d, r)$. Conversely, it is obvious that if $\overline{v} \in \mathrm{Supp}(d, r)$ then $\Pi(\overline{v}) \in \mathrm{Supp}(d, r-1)$. □

Lemma 2.6. *If* $P \in \mathbb{K}[x_1, \ldots, x_r]$ *has degree less or equal than* d *and vanishes on* $\mathrm{Supp}(d, r)$, *then* P *is the zero polynomial.*

Proof. We prove the statement by induction on r. For $r = 1$, it follows from the hypothesis that $P(x_1)$ vanishes over $\mathrm{Supp}(d, 1)$, of cardinal $d + 1$, and thus it has $d + 1$ different roots; hence it is identically zero. Let us assume that the lemma is true for $r = s - 1$, and that $P \in \mathbb{K}[x_1, \ldots, x_s]$ is such that $\deg(P) \leq d$ and $P(\overline{u}) = 0$ for all $\overline{u} \in \mathrm{Supp}(d, r)$. We consider the linear polynomials $L_k(x_1) = x_1 - k$, with $k \in \{0, \ldots, d\}$. Then, dividing w.r.t. x_1 we get that

$$P(x_1, \ldots, x_s) = Q(x_1, \ldots, x_s)L_k(x_1) + M(x_2, \ldots, x_s).$$

Since, $P(\overline{u}) = 0$ for all $\overline{u} \in \mathrm{Supp}(d, s)$, then $M(\Pi(\overline{u})) = 0$. By Lemma 2.5, we get that $M(\overline{v}) = 0$ for all $\overline{v} \in \mathrm{Supp}(d, s-1)$. So, by the induction hypothesis, M is identically 0. Thus, $\prod_{k=0}^{d} L_k$ divides P, which has degree at most d. Hence, P is also identically zero. □

In this situation, we are ready to prove the theorem.

Theorem 2.7. $\mathrm{Supp}(d, r)$ *is a* (d, r)*-test set of minimum cardinality.*

Proof. The fact that $\mathrm{Supp}(d, r)$ is a (d, r)-test set follows from Lemma 2.6 and Theorem 2.3. Let us prove the minimality. Let $N = \#(\mathrm{Supp}(d, r))$, and let us assume that there exists a (d, r)-test set A with $\#(A) = N^* < N$. A generic polynomial P in $\mathbb{K}[x_1, \ldots, x_r]$ of degree d has as many undetermined coefficients as elements in $\mathrm{Supp}(d, r)$; let us call them $\{a_i\}$. Now, since A is a (d, r)-test set, evaluating P at each element of A, we get an homogenous linear system $\{P(\overline{u}) = 0\}_{\overline{u} \in A}$ in the undetermined coefficients $\{a_i\}$. Since the rank of this system is at most N^*, that is smaller than N, there exists a nontrivial solution; in contradiction with the property of being a test set. □

Remark. As a consequence of this theorem it follows that, asymptotically, (d, r)-test sets have cardinality with lower bound $O(d^r)$ (if we consider d growing and r fixed) or $O(r^d)$ (if we rather consider r growing and d fixed). Thus, the result in Theorem 2.7 is, in some sense, not too different from the naive approach yielding $(d + 1)^r$ points (the cartesian product of sets of $d + 1$ points over each axis in $\mathbb{K}^r$), except if one is interested in the case of growing dimension and bounded degree, which, by the way, could be quite useful in automatic geometric reasoning (see, for example, the results in [12]), since statements therein involve several points (and, thus, many coordinates) but, generally, construction steps of low degree (involving several simple, linear or quadratic, operations such as building a line through two given points or intersecting a line and a circle, etc); note that

$$\lim_{r \to \infty} \frac{\binom{d+r}{r}}{(d + 1)^r} = 0.$$

The following theorem states that the property of being test-set is invariant under bijective affine transformations.

Theorem 2.8. *Let* A *be a* (d, r)*-test set, and* φ *a bijective affine transformation of* $\mathbb{K}^r$. *Then* $\varphi(A)$ *is a* (d, r)*-test set.*

Proof. Let us assume that $\varphi(A)$ is not a (d, r)-test set. Then, by Theorem 2.3, there exists a hypersurface $\mathcal{V} = \mathbb{V}(H)$, where $H(\mathbf{x}) = H(x_1, \ldots, x_r) \in \mathbb{K}[\mathbf{x}]$, of degree $\leq d$ such that $\varphi(A) \subset \mathcal{V}$. Let $F = H(\varphi^{-1}(\mathbf{x}))$, and let $\mathcal{W} = \mathbb{V}(F)$. Since φ is an affine transformation, $\deg(F) = \deg(H)$, and $A \subset \mathcal{W}$, which is a contradiction. □

In some cases it would be interesting to construct sets having stronger properties than that of being a test set, namely, such that any subset of cardinal greater than a fixed size is also a test set. More precisely, we introduce the following definition:

Definition 2.9. Let $d, r \in \mathbb{Z}_{>0}$, and $N = \#(\mathrm{Supp}(d, r))$. We say that a finite set A, with $\#(A) \geq N$, is a (d, r)-disjunctive test set if any subset of A of cardinal N is a (d, r)-test set.

The motivation of this notion is the following. Assume that A is disjunctive and $\#(A) \geq 2N - 1$ and $B \subseteq A$, then either B or $A \setminus B$ is a (d, r)-test set. Indeed, if $\#(B) \geq N$, the statement holds by the definition of disjunctive test set. Else, $\#(A \setminus B) \geq N$, and thus $A \setminus B$ is a (d, r)-test set.

In this context, the following holds.

Lemma 2.10. *For any given* $d, r \in \mathbb{Z}_{>0}$, *and* $N = \#(\mathrm{Supp}(d, r))$, *the following algorithm derives a* (d, r)*-disjunctive test set of any given cardinal* M *greater or equal to* N.

Proof. If $M = N$ then we can take $A = \text{Supp}(d, r)$ (see Theorem 2.7). We assume by induction that we know how to build a disjunctive test set, B of cardinal $M \geq N$, and let us build another one of cardinal $M + 1$. In fact, let us first remark that, for every subset C of B, of $N - 1$ elements, there exists a unique hypersurface in $H_C \subset \mathbb{K}^r$ of degree d, through these elements. This hypersurface can be constructed by solving a linear homogeneous system of $N-1$ equations in N unknowns, each equation being the generic polynomial of degree d in r variables, with undetermined coefficients, evaluated at one of the elements of C.

Notice that the rank of this linear system is $N - 1$, and thus it defines uniquely –except for multiplication by a common constant– the coefficients of a hypersurface. In fact, would the rank be strictly smaller than $N - 1$, we could add to C an extra point such that the rank of the extended system with the new equation for the extra point would be $N - 1$ or less and, therefore, it would have at least one solution. But this is a contradiction to the fact that B is disjunctive and all subsets of B with N elements (such as C plus the added point) must be (d, r)-test sets, implying that there is no hypersurface of degree d defined by these points.

Now consider all such hypersurfaces H_C for all different choices of $C \subset B$. Let $P \in \mathbb{K}^r$ be a point not in any of these hypersurfaces. Then we claim that $B^\star = B \cup \{P\}$ is also a (d, r)-disjunctive test set. In fact, if $A \subseteq B^\star$ has cardinal N and is a subset of B, it is obviously a (d, r)-test set, because B is disjunctive. On the other hand, if $P \in A$, then $A \cap B \subseteq B$ is of cardinal $N - 1$. By construction point P does not belong to the only hypersurface $H_{A\cap B}$ of degree d defined by $A \cap B$, and therefore A is a (d, r)-test set. □

The algorithm described in the proof of Lemma 2.10 can be outlined as follows.

Algorithm 1. Given $d, r \in \mathbb{Z}_{>0}$, and $N = \#(\text{Supp}(d, r))$, the following algorithm derives a (d, r)-disjunctive test set of any given cardinal M greater or equal to N.

(1) If $M = N$ Return $\text{Supp}(d, r)$.
(2) Set $B = \text{Supp}(d, r)$.
(3) For i from 1 to $M - N$ do
   (a) For any subset C of B with $\#(C) = N - 1$ determine the unique hypersurface H_C of $\mathbb{K}^r$ of degree d.
   (b) Compute a point $P \in \mathbb{K}^r$ not in any of the hypersurfaces obtained in the previous step.
   (c) Set $B = B \cup \{P\}$.
(4) Return B.

Example 2.11. We use the notation as in Algorithm 1. Let us consider $d = 2, r = 2 \in \mathbb{N}$, $\#(\text{Supp}(2, 2)) = 6$ and let $M = 7$. Then a $(2, 2)$-disjunctive test set of cardinal 7 can be build as follows.

$$\begin{aligned}\text{Supp}(2,2) &= \{P_1, P_2, P_3, P_4, P_5, P_6\} \\ &= \{(0,0), (0,1), (0,2), (1,0), (1,1), (2,0)\}.\end{aligned}$$

Let H_i be the unique conic passing through $\text{Supp}(2, 2) \setminus \{P_i\}$. More precisely, $H_1 = (x + y - 2)(x + y - 1), H_2 = x(x + y - 2), H_3 = x(x-1), H_4 = y(x+y-2), H_5 = xy$ and $H_6 = y(y-1)$. Then taking $P \notin \cup H_i$, for instance, $P = (2/3, 2/3)$, we have that $\text{Supp}(2, 2) \cup \{P\}$ is a $(2, 2)$-disjunctive test set of cardinal 7.

Remark. Given a (d, r)-disjunctive test set A of cardinal $M \geq N = \#(\text{Supp}(d, r))$, we have remarked –after Definition 2.9– that, if $M \geq 2N - 1$, it is true that, for every subset of $B \subseteq A$, at least one from B or its complement $A \setminus B$, must be a (d, r)- test set. Obviously $2N - 1$ is the minimum cardinal of sets A holding this property, since for $M < (2N - 1)$ we can always find subsets of A such that both the subset and its complement have cardinal strictly smaller than N. Now, since N is the minimum size of a (d, r)-test set (cf. Theorem 2.7), it is obvious that in this case neither A nor $A \setminus B$ can be (d, r)-test sets.

3 AN APPLICATION: TESTING THE NULLITY OF ELIMINATION IDEALS

In the sequel, we will denote by $\mathbf{x}_i = (x_1, \ldots, x_i)$ with $i \in \{1, \ldots, n\}$. Let us consider the ideal $\mathrm{I} \subset \mathbb{K}[\mathbf{x}_n]$ as well as its associated variety $\mathcal{V} = \mathbb{V}(\mathrm{I}) \subset \mathbb{K}^n$. In addition, we also consider the projection

$$\begin{array}{cccc}\pi_r: & \mathcal{V} \subseteq \mathbb{K}^n & \to & \mathbb{K}^r \\ & \mathbf{x}_n & \mapsto & \mathbf{x}_r\end{array}$$

and let I_r be the $\mathbf{x}_r$-elimination ideal, that is $\mathrm{I}_r = \mathrm{I} \cap \mathbb{K}[\mathbf{x}_r]$, and $\mathcal{V}_r = \mathbb{V}(\mathrm{I}_r) \subseteq \mathbb{K}^r$. By the Theorem of the Closure (see Theorem 3 pp. 125 in [2]) it holds that

$$\mathcal{V}_r = \overline{\pi_r(\mathcal{V})}.$$

We provide an algorithm that decides whether $\mathcal{V}_r$ is $\mathbb{K}^r$ or, equivalently, whether $\mathrm{I}_r = <0>$.

It holds that $\mathcal{V}_r \setminus \pi_r(\mathcal{V})$ is a constructible set. Let $\mathcal{W}_r$ be a subvariety of $\mathcal{V}_r$, of lower dimension, such that $\mathcal{V}_r \setminus \pi_r(\mathcal{V}) \subset \mathcal{W}_r$. The existence of $\mathcal{W}_r$ is also guaranteed by the Closure Theorem.

The algorithm is as follows

Algorithm 2. Given a bound d for the geometric degree of $\mathcal{V}$, the algorithm decides whether the ideal I_r is zero or not.

(1) Set $N = \binom{d+r}{r}$.
(2) Apply Algorithm 1 to N and (d, r) to get a (d, r)–disjunctive test set of cardinality $2N - 1$, say C.
(3) Using an oracle, decompose C as $C = A \cup B$, where for every $P \in A$ it holds that $P \in \pi_r(\mathcal{V})$ and for every $P \in B$ it holds that $P \notin \pi_r(\mathcal{V})$
(4) If $\#(A) \geq N$ then Return $\mathrm{I}_r = <0>$ else $\mathrm{I}_r \neq <0>$.

Theorem 3.1. *The previous algorithm is correct.*

Proof. By Lemma 2 in [6], we know that d also bounds the degree of $\mathcal{V}_r$. Moreover[2], the same bound applies to $\mathcal{W}_r$, that is to the closure of the "bad set" (i.e. the set of points that are in $\mathcal{V}_r$ but can not be lifted to $\mathcal{V}$). Assume $\#(A) \geq N$. By definition of disjunctive test set, A contains a (d, r)-test set. Now, since $A \subset \mathcal{V}_r$ and the degree of $\mathcal{V}_r$ is bounded by d, $\mathcal{V}_r$ must be $\mathbb{K}^r$. Thus, $\mathrm{I}_r = <0>$.

On the other hand if $\#(A) < N$, we prove that $\mathrm{I}_r \neq <0>$. Let us assume that $\mathrm{I}_r = <0>$. Since $\#(A) < N$, then $\#(B) \geq N$ and B contains a (d, r)-test set. Since B is included in $\mathcal{W}_r$ and its degree is also bounded by d, one concludes that $\mathcal{W}_r$ must be $\mathbb{K}^r$. But this

[2]Personal communication by prof. Martín Sombra, ICREA Research Professor at Universitat de Barcelona, Spain, to whom we would like to express our gratitude. Roughly, the idea is to reduce the general case to the case of irreducible varieties, then to the case in which both the given variety and the closure of its projection have the same dimension and, finally, work in a projective setting, studying the intersection of the variety with the hyperplane at infinity and project (yielding those points that can not be affinely lifted). See related ideas at [3].

is impossible, because, by construction, its dimension is strictly smaller than r. □

Remark.

(1) In Step 3 of Algorithm 2 we need to check through an oracle whether a point P is in the projection of the variety. This can be done, for example, by substituting the variables $x_1, \ldots, x_r$ by the corresponding coordinates of P in the generators of the ideal I to check afterwards whether the new variety in $\mathbb{K}^{n-r}$ is non-empty; this can be done by elimination theory techniques. In the context of the applications of these ideas to automatic theorem proving, the fiber of almost all points P is finite. Hence, the variety to be tested is zero-dimensional. Thus, the decision is faster.

(2) Note that the disjoint test-set C, appearing in Step 2 of Algorithm 2, only depends on d and r and not on the ideal I. Therefore, one may have a pre-computed data basis, for different values of d and r, to be used directly on Algorithm 2. Even, if one does not have at hand such a basis, one may combine Algorithms 1 and 2 as follows: whenever a point $P \in C$ is computed, one decides whether P belongs or not to $\pi_r(\mathcal{V})$. As soon as the cardinality of either A or B is greater or equal N, the process can be stopped, and one does not need to determine all elements in C.
A third option, probably the most efficient, is as follows. We compute a test-set T, via the support, with N elements and we apply a random linear transformation to T (see Theorem 2.8) to get T^*. In this situation, we check how many points in T^* can be lifted to $\mathcal{V}$. If this number is N, then we can conclude that $\mathrm{I}_r =< 0 >$. If not, we add to T^* a new point, as explained in Algorithm 1, to get T^{**} and we repeat the process.

Example 3.2. We illustrate Algorithm 2 by a toy example. We consider the ideal $\mathrm{I} \subset \mathbb{C}[x, y, z, w]$ defined by the generators

$$\begin{aligned}\mathrm{I} \;=<\; & -w^2x^2 + 2wx^3 - 2x^3z + 2x^2y^2 + 2x^2yz + x^2z^2 - 2\,xy^2z \\ & -2\,xyz^2 + y^4 + 2y^3z + y^2z^2 + 2w^2x - 2wx^2 - w^2, \\ & w^2x^2 - 2wx^3 + 2x^4 - 2x^3z + 2x^2y^2 + 2x^2yz + x^2z^2 - \\ & 2xy^2z - 2xyz^2 + y^4 + 2y^3z + y^2z^2 - 2w^2x + 2wx^2 + w^2 > .\end{aligned}$$

One may check that $\mathcal{V} = \mathbb{V}(\mathrm{I}) \subset \mathbb{C}^4$ has degree 4. Now, we consider the projection $\pi_2 : \mathcal{V} \subset \mathbb{C}^4 \longrightarrow \mathbb{C}^2; (x, y, z, w) \mapsto (x, y)$. We want to check whether $\overline{\pi_2(\mathcal{V})} = \mathbb{C}^2$ or, equivalently, whether $\mathrm{I} \cap \mathbb{C}[x, y] =< 0 >$. For this purpose, we apply Algorithm 2 with $N = 15$. So, we need a $(4, 2)$-disjoint test set of cardinality 29. Applying Algorithm 1 one get the following disjoint test set

$$\begin{aligned}C = \;& \{(-18, 28), (-15, -30), (-6, -5), (-5, 28), (-2, -17), \\ & (-2, 29), (0, 0), (0, 1), (0, 2), (0, 3), (0, 4), (1, 0), (1, 1), (1, 2), \\ & (1, 3), (2, 0), (2, 1), (2, 2), (3, -13), (3, 0), (3, 1), (4, 0), (9, 6), \\ & (11, 15), (12, -12), (13, -22), (16, -23), (19, 28), (21, 25)\}.\end{aligned}$$

Decomposing $C = A \cup B$, as in Step 3, by using some of the oracles described in the previous remark, we get that $\#(A) = 24$ and $\#(B) = 5$; Indeed, $B = \{(1, 0), (1, 1), (1, 2), (1, 3), (2, 2)\} \subset \mathbb{C}^2 \setminus \pi_2(\mathcal{V})$. Therefore, $\mathrm{I} \cap \mathbb{K}[x, y] =< 0 >$.

Now, we repeat the example but using the projection $\pi_2 : \mathcal{V} \subset \mathbb{C}^4 \longrightarrow \mathbb{C}^2; (x, y, z, w) \mapsto (x, w)$. So, C is as above but in this case it decomposes as $C = A \cup B$ with $\#(A) = 1$ and $\#(B) = 28$, being $A = \{(0, 0)\}$. Thus, in this case $\mathrm{I} \cap \mathbb{C}[y, z] \neq< 0 >$.

What could be the interest of having some test-by-examples of the nullity of an elimination ideal? Obviously, such tests could help computing the dimension of a polynomial ideal and selecting a collection of independent variables modulo the ideal. But, although our current work does not address this issue, the specific application of the zero-testing method we have in mind –and also the initial motivation for this work– is automated geometric theorem proving, within the realm of the "proof by exhaustion" method[3].

Without going into details, it happens that, for some approaches, the truth of a certain type of geometric statements involves checking that some multivariate polynomial is identically zero; and this is accomplished by verifying that the polynomial is zero on some sort of test set, where each element of the set corresponds to a geometric instance of the given statement (say, a particular position of a vertex on a triangle). Some attempts in this direction have been labeled as the method of *proving by examples.* We can find early occurrences of this approach in the works of [8],[9] and [25], while in [4] a survey of these early procedures for automatic theorem proving in geometry, till 1988, is presented. The dissertation of Kortenkamp [10] or the paper [11] provide a fine analysis on the advantages and limitations of this approach, in the context of Dynamic Geometry.

More recently, both the master dissertation of Weitzhofer [23] and the doctoral dissertation of Kovács [12], reconsider, extend, implement and test this technique in the popular program GeoGebra, following the completely general theorem proving and discovery approach of [21], that we can summarize as follows.

Let $\{H \Rightarrow T\}$ be a geometric statement, where $H = \{h_1, \ldots, h_\ell\}$ stands for the ideal of equations describing the geometric construction of the hypotheses and $T = (f)$ describes the thesis (or, more generally, the theses). Both ideals lie on a polynomial ring $\mathbb{K}[X]$, where the variables $X = \{x_1, \ldots, x_n\}$ refer to the coordinates involved in the algebraic description of the hypotheses, over a base field $\mathbb{K}$. Fix a maximum-size set $Y = \{x_1, \ldots, x_m\}$ of independent variables for the hypotheses ideal H (i.e. $m = \dim(H)$), and label as "non-degenerate" the irreducible components of H where Y remains independent. Consider $\mathbb{L}$, an algebraically closed extension on $\mathbb{K}$ (for instance $\mathbb{L} = \mathbb{C}$ and $\mathbb{K} = \mathbb{Q}$), and let the geometric instances verifying the hypotheses (respectively, the thesis) of the statement be the algebraic variety $\mathbb{V}(H)$ (respectively, $\mathbb{V}(T)$) in the affine space $\mathbb{L}^n$.

We say that a statement is "generally true" iff T holds over all non-degenerate components; and that it is "generally false" if it does not hold over any of them. Then it is shown that

a) The statement $\{H \Rightarrow T\}$ is generally true if and only if
$$\mathrm{I} \cap \mathbb{K}[Y] \neq \langle 0 \rangle .$$
where I is the ideal $\mathrm{I} = \langle h_1, \ldots, h_\ell, f \cdot t - 1 \rangle \subset \mathbb{K}[X, t]$.

b) The statement $\{H \Rightarrow T\}$ is generally false if and only if
$$\mathrm{I}^* \cap \mathbb{K}[Y] \neq \langle 0 \rangle .$$
where I^* is the ideal $\mathrm{I}^* = \langle h_1, \ldots, h_\ell, f \rangle \subset \mathbb{K}[X]$.

[3]"Proof by exhaustion, also known as proof by cases…is a method…in which the statement to be proved is split into a finite number of cases and each case is checked to see if the proposition in question holds". C.f. https://en.wikipedia.org/wiki/Proof_by_exhaustion

see [21].

Obviously, here the key tool is to decide -by dragging, on the GeoGebra window, the construction to a suitable number of positions, i.e. by considering some special values of $(x_1, \ldots, x_n)$ and verifying if the statement is false or true in these cases- if the elimination ideal of hypotheses and the negation of the theses or the ideal of hypotheses and theses is or not zero. See the above mentioned academic works for details of the excellent performance of this technique in the prototype version already implemented. Moreover, in [14], a detailed benchmark is presented on the comparative performance of different proving methods implemented in GeoGebra. The first column contains a list of ggb files describing geometric statements, alphabetically ordered. Then, there is a series of blocks (labeled as Recio, Botana, Botana D, BotanaGiac, etc.) referring to the considered theorem proving method, each one containing two columns: Result (true, false, empty, i.e. undefined for some reason) and Speed (in milliseconds, t/o means time-out!). Details about the different methods are provided in [13], although, concerning the method we are dealing with here, the reference in [13] is very limited: only the two-variables case is sketched, with some hints about its generalization for three variables. Notice that we are considering just a prototype implementation, thus it happens that, in many instances, some of the methods are not programmed to include some types of input (for example, in [13] the so called Recio's method -i.e. the one described in the current paper- is not yet programmed to deal with circles, thus it yields no answer in many cases!). Despite all these limitations it is clear that, when applicable, our method is much faster than any other one.

We finish with an example of the application of our algorithms to a geometric problem.

Example 3.3. In this example we illustrate how the ideas described above are applicable to prove that Simson's Theorem is generically true. The Theorem of Simson claims that

> *Given a triangle abc and a point d on its circumcircle, the feet e, f, g of the perpendiculars from d to the lines bc, ab, and ac, respectively, are collinear.*

We will follow the notation in [20] (subsections 1.4 and 1.5) but adding, as a non-degeneracy hypothesis, the condition h_6 below. Thus, the variables in the construction are $\{r, s, m, n, q, t, u, v, w\}$,

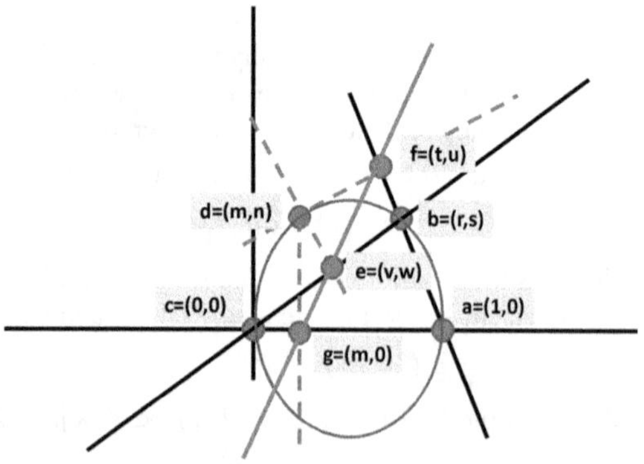

Figure 1: Illustration of Simson's Theorem

being $\{r, s, m\}$ a maximum size set of independent variables (see Fig. 1). The hypotheses are

$$
\begin{aligned}
h_1 &= s(t-1) - u(r-1) \ (f \text{ is on the line } ab).\\
h_2 &= (t-m)(r-1) + s(u-n) \ (df \text{ is perpendicular to } ab).\\
h_3 &= -rw + sv \ (e \text{ is on the line } cb).\\
h_4 &= r(m-v) + s(n-w) \ (de \text{ is perpendicular to } cb).\\
h_5 &= m^2 s - n^2 s + nr^2 + ns^2 + ms - nr \ (d \text{ is on the circumcircle}).\\
h_6 &= qs - 1 \ (abc \text{ does not degenerate as a triangle}).
\end{aligned}
$$

And the thesis

$$F = (w-u)(m-t) + u(v-t).$$

Therefore, we consider the ideal

$$\mathrm{I} =< h_1, \ldots h_6, zF - 1 >\subset \mathbb{C}[r, s, m, n, q, z, t, u, v, w].$$

The variety $\mathcal{V} = \mathbb{V}(\mathrm{I}) \subset \mathbb{C}^{10}$ has degree $d = 32$. In order to decide whether $\mathrm{I} \cap \mathbb{C}[r, s, m] =< 0 >$ we apply Algorithm 2 with the third optimization approach described in the remark after the algorithm, namely taking the support with $N = \binom{32+3}{3} = 6545$, applying a random bijective affine transformation and checking whether all elements are liftable. For the random affine transformation we have taken integers in $\{-10..10\}$, and we have consider an upper triangular matrix. The precise transformation $\mathcal{T}$ is

$$\mathrm{Y} = \begin{pmatrix} 7 & 0 & 9 \\ 0 & 2 & -3 \\ 0 & 0 & 6 \end{pmatrix} \mathrm{X} + \begin{pmatrix} -5 \\ 9 \\ 6 \end{pmatrix}.$$

The result is that none element in $\mathcal{T}(\mathrm{Supp}(N))$ can be lifted. Therefore, the conclusion is that elimination ideal is non-zero, and hence the theorem is generically true. The computation were performed with Maple 2017 on a PC with i7-5500U CPU 240GHz, and the 6545 lifting checks took 1.3 seconds.

REFERENCES

[1] Abánades, M., Botana, F., Kovács, Z., Recio, T., Sólyom-Gecse, C. Development of automatic reasoning tools in GeoGebra. *ACM Communications in Computer Algebra.* Volume 50 Issue 3, September 2016. Pages: 85-88.

[2] Cox, D., Little, J., O'Shea, D. (2012). Ideals, Varieties, and Algorithms. Springer, New York, third edition.

[3] D'Andrea C., Krick T. and Sombra M. (2013). Heights of varieties in multiprojective spaces and arithmetics Nullstellensätze. *Annales scientifiques de l'École Normale Supérieure.* Vol 46, issue 4, pp. 549–627.

[4] Ferro A. and Gallo G. (1988). Automated theorem proving in elementary geometry. *Le Matemathiche,* vol. XLIII, pp. 195–224.

[5] Gasca M. and Sauer T. (2000). Advances in Computational Mathematics (Special issue on Multivariate polynomial interpolation), vol. 12 (2000), pp. 377–410.

[6] Heintz J. (1983). Definability and fast quantifier elimination in algebraically closed fields. *Theoretical Computer Science,* 24, pp. 239-277.

[7] Heintz, J., Schnorr, C.P. (1982). Testing polynomials wich are easy to compute, *L'Enseignement Mathématique,* 30, 237–254.

[8] Hong J. (1986). Can we prove geometry theorems by computing an example?. *Science China Mathematics.* 29(8): 824-834.

[9] Hong J. (1986). Proving by example and gap theorems. *Proc. 27th Ann. Symp. Foundations Comp. Science.* 107–116. IEEE.

[10] Kortenkamp, U. (1999). Foundations of Dynamic Geometry. Ph. D. thesis. ETH Zürich. Available at http://citeseerx.ist.psu.edu/viewdoc/download?doi=10.1.1.100.2207&rep=rep1&type=pdf

[11] Kortenkamp, U., Richter-Gebert, J. (2004): Using automatic theorem proving to improve the usability of geometry software. Proceedings of MathUI, 2004. (Online publication available at https://www.researchgate.net/publication/215908130_Using_Automatic_Theorem_Proving_to_Improve_the_Usability_of_Geometry_Software).

[12] Kovács, Z. (2015). Computer based conjectures and proofs in teaching euclidean geometry. Ph. D. thesis. Johannes Kepler University, Linz. Available at http://www.jku.at/content/e263/e16099/e16086/e173791?view=PUBD&pub_id=51957

[13] Kovács, Z. (2015) Prover benchmark for GeoGebra 5.0.65.0 (r38763). http://test.geogebra.org/~kovzol/data/Prove-20150219b/

[14] Kovács, Z. (2018). Prover benchmark for GeoGebra 611. https://prover-test.geogebra.org/job/GeoGebra-provertest/ws/test/scripts/benchmark/prover/html/all.html
[15] Kounailis, E., Rusinowitch, M. (1990). Mechanizing inductive reasoning. In the*Eight National Conference on Artificial Intelligence.* AAAI-90 Proceedings. 240–245.
[16] Lipton, R. J.(2009). The curious history of the Schwartz-Zippel lema. In *Gödel's lost letter and P=NP*, Nov. 30, 2009. Available at https://rjlipton.wordpress.com/2009/11/30/the-curious-history-of-the-schwartz-zippel-lemma/
[17] Mora, T. (2003). De Nugis Groebnerialium 2: Applying Macaualay's Trick in order to easily write a Groebner basis, J. AAECC. 13 (2003) 437–446
[18] Pardo, L.M., (1995). How lower and upper complexity bounds meet in elimination theory, *Proc. AAECC–11*, (G. Cohen, M.Giusti, T. Mora, eds.), Springer LNCS. 948, 33–69.
[19] Pardo, L.M. (2012). La Conjetura de Cook (P = NP?). Parte II: Probabilidad, Interactividad y Comprobación Probabilística de Demostraciones. *La Gaceta de la Real Sociedad Matemática Española*, 15-2. 303–333.
[20] Recio, T. (1998). Cálculo simbólico y geométrico. *Editorial SÃŋntesis.* Madrid.
[21] Recio, T., Vélez, M.P. (1999(: Automatic discovery of theorems in elementary geometry, Journal of Automated Reasoning, 23, 63–82.
[22] Schwartz J.T. (1980). Fast probabilistic algorithms for verification of polynomial identities. *Journal of ACM.* 27: 701–717.
[23] Weitzhofer, S. (2013). Mechanic proof of theorems in plane geometry. Masterarbeit, Johannes Kepler University, Linz. Available at http://test.geogebra.org/%7Ekovzol/guests/SimonWeitzhofer/DiplArbeit.pdf
[24] Zariski, O. and Samuel, P. (1958). Commutative Algebra, Vol. 1, Van Nostrand.
[25] Zhang J., Yang L. and Deng M. (1990). The parallel numerical method of mechanical theorem proving. *Theoretical Computer Sience* 74:253–271.
[26] Zippel R. (1979). Probabilistic algorithms for sparse polynomials. In: Ng E.W. (eds) Symbolic and Algebraic Computation. EUROSAM 1979. Lecture Notes in Computer Science, vol 72. Springer, Berlin, Heidelberg.

Real Root Finding for Equivariant Semi-algebraic Systems

Cordian Riener
Department of Mathematics and Statistics
UiT The Arctic University of Norway
N-9037 Tromsø, Norway
cordian.riener@uit.no

Mohab Safey El Din
Sorbonne Université, CNRS, INRIA,
Laboratoire d'Informatique de Paris 6, LIP6, Équipe PolSys
F-75252, Paris Cedex 05, France
mohab.safey@lip6.fr

ABSTRACT

Let R be a real closed field. We consider basic semi-algebraic sets defined by n-variate equations/inequalities of s symmetric polynomials and an equivariant family of polynomials, all of them of degree bounded by $2d < n$. Such a semi-algebraic set is invariant by the action of the symmetric group. We show that such a set is either empty or it contains a point with at most $2d-1$ distinct coordinates. Combining this geometric result with efficient algorithms for real root finding (based on the critical point method), one can decide the emptiness of basic semi-algebraic sets defined by s polynomials of degree d in time $(sn)^{O(d)}$. This improves the state-of-the-art which is exponential in n. When the variables $x_1, \ldots, x_n$ are quantified and the coefficients of the input system depend on parameters $y_1, \ldots, y_t$, one also demonstrates that the corresponding one-block quantifier elimination problem can be solved in time $(sn)^{O(dt)}$.

KEYWORDS

Symmetric group, Semi-algebraic sets, Polynomial system solving

ACM Reference Format:
Cordian Riener and Mohab Safey El Din. 2018. Real Root Finding for Equivariant Semi-algebraic Systems . In *ISSAC '18: 2018 ACM International Symposium on Symbolic and Algebraic Computation, July 16–19, 2018, New York, NY, USA.* ACM, New York, NY, USA, 8 pages. https://doi.org/10.1145/3208976.3209023

1 INTRODUCTION

Let R be a real closed field. A *semi-algebraic set* is a subset of R^n defined by a boolean formula whose atoms are polynomial equalities and inequalities with coefficients in R. In this article, we consider basic semi-algebraic sets defined as follows. Given $F = (f_1, \ldots, f_k)$ and $G = (g_1, \ldots, g_s)$ in $R[x_1, \ldots, x_n]$, we denote by $S(F, G) \subset R^n$ the semi-algebraic set defined by $f_1 = \cdots = f_k = 0, g_1 \geq 0, \ldots, g_s \geq 0$. These sets arise in many areas of engineering sciences such as computational geometry, optimization, robotics (see e.g. [19, 28, 46, 63]). Algorithmic problems encompass real root finding, connectivity queries, or quantifier elimination.

Cordian Riener is supported by the Tromsø Research Foundation grant 17_matte_CR. Mohab Safey El Din is supported by the ANR grant ANR-17-CE40-0009 Galop and the PGMO grant Gamma.

ISSAC '18, July 16–19, 2018, New York, NY, USA

ACM ISBN 978-1-4503-5550-6/18/07...$15.00
https://doi.org/10.1145/3208976.3209023

Such problems are intrinsically hard [13]. In the worst case, solving quantifier elimination over the reals is doubly exponential in n and polynomial in the maximum degree of the input polynomials, see [25]. This complexity is achieved by the Cylindrical Algebraic Decomposition algorithm [17]. The idea of reducing real root finding to polynomial optimization in [57] is used in [37] to obtain the first algorithm with singly exponential complexity in n. This led to improvements for the decision problem [9, 20, 41, 49], quantifier elimination [8, 40, 44] and connectivity queries [7, 19, 21, 33, 42, 55]. Later, polar varieties are introduced in [2] for the decision problem [1, 3–5, 54], for computing roadmaps [55] or polynomial optimization [5, 34, 35, 39]. Complexity bounds are then cubic in some Bézout bound as well as practically efficient algorithms.

To break this curse of dimensionality, one exploits algebraic properties of systems defining semi-algebraic sets arising in applications. This has led to improvements, for e.g. the quadratic case [6, 36], the multi-homogeneous case [15, 43] and the important case of *symmetric semi-algebraic sets*.

Let $\mathscr{S}_n$ denote the group of permutations on a set of cardinality n. This group acts on R^n by permuting the coordinates. One says that a subset of R^n is symmetric when it is closed under this action.

Let now $f \in R[x_1, \ldots, x_n]$. One says that f is invariant under the action of $\mathscr{S}_n$ (or in short $\mathscr{S}_n$-invariant) when for all $\sigma \in \mathscr{S}_n$, $f(\sigma x) = f$ for $x = (x_1, \ldots, x_n)$. The following result summarizes the current state-of-the-art on symmetric semi-algebraic sets.

Theorem 1.1 ([50, 51, 65]). *Let $\{f, f_1, \ldots, f_s\} \subset R[x_1, \ldots, x_n]$ be $\mathscr{S}_n$-invariant polynomials of degree at most d.*

(A) *The real algebraic set $V_R(f)$ is not empty if and only if it contains a point with at most $\lfloor \frac{d}{2} \rfloor$ distinct coordinates.*
(B) *The semi-algebraic set in $S \subset R^n$ defined by $f_1 \geq 0, \ldots, f_s \geq 0$ is not empty if and only if it contains a point with at most d distinct coordinates.*

As a consequence, on input f, one can decide the emptiness of $V_R(f)$ by partitioning – up to symmetry – the set of variables $x_1, \ldots, x_n$ into $\lfloor \frac{d}{2} \rfloor$ subsets, say $\chi_1, \ldots, \chi_{\lfloor \frac{d}{2} \rfloor}$ and set $x_i = x_j$ in the input when x_i and x_j lie in the same set χ_ℓ. This way one is led to apply the aforementioned algorithms for deciding the emptiness of semi-algebraic sets to inputs involving at most $\lfloor \frac{d}{2} \rfloor$. Since the number of such partitions lies in $O(n^d)$, one finally obtains algorithms deciding the emptiness of $V_R(f)$ (resp. S) in time $n^{O(d)}$, hence polynomial time when d is fixed. The same reasoning holds for the case (B) of Theorem 1.1.

Of course, semi-algebraic sets defined by $\mathscr{S}_n$-invariant constraints define symmetric semi-algebraic sets but the reciprocal is not true as illustrated with the example $x_1 \geq 0, x_2 \geq 0$. A family F of constraints in $R[x_1, \ldots, x_n]$ is said to be $\mathscr{S}_n$-invariant when for all $f \in F$ and $\sigma \in \mathscr{S}_n$, $f(\sigma x) \in F$. Note that such families of constraints defined symmetric semi-algebraic sets. It is a major and longstanding challenge to obtain algorithms that, given a $\mathscr{S}_n$-invariant family of constraints, takes advantage of the symmetry invariance to decide if it is feasible over the reals.

The goal of this article is to *generalize* the results in [50, 51, 65] to the following special situation. Let $F = (f_1, \ldots, f_k)$ and $G = (g_1, \ldots, g_n)$ be in $\mathbf{R}[x_1, \ldots, x_n]$ and d be the maximum degree of those polynomials. Assume that for $1 \leq i \leq k$, f_i is $\mathscr{S}_n$-invariant and that G is $\mathscr{S}_n$-equivariant, i.e., we have $G(\sigma(x)) = (g_{\sigma(i)}(x))_{1\leq i\leq n}$ for all $\sigma \in \mathscr{S}_n$. The topical question we address is the following one. Can we decide the emptiness of the semi-algebraic set defined by $f_1 = \cdots = f_k = 0, g_1 \geq 0, \ldots, g_n \geq 0$ in time $n^{O(d)}$, i.e. polynomial in n and exponential in d? More generally, can we take advantage of equivariance for e.g. one-block quantifier elimination?

This latter question is important for a wide range of applications, in particular for the analysis of equivariant dynamical systems, which commonly appear in biology (see [60]). Those systems are of the form $\dot{\boldsymbol{x}} = f(\boldsymbol{x}, \lambda)$ where λ is a set of parameters and f is an equivariant family of polynomials for the action of the symmetric group on the $\boldsymbol{x}$ variables and the state variables $\boldsymbol{x}$ must be non-negative (see [60, Example 2]). When analyzing the equilibrium points of such systems w.r.t. parameters λ, we are led to solve equivariant semi-algebraic systems.

Main results. We provide a positive answer to this question. More precisely, the following holds.

(i) On input F and G as above, deciding the emptiness of $S(F, G) \cap \mathbf{R}^n$ can be done in time $n^{O(d)}$.

(ii) On input F and G in $\mathbf{R}[y_1, \ldots, y_t][x_1, \ldots, x_n]$ such that F and G satisfy the above $\mathscr{S}_n$-invariance and equivariance assumptions, the quantifier elimination problem $\exists x \in \mathbf{R}^n\ F = 0, G > 0$ can be solved in time $n^{O(dt)}$.

This result, which generalized Theorem 1.1, is of particular interest on families of systems where d is fixed and n grows. They are obtained by proving that $S(F, G)$ is not empty if and only if it contains a point with at most $2d - 1$ distinct coordinates. A key ingredient to establish such a property is the use of representation theory for equivariant maps and basic results from polynomial optimization. Combining such a geometric result with efficient algorithms for real root finding or one-block quantifier elimination yields the above complexity results. More accurate complexity results (with explicit constants in the exponent) are given under some assumptions which are proved to be generic.

We also report on practical experiments illustrating that algorithms described in this paper can tackle semi-algebraic systems which are out of reach of the current state-of-the-art.

Related works. We already mentioned several previous works which led to Theorem 1.1. More generally, the question of using symmetry in the context of real algebraic geometry is not new. Fundamental work started with [47, 48] which study the quotient of semi-algebraic sets, which are invariant under the action of a compact Lie group. In particular, Positivstellensätze for invariant polynomials which are non-negative on invariant semi-algebraic sets are derived. This line of work is further generalized by [16] and was applied for example in [23] to the context of the moment problem. A different line of work initiated by [32] consists in exploiting symmetries in the context of sums of squares relaxations of polynomial optimization. In particular, for optimization problems which are invariant by the symmetric group, a variety of strategies are exhibited in [52]. The topology of semi-algebraic sets defined by symmetric polynomials is also easier to understand: [11, 12] derived efficient algorithms to calculate e.g. their Euler-Poincaré characteristic.

With a more algebraic flavour, computer algebra has been developed to solve polynomial systems which are invariant under the action of some groups. Approaches for this longstanding problem focus on the zero-dimensional case and aim at describing algebraically the solution set. When all equations are invariant, invariants can be used for this purpose [24, 62]. Such an approach is completed by the use of SAGBI Gröbner bases techniques [29, 64]. When the system is globally invariant, [30, 31] provides an efficient dedicated Gröbner basis algorithm (see also [18, 59] for further developments).

Structure of the paper. Section 2 recalls properties of symmetric semi-algebraic sets and explains why a direct generalization of Theorem 1.1 is hopeless. Section 3 provides a proof that $S(F, G)$ is not empty iff it contains a point with at most $2d - 1$ distinct coordinates. Section 4 provides a description of the algorithms and the analysis of their complexity. Section 5 reports on practical performances.

2 PRELIMINARIES

A crucial condition in Theorem 1.1 is that all the polynomials defining the considered semi-algebraic sets are indeed symmetric. Such an assumption is easily bypassed in the case of real algebraic sets.

Corollary 2.1. *Let $f_1, \ldots, f_k \in \mathbf{R}[X_1, \ldots, X_n]$ with $\deg f_i \leq d$ for all i. Then $V_{\mathbf{R}}(f_1, \ldots, f_n)$ is not empty if and only if it contains a point with at most d distinct coordinates.*

Proof. Consider the polynomial $g := \sum_{i=1}^{k} \sum_{\sigma \in S_n} \sigma(f_i)^2$. Then we have an equality of the real varieties $V_{\mathbf{R}}(g) = V_{\mathbf{R}}(f_1, \ldots, f_n)$ and g is symmetric of degree $2d$ and in this situation statement (A) in Theorem 1.1 yields the result. □

However, in many applications the semi-algebraic set is defined by polynomials that are not themselves symmetric.

It is feasible to replace the non-invariant inequalities by a set of new inequalities which describe the same set but are invariant [16]: any symmetric semi-algebraic set defined by s inequalities can be defined with $s + 1$ inequalities which are invariant by the action of the symmetric group (see also [23, 45] for a constructive approach). However, such a "symmetrization" process comes at a price: In general it will increase the degree of the polynomials drastically. We illustrate this phenomenon in the following easy example.

Example 2.2. Consider the positive orthant $S := \{\boldsymbol{x} = (\mathbf{x}_1, \ldots, \mathbf{x}_n) \in \mathbf{R}^n\ :\ \mathbf{x}_1 \geq 0, \ldots, \mathbf{x}_n \geq 0\}$. Clearly, S is symmetric. By considering the map which sends the coordinates of $\boldsymbol{x} \in \mathbf{R}^n$ to the coefficients of the polynomial $h(t) := \prod_{i=1}^{n}(t - \mathbf{x}_i)$ one can prove that S is equivalently defined by $e_1(x) \geq 0, \ldots, e_n(x) \geq 0$ where e_i denotes the i-th elementary symmetric polynomial. One implication is immediate: $\boldsymbol{x} \in S$ clearly entails that $e_i(\boldsymbol{x}) \geq 0$ for $1 \leq i \leq n$. We prove the other implication by induction on n. The case $n = 1$ is clear. Now let $\boldsymbol{x} = (\mathbf{x}_1, \ldots, \mathbf{x}_n) \in \mathbf{R}^n$ be not in S, i.e., let one of its coordinates be negative. Besides, without loss of generality we can assume that all $\mathbf{x}_i \neq 0$ (since S has non-empty interior). We show further that this implies that there exists $1 \leq i \leq n$ such that $e_i(\boldsymbol{x}) < 0$. Clearly,

in the case when exactly one coordinate of $\boldsymbol{x}$ is negative we have $e_n(\boldsymbol{x}) < 0$ and hence our claim follows. Therefore, we assume that at least two coordinates are negative. We consider the polynomial $h(t)$ as defined above. i.e., $h(t) = t^n + \sum_{i=1}^{n}(-1)^i e_i(\boldsymbol{x})t^{n-i}$. Notice that, by construction, all roots of h are real. By Rolle's Theorem, there exists a root of its derivative $h' := \frac{\partial h}{\partial t}$ between every two roots of h. Since h has by construction at least two negative roots, h' has a negative root. Consider $(\tilde{\mathbf{x}}_1, \dots, \tilde{\mathbf{x}}_{n-1}) \in \boldsymbol{R}^{n-1}$ the $n-1$ roots of h' (ordered decreasingly). Since $(\tilde{\mathbf{x}}_1, \dots, \tilde{\mathbf{x}}_{n-1})$ is not in the $n-1$ dimensional positive orthant we can apply the induction hypothesis to the case $n-1$ to infer that at least for one $j \in \{1, \dots, n-1\}$ we have $e_j(\tilde{\mathbf{x}}_1, \dots, \tilde{\mathbf{x}}_{n-1}) < 0$. But since h' is the derivative of h this clearly implies $e_j(\mathbf{x}_1, \dots, \mathbf{x}_n) = \frac{1}{n-j} e_j(\tilde{\mathbf{x}}_1, \dots, \tilde{\mathbf{x}}_{n-1}) < 0$.
Of course, the description of S with symmetric polynomials is not unique. However, it follows from the equivalence shown above that no other description with symmetric polynomials can involve only symmetric polynomials of degree smaller than n.
Indeed, suppose that $S := \{\boldsymbol{x} \in \boldsymbol{R}^n : g_1(\boldsymbol{x}) \geq 0, \dots, g_m(\boldsymbol{x}) \geq 0\}$, where each g_i is a symmetric polynomial. It is classically known that each symmetric polynomial can be uniquely represented as a polynomial in the elementary symmetric polynomials, i.e. for each i we have a polynomial $\gamma_i \in \boldsymbol{R}[e_1, \dots, e_n]$ such that $g_i(x) = \gamma_i(e_1(x), \dots, e_n(x))$. Now suppose that for each i we have $\deg g_i < n$. Since the polynomials γ_i are unique and $\deg e_n = n$, it follows, that for each i we must have $\gamma_i(0, 0, \dots, 0, t) = 0$. Consider the point $\xi := (0, 1, 2, \dots, n-1)$. Similarly to the above reasoning, we consider a univariate polynomial $h(t) := \prod_{i=1}^{n}(t - \xi_i)$ (with $\xi_i = i - 1$). Note that $e_n(\xi) = 0$. Since all n roots of h are distinct, $h - \varepsilon$ has also n distinct real roots, for a small enough positive ε. Let $\zeta \in \boldsymbol{R}^n$ be one of the roots of $h - \varepsilon$. Then, $e_n(\zeta) < 0$ and thus $\zeta \notin S$. But $e_i(\xi) = e_i(\zeta)$ for all $1 \leq i \leq n-1$ and we deduce that $\gamma_j(\zeta) = \gamma_j(\xi)$ for $1 \leq j \leq m$. Hence, we get a contradiction with $\zeta \notin S$. Therefore, every representation of S in terms of symmetric polynomials must contain at least one polynomial of degree n, hence making useless Theorem 1.1 for algorithmic applications.

Notice that the semi-algebraic set S defined in the example above clearly contains points for which all coordinates are the same and we note the following generalization of Theorem 1.1 to basic convex semi-algebraic sets.

Proposition 2.3. *Let $S \subset \boldsymbol{R}^n$ be basic convex symmetric semi-algebraic set. Then S is not empty if and only if it contains a point for which all coordinates are equal.*

Proof. Suppose that S is not empty and let $x \in S$. Since S is symmetric, S also contains the orbit $\{\sigma(x) : \sigma \in \mathscr{S}_n\}$ of x. Since S is convex, it contains the point $y := \frac{1}{n!} \sum_{\sigma \in \mathscr{S}_n} \sigma(x)$ and clearly all coordinates of y are equal. □

Notice that the semi-algebraic set S defined in the example above contains points for which all coordinates are the same. In view of Proposition 2.3 it is natural to ask, to which extent it is possible to derive statements similar to Theorem 1.1 for symmetric semi-algebraic sets that are defined by polynomials of low degree, which are not invariant by the action of the symmetric group. The following example shows that for general semi-algebraic sets, such a generalization is not possible:

Example 2.4. Let $f := \sum_{i=1}^{n}(x_i - i)^2$ and its $\mathscr{S}_n$ orbit which we denote by $\mathcal{F}$. Let S be the semi-algebraic set $\{x \in \boldsymbol{R}^n : \exists g \in \mathcal{F}$ with $g(x) = 0\}$. By construction, S is a finite set which coincides with the orbit of $\xi = (1, \dots, n)$. Therefore, all points in S have distinct coordinates, but S is described by quadratic polynomials.

3 MAIN GEOMETRIC RESULT

One way to generalize Theorem 1.1 to semi-algebraic sets that are $\mathscr{S}_n$-invariant but not described by symmetric polynomials is to rely on results from the theory of finite reflection groups. A finite group is called a finite reflection group, if it is generated by orthogonal reflection on a finite set of hyperplanes. These groups are extensively studied and the particular case of the symmetric group acting by permuting the coordinates falls into this framework. We refer the interested reader to [38] for more details.

Definition 3.1. Let $\phi : \boldsymbol{R}^n \to \boldsymbol{R}^n$ be a morphism given by $\boldsymbol{x} \mapsto (\phi_1(\boldsymbol{x}), \dots, \phi_n(\boldsymbol{x}))$ and let G be a finite reflection group. Then ϕ is G-equivariant if we have $g(\phi) = \phi(g(x))$ for every $g \in G$. We will write $\mathrm{Mor}_G(\boldsymbol{R}^n, \boldsymbol{R}^n)$ for the set of G-equivariant morphisms.
We say that a sequence of polynomials of cardinality n is G-equivariant, if it defines a G-equivariant morphism.

Example 3.2. Let s be a bivariate symmetric polynomial and $d \in \mathbb{N}$. The map $(\mathbf{x}_1, \mathbf{x}_2, \mathbf{x}_3) \to (\mathbf{x}_1^d + s(\mathbf{x}_2, \mathbf{x}_3), \mathbf{x}_2^d + s(\mathbf{x}_1, \mathbf{x}_3), \mathbf{x}_3^d + s(\mathbf{x}_1, \mathbf{x}_2))$ is equivariant by the action of the symmetric group $\mathscr{S}_3$.

Let $\boldsymbol{R}[x_1, \dots, x_n]^G$ be the ring of polynomials in $\boldsymbol{R}[x_1, \dots, x_n]$ which are G-invariant. There is a natural action of $\boldsymbol{R}[x_1, \dots, x_n]^G$ on the set $\mathrm{Mor}_G(\boldsymbol{R}^n, \boldsymbol{R}^n)$ by multiplication: it clearly preserves the equivariance. In other words, the equivariant morphisms form a module over $\boldsymbol{R}[x_1, \dots, x_n]^G$. It follows from the work of Shchvartsman [58] that this module is a free module.

Theorem 3.3 (Shchwartsman). *For any finite reflection group G the set $\mathrm{Mor}_G(\boldsymbol{R}^n, \boldsymbol{R}^n)$ is a finite $\boldsymbol{R}[x_1, \dots, x_n]^G$-module of rank n. Furthermore, let $\psi_1, \dots, \psi_n$ be generators of $\boldsymbol{R}[x_1, \dots, x_n]^G$, then every equivariant morphism can uniquely be written as $f_i = \sum_{j=1}^{n} \frac{\partial \psi_j}{\partial x_i} s_j$ where $s_j \in \boldsymbol{R}[x_1, \dots, x_n]^G$.*

In the sequel we will be interested in basic semi-algebraic sets that are generated by polynomials which are $\mathscr{S}_n$ equivariant in the sense of Definition 3.1. The general machinery developed by Shchwartsman allows in the case of $\mathscr{S}_n$ for the following corollary, which gives a convenient description of such polynomials.

Corollary 3.4. *Let $\{f_1, \dots, f_n\}$ be a set of polynomials that define an $\mathscr{S}_n$ equivariant morphism and let $\deg f_i \leq d$. Then $f_i = \sum_{j=0}^{d} s_j \cdot x_i^j$, where $s_j \in \boldsymbol{R}[x_1, \dots, x_n]^{\mathscr{S}_n}$ is symmetric and of degree $\leq d-j+1$.*

Proof. It is classically known that every symmetric polynomial can be uniquely written in terms of the first n Newton sums $p_i := \sum_{j=1}^{n} x_j^i$. Thus, we can use these polynomials as generators of $\boldsymbol{R}[x_1, \dots, x_n]^{\mathscr{S}_n}$ and apply Theorem 3.3. Since $\mathrm{Mor}_{\mathscr{S}_n}(\boldsymbol{R}^n, \boldsymbol{R}^n)$ is a free module and the polynomials $p_1, \dots, p_n$ are algebraically independent, the degree restrictions follow at once, since we cannot have any cancellation of degrees in the representation. □

Let us denote by $A_{2d-1} \subset \boldsymbol{R}^n$ the subset of points with at most $2d-1$ distinct coordinates.

Theorem 3.5. *Let $F = (f_1, \dots, f_k)$ and $G = (g_1, \dots, g_n)$ be sequences of polynomials in $\mathbf{R}[x_1, \dots, x_n]$. Let d be the maximum of $\deg(f_i)$ and $\deg(g_j)$ for $1 \le i \le k$ and $1 \le j \le n$. Assume that for $1 \le i \le n$, f_i is $\mathscr{S}_n$ invariant, that G is $\mathscr{S}_n$-equivariant and that $\deg(g_j) \ge 2$ for $1 \le j \le n$. Then, the basic semi-algebraic set $S(F,G)$ is empty if and only if $S(F,G) \cap A_{2d-1} \neq \emptyset$.*

Recall that p_i denotes the Newton sum $\sum_{i=1}^n x_i^j$. For the proof of Theorem 3.5, we study some varieties defined by the p_i's. Let $\gamma := (\gamma_1, \dots, \gamma_d) \in \mathbf{R}^d$ then we denote by $\mathscr{N}_\gamma$ the real variety

$$\mathscr{N}_\gamma := \{x \in \mathbf{R}^n \ : \ p_1(x) = \gamma_1, \dots, p_d(x) = \gamma_d\}.$$

These varieties will play a crucial role for the proof of Theorem 3.5; the following lemma illustrates the importance of these sets.

Lemma 3.6. *Reusing the notations introduced above, consider a $\mathscr{S}_n$-invariant polynomial f in $\mathbf{R}[x_1, \dots, x_n]$ of degree d. Then f is constant over $\mathscr{N}_\gamma$.*

Proof. Since f is $\mathscr{S}_n$-invariant, one can write it as the composition $q(p_1, \dots, p_n)$ where q is a polynomial in $\mathbf{R}[u_1, \dots, u_n]$ ($u_1, \dots, u_n$ are new variables) and the p_i's are Newton polynomials as above. Since $\deg(f) = d$ and $\deg(p_i) = i$, one also deduces that $\deg(q, u_j) = 0$ for $d+1 \le j \le n$. This implies that q lies in $\mathbf{R}[u_1, \dots, u_d]$ and our claim follows immediately from the definition of $\mathscr{N}_\gamma$. □

Before going further, we first examine the possible roots of the polynomials g_j in an $\mathscr{S}_n$-equivariant system on the variety $\mathscr{N}_\gamma$.

Lemma 3.7. *Let $d \le n$, $\gamma \in \mathbf{R}^d$. Consider $(h_1, \dots, h_n)$ a sequence of polynomials of degree at most d in $\mathbf{R}[x_1, \dots, x_n]$ which are $\mathscr{S}_n$-equivariant and $\xi = (\xi_1, \dots, \xi_n) \in \mathscr{N}_\gamma$. Then, there exist $\{\alpha_1, \dots, \alpha_t\} \in \mathbf{R}^t$ with $t \le d-1$ such that $h_i(\xi) = 0$ if and only if $\xi_i \in \{\alpha_1, \dots, \alpha_t\}$.*

Proof. By Corollary 3.4, there exist symmetric polynomials s_i of degree at most d such that $h_i := \sum_{j=1}^d s_j \cdot \frac{\partial p_j}{\partial x_i}$, with $\deg(s_j) \le d$ for all $i \in \{1, \dots, n\}$. Since for $1 \le j \le d$, $\deg(s_j) \le d$ and s_j is symmetric, it follows that the value of s_j at ξ is determined by the value of the first d Newton sums at ξ (Lemma 3.6). Let $\gamma_i = p_i(\xi)$ for $1 \le i \le d$ and $\gamma = (\gamma_1, \dots, \gamma_d)$; besides, observe that, since $\xi \in \mathbf{R}^n$, we have $\gamma \in \mathbf{R}^d$. This implies that there exist $(b_1, \dots, b_d) \in \mathbf{R}^d$ such that for all $\zeta \in \mathscr{N}_\gamma \subset \mathbf{R}^n$, $s_1(\zeta) = b_1, \dots, s_d(\zeta) = b_d$. For $1 \le i \le n$, let us define the univariate polynomial $\tilde{h}_i = \sum_{j=1}^d b_j x_i^{j-1}$. As a consequence, the equality $h_i(\zeta) = \tilde{h}_i(\zeta)$ holds for all $\zeta \in \mathscr{N}_\gamma$. Now, consider the univariate polynomial $\delta(U) := \sum_{j=1}^d b_j U^{j-1}$ and let $\{\alpha_1, \dots, \alpha_t\}$ be its roots in $\mathbf{R}$. Since δ has degree $\le d-1$, we have $t \le d-1$. Observe that for every point $\xi \in \mathscr{N}_\gamma \subset \mathbf{R}^n$, $h_i(\xi) = 0$ iff $\tilde{h}_i(\xi) = 0$ and that $\tilde{h}_i(\xi) = \delta(\xi_i)$ where ξ_i is the i-th coordinate of ξ. In other words, $h_i(\xi) = 0$ iff $\xi_i \in \{\alpha_1, \dots, \alpha_{t-1}\}$. □

Proof of Theorem 3.5. Further S denotes $S(F,G)$. Note that it suffices to show that if $S \neq \emptyset$ then there exists a point in $S \cap A_{2d-1}$. So we assume that $S \neq \emptyset$ and pick $y \in S$. We set $p_1(y) = \gamma_1, \dots, p_d(y) = \gamma_d$ and we consider the corresponding real variety $\mathscr{N}_\gamma$ as defined above. We now take the intersection $S' := S \cap \mathscr{N}_\gamma$. Notice that $d \ge 2$ (by assumption) and hence $\mathscr{N}_\gamma$ is contained in a sphere. Thus, it follows that S' is closed and bounded. Further, we slightly abuse notation by using p_{d+1} to denote the map $x \to p_{d+1}(x)$ and its restrictions to subsets of $\mathbf{R}^n$. Moreover, since S' is closed and bounded, we deduce that $p_{d+1}(S')$ is closed and bounded too (see [14, Theorem 2.5.8]). Hence, we deduce that there exists $\xi = (\xi_1, \dots, \xi_n) \in S'$ with the property that $p_{d+1}(\xi)$ is maximal among all points in S'. We claim that $\xi \in A_{2d-1}$.
Let $\{i_1, \dots, i_\ell\}$ be the set of indices such that $g_i(\xi) = 0$ if and only if $i \in \{i_1, \dots, i_\ell\}$. By Lemma 3.7 applied to $G = (g_1, \dots, g_n)$, we deduce that there exists $\alpha = (\alpha_1, \dots, \alpha_t) \in \mathbf{R}^t$ with $t \le d-1$ such that for all $i \in \{i_1, \dots, i_\ell\}$, we have $\xi_i \in \{\alpha_1, \dots, \alpha_t\}$. Up to re-indexing the variables we can assume that $\{i_1, \dots, i_\ell\} = \{n-\ell+1, \dots, n\}$. For $i \in \{n-\ell+1, \dots, n\}$, we denote by $\kappa(i)$ the integer such that $\xi_i = \alpha_{\kappa(i)}$. This leads us to consider the intersection of S' with the affine linear space H of $\mathbf{R}^n$ defined by $x_{n-\ell+1} - \alpha_{\kappa(n-\ell+1)} = \dots = x_n - \alpha_{\kappa(n)} = 0$. We denote by S'_α the intersection of S' with the aforementioned hyperplanes.
Recall that ξ lies in S'_α and chosen to maximize p_{d+1} on S'. Then, ξ also maximizes the restriction of p_{d+1} to S'_α. Further, by construction, we have that $g_i(\xi) > 0$ for all $i \in \{1, \dots, n-\ell\}$. This shows that there exists a ball B centered at ξ, of radius small enough such that the following holds:
(i) for $i \in \{1, \dots, n-\ell\}$, g_i does not vanish in B;
(ii) the intersection of B with the real algebraic set defined by $f_1 = \dots = f_k = g_{n-\ell+1} = \dots = g_n = 0$ coincides with $S'_\alpha \cap B$.
Remark now that the real algebraic set defined by $f_1 = \dots = f_k = 0$ contains $\mathscr{N}_\gamma$. Also, applying Lemma 3.7 to G, one deduces that the real algebraic set defined by $g_{n-\ell+1} = \dots = g_n = 0$ coincides with the affine linear space H. We conclude that $S'_\alpha \cap B$ contains $\mathscr{N}_\gamma \cap H$. Besides, observe that ξ lies in $\mathscr{N}_\gamma \cap H$ and recall again that it maximizes the restriction of p_{d+1} to S'_α. We deduce that ξ maximizes the restriction of p_{d+1} to $\mathscr{N}_\gamma \cap H$.
Now, two situations may occur. Either, at ξ, the truncated Jacobian matrix associated to $(p_1, \dots, p_d)$ obtained by considering the partial derivatives w.r.t. $(x_1, \dots, x_{n-\ell})$ is full rank or it is not. In both cases, since $\xi = (\xi_1, \dots, \xi_n)$ maximizes the restriction of p_{d+1} to $\mathscr{N}_\gamma \cap H$, one deduces that there exists $(\lambda_0, \dots, \lambda_d) \in \mathbf{R}^{d+1} - \{0\}$ such that $0 = \lambda_0 \frac{\partial p_{d+1}}{\partial x_j}(\xi) - \sum_{i=1}^d \lambda_i \frac{\partial p_i}{\partial x_j}(\xi)$ for $1 \le j \le n-\ell$. This is rewritten as $0 = (d+1)\lambda_0 \xi_j^d - \sum_{i=1}^d (i) \lambda_i \xi_j^{i-1}$ for $1 \le j \le n-\ell$. The above algebraic relation entails that for $1 \le j \le n-\ell$, ξ_j is a root of the non-zero univariate polynomial $\eta(U) := \sum_{i=0}^d \lambda_i U^i$ of degree at most d (recall that $(\lambda_0, \dots, \lambda_d) \neq (0, \dots, 0)$). Therefore, at most d of the first $n-\ell$ coordinates of ξ can be distinct. Further, by construction, we have that there are at most $d-1$ possibilities for the last ℓ coordinates of ξ. Therefore, $\xi \in A_{2d-1}$ as claimed. □

Remark 1. *Observe that when F is $\mathscr{S}_n$-equivariant (instead of having all of its entries $\mathscr{S}_n$-invariant), the conclusions of Theorem 3.5 still hold. To see that it suffices to replace F be the sum of the squares of its entries. Also when the entries of F are subject to inequality constraints (instead of equality constraints), the conclusions of Theorem 3.5 still hold as one can replace inequalities by equations as in [7, Chap. 13].*

4 ALGORITHMS AND COMPLEXITY

4.1 Deciding emptiness

Further, we let $\mathbf{Q}$ be a real field, $\mathbf{R}$ be a real closed field containing $\mathbf{Q}$ and $\mathbf{C}$ be an algebraic closure of $\mathbf{R}$. We consider $F = (f_1, \dots, f_k)$ and $G = (g_1, \dots, g_n)$ be polynomial sequences in $\mathbf{Q}[x_1, \dots, x_n]$. As above, the semi-algebraic set of $\boldsymbol{R}^n$ defined by

$$f_1 = \cdots = f_k = 0, \qquad g_1 \geq 0, \ldots, g_n \geq 0$$

is denoted by $S(F, G)$. We start with a first complexity statement.

Theorem 4.1. *Let F and G be as above and d be an integer bounding the degrees of the polynomials in F and G. Assume that the polynomials in F are $\mathscr{S}_n$-invariant and that the map $\mathbf{x} \mapsto (g_1(\mathbf{x}), \ldots, g_n(\mathbf{x}))$ is $\mathscr{S}_n$-equivariant and that $d \leq n/2$.*
There exists an algorithm which, on input (F, G) decides whether $S(F, G)$ is empty using at most $n^{O(d)}$ arithmetic operations in $\boldsymbol{Q}$.

Proof. By Theorem 3.5, $S(F, G)$ is non-empty if and only if there exists $\boldsymbol{x} \in S(F, G)$ with at most $2d - 1$ distinct coordinates.
For $\boldsymbol{x} = (\mathbf{x}_1, \ldots, \mathbf{x}_n) \in \boldsymbol{R}^n$, we denote by $v(\boldsymbol{x}) = \{v_1, \ldots, v_p\}$ (with $p \leq n$ depending on $\boldsymbol{x}$) the set of values taken by the coordinates of $\boldsymbol{x}$ and by $\mathscr{P}(\boldsymbol{x}) = (\mathscr{P}_1, \ldots, \mathscr{P}_p)$ the partition given by the sets $\mathscr{P}_j = \{x_i \mid \mathbf{x}_i = v_j\}$. Up to renumbering, one assumes that the $\mathscr{P}_i$'s are given by ascending cardinality.
Hence, set $r = 2d-1$ and consider a partition $\gamma = [\gamma_1, \ldots, \gamma_r]$ of n of size r, i.e. $\gamma_1 + \cdots + \gamma_r = n$ with $\gamma_i \in \mathbb{N} - \{0\}$ for $1 \leq i \leq r$ and $\gamma_{i-1} \leq \gamma_i$ (by convention, $\gamma_0 = 0$). We say that a partition $\mathscr{P}_1, \ldots, \mathscr{P}_p$ of $(x_1, \ldots, x_n)$ is compatible with γ if $p \leq r$ and there exists an increasing sequence of integers s_i such that $|\mathscr{P}_i| = \gamma_{s_{i-1}} + \cdots + \gamma_{s_i}$.
We prove below that, given γ, one can decide in time $n^{O(r)}$ the existence of a real point $\boldsymbol{x}$ in $S(F, G)$ such that $\mathscr{P}(\boldsymbol{x})$ is compatible with γ. Bounding further the number of partitions of size r by n^r will establish the announced result (recall that $r = 2d - 1$).
Assume that such a point $\boldsymbol{x} = (\mathbf{x}_1, \ldots, \mathbf{x}_n)$ exists and consider $\mathscr{P}(\boldsymbol{x}) = (\mathscr{P}_1, \ldots, \mathscr{P}_p)$. For $\sigma \in \mathscr{S}_n$ we denote by $\sigma(\mathscr{P}_i)$ the set $\{x_{\sigma(j)} \mid x_j \in \mathscr{P}_i\}$. Let σ be a permutation of $\mathscr{S}_n$ such that $\sigma(\mathscr{P}_i) = \{x_{s_{i-1}}, \ldots, x_{s_i}\}$ and consider $\sigma(\boldsymbol{x}) = (\mathbf{x}_{\sigma(1)}, \ldots, \mathbf{x}_{\sigma(n)})$.
Now, remark that since all entries of F are invariant by the action of $\mathscr{S}_n$ and that G is $\mathscr{S}_n$-equivariant, $\sigma(\boldsymbol{x}) \in S(F, G)$. This leads us to associate to γ the partition $\Gamma = (\Gamma_1, \ldots, \Gamma_r)$ of $(x_1, \ldots, x_n)$ defined by $\Gamma_i = \{x_{\gamma_{i-1}+1}, \ldots, x_{\gamma_i}\}$ with $\gamma_0 = 0$ by convention.
Now, let $a_1, \ldots, a_r$ be new indeterminates. Next, we perform the substitution $x_{\gamma_{i-1}+1} = \cdots = x_{\gamma_i} = a_i$ for $1 \leq i \leq r$ in F and G. In the end, one obtains polynomial families in $\boldsymbol{R}[a_1, \ldots, a_r]$. The above discussion shows that we only need to decide the existence of real points to the new system one obtains this way. Using [10], this is done in time $n^{O(r)}$.
To finish the proof, it remains to count the number of partitions $\gamma = (\gamma_1, \ldots, \gamma_r)$ of n. The number $p(n, r)$ of partitions of n of size r satisfies the recurrence relation $p(n, r) = p(n-1, r) + p(n-r, r)$ with $p(n, r) = 0$ if $n < r$ and $p(n, n) = p(n, 1) = 1$. A simple induction establishes the inequality $p(n, r) \leq n^r$ which finishes the proof. □

The next result establishes a more precise complexity statement: we will actually identify the constant which is in the big-Oh exponent, when the input system satisfies some properties that we will prove to be generic. Further, given a polynomial family H in $\boldsymbol{R}[x_1, \ldots, x_n]$, $V(H) \subset \boldsymbol{C}^n$ denotes the set of common solutions to H in $\boldsymbol{C}^n$.
Hence, let as above $F = (f_1, \ldots, f_k)$ and $G = (g_1, \ldots, g_n)$ in $\boldsymbol{R}[x_1, \ldots, x_n]$. Further, for $\mathcal{I} = \{i_1, \ldots, i_\ell\} \subset \{1, \ldots, n\}$, we denote by $H_{\mathcal{I}}$ the set $F \cup \{g_{i_1}, \ldots, g_{i_\ell}\}$. We say that (F, G) satisfies the assumption R when

- the jacobian matrix of F has maximal rank at all points in $V(F)$;
- for all $\mathcal{I} \subset \{1, \ldots, n\}$, the jacobian matrix of $H_{\mathcal{I}}$ has maximal rank at any point of $V(H_{\mathcal{I}})$.

Now, let r in $\{1, \ldots, n\}$; we say that (F, G) satisfies assumption A_r if for any partition $\gamma = (\gamma_1, \ldots, \gamma_r)$ of n, when performing the substitution $x_{\gamma_{i-1}+1} = \cdots = x_{\gamma_i} = a_i$ $(1 \leq i \leq r)$ where $a_1, \ldots, a_r$ are new variables in (F, G), the obtained couple of polynomial sequences (F_γ, G_γ) satisfies R.
Further, the entries of F_γ (resp. G_γ) are denoted by $f_{1,\gamma}, \ldots, f_{k,\gamma}$ (resp. $g_{1,\gamma}, \ldots, g_{n,\gamma}$). We can now state our complexity result.

Theorem 4.2. *Let F and G be as above in $\boldsymbol{R}[x_1, \ldots, x_n]$, d be the maximum of the polynomials in F and G and E be the complexity of evaluating (F, G). Assume that for $1 \leq i \leq n$, f_i is $\mathscr{S}_n$ invariant, that $\boldsymbol{g}$ is $\mathscr{S}_n$-equivariant and that $\deg(g_j) \geq 2$ for $1 \leq j \leq n$ and that (F, G) satisfies assumption A_r.*
There exists an algorithm which on input (F, G) satisfying A, decides whether $S(F, G)$ is empty using $\tilde{O}\left(n^{2d}(2d)^{4d+1}(pE + d^2)\right)$ arithmetic operations in $\boldsymbol{Q}$.

Proof. Further we set $r = 2d - 1$. By Theorem 3.5, $S(F, G)$ is not empty if and only if $S(F, G)$ contains a point of $\boldsymbol{R}^n$ with at most r distinct coordinates. Besides, using the invariance of (F, G) under the action of $\mathscr{S}_n$ as in the proof of Theorem 4.1, deciding if $S(F, G)$ contains a real point with at most r distinct coordinates can be done by deciding if at least one of the semi-algebraic sets $S_\gamma = S(F_\gamma, G_\gamma)$ is non-empty when γ ranges of the set of partitions of n of length r. We already established that the number of such partitions is upper bounded by n^r at the end of the proof of Theorem 4.1.
Hence, let us focus on the complexity of deciding if S_γ is empty. We need to introduce some notation. For $\mathcal{I} = \{i_1, \ldots, i_\ell\} \subset \{1, \ldots, n\}$, we denote by $V_{\gamma, \mathcal{I}} \subset \boldsymbol{C}^n$ the algebraic set defined by $f_{1,\gamma} = \cdots = f_{k,\gamma} = g_{i_1,\gamma} = \cdots = g_{i_\ell,\gamma} = 0$. Further, we denote by $H = (h_1, \ldots, h_m) \subset \boldsymbol{R}[a_1, \ldots, a_r]$ these polynomials defining $V_{\gamma, \mathcal{I}}$.
Further, we use linear changes of variables. Hence for $\boldsymbol{A} \in \mathrm{GL}_n(\boldsymbol{R})$, we denote by $h_i^{\boldsymbol{A}}$ the polynomial obtained by performing the change of variables $\mathbf{a} \mapsto \boldsymbol{A}^{-1}\mathbf{a}$ in h_i and by $H^{\boldsymbol{A}}$ the sequence $(h_1^{\boldsymbol{A}}, \ldots, h_m^{\boldsymbol{A}})$.
Using [10], we deduce that, to decide the emptiness of S_γ, it suffices to compute sample points in each connected component of the real algebraic set $V_{\gamma, \mathcal{I}} \cap \boldsymbol{R}^n$ for all $\{i_1, \ldots, i_\ell\} \subset \{1, \ldots, n\}$ and filter out those points which lie in S_γ. Since (F, G) satisfies A, $V_{\gamma, \mathcal{I}}$ is either empty or smooth and equidimensional of co-dimension $k + \ell$ and the above polynomial system generates a radical ideal (by the Jacobian criterion [27, Theorem 16.19]). We conclude that we only need to consider subsets of cardinality $\ell \leq r - k$. We are in position to apply the results in [54].
Actually, we use a variant of the algorithm in [54], combining the geometric approach described therein with [56]. Let π_i be the canonical projection $(\mathbf{a}_1, \ldots, \mathbf{a}_r) \mapsto (\mathbf{a}_1, \ldots, \mathbf{a}_i)$ and, given an equidimensional and smooth algebraic set V, let $W(\pi_i, V)$ be the critical locus of the restriction of π_i to V. We will also consider the projections $\varphi_i : (\mathbf{a}_1, \ldots, \mathbf{a}_r) \mapsto \mathbf{a}_i$.
By [54, Theorem 2], in order to decide the emptiness of $V_{\gamma, \mathcal{I}}^{\boldsymbol{A}} \cap \boldsymbol{R}^n$, it suffices to perform a generic linear change of variables $\boldsymbol{A} \in \mathrm{GL}_r(\boldsymbol{R})$ and next compute rational parametrizations of all sets $\pi_{i-1}^{-1}(0) \cap W(\pi_i, V_{\gamma, \mathcal{I}}^{\boldsymbol{A}})$ for $1 \leq i \leq \dim(V_{\gamma, \mathcal{I}}^{\boldsymbol{A}}) + 1$. Technical but immediate computations show that $\pi_{i-1}^{-1}(0) \cap W(\pi_i, V_{\gamma, \mathcal{I}}^{\boldsymbol{A}}) = W(\varphi_i, Z_i)$

where $Z_i = \pi_{i-1}^{-1}(0) \cap V^A_{\gamma,I}$. Observe that in order to compute $Z_i = \pi_{i-1}^{-1}(0) \cap V^A_{\gamma,I}$ it suffices to solve the so-called Lagrange system $h^A_{1,i-1} = \cdots = h^A_{m,i-1} = 0, [\ell_1, \ldots, \ell_m]\text{jac}(H^A_{i-1}, i) = \mathbf{0}$ where $h^A_{j,i-1}$ (resp. H^A_{i-1}) is the polynomial obtained by setting $a_1 = \cdots = a_{i-1} = 0$ in h^A_j (resp. H^A), and $\text{jac}(H^A_{i-1}, 1)$ is the submatrix obtained by removing the first column of the Jacobian matrix associated with H^A_{i-1}. By [55, Proposition B.1], after performing a generic linear change of variables, assumptions needed to apply [56, Theorem 16]. This latter result shows that, letting E_H be the complexity of evaluating H and $r_i = r - (i-1)$, one can solve the above Lagrange system using $\tilde{O}\left(r_i^3\binom{r_i}{m}d^{2r_i+1}(pE_H + r_i d + r_i^2)\right)$ arithmetic operations in $\mathbf{Q}$. Hence, since $\dim(V_{\gamma,I}) = r - m$ the total cost of computing sample points in each connected component of $V_{\gamma,I} \cap \mathbf{R}^n$ uses $\tilde{O}\left(r^4 2^{2r} d^{2r+1}(pE_H + rd + r^2)\right)$ arithmetic operations in $\mathbf{Q}$. Finally, observe that E_H is bounded by the complexity of evaluating the input (F, G). Also, summing up this cost to take into account all possible subsets I (bounded by 2^r) and the number of partitions γ (bounded by n^r) ends the proof. □

It remains to establish the genericity of assumption A. To do that, we need to define the parameters'space in which the genericity statement will hold, i.e. the space of the coefficients of (F, G) where all entries of F are $\mathscr{S}_n$-invariant and G is $\mathscr{S}_n$-equivariant (recall also that all entries of (F, G) have degree bounded by d). Let $\mathfrak{R}$ be the Reynolds operator which sends $f \in \mathbf{C}[x_1, \ldots, x_n]$ to $\mathfrak{R}(f) = \frac{1}{n!}\sum_{\sigma \in \mathscr{S}_n} \sigma(f)$. Let now $\mathcal{M}$ be the set of all monomials of degree $\leq d$ in $\mathbf{C}[x_1, \ldots, x_n]$ and $\mathcal{M}_{\mathfrak{R}} = \mathfrak{R}(\mathcal{M})$, $c = |\mathcal{M}_{\mathfrak{R}}|$ and $T_i = (t_{i,1}, \ldots, t_{i,c})$ be new indeterminates for $1 \leq i \leq k$. we define now $\mathfrak{f}_i = \sum_{m_j \in \mathcal{M}_{\mathfrak{R}}} t_{i,j} m_j$ and $\mathfrak{f} = (\mathfrak{f}_1, \ldots, \mathfrak{f}_k)$ in $\mathbf{C}(T_1, \ldots, T_k)[x_1, \ldots, x_n]$. Observe that any sequence F such that all entries have degree bounded by d and are $\mathscr{S}_n$-invariant are obtained by specializing the indeterminates $(T_1, \ldots, T_k)$. Finally, we consider an additional sequence of indeterminates $T_{k+1} = (t_{k+1,1}, \ldots, t_{k+1,c})$ a polynomial $\mathfrak{g} = \sum_{m_j \in \mathcal{M}_{\mathfrak{R}}} t_{k+1,j} m_j$. Again, any sequence G which is $\mathscr{S}_n$-equivariant is obtained as the gradient vector of a polynomial obtained by instantiating T_{k+1} in $\mathfrak{g}$. Then, we set $N = c(k+1)$ and the parameters'space we consider is $\mathbf{C}^N$, i.e. the one endowed by the indeterminates $(T_1, \ldots, T_{k+1})$.

Theorem 4.3. *There exists a non-empty Zariski open set $\mathscr{O} \subset \mathbf{C}^N$ such that for (F, G) in $\mathscr{O}$, (F, G) satisfies assumption* A.

Proof. Let $I = \{i_1, \ldots, i_\ell\} \subset \{1, \ldots, n\}$, $r = 2d-1$, $\gamma = (\gamma_1, \ldots, \gamma_r)$ and $E_\gamma \subset \mathbf{C}^n$ be the linear subspace defined by $x_{\gamma_{i-1}+1} = \cdots = x_{\gamma_i}$ (for $1 \leq i \leq r$). We denote by Γ this set of linear equations which define Ext_γ. We consider the map $\Phi_{I,\gamma} : z = (\mathbf{x}, \mathbf{t}) \in E_\gamma \times \mathbf{C}^N \mapsto \left(\mathfrak{f}_1(z), \ldots, \mathfrak{f}_k(z), \frac{\partial \mathfrak{g}}{\partial x_{i_1}}(z), \ldots, \frac{\partial \mathfrak{g}}{\partial x_{i_\ell}}(z)\right)$. Assume for the moment that $\mathbf{0}$ is a regular value of Φ_I. Then, the algebraic version of Thom's weak transversality theorem (see e.g. [55, Proposition B.3]) states that there exists a non-empty Zariski open set $\mathscr{O}_I$ such that for any $\mathbf{t} \in \mathscr{O}_I$, $\mathbf{0}$ is a regular value for the specialized map $\mathbf{x} \mapsto \Phi_I(\mathbf{x}, \mathbf{t})$. In other words, at any $\mathbf{x} \in \mathbf{C}^N$ in the zero-set of the union of Γ with $\mathfrak{f}_1(., \mathbf{t}), \ldots, \mathfrak{f}_k(., \mathbf{t}), \frac{\partial \mathfrak{g}}{\partial x_{i_1}}(., \mathbf{t}), \ldots, \frac{\partial \mathfrak{g}}{\partial x_{i_\ell}}(., \mathbf{t})$, the Jacobian matrix of that polynomial family is full rank. By the Jacobian criterion [27, Theorem 16.19], we deduce that this polynomial family satisfies R.

Finally, we define $\mathscr{O}$ as the intersection of the finitely many non-empty Zariski open subsets $\mathscr{O}_I \subset \mathbf{C}^N$. Hence, $\mathscr{O}$ is a non-empty Zariski open set of $\mathbf{C}^N$ and for any $(F, G) \in \mathscr{O}$, (F, G) satisfies A. It remains to prove that for $I = \{i_1, \ldots, i_\ell\} \subset \{1, \ldots, n\}$, $\mathbf{0}$ is a regular value of the map $\Phi_{I,\gamma}$, i.e. the Jacobian matrix associated to $\Phi_{I,\gamma}$ is invertible at any point of $\Phi_{I,\gamma}^{-1}(\mathbf{0})$. To do that, we prove that the Jacobian matrix associated to Γ and $\left(\mathfrak{f}_1, \ldots, \mathfrak{f}_k, \frac{\partial \mathfrak{g}}{\partial x_{i_1}}, \ldots, \frac{\partial \mathfrak{g}}{\partial x_{i_\ell}}\right)$ is full rank at any point of $\Phi_{I,\gamma}^{-1}(\mathbf{0})$. We extract a full rank submatrix of that Jacobian matrix as follows:

- since Γ is a set of independent linear equations, one extracts a full rank square submatrix $\mathbf{J}$ with entries in $\mathbf{C}$ whose columns correspond to partial derivatives w.r.t. variables in $x_1, \ldots, x_n$;
- we select the columns corresponding to the partial derivatives w.r.t. indeterminates encoding the constant terms in $\mathfrak{f}_i$; this yields a diagonal submatrix Δ with 1's on the diagonal;
- we select the columns corresponding to the partial derivatives w.r.t. the indeterminate multiplying $(x_1 + \cdots + x_n)$ in $\mathfrak{g}$; this yields a diagonal submatrix Δ', with 1's on the diagonal.

In the end, the submatrix we have extracted is block-diagonal and these blocks on the diagonal are $\mathbf{J}$, Δ and Δ'. This ends the proof. □

4.2 One-block quantifier elimination

We now study the situation where $F = (f_1, \ldots, f_k)$ and $G = (g_1, \ldots, g_n)$ are polynomials in $\mathbf{Q}[x_1, \ldots, x_n, y_1, \ldots, y_t]$ such that *(i)* the action of $\mathscr{S}_n$ on $(x_1, \ldots, x_n)$ leaves invariant f_i ; *(ii)* the map $\mathbf{x} = (\mathrm{x}_1, \ldots, \mathrm{x}_n) \mapsto (g_1(\mathbf{x}, .), \ldots, g_n(\mathbf{x}, .))$ is $\mathscr{S}_n$ equivariant.
We consider the problem of computing a semi-algebraic description of the projection on the $(y_1, \ldots, y_t)$-space of the set $S(F, G) \subset \mathbf{R}^n \times \mathbf{R}^t$ defined by $f_1 = \cdots = f_k = 0, g_1 \geq 0, \ldots, g_n \geq 0$. This is equivalent to solve the one-block quantifier elimination problem:

$$\Phi : \quad \exists \mathbf{x} \in \mathbf{R}^n \quad f_1 = \cdots = f_k = 0, \quad g_1 \geq 0, \ldots, g_n \geq 0, \quad (4.1)$$

hence computing a quantifier-free formula which is equivalent to the quantified formula Φ. A geometric interpretation is that one aims at computing a semi-algebraic description of $\Pi(S(F, G))$ where Π is the projection $(\mathbf{x}, \mathbf{y}) \in \mathbf{R}^n \times \mathbf{R}^t \mapsto \mathbf{y}$.

Theorem 4.4. *Let F, G and Φ be as above, d be the maximum degree in the variables in $(x_1, \ldots, x_n)$ of the entries of F and G and assume that $d \leq \frac{n}{2}$. Then, there exists a quantifier-free formula $\Psi(Y) = \cup_{k=1}^K \Psi_k(Y)$ which is equivalent to Φ, and such that $K \leq n^{O(d)}$ and:*

$$\Psi_k(Y) = \vee_{i=1}^{\ell_k} \wedge_{j=1}^{\ell_{i,k}} (\vee_{u=1}^{\ell_{i,j,k}} \text{sign}(\varphi_{i,j,u,k}) = \sigma_{i,j,h,k})$$

$$\text{with} \quad \sigma_{i,j,h,k} \in \{0, 1, -1\}, \quad \ell_k \leq (n+k)^{d+1} n^{O(dt)}$$
$$\ell_{i,k} \leq (n+k)^{d+1} n^{O(d)}, \quad \ell_{i,j,k} \leq n^{O(d)}$$

and the degrees of the polynomials $\varphi_{i,j,u}$ are bounded by n^d. Moreover, there exists an algorithm which computes Ψ using at most $(k+n)^{dt} n^{O(dt)}$ arithmetic operations in $\mathbf{Q}$.

Proof. The proof is similar to the one of Theorem 4.1. We reduce the considered one-block quantifier elimination problem to solving finitely many one-block quantifier elimination problems.
Set $r = 2d-1$ and let $\Gamma(n, r)$ be the set of partitions $\gamma = (\gamma_1, \ldots, \gamma_r)$ of n of size r ($\gamma_0 = 0$ by convention). As in the proof of Theorem 4.1,

we associate to γ the substitution $x_{\gamma_{i-1}+1} = \cdots = x_{\gamma_i} = a_i$ for $1 \le i \le r$, where $a_1, \ldots, a_r$ are new variables. We denote by Φ_γ the formula obtained after performing this substitution in Φ and by $S_\gamma(F, G)$ the semi-algebraic set in $\boldsymbol{R}^r \times \boldsymbol{R}^t$ defined by the system obtained after applying the same substitution. Assume, for the moment, the following equality:

$$\Pi(S(F,G)) = \cup_{\gamma \in \Gamma(n,r)} \Pi(S_\gamma(F,G)). \qquad (4.2)$$

Then, performing quantifier elimination on formula Φ is equivalent to performing quantifier elimination on each formula Φ_γ – which yields a quantifier-free formula Ψ_γ defining $\Pi(S_\gamma(F,G))$ – and returning $\bigvee_{\gamma \subset \Gamma(n,r)} \Psi_\gamma$. Using [10, Theorem 14.16], one deduces that performing quantifier elimination on Φ_γ is done using $(k+n)^{dt} n^{O(dt)}$ arithmetic operations in $\boldsymbol{Q}$ and it yields a formula $\Psi_\gamma(Y) = \vee_{i=1}^{\ell} \wedge_{j=1}^{\ell_i} (\vee_{u=1}^{\ell_{i,j}} \mathrm{sign}(\varphi_{i,j,u}) = \sigma_{i,j,h})$ such that $\ell \le (n+k)^{d+1} n^{O(dt)}$, $\ell_i \le (n+k)^{d+1} n^{O(d)}$ and $\ell_{i,j} \le n^{O(d)}$. Now, recall that $\Gamma(n,r)$ has cardinality bounded by $n^{O(d)}$ (this bounds the integer K in the statement of the Theorem). Hence, runtime and degree bounds on the output formula are established.

Now, we prove that (4.2) holds which will end the proof. Let $\boldsymbol{y} \in \Pi(S(F,G))$ and $S_{\boldsymbol{y}} \subset \boldsymbol{R}^n$ be the projection of $S(F,G) \cap \Pi^{-1}(\boldsymbol{y})$ on the $(x_1, \ldots, x_n)$-space. Observe that $S_{\boldsymbol{y}}$ is defined by the polynomial system obtained by instantiating variables $(y_1, \ldots, y_t)$ to the coordinates of $\boldsymbol{y}$ in F and G ; we denote the obtained polynomial sequences by $F_{\boldsymbol{y}}$ and $G_{\boldsymbol{y}}$.

Observe that all entries of $F_{\boldsymbol{y}}$ are $\mathscr{S}_n$-invariant, the sequence $G_{\boldsymbol{y}}$ defines an equivariant map and all entries of $F_{\boldsymbol{y}}$ and $G_{\boldsymbol{y}}$ have degree $\le \frac{n}{2}$ by assumption. Hence, we can apply Theorem 3.5. It establishes that the semi-algebraic set $S_{\boldsymbol{y}}$ is empty if and only if it contains a point $\boldsymbol{x}$ with at most $2d-1$ coordinates. Now, observe, as in the proof of Theorem 4.1, thanks to the invariance of (F_γ, G_γ) that since under the action of $\mathscr{S}_n$, there exists a partition $\gamma = (\gamma_1, \ldots, \gamma_r)$ in $\Gamma(n,r)$ such that $S_{\boldsymbol{y}}$ has a non-empty intersection with the hyperplanes defined by $x_{\gamma_{i-1}+1} = \cdots = x_{\gamma_i}$ for $1 \le i \le r$. In other words, there exists $\gamma \in \Gamma(n,r)$ such that $\boldsymbol{y} \in \Pi(S_\gamma(F,G))$. We deduce that $\Pi(S(F,G)) \subset \cup_{\gamma \in \Gamma(n,r)} \Pi(S_\gamma(F,G))$. The reverse inclusion is immediate once we observe that $\cup_{\gamma \in \Gamma(n,r)} S_\gamma(F,G) \subset S(F,G)$. □

5 EXPERIMENTAL RESULTS

Our experiments make use of the following software

- RAGLIB. [53]. This is a Maple library, based on the FGB library by J.-C. Faugère. It implements algorithms based on the critical point method running in time singly exponential in n.
- MATHEMATICA-CAD [61], REALTRIANGULARIZE [22] which are packages computing Cylindrical Algebraic Decompositions (CAD) adapted to polynomial sequences.

We have considered the following test-suites:

- **S1**. We take the gradient of randomly chosen dense symmetric polynomials for G, letting F be the empty sequence; the coefficients of these polynomials are chosen between -2^{16} and 2^{16} using the random tool generator of MAPLE.
- **S2**. We take random dense systems of symmetric polynomials and equivariant families in $\mathbb{Q}[x_1, \ldots, x_n]$.

To solve these polynomial systems, we will use the following implementations of critical point method-based algorithms and CAD:

- **RAG** refers to the Real Algebraic Geometry library RAGLIB;

n	d	k	RS	RS-T	RAG	M	T
3	2	0	1.6	8	1.6	16	6.6
4	2	0	1.9	10	13	-	-
5	2	0	4.9	9	329	-	-
6	2	0	5	25	1577	-	-
7	2	0	6	1	39461	-	-
8	2	0	10	10	-	-	-
9	2	0	10	13	-	-	-

Table 1: Results obtained for test-suite S1

n	d	k	RS	RS-T	RAG	M	T
5	3	3	1762	-	1779	-	-
6	3	3	1583	-	376822	-	-
7	3	3	3135	-	-	-	-
8	3	3	4344	-	-	-	-
5	3	4	0.4	-	0.4	-	-
6	3	4	0.4	-	21	-	-
7	3	4	0.6	-	440	-	-
8	3	4	0.9	-	11686	-	-

Table 2: Results obtained for test-suite S2

- **M** refers to the CAD in MATHEMATICA;
- **T** refers to the CAD package in MAPLE.

The direct use of these polynomials will be compared with algorithms on which Theorems 4.1 and 4.2 rely. These consist in using critical point based algorithms to decide if the input system has a real solution with at most $2d-1$ distinct coordinates (where d bounds the degree of the inputs). Also we can substitute the use of those algorithms by ones that are based on CAD. This leads us to consider in our comparisons the following:

- **RS**: consists in using RAGLIB; this is an implementation of the algorithm on which Theorems 4.1 and 4.2 rely.
- **RS-T**: consists in using the CAD Maple package to look at solutions with at most $2d-1$ distinct coordinates.

The computations are performed on an Intel(R) Xeon(R) CPU E3-1505M v6 @ 3.00GHz with 32 Gb of RAM. Timings are given in seconds. The symbol '-' means that no result was obtained after 2 days of computation or because of a lack of memory. Tables 1 and 2 provide the results obtained for the test-suites **S1** and **S2**. One can see that the use of Theorem 3.5 allows us to tackle examples that are out of reach of other implementations.

We also observe that when $2d-1$ becomes larger than 4 or 5 implementations based on CAD cannot tackle most of the examples considered here while the critical point method based implementation RAGLIB scales far much better.

Finally, let us consider the following examples extracted from [26]:

- the problem **SWE** [26, p. 98] consists in proving that for $0 < a < b$, the semi-algebraic set defined by $m_2 > m_1^2 \frac{(a+b)^2}{4ab}$, $(b - x_1)(x_1 - a) \ge 0, \ldots, (b - x_n)(x_n - a) \ge 0$ is empty with
$$m_1 = \frac{1}{n}\sum_{i=1}^{n} x_i, \quad m_2 = \frac{1}{n}\sum_{i=1}^{n} x_i^2, \quad a = 1, \quad b = 2$$
- the problem 3.40.1 (referred to as **ROM**) in [26, p. 302] leads to decide the existence of real roots to the semi-algebraic system:
$$\sum_{i<j} x_i(x_i^2 + x_j^2) - \frac{1}{8}\left(\sum_{i=1}^{n} x_i\right)^4 > 0, x_1 > 0, \ldots, x_n > 0$$

The first (resp. second) table provides timings for **SWE** (resp. **ROM**). As observed previously, implementations based on the critical point methods scale way better than those based on CAD. Also our approach combined with critical point methods allows us to tackle problems which are out of reach of the state-of-the-art.

n	3	4	5	6	7	8	9
RS	0.12	0.14	0.3	0.5	0.6	0.74	1.2
RAG	0.2	0.3	0.5	1.6	9.8	131	1978
M	0.2	14.7	-	-	-	-	-

n	3	4	5	6	7	8	9
RS	0.25	0.8	4.2	95	6874	6902	14023
RAG	0.3	1	4.5	97	6664	-	-
M	0.04	0.5	1246	-	-	-	-

REFERENCES

[1] B. Bank, M. Giusti, J. Heintz, and G.M. Mbakop. 2001. Polar varieties and efficient real elimination. *Mathematische Zeitschrift* 238, 1 (2001), 115–144.

[2] B. Bank, M. Giusti, J. Heintz, and G.-M. Mbakop. 1997. Polar varieties and efficient real equation solving: the hypersurface case. *Journal of Complexity* 13, 1 (1997).

[3] B. Bank, M. Giusti, J. Heintz, and L.M. Pardo. 2005. Generalized polar varieties: Geometry and algorithms. *Journal of complexity* 21, 4 (2005), 377–412.

[4] B. Bank, M. Giusti, J. Heintz, and L.M. Pardo. 2010. Bipolar varieties and real solving of a singular polynomial equation. *Jaen Journal of Approximation* 2, 1 (2010), 65–77.

[5] B. Bank, M. Giusti, J. Heintz, and M. Safey El Din. 2014. Intrinsic complexity estimates in polynomial optimization. *Journal of Complexity* 30, 4 (2014), 430–443.

[6] A.I. Barvinok. 1993. Feasibility testing for systems of real quadratic equations. *Discrete & Computational Geometry* 10, 1 (1993), 1–13.

[7] S. Basu, R. Pollack, and M.-F. Roy. 1996. Computing Roadmaps of Semi-Algebraic Sets (Extended Abstract). In *STOC*. ACM, 168–173.

[8] S. Basu, R. Pollack, and M.-F. Roy. 1996. On the combinatorial and algebraic complexity of quantifier elimination. *Journal of ACM* 43, 6 (1996), 1002–1045.

[9] S. Basu, R. Pollack, and M.-F. Roy. 1998. A new algorithm to find a point in every cell defined by a family of polynomials. In *Quantifier elimination and cylindrical algebraic decomposition*. Springer-Verlag.

[10] S. Basu, R. Pollack, and M.-F. Roy. 2006. *Algorithms in real algebraic geometry* (2nd ed.). Algorithms and Computation in Mathematics, Vol. 10. Springer-Verlag.

[11] S. Basu and C. Riener. 2017. Bounding the equivariant Betti numbers of symmetric semi-algebraic sets. *Advances in Mathematics* 305 (2017), 803–855.

[12] S. Basu and C. Riener. 2017. Efficient algorithms for computing the Euler-Poincaré characteristic of symmetric semi-algebraic sets. In *Ordered Algebraic Structures and Related Topics*, Vol. 697. American Mathematical Soc., 51.

[13] L. Blum, F. Cucker, M. Shub, and S. Smale. 2012. *Complexity and real computation*. Springer Science & Business Media.

[14] J. Bochnak, M. Coste, and M.-F. Roy. 2013. *Real algebraic geometry*. Vol. 36. Springer Science.

[15] B. Bonnard, J.-C. Faugère, A. Jacquemard, M. Safey El Din, and T. Verron. 2016. Determinantal sets, singularities and application to optimal control in medical imagery. In *Proceedings of the ACM on International Symposium on Symbolic and Algebraic Computation*. ACM, 103–110.

[16] L. Bröcker. 1998. On symmetric semialgebraic sets and orbit spaces. *Banach Center Publications* 44, 1 (1998), 37–50.

[17] C.W. Brown and J.H Davenport. 2007. The complexity of quantifier elimination and cylindrical algebraic decomposition. In *Proceedings of the 2007 international symposium on Symbolic and algebraic computation*. ACM, 54–60.

[18] L. Busé and A. Karasoulou. 2016. Resultant of an equivariant polynomial system with respect to the symmetric group. *Journal of Symbolic Computation* 76 (2016), 142–157.

[19] J. Canny. 1987. *The complexity of robot motion planning*. MIT Press.

[20] J. Canny. 1988. Some algebraic and geometric computations in PSPACE. In *Proc. of the 20-th annual ACM symposium on Theory of computing*. ACM, 460–467.

[21] J. Canny. 1993. Computing roadmaps in general semi-algebraic sets. *Comput. J.* (1993).

[22] C. Chen, J.H. Davenport, F. Lemaire, M. Moreno Maza, B. Xia, R. Xiao, and Y. Xie. 2012. Computing the real solutions of polynomial systems with the RegularChains library in Maple. *ACM Communications in Computer Algebra* 45, 3/4 (2012), 166–168.

[23] J. Cimpric, S. Kuhlmann, and C. Scheiderer. 2009. Sums of Squares and Moment Problems in Equivariant Situations. *Trans. Amer. Math. Soc.* 361 (2009), 735–765.

[24] A. Colin. 1997. Solving a system of algebraic equations with symmetries. *Journal of Pure and Applied Algebra* 117 (1997), 195–215.

[25] J.H. Davenport and J. Heintz. 1988. Real quantifier elimination is doubly exponential. *Journal of Symbolic Computation* 5, 1-2 (1988), 29–35.

[26] D. Djukić, V. Janković, I. Matić, and N. Petrović. 2006. *The IMO compedium. A collection of problems suggested at the International Mathematical Olympiads: 1959–2004*. Springer.

[27] D. Eisenbud. 1995. *Commutative algebra with a view toward algebraic geometry*. Graduate Texts in Mathematics, Vol. 150. Springer-Verlag, New York.

[28] H. Everett, D. Lazard, S. Lazard, and M. Safey El Din. 2009. The Voronoi diagram of three lines. *Discrete & Computational Geometry* 42, 1 (2009), 94–130.

[29] J.-C. Faugère and S. Rahmany. 2009. Solving systems of polynomial equations with symmetries using SAGBI-Gröbner bases. In *Proceedings of the 2009 international symposium on Symbolic and algebraic computation*. ACM, 151–158.

[30] J.-C. Faugère and J. Svartz. 2012. Solving Polynomial Systems Globally Invariant Under an Action of the Symmetric Group and Application to the Equilibria of N vortices in the Plane. In *Proceedings of the 37th International Symposium on Symbolic and Algebraic Computation (ISSAC '12)*. ACM, 170–178.

[31] J.-C. Faugère and J. Svartz. 2013. Gröbner bases of ideals invariant under a commutative group: the non-modular case. In *Proceedings of the 38th International Symposium on Symbolic and Algebraic Computation*. ACM, 347–354.

[32] K. Gatermann and P.A. Parrilo. 2004. Symmetry groups, semidefinite programs, and sums of squares. *Journal of Pure and Applied Algebra* 192, 1 (2004), 95–128.

[33] L. Gournay and J.-J. Risler. 1993. Construction of roadmaps in semi-algebraic sets. *Appl. Alg. in Eng. Comm. and Comp.* 4, 4 (1993), 239–252.

[34] A. Greuet, F. Guo, M. Safey El Din, and L. Zhi. 2012. Global optimization of polynomials restricted to a smooth variety using sums of squares. *Journal of Symbolic Computation* 47, 5 (2012), 503–518.

[35] A. Greuet and M. Safey El Din. 2014. Probabilistic algorithm for polynomial optimization over a real algebraic set. *SIAM Journal on Optimization* 24, 3 (2014), 1313–1343.

[36] D. Grigoriev and D.V. Pasechnik. 2005. Polynomial-time computing over quadratic maps. *Computational complexity* 14, 1 (2005), 20–52.

[37] D. Grigoriev and N. Vorobjov. 1988. Solving systems of polynomials inequalities in subexponential time. *Journal of Symbolic Computation* 5 (1988), 37–64.

[38] L.C. Grove and C.T. Benson. 1996. *Finite reflection groups*. Vol. 99. Springer.

[39] F. Guo, M. Safey El Din, and L. Zhi. 2010. Global optimization of polynomials using generalized critical values and sums of squares. In *Proceedings of the 2010 International Symposium on Symbolic and Algebraic Computation*. ACM, 107–114.

[40] J. Heintz, M.-F. Roy, and P. Solernó. 1990. Sur la complexité du principe de Tarski-Seidenberg. *Bulletin de la Société mathématique de France* 118, 1 (1990), 101–126.

[41] J. Heintz, M.-F. Roy, and P. Solernò. 1993. On the theoretical and practical complexity of the existential theory of the reals. *Comput. J.* 36, 5 (1993), 427–431.

[42] J. Heintz, M.-F. Roy, and P. Solernó. 1994. Single exponential path finding in semi-algebraic sets II: The general case. In *Algebraic geometry and its applications*. Purdue University, West-Lafayette.

[43] D. Henrion, S. Naldi, and M. Safey El Din. 2016. Real root finding for determinants of linear matrices. *Journal of Symbolic Computation* 74 (2016), 205–238.

[44] H. Hong and M. Safey El Din. 2012. Variant quantifier elimination. *Journal of Symbolic Computation* 47, 7 (2012), 883–901.

[45] E. Hubert. 2017. Invariant Algebraic Sets and Symmetrization of Polynomial Systems. (April 2017). https://hal.inria.fr/hal-01254954 working paper or preprint.

[46] J.B. Lasserre. 2009. *Moments, positive polynomials and their applications*. World Scientific.

[47] C. Procesi. 1978. Positive symmetric functions. *Advances in Mathematics* 29, 2 (1978), 219–225.

[48] C. Procesi and G. Schwartz. 1985. Inequalities defining orbit spaces. *Invenciones mathmeaticae* 81 (1985), 539–554.

[49] J. Renegar. 1992. On the computational complexity and geometry of the first order theory of the reals. *Journal of Symbolic Computation* 13, 3 (1992), 255–352.

[50] C. Riener. 2012. On the degree and half-degree principle for symmetric polynomials. *Journal of Pure and Applied Algebra* 216, 4 (2012), 850–856.

[51] C. Riener. 2016. Symmetric semi-algebraic sets and non-negativity of symmetric polynomials. *Journal of Pure and Applied Algebra* 220, 8 (2016), 2809–2815.

[52] C. Riener, T. Theobald, L.J. Andrén, and J.-B. Lasserre. 2013. Exploiting Symmetries in SDP-Relaxations for Polynomial Optimization. *Mathematics of Operations Research* 38, 1 (2013), 122–141.

[53] M. Safey El Din. 2003. Raglib (real algebraic geometry library). `http://www-polsys.lip6.fr/~safey`. (2003).

[54] M. Safey El Din and É. Schost. 2003. Polar varieties and computation of one point in each connected component of a smooth real algebraic set. In *ISSAC'03*. ACM, 224–231.

[55] M. Safey El Din and É. Schost. 2017. A Nearly Optimal Algorithm for Deciding Connectivity Queries in Smooth and Bounded Real Algebraic Sets. *J. ACM* 63, 6 (2017), 48:1–48:37.

[56] M. Safey El Din and É. Schost. 2018. Bit complexity for multi-homogeneous polynomial system solving Application to polynomial minimization. *Journal of Symbolic Computation* 87 (2018).

[57] A. Seidenberg. 1954. A new decision method for elementary algebra. *Annals of Mathematics* 60 (1954), 365–374.

[58] O.V. Shchvartsman. 1982. Some remarks on the Chevalley theorem. *Functional Analysis and Its Applications* 16, 3 (1982), 237–238.

[59] S. Steidel. 2013. Gröbner bases of symmetric ideals. *Journal of Symbolic Computation* 54 (2013), 72 – 86.

[60] I. Stewart, T. Elmhirst, and J. Cohen. 2003. *Symmetry-Breaking as an Origin of Species*. Birkhäuser, Basel, 3–54.

[61] A.W. Strzeboński. 2006. Cylindrical algebraic decomposition using validated numerics. *Journal of Symbolic Computation* 41, 9 (2006), 1021–1038.

[62] B. Sturmfels. 2008. *Algorithms in invariant theory*. Springer Science.

[63] A. Tannenbaum and Y. Yomdin. 1987. Robotic manipulators and the geometry of real semialgebraic sets. *IEEE Journal on Robotics and Automation* 3, 4 (1987), 301–307.

[64] N.M. Thiéry. 2001. Computing minimal generating sets of invariant rings of permutation groups with sagbi-grobner basis. *Discrete Mathematics and Theoretical Computer Science* 315 (2001), 328.

[65] V. Timofte. 2003. On the positivity of symmetric polynomial functions.: Part I: General results. *J. Math. Anal. Appl.* 284, 1 (2003), 174–190.

Error Correction in Fast Matrix Multiplication and Inverse

Daniel S. Roche
United States Naval Academy
Annapolis, Maryland, U.S.A.
roche@usna.edu

ABSTRACT

We present new algorithms to detect and correct errors in the product of two matrices, or the inverse of a matrix, over an arbitrary field. Our algorithms do not require any additional information or encoding other than the original inputs and the erroneous output. Their running time is softly linear in the number of nonzero entries in these matrices when the number of errors is sufficiently small, and they also incorporate fast matrix multiplication so that the cost scales well when the number of errors is large. These algorithms build on the recent result of Gasieniec et al. [18] on correcting matrix products, as well as existing work on verification algorithms, sparse low-rank linear algebra, and sparse polynomial interpolation.

KEYWORDS

error correction, matrix multiplication, linear algebra, sparse interpolation, algorithms

ACM Reference Format:
Daniel S. Roche. 2018. Error Correction in Fast Matrix Multiplication and Inverse. In *ISSAC '18: 2018 ACM International Symposium on Symbolic and Algebraic Computation, July 16–19, 2018, New York, NY, USA.* ACM, New York, NY, USA, 8 pages. https://doi.org/10.1145/3208976.3209001

1 INTRODUCTION

Efficiently and gracefully handling computational errors is critical in modern computing. Such errors can result from short-lived hardware failures, communication noise, buggy software, or even malicious third-party servers.

The first goal for fault-tolerant computing is *verification.* The groundbreaking work of Freivalds [17] presented a linear-time algorithm to verify the correctness of a single matrix product. Recently, efficient verification algorithms for a wide range of computational linear algebra problems have been developed [13, 15, 16, 27].

A higher level of fault tolerance is achieved through *error correction*, which is the goal of the present study. This is a strictly stronger model than verification, where we seek not only to identify when a result is incorrect, but also to compute the correct result if it is "close" to the given, incorrect one. Some recent error-correction problems considered in the computer algebra literature include Chinese remaindering [5, 19, 29], system solving [8, 28], and function recovery [12, 26].

A generic approach to correcting errors *in transmission* would be to use an error-correcting code, writing the result with some redundancy to support transmission over a noisy channel. But this approach requires extra bandwidth, is limited to a fixed number of errors, and does not account for malicious alterations or mistakes in the computation itself.

Instead, we will use the information in the problem itself to correct errors. This is always possible by re-computing the result, and so the goal is always to correct a small number of errors in (much) less time than it would take to do the entire computation again. Our notion of error correction makes it possible to correct an unbounded number of mistakes that occur either in computation or transmission, either at random or by a malicious party.

Some other applications of error correction have nothing to do with alterations or mistakes. One example is sparse matrix multiplication, which can be solved with an error-correction algorithm by simply assuming the "erroneous" matrix is zero. Another example is computing a result over $\mathbb{Z}$ using Chinese remaindering modulo small primes, where the entries have varying bit lengths. The small entries are determined modulo the first few primes, and the remaining large entries are found more quickly by applying an error correction algorithm using (known) small entries.

1.1 Our results

Matrix multiplication with errors. The first problem we consider is the same as in Gasieniec et al. [18], correcting a matrix product. Given $A, B, C \in \mathsf{F}^{n\times n}$, the task is to compute the unique error matrix $E \in \mathsf{F}^{n\times n}$ such that $AB = C - E$.

Algorithm 5 solves this problem using

$$\widetilde{O}\left(t + k \cdot \min\left(\left\lceil \tfrac{t}{r} \right\rceil, n/\min(r, \tfrac{k}{r})^{3-\omega}\right)\right)$$

field operations, where

- $t = \#A + \#B + \#C$ is the number of nonzero entries in the input matrices, at most $O(n^2)$;
- $k = \#E$ is the number of errors in the given product C; and
- $r \le n$ is the number of distinct rows (or columns) in which errors occur, whichever is larger.

An even more detailed complexity statement, incorporating rectangular matrices and a failure probability, can be found in Theorem 7.1. To understand the implications of this complexity, consider six cases, as summarized in Table 1.

The cost of our algorithm depends on the locations of the errors. If there are a constant number of errors per row or column, we can use sparse multiplication to achieve softly-linear complexity $\widetilde{O}(t + n + k)$. This is similar to [18] except that we do not require the input matrices to be dense.

If $k > n$ errors are spread out among all rows and columns, the worst-case cost using dense multiplication is $\widetilde{O}(k^{0.38}n^{1.63})$. As the number of errors grows to n^2, this cost approaches that of normal matrix multiplication without error correction.

ISSAC '18, July 16–19, 2018, New York, NY, USA
2018. ACM ISBN 978-1-4503-5550-6/18/07.
https://doi.org/10.1145/3208976.3209001

	Spread-out errors $r = \min(n, k)$		Compact errors $r = \sqrt{k}$
	$k \leq n$	$k > n$	
Sparse	$t + k + n$	$k\lceil \frac{t}{n} \rceil + n$	$\sqrt{kt} + k + n$
Dense	$t + kn$	$k^{\omega-2}n^{4-\omega}$ $k^{0.38}n^{1.63}$	$t + k^{(\omega-1)/2}n$ $t + k^{0.69}n$

Table 1: Soft-oh cost of Algorithm 5 in several cases, for correcting up to k errors (which appear in r rows) in the product of two $n \times n$ matrices with at most t nonzero entries. The two rows indicate whether sparse or dense rectangular multiplication is used as a subroutine.

In the other extreme, if the errors are isolated to a square (but not necessarily contiguous) submatrix, then the worst-case cost using dense multiplication is $\widetilde{O}(t = k^{0.69}n)$. Again this scales to n^ω as $k \to n^2$, but the cost is better for $k < n^2$. This situation may also make sense in the context of distributed computing, where each node in a computing cluster might be assigned to compute one submatrix of the product.

Our algorithm is never (asymptotically) slower than that of [18] or the $O(n^\omega)$ cost of naïve recomputation, but it is faster in many cases: for example when the inputs are sparse, when there are many errors, and when the errors are compactly located.

Matrix inverse with errors. The second problem we consider is that of correcting computational errors in a matrix inverse. Formally, given $A, B \in \mathsf{F}^{n \times n}$, the task is to compute the unique error matrix $E \in \mathsf{F}^{n \times n}$ such that $A^{-1} = B + E$.

Algorithm 6 shows how to solve this problem using

$$\widetilde{O}\left(t + nk/\min(r, \tfrac{k}{r})^{3-\omega} + r^\omega\right)$$

field operations, where the parameters t, k, n are the same as before, and r is the number of rows or columns which contain errors, whichever is *smaller*. This is the same complexity as our algorithm for matrix multiplication with errors, plus an additional r^ω term.

The additional r^ω term makes the situation here less fractured than with the multiplication algorithm. In the case of spread-out errors, the cost is $\widetilde{O}(t + nk + k^\omega)$, which becomes simply $\widetilde{O}(n^2 + k^\omega)$ when the input matrices are dense. The case of compact errors is better, and the complexity is just $\widetilde{O}\left(t + nk^{(\omega-1)/2}\right)$, the same as that of our multiplication algorithm

As before, the cost of this algorithm approaches the $O(n^\omega)$ cost of the naïve inverse computation as the number of errors k grows to n^2.

Domains. The algorithms we present work over any field and require only that a field element of order larger than n can be found. Because our algorithms explicitly take $O(n)$ time to compute the powers of this element anyway, the usual difficulties with efficiently generating high-order elements in finite fields do not arise.

Over the integers $\mathbb{Z}$ or rationals $\mathbb{Q}$, the most efficient approach would be to work modulo a series of primes and use Chinese remaindering to recover the result. A similar approach could be used over polynomial rings.

Over the reals $\mathbb{R}$ or complex numbers $\mathbb{C}$, our algorithms work only under the unrealistic assumption of infinite precision. We have not considered the interesting question of how to recover from the two types of errors (noise and outliers) that may occur in finite precision.

1.2 Related work

Let ω be a constant between 2 and 3 such that two $n \times n$ matrices can be multiplied using $O(n^\omega)$ field operations. In practice, $\omega = 3$ for dimensions n up to a few hundred, after which Strassen-Winograd multiplication is used giving $\omega =< 2.81$. The best asymptotic algorithm currently gives $\omega < 2.3728639$ [31].

Even though the practical value of ω is larger than the asymptotic one, matrix multiplication routines have been the subject of intense implementation development for decades, and highly-tuned software is readily available for a variety of architectures [14, 35]. Running times based on n^ω have practical as well as theoretical significance; the ω indicates where an algorithm is able to take advantage of fast low-level matrix multiplication routines.

Special routines for multiplying sparse matrices have also been developed. Writing t for the number of nonzero entries in the input, the standard row- or column-wise sparse matrix multiplication costs $O(tn)$ field operations. Yuster and Zwick [36] improved this to $\widetilde{O}(n^2 + t^{0.697}n^{1.197})$. Later work also incorporates the number k of nonzeros in the product matrix. Lingas [32] gave an output-sensitive algorithm with running time $O(k^{0.186}n^2)$. Amossen and Pagh [1] have another with complexity $\widetilde{O}(t^{0.667}k^{0.667} + t^{0.862}k^{0.408})$, an improvement when the outputs are not too dense. Pagh [33] developed a different approach with complexity $\widetilde{O}(t + kn)$; that paper also includes a nice summary of the state of the art. Our multiplication with errors algorithm can also be used for sparse multiplication, and it provides a small improvement when the input and output are both not *too* sparse.

The main predecessor to our work is the recent algorithm of Gasieniec et al. [18], which can correct up to k errors in the product of two $n \times n$ matrices using $\widetilde{O}(n^2 + kn)$ field operations. Their approach is based in part on the earlier work of Pagh [33] and makes clever use of hashing and fast Fourier transforms in order to achieve the stated complexity.

We not only improve on the complexity of that problem, but also consider related problem of correcting errors in a matrix inverse. Computing the inverse of a matrix (without errors) has the same asymptotic complexity $O(n^\omega)$ as fast matrix multiplication [9].

2 OVERVIEW

Multiplication with errors. A high-level summary of our multiplication algorithm is as follows:

(1) Determine which rows in the product contain errors.
(2) Write the unknown sparse matrix of errors as $E = C - AB$. Remove the rows with no errors from E, C, and A, so we have $E' = C' - A'B$.
(3) Treating the rows of E' as sparse polynomials, use structured linear algebra and fast matrix multiplication to evaluate each row polynomial at a small number of points.
(4) Use sparse polynomial interpolation to recover at least half of the rows from their evaluations.

(5) Update C and iterate $O(\log k)$ times to recover all k errors.

To determine the rows of E which are nonzero in Step 1, we apply a simple variant of Frievalds' verification algorithm: for a random vector $\mathbf{v}$, the nonzero rows of $E\mathbf{v}$ are probably the same as the nonzero rows of E itself.

The evaluation/interpolation approach that follows is reminiscent of that in Gasieniec et al. [18], with two important differences. First, using sparse polynomial techniques rather than hashing and FFTs means the complexity scales linearly with the number of nonzeros t in the input rather than the dense matrix size n^2. Second, by treating the rows separately rather than recovering all errors at once, we are able to incorporate fast matrix multiplication so that our worst-case cost when all entries are erroneous is never more than $O(n^\omega)$, the same as that of naïve recomputation.

Section 4 provides details on the Monte Carlo algorithm to determine the rows and columns where errors occur (Step 1 above), Section 5 presents a variant of sparse polynomial interpolation that suits our needs for Step 4, and Section 6 explains how to perform the row polynomial evaluations in Step 3. A certain rectangular matrix multiplication in this step turns out to dominate the overall complexity. We connect all these pieces of the multiplication algorithm in Section 7.

Inverse with errors. Our algorithm for correcting errors in a matrix inverse is based on the multiplication algorithm, but with two complications. Writing A for the input matrix, B for the erroneous inverse, and E for the (sparse) matrix of errors in B, we have:

$$AE = I - AB, \qquad EA = I - BA.$$

We want to compute $E\mathbf{v}$ for a random vector $\mathbf{v}$ in order to determine which rows of E are nonzero. This is no longer possible directly, but using the second formulation as above, we can compute $EA\mathbf{v}$. Because A must be nonsingular, $A\mathbf{v}$ has the same distribution as a random vector, so this approach still works.

The second complication is that removing zero rows of E does not change the dimension of the right-hand side, but only removes corresponding *columns* from A on the left-hand side. We make use of the recent result of Cheung et al. [11], which shows how to quickly find a maximal set of linearly independent rows in a sparse matrix. This allows us to find a small submatrix X of A such that $XE' = I' - A'B$, with E', I', A' being compressed matrices as before. Because the size of X depends on the number of errors, it can be inverted much more quickly than re-computing the entire inverse of A.

The dominating cost in most cases is the same rectangular matrix product as needed as in matrix multiplication with error correction. However, here we also have the extra cost of finding X and computing its inverse, which dominates the complexity when there are a moderate number of errors and their locations are spread out.

This algorithm — which depends on the subroutines of Sections 4 to 6 — is presented in detail in Section 8. .

3 NOTATION AND PRELIMINARIES

The soft-oh notation $\widetilde{O}(\cdots)$ is the same as the usual big-oh notation but ignoring sub-logarithmic factors: $f \in \widetilde{O}(g)$ if and only if $f \in O\left(g \log^{O(1)} g\right)$, for some runtime functions f and g.

We write $\mathbb{N}$ for the set of nonnegative integers and $\mathbb{F}_q$ for the finite field with q elements.

For a finite set $\mathcal{S}$, the number of elements in $\mathcal{S}$ is denoted $\#\mathcal{S}$, and $\mathbb{P}(\mathcal{S})$ is the powerset of $\mathcal{S}$, i.e., the set of subsets of $\mathcal{S}$.

The number of nonzero entries in a matrix $M \in \mathsf{F}^{m\times n}$ is written as $\#M$. Note that $\#M \le mn$, and if M has rank k then $\#M \ge k$.

For a univariate polynomial $f \in \mathsf{F}[x]$, $\operatorname{supp}(f) \subseteq \mathbb{N}$ denotes the exponents of nonzero terms of f. Note that $\#\operatorname{supp}(f) \le \deg f + 1$.

We assume that the number of field operations to multiply two (dense) polynomials in $\mathsf{F}[x]$ with degrees less than n is $\widetilde{O}(n)$. This is justified by the generic algorithm from Cantor and Kaltofen [10] which gives $O(n \log n \operatorname{loglog} n)$, or more result results of Harvey et al. [20] which improve this to $O\left(n \log n \, 8^{\log^* n}\right)$ for finite fields.

As discussed earlier, we take ω with $2 \le \omega \le 3$ to be any feasible exponent of matrix multiplication. By applying fast matrix multiplication in blocks, it is also possible to improve the speed of rectangular matrix multiplication in a straightforward way. In particular:

Fact 3.1. *The product of any $m \times \ell$ matrix times a $\ell \times n$ matrix can be found using $O\left(m\ell n/\min(m, \ell, n)^{3-\omega}\right)$ ring operations.*

Note that it might be possible to improve this for certain values of m, ℓ, n using [30], but that complexity is much harder to state and we have not investigated such an approach.

We restate two elementary facts on sparse matrix multiplication.

Fact 3.2. *For any $M \in \mathsf{F}^{m\times n}$ and $\mathbf{v} \in \mathsf{F}^n$, the matrix-vector product $M\mathbf{v}$ can be computed using $O(\#M)$ field operations.*

Corollary 3.3. *For any $A \in \mathsf{F}^{m\times \ell}$ and $B \in \mathsf{F}^{\ell\times n}$, their product AB can be computed using $O(\#A \cdot n)$ field operations.*

4 IDENTIFYING NONZERO ROWS AND COLUMNS

Our algorithms for error correction in matrix product and inverse computation both begin by determining which rows and columns contain errors. This is accomplished in turn by applying a random row or column vector to the unknown error matrix E.

For now, we treat the error matrix E as a *black box*, i.e., an oracle matrix which we can multiply by a vector on the right or left-hand side. The details of the black box construction differ for the matrix multiple and inverse problem, so we delay those until later.

The idea is to apply a row or column vector of random values to the unknown matrix E, and then examine which entires in the resulting vector are zero. This is exactly the same idea as the classic Monte Carlo verification algorithm of Freivalds [17], which we extend to which rows or columns in a matrix are nonzero. This black-box procedure is detailed in Algorithm 1 `FindNonzeroRows`.

The correctness of `FindNonzeroRows` depends on the parameter ϵ. The running time depends on this ϵ, the size of F, and the cost of performing matrix-vector products with the black-box matrix M.

Lemma 4.1. `FindNonzeroRows` *always returns a list of nonzero row indices in M With probability at least $1 - \epsilon$, it returns the index of* every *nonzero row in M.*

Proof. Consider a single row $\mathbf{u}^T$ of M. If $\mathbf{u}$ is zero, then the corresponding row of MV will always be zero; hence every index returned must be a nonzero row.

Algorithm 1: `FindNonzeroRows`($V \mapsto MV, \epsilon$)

Input: Black box for right-multiplication by an unknown matrix $M \in \mathsf{F}^{m\times n}$ and error bound $\epsilon \in \mathbb{R}, 0 < \epsilon < 1$

Output: Set $\mathcal{J} \subseteq \{0, \ldots, m-1\}$ that with probability at least $1 - \epsilon$ consists of the indices of nonzero rows in M

$\ell \leftarrow \lceil \log_{\#\mathsf{F}} \frac{m}{\epsilon} \rceil$
$V \leftarrow$ matrix in $\mathsf{F}^{n\times\ell}$ with uniform random entries from F
$B \leftarrow MV$ using the black box
return *Indices of rows of B which are not all zeros*

Next assume $\mathbf{u}^T$ has at least one nonzero entry, say at index i, and consider one row $\mathbf{v} \in \mathsf{F}^n$ of the random matrix V. Whatever the other entries in $\mathbf{u}$ and $\mathbf{v}$ are, there is exactly one value for the i'th entry of v such that $\mathbf{u}^T\mathbf{v} = 0$. So the probability that $\mathbf{u}^T\mathbf{v} = 0$ is $\frac{1}{\#\mathsf{F}}$, and by independence the probability that $\mathbf{u}^T V = \mathbf{0}^{1\times\ell}$ is $1/(\#\mathsf{F})^\ell$.

Because M has at most m nonzero rows, the union bound tells us that the probability *any one* of the corresponding rows of MV is zero is at most $m/(\#F)^\ell$. From the definition of ℓ, this ensures a failure probability of at most ϵ. □

Because we mostly have in mind the case that F is a finite field, we assume in `FindNonzeroRows` and in the preceding proof that it is possible to sample uniformly from the entire field F. However, the same results would hold if sampling from any fixed subset of F (perhaps increasing the size of ℓ if the subset is small).

5 BATCHED LOW-DEGREE SPARSE INTERPOLATION

Our algorithms use techniques from sparse polynomial interpolation to find the locations and values of erroneous entries in a matrix product or inverse.

Consider an unknown univariate polynomial $f \in \mathsf{F}[x]$ with degree less than n and at most s nonzero terms. The nonzero terms of f can be uniquely recovered from evaluations $f(\theta^0), \ldots, f(\theta^{2s-1})$ at $2s$ consecutive powers [3, 24].

Doing this efficiently in our context requires a few variations to the typical algorithmic approach. While the state of the art seen in recent papers such as [2, 22, 23, 25] achieves softly-linear complexity in terms of the sparsity t, there is either a higher dependency on the degree, a restriction to certain fields, or both.

Here, we show how to take advantage of two unique aspects of the problem in our context. First, we will interpolate a *batch* of sparse polynomials at once, on the same evaluation points, which allows for some useful precomputation. Secondly, the maximum degree of any polynomial we interpolate is n, the column dimension of the unknown matrix, and we are allowed linear-time in n.

The closest situation in the literature is that of van der Hoeven and Lecerf [21], who show how to recover a sparse polynomial if the exponents are known. In our case, we can tolerate a much larger set containing the possible exponents by effectively amortizing the size of this exponent set over the group of batched sparse interpolations.

Recall the general outline of Prony's method for sparse interpolation of $f \in \mathsf{F}[x]$ from evaluations $(f(\theta^i))_{0\le i<2s}$:

(1) Find the minimum polynomial $\Gamma \in \mathsf{F}[z]$ of the sequence of evaluations.
(2) Find the roots $v_1, \ldots, v_s$ of Γ.
(3) Compute the discrete logarithm base θ of each v_i to determine the exponents of f.
(4) Solve a transposed Vandermonde system built from v_i and the evaluations to recover the coefficients of f.

Steps 1 and 4 can be performed over any field using fast multipoint evaluation and interpolation in $\widetilde{O}(s)$ field operations [24]. However, the other steps depend on the field and in particular Step 3 can be problematic over large finite fields.

To avoid this issue, we first pre-compute all possible roots θ^{e_i} for any minpoly Γ_i in any of the batch of r sparse interpolations that will be performed. Although the set of possible roots is larger than the degree of any single minpoly Γ_i, in our case the set is always bounded by the dimension of the matrix, so performing this precomputation once is worthwhile.

5.1 Batched root finding

While fast root-finding procedures over many fields have already been developed, we present a simple but efficient root-finding procedure for our specific case that has the advantage of running in softly-linear time over any coefficient field. The general idea is to first compute a coprime basis (also called a gcd-free basis) for the minpolys Γ_i, then perform multi-point evaluation with the precomputed list of possible roots.

The details of procedure `FindRoots` are in Algorithm 2 below. In the algorithm, we use a *product tree* constructed from a list of t polynomials. This is a binary tree of height $O(\log t)$, with the original polynomials at the leaves, and where every internal node is the product of its two children. In particular, the root of the tree is the product of all t polynomials. The total size of a product tree, and the cost of computing it, is softly-linear in the total size of the input polynomials; see Borodin and Munro [6] for more details.

Lemma 5.1. *Given a set $Q \subseteq \mathsf{F}$ with of size $\#Q = c$ and a list of r polynomials $\Gamma_1, \ldots, \Gamma_r \in \mathsf{F}[z]$ each with degree at most s, Algorithm 2* `FindRoots` *correctly determines all roots of all Γ_i's which are in Q using $\widetilde{O}(rs + c)$ field operations*

Proof. Algorithms 18.1 and 21.2 of Bernstein [4] are deterministic and compute (respectively) a coprime basis and then a factorization of the Γ_i's according to the basis elements.

The polynomials $M_{i,j}$ form a standard product tree from the polynomials in the coprime basis. For any element of the product tree, its roots must be a subset of the roots of its parent node. So the multi-point evaluations on Line 9 determine, for every polynomial in the tree, which elements of Q are roots of that polynomial.

The cost of computing the coprime basis using Algorithm 18.1 in [4] is $\widetilde{O}(rs)$ with at least a $\log^5(rs)$ factor. This gives the first term in the complexity (and explains our use of soft-oh notation throughout). This cost dominates the cost of constructing the product tree and factoring the Γ_i's on Line 11.

Using the standard product tree algorithm [6], the cost of multipoint evaluation of a degree-n polynomial at each of n points is $\widetilde{O}(n)$ field operations. In our algorithm, this happens at each level down the product tree. At each of $\lceil \log_2 t \rceil \in O(\log(rs))$ levels there are

Algorithm 2: FindRoots($Q, [\Gamma_1, \ldots, \Gamma_r]$)

Input: Set of possible roots $Q \subseteq \mathsf{F}$ and r polynomials $\Gamma_1, \ldots, \Gamma_r \in \mathsf{F}[z]$

Output: A list of sets $[\mathcal{R}_1, \ldots, \mathcal{R}_r] \in \mathbb{P}(Q)^r$ such that $g_i(\alpha_j) = 0$ for every $1 \le i \le r$ and $\alpha_j \in \mathcal{R}_i$

$\{g_0, \ldots, g_{t-1}\} \leftarrow$ coprime basis of $\{\Gamma_i\}_{1 \le i \le r}$ using Algorithm 18.1 of Bernstein [4]

/* Compute product tree from bottom-up */

for $j \leftarrow 0, 1, \ldots, t-1$ **do** $M_{0,j} \leftarrow g_j$

for $i \leftarrow 1, 2, \ldots, \lceil \log_2 t \rceil$ **do**

  for $j \leftarrow 0, 1, \ldots, \lceil t/2^i \rceil - 1$ **do**

    $M_{i,j} \leftarrow M_{i-1,2j} \cdot M_{i-1,2j+1}$

/* Find roots of basis elements */

$S_{\lceil \log_2 t \rceil + 1, 0} \leftarrow Q$

for $i \leftarrow \lceil \log_2 t \rceil, \lceil \log_2 t \rceil - 1, \ldots, 0$ **do**

  for $j \leftarrow 0, 1, \ldots, \lceil t/2^i \rceil - 1$ **do**

    Evaluate $M_{i,j}$ at each point in $S_{i+1, \lfloor j/2 \rfloor}$ using fast multipoint evaluation

    $S_{i,j} \leftarrow$ roots of $M_{i,j}$ found on previous step

/* Determine roots of original polynomials */

Compute exponents $(e_{i,j})_{1 \le i \le r, 0 \le j < t}$ such that $\Gamma_i = g_0^{e_{i,0}} \cdots g_{t-1}^{e_{i,t-1}}$ for all i, using algorithm 21.2 of Bernstein [4]

for $i \leftarrow 1, 2, \ldots, r$ **do** $\mathcal{R}_i \leftarrow \bigcup_{0 \le j < t, e_{i,j} \ge 1} S_{0,j}$

at most c points (since the polynomials at each level are relatively prime). The total degree at each level is at most $\deg \prod_i \Gamma_i \le rs$. If $rs > c$, then this cost is already bounded by that of determining the coprime basis. Otherwise, the multi-point evaluations occur in $O(c/(rs))$ batches of rs points each, giving the second term in the complexity statement. □

5.2 Batched sparse interpolation algorithm

We are now ready to present the full algorithm for performing simultaneous sparse interpolation on r polynomials based on $2s$ evaluations each.

Note that, in the case of very small fields with no order-n elements, this approach can still by used by working over an extension of order at most $O(\log n)$. In our application n is actually the dimension of the erroneous matrix, so this does not change the overall complexity by more than a logarithmic factor.

Theorem 5.2. *Let* F *be a field with an element* $\theta \in \mathsf{F}$ *whose multiplicative order is at least n, and suppose* $f_1, \ldots, f_r \in \mathsf{F}[x]$ *are unknown univariate polynomials. Given bounds* $n, s \in \mathbb{N}$*, a set* $\mathcal{S} \subseteq \mathbb{N}$ *of possible exponents, and evaluations* $f_i(\theta^j)$ *for all* $1 \le i \le r$ *and* $0 \le j < 2s$*, Algorithm 3* MultiSparseInterp *requires* $\widetilde{O}(rs + \#\mathcal{S} \log n)$ *field operations in the worst case.*

The algorithm correctly recovers every polynomial f_i *such that* $\#\mathrm{supp} f_i \le s$*,* $\mathrm{supp} f_i \subseteq \mathcal{S}$*, and* $\deg f_i < n$*.*

Proof. From Lemma 5.1, the cost of FindRoots is $\widetilde{O}(rs + \#\mathcal{S})$. This dominates the cost of the minpoly and transposed Vandermonde computations, which are both $\widetilde{O}(rs)$ [24]. Using binary

Algorithm 3: MultiSparseInterp($r, n, s, \mathcal{S}, \theta, Y$)

Input: Bounds $r, n, s \in \mathbb{N}$, set $\mathcal{S} \subseteq \{0, \ldots, n-1\}$ of possible exponents, high-order element $\theta \in \mathsf{F}$, and evaluations $Y_{i,j} \in \mathsf{F}$ such that $f_i(\theta^j) = Y_{i,j}$ for all $1 \le i \le r$ and $0 \le j < 2s$

Output: Nonzero coefficients and corresponding exponents of $f_i \in \mathsf{F}[x]$ or 0 indicating failure, for each $1 \le i \le r$

1 **for** $i = 1, 2, \ldots, r$ **do**

2   $\Gamma_i \leftarrow$MinPoly($Y_{i,0}, \ldots, Y_{i,2s-1}$) using fast Berlekamp-Massey algorithm

3 $\mathcal{R}_1, \ldots, \mathcal{R}_r \leftarrow$ FindRoots($\{\, \theta^d \mid d \in \mathcal{S} \,\}, \Gamma_1, \ldots, \Gamma_r$)

4 **for** $i = 1, 2, \ldots, r$ **do**

5   **if** $\#\mathcal{R}_i \ne \deg \Gamma_i$ **then** $f_i \leftarrow 0$

6   **else**

7     $t_i \leftarrow \#\mathcal{R}_i$

8     $\{e_{i,1}, \ldots, e_{i,t_i}\} \leftarrow \{\, d \in \mathcal{S} \mid \theta^d \in \mathcal{R}_i \,\}$

9     $[a_{i,1}, \ldots, a_{i,t_i}] \leftarrow$ solution of transposed Vandermonde system from roots $[\theta^{e_{i,1}}, \ldots, \theta^{e_{i,t_t}}]$ and right-hand vector $[Y_{i,0}, \ldots, Y_{i,t_i-1}]$

10     $f_i \leftarrow a_{i,1} x^{e_{i,1}} + \cdots + a_{i,t_i} x^{e_{i,t_i}}$

powering, computing the set $\{\, \theta^d \mid d \in \mathcal{S} \,\}$ on Line 3 requires $O(\#\mathcal{S} \log n)$ field operations.

If f_i has at most $t_i \le s$ nonzero terms, then the minpoly Γ_i computed on Line 2 is a degree-t_i polynomial with exactly t_i distinct roots. If $\mathrm{supp}(f_i) \subseteq \mathcal{S}$, then by Lemma 5.1, FindRoots correctly finds all these roots. Because these are the only terms in f_i, solving the transposed Vandermonde system correctly determines all corresponding coefficients; see [24] or [21] for details. □

6 PERFORMING EVALUATIONS

Consider the matrix multiplication with errors problem, recovering a sparse error matrix $E \in \mathsf{F}^{r \times n}$ according to the equation $E = C - AB$. In this section, we show how to treat each row of E as a sparse polynomial and evaluate each of these at consecutive powers of a high-order element θ, as needed for the sparse interpolation algorithm from Section 5. The same techniques will also be used in the matrix inverse with errors algorithm.

Consider a column vector of powers of an indeterminate, $\mathbf{x} = [1, x, x^2, \ldots, x^{n-1}]^T$. The matrix-vector product $E\mathbf{x}$ then consists of m polynomials, each degree less than n, and with a 1-1 correspondence between nonzero terms of the polynomials and nonzero entries in the corresponding row of E.

Evaluating every polynomial in $E\mathbf{x}$ at a point $\theta \in \mathsf{F}$ is the same as multiplying E by a vector $\mathbf{v} = [1, \theta, \theta^2, \ldots, \theta^{n-1}]^T$. Evaluating each polynomial in $E\mathbf{x}$ at the first $2s$ powers $1, \theta, \theta^2, \ldots, \theta^{2s-1}$ allows for the unique recovery of all t-sparse rows, according to Theorem 5.2. This means multiplying E times an *evaluation matrix* $V \in \mathsf{F}^{n \times 2s}$ such that $V_{i,j} = \theta^{ij}$.

Consider a single row vector $\mathbf{u} \in \mathsf{F}^{1 \times n}$ with c nonzero entries. Multiplying $\mathbf{u}V$ means evaluating a c-sparse polynomial at the first $2s$ powers of θ; we can view it as removing the $n - c$ zero entries from $\mathbf{u}$ to give $\mathbf{u}' \in \mathsf{F}^{1 \times c}$, and removing the same $n - c$ rows from

Algorithm 4: $\texttt{DiffEval}(A, B, C, \theta, s)$

Input: Matrices $A \in \mathsf{F}^{r\times\ell}$, $B \in \mathsf{F}^{\ell\times n}$, $C \in \mathsf{F}^{r\times n}$, high-order element $\theta \in \mathsf{F}$, and integer $s \in \mathbb{N}$

Output: Matrix $Y = (C - AB)V \in \mathsf{F}^{r\times 2s}$, where V is the $r \times 2s$ evaluation matrix given by $(\theta^{ij})_{0\le i<n, 0\le j<2s}$.

1 Pre-compute θ^j for all indices j of nonzero columns in B or C

2 $Y_C \leftarrow CV$ using the pre-computed θ^j's and fast transposed Vandermonde applications row by row

3 $Y_B \leftarrow BV$ similarly

4 $Y_{AB} \leftarrow AY_B$ using dense or sparse multiplication, whichever is faster

5 **return** $Y_C - Y_{AB}$

V to get $V' \in \mathsf{F}^{c\times 2s}$, and then computing the product $\mathbf{u}'V'$. This evaluation matrix with removed rows V' is actually a *transposed Vandermonde matrix* built from the entries θ^i for each index i of a nonzero entry in $\mathbf{u}$.

An explicit algorithm for this transposed Vandermonde matrix application is given in Section 6.2 of Bostan et al. [7], and they show that the complexity of multiplying $\mathbf{u}'V'$ is $\widetilde{O}(c + s)$ field operations, and essentially amounts to a power series inversion and product tree traversal. (See also Section 5.1 of van der Hoeven and Lecerf [21] for a nice description of how this approach is used for fast evaluation of a sparse polynomial at consecutive powers.) We repeat this for each row in a given matrix M to compute AV.

Now we are ready to show how to compute $EV = (C - AB)V$ efficiently, using the approach just discussed to compute CV and BV before multiplying A times BV and performing a subtraction. As we will show, the rectangular multiplication of A times BV is the only step which is not softly-linear time, and this dominates the complexity.

Lemma 6.1. *Algorithm 4* $\texttt{DiffEval}$ *always returns the correct matrix of evaluations* $(C - AB)V$ *and uses*

$$\widetilde{O}\left(\#B + \#C + n + s \cdot \min\left(\#A + r, \frac{r\ell}{\min(r, s, \ell)^{3-\omega}}\right)\right)$$

field operations.

Proof. Correctness comes from the discussion above and the correctness of the algorithm in section 6.2 of Bostan et al. [7] which is used on Lines 2 and 3.

The cost of pre-computing all powers θ^j using binary powering is $O(n \log n)$ field operations, since the number of nonzero columns in B or C is at most n. Using these precomputed values, each transposed Vandermonde apply costs $\widetilde{O}(k + s)$, where k is the number of nonzero entries in the current row. Summing over all rows of C and B gives $\widetilde{O}(\#B + \#C + rs + \ell s)$ for these steps.

The most significant step is the rectangular multiplication of $A \in \mathsf{F}^{r\times\ell}$ times $Y_B \in \mathsf{F}^{\ell\times s}$. Using sparse multiplication, the cost is $O(\#A \cdot s)$, by Corollary 3.3. Using dense multiplication, the cost is $O\left(r\ell s/\min(r, \ell, s)^{\omega-3}\right)$ according to Fact 3.1.

Because all the relevant parameters $\#A, s, r, \ell$ are known before the multiplication, we assume that the underlying software makes the best choice among these two algorithms.

Note that rs and ℓs are definitely dominated by the cost of the dense multiplication. In the sparse multiplication case, the situation is more subtle when $\#A < \ell$. But in this case, we just suppose that rows of BV which are not used in the sparse multiplication $A(BV)$ are never computed, so the complexity is as stated. □

7 MULTIPLICATION WITH ERROR CORRECTION ALGORITHM

We now have all the necessary components to present the complete multiplication algorithm, Algorithm 5 $\texttt{MultiplyEC}$. The general idea is to repeatedly use $\texttt{FindNonzeroRows}$ to determine the locations on nonzeros in E, then $\texttt{DiffEval}$ and $\texttt{MultiSparseInterp}$ to recover half of the nonzero rows at each step.

Setting the target sparsity of each recovered row to $s = \lceil 2k/r \rceil$, where r is the number of nonzero rows, ensures that at least half of the rows are recovered at each step. To get around the fact that the number of errors k is initially unknown, we start with an initial guess of $k = 1$, and double this guess whenever fewer than half of the remaining rows are recovered.

The procedure is probabilistic of the Monte Carlo type *only* because of the Monte Carlo subroutine $\texttt{FindNonzeroRows}$ to determine which rows are erroneous. The other parts of the algorithm — computing evaluations and recovering nonzero entries — are deterministic based on the bounds they are given.

Theorem 7.1. *Algorithm 5* $\texttt{MultiplyEC}$ *finds all errors in* C *with probability at least* $1 - \epsilon$ *and always uses*

$$\widetilde{O}\left(m + \left\lceil \log_{\#\mathsf{F}} \tfrac{1}{\epsilon} \right\rceil (n + t) + k \cdot \min\left(\left\lceil \tfrac{t}{r} \right\rceil, \ell/\min(\ell, r, \tfrac{k}{r})^{3-\omega}\right)\right)$$

field operations, where k *is the* actual *number of errors in the given product* C*. Otherwise, it uses* $\widetilde{O}(m\ell n/\min(m, \ell, n)^{3-\omega})$ *field operations and may return an incorrect result.*

Proof. The only probabilistic parts of the algorithm are the calls to $\texttt{FindNonzeroRows}$, which can only fail by incorrectly returning too few rows. If this never happens, then each iteration through the while loop either (a) discovers that the value of k was too small and increases it, or (b) recovers half of the rows or columns of E.

So the total number of iterations of the while loop if the calls to $\texttt{FindNonzeroRows}$ are never incorrect is at most $\lceil \log_2 k \rceil + \lceil \log_2 m \rceil + \lceil \log_2 n \rceil$. By the union bound, from the way that ϵ' is computed and the fact that there are two calls to $\texttt{FindNonzeroRows}$ on every iteration, the probability that $\texttt{FindNonzeroRows}$ is never incorrect is at least $1 - \epsilon$.

In this case, the rest of the correctness and the running time follow directly from Lemmas 4.1 and 6.1 and Theorem 5.2.

If a call to $\texttt{FindNonzeroRows}$ returns an incorrect result, two bad things can happen. First, if $\mathcal{J}$ is too small during some iteration, all of the evaluations may be incorrect, leading to k being increased. In extremely unlucky circumstances, this may happen $O(\log(rn))$ times until the product is naïvely recomputed on Line 19, leading to the worst-case running time.

The second thing that can occur when a call to $\texttt{FindNonzeroRows}$ fails is that it may incorrectly report all errors have been found,

Algorithm 5: `MultiplyEC`$(A, B, C, \theta, \epsilon)$

Input: Matrices $A \in \mathsf{F}^{m\times\ell}$, $B \in \mathsf{F}^{\ell\times n}$, $C \in \mathsf{F}^{m\times n}$, high-order element $\theta \in \mathsf{F}$, and error bound $0 < \epsilon < 1$

Output: Matrix $E \in \mathsf{F}^{m\times n}$ such that, with probability at least $1-\epsilon$, $AB = C - E$

$k \leftarrow 1$
$E \leftarrow \mathbf{0}^{m\times n}$
$\epsilon' \leftarrow \epsilon/(4\lceil\log_2(mn)\rceil + 1)$
$\mathcal{J} \leftarrow$ `FindNonzeroRows`$(V \mapsto CV - A(BV), \epsilon')$
while $\#\mathcal{J} \geq 1$ **do**
  if #`FindNonzeroRows`$(V \mapsto (V^T(C-E) - (V^TA)B)^T, \epsilon') > \#\mathcal{J}$ **then**
    Transpose C and E, swap and transpose A and B, replace $\mathcal{J}$
  $r \leftarrow \#\mathcal{J}$
  $A' \leftarrow$ submatrix of A from rows in $\mathcal{J}$
  $C' \leftarrow$ submatrix of $(C-E)$ from rows in $\mathcal{J}$
  $s \leftarrow \lceil 2(k - \#E)/r\rceil$
  $Y \leftarrow$ `DiffEval`(A', B, C', θ, s)
  $f_1, \ldots, f_r \leftarrow$ `MultiSparseInterp`(r, n, s, θ, Y)
  for $i \leftarrow 1, 2, \ldots, r$ **do**
    Set $(\mathcal{J}_i, e)$th entry of E to c for each term cx^e of f_i
  $\mathcal{J} \leftarrow$ `FindNonzeroRows`$(V \mapsto (C-E)V - A(BV), \epsilon')$
  if $\#\mathcal{J} > r/2$ **then**
    $k \leftarrow 2k$
    if $k \geq 2n\#J$ **then return** $C - AB$
  foreach $i \in \mathcal{J}$ **do**
    Clear entries from row i of E added on this iteration
return E

leading to the small $1-\epsilon$ chance that the algorithm returns an incorrect result. □

8 INVERSE ERROR CORRECTION ALGORITHM

As discussed in Section 2, our algorithm for correcting errors in a matrix inverse follows mostly the same outline as that for correcting a matrix product, with two important changes. These are the basis for the next two lemmas.

Lemma 8.1. *For any matrices $E, A \in \mathsf{F}^{n\times n}$ where A is invertible, a call to* `FindNonzeroRows`$(V \mapsto EAV, \epsilon)$ *correctly returns the nonzero rows of E with probability at least $1-\epsilon$.*

Proof. Recall from the proof of Lemma 4.1 that the correctness of `FindNonzeroRows` depends on applying a matrix $V \in \mathsf{F}^{n\times\ell}$ of random entries to the unknown matrix E.

In the current formulation, instead of applying the random matrix V directly to E, instead the product AV is applied. But because A is nonsingular, there is a 1-1 correspondence between the set of all matrices $V \in \mathsf{F}^{n\times\ell}$ and matrices the set $\{AV \mid V \in \mathsf{F}^{n\times\ell}\}$. That is, applying a random matrix to EA is the same as applying a random matrix to E itself, and therefore the same results hold. □

Algorithm 6: `InverseEC`(A, B, θ, ϵ)

Input: Matrices $A, B \in \mathsf{F}^{n\times n}$, high-order element $\theta \in \mathsf{F}$, and error bound $0 < \epsilon < 1$

Output: Matrix $E \in \mathsf{F}^{n\times n}$ such that, with probability at least $1-\epsilon$, $A^{-1} = B + E$

$k \leftarrow 1$
$E \leftarrow \mathbf{0}^{n\times n}$
$\epsilon' \leftarrow \epsilon/(8\lceil\log_2 n\rceil + 1)$
$\mathcal{J} \leftarrow$ `FindNonzeroRows`$(V \mapsto V - B(AV), \epsilon')$
while $\#\mathcal{J} \geq 1$ **do**
  if #`FindNonzeroRows`$(V \mapsto V - A((B+E)V), \epsilon') > \#\mathcal{J}$ **then**
    Transpose A, B, and E, and replace $\mathcal{J}$
  $r \leftarrow \#\mathcal{J}$
  $A' \leftarrow$ submatrix of A from columns in $\mathcal{J}$
  $\mathcal{J}' \leftarrow$ set of r linearly independent rows in A' according to Lemma 8.2
  $I', A'' \leftarrow$ submatrices of I, A from the rows chosen in $\mathcal{J}'$
  $X^{-1} \leftarrow$ inverse of submatrix of A' according to Lemma 8.2
  $s \leftarrow \lceil 2(k - \#E)/r\rceil$
  $Y \leftarrow$ `DiffEval`(A'', B, I', θ, s)
  $Y' \leftarrow X^{-1}Y$
  $f_1, \ldots, f_r \leftarrow$ `MultiSparseInterp`(r, n, s, θ, Y')
  for $i \leftarrow 1, 2, \ldots, r$ **do**
    Set $(\mathcal{J}_i, e)$th entry of E to c for each term cx^e of f_i
  $\mathcal{J} \leftarrow$ `FindNonzeroRows`$(V \mapsto V - (B+E)(AV), \epsilon')$
  if $\#\mathcal{J} > r/2$ **then**
    $k \leftarrow 2k$
    if $k \geq 2n\#J$ **then return** $A^{-1} - B$
  foreach $i \in \mathcal{J}$ **do**
    Clear entries from row i of E added on this iteration
return E

Lemma 8.2. *Given any rank-r matrix $A \in \mathsf{F}^{n\times r}$, it is possible to compute a matrix $X \in \mathsf{F}^{r\times r}$ formed from a subset of the rows of A, and its inverse X^{-1}, using $\widetilde{O}(\#A + r^\omega)$ field operations.*

Proof. This is a direct consequence of [11, Theorem 2.11], along with the classic algorithm of [9] for fast matrix inversion. Alternatively, one could use the approach of [34] to compute the lexicographically minimal set of linearly independent rows in A, as well as a representation of the inverse, in the same running time. □

The resulting algorithm for matrix inversion with errors is presented in Algorithm 6 `InverseEC`.

Theorem 8.3. *Algorithm 6* `InverseEC` *finds all errors in B with probability at least $1-\epsilon$, and always uses*

$$\widetilde{O}\left(\left\lceil \log_{\#\mathsf{F}} \tfrac{1}{\epsilon}\right\rceil t + nk/\min(r, \tfrac{k}{r})^{3-\omega} + r^\omega\right)$$

field operations, where k is the actual *number of errors in the given product C. Otherwise, it uses $\widetilde{O}(n^\omega)$ field operations and may return an incorrect result.*

Proof. In this algorithm, we make use of two different formulas for E:

$$EA = I - BA \quad (1)$$

$$AE = I - AB \quad (2)$$

The first formula (1) is used to determine the nonzero rows of E on Lines 4 and 19, and the second formula (2) is used to evaluate the rows of XE on Line 14.

The main difference in this algorithm compared to `MultiplyEC` is the need to find r nonzero rows of A' to constitute the matrix X and compute its inverse X^{-1}. According to Lemma 8.2 these both cost $\widetilde{O}(r^\omega)$, which gives the additional term in the complexity statement. Note that this also eliminates the utility of sparse multiplication in all cases, simplifying the complexity statement somewhat compared to that of `MultiplyEC`.

The rest of the proof is identical to that of Theorem 7.1. □

ACKNOWLEDGMENTS

This work was performed while the author was graciously hosted by the Laboratoire Jean Kuntzmann at the Université Grenoble Alpes. Thanks to many colleagues for fruitful discussions on these topics, especially Clément Pernet and Jean-Guillaume Dumas.

This work was supported in part by the National Science Foundation under grants 1319994 (https://www.nsf.gov/awardsearch/showAward?AWD_ID=1319994) and 1618269 (https://www.nsf.gov/awardsearch/showAward?AWD_ID=1618269).

REFERENCES

[1] R. R. Amossen and R. Pagh. Faster join-projects and sparse matrix multiplications. In *ICDT '09*, pages 121–126, New York, NY, USA, 2009. ACM. doi:10.1145/1514894.1514909.

[2] A. Arnold, M. Giesbrecht, and D. S. Roche. Faster sparse multivariate polynomial interpolation of straight-line programs. *J. Symbolic Computation*, 2015. doi:10.1016/j.jsc.2015.11.005.

[3] M. Ben-Or and P. Tiwari. A deterministic algorithm for sparse multivariate polynomial interpolation. In *STOC '88*, pages 301–309, New York, NY, USA, 1988. ACM. doi:10.1145/62212.62241.

[4] D. J. Bernstein. Factoring into coprimes in essentially linear time. *J. Algorithms*, 54(1):1–30, 2005. doi:10.1016/j.jalgor.2004.04.009.

[5] J. Böhm, W. Decker, C. Fieker, and G. Pfister. The use of bad primes in rational reconstruction. *Math. Comp.*, 84(296):3013–3027, 2015. doi:10.1090/mcom/2951.

[6] A. Borodin and I. Munro. *The computational complexity of algebraic and numeric problems*. Number 1 in Elsevier Computer Science Library; Theory of Computation Series. American Elsevier Pub. Co., New York, 1975.

[7] A. Bostan, G. Lecerf, and E. Schost. Tellegen's principle into practice. In *ISSAC '03*, pages 37–44. ACM, 2003. doi:10.1145/860854.860870.

[8] B. Boyer and E. L. Kaltofen. Numerical linear system solving with parametric entries by error correction. In *SNC '14*, pages 33–38. ACM, 2014. doi:10.1145/2631948.2631956.

[9] J. R. Bunch and J. E. Hopcroft. Triangular factorization and inversion by fast matrix multiplication. *Mathematics of Computation*, 28(125):231–236, 1974. URL http://www.jstor.org/stable/2005828.

[10] D. G. Cantor and E. Kaltofen. On fast multiplication of polynomials over arbitrary algebras. *Acta Informatica*, 28:693–701, 1991. doi:10.1007/BF01178683.

[11] H. Y. Cheung, T. C. Kwok, and L. C. Lau. Fast matrix rank algorithms and applications. *J. ACM*, 60(5):31:1–31:25, Oct. 2013. doi:10.1145/2528404.

[12] M. T. Comer, E. L. Kaltofen, and C. Pernet. Sparse polynomial interpolation and Berlekamp/Massey algorithms that correct outlier errors in input values. In *ISSAC '12*, pages 138–145, New York, NY, USA, 2012. ACM. doi:10.1145/2442829.2442852.

[13] J.-G. Dumas and E. Kaltofen. Essentially optimal interactive certificates in linear algebra. In *ISSAC '14*, pages 146–153. ACM, 2014. doi:10.1145/2608628.2608644.

[14] J.-G. Dumas, P. Giorgi, and C. Pernet. Dense linear algebra over word-size prime fields: the FFLAS and FFPACK packages. *ACM Trans. Math. Softw.*, 35:19:1–19:42, October 2008. doi:10.1145/1391989.1391992.

[15] J.-G. Dumas, E. Kaltofen, E. Thomé, and G. Villard. Linear time interactive certificates for the minimal polynomial and the determinant of a sparse matrix. In *ISSAC '16*, pages 199–206. ACM, 2016. doi:10.1145/2930889.2930908.

[16] J.-G. Dumas, D. Lucas, and C. Pernet. Certificates for triangular equivalence and rank profiles. In *ISSAC '17*, pages 133–140. ACM, 2017. doi:10.1145/3087604.3087609.

[17] R. Freivalds. Fast probabilistic algorithms. In J. Bečvář, editor, *Mathematical Foundations of Computer Science 1979*, pages 57–69. Springer Berlin Heidelberg, 1979.

[18] L. Gasieniec, C. Levcopoulos, A. Lingas, R. Pagh, and T. Tokuyama. Efficiently correcting matrix products. *Algorithmica*, 79(2):428–443, Oct 2017. doi:10.1007/s00453-016-0202-3.

[19] O. Goldreich, D. Ron, and M. Sudan. Chinese remaindering with errors. In *STOC '99*, pages 225–234. ACM, 1999. doi:10.1145/301250.301309.

[20] D. Harvey, J. van der Hoeven, and G. Lecerf. Faster polynomial multiplication over finite fields. *J. ACM*, 63(6):52:1–52:23, Jan. 2017. doi:10.1145/3005344.

[21] J. van der Hoeven and G. Lecerf. On the bit-complexity of sparse polynomial and series multiplication. *J. Symbolic Computation*, 50:227–0254, 2013. doi:10.1016/j.jsc.2012.06.004.

[22] Q. Huang and X. Gao. Faster deterministic sparse interpolation algorithms for straight-line program multivariate polynomials. *CoRR*, abs/1709.08979, 2017. URL http://arxiv.org/abs/1709.08979.

[23] S. M. M. Javadi and M. Monagan. Parallel sparse polynomial interpolation over finite fields. In *PASCO '10*, pages 160–168, New York, NY, USA, 2010. ACM. doi:10.1145/1837210.1837233.

[24] E. Kaltofen and L. Yagati. Improved sparse multivariate polynomial interpolation algorithms. In P. Gianni, editor, *Symbolic and Algebraic Computation*, volume 358 of *Lecture Notes in Computer Science*, pages 467–474. Springer Berlin / Heidelberg, 1989. doi:10.1007/3-540-51084-2_44.

[25] E. L. Kaltofen. Fifteen years after DSC and WLSS2: What parallel computations I do today [invited lecture at PASCO 2010]. In *PASCO '10*, pages 10–17, New York, NY, USA, 2010. ACM. doi:10.1145/1837210.1837213.

[26] E. L. Kaltofen and Z. Yang. Sparse multivariate function recovery from values with noise and outlier errors. In *ISSAC '13*, pages 219–226. ACM, 2013. doi:10.1145/2465506.2465524.

[27] E. L. Kaltofen, M. Nehring, and B. D. Saunders. Quadratic-time certificates in linear algebra. In *ISSAC '11*, pages 171–176. ACM, 2011. doi:10.1145/1993886.1993915.

[28] E. L. Kaltofen, C. Pernet, A. Storjohann, and C. Waddell. Early termination in parametric linear system solving and rational function vector recovery with error correction. In *ISSAC '17*, pages 237–244. ACM, 2017. doi:10.1145/3087604.3087645.

[29] M. Khonji, C. Pernet, J.-L. Roch, T. Roche, and T. Stalinski. Output-sensitive decoding for redundant residue systems. In *ISSAC '10*, pages 265–272. ACM, 2010. doi:10.1145/1837934.1837985.

[30] F. Le Gall. Faster algorithms for rectangular matrix multiplication. In *FOCS '12*, pages 514–523, Oct 2012. doi:10.1109/FOCS.2012.80.

[31] F. Le Gall. Powers of tensors and fast matrix multiplication. In *ISSAC '14*, pages 296–303, New York, NY, USA, 2014. ACM. doi:10.1145/2608628.2608664.

[32] A. Lingas. A fast output-sensitive algorithm for boolean matrix multiplication. In A. Fiat and P. Sanders, editors, *Algorithms - ESA 2009*, pages 408–419. Springer Berlin Heidelberg, 2009. doi:10.1007/978-3-642-04128-0_37.

[33] R. Pagh. Compressed matrix multiplication. *ACM Trans. Comput. Theory*, 5(3): 9:1–9:17, Aug. 2013. doi:10.1145/2493252.2493254.

[34] A. Storjohann and S. Yang. A relaxed algorithm for online matrix inversion. In *ISSAC '15*, pages 339–346, New York, NY, USA, 2015. ACM. doi:10.1145/2755996.2756672.

[35] Q. Wang, X. Zhang, Y. Zhang, and Q. Yi. Augem: Automatically generate high performance dense linear algebra kernels on x86 cpus. In *Proc. Int'l Conference on High Performance Computing, Networking, Storage and Analysis*, SC '13, pages 25:1–25:12. ACM, 2013. doi:10.1145/2503210.2503219.

[36] R. Yuster and U. Zwick. Fast sparse matrix multiplication. *ACM Trans. Algorithms*, 1(1):2–13, July 2005. doi:10.1145/1077464.1077466.

On the complexity of computing real radicals of polynomial systems

Mohab Safey El Din
Sorbonne Université, CNRS, INRIA, Laboratoire d'Informatique de Paris 6, LIP6, Équipe PolSys
F-75252, Paris Cedex 05, France
mohab.safey@lip6.fr

Zhi-Hong Yang
KLMM, Academy of Mathematics and Systems Science, Chinese Academy of Sciences, Beijing 100190, China
University of Chinese Academy of Sciences, Beijing 100049, China
zhyang@amss.ac.cn

Lihong Zhi
KLMM, Academy of Mathematics and Systems Science, Chinese Academy of Sciences, Beijing 100190, China
University of Chinese Academy of Sciences, Beijing 100049, China
lzhi@mmrc.iss.ac.cn

ABSTRACT

Let $f = (f_1, \ldots, f_s)$ be a sequence of polynomials in $\mathbb{Q}[X_1, \ldots, X_n]$ of maximal degree D and $V \subset \mathbb{C}^n$ be the algebraic set defined by f and r be its dimension. The real radical $\sqrt[re]{\langle f\rangle}$ associated to f is the largest ideal which defines the real trace of V. When V is smooth, we show that $\sqrt[re]{\langle f\rangle}$, has a finite set of generators with degrees bounded by $\deg V$. Moreover, we present a probabilistic algorithm of complexity $(snD^n)^{O(1)}$ to compute the minimal primes of $\sqrt[re]{\langle f\rangle}$.

When V is not smooth, we give a probabilistic algorithm of complexity $s^{O(1)}(nD)^{O(nr2^r)}$ to compute rational parametrizations for all irreducible components of the real algebraic set $V \cap \mathbb{R}^n$. Experiments are given to show the efficiency of our approaches.

KEYWORDS

Polynomial system; Real radical; Real Algebraic Geometry

ACM Reference Format:
Mohab Safey El Din, Zhi-Hong Yang, and Lihong Zhi. 2018. On the complexity of computing real radicals of polynomial systems. In *ISSAC '18: 2018 ACM International Symposium on Symbolic and Algebraic Computation, July 16–19, 2018, New York, NY, USA.* ACM, New York, NY, USA, 8 pages. https://doi.org/10.1145/3208976.3209002

1 INTRODUCTION

Let $\mathbb{Q}$, $\mathbb{R}$ and $\mathbb{C}$ be the fields of rational, real and complex numbers and $X = (X_1, \ldots, X_n)$ be a sequence of variables.

For $f = (f_1, \ldots, f_s)$ in $\mathbb{Q}[X] := \mathbb{Q}[X_1, \ldots, X_n]$, we denote by $\langle f\rangle$ the ideal generated by f in $\mathbb{Q}[X]$. For $\mathbb{K} = \mathbb{C}$ or $\mathbb{R}$, we let $V_{\mathbb{K}}(f) := \{x \in \mathbb{K}^n \mid f_1(x) = 0 \ldots, f_s(x) = 0\}$. The radical ideal of $\langle f\rangle$ is the vanishing ideal of the algebraic set $V_{\mathbb{C}}(f) \subset \mathbb{C}^n$.

The real radical $\sqrt[re]{\langle f\rangle}$ of $\langle f\rangle$ in $\mathbb{Q}[X]$ is defined as the set of polynomials $g \in \mathbb{Q}[X]$ such that $g^{2m} + \sum_{i=1}^{l} a_i^2 \in \langle f\rangle$ for $m, l \in \mathbb{N}$, $a_i \in \mathbb{Q}[X]$. An ideal is said to be real if it equals its real radical. The Real Nullstellensatz (see e.g. [31]) states that $\sqrt[re]{\langle f\rangle}$ is equal to the vanishing ideal of $V_{\mathbb{R}}(f)$. Hence, representing the real radical associated to f provides some insight on the geometry of $V_{\mathbb{R}}(f)$.

Computing real radicals has attracted much attention both on the symbolic and numerical side. Symbolic algorithms were developed at first in [2]. Later [31] proposed a revised form of this algorithm and gave an upper bound $D^{2^{O(n^2)}}$ for the degree of the generators of $\sqrt[re]{\langle f\rangle}$, where $D = \max\{\deg f_1, \ldots, \deg f_s\}$. [40, 41] implemented this algorithm and improved its efficiency by avoiding some linear changes of coordinates. This algorithm is based on properties of isolated points of real algebraic sets and computation of real radicals of zero-dimensional ideals. Instead of computing real radicals, [6–8] give a method to decompose semi-algebraic systems into regular semi-algebraic systems.

On the numerical side, [22, 23] presented an algorithm based on moment relaxations to compute zero-dimensional real radicals in $\mathbb{R}[X]$. Subsequently, [28] generalized this algorithm to positive dimensional cases. [5] gave a method based on numerical algebraic geometry and sums of squares programming to certify that a set of polynomials generates the real radical. We emphasize that these algorithms compute real radicals in $\mathbb{R}[X]$ and hence return approximate encodings of those radicals. To see this, consider a univariate polynomial $f \in \mathbb{Q}[X_1]$ with a single irrational real root ρ. The real radical of $\langle f\rangle$ is generated by $X_1 - \rho$. The aforementioned algorithms based on numerical computations use an approximation of ρ to encode the output. By contrast, symbolic algorithms return real radicals with base field $\mathbb{Q}$ and in the example we just considered would simply return f.

In this paper, we focus on symbolic algorithms for computing generators or *lazy representations* (see Definition 1.2) for real radicals in $\mathbb{Q}[X]$ with a focus on complexity issues.

Main results. All in all, we improve the complexity bound $D^{2^{O(n^2)}}$ for computing real radicals. When $V_{\mathbb{C}}(f)$ is smooth, we use polynomial system solving techniques in [3, 16, 33] to obtain an algorithm running in time polynomial in snD^n.

Theorem 1.1. *Let $f = (f_1, \ldots, f_s) \subset \mathbb{Q}[X_1, \ldots, X_n]$ with $D = \max(\deg(f_i), i = 1, \ldots, s)$ encoded by a straight-line program Γ. Assume that $V_{\mathbb{C}}(f)$ is smooth, of dimension r and of degree δ. There exists a probabilistic algorithm which takes as input Γ and returns generators of each minimal associated prime of $\sqrt[re]{\langle f\rangle}$ with maximum degree δ. In case of success, the algorithm uses $(snD^n)^{O(1)}$ arithmetic operations in $\mathbb{Q}$.*

Mohab Safey El Din is supported by the ANR grant ANR-17-CE40-0009 Galop and the PGMO grant Gamma. Zhi-Hong Yang and Lihong Zhi are supported in part by the National Natural Science Foundation of China under Grants 11571350 and the National Key Research Project of China 2016YFB0200504.

ACM ISBN 978-1-4503-5550-6/18/07…$15.00
https://doi.org/10.1145/3208976.3209002

When $V = V_{\mathbb{C}}(f)$ is not smooth and has dimension r, we obtain an algorithm using $s^{O(1)}(nD)^{O(nr2^r)}$ arithmetic operations in $\mathbb{Q}$ to represent the irreducible components of $\sqrt[re]{\langle f \rangle}$. Hence for fixed r, it is singly exponential in n by contrast to previous results.

The difficulty in the non-smooth case is that the real algebraic set $V_{\mathbb{R}}(f)$ might be embedded in the singular locus of V, or even worse, in the singular locus of the singular locus of V, etc. Using the Jacobian criterion and Gröbner bases to compute the vanishing ideal of the singular locus of V, would result in the complexity $D^{2^{O(n^2)}}$ as in [31]. To bypass complexity issues, we use techniques developed in the last decades to represent algebraic sets. Such techniques, which are now standard in computer algebra, consist in representing an equidimensional algebraic set $V \subset \mathbb{C}^n$ *outside* a Zariski closed set, hence often restricting to a subset of V which is a complete intersection. There are two main such representations, either triangular sets[42, 43] (also known as regular chains[17], tower of simple extensions[25], regular set[30]) or rational parametrizations (also known as geometric resolutions)(see e.g.[15, 27, 38, 39]). The following definition is folkore.

Definition 1.2. An r-dimensional rational parametrization $\mathscr{Q} = ((w, v_1, \ldots, v_n), \boldsymbol{\ell})$ in $\mathbb{Q}[T_1, \ldots, T_{r+1}]$ of degree δ consists of the following:

- a sequence of polynomials $(w, v_1, \ldots, v_n)$ in $\mathbb{Q}[T_1, \ldots, T_{r+1}]$ such that the following holds: the variables $T_1, \ldots, T_{r+1}$ are new and w is square-free and monic and of degree δ in each variable $T_1, \ldots, T_{r+1}$ and, for $1 \leq i \leq n$, $\deg(v_i, T_{r+1}) < \deg(w, T_{r+1})$.
- $\boldsymbol{\ell} = (\lambda_1, \ldots, \lambda_{r+1})$ is a sequence of linear forms in variables $X_1, \ldots, X_n$ such that $\lambda_i(v_1, \ldots, v_n) = T_i \frac{\partial w}{\partial T_{r+1}} \mod w$.

The corresponding algebraic set $Z(\mathscr{Q}) \subset \mathbb{C}^n$ is the Zariski closure of the locally closed set of points $(x_1, \ldots, x_n) \in \mathbb{C}^n$ such that $\exists \vartheta \in \mathbb{C}^{r+1}, w(\vartheta) = 0, \frac{\partial w}{\partial T_{r+1}}(\vartheta) \neq 0, x_i = \frac{v_i}{\partial w / \partial T_{r+1}}(\vartheta)$. Observe that $Z(\mathscr{Q})$ is equidimensional (using the Jacobian criterion) and that the Zariski closure of the image of $Z(\mathscr{Q})$ by the map $x \to (\lambda_1(x), \ldots, \lambda_{r+1}(x))$ is defined by $w = 0$. Furthermore, the polynomial w is called the eliminating polynomial of the parametrization. Besides, the degree of w coincides with the degree of $Z(\mathscr{Q})$ (see [15, 27]). Finally, observe also that the parametrization ((1)) encodes the empty set. Equidimensional decompositions of algebraic sets whose components are represented by such parametrizations can be efficiently computed using [26]. This is a key ingredient for the proof of the result below.

THEOREM 1.3. *Let $f = (f_1, \ldots, f_s) \subset \mathbb{Q}[X_1, \ldots, X_n]$ of degrees bounded by D. Let r be the maximum of 1 and the dimension of the algebraic set $V_{\mathbb{C}}(f)$. Then, there exists a probabilistic algorithm* LazyRealRadical *which takes as input f and returns rational parametrizations of the minimal associated primes of $\sqrt[re]{\langle f \rangle}$ using $s^{O(1)}(nD)^{O(nr2^r)}$ arithmetic operations in $\mathbb{Q}$.*

Plan of the paper. In Section 2, we introduce some basic notions that will be used throughout the paper. In Section 3, we present an algorithm for computing generators of real radicals under the smoothness assumption and show the correctness and the complexity of the algorithm. In Section 4, we give a probabilistic algorithm to compute rational parametrizations for all irreducible components of an arbitrarily given real algebraic set. The last section is devoted to practical experiments.

2 PRELIMINARIES

2.1 Ideals and varieties

For basic notions related to affine and projective spaces, ideals and algebraic sets (and their irreducible components), as well as equidimensionality we refer to [9]. For basic definitions on real algebraic sets and semi-algebraic sets, we refer to [4]. In the sequel, we use the following notations.

We denote by $\mathbb{P}^n(\mathbb{C})$ the n-dimensional *projective space* over $\mathbb{C}$. A subset of $\mathbb{P}^n(\mathbb{C})$ is called a *projective algebraic set* if it is the set of common zeros of some homogeneous polynomials in $\mathbb{Q}[X_0, X_1, \ldots, X_n]$.

Let $S \subset \mathbb{C}^n$, we denote by $\overline{S}$ the Zariski closure of S which is the smallest algebraic set containing S; we denote by $I(S)$ the *vanishing ideal* of S which is the set of all polynomials in $\mathbb{Q}[X_1, \ldots, X_n]$ vanishing identically over S.

Let $V \subset \mathbb{C}^n$ be an algebraic set. Let $I(V) = \langle f_1, \ldots, f_s \rangle \subset \mathbb{Q}[X]$ and p be a point of V. The *tangent space* of V at p, denoted by $T_p(V)$, is given by $T_p(V) := \bigcap_{j=1}^{s} \left\{ x \in \mathbb{C}^n \,\middle|\, \sum_{i=1}^{n} \frac{\partial f_j}{\partial X_i}(p) x_i = 0 \right\}$. The dimension of V at p, denoted by $\dim_p V$, is the maximum dimension of an irreducible component of V containing p. The point p is said to be *non-singular* (or *regular*) at V if $\dim T_p(V) = \dim_p V$. Otherwise, p is called a *singular point* of V. The *singular locus* of V is the set $\mathrm{Sing}(V) := \{p \in V \mid p \text{ is a singular point of } V\}$. We say that V is *smooth* if V has no singular point, that is, $\mathrm{Sing}(V) = \emptyset$.

All the notions above can be similarly defined for real algebraic sets in $\mathbb{R}^n$ and projective algebraic sets in $\mathbb{P}^n(\mathbb{C})$.

Let $W \subset \mathbb{C}^n$ be an irreducible algebraic set and $r := \dim W$. The *degree* $\deg W$ of W is $\sup\{\#(H_1 \cap \ldots \cap H_r \cap W)\}$ where $H_1, \ldots, H_r$ are hyperplanes in $\mathbb{C}^n$ meeting W at finitely many points. If W is not irreducible, then its *degree* is defined to be the sum of the degrees of all its irreducible components.

2.2 Chow forms

We recall the definition of Chow forms [14, Chapter 3]. Let $V \subset \mathbb{P}^n(\mathbb{C})$ be an irreducible projective set, where $\dim V = r$. For $i = 0, \ldots, r$, we denote by $U_i = (U_{i0}, \ldots, U_{in})$ a group of $n+1$ variables and $U := (U_0, \ldots, U_r)$. Let $L_i = U_{i0}X_0 + \ldots + U_{in}X_n$, $i = 0, \ldots, r$. The *Chow form* of the projective set V is the unique (up to a scalar factor) irreducible polynomial $\mathcal{F}_V \in \mathbb{Q}[U]$ such that for any $u_0, \ldots, u_r \in \mathbb{C}^{n+1}$,

$$\mathcal{F}_V(u_0, \ldots, u_r) = 0 \Leftrightarrow V \cap \{L_0(u_0, X) = 0, \ldots, L_r(u_r, X) = 0\} \neq \emptyset$$

where $L_i(u_i, X) = u_{i0}X_0 + \cdots + u_{in}X_n$, $i = 0, \ldots, r$.

Let $W \subset \mathbb{P}^n(\mathbb{C})$ be an equidimensional projective set and W_i be its irreducible components ($1 \leq i \leq \ell$). The Chow form of W is defined as $\mathcal{F}_W = \prod_{i=1}^{\ell} \mathcal{F}_{W_i}$, where $\mathcal{F}_{W_i}$ is the Chow form of W_i.

This definition can be extended to equidimensional affine algebraic sets in $\mathbb{C}^n$. Assume that we are given a finite sequence of polynomials $f = (f_1, \ldots, f_s)$ in $\mathbb{Q}[X_1, \ldots, X_n]$ and let f_i^h be the homogenization of f_i using the new variable X_0. Denote $f^h = (f_1^h, \ldots, f_s^h)$. Then the affine algebraic set $V := V_{\mathbb{C}}(f)$ can be identified with a subset of $\mathbb{P}^n(\mathbb{C})$ which is $V_{\mathbb{C}}(f^h) \setminus V_{\mathbb{C}}(X_0)$, and the *projective closure* of V is the smallest projective algebraic set containing $V_{\mathbb{C}}(f^h) \setminus V_{\mathbb{C}}(X_0)$ [see 9, Chapter 8]. The Chow form of V is defined to be the Chow form of its projective closure in $\mathbb{P}^n(\mathbb{C})$ [see 16, Section 1.1].

3 ALGORITHM FOR THE SMOOTH CASE

3.1 Preliminary results

Let V be a smooth and equidimensional algebraic set in $\mathbb{C}^n$ defined by polynomials in $\mathbb{Q}[X]$ and let $m := (n - \dim V)(1 + \dim V)$. It has been shown in [3, Theorem 10 and Corollary 17] that there exist polynomials $g_1, \ldots, g_m$ with $\deg g_i \le \deg V$ such that $g_1, \ldots, g_m$ generate the ideal $I(V)$. Moreover, the polynomials $g_1, \ldots, g_m$ can be obtained by specializing the Chow form of V at some generic linear forms with rational coefficients (see [3, Section 4] for details). We slightly generalize this result.

Theorem 3.1. *Let V be a smooth algebraic set in $\mathbb{C}^n$ of degree δ. There exists a finite set of polynomials $G = (g_1, \ldots, g_s) \subset \mathbb{Q}[X]$ with $\max(\deg(g_i), i = 1, \ldots, s) \le \delta$ such that $\langle G \rangle = I(V)$.*

Proof. Set $r = \dim(V)$ and $V = \bigcup_{i=0}^r V_i$ be the minimal equidimensional decomposition of V, where V_i is either empty or i-equidimensional. Let $m_i := (n - i)(i + 1)$, for $i = 0, \ldots, r$. By [3, Theorem 10 and Corollary 17], there exist polynomials $g_1^{(i)}, \ldots, g_{m_i}^{(i)}$ with degrees bounded by $\deg V_i$ such that $I(V_i) = \langle g_1^{(i)}, \ldots, g_{m_i}^{(i)} \rangle$, for $i = 0, \ldots, r$. Since V is smooth, according to [9, §9.6, Theorem 8], we have $V_i \cap V_j = \emptyset$ for any $0 \le i < j \le r$. Then $I(V_i) + I(V_j) = \langle 1 \rangle$ for all $0 \le i < j \le r$ and therefore $I(V) = \bigcap_{i=0}^r I(V_i)$ which equals $\left\langle \left\{ g_{j_0}^{(0)} \cdots g_{j_r}^{(r)} \mid 1 \le j_0 \le m_0, \ldots, 1 \le j_r \le m_r \right\} \right\rangle$.

Moreover, $\deg\left(g_{j_0}^{(0)} \cdots g_{j_r}^{(r)}\right) \le \deg V_0 + \cdots + \deg V_r = \delta$. Let $G := \left\{ g_{j_0}^{(0)} \cdots g_{j_r}^{(r)} \mid 1 \le j_0 \le m_0, \ldots, 1 \le j_r \le m_r \right\}$, we have $\langle G \rangle = I(V) = \sqrt{I}$ and $\deg(g) \le \delta$ for all $g \in G$. □

We recall now a well-known criterion for testing whether a given prime ideal is real.

Proposition 3.2. *[29, Theorem 12.6.1] Let I be a prime ideal in $\mathbb{Q}[X]$, then I is real if and only if I has a non-singular real zero.*

Theorem 3.3. *Let f be a finite polynomial sequence of $\mathbb{Q}[X]$ and $V := V_{\mathbb{C}}(f)$ of degree δ. If V is smooth, then $\sqrt[re]{\langle f \rangle}$ has a finite set of generators $G \subset \mathbb{Q}[X]$ with $\deg(g) \le \delta$ for $g \in G$.*

Proof. Let $V = \bigcup_{i=1}^s V_i$ be the minimal irreducible decomposition of V. Note that for $i = 1, \ldots, s$, V_i is smooth (because V is) and $I(V_i)$ is prime. W.l.o.g. we assume that $V \cap \mathbb{R}^n \ne \emptyset$ since otherwise the conclusion is trivial. Let $\Omega := \left\{ V_j \mid V_j \cap \mathbb{R}^n \ne \emptyset,\ 1 \le j \le s \right\}$. If $V_j \in \Omega$, then the prime ideal $I(V_j)$ has at least one non-singular real zero because V_j is smooth and $V_j \cap \mathbb{R}^n \ne \emptyset$. Therefore, according to Proposition 3.2, $I(V_j)$ is real for every $V_j \in \Omega$. Now we have $I\left(\overline{V \cap \mathbb{R}^n}\right) = I(V \cap \mathbb{R}^n) = I\left(\bigcup_{V_j \in \Omega} \left(V_j \cap \mathbb{R}^n\right)\right)$ which equals $\bigcap_{V_j \in \Omega} I\left(V_j \cap \mathbb{R}^n\right) = \bigcap_{V_j \in \Omega} I\left(V_j\right)$, where $\overline{V \cap \mathbb{R}^n}$ is the Zariski closure of $V \cap \mathbb{R}^n$ in $\mathbb{C}^n$, and the last equality follows from the fact that $I(V_j)$ is real. Note that the first equality holds because for any subset S of $\mathbb{C}^n$, S and its Zariski closure $\overline{S}$ have the same vanishing ideal [see 9, §4.4]. It follows that $I\left(\overline{V \cap \mathbb{R}^n}\right)$ and $\bigcap_{V_j \in \Omega} I\left(V_j\right)$ define the same algebraic set, that is, $\overline{V \cap \mathbb{R}^n} = \bigcup_{V_j \in \Omega} V_j$. Then,

$$\deg(\overline{V \cap \mathbb{R}^n}) = \sum_{V_j \in \Omega} \deg V_j \le \sum_{i=1}^{s} \deg V_i = \deg V. \quad (1)$$

By the Real Nullstellensatz, $\sqrt[re]{\langle f \rangle} = I(V \cap \mathbb{R}^n)$. We already observed that $I\left(\overline{V \cap \mathbb{R}^n}\right) = I(V \cap \mathbb{R}^n)$. Hence, we have $\sqrt[re]{\langle f \rangle} = I\left(\overline{V \cap \mathbb{R}^n}\right)$. Moreover, $\overline{V \cap \mathbb{R}^n}$ is smooth because V is smooth. The conclusion follows from Theorem 3.1 and the inequality (1). □

3.2 Algorithm description

Let $f = (f_1, \ldots, f_s) \subset \mathbb{Q}[X]$, and assume that $V = V_{\mathbb{C}}(f)$ is smooth of dimension r. Write the minimal equidimensional decomposition of V as $V = \bigcup_{i=1}^r V_i$, where V_i is either empty or is i-equidimensional. Denote by $f_1^h, \ldots, f_s^h$ the homogenizations of $f_1, \ldots, f_s$ using the new variable X_0. Our algorithm uses several subroutines for computing generators of real radicals when $V = V_{\mathbb{C}}(f)$ is smooth.

- PointsPerComponents. It takes as input polynomials $f_1 = 0, \ldots, f_s = 0$ and returns a set of real points meeting every connected component of $V_{\mathbb{R}}(f_1, \ldots, f_s)$ [see 33].
- Equidim. It takes as input homogeneous polynomials $f_1^h, \ldots, f_s^h, g \in \mathbb{Q}[X_0, \ldots, X_n]$ and returns the Chow forms of all equidimensional components of $V_{\mathbb{C}}(f_1^h, \ldots, f_s^h) \setminus V_{\mathbb{C}}(g)$ [see 16]).
- Generators. It takes as input a Chow form $\mathcal{F}_{V_i}$ of some equidimensional algebraic set V_i and returns a set of generators of the radical ideal $I(V_i)$ [see 3].

Let $V_i \subset \mathbb{C}^n$ be an equidimensional component of V and $V_i^h \subset \mathbb{P}^n$ denote the projective closure of V_i. Let $V_i = \bigcup_{j=1}^{m_i} V_{ij}$ be the minimal irreducible decomposition of V_i. Then $V_i^h = \bigcup_{j=1}^{m_i} V_{ij}^h$, where V_{ij}^h is the projective closure of V_{ij}. We can compute the Chow form $\mathcal{F}_{V_i}$ of V_i by the subroutine Equidim. According to the definition of the Chow form, $\mathcal{F}_{V_i} = \prod_{j=1}^{m_i} \mathcal{F}_{V_{ij}}$. Therefore we can compute the Chow forms of all the irreducible components of V_i by factorizing $\mathcal{F}_{V_i}$ over $\mathbb{Q}$. The following is the algorithm mentioned in Theorem 1.1.

RealRadicalSmooth(f)

(1) S = PointsPerComponents($f = 0$);
(2) if $S = \emptyset$, then return $\{1\}$;
(3) $\left\{\mathcal{F}_{V_0}, \ldots, \mathcal{F}_{V_r}\right\}$ = Equidim(f^h, X_0);
(4) for $0 \le i \le r$ do
 $\{\mathcal{F}_{V_{i1}}, \ldots, \mathcal{F}_{V_{im_i}}\} \leftarrow$ irreducible factors of $\mathcal{F}_{V_i}$;
(5) $\Omega = \{\}$;
(6) for $0 \le i \le r$ and $1 \le j \le m_i$ do
 G_{ij} = Generators($\mathcal{F}_{V_{ij}}$);
 if $V_{\mathbb{C}}(G_{ij}) \cap S \ne \emptyset$ then $\Omega = \Omega \cup \left\{G_{ij}\right\}$;
(7) return Ω.

3.3 Proof of Theorem 1.1

Probabilistic aspects. The algorithms used in Step 1,3,4,6 are probabilistic. The probability of success of these algorithms depends on choices of points in $\mathbb{Q}^{n^{O(1)}}$, and there exist a Zariski open set in $\mathbb{Q}^{n^{O(1)}}$ such that for all choices in this set yield correct answers for these algorithms in RealRadicalSmooth. In the following, we assume that all the probabilistic calls mentioned above perform correctly.

Correctness of algorithm RealRadicalSmooth. Let $V_{ij} := V_{\mathbb{C}}(G_{ij})$. Since V is smooth, by [9, §9.6, Theorem 8], its irreducible components V_{ij} do not intersect each other. Hence for each nonempty real algebraic set $V_{ij} \cap \mathbb{R}^n$, it contains at least one connected component of $V_{\mathbb{R}}(f)$, which implies that $V_{ij} \cap \mathbb{R}^n \neq \emptyset$ if and only if $V_{ij} \cap S \neq \emptyset$. On the other hand, the prime ideal $I\left(V_{ij}\right)$ is real if and only if $V_{ij} \cap \mathbb{R}^n \neq \emptyset$ (see the proof of Theorem 3.3). Thus, $I\left(V_{ij}\right)$ is real if and only if $V_{ij} \cap S \neq \emptyset$. Then we have $\sqrt[re]{\langle f\rangle} = \bigcap_{V_{ij}\cap S\neq\emptyset} I\left(V_{ij}\right)$[31, Lemma 2.2(a)]. Finally, the ideals $I\left(V_{ij}\right)$ are exactly the prime components of $\sqrt[re]{\langle f\rangle}$ since V_{ij} are irreducible components of $V_{\mathbb{C}}(f)$. The correctness of the algorithm is proved.

Complexity analysis. The first step of RealRadicalSmooth computes a finite set S of real points meeting every connected component of the real algebraic set $V_{\mathbb{R}}(f)$. Many algorithms can be used (see [33–37]). Using [34] and by the complexity analysis in [33], Step 1 uses $sL(nD^n)^{O(1)}$ arithmetic operations in $\mathbb{Q}$ where L is the length of the straight-line program Γ.

Next, by [16, Theorem 1], computing the Chow forms of all equidimensional components of $V_{\mathbb{C}}(f_1^h, \ldots, f_s^h) \setminus V_{\mathbb{C}}(X_0)$ requires at most $sL(nD^n)^{O(1)}$ arithmetic operations in $\mathbb{Q}$. The Chow forms $\left\{\mathcal{F}_{V_0}, \ldots, \mathcal{F}_{V_r}\right\}$ computed in Step 3 are encoded by straight-line programs of length bounded by $sL(nD^n)^{O(1)}$ [16, Section 3.5].

Suppose that the straight-line program encoding $\mathcal{F}_{V_i}$ has length L_i, then the cost of factorizing $\mathcal{F}_{V_i}$ over $\mathbb{Q}$ is polynomial in L_i and the total degree of $\mathcal{F}_{V_i}$ [18, 20]. Note that the total degree of $\mathcal{F}_{V_i}$ is bounded by $(i+1)D^n$, so Step 4 can be done using at most $(sLn(r+1)D^n)^{O(1)}$ arithmetic operations in $\mathbb{Q}$. Observe that $r \leq n-1$, we can bound $(sLn(r+1)D^n)^{O(1)}$ by $(sLnD^n)^{O(1)}$.

The cost of computing generators G_{ij} of $I\left(V_{ij}\right)$ from the Chow form $\mathcal{F}_{V_{ij}}$ does not increase the order of the complexity of Step 4 [3, Section 5.5]. Deciding the emptiness of $V_{\mathbb{C}}(G_{ij}) \cap S$ is done by evaluating the polynomials of G_{ij} at all points of S, and its cost is negligible. Observe that L is bounded by $O(s(nD)^n)$ (see e.g. [21]). Therefore, in case of success, the algorithm RealRadicalSmooth uses $(snD^n)^{O(1)}$ arithmetic operations in $\mathbb{Q}$.

4 LAZY REPRESENTATIONS AND NON-SMOOTH CASE

4.1 Preliminary results

The following result is folklore and extracted from [10, 27].

Lemma 4.1. *Let $V \subset \mathbb{C}^n$ be an equi-dimensional algebraic set defined over $\mathbb{Q}$ of dimension r. There exists a non-empty Zariski open set $\mathscr{G}(V) \subset \mathbb{C}^{n\times(r+1)}$ such that for $\boldsymbol{\ell} \in \mathscr{G}(V) \cap \mathbb{Q}^{n\times(r+1)}$ the following holds. There exists a sequence of polynomials $(w, v_1, \ldots, v_n)$ in $\mathbb{Q}[T_1, \ldots, T_{r+1}]$ such that $Z(\mathscr{Q}) = V$ with $\mathscr{Q} = ((w, v_1, \ldots, v_n), \boldsymbol{\ell})$.*

Let $\mathscr{Q} = ((w, v_1, \ldots, v_n), \boldsymbol{\ell} = (\lambda_1, \ldots, \lambda_{r+1}))$ be a rational parametrization. We define the polynomial $\sigma_{\mathscr{Q}}$ as the one obtained by substituting the variables $T_1, \ldots, T_{r+1}$ with the $\lambda_1, \ldots, \lambda_{r+1}$ in $\frac{\partial w}{\partial T_{r+1}}$. We denote by $\mathcal{S}(\mathscr{Q})$ the intersection of $Z(\mathscr{Q})$ with $V_{\mathbb{C}}(\sigma_{\mathscr{Q}})$. The following lemma is pointed out as a remark in the conclusion of [26].

Lemma 4.2. *Under the above notations, the ideal associated to $Z(\mathscr{Q})$ in $\mathbb{Q}[X_1, \ldots, X_n]$ is prime if and only if w is irreducible over $\mathbb{Q}$.*

Lemma 4.3. *Assume that the vanishing ideal of $Z(\mathscr{Q})$ in $\mathbb{Q}[X]$ is prime. Then, it is real if and only if one of the following equivalent conditions are satisfied:*

(i) $Z(\mathscr{Q})$ contains a real regular point;

(ii) the semi-algebraic set defined by $w = 0$, $\frac{\partial w}{\partial T_{r+1}} \neq 0$ is non-empty.

In particular, if the vanishing ideal of $Z(\mathscr{Q})$ is not real, then $Z(\mathscr{Q}) \cap \mathbb{R}^n$ coincides with $\mathcal{S}(\mathscr{Q}) \cap \mathbb{R}^n$.

Proof. We denote $h = \frac{\partial w}{\partial T_{r+1}}$ and I the vanishing ideal of $Z(\mathscr{Q})$. By [29, Theorem 12.6.1] I is real if and only if it has a regular real zero which is equivalent to the assertion that $Z(\mathscr{Q})$ contains a regular real point.

Now we prove that the condition (ii) holds if and only if I is real. Without loss of generality, we assume that the linear forms $\lambda_i = X_i$ for $i = 1, \ldots, r+1$. Then $T_i = X_i$ for $i = 1, \ldots, r+1$.

If the semi-algebraic set defined by $w = 0, h \neq 0$ is not empty, that is, there exists $\vartheta \in \mathbb{R}^{r+1}$ such that $w(\vartheta) = 0$ and $h(\vartheta) \neq 0$, then we have a real point $x = \left(\frac{v_1}{h}(\vartheta), \ldots, \frac{v_n}{h}(\vartheta)\right) \in Z(\mathscr{Q})$. It follows from the definition of $Z(\mathscr{Q})$ and the Hilbert Nullstellensatz that the polynomials $w, hX_{r+2} - v_{r+2}, \ldots, hX_n - v_n$ belong to I. Then x is a regular real zero of I because the Jacobian matrix of $w, hX_{r+2} - v_{r+2}, \ldots, hX_n - v_n$ has rank $n-r$ at the point x. Thus the ideal I is real.

Conversely, if the set $\left\{\vartheta \in \mathbb{R}^{r+1} \mid w(\vartheta) = 0, h(\vartheta) \neq 0\right\}$ is empty, then we have $Z(\mathscr{Q}) \cap \mathbb{R}^n \subset Z(\mathscr{Q}) \cap V_{\mathbb{C}}(\sigma_{\mathscr{Q}})$. On the other hand, $Z(\mathscr{Q}) \cap V_{\mathbb{C}}(\sigma_{\mathscr{Q}})$ has dimension less than $\dim(Z(\mathscr{Q}))$ (since $Z(\mathscr{Q})$ is irreducible and $Z(\mathscr{Q}) \cap V_{\mathbb{C}}(\sigma_{\mathscr{Q}})$ is strictly contained in $Z(\mathscr{Q})$). Hence $Z(\mathscr{Q}) \cap \mathbb{R}^n$ has dimension less than $\dim(Z(\mathscr{Q}))$, which implies that the vanishing ideal of $Z(\mathscr{Q})$ is not real. □

From the proof of Lemma 4.3, we immediately have the following corollary:

Corollary 4.4. *Under the above notations, assume that $Z(\mathscr{Q})$ is irreducible, then $\mathcal{S}(\mathscr{Q})$ has dimension strictly less than* $\dim(Z(\mathscr{Q}))$.

4.2 Subroutines

In this paragraph, we describe the subroutines used in the main algorithm.

Subroutine IrreducibleDecomposition. This subroutine aims at performing the following. Given a straight-line program of length L which evaluates a sequence of polynomials $f = (f_1, \ldots, f_s)$ in $\mathbb{Q}[X]$, it outputs a list of rational parametrizations encoding the irreducible components of $V_{\mathbb{C}}(f)$. This computation simply consists of calling the equidimensional decomposition algorithm in [26] which uses $(sLnD^n)^{O(1)}$ operations in $\mathbb{Q}$ to return zero-dimensional parametrizations of generic points in $V_{\mathbb{C}}(f)$. Combined with the Hensel lifting technique in [15] (which are actually used in [26]), that algorithm allows to recover r-equidimensional parametrizations for the components of dimension r. The total cost becomes $(snD^{n\max(1,r)})^{O(1)}$. Deducing from this the irreducible components is then easily done by factoring the eliminating polynomials of the parametrizations (the one which vanishes in the representation); the cost of this latter step is negligible [18, 20].)

Lemma 4.5. *Let $f = (f_1, \ldots, f_s)$ be a sequence of polynomials in $\mathbb{Q}[X]$ of degree bounded by D and V be the algebraic set defined by f with $r = \dim(V)$. There exists a probabilistic algorithm which computes a list of rational parametrizations encoding the irreducible components of V using $(snD^{n\max(1,r)})^{O(1)}$ operations in $\mathbb{Q}$.*

Subroutine IsReal. Let $\mathscr{Q}$ be a rational parametrization in $\mathbb{Q}[T_1, \ldots, T_{r+1}]$ of degree δ with $Z(\mathscr{Q})$ irreducible, the subroutine IsReal decides if $Z(\mathscr{Q})$ contains a real regular point in time $\delta^{O(r)}$.

Lemma 4.6. *Let $\mathscr{Q} = (w, v_1, \ldots, v_n, \boldsymbol{\ell})$ be a rational parametrization in $\mathbb{Q}[T_1, \ldots, T_{r+1}]$ of degree δ such that $Z(\mathscr{Q})$ is irreducible. There exists an algorithm* IsReal *which returns* true *if $Z(\mathscr{Q})$ contains real regular points or* false *otherwise. It uses $\delta^{O(\max(1,r))}$ arithmetic operations in $\mathbb{Q}$.*

Proof. By Lemma 4.3, it suffices to decide if the semi-algebraic system $w = 0$, $\frac{\partial w}{\partial T_{r+1}} \neq 0$ has a real solution. Using [1, Chapter 14], this can be done using $\delta^{O(\max(1,r))}$ arithmetic operations in $\mathbb{Q}$. □

Subroutine ChangeSeparatingElement. We describe now a subroutine which takes as input a rational parametrization encoding an equidimensional algebraic set Z using linear forms $\boldsymbol{\ell}$ and returns a new sequence of linear forms $\boldsymbol{\ell}'$ and which computes a new rational parametrization still encoding Z but using $\boldsymbol{\ell}'$.

Lemma 4.7. *Let $\mathscr{Q} = ((w, v_1, \ldots, v_n), \boldsymbol{\ell})$ be a rational parametrization of degree δ encoding a r-equidimensional algebraic set Z and $\boldsymbol{\ell}$ in the non-empty Zariski open set $\mathscr{G}(Z)$ defined in Lemma 4.1.*

Then, there exists a routine ChangeSeparatingElement *which computes a rational parametrization $\mathscr{Q} = ((w', v'_1, \ldots, v'_n), \boldsymbol{\ell}')$ using $(r+1)(n\delta)^{O(\max(1,r))}$ arithmetic operations in $\mathbb{Q}$.*

Proof. The algorithm for changing one linear form works as in the proof of [38, Lemma J.8 of the electronic Appendix]. It simply consists in using the algorithm underlying [32, Lemma 2] which performs this operation in the zero-dimensional case in time $(n\delta)^{O(1)}$.

Here, we deal with positive dimensional situations. In [38, Lemma J.8 of the Appendix], the one dimensional situation is tackled by performing operations in a univariate power series ring $\mathbb{Q}[[T_1 - y_1]]$ (where y_1 is chosen randomly) by applying [32, Lemma 2]. Doing this allows us to use the algorithm designed for the zero-dimensional case but performing operations in $\mathbb{Q}[[T_1 - y_1]]$ and truncate computations up to $\deg(\mathscr{Q})+1$. The extra cost of such a strategy is just the extra cost induced by the arithmetics in $\mathbb{Q}[[T_1 - y_1]]$.

To tackle the r-dimensional case, we do the same but using power series ring $\mathbb{Q}[[T_1 - y_1, \ldots, T_r - y_r]]$ where $y_1, \ldots, y_r$ are chosen randomly and truncating computations again up to the degree of $\mathscr{Q}$. Again the extra cost comes from arithmetic operations in $\mathbb{Q}[[T_1 - y_1, \ldots, T_r - y_r]]$ which is dominated by $(n\delta)^{O(r)}$ since computations are truncated up to $\deg(\mathscr{Q}) + 1$.

Now, changing $r + 1$ linear forms requires to perform the above operations $r + 1$ times. □

Subroutine Intersect. Let $\mathscr{Q} = ((w, v_1, \ldots, v_n), \boldsymbol{\ell})$ with $\boldsymbol{\ell} = (\lambda_1, \ldots, \lambda_{r+1})$ be a rational parametrization in $\mathbb{Q}[T_1, \ldots T_{r+1}]$ and $g \in \mathbb{Q}[T_1, \ldots T_{r+1}]$. We denote by $g_{\mathscr{Q}}$ the polynomial $g(\lambda_1, \ldots, \lambda_{r+1}) \in \mathbb{Q}[X]$. A key step for our algorithm is to compute $Z(\mathscr{Q}) \cap V_{\mathbb{C}}(g_{\mathscr{Q}})$

Lemma 4.8. *Let $\mathscr{Q} = ((w, v_1, \ldots, v_n), \boldsymbol{\ell})$ be a rational parametrization in $\mathbb{Q}[T_1, \ldots, T_{r+1}]$ encoding an equidimensional algebraic set $Z = Z(\mathscr{Q}) \subset \mathbb{C}^n$ of dimension $r \geq 1$ and degree δ and let g be a polynomial in $\mathbb{Q}[T_1, \ldots, T_{r+1}]$ of degree δ'. Assume that the intersection of Z with $V_{\mathbb{C}}(g_{\mathscr{Q}})$ has dimension $r - 1$. There exists an algorithm* Intersect *which on input $(\mathscr{Q}, g)$ outputs a list of rational parametrizations encoding the irreducible components of $Z \cap V_{\mathbb{C}}(g_{\mathscr{Q}})$ in time $(n\max(\delta, \delta'))^{O(r)}$.*

Proof. The algorithm starts by choosing randomly a sequence of $r + 1$ linear forms $\boldsymbol{\ell}' = (\lambda'_1, \ldots, \lambda'_{r+1})$ in $X_1, \ldots, X_n$ assuming that $\boldsymbol{\ell}'$ lies in the non-empty Zariski open set $\mathscr{G}(Z)$ (defined in Lemma 4.1).

Recall that Z is r-equidimensional. Observe that by Krull's theorem [11], $Z \cap V_{\mathbb{C}}(g_{\mathscr{Q}})$ is either empty or has dimension greater than or equal to $r - 1$ and hence none of its irreducible components has dimension less than $r-1$. Since, by assumption, $\dim(Z \cap V_{\mathbb{C}}(g_{\mathscr{Q}})) = r - 1$, we deduce that it is equidimensional (of dimension $r - 1$).

Hence, it makes sense to assume additionally that the first r linear forms of $\boldsymbol{\ell}'$ lie in the non-empty Zariski open set $\mathscr{G}(Z \cap V_{\mathbb{C}}(g_{\mathscr{Q}}))$ (see again Lemma 4.1). Another assumption of the same nature will be done and stated precisely below.

Next, one computes a rational parametrization $\mathscr{Q}' = ((w', v'_1, \ldots, v'_n), \boldsymbol{\ell}')$ defining Z. For clarity, we denote by $T'_1, \ldots, T'_{r+1}$ the variables involved in $\mathscr{Q}'$. Lemma 4.7 establishes that this step can be performed using $(r+1)(n\delta)^{O(r)}$ arithmetic operations in $\mathbb{Q}$.

Now, we want to compute a rational parametrization of the intersection of $Z = Z(\mathscr{Q}')$ with $V_{\mathbb{C}}(g_{\mathscr{Q}})$. The process we would like to mimic is as follows:

(1) substitute in g the variables $T_1, \ldots, T_{r+1}$ by the linear forms $\lambda_1, \ldots, \lambda_{r+1}$ used in $\mathscr{Q}$ (hence yielding an explicit representation of $g_{\mathscr{Q}}$);
(2) substitute the X_i's by their parametrizations in $\mathscr{Q}'$, hence obtaining a rational fraction g' (it lies in $\mathbb{Q}(T'_1, \ldots, T'_{r+1})$);
(3) compute a representation of the intersection of the vanishing sets of the numerator of g' and w' (through subresultant computations as in [15]) and deduce from that a rational representation of $Z \cap V_{\mathbb{C}}(g_{\mathscr{Q}})$.

Carrying out directly these steps without taking care of denominators does not allow us to obtain the announced complexity statement.

To achieve the announced complexity bound, we use a classical evaluation interpolation technique: that will allow us to obtain a better control on the monomial combinatorics and handle the presence of denominators.

Instead of computing an explicit representation of $g_{\mathscr{Q}}$, we will actually build a straight-line program Γ evaluating it. Since g is a polynomial of degree δ' involving $r + 1$ variables and since $\boldsymbol{\ell}$ is composed of $r + 1$ linear forms in $X_1, \ldots, X_n$ which are equal to

$T_1, \ldots, T_{r+1}$, the length of such a straight-line program is bounded by $(r\delta')^{O(r)} + O(nr)$.

Evaluating the rational fraction g' defined above is then obtained by stacking to Γ the parametrizations $X_i = \frac{v_i'}{\partial w'/\partial T_{r+1}'}$. Evaluating all parametrizations can be done using $(n\delta)^{O(r)}$ operations in $\mathbb{Q}$ (because the polynomials in $\mathscr{Q}'$ have degree $\leq \delta$ and involve $r+1$ variables). In the end, one can evaluate g' using $(r\delta')^{O(r)} + O(nr) + (n\delta)^{O(r)}$ arithmetic operations in $\mathbb{Q}$.

Now take $y = (y_1, \ldots, y_{r-1})$ in $\mathbb{Q}^{r-1}$. Substituting the variables $T_1', \ldots, T_{r-1}'$ by $y_1, \ldots, y_{r-1}$ in g' is done thanks to the procedure described above in time $(r\delta')^{O(r)} + O(nr) + (n\delta)^{O(r)}$.

For y as above, we denote by g_y' the obtained rational fraction. Similarly, $\mathscr{Q}_y'$ denotes the rational parametrization obtained by substituting the variables $T_1', \ldots, T_{r-1}'$ with $y_1, \ldots, y_{r-1}$ in $\mathscr{Q}'$.

Using the intersection algorithm of [15] with input $\mathscr{Q}_y'$ and the numerator of g_y', one computes a zero-dimensional rational parametrization encoding $Z \cap V_{\mathbb{C}}(g_{\mathscr{Q}}) \cap V_{\mathbb{C}}(\ell_y')$.

Since, by Bézout's theorem, the intersection of Z with $V_{\mathbb{C}}(g_{\mathscr{Q}})$ has degree bounded by $\delta'\delta$, it is sufficient to repeat this process $(\delta'\delta)^{O(r)}$ times to interpolate a rational parametrization for $Z \cap V_{\mathbb{C}}(g_{\mathscr{Q}})$. The last step consists in extracting from that parametrization the irreducible components of $Z \cap V_{\mathbb{C}}(g_{\mathscr{Q}})$ by factoring the eliminating polynomial of $\mathscr{Q}$. The complexity statement follows easily. □

Subroutine RemoveRedundantComponents. Let $\mathscr{L} = (\mathscr{Q}_1, \ldots, \mathscr{Q}_t)$ be a list of rational parametrizations such that, for $1 \leq i \leq t$, $Z(\mathscr{Q}_i)$ is irreducible. The routine RemoveRedundantComponents returns a subset of $\mathscr{L}$ say, $\mathscr{Q}_{i_1}, \ldots, \mathscr{Q}_{i_k}$ such that, $Z(\mathscr{Q}_{i_1} \cup \cdots \cup Z(\mathscr{Q}_{i_k}) = Z(\mathscr{Q}_1) \cup \cdots \cup Z(\mathscr{Q}_t)$ and, for $u \neq v$, $Z(\mathscr{Q}_{i_u}) \not\subset Z(\mathscr{Q}_{i_v})$.

Lemma 4.9. *Let $\mathscr{L} = (\mathscr{Q}_1, \ldots, \mathscr{Q}_t)$ be a list of rational parametrizations with δ_i being the degree of $\mathscr{Q}_i$ and δ be the maximum of $\delta_1, \ldots, \delta_t$. Assume that for $1 \leq i \leq t$, $Z(\mathscr{Q}_i)$ is irreducible of dimension r_i; let r be the maximum of 1 and $r_1, \ldots, r_t$.*
There exists an algorithm RemoveRedundantComponents *which on input $\mathscr{L}$ returns a subset $\mathscr{Q}_{i_1}, \ldots, \mathscr{Q}_{i_k}$ of $\mathscr{L}$ such that, the following holds:*

- $Z(\mathscr{Q}_{i_1}) \cup \cdots \cup Z(\mathscr{Q}_{i_k}) = Z(\mathscr{Q}_1) \cup \cdots \cup Z(\mathscr{Q}_t)$;
- *for $u \neq v$, $Z(\mathscr{Q}_{i_u}) \not\subset Z(\mathscr{Q}_{i_v})$.*

It uses $t(r+1)(n\delta)^{O(r)}$ operations in $\mathbb{Q}$.

Proof. The algorithm starts by sorting (in ascending order) the rational parametrizations according to their dimension. Up to renumbering, one may assume that $\mathscr{Q}_1, \ldots, \mathscr{Q}_t$ are already sorted by nondecreasing dimension (i.e. $r_i \leq r_{i+1}$). The algorithm starts by choosing randomly $r+1$ linear forms $\boldsymbol{\ell} = (\lambda_1, \ldots, \lambda_{r+1})$ and call the routine ChangeSeparatingElement with input $\mathscr{Q}_i$ and $(\lambda_1, \ldots, \lambda_{r_i+1})$. According to Lemma 4.7, this step uses $t(r+1)(n\delta)^{O(r)}$ operations in $\mathbb{Q}$. To keep notations simple, we keep on naming $\mathscr{Q}_1, \ldots, \mathscr{Q}_t$ for the obtained rational parametrizations. Since, by assumption, the rational parametrizations define irreducible algebraic sets, one only needs to decide if $Z(\mathscr{Q}_i) \subset Z(\mathscr{Q}_j)$ for $i < j$ and $r_i < r_j$. Thanks to the change of separating element, it then suffices to pick a random rational point in $\mathbb{Q}^{r_i - 1}$ and specialize both in $\mathscr{Q}_i$ and $\mathscr{Q}_j$ the parameters corresponding to $\lambda_1, \ldots, \lambda_{r_i}$. Hence, we are led to decide the inclusion of a finite set of points in an algebraic set ; both are given by a rational parametrization. This boils down to standard Euclidean remainder computations (see [27]). □

4.3 Description of main algorithm

The algorithm takes as input a sequence $f = (f_1, \ldots, f_s)$ of polynomials in $\mathbb{Q}[X_1, \ldots, X_n]$ of degree bounded by D.
It returns a list of rational parametrizations, each of which defining a prime component of the real radical ideal generated by f.

The algorithm starts by calling IrreducibleDecomposition to compute a finite sequence of rational parametrizations $\mathscr{R}_1, \ldots, \mathscr{R}_t$ encoding the irreducible components of $V_{\mathbb{C}}(f)$. Next, for $1 \leq i \leq t$, one computes a list of rational parametrizations encoding the irreducible components of the real radical associated to $Z(\mathscr{R}_i)$. This is done by calling a routine called LazyRealRadicalRec which is described further. Finally, the routine RemoveRedundantComponents is called with input the list of all previously computed rational parametrizations to remove redundancies.

LazyRealRadical(f)

(1) $(\mathscr{R}_1, \ldots, \mathscr{R}_t)$ = IrreducibleDecomposition(f);
(2) if $t = 1$ and $\mathscr{R}_1 = (1)$ then return ((1));
(3) res = {};
(4) for $1 \leq j \leq t$ do
 - res = res ∪ LazyRealRadicalRec($\mathscr{R}_i$);

(5) return RemoveRedundantComponents(res).

We describe now the routine LazyRealRadicalRec. It takes as input a rational parametrization $\mathscr{Q}$ and outputs a list of rational parametrizations encoding the irreducible algebraic sets defined by the prime components of the real radical associated to $Z(\mathscr{Q})$.

It works as follows. First, it decides if $Z(\mathscr{Q})$ contains real regular points using the routine IsReal. If this is the case, then it returns $\mathscr{Q}$, else it computes rational parametrizations encoding the prime components of the set $S(\mathscr{Q})$ and performs a recursive call with input these parametrizations.

LazyRealRadicalRec($\mathscr{Q}$)

(1) if $\mathscr{Q} = (1)$ then return (1);
(2) if IsReal($\mathscr{Q}$) then return ($\mathscr{Q}$);
(3) let w be the eliminating polynomial of $\mathscr{Q}$ in $\mathbb{Q}[T_1, \ldots, T_{r+1}]$;
(4) $(\mathscr{Q}_1', \ldots, \mathscr{Q}_k')$ = Intersect($\mathscr{Q}, \frac{\partial w}{\partial T_{r+1}}$);
(5) for $1 \leq \ell \leq k$ do
 - res = res ∪ LazyRealRadicalRec($\mathscr{Q}_\ell'$);

(6) return RemoveRedundantComponents(res).

4.4 Proof of Theorem 1.3

We start by proving correctness and termination.

Proof. On input f, LazyRealRadical starts by computing an irreducible decomposition of the algebraic set defined by f by means of rational parametrizations $\mathscr{R}_1, \ldots, \mathscr{R}_t$. The next step consists in computing rational parametrizations encoding the prime components of the real radical associated to $Z(\mathscr{R}_i)$ for $1 \leq i \leq t$.

This is done through the call to the routine LazyRealRadicalRec. Hence, the main step for proving correctness of LazyRealRadical consists in proving the correctness of LazyRealRadicalRec. Recall that it takes as input a rational parametrization $\mathscr{Q}$ encoding an irreducible algebraic set. We prove its correctness by decreasing induction on the dimension of $Z(\mathscr{Q})$. The case where the $Z(\mathscr{Q})$ is finite is immediate; hence we assume below that $Z(\mathscr{Q})$ has positive dimension, say r, and terminates and is correct on inputs encoding algebraic sets of dimension less than r.

The routine LazyRealRadicalRec decides if the prime ideal associated to $Z(\mathscr{Q})$ is real by calling the routine IsReal. If this is the case, $\mathscr{Q}$ is returned as expected. Else, it computes a decomposition of $\mathcal{S}(\mathscr{Q})$ following Lemma 4.3. Besides, Corollary 4.4 establishes that $\mathcal{S}(\mathscr{Q})$ has dimension strictly less than $\dim(Z(\mathscr{Q}))$. Termination and correctness follow by the induction assumption. □

We can now prove the complexity statement.

Proof. The first step of LazyRealRadical consists in calling the routing IrreducibleDecomposition which uses $(snD^{nr})^{O(1)}$ arithmetic operations in $\mathbb{Q}$ (Lemma 4.5) where r is the the maximum of 1 and the dimension of the algebraic set defined by the input f. By Bézout's theorem, the sum of the degrees of the irreducible components encoded by the output is bounded by D^n. Hence, we have $t \leq D^n$ and for $1 \leq i \leq t$, the degree of $\mathscr{R}_i$ is bounded by D^n.

Next, one enters in the loop and call t times LazyRealRadicalRec with $\mathscr{R}_i$ as input (for $1 \leq i \leq t$). Below, we prove that running LazyRealRadicalRec with input a rational parametrization, say $\mathscr{Q}$, of degree δ encoding an irreducible algebraic set of dimension ρ takes $(n\delta)^{O(2^\rho)}$ arithmetic operations in $\mathbb{Q}$ and the sum of the degrees of the rational parametrizations it outputs lies in $(n\delta)^{O(2^\rho)}$ Hence, the whole cost of the "for loop" is $(nD)^{O(n2^r)}$.

The last step consists in calling the routine RemoveRedundantComponents. Lemma 4.9 allows to estimate the complexity of this step. All in all, the total cost is bounded by $s^{O(1)}(nD)^{O(nr2^r)}$.

We prove now the claim on the complexity of LazyRealRadicalRec. The first step consists in calling subroutine IsReal on input $\mathscr{Q}$. This call takes $\delta^{O(\rho)}$ arithmetic operations in $\mathbb{Q}$ (Lemma 4.6). When it returns true, $\mathscr{Q}$ is returned else a call to Intersect is performed with input $\mathscr{Q}$ and $\frac{\partial w}{\partial T_{\rho+1}}$ where w is the eliminating polynomial of $\mathscr{Q}$. By Lemma 4.8, this uses $(n\delta)^{O(\rho)}$ arithmetic operations in $\mathbb{Q}$.

The sum of the degrees of the output is bounded by δ^2 but the dimension of these output rational parametrizations is $\rho - 1$. Hence, denoting by $T(\delta, \rho)$ the cost of LazyRealRadicalRec on input a rational parametrization of degree δ encoding an irreducible algebraic set of dimension ρ, the following recursive formula holds:

$$T(\delta, \rho) \leq (n\delta)^{O(\rho)} + T(\delta^2, \rho - 1).$$

Solving this recurrence formula yields a complexity $(n\delta)^{O(2^\rho)}$. The same formula occurs for the degree bounds on the output. Hence, we are done. □

As for algorithm RealRadicalSmooth, most of subroutines which are used in LazyRealRadical are probabilistic: they rely on either generic specialization points or generic choices of linear changes of variables (or linear forms).

5 EXPERIMENTS

We give several examples to show the efficiency of our approach. All the examples given below are beyond the reach of the Singular library realrad implemented by Spang [40] which is, up to our knowledge, the single available implementation of the algorithm given by [2, 31]. That implementation is based on Gröbner bases.

Observe that one can use Singular functionalities to compute equidimensional/prime decompositions and intersections of ideals as well as elimination ideals, by means of Gröbner bases. Hence, one can "simulate" LazyRealRadical using those functionalities combined with the HasRealSolutions function in the Maple library RAGlib [34].

In a word, taking a polynomial sequence f as input, we will obtain generators of the minimal associated primes of $\sqrt[re]{\langle f\rangle}$.

The computations were performed on an Intel(R) Xeon(R) CPU E7-4809 v2 @ 1.90GHz and 756GB of RAM.

Example 5.1 (Vor1). The following polynomial comes form [12]:

$$\begin{aligned}\mathrm{Vor1} =& (\alpha^2 + \beta^2 + 1)a^2\lambda^4 - 2a(2a\beta^2 + ay\beta + a\alpha x - \beta\alpha + 2a + 2a\alpha^2 - \beta\alpha a^2)\lambda^3 \\ &+ (\beta^2 + 6a^2\beta^2 - 2\beta x a^3 - 6\beta\alpha a^3 + 6y\beta a^2 - 6a\beta\alpha - 2a\beta x + 6\alpha x a^2 + y^2a^2 \\ &- 2a\alpha y + x^2a^2 - 2y\alpha a^3 + 6a^2\alpha^2 + a^4\alpha^2 + 4a^2)\lambda^2 \\ &- 2(xa - ya^2 - 2\beta a^2 - \beta + 2a\alpha + \alpha a^3)(xa - y - \beta + a\alpha)\lambda + (1 + a^2)(xa - y - \beta + a\alpha)^2.\end{aligned}$$

This polynomial is a sum of squares [19], thus the ideal $\langle \mathrm{Vor1}\rangle$ is not real. Take Vor1 as input and we obtain in 9 sec. the minimal primes of the real radical $\sqrt[re]{\langle \mathrm{Vor1}\rangle}$:

$$P_1 = \langle a\alpha - ax + \beta - y, \lambda + 1\rangle, P_2 = \langle a\alpha + ax - \beta - y, \lambda\rangle, P_3 = \langle 2\beta\lambda + \beta + y, a\rangle.$$

Example 5.2. Consider the discriminant $\mathcal{D}$ of the characteristic polynomial of the following linear symmetric matrix:

$$\begin{pmatrix} x & 1 & 1 \\ 1 & y & 1 \\ 1 & 1 & z \end{pmatrix}.$$

It has been proved that $\mathcal{D}$ is a sum of squares [24]. On input $\mathcal{D}$, our algorithm computed in 4 sec. the real radical $\sqrt[re]{\langle \mathcal{D}\rangle}$. It has only one minimal prime which is $\langle y - z, g\rangle$ where

$$\begin{aligned} g =& -19y^{12} + 228y^{11}z - 1254y^{10}z^2 + 4180y^9z^3 - 9405y^8z^4 + 15048y^7z^5 - 17556y^6z^6 + 15048y^5z^7 \\ &- 9405y^4z^8 + 4180y^3z^9 - 1254y^2z^10 + 228yz^11 - 19z^12 - 606y^10 + 6060y^9z - 27270y^8z^2 \\ &+ 72720y^7z^3 - 127260y^6z^4 + 152712y^5z^5 - 127260y^4z^6 + 72720y^3z^7 - 27270y^2z^+ 6060yz^9 \\ &- 606z^10 - 6732y^8 + 53856y^7z - 188496y^6z^2 + 376992y^5z^3 - 471240y^4z^4 + 376992y^3z^5 \\ &- 188496y^2z^6 + 53856yz^7 - 6732z^8 - 35370y^6 + 212220y^5z - 530550y^4z^2 + 707400y^3z^3 \\ &- 530550y^2z^4 + 212220yz^5 - 35370z^6 - 116073y^4 + 464292y^3z - 696438y^2z^2 + 464292yz^3 \\ &- 116073z^4 - 77760y^2 + 155520yz - 77760z^2 + 139968x - 69984y - 69984z. \end{aligned}$$

Example 5.3 (Homotopy-1). This example is taken from [7]:

$$f_1 = x^3y^2 + c_1x^3y + y^2 + c_2x + c_3,\ f_2 = c_4x^4y^2 - x^2y + y + c_5,\ f_3 = c_4 - 1.$$

Take the sequence $f = (f_1, f_2, f_3)$ as input and we obtain in a single second that $\sqrt[re]{\langle f\rangle}$ has only one minimal prime which is the ideal $\langle f\rangle$. This shows that the ideal $\langle f\rangle$ is prime and real.

Example 5.4 (Cinquin-3-4). This is also an example taken from [7]:

$$f_1 = s - x_1(1 + x_2^4 + x_3^4),\ f_2 = s - x_2(1 + x_1^4 + x_3^4),\ f_3 = s - x_3(1 + x_1^4 + x_2^4).$$

We obtain in 47 sec. the minimal primes of $\sqrt[re]{\langle f\rangle}$ for $f = (f_1, f_2, f_3)$:

$$\begin{aligned} P_1 &= \langle x_3 - x_1, x_2 - x_1, -x_3^4x_1 - x_2^4x_1 - x_1 + s\rangle, \\ P_2 &= \langle x_3 - x_1, x_2^3x_1 + x_2^2x_1^2 + x_2x_1^3 - x_1^4 - 1, -x_3^4x_1 - x_2^4x_1 - x_1 + s\rangle, \\ P_3 &= \langle x_2 - x_1, x_3^3x_1 + x_3^2x_1^2 + x_3x_1^3 - x_1^4 - 1, -x_3^4x_1 - x_2^4x_1 - x_1 + s\rangle, \\ P_4 &= \langle x_3 - x_2, x_2^4 - x_2^3x_1 - x_2^2x_1^2 - x_2x_1^3 + 1, -x_3^4x_1 - x_2^4x_1 - x_1 + s\rangle. \end{aligned}$$

Example 5.5 (Essential Variety). This is an example taken from [13]. Let $\mathcal{E}$ be the essential variety defined as:

$$\mathcal{E} = \left\{ M \in \mathbb{R}^{3\times 3} \mid \det(M) = 0,\ 2(MM^T)M - \mathrm{tr}(MM^T)M = 0 \right\},$$

where $\det(M)$ is the determinant of M and $\mathrm{tr}(MM^T)$ is the trace of MM^T.

If we write the matrix M as

$$\begin{pmatrix} a & b & c \\ u & v & w \\ x & y & z \end{pmatrix},$$

then the 10 cubics defining $\mathcal{E}$ are:

$$avz - awy - buz + bwx + cuy - cvx,$$
$$(2a^2 + 2b^2 + 2c^2)a + (2au + 2bv + 2cw)u + (2ax + 2by + 2cz)x - ga,$$
$$(2a^2 + 2b^2 + 2c^2)b + (2au + 2bv + 2cw)v + (2ax + 2by + 2cz)y - gb,$$
$$(2a^2 + 2b^2 + 2c^2)c + (2au + 2bv + 2cw)w + (2ax + 2by + 2cz)z - gc,$$
$$(2au + 2bv + 2cw)a + (2u^2 + 2v^2 + 2w^2)u + (2ux + 2vy + 2wz)x - gu,$$
$$(2au + 2bv + 2cw)b + (2u^2 + 2v^2 + 2w^2)v + (2ux + 2vy + 2wz)y - gv,$$
$$(2au + 2bv + 2cw)c + (2u^2 + 2v^2 + 2w^2)w + (2ux + 2vy + 2wz)z - gw,$$
$$(2ax + 2by + 2cz)a + (2ux + 2vy + 2wz)u + (2x^2 + 2y^2 + 2z^2)x - gx,$$
$$(2ax + 2by + 2cz)b + (2ux + 2vy + 2wz)v + (2x^2 + 2y^2 + 2z^2)y - gy,$$
$$(2ax + 2by + 2cz)c + (2ux + 2vy + 2wz)w + (2x^2 + 2y^2 + 2z^2)z - gz,$$

where $g = (a^2 + b^2 + c^2 + u^2 + v^2 + w^2 + x^2 + y^2 + z^2)$. Let I denote the ideal generated by these 10 cubics. Take these 10 cubics as input and we obtain in 800 sec. only one minimal prime of $\sqrt[r]{I}$, which is the ideal I itself. Thus I is a real ideal.

ACKNOWLEDGMENT

We thank Yue Ren for his help with the implementation of our algorithms. We also thank Erich L. Kaltofen for his valuable suggestions on the complexity of factorizing multivariate polynomials.

REFERENCES

[1] Basu, S., Pollack, R., Roy, M.-F., 2006. Algorithms in Real Algebraic Geometry. Springer Berlin Heidelberg, Berlin, Heidelberg.

[2] Becker, E., Neuhaus, R., 1993. Computation of real radicals of polynomial ideals. In: Eyssette, F., Galligo, A. (Eds.), Computational Algebraic Geometry. Vol. 109. Birkhäuser, Boston, MA, pp. 1–20.

[3] Blanco, C., Jeronimo, G., Solernó, P., 2004. Computing generators of the ideal of a smooth affine algebraic variety. Journal of Symbolic Computation 38 (1), 843–872.

[4] Bochnak, J., Coste, M., Roy, M.-F., 1998. Real algebraic geometry. Vol. 36. Springer, Berlin, Heidelberg.

[5] Brake, D. A., Hauenstein, J. D., Liddell, Jr., A. C., 2016. Validating the completeness of the real solution set of a system of polynomial equations. In: Proceedings of the 2016 International Symposium on Symbolic and Algebraic Computation. ISSAC'16. ACM, New York, NY, USA, pp. 143–150.

[6] Chen, C., Davenport, J. H., May, J. P., Maza, M. M., Xia, B., Xiao, R., 2010. Triangular decomposition of semi-algebraic systems. In: Proceedings of the 2010 International Symposium on Symbolic and Algebraic Computation. ISSAC'10. ACM, New York, NY, USA, pp. 187–194.

[7] Chen, C., Davenport, J. H., May, J. P., Maza, M. M., Xia, B., Xiao, R., 2013. Triangular decomposition of semi-algebraic systems. Journal of Symbolic Computation 49, 3–26.

[8] Chen, C., Davenport, J. H., Moreno Maza, M., Xia, B., Xiao, R., 2011. Computing with semi-algebraic sets represented by triangular decomposition. In: Proceedings of the 36th International Symposium on Symbolic and Algebraic Computation. ISSAC'11. ACM, New York, NY, USA, pp. 75–82.

[9] Cox, D., Little, J., O'shea, D., 1992. Ideals, varieties, and algorithms. Vol. 3. Springer.

[10] Durvye, C., Lecerf, G., 2008. A concise proof of the Kronecker polynomial system solver from scratch. Expositiones Mathematicae 26 (2), 101–139.

[11] Eisenbud, D., 1995. Commutative Algebra: with a View Toward Algebraic Geometry. Vol. 150. Springer New York, New York, NY.

[12] Everett, H., Lazard, D., Lazard, S., Safey El Din, M., 2009. The Voronoi diagram of three lines. Discrete & Computational Geometry 42 (1), 94–130.

[13] Fløystad, G., Kileel, J., Ottaviani, G., 2017. The Chow form of the essential variety in computer vision. Journal of Symbolic Computation.

[14] Gelfand, I. M., Kapranov, M. M., Zelevinsky, A. V., 1994. Discriminants, Resultants, and Multidimensional Determinants. Birkhäuser Boston, Boston, MA.

[15] Giusti, M., Lecerf, G., Salvy, B., 2001. A Gröbner free alternative for polynomial system solving. Journal of complexity 17 (1), 154–211.

[16] Jeronimo, G., Krick, T., Sabia, J., Sombra, M., 2004. The computational complexity of the Chow form. Foundations of Computational Mathematics 4 (1), 41–117.

[17] Kalkbrener, M., 1991. Three contributions to elimination theory. Ph.D. thesis, Johannes Kepler University, Linz.

[18] Kaltofen, E., 1989. Factorization of polynomials given by straight-line programs. Randomness and Computation 5, 375–412.

[19] Kaltofen, E., Li, B., Yang, Z., Zhi, L., 2008. Exact certification of global optimality of approximate factorizations via rationalizing sums-of-squares with floating point scalars. In: Proceedings of the Twenty-first International Symposium on Symbolic and Algebraic Computation. ISSAC'08. ACM, New York, NY, USA, pp. 155–164.

[20] Kaltofen, E., Trager, B. M., 1990. Computing with polynomials given by black boxes for their evaluations: greatest common divisors, factorization, separation of numerators and denominators. Journal of Symbolic Computation 9 (3), 301–320.

[21] Krick, T., 2002. Straight-line programs in polynomial equation solving. Foundations of computational mathematics: Minneapolis 312, 96–136.

[22] Lasserre, J.-B., Laurent, M., Mourrain, B., Rostalski, P., Trébuchet, P., 2013. Moment matrices, border bases and real radical computation. Journal of Symbolic Computation 51, 63–85.

[23] Lasserre, J. B., Laurent, M., Rostalski, P., 2008. Semidefinite characterization and computation of zero-dimensional real radical ideals. Foundations of Computational Mathematics 8 (5), 607–647.

[24] Lax, P., 2005. On the discriminant of real symmetric matrices. Selected Papers Volume II, 577–586.

[25] Lazard, D., 1991. A new method for solving algebraic systems of positive dimension. Discrete Applied Mathematics 33 (1-3), 147–160.

[26] Lecerf, G., 2000. Computing an equidimensional decomposition of an algebraic variety by means of geometric resolutions. In: Proceedings of the 2000 International Symposium on Symbolic and Algebraic Computation. ISSAC'00. ACM, New York, NY, USA, pp. 209–216.

[27] Lecerf, G., 2003. Computing the equidimensional decomposition of an algebraic closed set by means of lifting fibers. Journal of Complexity 19 (4), 564–596.

[28] Ma, Y., Wang, C., Zhi, L., 2016. A certificate for semidefinite relaxations in computing positive-dimensional real radical ideals. Journal of Symbolic Computation 72, 1–20.

[29] Marshall, M., 2008. Positive polynomials and sums of squares. No. 146. American Mathematical Soc.

[30] Moreno Maza, M., 1997. Calculs de pgcd au-dessus des tours d'extensions simples et résolution des systèmes d'équations algébriques. Ph.D. thesis, Université Paris 6.

[31] Neuhaus, R., 1998. Computation of real radicals of polynomial ideals – II. Journal of Pure and Applied Algebra 124 (1), 261–280.

[32] Poteaux, A., Schost, É., 2013. On the complexity of computing with zero-dimensional triangular sets. Journal of Symbolic Computation 50 (Supplement C), 110 – 138.

[33] Safey El Din, M., 2005. Finding sampling points on real hypersurfaces is easier in singular situations. MEGA (Effective Methods in Algebraic Geometry) Electronic proceedings.

[34] Safey El Din, M., 2007. RAGLib (Real Algebraic Geometry Library), Maple package.

[35] Safey El Din, M., 2007. Testing sign conditions on a multivariate polynomial and applications. Mathematics in Computer Science 1 (1), 177–207.

[36] Safey El Din, M., Schost, É., 2003. Polar varieties and computation of one point in each connected component of a smooth real algebraic set. In: Proceedings of the 2003 International Symposium on Symbolic and Algebraic Computation. ISSAC'03. ACM, New York, NY, USA, pp. 224–231.

[37] Safey El Din, M., Schost, É., 2004. Properness defects of projections and computation of at least one point in each connected component of a real algebraic set. Discrete & Computational Geometry 32 (3), 417–430.

[38] Safey El Din, M., Schost, É., 2017. A nearly optimal algorithm for deciding connectivity queries in smooth and bounded real algebraic sets. Journal of the ACM 63 (6), 48:1–48:37.
URL http://doi.acm.org/10.1145/2996450

[39] Schost, É., 2003. Computing parametric geometric resolutions. Applicable Algebra in Engineering, Communication and Computing 13 (5), 349–393.

[40] Spang, S. J., 2007. On the computation of the real radical. Ph.D. thesis, Technische Universität Kaiserslautern.

[41] Spang, S. J., 2008. A zero-dimensional approach to compute real radicals. The Computer Science Journal of Moldova 16 (1), 64–92.

[42] Wang, D., 1998. Decomposing polynomial systems into simple systems. Journal of Symbolic Computation 25 (3), 295–314.

[43] Wu, W.-T., 1984. Basic principles of mechanical theorem proving in elementary geometries. Journal of Systems Science and Mathematical Sciences 4, 207–235.

On Continuity of the Roots of a Parametric Zero Dimensional Multivariate Polynomial Ideal

Yosuke Sato
Tokyo University of Science
Tokyo, Japan
ysato@rs.kagu.tus.ac.jp

Ryoya Fukasaku
Tokyo University of Science
Tokyo, Japan
fukasaku@rs.tus.ac.jp

Hiroshi Sekigawa
Tokyo University of Science
Tokyo, Japan
sekigawa@rs.tus.ac.jp

ABSTRACT

Let $F = \{f_1(\bar{A},\bar{X}),\dots,f_l(\bar{A},\bar{X})\}$ be a finite set of polynomials in $\mathbb{Q}[\bar{A},\bar{X}]$ with variables $\bar{A} = A_1,\dots,A_m$ and $\bar{X} = X_1,\dots,X_n$. We study the continuity of the map θ from an element $\bar{a}$ of $\mathbb{C}^m$ to a subset of $\mathbb{C}^n$ defined by $\theta(\bar{a})$ = " the zeros of the polynomial ideal $\langle f_1(\bar{a},\bar{X}),\dots,f_l(\bar{a},\bar{X})\rangle$ ". Let $\mathcal{G} = \{(G_1,\mathcal{S}_1),\dots,(G_k,\mathcal{S}_k)\}$ be a comprehensive Gröbner system of $\langle F\rangle$ regarding $\bar{A}$ as parameters. By a basic property of a comprehensive Gröbner system, when the ideal $\langle f_1(\bar{a},\bar{X}),\dots,f_l(\bar{a},\bar{X})\rangle$ is zero dimensional for some $\bar{a} \in \mathcal{S}_i$, it is also zero dimensional for any $\bar{a} \in \mathcal{S}_i$ and the cardinality of $\theta(\bar{a})$ is identical on $\mathcal{S}_i$ counting their multiplicities. In this paper, we prove that θ is also continuous on $\mathcal{S}_i$. Our result ensures the correctness of an algorithm for real quantifier elimination one of the authors has recently developed.

CCS CONCEPTS

• **Computing methodologies → Equation and inequality solving algorithms;**

KEYWORDS

parametric polynomial system; continuity; comprehensive Gröbner system; real quantifier elimination

ACM Reference Format:
Yosuke Sato, Ryoya Fukasaku, and Hiroshi Sekigawa. 2018. On Continuity of the Roots of a Parametric Zero Dimensional Multivariate Polynomial Ideal. In *ISSAC'18: 2018 ACM International Symposium on Symbolic and Algebraic Computation, July 16–19, 2018, New York, NY, USA.* ACM, New York, NY, USA, 7 pages. https://doi.org/10.1145/3208976.3209004

1 INTRODUCTION

Continuity of the roots of a parametric unary polynomial is easily obtained using Rouche's theorem. In complex numbers $\mathbb{C}$, the roots of a unary polynomial equation $X^n + A_{n-1}X^{n-1} + \cdots + A_1X + A_0 = 0$ is continuous with respect to the values of the parameters $A_{n-1},\dots,A_0$. This fact is precisely described as follows. The equation $X^n + a_{n-1}X^{n-1} + \cdots + a_1X + a_0 = 0$ has n number of roots counting their multiplicities for each $(a_{n-1},\dots,a_1,a_0) \in \mathbb{C}^n$. We can regard them as an n-size multiset of elements of $\mathbb{C}$ and introduce a natural topology on the set of such multisets. Then the map θ from an element $(a_{n-1},\dots,a_1,a_0)$ of $\mathbb{C}^n$ to a multiset defined by $\theta(a_{n-1},\dots,a_1,a_0)$ = " an n-size multiset consisting of the roots of the equation $X^n + a_{n-1}X^{n-1} + \cdots + a_1X + a_0 = 0$ " is continuous.

For a system of multivariate parametric polynomial equations, however, its continuity becomes much subtler. Consider the following system of equations with a parameter A:

$$X_1X_2 + AX_2 - 1 = 0, X_1^2 + AX_2 - 1 = 0.$$

When $A \neq 0$, it has the following three roots for (X_1,X_2):

$$(0,\frac{1}{A}),(\frac{-A \pm \sqrt{4+A^2}}{2},\frac{-A \pm \sqrt{4+A^2}}{2}).$$

On the other hand, it has only two roots $(\pm1,\pm1)$ for $A = 0$. Let $I = \langle X_1X_2 + AX_2 - 1, X_1^2 + AX_2 - 1\rangle$ be a parametric ideal in $\mathbb{C}[X_1,X_2]$ with a parameter A. When $A \neq 0$, the residue class ring $\mathbb{C}[X_1,X_2]/I$ has dimension 3 as a $\mathbb{C}$-vector space, hence I has three zeros. (We actually have no multiple roots.) While on the other hand, the residue class ring has dimension 2 for $A = 0$, hence I has only two zeros even if we count multiplicity. In order to discuss the continuity of a system of multivariate parametric polynomial equations in some region of the parameters, we need that the residue class ring by its associated parametric ideal has the same dimension for any specialization with an element of the region. In the above example, the dimension is not invariant in any neighborhood of $A = 0$ and the value of $\frac{1}{A}$ actually diverges at $A = 0$.

A comprehensive Gröbner system is an ideal tool for handling parametric polynomial ideals. Let $F = \{f_1(\bar{A},\bar{X}),\dots,f_l(\bar{A},\bar{X})\}$ be a finite set of polynomials in $\mathbb{Q}[\bar{A},\bar{X}]$ with variables $\bar{A} = A_1,\dots,A_m$ and $\bar{X} = X_1,\dots,X_n$. Let $\mathcal{G} = \{(G_1,\mathcal{S}_1),\dots,(G_k,\mathcal{S}_k)\}$ be a comprehensive Gröbner system of $\langle F\rangle$ regarding $\bar{A}$ as parameters. By a basic property of a comprehensive Gröbner system, when the ideal $\langle F(\bar{a},\bar{X})\rangle = \langle f_1(\bar{a},\bar{X}),\dots,f_l(\bar{a},\bar{X})\rangle$ in $\mathbb{C}[\bar{X}]$ is zero dimensional for some $\bar{a} \in \mathcal{S}_i$, it is also zero dimensional for any $\bar{a}$ of $\mathcal{S}_i$, furthermore the dimension of the residue class ring $\mathbb{C}[\bar{X}]/\langle F(\bar{a},\bar{X})\rangle$ as a $\mathbb{C}$-vector space is identical on $\mathcal{S}_i$. Hence, we can discuss the continuity of the roots of the system of parametric polynomial equations $f_1(\bar{A},\bar{X}) = 0,\dots,f_l(\bar{A},\bar{X}) = 0$ on such $\mathcal{S}_i$. Let d be the dimension of $\mathbb{C}[\bar{X}]/\langle F(\bar{a},\bar{X})\rangle$ for every $\bar{a} \in \mathcal{S}_i$. Define a map θ from an element $\bar{a} \in \mathcal{S}_i$ to a d-size multiset of elements of $\mathbb{C}^n$ by $\theta(\bar{a})$ = " a d-size multiset consisting of the zeros of the ideal $\langle F(\bar{a},\bar{X})\rangle$ ". In this paper, we prove that θ is continuous on $\mathcal{S}_i$ w.r.t. a natural topology introduced on the set of d-size multisets of elements of $\mathbb{C}^n$.

The most important motivation of our work is to give a correctness proof for an algorithm one of the authors has recently developed for real quantifier elimination in [9] and embedded in

ISSAC'18, July 16–19, 2018, New York, NY, USA

ACM ISBN 978-1-4503-5550-6/18/07...$15.00
https://doi.org/10.1145/3208976.3209004

the real quantifier elimination program released as free software in [6], which brings us a drastic improvement of the work introduced in [7].

The paper is organized as follows. In section 2, we give a minimal review of the theory of a comprehensive Gröbner system we need for understanding the paper. Section 3 is devoted to our main result. In section 4, as an application of our result we give a correctness proof for the algorithm used in the program of [6].

2 COMPREHENSIVE GRÖBNER SYSTEM

In the rest of the paper, $\mathbb{Q}$, $\mathbb{R}$ and $\mathbb{C}$ denote the field of rational numbers, real numbers and complex numbers. The symbols $\bar{A}$ and $\bar{X}$ denote some variables $A_1,\ldots,A_m$ and $X_1,\ldots,X_n$. $T(\bar{X})$ denote the set of terms of $\bar{X}$. The symbol $>$ denotes an admissible term order on $T(\bar{X})$. For a polynomial f in $\mathbb{Q}[\bar{A},\bar{X}]$, $LM(f)$, $LT(f)$ and $LC(f)$ denote the leading monomial, the leading term and the leading coefficient of f respectively regarding f as a member of the polynomial ring over the coefficient ring $\mathbb{Q}[\bar{A}]$, i.e. $f \in (\mathbb{Q}[\bar{A}])[X]$. (Note that $LM(f) = LC(f)LT(f)$ and $LC(f) \in \mathbb{Q}[\bar{A}]$.)
For an ideal I of a polynomial ring over a field K, $V_{K'}(I)$ denotes the variety of I in an extension field K' of K.

Definition 1 (Algebraic partition). Let S be an algebraically constructible subset of an affine space $\mathbb{C}^m$ for some natural number m. A finite set $\{\mathcal{S}_1,\ldots,\mathcal{S}_k\}$ of non-empty subsets of S is called an algebraic partition of S if it satisfies the following properties 1, 2 and 3:

(1) $\cup_{i=1}^k \mathcal{S}_i = S$.
(2) $\mathcal{S}_i \cap \mathcal{S}_j = \emptyset$ if $i \neq j$.
(3) $\mathcal{S}_i$ is a locally closed set for each i, that is $\mathcal{S}_i = V_{\mathbb{C}}(I_1)\backslash V_{\mathbb{C}}(I_2)$ for some ideals I_1,I_2 of $\mathbb{Q}[\bar{A}]$.

Each $\mathcal{S}_i$ is called a segment.

Definition 2 (Comprehensive Gröbner system). Let S be an algebraically constructible subset of $\mathbb{C}^m$. For an ideal I of $\mathbb{Q}[\bar{A},\bar{X}]$, a finite set $\mathcal{G} = \{(\mathcal{S}_1,G_1),\ldots,(\mathcal{S}_k,G_k)\}$ satisfying the following properties 1, 2, 3 and 4 is called a comprehensive Gröbner system of I over S with parameters $\bar{A}$ w.r.t. $>$:

(1) Each G_i is a finite subset of $\mathbb{Q}[\bar{A},\bar{X}]$.
(2) $\{\mathcal{S}_1,\ldots,\mathcal{S}_k\}$ is an algebraic partition of S.
(3) For each $\bar{a} \in \mathcal{S}_i$, $G_i(\bar{a}) = \{g(\bar{a},\bar{X}) : g(\bar{A},\bar{X}) \in G_i\}$ is a Gröbner basis of the ideal $I(\bar{a})$ of $\mathbb{C}[\bar{X}]$ with respect to $>$, where $I(\bar{a})$ denotes an ideal of $\mathbb{C}[\bar{X}]$ generated by $\{f(\bar{a},\bar{X}) : f(\bar{A},\bar{X}) \in I\}$.
(4) For each $\bar{a} \in \mathcal{S}_i$, $LC(g)(\bar{a}) \neq 0$ for any element g of G_i.

In addition, if each $G_i(\bar{a})$ is a minimal (reduced) Gröbner basis, $\mathcal{G}$ is said to be minimal (reduced). Being monic is not required. When $\mathcal{S}$ is a whole space $\mathbb{C}^m$, the words "over $\mathcal{S}$" is usually omitted.

Remark 1. *The set of leading terms of $G_i(\bar{a})$ is invariant for each $\bar{a} \in \mathcal{S}_i$, hence the dimension of the residue class ring $\mathbb{C}[\bar{X}]/\langle G_i(\bar{a})\rangle$ as a $\mathbb{C}$-vector space is also invariant. Accordingly, when it has a finite dimension, say l, the ideal $\langle G_i(\bar{a})\rangle$ has l number of zeros in $\mathbb{C}$ counting their multiplicities.*

3 CONTINUITY OF PARAMETRIC POLYNOMIAL SYSTEM

We begin with defining a topology on a set of multisets.

Definition 3 (Distance of points). *For two points $\bar{a} = (a_1,\ldots,a_m)$ and $\bar{b} = (b_1,\ldots,b_m)$ in $\mathbb{C}^m$, we define a distance $d(\bar{a},\bar{b})$ between $\bar{a}$ and $\bar{b}$ to be* $\max(|a_1 - b_1|,\ldots,|a_m - b_m|)$.

Definition 4 (Multiset). *For a set of finite ordered sets $S^v = \{(s_1,\ldots,s_v) : s_1,\ldots,s_v \in S\}$, define an equivalence relation $\sim$ by $(s_1,\ldots,s_v) \sim (t_1,\ldots,t_v)$ iff $s_1 = t_{\sigma(1)},\ldots,s_v = t_{\sigma(v)}$ for some permutation σ. Its equivalent class is called a v-size multiset. The equivalent class of an element $(s_1,\ldots,s_v)$ is denoted by $(s_1,\ldots,s_v)_M$.*

Example 1. *$(a,a,b)_M = (a,b,a)_M = (b,a,a)_M$, but $(a,a,b)_M \neq (a,b,b)_M$.*

Definition 5 (Distance of multisets). *Let S be a metric space with a distance d. For two v-size multisets $\alpha = (\alpha_1,\ldots,\alpha_v)_M$ and $\beta = (\beta_1,\ldots,\beta_v)_M$ of elements of S, we define a distance $D(\alpha,\beta)$ by*

$$\min(\{\max(d(\alpha_1,\beta_{\sigma(1)}),\ldots,d(\alpha_n,\beta_{\sigma(n)})) : \sigma \in S_n\}),$$

where S_n denotes the symmetric group of degree n.

We define continuity of the roots of a zero dimensional parametric ideal as follows.

Definition 6 (Continuity of roots). *Let I be an ideal of $\mathbb{Q}[\bar{A},\bar{X}]$. Suppose that the residue class ring $\mathbb{C}[\bar{X}]\ /I(\bar{a})$ has a uniform dimension l as a $\mathbb{C}$-vector space for each element $\bar{a}$ of a subset $S \subset \mathbb{C}^m$. Let $\theta(\bar{a})$ be the l-size multiset of the zeros of the ideal $I(\bar{a})$. We say I has continuous roots on S, if θ is continuous w.r.t. the topology on the set of multisets induced by the distance D and the topology of the subspace S of $\mathbb{C}^m$ induced by the distance d.*

Example 2. *Let $I = \langle X_1X_2 + AX_2 - 1, X_1^2 + AX_2 - 1\rangle$ be an ideal of $\mathbb{Q}[A,X_1,X_2]$ treated in the introduction. Let $S_1 = \{a \in \mathbb{C} : a \neq 0\}$ and $S_2 = \{0\}$. I is continuous on S_1. Note that I is also continuous on S_2, since every map is continuous on a subspace consisting of isolated points.*

For a unary polynomial ideal we can easily obtain the following fact using Rouche's theorem.

Theorem 1. *Let $I = \langle X^m + A_{m-1}X^{m-1} + \cdots + A_1X + A_0\rangle$ be an ideal in $\mathbb{Q}[A_0,\ldots,A_{m-1},X]$. Then I is continuous on $\mathbb{C}^m$.*

The following well-known fact plays an important role for showing our result. (Its proof can be found in Theorem (4.5) of [3] for example.)

Theorem 2. *Let I be a zero dimensional ideal in $\mathbb{C}[\bar{X}]$. Let l be the dimension of the residue class ring $\mathbb{C}[\bar{X}]/I$ as a $\mathbb{C}$-vector space and $\alpha_1,\ldots,\alpha_l \in \mathbb{C}^n$ be the zeros of I counting multiplicity. For a polynomial $h \in \mathbb{C}[\bar{X}]$, define a linear map ϕ_h from the residue class ring $\mathbb{C}[\bar{X}]/I$ to itself by $\phi_h(f) = hf$ for each $f \in \mathbb{C}[\bar{X}]/I$. Then, the eigenvalues of ϕ_h are $h(\alpha_1),\ldots,h(\alpha_l)$ counting multiplicity.*

Combining them together with properties of a comprehensive Gröbner system, we have the following fact.

Lemma 1. *Let $\mathcal{G} = \{(\mathcal{S}_1,G_1),\ldots,(\mathcal{S}_k,G_k)\}$ be a minimal comprehensive Gröbner system of an ideal I of $\mathbb{Q}[\bar{A},\bar{X}]$ with parameters $\bar{A}$ w.r.t. some term order. Let $h(\bar{X})$ be an arbitrary polynomial* *in* $\mathbb{Q}[\bar{X}]$. *If the ideal* $\langle G_i(\bar{a})\rangle$ *is zero dimensional for each* $\bar{a} \in \mathcal{S}_i$, *then the residue class ring* $\mathbb{C}[\bar{X}]/I(\bar{a})$ *as a* $\mathbb{C}$*-vector space has a uniform dimension* l *for each* $\bar{a} \in \mathcal{S}_i$. *Define a map* θ_h *from an element* $\bar{a} \in \mathcal{S}_i$ *to the* l*-size multiset* $(h(\alpha_1),\ldots,h(\alpha_l))_M$ *of elements of* $\mathbb{C}$, *where* $\alpha_1,\ldots,\alpha_l$ *are zeros of* $I(\bar{a})$ *counting multiplicity. Then,* θ_h *is continuous.*

Proof. The first assertion follows from REMARK 1. For readability, we simply denote G for G_i and $\mathcal{S}$ for $\mathcal{S}_i$. For each $\bar{a} \in \mathcal{S}$ let $\phi_{h,\bar{a}}$ denote a linear map from $\mathbb{C}[\bar{X}]/I(\bar{a})$ to itself defined by $\phi_{h,\bar{a}}(f) = hf$ for each $f \in \mathbb{C}[\bar{X}]/I(\bar{a})$. Using a canonical basis $\{t \in T(\bar{X}) : t$ is not dividable by any $LT(g)$ of $g \in G\}$ of a $\mathbb{C}$-vector space $\mathbb{C}[\bar{X}]/I(\bar{a})$ for each $\bar{a} \in \mathcal{S}$ and monomial reductions by $G(\bar{a})$ which are also performed uniformly for each $\bar{a} \in \mathcal{S}$, we can obtain a uniform representation matrix of $\phi_{h,\bar{a}}$ such that each component is represented by $\frac{p(\bar{a})}{q(\bar{a})}$ with some polynomials $p,q \in \mathbb{Q}[\bar{A}]$, where $q(\bar{a}) \neq 0$ is guaranteed for any $\bar{a} \in \mathcal{S}$. Hence, we have a uniform representation of the characteristic polynomial of $\phi_{h,\bar{a}}$ for each $\bar{a} \in \mathcal{S}$ in a form of

$$X^l + \frac{p_{l-1}(\bar{a})}{q_{l-1}(\bar{a})}X^{l-1} + \cdots + \frac{p_1(\bar{a})}{q_1(\bar{a})}X + \frac{p_0(\bar{a})}{q_0(\bar{a})},$$

with some polynomials $p_{l-1}(\bar{A}),q_{l-1}(\bar{A}), \ldots, p_0(\bar{A}),q_0(\bar{A}) \in \mathbb{Q}[\bar{A}]$ such that $q_{l-1}(\bar{a}) \neq 0,\ldots, q_0(\bar{a}) \neq 0$ for any $\bar{a} \in \mathcal{S}$. By Theorem 2, $\theta_h(\bar{a})$ is the l-size multiset consisting the roots of this characteristic polynomial. Hence, the continuity of θ_h follows from Theorem 1. □

Before showing our main result, we need one more well-known fact. (Its proof can be found in Lemma 8.75 of [2] for example.)

Lemma 2. *For an arbitrary finite set* $P \subset \mathbb{C}^n$, *there exists a linear polynomial* $h(\bar{X}) = c_1X_1+\cdots+c_nX_n \in \mathbb{Q}[\bar{X}]$ *such that* $h(\alpha) \neq h(\alpha')$ *for any pair of distinct elements* α, α' *of* P.

Now we are ready to show our main result.

Theorem 3. *Let* $\mathcal{G} = \{(\mathcal{S}_1,G_1),\ldots,(\mathcal{S}_k,G_k)\}$ *be a minimal comprehensive Gröbner system of an ideal* I *of* $\mathbb{Q}[\bar{A},\bar{X}]$ *with parameters* $\bar{A}$ *w.r.t. some term order. Suppose that the ideal* $\langle G(\bar{a})\rangle$ *is zero dimensional for each* $\bar{a} \in \mathcal{S}_i$, *then* I *has continuous roots on* $\mathcal{S}_i$.

Proof. For readability, we also simply denote G for G_i and $\mathcal{S}$ for $\mathcal{S}_i$. θ denotes the same map given in Definition 6. θ_h denotes the same map given in Lemma 1 for $h \in \mathbb{Q}[\bar{X}]$. Take an arbitrary element $\bar{a} \in \mathcal{S}$ and let l be the dimension of $\mathbb{C}[\bar{X}]/I(\bar{a})$. Let α_1, …, $\alpha_l \in \mathbb{C}^n$ be the zeros of $I(\bar{a})$ counting multiplicity. For each $j = 1, \ldots, n$ and $\alpha \in \mathbb{C}^n$ let $p_j(\alpha)$ be the j-th projection of α, i.e., $p_j(\alpha) = c_j$ for $\alpha = (c_1,\ldots,c_n) \in \mathbb{C}^n$. Regarding p_j as a polynomial $p_j(\bar{X}) = X_j$ in $\mathbb{Q}[\bar{X}]$, and applying Lemma 1 for $h = p_j$, the map π_j from an element $\bar{a}$ of $\mathcal{S}$ to a multiset of elements of $\mathbb{C}$ defined by $\pi_j(\bar{a}) = (p_j(\alpha_1),\ldots,p_j(\alpha_l))_M$, that is $\pi_j = \theta_{p_j}$, is continuous for each j. We will show that θ is continuous at $\bar{a}$.
We first consider the case where $\alpha_1 = \cdots = \alpha_l$. Set $\alpha = \alpha_1 = \cdots = \alpha_l$ and take an arbitrary $\varepsilon > 0$. Since each map π_j is continuous in $\mathcal{S}$, there exists a positive δ such that for each j, $D(\pi_j(\bar{b}),\pi_j(\bar{a})) < \varepsilon$ holds for any $\bar{b} \in \mathcal{S}$ with $d(\bar{a},\bar{b}) < \delta$. Let $\beta_1,\ldots,\beta_l$ be the zeros of $I(\bar{b})$ counting multiplicity, in other words $\theta(\bar{b}) = (\beta_1,\ldots,\beta_l)_M$. By the definition of D, the inequality $D(\pi_j(\bar{b}),\pi_j(\bar{a})) < \varepsilon$ implies $|p_j(\beta_i) - p_j(\alpha)| < \varepsilon$ for each $i = 1,\ldots,l$. Hence, $d(\beta_i,\alpha) < \varepsilon$ for each $i = 1,\ldots,l$. Since $\theta(\bar{a}) = (\alpha,\ldots,\alpha)_M$, $D(\theta(\bar{b}),\theta(\bar{a})) < \varepsilon$ by the definition of D. Therefore, θ is continuous at $\bar{a}$.

Next, we consider the case where $\alpha_j \neq \alpha_k$ for some $j \neq k$. Set $B_i(\bar{a}) = \{p_i(\alpha_1),\ldots,p_i(\alpha_l)\}$ for each $i = 1,\ldots,n$ and $B(\bar{a}) = B_1(\bar{a})\times\cdots\times B_n(\bar{a})$. Note that $2 \leq |B(\bar{a})|$. Lemma 2 guarantees that we can have a linear polynomial $h(\bar{X}) = c_1X_1 + \cdots + c_nX_n \in \mathbb{Q}[\bar{X}]$ such that $h(\alpha) \neq h(\alpha')$ for any pair of distinct elements α, α' of $B(\bar{a})$. By multiplying a constant if necessary, we can assume that $\max(|c_1|,\ldots,|c_n|) \leq 1/n$. Take ε_0 such that $0 < \varepsilon_0 < \frac{1}{2}\min(\{|h(\alpha) - h(\alpha')| : \alpha, \alpha' \in B(\bar{a}), \alpha \neq \alpha'\})$. Then, for any pair α,α' of distinct elements of $B(\bar{a})$ and $\varepsilon \leq \varepsilon_0$,

$$\{z \in \mathbb{C} : |z - h(\alpha)| < \varepsilon\} \cap \{z \in \mathbb{C} : |z - h(\alpha')| < \varepsilon\} = \emptyset.$$

For any two points $\gamma = (\gamma_1,\ldots,\gamma_n)$ and $\gamma' = (\gamma_1',\ldots,\gamma_n')$ in $\mathbb{C}^n$, we have

$$|h(\gamma')-h(\gamma)| \leq \sum_{j=1}^{n} |c_j(\gamma_j'-\gamma_j)| \leq \frac{1}{n}\sum_{j=1}^{n} |\gamma_j'-\gamma_j| \leq d(\gamma,\gamma').$$

Thus, $d(\gamma,\gamma') < \varepsilon$ implies that $|h(\gamma') - h(\gamma)| < \varepsilon$.
Take any positive ε with $\varepsilon \leq \varepsilon_0$. Since the map $\theta_h(\bar{a}) = (h(\alpha_1),\ldots, h(\alpha_l))_M$ is continuous in $\mathcal{S}$, there exists a positive δ such that $D(\theta_h(\bar{a}),\theta_h(\bar{b})) < \varepsilon$ holds for any $\bar{b} \in \mathcal{S}$ with $d(\bar{a},\bar{b}) < \delta$. Since each map $\pi_j(\bar{a})$ is also continuous in $\mathcal{S}$, there exists a positive δ' ($\leq \delta$) such that $D(\pi_j(\bar{a}),\pi_j(\bar{b})) < \varepsilon$ holds for any $j = 1,\ldots, n$ and $\bar{b} \in \mathcal{S}$ with $d(\bar{a},\bar{b}) < \delta'$. This means that for any zero β of $\langle G(\bar{b})\rangle$ with $d(\bar{a},\bar{b}) < \delta'$, there exists $\alpha' \in B(\bar{a})$ such that $|p_j(\beta)-p_j(\alpha')| < \varepsilon$ holds for any $j = 1, \ldots, n$, that is, $\beta \in \{z \in \mathbb{C}^n : d(\alpha',z) < \varepsilon\}$.
We show that α' is a zero of $\langle G(\bar{a})\rangle$ by contradiction. Assume that α' is not a zero of $\langle G(\bar{a})\rangle$ and let α be any zero of $\langle G_i(\bar{a})\rangle$. Then, $|h(\alpha') - h(\alpha)| > 2\varepsilon$ holds. On the other hand, $|h(\beta) - h(\alpha')| < \varepsilon$ because $d(\alpha',\beta) < \varepsilon$. Thus,

$$|h(\beta) - h(\alpha)| \geq |h(\alpha') - h(\alpha)| - |h(\beta) - h(\alpha')| > \varepsilon.$$

This implies that $D(\theta_h(\bar{a}),\theta_h(\bar{b})) > \varepsilon$. This is a contradiction.
Let α be a zero of $\langle G_i(\bar{a})\rangle$ and let μ be its multiplicity. Take any positive ε ($\leq \varepsilon_0$) and positive δ' for ε as above. Take $\bar{b}$ with $d(\bar{a},\bar{b}) < \delta'$. Now, we prove that there are exactly μ zeros of $\langle G_i(\bar{b})\rangle$ in the region:

$$\{z \in \mathbb{C}^n : d(\alpha,z) < \varepsilon\} \tag{1}$$

counting multiplicity. It is also shown by contradiction.
Assume that ν ($> \mu$) zeros belong to the region (1). Without loss of generality, we can assume that $\alpha = \alpha_1 = \cdots = \alpha_\mu$ among the zeros $\alpha_1, \ldots, \alpha_l$ of $\langle G_i(\bar{a})\rangle$, and ν zeros of $\langle G_i(\bar{b})\rangle$ in the region (1) are $\beta_1,\ldots,\beta_\nu$. Then, for any $\sigma \in S_l$, there exists a number k ($1 \leq k \leq \nu$) such that $\sigma(k) > \mu$. Thus, $d(\beta_k,\alpha_{\sigma(k)}) > \varepsilon$ because $d(\alpha,\beta_k) < \varepsilon$ and $d(\alpha,\alpha_{\sigma(k)}) \geq |h(\alpha_{\sigma(k)}) - h(\alpha)| > 2\varepsilon$. Therefore, there exists j ($1 \leq j \leq n$) such that $|p_j(\beta_k) - p_j(\alpha_{\sigma(k)})| > \varepsilon$, which contradicts the condition $D(\pi_j(\bar{a}),\pi_j(\bar{b})) < \varepsilon$.
Assume that only ν ($< \mu$) zeros belong to the region (1), then there exists a zero α' of $\langle G_i(\bar{a})\rangle$ such that its multiplicity μ' is larger than the number of zeros of $\langle G_i(\bar{b})\rangle$ in the region:

$$\{z \in \mathbb{C}^n : d(\alpha',z) < \varepsilon\},$$

because the number of zeros of $\langle G_i(\bar{a})\rangle$ is equal to that of $\langle G_i(\bar{b})\rangle$ and the zeros of $\langle G_i(\bar{b})\rangle$ belong to

$$\cup_{j=1}^{l}\{z \in \mathbb{C}^n : d(z,\alpha_j) < \varepsilon\}.$$

Thus, there exist a zero α' of $\langle G_i(\bar{a})\rangle$ such that the number of zeros of $\langle G_i(\bar{b})\rangle$ is larger than the multiplicity of α', which leads to a contradiction as shown above. □

4 APPLICATION

In this section, as an application of the above theorem, we give a correctness proof of an algorithm for real quantifier elimination one of the authors has recently developed in [9] and embedded in his free software [6].

Based on the real root counting theorem introduced in [14], a real quantifier elimination method using the computation of comprehensive Gröbner systems is introduced in [17]. The method is further improved in [4, 7–9]. Main parts of these methods are the algorithms which eliminate all quantifiers $\exists\bar{X}$ from the following basic first order formula:

$$\phi(\bar{A}) \wedge \exists\bar{X}\ (f_1(\bar{A},\bar{X}) = 0 \wedge \cdots \wedge f_s(\bar{A},\bar{X}) = 0 \\ \wedge h_1(\bar{A},\bar{X}) > 0 \wedge \cdots \wedge h_t(\bar{A},\bar{X}) > 0),$$

where $\phi(\bar{A})$ is a quantifier free first order formula consisting only of equality = and disequality $\neq$, $f_1,\ldots,f_s$, $h_1,\ldots,h_t$ are polynomials in $\mathbb{Q}[\bar{A},\bar{X}]$ such that a specialized ideal $I(\bar{a})$ of the parametric ideal $I = \langle f_1(\bar{A},\bar{X}),\ldots,f_s(\bar{A},\bar{X})\rangle$ is zero dimensional for any $\bar{a} \in \mathbb{C}^m$ satisfying $\phi(\bar{a})$.

One of the most important facts introduced in [7] is that we can have an efficient algorithm for the quantifier elimination of a slightly different formula:

$$\phi(\bar{A}) \wedge \exists\bar{X}\ (f_1(\bar{A},\bar{X}) = 0 \wedge \cdots \wedge f_s(\bar{A},\bar{X}) = 0 \\ \wedge h_1(\bar{A},\bar{X}) \geq 0 \wedge \cdots \wedge h_t(\bar{A},\bar{X}) \geq 0).$$

In order to use this algorithm, we need to compute a minimal comprehensive Gröbner system of the saturation ideal $I : h^\infty$ with $h = h_1 \cdots h_t$ over $\mathcal{S} = \{\bar{a} \in \mathbb{C}^m : \phi(\bar{a})\}$. Computation of a Gröbner basis of a saturation ideal is generally much heavier than that of its original ideal. This phenomenon is especially prominent for a parametric ideal. In [8, 9] we introduced a method to obtain an algebraically constructible subset $\mathcal{S}' \subseteq \mathcal{S}$ such that $I(\bar{a}) = I(\bar{a}) : h(\bar{a},\bar{X})^\infty$ for any $\bar{a} \in \mathcal{S}' \cap \mathbb{R}^m$ by using only a minimal comprehensive Gröbner system of I. The method is further improved and embedded in the real quantifier elimination program released as free software in [6]. In order to ensure its correctness, we need Theorem 3 shown in the previous section. In this section, we first give a minimal background for understanding our correctness proof, then give a rough sketch of the above work of [8, 9], and finally introduce the new method together with its correctness proof.

4.1 Multivariate Hermitian quadratic forms

Let I be a zero dimensional ideal in a polynomial ring $\mathbb{R}[\bar{X}]$. Considering the residue class ring $\mathbb{R}[\bar{X}]/I$ as a $\mathbb{R}$-vector space, let $\{v_1, \ldots, v_d\}$ be its basis. For an arbitrary $h \in \mathbb{R}[\bar{X}]/I$ and each i,j ($1 \leq i,j \leq d$) we define a linear map $\theta_{h,i,j}$ from $\mathbb{R}[\bar{X}]/I$ to $\mathbb{R}[\bar{X}]/I$ by $\theta_{h,i,j}(f) = hv_iv_jf$ for $f \in \mathbb{R}[\bar{X}]/I$. Let $q_{h,i,j}$ be the trace of $\theta_{h,i,j}$ and M_h^I be a real symmetric matrix such that the (i,j)-th component is given by $q_{h,i,j}$. Regarding a real symmetric matrix as a quadratic form, M_h^I is called a *multivariate Hermitian quadratic form*. The characteristic polynomial of M_h^I is denoted by $\chi_h^I(x)$. We have the following properties.

Lemma 3. *Suppose I has l zeros in $\mathbb{C}^n$ without counting multiplicity and set $V_\mathbb{C}(I) = \{\bar{\alpha}_1,\ldots,\bar{\alpha}_l\}$. Then $\mathrm{rank}(M_1^I) = l$ and $\chi_1^I(x)$ has the following form:*

$$\chi_1^I(x) = x^d + a_1x^{d-1} + \cdots + a_lx^{d-l}$$

for some $a_1,\ldots,a_l \in \mathbb{R}$ such that $a_l \neq 0$. For each $h \in \mathbb{R}[\bar{X}]$, we have $\mathrm{rank}(M_h^I) \leq l$ and $\chi_h^I(x)$ has the following form:

$$\chi_h^I(x) = x^d + b_1x^{d-1} + \cdots + b_lx^{d-l}.$$

Furthermore the following relation between a_l and b_l holds:

$$b_l = h(\bar{\alpha}_1)\cdots h(\bar{\alpha}_l)a_l.$$

As a direct consequence, we have the following fact.

Corollary 1. *$b_l \neq 0$ if and only if $I = I : h^\infty$.*

4.2 Computation of saturation ideal

Once we obtain a minimal comprehensive Gröbner system $\mathcal{G} = \{(\mathcal{S}_1,G_1),\ldots,(\mathcal{S}_k,G_k)\}$ of the parametric ideal I over $\mathcal{S}$, the above properties enable us to compute an algebraically constructible subset $\mathcal{S}' \subseteq \mathcal{S}$ such that $I(\bar{a}) = I(\bar{a}) : h(\bar{a},\bar{X})^\infty$ for any $\bar{a} \in \mathcal{S}'$ using $\mathcal{G}$ as follows.

For readability and to avoid confusion, we fix i and denote $\mathcal{S}_i$ and G_i simply by $\mathcal{S}$ and G. By a similar reason as we have observed in the proof of Lemma 1, we can get uniform representations of $\chi_1^I(x)$ and $\chi_h^I(x)$ on $\mathcal{S} \cap \mathbb{R}^m$. That is $\chi_1^I(x) = x^d + a_1x^{d-1} + \cdots + a_{d-1}x + a_d$ and $\chi_h^I(x) = x^d + b_1x^{d-1} + \cdots + b_{d-1}x + b_d$ for some $a_1,\ldots,a_d,b_1,\ldots,b_d \in \mathbb{Q}(\bar{A})$ such that their denominators are guaranteed not to vanish on $\mathcal{S}$, where d is the dimension of $\mathbb{C}[\bar{X}]/I(\bar{a})$ determined uniquely for every $\bar{a} \in \mathcal{S}$. Let r be the least integer such that $a_{d-r} \neq 0$ as an element of $\mathbb{Q}(\bar{A})$. Then, $\mathrm{rank}(M_1^I) \leq d-r$ and $\mathrm{rank}(M_h^I) \leq \mathrm{rank}(M_1^I) \leq d-r$ by Lemma 3. Therefore, we have the following uniform representations:

$$\begin{aligned} \chi_1^I(x) &= x^d + a_1x^{d-1} + \cdots + a_{d-r}x^r, \\ \chi_h^I(x) &= x^d + b_1x^{d-1} + \cdots + b_{d-r}x^r. \end{aligned}$$

Using them, we can construct an algebraically constructible subset $\mathcal{S}' \subseteq \mathcal{S}$ such that $I(\bar{a}) = I(\bar{a}) : h(\bar{a},\bar{X})^\infty$ for each $\bar{a} \in \mathcal{S}' \cap \mathbb{R}^m$ as follows.

For each $i = 1,\ldots,d-r$, let $p_i^a, p_i^b \in \mathbb{Q}[\bar{A}]$ be the numerators of a_i, b_i respectively.

Let $\mathcal{S}_0,\mathcal{S}_1,\ldots,\mathcal{S}_{d-r},\mathcal{T}_1,\ldots,\mathcal{T}_{d-r} \subset \mathcal{S}$ be defined as follows:

$$\begin{aligned} \mathcal{S}_0 &= (V_\mathbb{C}(p_1^a,p_2^a,\ldots,p_{d-r}^a) \cap \mathcal{S}, \\ \mathcal{S}_1 &= (V_\mathbb{C}(p_2^a,\ldots,p_{d-r}^a) \setminus V_\mathbb{C}(p_1^b)) \cap \mathcal{S}, \\ \mathcal{T}_1 &= (V_\mathbb{C}(p_1^b,p_2^a,\ldots,p_{d-r}^a) \setminus V_\mathbb{C}(p_1^a)) \cap \mathcal{S}, \\ \mathcal{S}_2 &= (V_\mathbb{C}(p_3^a,\ldots,p_{d-r}^a) \setminus V_\mathbb{C}(p_2^b)) \cap \mathcal{S}, \\ \mathcal{T}_2 &= (V_\mathbb{C}(p_2^b,p_3^a,\ldots,p_{d-r}^a) \setminus V_\mathbb{C}(p_2^a)) \cap \mathcal{S}, \\ &\vdots \\ \mathcal{S}_{d-r-1} &= (V_\mathbb{C}(p_{d-r}^a) \setminus V_\mathbb{C}(p_{d-r-1}^b)) \cap \mathcal{S}, \\ \mathcal{T}_{d-r-1} &= (V_\mathbb{C}(p_{d-r-1}^b,p_{d-r}^a) \setminus V_\mathbb{C}(p_{d-r-1}^a)) \cap \mathcal{S}, \\ \mathcal{S}_{d-r} &= (V_\mathbb{C}(0) \setminus V_\mathbb{C}(p_{d-r}^b)) \cap \mathcal{S}, \\ \mathcal{T}_{d-r} &= (V_\mathbb{C}(p_{d-r}^b) \setminus V_\mathbb{C}(p_{d-r}^a)) \cap \mathcal{S}. \end{aligned}$$

Note first that $(V_{\mathbb{C}}(p^a_{i+1},\ldots,p^a_{d-r})\setminus V_{\mathbb{C}}(p^a_i))\cap\mathcal{S}=\mathcal{S}_i\cup\mathcal{T}_i$ for each $i=1,\ldots,d-r$, since if $p^a_{i+1}=0,\ldots,p^a_{d-r}=0$ then $p^a_i=0$ implies $p^b_i=0$ by LEMMA 3. (When $i=d-r$, $V_{\mathbb{C}}(p^a_{i+1},\ldots,p^a_{d-r})$ denotes $V_{\mathbb{C}}(0)$.) Hence $\{\mathcal{S}_0,\mathcal{S}_1,\ldots,\mathcal{S}_{d-r},\mathcal{T}_1,\ldots,\mathcal{T}_{d-r}\}$ forms a partition of $\mathcal{S}$. Secondly note that $I(\bar{a})=I(\bar{a}):h(\bar{a},\bar{X})^\infty$ for any $\bar{a}\in\mathcal{S}_i\cap\mathbb{R}^m$ for $i=1\ldots,d-r$ by COROLLARY 1. The corollary also implies $I(\bar{a})\neq I(\bar{a}):h(\bar{a},\bar{X})^\infty$ for each $\bar{a}\in\mathcal{T}_i\cap\mathbb{R}^m$ for $i=1,\ldots,d-r$. Finally note that $\mathrm{rank}(M^I_1)=0$ on $\mathcal{S}_0\cap\mathbb{R}^m$, that is $V_{\mathbb{C}}(I(\bar{a}))=\emptyset$ for each $\bar{a}\in\mathcal{S}_0\cap\mathbb{R}^m$ by LEMMA 3. It follows that $I(\bar{a})=\langle 1\rangle$ hence $I(\bar{a})=I(\bar{a}):h(\bar{a},\bar{X})^\infty$. Consequently we have a desired subset $\mathcal{S}'=\mathcal{S}_0\cup\ldots\cup\mathcal{S}_{d-r}$. Note also that $I(\bar{a})\neq I(\bar{a}):h(\bar{a},\bar{X})^\infty$ for each $\bar{a}\in\mathcal{T}'\cap\mathbb{R}^m=\mathbb{R}^m\setminus\mathcal{S}'$, where $\mathcal{T}'=\mathcal{T}_1\cup\ldots\cup\mathcal{T}_{d-r}$. If $\mathcal{T}'\neq\emptyset$, we need to compute a minimal comprehensive Gröbner basis of $I:h^\infty$ over $\mathcal{T}'$ for our real quantifier elimination. One of the most important properties of the algorithm for the computation of comprehensive Gröbner systems introduced in [16] and improved by the successive works such as [10–13] is that the computation of a comprehensive Gröbner system of a parametric ideal over an algebraically constructible set tends to be much lighter when the algebraically constructible set becomes smaller. As a consequence, the computation of a minimal comprehensive Gröbner system of the saturation ideal $I:h^\infty$ over $\mathcal{T}'$ is generally much lighter than that of $\mathcal{S}$.

4.3 New method and its correctness

From a theoretical point of view, the subsets $\mathcal{S}'$ and $\mathcal{T}'$ give us a perfect information for checking whether $I(\bar{a})$ is equal to $I(\bar{a}):h(\bar{a},\bar{X})$ or not for each $\bar{a}\in\mathcal{S}\cap\mathbb{R}^m$. From a practical point of view, however, their representation formulas tend to be very complicated when d is not small. In order to use them for quantifier elimination, such complicated formulas are not desirable since they cause us to produce a complicated quantifier free formula. Using THEOREM 3, we can improve the above method as follows.

THEOREM 4. *Using the same notations in the previous subsection, suppose that $\mathcal{S}\cap\mathbb{R}^m$ does not contain isolated points and p^a_{d-r} does not vanish on $\mathcal{S}\cap\mathbb{R}^m$ that is $\{\bar{a}\in\mathcal{S}\cap\mathbb{R}^m:p^a_{d-r}(\bar{a})=0\}\neq\mathcal{S}\cap\mathbb{R}^m$. Let $c_{d-r}=b_{d-r}/a_{d-r}\in\mathbb{Q}(\bar{A})$ and $p^c_{d-r}\in\mathbb{Q}(\bar{A})$ be its numerator. If $p^c_{d-r}(\bar{a})\neq 0$ for $\bar{a}\in\mathcal{S}\cap\mathbb{R}^m$, then $I(\bar{a})=I(\bar{a}):h(\bar{a},\bar{X})^\infty$. On the other hand, if $p^c_{d-r}(\bar{a})=0$ for $\bar{a}\in\mathcal{S}\cap\mathbb{R}^m$, then $I(\bar{a})\neq I(\bar{a}):h(\bar{a},\bar{X})^\infty$.*

PROOF. If $p^a_{d-r}(\bar{a})\neq 0$, then the assertion follows directly from LEMMA 3. For each $\bar{a}\in\mathcal{S}\cap\mathbb{R}^m$ let $(\alpha_1(\bar{a}),\ldots,\alpha_d(\bar{a}))_M$ denote the multiset of the zeros of $I(\bar{a})$. When $p^a_{d-r}(\bar{a})\neq 0$, by LEMMA 3, the ideal $I(\bar{a})$ has r zeros without counting continuity. Let it be $\{\alpha'_1(\bar{a}),\ldots,\alpha'_r(\bar{a})\}$. By LEMMA 3, we also have $c_{d-r}(\bar{a})=h(\bar{a},\alpha'_1(\bar{a}))\cdots h(\bar{a},\alpha'_r(\bar{a}))$. Suppose now that $p^a_{d-r}(\bar{a})=0$, then by our assumptions there exists an infinite sequence $\bar{a}_1,\bar{a}_2,\ldots,\bar{a}_k,\ldots$ of points of $\mathcal{S}\cap\mathcal{R}^m$ such that $p^a_{d-r}(\bar{a}_k)\neq 0$ for each k and $\lim_{k\to\infty}d(\bar{a}_k,\bar{a})=0$. Hence, $\lim_{k\to\infty}c_{d-r}(\bar{a}_k)=\lim_{k\to\infty}h(\bar{a},\alpha'_1(\bar{a}_k))\cdots h(\bar{a},\alpha'_r(\bar{a}_k))$. Since $\lim_{k\to\infty}(\alpha_1(\bar{a}_k),\ldots,\alpha_d(\bar{a}_k))_M=(\alpha_1(\bar{a}),\ldots,\alpha_d(\bar{a}))_M$ w.r.t. the distance D by THEOREM 3, we have $c_{d-r}(\bar{a})=\lim_{k\to\infty}c_{d-r}(\bar{a}_k)$ $=h(\bar{a},\alpha_{n_1}(\bar{a}))\cdots h(\bar{a},\alpha_{n_r}(\bar{a}))$ for some multiset $(n_1,\ldots,n_r)_M$ such that $\{\alpha_{n_1}(\bar{a}),\ldots,\alpha_{n_r}(\bar{a})\}=\{\alpha_1(\bar{a}),\ldots,\alpha_d(\bar{a})\}$. Therefore, if $p^c_{d-r}(\bar{a})\neq 0$ which implies $c_{d-r}(\bar{a})\neq 0$, we have $h(\bar{a},\alpha(\bar{a}))\neq 0$ for any zero $\alpha(\bar{a})$ of $I(\bar{a})$, that is $I(\bar{a})=I(\bar{a}):h(\bar{a},\bar{X})^\infty$. The second assertion is a direct consequence of by LEMMA 3. □

By this theorem, we can simply put $\mathcal{S}'=\{\bar{a}\in\mathcal{S}:p^c_{d-r}(\bar{a})\neq 0\}$ and $\mathcal{T}'=\{\bar{a}\in\mathcal{S}:p^c_{d-r}(\bar{a})=0\}$, then proceed the computation of a minimal comprehensive Gröbner system of the saturation ideal $I:h^\infty$ over $\mathcal{T}'$ for our real quantifier elimination.

REMARK 2. *Two assumptions of the above theorem are natural requirements for our real quantifier elimination. If $\mathcal{S}\cap\mathbb{R}^m$ contains isolated points, such points are finite and we do not need to handle them symbolically. If p^a_{d-r} vanishes on $\mathcal{S}\cap\mathbb{R}^m$, we actually do not need p^a_{d-r} and assume that $\chi^I_1(x)=x^d+a_1x^{d-1}+\cdots+a_{d-r-1}x^{r+1}$.*

The following example is too simple for applying our real quantifier elimination method. There are more practical algorithms for it. Our algorithm is efficient only for a basic formula such that the structure of the underlying parametric ideal is not clear. We use it only for the reason that we can easily explain how the improved method works.

EXAMPLE 3. *Consider the basic first order formula*

$$\exists X(X^2+AX+B=0\wedge X>0).$$

Let $f_1=f=X^2+AX+B, h_1=h=X, I=\langle X^2+AX+B\rangle$ in $\mathbb{Q}[A,B,X]$ with parameters A,B and $\phi(A,B)$ is 'true'. Obviously $\mathcal{G}=\{(\mathcal{S}_1,G_1)\}$ with $G_1=\{f\}$ and $\mathcal{S}_1=\mathbb{C}^2$ is a reduced comprehensive Gröbner system of I. For $(A,B)\in\mathbb{R}^2$, we have the following uniform representations:

$$\begin{aligned}M^I_1&=\begin{pmatrix}2&-A\\-A&A^2-2B\end{pmatrix},\\ M^I_h&=\begin{pmatrix}-A&A^2-2B\\A^2-2B&-A^3+3AB\end{pmatrix},\\ \chi^I_1(x)&=x^2+(-A^2+2B-2)x+A^2-4B,\\ \chi^I_h(x)&=x^2+(A^3+A-3AB)x+A^2B-4B^2.\end{aligned}$$

Hence, we have $p^a_1(A,B)=-A^2+2B-2, p^a_2=A^2-4B, p^b_1=A^3+A-3AB, p^b_2=A^2B-4B^2$ and $p^c_2(A,B)=B$.

If we use the method described in the previous subsection, we have $\mathcal{S}'=\mathcal{S}_0\cup\mathcal{S}_1\cup\mathcal{S}_2$ and $\mathcal{T}'=\mathcal{T}_1\cup\mathcal{T}_2$ with $\mathcal{S}_0=\{(A,B)\in\mathbb{C}^2:-A^2+2B-2=0,A^2-4B=0\}$, $\mathcal{S}_1=\{(A,B)\in\mathbb{C}^2:A^2-4B=0,A^3+A-3AB\neq 0\}$, $\mathcal{S}_2=\{(A,B)\in\mathbb{C}^2:A^2B-4B^2\neq 0\}$, $\mathcal{T}_1=\{(A,B)\in\mathbb{C}^2:A^3+A-3AB=0,A^2-4B=0,-A^2+2B-2\neq 0\}$, and $\mathcal{T}_2=\{(A,B)\in\mathbb{C}^2:A^2B-4B^2=0,A^2-4B\neq 0\}$, such that $I=I:h^\infty$ on $\mathcal{S}'\cap\mathbb{R}^2$ and $I\neq I:h^\infty$ on $\mathcal{T}'\cap\mathbb{R}^2$. Using them we have the following rather complicated representation formulas of $\mathcal{S}'$ and $\mathcal{T}'$:

$$\begin{aligned}\mathcal{S}'=\{(A,B)\in\mathbb{C}^2:&(-A^2+2B-2=0\wedge A^2-4B=0)\vee\\&(A^2-4B=0\wedge A^3+A-3AB\neq 0)\vee(A^2B-4B^2\neq 0)\},\\ \mathcal{T}'=\{(A,B)\in\mathbb{C}^2:&(A^3+A-3AB=0\wedge A^2-4B=0\wedge\\&-A^2+2B-2\neq 0)\vee(A^2B-4B^2=0\wedge A^2-4B\neq 0)\}.\end{aligned}$$

On the other hand, if we use the new method, we have the following much simpler representation formulas:

$$\mathcal{S}'=\{(A,B)\in\mathbb{C}^2:B\neq 0\},\mathcal{T}'=\{(A,B)\in\mathbb{C}^2:B=0\}.$$

Note also that we have $B=\alpha\beta=h(\alpha)h(\beta)$ for the zeros α and β of the equation $X^2+AX+B=0$. The essential point of THEOREM 4 is that this relation always holds even when $\alpha=\beta$.

Remark 3. *Theorem 4 ensures that the obtained sets $\mathcal{S}' \cap \mathbb{R}^m$ and $\mathcal{T}' \cap \mathbb{R}^m$ by the both methods are identical. As long as the computation of a minimal comprehensive Gröbner system of the saturation ideal $I : h^\infty$ over $\mathcal{T}'$ obtained by the new method terminates, it produces a simpler quantifier free formula in general.*

4.4 Computation data

The new method is used for the implementation [6] of the improved algorithm introduced in [9]. We conclude this section with some computation data we have obtained using the implementation [6] and the previous implementation [5] which uses a naive method for computing a saturation ideal. The following table **Table 1** contains some computation data we have obtained using both implementations. The table contains computation time measured in seconds. All the computations were done by the same computer environment with an Intel(R) Core(TM) i7-3635QM CPU @ 2.40GHz with 16 GB memory working on Ubuntu14.04. ∞ means that the computation does not terminate within 1 hour. The treated problems, i1, i2, ..., i8 and i9 are among the real QE problems we have encountered in the ongoing research project of artificial intelligence [1]. They are typical problems for which our new method is efficient, that is we need computation of saturation ideals in some step. A naive method implemented in [5] cannot handle some of them except for the problem i4, meanwhile the new method implemented in [6] successfully computes all of them.

i1 $\exists x_1 \exists x_2 \exists x_6 \exists x_7 (\bigwedge_{i=1}^{6} F_i = 0 \wedge \bigwedge_{i=1}^{7} P_i \neq 0 \wedge Q > 0)$.

$F_1 = x_5 x_1 x_4^2 + x_4^2 - x_1 x_2 x_4 - x_2 x_4 + x_1 x_2 + 3x_2,$
$F_2 = x_1 x_4 + x_3 - x_1 x_2,$
$F_3 = x_3 x_4 - 2x_2^2 - x_1 x_2 - 1,$
$F_4 = x_1 x_3^2 + x_3^2 - x_1^2 x_2 x_3 - x_1 x_2 x_3 + x_1^3 x_2 + 3x_1^2 x_2,$
$F_5 = (-x_3) + x_1 x_2 x_3 - 2x_1 x_2^2 - x_1^2 x_2 - x_1,$
$F_6 = 2x_1 x_2^2 + 2x_1^2 x_2^2 - 2x_1^2 x_2 + x_1^2 + x_1,$
$P_1 = x_1^2 + x_2 + x_3^2 + x_4,$
$P_2 = x_1 x_7 + x_2 x_6 - x_3,$
$P_3 = x_2 - x_1^5,$
$P_4 = x_2 - x_3^5,$
$P_5 = x_7^5 - x_1,$
$P_6 = x_6 - x_2^2,$
$P_7 = x_3 - (x_6^{21} - 1),$
$Q = x_8^7 x_1 + x_8^6 x_2 + x_8^5 x_3 + x_8^4 x_4 + x_8^3 x_5 + x_8^2 x_6 + x_8 x_7 - (x_1 + x_2 + x_3 + x_4 + x_5 + x_6 + x_7^3).$

i2 $\exists v_1 \exists v_2 (F = 0 \wedge P \neq 0)$.

$F = av_1^3 + 3v_1^3 v_2 + 2v_1 v_2 + bv_2^3,$
$P = v_1 v_2 (v_2 - 1)(3v_1 - v_2)(v_1 + v_2)(av_1 + 27bv_1 + 9v_1^2 + 6)(av_1^3 + 3v_1^3 + b + 2v_1)(av_1 - bv_1 - 3v_1^2 - 2).$

i3 $\exists c_2 \exists s_2 \exists c_1 \exists s_1 \exists t (\bigwedge_{i=1}^{4} F_i = 0 \wedge \bigwedge_{i=1}^{2} P_i \neq 0 \wedge Q > 0)$.

$F_1 = r - c_1 + l(s_1 s_2 + c_1 c_2),$
$F_2 = z - s_1 - l(s_1 c_2 - s_2 c_1) - c_1,$
$F_3 = s_1^2 + c_1^2 - 1,$
$F_4 = s_2^2 + c_2^2 - 1,$
$P_1 = l^2 - r^2 - z^2 + t - 4,$
$P_2 = 9r^2 - 8zr + 5z^2 - t,$
$Q = 4c_1 r + 2c_1 z + 2c_2 l + 5s_1^2 - t.$

i4 $\exists x \exists y \exists z \exists w (\bigwedge_{i=1}^{5} F_i = 0 \wedge P \neq 0 \wedge Q > 0)$.

$F_1 = xyw + axz + yz - 1,$
$F_2 = xyz + xz + xy - a,$
$F_3 = xz + yz - az - x - y - 1,$
$F_4 = axy - byz,$
$F_5 = ayz - bzx,$
$P = w((-w^6) - 9w^4 - 135w^2 - 27),$
$Q = w - c.$

i5 $\exists x \exists y (F = 0 \wedge P \neq 0)$.

$F = ax^3 - (x^2 y^3 + bxy + x + y),$
$P = (x+1)(y+1)xy(x+y)(x-y)(ax^2-1)(x^3+ax+b)((-x^4) + ax^2 - bx - 2)(ax^3 + bx + x^2 - x + 1).$

i6 $\exists x \exists y \exists z (\bigwedge_{i=1}^{4} F_i = 0 \wedge \bigwedge_{i=1}^{2} P_i \neq 0)$.

$F_1 = xy + axz + yz - 1,$
$F_2 = xyz + xz + xy - a,$
$F_3 = xz + yz - az - x - y - 1,$
$F_4 = axy - byz,$
$P_1 = ayz - bzx,$
$P_2 = azx - bxy.$

i7 $\exists x \exists y \exists z \exists u \exists v \exists w (\bigwedge_{i=1}^{8} F_i = 0 \wedge P \neq 0 \wedge \bigwedge_{i=1}^{3} Q_i > 0)$.

$F_1 = xyu + axz + yz - 1,$
$F_2 = xyzv + xz + xy - b,$
$F_3 = axy - byz,$
$F_4 = ayz - bzx,$
$F_6 = azu - buv,$
$F_7 = auv - bvx,$
$F_8 = avx - bxy,$
$P = axy - wy + y^2 + b,$
$Q_1 = axyz - bcuv,$
$Q_2 = ax + y + bz - c^3 w,$
$Q_3 = (-b)uv + ax.$

i8 $\exists s \exists t (F = 0 \wedge \bigwedge_{i=1}^{3} P_i \neq 0)$.

$F = (t - a)(s - b) + (t^4 - a^4)(s^4 - b^4) - 1,$
$P_1 = t - a,$
$P_2 = s - b,$
$P_3 = a - b.$

i9 $\exists b_1 \exists b_2 \exists c_1 \exists c_2 \exists d_1 \exists d_2 \exists e_1 \exists e_2 \exists f_1 \exists f_2 \exists h_1 \exists h_2 \exists k_1 \exists k_2 \exists o_1 \exists o_2$
$(\bigwedge_{i=1}^{19} F_i = 0 \wedge \bigwedge_{i=1}^{3} P_i \neq 0, \wedge Q > 0).$

$F_1 = b_1,$
$F_2 = b_2,$
$F_3 = c_1 - 1,$
$F_4 = c_2,$
$F_5 = (a_1 - d_1)(b_1 - c_1) + (a_2 - d_2)(b_2 - c_2),$
$F_6 = (b_1 - e_1)(a_1 - c_1) + (b_2 - e_2)(a_2 - c_2),$
$F_7 = (c_1 - f_1)(a_1 - b_1) + (c_2 - f_2)(a_2 - b_2),$
$F_8 = a_1 - h_1 - k_1(a_1 - d_1),$
$F_9 = a_2 - h_2 - k_1(a_2 - d_2),$
$F_{10} = b_1 - h_1 - k_2(b_1 - e_1),$
$F_{11} = b_2 - h_2 - k_2(b_2 - e_2),$
$F_{12} = (o_1 - b_1)^2 + (o_2 - b_2)^2 - r,$
$F_{13} = (o_1 - c_1)^2 + (o_2 - c_2)^2 - r,$
$F_{14} = (o_1 - e_1)^2 + (o_2 - e_2)^2 - r,$
$F_{15} = (o_1 - f_1)^2 + (o_2 - f_2)^2 - r,$

$$F_{16} = (o_1 - a_1)^2 + (o_2 - a_2)^2 - r,$$
$$F_{17} = (o_1 - f_1)^2 + (o_2 - f_2)^2 - r,$$
$$F_{18} = (o_1 - h_1)^2 + (o_2 - h_2)^2 - r,$$
$$F_{19} = (o_1 - e_1)^2 + (o_2 - e_2)^2 - r,$$
$$P_1 = o_1 o_2^5 - k_1^5 k_2,$$
$$P_2 = o_1,$$
$$P_3 = o_2,$$
$$Q = 16r^2 - 1.$$

Table 1: Computation Time of 9 QE problems

	i1	i2	i3	i4	i5	i6	i7	i8	i9
CGSQE2016	48	2	2	40	1	40	7	8	27
CGSQE2017	∞	∞	∞	118	∞	∞	∞	∞	∞

More information including computation date by other existing real QE implementations can be found in the website of [6].

5 CONCLUSION AND REMARKS

Given a parametric ideal I of $\mathbb{Q}[\bar{A},\bar{X}]$ and an algebraically constructible subset $\mathcal{S} \subseteq \mathbb{C}^m$ such that $I(\bar{a})$ is zero dimensional for each $\bar{a} \in \mathcal{S}$. In order to divide $\mathcal{S}$ into its partition $\{\mathcal{S}_1,\ldots,\mathcal{S}_k\}$ such that the roots of I is continuous on each $\mathcal{S}_i$, Theorem 3 does not provide us a canonical form of such a partition. Consider the parametric ideal $I = \langle X^2 + AX + B\rangle$ in $\mathbb{Q}[A,B,X]$ with parameters A, B. Besides an obvious minimal comprehensive Gröbner system $\mathcal{G} = \{(\{X^2 + AX + B\},\mathbb{C}^2)\}$, we also have its minimal comprehensive Gröbner system $\mathcal{G} = \{(\{X^2+AX+B\},\mathcal{S}_1),(\{X^2+AX+B\},\mathcal{S}_2)\}$ where $\{\mathcal{S}_1,\mathcal{S}_2\}$ is any algebraic partition of $\mathbb{C}^2$. Though I has continuous roots on each $\mathcal{S}_i$, $\mathcal{S}_1 \cup \mathcal{S}_2$ is a connected subspace and I also has continuous roots on $\mathcal{S}_1 \cup \mathcal{S}_2$. We think that a desired canonical form of a partition should not contain any pair of disjoint subsets $\mathcal{S}_1,\mathcal{S}_2$ such that $\mathcal{S}_1$ and $\mathcal{S}_2$ is path-connected and the roots of I is continuous on $\mathcal{S}_1 \cup \mathcal{S}_2$. A comprehensive Gröbner system constructed as a stratified Gröbner basis of I in $R[\bar{X}]$ with a coefficient ring R which is the smallest commutative von Neumann regular ring containing $\mathbb{Q}[\bar{A}]$ introduced in [15] may provide us such a canonical form of an algebraic partition.

It might be possible to define continuity for the roots of a non zero dimensional parametric ideal. For such a definition, however, we must start with defining a topology on a set of infinite varieties then discuss the way to apply the theory of comprehensive Gröbner systems. It is certainly beyond the scope we have presented in the paper.

ACKNOWLEDGMENTS

This work was partially supported by JSPS KAKENHI Grant Numbers 17K12642, 18K03426, and 18K11172.

REFERENCES

[1] N. H. Arai, T. Matsuzaki, H. Iwane, and H. Anai. 2014. Mathematics by Machine. In *Proceedings of International Symposium on Symbolic and Algebraic Computation*. ACM Press, 1–8.

[2] T. Becker and V Weispfenning. 1993. *Gröbner Bases, GTM 141*. Springer.

[3] D. Cox, Little. J., and D. O'Shea. 1997. *Using Algebraic Geometry, GTM 185*. Springer.

[4] R. Fukasaku. 2014. QE Software Based on Comprehensive Gröbner Systems. In *Proceedings of Mathematical Software - ICMS 2014 - 4th International Congress, LNCS Vol. 8592*. Springer, 512–517.

[5] R. Fukasaku. 2016. 2016 Version of **CGSQE** Package. http://www.rs.tus.ac.jp/fukasaku/software/CGSQE-20160509/

[6] R. Fukasaku. 2017. 2017 Version of **CGSQE** Package. http://www.rs.tus.ac.jp/fukasaku/software/CGSQE-2017/

[7] R. Fukasaku, H. Iwane, and Y. Sato. 2015. Real Quantifier Elimination by Computation of Comprehensive Gröbner Systems. In *Proceedings of International Symposium on Symbolic and Algebraic Computation*. ACM Press, 173–180.

[8] R. Fukasaku, H. Iwane, and Y. Sato. 2016. On the Implementation of CGS Real QE. In *Proceedings of Mathematical Software - ICMS 2016 - 5th International Conference, LNCS Vol. 9725*. Springer, 165–172.

[9] R. Fukasaku, H. Iwane, and Y. Sato. to appear. On Multivariate Hermitian Quadratic Forms. *Mathematics in Computer Science* (to appear).

[10] D. Kapur, Y. Sun, and D. Wang. 2010. A New Algorithm for Computing Comprehensive Gröbner Systems. In *Proceedings of International Symposium on Symbolic and Algebraic Computation*. ACM Press, 29–36.

[11] Y. Kurata. 2011. Improving Suzuki-Sato's CGS Algorithm by Using Stability of Gröbner Bases and Basic Manipulations for Efficient Implementation. *Communications of the Japan Society for Symbolic and Algebraic Computation* 1 (2011), 39–66.

[12] K. Nabeshima. 2007. A Speed-Up of the Algorithm for Computing Comprehensive Gröbner Systems. In *Proceedings of International Symposium on Symbolic and Algebraic Computation*. ACM Press, 299–306.

[13] K. Nabeshima. 2012. Stability Conditions of Monomial Bases and Comprehensive Gröbner systems. In *Proceedings of Computer Algebra in Scientific Computing, LNCS Vol. 7442*. Springer, 248–259.

[14] P. Pedersen, M.-F. Roy, and A. Szpirglas. 1993. Counting real zeros in the multivariate case. In *Proceedings of Effective Methods in Algebraic Geometry, Progress in Mathematics Vol. 109*. Birkhäuser, 203–224.

[15] A. Suzuki and Y. Sato. 2003. An Alternative Approach to Comprehensive Gröbner Bases. *Journal of Symbolic Computation* 36, 3-4 (2003), 649–667.

[16] A. Suzuki and Y. Sato. 2006. A Simple Algorithm to Compute Comprehensive Gröbner Bases Using Gröbner Bases. In *Proceedings of International Symposium on Symbolic and Algebraic Computation*. ACM Press, 326–331.

[17] V. Weispfenning. 1998. A New Approach to Quantifier Elimination for Real Algebra. In *Quantifier Elimination and Cylindrical Algebraic Decomposition*. Springer, 376–392.

Fast Straightening Algorithm for Bracket Polynomials Based on Tableau Manipulations*

Changpeng Shao
Key Lab of System Control, AMSS; UCAS
Beijing 100190, China
shaochangpeng11@mails.ucas.ac.cn

Hongbo Li†
Key Lab of Math. Mechanization, AMSS; UCAS
Beijing 100190, China
hli@mmrc.iss.ac.cn

ABSTRACT

Straightening is the most fundamental symbolic manipulation in bracket algebra. Young's classical algorithm and White's more recent algorithm have poor performance in straightening bracket polynomials of degree > 4. Rota's straightening algorithm based on Capelli operator is generally superior to the former two in speed, but still performs badly when the degree reaches 5.

In this paper, a new operator is defined in bracket algebra based on tableau manipulations, and is simpler than Capelli operator. A new straightening algorithm is then proposed, and is superior to the above three algorithms by a speedup of two order of magnitude on average by testing over 500 examples in the past two years.

CCS CONCEPTS

• **Computing methodologies** → **Symbolic and algebraic algorithms**; *Combinatorial algorithms*;

KEYWORDS

Young Tableau; Bracket algebra; Straightening algorithm; Classical invariant theory; Capelli operator

ACM Reference Format:

Changpeng Shao, Hongbo Li. 2018. Fast Straightening Algorithm for Bracket Polynomials Based on Tableau Manipulations. In *Proceedings of 2018 ACM International Symposium on Symbolic and Algebraic Computation (ISSAC'18)*, ACM, New York, NY, USA, 8 pages.
https://doi.org/10.1145/3208976.3208978

*The paper is supported by NSFC Project 11671388 and CAS Project QYZDJ-SSW-SYS022.
†Correspondence author.

ISSAC'18, July 16–19, 2018, New York, NY, USA

ACM ISBN 978-1-4503-5550-6/18/07.
https://doi.org/10.1145/3208976.3208978

1 INTRODUCTION

Bracket algebra grows out of classical invariant theory [14] and combinatorics [7], and has important applications in representation theory [9], projective geometry [15], algebraic geometry [4], automated theorem proving [12], robotics [16], mechanism design [11], etc.

Changing a bracket polynomial into its normal form, called *straightening*, is a basic symbolic manipulation in bracket algebra. The first method is due to A. Young [18] in 1928. In 1991, N. White [17] presented an improved method. Each method relies on a set of **quadratic** bracket polynomials for elimination. With the increase of the degree of the bracket polynomial, both methods quickly become inefficient.

During 1978-80, J. Désarménien et al. [5], [6] proposed a straightening algorithm based on solving a linear triangular system obtained by Capelli operations [2], called *Rota's algorithm*. This algorithm can handle bracket polynomials much more efficiently in general. There are various developments and generalizations of Rota's algorithm, *e.g.*, in the work of A. Brini [1], M. Clausen [3], R. Huang and N. White [10], to name a few.

However, Rota's algorithm still performs badly when the degree of bracket polynomial reaches 5. One reason is its demand for almost all straight bracket monomials having the same content with the input, the number of which grows quickly with the increase of the degree. Another reason is that the evaluation of Capelli operator is time-consuming. There is the need to further improve Rota's algorithm from the two aspects.

In this paper, we propose a new operator upon rectangular Young tableaux, called *straight roll-and-sort* (abbr. `Sros`), and prove its well-definedness in bracket algebra. This operator involves much fewer straight bracket monomials than in Rota's algorithm, and is easier to implement than Capelli operator. We further disclose the connection of this operator with Capelli operator. Then we come up with an algorithm to straighten bracket polynomials based on this operator.

We test the four straightening algorithms: Young's, White's, Rota's, and ours, with over 500 examples in the past two years. The tests show that `Sros` outperforms the other three algorithms by achieving a speedup of one to three order of magnitude.

2 TABLEAU RING AND ROLL-AND-DIVE OPERATOR

Let A be a finite alphabet of letters. A *tableau* (shorthand of *rectangular Young tableau*) [8] of *dimension n and degree d* refers to a $d \times n$ array of letters in A. All the entries of a tableau T form a multiset, called the *content* of the tableau. In this paper we always fix the dimension n. We assume that an order exists among the letters of alphabet A.

For example, we always assume $\mathbf{a}_1 \prec \mathbf{a}_2 \prec \ldots \prec \mathbf{a}_m$. Tableau $\begin{matrix} \mathbf{a}_1 & \mathbf{a}_4 & \mathbf{a}_5 \\ \mathbf{a}_2 & \mathbf{a}_3 & \mathbf{a}_4 \end{matrix}$ has dimension 3 and degree 2; its content is $\mathbf{a}_1, \mathbf{a}_2, \mathbf{a}_3, \mathbf{a}_4^{(2)}, \mathbf{a}_5$, where $\mathbf{a}_4^{(2)}$ denotes that letter $\mathbf{a}_4$ occurs twice in the tableau.

The *i-th row* (from left to right) and j-th column (from top to bottom) of a tableau have the same meaning as their matrix counterparts. The columns of a tableau T can be connected to form a single sequence of letters, called the *column sequence* of the tableau, denoted by $col(T)$.

The reason why we distinguish tableau from matrix is that they have different multiplications. Two tableaux of the same dimension can be multiplied together: by putting the first tableau on top of the second one, so that their columns are connected one by one, a larger tableau is formed, called the *product* of two tableaux.

By introducing an abstract zero tableau, all tableaux of the same dimension n generate an associative ring, called the *tableau ring* with dimension n. As a $\mathbb{Z}$-module the tableau ring is free. A general element of the tableau ring is called a *tableau polynomial*. A tableau polynomial is said to be *homogeneous* if every term has the same content. In other words, in a homogeneous tableau/bracket polynomial, every letter occurs the same number of times in different terms. As straightening a bracket polynomial is equivalent to straightening its different homogeneous groups of terms, in this paper all bracket polynomials under consideration are homogeneous.

An order among letters induces many different orders among tableaux. The following order, called the *negative column order*, is a total order among tableaux, and is the only order we use throughout this paper. For two tableaux T_1, T_2 of degree d_1, d_2 respectively, $T_1 \succ T_2$ if and only if either $d_1 > d_2$, or $d_1 = d_2$ but $col(T_1)$ has **lower** lexicographical order than $col(T_2)$.

A tableau is said to be *straight* if along every row the letters are increasing, and along every column the letters are non-decreasing. A *straight tableau polynomial* is a $\mathbb{Z}$-linear combination of straight tableaux. The $\mathbb{Z}$-module of all straight tableau polynomials is denoted by $STAB$. All tableaux of degree d and dimension n span another $\mathbb{Z}$-module, denoted by $TAB_{d\times n}$.

Upon $TAB_{d\times n}$ the Cartesian product of d symmetric groups of n letters, denoted by $(S_n)^d$, acts in the following way: for i from 1 to d, the i-th factor group S_n acts on the i-th row of a tableau. This action, called the *row action*, is denoted as a left action. Similarly, the Cartesian product of n symmetric groups of d letters, denoted by $(S_d)^n$, acts on $TAB_{d\times n}$ in the following way: for i from 1 to n, the i-th factor group S_d acts on the i-th column of a tableau. This action, called the *column action*, is denoted as a right action.

The *row-column action* by the two groups $(S_n)^d$ and $(S_d)^n$ upon a tableau T is defined as follows: given elements $\sigma \in (S_n)^d$ and $\tau \in (S_d)^n$, first σ acts on T from the left as the row action, then τ acts on σT from the right as the column action; the action is denoted by $(\sigma T)\tau$. Notice that in [6], this action is written as $\sigma \leftrightarrow T \updownarrow \tau$; in [7], this action is written as ${}^{\tau}({}^{\sigma}T)$. It is not a group action.

Two linear operations upon tableau polynomials:

- *Column-wise sorting*: Given a tableau T of degree d, if within each column we permute its d entries to get a non-decreasing sequence, then we get a new tableau composed of n non-increasing sequences. The operation is called the *column-wise sorting* of T, denoted by $T^{\downarrow\downarrow}$. It is a column action.
- *Lex-column sorting*: Given a tableau T of degree d, when the n columns are permuted according to the lexicographical order among length-n sequences, we get a non-descending sequence of the n columns, which forms a new tableau. The operation is called the *lex-column sorting* of T, denoted by ${}^{\rightarrow}T$. It is a row action.

The following linear operator upon $\mathbb{Z}$-module $TAB_{d\times n}$ is called the *roll-and-sort operator*, denoted by Ros_d: for any tableau T of degree d,

$$Ros_d(T) := \sum_{\sigma\in(S_n)^d} \operatorname{sign}(\sigma)\,(\sigma T)^{\downarrow\downarrow}, \tag{2.1}$$

where for $\sigma = (\sigma_1, \ldots, \sigma_d) \in (S_n)^d$, $\operatorname{sign}(\sigma) = \operatorname{sign}(\sigma_1) \times \cdots \times \operatorname{sign}(\sigma_d)$. The operator "*Ros*" can be extended to the whole tableau ring as following: any tableau polynomial can be written as $\sum_i f_i$, where $f_i \in TAB_{i\times n}$; then

$$Ros(\sum_i f_i) := \sum_i Ros_i(f_i).$$

The *straight roll-and-sort operator*, denoted by "*Sros*", is a linear map from the tableau ring to $STAB$, the set of straight tableau polynomials: for any tableau polynomial f,

$$Sros(f) := Ros(f)\,|_{STAB}, \quad \text{i.e., throwing away all terms not lying in } STAB. \tag{2.2}$$

For example, for $T = \begin{matrix} \mathbf{a}_1 & \mathbf{a}_3 & \mathbf{a}_5 \\ \mathbf{a}_2 & \mathbf{a}_4 & \mathbf{a}_6 \end{matrix}$, we have

$$Sros(T) = \begin{matrix} \mathbf{a}_1 & \mathbf{a}_3 & \mathbf{a}_5 \\ \mathbf{a}_2 & \mathbf{a}_4 & \mathbf{a}_6 \end{matrix} + \begin{matrix} \mathbf{a}_1 & \mathbf{a}_2 & \mathbf{a}_3 \\ \mathbf{a}_4 & \mathbf{a}_5 & \mathbf{a}_6 \end{matrix}.$$

For a tableau T of degree d, computing $Sros(T)$ directly by definition (2.1) is inefficient. The following conclusion, which is easy to derive by the definition of straight tableau, provides a better formula to compute $Sros(T)$.

PROPOSITION 2.1. For any tableau T of degree d,

$$Sros(T) = \sum_{\sigma=(\mathrm{id},\sigma_2,\sigma_3,\ldots,\sigma_d)\in(S_n)^d} \operatorname{sign}(\sigma)\operatorname{sign}(\tau)^d \; {}^{\rightarrow}((\sigma T)^{\downarrow\downarrow})|_{STAB}, \tag{2.3}$$

where "id" is the identity of S_n, and $\tau \in S_n$ is the column permutation changing $(\sigma T)^{\downarrow\downarrow}$ into ${}^{\rightarrow}((\sigma T)^{\downarrow\downarrow})$.

3 BRACKET RING AND STRAIGHTENING

Define a two-sided ideal $\mathcal{I}$ of the tableau ring generated by the tableau polynomials in the following equalities:

Comm: For any tableau T, if $T\tau_{1,2}$ is the tableau obtained from T by switching the first row and the second row, then $T - T\tau_{1,2} = 0$.

Asym: For any tableau R of degree 1, if $\sigma_{i,j}R$ is obtained from R by switching the two letters of position i and j respectively, then $R + \sigma_{i,j}R = 0$; in particular, if the two letters are identical, then $R = 0$.

GP: For any pairwise different letters $\mathbf{a}_1, \mathbf{a}_2, \ldots, \mathbf{a}_{n-1}$, and another pairwise different letters $\mathbf{b}_1, \mathbf{b}_2, \ldots, \mathbf{b}_{n+1}$ of A,

$$\sum_{k=1}^{n+1}(-1)^{k-1} \begin{matrix} \mathbf{a}_1 & \mathbf{a}_2 & \ldots & \mathbf{a}_{n-1} & \mathbf{b}_k \\ \mathbf{b}_1 & \ldots & \check{\mathbf{b}}_k & \ldots & \mathbf{b}_{n+1} \end{matrix} = 0, \quad (3.1)$$

where $\check{\mathbf{b}}_k$ denotes that $\mathbf{b}_k$ does not occur in the row.

The quotient of the tableau ring by ideal $\mathcal{I}$ is called the *bracket ring* of dimension n. The equivalence class of a tableau modulo $\mathcal{I}$ is called a *bracket monomial*, and the equivalence class of a tableau of degree 1 is called a *bracket*. A general element of the bracket ring is called a *bracket polynomial*. The bracket ring is commutative.

The canonical projection from the tableau ring to the bracket ring is denoted by a pair of brackets "[ ]", called the *bracket operator*. In classical invariant theory, a bracket is the determinant of n vectors; in our notation, the n vectors are denoted by the n letters in the bracket. A bracket is usually written as $[T]$, where T is a tableau. The bracket in this form is said to have T as its *tableau form*. The *tableau polynomial form* of a bracket polynomial is defined similarly.

A tableau of degree d is said to be *pre-normal*, if along each row the entries are increasing in order, and the d rows are non-decreasing in the lexicographical order among length-n sequences. Any bracket polynomial can be changed into a unique pre-normal tableau form, called the *pre-normal form*.

The pre-normal form of a tableau can be obtained as follows: first sort the letters in each row by relation **Asym**, then permute the rows non-decreasingly by relation **Comm**.

A bracket polynomial is said to be *straight* if so is its tableau form. The first main theorem of classical invariant theory [14] states that the $\mathbb{Z}$-module of straight bracket polynomials is free, and for any bracket polynomial f, there is a unique straight tableau polynomial T such that $f = [T]$. T is called the *straight tableau form* of f, and the term *straightening* refers to a procedure of finding T from f.

In the literature there are three major straightening algorithms. A. Young [18] proposed to use the following *van der Waerden relations* for straightening: for any $0 \leq r < n$, let $s = n-1-r$, and let $P(n-r, n-s)$ be the set of partitions of the sequence $1, 2, \ldots, n+1$ into two subsequences of length $n-r$ and $n-s$ respectively, then for any three groups of letters $\mathbf{a}_1, \mathbf{a}_2, \ldots, \mathbf{a}_r$, and $\mathbf{b}_1, \mathbf{b}_2, \ldots, \mathbf{b}_{n+1}$, and $\mathbf{c}_1, \mathbf{c}_2, \ldots, \mathbf{c}_s$,

$$\sum_{\sigma \in P(n-r,n-s)} \operatorname{sign}(\sigma) \begin{bmatrix} \mathbf{a}_1 & \ldots & \mathbf{a}_r & \mathbf{b}_{\sigma(1)} & \ldots & \mathbf{b}_{\sigma(n-r)} \\ \mathbf{b}_{\sigma(s+2)} & \ldots & \mathbf{b}_{\sigma(n+1)} & \mathbf{c}_1 & \ldots & \mathbf{c}_s \end{bmatrix} = 0. \quad (3.2)$$

N. White [17] proposed to use the following *multiple relations* for straightening besides the van der Waerden relations: for any $0 < r < n$, let $s = n - r$, and let $P(n-r, n-s)$ be the set of partitions of the sequence $1, 2, \ldots, n$ into two subsequences of length $n-r$ and $n-s$ respectively, then for any three groups of letters $\mathbf{a}_1, \mathbf{a}_2, \ldots, \mathbf{a}_r$, and $\mathbf{b}_1, \mathbf{b}_2, \ldots, \mathbf{b}_n$, and $\mathbf{c}_1, \mathbf{c}_2, \ldots, \mathbf{c}_s$,

$$\sum_{\sigma \in P(n-r,n-s)} \operatorname{sign}(\sigma) \begin{bmatrix} \mathbf{a}_1 & \ldots & \mathbf{a}_r & \mathbf{b}_{\sigma(1)} & \ldots & \mathbf{b}_{\sigma(n-r)} \\ \mathbf{b}_{\sigma(s+1)} & \ldots & \mathbf{b}_{\sigma(n)} & \mathbf{c}_1 & \ldots & \mathbf{c}_s \end{bmatrix} = \begin{bmatrix} \mathbf{a}_1 & \ldots & \mathbf{a}_r & \mathbf{c}_1 & \ldots & \mathbf{c}_s \\ \mathbf{b}_1 & \ldots & \mathbf{b}_r & \mathbf{b}_{r+1} & \ldots & \mathbf{b}_n \end{bmatrix}.$$

G.-C. Rota [5] proposed to use the *Capelli operator* for straightening. To introduce this operator we need the following *polarization operator* of a letter $\mathbf{a}$ by letter $\mathbf{d}$: for any tableau T whose every row contains at most one copy of letter $\mathbf{a}$, let d be the degree of T, then

$$D_{\mathbf{d},\mathbf{a}}T := \sum_{i=1}^{d} (T \text{ after replacing } \mathbf{a} \text{ by } \mathbf{d} \text{ in row } i). \quad (3.3)$$

For any $l \geq 0$, the *l-th order polarization operator* of letter $\mathbf{a}$ by letter $\mathbf{d}$, denoted by $D^l_{\mathbf{d},\mathbf{a}}$, is

$$D^l_{\mathbf{d},\mathbf{a}}T := \begin{cases} T, & \text{if } l = 0; \\ D_{\mathbf{d},\mathbf{a}}(D^{l-1}_{\mathbf{d},\mathbf{a}}T), & \text{if } l > 0. \end{cases}$$

It is easy to see that when $D^l_{\mathbf{d},\mathbf{a}}$ acts on a tableau, the result is the sum of all possible replacements of letter $\mathbf{a}$ at l different positions in the tableau by letter $\mathbf{d}$.

Let T be a tableau whose letters are $\mathbf{a}_i \in A$, where $i = 1, \ldots, m$. For any $i = 1, \ldots, m$, any $j = 1, \ldots, n$, let α_{ij} be the multiplicity of letter $\mathbf{a}_i$ in the j-th column of T. Let $\mathbf{u}_1, \mathbf{u}_2, \ldots, \mathbf{u}_n$ be n letters in another alphabet U. The following linear map from the tableau ring with alphabet A to the tableau ring with alphabet $A \cup U$ is called the *Capelli operator* [3] associated with T, denoted by C_T:

$$C_T := \text{composition of } D^{\alpha_{ij}}_{\mathbf{u}_j,\mathbf{a}_i} \text{ for all } 1 \leq i \leq m,\ 1 \leq j \leq n. \quad (3.4)$$

Lemma 3.1. [2], [5] Let $S \succ T$ be two tableaux of the same content, then $C_S S \neq 0$ but $C_S T = 0$.

Given a tableau T, there are finitely many straight tableaux having the same content with it; assume that $S_1, S_2, \ldots, S_t$ are all these straight tableaux. By the first main theorem of classical invariant theory,

$$[T] = \sum_{i=1}^{t} \lambda_i [S_i], \quad \text{for some } \lambda_i \in \mathbb{Z}. \quad (3.5)$$

For $i = 1, \ldots, t$, when C_{S_i} acts on the two sides of (3.5), a linear equation in the λ's is obtained. There are t such equations in t unknowns. By Lemma 3.1, the coefficient matrix of the linear system is triangular and nondegenerate. Solving the linear system, one gets the straight tableau form of $[T]$. This is Rota's straightening algorithm.

4 STRAIGHT ROLL-AND-SORT OPERATOR FOR BRACKET RING

A tableau is said to have *multilinear multiplicity*, or to be *multilinear*, if all its entries have multiplicity 1, *i.e.*, each letter in the tableau occurs only once. If a tableau does not have multilinear multiplicity, it can be polarized to a linear combination of multilinear tableaux. This is done as follows.

Given a tableau T whose content is $\{\mathbf{b}_i^{(m_i)} \mid i = 1, \ldots, N\}$, where $\mathbf{b}_1 \prec \mathbf{b}_2 \prec \ldots \prec \mathbf{b}_N$, and for $i = 1, \ldots, N$, $m_i > 0$ is the multiplicity of $\mathbf{b}_i \in A$. Introduce an alphabet V containing the following new letters, together with the *induced order* among them:

$$\begin{array}{ccccccccc} \mathbf{v}_{1,1} & \prec & \mathbf{v}_{1,2} & \prec & \cdots & \prec & \mathbf{v}_{1,m_1} & \prec \\ \mathbf{v}_{2,1} & \prec & \mathbf{v}_{2,2} & \prec & \cdots & \prec & \mathbf{v}_{2,m_2} & \prec \\ \vdots & & \vdots & & \ddots & & \vdots & \prec \\ \mathbf{v}_{N,1} & \prec & \mathbf{v}_{N,2} & \prec & \cdots & \prec & \mathbf{v}_{N,m_N}. & \end{array} \tag{4.1}$$

The *multilinear polarization operator* is

$$Pol := \text{composition of } D_{\mathbf{v}_{i,j},\mathbf{b}_i} \text{ for all } i = 1..N,\ j = 1..m_i. \tag{4.2}$$

The following conclusion is obvious by the definitions of *Ros* and *Pol*.

LEMMA 4.1. *Let T be a tableau of degree d, whose different letters are $\mathbf{b}_1 \prec \mathbf{b}_2 \prec \ldots \prec \mathbf{b}_N$. For the letters $\mathbf{v}_{i,j}$ with order (4.1), let $Eval_{\mathbf{v},\mathbf{b}}$ be the evaluation changing $\mathbf{v}_{i,j}$ into $\mathbf{b}_i$ for $i = 1, \ldots, N$. Set $M := m_1!m_2! \cdots m_N!$. Then*

$$Eval_{\mathbf{v},\mathbf{b}}(Ros(Pol(T))) = M \times Ros(T). \tag{4.3}$$

THEOREM 4.2. *If f_1, f_2 are two homogeneous tableau polynomials and $[f_1] = [f_2]$, then $Ros(f_1) = Ros(f_2)$.*

Proof. By the definition (2.1) of roll-and-sort operator, the proofs of the following results are trivial:

- If T is a tableau, and $T\tau_{i,j}$ is the result of switching the i-th row and the j-th row, then $Ros(T\tau_{i,j}) = Ros(T)$.
- If $\sigma_i T$ is the result of acting $\sigma_i \in S_n$ upon the i-th row of T, then $Ros(\sigma_i T) = \text{sign}(\sigma_i) Ros(T)$.

Then the theorem is proved if for any tableau T of degree d, any letters $\mathbf{a}_1, \ldots, \mathbf{a}_{n-1}$ and $\mathbf{b}_1, \ldots, \mathbf{b}_{n+1}$,

$$\sum_{k=1}^{n+1} (-1)^{k-1} Ros(Y_k T) = 0, \tag{4.4}$$

where $Y_k = \begin{array}{ccccc} \mathbf{a}_1 & \ldots & \ldots & \mathbf{a}_{n-1} & \mathbf{b}_k \\ \mathbf{b}_1 & \ldots & \check{\mathbf{b}}_k & \ldots & \mathbf{b}_{n+1} \end{array}$.

First assume that $Y_1 T$ is multilinear. Suppose ϵZ is a term of (4.4), where ϵ is the coefficient. Then there is only one column of Z having two letters of the $\mathbf{b}$'s, all other columns have one letter $\mathbf{a}_i$ and one letter $\mathbf{b}_j$. Suppose the two letters are $\mathbf{b}_u, \mathbf{b}_v$, where $u < v$. By definition (2.1), Z can only be obtained from $Ros(Y_u T)$ or $Ros(Y_v T)$.

If Z is from $Ros(Y_u T)$, say

$$\begin{aligned} \epsilon Z &= (-1)^{u-1} \text{sign}(\sigma_1)\text{sign}(\sigma_2) \cdots \text{sign}(\sigma_{d+2}) \\ &\quad \Big(((\sigma_1, \sigma_2) Y_u)((\sigma_3, \ldots, \sigma_{d+2})T) \Big)^{\downarrow\downarrow}, \end{aligned}$$

where the $\sigma_i \in S_n$, then

- set $\mathbf{A}$ to be the sequence $\mathbf{a}_1 \ldots \mathbf{a}_{n-1}$ of $n-1$ letters;
- set $\mathbf{B}$ to be the sequence $\mathbf{b}_1 \ldots \check{\mathbf{b}}_u \ldots \check{\mathbf{b}}_v \ldots \mathbf{b}_{n+1}$ of $n-1$ letters;
- set $\beta_{2v} \in S_n$ to be the permutation in the second row changing $(\mathbf{B}\ \mathbf{b}_v)$ to the second row of Y_u;
- set $\beta_{2u} \in S_n$ to be the permutation in the second row changing the second row of Y_v to $(\mathbf{B}\ \mathbf{b}_u)$.

We have

$$\begin{aligned} \epsilon Z &= (-1)^{u-1} \text{sign}(\sigma_1)\text{sign}(\sigma_2) \cdots \text{sign}(\sigma_{d+2}) \\ &\quad \Big(((\sigma_1, \sigma_2\beta_{2v}) \begin{array}{cc} \mathbf{A} & \mathbf{b}_u \\ \mathbf{B} & \mathbf{b}_v \end{array})((\sigma_3, \ldots, \sigma_{d+2})T) \Big)^{\downarrow\downarrow} \\ &= (-1)^{u-1} \text{sign}(\sigma_1)\text{sign}(\sigma_2) \cdots \text{sign}(\sigma_{d+2}) \\ &\quad \Big(((\sigma_1, \sigma_2\beta_{2v}) \begin{array}{cc} \mathbf{A} & \mathbf{b}_v \\ \mathbf{B} & \mathbf{b}_u \end{array})((\sigma_3, \ldots, \sigma_{d+2})T) \Big)^{\downarrow\downarrow} \\ &= (-1)^{u-1} \text{sign}(\sigma_1)\text{sign}(\sigma_2) \cdots \text{sign}(\sigma_{d+2}) \\ &\quad \Big(((\sigma_1, \sigma_2\beta_{2v}\beta_{2u}) Y_v((\sigma_3, \ldots, \sigma_{d+2})T) \Big)^{\downarrow\downarrow}. \end{aligned}$$

Since

$$\begin{aligned} \epsilon' Z' = (-1)^{v-1} &\text{sign}(\sigma_1)\text{sign}(\sigma_2\beta_{2v}\beta_{2u})\text{sign}(\sigma_3) \cdots \text{sign}(\sigma_{d+2}) \\ &\Big(((\sigma_1, \sigma_2\beta_{2v}\beta_{2u}) Y_v((\sigma_3, \ldots, \sigma_{d+2})T) \Big)^{\downarrow\downarrow} \end{aligned}$$

is a term of $Ros(Y_v T)$, by $\text{sign}(\beta_{2v})\text{sign}(\beta_{2u}) = (-1)^{u+v}$, we get $\epsilon' Z' = -\epsilon Z$. So ϵZ is canceled by a term from $Ros(Y_v T)$.

Similarly, if ϵZ is from $Ros(Y_v T)$, it is canceled by a term from $Ros(Y_u T)$. Now that the terms on the left side of (4.4) cancel pairwise, (4.4) holds in the multilinear case.

In the general case, we have $\sum_{k=1}^{n+1} (-1)^{k-1} Ros(Pol(Y_k T)) = 0$. By Lemma 4.1, applying the $Eval_{\mathbf{v},\mathbf{b}}$ operator to the equality leads to $\sum_{k=1}^{n+1} (-1)^{k-1} Ros(Y_k T) = 0$. □

COROLLARY 4.3. *Ros and Sros are both linear maps from the bracket ring to the tableau ring.*

LEMMA 4.4. [13] *Let T be a tableau in pre-normal form, then $T^{\downarrow\downarrow}$ is straight, and is the leading term of the straight tableau form of $[T]$.*

LEMMA 4.5. *For any two columns C_1, C_2 of degree d, if there is a 1-to-1 correspondence between their entries, such that any entry of $C_1 \preceq$ the counterpart of C_2, and at least one entry of $C_1 \prec$ its counterpart of C_2, then $C_1^{\downarrow\downarrow} \succ C_2^{\downarrow\downarrow}$.*

THEOREM 4.6. *Let T be a tableau in pre-normal form, then in both $Ros(T)$ and $Sros(T)$, the leading term is $T^{\downarrow\downarrow}$.*

Proof. Obviously $T^{\downarrow\downarrow}$ is a term of T. By Lemma 4.4, we only need to prove the statement for $Ros(T)$. For simplicity, we only assume that the letters in each row of T are increasing in order, but **do not assume** that the letters in the first column of T are non-decreasing in order.

For any tableau C of dimension 1, *i.e.*, a column, obviously $C^{\downarrow\downarrow}$ has the maximal negative column order among all the permutations of the letters in the column.

Suppose $Y = \text{sign}(\sigma)(\sigma T)^{\downarrow\downarrow}$ is a term of $Ros(T)$, and $Y \succeq T^{\downarrow\downarrow}$. Let the first column of T be L_T, and let the first column of Y be L_Y. Then by Lemma 4.5, $L_T^{\downarrow\downarrow} \succeq L_Y^{\downarrow\downarrow}$, and the equality holds if and only if $L_T = L_Y$. As $Y \succeq T^{\downarrow\downarrow}$, it must be that $L_T^{\downarrow\downarrow}$ is the first column of Y. So σ fixes the first column of T.

Removing the first columns from both Y and T, we get two tableaux Y' and T' of dimension $n-1$, such that $Y = \text{sign}(\sigma')(\sigma' T')^{\downarrow\downarrow}$ for some $\sigma' \in (S_{n-1})^d$, and the letters in each row of T' are increasing in order, and $Y' \succeq T'^{\downarrow\downarrow}$. By induction on n, it can be proved that $Y = T^{\downarrow\downarrow}$, and σ is the identity of $(S_n)^d$. Hence $T^{\downarrow\downarrow}$ is the leading term of $Ros(T)$; it has no like term on the right side of (2.1). □

Corollary 4.7. Let f be a homogeneous bracket polynomial in pre-normal form, then $Sros(f)$ and the straight tableau form of f have the same leading term.

Proof. Let F be the tableau form of f, and let the straight form of F be $\sum_i \lambda_i T_i$, where the $\lambda_i \in \mathbb{Z}$, the T_i are straight and are pairwise different, and T_1 is the leading tableau among the T_i. Since $[\sum_i \lambda_i T_i] = [F]$, by Theorem 4.2, $Sros(f) = Sros(F) = \sum_i \lambda_i Sros(T_i)$.

By Theorem 4.6, the leading term of $Sros(T_i)$ is $T_i^{\downarrow\downarrow} = T_i$. So T_1 is the unique leading tableau among the tableaux of $Sros(T_i)$. Then $\lambda_1 T_1$ is the leading term of both $Sros(f)$ and $\sum_i \lambda_i T_i$. □

Algorithm 1 "Sros": straightening homogeneous bracket polynomial by successive straight roll-and-sort operations

Input: A homogeneous tableau polynomial F
Output: The straight tableau form of $[F]$

1: Replace F by its pre-normal form.
   If F is straight then return F and exit.
2: Set $g :=$ leading term of $F^{\downarrow\downarrow}$.
   If $g \prec T^{\downarrow\downarrow}$ for some term T of F, then set $g := 0$.
3: Compute $q := Sros(F - g)$ by formula (2.3).
4: While $q \neq 0$ do
      Set $h :=$ leading term of q.
      Set $g := g + h$.
      Set $q := q - Sros(h)$.
   End do.
5: **return** g.

Algorithm 1 is based on Corollary 4.7. For a bracket polynomial f, the algorithm first finds the leading term h_1 of the straight tableau form of f by computing $Sros(f)$, then finds the leading term h_2 of the straight tableau form of $f - h_1$ by computing $Sros(f) - Sros(h_1)$, and then repeats this procedure until for some s, $Sros(f) - Sros(h_1) - \cdots - Sros(h_s) = 0$. It returns $h_1 + \ldots + h_s$ as the straight tableau form of f.

Illustrative example. The input is $f = \left[\begin{array}{ccc} \mathbf{a}_1 & \mathbf{a}_4 & \mathbf{a}_6 \\ \mathbf{a}_2 & \mathbf{a}_3 & \mathbf{a}_5 \end{array}\right]$.

Round 1. $g = f^{\downarrow\downarrow} \neq f$, and

$$q = Sros(f - f^{\downarrow\downarrow}) = - \begin{array}{ccc} \mathbf{a}_1 & \mathbf{a}_2 & \mathbf{a}_5 \\ \mathbf{a}_3 & \mathbf{a}_4 & \mathbf{a}_6 \end{array} - \begin{array}{ccc} \mathbf{a}_1 & \mathbf{a}_2 & \mathbf{a}_3 \\ \mathbf{a}_4 & \mathbf{a}_5 & \mathbf{a}_6 \end{array}.$$

The leading term of q is $h_2 = - \begin{array}{ccc} \mathbf{a}_1 & \mathbf{a}_2 & \mathbf{a}_5 \\ \mathbf{a}_3 & \mathbf{a}_4 & \mathbf{a}_6 \end{array}$.

Round 2. $g = g + h_2$, and

$$q = q - Sros(h_2) = - \begin{array}{ccc} \mathbf{a}_1 & \mathbf{a}_2 & \mathbf{a}_3 \\ \mathbf{a}_4 & \mathbf{a}_5 & \mathbf{a}_6 \end{array} := h_3.$$

The leading term of q is h_3.

Round 3. $g = g + h_3$, and

$$q = q - Sros(h_3) = 0.$$

Return.

$$f = \left[\begin{array}{ccc} \mathbf{a}_1 & \mathbf{a}_3 & \mathbf{a}_5 \\ \mathbf{a}_2 & \mathbf{a}_4 & \mathbf{a}_6 \end{array}\right] - \left[\begin{array}{ccc} \mathbf{a}_1 & \mathbf{a}_2 & \mathbf{a}_5 \\ \mathbf{a}_3 & \mathbf{a}_4 & \mathbf{a}_6 \end{array}\right] - \left[\begin{array}{ccc} \mathbf{a}_1 & \mathbf{a}_2 & \mathbf{a}_3 \\ \mathbf{a}_4 & \mathbf{a}_5 & \mathbf{a}_6 \end{array}\right].$$

There are altogether 5 straight tableaux having the same content with the input f in the above example:

$$S_1 := \begin{array}{ccc} \mathbf{a}_1 & \mathbf{a}_3 & \mathbf{a}_5 \\ \mathbf{a}_2 & \mathbf{a}_4 & \mathbf{a}_6 \end{array}, \quad S_2 := \begin{array}{ccc} \mathbf{a}_1 & \mathbf{a}_3 & \mathbf{a}_4 \\ \mathbf{a}_2 & \mathbf{a}_5 & \mathbf{a}_6 \end{array}, \quad S_3 := \begin{array}{ccc} \mathbf{a}_1 & \mathbf{a}_2 & \mathbf{a}_5 \\ \mathbf{a}_3 & \mathbf{a}_4 & \mathbf{a}_6 \end{array},$$

$$S_4 := \begin{array}{ccc} \mathbf{a}_1 & \mathbf{a}_2 & \mathbf{a}_4 \\ \mathbf{a}_3 & \mathbf{a}_5 & \mathbf{a}_6 \end{array}, \quad S_5 := \begin{array}{ccc} \mathbf{a}_1 & \mathbf{a}_2 & \mathbf{a}_3 \\ \mathbf{a}_4 & \mathbf{a}_5 & \mathbf{a}_6 \end{array},$$

where $S_i \succ S_j$ for $i < j$.

In algorithm **Sros**, all together 3 straight tableaux are generated: S_2, S_4, S_5. In comparison, Rota's algorithm requires at least the following tableaux: S_2, S_3, S_4, S_5, as S_1 can be dismissed because $S_1 \succ f^{\downarrow\downarrow}$.

Ros and the Capelli operator are related as following, whose proofs have no space to present here.

Proposition 4.8. Let S be a tableau of degree d, and let f be a tableau polynomial whose tableaux all have the same content with S, then

- $[C_S f] = \lambda [I_d]$, where $\lambda \in \mathbb{Z}$, and I_d is the tableau of degree d whose every row is $\mathbf{u}_1\ \mathbf{u}_2 \ldots \mathbf{u}_n$. Denote $[C_S f]/[I_d] := \lambda$.
- λS is the sum of all the terms of the form μS in $Ros(f)$, where $\mu \in \mathbb{Z}$.

Corollary 4.9. Let T be a tableau of degree d. Let $S_1, S_2, \cdots, S_t$ be all the tableaux of the same content with T. Then

$$\begin{array}{rcl} Ros(T) & = & \displaystyle\sum_{i=1}^{t} \frac{[C_{S_i} T]}{[I_d]} S_i, \\ Sros(T) & = & \displaystyle\sum_{i=1}^{t} \frac{[C_{S_i} T]}{[I_d]} (S_i \mid_{STAB}). \end{array} \quad (4.5)$$

5 TESTS AND COMPARISON

We test the following straightening algorithms:

1. Young's algorithm (**Young**):
This algorithm reduces the *row sequence order* of the tableau polynomial at each step.

2. White's algorithm version C (**White**):

N. White [17] proposed five different versions of his straightening algorithm. By our tests, his algorithm C is the most efficient among the five, and is denoted by `White`.

3. Rota's algorithm (`Rota`):

Let $[F]$ be the input bracket monomial. The original version of Rota's algorithm consists of three stages:

- set up the set $STAB(F)$ of straight tableaux having the same content with F;
- for each $S_i \in STAB(F)$, act Capelli operator C_{S_i} upon F, and upon all $S_j \succeq S_i$ in $STAB(F)$; a linear triangular system is then generated;
- solve the linear system to get the normal form; in our implementation, the `ReducedRowEchelonForm` command of Maple is used.

`Rota+`: To improve the efficiency of `Rota`, we integrate the Capelli operations with the triangular system solving to get a new version of Rota's algorithm, denoted by `Rota+`.

4. `Sros` algorithm:

In Algorithm 1, computing *Sros* by (2.3) is still inefficient. We propose a recursive algorithm to compute *Sros*.

Assume that X and Y are two tableaux of the same degree. By putting X on the left side of Y and connecting their corresponding rows, a new tableau is obtained, called the *join* of X, Y, denoted by $X \mid Y$. The join operator can be extended by multilinearity and associativity to finitely many linear combinations of tableaux of the same degree.

Definition 5.1. Assume that X, Y are tableaux of degree d, where X is straight, and the connent of Y is $\{\mathbf{v}_1^{(\alpha_1)}, \mathbf{v}_2^{(\alpha_2)}, \cdots, \mathbf{v}_m^{(\alpha_m)}\}$, where α_i is the multiplicity of letter $\mathbf{v}_i$, and $\mathbf{v}_1 \prec \mathbf{v}_2 \prec \cdots \prec \mathbf{v}_m$. Let the dimension of Y be n.

Let $C = (\mathbf{v}_{i_1}, \mathbf{v}_{i_2}, \ldots, \mathbf{v}_{i_d})^T$, where for $1 \le h \le d$, $\mathbf{v}_{i_h}$ is the (p_h, q_h) entry of Y with the following properties:

(1) the p_h are pairwise different;

(2) $i_1 \le i_2 \le \ldots \le i_d$;

(3) $\mathbf{v}_{i_h} \succ$ the last entry of row h of X, for all $1 \le h \le d$;

(4) denote the entries of C with multiplicity by $\mathbf{v}_{j_1}^{(\gamma_1)}, \mathbf{v}_{j_2}^{(\gamma_2)}, \ldots, \mathbf{v}_{j_k}^{(\gamma_k)}$, such that $j_1 < j_2 < \ldots < j_k$ and $\gamma_1 + \gamma_2 + \cdots + \gamma_k = d$, then $j_1 = i_1 = \ldots = i_{\alpha_1} = 1$ and $\gamma_1 = \alpha_1$;

(5) for any $1 < s \le k$, for any $j_{s-1} < t \le m$, let X_{-1} be the last row of X, set $L(t) :=$ row number of the first entry of X_{-1} that is $\succeq \mathbf{v}_t$, and if all entries of X_{-1} are $\prec \mathbf{v}_t$, set $L(t) := d+1$;
if $t < j_s$, then $\alpha_t \le \gamma_1 + \gamma_2 + \cdots + \gamma_{s-1}$; if $t = j_s$, then

$$\begin{aligned} &\max(1, \alpha_t - (\gamma_1 + \gamma_2 + \cdots + \gamma_{s-1})) \\ \le\ & \gamma_s \\ \le\ & \min(\alpha_t, L(t) - 1 - (\gamma_1 + \gamma_2 + \cdots + \gamma_{s-1})); \end{aligned}$$

(6) for any $1 < s \le k$,
$\alpha_1 + \alpha_2 + \cdots + \alpha_{j_s} \le n(\gamma_1 + \gamma_2 + \cdots + \gamma_{s-1}) + \gamma_s$;

(7) $m - j_s \ge n$ for any $1 < s < k$, while $m - j_k \ge n - 1$.

The set of C's with the above properties is denoted by $Fcol(X \mid Y)$, called the *first-column candidates* of Y in $X \mid Sros(Y)$. The *column sign* of C is defined as

$$sign(C) = (-1)^{\sum_{j=1}^{d}(q_j - 1)}. \tag{5.1}$$

Lemma 5.2. Assume that X, Y are tableaux of the same degree. Further assume that $Sros(X \mid Y) = \sum_l \lambda_l X \mid T_l$, where $\lambda_l \in \mathbb{Z}$, and $X \mid T_l$ is straight. If C_l is the first column of T_l, then $C_l \in Fcol(X \mid Y)$.

Proof. Let d be the degree of both X and Y, and let n be the dimension of Y. Let the content of Y be $\{\mathbf{v}_1^{(\alpha_1)}, \mathbf{v}_2^{(\alpha_2)}, \cdots, \mathbf{v}_m^{(\alpha_m)}\}$, where $\mathbf{v}_1 \prec \mathbf{v}_2 \prec \cdots \prec \mathbf{v}_m$. Let $C_l = (\mathbf{v}_{i_1}, \ldots, \mathbf{v}_{i_d})^T$, where for $1 \le h \le d$, $\mathbf{v}_{i_h}$ is the (p_h, q_h) entry of Y. Denote the entries of C_l with multiplicity by $\mathbf{v}_{j_1}^{(\gamma_1)}, \mathbf{v}_{j_2}^{(\gamma_2)}, \ldots, \mathbf{v}_{j_k}^{(\gamma_k)}$, such that $j_1 < j_2 < \ldots < j_k$ and $\gamma_1 + \gamma_2 + \cdots + \gamma_k = d$. There exists a straight tableau D_l such that $X \mid C_l \mid D_l$ is straight and is a term of $Sros(X \mid Y)$. Below we verify that C_l satisfies (1) – (7) of Definition 5.1.

(1) By the definition of *Sros*, no two entries in the same row of $X \mid Y$ can lie in the same column of $X \mid C_l \mid D_l$, so the p_h are pairwise different.

(2) and (3) are obvious by the straightness of $X \mid C_l$.

(4) Since letter $\mathbf{v}_1$ has the smallest order in Y, it can only occur in the first column of straight tableau $C_k \mid D_k$, so $j_1 = i_1 = \ldots = i_{\alpha_1} = 1$ and $\gamma_1 = \alpha_1$.

(5) For any $1 < s \le k$, denote

$$\beta := \gamma_1 + \gamma_2 + \cdots + \gamma_{s-1}.$$

Then the first β rows of C_l are occupied by letters $\preceq \mathbf{v}_{j_{s-1}}$. For any $j_{s-1} < t < j_s$, letter $\mathbf{v}_t$ does not occur in C_l, so all copies of $\mathbf{v}_t$ of Y must occur in the first β rows of D_l, and $\alpha_t \le \beta$ follows.

For the multiplicity γ_s of $\mathbf{v}_{j_s}$ in C_l, let its lower bound and upper bound be $\min_s$ and $\max_s$ respectively. Then $\min_s = 1$ is realized when $\alpha_{j_s} - 1$ copies of $\mathbf{v}_{j_s}$ of Y are in the first β rows of D_l, *i.e.*, when $\alpha_{j_s} - \beta \le 1$; $\min_s = \alpha_{j_s} - \beta > 0$ is realized when the first β rows of D_l each occupy a copy of $\mathbf{v}_{j_s}$, *i.e.*, when $\alpha_{j_s} - \beta > 0$. Hence $\gamma_s \ge \max(1, \alpha_{j_s} - \beta)$.

By the definition of $L(j_s)$, only in the first $L(j_s) - 1$ rows of X is every entry $\prec \mathbf{v}_{j_s}$. So in C_l, letter $\mathbf{v}_{j_s}$ can occur only in the region from row $\beta + 1$ to row $L(j_s) - 1$. Then $\max_s = L(j_s) - 1 - \beta$ is realized when $\alpha_{j_s} \ge L(j_s) - 1 - \beta$ and the region of C_l from row $\beta + 1$ to row $L(j_s) - 1$ is occupied by copies of $\mathbf{v}_{j_s}$.

(6) Denote $\delta := \alpha_1 + \alpha_2 + \cdots + \alpha_{j_s}$. It is the number of entries of Y that are $\preceq \mathbf{v}_{j_s}$. In $C_l \mid D_l$, these entries must lie in the union of two regions: the region of C_l from row 1 to row $\beta + \gamma_s$, and the region of D_l from row 1 to row β. The number of positions of the two regions is $n\beta + \gamma_s$. So $\delta \le n\beta + \gamma_s$.

(7) The number of different letters in Y that are $\succ \mathbf{v}_{j_s}$ is $m - j_s$. When $s = k$, then in row d of D_l there are $n - 1$ different letters $\succ \mathbf{v}_{j_s}$; when $s < k$, then in row d of $C_l \mid D_l$ there are n different letters $\succ \mathbf{v}_{j_s}$. So $m - j_s \ge n$ for any $1 < s < k$, and $m - j_k \ge n - 1$. □

In implementing $Fcol(X \mid Y)$, the entries of each column $C \in Fcol(X \mid Y)$ are constructed one by one. If we use the same symbol C to denote the unfinished column at an instance of the construction, then each time an entry of Y that is not in C is tested to meet all the seven requirements in Definition 5.1 successfully, C gets a prolongation by attaching the entry to it. C can have more than one possible prolongation at an instance, so the construction of $Fcol(X \mid Y)$ is a bifurcation procedure. The seven requirements in Definition 5.1 provide tight control of the bifurcation.

Based on Definition 5.1 and Lemma 5.2, the following conclusion can be derived:

THEOREM 5.3. Let Y be a tableau. For any set of entries D of Y, let $Y \backslash D$ denote the pre-normal form of the remainder of Y after deleting D and then compressing each row to the left. Then

$$Sros(Y) = \sum_{C \in Fcol(Y)} \mathrm{sign}(C)\; C \mid Sros(Y \backslash C). \qquad (5.2)$$

Algorithm 2 `RSros`: Recursively computing *Sros*

Input: A tableau Y of dimension n in pre-normal form.
Output: $Sros(Y)$

```
Set g := 0.
If n = 1, then set g := Y, else
    Compute Fcol(Y) = {C_i | 1 ≤ i ≤ h} by Def. 5.1.
    For i from 1 to h do
        Set D_i := C_i | RSros(Y\C_i).
        Set g := g + sign(C_i)D_i.
    End do.
End if.
return g.
```

We have tested the algorithms with over 500 examples. In these examples, the dimension n is 3 or 4, and the degree d ranges from 3 to 7. The algorithms are implemented in Maple 13 on Windows 7. The tests are run on a DELL workstation with specifications Intel(R) Xeon(R) CPU E5-2630v3 @ 2.40 GHz RAM @ 32 G.

Below we present 12 examples in the tests.

$$(1): \begin{bmatrix} \mathbf{a}_1 & \mathbf{a}_{10} & \mathbf{a}_{15} \\ \mathbf{a}_2 & \mathbf{a}_9 & \mathbf{a}_{14} \\ \mathbf{a}_3 & \mathbf{a}_8 & \mathbf{a}_{13} \\ \mathbf{a}_4 & \mathbf{a}_7 & \mathbf{a}_{12} \\ \mathbf{a}_5 & \mathbf{a}_6 & \mathbf{a}_{11} \end{bmatrix}, \quad (2): \begin{bmatrix} \mathbf{a}_1 & \mathbf{a}_6 & \mathbf{a}_{13} \\ \mathbf{a}_2 & \mathbf{a}_7 & \mathbf{a}_{15} \\ \mathbf{a}_3 & \mathbf{a}_8 & \mathbf{a}_{12} \\ \mathbf{a}_4 & \mathbf{a}_9 & \mathbf{a}_{14} \\ \mathbf{a}_5 & \mathbf{a}_{10} & \mathbf{a}_{11} \end{bmatrix},$$

$$(3): \begin{bmatrix} \mathbf{a}_1 & \mathbf{a}_{18} & \mathbf{a}_{19} & \mathbf{a}_{20} \\ \mathbf{a}_2 & \mathbf{a}_{15} & \mathbf{a}_{16} & \mathbf{a}_{17} \\ \mathbf{a}_3 & \mathbf{a}_{12} & \mathbf{a}_{13} & \mathbf{a}_{14} \\ \mathbf{a}_4 & \mathbf{a}_9 & \mathbf{a}_{10} & \mathbf{a}_{11} \\ \mathbf{a}_5 & \mathbf{a}_6 & \mathbf{a}_7 & \mathbf{a}_8 \end{bmatrix}, (4): \begin{bmatrix} \mathbf{a}_1 & \mathbf{a}_{18} & \mathbf{a}_{19} & \mathbf{a}_{20} \\ \mathbf{a}_2 & \mathbf{a}_{12} & \mathbf{a}_{14} & \mathbf{a}_{15} \\ \mathbf{a}_3 & \mathbf{a}_{10} & \mathbf{a}_{16} & \mathbf{a}_{17} \\ \mathbf{a}_4 & \mathbf{a}_8 & \mathbf{a}_{11} & \mathbf{a}_{13} \\ \mathbf{a}_5 & \mathbf{a}_6 & \mathbf{a}_7 & \mathbf{a}_9 \end{bmatrix},$$

$$(5): \begin{bmatrix} \mathbf{a}_1 & \mathbf{a}_{17} & \mathbf{a}_{18} \\ \mathbf{a}_2 & \mathbf{a}_{15} & \mathbf{a}_{16} \\ \mathbf{a}_3 & \mathbf{a}_{13} & \mathbf{a}_{14} \\ \mathbf{a}_4 & \mathbf{a}_{11} & \mathbf{a}_{12} \\ \mathbf{a}_5 & \mathbf{a}_9 & \mathbf{a}_{10} \\ \mathbf{a}_6 & \mathbf{a}_7 & \mathbf{a}_8 \end{bmatrix}, \quad (6): \begin{bmatrix} \mathbf{a}_1 & \mathbf{a}_{12} & \mathbf{a}_{18} \\ \mathbf{a}_2 & \mathbf{a}_{11} & \mathbf{a}_{17} \\ \mathbf{a}_3 & \mathbf{a}_{10} & \mathbf{a}_{16} \\ \mathbf{a}_4 & \mathbf{a}_9 & \mathbf{a}_{15} \\ \mathbf{a}_5 & \mathbf{a}_8 & \mathbf{a}_{14} \\ \mathbf{a}_6 & \mathbf{a}_7 & \mathbf{a}_{13} \end{bmatrix},$$

$$(7): \begin{bmatrix} \mathbf{a}_1 & \mathbf{a}_7 & \mathbf{a}_{10} \\ \mathbf{a}_1 & \mathbf{a}_6 & \mathbf{a}_9 \\ \mathbf{a}_1 & \mathbf{a}_5 & \mathbf{a}_8 \\ \mathbf{a}_2 & \mathbf{a}_5 & \mathbf{a}_8 \\ \mathbf{a}_2 & \mathbf{a}_4 & \mathbf{a}_7 \\ \mathbf{a}_3 & \mathbf{a}_4 & \mathbf{a}_7 \end{bmatrix}, \quad (8): \begin{bmatrix} \mathbf{a}_1 & \mathbf{a}_{11} & \mathbf{a}_{12} \\ \mathbf{a}_2 & \mathbf{a}_{10} & \mathbf{a}_{11} \\ \mathbf{a}_2 & \mathbf{a}_9 & \mathbf{a}_{10} \\ \mathbf{a}_3 & \mathbf{a}_8 & \mathbf{a}_9 \\ \mathbf{a}_4 & \mathbf{a}_7 & \mathbf{a}_8 \\ \mathbf{a}_5 & \mathbf{a}_6 & \mathbf{a}_7 \end{bmatrix},$$

$$(9): \begin{bmatrix} \mathbf{a}_1 & \mathbf{a}_{14} & \mathbf{a}_{15} \\ \mathbf{a}_1 & \mathbf{a}_{13} & \mathbf{a}_{14} \\ \mathbf{a}_2 & \mathbf{a}_{11} & \mathbf{a}_{12} \\ \mathbf{a}_2 & \mathbf{a}_{10} & \mathbf{a}_{11} \\ \mathbf{a}_3 & \mathbf{a}_9 & \mathbf{a}_{10} \\ \mathbf{a}_3 & \mathbf{a}_8 & \mathbf{a}_9 \\ \mathbf{a}_4 & \mathbf{a}_5 & \mathbf{a}_6 \end{bmatrix}, \quad (10): \begin{bmatrix} \mathbf{a}_1 & \mathbf{a}_{11} & \mathbf{a}_{12} \\ \mathbf{a}_2 & \mathbf{a}_{10} & \mathbf{a}_{11} \\ \mathbf{a}_2 & \mathbf{a}_9 & \mathbf{a}_{10} \\ \mathbf{a}_3 & \mathbf{a}_8 & \mathbf{a}_9 \\ \mathbf{a}_3 & \mathbf{a}_7 & \mathbf{a}_8 \\ \mathbf{a}_4 & \mathbf{a}_6 & \mathbf{a}_7 \\ \mathbf{a}_4 & \mathbf{a}_5 & \mathbf{a}_6 \end{bmatrix},$$

$$(11): \begin{bmatrix} \mathbf{a}_1 & \mathbf{a}_{14} & \mathbf{a}_{15} \\ \mathbf{a}_1 & \mathbf{a}_{13} & \mathbf{a}_{14} \\ \mathbf{a}_2 & \mathbf{a}_{11} & \mathbf{a}_{12} \\ \mathbf{a}_2 & \mathbf{a}_{10} & \mathbf{a}_{11} \\ \mathbf{a}_3 & \mathbf{a}_9 & \mathbf{a}_{10} \\ \mathbf{a}_3 & \mathbf{a}_6 & \mathbf{a}_8 \\ \mathbf{a}_4 & \mathbf{a}_5 & \mathbf{a}_7 \end{bmatrix}, \quad (12): \begin{bmatrix} \mathbf{a}_1 & \mathbf{a}_8 & \mathbf{a}_{11} \\ \mathbf{a}_1 & \mathbf{a}_9 & \mathbf{a}_{10} \\ \mathbf{a}_2 & \mathbf{a}_7 & \mathbf{a}_8 \\ \mathbf{a}_2 & \mathbf{a}_6 & \mathbf{a}_{10} \\ \mathbf{a}_3 & \mathbf{a}_5 & \mathbf{a}_9 \\ \mathbf{a}_3 & \mathbf{a}_4 & \mathbf{a}_7 \\ \mathbf{a}_4 & \mathbf{a}_5 & \mathbf{a}_6 \end{bmatrix}.$$

In the following, "–" indicates **failure**: either the test does not finish in 24 hours, or Maple returns "Memory allocation failed".

Table 1: Time (seconds) consumed in straightening

NO.	Young	White	Rota	Rota+	Sros
(1)	–	30240.57	43116.46	16070.75	13.07
(2)	–	35326.12	43095.52	13495.11	9.66
(3)	–	–	–	–	128.83
(4)	–	–	–	–	3798.29
(5)	–	64245.62	–	–	43.95
(6)	–	–	–	–	16417.88
(7)	35624.27	13712.12	8684.90	5721.24	38.13
(8)	39241.46	15328.91	28705.62	8245.29	49.51
(9)	–	56019.29	–	67958.13	3028.11
(10)	–	33261.75	–	23134.19	911.67
(11)	–	–	–	–	7824.91
(12)	–	–	70785.71	36726.39	8167.86

As in [17], we can use the *total number of steps* and the *total number of terms* to measure the complexity of an algorithm when straightening a bracket polynomial:

Table 2: Total number of steps

NO.	Young	White	Rota	Rota+	Sros
(1)	–	11020	18050489	1486066	1718
(2)	–	11581	18050489	982509	1396
(3)	–	–	–	–	3487
(4)	–	–	–	–	11338
(5)	–	19853	–	–	2037
(6)	–	–	–	–	26093
(7)	1682	935	306345	182041	77
(8)	18635	5173	7672345	472412	418
(9)	–	21566	–	403788272	1935
(10)	–	19886	–	89831247	1713
(11)	–	–	–	–	4111
(12)	–	–	46807984	20793721	4799

Total number of steps: Each step is either the generation of a sequence of tableaux from a tableau, or the clearance of a column by the diagonal entry of the column in a triangular matrix.

Total number of terms: Each step in a saved variable, the number of terms after the combination of like terms is taken down; the sum of the numbers of terms over all the variables and steps is the total number of terms.

Table 3: Total number of terms

NO.	Young	White	Rota	Rota+	Sros
(1)	–	24345233	260206664	2133228	856398
(2)	–	35537137	259821978	2023092	634952
(3)	–	–	–	–	4913519
(4)	–	–	–	–	50265949
(5)	–	42898729	–	–	1802416
(6)	–	–	–	–	220261416
(7)	8361222	2108691	13238968	71341	3637
(8)	92634585	12046158	40411868	116173	78849
(9)	–	49019189	–	23695787	1565798
(10)	–	44229315	–	9408518	1568021
(11)	–	–	–	–	6480851
(12)	–	–	934535234	17634525	9007292

The following data discloses one reason why `Rota` and `Rota+` are less efficient than `Sros`: the former two need a lot more straight tableaux than the latter one.

Table 4: Numbers of straight tableaux involved

NO.	Rota / Rota+	Sros	Final
(1)	6006	2384	1718
(2)	6006	2782	1396
(3)	1662804	10204	3487
(4)	1662804	21961	11338
(5)	87516	7092	2037
(6)	87516	62623	26093
(7)	782	233	77
(8)	3915	852	418
(9)	41688	4546	1935
(10)	15711	2832	1713
(11)	68151	7293	4111
(12)	9675	6295	4799

The following table discloses that Capelli operations are time-consuming, and cost about 98% of the total time in `Rota`. It indicates that replacing Capelli operator by *Sros* has significant advantage.

Table 5: Time (sec.) consumed at each stage of `Rota`

NO.	Straight tableaux enumeration	Capelli operation	Linear equation solving
(1)	16.72	42243.49	856.25
(2)	16.72	42243.49	835.31
(7)	27.13	8415.86	241.91
(8)	42.41	28211.92	451.29
(12)	504.98	69182.54	1098.19

REFERENCES

[1] Brini, A. and Teolos, A. Young-Capelli Symmetrizers in Superalgebras. *PNAS USA* **86**, 775-778, 1989.

[2] Capelli, A. Über die Zurückführung der Cayley'schen Operation Ω auf Gewöhnliche Polar-Operationen. *Mathematische Annalen* **29**(3): 331-338, 1887.

[3] Clausen, M. Dominance Orders, Capelli Operators, and Straightening of Bideterminants. *European Journal of Combinatorics* **5**: 207-222, 1984.

[4] De Concini, C., Eisenbud, D. and Procesi, C. Young Diagrams and Determinantal Varieties. *Invent. Math.* **56**, 129-165, 1980.

[5] Désarménien, J., Kung, J.P.S. and Rota, G.-C. Invariant Theory, Young Bitableaux, and Combinatorics. *Advances in Mathematics* **27**: 63-92, 1978.

[6] Désarménien, J. An algorithm for the Rota Straightening Formula. *Discrete Mathematics* **30**: 51-68, 1980.

[7] Doubilet, P., Rota, G.-C. and Stein, J. On the Foundations of Combinatorial Theory: IX Combinatorial Methods in Invariant Theory. *Studies in Applied Math.* **53**: 185-216, 1974.

[8] Fulton, W. *Young Tableaux, with Applications to Representation Theory and Geometry.* Cambridge University Press, Cambridge, 1997.

[9] Grosshans, F.D., Rota, G.-C. and Stein, J.A. *Invariant Theory and Superalgebras.* AMS, 1987.

[10] Huang, R.Q. and White, N.L. Straightening Coefficients in the Supersymmetric Letter-Place Algebra. *Journal of Algebra* **171**: 655-675, 1995.

[11] Lee-St.John, A. and Sidman, J. Combinatorics and the Rigidity of CAD Systems. *CAD* **45**(2), 473-482, 2013.

[12] Li, H. *Invariant Algebras and Geometric Reasoning.* World Scientific, Singapore, 2008.

[13] Li, H., Shao, C., Huang, L. and Liu, Y. Reduction among Bracket Polynomials. *In: Proc. ISSAC'14*, ACM Press, New York, pp. 304-311, 2014.

[14] Olver, P.J. *Classical Invariant Theory.* Cambridge University Press, Cambridge, 1999.

[15] Richter-Gebert, J. *Perspectives on Projective Geometry.* Springer, Heidelberg, 2011.

[16] Sitharam, M. Combinatorial Approaches to Geometric Constraint Solving: Problems, Progress, and Directions. In: *DIMACS: Series in Discrete Mathematics and Theoretical Computer Science* **67** (2005), 117.

[17] White, N. Implementation of the Straightening Algorithm of Classical Invariant Theory. In: Staton, D. (*ed.*), *Invariant Theory and Tableaux.* Springer, New York, pp. 36-45, 1990.

[18] Young, A. On quantitative substitutional analysis (3rd paper). *Proc. London Mathematical Society Series* **2**(28): 255-292, 1928.

Comparison of CAD-based Methods for Computation of Rational Function Limits

Adam Strzeboński
Wolfram Research Inc.
Champaign, Illinois
adams@wolfram.com

ABSTRACT

We present five methods for computation of limits of real multivariate rational functions. The methods do not require any assumptions about the rational function and compute the lower limit and the upper limit. All methods are based on the cylindrical algebraic decomposition (CAD) algorithm, but use different formulations of the problem. We give an empirical comparison of the methods on a large set of examples.

ACM Reference Format:
Adam Strzeboński. 2018. Comparison of CAD-based Methods for Computation of Rational Function Limits. In *ISSAC '18: 2018 ACM International Symposium on Symbolic and Algebraic Computation, July 16–19, 2018, New York, NY, USA.* ACM, New York, NY, USA, 8 pages. https://doi.org/10.1145/3208976.3208982

Keywords: multivariate rational function limit; cylindrical algebraic decomposition; symbolic limit computation.

1 INTRODUCTION

Computation of limits is one of the basic problems of computational calculus. In the univariate case computing limits of rational functions is easy, and the state of the art limit computation algorithms [9, 13] are applicable to large classes of functions. In the multivariate case computing limits of real rational functions is a nontrivial problem that has been a subject of recent research [1, 5, 21–23].

The limit of a rational function may not exist, however the lower limit and the upper limit always exist. A weak version of the limit computation problem consists of deciding whether the limit exists and, if it does, finding the value of the limit. A strong version consists of finding the values of the lower limit and the upper limit. In this paper we consider rational functions with rational number coefficients and compute limits at points with rational coordinates. Instead of rational numbers we could use any computable subfield K of $\mathbb{R}$, as long as polynomials with coefficients in K are accepted by the CAD algorithm (e.g. K could be the field of real algebraic numbers).

Let us state the problems precisely. Denote $x = (x_1, \ldots, x_n)$ and $\bar{\mathbb{R}} = \mathbb{R} \cup \{-\infty, \infty\}$. Let $g \in \mathbb{Q}[x]$, $h \in \mathbb{Q}[x] \setminus \{0\}$, $D = \{u \in \mathbb{R}^n : h(u) \neq 0\}$, $f : D \ni u \to \frac{g(u)}{h(u)} \in \mathbb{R}$, and let $c \in \mathbb{Q}^n$.

ISSAC '18, July 16–19, 2018, New York, NY, USA

ACM ISBN 978-1-4503-5550-6/18/07...$15.00
https://doi.org/10.1145/3208976.3208982

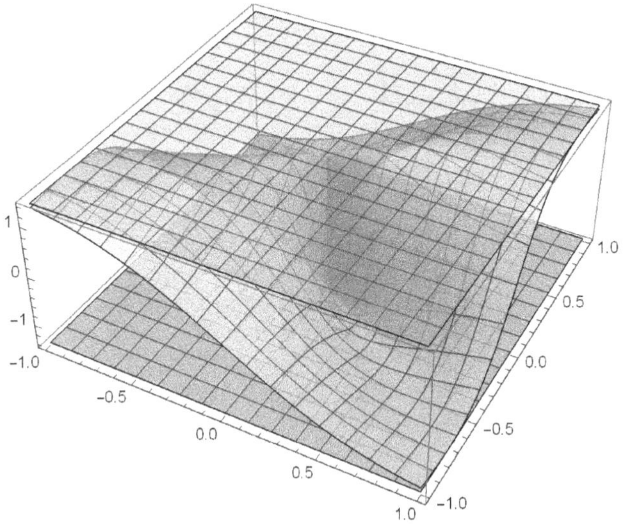

Figure 1.1: The lower and the upper limit of $z = \frac{4xy}{x^2+2y^2}$ at 0.

Problem 1. Find $l \in \bar{\mathbb{R}}$ such that $l = \lim_{u \to c} f(u)$ or prove that such l does not exist.

Problem 2. Find $l_1, l_2 \in \bar{\mathbb{R}}$ such that $l_1 = \liminf_{u \to c} f(u)$ and $l_2 = \limsup_{u \to c} f(u)$.

Example 3. Let $g = x^2(x + y + z)$ and $h = x^2 + (y - z)^2$. Then the zero of h at 0 is not isolated, however $h^{-1}(0) \subset g^{-1}(0)$ and

$$\lim_{(x,y,z) \to 0} \frac{g(x,y,z)}{h(x,y,z)} = 0$$

Example 4. Let $g = 2x(y - z)$ and $h = x^2 + (y - z)^2$. Then

$$\liminf_{(x,y,z) \to 0} \frac{g(x,y,z)}{h(x,y,z)} = -1$$

$$\limsup_{(x,y,z) \to 0} \frac{g(x,y,z)}{h(x,y,z)} = 1$$

and $\lim_{(x,y,z) \to 0} \frac{g(x,y,z)}{h(x,y,z)}$ does not exist.

Example 5. If the limit exists and is finite then it is a rational number (it is equal to the limit of a univariate rational function obtained by replacing all variables with integer multiples of one variable). The upper limit and the lower limit do not need to be rational. They do need to be algebraic (by Tarski's theorem [20]; algorithms presented here give a constructive proof). Let $g = 4xy$

and $h = x^2 + 2y^2$. Then

$$\liminf_{(x,y)\to 0} \frac{g(x,y)}{h(x,y)} = -\sqrt{2}$$

$$\limsup_{(x,y)\to 0} \frac{g(x,y)}{h(x,y)} = \sqrt{2}$$

The plot of $z = g(x,y)/h(x,y)$ and the planes $z = -\sqrt{2}$ and $z = \sqrt{2}$ is shown in Figure 1.1.

Recently two algorithms partially solving Problem 1 have been proposed. The algorithm presented in [22] solves a modified version of the problem, namely it decides whether the limit exists and is finite. The negative answer includes both the case when the limit does not exist and the case when the limit exists and is infinite. The algorithm uses Wu's elimination method, rational univariate representations, and requires adjoining two infinitesimal elements to the field. The algorithm presented in [1] (which generalizes algorithms of [5, 21]) solves Problem 1 under the additional assumption that c is an isolated zero of h. The authors use the theory of Lagrange multipliers to reduces the problem to computing the limit along a real algebraic set, and solve the reduced problem using regular chains methods.

In this paper we investigate application of the cylindrical algebraic decomposition (CAD) methods to computation of limits of real rational functions. Since definitions of limit, lower limit, and upper limit of rational functions can be written as quantified polynomial formulas, real quantifier elimination, and in particular CAD, can be used to solve both Problem 1 and Problem 2. However, since the CAD algorithm has doubly exponential complexity in the number of variables, it is very important in practice to find a formulation of the problem which introduces as few variables as possible, and which can be solved using a customized simpler version of the CAD algorithm. We propose five such formulations and compare their efficiency on examples form literature and a large set of examples extracted from inputs submitted to the Wolfram Alpha website.

We describe algorithms computing the lower limit. This is sufficient to solve both Problem 2 and Problem 1, since

$$\limsup_{u\to c} f(u) = -\liminf_{u\to c} -f(u)$$

and the limit exists iff

$$\limsup_{u\to c} f(u) = \liminf_{u\to c} f(u)$$

However, when both the lower limit and the upper limit are needed certain steps of the computation can be shared, and if only a solution of Problem 1 is required, it can often be obtained in a simpler way. After each algorithm we remark on how it can be adjusted to efficiently obtain the required goal.

Without loss of generality we will assume that $c = 0$. If $h(0) \neq 0$ then f is continuous at 0, and hence the limit can be obtained by evaluation. Therefore w.l.o.g. we will assume that $h(0) = 0$, in particular $0 \notin D$. Canceling common factors of g and h does not affect the limits, hence w.l.o.g. we will assume that g and h are relatively prime.

2 CYLINDRICAL ALGEBRAIC DECOMPOSITION

In this paper we assume reader's familiarity with the CAD algorithm. Here we give a very brief introduction to CAD, aimed mainly at introducing terminology and notation that we will use in the description of the algorithms. For more details see [6]. Detailed descriptions of the CAD variant we use here are given in [17, 18].

A subset of $\mathbb{R}^n$ is *semialgebraic* if it is the solution set of a Boolean formula whose atoms are polynomial equations and inequalities with real coefficients. For an introduction to semialgebraic set theory see e.g. [2, 3].

Every semialgebraic set can be represented as a finite union of disjoint *cells* (see [10]), defined recursively as follows.

(1) A cell in $\mathbb{R}$ is a point or an open interval.
(2) A cell in $\mathbb{R}^{k+1}$ has one of the two forms

$$\{(\overline{a}, a_{k+1}) : \overline{a} \in C_k \wedge a_{k+1} = r(\overline{a})\}$$
$$\{(\overline{a}, a_{k+1}) : \overline{a} \in C_k \wedge r_1(\overline{a}) < a_{k+1} < r_2(\overline{a})\}$$

where C_k is a cell in $\mathbb{R}^k$, r is a continuous real algebraic function, and r_1 and r_2 are continuous real algebraic functions, $-\infty$, or ∞, and $r_1 < r_2$ on C_k.

The Cylindrical Algebraic Decomposition (CAD) algorithm [6, 8, 17] can be used to compute a cell decomposition of any semialgebraic set presented by a quantified system of polynomial equations and inequalities. An alternative method of computing cell decompositions is given in [7]. Cell decompositions computed by the CAD algorithm can be represented directly [4, 17] as cylindrical algebraic formulas (CAF; for a precise definition see [18]).

A *real algebraic function* given by the *defining polynomial* $p \in \mathbb{Z}[x_1, \ldots, x_k, y]$ and a *root number* $\lambda \in \mathbb{N}_+$ is the function

$$Root_{y,\lambda}p : \mathbb{R}^k \ni \overline{a} \longrightarrow Root_{y,\lambda}p(\overline{a}) \in \mathbb{R} \tag{2.1}$$

where $Root_{y,\lambda}p(\overline{a})$ is the λ-th real root of $p(\overline{a}, y) \in \mathbb{R}[y]$. The function is defined for those values of $\overline{a}$ for which $p(\overline{a}, y)$ has at least λ real roots. The real roots are ordered by the increasing value and counted with multiplicities. A real algebraic number $Root_{y,\lambda}p \in \mathbb{R}$ given by a *defining polynomial* $p \in \mathbb{Z}[y]$ and a *root number* λ is the λ-th real root of p.

A cell C in $\mathbb{R}^n$ computed by the CAD algorithm applied to a formula with free variables $(x_1, \ldots, x_n)$ has a description of the form

$$b_1(x_1) \wedge b_2(x_1, x_2) \wedge \ldots \wedge b_n(x_1, \ldots, x_n)$$

where the formula $b_k(x_1, \ldots, x_k)$, which we will call *the bounds on* x_k *in* C is either

$$x_k = r(x_1, \ldots, x_{k-1})$$

or

$$r_1(x_1, \ldots, x_{k-1}) < x_k < r_2(x_1, \ldots, x_{k-1})$$

where r, r_1, and r_2 are $-\infty$, ∞, or continuous real algebraic functions whose defining polynomials are k-variate CAD projection polynomials. The *lower bound on* x_k *in* C is r or r_1 and *the upper bound on* x_k *in* C is r or r_2. The the *projection* of C on $\mathbb{R}^k$ is the cell $\Pi_k(C)$ in $\mathbb{R}^k$ given by

$$\Pi_k(C) = \{(a_1, \ldots, a_k) \in \mathbb{R}^k : b_1(a_1) \wedge \ldots \wedge b_k(a_1, \ldots, a_k)\}$$

A finite collection Δ of cells in $\mathbb{R}^n$ is *cylindrically arranged* if for any $C_1, C_2 \in \Delta$ and any $k \leq n$ $\Pi_k(C_1)$ and $\Pi_k(C_2)$ are either disjoint or identical. A *cylindrical algebraic decomposition (CAD) of* $\mathbb{R}^n$ is a finite collection Δ of pairwise disjoint cylindrically arranged cells in $\mathbb{R}^n$ such that $\bigcup_{C\in\Delta} C = \mathbb{R}^n$.

Some of the algorithms presented here use the algorithm described in [19], which computes cell adjacencies for well-based CAD. Cells C_1 and C_2 of a CAD Δ are *adjacent* if $C_1 \neq C_2$ and $C_1 \cup C_2$ is connected. A CAD is *well-based* if none of the polynomials whose roots appear in cell description vanishes identically at any point (see [14, 19] for more details). If Δ is well-based then C_1 and C_2 are adjacent iff $C_1 \subseteq \overline{C_2}$ or $C_2 \subseteq \overline{C_1}$.

For a finite set of polynomials $F \subset \mathbb{Q}[x_1, \ldots, x_{k+1}]$ let

$$GP(F, x_{k+1}) \subset \mathbb{Q}[x_1, \ldots, x_k]$$

denote the set of irreducible factors of the leading coefficients, discriminants, and pairwise resultants of the elements of F treated as polynomials in x_{k+1}.

3 METHODS BASED ON OPTIMIZATION

For $u \in \mathbb{R}^n$ let $\|u\| := \max_{1\leq i\leq n}|u_i|$. The lower limit and the upper limit are defined as follows

$$\liminf_{u\to 0} f(u) = \lim_{\epsilon\to 0^+} \inf_{u\in D\wedge \|u\|<\epsilon} f(u)$$

$$\limsup_{u\to 0} f(u) = \lim_{\epsilon\to 0^+} \sup_{u\in D\wedge \|u\|<\epsilon} f(u)$$

Let us first introduce a subalgorithm that will be used in the algorithms described in this section.

Algorithm 6. *(UALimit)*
Input: A univariate real algebraic function $Root_{y,\lambda}p(z)$ *defined in* $(a, b) \subseteq \mathbb{R}$.
Output: $\lim_{z\to a^+} Root_{y,\lambda}p(z)$.

Limits of univariate real algebraic functions can be computed using a specialized version of the CAD cell adjacency computation algorithm described in [19]. Note that a bivariate CAD is always well-based and the (one-sided) limit always exists.

The following algorithm makes the most direct use of the definition. It introduces two variables z and y in addition to the variables x, however it constructs only one cell in z and treats the variables x as existentially quantified. The formula for which CAD is constructed always contains an equational constraint and hence the variant of CAD making use of equational constraints [11, 12] is used. The variable z corresponds to ϵ from the definition of lower limit and the variable y is constrained to be equal to $f(u)$ with $\|u\| < z$. Hence the lower limit of $f(u)$ at zero is equal to the limit of the infimum of y as z tends to zero through positive values. Since the constraints are semialgebraic, the infimum of y will be a continuous real algebraic function of z (or an infinity) on an interval $(0, e)$, for some positive e.

Algorithm 7. *(OLIM1)*
Input: $g \in \mathbb{Q}[x]$, $h \in \mathbb{Q}[x] \setminus \{0\}$.
Output: $\liminf_{u\to 0} \frac{g(u)}{h(u)}$.

(1) *Set*

$$S(z, y, x) := z > 0 \wedge \|x\| < z \wedge h \neq 0 \wedge g = yh$$

(2) *Compute the CAD projection for S, with variables ordered* $z < y < x_1 < \ldots < x_n$. *Let* F_v *be the set of projection polynomials with the "largest" variable* v.
(3) *Choose a positive rational number e smaller than all positive roots of elements of* F_z.
(4) *Construct cells extending the open cell with sample point* (e), *starting with the smallest values of* y, *until the first cell C on which S is true is found. Let r be the lower bound on* y *in C*.
(5) *If* $r = -\infty$, *return* $-\infty$.
(6) *Let* $p \in F_y$ *and* $\lambda \in \mathbb{N}$ *be such that* $r = Root_{y,\lambda}p(z)$.
(7) *Use UALimit to compute* $l = \lim_{z\to 0^+} Root_{y,\lambda}p(z)$.
(8) *Return l.*

Proof. To prove correctness of Algorithm 7 put

$$L(\epsilon) := \inf_{u\in D\wedge \|u\|<\epsilon} f(u)$$

and note that

$$L(\epsilon) = \inf_{a\in A(\epsilon)} a$$

where

$$A(\epsilon) := \{a : \exists_{u\in D}\|u\| < \epsilon \wedge a = f(u)\}$$

For each $\epsilon > 0$

$$A(\epsilon) = \{a : \exists_{u\in\mathbb{R}^n} S(\epsilon, a, u)\}$$

In particular, if r is the lower bound on y in the cell C constructed in step (4) then, for $0 < \epsilon \leq e$, $L(\epsilon) = r(\epsilon)$. Since

$$\liminf_{u\to 0} f(u) = \lim_{\epsilon\to 0^+} L(\epsilon)$$

Algorithm 7 returns $\liminf_{u\to 0} f(u)$ as required. □

The upper limit can be computed in a similar way, and when both the lower limit and the upper limit are needed, steps (1)-(3) of Algorithm 7 can be shared.

Example 8. Let $g = x_1(x_2 - x_3 + x_1x_3)$ and $h = x_1^2 + (x_2 - x_3)^2$. In step (3) F_z consists of 1798 polynomials that have 1604 real roots. The 911-th root is the first positive one and it is greater than $e = 5/4096$. In step (4) F_y consists of 95 polynomials that have 93 real roots for $z = e$, and hence there are 187 cells in y to check. The first cell on which S is true is found when lifting the the 11-th cell in y, which is a sector with the lower bound

$$r = Root_{y,1}4y^2 + 4yz - 1 = -\frac{z + \sqrt{z^2 + 1}}{2}$$

Hence $l = \lim_{z\to 0^+} r = -\frac{1}{2}$. The computation takes 1.76 seconds.

The following algorithm computes the lower limit using a specialized version of CAD which uses the "generic" projection operator of [15, 16] and constructs only open cells. The algorithm introduces two variables z and y in addition to the variables x, however it constructs only one cell in z, performs a binary search on cells in y, and treats variables x as existentially quantified. As in Algorithm 7, the variable z corresponds to ϵ from the definition of lower limit. The variable y is constrained to be greater than $f(u)$ with $\|u\| < z$. As before, the lower limit of $f(u)$ at zero is equal to the limit of the infimum of y as z tends to zero through positive values. However, since all constraints are strict inequalities, the infimum of y as a function of z can be determined by analysing only open CAD cells.

Algorithm 9. *(OLIM2)*
Input: $g \in \mathbb{Q}[x]$, $h \in \mathbb{Q}[x] \setminus \{0\}$.
Output: $\liminf_{u \to 0} \frac{g(u)}{h(u)}$.

(1) *Set* F_{x_n} *to the set of irreducible factors of*
$$\bigcup_{i=1}^{n} \{x_i + z, x_i - z\} \cup \{g - yh, h, z\}$$
(2) *For* $i = n - 1$ *to* 1 *set* $F_{x_i} := GP(F_{x_{i+1}}, x_{i+1})$.
(3) *Set* $F_y := GP(F_{x_1}, x_1)$ *and* $F_z := GP(F_y, y)$.
(4) *Choose a positive rational number* e *smaller than all positive roots of elements of* F_z.
(5) *Compute the real roots* $r_1 < \ldots < r_m$ *of* $p(e, y)$ *for* $p \in F_y$.
(6) *For* $0 \leq i \leq m$ *find a rational number* $r_i < a_i < r_{i+1}$, *where* $r_0 = -\infty$ *and* $r_{m+1} = \infty$.
(7) *Compute the minimal* $0 \leq i_0 \leq m$ *such that*
$$\varphi_i := \exists_x \|x\| < e \wedge ((h > 0 \wedge g < a_i h) \vee (h < 0 \wedge g > a_i h))$$
is true.
(8) *If* $i_0 = 0$, *return* $-\infty$.
(9) *Let* $p \in F_y$ *and* $\lambda \in \mathbb{N}$ *be such that* $r_{i_0} = Root_{y,\lambda} p(e)$.
(10) *Use UALimit to compute* $l = \lim_{z \to 0^+} Root_{y,\lambda} p(z)$.
(11) *Return* l.

Proof. To prove correctness of Algorithm 9 put
$$L(\epsilon) := \inf_{u \in D \wedge \|u\| < \epsilon} f(u)$$
and note that
$$L(\epsilon) = \inf_{a \in A(\epsilon)} a$$
where
$$A(\epsilon) := \{a \;:\; \exists_{u \in D} \|u\| < \epsilon \wedge a > f(u)\}$$
For each $\epsilon > 0$, $L(\epsilon) \in \mathbb{R} \cup \{-\infty\}$ and $A(\epsilon) = (L(\epsilon), \infty)$. Steps (1)-(3) of Algorithm 9 construct the projection used in the algorithm GCAD of [16] for the input system
$$S(z, y, x) = z > 0 \wedge \|x\| < z \wedge ((h > 0 \wedge g < yh) \vee (h < 0 \wedge g > yh))$$
In particular, in step (7) the truth value of φ_i can be determined by running the lifting phase of GCAD for the open cell with the sample point (e, a_i), until either an open cell on which $S(z, y, x)$ is true is found, or it is shown that such cell does not exist. The value of i_0 can be determined by binary search in the set $0 \leq i \leq m$.

For each $\epsilon > 0$
$$A(\epsilon) = \{a \;:\; \exists_{u \in \mathbb{R}^n} S(\epsilon, a, u)\}$$
In particular, $L(e) = r_{i_0}$.

The union of the open cells constructed by the algorithm GCAD differs from the solution set of $S(z, y, x)$ by a lower-dimensional set. Hence, for each open interval I obtained by subdividing $\mathbb{R}_+$ with positive roots of elements of F_z, $L(\epsilon)$ is either identically $-\infty$ on I or there exist $p_I \in F_y$ and $\lambda_I \in \mathbb{N}$ such that $L(\epsilon) = Root_{y,\lambda_I} p_I(\epsilon)$ on I.

In particular, if $i_0 = 0$, then $L(\epsilon) = -\infty$ for $0 < \epsilon \leq e$, otherwise $L(\epsilon) = Root_{y,\lambda} p(\epsilon)$ for $0 < \epsilon \leq e$, where $p \in F_y$ and $\lambda \in \mathbb{N}$ are such that $r_{i_0} = Root_{y,\lambda} p(e)$. Since
$$\liminf_{u \to 0} f(u) = \lim_{\epsilon \to 0^+} L(\epsilon)$$
Algorithm 9 returns $\liminf_{u \to 0} f(u)$ as required. □

The upper limit can be computed in a similar way, and when both the lower limit and the upper limit are needed, steps (1)-(6) of Algorithm 9 can be shared.

Example 10. Let $g = x_1(x_2 - x_3 + x_1 x_3)$ and $h = x_1^2 + (x_2 - x_3)^2$, as in Example 8. In step (4) F_z consists of 262 polynomials that have 105 real roots. The 54-th root is the first positive one and it is greater than $e = 5/64$. In step (5) F_y consists of 39 polynomials that have 33 real roots for $z = e$, and hence in step (6) there are 34 sectors with sample points a_i. Step (7) uses binary search to find the smallest i such that φ_i is true. The truth values computed using the algorithm of [15, 16] are: $\varphi_0 = false$, $\varphi_{33} = true$, $\varphi_{17} = true$, $\varphi_9 = true$, $\varphi_5 = true$, $\varphi_3 = true$, $\varphi_1 = false$, and $\varphi_2 = false$, which shows that $i_0 = 3$. The lower bound of the 4-th sector is
$$r_{i_0} = Root_{y,1} 4y^2 + 4yz - 1 = -\frac{z + \sqrt{z^2 + 1}}{2}$$
Hence $l = \lim_{z \to 0^+} r_{i_0} = -\frac{1}{2}$. The computation takes 0.22 seconds.

4 METHODS BASED ON TOPOLOGICAL PROPERTIES

For a subset Z of $\mathbb{R}^n$, let $\overline{Z}$ denote the closure of Z in the Euclidean topology. The algorithms presented in this section use the following characterization of the lower limit and the upper limit.

Proposition 11. *Let*
$$\begin{aligned} l_1 &:= \liminf_{u \to 0} f(u) \\ l_2 &:= \limsup_{u \to 0} f(u) \\ S_1(y, x) &:= (h > 0 \wedge g < yh) \vee (h < 0 \wedge g > yh) \\ S_2(y, x) &:= (h > 0 \wedge g > yh) \vee (h < 0 \wedge g < yh) \\ Z_1 &:= \{(a, u) \in \mathbb{R}^{n+1} \;:\; S_1(a, u)\} \\ Z_2 &:= \{(a, u) \in \mathbb{R}^{n+1} \;:\; S_2(a, u)\} \end{aligned}$$
and, for $a \in \mathbb{R}$, *let*
$$\begin{aligned} Z_1(a) &:= \{u \in \mathbb{R}^n \;:\; S_1(a, u)\} \\ Z_2(a) &:= \{u \in \mathbb{R}^n \;:\; S_2(a, u)\} \end{aligned}$$
Then if $a > l_1$ *then* $0 \in \overline{Z_1(a)}$ *and if* $a < l_1$ *then* $(a, 0) \notin \overline{Z_1}$. *Similarly, if* $a < l_2$ *then* $0 \in \overline{Z_2(a)}$ *and if* $a > l_2$ *then* $(a, 0) \notin \overline{Z_2}$. *Note that we assume that* $h(0) = 0$ *and hence neither* $Z_1(a)$ *nor* $Z_2(a)$ *contain* 0.

Proof. If $a > l_1$ then
$$\forall_{\epsilon > 0} \exists_u \|u\| < \epsilon \wedge h(u) \neq 0 \wedge \frac{g(u)}{h(u)} < a$$
which is equivalent to
$$\forall_{\epsilon > 0} \exists_u \|u\| < \epsilon \wedge S_1(a, u)$$
which in turn is equivalent to $0 \in \overline{Z_1(a)}$.

If $a < l_1$ then for some $\epsilon > 0$
$$\inf_{u \in D \wedge \|u\| < \epsilon} f(u) > \frac{a + l_1}{2}$$
Hence
$$\forall_u (\|u\| < \epsilon \wedge h(u) \neq 0) \Rightarrow \frac{g(u)}{h(u)} > \frac{a + l_1}{2}$$
and therefore
$$\{(b, u) \in \mathbb{R}^{n+1} \;:\; |b - a| < \frac{l_1 - a}{2} \wedge \|u\| < \epsilon\} \cap Z_1 = \emptyset$$

which shows that $(a, 0) \notin \overline{Z_1}$. The proof of the second part of the proposition is similar. □

Let us first introduce terminology and subalgorithms that will be used in the limit computation algorithm described in this section.

Let $p \in \mathbb{Q}[y, x_1, \ldots, x_n]$. We will say that p is *regular in* x_k if either p does not depend on x_k or the leading coefficient of p treated as a polynomial in x_k belongs to $\mathbb{Q}[y]$. We say that a finite set $P \subset \mathbb{Q}[y, x_1, \ldots, x_n]$ is *regular in* x_k if all elements of P are regular in x_k.

For a matrix $M \in \mathbb{R}^{n \times n}$ by M_i we denote the i-th row of M, so that $M_i x$ is the i-th component of the vector Mx. If we specify a matrix M by giving values of $M_i x$ for some of the i, we assume that for the remaining i, $M_i x = x_i$.

Algorithm 12. *(RPROJ)*
Input: A finite set $F \subset \mathbb{Q}[y, x_1, \ldots, x_n]$.
Output: $(P_0, \ldots, P_n)$ *and an invertible matrix* $M \in \mathbb{Z}^{n \times n}$ *such that* P_n *is the set of irreducible factors of* $F(y, M_1 x, \ldots, M_n x)$ *and, for* $1 \leq k \leq n$, P_k *is regular in* x_k *and* $P_{k-1} = GP(P_k, x_k)$.

(1) *Set* M *to the identity matrix.*
(2) *For* $k = n$ *to* 1 *do:*
  (a) *If* $k = n$ *let* P_k *be the set of irreducible factors of* F, *else let* $P_k := GP(P_{k+1}, x_{k+1})$.
  (b) *If there exists* $1 \leq i \leq k$ *such that* P_k *is regular in* x_i, *let* $M'_i x = x_k$ *and* $M'_k x = x_i$.
  (c) *Otherwise*
    (i) *Let* q *be the product of lead homogeneous forms in* $$(x_1, \ldots, x_k)$$ *of elements of* P_k.
    (ii) *Find an integer vector* $a = (a_1, \ldots, a_{k-1}, 1)$ *such that* $q(a) \in \mathbb{Q}[y] \setminus \{0\}$.
    (iii) *Let* $M'_i x = x_i + a_i x_k$ *for* $1 \leq i \leq k-1$.
  (d) *Set* $M := MM'$ *and* $P_i := P_i(y, M'_1 x, \ldots, M'_n x)$ *for* $k \leq i \leq n$.
(3) *Compute* $P_0 := GP(P_1, x_1)$.
(4) *Return* $(P_0, \ldots, P_n)$ *and* M.

In step (2c) $q(x_1, \ldots x_{k-1}, 1) \in \mathbb{Q}[y][x_1, \ldots x_{k-1}]$ is a nonzero polynomial, hence we can find integer values $(a_1, \ldots, a_{k-1})$ for which it is nonzero. If $p \in P_k$ has a lead homogeneous form ω of degree d in $(x_1, \ldots, x_k)$, then $p(y, M'_1 x, \ldots, M'_k x) = \omega(a) x_k^d + r$ where the degree of r in x_k is less than d. This shows that $P_k(y, M'_1 x, \ldots, M'_k x)$ is regular in x_k.

In step (2d), $M'_i x = x_i$ for $k < i \leq n$, hence the transformation $P_i := P_i(y, M'_1 x, \ldots, M'_n x)$ preserves the regularity of P_i in x_i and the property $P_{i-1} = GP(P_i, x_i)$ for $k < i \leq n$. This shows correctness of Algorithm 12.

The following two subalgorithms decide whether 0 belongs to the closure of the solution set of the input system. Here a system of inequalities is a disjunction of conjunctions of inequalities. Depending on which of the two subalgorithms is used in Algorithm 15, we get two versions of the limit computation algorithm.

Algorithm 13. *(ZCQ1)*
Input: A system $S(x)$ *of strict polynomial inequalities.*
Output: true or $false$ *depending on whether* 0 *belongs to the closure of the solution set of* $S(x)$.

(1) *If* $S(0)$ *is true return true.*
(2) *Let* $T(z, x) := \|x\| < z \wedge S(x)$, *and let* F_{x_n} *be the set of all irreducible factors of polynomials that appear in* T.
(3) *For* $i = n-1$ *to* 1 *set* $F_{x_i} := GP(F_{x_{i+1}}, x_{i+1})$.
(4) *Set* $F_z := GP(F_{x_1}, x_1)$.
(5) *Choose a positive rational number* e *smaller than all positive roots of elements of* F_z.
(6) *Run the lifting phase of the algorithm GCAD of [16] with the projection set* $(F_z, F_{x_1}, \ldots, F_{x_n})$ *for the open cell with the sample point* (e).
(7) *Return true if an open cell on which* $T(z, x)$ *is true is found, and return* $false$ *otherwise.*

Proof. To prove correctness of Algorithm 13 note that 0 belongs to the closure of the solution set of $S(x)$ iff

$$\forall_{z>0} \exists_x T(z, x) \tag{4.1}$$

Steps (2)-(4) of Algorithm 13 construct the projection used in the algorithm GCAD of [16] for the input system $T(z, x)$. Let Δ be the collection of open cells returned by the algorithm GCAD. The union of cells of Δ differs from the solution set of $T(z, x)$ by a lower dimensional set. Note that the solution set of $T(z, x)$ is open and hence (4.1) is true iff there is an open cell C in Δ such that the projection $\Pi_1(C)$ on $\mathbb{R}^1$ contains an open interval $(0, \epsilon)$. Since the endpoints of $\Pi_1(C)$ are infinite or roots of elements of F_z, (4.1) is true iff Δ contains a cell which extends the open cell with the sample point (e). This can be determined by running the lifting phase of GCAD for the open cell with the sample point (e) until either an open cell on which $T(z, x)$ is true is found, or it is shown that such cell does not exist. □

The next subalgorithm requires the ability to compute a well-based CAD Δ of $\mathbb{R}^n$ such that the solution set of $S(x)$ is a union of cells of Δ. In the proof of correctness of Algorithm 15 we show that this requirement is satisfied.

Algorithm 14. *(ZCQ2)*
Input: A system $S(x)$ *of polynomial inequalities.*
Output: true or $false$ *depending on whether* 0 *belongs to the closure of the solution set of* $S(x)$.

(1) *If* $S(0)$ *is true return true.*
(2) *Compute a well-based CAD* Δ *of* $\mathbb{R}^n$ *such that the solution set of* $S(x)$ *is a union of cells of* Δ.
(3) *Use the algorithm CADAdjacency of [19] to compute adjacencies between cells of* Δ.
(4) *Return true if the cell containing* 0 *is adjacent to a cell on which* $S(x)$ *is true, and return* $false$ *otherwise.*

The following algorithm computes the lower limit using Proposition 11. The algorithm introduces a new variable y in addition to the variables x. The variable y is used only in one CAD projection computation needed to determine a finite number of possible values for the lower limit. The lower limit is then determined by a binary search among the possible values.

Algorithm 15. *(TLIM)*
Input: $g \in \mathbb{Q}[x]$, $h \in \mathbb{Q}[x] \setminus \{0\}$.
Output: $\liminf_{u \to 0} \frac{g(u)}{h(u)}$.

(1) *Set* $F = \{g - yh, h, x_1, \ldots, x_n\}$ *and compute*
$$((P_0, \ldots, P_n), M) = RPROJ(F; y; x_1, \ldots, x_n)$$
(2) *Compute the real roots* $r_1 < \ldots < r_m$ *of elements of* P_0.
(3) *For* $0 \le i \le m$ *find a rational number* $r_i < a_i < r_{i+1}$, *where* $r_0 = -\infty$ *and* $r_{m+1} = \infty$.
(4) *Use binary search and Algorithm 13 or 14 to find* i_0 *defined as the minimal* $0 \le i \le m$ *such that* $0 \in \overline{Z_1(a_i)}$ *or* $m+1$ *if* $0 \notin \overline{Z_1(a_i)}$ *for all* $0 \le i \le m$.
(5) *Return* r_{i_0}.

Proof. Put $l := \liminf_{u \to 0} f(u)$. To show that $r_{i_0} = l$ we will prove that for any fixed $0 \le i \le m$ either $r_i \ge l$ (and hence $0 \in \overline{Z_1(b)}$ for all $r_i < b < r_{i+1}$) or $r_{i+1} \le l$ (and hence $0 \notin \overline{Z_1(b)}$ for all $r_i < b < r_{i+1}$).

Fix $0 \le i \le m$ and $r_i < \alpha < r_{i+1}$ and put
$$\sigma(t) := \begin{cases} \alpha - t^2 & i = 0 \\ \frac{\alpha + t^2 r_{i+1}}{t^2+1} & 1 \le i < m \\ \alpha + t^2 & i = m \end{cases}$$
We will show that either $\sigma(a) \ge l$ for all $a \in \mathbb{R}$ or $\sigma(a) \le l$ for all $a \in \mathbb{R}$. This is sufficient to prove that either $r_i \ge l$ or $r_{i+1} \le l$ since
$$\sigma((-\infty, \infty)) = \begin{cases} (r_i, \alpha] & i = 0 \\ [\alpha, r_{i+1}) & 1 \le i \le m \end{cases} \tag{4.2}$$
and α is an arbitrary number in (r_i, r_{i+1}).

Let $(Q_0, \ldots, Q_n)$ be $(P_0, \ldots, P_n)$ with y replaced with $\sigma(t)$ and with all polynomials multiplied by suitable powers of $t^2 + 1$ to remove the denominators. Since, for $1 \le k \le n$, P_k is regular in x_k, all factors of the leading coefficients of elements of P_k that depend on x_k belong to P_0. Hence the leading coefficients of elements of Q_k that depend on x_k belong to $\mathbb{R}[t]$ and have no real roots, and $Q_{k-1} = GP(Q_k, x_k)$. Therefore $(Q_0, \ldots, Q_n)$ is a valid CAD projection set and a $(Q_0, \ldots, Q_n)$-invariant CAD is well-based in the sense of [14, 19].

Fix a $(Q_0, \ldots, Q_n)$-invariant CAD Δ of $\mathbb{R}^{n+1}$. Q_n is equal to the set of irreducible factors of $F(\sigma(t), M_1x, \ldots, M_nx)$ up to multiplication by powers of t^2+1 and $x_1, \ldots, x_n \in F$, hence $M_1x, \ldots, M_nx \in Q_n$. Since M is invertible, $x_1 = 0 \wedge \ldots \wedge x_n = 0$ is the only solution of $M_1x = 0 \wedge \ldots \wedge M_nx = 0$. Since the elements of Q_0 have no real roots, the projection $\Pi_1(C)$ on $\mathbb{R}^1$ is equal to $\mathbb{R}^1$ for any cell $C \in \Delta$. Therefore $C_0 = \mathbb{R} \times \{(0, \ldots, 0)\}$ is a cell of Δ.

Since $g - yh, h \in F$, the solution set W of $S_1(\sigma(t), Mx)$ is a union of cells of Δ. Since Δ is well-based, either $C_0 \subseteq \overline{W}$ or $C_0 \cap \overline{W} = \emptyset$.

The mapping
$$\Phi_M : \mathbb{R}^n \ni u \longrightarrow M.u \in \mathbb{R}^n$$
is a homeomorphism which maps zero to zero, hence
$$\liminf_{u \to 0} f(Mu) = l$$
For $a \in \mathbb{R}$ put
$$W(a) := \{u \in \mathbb{R}^n \ : \ S_1(\sigma(a), Mu)\}$$
If $\sigma(a) > l$ then, by Proposition 11, $0 \in \overline{W(a)}$, and hence $C_0 \subseteq \overline{W}$. If $\sigma(a) < l$ then, by Proposition 11,
$$(\sigma(a), 0) \notin \overline{\{(b, u) \in \mathbb{R}^{n+1} \ : \ S_1(b, Mu)\}}$$
hence, by continuity of σ, $(a, 0) \notin \overline{W}$, and so $C_0 \cap \overline{W} = \emptyset$.

Therefore either $\forall_{a \in \mathbb{R}} \sigma(a) \ge l$ or $\forall_{a \in \mathbb{R}} \sigma(a) \le l$, which completes the proof of the equality $r_{i_0} = l$.

To complete the proof of correctness of Algorithm 15 we need to show that both Algorithm 13 and Algorithm 14 can be used in step (4) to decide whether $0 \in \overline{Z_1(a_i)}$.

Algorithm 13 can be used with $S_1(a_i, x)$ as the input, since $S_1(a_i, x)$ contains only strict inequalities.

To show that Algorithm 14 can be used in step (4), note that since Φ_M is a homeomorphism which maps zero to zero, $0 \in \overline{Z_1(a_i)}$ iff 0 belongs to the closure of the solution set $S_1(a_i, Mx)$. Since, for $1 \le k \le n$, P_k is regular in x_k, all factors of the leading coefficients of elements of P_k that depend on x_k belong to P_0. Since all elements of P_0 are nonzero at a_i, $(P_1(a_i, x), \ldots, P_n(a_i, x))$ is a valid CAD projection set, a $(P_1, \ldots, P_n)$-invariant CAD Δ is well-based in the sense of [14, 19], and the solution set of $S_1(a_i, Mx)$ is a union of cells of Δ. Hence Algorithm 14 can be used in step (4) with $S_1(a_i, Mx)$ as the input. □

The upper limit can be computed in a similar way, and when both the lower limit and the upper limit are needed, steps (1)-(3) of Algorithm 15 can be shared. Computing univariate limits along curves provides an upper bound on the lower limit and a lower bound on the upper limit, thus reducing the search space in step (4). If only a solution of Problem 1 is needed, univariate limit computations provide a limit value candidate (or disprove the existence of limit). To decide whether the limit exists it is sufficient to check at most two values of a_i in step (4). If the limit candidate is not one of the r_i the limit does not exist. If the limit candidate is equal to r_i then it suffices to check whether a_{i-1} is greater than the lower limit or a_i is less than the upper limit.

Example 16. Let $g = x_1(x_2 - x_3 + x_1x_3)$ and $h = x_1^2 + (x_2 - x_3)^2$, as in Example 8. The matrix M computed in step (1) is the permutation matrix $((1,0,0),(0,0,1),(0,1,0))$. In step (2) P_0 consists of 14 polynomials that have 7 real roots, and hence in step (6) there are 8 sectors with sample points a_i. Step (4) uses binary search to find i_0. The conditions verified using Algorithm 13 or 14 are: $0 \in \overline{Z_1(a_7)}$, $0 \notin \overline{Z_1(a_0)}$, $0 \in \overline{Z_1(a_3)}$, $0 \notin \overline{Z_1(a_1)}$, and $0 \notin \overline{Z_1(a_2)}$. Hence $i_0 = 3$ and the algorithm returns $r_{i_0} = -\frac{1}{2}$. The computation takes 0.375 seconds when Algorithm 13 is used and 0.11 seconds when Algorithm 14 is used.

When the algorithm uses univariate limit computations to obtain an upper bound for the lower limit, the algorithm only needs to check a_i such that r_{i+1} does not exceed the bound. In this example the obtained upper bound is 0 and $r_4 = 0$, hence the algorithm only verifies $0 \in \overline{Z_1(a_3)}$, $0 \notin \overline{Z_1(a_0)}$, $0 \notin \overline{Z_1(a_1)}$, and $0 \notin \overline{Z_1(a_2)}$. The computation takes 0.297 seconds when Algorithm 13 is used and 0.0804 seconds when Algorithm 14 is used.

5 EMPIRICAL RESULTS

We compare five CAD-based methods for computation of limits of real multivariate rational functions. OLIM1 uses Algorithm 7, OLIM2 uses Algorithm 9, TLIM1 uses Algorithm 15 with Algorithm 13 used in step (4), TLIM2 uses Algorithm 15 with Algorithm 14 used in step (4), and TLIM3 uses Algorithm 15 with step (4) using Algorithm 14 if the matrix M computed in step (1) is an identity matrix or a permutation matrix, and using Algorithm 13 otherwise.

Table 1: Example 17 timings for Problem 2

n	d	OLIM1	OLIM2	TLIM1	TLIM2	TLIM3
2	2	0.018	0.021	0.021	0.021	0.021
2	3	0.055	0.094	0.038	0.099	0.092
2	4	0.212	10.4	0.036	0.050	0.040
2	5-6	20.2	28.1	0.517	0.174	0.147
2	7-8	11.9	49.1	0.156	0.102	0.090
2	9-200	67.9	71.4	3.33	11.0	10.9
3	2	11.5	0.979	0.359	0.110	0.110
3	3-4	221	97.6	4.85	7.56	1.85
3	5-23	245	209	84.9	53.3	18.2

The motivation for the criterion used in TLIM3 is that Algorithm 14 uses $S_1(a_i, Mx)$ as the input and Algorithm 13 uses $S_1(a_i, x)$ as the input, so using Algorithm 13 may be preferable if the linear transformation represented by M may destroy the sparsity of the input. The algorithms have been implemented in *Mathematica*, as a part of the Limit command, using the built-in C implementation of the CAD algorithm. The experiments have been conducted on a Linux server with four 8-core 2.4 GHz Intel Xeon E5 processors and 378 GB of RAM. The reported CPU time is the total from all cores used. Each computation was given a 600 second time limit.

Example 17. In this example we used inputs selected from 120000 multivariate limit problems submitted to Wolfram Alpha. We have run the problems through the *Mathematica* built-in Limit and MinLimit commands, and selected the multivariate rational function limit inputs for which *Mathematica* was using a CAD-based method. *Mathematica* first tries to determine the limit by applying structural criteria and by computing univariate limits along curves. CAD-based methods are used only if the simpler methods fail. We have obtained 4818 distinct rational function inputs for which solving of Problem 2 required a CAD-based method. In 4793 of these at least one of the methods finished in under 600 seconds. For Problem 1 we obtained 612 inputs that required a CAD-based method. The large difference in the number of examples comes from the fact that *Mathematica* uses criteria that can prove non-existence of limit, but do not provide the value of the lower limit. Table 1, Table 2, and Table 3 give results for the lower limit computation. Table 4, Table 5, and Table 6 give results for solving Problem 1. Table 1 and Table 4 give the average timings in seconds (timeouts are counted as 600 seconds). Table 2 and Table 5 give the percentages of timeouts. Columns n and d give the number of variables and the total degree for the given group of examples. Table 3 and Table 6 show the number of times each algorithm was the fastest. Column $Total$ gives the total number of examples in the given group. For some examples more than one method achieved the winning time, in particular, since for a given example TLIM3 is the same as either TLIM1 or TLIM2, each win for TLIM3 was also a win for TLIM1 or TLIM2.

In Example 17 TLIM1 has the best average timing for 6 sets of Problem 1 examples and 3 sets of Problem 2 examples. TLIM3 has the best average timing for 2 sets of Problem 1 examples and 5 sets of Problem 2 examples. OLIM1 has the best average time in one set of Problem 2 examples. TLIM3 is at least as fast as TLIM2 for all sets of examples. TLIM1 and OLIM2 were the fastest methods for the largest number of Problem 1 examples. TLIM3 and OLIM1 were the fastest methods for the largest number of Problem 2 examples. However, each of the methods was the fastest for a significant

Table 2: Example 17 timeout percentages for Problem 2

n	d	OLIM1	OLIM2	TLIM1	TLIM2	TLIM3
2	2	0	0	0	0	0
2	3	0	0	0	0	0
2	4	0	1.68	0	0	0
2	5-6	2.70	4.04	0	0	0
2	7-8	1.52	7.86	0	0	0
2	9-200	10.1	9.07	0.27	1.60	1.60
3	2	0	0	0	0	0
3	3-4	12.6	13.5	0.47	0.93	0
3	5-23	36.6	29.3	9.76	7.32	0

Table 3: Example 17 win counts for Problem 2

n	d	Total	OLIM1	OLIM2	TLIM1	TLIM2	TLIM3
2	2	1213	614	35	9	613	613
2	3	139	45	39	59	3	8
2	4	1191	487	101	257	385	400
2	5-6	742	317	31	205	213	228
2	7-8	394	138	14	85	176	177
2	9-200	375	100	12	62	213	213
3	2	483	7	7	28	445	445
3	3-4	215	23	14	19	160	168
3	5-23	41	5	6	5	26	29

Table 4: Example 17 timings for Problem 1

n	d	OLIM1	OLIM2	TLIM1	TLIM2	TLIM3
2	2	0.046	0.030	0.019	0.043	0.041
2	3	0.107	0.076	0.027	0.083	0.078
2	4	1.31	9.00	0.044	0.109	0.083
2	5-6	51.3	21.2	0.183	0.275	0.229
2	7-8	25.5	68.6	0.129	0.261	0.221
2	9-100	101	89.6	2.95	44.8	44.7
3	2-3	80.1	120	0.451	0.546	0.397
3	4-12	74.2	148	24.2	101	19.1

Table 5: Example 17 timeout percentages for Problem 1

n	d	OLIM1	OLIM2	TLIM1	TLIM2	TLIM3
2	2	0	0	0	0	0
2	3	0	0	0	0	0
2	4	0	1.25	0	0	0
2	5-6	5.92	2.63	0	0	0
2	7-8	3.00	11.0	0	0	0
2	9-100	16.0	10.7	0	7.14	7.14
3	2-3	13.3	20.0	0	0	0
3	4-12	7.69	23.1	0	15.4	0

Table 6: Example 17 win counts for Problem 1

n	d	Total	OLIM1	OLIM2	TLIM1	TLIM2	TLIM3
2	2	25	0	3	24	0	1
2	3	91	0	12	80	1	3
2	4	160	14	28	118	4	19
2	5-6	152	9	16	121	6	9
2	7-8	100	15	12	68	6	8
2	9-100	56	3	3	38	12	12
3	2-3	15	0	5	9	1	3
3	4-12	13	1	6	4	2	4

Table 7: Example 18 timings

p	n	d	OLIM1	OLIM2	TLIM1	TLIM2	TLIM3	LT
1*a*	3	3	> 600	> 600	3.66	0.263	0.263	2.63
1*b*	3	3	> 600	> 600	6.74	0.406	0.406	2.63
2	4	2	4.79	1.17	0.247	0.084	0.084	0.144
3	4	4	> 600	> 600	59.7	1.16	1.16	1.38
4	3	2	1.66	0.343	0.204	0.111	0.111	0.080
5	3	3	0.105	0.044	0.030	0.017	0.017	0.372
6	6	6	10.9	3.03	0.156	0.038	0.038	1.02

number of examples of each problem. OLIM1 and OLIM2 timed out more frequently than TLIM1, TLIM2, and TLIM3, likely due to the fact that they require projection computation with one variable more.

Example 18. The functions in this example were selected from examples in [1, 22], using the same procedure as in Example 17, that is functions for which *Mathematica* solves both Problem 1 and Problem 2 without using CAD-based methods were not selected. For the first function, selected from [22], CAD-based methods were needed for solving of both Problem 1 (1*a* in Table 7) and Problem 2 (1*b* in Table 7). For the other five functions, selected from [1], CAD-based methods were needed only for solving of Problem 2.

(1) $(x^2y - x^2z + 2yz^2 - z^3)/(x^2 - xy + y^2 + xz - 2yz + z^2)$
(2) $(x^2 + y^2 + wz)/(w^2 + x^2 + y^2 + z^2)$
(3) $wxyz/(w^4 + x^4 + y^4 + z^4)$
(4) $(xy + xz - yz)/(x^2 + y^2 + z^2)$
(5) $(2x^3 + 4y^2)/(3x^2 + y^2 + 4z^2)$
(6) $t^2/(l^2 + t^2 + w^6 + x^2 + y^2 + z^2)$

All limits were computed at 0. The results are given in Table 7. Columns p, n, and d give the example number, the number of variables, and the total degree. Columns marked with the algorithm names give timings in seconds. The column marked LT gives the timings for algorithms presented in [1, 22]. Note that these algorithms solve Problem 1, so the timings are not directly comparable, except for row (1*a*). For the algorithm presented in [22] we use the timing reported in the paper. The timings for the algorithm RationalFunctionLimit presented in [1] were obtained by running the algorithm in Maple 18 with RegularChains library, on the computer used for the other experiments.

In Example 18 methods TLIM2 and TLIM3 were identical (because the matrix M computed in step (1) of Algorithm 15 was always an identity matrix or a permutation matrix) and were faster than all other methods.

6 CONCLUSION

We have present five CAD-based methods for computation of limits of real multivariate rational functions. The methods can be used for determining whether the limit exists and, if it does, computing the value of the limit. They can also be used to solve a more general problem of computing lower and upper limits. The algorithms do not require any assumptions about the rational function. Experimental results suggest that for problems with at least three variables algorithm TLIM3 gives the best average timings. However, since each of the methods was the fastest for a significant number of examples, finding a good automatic method selection heuristic is a nontrivial problem for future research.

REFERENCES

[1] P. Alvandi, M. Kazemi, and M. Moreno Maza. 2016. Computing Limits of Real Multivariate Rational Functions. In *Proceedings of the International Symposium on Symbolic and Algebraic Computation, ISSAC 2016*. ACM, 39–46.
[2] S. Basu, R. Pollack, and M.F. Roy. 2006. *Algorithms in real algebraic geometry*. Vol. 10. Springer-Verlag New York Inc.
[3] J. Bochnak, M. Coste, and M.F. Roy. 1998. *Real Algebraic Geometry*. Springer.
[4] C. W. Brown. 2003. QEPCAD B - a program for computing with semi-algebraic sets using CADs. *ACM SIGSAM Bulletin* 37 (2003), 97–108.
[5] C. Cadavid, S. Molina, and J. D. Velez. 2013. Limits of quotients of bivariate real analytic functions. *J. Symbolic Comp.* 50 (2013), 197–207.
[6] B. Caviness and J. Johnson (Eds.). 1998. *Quantifier Elimination and Cylindrical Algebraic Decomposition*. Springer Verlag, New York.
[7] C. Chen, M. Moreno Maza, B. Xia, and L. Yang. 2009. Computing Cylindrical Algebraic Decomposition via Triangular Decomposition. In *Proceedings of the International Symposium on Symbolic and Algebraic Computation, ISSAC 2009*. ACM, 95–102.
[8] G. E. Collins. 1975. Quantifier Elimination for the Elementary Theory of Real Closed Fields by Cylindrical Algebraic Decomposition. *Lect. Notes Comput. Sci.* 33 (1975), 134–183.
[9] D. Gruntz. 1996. *On computing limits in a symbolic manipulation system*. Ph.D. Dissertation. ETH.
[10] S. Łojasiewicz. 1964. *Ensembles semi-analytiques*. I.H.E.S.
[11] S. McCallum. 1999. On Projection in CAD-Based Quantifier Elimination with Equational Constraint. In *Proceedings of the International Symposium on Symbolic and Algebraic Computation, ISSAC 1999*. ACM, 145–149.
[12] S. McCallum. 2001. On Propagation of Equational Constraints in CAD-Based Quantifier Elimination. In *Proceedings of the International Symposium on Symbolic and Algebraic Computation, ISSAC 2001*. ACM, 223–230.
[13] B. Salvy and J. Shackell. 1999. Symbolic asymptotics: Multiseries of inverse functions. *J. Symb. Comput.* 27 (1999), 543–563.
[14] J. T. Schwartz and M. Sharir. 1983. On the Piano Movers Problem II. General Techniques for Computing Topological Properties of Real Algebraic Manifolds. *Advances in Applied Mathematics* 4 (1983), 298–351.
[15] A. Strzeboński. 1997. Computing in the Field of Complex Algebraic Numbers. *J. Symbolic Comp.* 24 (1997), 647–656.
[16] A. Strzeboński. 2000. Solving Systems of Strict Polynomial Inequalities. *J. Symbolic Comp.* 29 (2000), 471–480.
[17] A. Strzeboński. 2006. Cylindrical Algebraic Decomposition using validated numerics. *J. Symbolic Comp.* 41 (2006), 1021–1038.
[18] A. Strzeboński. 2010. Computation with Semialgebraic Sets Represented by Cylindrical Algebraic Formulas. In *Proceedings of the International Symposium on Symbolic and Algebraic Computation, ISSAC 2010*. ACM, 61–68.
[19] A. Strzeboński. 2017. CAD Adjacency Computation Using Validated Numerics. In *Proceedings of the International Symposium on Symbolic and Algebraic Computation, ISSAC 2017*. ACM, 413–420.
[20] A. Tarski. 1951. *A decision method for elementary algebra and geometry*. University of California Press.
[21] J. D. Velez, J. P. Hernandez, and C. A. Cadavid. 2015. Limits of quotients of real polynomial functions of three variables. arXiv 1505.04121.
[22] S. J. Xiao and G. X. Zeng. 2014. Determination of the limits for multivariate rational functions. *Science China Mathematics* 57, 2 (2014), 397–416.
[23] S. J. Xiao, X. N. Zeng, and G. X. Zeng. 2015. Real valuations and the limits of multivariate rational functions. *Journal of Algebra and Its Applications* 14, 5 (2015), 1550–1567.

On Affine Tropical F5 Algorithms

Tristan Vaccon
Université de Limoges; CNRS, XLIM UMR 7252
Limoges, France
tristan.vaccon@unilim.fr

Thibaut Verron
Johannes Kepler University
Institute for Algebra
Linz, Austria
thibaut.verron@jku.at

Kazuhiro Yokoyama
Departement of Mathematics, Rikkyo University
Tokyo, Japan
kazuhiro@rikkyo.ac.jp

ABSTRACT

Let K be a field equipped with a valuation. Tropical varieties over K can be defined with a theory of Gröbner bases taking into account the valuation of K. Because of the use of the valuation, the theory of tropical Gröbner bases has proved to provide settings for computations over polynomial rings over a p-adic field that are more stable than that of classical Gröbner bases.

Beforehand, these strategies were only available for homogeneous polynomials. In this article, we extend the F5 strategy to a new definition of tropical Gröbner bases in an affine setting.

We provide numerical examples to illustrate time-complexity and p-adic stability of this tropical F5 algorithm. We also illustrate its merits as a first step before an FGLM algorithm to compute (classical) lex bases over p-adics.

CCS CONCEPTS

• **Computing methodologies → Algebraic algorithms**;

KEYWORDS

Algorithms, Tropical geometry, Gröbner bases, F5 algorithm, p-adic precision

ACM Reference Format:
Tristan Vaccon, Thibaut Verron, and Kazuhiro Yokoyama. 2018. On Affine Tropical F5 Algorithms. In *ISSAC '18: 2018 ACM International Symposium on Symbolic and Algebraic Computation, July 16–19, 2018, New York, NY, USA.* ACM, New York, NY, USA, 8 pages. https://doi.org/10.1145/3208976.3209012

1 INTRODUCTION

Tropical geometry as we understand it has not yet reached half a century of age. It has nevertheless spawned significant applications to very various domains, from algebraic geometry to combinatorics, computer science, economics, non-archimedean geometry (see [MS15], [EKL06]) and even attempts at proving the Riemann hypothesis (see [C15]).

Effective computation over tropical varieties make decisive use of Gröbner bases. Since Chan and Maclagan's definition of tropical Gröbner bases taking into account the valuation in [C13, CM13], computations of tropical Gröbner bases are available over fields with trivial or non-trivial valuation, but only in a context of homogeneous ideals.

On the other hand, for classical Gröbner bases, numerous algorithms have been developed allowing for more and more efficient computations. The latest generation of algorithms for computing Gröbner bases is the family of signature-based algorithms, which keep track of where the polynomials come from in order to anticipate useless reductions. This idea was initiated in Algorithm F5 [F02], and has since then been widely studied and generalized ([BFS14, EF17]).

Most of those algorithms, including the original F5 algorithm, are specifically designed for homogeneous systems, and adapting them to affine (or inhomogeneous) systems requires special care (see [E13]).

An F5 algorithm computing tropical Gröbner bases without any trivial reduction to 0, inspired by the classical F5 algorithm, has been described in [VY17]. The goal of this paper is to extend the definition of tropical Gröbner bases to inhomogeneous ideals, and describe ways to adapt the F5 algorithm in this new setting.

The core motivation is the following. It has been proved [V15] that computing tropical Gröbner bases, taking into account the valuation, is more stable for polynomial ideals over a p-adic field than classical Gröbner bases.

Thus, an affine variant of tropical Gröbner bases is highly desirable to handle non-homogeneous ideals over p-adics. For classical Gröbner bases, it is always possible to homogenize the input ideal, compute a homogeneous Gröbner basis, and dehomogenize the result. This technique is not always optimal, because the algorithm may end up reaching a higher degree than needed, computing points at infinity of the system, but it always gives a correct result and, in the case of signature Gröbner basis algorithms, is able to eliminate useless reductions. However, in a tropical setting, terms are ordered with a tropical term order, taking into account the valuation of the coefficients. As far as we know it, there is no way to dehomogenize a system in a way that would preserve the tropical term order. Indeed, no tropical term order can be an elimination order.

Moreover, the FGLM algorithm can be adapted to the tropical case (see Chap. 9 of [V*]), making it possible to compute a lexicographical (classical) Gröbner basis from a tropical one. We provide numerical data to estimate the loss in precision for the computation of a lex Gröbner basis using a tropical F5 algorithm followed by an FGLM algorithm, in an affine setting.

1.1 Related works

A canonical reference for an introduction to computational tropical algebraic geometry is the book of Maclagan and Sturmfels [MS15].

The computation of tropical varieties over $\mathbb{Q}$ with trivial valuation is available in the Gfan package by Anders Jensen (see [Gfan]), by using standard Gröbner bases computations. Chan and Maclagan have developed in [CM13] a Buchberger algorithm to compute

The second author is supported by the Austrian FWF grant F5004.

ISSAC '18, July 16–19, 2018, New York, NY, USA

ACM ISBN 978-1-4503-5550-6/18/07...$15.00
https://doi.org/10.1145/3208976.3209012

tropical Gröbner bases for homogeneous entry polynomials (using a special division algorithm). Following their work, still for homogeneous polynomials, a Matrix-F5 algorithm has been proposed in [V15] and a Tropical F5 algorithm in [VY17]. Markwig and Ren have provided a completely different technique of computation using projection of standard bases in [MY16], again only for homogeneous entry polynomials.

In the classical Gröbner basis setting, many techniques have been studied to make the computation of Gröbner bases more efficient. In particular, Buchberber's algorithm is frequently made more efficient by using the *sugar-degree* (see [GMNRT91, BCM11]) instead of the actual degree for selecting the next pair to reduce. This technique was a precursor of modern signature techniques, in the sense that the sugar-degree of a polynomial is exactly the degree of its signature. General signature-based algorithms for computing classical Gröbner bases of inhomogeneous ideals have been extensively studied in [E13].

1.2 Specificities of computating tropical GB

The computation of tropical GB, even by a Buchberger-style algorithm, is not as straightforward as for classical Gröbner bases. One way to understand this is the following: even for homogeneous ideals, there is no equivalence between tropical Gröbner bases and row-echelon linear bases at every degree. Indeed,we can remark that $(f_1, f_2) = (x + y, 2x + y)$ is a tropical GB over $\mathbb{Q}[x, y]$ with 2-adic valuation, $w = [0, 0]$ and grevlex ordering. Nevertheless, the corresponding 2×2 matrix in the vector space of homogeneous polynomials of degree 2 is not under tropical row-echelon form.

As a consequence, reduction of a polynomial by a tropical GB is not easy. In [C13, CM13], Chan and Maclagan relied on a variant of Mora's tangent cone algorithm to obtain a division algorithm. In [V15, VY17], the authors relied on linear algebra and the computation of (tropical) row-echelon form. In this article, we extend their method to the computation of tropical Gröbner bases in an affine setting, through an F5 algorithm.

1.3 Main idea and results

Extending the tropical F5 algorithm to inhomogeneous inputs poses two difficulties. First, as mentioned, tropical Gröbner bases used to be only defined and computed for homogeneous systems. Even barebones algorithms such as Buchberger's algorithm are not available for inhomogeneous systems. The second problem is a general problem of signature Gröbner bases with inhomogeneous input. The idea of signature algorithms is to compute polynomials with increasing signatures, and the F5 criterion detects trivial reductions to 0 by matching candidate signatures with existing leading terms. For homogeneous ideals, the degree of the signature of a polynomial and the degree of the polynomial itself are correlated. This is what makes the F5 criterion applicable.

The survey paper [E13] has shown that Algorithm F5, using the *position over term* ordering on the signatures, has to reach a tradeoff between eliminating all reductions to 0 and performing other useless reductions.

More precisely, let $f_1, \dots, f_m$ be homogeneous polynomials with coefficients in a field with valuation K, and define $I_{k,d}$ the vector space of polynomials in $\langle f_1, \dots, f_k \rangle$ with degree at most d. With the usual computational strategy, the algorithm computes a basis of $I_{1,1}$, then $I_{2,1}$, and so on until $I_{m,1}$, and then $I_{1,2}$, and so on. In a lot of situations [BFS04] ideals with more generators have a Gröbner basis with lower degree, and this strategy ensures that the algorithm does not reach a degree higher than needed.

However, the same algorithm for affine system will, at each step, merely compute a *set of polynomials* in each $I_{k,d}$. This set needs not be a generating set because of degree falls. To obtain a basis instead, one has to proceed up to some $I_{k,\delta}$ with $\delta \geq d$. When $\delta > d$, some polynomials will be missing for the F5 criterion in degree less than δ, and the corresponding trivial reductions to 0 will not be eliminated.

In this paper, we show that the tropical F5 algorithm [VY17] works in an affine setting, and we characterize those trivial reductions to 0 which are eliminated by the F5 criterion. In particular, we show that the Macaulay matrices built at each step of the computations are Macaulay matrices of all polynomials with a given *sugar-degree*.

Compared to [VY17], the overall presentation of the F5 algorithms is clarified. It can now be summarized as the following strategy: filtration, signature, F5 elimination criterion, Buchberger-F5 criterion and finally the F5 algorithm.

Theorem 1.1. *Given a set of (non-necessarily homogeneous) polynomials $f_1, \dots, f_m \in K[X_1, \dots, X_n]$, the Tropical F5 algorithm (Algorithm 3) computes a tropical Gröbner basis of I, without reducing to 0 any trivial tame syzygy (Def. 3.1).*

We also examine an incremental affine version of the homogeneous tropical F5-algorithm and an affine tropical F4, and we compare their performances on several examples. Even in a non-homogeneous setting, the loss in precision of the tropical F5 algorithm remains satisfyingly low.

1.4 Organization of the paper

Section 2 introduces notations and nonhomogeneous tropical Gröbner bases. Section 3 then introduces the filtration on ideals necessary for F5 algorithms in this context. Section 4 is devoted to provide a Buchberger-F5 criterion on which Section 5 elaborates a first tropical F5 algorithm. Section 6 briefly presents other methods for the computation of nonhomogeneous tropical Gröbner bases. Finally, Section 7 displays numerical results related to the precision behaviour and time-complexity of the algorithms we have described.

Acknowledgements

We thank Jean-Charles Faugère, Marc Mezzarobba, Pierre-Jean Spaenlehauer, Masayuki Noro, and Naoyuki Shinohara for fruitful discussions.

2 AFFINE TROPICAL GB

2.1 Notations

Let k be a field with valuation val. The polynomial ring $k[X_1, \dots, X_n]$ will be denoted by A. Let T be the set of monomials of A. For $u = (u_1, \dots, u_n) \in \mathbb{Z}^n_{\geq 0}$, we write x^u for $X_1^{u_1} \dots X_n^{u_n}$ and $|f|$ for the degree of $f \in A$. In A^s, $(e_i)_{i=1}^s$ is the canonical basis.

The matrix of a list of polynomials written in a basis of monomials is called a *Macaulay matrix*.

Given a mapping $\phi : U \to V$, $Im(\phi)$ denotes the image of ϕ. For a matrix M, $Rows(M)$ is the list of its rows, and $Im(M)$ denotes the left-image of M (*i.e.* $Im(M) = span(Rows(M))$). For $w \in Im(val)^n \subset \mathbb{R}^n$ and $\leq_1$ a monomial order on A, we define $\leq$ a tropical term order as in the following definition:

Definition 2.1. Given $a, b \in k^*$ and x^α and x^β two monomials in A, we write $ax^\alpha < bx^\beta$ if:

- $|x^\alpha| < |x^\beta|$, or
- $|x^\alpha| = |x^\beta|$, and $val(a) + w \cdot \alpha > val(b) + w \cdot \beta$, or $val(a) + w \cdot \alpha = val(b) + w \cdot \beta$ and $x^\alpha <_1 x^\beta$.

For u of valuation 0, we write $ax^\alpha =_\leq uax^\alpha$. Accordingly, $ax^\alpha \leq bx^\beta$ if $ax^\alpha < bx^\beta$ or $ax^\alpha =_\leq bx^\beta$.

Throughout this article, we are interested in computing a tropical Gröbner basis of $I = \langle f_1, \dots, f_s \rangle$ for some given $f_1, \dots, f_s \in A$ (ordered increasingly by degree).

2.2 Tropical GB

A tropical term order provides an order on the terms of the polynomials $f \in A$.

Definition 2.2. For $f \in A$, we define $LT(f)$ to be the biggest term of f. We define $LM(f)$ to be the monomial corresponding to $LT(f)$ and $LC(f)$ the corresponding coefficient.

We define $LM(I)$ to be the monomial ideal generated by the monomials $LM(f)$ for $f \in I$.

We can then naturally define what is a tropical Gröbner basis (*tropical GB* for short):

Definition 2.3. $G \subset I$ is a tropical GB of I if span($LM(g)$ for $g \in G$) $= LM(I)$.

We can remark that for homogeneous polynomials this definition coincide with that given in [VY17].

3 FILTRATION AND $\mathfrak{S}$-GB

3.1 Definition and elimination criterion

One of the main ingredient for F5 algorithms is the definition of a vector space filtration of the ideal I. It is defined from the initial polynomials $F = (f_1, \dots, f_s)$ generating I. For simplicity, we assume that they are ordered by increasing degree.

First, we extend $\leq$ to the monomials of the vector space A^s. To that intent, we highlight some monomials that appear as leading monomial of a syzygy.

Definition 3.1. Let $(a_1, \dots, a_s) \in A^s$ and $i \in \{1, \dots, s\}$ be such that: (1) $\sum_j a_j f_j = 0$. (2) $a_i \neq 0$ and $a_j = 0$ for $j > i$. (3) for all $j < i$, $|a_j f_j| \leq |a_i f_i|$.

We call such a syzygy a *tame syzygy* and we define $LM(a_i)e_i$ to be its leading monomial. We define $LM(TSyz(F))$ as the module in A^s generated by the leading monomials of the tame syzygies. Trivial tame syzygies are the tame syzygies that are also trivial (*i.e.* in the module generated by the $f_i e_j - f_j e_i$).

The F5 criterion that we use in this article is designed to recognize some of the tame syzygies and use this knowledge to avoid useless reduction to zero of some polynomials. It is the main motivation for defining a filtration on the vector space A^s. We use a degree-refining monomial ordering $\leq_m$ on A.[1] We define a total order on the monomials of A^s.

Definition 3.2. We write that $x^\alpha e_i \leq_{sign} x^\beta e_j$ if:

(1) if $i < j$, or
(2) if $i = j$ and $|x^\alpha f_i| < |x^\beta f_j|$, or
(3) if $i = j$ and $|x^\alpha f_i| = |x^\beta f_j|$, and
- $x^\alpha \notin LM(TSyz(F))$ and $x^\beta \in LM(TSyz(F))$, or
- both $x^\alpha, x^\beta \in LM(TSyz(F))$ and $x^\alpha \leq_m x^\beta$, or
- both $x^\alpha, x^\beta \notin LM(TSyz(F))$ and $x^\alpha \leq_m x^\beta$.

Definition 3.3. We consider the vector space

$$I_{\leq_{sign} x^\alpha e_i} := Span(\{x^\beta f_j, \text{ s.t. } x^\beta e_j \leq_{sign} x^\alpha e_i\})$$

and the vector space $I_{<_{sign} x^\alpha e_i}$ defined accordingly. We define $I = \bigcup_{\uparrow x^\alpha e_i} I_{\leq_{sign} x^\alpha e_i}$ as an increasing vector space filtration of I.

We then have a very natural definition of signature. In litterature, this notion of signature is sometimes called *minimal signature.*

Definition 3.4. For $f \in I$, the smallest $x^\alpha e_i$ such that $f \in I_{\leq_{sign} x^\alpha e_i}$ is called the **signature** of f and noted $S(f)$.

The degree $|x^\alpha f_i|$ is called the **sugar-degree** of $x^\alpha e_i$.[2] For the purpose of Algorithm 3, we design a filtration compatible with the sugar-degree.

Definition 3.5. We consider the vector space

$$I^{\leq d} = Span(\{x^\beta f_j, \text{ s.t. } |x^\beta e_j| \leq d\})$$

We then define, for $x^\alpha e_i$ with sugar-degree d, the vector space $I^{\leq d}_{\leq_{sign} x^\alpha e_i} = Span(\{x^\beta f_j, \text{ s.t. } x^\beta e_j \leq_{sign} x^\alpha e_i \text{ and } |x^\beta f_j| \leq d\})$.

$I = \bigcup_{\uparrow d} I^{\leq d}$ is also a vector space filtration. $I^{\leq d}$ can itself be filtrated by the $I^{\leq d}_{\leq_{sign} x^\alpha e_i}$. We have a compatible notion of signature:

Definition 3.6. For $d \in \mathbb{Z}_{>0}$ and $f \in I^{\leq d}$, the smallest $x^\alpha e_i$ such that $f \in I^{\leq d}_{\leq_{sign} x^\alpha e_i}$ is called the d-**signature** of f and noted $S_d(f)$.

We remark that $S_d(f)$ can be different from $S(f)$ for small f, but all $S_d(f)$ are equal when d is large.

The main motivation for defining the vector spaces $I^{\leq d}_{\leq_{sign} x^\alpha e_i}$ is their finite dimension. Their compatibility with the sugar-degree allows the F5 algorithm to compute only one Macaulay matrix by sugar-degree d.

The goal of the F5 criterion is to recognize some $x^\alpha e_i$ such that the filtration is constant at $I^{\leq d}_{\leq_{sign} x^\alpha e_i}$. As a consequence, this knowledge allows to skip some calculation as, because of this constancy, they will not provide any new leading monomial. We can then state a first version of the F5 elimination criterion:

Proposition 3.7 ([F02]). *If x^α is such that $x^\alpha e_i \in LM(Tsyz(F))$, $d \geq |x^\alpha f_i|$, then the filtration is constant at $I^{\leq d}_{\leq_{sign} x^\alpha e_i}$. If $x^\alpha \in LM(I^{\leq d}_{\leq_{sign} x^\beta e_j})$ for some x^β and j such that $|x^\beta f_j| \leq |x^\alpha|$, then $x^\alpha e_i \in LM(Tsyz(F))$ for any $i > j$.*

Proof. For the first part, we can write $(x^\alpha + g) f_i = \sum_{j<i} a_j f_j$, with $LT(g) < x^\alpha$ and for all $j < i$, $|a_j f_j| \leq |x^\alpha f_i|$. Then:

$$x^\alpha f_i = (-g) f_i + \sum_{j=1}^{i-1} a_j f_j.$$

By linear algebra and a complete reduction using as pivot the $x^\beta e_j \in LM(Tsyz(F))$, we can assume that g has no monomial in

[1] $\leq_m$ is not necessarily related to $\leq_1$ and $\leq$.

[2] Sugar-degree has been introduced and explored in [GMNRT91, BCM11].

$LM(TSyz(F))$ and obtain: $x^\alpha f_i \in I^{\leq d}_{<x^\alpha e_i}$, and therefore, the filtration is constant at $I^{\leq d}_{\leq x^\alpha e_i}$.

For the second part, we can write $x^\alpha + g = \sum_{k \leq j} a_k f_k$, with $LT(g) < x^\alpha$ and for all $k \leq j$, $|a_j f_j| \leq |x^\beta f_j| \leq |x^\alpha|$. Then $(x^\alpha + g)f_i - \sum_{k \leq j}(a_k f_i) f_k = 0$ and we do have $|x^\alpha f_i| \geq |(a_k f_i) f_k|$ for all $k \leq j$. □

If all the f_i's are homogeneous, this coincides with the usual F5 elimination criterion, as for example stated in [VY17], which eliminates all trivial reductions to zero in the course of the algorithm. For affine polynomials, the F5 criterion only eliminates those trivial reductions which are tame.

3.2 Tropical $\mathfrak{S}$-GB

In order to take advantage of the F5 elimination criterion to compute tropical Gröbner bases, we focus on the computation of tropical Gröbner bases which are compatible with the filtration: tropical $\mathfrak{S}$-GB. We first need the definition of reductions compatible with the filtration and the corresponding irreducible polynomials.

Definition 3.8 ($\mathfrak{S}$-reduction). Let $e, g \in I$, $h \in I$. We say that e $\mathfrak{S}$**-reduces** to g with h, $e \xrightarrow[\mathfrak{S}]{h} g$, if there are $t \in T$ and $\alpha \in k^*$ such that:

- $LT(g) < LT(e)$, $LM(g) \neq LM(e)$ and $e - \alpha t h = g$ and
- $S(th) <_{sign} S(e)$.

It is then natural to define what is an $\mathfrak{S}$-irreducible polynomial.

Definition 3.9 ($\mathfrak{S}$-irreducible polynomial). We say that $g \in I$ is $\mathfrak{S}$-irreducible if there is no $h \in I$ which $\mathfrak{S}$-reduces g. If there is no ambiguity, we might omit the $\mathfrak{S}$ – .

Definition 3.10 (Tropical $\mathfrak{S}$-Gröbner basis). We say that $G \subset I$, a set of $\mathfrak{S}$-irreducible polynomials, is a **tropical $\mathfrak{S}$-Gröbner basis** (or tropical $\mathfrak{S}$–GB, or just $\mathfrak{S}$–GB for short when there is no ambiguity) of I with respect to a given tropical term order, if for each $\mathfrak{S}$-irreducible polynomial $h \in I$, there exist $g \in G$ and $t \in T$ such that $LM(tg) = LM(h)$ and $tS(g) = S(h)$.

Definition 3.11. Definitions 3.8, 3.9 and 3.10 have natural analogues when one restricts to the vector space $I^{\leq d}$ and S_d with $\mathfrak{S}_d$-reduction, $\mathfrak{S}_d$-irreducible polynomial and tropical $\mathfrak{S}_d$-GB.

Proposition 3.12. *If G is a tropical $\mathfrak{S}$-Gröbner basis, then for any nonzero $h \in I$, there exist $g \in G$ and $t \in T$ such that:*

- *$LM(tg) = LM(h)$*
- *$S(tg) = tS(g) = S(h)$ if h is irreducible, and $S(tg) = tS(g) <_{sign} S(h)$ otherwise.*

Hence, there is an $\mathfrak{S}$-reductor for h in G when h is not irreducible.

Corollary 3.13. *If G is a tropical $\mathfrak{S}$-Gröbner basis, then G is a tropical Gröbner basis of I, for $<$.*

As a consequence computing a tropical $\mathfrak{S}$-GB provides a tropical GB, and we can use the F5 elimination criterion 3.7 to our advantage when computing these tropical $\mathfrak{S}$-GB. Moreover, we also have the following finiteness result:

Proposition 3.14. *Every tropical $\mathfrak{S}$-Gröbner basis contains a finite tropical $\mathfrak{S}$-Gröbner basis.*

Proof. We refer to the proof of Proposition 14 of [AP]. It uses an adapted Dickson's Lemma and since it is mostly a question of monomial ideals, the transposition to the tropical setting is direct. □

3.3 Linear algebra and existence

For $x^\alpha \in T$ and $1 \leq i \leq n$, let us denote by $Mac_{\leq_{sign} x^\alpha e_i}(F)$ the Macaulay matrix of the polynomials $x^\beta f_j$ such that $x^\beta f_j \leq x^\alpha f_i$, ordered increasingly for the order on the $x^\beta e_j$'s. One can perform a tropical LUP algorithm on $Mac_{\leq d}(F)$ (see Algo. 2) and obtain all the leading monomials in $I_{\leq_{sign} x^\alpha e_i}$. This can be (theoretically) performed for all $x^\alpha e_i$ to obtain the existence of an $\mathfrak{S}$-GB of I.

3.4 More on signatures

We define Σ to be the set of signatures.

Thanks to Proposition 3.7, not all $x^\alpha e_i$ can be a signature:

Remark 3.15. If $x^\alpha e_i \in LM(TSyz(F))$ then $x^\alpha e_i \notin \Sigma$.

We provide two lemmata to understand the compatibility of Σ with basic operations on polynomials.

Lemma 3.16. *If $f, g \in I$ are such that $S(f) = S(g)$ and $LM(f) \neq LM(g)$, then there exist $a, b \in k^*$ such that $S(af + bg) < S(f)$ and $af + bg \neq 0$.*

If one takes the point of view of linear algebra, the proof is direct.

Lemma 3.17. *If $g \in I$ and $\tau \in T$ then $S(\tau g) \leq \tau S(g)$. If moreover $\tau S(g) \in \Sigma$, then $S(\tau g) = \tau S(g)$ and for all $\mu \in T$ such that μ divides τ, $S(\mu g) = \mu S(g)$.*

Proof. The first part is direct. For the second part, one can show that it is possible to write that $\tau g = h + r$ for some $h \in I$ of signature $\tau S(g)$, irreducible, and $r \in I_{<_{sign} \tau S(g)}$ and conclude that $S(\tau g) = \tau S(g)$.

For the last statement, assume that there exists a $\mu \in T$ dividing τ such that $S(\mu g) < \mu S(g)$. Then $S(\tau g) = S(\frac{\tau}{\mu}\mu g) \leq \frac{\tau}{\mu} S(\mu g) < \frac{\tau}{\mu}\mu S(g) = \tau S(g)$, which is a contradiction. □

4 BUCHBERGER-F5 CRITERION

In this section, we explain a criterion, the Buchberger-F5 criterion, on which we build our F5 algorithm to compute tropical $\mathfrak{S}$-Gröbner bases. It is an analogue of the Buchberger criterion which includes the F5 elimination criterion.

We need a slightly different notion of S-pairs, called here normal pairs and can then state the Buchberger-F5 criterion.

Definition 4.1 (Normal pair). Given $g_1, g_2 \in I$, let $Spol(g_1, g_2) = u_1 g_1 - u_2 g_2$ be the S-polynomial of g_1 and g_2, with for $i \in \{1, 2\}$, $u_i = \frac{lcm(LM(g_1), LM(g_2))}{LT(g_i)}$. We say that (g_1, g_2) is a **normal pair** if:

(1) the g_i's are $\mathfrak{S}$-irreducible polynomials.
(2) $S(u_i g_i) = LM(u_i) S(g_i)$ for $i = 1, 2$.
(3) $S(u_1 g_1) \neq S(u_2 g_2)$.

We define accordingly d-normal pairs in $I^{\leq d}$.

Theorem 4.2 (Buchberger-F5 criterion). *Suppose that G is a finite set of $\mathfrak{S}$-irreducible polynomials of $I = \langle f_1, \dots, f_s \rangle$ such that:*

(1) for all $\forall i \in [\![1, s]\!]$, there exists $g \in G$ such that $S(g) = e_i$.
(2) for any $g_1, g_2 \in G$ such that (g_1, g_2) is a normal pair, there exists $g \in G$ and $t \in T$ such that tg is $\mathfrak{S}$-irreducible and $tS(g) = S(tg) = S(Spol(g_1, g_2))$.

Then G is a $\mathfrak{S}$-Gröbner basis of I. The analogue result using d-normal pairs to recognize an $\mathfrak{S}_d$-GB in $I^{\leq d}$ is also true.

Remark 4.3. The converse of this result is clear.

Theorem 4.2 is an analogue of the Buchberger criterion for tropical $\mathfrak{S}$-Gröbner bases. To prove it, we adapt the classical proof of the Buchberger criterion and the proof of the tropical Buchberger algorithm of Chan and Maclagan (Algorithm 2.9 of [C13]). We need two lemmata, the first one being elementary.

Lemma 4.4. *Let $x^\alpha, x^\beta, x^\gamma, x^\delta \in T$ and $P, Q \in A$ be such that $LM(x^\alpha P) = LM(x^\beta Q) = x^\gamma$ and $x^\delta = lcm(LM(P), LM(Q))$. Then*

$$Spol(x^\alpha P, x^\beta Q) = x^{\gamma-\delta} Spol(P, Q).$$

Lemma 4.5. *Let G be an $\mathfrak{S}$-Gröbner basis of I up to some signature σ. Let $h \in I$, be such that $S(h) \leq \sigma$. Then there exist $r \in \mathbb{N}$, $g_1, \dots, g_r \in G$, $Q_1, \dots, Q_r \in A$ such that for all i and x^α a monomial of Q_i, $S(x^\alpha g_i) = x^\alpha S(g_i) \leq S(h)$ and $LT(Q_i g_i) \leq LT(h)$, the $x^\alpha S(g_i)$'s are all distinct and non-zero, and, finally, we have*

$$h = \sum_{i=1}^{r} Q_i g_i.$$

Proof. It is clear by linear algebra. One can form a Macaulay matrix whose rows correspond to polynomials $c\tau g$ with $\tau \in T, c \in k^*, g \in G$ such that $S(\tau g) = \tau S(g) \leq S(h)$. Only one row is possible per non-zero signature, and each monomial in $LM(I_{\leq \sigma})$ is reached as leading term by only one row. It is then enough to stack h at the bottom of this matrix and perform a tropical LUP form computation (see Algorithm 2) to read the Q_i's on the reduction of h. □

Proof of Theorem 4.2. We prove the main result by induction on the signature. We follow the order $\leq_{sign}$ for the induction. It is clear for $\sigma = e_1$ and also for the fact we can pass from an $\mathfrak{S}$-GB up to $<_{sign} e_i$ to $\leq_{sign} e_i$. We write the elements of G as $g_1, \dots, g_r$ for some $r \in \mathbb{Z}_{>0}$.

Let us assume that G is an $\mathfrak{S}$-GB up to signature $<_{sign} \sigma$ for some signature σ and let us prove it is a $\mathfrak{S}$-GB up to $\leq_{sign} \sigma$. We can assume that all $g \in G$ satisfy $LC(g) = 1$. Let $P \in I$ be irreducible, with $LC(P) = 1$ and such that $S(P) = \sigma$. We prove that there is $\tau \in T, g \in G$ such that $LM(P) = LM(\tau g)$ and $S(\tau g) = \tau S(g) = \sigma$.

Our first assumption for G implies that there exist at least one $g \in G$ and some $\tau \in T$ such that $\tau S(g) = S(P) = \sigma$.

If $LM(\tau g) =_{\leq} LM(P)$ we are done. Otherwise, by Lemma 3.16, there exist some $a, b \in k^*$ such that $S(aP + b\tau g) = \sigma'$ for some $\sigma' <_{sign} \sigma$.

We can apply Lemma 4.5 to $aP + b\tau g$ and obtain that there exist $h_1, \dots, h_r \in A$, such that $P = \sum_{i=1}^r h_i g_i$, and for all i, and x^γ monomial of h_i, the $x^\gamma S(g_i) = S(x^\gamma g_i) \leq_{sign} \sigma$ are all distincts. We remark that $LT(P) \leq \max_i(LT(g_i h_i))$. We denote by $m_i := LT(g_i h_i)$.

Among all such possible ways of writing P as $\sum_{i=1}^r h_i g_i$, we define β as the **minimum** of the $\max_i(LT(g_i h_i))$'s. Such a β exists thanks to Lemma 2.10 in [CM13] (adaptation to the non-homogeneous setting is for free). We write $x^u = LM(\beta)$.

If $LT(P) =_{\leq} \beta$, then we are done. Indeed, there is then some i and τ in the terms of h_i such that $LM(\tau g_i) = LM(P)$ and $S(\tau g_i) = \tau S(g_i) \leq_{sign} \sigma$.

We now show that $LT(P) < \beta$ leads to a contradiction.

We can renumber the g_i's so that:

- $\beta =_{\leq} m_1 =_{\leq} \cdots =_{\leq} m_d$.
- $\beta > m_i$ for $i > d$.

We can assume that among the set of possible $(h_1, \dots, h_r)$ that reaches β, we take one such that this d is minimal.

Since $LT(P) < \beta$, then we have $d \geq 2$.

We can write

$$Spol(g_1, g_2) = LC(g_2) \frac{lcm(LM(g_1), LM(g_2))}{LM(g_1)} g_1 - LC(g_1) \frac{lcm(LM(g_1), LM(g_2))}{LM(g_2)} g_2.$$

By construction, $LM(h_1)S(g_1) \neq LM(h_2)S(g_2)$, so $(LM(h_1)g_1, LM(h_2 g_2))$ is a normal pair. By Lemma 4.4, there exists a term μ such that $\mu \frac{lcm(LM(g_1), LM(g_2))}{LM(g_i)} = LM(h_i)$ for $i \in \{1, 2\}$. So by Lemma 3.17, (g_1, g_2) is a normal pair as well.

If $S(Spol(g_1, g_2)) = \sigma$, by the second property of the F5 criterion, we are done.

Otherwise, $S(Spol(g_1, g_2)) <_{sign} \sigma$. Moreover, let

$$L = \frac{LC(h_1 g_1)}{LC(g_1)LC(g_2)} \frac{x^u}{lcm(LM(g_1), LM(g_2))}.$$

Then we have $S(L \cdot Spol(g_1, g_2)) \leq_{sign} \sigma$ thanks to Lemma 4.4. Using the same construction as before with the first assumption of the F5 criterion and Lemmata 3.16 and 4.5, we obtain some h_i''s such that $L \cdot Spol(g_1, g_2) = \sum_{i=1}^r h_i' g_i$, $LT(h_i' g_i) \leq LT(L \cdot Spol(g_1, g_2)) < \beta$ for all i. Furthermore, the signatures $S(x^\alpha g_i) = x^\alpha S(g_i)$ for $i \in \{1, \dots, r\}$ and x^α in the support of h_i' are all distincts.

We then get:

$$\begin{aligned} P &= \sum_{i=1}^r h_i g_i, \\ &= \sum_{i=1}^r h_i g_i - L \cdot Spol(g_1, g_2) + \sum_{i=1}^r h_i' g_i, \\ &= \left(h_1 - \frac{LC(h_1 g_1)}{LC(g_1)} \frac{x^u}{LM(g_1)} + h_1'\right) g_1 \\ &\quad + \left(h_2 - \frac{LC(h_1 g_1)}{LC(g_2)} \frac{x^u}{LM(g_2)} + h_2'\right) g_2 + \sum_{i=3}^r (h_i + h_i') g_i, \\ &=: \sum_{i=1}^r \widetilde{h}_i g_i, \end{aligned}$$

where the $\widetilde{h}_i$'s are defined naturally.

By construction, $LT(\widetilde{h}_1 g_1) < LT(h_1 g_1) = \beta$ and $LT(\widetilde{h}_i) \leq \beta$ for $i \leq d$ and $LT(\widetilde{h}_i) < \beta$ for $i > d$.

As a consequence, we have obtained a new expression for f with either $max_i(LT(\widetilde{h}_i)) < \beta$ or this term attained stricly less than d times, which is in either case a contradiction with their definitions as minima. So $LT(P) =_{\leq} \beta$, which concludes the proof of the main result. It is then direct to adapt the previous proof to the case of an $\mathfrak{S}_d$-GB. □

This theorem holds also for $\mathfrak{S}$-GB (or $\mathfrak{S}_d$-GB) up to a given signature. We have the following variant as a corollary for compatibility with sugar-degree:

Proposition 4.6. *Suppose that $d \in \mathbb{Z}_{>0}$, and G is a finite set of polynomials of I such that:*

(1) Any $g \in G$ is $\mathfrak{S}_d$-irreducible in $I^{\leq d}$.
(2) For all $g_1, g_2 \in G$ we have g_1, g_2 and $Spol(g_1, g_2)$ in $I^{\leq d}$.
(3) For all $i \in [\![1, s]\!]$, there exists $g \in G$ such that $S_d(g) = e_i$.

(4) for any $g_1, g_2 \in G$ such that (g_1, g_2) is a d-normal pair, there exists $g \in G$ and $t \in T$ such that tg is $\mathfrak{S}_d$-irreducible and $tS_d(g) = S_d(tg) = S_d(Spol(g_1, g_2))$.

Then G is an $\mathfrak{S}$-Gröbner basis of I.

5 F5 ALGORITHM

In this section, we present our F5 algorithm. To this intent, we need to discuss some crucial algorithmic points: how to recognize with which pairs to proceed and how to build the Macaulay matrices and reduce them. Some algorithms are on the following page.

5.1 Admissible pairs and guessed signatures

The second condition in the Definition 4.1 of normal pairs is not possible to check in advance in an F5 algorithm. One needs an $\mathfrak{S}$-Gröbner basis up to the corresponding signature to be able to certify it. To circumvent this issue, we use the weaker notion of admissible pair.

Definition 5.1 (d-Admissible pair). Given $g_1, g_2 \in I^{\leq d}$, let $Spol(g_1, g_2) = u_1 g_1 - u_2 g_2$ be the S-polynomial of g_1 and g_2. We have

$$u_i = \frac{lcm(LM(g_1), LM(g_2))}{LT(g_i)}.$$

We say that (g_1, g_2) is a d-**admissible pair** if:

(1) $LM(u_i)S_d(g_i) = x_i^{\alpha} e_{j_i} \notin LM(TSyz)$.
(2) $LM(u_1)S_d(g_1) \neq LM(u_2)S_d(g_2)$.

To certify that a set is an $\mathfrak{S}_d$-GB, handling d-admissible pairs instead of d-normal pairs is harmless. Indeed, d-normal pairs in $I^{\leq d}$ are contained inside the d-admissible pairs. Whether a pair is d-admissible can be checked easily before proceeding to reduction.

During the execution of the algorithm, when a polynomial $x^\alpha g$ is processed, it is at first not possible to know what is its signature. Algorithm 3 has computed $S_d(g)$ beforehand. Thanks to the F5 elimination criterion (Prop 3.7), we can detect some of the $x^\alpha g$ such that $S(x^\alpha g) \neq x^\alpha S(g)$ and eliminate them. For the processed polynomials, we use $x^\alpha S_d(g)$ as a **guessed signature** in the algorithm. Once an $\mathfrak{S}$-GB up to signature $< x^\alpha S_d(g)$ is computed, we have the following alternative. First case: $S_d(x^\alpha g) < x^\alpha S_d(g)$ and $x^\alpha g$ reduces to zero (by the computed $\mathfrak{S}_d$-GB up to d-signature $< x^\alpha S_d(g)$). The guessed signature was wrong but it is harmless as the polynomial is useless anyway. Second case: $S_d(x^\alpha g) = x^\alpha S_d(g)$, and then the guessed signature is certified. Once the criterion of Proposition 4.6 is satisfied, all signatures are certified.

What happens when we can obtain f with signature $S_d(f) = x^\alpha e_i$ in degree d, and $S_{d+1}(f) = x^\beta e_j <_{sign} x^\alpha e_i$ in degree $d+1$? Thanks to the way Algorithm 1 handles polynomials, always looking for smallest signature available, f and its multiples will then be built using only the second way. The first way of writing will at most appear so as to be reduced by the second one.

5.2 Symbolic Preprocessing and Rewritten criterion

One of the main parts of the F5 algorithm 3 is the Symbolic Preprocessing : Algorithm 1. From the current set of S-pairs, sugar-degree d, and the current $\mathfrak{S}_{d-1}$-GB, it produces a Macaulay matrix. One can read on the tropical reduction of this matrix new polynomials to append to the current basis to obtain an $\mathfrak{S}_d$-GB. It mostly consists of detecting which pairs are admissible and selecting a (complete) set of reductors.

A special part of the algorithm is the use of Rewritten techniques (due to Faugère (see [F02])).

The idea is the following. Once a polynomial has passed the F5 elimination criterion and is set to appear in a Macaulay matrix, it can be replaced by any other multiple of an element of G of the same d-signature. Indeed, assuming correctness of the algorithm without any rewriting technique, if one of them, h, is of d-signature $x^\alpha e_i$, the algorithm computes a tropical $\mathfrak{S}$-Gröbner basis up to d-signature $<_{sign} x^\alpha e_i$. Hence, h can be replaced by any other polynomial of same signature: it would be reduced to the same polynomial. By induction, one can prove that all of them can be replaced at the same time. We also remark that this is still valid for replacing a row of a given guessed d-signature by another of the same guessed d-signature.

One efficient way is to replace a polynomial $t \times g$ by the polynomial $x^\beta h$ ($h \in G$) of same (guessed) d-signature $tS_d(g)$ such that x^β has smallest degree.[3] Taking the sparsest available is another possibility. It actually leads to a substantial reduction of the running time of the F5 algorithm.

Algorithm 1: Symbolic-Preprocessing-Rewritten

input : P, a set of $d-1$-admissible pairs of sugar-degree d and G such that $G \cap I^{\leq d-1}$ is an $\mathfrak{S}_{d-1}$-GB
output: A Macaulay matrix of degree d

```
for Q polynomial in P do
    Replace Q in P by the polynomial (uS(g), u × g) with g
    latest added to G reaching the same guessed signature ;
C ← the set of the monomials of the polynomials in P ;
U ← the polynomials of P with their signature, except
    only one polynomial is taken by guessed signature ;
D ← ∅ ;
while C ≠ D do
    m ← max(C \ D) ;
    D ← D ∪ {m} ;
    V ← ∅ ;
    for g ∈ G do
        if LM(g) | m then
            V ← V ∪ {(g, m/LM(g))} ;
    (g, δ) ← the element of V with δ × g of smallest
        guessed signature not already in the signatures of U,
        with tie-breaking by taking minimal δ (for degree
        then for ≤_sign) ;
    U ← U ∪ {δ × g} ;
    C ← C ∪ {monomials of δ × g} ;
M ← the polynomials of U, written in a Macaulay matrix
    and ordered by increasing guessed signature ;
Return M ;
```

[3] Indeed, such an h can be considered as one of the most reduced possible.

5.3 Linear algebra

To reduce the Macaulay matrices while respecting the signatures, we use the following tropical LUP algorithm from [V15]: Algorithm 2. If the rows correspond to polynomials ordered by increasing signature, it computes a row-reduction, respecting the signatures with each non-zero row with a different leading monomial.

Algorithm 2: The tropical LUP algorithm

input : M, a Macaulay matrix of degree d in A, with n_{row} rows and n_{col} columns, and *mon* a list of monomials indexing the columns of M.
output : $\widetilde{M}$, the U of the tropical LUP-form of M

- $\widetilde{M} \leftarrow M$;
- **if** $n_{col} = 1$ *or* $n_{row} = 0$ *or* M *has no non-zero entry* **then**
  - Return $\widetilde{M}$;
- **else**
  - **for** $i = 1$ *to* n_{row} **do**
    - **Find** j such that $\widetilde{M}_{i,j}$ has the greatest term $\widetilde{M}_{i,j} x^{mon_j}$ for $\leq$ of the row i;
    - **Swap** the columns 1 and j of $\widetilde{M}$, and the 1 and j entries of *mon*;
    - By **pivoting** with the first row, eliminates the coefficients of the other rows on the first column;
    - **Proceed recursively** on the submatrix $\widetilde{M}_{i \geq 2, j \geq 2}$;
  - **Return** $\widetilde{M}$;

5.4 A Complete Algorithm

We now provide with Algorithm 3 a complete version of an F5 algorithm wich uses Buchberger-F5 criterion and all the techniques introduced in this section.

Theorem 5.2. *Algorithm 3 computes an $\mathfrak{S}$-GB of I. It avoids trivial tame syzygies.*

Proof. It relies on Theorem 4.2 and then Proposition 4.6. The proof is by induction on the sugar-degree, then i, then the $x^\alpha e_i$. One first proves that at the end of the main *while* loop any guessed signature is correct, or its row has reduced to zero, and then that $\mathfrak{S}_d$-GB are computed, signature by signature. One can then apply 4.6 on the output to conclude. Termination is a consequence of correctness and Prop. 3.14. For the syzygies, it is a consequence of Prop. 3.7 and the fact that trivial syzygies of leading monomial $x^\alpha e_i$ are such that $x^\alpha \in LM(\langle f_1, \dots, f_{i-1} \rangle)$. □

Remark 5.3. Condition 1 of 4.2 and 3 of 4.6 is not satisfied when for some i, $f_i \in \langle f_1, \dots, f_{i-1} \rangle$. This is harmless as: (1) As soon as it is found by computation, no signature in e_i will appear anymore. (2) The Buchberger-F5 criterion can be applied omitting f_i.

6 OTHER ALGORITHMS

6.1 Iterative F5

In this subsection, we present briefly another way of extending the F5 algorithm to the affine setting: a completely iterative way in the initial polynomials. The idea is to compute tropical Gröbner bases for $\langle f_1 \rangle, \langle f_1, f_2 \rangle, \dots, \langle f_1, \dots, f_s \rangle$.

Algorithm 3: A complete F5 algorithm

input : $f_1, \dots, f_s$ polynomials, ordered by degree
output : A tropical $\mathfrak{S}$-GB G of $\langle f_1, \dots, f_s \rangle$

- $G \leftarrow \{(e_i, f_i) \text{ for i in } [\![1, s]\!]\}$;
- $B \leftarrow \{\text{S-pairs of } G\}$; $d \leftarrow 1$;
- **while** $B \neq \emptyset$ **do**
  - **if** *there is* i *s.t.* $|f_i| = d$ **then**
    - Replace the occurence of f_i in G by its reduction modulo $G \cap \langle f_1, \dots, f_{i-1} \rangle$;
  - P **receives** the pop of the $d-1$-admissible pairs in B of sugar-degree d. Suppress from B the others of sugar-degree d;
  - **Write** them in a Macaulay matrix M_d, along with their $\mathfrak{S}_d$-reductors obtained from G (one per signature) by **Symbolic-Preprocessing-Rewritten**(P, G) (Algorithm 1);
  - **Apply** Algorithm 2 to compute the U in the tropical LUP form of M (no choice of pivot) ;
  - **Add** to G all the polynomials obtained from $\widetilde{M}$ that provide new leading monomial up to their d-signature ;
  - **Add** to B the corresponding new d-admissible pairs ;
  - $d \leftarrow d + 1$;
- **Return** G ;

This corresponds to using the position over term ordering on the signatures, or in terms of filtration, to the following filtration on A^s:

Definition 6.1. We write that $x^\alpha e_i \leq_{incr} x^\beta e_j$ if:

(1) if $i < j$.
(2) if $i = j$ and $|x^\alpha f_i| < |x^\beta f_j|$.
(3) if $i = j$ and $|x^\alpha f_i| = |x^\beta f_j|$, and
- $x^\alpha \notin LM(I_{i-1})$ and $x^\beta \in LM(I_{i-1})$, or
- both $x^\alpha, x^\beta \in LM(I_{i-1})$ and $x^\alpha \leq x^\beta$, or
- both $x^\alpha, x^\beta \notin LM(I_{i-1})$ and $x^\alpha \leq x^\beta$.

Proposition 6.2 ([F02]). *If $x^\alpha \in LM(I_{i-1})$, then the filtration is constant at*

$$I_{\leq x^\alpha e_i}.$$

Proof. We can write $x^\alpha + g = \sum_{j<i} a_j f_j$, with for all j $a_j \in I$, and $g \in I$ with no monomial in $LM(I_{i-1})$. Then: $x^\alpha f_i = (-g) f_i + \sum_{j=1}^{i-1} (a_j f_i) f_j$, and the filtration is constant at $I_{\leq x^\alpha e_i}$. □

It is then possible to state a Buchberger-F5 criterion and provide an adapted F5 algorithm. The two algorithms will then differ in the following way. **1.** For a given x^α and e_i, the vector space $I_{<x^\alpha e_i}$ is much bigger in the iterative setting, often of infinite dimension. Thus, polynomials of signature $x^\alpha e_i$ can be more deeply reduced. **2.** More syzygies can be avoided in the iterative setting. **3.** However, many more matrices are to be produced: one for each i and each necessary degree. Construction of the matrices is not mutualised by degree anymore.

6.2 F4

Another way to compute tropical Gröbner bases for affine polynomials is to adapt Faugère's F4 algorithm [F99]

Roughly, the F4 algorithm is an adaptation of Buchberger's algorithm such that: all S-polynomials of a given degree are processed and reduced together in a big Macaulay matrix, along with their reducers. The algorithm carries on the computation until there is no S-polynomials to reduce.

In a tropical setting, we have adapted the so-called "normal strategy" of F4 using the tropical LUP algorithm to reduce the Macaulay matrices. We have used Algorithm 2 to reduce the Macaulay matrices. So-called tropical row-echelon forms (Algorithm 3.2.2 and 3.7.3 of [V15]) are also possible, enabling a trade-off between speed, thoroughness of the reduction and loss in precision.

7 NUMERICAL EXPERIMENTS

A toy implementation of our algorithms in Sagemath [Sage] is available on https://gist.github.com/TristanVaccon. We have gathered some numerical results in the following arrays. Timings are in seconds of CPU time.[4]

7.1 Benchmarks

Here, the base field is $\mathbb{Q}$ with 2-adic valuation. We have applied the tropical F5 algorithm, Algorithm 3, an iterative tropical F5, and a tropical F4 algorithm on the Katsura n and Cyclic n systems for varying n. Dots mean no conclusion in decent time.

w=[0,...,0]	Katsura 4	5	6	7	Cyclic 4	5	6
Trop F5	.16	1.2	1371	•	0.4	21	•
Iterative trop F5	0.3	1.9	1172	•	0.4	21	•
Trop F4	.5	5	30	•	1.7	112	•

$w = [(-2)^{i-1}]$	Katsura 4	5	6	7	Cyclic 4	5	6
Trop F5	0.15	0.8	17	•	0.18	11	•
Iterative trop F5	0.18	1.1	20	•	0.18	11	•
Trop F4	0.2	1.7	15	•	1	65	•

7.2 Trop. F5+FGLM

For a given p, we take three polynomials with random coefficients in $\mathbb{Z}_p$ (using the Haar measure) in $\mathbb{Q}_p[x, y, z]$ of degree $2 \leq d_1 \leq d_2 \leq d_3 \leq 4$. We first compute a tropical Gröbner basis for the weight $w = [0, 0, 0]$[5] and the grevlex monomial ordering, and then apply an FGLM algorithm (tropical to classical as in Chapter 9 of [V*]) to obtain a lex GB. For any given choice of d_i's, we repeat the experiment 50 times. Coefficients of the initial polynomials are all given at some high-enough precision $O(p^N)$ for no precision issue to appear. We can not provide a certificate on the monomials of the output basis though. Results are compiled in the following arrays.

Firstly, an array for timings given as couples: average of the timings for the tropical F5 part and for the FGLM part, with $D = d_1 + d_2 + d_3 - 2$, the Macaulay bound. We add that for $p = 2, 3$, there is often a huge standard deviation on the timings of the F5 part.

	$D = 4$		5		6		7		8		9	
$p = 2$	.7	0.2	2.5	0.5	18	2.3	300	11	50	37	145	138
3	.8	.2	.9	.5	4	2	9	11	16	37	80	144
101	0.3	.2	.5	.5	1	2	3	10	4.6	37	11	150
65519	.4	.2	.6	.6	1.3	2.6	3.5	11	5	39	10	132

Coefficients of the output tropical GB or classical GB are known at individual precision $O(p^{N-m})$. We compute the total mean and max on those m's on the obtained GB. Results are compiled in the following array as couples of mean and max. The first array is for the F5 part and the second for the precision on the final result.

	$D = 4$		5		6		7		8		9	
$p = 2$	1.3	13	1.3	13	1.3	14	1.5	13	1.4	17	1.3	15
3	.6	6	.7	8	.7	7	.6	7	.6	7	.6	10
101	0	1	0	1	0	1	0	2	0	2	0	1
65519	0	0	0	0	0	1	0	0	0	0	0	0

	$D = 4$		5		6		7		8		9	
$p = 2$	8	71	17	170	58	393	167	913	290	1600	570	3900
3	5	38	13	114	27	230	81	640	167	1600	430	3100
101	.2	11	0	2	1.3	80	4	210	8	407	0	2
65519	0	0	0	0	0	0	0	0	0	0	0	0

Most of the loss in precision appears in the FGLM part. In comparison, the F5 part is quite stable, and hence, our goal is achieved.

[4]Everything was performed on a Ubuntu 16.04 with 2 processors of 2.6GHz and 16 GB of RAM.

[5]Efficiency of this choice regarding to the loss in precision was studied in the extended version of [V15]

REFERENCES

[AP] Alberto Arri and John Perry. The F5 criterion revised. Journal of Symbolic Computation, 2011, plus *corrigendum* in 2017.

[BFS04] Magali Bardet, Jean-Charles Faugère and Bruno Salvy. On the complexity of Gröbner basis computation of semi-regular overdetermined algebraic equations Proceeding of the 2004 International Conference on Polynomial System Solving (ICPSS'04), Paris, France, pages 71–75, 2004.

[BFS14] Magali Bardet, Jean-Charles Faugère, and Bruno Salvy. On the Complexity of the F5 Gröbner basis Algorithm. Journal of Symbolic Computation, pages 1–24, September 2014. 24 pages.

[BCM11] Bigatti A.M. and Caboara M. and Robbiano L. Computing inhomogeneous Gröbner bases, Journal of Symbolic Computation, 2011.

[C13] Chan, Andrew J., Gröbner bases over fields with valuations and tropical curves by coordinate projections, PhD Thesis, University of Warwick, August 2013.

[CM13] Chan, Andrew J. and Maclagan, Diane Gröbner bases over fields with valuations, to appear in Mathematics of Computation.

[C15] Connes, Alain, An essay on the Riemann Hypothesis, http://arxiv.org/pdf/1509.05576, 2015.

[E13] Eder Christian An analysis of inhomogeneous signature-based Gröbner basis computations, Journal of Symbolic Computation, 2013

[EF17] Eder Christian and Faugère Jean-Charles A survey on signature-based algorithms for computing Gröbner bases, Journal of Symbolic Computation, 2017

[EKL06] Einsiedler, Manfred and Kapranov, Mikhail and Lind, Douglas Non-archimedean amoebas and tropical varieties, Journal für die reine und angewandte Mathematik (Crelles Journal), 2006.

[F99] Faugère, Jean-Charles, A new efficient algorithm for computing Gröbner bases (F4), Journal of Pure and Applied Algebra, 1999

[F02] Faugère, Jean-Charles, A new efficient algorithm for computing Gröbner bases without reduction to zero (F5), Proceedings of the 2002 international symposium on Symbolic and algebraic computation, ISSAC '02, Lille, France.

[GMNRT91] Giovini Alessandro, Mora Teo, Niesi Gianfranco, Robbiano Lorenzo, and Traverso Carlo. "One sugar cube, please" or selection strategies in the Buchberger algorithm. In Proceedings of the 1991 international symposium on Symbolic and algebraic computation (ISSAC '91).

[Gfan] Jensen, Anders N. Gfan, a software system for Gröbner fans and tropical varieties, Available at http://home.imf.au.dk/jensen/software/gfan/gfan.html.

[MS15] Maclagan, Diane and Sturmfels, Bernd, Introduction to tropical geometry, Graduate Studies in Mathematics, volume 161, American Mathematical Society, Providence, RI, 2015, ISBN 978-0-8218-5198-2.

[MY16] Markwig, Thomas and Ren, Yue Computing tropical varieties over fields with valuation, http://arxiv.org/pdf/1612.01762, 2016.

[Sage] SageMath, the Sage Mathematics Software System (Version 8.3.beta1), The Sage Development Team, 2018, http://www.sagemath.org.

[V14] Vaccon Tristan, Matrix-F5 algorithms over finite-precision complete discrete valuation fields, Proceedings of 39th International Symposium on Symbolic and Algebraic Computation, ISSAC'14, Kobe, Japan.

[V*] Vaccon Tristan, Précision p-adique, thèse de l'Université de Rennes 1, https://tel.archives-ouvertes.fr/tel-01205269.

[V15] Vaccon Tristan, Matrix-F5 Algorithms and Tropical Gröbner Bases Computation, Proceedings of the 40th International Symposium on Symbolic and Algebraic Computation, ISSAC 2015, Bath, United Kingdom. Extended version in the Journal of Symbolic Computation, Dec. 2017.

[VY17] Vaccon Tristan and Yokoyama Kazuhiro, A Tropical F5 algorithm, Proceedings of the 42th International Symposium on Symbolic and Algebraic Computation, ISSAC 2017, Kaiserslautern, Germany.

On Computing the Resultant of Generic Bivariate Polynomials

Gilles Villard

Univ Lyon, CNRS, ENS de Lyon, Inria, Université Claude Bernard Lyon 1, LIP UMR 5668, F-69007 Lyon, France

ABSTRACT

An algorithm is presented for computing the resultant of two generic bivariate polynomials over a field K. For such p and q in K$[x, y]$ both of degree d in x and n in y, the algorithm computes the resultant with respect to y using $(n^{2-1/\omega}d)^{1+o(1)}$ arithmetic operations in K, where two $n \times n$ matrices are multiplied using $O(n^{\omega})$ operations. Previous algorithms required time $(n^2 d)^{1+o(1)}$.

The resultant is the determinant of the Sylvester matrix $S(x)$ of p and q, which is an $n \times n$ Toeplitz-like polynomial matrix of degree d. We use a blocking technique and exploit the structure of $S(x)$ for reducing the determinant computation to the computation of a matrix fraction description $R(x)Q(x)^{-1}$ of an $m \times m$ submatrix of the inverse $S(x)^{-1}$, where $m \ll n$. We rely on fast algorithms for handling dense polynomial matrices: the fraction description is obtained from an x-adic expansion via matrix fraction reconstruction, and the resultant as the determinant of the denominator matrix.

We also describe some extensions of the approach to the computation of generic Gröbner bases and of characteristic polynomials of generic structured matrices and in univariate quotient algebras.

ACM Reference Format:

Gilles Villard. 2018. On Computing the Resultant of Generic Bivariate Polynomials. In *ISSAC'18: 2018 ACM International Symposium on Symbolic and Algebraic Computation, July 16–19, 2018, New York, NY, USA*. ACM, New York, NY, USA, 8 pages. https://doi.org/10.1145/3208976.3209020

1 INTRODUCTION

Given two bivariate polynomials p and q in K$[x, y]$ where K is a commutative field, we address the question of computing the resultant $\mathrm{Res}_y(p, q) \in \mathrm{K}[x]$ of p and q with respect to y. We take $p = \sum_{i=0}^{n} p_i(x)y^i$ and $q = \sum_{i=0}^{n} q_i(x)y^i$ of degree d in x and n in y. The Sylvester matrix $S(x) \in \mathrm{K}[x]^{2n \times 2n}$ associated to p and q is defined by $s_{i,j} = p_{n+j-i}$ and $s_{i,j+n} = q_{n+j-i}$, for $1 \leq i \leq 2n$ and $1 \leq j \leq n$ (where $p_k = q_k = 0$ when $k < 0$ or $k > n$). The resultant of p and q with respect to y is the determinant of S.

Since the early 1970's it is known that the bivariate resultant can be computed in $(n^2 d)^{1+o(1)}$ arithmetic operations in K. This complexity bound is obtained by combining an evaluation-interpolation approach à la Collins and Brown for the multivariate resultant [8, 10], and the half-gcd algorithm resulting from the works of Knuth [30] and Schönhage [45] for the integers, and of Moenck [39] for the univariate polynomials. We refer to [16, Chap. 11] for more

ISSAC'18, July 16–19, 2018, New York, NY, USA
© 2018 Copyright held by the owner/author(s). Publication rights licensed to ACM.
ACM ISBN 978-1-4503-5550-6/18/07...$15.00
https://doi.org/10.1145/3208976.3209020

details and references. More precisely, on the one hand, the resultant of two univariate polynomials of degree n (taking $d = 0$ in above definition) can be computed in $O(\mathsf{M}(n) \log n)$ arithmetic operations in K using the Knuth-Schönhage-Moenck algorithm. We use $\mathsf{M}(n)$ for a multiplication time for univariate polynomials of degree bounded by n over K (see for instance [16, Chap. 8]). On the other hand, in our case the resultant has degree at most $2nd$, hence an extra factor nd appears for the evaluation-interpolation cost. In total, it can be shown that the bivariate resultant can be computed using $O(n \mathsf{M}(nd) \log(nd))$ arithmetic operations [16, Chap. 11], which is $(n^2 d)^{1+o(1)}$ using $\mathsf{M}(n) = O(n \log n \log \log n)$ with Cantor and Kaltofen's polynomial multiplication [9].

Before giving an overview of our approach let us mention some important results that have been obtained since the initial results cited above. For comprehensive presentations of the resultant and subresultant problem, and detailed history and complexity analyses, the reader may refer to [16, 17, 36]. Especially for avoiding modular methods over $\mathbb{Z}$, recursive subresultant formulas have been given in [17, 38, 43] that allow half-gcd schemes for computing the resultant of polynomials in D$[y]$ where D is a domain such that the exact division can be performed.

The complexity bound $(n^2 d)^{1+o(1)}$ has not been improved in the general case. In some special cases much better complexity bounds are known [5, Sec. 5]. In particular, for univariate f and g of degree n in K$[y]$, the composed sum $(f \oplus g)(x) = \mathrm{Res}_y(f(x - y), g(y))$ and the composed product $(f \otimes g)(x) = \mathrm{Res}_y(y^n f(x/y), g(y))$ can be computed using $n^{2+o(1)}$ operations in K [5]. (The restrictions in [5] for fields of small characteristic may be bypassed by techniques such as those in [33] and references therein.) The latter bound improves upon $n^{3+o(1)}$ (taking $d = n$, $p(x, y) = f(x - y)$, and $q(x, y) = g(y)$) and is essentially optimal since the composed sum and product have degree n^2.

Another special bivariate case concerns particular resultants that are linear with respect to one of the variables. The question is related to characteristic polynomials of special structured matrices. For a and g monic of degree n in K$[y]$, the characteristic polynomial of a in the quotient algebra $\mathcal{A} = \mathrm{K}[y]/\langle g(y) \rangle$ is given by $\chi(x) = \mathrm{Res}_y(x - a(y), g(y))$ (see for instance [13, Chap. 4, Proposition (2.7)]). Representing the endomorphism of the multiplication by a by an appropriate $n \times n$ matrix A, χ is the characteristic polynomial $\det(xI - A)$ of A. Let ω be the exponent of fast matrix multiplication. In [46, Theo. 3.4] (see also [47] and [28, Sec. 6]), with a formulation that uses mainly polynomials, it is shown that an algorithm exists for computing the minimal polynomial μ of a using $n^{1.5+o(1)} + O(n^{(\omega+1)/2})$ operations in K. Using $\omega = 2.373$ [12, 34], the latter bound is $O(n^{1.687})$. The resultant point of view is adopted in [5] where an approach using similar tools than in [46, 47] leads to the same exponent for the characteristic polynomial, hence the special resultant χ (see above for fields of small characteristic). With $\omega < 3$, the bound $O(n^{(\omega+1)/2})$ is better than $n^{2+o(1)}$ for a general resultant (taking $d = 1$, $p(x, y) = x - a(y)$, and $q(x, y) = g(y)$).

Both methods in [46] and [5] use a K-linear map $\pi : \mathcal{A} \to \mathsf{K}$. The map in [46] allows to reduce the minimal polynomial problem to the one of computing generators of linearly generated sequences [44, 50]. The trace is used in [5], and allows via Le Verriers's approach to compute the characteristic polynomial using Newton identities. With a linear algebra point of view we note that those latter algorithms could compare to a structured version of the one in [26]. Using Wiedemann's method [53], the minimal polynomial computation can be reduced to the computation of generators of linearly generated sequences with $\pi : A \mapsto X^T AY \in \mathsf{K}$ where X and Y are vectors.

We also mention the particular situation where only a few terms of the resultant are needed. The algorithm of [40] computes the truncated resultant $\mathrm{Res}_y(p, q) \bmod x^k$ in $(nk)^{1+o(1)}$ operations in K. The latter bound improves upon a division-free computation of the resultant over $\mathsf{K}[x]/\langle x^k\rangle$ in time $(n^2k)^{1+o(1)}$. For a division-free univariate resultant over K in $n^{2+o(1)}$ operations one can indeed apply Strassen's removal of divisions to polynomials defined by: $p_0(x) = 1, p_1(x) = x$, and $p_k(x) = xp_{k-1}(x) + p_{k-2}(x)$ for $k \geq 2$[1].

Our contribution. The complexity bound $(n^2d)^{1+o(1)}$ for the bivariate resultant is roughly speaking the product of the essentially linear time for the half-gcd over K by the degree $O(nd)$ of the answer. For generic input polynomials p and q, we reduce the complexity bound below this product. We are going to prove the following theorem.

THEOREM 1.1. (Proven in Section 6.) *Let p and q in $\mathsf{K}[x, y]$ be of degree d in x and n in y. Except if (p, q) is on a certain hypersurface of $\mathsf{K}^{2(n+1)(d+1)}$ the resultant $\mathrm{Res}_y(p, q) \in \mathsf{K}[x]$ of p and q can be computed using $(n^{2-1/\omega}d)^{1+o(1)}$ operations in K*[2,3].

For two generic polynomials p and q of degree n the best known bound was $n^{3+o(1)}$, we obtain $n^{8/3+o(1)}$ with $\omega = 3$, and $O(n^{2.58})$ asymptotically. Our approach can be used for other types of structured matrices, such as those with small displacement rank [25]. For example, an immediate consequence is the computation of the characteristic polynomial of a Toeplitz matrix (see Section 7). The best known bound was $n^{2+o(1)}$ [42]. We obtain $n^{5/3+o(1)}$ or $O(n^{1.58})$ for the characteristic polynomial of a generic Toeplitz matrix. Another case linear in x has been mentioned above: characteristic polynomials in univariate quotient algebras can also be computed in a generic case in $O(n^{1.58})$ operations, which improves upon previous methods whose cost is $O(n^{1.687})$. Note that, already for $\omega = 3$, the bound $n^{5/3+o(1)}$ improves upon $n^{2+o(1)}$. In view of the above discussion concerning the algorithms in [5, 26, 46] we are going to see that our approach may be seen as using several maps simultaneously, somewhat in the spirit of the blocked version [29] of [26].

Overview of the approach. An often successful idea for computing the determinant of a matrix M over $\mathsf{K}[x]$ or $\mathbb{Z}$, is to reduce the problem using Cramer's rule to the solution of one or a few linear systems $M^{-1}y$ for well chosen vectors y [41]. For example in the integer case, the determinant (or, for a non generic M, the largest invariant factor) can be recovered from the denominators of the entries of a few random system solutions [1, 15, 49]. The latter approach works in three phases: (i) use lifting for computing truncated p-adic expansions of system solutions $M^{-1}y$; (ii) reconstruct corresponding (scalar) fractions for the entries of the solutions; (iii) deduce the determinant (or the largest invariant factor) of M from denominators. The polynomial matrix case is studied in [48] and follows analogous steps starting instead with x-adic expansions.

Our resultant algorithm is given in Section 6. It generalizes the three phases (i)-(ii)-(iii) for computing the determinant of the Sylvester matrix $S(x)$, and some major changes are required. The improvement is obtained thanks to: a block approach—instead of linear system solving; the expansion and reconstruction of matrix polynomial fractions—instead of scalar polynomial fractions; the replacement of system solution lifting by a specific expansion phase that takes advantage of the structure of the input matrix.

Indeed, reducing the determinant problem to system solution is an appropriate strategy in many cases, however, given a $2n \times 2n$ Sylvester matrix $S(x)$ of degree d, a linear system solution $S(x)^{-1}y$ will have size $\Omega(n^2d)$ in a generic sense, which is too large for the objective of improving the resultant complexity bound. Inspiration may be gained from block Krylov subspace techniques—see [29] and references therein—for the determinant of a characteristic matrix $M = xI - A$. Rather than fully solving systems $S(x)^{-1}y$, a first idea is to circumvent the difficulty by computing only several entries of several linear system solutions. "Several" here means $m \ll n$ where m is chosen as a function of n in Section 6 for minimizing the overall cost. More precisely, we consider the $m\times m$ north-eastern submatrix

$$H(x) = X^T S(x)^{-1} Y \in \mathsf{K}(x)^{m\times m}$$

of $S(x)^{-1}$, where $X = [I_m, 0, \ldots, 0]^T$ and $Y = [0, 0, \ldots, I_m]^T$ are $(2n)\times m$ matrices, and I_m is the identity matrix of dimension m. We are going to see that generically this $m\times m$ submatrix of the inverse of $S(x)$ has a (right) fraction description (among other properties, see further below)

$$H(x) = R(x)Q(x)^{-1} \qquad (1)$$

that can be computed fast, where R and Q are polynomial matrices of dimension m and degree at most $2\lceil n/m\rceil d$. The necessary background on fraction descriptions will be given in Section 2. Our choice of X and Y will in particular simplify the presentation for Gröbner bases in Section 7. Different and more general choices could however be made. For instance, with $X = Y = [0, 0, \ldots, I_m]^T$ the fraction H could be seen as the inverse of a Schur complement.

Once the description (1) is available the resultant is deduced from the denominator matrix (generalization of Cramer's rule, see Lemma 2.1) since generically we will have

$$\mathrm{Res}_y(p, q)(x) = \det S(x) = s \det Q(x), \text{ for some } s \in \mathsf{K} \setminus \{0\}.$$

The leading term of the resultant, depending here on the scalar s, will be computed separately. In order to prove the degree bound on R and Q, we first identify in Section 3 special polynomials $\bar{p}$ and $\bar{q}$ whose Sylvester matrix leads to a (sufficiently) generic degree behaviour. We then show in Section 4 that the generic behaviour corresponds to (p, q)'s not on a certain hypersurface. The polynomials $\bar{p}$ and $\bar{q}$ will be $\bar{p}(x, y) = x^d y^n + y^m$ and $\bar{q}(x, y) = y^n + x^d$, where $1 \leq m \leq n$. For example, with input degrees $n = 8$ and $d = 1$, and blocking factor $m = 3$, consider the polynomials $\bar{p}(x, y) = xy^8 + y^3$ and $\bar{q}(x, y) = y^8 + x$. The 3×3 north-eastern submatrix of the

[1]The author thanks E. L. Kaltofen for showing this construction.
[2]One should expect a slight exponent improvement by employing fast rectangular matrix multiplication [11, 22, 35].
[3]Links to Maple worksheets with some constructions of the paper and examples are provided on the page http://perso.ens-lyon.fr/gilles.villard/mws/issac18.

inverse of their 16×16 Sylvester matrix $\bar{S}(x)$ satisfies

$$\bar{H}(x) = \bar{R}(x)\bar{Q}(x)^{-1} = -\begin{bmatrix} 1 & 0 & 0 \\ 0 & 1 & 0 \\ 0 & 0 & 1 \end{bmatrix}\begin{bmatrix} x & 0 & x^4 \\ x^6 & x & 0 \\ 0 & x^6 & x \end{bmatrix}^{-1},$$

with $\bar{Q}$ of degree $2\lceil 8/3 \rceil = 6$, and we have $\mathrm{Res}_y(xy^8 + y^3, y^8 + x) = \det \bar{Q}(x) = x^{16} + x^3$.

The size of the description RQ^{-1} will be generically $O(mnd)$, hence smaller than the size of a system solution, hence the description can be handled with fewer operations. Furthermore, in the same Section 4 we also make use of a small (left) description $H = Q_L^{-1}R_L$. The existence of both a small left and a small right description implies that only $O(nd/m)$ terms of an x-adic expansion of H suffice for computing the denominator Q using matrix fraction reconstruction (see Lemma 2.5 and Corollary 4.2).

Another issue then arises for computing the initial x-adic expansion of H. The immediate approach that would compute an expansion of $S(x)^{-1}Y$ and in the end keep only $XS(x)^{-1}Y$ would have prohibitive cost. Computing only selected entries of the inverse therefore requires a modification of the expansion step. We circumvent the difficulty by making use of the Toeplitz-like structure of the Sylvester matrix. One will find the necessary reminders concerning dense structured matrices in Section 5. The reader may refer for example to [3, 21] for an insight into the subject. As well as S, the inverse S^{-1} is Toeplitz-like. With our choice of X and Y what follows is essentially the fact that H, as a special submatrix of S^{-1}, is also Toeplitz-like. One can write S^{-1} in ΣLU form [25, 27], we mean:

$$S(x)^{-1} = \sum_{i=1}^{2} L_i(x)U_i(x) \in \mathsf{K}(x)^{(2n)\times(2n)} \quad (2)$$

for some lower triangular Toeplitz matrices L_1 and L_2 and some upper triangular Toeplitz matrices U_1 and U_2. We will then use the fact that thanks to the triangular structure of L_1 and L_2 one has

$$H(x) = \sum_{i=1}^{2} L_i^{(m)}(x)T_i^{(m)}(x) \in \mathsf{K}(x)^{m\times m} \quad (3)$$

where the $L_i^{(m)}$'s and $T_i^{(m)}$'s are Toeplitz submatrices of the L_i's and U_i's. A key point is that from the ΣLU representation of S^{-1} the computation of H will involve two multiplications of Toeplitz matrices of dimension only $m \times m$.

Structured matrix inversion has been well studied. Over a field, a randomized divide-and-conquer approach allows to compute—via Schur complements—a ΣLU representation of the inverse of a Toeplitz-like matrix using $O(\mathsf{M}(n)\log n)$ arithmetic operations, see [4, 27] and [3, Chap. 2, Sec. 13]. The Sylvester matrix is block Toeplitz (after a colum permutation, with 1×2 rectangular blocks), which is a special Toeplitz-like case. Therefore we will rather follow the path of [31] for reducing the problem to matrix Padé approximation and to the use of the half-gcd algorithm.

For the sake of completeness we propose a specific study of the Sylvester matrix case in Section 5. We use known techniques for deriving an explicit formula for a ΣLU representation (2) of its inverse over a field. Such a formula allows to compute a ΣLU representation essentially via the half-gcd algorithm in time $O(\mathsf{M}(n)\log n)$. With operations on truncated power series a corresponding expansion of order $O(nd/m)$ is therefore obtained using $(n^2d/m)^{1+o(1)}$ operations. Finally, taking advantage of Toeplitz structures in (3), an appropriate expansion of the $m\times m$ matrix H is obtained via Toeplitz matrix multiplication using $(m^2 \times nd/m)^{1+o(1)}$ operations. For instance, taking $m = \sqrt{n}$, we see that computing an order $O(\sqrt{n}d)$ expansion of a $\sqrt{n} \times \sqrt{n}$ submatrix of $S(x)^{-1}$ (hence n entries) has cost $(n^{3/2}d)^{1+o(1)}$, while solving a linear system (n entries also) via an expansion of order $O(nd)$ would require $(n^2d)^{1+o(1)}$ operations.

Dense linear algebra for reconstructing $H = RQ^{-1}$ from its expansion [2, 19] and for computing the determinant of Q [32, 48] can be performed using $(m^\omega \times nd/m)^{1+o(1)}$ operations. We will see in Section 6 that it follows that the overall cost for the resultant is minimized by choosing $m \sim n^{1/\omega}$.

Some consequences: generic bivariate ideals and characteristic polynomials. In Section 7 we discuss some corollaries and extensions of the above approach. For instance, from the structure of the Sylvester matrix, we notice that the entries of Q give the coefficients in $\mathsf{K}[x]$ of polynomials in the ideal $\mathcal{I}$ generated by p and q. Those polynomials have degree less than m in y, and a Gröbner basis of $\mathcal{I}$ can be deduced for the lexicographic order within the complexity bound of Theorem 1.1. We will also discuss the case of polynomials linear in one of the variables and compute characteristic polynomials.

2 MATRIX FRACTIONS

We give the basic notions and results we need in the rest of the text concerning matrix fraction descriptions. The reader may refer to the comprehensive material in [24]. By analogy with scalar polynomial fractions, an $n \times m$ rational matrix $H(x)$ over $\mathsf{K}(x)$ can be written as a fraction of two polynomial matrices. A right fraction description is given by $R(x) \in \mathsf{K}[x]^{n\times m}$ and $Q(x) \in \mathsf{K}[x]^{m\times m}$ such that

$$H(x) = R(x)Q(x)^{-1} \in \mathsf{K}(x)^{n\times m},$$

and a left description by $R_L(x) \in \mathsf{K}[x]^{n\times m}$ and $Q_L(x) \in \mathsf{K}[x]^{n\times n}$ such that

$$H(x) = Q_L(x)^{-1}R_L(x) \in \mathsf{K}(x)^{n\times m}.$$

Degrees of denominator matrices are minimized using column reduced forms. A non singular polynomial matrix is said to be column reduced if its leading column coefficient matrix is non singular [24, Sec. 6.3].

This leads us to the definition of *irreducible and minimal fraction descriptions.* If R and Q (resp. R_L and Q_L) have unimodular right (resp. left) matrix gcd's [24, Sec. 6.3] then the description is called irreducible. If in addition Q (resp. Q_L) is column reduced then the description is called minimal. Our determinant algorithm relies on the following lemma that we will use as a generalization of Cramer's rule.

LEMMA 2.1. ([24, Lemma 6.5-9].) *The denominators of irreducible matrix fraction descriptions all have the same non unity invariant factors (non unity entries in the Smith normal form). They all have in particular the same determinant up to a non zero element of* K.

We also have a multiplicative property for the denominators.

LEMMA 2.2. ([24, Lemma 6.5-5].) *Let $Q \in \mathsf{K}[x]^{m\times m}$ be the denominator of an irreducible right description of H and $Q' \in \mathsf{K}[x]^{m\times m}$ be the denominator of an arbitrary right description of H. There exists a polynomial matrix M such that $Q' = QM$.*

For a non singular square polynomial matrix M, we now study the special fraction $H = X^T M(x)^{-1} Y$, where for $1 \le m \le n$, $X = [I_m, 0, \ldots, 0]^T$ and $Y = [0, 0, \ldots, I_m]^T$ are in $\mathsf{K}^{n \times m}$. Let M_{NE} be the square submatrix of dimension $2n - m$ given by rows $1, \ldots, 2n - m$ and columns $m + 1, \ldots, 2n$ of M, let also M^* be the adjoint matrix of M. From the Schur complement formula, $g(x) = \det M_{\text{NE}}(x) = (\det(X^T M^*(x) Y))/(\det M(x))^{m-1}$ is a polynomial in $\mathsf{K}[x]$. Then if $X^T M^{-1} Y = RQ^{-1}$, taking determinants in both sides we obtain

$$g(x)/\det M(x) = \det R(x)/\det Q(x). \tag{4}$$

Hence $\det Q$ divides $\det M$ whenever RQ^{-1} is irreducible and we have the next lemma.

Lemma 2.3. (Compare with [29, Theorem 2.12].) *The denominators of irreducible matrix fraction descriptions of $X^T M^{-1} Y$ all have same determinant up to a non zero element of K, which is a divisor of $\det M$.*

The next thing we need is a characterization of the link between the degree of fraction descriptions and the number of terms required for reconstructing the fraction from its expansion. In the matrix case the number of terms depends on both the left and right degrees since those degrees may be different. A matrix fraction is said to be strictly proper if it tends to zero when x tends to infinity. The material of next lemma can be found along the lines of [24], or [52, Sec. 4] and [29, Sec. 2]. The two latter references illustrate the links of our algorithm with block Krylov methods.

Lemma 2.4. *Let $H \in \mathsf{K}(x)^{m \times m}$ be a strictly proper fraction, and write $H(x) = \sum_{k \ge 0} H_k x^{-1-k}$. For any integer $\delta \ge 0$, let also $\mathcal{H}$ be the following block Hankel matrix:*

$$\mathcal{H} = \begin{bmatrix} H_0 & H_1 & \cdots & H_{\delta-1} \\ H_1 & \iddots & \iddots & H_\delta \\ \vdots & \iddots & \iddots & \vdots \\ H_{\delta-1} & H_\delta & & H_{2\delta-2} \end{bmatrix} \in \mathsf{K}^{(m\delta) \times (m\delta)},$$

and denote by $\mathcal{H}_\infty$ the corresponding infinite block Hankel matrix. The rank of $\mathcal{H}_\infty$ is the determinantal degree ν of denominators of irreducible fraction descriptions of H; $\operatorname{rank} \mathcal{H} = \operatorname{rank} \mathcal{H}_\infty$ if and only if H has left and right fraction descriptions of degree at most δ.

Proof. *(Brief outline.)* One has a correspondence between denominators of descriptions and minimum generators of the sequence $\{H_i\}_{i \ge 0}$ [29, Lemma 2.8]. The fact that the rank of $\mathcal{H}_\infty$ is ν is by applying [29, (2.6)] both on the left and right side, as well as the fact that $\operatorname{rank} \mathcal{H} = \nu$ as soon as descriptions have degree at most δ. Conversely, if $\operatorname{rank} \mathcal{H} = \operatorname{rank} \mathcal{H}_\infty$ then, arguing in a similar way than in [29, Cor. 3.8], relations between columns (resp. rows) in $\mathcal{H}_\infty$ provide right (resp. left) descriptions of degree at most δ. □

We will use Lemma 2.4 for showing in the next two sections that small degree descriptions exist in the generic case. Among the methods for matrix fraction reconstruction from the expansion of H (see for instance [29, Sec. 2]), the proof of Lemma 2.4 indicates that one could use block-Hankel system solving. We will rather use a deterministic approach based on polynomial matrices and order bases computation [2, 19].

Generically we will be in the situation where $H \in \mathsf{K}(x)^{m \times m}$ has a power series expansion. An order basis (also known as minimal approximant basis or σ-basis) [2] of $[H(x) \ \ -I_m] \in \mathsf{K}[[x]]^{m \times (2m)}$ with order σ, is a minimal (column reduced) basis of the module of vectors $u \in \mathsf{K}[x]^{2m}$ such that $[H(x) \ \ -I_m]\, u(x) \equiv 0 \mod x^\sigma$. In particular, an order basis is a polynomial matrix in $\mathsf{K}[x]^{(2m) \times (2m)}$.

Lemma 2.5. Matrix fraction reconstruction. *([19, Lemma 3.7].) Let $H \in \mathsf{K}(x)^{m \times m}$ be a strictly proper power series, with left and right matrix fractions descriptions of degree at most δ. The m columns $[Q^T \ R^T]^T$ of degree at most δ of an order basis of $[H \ \ -I_m]$ with order $2\delta + 1$ define a minimal description RQ^{-1} of H.*

We use order bases in a special case. For more recent results on the problem the reader may refer to [23, 54].

3 A SPECIAL SYLVESTER MATRIX

For polynomials p and q in $\mathsf{K}[x, y]$ with non singular Sylvester matrix S, we consider the $m \times m$ north-eastern submatrix H of S^{-1}. In this section we construct special polynomials $\bar{p}$ and $\bar{q}$ such that the corresponding $\bar{H}$ has small degree—we mean in $O(nd/m)$—minimal descriptions; the latter having denominators whose determinant is equal to the one of the Sylvester matrix $\bar{S}$ of $\bar{p}$ and $\bar{q}$ up to a non zero constant. Note that we know by Lemma 2.3 that the determinant of such a denominator is a divisor of the resultant. The properties of $\bar{p}$ and $\bar{q}$ will allow us in the next section to identify the degree behaviour for descriptions associated to generic polynomials.

For integers $l, m \ge 1$, consider $B \in \mathsf{K}[x]^{l \times (l+m)}$ such that

$$b_{i,i} = x^d \text{ and } b_{i,i+m} = -1 \text{ for } 1 \le i \le l, \tag{5}$$

and $b_{i,j} = 0$ otherwise. We construct m vectors that form the columns of a nullspace basis $P \in \mathsf{K}[x]^{(l+m) \times m}$ of B. Among those vectors, m_1 are of degree $\delta = \lceil l/m \rceil d$ and $m_2 = m\lceil l/m \rceil - l$ are of degree $\delta - d = \lfloor l/m \rfloor d$, such that the sum of the degrees is ld. If m divides l then the m vectors are of degree $\delta = ld/m$. Those vectors have zero entries but for $p_{k,k} = 1, 1 \le k \le m$, and in each column $1 \le j \le m$ for $p_{k+m,j} = x^d p_{k,j}, 1 \le k \le l$. The columns of P are in the nullpace of B, one can check that $\sum_k b_{i,k} p_{k,j} \stackrel{?}{=} 0$. Indeed if for some ξ, $b_{i,\xi} = x^d$ then the only other non zero entry in row i is $b_{i,\xi+m} = -1$, and $\sum_k b_{i,k} p_{k,j} = b_{i,\xi} p_{\xi,j} + b_{i,\xi+m} p_{\xi+m,j} = x^d p_{\xi,j} - p_{\xi+m,j} = 0$. Then we note that P is a basis of the nullspace since it admits I_m as uppermost submatrix, hence it cannot be divided by a non unimodular matrix. The entries of P with highest column degrees are in its lowest submatrix, which is say $D_{\delta,d}(x) = \operatorname{diag}(x^\delta, \ldots, x^\delta, x^{\delta-d}, \ldots, x^{\delta-d}) \cdot C$ for a C column permutation:

$$P(x) = \begin{bmatrix} I_m \\ \text{degrees} < \delta \text{ or } \delta - d \\ D_{\delta,d}(x) \end{bmatrix} \in \mathsf{K}[x]^{(l+m) \times m}. \tag{6}$$

We then consider $\bar{p}(x, y) = x^d y^n + y^m$ and $\bar{q}(x, y) = y^n + x^d$, $1 \le m \le n$. The corresponding Sylvester matrix is

$$\bar{S}(x) = \begin{bmatrix} x^d I_n + I'_{n|m-n} & I_n \\ I'_{n|m} & x^d I_n \end{bmatrix} \in \mathsf{K}[x]^{(2n) \times (2n)}, \tag{7}$$

where $I'_{n|k} \in \mathsf{K}^{n \times n}$ has 1's on the upper diagonal starting at entry $(1, k+1)$ if $k \ge 0$, or on the lower diagonal starting at entry $(-k+1, 1)$

otherwise. We then introduce P_1 such that $\bar{S}P_1 \in \mathsf{K}[x]^{(2n)\times n}$ is:

$$\bar{S}(x)\begin{bmatrix} -I_n \\ x^d I_n + I'_{n|m-n} \end{bmatrix} = \begin{bmatrix} 0 \\ x^{2d} I_n - I'_{n|m} + x^d I'_{n|m-n} \end{bmatrix}.$$

Rows $n+1$ to $2n-m$ of $\bar{S}P_1$ form a matrix as in (5) with $l = n-m$, whose nullspace is described by a matrix P_2 as in (6), with $\delta_0 = 2\lceil (n-m)/m \rceil d$. The first $2n-m$ rows of $\bar{S}$ can therefore be annihilated using:

$$P_1(x)P_2(x) = \begin{bmatrix} -I_m \\ \text{degrees} < \delta_0 + d \text{ or } \delta_0 - d \\ D_{\delta_0+d,2d}(x) + I_m \end{bmatrix} \in \mathsf{K}[x]^{(2n)\times m}.$$

Now, applying P_1P_2 to $\bar{S}$ given by (7) we arrive at:

$$\bar{S}(x)P_1(x)P_2(x) = \begin{bmatrix} 0 \\ D_{\delta_0+2d,2d}(x) + I_m \end{bmatrix} \in \mathsf{K}[x]^{(2n)\times m}.$$

Taking $\delta = \delta_0 + 2d$ and $\bar{Q}(x) = D_{\delta,2d}(x) + x^d I_m \in \mathsf{K}[x]^{m\times m}$, with

$$X = \begin{bmatrix} I_m, 0, \dots, 0 \end{bmatrix}^T,\ Y = \begin{bmatrix} 0, \dots, 0, I_m \end{bmatrix}^T \in \mathsf{K}^{(2n)\times m}, \quad (8)$$

we are led to $P_1(x)P_2(x) = \bar{S}(x)^{-1}Y\bar{Q}(x)$. This gives

$$\bar{H}(x) = X^T \bar{S}(x)^{-1} Y = -\bar{Q}(x)^{-1} \in \mathsf{K}(x)^{m\times m}. \quad (9)$$

The right and left descriptions $\bar{Q}^{-1} = -I_m\bar{Q}^{-1} = -\bar{Q}^{-1}I_m$ are irreducible, therefore by Lemma 2.3 $\det \bar{Q}$ is a divisor of $\det \bar{S}$. Both determinants have leading coefficient ± 1, and $\deg \det \bar{Q} = 2nd$. In terms of determinants (4) and (9) can be rewritten as

$$\det(X^T \bar{S}(x)^{-1} Y) = \pm 1/\det \bar{Q}(x) = \pm 1/\det \bar{S}(x). \quad (10)$$

As announced at the beginning of the section, $\bar{Q}$ has degree in $O(nd/m)$ and its determinant gives the resultant.

Writing $\bar{H}(x) = \sum_{k\geq 0} \bar{H}_k x^{-1-k}$, we consider the Hankel matrices $\bar{\mathcal{H}} \in \mathsf{K}^{(m\delta)\times(m\delta)}$, where $\delta = 2\lceil n/m \rceil d$, and $\bar{\mathcal{H}}_\infty$ as in Lemma 2.4. Applying the latter lemma, since we have left and right descriptions of degree at most δ we know that

$$\operatorname{rank} \bar{\mathcal{H}} = \deg \det \bar{Q} = 2nd. \quad (11)$$

We have proceeded by block elimination for studying submatrices of S^{-1}. Direct inversion could have been used also.

4 DEGREES IN THE GENERIC CASE

Using the special Sylvester matrix of previous section, we now show that submatrices of S^{-1} have small descriptions generically. We consider generic bivariate polynomials p and q of degree d in x and n in y, we mean whose coefficients are distinct indeterminates $\alpha_{i,j}$ and $\beta_{i,j}$, for $0 \leq i \leq n$ and $0 \leq j \leq d$. We denote the polynomial ring $\mathsf{K}[\alpha_{0,0}, \dots, \alpha_{n,d}, \beta_{0,0}, \dots, \beta_{n,d}]$ by $\mathcal{R}_{\alpha,\beta}$, and the corresponding field of fractions by $\mathcal{F}_{\alpha,\beta}$. By genericity, the Sylvester matrix S associated to p and q is non singular (see also Φ_2 further below). Let Q be the denominator of a minimal description such that:

$$H(x) = X^T S(x)^{-1} Y = R(x)Q(x)^{-1}, \quad (12)$$

where X and Y are as in (8).

We first show that $\det Q$ is $\det S$ up to the leading coefficient. Then we show that Q has small column degrees, we mean in $O(n/m)$, hence Q can be computed from $O(n/m)$ terms of an expansion of H by Lemma 2.5. We may draw a parallel with the study of "lucky" projections X and Y in Coppersmith's block Wiedemann algorithm [29, 51]: unlucky projections may cause a drop in the determinantal degree of the minimal sequence generator, and/or increase the required length of the sequence.

Using Lemma 2.3 we know that $\det Q$ is a divisor of $\det S$. The fractions in (4) with $M = S$ are irreducible since they are irreducible in the special case (10). It follows that $\det Q$ is $\det S$ up to the leading term, and the polynomial $\Phi_1 = \operatorname{Res}_x(g, \det S) \in \mathcal{R}_{\alpha,\beta}$, where g has been define at (4), is non identically zero. Next, write $H(x) = \sum_{k\geq 0} H_k x^{-1-k}$, and, with $\delta = 2\lceil n/m \rceil d$ used for (11), consider the Hankel matrix $\mathcal{H} \in \mathcal{F}_{\alpha,\beta}^{(m\delta)\times(m\delta)}$ as in Lemma 2.4. Defining $\Phi_2 \in \mathcal{R}_{\alpha,\beta}$ to be the determinant of the coefficient matrix of degree d of S, the entries of $\mathcal{H}$ can be written as fractions with denominators being powers of Φ_2. In particular, $\mathcal{H}$ is well defined for $\bar{S}$ in (7) whose coefficient of degree d is the identity. Therefore Φ_2 is non trivial, which implies that H is strictly proper and $\deg \det S = 2nd$. Finally using (11) we know that $\operatorname{rank} \mathcal{H} \geq 2nd$, and $\operatorname{rank} \mathcal{H} = 2nd$ since $2nd$ is the maximum possible value. Therefore, $\operatorname{rank} \mathcal{H}_\infty = \operatorname{rank} \mathcal{H}$, and by Lemma 2.4 the fraction H has descriptions of degree at most δ . Let $\Phi_3 \in \mathcal{R}_{\alpha,\beta}$ be the non zero determinant of a submatrix of $\mathcal{H}$ of rank $2nd$ multiplied by an appropriate power of Φ_2.

We identify the set of ordered pairs (p, q) of bivariate polynomials p and q of degree at most d in x and n in y with the space $\mathsf{K}^{2(n+1)(d+1)}$, of which $\Phi = \Phi_1\Phi_2\Phi_3 \in \mathcal{R}_{\alpha,\beta}$ defines a hypersurface. Using the special polynomials $\bar{p}$ and $\bar{q}$ of Section 3 we have proven that Φ is not identically zero, and the construction of Φ ensures appropriate properties for computing the resultant outside the hypersurface. Indeed, $\Phi_1 \neq 0$ ensures that $\det Q$ is not a strict divisor or the resultant; $\Phi_2 \neq 0$ provides invertibility of S and strict properness of S^{-1}; $\Phi_3 \neq 0$ leads to denominators Q with small column degrees.

Proposition 4.1. *Let p and q in $\mathsf{K}[x, y]$ be of degree d in x and n in y. If the coefficients of p and q do not form a zero of $\Phi = \Phi_1\Phi_2\Phi_3$ then, for $1 \leq m \leq n$ and X, Y as in (8), the Sylvester matrix S of p and q satisfies*

$$X^T S(x)^{-1} Y = Q_L(x)^{-1} R_L(x) = R(x)Q(x)^{-1} \in \mathsf{K}(x)^{m\times m}$$

for some matrices Q_L, R_L, R and Q of degree at most $\delta = 2\lceil n/m \rceil d$. When the latter descriptions are taken minimal the denominator Q satisfies $\det Q = s \operatorname{Res}_y(p, q)$ for some non zero $s \in \mathsf{K}$.

For more insight about the hypersurface to avoid in the space of bivariate polynomials, we note that the (total) degree of Φ in the $\alpha_{i,j}$'s and $\beta_{i,j}$'s is dominated by the degree of Φ_3. The numerators in $\mathcal{H}$ have degree $O(n\delta)$, hence $\deg \Phi_3$ is $O(n\delta \times m\delta)$ and $\deg \Phi$ is $O(n^3d^2/m)$.

The degree bound $2\lceil n/m \rceil d$ in x we consider for Q is sufficient for our purpose since in $O(nd/m)$, and is generically the smallest possible value when m divides n exactly. We note however that a different proof could certainly lead to the sharper bound $\lceil 2nd/m \rceil$.

In the resultant algorithm we will also use the fact that S^{-1} and H are power series since generically $\det S(0) \neq 0$. Proposition 4.1 and Lemma 2.5 then give the following.

Corollary 4.2. *Let p and q generic in $\mathsf{K}[x, y]$ be of degree d in x and n in y. Take $1 \leq m \leq n$, $\delta = 2\lceil n/m \rceil d$, and X, Y as in (8). The first m rows of the m columns of degree at most δ of an order basis of*

$[X^T S^{-1} Y - I_m]$ *with order* $2\delta + 1$ *define a matrix* Q *such that* $\det Q$ *is* $\mathrm{Res}_y(p, q)$ *up to the leading coefficient.*

Note that the specialization $\bar{p}(x, y)$ and $\bar{q}(x, y)$ of Section 3 (used for bounding the generic degree) can be shifted to $\bar{p}(x + \alpha, y)$ and $\bar{q}(x + \alpha, y)$ with an appropriate $\alpha \in \mathsf{K}$ in order to also satisfy also the power series assumption. A different choice of algorithm for the reconstruction could rely simply on the properness of H and handle its expansion at $x = \infty$; see the discussion before Lemma 2.5.

5 TOEPLITZ-LIKE MATRICES

The resultant algorithm given in next section works by reconstructing a matrix fraction from its expansion. In this section we see how to compute a ΣLU (Toeplitz-like) representation [25] of the inverse of a Sylvester matrix. This representation will allow to minimize the cost of the expansion step. For the resultant computation, operations will be on truncated power series with adequate invertibility conditions, hence below we simply consider we are over a field K.

The Sylvester matrix can be seen as a block Toeplitz matrix: after a column permutation, with rectangular 1×2 blocks. As stated in the introduction an appropriate representation of S^{-1} over a field could therefore be computed using the randomized divide and conquer approaches in [27] and [3, Chap. 2, Sec. 13]. For the specific Sylvester matrix case we detail below an alternative (deterministic) solution. Using widely used techniques we derive an explicit formula for S^{-1}; see (16). The formula is in the spirit of those in [31, 37] and slightly more compact (since specific to the Sylvester case). Then we briefly recall how matrix Padé approximation [2] and the half-gcd algorithm can be combined, as suggested in [31], with the formula, for computing a ΣLU representation of S^{-1}. About the relation between the extended Euclidean scheme and structured matrices the reader may also refer to [3, Chap. 2, Sec. 9].

For two coprime univariate polynomials p and q, consider their Sylvester matrix $S \in \mathsf{K}^{(2n)\times(2n)}$. Following the definitions and results of [25], we let Z be the lower shift matrix (ones on the subdiagonal and zeroes elsewhere) and J be the reversal matrix (ones on the antidiagonal and zeroes elsewhere). Since $\mathrm{rank}(S - ZSZ^T) \le 2$, the (+)-displacement rank of S is $\alpha \le 2$, therefore we can write

$$S^{-1} = \sum_{i=1}^{2} L_i U_i \in \mathsf{K}^{(2n)\times(2n)}$$

for some lower triangular Toeplitz matrices L_1 and L_2 and some upper triangular Toeplitz matrices U_1 and U_2. Applying the techniques in [21] and [3, Chap 2, Sec. 11] the L_i's and the U_i's can be expressed as Krylov matrices, using iterated powers of Z. For a square matrix M we define the displacement operator

$$\varphi(M) = MZ - ZM. \qquad (13)$$

Let e_i denote the ith canonical vector. For the Sylvester matrix one can write $\varphi(S) = \mathcal{V}\mathcal{W}^T$, where $\mathcal{V}$ and $\mathcal{W}$ are matrices with two columns in $\mathsf{K}^{2n\times 2}$ defined by:

$$\varphi(S) = \mathcal{V}\mathcal{W}^T = [\ Se_{n+1} - Z^n Se_1, -Z^n Se_{n+1}\ ] \begin{bmatrix} e_n^T \\ e_{2n}^T \end{bmatrix}.$$

Multiplying $\varphi(S)$ in (13) by S^{-1} on the left and the right we obtain

$$\varphi(S^{-1}) = \mathcal{X}\mathcal{Y}^T, \text{ with } \mathcal{X} = -S^{-1}\mathcal{V}, \text{and } \mathcal{Y}^T = \mathcal{W}^T S^{-1}.$$

Using [3, Chap. 2, Theorem 11.3] and the notation $\mathcal{X} = [x_1, x_2]$ and $\mathcal{Y} = [y_1, y_2]$, it follows that

$$S^{-1} = \mathcal{L}(JS^{-T} e_{2n}) - \sum_{i=1}^{2} \mathcal{U}(ZJx_i)\,\mathcal{L}(Jy_i), \qquad (14)$$

where for a vector v of dimension $2n$, $\mathcal{L}(v)$ and $\mathcal{L}(v)$ are the square Krylov matrices of dimension $2n$:

$$\mathcal{L}(v) = [v, Zv, \dots, Z^{2n-1}v],\ \mathcal{U}(v) = \mathcal{L}(v)^T.$$

Note that since Z is the lower-shift matrix, then $\mathcal{L}(\cdot)$ is Toeplitz lower triangular and $\mathcal{U}(\cdot)$ is Toeplitz upper triangular. Using that $J\mathcal{U}(\cdot)J = \mathcal{V}(\cdot)$, from (14) we derive

$$JS^{-1}J = \mathcal{U}(JS^{-T} e_{2n}) - \sum_{i=1}^{2} \mathcal{L}(ZJx_i)\,\mathcal{U}(Jy_i),$$

and since $y_2 = S^{-T} e_{2n}$,

$$JS^{-1}J = -\mathcal{L}(ZJx_1)\,\mathcal{U}(Jy_1) + \mathcal{L}(-ZJx_2 + I_{2n})\,\mathcal{U}(Jy_2).$$

Rewriting the above for $\varphi(JSJ)$ and $\varphi(JS^{-1}J)$ we obtain:

Proposition 5.1. (Deduced from [21] and [3, Chap. 2, Sec. 11].) *Let* p *and* q *be coprime univariate polynomial over* K *of degree* n, *let* $S \in \mathsf{K}[x]^{(2n)\times(2n)}$ *be their Sylvester matrix. Define the following vectors in* K^{2n}:

$$s = [-q_{n-1}, \dots, -q_1, p_n - q_0, p_{n-1}, \dots, p_0]^T,$$
$$t = [-p_{n-1}, \dots, -p_1, -p_0, 0, \dots, 0]^T,$$

and

$$x_1 = S^{-1}s, x_2 = S^{-1}t, y_1 = S^{-T} e_{n+1}, y_2 = S^{-T} e_1. \qquad (15)$$

The inverse of the Sylvester matrix then satisfies:

$$S^{-1} = \sum_{i=1}^{2} L_i U_i = \mathcal{L}(Zx_1)\,\mathcal{U}(y_1) + \mathcal{L}(Zx_2 + I_{2n})\,\mathcal{U}(y_2). \qquad (16)$$

Representation (16) is slightly more compact than the representations in [31, 37] for general block-Toeplitz matrices. The latter representations could however be compressed into (16) using for instance the solutions of [27, Prop. 4] and [3, Chap. 2, Prob. 2.11b].

We use (16) for representing S^{-1} with $O(n)$ elements of K that are given by the first columns of L_1 and L_2, and first rows of U_1 and U_2. The latter vectors are obtained by solving the linear systems in (15). The first two equations in (15) can be rewritten as polynomial Diophantine equations (for instance see [16, Chap. 4]), and the last two as simultaneous Padé approximation problems [31] that can be solved at essentially the cost $O(\mathsf{M}(n)\log n)$ of the half-gcd [2].

6 THE GENERIC RESULTANT ALGORITHM

The resultant algorithm is given at Figure 1. We use FFT-based polynomial and truncated power series arithmetic [16, Chap. 8,9]. Power series are all truncated at the same order, for a rational matrix M we use $\tilde{M}$ to denote the truncated expansion. For the moment let the blocking factor be $m = \lceil n^{\sigma} \rceil$ for some $\sigma \ge 0$.

Generically the power series expansions are well defined, in particular $\det S(x) \not\equiv 0 \mod x$; see the comment before Corollary 4.2. Using Proposition 5.1 over truncated power series modulo $x^{2\delta+1}$, Step 3 has cost $(n \times \delta)^{1+o(1)} = (n^{2-\sigma} d)^{1+o(1)}$. We then proceed with the first m entries of the first columns or rows of the truncated L_i's and U_i's. Since the multiplication $m \times m$ Toeplitz matrix times vector is done over a field with $O(\mathsf{M}(m))$ operations, Step 4 has cost $(m^2 \times \delta)^{1+o(1)} = (n^{1+\sigma} d)^{1+o(1)}$. Using the order basis algorithm of [2, 19], Step 5 can be performed in time $(m^{\omega} \times \delta)^{1+o(1)} =$

Algorithm *Generic block resultant for p and q in* $\mathsf{K}[x,y]$.

Input: generic polynomials p and q of degree d in x and n in y.
Output: the resultant $\mathrm{Res}_y(p,q)$ of p and q with respect to y.

/* *The* $\tilde{}$ *notation stands for truncated power series matrices* */

1. $m := \lceil n^{1/\omega} \rceil$. /* *Blocking factor* */
2. $\delta = 2\lceil n/m \rceil d$. /* *Intermediary degree bound* */
3. /* *Expansion step 1. Structured representation of the inverse* */
   Compute the first columns of $\tilde{L}_1$ and $\tilde{L}_2$, and first rows of $\tilde{U}_1$ and $\tilde{U}_2$ using Proposition 5.1 such that
   $$S(x)^{-1} \equiv \sum_{i=1}^{2} \tilde{L}_i(x)\tilde{U}_i(x) \mod x^{2\delta+1} \in \mathsf{K}[x]^{(2n)\times(2n)}.$$
4. /* *Expansion step 2. Submatrix of* S^{-1} */
   Using the $m \times m$ Toeplitz submatrices $\tilde{L}_i^{(m)}$'s and $\tilde{T}_i^{(m)}$'s of the $\tilde{L}_i$'s and $\tilde{U}_i$'s such that
   $$\tilde{H}(x) \equiv \sum_{i=1}^{2} \tilde{L}_i^{(m)}(x)\tilde{T}_i^{(m)}(x) \mod x^{2\delta+1},$$
   compute
   $$\tilde{H}(x) \equiv H(x) \equiv X^T S(x)^{-1} Y \mod x^{2\delta+1} \in \mathsf{K}[x]^{m\times m}.$$
5. /* *Matrix fraction reconstruction, see Corollary 4.2* */
   Compute an order basis $P(x) \in \mathsf{K}[x]^{2m\times 2m}$ of $[\tilde{H}(x) \ -I_m]$ with order $2\delta + 1$.
   $Q(x)$:= the first m rows of the m columns of $P(x)$ of degree $\leq \delta$.
6. /* *Determinant computation* */
   S_d :=leading matrix of S, $S_d \in \mathsf{K}^{(2n)\times(2n)}$.
   $s := \det S_d \in \mathsf{K} \setminus \{0\}$.
   $r(x) := \det Q(x)$.
   Return $(s/r_{2n}) \cdot r(x)$.

Figure 1: Computation of the resultant.

$(n^{1+(\omega-1)\sigma}d)^{1+o(1)}$. Using Corollary 4.2 the matrix Q is well defined, its determinant can then be computed using dense $m \times m$ linear algebra for polynomial matrices of degree δ. The cost of Step 6 is bounded by $(m^\omega \times \delta)^{1+o(1)} = (n^{1+(\omega-1)\sigma}d)^{1+o(1)}$ using the randomized algorithm of [48] or the deterministic one in [32]. The correctness of the algorithm follows from Corollary 4.2. By equalizing $2-\sigma$ and $1+(\omega-1)\sigma$ we take $\sigma = 1/\omega$ for minimizing the overall cost, and Theorem 1.1 is proven.

Since we have genericity assumptions we could rely either on randomized or deterministic algorithms at every stages of the resultant algorithm. For example, thanks to the genericity, the randomized approaches of [27] and [3, Chap. 2, Sec. 13] would behave deterministically at Step 3. The same is true for the randomized algorithm of [48] for the final determinant computation. We remark however that our complexity bound has been derived using deterministic solutions. As far as we know, the use of the best known randomized strategies would lead to an improvement restricted to log factors.

7 EXTENSIONS

We present here some consequences of our approach.

Generic bivariate ideals. By Proposition 4.1 we have $X^T S^{-1} Y = RQ^{-1}$ with $\det Q = s \det S$ where $s \in \mathsf{K} \setminus \{0\}$. If Q' is the right denominator of a minimal description of $S^{-1}Y$ then it is also a denominator for $X^T S^{-1} Y$ and by Lemma 2.2 we know that Q' is a multiple of Q. Applying Lemma 2.1 to left and right descriptions of $S^{-1}Y$ we see that $\det Q'$ divides $\det S$, hence $\det Q$, it follows that $Q' = QU$ with U unimodular, and Q is also a denominator for a minimal description of $S^{-1}Y$. Consequently, for some some polynomial matrix P one has $S(x)P(x) = \left[0,\ldots,0,Q(x)^T\right]^T \in \mathsf{K}[x]^{(2n)\times m}$. Thanks to the form of S, the polynomials $\sum_{i=1}^m q_{i,j}(x)y^{m-i}$, $1 \leq j \leq m$, constructed from the entries of Q, are in the ideal I generated by p and q. If by right unimodular equivalence we compute the Hermite normal form G of Q as a lower triangular matrix, the last two columns of G give two polynomials $\gamma_1(x,y) = g_{m-1,m-1}(x)y + g_{m,m-1}(x)$ and $\gamma_2(x) = g_{m,m}(x)$ in the ideal I. The polynomial γ_2 divides $\det Q$, hence $\det S$. Further, from the Hermite form of the Sylvester matrix of $\bar{p}$ and $\bar{q}$ in Section 3 with $m = 1$, one can see that generically one must have $\gamma_2 = s \det S$ for $s \neq 0 \in \mathsf{K}$, which implies that $g_{m-1,m-1}$ is an element in K.

Since the Hermite form is normalized with monic diagonal entries we have $\gamma_1(x,y) = y - g_{m,m-1}(x)$ and $\gamma_2(x) = s \det S$. This is also the fact that generically I is generated by $\det S = \mathrm{Res}_y(p,q)$ and a polynomial $y - g(x)$ that form a Gröbner basis of I for the lexicographic order with $y > x$ [18].

We see that the computation of the Hermite form of Q provides a Gröbner basis of the ideal generated by p and q. Using the notations of previous sections, Q is $m \times m$ of degree δ, its Hermite form can be computed in $(m^\omega \times \delta)^{1+o(1)}$ operations using the randomized algorithm of [20] or the deterministic one in [32]. The complexity bound of Theorem 1.1 remains valid for the computation of a Gröbner basis of the ideal $\langle p, q \rangle$.

Characteristic polynomial of a generic structured matrix. Parallel to the construction of Section 3, for $1 \leq m \leq n$ let us consider the two matrices: $B' \in \mathsf{K}[x]^{m\times n}$ such that $B'_{i,i} = x$ and $B'_{i,i+n-m} = -1$ for $1 \leq i \leq m$, and $B'_{i,j} = 0$ otherwise; $B'' \in \mathsf{K}[x]^{(n-m)\times n}$ such that $B''_{i,i} = 1$ and $B''_{i,i+m} = x$ for $1 \leq i \leq n-m$, and $B''_{i,j} = 0$ otherwise. Consider also $\bar{T}(x) = \left[(B'(x))^T, (B''(x))^T\right]^T \in \mathsf{K}[x]^{n\times n}$. One can check that $X^T \bar{T}^{-1} Y$ can be described in a manner similar to (9). The fraction descriptions now have degree bounded by $\delta = \lceil n/m \rceil$. Since $\bar{T} = xI_n - \bar{T}_0$, the determinant of $\bar{T}$ is the characteristic polynomial of $\bar{T}_0$, and note that $\bar{T}_0$ is Toeplitz.

This shows that for a generic Toeplitz matrix T_0, a modification of the algorithm of Section 6 using a ΣLU representation of $T^{-1} = (xI_n - T_0)^{-1}$ will compute the characteristic polynomial within the complexity bound of Theorem 1.1 with $d = 1$. One may expect to have analogous results for more general classes of structured matrices [6, 14].

Characteristic polynomials in univariate quotient algebras. We consider a slight modification of $\bar{p}$ and $\bar{q}$ of Section 3. For $1 \leq m \leq n$ take $\bar{p}(x,y) = y^n + y^m$ (or $\bar{p}(x,y) = y^n$ for $m = n$ in characteristic 2) and $\bar{q}(x,y) = y^n + x$. With $\bar{S}$ the Sylvester matrix of $\bar{p}$ and $\bar{q}$ the fraction $X^T \bar{S}^{-1} Y$ can be described similarly to (9), with $\delta = \lceil n/m \rceil$.

Note that we are not in a generic Sylvester case since for instance the coefficient matrix of degree one of $\bar{S}$ is singular. We are however in a generic situation for the special resultant of polynomials $x - a(y)$ and $g(y)$ of degree n in y. The arguments of Sections 3 and 4 can be extended to the situation here. The special Sylvester matrix has dimensions $(2n) \times (2n)$ and for generic a and g the resultant has degree n. Modified Φ_2 and Φ_3 have to be used for an appropriate extension of Proposition 4.1, H remains strictly proper (which is not true anymore for S^{-1} in general).

This shows that the complexity bound $O(n^{1.58})$ of Theorem 1.1 with $d = 1$ is valid generically for computing the characteristic polynomial χ of the multiplication by a in $\mathcal{A} = \mathsf{K}[y]/\langle g(y)\rangle$.

Previously existing general resultant algorithms compute the characteristic polynomial in $\mathcal{A}$ at cost $n^{2+o(1)}$. However, in this special resultant case, the minimal and characteristic polynomial problems, respectively in [46] and [5], are reduced to the modular power projection problem, and by duality to the modular composition problem [28, 46]. With an adaptation of the composition algorithm of [7] this leads to algorithms using $n^{1.5+o(1)} + O(n^{(\omega+1)/2})$ operations in K for the minimal and characteristic polynomials [5, 46]. Note that for small characteristic fields the approach in [5] asks the root multiplicity of χ to be less than the characteristic of K; small fields can be handled using p-adic techniques such as in [33].

Our bound $n^{2-1/\omega+o(1)}$ shows that in the generic case with $\omega > 2$ the composition algorithm of [7] can be bypassed. As evoked above, composition is dual to power projection. The algorithms of [5, 46] rely on particular K-linear maps $\pi : \mathcal{A} \rightarrow \mathsf{K}$ for the projections. The same is true for our algorithm. Since special maps can be used, the characteristic polynomial problem may not be as difficult as the general composition problem.

Acknowledgements. The author is grateful to the referees for their careful readings and helpful comments; to E. L. Kaltofen for his motivating questions; to J.-C. Faugère, A. Galligo, V. Neiger, M. Safey El Din and B. Salvy for rich discussions on Gröbner bases.

REFERENCES

[1] J. Abbott, M. Bronstein, and T. Mulders. 1999. Fast deterministic computation of determinants of dense matrices. In *Proc. ISSAC*. ACM Press.
[2] B. Beckermann and G. Labahn. 1994. A uniform approach for the fast computation of matrix-type Padé approximants. *SIAM J. Math. Anal. Appl.* 15, 3 (1994).
[3] D. Bini and V.Y. Pan. 1994. *Polynomial and matrix computations*. Birkhäuser.
[4] R.R. Bitmead and B.D.O. Anderson. 1980. Asymptotically fast solution of Toeplitz and related systems of linear equations. *Linear Algebra Appl.* 34 (1980).
[5] A. Bostan, P. Flajolet, B. Salvy, and É. Schost. 2006. Fast computation of special resultants. *J. Symbolic Computation* 41, 1 (2006).
[6] A. Bostan, C.-P. Jeannerod, C. Mouilleron, and É. Schost. 2017. On matrices with displacement structure: generalized operators and faster algorithms. *SIAM J. Math. Anal. Appl.* 38, 3 (2017).
[7] R.P. Brent and H.T. Kung. 1978. Fast algorithms for manipulating formal power series. *J. ACM* 25, 4 (1978).
[8] W.S. Brown. 1971. On Euclids algorithm and the computation of polynomial greatest common divisors. *J. ACM* 18, 4 (1971).
[9] D.G. Cantor and E. Kaltofen. 1991. On fast multiplication of polynomials over arbitrary algebras. *Acta Informatica* 28, 7 (1991).
[10] G.E. Collins. 1971. The Calculation of Multivariate Polynomial Resultants. *J. ACM* 18, 4 (1971).
[11] D. Coppersmith. 1997. Rectangular matrix multiplication revisited. *J. Complexity* 13 (1997).
[12] D. Coppersmith and S. Winograd. 1990. Matrix multiplication via arithmetic progressions. *J. Symbolic Computation* 9, 3 (1990).
[13] D. Cox, J. Little, and D. O'Shea. 1998. *Using Algebraic Geometry*. Springer-Verlag, New-York. 2nd edition 2005.
[14] C. De Sa, A. Cu, R. Puttagunta, C. Ré, and A. Rudra. 2018. A two-pronged progress in structured dense matrix vector multiplication. In *Proc. ACM-SIAM SODA*.
[15] W. Eberly, M. Giesbrecht, and G. Villard. 2000. Computing the determinant and Smith form of an integer matrix. In *Proc. FOCS*. IEEE.
[16] J. von zur Gathen and J. Gerhard. 1999. *Modern Computer Algebra*. Cambridge University Press. Third edition 2013.
[17] J. von zur Gathen and T. Lücking. 2003. Subresultants revisited. *Theoretical Computer Science* 297, 1-3 (2003).
[18] P. Gianni and T. Mora. 1987. Algebraic solution of systems of polynomial equations using Gröbner bases. In *Proc. AAECC (LNCS 536)*.
[19] P. Giorgi, C.-P. Jeannerod, and G. Villard. 2003. On the complexity of polynomial matrix computations. In *Proc. ISSAC*. ACM Press.
[20] S. Gupta. 2011. *Hermite forms of polynomial matrices*. Master Thesis. University of Waterloo. http://hdl.handle.net/10012/6108
[21] G. Heinig and K. Rost. 1984. *Algebraic Methods for Toeplitz-like Matrices and Operator*. Springer, Birkhäuser Basel.
[22] X. Huang and V.Y. Pan. 1998. Fast rectangular matrix multiplication and applications. *J. of Complexity* 14, 2 (1998).
[23] C.-P. Jeannerod, V. Neiger, É. Schost, and G. Villard. 2016. Fast computation of minimal interpolation bases in Popov form for arbitrary shifts. In *Proc. ISSAC*. ACM Press.
[24] T. Kailath. 1980. *Linear Systems*. Prentice-Hall.
[25] T. Kailath, S.Y. Kung, and M. Morf. 1979. Displacement ranks of matrices and linear equations. *J. Mathematical Analysis and Applications* 68, 2 (1979).
[26] E. Kaltofen. 1992. On computing determinants without divisions. In *Proc. ISSAC*. ACM Press.
[27] E. Kaltofen. 1994. Asymptotically fast solution of Toeplitz-like singular linear systems. In *Proc. ISSAC*. ACM Press.
[28] E. Kaltofen. 2000. Challenges of symbolic computation: my favorite open problems. *J. Symbolic Computation* 29, 6 (2000).
[29] E. Kaltofen and G. Villard. 2005. On the complexity of computing determinants. *Computational Complexity* 13, 3 (2005).
[30] D. E. Knuth. 1971. The analysis of algorithms. In *Actes, Congrès int. math. (Nice, 1970)*. Tome 3. Gauthier-Villars, 269–274. http://perso.ens-lyon.fr/gilles.villard/BIBLIOGRAPHIE/Knuth-ICM-1970.pdf
[31] G. Labahn. 1992. Inversion components of block Hankel-like matrices. *Linear Algebra Appl.* 177 (1992).
[32] G. Labahn, V. Neiger, and W. Zhou. 2017. Fast deterministic computation of the Hermite normal form and determinant of a polynomial matrix. *J. Complexity* 42 (2017).
[33] P. Lairez and T. Vaccon. 2016. On p-adic differential equations with separation of variables. In *Proc. ISSAC*. ACM Press.
[34] F. Le Gall. 2014. Powers of Tensors and Fast Matrix Multiplication. In *Proc. ISSAC*. ACM Press.
[35] F. Le Gall and F. Urrutia. 2018. Improved rectangular matrix multiplication using powers of the Coppersmith-Winograd tensor. In *Proc. ACM-SIAM SODA*.
[36] G. Lecerf. 2017. *On the complexity of the Lickteig-Roy subresultant algorithm*. HAL report. CNRS & École Polytechnique.
[37] L. Lerer and M. Tismenetsky. 1986. Generalized Bezoutian and the inversion problem for block matrices I. General scheme approximants. *Integral Equations and Operator Theory* 9, 6 (1986).
[38] T. LickteigandM.-F. Roy. 1996. Cauchy index computation. *Calcolo* 33, 3-4 (1996).
[39] R. T. Moenck. 1973. Fast computation of GCDs. In *Proc. STOC*. ACM Press.
[40] G. Moroz and É. Schost. 2016. A fast algorithm for computing the truncated resultant. In *Proc. ISSAC*. ACM Press.
[41] V. Pan. 1988. Computing the determinant and the characteristic polynomial of a matrix via solving linear systems of equations. *Inf. Process. Lett.* 28, 2 (1988).
[42] V. Pan. 1992. Parametrization of Newtons iteration for computations with structured matrices and applications. *Comp. Math. Appl.* 24, 3 (1992).
[43] D. Reischert. 1997. Asymptotically fast computation of subresultants. In *Proc. ISSAC*. ACM Press.
[44] J. Rifà and J. Borrell. 1991. Improving the time complexity of the computation of irreducible and primitive polynomials in finite fields. In *Proc. AAECC(LNCS 539)*.
[45] A. Schönhage. 1971. Schnelle Berechnung von Kettenbruchentwicklungen. *Acta Informatica* 1 (1971).
[46] V. Shoup. 1994. Fast construction of irreducible polynomials over finite fields. *J. Symbolic Computation* 17, 5 (1994).
[47] V. Shoup. 1995. A New Polynomial Factorization Algorithm and its Implementation. *J. Symbolic Computation* 20, 4 (1995).
[48] A. Storjohann. 2003. High-order lifting and integrality certification. *J. Symbolic Computation* 36, 3-4 (2003).
[49] A. Storjohann. 2005. The shifted number system for fast linear algebra on integer matrices. *J. Complexity* 21, 4 (2005).
[50] J.A. Thiong Ly. 1989. Note for computing the minimun polynomial of elements in large finite fields. In *Proc. Coding Theo. App. (LNCS 388)*.
[51] G. Villard. 1997. Further analysis of Coppersmiths block Wiedemann algorithm for the solution of sparse linear systems. In *Proc. ISSAC*. ACM Press.
[52] G. Villard. 1997. *A study of Coppersmith's block Wiedemann algorithm using matrix polynomials*. RR 975 IM IMAG Grenoble.
[53] D. Wiedemann. 1986. Solving sparse linear equations over finite fields. *IEEE Trans. Information Theory* 32, 1 (1986).
[54] W. Zhou and G. Labahn. 2012. Efficient Algorithms for Order Basis Computation. *J. Symbolic Computation* 47, 7 (2012).

An Approach for Certifying Homotopy Continuation Paths: Univariate Case

Juan Xu
Beihang University
Beijing, China
xujuan0505@126.com

Michael Burr*
Clemson University
Clemson, SC
burr2@clemson.edu

Chee Yap†
Courant Institute, NYU
New York, NY
yap@cs.nyu.edu

ABSTRACT

Homotopy continuation is a well-known method in numerical root-finding. Recently, certified algorithms for homotopy continuation based on Smale's alpha-theory have been developed. This approach enforces very strong requirements at each step, leading to small step sizes. In this paper, we propose an approach that is independent of alpha-theory. It is based on the weaker notion of well-isolated approximations to the roots. We apply it to univariate polynomials and provide experimental evidence of its feasibility.

CCS CONCEPTS

• **Computing methodologies → Hybrid symbolic-numeric methods**; *Equation and inequality solving algorithms*;

KEYWORDS

Homotopy Continuation; Certified Computation; Interval Arithmetic; Well-Isolated Roots

ACM Reference Format:
Juan Xu, Michael Burr, and Chee Yap. 2018. An Approach for Certifying Homotopy Continuation Paths: Univariate Case. In *ISSAC '18: 2018 ACM International Symposium on Symbolic and Algebraic Computation, July 16–19, 2018, New York, NY, USA.* ACM, New York, NY, USA, 8 pages. https://doi.org/10.1145/3208976.3209010

1 INTRODUCTION

Homotopy continuation is a method for approximating the solutions of a system of polynomials f by tracking and deforming the approximate solutions of an easier system of polynomials g. We call f the target system and g the start system. We are given f while the homotopy method chooses g as well as the homotopy $H(z, t)$ such that $H(z, 0) = g$ and $H(z, 1) = f$. We focus on linear homotopies of the form $H(z, t) = (1 - t)\gamma g(z) + tf(z)$ for some $\gamma \in \mathbb{C} \setminus \{0\}$. The recent development of software packages for homotopy continuation has led to significant interest and development of these techniques both within the mathematics community as well as for their applications. Some of the main homotopy continuation packages include `Bertini` [1], `PHCpack` [24], `Hom4PS` [18], and `NAG4M2` [19], see also the references therein. Homotopy continuation methods (broadly speaking) consist of three phases: (1) choosing an appropriate start system g and approximating its roots, (2) tracking the roots as g is deformed to the target system f, and (3) applying end-game techniques to analyze singular solutions.

In this paper, we provide a certified version of Phase (2) for univariate polynomials using well-isolated approximations to roots, subdivisions, and interval methods. To this end, we assume that f has only simple roots in order to avoid the end-game issues in Phase (3). Approximating the roots of the start system g in Phase (1) is also not an issue, especially when discussing univariate roots. In this case, it is standard to choose $g(z) = z^n - 1$ when $\deg(f) = n$. Next, we describe the central problem of Phase (2).

A **solution path** for a homotopy is a continuous function $\alpha(t)$ such that $H(\alpha(t), t) = 0$ for all $t \in [0, 1]$. We call $H(z, t)$ a **good homotopy** if the n solution paths $\{\alpha^i : i = 1, \ldots, n\}$ are non-singular and do not diverge to infinity. We restrict our attention to good homotopies in this paper.

In general, path tracking consists of the following iterative procedure: to track the ith path, assume we are given an approximation z_0^i to $\alpha^i(0)$. Starting with $(z_0^i, t_0^i = 0)$, for $j \geq 0$, assume we can generate a pair (z_{j+1}^i, t_{j+1}^i) from (z_j^i, t_j^i) such that $1 \geq t_{j+1}^i > t_j^i$. Intuitively, each z_j^i is an approximation to $\alpha^i(t_j)$. If z_{j+1}^i is not an approximation to $\alpha^i(t_{j+1})$, we say that **path jumping** has occurred. Such errors are the central concern in Phase (2). Although the sequence $\{z_j^i : j \geq 0\}$ is explicit, the solution path $\alpha^i(t)$ is only implicit. The main problem is to ensure correctness without direct access to $\alpha^i(t)$. The preceding discussions are quite informal, as the notion "z_j^i is (or is not) an approximation of $\alpha^i(t_j)$" is imprecise. We now turn to ways to make these statements precise and effective.

The key idea, which also applies in multivariate setting, lies in defining what it means for $z_0 \in \mathbb{C}^m$ to identify a unique root z_* of $h : \mathbb{C}^m \to \mathbb{C}^m$. It is tempting to choose z_* to be the root of h closest to z_0, but this idea is not effective. Typically, this identification is done via Newton iteration because, until the current paper, the corrector steps of homotopy continuation use Newton iteration. In the literature, $z_0 \in \mathbb{C}^m$ typically identifies a root z_* of h in one of two ways: (i) z_0 lies in the Newton basin of z_*, or (ii) z_0 converges quadratically (from the start) towards z_*. Note that Condition (ii) is stricter than Condition (i). By applying Newton iteration to z_0 sufficiently many times, we can (eventually) confirm these conditions, but this is not effective. Smale's α-theory [10] provides a way to check Condition (ii) without applying the Newton operator. In

*Partially supported by a grant from the Simons Foundation (#282399 to Michael Burr) and NSF Grant CCF-1527193.
†Partially supported NSF Grants Nos. CCF-1423228 and CCF-1564132.

ISSAC '18, July 16–19, 2018, New York, NY, USA
© 2018 Association for Computing Machinery.
ACM ISBN 978-1-4503-5550-6/18/07...$15.00
https://doi.org/10.1145/3208976.3209010

particular, one can effectively evaluate the function[1] α_h such that if this function at z_0 is less than some universal constant (e.g., 0.158), then z_0 satisfies Condition (ii). The certified homotopy methods of Beltran-Leykin [6] and Bürgisser-Cucker [11] avoid path jumping by ensuring that the z_j^i's satisfy some strong form of this alpha test.

In this paper, we develop a weaker way for z_0 to identify a root z_* that can be used to track a path $\alpha(t)$: we say that $z_0 \in \mathbb{C}$ is a **well-isolated approximation** of h if its distance to the closest root of h is at most one-third the distance to the second closest root of h. To make this effective, assume that such a z_0 comes with a witness radius r_0. That is, we have a disc $\Delta(z_0, r_0)$ centered at z_0 of radius r_0 with the following property: $\Delta(z_0, r_0)$ contains a unique root of $h(z)$, and $\Delta(z_0, 3r_0)$ contains no additional roots of $h(z)$. In this case, we call $\Delta(z_0, r_0)$ a **well-isolator** of a root of h. A key contribution of this paper is to show how, given a well-isolator $\Delta(z_j, r_j)$ for $h_j(z) = H(z, t_j)$, we can compute a time $t_{j+1} \in (t_j, 1]$ and a well-isolator $\Delta(z_{j+1}, r_{j+1})$ for h_{j+1}, such that both well-isolators identify the same solution path $\alpha(t)$. We use the recently developed soft Graeffe-Pellet tests [3, 4] to verify a well-isolator $\Delta(z, r)$.

The motivation for our approach comes from an intuition that using the approximate roots of α-theory is unnecessarily strong for the goal of avoiding path jumping. We show that the weaker notion of well-isolated approximations is sufficient for our purposes. Consequently, we expect our approach takes fewer steps. This is supported by **Table 1** which compares the number of time steps using α-theory versus our well-approximated root approach. The data for α-based tracking is from Beltrán and Leykin [5, Section 9.1 and Table 3]. We run our tracker on $H_m(x, t) = (1-t)\gamma(x^2 - 1) + t(x^2 - (1+m))$ using $\gamma = 1$ or $\boldsymbol{i}$ (the $\gamma = 1$ case was used in the previous work). Overall, our well-isolated tracker uses 4 to 8 times fewer steps than the alpha-based tracker. Hauenstein and Liddle [13] use a specialized[2] homotopy to track a single root of f. Our performance is comparable to the `ModifiedNewton` tracker in their Table A.1. Their other trackers use about half as many steps.

α-theory has been employed in previous certified algorithms because it pairs well with Newton iteration, the typical corrector in homotopy continuation. Our approach, however, does not use Newton iteration – this is an intended (possibly surprising) feature of our approach. We design our time steps $\delta t_j := t_{j+1} - t_j$ to be correlated with r_0, and so a larger r_0 allows us to take larger time steps. Newton iteration, on the other hand, would result in more steps if r_0 were very small.

Since these ideas are new and the univariate case already has various subtleties, we focus on the univariate case in this paper.

1.1 Literature Survey.

There are various approaches to certify the output of a homotopy continuation algorithm: see [5–7, 11–14, 16, 17, 20], and the references therein. The first rigorously justified algorithm in the Bit Model of computation (including Turing Machines) is from Beltran and Leykin [6] with implementation in [5]. The emphasis on a computational model is important: most algorithms are described in an Algebraic Model (e.g., the Real RAM Model or BSS Model) where each algebraic operation is treated as a primitive operation. It is well-known that the correct implementation of algebraic algorithms is highly nontrivial. Conversely, the correct implementation of bit model algorithms is comparatively easy.

It is generally understood that certified homotopy algorithms mean that each path is correctly tracked. But there is a weaker notion of simply certifying the output as in [14]. Strictly speaking, this type of certification is not specific to homotopy continuation (since we can use the method to certify the output of any root finding algorithm). This method amounts to checking that the final root is actually an approximate zero, but it is helpless to recover any lost roots due to path jumping. On the other hand, certifying the paths ensures that no roots are lost.

In [5–7, 11, 13, 21–23], the authors present certified complexity analyses or homotopy continuation algorithms which remain very close to the path, such as near the *alpha*-region of convergence. In [12] the authors use an *a posteriori* approach to certify the correctness of a path by reversing a non-certified homotopy step. In [15–17, 20] the authors present algorithms for path tracking using interval arithmetic. These papers track general curves and are not tuned to studying homotopy continuation-based paths.

1.2 Overview of Paper

In Section 2 we establish some common notation, including clarifying the good homotopy assumption of this work.

In Section 3, we give an overview of our main algorithm, the Well-Isolated Tracker. Couched in the familiar predictor-correct framework of homotopy continuation, we expose the details of our predictor and corrector modules. We develop well-isolated approximations into a tool for correct path tracking. Our predictor uses classical Euler steps (this is absent in current α-theory approaches). Instead of Newton iteration, we use bisection using a recently developed soft Graeffe-Pellet test.

Sections 4 and 5 provide technical details of the Update Subroutine, which is a loop describing the interaction between the predictor and corrector. The main algorithm consists of an outer loop around this inner loop. Section 4 presents a slightly abstract view (the "geometric meaning") of the Update Subroutine, and Section 5 instantiates these with explicit formulas necessary for implementation. Also in Section 5, we address issues of numerical approximations using interval methods. Because of the intricate predictor-corrector interaction, the correctness of the overall algorithm is nontrivial. We first prove the termination of the inner loop (`Update` Subroutine). The termination of the outer loop (the main algorithm) requires an improved corrector strategy. In Section 6, we present experimental results and conclude in Section 7.

2 BASIC SETUP AND NOTATION

In this paper, we follow many of the standard conventions used in homotopy continuation, e.g., see [2]. Our goal is to find the roots of a given target univariate polynomial $f \in \mathbb{Q}[x]$. Suppose that $g \in \mathbb{Q}[x]$ is the starting polynomial of the same degree as f and whose roots we already know. We connect f and g using a linear homotopy with the standard γ-trick, i.e., for $\gamma \in \mathbb{C}$, $H(x, t) = H_\gamma(x, t) := tf(x) + \gamma(1-t)g(x)$. We observe that $H(x, 0) = \gamma g(x)$

[1] The α_h function is from Smale's *alpha*-theory. It is defined for the polynomial h and should not be confused with the solution paths α^i.

[2] They then exploit the fact that $\frac{\partial H}{\partial t} = -f(x_1)$ is constant. We expect our performance to also improve if we exploit this special case.

Parameter m:	10	40	70	100	1000	2000	3000	4000	5000	10000	20000	30000
# of Alpha Steps (from [5, p. 288]):	184	250	276	292	395	426	446	457	468	499	530	547
# of Well-Isolated Steps: ($\gamma = 1$)	12	18	20	21	32	36	36	39	41	44	48	48
# of Well-Isolated Steps: ($\gamma = \mathbf{i}$)	25	30	33	36	46	49	50	53	53	56	60	62

Table 1: Comparison with Alpha Tracking for $H(x, t) = x^2 - (1 + mt)$. The number of steps are the same for both roots.

and $H(x, 1) = f(x)$. Given a root $z \in \mathbb{C}$ of g, the **solution path** for z is a continuous function $\alpha : [0, 1] \to \mathbb{C}$ where $\alpha(0) = z$ and $H(\alpha(t), t) = 0$ for all $t \in [0, 1]$.

Good Homotopy Assumption: *all solution paths are nonsingular and none diverge to infinity.* The results of this paper depend on this assumption, so we clarify the phrase "non-singularity of solution paths". Non-singularity implies that the solution paths are pairwise disjoint. The algebraic set $\{\alpha(t) : t \in [0, 1]\}$ might be regular, yet its parametrization $\alpha(t)$ might be singular, i.e., $\alpha'(t)$ might not be defined for some t. We interpret the Good Homotopy Assumption to mean that the parametrization $\alpha(t)$ itself is well-defined. To see what this entails, we differentiate $H(\alpha(t), t) = 0$ with respect to t:

$$\alpha'(t)\frac{\partial H}{\partial x}(\alpha(t), t) + \frac{\partial H}{\partial t}(\alpha(t), t) = 0.$$

Thus $\alpha'(t)$ is well-defined *provided* $\frac{\partial H}{\partial x}(\alpha(t), t)$ *does not vanish.* So we assume that the function $\frac{\partial H}{\partial x}(\alpha(t), t) \neq 0$ for all $t \in [0, 1]$, viewed as part of our good homotopy assumption. Note that the non-vanishing of $\alpha'(t)$ for all $t \in [0, 1]$ is the typical case for a random choice of γ. We define the function

$$G(x, t) = -\frac{\frac{\partial H}{\partial t}(x, t)}{\frac{\partial H}{\partial x}(x, t)} = \frac{\gamma g(x) - f(x)}{(1 - t)\gamma g'(x) + t f'(x)}. \tag{1}$$

Observe that $\alpha'(t) = G(\alpha(t), t)$ for any solution path $\alpha(t)$.

Our algorithm proceeds by maintaining closed disks isolating the roots of $H(x, t_0)$ for $t_0 \in [0, 1]$. We denote disks as follows: $\Delta(m, r) \subseteq \mathbb{C}$ denotes the closed complex disk centered at $m \in \mathbb{C}$ of radius $r > 0$. Additionally, for any real $k > 0$, let $k\Delta(m, r) := \Delta(m, kr)$, and, for any $t \in [0, 1]$, let $\Delta(m, r, t) := \Delta(m, r) \times \{t\} \subseteq \mathbb{C} \times [0, 1]$. For a polynomial $h \in \mathbb{Q}[x]$, $\Delta(m, r)$ is **well-isolating** (for h) if both $\Delta(m, r)$ and $3\Delta(m, r)$ contain a unique root of h.

3 OVERVIEW OF ALGORITHM

In this section, we provide a high-level overview overview of our homotopy algorithm. We frame our algorithm in the standard predictor-corrector framework. Throughout this section, we fix a solution path $\alpha(t)$ from our homotopy.

3.1 Update Subroutine

Our homotopy algorithm maintains and updates a state during its algorithm. A **state** consists of the following data:

$$\sigma_0 = (m_0, r_0, t_0, \delta t_0) \in \mathbb{C} \times \mathbb{R}_{>0} \times [0, 1]^2. \tag{2}$$

This state is a **valid state** relative to a solution path $\alpha(t)$ provided $\Delta(m_0, r_0)$ is well-isolating for the root $\alpha(t_0)$ of the polynomial $H(x, t_0)$. Thus, m_0 is a well-isolated approximation of the root $\alpha(t_0)$. Additionally, δt_0 provides a suggestion for the next time step. In our algorithm, we assume that we begin with a valid initial state for $\gamma g(x) = H(x, 0)$, and, in this section, we focus on the update step that transforms σ_0 to a valid state σ_1 at time $t_1 > t_0$.

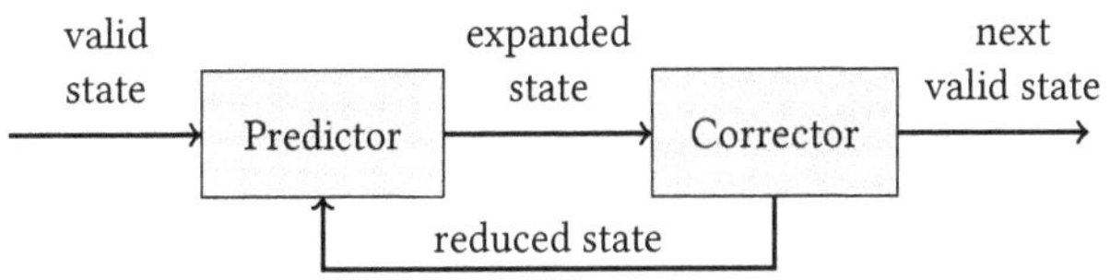

Figure 1: Update Subroutine

Figure 1 is a schematic for our Update Subroutine that converts a valid state into another valid state at the next time instance. It has two modules, a predictor and a corrector. Starting with a valid state σ_0, the predictor produces an "expanded" state σ_1 and sends it to the corrector module. The corrector module either confirms that σ_1 is valid, or sends a "reduced" state back to the predictor. The "expanded" and "reduced" terminology is clarified below.

Well-Isolated Tracker Algorithm
Input: Well-isolator $\Delta(m_0, r_0)$ for start polynomial g
Output: Well-isolator of the valid state σ at time $t = 1$.
  Initialize state $\sigma \leftarrow (m_0, r_0, 0, 2r_0)$
  While (the time of σ is less than 1)
    $\sigma \leftarrow$ Update(σ)
  Return the well-isolator σ.

Figure 2: Main Algorithm for path tracking

Our main algorithm is the path tracker shown in Figure 2. It is a while-loop around the Update Subroutine called the **outer loop**. The loop in Update is called the **inner loop**. The tracker terminates when the outer loop reaches a valid state at time $t = 1$. The input $\Delta(m_0, r_0)$, being a well-isolator of the starting polynomial g, defines a unique solution path $\alpha(t)$. Validity of states refers to this path. And the final valid state represents a well-isolated approximation of the root $\alpha(1)$ of the final polynomial f.

3.2 Corrector Module

In this section, we provide an overview of the corrector module of the predictor-corrector loop. The corrector module has three tests, called the Bounded, On-Track, and Isolated tests. The first two tests are computed on the "transition region" T between the valid state and the expanded state, i.e., $T \cap \mathbb{C} \times \{t_0\}$ is the starting valid disk $\Delta(m_0, r_0, t_0)$ and $T \cap \mathbb{C} \times \{t_1\}$ is the disk $\Delta(m_1, r_1, t_1)$ corresponding to the expanded state. If all the tests pass, the corrector sends σ_1 to the output of the Update Subroutine; otherwise, it reduces the valid disk $\Delta(m_0, r_0)$ and/or the step size δt_0. The construction of T and the details of the correctors are discussed in Section 4.

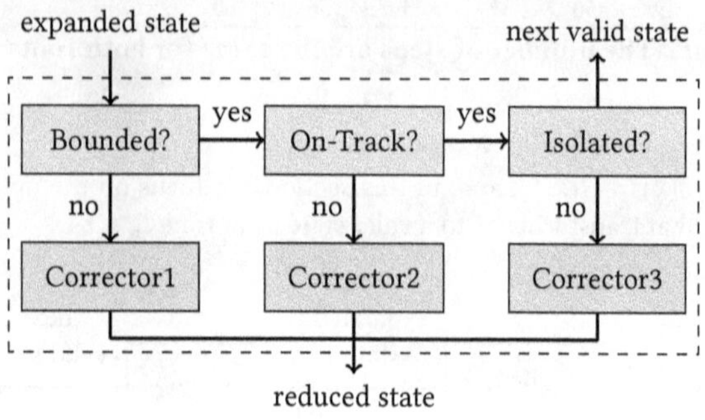

Figure 3: Schematic of Corrector Module

The Good Homotopy Assumption implies $\frac{\partial H}{\partial x}(\alpha(t), t)$ is never zero for any solution path $\alpha(t)$. However, it is possible that this derivative vanishes for some $(x, t) \in T$. The Bounded test assures that $\frac{\partial H}{\partial x}(x, t)$ never vanishes within T, i.e., $|G(x, t)|$ is bounded.

The On-Track test guarantees that the region T contains the portion of the solution path α between t_0 and t_1, i.e., $\alpha([t_0, t_1]) \subseteq T$. This test assumes that the Bounded test has passed. The On-Track test checks that $\delta t = t_1 - t_0$ is sufficiently small.

The Isolated test guarantees that the disk $3\Delta(m_1, r_1)$ isolates a unique root of $H(x, t_1)$. If both the Bounded and On-Track tests are passed, we know that this unique root is actually $\alpha(t_1)$, and $\alpha(t_1)$ lies in $\Delta(m_1, r_1)$. Thus σ_1 is a valid state relative to the path $\alpha(t)$.

At a high level, the corrector module is described by the following pseudo-code: In this code, the Reduce function serves as the corrector function, and details on this function are provided in the next section. The parameters ε and ε' are often set to $\frac{1}{2}$ or $\frac{3}{4}$.

Corrector Module
Input: Valid state σ_0 and expanded state σ_1
Output: Send a reduced state to the Predictor or output σ_1 as a valid state
If the Bounded(σ_0, σ_1) fails,
send Reduce($\sigma_0, \varepsilon, \varepsilon'$) to Predictor
Else if On-Track(σ_0, σ_1) fails,
send Reduce($\sigma_0, \varepsilon, 1$) to Predictor
Else if Isolated(σ_1) fails,
send Reduce($\sigma_0, 1, \varepsilon'$) to Predictor
Else output σ_1.

Figure 4: Corrector Module. $\varepsilon, \varepsilon' \in \{\frac{1}{2}, \frac{3}{4}\}$.

4 DETAILS OF THE MODULES

In this section, we describe the details of the predictor and corrector modules. The predictor is designed to be optimistic and encourages larger disks and step sizes. The corrector reduces a valid state by reducing r_0 or δt_0. The adaptivity of our algorithm is based on a balance between these two opposing goals.

4.1 Predictor Module

For a given valid state σ_0, the predictor module suggests a new state σ_1 at time $\min\{t_0 + \delta t_0, 1\}$ by approximating the path $\alpha(t)$ with (an approximation to) the tangent line to the curve at t_0. In particular, we observe that, on small scales, the path $\alpha(t)$ starting at t_0 can be approximated by the tangent line to the curve $\alpha'(t_0)(t - t_0) + \alpha(t_0)$ at t_0. Since we do not know the root $\alpha(t_0)$, we approximate $\alpha(t_0)$ with m_0 and $\alpha'(t_0)$ with $G(m_0, t_0)$. This approximation is the point m_1 (known as the Euler step) in Figure 5: Note that we define r_1 and δt_1 to be twice their previous values. These choices are optimistic and are designed to bias the algorithm towards using larger disks and taking larger steps. Hence σ_1 is called an "expanded state".

Subroutine Predict(σ_0)
Input: Valid state σ_0
Output: Expanded state σ_1
$m_1 \leftarrow m_0 + G(m_0, t_0) \min\{\delta t_0, 1 - t_0\}$
$r_1 \leftarrow 2r_0$
$t_1 \leftarrow \min\{1, t_0 + \delta t_0\}$
$\delta t_1 \leftarrow 2\delta t_0$.

Figure 5: Predictor Subroutine

By a **transition**, we mean a pair of states written in the form "$\sigma_0 \to \sigma_1$" where σ_0 is valid, σ_1 is not necessarily valid, but $t_0 < t_1$.

4.2 Bounded Test

Given σ_0 and an expanded state σ_1, we consider the convex hull of $\Delta(m_0, r_0, t_0)$ and $\Delta(m_1, r_1, t_1)$, denoted

$$T := \text{Chull}(\Delta(m_0, r_0, t_0), \Delta(m_1, r_1, t_1)).$$

T is frustum in the three-dimensional space $\mathbb{C} \times [0, 1]$ illustrated in Figure 6. Since the function $G(x, t)$ is a rational function, its value is bounded if and only if the denominator never vanishes. The success of the Bounded implies the denominator $\frac{\partial H}{\partial x}(x, t)$ does not vanish in the frustum T.

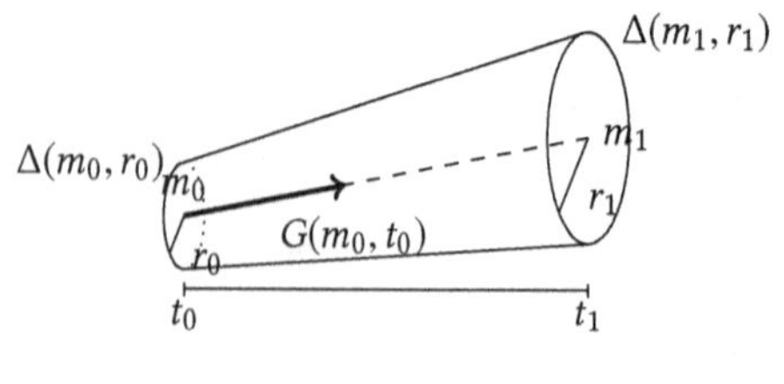

Figure 6: The frustum T is the convex hull of $\Delta(m_0, r_0, t_0)$ and $\Delta(m_1, r_1, t_1)$.

To verify that $\frac{\partial H}{\partial x}$ does not vanish on T, it is easier to show that it does not vanish on a cylinder $\widehat{T}$ containing T. We may define $\widehat{T} := \Delta(m_0, R) \times [t_0, t_1]$ where R is chosen as

$$R := 3r_0 + |G(m_0, t_0)|\delta t_0. \tag{3}$$

Suppose that we can find an $\mathcal{R}_x$ so that the following holds:

$$\left(\frac{\partial H}{\partial x}\right)(\Delta(m_0, R) \times [t_0, t_1]) \subseteq \frac{\partial H}{\partial x}(m_0, t_0) + \Delta(0, \mathcal{R}_x)$$

for some positive real number $\mathcal{R}_x$ (see Equation (8) in Section 5 below). In this case, for all $(x, t) \in \Delta(m_0, R) \times [t_0, t_1]$,

$$\left|\frac{\partial H}{\partial x}(x, t)\right| \geq \left|\frac{\partial H}{\partial x}(m_0, t_0)\right| - \mathcal{R}_x. \quad (4)$$

If the right-hand-side of Inequality (4) is positive, $\frac{\partial H}{\partial x}$ does not vanish on T. For our correctness proof below, we need the slightly stronger condition that the right hand side of (4) is larger than $\frac{1}{4}\frac{\partial H}{\partial x}(m_0, t_0)$, which is equivalent to

$$\mathcal{R}_x \leq \frac{3}{4}\left|\frac{\partial H}{\partial x}(m_0, t_0)\right|. \quad (5)$$

In particular, if Inequality (5) holds then $\frac{\partial H}{\partial x}$ is bounded in T. A formula for $\mathcal{R}_x$ is given in Equation (8).

4.3 On-Track Test

Suppose that the bounded condition is satisfied for transition $\sigma_0 \to \sigma_1$, so that G is bounded on $\widehat{T}$. We can then define

$$\max_{(x,t)\in\widehat{T}} |G(x, t) - G(m_0, t_0)|$$

to be the **relative variation** of G on $\widehat{T}$. Let $\mathcal{R}^*$ be any upper bound on the relative variation on $\widehat{T}$ (see Equation (9) in Section 5 below), and define

$$\delta t^* := \frac{r_0}{\mathcal{R}^*}. \quad (6)$$

This quantity describes how much a solution path α starting within $\Delta(m_0, r_0)$ can bend away from $G(m_0, t_0)$. This is made precise in the following lemma:

Lemma 4.1 (On-Track Condition). *If $\delta t^* \geq \delta t_0$ and σ_0 is a valid state for $\alpha(t_0)$, then α remains within T.*

Proof. Let $m(t) := m_0 + G(m_0, t_0)(t - t_0)$ be the path connecting the centers of $\Delta(m_0, r_0) \times \{t_0\}$ and $\Delta(m_1, r_1) \times \{t_1\}$ and $\gamma(t) := \alpha(t) - m(t)$. Observe that by our choice of R, for all $t \in [t_0, t_1)$, $T \cap \{t\}$ is contained within the relative interior of $\widehat{T} \cap \{t\}$. Since $\Delta(m_0, r_0)$ is valid for $\alpha(t_0)$, we know that $|\gamma(t_0)| \leq r_0$. Suppose, for contradiction, that α leaves T. By our observation, there is some time $t' \in (t_0, t_1)$ so that $\alpha(t') \notin T$ but $\alpha(t) \in \widehat{T}$ for all $t \in [t_0, t']$. We observe that $|\gamma(t')| > r_0\left(1 + \frac{t'-t_0}{\delta t_0}\right)$. Therefore, by the reverse triangle inequality, it follows that

$$\frac{|\gamma(t') - \gamma(t_0)|}{t' - t_0} \geq \frac{|\gamma(t')| - |\gamma(t)|}{t' - t_0} > \frac{r_0}{\delta t_0}. \quad (7)$$

However, by the mean value theorem for paths, the quantities in Inequality (7) are bounded above by $|\gamma'(t'')| \leq \mathcal{R}^* = \frac{r_0}{\delta t^*}$ for some $t'' \in (t_0, t')$. This contradicts the given inequality. Q.E.D.

Therefore, we define the `On-Track` test to be true if the inequality in Lemma 4.1 holds.

4.4 Isolated Test

The Isolated Test verifies that $\Delta(m_1, r_1)$ is a well-isolator. If the transition $\sigma_0 \to \sigma_1$ satisfies both the `Bounded` and `On-Track` tests, then the solution path α must pass through $\Delta(m_1, r_1)$. Therefore $\Delta(m_1, r_1)$ is a well-isolator if and only if $3\Delta(m_1, r_1)$ contains exactly one root of $H(x, t_1)$. We use the soft-variant of the Graeffe-Pellet test $\widetilde{T}_1^G(\Delta, h(x))$ in [4, Algorithm 5 in Section 3], which returns true only if $\Delta \subseteq \mathbb{C}$ has exactly one root. Thus, we define the `Isolated` test to be true if the Graeffe-Pellet test $\widetilde{T}_1^G(3\Delta(m_1, r_1), H(x, t_1))$ succeeds.

4.5 Corrector

The corrector module is based on the `Reduce` function, where `Reduce`$(\sigma_0, \varepsilon, \varepsilon')$ reduces the step size by a factor of ε and replaces the isolating disk $\Delta(m_0, r_0)$ with a new disk which is a subset of $\Delta(m_0, r_0)$ of radius at most $\varepsilon' r_0$. Reducing the step size is straightforward since we replace δt_0 with $\varepsilon\delta t_0$. We now reduce the radius by following the approach in [4, Algorithm 8].

Since σ_0 is known to be isolating, it is enough to cover $\Delta(m_0, r_0)$ by smaller disks and confirm that one of these disks is isolating. In particular, let B be the circumscribing square of $\Delta(m_0, r_0)$, treating $\mathbb{C}$ as $\mathbb{R}^2$. We then split B into four equal boxes $B_1, \ldots, B_4$ by bisecting each of the sides of B. For each B_i, let m_i be the midpoint of B_i and consider $\Delta\left(m_i, \frac{3}{4}r_0\right)$. We show that for one of these disks the Graeffe-Pellet test succeeds as follows, see also Figure 8: The disk $\Delta\left(m_i, \frac{\sqrt{2}}{2}r_0\right)$ contains the box B_i and $\Delta\left(m_i, \frac{3}{2}r_0\right)$ is contained within $3\Delta(m_0, r_0)$. If $\alpha(t_0) \in B_i$, then the Graeffe-Pellet test succeeds on $\Delta\left(m_i, \frac{3}{4}r_0\right)$ by [4, Lemma 4]. Moreover, the disk $3\Delta\left(m_i, \frac{3}{4}r_0\right)$ is contained in $3\Delta(m_0, r_0)$, so $\Delta\left(m_i, \frac{3}{4}r_0\right)$ is valid. This construction is made explicit in the `Bisect` subroutine. We summarize this argument in the following lemma:

Lemma 4.2. *The* `Bisect` *subroutine returns a valid state for $\alpha(t)$.*

Subroutine `Bisect`$(\Delta(m_0, r_0))$
Input: Well-isolator $\Delta(m_0, r_0)$
Output: Well-isolator $\Delta(m_0', r_0')$ of radius $3r_0/4$.
  Let B be circumscribing square of $\Delta(m_0, r_0)$
    Split B into 4 congruent subboxes $B_1, \ldots, B_4$
  For $j = 1$ to 4:
    Let m_j be the center of B_j
    If $\widetilde{T}_1^G(\Delta(m_j, \frac{3}{4}r_0), H(x, t_0))$ succeeds
      $m_0' \leftarrow m_j$ and $r_0' \leftarrow \frac{3}{4}r_0$
      Return $\Delta(m_0', r_0')$.

Figure 7: The Bisection Subroutine

4.6 Correctness of the Algorithm

The main issue of correctness is halting: this is proved in two parts. Here, we prove that the inner loop halts (i.e., `Update` halts). The halting of the outer loop (i.e., the main tracker) is more intricate, and awaits additional development in Section 5.

www.ingramcontent.com/pod-product-compliance
Lightning Source LLC
Chambersburg PA
CBHW080651220326
41598CB00033B/5165